July 15 – 17, 2019
Aberdeen, Scotland, UK

Association for Computing Machinery

Advancing Computing as a Science & Profession

ITiCSE '19

Proceedings of the 2019 ACM Conference on Innovation and Technology in Computer Science Education

Conference Chairs:
Bruce Scharlau (University of Aberdeen, UK)
Roger McDermott (Robert Gordon University, UK)

Programme Chairs:
Arnold Pears (KTH Royal Institute of Technology, Sweden)
Mihaela Sabin (University of New Hampshire, USA)

Sponsored by:
ACM SIGCSE

Association for
Computing Machinery

Advancing Computing as a Science & Profession

The Association for Computing Machinery
1601 Broadway, 10th Floor
New York, NY 10019-7434

ISBN: 978-1-4503-6301-3 (Digital)

ISBN: 978-1-4503-7063-9 (Print)

Additional copies may be ordered prepaid from:

ACM Order Department
PO Box 30777
New York, NY 10087-0777, USA

Phone: 1-800-342-6626 (USA and Canada)
+1-212-626-0500 (Global)
Fax: +1-212-944-1318
E-mail: acmhelp@acm.org
Hours of Operation: 8:30 am – 4:30 pm ET

Foreword

Welcome to ITiCSE 2019 at the University of Aberdeen! The university was founded in 1495 by Bishop Elphinstone, and is Scotland's third oldest university, as well as the fifth oldest university in the English-speaking world. This year it was acclaimed as the 'Scottish University of the Year' by the Times and Sunday Times Good University Guide.

Aberdeen is a medieval university city of about 250,000 people, which sits on the east coast of the North Sea between the River Dee and the River Don, and is Scotland's third largest city. The city is known for its energy related business, and is at the heart of an area of outstanding natural beauty which includes Royal Deeside, the Grampian mountains, and the Aberdeenshire coast. It is also less than 50 miles from Speyside, the heart of the Scotch malt whisky industry, and a departure point to visit the historic and prehistoric sites on the islands of Orkney and Shetland. We also have the world's busiest heliport, which annually ferries 500,000 staff to and from the oil rigs in the North Sea. This is why you'll regularly hear helicopters during your visit.

This year, an ITiCSE record of 243 papers were submitted, of which 66 were accepted, giving an acceptance rate of 27%. Of these papers, just over half had an author from the United States or Canada, while European authors were represented in about 40% of the papers. We also accepted papers with authors from Central and South America, China, Japan, Australia, and the Middle East, giving us a truly international flavour of current Computer Science Education research and practice.

In addition to the Paper, Poster and Panel submissions, and Tips, Techniques and Courseware presentations, we have ten Working Groups investigating these topics: the pacing of introductory CS courses; fostering program comprehension for novice programmers; exploring pass rates in computing and other STEM subjects; sustainability issues in CS; diversity in the cybersecurity field; data science education; benchmarking K-12 CS education in schools; developing a model curriculum for cloud computing; and designing better compiler error messages. The reports from these groups will be published in a companion volume to the final proceedings, but we look forward to the working groups presenting preliminary findings during the conference.

We are introducing a Doctoral Consortium over the weekend ahead of the conference in order to provide PhD students studying computing science education an opportunity to explore and develop their research interests in a workshop environment with a panel of established researchers. We hope this encourages new members into our academic community where they can feel welcome, and contribute to ongoing work in our area.

We have two keynote speakers. Dr Kate Stone, the founder of Novalia, will talk about her work making technology disappear though the power of digital ink. Marian Petre, Professor of Computing at the Open University in the UK, will reflect on long-term empirical research on software design and consider how expert practice can inform how we teach the subject.

The daily social activities will be held in the university's Elphinstone Hall, which is where student graduation ceremonies take place each June and November. Naturally, for 'castle country' you'll have the chance to visit a castle, and taste some whisky too as part of the excursions.

We look forward to talking to you while you're here. We know you'll have fun making new friends, and reacquainting yourself with old ones too, as you fill up on new ideas and innovations to take home to your classroom. We hope you'll also take home some wonderful memories of our lovely surrounding countryside and the beautiful Aberdeenshire coast.

Slàinte!

Bruce Scharlau and
Roger McDermott
ITiCSE 2019 Conference Chairs

Arnold Pears and
Mihaela Sabin
ITiCSE 2019 Program Chairs

Table of Contents

- **ITiCSE 2019 Organization List** xv
- **ITiCSE 2019 Sponsors & Supporters** xxi

Keynote 1

- **Designing for a Connected World** 1
  Kate Stone *(Novalia Ltd.)*

Session 1A: Identity

- **Identity and Belonging for Graduate Apprenticeships in Computing: The experience of first cohort degree apprentices in Scotland** 2
  Ella Taylor-Smith, Sally Smith, Colin Smith *(Edinburgh Napier University)*
- **Understanding CS Undergraduate Students' Professional Identity through the lens of their Professional Development** 9
  Amanpreet Kapoor, Christina Gardner-McCune *(University of Florida)*
- **The Impact of Self-Theories to Academic Achievement and Soft Skills in Undergraduate CS Studies: First Findings** 16
  Mikko-Ville Apiola, Mikko-Jussi Laakso *(University of Turku)*

Session 1B: Novice Programmers

- **Identifying and Validating Java Misconceptions Toward a CS1 Concept Inventory** 23
  Ricardo Caceffo *(State University of Campinas)*, Pablo Frank-Bolton *(The George Washington University)*, Renan Souza, Rodolfo Azevedo *(State University of Campinas)*
- **Explaining Novice Programmer's Struggles, in Two Parts: Revisiting the ITiCSE 2004 working group's study using dual process theory** 30
  Tony A. Lowe *(Purdue University)*
- **Novice Rationales for Sketching and Tracing, and How They Try to Avoid It** 37
  Kathryn Cunningham *(University of Michigan)*, Shannon Ke *(Georgia Institute of Technology)*, Mark Guzdial, Barbara Ericson *(University of Michigan)*

Session 1C: Curriculum

- **Non-restricted Access to Model Solutions: A Good Idea?** 44
  Henrik Nygren, Juho Leinonen, Arto Hellas *(University of Helsinki)*
- **Visual Portrayals of Data and Results at ITiCSE** 51
  Simon *(University of Newcastle)*, Brett A. Becker *(University College Dublin)*, Sally Hamouda *(Rhode Island College)*, Robert McCartney *(University of Connecticut)*, Kate Sanders *(Rhode Island College (Emerita))*, Judy Sheard *(Monash University)*
- **A Survey of Introductory Programming Courses in Ireland** 58
  Brett A. Becker *(University College Dublin)*

Session 1D: Pedagogy

- **Helping Students Solve Parsons Puzzles Better** 65
  Amruth N. Kumar *(Ramapo College of New Jersey)*

- **The Relationship Between Students' Engagement and the Development of Transactive Memory Systems in MUVE:: An Experience Report** 71
  Louis Nisiotis *(Faculty of Science, Technology and Arts (STA), Sheffield Hallam University)*,
  Styliani Kleanthous *(Cyprus Center for Algorithmic Transparency, Open University of Cyprus)*
- **Are There Differences in Learning Gains When Programming a Tangible Object or a Simulation?** 78
  Grégoire Fessard, Patrick Wang, Ilaria Renna *(Institut Supérieur d'Électronique de Paris)*

Session 2A: Expectation and Experience

- **New Entrants' Expectations of the First Year Computer Science Experience in the Context of a New National High School Curriculum** 85
  Jyoti Bhardwaj *(Edinburgh Napier University)*
- **Applying Gamification to Motivate Students to Write High-Quality Code in Programming Assignments** 92
  Remin Kasahara, Kazunori Sakamoto, Hironori Washizaki, Yoshiaki Fukazawa *(Waseda University)*
- **Paper or Online? A Comparison of Exam Grading Techniques** 99
  Yingjun Cao, Leo Porter, Soohyun Nam Liao, Rick Ord *(University of California, San Diego)*

Session 2B: Programming

- **Measuring Instruction Comprehension by Mining Memory Traces for Early Formative Feedback in Java Courses** 105
  Frank Höppner *(Ostfalia University of Applied Sciences)*,
- **Quantifying Activity and Collaboration Levels in Programming Assignments** 112
  James F. Power *(Maynooth University)*, John Waldron *(Trinity College Dublin)*
- **How Teachers Would Help Students to Improve Their Code** 119
  Hieke Keuning *(Open University of the Netherlands and Windesheim University of Applied Sciences)*,
  Bastiaan Heeren *(Open University of the Netherlands)*,
  Johan Jeuring *(Utrecht University and Open University of the Netherlands)*

Session 2C: Curriculum

- **Bridging the Digital Skills Gap: Are computing degree apprenticeships the answer?** 126
  Ella Taylor-Smith, Sally Smith, Khristin Fabian *(Edinburgh Napier University)*, Tessa Berg *(Heriot-Watt University)*,
  Debbie Meharg, Alison Varey *(Edinburgh Napier University)*
- **Programme Integrating Courses Fighting to Get Engineers to Reflect on Non-technical Topics** 133
  Emma Riese, Olle Bälter, Björn Hedin, Viggo Kann *(KTH Royal Institute of Technology)*
- **Digital Storytelling and Group Work: Integrating the Narrative Approach into a Higher Education Computer Science Course** 140
  Ari Korhonen *(Aalto University)*, Marianna Vivitsou *(University of Helsinki)*

Session 2D: Pedagogy

- **Does Studying CS Automatically Foster a Growth Mindset?** 147
  Michael Lodi *(University of Bologna & INRIA)*
- **Understanding How Work Habits influence Student Performance** 154
  Seth Copen Goldstein *(Carnegie Mellon University)*, Hongyi Zhang *(Peking University)*,
  Majd Sakr, Haokang An, Cameron Dashti *(Carnegie Mellon University)*
- **Making CS Learning Visible: Case Studies on How Visibility of Student Work Supports a Community of Learners in CS Classrooms** 161
  Amber Solomon, Vanessa Oguamanam *(Georgia Institute of Technology)*, Mark Guzdial *(University of Michigan)*,
  Betsy DiSalvo *(Georgia Institute of Technology)*

Session 3A: Panel 1

- **Perspectives on the Student Transition into CS1** 168
  Angela A. Siegel *(Dalhousie University)*, Mark Zarb *(Robert Gordon University)*,
  Richard Glassey *(KTH Royal Institute of Technology)*, Janet Hughes *(The Open University)*

Session 3B: Pair Programming

- **How Prior Programming Experience Affects Students' Pair Programming Experiences and Outcomes** 170
  Nicholas A. Bowman, Lindsay Jarratt, K.C. Culver, Alberto Maria Segre *(University of Iowa)*
- **A Large-Scale Experimental Study of Gender and Pair Composition in Pair Programming** ... 176
  Lindsay Jarratt, Nicholas A. Bowman, K.C. Culver, Alberto Maria Segre *(University of Iowa)*
- **More Effective Contextualization of CS Education Research: A Pair-Programming Example** 182
  Briana Bettin, Linda Ott, Leo Ureel *(Michigan Technological University)*

Session 3C: CS1

- **Instructional Framework for CS1 Question Activities** 189
  Rita Garcia, Katrina Falkner, Rebecca Vivian *(University of Adelaide)*
- **Behaviors of Higher and Lower Performing Students in CS1** 196
  Soohyun Nam Liao, Sander Valstar, Kevin Thai, Christine Alvarado *(University of California, San Diego)*,
  Daniel Zingaro *(University of Toronto, Mississauga)*,
  William G. Griswold, Leo Porter *(University of California, San Diego)*
- **Experience Report: Thinkathon – Countering an "I Got It Working" Mentality with Pencil-and-Paper Exercises** 203
  Quintin Cutts, Matthew Barr, Mireilla Bikanga Ada, Peter Donaldson, Steve Draper, Jack Parkinson,
  Jeremy Singer, Lovisa Sundin *(University of Glasgow)*

Session 3D: Student Reasoning

- **A Multi-Level Study of Undergraduate Computer Science Reasoning about Concurrency** 210
  Aubrey Lawson, Eileen T. Kraemer, S. Megan Che, Cazembe Kennedy *(Clemson University)*
- **Final Year Students' Approaches to Implementing Complex Distributed Systems** 217
  Claudia Szabo, Michael Scott Pointon *(University of Adelaide)*
- **Qualitative Observations of Student Reasoning: Coding in the Wild** 224
  Cazembe Kennedy, Eileen Kraemer *(Clemson University)*

Session 4A: Panel 2

- **Resources for Researching and Teaching Computing Education in Primary and Secondary Schools: What Exists and What is Still Needed** 231
  Monica McGill *(Knox College)*, Miles Berry *(University of Roehampton)*, Leigh Ann DeLyser *(CSforAll Consortium)*,
  Briana Morrison *(University of Nebraska at Omaha)*

Session 4B: Tips, Techniques and Courseware

- **Teaching AVR Assembly by Building an Arduino Arcade Machine** 233
  Michael Black, Joseph Matta *(Bridgewater State University)*
- **Connecting Majors/Non-Majors Courses Via Tabular Data** 235
  Ali Erkan, Adam Lee *(Ithaca College)*
- **Automatic Evaluation of the Quality of Solutions for an Open Programming Task** 237
  Stephan Euler *(TH Mittelhessen University of Applied Sciences)*
- **csedresearch.org: Resources for Primary and SecondaryComputer Science Education Research** 239
  Monica M. McGill *(Knox College)*, Adrienne Decker *(University at Buffalo)*

- **If Memory Serves: A Game to Supplement the Instruction of Concepts Related to Pointers** .. 241
  Monica M. McGill *(Knox College)*, Ian Pollock *(California State University, East Bay)*
- **In-Depth Feedback on Programming Assignments Using Pattern Recognition and Real-Time Hints** 243
  Amir Rubinstein, Noam Parzanchevski, Yossi Tamarov *(Tel-Aviv University)*
- **Teaching Self-Balancing Trees Using a Beauty Contest** 245
  Samah Senbel *(Sacred Heart University)*
- **Exploring the Potential of Social Annotations for Predictive and Descriptive Analytics** 247
  Shaveen Singh *(Monash University)*
- **Laughter over Dread: Early Collaborative Problem Solving through an Extended Induction using Robots** 249
  Mark Zarb *(Robert Gordon University)*, Michael Scott *(Falmouth University)*

Session 5A: Working Groups Presentations

- **Securing the Human: Broadening Diversity in Cybersecurity** 251
  Mohammad Azhar *(Borough Of Manhattan Community College)*, Sajal Bhatia *(Sacred Heart University)*, Greg Gagne *(Westminster College)*, Chadi Kari *(University of the Pacific)*, Joseph Maguire *(University of Glasgow)*, Xenia Mountrouidou *(College of Charleston)*, Liviana Tudor *(Politehnica University of Bucharest & Petroleum-Gas University of Ploiesti)*, David Vosen *(College of St. Scholastica)*, Timothy T. Yuen *(University of Texas at San Antonio)*
- **Unexpected Tokens: A Review of Programming Error Messages and Design Guidelines for the Future** 253
  Brett A. Becker *(University College Dublin)*, Paul Denny *(University of Auckland)*, Raymond Pettit *(University of Virginia)*, Durell Bouchard *(Roanoke College)*, Dennis J. Bouvier *(Southern Illinois University Edwardsville)*, Brian Harrington *(University of Toronto Scarborough)*, Amir Kamil *(University of Michigan)*, Amey Karkare *(Indian Institute of Technology Kanpur)*, Chris McDonald *(University of Western Australia)*, Peter-Michael Osera *(Grinnell College)*, Janice L. Pearce *(Berea College)*, James Prather *(Abilene Christian University)*
- **Toward Developing a Cloud Computing Model Curriculum** 255
  D. Cenk Erdil *(Sacred Heart University)*, Laurie White *(Google)*, Derek Foster *(University of Lincoln)*, Joshua Adams *(Saint Leo University)*, Amadeo Jose Arguelles Cruz *(Instituto Politecnico Nacional)*, Brian Hainey *(Glasgow Caledonian University)*, Harvey Hyman *(University of South Florida)*, Gareth Lewis *(Falmouth University)*, Sajid Nazir *(Glasgow Caledonian University)*, Manh Van Nguyen *(Saint Leo University)*, Majd Sakr *(Carnegie Mellon University)*, Lee Stott *(Microsoft)*
- **An International Benchmark Study of K-12 Computer Science Education in Schools** 257
  Katrina Falkner *(University of Adelaide)*, Sue Sentance *(Raspberry Pi Foundation)*, Rebecca Vivian *(University of Adelaide)*, Sarah Barksdale *(University of Minnesota)*, Leonard Busuttil *(University of Malta)*, Elizabeth Cole *(University of Glasgow)*, Christine Liebe *(Lotus Education Institute)*, Francesco Maiorana *(University of Catania)*, Monica M. McGill *(Knox College)*, Keith Quille *(Technological University Dublin)*
- **Towards an Ability to Direct College Students to an Appropriately Paced Introductory Computer Science Course** 259
  James Heliotis *(Rochester Institute of Technology)*, Leo C. Ureel *(Michigan Technological University)*, Mireilla Bikanga Ada *(University of Glasgow)*, Mohsen Dorodchi *(University of North Carolina)*, Victoria Eisele *(Front Range Community College)*, Megan E. Lutz *(University of Georgia)*, Ethel Tshukudu *(University of Glasgow)*
- **Program Comprehension: Identifying Learning Trajectories for Novice Programmers** 261
  Cruz Izu *(University of Adelaide)*, Carsten Schulte *(Paderborn University)*, Ashish Aggarwal *(University of Florida)*, Quintin Cutts *(University of Glasgow)*, Rodrigo Duran *(Aalto University)*, Mirela Gutica *(British Columbia Institute of Technology)*, Birte Heinemann *(Paderborn University)*, Eileen Kraemer *(Clemson University)*, Violetta Lonati *(University of Milan)*, Claudio Mirolo *(University of Udine)*, Renske Weeda *(Radboud University)*

- **1.5 Degrees of Separation: Computer Science Education in the Age of the Anthropocene** 263
  Ian Pollock *(California State University East Bay)*, Bedour Alshaigy, Andrew Bradley *(Oxford Brookes University)*, Birgit R. Krogstie *(Norwegian University of Science and Technology)*, Viraj Kumar *(Indian Institute of Science)*, Linda Ott *(Michigan Technological University)*, Anne-Kathrin Peters *(Uppsala University)*, Charles Riedesel *(University of Nebraska - Lincoln)*, Charles Wallace *(Michigan Technological University)*
- **Data Science Education: Global Perspectives and Convergence** 265
  Rajendra K. Raj *(Rochester Institute of Technology)*, Allen Parrish *(Mississippi State University)*, John Impagliazzo *(Hofstra University)*, Carol J. Romanowski *(Rochester Institute of Technology)*, Sherif Aly Ahmed *(The American University in Cairo)*, Casey C. Bennett *(DePaul University)*, Karen C. Davis *(Miami University)*, Andrew McGettrick *(Strathclyde University)*, Teresa Susana Mendes Pereira *(Instituto Politécnico de Viana do Castelo)*, Lovisa Sundin *(University of Glasgow)*
- **Pass Rates in STEM Disciplines Including Computing** 267
  Simon *(University of Newcastle)*, Andrew Luxton-Reilly *(University of Auckland)*, Vangel Ajanovski *(Ss Cyril and Methodius University)*, Eric Fouh *(University of Pennsylvania)*, Chris Gonsalvez *(Monash University)*, Juho Leinonen *(University of Helsinki)*, Jack Parkinson *(University of Glasgow)*, Matthew Poole *(University of Portsmouth)*, Neena Thota *(University of Massachusetts, Amherst)*
- **A Periodic Table of Computing Education Learning Theories** 269
  Claudia Szabo, Nickolas Falkner *(University of Adelaide)*, Andrew Petersen *(University of Toronto Mississauga)*, Heather Bort *(Marquette University)*, Cornelia Connolly *(NUI Galway)*, Kathryn Cunningham *(University of Michigan)*, Peter Donaldson *(University of Glasgow)*, Arto Hellas *(University of Helsinki)*, James Robinson *(Raspberry PI Foundation)*, Judy Sheard *(Monash University)*

Session 5B: Professional Development

- **Effective Computer Science Teacher Professional Development: Beauty and Joy of Computing 2018** 271
  Alexandra Milliken, Christa Cody, Veronica Catété, Tiffany Barnes *(North Carolina State University)*
- **Infusing Computing: Analyzing Teacher Programming Products in K-12 Computational Thinking Professional Development** 278
  Yihuan Dong, Veronica Catété, Nicholas Lytle, Amy Isvik, Tiffany Barnes *(North Carolina State University)*, Robin Jocius, Jennifer Albert, Deepti Joshi, Richard Robinson, Ashley Andrews *(The Citadel)*
- **Impact of HFOSS on Education on Instructors** 285
  Lori Postner, Darci Burdge *(Nassau Community College)*, Heidi J. C. Ellis, Stoney Jackson *(Western New England University)*, Gregory W. Hislop *(Drexel University)*

Session 5C: Poster Presentations

- **Evaluating the Effectiveness of Explicit Instruction in Reducing Program Reasoning Fallacies in Elementary Level Students** 292
  Ashish Aggarwal, Christina Gardner-McCune, David S. Touretzky *(Carnegie Mellon University)*
- **A Conceptual Framework for Identifying Emotional Factors Leading to Student Disengagement in VLEs** 293
  Lubna Alharbi, Floriana Grasso, Phil Jimmieson *(University of Liverpool)*
- **A Framework for Improving the Sharing of Teaching Practices among Computer Science Instructors** 294
  Nouf Almujally, Mike Joy *(University of Warwick)*
- **A Reflective Writing Framework for Computing Education** 295
  Huda Alrashidi, Mike Joy *(University of Warwick)*, Thomas Daniel Ullmann *(Open University)*
- **Eye Tracking to Evaluate Comprehension of Computational Thinking** 296
  Abdurrahman Arslanyilmaz, Kendra Corpier *(Youngstown State University)*
- **The Use of Gamification to Support the Process of Teaching Scrum** 297
  Luiz Ricardo Begosso, Luis Henrique Buzzo Franco, Douglas Sanches Cunha *(FEMA)*, Luiz Carlos Begosso *(FATEC, FEMA)*

- **OurKidsCode: A National Programme to get Families Involved in CS Education** 298
  Nina Bresnihan, Glenn Strong, Lorraine Fisher, Richard Millwood *(Trinity College Dublin)*,
  Aine Lynch *(National Parents Council Primary)*
- **Student Motivation and Engagement in STEM Courses: Exploring the Potential Impact of Gamification** 299
  Lillian Cassel, Darina Dicheva, Christo Dichev, Breonte Guy, Keith Irwin *(Winston-Salem State University)*
- **Computing Ipsative Assessment. Improving the Student Experience in Higher Education Using Personalised Assessment and Feedback** 300
  Ryan Crosby, Marie Devlin, Lindsay Marshall *(Newcastle University)*
- **Development of a Checklist Tool for Teaching Problem-Solving Skills** 301
  Hillary Dawkins, Grant Douglas, Kevin Glover-Netherton, David Hudec, Sean Lunt, Dalton Polhill, Mostafa Rashed, Matthew Sampson, Alliyya Mohammed, James Mosley, Rhys Young, Judi McCuaig *(University of Guelph)*
- **Infusing Data Science Across Disciplines** 302
  Debzani Deb, Russell M. Smith, Muztaba Fuad *(Winston-Salem State University)*
- **Idempotent Factorizations: A New Addition to the Cryptography Classroom** 303
  Barry Fagin *(US Air Force Academy)*
- **Improving Functional Programming Understanding through Student-Created Instructional Videos** 304
  Pedro G. Feijóo-García *(University of Florida & Universidad El Bosque)*, Christina Gardner-McCune *(University of Florida)*
- **We Need to Talk!! – A Chatroom Application Using a Student-Designed Protocol** 305
  Greg Gagne *(Westminster College)*,
- **The Peanut Butter and Jelly Sandwich Challenge as an Approach to Improve Students Abilities in Test Case Writing** 306
  Kiev Gama *(Universidade Federal de Pernambuco)*, Andrew Diniz, Ricardo Almeida, Hendi Coelho *(PUC-Rio)*
- **Teaching Logic with Iltis: an Interactive, Web-Based System** 307
  Gaetano Geck, Artur Ljulin, Jonas Haldimann, Johannes May, Jonas Schmidt, Marko Schmellenkamp, Daniel Sonnabend, Felix Tschirbs, Fabian Vehlken, Thomas Zeume *(TU Dortmund)*
- **Adapting the IT2017 Curricula for Two Year Transfer Programs: Determining Appropriate Competencies for the First Two Years of a Baccalaureate IT Program** 308
  Markus Geissler *(Cosumnes River College)*, Cindy S. Tucker *(Bluegrass Community and Technical College)*, Christian Servin *(El Paso Community College)*, Cara Tang *(Portland Community College)*, Melissa Stange *(Lord Fairfax Community College)*
- **Unplugged Activities to Introduce Parallel Computing in Introductory Programming Classes: an Experience Report** 309
  Sheikh K. Ghafoor, David W. Brown, Mike Rogers, Thomas Hines *(Tennessee Tech University)*
- **From Data To Insights in CS1** 310
  Ananda Gunawardena *(Rutgers University / Princeton University)*
- **Motivating High School Girls to Study Computer Science** 311
  Mirela Gutica *(British Columbia Institute of Technology)*
- **Findings from a Multi-year Study of CT in K-2 Students in Formal and Informal Settings** 312
  Tony Lowe, Sean Brophy, Monica Cardella *(Purdue University)*
- **Devising Work-based Learning Curricula with Apprentice Research Software Engineers** 313
  Joseph Maguire, Quintin Cutts, Jack Parkinson, Matthew Barr, Derek Somerville *(University of Glasgow)*
- **Insights from using Supplemental Instruction (SI) in Data Structures Course to Increase Retention** 314
  Aparna Mahadev *(Worcester State University)*
- **Exploring the Correlation Between Teacher Pedagogical Content Knowledge and Content Knowledge in Computer Science Classrooms** 315
  Tom McKlin, Taneisha Lee, Dana Wanzer *(The Findings Group)*,
  Brian Magerko, Doug Edwards, Sabrina Grossman *(Georgia Institute of Technology)*,
  Emily Bryans *(The Findings Group)*, Jason Freeman *(Georgia Institute of Technology)*

- **A Proposal for Recognizing Skills in Data Science Using Open Badges** 316
  Ernestina Menasalvas, Ana M. Moreno, Nik Swoboda *(Universidad Politécnica de Madrid)*
- **A Gamification Pathway for Computer Science Student Success** 317
  Patricia Morreale, Nohelia Diplan *(Kean University)*, Dustin York *(Maryville University)*
- **Impact of Part-Time CS Engineering Internships on Workload** 318
  Juan J. Olarte, César Domínguez, Arturo Jaime, Francisco J. García-Izquierdo *(University of La Rioja)*
- **Instructional Pseudocode Guide to Teach Problem-Solving** 319
  Svetlana Peltsverger, Sourav Debnath *(Kennesaw State University)*
- **Supporting Abstraction Skills Using Augmented Reality?** 320
  Rebecca Reuter, Marco Knietzsch, Florian Hauser, Jürgen Mottok *(OTH Regensburg)*
- **COOL: Cooperative Open Learning for Beginning Programmers** 321
  Barbara Sabitzer, Iris Groher, Johannes Sametinger *(Johannes Kepler Universität)*
- **Designing Engaging Learning Experiences** 322
  Raghav V. Sampangi, Angela A. Siegel *(Dalhousie University)*
- **Shaping Curricular Guidelines for Associate-Degree Cybersecurity Programs** 323
  Melissa Stange *(Lord Fairfax Community College)*, Cara Tang *(Portland Community College)*,
  Christian Servin *(El Paso Community College)*, Cindy Tucker *(Bluegrass Community & Technical College)*,
  Markus Geissler *(Cosumnes River College)*
- **Computing Opportunities for Students of Color** 324
  Gloria Townsend, Khadija Stewart *(DePauw University)*
- **A Prototype MATLAB Code Critiquer** 325
  Marissa Walther, Leo C. Ureel, Charles Wallace *(Michigan Technological University)*
- **How Can Children Express Their Intentions Through Coding?**
  – Analysis of Viscuit Programs in Kindergarten – 326
  Takeshi Watanabe *(The University of Electro-Communications & Digitalpocket LLC)*,
  Yuriko Nakayama *(Kagawa-fujimigaoka Kindergarten)*, Yasunori Harada *(Digitalpocket LLC)*,
  Yasushi Kuno *(The University of Electro-Communications)*
- **Challenges of Delivering a Graduate Apprenticeship** 327
  Tiffany Young, Mark Zarb *(Robert Gordon University)*
- **Incorporating On-Campus Days in a Graduate Apprenticeship** 328
  Tiffany Young, Mark Zarb *(Robert Gordon University)*
- **Integrating Real-World Clients in a Project Management Module** 329
  Mark Zarb, Tiffany Young *(Robert Gordon University)*, William Ballew *(James Fisher Digital)*

Keynote 2

- **Lessons from Experts: Software Design Dialogues** 331
  Marian Petre *(Open University)*

Session 6A: Panel 3

- **Interdisciplinary Computer Science Pre-service TeacherPreparation: Panel** 332
  Francesco Maiorana *(University of Catania)*, Gretchen Richards *(Jacksonville State University)*,
  Chery Lucarelli *(The College of St. Scholastica)*, Miles Berry *(University of Roehampton)*,
  Barbara Ericson *(University of Michigan)*

Session 6B: Doctoral Consortium Preseentations

- **A Grounded Theory of Computing Professional Identity Formation** 334
  Amanpreet Kapoor *(University of Florida)*
- **Investigating Novice Programmers' Interaction with Programming Environments** 336
  Ioannis Karvelas *(University College Dublin)*

- **From Studying to Learning Computer Science: A study of the first-year experience of computer science education at university** 338
  Madeleine Lorås *(Norwegian University of Science and Technology)*
- **A Theory of Applied Mind of Programming: Understanding the challenges in learning to program** 340
  Tony Lowe *(Purdue University)*
- **Gamification and Collaboration to Evaluate and Improve the Security Mindset of Developers** 342
  Léon McGregor *(Heriot-Watt University)*
- **Computational Thinking At Primary School: Didactical and Psychological Aspects** 344
  Marialaura Moschella *(Free University of Bolzano)*
- **Pattern-Oriented Instruction and its Influence on Meaningful Learning of Algorithmic Patterns and Acquiring Fundamental Skills in Computer Science** 346
  Liat Nakar *(Weizmann Institute of Science)*
- **Learning through Construction's Influence on IT Students' Identity Formation** 348
  Justyna Szynkiewicz *(NORD University)*
- **"I Don't Know Too Much About It": On the Security Mindsets of Future Software Creators** .. 350
  Mohammad Tahaei *(University of Edinburgh)*
- **Utilising Game Design to Create Engaging Education: A framework for Gameful Learning** 351
  David Williams *(Dublin Business School)*

Session 6C: Programming

- **Direct Manipulation versus Text-based Programming: An experiment report** 353
  Michel Adam, Moncef Daoud *(Université Bretagne Sud)*, Patrice Frison *(IRISA lab - Université Bretagne Sud)*,
- **Auto-Generating Visual Exercises for Learning Program Semantics** 360
  Rebecca Smith, Terry Tang, Joe Warren, Scott Rixner *(Rice University)*
- **Identifying Predictors for Code Highlighting Skills: A Regressional Analysis of Knowledge, Syntax Abilities and Highlighting Skills** 367
  Matthias Kramer, Mike Barkmin, Torsten Brinda *(University of Duisburg-Essen)*

Session 6D: Experience

- **Teaching Electronics and Programming in Norwegian Schools Using the air:bit Sensor Kit** 374
  Bjørn Fjukstad, Nina Angelvik, Morten Grønnesby, Maria Wulff Hauglann *(The Arctic University of Norway)*,
  Hedinn Gunhildrud *(Science Centre of Northern Norway)*,
  Fredrik Høisæther Rasch, Julianne Iversen, Margaret Dalseng, Lars Ailo Bongo *(The Arctic University of Norway)*
- **Below C Level: A Student-Centered x86-64 Simulator** 381
  Caitlin Fanning, Saturnino Garcia *(University of San Diego)*
- **Developing Course Projects in a Hack Day: An Experience Report** 388
  Kiev Gama *(Universidade Federal de Pernambuco)*

Session 7A: Secondary School

- **Use, Modify, Create: Comparing Computational Thinking Lesson Progressions for STEM Classes** 395
  Nicholas Lytle, Veronica Catete, Danielle Boulden, Yihuan Dong, Jennifer Houchins, Alexandra Milliken, Amy Isvik, Dolly Bounajim, Eric Wiebe, Tiffany Barnes *(North Carolina State University)*

- **Text-based Programming in Elementary School: A Comparative Study of Programming Abilities in Children with and without Block-based Experience** 402
  Marcos J. Gomez, Marco Moresi *(Universidad Nacional de Cordoba)*,
  Luciana Benotti *(Universidad Nacional de Cordoba / CONICET)*
- **Exploring Differences in Minority Students' Attitudes towards Computing after a One-Day Coding Workshop** 409
  Michael J. Lee *(New Jersey Institute of Technology)*

Session 7B: Computational Thinking

- **A Framework for Decomposition in Computational Thinking** 416
  Peter J. Rich, Garrett Egan, Jordan Ellsworth *(Brigham Young University)*
- **Making Computer Science Education Mandatory: Exploring a Demographic Shift in Switzerland** 422
  Alexander Repenning, Anna Lamprou, Serge Petralito *(Northwestern Switzerland (PH FHNW))*,
  Ashok Basawapatna *(SUNY Old Westbury)*
- **Pedagogical Content for Professors of Introductory Programming Courses** 429
  Yorah Bosse *(University of Sao Paulo (USP) & Federal University of Mato Grosso do Sul (UFMS))*,
  David Redmiles *(University of California, Irvine (UCI))*,
  Marco A. Gerosa *(Northern Arizona University (NAU) & University of Sao Paulo (USP))*

Session 7C: Programming

- **An Exploration of Novice Programmers' Comprehension of Conditionals in Imperative and Functional Programming** 436
  Claudio Mirolo *(University of Udine)*, Cruz Izu *(The University of Adelaide)*
- **Towards a Common Instrument for Measuring Prior Programming Knowledge** 443
  Rodrigo Silva Duran, Jan-Mikael Rybicki *(Aalto University)*, Arto Hellas *(University of Helsinki)*,
  Sanna Suoranta *(Aalto University)*
- **Copying Can Be Good: How Instructors Use Imitation in Teaching Programming** 450
  Carol Zander *(University of Washington, Bothell)*, Anna Eckerdal *(Uppsala University)*,
  Robert McCartney *(University of Connecticut)*, Jan Erik Moström *(Umea University)*,
  Kate Sanders *(Rhode Island College)*, Lynda Thomas *(Aberystwyth University)*

Session 7D: Software Architecture and Algorithms

- **Applying Case-Based Learning for a Postgraduate Software Architecture Course** 457
  Eng Lieh Ouh *(Singapore Management University)*, Yunghans Irawan *(National University of Singapore)*
- **Students' Misconceptions of Optimization Algorithms** 464
  J. Ángel Velázquez-Iturbide *(Universidad Rey Juan Carlos)*
- **AlgoBOWL: A Competition-Based Group Project for Algorithms Courses** 471
  Dinesh P. Mehta, Jack Rosenthal *(Colorado School of Mines)*

Session 8A: School

- **The Effectiveness of Creating Localized Content for Middle School Computing Curriculum** 478
  Huda Gedawy, Saquib Razak, Hanan Alshikhabobakr *(Carnegie Mellon University Qatar)*
- **Using Action Research to Distill Research-Based Segments of Pedagogical Content Knowledge of K-12 Computer Science Teachers** 485
  Ofra Brandes, Michal Armoni *(Weizmann Institute of Science)*
- **A Systems Change Approach to CS Education: Creating Rubrics for School System Implementation** 492
  Leigh Ann DeLyser, Lauren Wright *(CSforALL)*

Session 8B: Operating Systems and Security

- **Effect of Native Language on Student Learning and Classroom Interaction in an Operating Systems Course** 499
  Adalbert Gerald Soosai Raj, Eda Zhang *(University of Wisconsin-Madison)*,
  Saswati Mukherjee *(College of Engineering Guindy, Anna University)*,
  Jim Williams, Richard Halverson, Jignesh M. Patel *(University of Wisconsin-Madison)*
- **Using Automated Prompts for Student Reflection on Computer Security Concepts** 506
  Hui Chen *(Brooklyn College of the City University of New York)*,
  Agnieszka Ciborowska, Kostadin Damevski *(Virginia Commonwealth University)*
- **Teaching Integer Security Using Simple Visualizations** 513
  James Walker, Man Wang *(Michigan Technological University)*, Steven Carr *(Western Michigan University)*,
  Jean Mayo, Ching-Kuang Shene *(Michigan Technological University)*

Session 8C: Learning Environments

- **The Impact of Adding Textual Explanations to Next-step Hints in a Novice Programming Environment** 520
  Samiha Marwan, Nicholas Lytle *(North Carolina State University)*, Joseph Jay Williams *(University of Toronto)*,
  Thomas Price *(North Carolina State University)*
- **Using Social Annotations to Augment the Learning Space and Learner Experience** 527
  Shaveen Singh, Bernd Meyer *(Monash University)*
- **RepoBee: Developing Tool Support for Courses using Git/GitHub** 534
  Simon Larsén, Richard Glassey *(KTH: Royal Institute of Technology)*

Session 8D: Evaluation and Analytics

- **Evaluating Instructors' Classification of Programming Exercises Using the Revised Bloom's Taxonomy** 541
  Susana Masapanta-Carrión *(Pontificia Universidad Católica del Ecuador)*,
  J. Ángel Velázquez-Iturbide *(Universidad Rey Juan Carlos)*
- **Design and Pilot Testing of Subgoal Labeled Worked Examples for Five Core Concepts in CS1** 548
  Lauren E. Margulieux *(Georgia State University)*, Briana B. Morrison *(University of Nebraska Omaha)*, Adrienne Decker *(University at Buffalo)*
- **Syntax-based Improvements to Plagiarism Detectors and their Evaluations** 555
  Lawton Nichols *(University of California, Santa Barbara)*, Kyle Dewey *(California State University Northridge)*,
  Mehmet Emre, Sitao Chen, Ben Hardekopf *(University of California, Santa Barbara)*

Author Index 562

ITiCSE 2019 Conference Organization

Conference Chairs:	Bruce Scharlau *(University of Aberdeen, UK)* Roger McDermott *(Robert Gordon University, UK)*
Programme Chairs:	Arnold Pears *(KTH Royal Institute of Technology, Sweden)* Mihaela Sabin *(University of New Hampshire, USA)*
Treasurer/Registrar:	Bruce Scharlau *(University of Aberdeen, UK)* Julie Dixon *(University of Aberdeen, UK)*
Working Group Chairs:	Guido Rößling *(Technische Universität Darmstadt, Germany)* Michail Giannakos *(Norwegian University of Science and Technology, Norway)*
Database Coordinator:	Janet Carter *(University of Kent, UK)* Simon *(University of Newcastle, Australia)*
Web Page Coordinator:	Dennis Bouvier *(Southern Illinois University Edwardsville, USA)*
Tips, Techniques & Courseware:	Jane Sinclair *(University of Warwick)*
Posters and Panels:	Bedour Alshaigy *(Oxford Brookes University, UK)*
Doctoral Consortium:	Mark Zarb *(Robert Gordon University, UK)* Angela Siegel *(Dalhousie University, Canada)*
Student Coordinator:	David Corsar *(Robert Gordon University, UK)*
Proceedings:	Stan Kurkovsky *(Central Connecticut State University, USA)* Jim Paterson *(Glasgow Caledonian University, UK)*
Event Organisation and Evaluations:	Julie Dixon *(University of Aberdeen, UK)*

Associate Program Chairs:

Michal Armoni *(Weizmann Institute of Science, Israel)*
Brett Becker *(University College Dublin, Ireland)*
Bo Brinkman *(Google, Inc, USA)*
Kevin Buffardi *(California State University – Chico, USA)*
Sridhar Chimalakonda *(Indian Institute of Technology Tirupati, India)*
James Davenport *(University of Bath, United Kingdom)*
Nick Falkner *(The University of Adelaide, Australia)*
Cruz Izu *(The University of Adelaide, Australia)*
Meena Jha *(Central Queensland University, Australia)*
Carsten Kleiner *(University of Applied Sciences & Arts Hannover, Germany)*
Daniel Krutz *(Rochester Institute of Technology, USA)*
David Levine *(St Bonaventure University, USA)*
Violetta Lonati *(Università degli Studi di Milano, Italy)*
Andrew Luxton-Reilly *(University of Auckland, New Zealand)*
Larry Merkle *(Air Force Institute of Technology, USA)*
Gabriela Moise *(PG University of Ploiesti, Romania)*
Mattia Monga *(Università degli Studi di Milano, Italy)*
Christopher Moretti *(Princeton University, USA)*
James Paterson *(Glasgow Caledonian University, United Kingdom)*
Keith Quille *(Technological University Dublin, Ireland)*
Saquib Razak *(Carnegie Mellon University, Qatar)*
Guido Rößling *(Technische Universität Darmstadt, Germany)*
Claudia Szabo *(The University of Adelaide, Australia)*
Cynthia Taylor *(Oberlin College, USA)*
Troy Vasiga *(University of Waterloo, Canada)*

Reviewers: Ashish Aggarwal *(University of Florida, USA)*
Marzieh Ahmadzadeh *(University of Toronto, Scarborough, Canada)*
Vangel Ajanovski *(Ss Cyril and Methodius University, Macedonia)*
Ibrahim Al-Bluwi *(Princeton University, USA)*
Meghan Allen *(University of British Columbia, Canada)*
Huda Alrashidi *(University of Warwick, UK)*
Eliane Cristina Araujo *(SPLAB/UFCG, Brazil)*
John Barr *(Ithaca College, USA)*
João Paulo Barros *(Instituto Politecnico de Beja, Portugal)*
Lina Battestilli *(North Carolina State University, USA)*
Leland Beck *(San Diego State University, USA)*
Marjahan Begum *(Copenhagen Business School, Denmark)*
Marta Beltrán Pardo *(Universidad Rey Juan Carlos, Spain)*
Moti Ben-Ari *(Weizmann Institute of Science, Israel)*
Luciana Benotti *(Universidad Nacional de Cordoba, Argentina)*
Marc Berges *(Technical University of Munich, Germany)*
Bradley Beth *(The University of Texas at Austin, USA)*
William Billingsley *(University of New England, Australia)*
Andreas Bollin *(University of Klagenfurt, Austria)*
João Marcelo Borovina Josko *(Federal University of ABC, Brazil)*
Dennis Bouvier *(Southern Illinois University Edwardsville, USA)*
David Brown *(Tennessee Technological University, USA)*
Robert Buchmann *(Babeș-Bolyai University of Cluj Napoca, Romania)*
David Bunde *(Knox College, USA)*
Paul Cao *(University of California – San Diego, USA)*
Lillian Cassel *(Villanova University, USA)*
Francisco Enrique Vicente Castro *(Worcester Polytechnic Institute, USA)*
Veronica Catete *(North Carolina State University, USA)*
Thea Charles *(Siegel Family Endowment, USA)*
Jacqui Chetty *(University of Kent, UK)*
Donald Chinn *(University of Washington Tacoma, USA)*
Vanea Chiprianov *(University of Pau & Pays Adour, France)*
Stephen Cooper *(University of Nebraska Lincoln, USA)*
Michelle Craig *(University of Toronto, Canada)*
Quintin Cutts *(University of Glasgow, UK)*
Marian Daun *(University of Duisburg-Essen, Germany)*
Renzo Davoli *(University of Bologna, Italy)*
Giuseppe De Ruvo *(Independent, Italy)*
Josh Dehlinger *(Towson University, USA)*
Leigh Ann DeLyser *(CSNYC, USA)*
Mario Di Francesco *(Aalto University, Finland)*
Zachary Dodds *(Harvey Mudd College, USA)*
Toby Dragon *(Ithaca College, USA)*
Dimitris Dranidis *(University of Sheffield, Greece)*
Bob Edmison *(Virginia Tech, USA)*
Stephen H Edwards *(Virginia Tech, USA)*

Matthias Ehlenz *(RWTH Aachen University, Germany)*
Yasmine El-Glaly *(Rochester Institute of Technology, USA)*
Kiran Eranki *(Indian Institute of Technology, Bombay, India)*
Barry Fagin *(US Air Force Academy, USA)*
Mohammed Farghally *(Assiut University, Egypt)*
Pedro Guillermo Feijóo García *(Universidad El Bosque, Colombia, and University of Florida, U*
Alan Fekete *(University of Sydney, Australia)*
Maria Lydia Fioravanti *(University of São Paulo, Brazil)*
Gene Fisher *(Cal Poly University, USA)*
Gordon Fraser *(University of Passau, Germany)*
Adam Gaweda *(NC State University, USA)*
Katharina Geldreich *(Technische Universität München, Germany)*
Paul Gestwicki *(Ball State University, USA)*
Ana-Maria Ghiran *(Babeș-Bolyai University of Cluj Napoca, Romania)*
Nasser Giacaman *(University of Auckland, New Zealand)*
Richard Glassey *(KTH: Royal Institute of Technology, Sweden)*
Jean Goulet *(Université de Sherbrooke, Canada)*
Marco Aurélio Graciotto Silva *(Universidade Tecnológica Federal do Paraná, Brazil)*
Rebecca Grasser *(Lakeland Community College, USA)*
Francisco J Gutierrez *(University of Chile, Chile)*
Juan Manuel Gutiérrez Cárdenas *(Universidad de Lima, Perú)*
Margaret Hamilton *(RMIT University, Australia)*
Brian Harrington *(University of Toronto Scarborough, Canada)*
Matthias Hauswirth *(University of Lugano, Switzerland)*
Cecily Heiner *(Southern Utah University, USA)*
Arto Hellas *(University of Helsinki, Finland)*
Cay Horstmann *(San José State University, USA)*
David Hovemeyer *(York College of Pennsylvania, USA)*
Janet Hughes *(The Open University, UK)*
Harvey Hyman *(USF, USA)*
Jana Jackova *(Matej Bel University, Slovakia)*
Chris Johnson *(University of Wisconsin, Eau Claire, USA)*
Colin Johnson *(University of Kent, UK)*
Viggo Kann *(Royal Institute of Technology, Sweden)*
Beth Katz *(Millersville University, USA)*
Aaron Keen *(Cal Poly University, USA)*
Petros Kefalas *(University of Sheffield, Greece)*
Bill Kerney *(Clovis Community College, USA)*
Hieke Keuning *(Windesheim University of Applied Sciences, The Netherlands)*
Hassan Khosravi *(University of Queensland, Australia)*
Michael Kirkpatrick *(James Madison University, USA)*
Antti Knutas *(Lappeenranta University of Technology, Finland)*
Eileen Kraemer *(Clemson University, USA)*
Viraj Kumar *(Indian Institute of Science, India)*
Bastian Küppers *(RWTH Aachen University, Germany)*
Stan Kurkovsky *(Central Connecticut State University, USA)*

Zachary Kurmas *(Grand Valley State University, USA)*
Angelo Kyrilov *(University of California, Merced, USA)*
Lisa Lacher *(University of Houston-Clear Lake, USA)*
Dieter Landes *(Hochschule Coburg, Germany)*
Joan Langdon *(Bowie State University, USA)*
David Largent *(Ball State University, USA)*
Chi-Un Lei *(University of Hong Kong, Hong Kong)*
Juho Leinonen *(University of Helsinki, Finland)*
Michael Lodi *(Università di Bologna, Italy)*
Matija Lokar *(University of Ljubljana, Slovenia)*
Nicholas Lytle *(North Carolina State University, USA)*
Manuel Maarek *(Heriot-Watt University, UK)*
Joseph Maguire *(University of Glasgow, UK)*
Francesco Maiorana *(University of Catania, Italy)*
Chao Mbogo *(Kenya Methodist University, Kenya)*
Lester I McCann *(The University of Arizona, USA)*
Sean McCulloch *(Ohio Wesleyan University, USA)*
Chris McDonald *(University of Western Australia, Australia)*
Charlie McDowell *(University of California Santa Cruz, USA)*
António José Mendes *(University of Coimbra, Portugal)*
Joe Miró Julià *(Universitat de les Illes Balears, Spain)*
Shitanshu Mishra *(Indian Institute of Technology Bombay, India)*
Marcello Missiroli *(University of Bologna, Italy)*
Karina Mochetti *(UFF, Brazil)*
Srikanth Mudigonda *(Saint Louis University, USA)*
Brandon D Myers *(University of Iowa, USA)*
Emma Norling *(The University of Sheffield, UK)*
Ola Oluwakemi *(University of British Columbia, Canada)*
Linda Ott *(Michigan Technological University, USA)*
Eng Lieh Ouh *(Singapore Management University, Singapore)*
Diana Pérez Marin *(Universidad Rey Juan Carlos, Spain)*
Andrew Petersen *(University of Toronto, Canada)*
Irene Polycarpou *(University of Central Lancashire Cyprus, Cyprus)*
Leo Porter *(UC San Diego, USA)*
Prajish Prasad *(Indian Institute of Technology Bombay, India)*
Thomas Price *(North Carolina State University, USA)*
Yizhou Qian *(Purdue University, USA)*
Jean-Baptiste Raclet *(IRIT, France)*
Samuel Rebelsky *(Grinnell College, USA)*
Chuck Riedesel *(University of Nebraska – Lincoln, USA)*
Adrián Riesco *(Universidad Complutense de Madrid, Spain)*
Emma Riese *(KTH Royal Institute of Technology, Sweden)*
Susan Rodger *(Duke University, USA)*
Rubén Rafael Rubio Cuéllar *(Universidad Complutense de Madrid, Spain)*
Daniel Russo *(Università di Bologna, Italy)*
André Santos *(ISCTE – Instituto Universitário de Lisboa, Portugal)*

Stephanie Elzer Schwartz *(Millersville University, USA)*
Yvonne Sedelmaier *(Hochschule Coburg, Germany)*
Camelia Serban *(Babeș-Bolyai University, Romania)*
Cliff Shaffer *(Virginia Tech, USA)*
Mark Sherriff *(University of Virginia, USA)*
Kalpathi Subramanian *(The University of N Carolina at Charlotte, USA)*
Anya Tafliovich *(University of Toronto Scarborough, Canada)*
Toni Taipalus *(University of Jyväskylä, Finland)*
Burcin Tamer *(Computing Research Association, USA)*
Sheng Tan *(Florida State University, USA)*
Terry Tang *(Rice University, Facebook Inc., USA)*
Neena Thota *(UMass Amherst, USA)*
Daniel Toll *(Linnaeus University, Sweden)*
Ian Utting *(University of Kent, UK)*
Tullio Vardanega *(University of Padua, Italy)*
J Ángel Velázquez Iturbide *(Universidad Rey Juan Carlos, Spain)*
Andreea Vescan *(Babeș-Bolyai University, Romania)*
Giovanni Vincenti *(Baltimore University, USA)*
David Voorhees *(Le Moyne College, USA)*
Sally Wahba *(Clemson University, USA)*
Henry Walker *(Grinnell College, USA)*
Charles Wallace *(Michigan Technological University, USA)*
Patrick Wang *(Institut Supérieur d'Electronique de Paris, France)*
Monica Ward *(Dublin City University, Ireland)*
Joshua Levi Weese *(Kansas State University, USA)*
Victor Winter *(University of Nebraska at Omaha, USA)*
Chris Wong *(University of Technology, Sydney, Australia)*
Arthur Yanushka *(Christian Brothers University, USA)*
Chen-Hsiang (Jones) Yu *(Wentworth Institute of Technology, USA)*
Timothy Yuen *(University of Texas at San Antonio, USA)*
Carol Zander *(University of Washington Bothell, USA)*

ITiCSE 2019 Sponsors and Supporters

Designing for a Connected World

Kate Stone
Novalia Ltd.
kate.stone@novalia.co.uk

ABSTRACT

The march of the digital frontline seems to have relentlessly vaporised so much of what is around us and sent it to the cloud. With our heads now so often stuck in those clouds we seem to be losing touch of what is physically around us; including each other. What if we could add a digital soul to everyday objects and design, prototype and manufacture physical products almost as quickly as digital experiences? My work is a journey towards attempting to let some of this happen.

CCS CONCEPTS

• **Human-centered computing**;

KEYWORDS

Internet of things, print, capacitive touch, conductive ink, disappearing technology, magical

ACM Reference Format:

Kate Stone. 2019. Designing for a Connected World. In *Innovation and Technology in Computer Science Education (ITiCSE '19), July 15–17, 2019, Aberdeen, Scotland Uk.* ACM, New York, NY, USA, 1 page. https://doi.org/10.1145/3304221.3319795

BIOGRAPHY

Kate has spent the last decade on a journey of discovery from the world of science to creative design. Kate and her team at Novalia have developed a new technology platform with which they create products that are a delightful blend of being magical, old fashioned and futuristic. Kate believes the future will look more like the past than the present due to our natural mix of nostalgia and futuristic stargazing. Over the last few years with her team she has created experiences for large brands as part of advertising campaigns, working with Pizza Hut, McDonalds, Bud Light, Hersheys and IKEA. They are presently working on a children's toy called 'Touchscape' that is a board game like surface that connects to Amazon's Alexa.

Kate is from the UK however now lives in Woodstock, New York and has a degree in electronics from Salford University and PhD in physics from Cambridge University but believes the most useful things she learnt in life were discovered during four years of travel through Australia and Asia and in particular working on a sheep farm for two years in the Australian outback.

Kate has spoken at TED twice and both talks can be found online on TED.com.

ITiCSE '19, July 15–17, 2019, Aberdeen, Scotland UK

ACM ISBN 978-1-4503-6301-3/19/07.
https://doi.org/10.1145/3304221.3319795

Identity and Belonging for Graduate Apprenticeships in Computing*

The experience of first cohort degree apprentices in Scotland

Ella Taylor-Smith†
School of Computing
Edinburgh Napier University
Edinburgh, Scotland, UK
e.taylor-smith@napier.ac.uk

Sally Smith†
School of Computing
Edinburgh Napier University
Edinburgh, Scotland, UK
s.smith@napier.ac.uk

Colin Smith†
School of Computing
Edinburgh Napier University
Edinburgh, Scotland, UK
cf.smith@napier.ac.uk

ABSTRACT

In September 2017, our university's first graduate apprentices began degrees in Software Development, Cybersecurity, and Information Technology Management for Business. This study explores how apprentices experience their association with the university and identities as students, but also employees. In Scotland, Graduate Apprenticeships (GAs) are undergraduate degrees in which the students are in full-time employment, while completing degree modules over four years, as for a traditional full-time degree. The curriculum follows a skills framework designed by employers so that graduates have the professional and technical attributes required by the industry. The degrees parallel Degree Apprenticeships in England, though there are national differences in implementation.

Themes of identity and belonging are central to current investigations of the experience of STEM students, especially computing students, as fewer students choose STEM courses, and many transfer out of their subjects or do not complete their degrees. The research hypothesis is that the apprentices' employment will provide a strong IT professional identity supports their progress at university.

Semi-structured interviews with apprentices in the first computing cohorts explored their situated perspectives. Responses were identified which concerned the apprentices' identity as students or employees, including themes around belonging. Thematic analysis of these responses revealed that apprentices defined themselves in opposition to traditional student identities and did draw strength from their identity as employees. They experienced belonging specifically within their GA cohort—the first of its kind in the university. A better understanding of identity and belonging can be used by universities to address the challenges of retention.

* Identity and belonging for Graduate Apprenticeships in Computing

ITiCSE '19, July 15–17, 2019, Aberdeen, Scotland UK

ACM ISBN 978-1-4503-6301-3/19/07...$15.00 https://doi.org/10.1145/3304221.3319753

CCS CONCEPTS

• Social and professional topics → Computing education

KEYWORDS

Graduate apprenticeship, degree apprenticeship, work-based learning, identity, belonging.

ACM Reference format:

Ella Taylor-Smith, Sally Smith, Colin Smith. 2019. Identity and belonging for Graduate Apprenticeships in Computing: The experience of first cohort degree apprentices in Scotland. In *Proc. of the 24th Annual Conf. on Innovation & Technology in Computer Science Education (ITiCSE'19). ACM, NY, NY, USA, 7 pages.* https://doi.org/10.1145/3304221.3319753

1 Introduction

Graduate and degree apprenticeships in computing provide new opportunities for Higher Education Institutions (HEIs) to implement degrees that are aligned to contemporary industry and the digital needs of the public sector, leading to appropriately-skilled and experienced graduates. The degrees can also provide opportunities to widen access and diversify the student population, as apprentices do not need to take on student debt. As the apprentices are working in the industry, they are likely to have conceptualisations of computing and IT professions that, situated in their own experience, are grounded and more nuanced than those of a first year on-campus student. This may be helpful in their studies, in terms of personal and subject-specific engagement.

Research in European and North American countries indicates a shortfall of young people intending to become scientists, and engagement problems for students studying STEM subjects [16]. In computing, this is reflected in retention problems. Data about UK students, for example, records that 10.5% of undergraduates who started computing degrees in 2015/16 left higher education without achieving any awards, compared to 6.4% across all subjects [10]. Biggers, Brauer, and Yilmaz [1] highlight the parallel issue of students who stay in higher education, but transfer out of Computer Science majors. Various studies have hypothesised that these retention problems have their roots in students' conceptions of computing, especially in narrow predictions of the activities they will encounter while studying computing and in future careers [1, 16, 19, 20]. In the early years of their degrees, students expect a focus on programming, which is creative and rewarding for some, but lacking in human contact and meaning for others [1, 16, 19]. This study investigates the experience of first year graduate apprentices [GAs], studying computing subjects, in Scotland. As full-time employees, these GAs have situated experience of computing and IT in the workplace. They may also have established IT-identities as IT-admin, helpdesk, QA testers, or even developers. The research hypothesis is that *the apprentices' employment status will lead to the construction of a salient IT-professional identity that supports their progress at university.* The GAs' experiences and perceptions are gathered through narrative interviews, which are analysed using themes of identity and belonging in order to understand the relationships between the individual contexts of the apprentices and their experiences of studying on these innovative degrees.

2 Graduate Apprenticeships in Scotland

The degree apprenticeship agenda in the UK aims to improve the match between graduates' skills and employers' needs, by adapting and extending apprenticeship schemes into higher education [17]. The Richard Review [23] recognised the favourable public opinion of apprenticeships ("people react warmly", p3) and suggested ways to adapt the concept to contemporary needs. Employers would have a central role in designing the new apprenticeships through creating the standards (lists of required competencies) that would guide content and assessment in each subject [11, 12]. The apprenticeships would be funded through the new apprenticeship levy: all large employers have been liable for 0.5% of their salary costs, from April 2017" [21].

In Scotland, these higher-level apprenticeships are called Graduate Apprenticeships and the process is administered by Skills Development Scotland (SDS), an executive public body of the Scottish Government. SDS brings employers together to develop the frameworks that define graduate apprenticeships, currently in twelve, mostly STEM, areas [24]. HEIs propose implementations for each degree and bid for places, responding to SDS tenders. Successful HEIs promote their courses to employers and potential apprentices. Interested employers either identify potential apprentices in their staff or recruit people directly into the GA role and degree. In this way, the Graduate Apprenticeships are designed and implemented by a partnership of SDS, employers, and HEIs. As the partnership is embodied in the apprentices [4], their experiences and perspectives are of key value in examining the implementation of the degrees, especially efforts to identify what is working well or any emerging problems, and to suggest areas for improvement. The apprentices' perspectives can also reveal links between their individual contexts and their progress with the course. As apprentices are employed in various roles by diverse employers (from local start-ups to international companies to the public sector), they bring different experiences, opportunities, and challenges to their studies, especially work-based learning elements.

These new partnerships to create appropriately-skilled graduates are particularly important in computing, where there is a high demand for digitally-skilled employees, while, paradoxically, the transition from university study into graduate employment has seemed to be more challenging than for other subjects [25]. While more recent graduate destination data [9] shows UK IT graduate unemployment to be still relatively high, six months after graduation, at 9.2%, the HESA data also shows that few IT graduates are taking on non-professional (stop-gap) roles, such as hospitality or retail, and suggests that they hold out for the right professional role [8, 9]. The Shadbolt Review [25] noted the importance of work experience in bridging the gap between study and professional employment; Graduate Apprenticeships extend work experience into credit-bearing work-based learning, unambiguously defining the place of employment as a place of learning. GA degrees need to be carefully designed to enable apprentices to apply their developing skills and knowledge in their workplace, to allow them to master the learning outcomes outlined in the degree frameworks. The university also facilitates workshops for employer-mentors to support them in determining the context and scope of work-based learning.

As apprentices are salaried employees and their fees are paid, the scheme also has the potential to widen participation in higher education, though this may require specific strategies from employers as recruiters [e.g., see 18, 28, 29]. A deep exploration of the challenges and potential impacts of these degrees is essential if the scheme is to be successfully scaled up. This paper reports one such research implementation—interviews with first year graduate apprentices. The focus here is data concerning the apprentices' identities as employees and students, including where they experienced a sense of belonging—at university or at work.

3 Belonging and identity

Our university implements Graduate Apprenticeship degrees through teaching apprentices on campus one day per week (in the first two years), running modules through three trimesters (including the summer). On-campus learning provides important elements of the traditional university experience, including access to learning facilities, such as the computing labs and the library, and some shared sessions with on-campus students. Physical co-presence can help to develop the cohort as a learning community, including face-to-face relationships with staff [7, 30]. Pizza lunches are provided for apprentices and staff to further this process and to help monitor student experience. With dual roles as student and employee, this study set out to explore self-identification and sense of belonging in this new apprenticeship context.

Identity is considered to comprise a sense of self in relation to the multiple roles people hold, together with notions of value and meaning attached to such roles [26, 30]. For this study, the role of student and employee are significant. Identity within roles influences social interactions and thus impacts on relationships and behaviour: at university and in the workplace. Formulating a new identity, or identity construction, is the result of social processes such as following role models, interacting with networks, and imagining (or acting) in a role [26]. Identity also affects a sense of belonging, where belonging is feeling at home, being respected, being welcomed [31], and a sense of connection [14]. Students' success and well-being at university depend on both academic and social factors, from the institution and the students, combined with the students' background and external influences [e.g., 15, 22]. Kahu and Nelson describe students' agency in terms of self-efficacy, emotion, belonging, and well-being [15]. For apprentices, these factors, especially self-efficacy and belonging, are likely to be influenced by both their employment contexts and their comparatively limited time on campus. The apprentice is the only stakeholder who can fully appreciate this: "Since there are at least two 'realities' involved (company and higher education institution) nobody except the student has a complete overview" [4, p.29].

Researchers have called for a greater understanding of identity construction among computing students [e.g. 1, 16, 19, 20], suggesting that undergraduate students' perceptions of the computing field may be misaligned to their personal identities and values. For example, Biggers, Brauer, and Yilmaz [1] are concerned with the social and academic integration of computing students. They compare students who leave a Computer Science (CS) major in a U.S. college, with those who stay, gathering their perspectives on the field and the course. They found that the leavers were frustrated by the lack of human interaction, perhaps because their courses were intensely programming-focused in the first year. Kinnunen et al. [16], studying undergraduate computing students in Finland, Sweden, and UK, suggest that students' perceptions of their current and future CS identities influence their propensity to enjoy or leave the subject. They noted a disparity between the students' expectations of the course (lots of programming) and their career aspirations (including managing their own companies). Enthusiastic students in both studies conceived of programming in terms of creating and problem solving.

This conceptualisation of computing/IT is elaborated more fully in Peters et al. [19, 20], where students' perceptions of coding and solving problems as creative and collaborative are understood in terms of *participation* as an essential attribute of learning and identity development, from Wenger's work on Communities of Practice [30]. For Wenger, negotiation of meaning is at the centre of identity development and this takes place through (ideally collaborative) participation and reification. Peters et al. identify this participation in computing students' narratives of creating through coding and collaborative problem-solving. They also find that computing students who do not experience this feel isolated in the human-computer dyad. These students foresee a future "hammering on the keyboard" [19, p. 7] and leave their computing course. Peters et al. suggest that their students' narrow concept of computing may reflect their rather homogenous CS student group and that education needs to support more advanced experiences of participation and richer ways of negotiating meaning. Apprenticeships would seem to be ideal contexts for this.

However, Graduate Apprenticeships present identity challenges for the apprentices, as they are regarded as having dual identities: employee and student. The apprenticeships are an intense combination of work and study, which is likely to challenge the apprentices [29], so it is vital for HEIs to understand their experience. Such insights are useful to HEIs who are currently planning or already running higher apprenticeships, as implementations need to be designed or adjusted to support this new type of student. This study explores the how the apprentices experience their dual identity. Does their work identity support or antagonise their student identity? Does their experience of IT in the workplace create a participatory IT-identity that supports and motivates the apprentices in their studies? To this end, we interviewed fifteen computing apprentices, halfway through their first year.

4 Methodology

The research aim of the interviews was to investigate the contexts of the apprentices: their backgrounds, their employment, their family lives, and their lived experience of being an apprentice. Semi-structured interviews were conducted with fifteen graduate apprentices studying Software Development, Cybersecurity, or Information Technology Management for Business, within the university's first cohort (of 26). The apprentices were encouraged to volunteer and all volunteers were interviewed. The interviews aimed to uncover the apprentices' backgrounds, especially their paths into IT and the Graduate Apprenticeship, as well as their experience of the degrees, once they had settled in. The approach reflected that of narrative interviews, which encourage interviewees to describe their lives as a series of events, thinking aloud about their trajectories [5, 13]. The narrative method was adapted to restrict interviews to an hour, given the pressure on the apprentices' time. The interview protocol focused on their experience of education and work, from school to the present, including their paths into working in IT. The apprentices were interviewed in their second or third trimester and asked about their experiences of the degree, in the contexts of their work-life and university study, including questions around identity and belonging. Of the fifteen interviewees, four were female; twelve were interviewed at their workplace and three at the university. Interviews were audio-recorded and transcribed. Following university ethics procedures, participants had been informed about the use of anonymised data from interviews and signed informed consent forms.

A dataset was created of transcript texts concerned with participants' experience of the apprenticeship, especially the integration between their studies and employment. This dataset was analysed using *thematic analysis*, following the processes described by Braun and Clarke [2]. Comments or narratives concerned with identity and/or belonging were identified by two researchers individually. Each researcher identified themes within these texts and coded the texts accordingly. Braun and Clark describe the identification of themes: "A theme captures something important about the data in relation to the research question, and represents some level of patterned response or meaning within the data set" [2]. The researchers resolved the themes, including hierarchical relationships between the themes, by discussion. This hierarchical thematic coding enabled related ideas to be surfaced across the interview transcripts and meaningfully grouped together providing a summary of the responses of the participants, including areas where their experiences diverged. The resulting *map* of the apprentices' contexts and experiences highlights the strengths and challenges of the current implementation for this cohort.

5 Findings

5.1 Overview

Most of the interviewees talked about the links between what they were studying at university and what they did at work or the wider business or future needs of their organisations. However, this was one factor among many contributing to a graduate apprentice identity that supported their university study. There were many strong connections between their work identity and student identity and they specifically distinguished themselves from full-time students [Figure 1].

All the quotations have been lightly edited to remove grace phrases and repetition. Gender-neutral pronouns are used below to protect the students' anonymity. While the interactions between gender identities and work or student identities are important in this context, the small sample size, including four women, means that we cannot discuss gendered experiences here without comprising the participants' anonymity. The prevalence of themes in the interview texts is indicated by phrases such as "most of the participants" or "some interviewees", following the conventions for thematic analysis [2, p83] and providing some indication of the generality of experience among the participants, without providing specific percentages, which could be misleading.

5.2 Contextualising computing

Most of the participants experienced a positive connection between what they did at work and what they learned at university: "Like, everything we do in uni, I can relate back to my work. And stuff that we do at work, I can relate to uni as well. So it's good that way." For some, university study helped them to understand workplace processes: "[In class] I'll be thinking 'Well, we use that'' and when he's explaining it, I can see why we do certain things here that way." And "I then knew that's how you have your office system; that's our main system; this is what, all the things it can do. I think that was sort of a turning point. I realised what I was learning was actually helpful in here."

Some interviewees specifically noted the importance of this connection with their work, in contrast to on-campus degrees: "I'll learn stuff in uni and I'll come back and I'll say 'That's what that is' and things like that. So it's great to be able to sort of put the two together. I think that's more beneficial than sitting in a lecture all day and just having notes and stuff, but not actually having that sort of real world experience of it." One interviewee recognised how their interest in IT, developed at work, supported their study and how different this context was to starting a computing degree previously, on leaving school: "I'm more focused and doing quite well on the degree so far, I think...It's because it's something I'm wholly interested in and involved in on a day-to-day basis at work. But back then, it was: choosing computing because I thought it was the right thing to do, not because I wanted to specifically do it."

However, two interviewees, who were self-taught developers, had narrower conceptions of their work, which limited the potential for links with university. One was open to the relevance of learning Human-Computer Interaction and systems design, but noted "We don't get to decide how things are going to be started, how things are designed here." Another, for various reasons, experienced a total disconnect between their work and study, for example: "At this level or at this point, what we're learning currently here is not like directly applicable to my workplace. Because we're not going to learn about web development, especially not a specific area of web development that we do."

Several interviewees interacted with their work colleagues around their university coursework. Some inspired conversations between their workplace's developers about what they were studying at university. Some received practical help, for example colleagues helped them to understand a study topic by providing local examples: "Since starting, I've actually learnt other stuff as well from other members of the team. So, the software development module, I got to speak to [our Java developer] and he was helping me out...and explaining what things were in a work context, rather than just out of books and things like that. It's been great." This could involve help to get to grips with programming and even strengthen relationships in the workplace: "So, [my work colleague], one night we were here until 7 o'clock, just pinpointing everything that I was struggling with...And just getting that work-based knowledge of it helped apply what I was learning."

The link between work and study ran both ways and one interviewee described providing a real-world example of good system design in response to a lecturer's question. The apprentice worked as a developer in the public sector and had created a system based on in-situ observations of a daily problem: "In the lecture, somebody was talking about system design.. and I explained one of the things that we'd done...it's basically just sitting down watching what the problem was, coming up with solutions, agreeing it, doing test pilots, and then we went for it. And now they're doing it and we're nearly at a *million* requests, in four years." This example was provided in a large lecture, attended by both on-campus students and GAs, demonstrating how the lecturers are beginning to benefit from teaching the GA cohorts.

Many of the interviewees seemed to have entered IT careers tangentially, rather than fulfilling long-established ambitions, and a few spoke about finding their work rewardingly people-centric: "Certainly, the roles we're in just now, communicating with other teams and working closely with other teams, I would say is a big part of the job, and I think that's why I liked it the most. It's like building relationships with people, and working closely with other people." Several had started on-campus computing degrees, but not completed them. They valued this new opportunity to study, while engaged in practical, rewarding, and collaborative work, rather than the potentially isolating experience of leaving home and studying computing: "You're supposed to be getting your uni experience, but software engineering– if you want to sit and study and everything, it's not a very social activity to sit in your room and code."

So, with one exception, the apprentices experienced a strong positive connection between what they did at work and what they studied at university. Their work also provided full, lived experiences of computing, including collaboration and (for those working in a helpdesk role) solving people's IT problems. How did this influence their GA identities, as both students and employees?

5.3 Graduate apprentices' identities

Figure 1 summarises the identities of the graduate apprentices as students: i.e., at university and when working on their coursework elsewhere. This "GAs at-uni" identity draws on the specific nature of the cohort, as they band together as a group and are nurtured by university staff (the upper circle within their at-uni identity). They also bring confidence, support and, as discussed above, applied subject knowledge from their work role (the lower circle in their at-uni identity). However, they specifically distinguish themselves (the blue water) from "normal", full-time, on-campus students, and this becomes part of their identity.

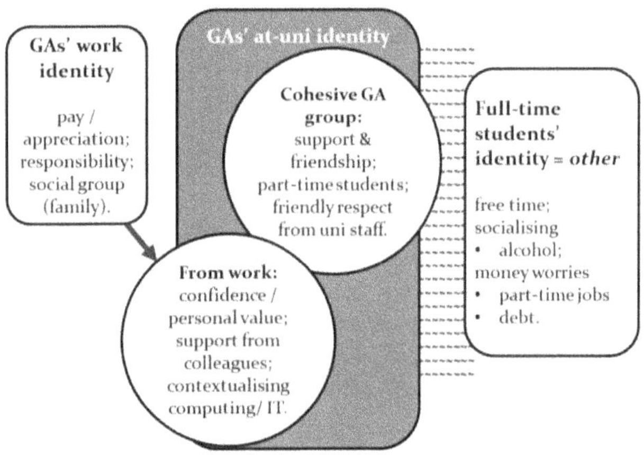

Figure 1: Graduate apprentices' identities (theme map)

Most of the interviewees conceived of themselves as employees, even when at university. Their employers paid their salary for their university day ("I get paid to do a degree") and their responsibilities continued through it: "I feel that weird disconnect, because you're still working and while you're at uni, your mind's still at work." While most of the interviewees had been in post with their employer prior to starting the Graduate Apprenticeship, two had been taken on specifically for this role and a few others had recently completed Modern Apprenticeships with their companies. (Modern Apprenticeships are shorter apprenticeships, primarily designed for young people). In this context, the nature of their identity as employees varied from people with established roles and expertise, even management responsibilities, to people new to their companies and in their first office job. One interviewee described their team as "a kind of larger family", while another called themself "so ingrained".

The apprentices conceptualised a traditional (full-time) student identity, which they did not share, with abundant unstructured time and alcohol-centred socialising. Several had started or completed traditional degrees and experienced this student identity: "I wasn't under any illusions that it was going to be like what a student life was before, because obviously people have jobs and it's not like we're going to be out boozing all the time." Some described themselves as part-time students. They also contrasted their financial status with traditional students' worries about money and debt. Interviewees recalled the experiences of relatives and friends doing traditional degrees: "having a part-time job and all that balance and moneys and loans and debts."

Although the apprentices defined themselves in contrast to the other students on campus, few expressed alienation. Rather, three factors supported their confidence at university. First, their job: they drew on their employee identity (status) as a strength. Some interviewees had established roles, skills, and responsibilities, which seemed to be important parts of their identity. Others were nearer the beginning of their IT careers and valued their employers' faith in them: "We'll pay your salary whilst you're out for that day, to get you trained up to come to work with us, because we feel like you deserve it and are capable of doing it." Several interviewees described work colleagues helping them with their university study, especially developers helping with programming challenges, as described above. Many interviewees described their managers as supportive, offering encouragement and practical support—even time and space to study if work downtime coincided with module deadlines.

Secondly, they experienced their cohort as a cohesive and supportive group. They shared their workplace experiences across organisations, helped each other, and enjoyed new friendships: "the people on the course generally, probably have made it easier, because you're like friends"; "If you're struggling, there's always somebody there to help you...that may know—will know something you don't know and vice versa."

Third, while there were some specific communication problems, interviewees also described the university staff as friendly and helpful, beyond their expectations. "I think what's been done well is the kind of pizza lunches, where we kind of get to actually talk to people, because it can be very difficult to have an actual chat about how things are going"; "I feel everybody's really nice, at the university. I think they're all—like you're all trying to help us." This raises questions about how these conditions will change over time, as the Graduate Apprenticeships become less novel and cohorts increase in size.

6 Outcomes, future work, and challenges

Instrumental outcomes of the first year included exceptional academic results and a 100% retention rate. In terms of this study, multiple identities as part-time students and employees were observed. The employee identity was most salient and impacted positively on their university study, through support from their employers and co-workers, as well as including a contextualised understanding of computing at the centre of their working worlds. Further, their employment provided motivation to study to fulfil their employers' expectations. Clearly, the GAs benefited from the integration between their study topics and work experience. They had a broad understanding of computing, including real-world goals and, in many cases, the importance of collaboration, whether developing in teams or using IT to support collaborative work. Given the 100% retention rate, is our hypothesis supported? *Does the apprentices' employment lead to the construction of a salient IT-professional identity that supports their progress at university?* Yes. However, their IT-identity is not their only support mechanism, as they have banded together as a group and support each other and are also specifically supported by university staff implementing this new degree. So, there are important, additional factors to their IT-identity in their progress through their first year.

Their student identity was described in terms of otherness, difference from perceived on-campus student behaviour and values. This could signal the emergence of a new *professional* identity on the part of the Graduate Apprentice; whereby a combination of technical skills, capabilities, status and roles merge with work and life experiences into a "coherent image of self" [3]. A professional identity that values skills acquisition and application within a workplace context would certainly align with the aims of apprenticeship degrees. Fuller and Unwin [7] describe how even highly skilled knowledge workers may go on "an extensive learning journey" [p.218] and suggest that apprenticeships are stronger and richer learning environments when organisations support this journey [6]. However, the apprentices' conceptualisation of the school's on-campus students tends towards caricature, rather than representation, neglecting the proportions of our students that are older (e.g. 23% over 25) and the prevalence of work experience [27].

Belonging was expressed in two ways. The first, and strongest, sense of belonging to emerge from the narratives was that of belonging to the cohort of apprentices. A strong bond had been established between apprentices through shared but unique experience. The apprentices experienced their cohort as a locus for support, guidance, and light relief, with the underlying recognition that they were part of something new, with somewhat uncertain boundaries and expectations. The second was a sense of belonging to the university, demonstrated, for example, in recognising the respect shown by university tutors.

This consideration of identity and belonging will inform the course team's review of the way the apprenticeship course is structured and delivered, including implementation plans for later years. The findings raise questions for the team: if student identity is the less salient identity, what will happen as the university study course components reduce in favour of the work-based learning component? Will the university degree award begin to seem less valuable to the apprentices than at the beginning? If the work-identity is the main source of the apprentices' strength, is it vulnerable to changes in the workplace? Furthermore, the sense of belonging facilitated by the cohesion of the apprentices as a cohort may be challenged when work-based learning diverges through differing employment contexts, with consequently fewer opportunities to relate and share, even potential for jealousy. Future work will examine these tentative predications of experiences, through research with apprentices as they continue their degrees. This research will be carefully planned to respect the time of the apprentices, both as employees and time-pressured students. Employers will also be involved in the research programme, both to gather their perspectives and to ensure that they understand how this fits with the ongoing development of the Graduate Apprenticeship scheme.

7 Impact

Apprenticeships represent a new and significant investment in skills, funded through the Apprenticeship Levy. The stakes are high for these apprenticeships to fill the skills gaps, as articulated earlier. As increasing numbers of universities start to implement higher apprenticeships, they share a desire for apprentices to successfully achieve their degrees and add value to their employing organisations. Increasing awareness of apprentices' lived experiences, through exploring their self-identification and the roots of their sense of belonging, can usefully influence the approaches universities take to supporting these new learners. The National Student Survey (funded by the UK government) now includes a question relating to being part of a community of students and academic staff, which is likely to encourage universities to develop their understanding of notions of belonging, especially through the perceptions of diverse types of students. However, given the importance of students' conceptualisations of computing and their growing IT-identities to their progress through computing degrees, researchers need to continue to explore identity and belonging at a school or subject level in computing.

The insights from this study of apprentices, revealing some of the factors influencing their sense of belonging as students and its impact on their studies, are also likely to be relevant for certain groups of on-campus students. Universities interested in the sense of community amongst their students can benefit from exploring the perspectives of students on diverse learner journeys. Computing departments in particular can usefully find ways to strengthen and deepen their students' conceptualisation of computing and their personal and collaborative IT-identities.

ACKNOWLEDGMENTS

The first Graduate Apprenticeships were funded by Skills Development Scotland and European Social Fund.

REFERENCES

[1] Maureen Biggers, Anne Brauer, and Tuba Yilmaz. 2008. Student Perceptions of Computer Science: A Retention Study Comparing Graduating Seniors with CS Leavers. *ACM SIGCSE Bulletin*, ACM 40, 1, 402–406.

[2] Virginia Braun and Victoria Clarke. 2006. Using thematic analysis in psychology. *Qualitative Research in Psychology* 3, 2, 77–101.

[3] Toni Cascio and Janice Gasker, 2001. Everyone has a shining side: Computer-mediated mentoring in social work education. *Journal of Social Work Education* 37, 2, 283-293.

[4] CWIHE, 2016. *EU-Coop – Cooperative And Work Integrated Higher Education: A Handbook for Implementing Co-Op Education Model.* CWIHE. Retrieved 24 January 2019 from https://cwihe.com/multimedia/documentation/

[5] Sebastian Dziallas and Sally Fincher, 2016. Aspects of Graduateness in Computing Students' Narratives. In *Proceedings of the 2016 ACM Conference on International Computing Education Research* (ICER '16). ACM. DOI: http://dx.doi.org/10.1145/2960310.2960317.

[6] Alison Fuller and Lorna Unwin, 2003. Learning as Apprentices in the Contemporary UK Workplace: creating and managing

expansive and restrictive participation, *Journal of Education and Work* 16, 4, 407-426. doi: 10.1080/1363908032000093012c

[7] Alison Fuller and Lorna Unwin, 2010. 'Knowledge Workers' as the New Apprentices: The Influence of Organisational Autonomy, Goals and Values on the Nurturing of Expertise. *Vocations and Learning* 3, 3, 203-222.

[8] Laura Greaves, Jane Howie, Barrie Grey, Helen Kempster, Claire Guy, Nikki Abbott, and Pamela Kelly. 2018. *What do graduates do?* Manchester: Higher Education Careers Services Unit (HECSU). Retrieved 22 January 2019 from https://luminate.prospects.ac.uk/what-do-graduates-do

[9] HESA. 2017. *Destinations of Leavers from Higher Education Longitudinal survey.* Retrieved 21 January 2019 from https://www.hesa.ac.uk/data-and-analysis/publications/long-destinations-2012-13

[10] HESA. 2018. *Non-continuation: UK Performance Indicators 2016/17 (March 2018).* Retrieved 21 January 2019 from https://www.hesa.ac.uk/news/08-03-2018/non-continuation-tables

[11] Ann Hodgson, Ken Spours, and David Smith, 2017. Future apprenticeships in England: the role of mediation in the new model. *Journal of Education and Work* 30, 6, 653-668. DOI: 10.1080/13639080.2017.1349299

[12] Institute for Apprenticeships, 2017. *'How to' guide for trailblazers.* UK: Institute for Apprenticeships. Retrieved 24 January 2019 from https://www.instituteforapprenticeships.org/media/1033/how_to__guide_for_trailblazers_-_v2.pdf

[13] Sandra Jovchelovitch and Martin W Bauer, 2000. Narrative interviewing. In: Martin W Bauer and George Gaskell (eds.) *Qualitative Researching With Text, IMAge and Sound: a Practical Handbook*, (pp. 57-74) London: SAGE.

[14] Ella Kahu, 2014. Increasing the emotional engagement of first year mature-aged distance students: Interest and belonging. *International Journal of the First Year in Higher Education* 5,2, 45-55.

[15] Ella Kahu and Karen Nelson, 2018. Engagement in the Educational Interface: Understanding the Mechanisms of Student Success. *Higher Education Research and Development* 37,1, 58-71. DOI: 10.1080/07294360.2017.1344197

[16] Päivi Kinnunen, Matthew Butler, Michael Morgan, Aletta Nylen, Anne-Kathrin Peters, Jane Sinclair, Sara Kalvala, and Erkki Pesonen, 2018. Understanding initial undergraduate expectations and identity in computing studies. *European Journal of Engineering Education* 43, 2, 201-218, DOI: 10.1080/03043797.2016.1146233

[17] Steve Lambert, 2016. Are current accountability frameworks appropriate for degree apprenticeships? *Higher Education, Skills and Work-Based Learning* 6, 4, 345–356. DOI: 10.1108/HESWBL-05-2016-0027

[18] NCUB. 2018. *Degree Apprenticeships: impacts, challenges, future opportunities*, National Centre for Universities and Business. Retrieves 22 January 2019 from http://www.ncub.co.uk/images/reports/NCUB-Degree-Apprenticeships-Report-Mar-18-WEB.pdf

[19] Anne-Kathrin Peters, Anders Berglund, Anna Eckerdal, and Arnold Pears. 2014. First Year Computer Science and IT Students' Experience of Participation in the Discipline. In *proceedings of 2014 International Conference on teaching and learning in computing and engineering (LaTiCE), Kuching, April 11–13*, 1–8. IEEE.

[20] Anne-Kathrin Peters, Anders Berglund, Anna Eckerdal, and Arnold Pears. 2015. Second Year Computer Science and IT Students' Experience of Participation in the Discipline. In *proceedings of the 15th Koli calling conference on computing education research, November 19–22*, ACM, 68–76.

[21] Philip Powell and Anita Walsh, 2018. Whose curriculum is it anyway? Stakeholder salience in the context of Degree Apprenticeships. *Higher Education Quarterly* 72, 2, 90-106. DOI: 10.1111/hequ.12149

[22] Dianne Reay, Gill Crozier, and John Clayton, 2010. "Fitting in" or "standing out': working-class students in UK higher education. *British Educational Research Journal* 32, 1, 1–19.

[23] Doug Richard, 2012. *The Richard Review of Apprenticeships.* London: BIS. Retrieved 24 January 2019 from https://assets.publishing.service.gov.uk/government/uploads/system/uploads/attachment_data/file/34708/richard-review-full.pdf

[24] SDS, 2018. *Graduate Apprenticeships.* Skills Development Scotland. https://www.skillsdevelopmentscotland.co.uk/what-we-do/apprenticeships/graduate-apprenticeships/

[25] Nigel Shadbolt, 2016. *Shadbolt Review of Computer Sciences Degree Accreditation and Graduate Employability.* London: BIS. Retrieved 24 January 2019 from https://www.gov.uk/government/publications/computer-science-degree-accreditation-and-graduate-employability-shadbolt-review

[26] Sheldon Stryker and Peter J Burke, 2000. The past, present, and future of an identity theory. *Social Psychology Quarterly*, 63(4), 284-297.

[27] Sally Smith, Ella Taylor-Smith, Liz Bacon, and Lachlan Mackinnon, 2019. Equality of opportunity for work experience? Computing students at two UK universities "play the game". *British Journal of Sociology of Education.* https://doi.org/10.1080/01425692.2018.1489219

[28] Ella Taylor-Smith, Sally Smith, and Alison Varey, 2018. Graduate apprenticeships are great opportunities for individuals, but are they inclusive? In *proceedings of Society for Research into Higher Education (SRHE) Annual Conference, Newport, Wales, December 2018.* http://srhe.ac.uk/conference2018/abstracts/0273.pdf

[29] UCAS. 2017. *Progression Pathways 2017: Pathways through higher education.* UCAS. Retrieved 22 January 2019 from https://www.ucas.com/files/progression-pathways-2017-report

[30] Etienne Wenger, 1998. *Communities of practice: Learning meaning and identity.* Cambridge: Cambridge University Press.

[31] Mantze Yorke, 2016. The development and initial use of a survey of student 'belongingness', engagement and self-confidence in UK higher education. *Assessment & Evaluation in Higher Education* 41, 1, 154-166.

Understanding CS Undergraduate Students' Professional Identity through the lens of their Professional Development

Amanpreet Kapoor
Computer & Info. Science & Engineering
University of Florida, Gainesville, FL, USA 32611
kapooramanpreet@ufl.edu

Christina Gardner-McCune
Computer & Info. Science & Engineering
University of Florida, Gainesville, FL, USA 32611
gmccune@ufl.edu

ABSTRACT

Academic institutions play a crucial role in the development of students' professional identities. However, we have limited knowledge of how computing professional identity develops. This paper aims to understand how CS undergraduate students develop their professional identity through analyzing students' reflection on their career goals, experiences in CS degree programs, and engagement in professional development. We present findings from qualitative analysis of 14 semi-structured interviews with CS undergraduate students in the United States. We found that CS undergraduates form their computing professional identity typically between Years 2-3 of their degree programs. We identified several reasons students are committed to a computing profession: intrinsic factors (e.g., interest and perception of ability), and discipline-specific factors (e.g. utility and growth). We also found several factors that shape their professional identity: coursework, informal activities like hackathons, and professional development activities including internships and conferences. These findings suggest that the development of computing professional identity is not limited to students' involvement in the academic degree programs but the engagement they have with the broader computing community.

CCS CONCEPTS

- **Social and professional topics** → Computing education

KEYWORDS

Professional identity, Professional development, Career choices

ACM Reference format:

Amanpreet Kapoor, and Christina Gardner-McCune. 2019. Understanding CS Undergraduate Students' Professional Identity through the lens of their Professional Development. In *Proceedings of 24th Annual ACM Conference on Innovation and Technology in Computer Science Education (ITiCSE'19)*. ACM, New York, NY, USA, 7 pages. https://doi.org/10.1145/3304221.3319764

ITiCSE '19, July 15–17, 2019, Aberdeen, Scotland UK.

ACM ISBN 978-1-4503-6301-3/19/07...$15.00
https://doi.org/10.1145/3304221.3319764

1 INTRODUCTION

Professional identity enables a person to be technically competent, self-confident, and experience a sense of belongingness to the profession [9,26,34]. As academic institutions, our role is to create pathways for professional identity development through our degree programs to ensure students' have a solidified computing professional identity before they graduate. However, we have limited knowledge of factors that contribute to computing professional identity development and the role played by degree programs in supporting this process. Thus, CS Education researchers have expressed the need for a theory of computing identity development [33] and argued for domain-specific theories in computing [29]. Our broader research goal is to fill this gap by developing a grounded theory on the formation of computing professional identity. We defined computing professional identity as "*the transformation of a person's interest in computing into a person's self-identification as someone who engages in computing professionally through one or more computing sub-disciplines and career paths*" [17].

In this paper, we present findings from our exploratory study that answers the following research questions:

RQ1. To what extent do CS undergraduates feel committed to a computing profession?

RQ2. What factors contribute to CS students' exploration or commitment to a CS profession?

RQ3. What factors influence the process of computing professional identity formation in CS undergraduate students?

2 CONCEPTUAL FRAMEWORK

Identity theory research describes identity and identity development as multi-dimensional. The operational definition of identity put forth in the Handbook of Identity Development by Schwartz, Luyckx, and Vignoles [34] frames personal identity as "*the confluence of the person's self-chosen or ascribed commitments, personal characteristics, and beliefs about themself; roles and positions in relation to significant others; and their membership in social groups and categories*". Theories of personal identity tend to focus on individual-level processes and emphasize the agentic role of the individual in creating or discovering his or her own identity [21]. Social learning theories suggest that identity is constructed through the interactions an individual has with the community [22]. We use the following theories as a conceptual framework: James Marcia's *Identity Status Theory* [25] and Lent, Brown, and Hackett's *Social*

Cognitive Career Theory [23] to understand CS undergraduate students' career choices through social interactions and agency.

Marcia's Identity Status Theory suggests that professional identity is one facet of an individual's identity that forms usually between the ages of 17-23 and includes an individual's social, personal, and cultural identity [25]. Identity Status Theory suggests that identity changes over time based on a person's active or passive exploration and commitment to their chosen profession. The theory identifies four statuses to characterize individuals in identity development: (1) *Identity Diffusion*, when an individual is neither exploring nor committed to a career choice; (2) *Identity Foreclosure*, when an individual has not explored career options but is committed to a career due to influence or expectations of an external agent; (3) *Identity Moratorium*, when an individual is exploring career options but is not committed to a career choice; and (4) *Identity Achievement*, when an individual has explored career options and is committed to an identity after the exploration process. The theory proposes that identity development happens during active exploration highlighted by the *Moratorium* and *Achievement* statuses.

Social Cognitive Career Theory (SCCT) provides a framework for understanding three intricately woven aspects of career development through the lens of an individual's agency as well as factors that enhance or hinder this agency. These aspects include: (1) the formation and elaboration of career-relevant interests; (2) selection of academic and career choice options; and (3) performance and persistence in educational and occupational pursuits [23]. SCCT posits that people are likely to develop interest and pursue a career if they have strong self-efficacy beliefs, outcome expectations, and environmental support for gaining professional competence. We believe these theories offer insight into the development of computing professional identity and hence they guided our research.

3 RELATED WORK

3.1 Computing Professional Identity

Research on computing identity is limited [33] and is largely focused on CS students' characteristics, attitudes, and interests in learning to program [32]. However, recent work on computing identity formation by Peter's study at Uppsala University [32] found that students begin degree programs with broader social interests and identities but end with strict technical identities, thus rejecting their broader identities.

Research on computing *professional* identity includes our prior work that found CS undergraduate students identifying themselves professionally as software development professionals, specialized CS professionals, and by their majors [17]. Other work in this domain includes McCartney and Sanders' case study which investigated significant school- and job-related events that affect computing students' professional identity [26]. They found peer interactions, courses, internships, and jobs influencing students' professional identity. In addition, Tomer and Mishra's found that software engineering students reported a major disconnect between their academic learning and their learning in industry. This experience in the industry "*morphed*" their professional identities [36]. In this paper, we aim to extend the computing identity literature with details of how CS students are developing their professional identity through exploration and commitment to computing professions.

3.2 Undergraduate Students' Choices in CS

While there is a lack of research on how CS students' make choices regarding computing professions, there has been significant research on CS undergraduate students' choices regarding computing major [2,4,11,24,28], specializations [15], learning resources [19], and coursework [14]. Prominent research includes Lewis, Yasuhara, and Anderson's paper on students' decision to major in CS. They found five factors using a grounded theory approach that contributes to this decision: ability, enjoyment, fit, utility, and opportunity cost [24]. Hewner and Guzdial found that CS students' pick a specialization based on enjoyment, misconceptions of a field, and lack of vision for their career [15]. Thus, in this paper, we focus on understanding the role of students' choices in their exploration of computing disciplines and their commitment to computing careers.

3.3 Professional Development in CS

Previous work on professional development in CS has largely focused on the professional development of teachers [13,27,30] and professional development of undergraduates through interventions including research [3,7], industry experiences [10,16,18], project-based courses [8], academic scaffolded professional development programs [1,5,12,20], and capstone projects [31]. However, most of this research focused on the implications of professional development on broadening participation, reducing student misconceptions of computing, or improving students' competence in computing. Thus, there is a lack of empirical studies that determine the role played by students' involvement in professional development activities on their computing identity formation and career choices. Our study tries to fill this gap by understanding the experiences of CS students' in various professional development activities.

4 METHODS

4.1 Study Design

We designed a cross-sectional mixed-method study using a Concurrent Triangulation Design [6] to understand how CS undergraduate students form their professional identity. In this design, both qualitative and quantitative data is collected concurrently. In addition, the data is analyzed separately for each phase and then compared and combined [6]. We used this study design to (1) recruit a mix of interview participants equally representing gender and academic standing from our survey participants to gather information-rich cases through purposeful sampling [6], (2) triangulate the data to ensure reliability, and (3) understand the research problem through exploration [6] before we collect data from multiple institutions on developing a computing professional identity theory.

4.2 Research Site

The study was conducted at the University of Florida in the United States in Spring 2016 after receiving the Institutional Review Board approval. At the time of the study, the university had a population of 1519 undergraduate CS and Computer Engineering (CE) majors. The CS undergraduate program allows students to major in CS or CE, but at the time did not offer a specialized track in any subdisciplines of CS. The students can choose a major when they start college but can change it at any time. The CS/CE undergraduate program offers tech electives which students choose during their Years 3-4.

4.3 Participants

We interviewed 14 CS/CE undergraduate students in this study. All participants were between the ages of 18 to 23 based on the average age range of enrolled undergraduate students at our university. We recruited participants by email, flyers, and a separate question at the end of our survey asking, *"If you are interested in being interviewed for the study, please provide your email address. If selected, you will be compensated $10"*. A pool of 14 students was chosen from 56 students, ensuring that we had equal representation of gender, academic standing, and degree program (see Table 1). The participants were compensated with a $10 gift card. The 14 interviewed participants were CS majors (50.0%, n=7), CE majors (42.9%, n=6) or CS minors (7.1%, n=1). In addition, ten out of 14 interview participants felt they belonged to a computing major in the survey and one student felt she did not belong. The other three students in the interview sample did not complete this question on the survey. However, we gauged from the experiences shared during the interview that the remaining three students' felt they belonged to computing.

Table 1: Demographics of Study Participants (N=14)

Academic Standing (By Year)				Gender	
Year 1	Year 2	Year 3	Year 4	Male	Female
21.4%, n=3	21.4%, n=3	21.4%, n=3	35.7%, n=5	57.1%, n=8	42.9%, n=6

4.4 Data Collection

The interview participants were asked 27 open-ended questions regarding their professional goals and identity, degree experience, professional experience, skills and social supports in an in-person interview by the first author. These interviews were semi-structured and guided by the research questions but were unstructured enough to allow the discovery of new information [35]. Some sample questions from the interview are shown in Table 2. The interviews were completed in 25 to 48 minutes (Mean=33.5, SD=6.7). The interviews were transcribed by a commercial transcription service and reviewed for accuracy by the first author. The generated transcripts resulted in a corpus consisting of 3357 to 9444 words per transcript (Mean=5474, SD=1424). We anonymized all participant names and student organization/club names to ensure confidentiality.

4.5 Data Analysis

We deductively coded the data for RQ1 to test the validity of Marcia's Identity Statuses [25] on CS undergraduate students' professional identity. We used Marcia's Identity Statuses and interpreted the students' commitment to a CS profession through their (1) association with a computing profession; (2) confidence in pursuing a computing profession; and (3) professional development and exploration. Since there is a lack of literature on how CS students explore and commit to computing professions, we coded the data for RQ2 and RQ3 using inductive content analysis and thematic analysis based on grounded theory (see Table 3) [35]. The primary codes were clustered to form categories, and these categories formed the basis of our codebook. After coding the data for each participant, we wrote memos regarding the participant's characteristics and compared the participant's categories with our existing categories. The codes and the categories were continually compared following the constant comparison method in grounded theory [35]. Through this process, we found that we reached theoretical saturation of our categories after coding 9 of our 14 interviews. This means that no new categories emerged after we coded the first nine transcripts at random.

Table 2: Some Questions from Interview Script that guided the Inquiry

Questions
How do you identify yourself professionally? Clarification: With many sub-disciplines in CS emerging like User Experience (UX), Web Development, etc., which discipline do you associate with?
Where do you see your career going in 3-5 years after graduation? Follow-up: What area do you want to work in? (e.g., Software, UX)
How are you preparing yourself to achieve your professional goals?

Table 3: Example of Inductive Content and Thematic Analysis (RQ2)

RQ2: What factors contribute to CS students' exploration or commitment to a CS profession?			
Raw Data	P1, male, senior: Because it's [Software Engineering] fulfilling and it's interesting and I think there's a lot of *growth* for that.	P5, female, junior: I like being able to *create something and see it happen*, like right away, immediately, when I'm making an app, it's just like it's there.	P12, male, sophomore: It's just cool [Augmented Reality]. I think people, in general, are really bad at everything. I think technology is cool, so *why not make people less inefficient.*
Primary Code	growth in discipline	Creating tangible artifacts	Improve people's efficiency
Categor y	growth	utility	
Theme	discipline specific factors		

We identified a total of 62 unique categories through our analysis. From these categories, two themes emerged for RQ1, two themes for RQ2, and four themes for RQ3. To ensure the reliability of these themes, the second author reviewed the first author's codebook until a consensus was reached about the categories, theme description, and accuracy. To validate our themes, we invited three researchers not associated with this project to code the interview data. Each researcher was assigned a random transcript, a codebook, and asked to identify the themes for RQ1 based on the codebook. They were asked to highlight the excerpts in their transcript which led to their assumption. All three researchers identified the themes in agreement with the first author. Their highlighted excerpts further helped us to better describe our themes in the codebook.

4.6 Positionality

An important aspect of qualitative research is to recognize the researcher's positionality to present their biases for ensuring transparency and validity of coded data [6]. The first author who coded the data is a doctoral student in Human-Centered Computing and holds bachelors and masters degree in CS. He has worked in the tech industry for multiple years and was actively involved in various student clubs during his education. This proactive involvement helped him in networking, learning, and gaining employment. Therefore, he believes there is value in active involvement outside the classroom.

The second author is an Assistant Professor at the University of Florida. Her research focuses on advancing the science of how people learn to program and develop computing identities. She is the Principal Investigator of the CS Identity project and reviewed the first author's coding scheme. From her interactions with students, she has noticed a trend towards working outside the curriculum for professional development and advancement.

The perspectives held by the authors might have influenced the data collection process as well as the potential representation of the findings. However, they have diligently tried to avoid confirmation bias by using rigorous qualitative research techniques and outside reviewers.

5 FINDINGS AND DISCUSSION

5.1 Commitment to one or more professions (RQ1)

Overall students were either interested or committed to becoming Computer Scientists/Computer Engineers (n=6), Software Development Professionals (n=7) or Specialized CS/CE Professionals (e.g., UX, Cyber Security, etc., n=7). Eight out of 14 students identified their interest or commitment to one profession and the remaining students indicated two professions. Using deductive coding categories derived from Marcia's Identity Status Theory, we interpreted the students' exploration of and commitment to a computing profession, i.e., their identity status. This analysis answers RQ1. *To what extent do CS undergraduates feel committed to a computing profession?* Two themes emerged from our analysis: *Moratorium* and *Achieved.*

5.1.1 Themes

Moratorium. In this theme, 57.1% of 14 CS students (n=8) had no or low commitment to a computing profession but were exploring various computing disciplines. Five students described their interest in two or more computing disciplines and three students shared that they had limited knowledge of computing professions. Students in this theme were involved in campus activities or were exploring computing disciplines to understand their likes and dislikes. Despite their exploration of their computing interest, students in this theme used low confidence phrases such as "not sure", "hopefully", "at this point", etc. when describing their career goals or commitment to a specific computing profession. These behaviors are characteristic of most students categorized as moratorium (high exploration and low commitment) [25]. We also noticed this trend among students in the early years (Years 1-2) of their computing programs. Responses from all three freshmen and all three sophomores were categorized to this theme. However, responses from one male junior and one female senior were categorized in this theme. P13, the male junior, was a transfer student who recently completed his two-year associate degree. He indicated that he had less experience in the degree program since he had only taken one computing course. On the other hand, P14, the female senior, was unsure of what she wanted to do after graduation. When asked about her career plans, she stated,

> *"That's a question I've just been asking myself recently as I near graduation and as of right now, I find it kind of hard to decide. I would say I might be more interested in project management side if I go into industry. If I decide to go into a graduate school, I think I'm leaning more towards like human-computer interaction (HCI)."*

P14 chose a CS major through a process of elimination during her exploration in engineering disciplines. She looked at courses in mechanical engineering and recalled that "*they didn't seem very fun*". She had been exploring different disciplines in computing and had interests in natural sciences, HCI and project management. Her interest in natural sciences stemmed from her research experience at one of our university's research labs which subsequently led her to secure an internship at a national research lab in her last summer before she graduated. She came across HCI through a conference at the end of her junior year and got interested in the field's focus on "*constant thought for users*". In addition, she got interested in project management because she was not confident in her programming abilities but got a chance to manage a team. This interest was strengthened when she managed a team in a software engineering course. She concludes that she enjoys "*managing a project versus actually developing it*". Thus, she was exploring several computing career paths despite her upcoming graduation in less than six months. She argued that this uncertainty is due to her lack of exposure to various computing disciplines earlier in her degree program,

> *"The track that I took as far as where I've been taking my classes, I feel that it's kind of too late, too late for me to get exposed to like different fields, so basically, I took most of my major course work and then left my tech electives for the end and I feel that that has hindered me because tech electives help you better understand like what track you wanna go into, in my opinion."*

Achieved. In this theme, 42.9% of 14 CS students (n=6) were committed to a specific computing profession. Three of the six students were committed to a specific area (e.g. back-end programming) within a sub-discipline of computing (e.g. software engineering). Students in this theme talked about their engagement in their chosen discipline throughout the interview. They were focused on gaining technical competence through reading books, internships, hackathons, or other professional development activities. Further, they were confident about their career choices. These behaviors are characteristic of most students categorized as achieved (high exploration and high commitment) [25]. We also noticed this trend among students in the later years (Years 3-4) of their computing programs. Thus, they had a high commitment to a CS profession and explored the committed discipline to ensure competence. Responses from two of the three juniors and four of the five seniors were categorized in this theme. For example, P3, the female senior, identified herself as a "*software developer*" interested in "*work[ing] in back end development, especially web programming, APIs and lower level socket programming*". During the interview, she indicated that she intentionally selected this career path and described her deliberate preparation process for achieving her career goals which included courses, reading documentation, and canonical developer books:

"I'm taking courses like object-oriented programming and design patterns that mainly focus on back-end development. [I use] Stack Overflow, the Javadocs, especially when I'm working with Java. I try to mostly understand the API that Java intended to put out, learn how to use it through them and actually use it. And the other thing I do is books. I have the Gang of Four Design patterns book and Meyer's Object-Oriented Programming, Martin Fowler's UML Distilled, so I like to keep my textbooks and refer back."

5.1.2 Discussion

This section demonstrates the utility of Marcia's Identity Status Theory [25] in understanding students' computing professional identity development. It also provides us with insights into the extent to which students are committed to a specific computing career. We found that CS undergraduates form their computing professional identity typically between Years 2-3 of their degree programs. As expected, most freshmen and sophomores are exploring computing professions but are not committed to a computing profession; and as hoped most juniors and seniors are committed to a specific computing profession and are focused on gaining technical competence in their career choice. However, we also found that transfer students, as well as some graduating students like P14, may be developing their computing professional identity later in their degree programs. There are multiple reasons for this delay including lack of exposure to different computing disciplines earlier in their degree programs, delayed course enrollment due to transferring, lack of confidence in their technical competencies, and/or indecision about committing to one specific computing profession. This poses an interesting problem for departments and for students if our goal is to ensure that students are developing appropriate technical skills and knowledge and are prepared for their careers upon graduation. If students are not being exposed to various computing disciplines until their junior and senior year when they take technical electives, then departments need to find ways to address these issues so that all students have a conducive environment for developing their computing professional identities.

5.2 Reasons for association with a profession (RQ2)

In the interview, we asked the students to explain their reasons for exploring or committing to a computing profession. This qualitative data was relevant for answering RQ2: *What factors contribute to CS students' exploration or commitment to a CS profession?* Two themes emerged from nine categories in our data analysis: *intrinsic factors* and *discipline-specific factors.*

5.2.1 Themes

Intrinsic factors. In this theme, 92.9% of the 14 students (n=13) stated that they were exploring or committed to a computing profession because of intrinsic characteristics. The five categories in this theme were self-interest (10), ability (6), personality (4), enjoyment (3), and satisfaction (3). Students self-evaluated their *abilities* through the lens of coursework, completion of projects, or performance in internships. We also found that CS students associated themselves with specific computing disciplines if they found the discipline "*fun*" or enjoyed working in an area. Students' perception of *self-interest* was based on their like or dislike for a certain computing discipline. In addition, three students stated that their *personality* matched or did not match a specific computing profession using phrases such as "*detailed-oriented*" for interest in product management or "*lack of patience*" for dealing with hardware. Three students also suggested that they were interested or committed to a specific computing discipline as their experience was "*fulfilling*" or satisfying. P1, a senior male, who belonged to the *satisfaction* and *self-interest* category said that he wanted to pursue software development after he graduates "*because it's fulfilling and interesting*".

Discipline-specific factors. In this theme, 85% of the 14 students (n=12) stated that they were committed to or exploring a specific computing profession because of factors pertinent to a computing profession. The four categories in this theme were applicability of multidisciplinary knowledge (7), utility (5), perception of disciplines' coolness (3), and growth (1). Seven students stated that they were exploring or committed to a computing profession as the discipline was at an intersection of multiple areas and offered them an opportunity to employ their *multidisciplinary knowledge.* Five students stated they associated with a discipline because of the field's *utility* in creating tangible artifacts or contribution to society. Three students associated with a computing profession because of the field's *coolness* and one student for opportunities to grow. Consider P2, a sophomore female interested in software engineering, web development and UX due to discipline-specific factors (applicability of multidisciplinary knowledge) as well as intrinsic factors (enjoyment, satisfaction, personality, and self-interest).

*"I've always been an **artsy** type of person, so I **love** design and all that stuff. I really **enjoyed** it, like I love Photoshop and Adobe Illustrator. So just the chance to kind of **integrate** what I know now with coding to those design things is a really **exciting** possibility for me. So, I hope to find like a career I can do a lot of that stuff. I mean ideally, I'd really like to do stuff with design. And like get my arts **fulfillment** in".*

5.2.2 Discussion

Our analysis was focused on understanding how CS students' make choices regarding computing professions throughout their exploration process. We found that students take into account both intrinsic as well as discipline-specific factors when exploring or committing to a specific computing discipline. Overall, we found 78.6% of 14 students (n=11) considered both types of factors when associating with a computing discipline. Two students explored or committed to a computing profession due to intrinsic factors and one student due to discipline-specific factors. Our study contributes to the CS Education literature an understanding of factors that impact students' choices to explore or commit to computing careers. Similar to the factors identified by Lewis et al. on how students pick a computing major [24], our findings confirm that CS students also take into account *ability, enjoyment,* and *utility* when exploring or committing to a computing profession. However, unlike previous work [24], we also find that CS students decide to explore a computing profession based on the *applicability of multidisciplinary knowledge* and *growth* in a specific computing profession.

5.3 Factors influencing professional identity (RQ3)

We asked the 14 interviewed students to describe their experiences in degree program and involvement in professional development activities. This qualitative data was relevant for analyzing RQ3. *What factors influence the process of computing professional identity formation in CS undergraduate students?* We found four themes that shaped students' computing professional identity development: *Coursework, People, Informal activities,* and *Professional development opportunities.*

5.3.1 Themes

Coursework. We found mixed responses regarding the role of coursework in shaping CS students' professional interests. For some students' courses played a key role in deciding their professional interests and career goals through exploration of different computing disciplines, development of their likes and dislikes, recognition of the utility of the discipline, and evaluation of their ability in a computing discipline. While for other CS/CE students the courses had a limited impact on their career choices or led them not to pursue a CS area. In addition, two students suggested a need for a course in freshman year to introduce students to various computing disciplines.

People. CS students were influenced by mentors, friends, parents, relatives, industry professionals, or other people in their broader support network regarding decisions related to their professional interests. Students suggested that parents and relatives advised them to pursue a computing major which further led to the development of interest in computing. Further, advice from elements of the support network led them to choose courses, prepare for professional development, and recognize expectancies in the industry regarding computing professions.

Informal activities (Clubs, Projects, and Hackathons). In this theme, CS students indicated that informal activities including clubs, personal projects, and hackathons shaped their professional choices. Students' got an opportunity to explore an unfamiliar computing discipline through participation in one or more informal activities. Students also mentioned that clubs helped them in developing their skills, meeting people and collaborating, finding mentors, or knowing professional expectations. Hackathons helped them in exploring the discipline and learning at a fast pace.

Professional development opportunities (Conferences, Internships, and Research). CS students in this theme shared vivid descriptions of how professional development activities influenced their career choices. Students described that internships reaffirmed their ability to continue pursuing a CS major and allowed them to explore new computing sub-disciplines. Similar to internships, other professional development opportunities including conferences and research also broadened students' understanding or perspective on the breadth of computing and led to their involvement in computing sub-disciplines which they were earlier unfamiliar with. P14, a female in her senior year explained that she came across "*human-centered computing*" through a computing conference for women at the end of her junior year and how it was "*an eye-opener*" for her. Another student, P10, a senior male who interned as a Software Test Engineering intern, explained that his internship took him "*from a computer science student to someone who has a bigger view, a bigger scope of the whole software development process*" and he realized that CS is not about "*sitting behind a computer all day and coding*".

5.3.2 Discussion

Our data analysis for RQ3 yields two contributions. First, the development of computing professional identity is influenced by students' engagement in informal and professional development activities outside of the classroom in the broader computing community. Second, early coursework in computing degree programs provide students with opportunities to evaluate intrinsic factors such as enjoyment and ability in programming but provide limited opportunities for students to explore discipline-specific factors such as the utility of various computing disciplines or to develop a broader view of computing. Students' recognize this broader view in the latter part of their degree programs through technical electives, industry experiences, or involvement in professional development activities. Thus, we suggest that CS departments include a preliminary course that provides students an opportunity to get an overview of the breadth of CS disciplines.

6 IMPLICATIONS

The findings from this research highlight the need for building students' confidence through course interventions or projects during Years 1-2 of computing degree programs. These interventions should provide students with opportunities to (1) learn different computing areas, (2) understand various computing careers, and (3) develop technical skills. Interventions in Years 2-3 should provide opportunities for job shadowing or mentoring that allow students to gain a greater understanding of computing careers and their interests. Programs like these need to target transfer students and students who are unclear about their computing career path. We recommend that departments allocate additional funds for professional development activities for students at every stage of their degree program so that they can participate in hackathons, conferences, and internships. Finally, we suggest that researchers studying computing professional identity focus on intrinsic and discipline-specific factors as they both influence students' professional identity development process.

7 LIMITATIONS

We attempt to address the validity of our qualitative inquiry through the transparency of our research process as well as recognizing the researcher's biases. Our findings represent a snapshot of the students' experiences taken from a small sample at a US-based university. Our findings may not generalize to large populations of students at similar or different institutions or experiences of CS students in other countries. We provided a description of our university to help the readers understand the context in which the findings were applicable.

REFERENCES

[1] Lingma Acheson and Ryan Rybarczyk. 2016. Integrating career development into computer science undergraduate curriculum. In *2016 11th International Conference on Computer Science & Education (ICCSE)*, 177–181. DOI:https://doi.org/10.1109/ICCSE.2016.7581576

[2] Amnah Alshahrani, Isla Ross, and Murray I. Wood. 2018. Using Social Cognitive Career Theory to Understand Why Students Choose to Study Computer Science. In *Proceedings of the 2018 ACM Conference on International Computing Education Research - ICER '18*, 205–214. DOI:https://doi.org/10.1145/3230977.3230994

[3] Christine Alvarado and Neil Spring. 2018. Successfully Engaging Early Undergraduates in CS Research. In *Proceedings of the 49th ACM Technical Symposium on Computer Science Education - SIGCSE '18*, 1050–1050. DOI:https://doi.org/10.1145/3159450.3162365

[4] Lecia J. Barker, Charlie McDowell, and Kimberly Kalahar. 2009. Exploring factors that influence computer science introductory course students to persist in the major. In *Proceedings of the 40th ACM technical symposium on Computer science education - SIGCSE '09*, 153. DOI:https://doi.org/10.1145/1508865.1508923

[5] Kristy Elizabeth Boyer, E. Nathan Thomas, Audrey S. Rorrer, Deonte Cooper, and Mladen A. Vouk. 2010. Increasing technical excellence, leadership and commitment of computing students through identity-based mentoring. In *Proceedings of the 41st ACM technical symposium on Computer science education - SIGCSE '10*, 167. DOI:https://doi.org/10.1145/1734263.1734320

[6] John W. Creswell and J. David Creswell. 2017. *Research Design: Qualitative, Quantitative, and Mixed Methods Approaches.*

[7] Teresa Dahlberg, Tiffany Barnes, Audrey Rorrer, Eve Powell, and Lauren Cairco. 2008. Improving retention and graduate recruitment through immersive research experiences for undergraduates. In *Proceedings of the 39th SIGCSE technical symposium on Computer science education - SIGCSE '08*, 466. DOI:https://doi.org/10.1145/1352135.1352293

[8] Christopher Dean, Thomas D. Lynch, and Rajiv Ramnath. 2011. Student perspectives on learning through developing software for the real world. In *2011 Frontiers in Education Conference (FIE)*. DOI:https://doi.org/10.1109/FIE.2011.6142904

[9] Jennifer Dempsey, Richard T. Snodgrass, Isabel Kishi, and Allison Titcomb. 2015. The Emerging Role of Self-Perception in Student Intentions. In *Proceedings of the 46th ACM Technical Symposium on Computer Science Education - SIGCSE '15*, 108–113. DOI:https://doi.org/10.1145/2676723.2677305

[10] Sebastian Dziallas and Sally Fincher. 2016. Aspects of Graduateness in Computing Students' Narratives. In *Proceedings of the 2016 ACM Conference on International Computing Education Research - ICER '16*, 181–190. DOI:https://doi.org/10.1145/2960310.2960317

[11] Sebastian Dziallas and Sally Fincher. 2018. "I told you this last time, right?": Re-visiting narratives of STEM education. In *Proceedings of the 2018 ACM Conference on International Computing Education Research - ICER '18*, 223–231. DOI:https://doi.org/10.1145/3230977.3230989

[12] Meg Fryling, MaryAnne Egan, Robin Y. Flatland, Scott Vandenberg, and Sharon Small. 2018. Catch 'em Early: Internship and Assistantship CS Mentoring Programs for Underclassmen. In *Proceedings of the 49th ACM Technical Symposium on Computer Science Education - SIGCSE '18*, 658–663. DOI:https://doi.org/10.1145/3159450.3159556

[13] Joanna Goode, Jane Margolis, and Gail Chapman. 2014. Curriculum is not enough. In *Proceedings of the 45th ACM technical symposium on Computer science education - SIGCSE '14*, 493–498. DOI:https://doi.org/10.1145/2538862.2538948

[14] Michael Hewner. 2014. How CS undergraduates make course choices. In *Proceedings of the tenth annual conference on International computing education research - ICER '14*, 115–122. DOI:https://doi.org/10.1145/2632320.2632345

[15] Michael Hewner and Mark Guzdial. 2011. How CS majors select a specialization. In *Proceedings of the seventh international workshop on Computing education research - ICER '11*, 11. DOI:https://doi.org/10.1145/2016911.2016916

[16] Amanpreet Kapoor. 2019. Deconstructing Successful and Unsuccessful Computer Science Undergraduate Interns. In *Proceedings of the 50th ACM Technical Symposium on Computer Science Education - SIGCSE '19*, 1297–1297. DOI:https://doi.org/10.1145/3287324.3293711

[17] Amanpreet Kapoor and Christina Gardner-McCune. 2018. Understanding Professional Identities and Goals of Computer Science Undergraduate Students. In *Proceedings of the 49th ACM Technical Symposium on Computer Science Education - SIGCSE '18*, 191–196. DOI:https://doi.org/10.1145/3159450.3159474

[18] Amanpreet Kapoor and Christina Gardner-McCune. 2019. Understanding CS Undergraduate Students' Professional Development through the Lens of Internship Experiences. In *Proceedings of the 50th ACM Technical Symposium on Computer Science Education - SIGCSE '19*, 852–858. DOI:https://doi.org/10.1145/3287324.3287408

[19] Daniel Knox and Sally Fincher. 2013. Where students go for knowledge and what they find there. In *Proceedings of the ninth annual international ACM conference on International computing education research - ICER '13*, 35. DOI:https://doi.org/10.1145/2493394.2493399

[20] Deborah Knox. 2016. Guiding Career Development Prior to Capstone Experiences (Abstract Only). In *Proceedings of the 47th ACM Technical Symposium on Computing Science Education - SIGCSE '16*, 698–698. DOI:https://doi.org/10.1145/2839509.2850571

[21] Jane Kroger and Kathy E. Green. 1996. Events associated with identity status change. *J. Adolesc.* 19, (1996), 359–380. DOI:https://doi.org/10.1006/jado.1996.0045

[22] Jean Lave and Etienne Wenger. 1991. *Situated learning: legitimate peripheral participation.* Cambridge University Press.

[23] Robert W. Lent, Steven. D. Brown, and Gail Hackett. 2004. Towards a Unifying Social Cognitive Theory of Career and Academic Interest, Choice, and Performance. *J. Vocat. Behav.* 45, (2004), 79–122.

[24] Colleen M. Lewis, Ken Yasuhara, and Ruth E. Anderson. 2011. Deciding to major in computer science. In *Proceedings of the seventh international workshop on Computing education research - ICER '11*, 3. DOI:https://doi.org/10.1145/2016911.2016915

[25] James E. Marcia. 1966. Development and validation of ego-identity status. *J. Pers. Soc. Psychol.* 3, 5 (1966), 551–558. DOI:https://doi.org/10.1037/h0023281

[26] Robert McCartney and Kate Sanders. 2015. School/Work: Development of Computing Students' Professional Identity at University. In *Proceedings of the eleventh annual International Conference on International Computing Education Research - ICER '15*, 151–159. DOI:https://doi.org/10.1145/2787622.2787732

[27] J. McGrath Cohoon and Feng Raoking. 2013. Professional development for mid-career women in computer science and engineering. In *2013 IEEE Frontiers in Education Conference (FIE)*, 618–622. DOI:https://doi.org/10.1109/FIE.2013.6684899

[28] Catherine Mooney, Brett A. Becker, Lana Salmon, and Eleni Mangina. 2018. Computer science identity and sense of belonging. In *Proceedings of the 1st International Workshop on Gender Equality in Software Engineering - GE '18*, 1–4. DOI:https://doi.org/10.1145/3195570.3195575

[29] Greg L. Nelson and Andrew J. Ko. 2018. On Use of Theory in Computing Education Research. In *Proceedings of the 2018 ACM Conference on International Computing Education Research - ICER '18*, 31–39. DOI:https://doi.org/10.1145/3230977.3230992

[30] Lijun Ni and Mark Guzdial. 2012. Who AM I?: understanding high school computer science teachers' professional identity. In *Proceedings of the 43rd ACM technical symposium on Computer Science Education - SIGCSE '12*, 499. DOI:https://doi.org/10.1145/2157136.2157283

[31] Rick Parker. 2018. Developing Software Engineers: A study of professionalization in a CS Senior Capstone. In *Proceedings of the 49th ACM Technical Symposium on Computer Science Education - SIGCSE '18*, 276–276. DOI:https://doi.org/10.1145/3159450.3162326

[32] Anne-Kathrin Peters. 2018. Students' Experience of Participation in a Discipline—A Longitudinal Study of Computer Science and IT Engineering Students. *ACM Trans. Comput. Educ.* 19, 1 (September 2018), 1–28. DOI:https://doi.org/10.1145/3230011

[33] Sarah L. Rodriguez and Kathleen Lehman. 2017. Developing the next generation of diverse computer scientists: the need for enhanced, intersectional computing identity theory. *Comput. Sci. Educ.* 27, 3–4 (October 2017), 229–247. DOI:https://doi.org/10.1080/08993408.2018.1457899

[34] Seth J. Schwartz, Koen Luyckx, and Vivian L. Vignoles. 2011. *Handbook of Identity Theory and Research.* Springer Science & Business Media.

[35] Anselm Strauss and Juliet Corbin. 2008. *Basics of Qualitative Research.* SAGE Publications, Inc.

[36] Gunjan Tomer and Sushanta Kumar Mishra. 2016. Professional identity construction among software engineering students. *Inf. Technol. People* 29, 1 (March 2016), 146–172. DOI:https://doi.org/10.1108/ITP-10-2013-0181

The Impact of Self-Theories to Academic Achievement and Soft Skills in Undergraduate CS Studies: First Findings

Mikko-Ville Apiola
University of Turku, Finland
Department of Future Technologies
mikko.apiola@ieee.org

Mikko-Jussi Laakso
University of Turku, Finland
Department of Future Technologies
mikko.laakso@utu.fi

ABSTRACT

There is strong evidence of the impact of self-theories to students' academic achievement and behavior in many domains of education, including CS. However, the research on self-theories in CSE are far from conclusive. In this research, we studied 1st year CS and CE students' self-theories and looked at associations to academic achievement in their first courses, as well as the students' conceptualisations of intelligence. Contradictory to previous research, students with a fixed view on intelligence received the best exam scores. Students' conceptualisations of intelligence were found to lean towards cognitive g-theories of intelligence. These initial findings show a number of crucially important future research directions in relation to self-theories, soft skills development, and academic achievement in CS studies.

CCS CONCEPTS

• **Social and professional topics → Computer science education; Computational science and engineering education.**

ACM Reference Format:
Mikko-Ville Apiola and Mikko-Jussi Laakso. 2019. The Impact of Self-Theories to Academic Achievement and Soft Skills in Undergraduate CS Studies: First Findings. In *Innovation and Technology in Computer Science Education (ITiCSE '19), July 15–17, 2019, Aberdeen, Scotland, UK.* ACM, New York, NY, USA, 7 pages. https://doi.org/10.1145/3304221.3319766

1 INTRODUCTION

One important source of error and bias in thinking originates from self-theories [10]. It has been shown that people's beliefs about themselves radically shape their actions and thinking in otherwise identical situations [10]. Moreover, extensive research shows that self-theories can explain—often to a greater extent than popular constructs such as confidence, self-esteem, or past success—why some people exceed in their expectations, while some fail to fulfil their potential [10]. In addition to academic achievement, in many cases, self-theories have a fundamental impact to social behaviour, judgment of self and others, and stereotyping of groups [10].

Studies about expertise suggest that deliberate practice, willpower and love of learning explain success to a greater extent than any fixed entity such as genetic capability, intelligence, or talent [10, 16],[35, pp. 115]. Theories that people hold about themselves and others are better predictors of success or failure than individual stable traits [10, 35]. One important type of self-theory for learning is one's perceptions about the general nature of intellectual capacities, which has, according to an impressive number of studies, a direct impact to the amount of effort in challenging tasks [10, 13].

According to the theories of Dweck [10], believers in an "entity theory" of intelligence think that intelligence is a fixed trait: you have a certain amount and that's it. This leads students to try to look smart, and to see challenges as threats to self-esteem. In contrast, those who have an "incremental theory" of intelligence believe that intelligence can be increased through effort [10]. Then, if intelligence can be increased, why not do it? These two self-theories have been demonstrated to have radical repercussions for students' motivation and academic achievement [10, 12, 13, 45].

The theory of self-theories [10] has sparked an extensive amount of experiments on a variety of domains. What makes self-theories in learning particularly interesting is, that in many cases, relatively small interventions have succeeded to positively alter students' mindsets, leading to increased academic achievement [45]. Self-theories is a recognised research domain in CSE, too. However the extent of self-theory research in CSE is relatively small, and the results are inconclusive. Research suggests a possible existence of a domain-specific and separate mindset-construct in CS, and calls for more research in order to understand self-theories and conceptualisations of intelligence in CSE with more depth.

In this research, data was collected from a comprehensive sample of 1st year CS or computer engineering (CE) students in University of Turku, Finland. Mindset-scales were developed for general intelligence, mathematics intelligence, and computing intelligence. Statistical associations between the students' mindset scores on these distinct scales, and academic achievement in the students' first CS courses were investigated. In addition, students' perceptions of intelligence and ability were analysed qualitatively.

The research questions of this study were set as follows:

(1) What are the 1st year CS and CE students' self-theories in intelligence, mathematics, and computing in Department of Future Technologies, University of Turku, Finland?
(2) What statistical associations can be found between students' self-theories and academic achievement in first CS courses?
(3) How do 1st year CS/CE students conceptualise intelligence?

This research is part of our wider research efforts to understand the role of educational psychology in CSE, and to design related interventions and teaching methods to support the growth of intellectual capacities, collaboration skills, creativity, and other "soft skills", which are all increasingly advocated for CS programs [33].

ITiCSE '19, July 15–17, 2019, Aberdeen, Scotland, UK

ACM ISBN 978-1-4503-6301-3/19/07...$15.00
https://doi.org/10.1145/3304221.3319766

2 BACKGROUND: SELF-THEORIES

Beliefs about the fixed or malleable nature of personal attributes—such as personality, social behaviour, or intelligence—has fundamental implications to thinking and behaviour [10]. For example, research shows that pupils behave differently in social situations in relation to what extent they attribute social rejection as a lack of personal social ability [10, page 67]. After social rejection, people with fixed self-theories of personality tend to judge and label themselves as deficient [10, page 68]. Also, fixed theories of personal attributes leads students to see performance as a direct reflection of intelligence, resulting in judgments of low ability in case of failure both in regards of themselves, and of others, which is not the case of those who see personal attributes as dynamic [10, p 73-81].

Students with fixed orientations are also significantly more eager to perceive group differences in behaviour as evidence of deeply rooted characteristic truths [10, p. 93]. The most extensively researched domain in self-theories is intelligence, and it's relation to academic achievement. The extensive research of Carol Dweck [10] challenges the common beliefs in our western societies that prior knowledge and skills, prior success, praise of traits, or confidence in one's intellectual abilities explain success [10, 13, 45].

2.1 Mindset and academic achievement

There exists an impressive amount of research about mindset and academic achievement at university and school levels, in a variety of topics of study. For example, an extensive study in Chile [4], showed that *growth mindset* is a strong predictor of academic achievement across all socioeconomic strata in Chile: those who hold a growth mindset consistently outperform those who do not. The results were found to be valid across all Chile's schools and across all levels of family income [4]. In another study, growth mindset predicted an upward trajectory in high school grades, and a mindset-intervention promoted positive change in classroom motivation [2].

In one study, mindset-interventions were delivered to $n = 1594$ students, and especially at-risk-students were found to benefit from the interventions, as demonstrated by significant GPA increases [28]. Another research [30] found that in a sample of $n = 150$ middle school students, those who believed that intelligence could be developed earned higher grades and were more likely to move to advanced math courses. In five studies [18], it was found that learning goals predicted achievement, while ability-linked goals predicted withdrawal and poorer performance in face of challenge.

In one study [1], it was found that a mindset-intervention had the power to override a powerful phenomenon known as stereotype-threat that specifically has an impact on African-American college students. The growth-mindset was connected to greater enjoyment of academic process, greater academic engagement, and higher GPA as compared to counterparts in control groups [1]. A review of social-psychological interventions [45] shows that interventions, including mindset-interventions, have produced long-lasting gains in academic achievement in multiple contexts.

A growing body of evidence suggests that students' mindsets play a key role in math achievement [12]. In general, students tend to have more of a fixed view of math skills than of other intellectual domains [12]. A study in Russia found that for certain types of math problems, students' persistence may vary as a function of mindset and previous math success [36]. Thus, several studies show that mindset is often associated with higher academic achievement, and that mindsets can be positively altered with interventions.

2.2 Mindset in CSE

Some ten years ago, Murphy [26] wrote about the importance of launching studies about self-theories in CS, proposing large-scale quantitative assessments and qualitative studies on how students perceive intelligence and how that reflects on behaviour [26]. A number of research studies have followed, with mixed results.

Research in Scotland [6] used a mixture of mindset-interventions in an introductory programming course in Python. It was found that the applied mindset-interventions had a positive impact on students' mindsets and corresponding significant change in class tests as well as end-of-year exams [6]. It was also found that previous programming experience ranged a lot, which is a common issue in CS studies (eg. [42]), and complicates data analysis. The authors suspect that CS teachers' mindsets and their instructional practices may, in too many cases, foster a fixed mindset [7], which is backed up by results from one institution, where 77% of surveyed faculty members disagreed with the statement *"Nearly everyone is capable of succeeding in the computer science curriculum if they work at it."*, suggesting a fixed mindsets among CS educators [25]. In similar lines, one study found that CS tutors held a fixed mindset [6].

In another research [37] the impact of mindset-interventions for a CS1 course did not succeed in altering students' mindsets. Possible reasons given were the relatively small scale of the intervention and validity of the used scales. Another research [34] studied mindset in a population of undergraduate software engineering students and found evidence for domain-specific mindset in programming, which differed significantly from a general intelligence-related mindset. The authors [34] suggest that programming mindset might be a better predictor than general mindset. In regards of digital learning, one research project [14] developed a set of progress indicators for the purpose of assessing students' programming effort independently of the correctness of their code, for the purpose of automatically generating growth-mindset promoting feedback.

2.3 Conceptualisations of intelligence

The original IQ test was invented in order to identify pupils who are not thriving in public schools of Paris in order to "get them back on track", not to measure children's fixed entities [10, page 59]. A number of scholars agree that measuring IQ in order to predict potential is pointless, as IQ does not determine a person's potential for accomplishment with the right kind of motivation and instruction (for references, see [10, page 60]). While IQ may be an indicator of people's cognitive abilities, it's usefulness is debatable, and over the last decades, more general conceptualisations of intelligence have gained prominence [21]. One well developed example is Howard Gardner's view of intelligence as a rich and varied capacity that can be developed, and is not fixed [17]. Conceptualisations of intelligence range from general-ability (g) theories to theories of multiple intelligencies [39]. Modern conceptualisations include collective intelligence [44] and systems intelligence [21, 41].

In extensive studies of the lives of great historical figures in sciences, arts, and business, social intelligence is identified as a crucial component in success [19, pages 125–164]. Greene argues that *"Often the greatest obstacle to our pursuit of mastery comes from the emotional drain we experience in dealing with the resistance and manipulations of the people around us."* [19, p. 125]. The importance of social abilities is dealt extensively in systems intelligence (SI), a holistic conceptualisation of intelligence[1]. SI is defined as an *"ability to act intelligently within complex systems involving interaction and feedback"* [41], and is grounded on the premise that skills, orientations and qualities can be developed with effort [21].

Research shows that people's descriptions and evaluations of themselves and of others are too often fixed and static [10], which is acknowledged well in SI: *"Just as we tend to fix a version of ourselves, we are also prone to fixing a version of the systems we live in in our own minds, and then we tend to assume that our version is shared by others. We think we know how our relatives see the family systems, our friends see our friendships, our colleagues see our workplace, and so on."* [21, page 18] A person with high SI avoids fixed thinking, and fosters the development potential in people's qualities [41].

SI research shows that in contexts, such as large technology corporations, a person's beliefs about co-operation can act as a limiting factor in human interaction [31, 32], and may influence how individuals act, approach and frame themselves in situations. SI as a concept has evolved over decades of research and includes a range of crucial forms of action that is beneficial from personal, holistic, and systemic viewpoints [21]. SI is a practical concept that may be valuable in fostering the crucial future soft-skills competencies required from tomorrow's computer scientists and engineers [23].

3 METHODS AND DATA

This is a mixed-methods study [5]. The quantitative data, which consists of the mindset-scales and course data is described in section 3.1. The qualitative data consists of students' conceptualisations of intelligence, and is described in section 3.2. All used data and analysis methods are summarised in Table 1.

Table 1: Summary of data and research methods

Instrument	Quantitative	Qualitative
Self-theory scales (Data A)		
Intelligence scale	✓	
Math intelligence scale	✓	
Computing intelligence scale	✓	
Self-theory questions (Data B)		
Social skills	✓	
Sports	✓	
Programming	✓	
Languages	✓	
Intelligence	✓	
Mathematics	✓	
Course data (Data C)		
Final grades	✓	
No. of ass. submissions	✓	
Time of ass. submissions	✓	
Conceptualisations of intelligence (Data D)		
Free-form written answers		✓

3.1 Mindset scales and course data

Quantitative data was collected from a comprehensive sample of 1st year students of CE or CS. The data was collected by using a paper-based questionnaire, which was based on the *"Theories of Intelligence Scale–Self Form for Adults"* [10, page 178]. This instrument contains eight items, such as *"You have a certain amount of intelligence, and you can't really do much to change it."* In addition, by following the recommendations of Dweck [12], as well as observations from previous research suggesting the need for computing-specific mindset-measures [34], separate versions of the instrument were created for self-theories of intelligence in mathematics and computing. In addition, the questionnaire contained a section with six questions that measured the extent to which students perceived success in different domains to result from deliberate practice versus inborn capacities. A total of 86 ($n = 86$) responses were returned, reaching a 96% (86/90) response rate.

The set of eight questions in the *"Theories of Intelligence Scale–Self Form for Adults"* includes—on a six point likert-scale—four questions (Q1,Q2,Q4,Q6) that measure the incremental theory of intelligence, and four questions (Q3,Q5,Q7,Q8) that measure the entity theory of intelligence. Two sum variables were generated, one for incremental theory of intelligence (growth mindset), and another for entity theory of intelligence (fixed mindset). A combined score for each student was then computed by using the formula $ms = (fix + (24 - gro))/8$, resulting in a mindset-score for each student that ranges from 0.5 to 5.5, where values above 3 suggest an entity theory, and values below 3 suggest an incremental theory of intelligence. Separate scores were calculated for self-theories of intelligence, mathematical intelligence, and computing intelligence.

In addition to the three scales (Data A), the questionnaire contained a section, which asked the respondents to rate their perceptions about the stable or dynamic nature of performance in the domains of social skills, sports, programming, languages, intelligence and mathematics, each with one question. For each item, students were asked to rate if succeeding in the domain was—according to them—more due to inborn and stable capabilities, or due to effortful practice. The scale included five options: (100%/0%), (75%/25%), (50%/50%), (25%/75%), (0%/100%). This constitutes Data B.

Data from first CS courses was collected. In the first period, students of CS and CE complete the course Basics of Computer Science I (BCS), followed by Basics of Algorithms and Programming (BAP) in the second period. While and after these courses were taught, students' performance data was collected from all course assignments, as well as their final grades. A specific learning management system (LMS) is used in these courses, which also collects data about students' time usage and resubmission patterns in different learning tasks. On a scale from 0 to 5, the average grade in the BCS course was 4.622. Thus, the course was too easy to reveal differences in performance of students, and thus all data from BCS was dropped from data analysis. BAP is the first "serious" CS course and it is much more challenging and divisive. Thus, data from the BAP-course was selected for data analysis, including grades and submission data, which constitutes Data C.

The internal consistency of the mindset-scales (Data A) was investigated by using Cronbach's α. After this, the collected quantitative data, including the mindset scales and course performance data was analysed for descriptive statistics, and basic measures of statistical association. All data analysis was performed in R[2].

[1] See http://systemsintelligence.aalto.fi and https://salserver.org.aalto.fi/sitest/en/

[2] https://www.r-project.org

3.2 Conceptualisations of intelligence

In addition to quantitative data, the questionnaire contained the following two free-form questions, *"What is intelligence? Define in your own terms with a few sentences."*, and *"What is math intelligence? Define in your own terms with a few sentences."* This data was typed into a word processor, then imported into ATLAS.ti qualitative analysis tool, and the data was coded by following the guidelines of qualitative content analysis [9, p. 281]. This constitutes Data D.

4 QUANTITATIVE RESULTS

4.1 Internal consistency of mindset-scales

The consistency of the mindset-scales of intelligence, math intelligence and computing intelligence were inspected by using Cronbach's α. For each respondent of the mindset-questionnaire ($n = 86$), a total of six scales were computed, two for each three types of intelligence, one for fixed mindset, and one for growth mindset. Each scale consisted of four variables, each representing one question in the questionnaire. For example, the growth-scale for intelligence consisted of questions Q1,Q2,Q4,Q6, and the fixed-scale of intelligence consisted of questions Q3,Q5,Q7,Q8 in the original mindset instrument [10, page 178]. The α-scores were calculated with the *psych*-package[3] of *R*. The α-scores were as follows: 0.96 (growth intelligence), 0.92 (fixed intelligence), 0.96 (growth mathintel), 0.93 (fixed mathintel), 0.96 (growth compintel), 0.94 (fixed compintel). Thus, high internal consistency was found in all six scales.

4.2 Self-theories scales: descriptives

A total of $n = 86$ responses were received to the self-theory questionnaire. Out of these, each 86 responded to all questions from the intelligence scale, and math intelligence scale. Two respondents did not respond to the computing intelligence scale questions. The descriptives for the three self-theory-scales were $\overline{intel} = 2.57, s = 1.1$ (intelligence), $\overline{mintel} = 2.47, s = 0.99$ (mathematics intelligence), and $\overline{cintel} = 2.26, s = 0.93$ (computing intelligence). Since values below 3 indicate an incremental self-theory of intelligence, this sample leans towards the incremental theory of intelligence (growth mindset) in all three scales. The density-plots for all three scales are shown in Figure 1. Values on the left side of the blue vertical line indicate a growth mindset, and values on the right side of the blue line indicate a fixed mindset. It can be observed that—on average—students' considered computing intelligence to be of a more dynamic nature than intelligence. This difference in means was statistically significant at $p = 0.046$ level (Student's t-test).

In regards of research on self-theory scales, it is often the case that students are divided to three classes: those with a fixed mindset, those with a growth mindset, and those with a "mixed" mindset (eg. [4]). If we do this and assign people to three classes with the ranges $[0.5, 2.5)$ for growth self-theory, $[2.5, 3.5]$ for mixed self-theory, and $(3.5, 5.5]$ for a fixed self-theory, the division of students to the three categories according to the three scales are found in Table 2

4.3 Stable versus dynamic nature of skills

In regards of Data B, students rated their perceptions as to what extent performance in different domains is due to inborn and stable

Figure 1: Density plots of the three self-theory scales

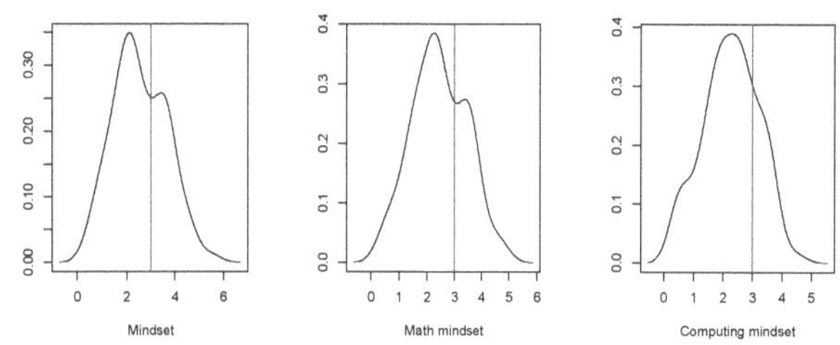

Table 2: Categorisations of students to scales

	Fixed	Mixed	Growth
Intelligence	21	22	43
Math intelligence	13	27	46
Computing intelligence	6	33	45

capabilities versus deliberate practice and effort. On a range from 1 to 5—where 1 indicates deliberate practice and dynamic nature of the ability, and 5 indicates a stable and inborn nature of the ability—the descriptives show the following: *intelligence* $\overline{x} = 3.12, s = 0.92$, *mathematics* $\overline{x} = 2.86, s = 0.84$, *social skills* $\overline{x} = 2.7, s = 0.91$, *sports* $\overline{x} = 2.37, s = 0.86$, *languages* $\overline{x} = 2.35, s = 0.74$, and *programming* $\overline{x} = 2.21, s = 0.73$. Thus, intelligence was, in this sample, considered to be the most stable property, followed by mathematics skills, social skills, sports, languages, and programming. Programming was considered to be the skill least dependent on stable or inborn capabilities, and the skill which mostly depends on effort and deliberate practice. It is noteworthy that social skills were considered to be statistically significantly more stable than skills in languages, programming, and sports (for each: $p < 0.02$, Student's t-test).

4.4 Performance in first CS courses

Basics of Algorithms and Programming (BAP) is a second period course, which is the first really challenging CS course. All CS and CE students must attend the course. The course is also attended by a high number of students of CS minors, who study other topics as their majors. In autumn 2018 BAP-course was attended by 336 students, and completed by 238 students (161 males, 77 females). Out of the $n = 86$ 1st year CS and CE students who completed the self-theory questionnaire, $n = 65$ attended the BAP course (49 males, 16 females), and $n = 55$ received a passing grade (41 males, 14 females). As shown in Section 3.1, this sample consisted only of first year CS and CE students, and did not consider students from other disciplines. The mean grade of this sample of $n = 65$ students was $\overline{x} = 2.89$ with standard deviation $s = 1.78$.

4.5 Correlational analysis

A correlational analysis (Pearson's, see Table 3) revealed the following. The three mindset-scales were associated, but not too strongly, indicating that the constructs are separate. For example, mindset (intel) associated with mindset (computing) by ($r = .57, p < .01, df = 82$). In regards of Data B (perceptions of stable or dynamic nature

[3] https://personality-project.org/r/

of skill domains), it is noteworthy that mindset-scales correlated rather strongly with the intelligence, mathematics, and programming variables, but only mildly with languages or social skills. Thus, e.g. those with a fixed view on intelligence seem not to be the same persons who have a fixed view on social skills. For those mindsetters who attended BAP ($n = 56$), exam scores and mindset were not associated ($r = .17, p = .2, df = 63$, intel), ($r = .16, p = .2, df = 63$, math intel), ($r = .06, p = .6, df = 61$, computing intel). There were no associations (Pearson's) between mindset-scales and submission times, or number of assignment submissions.

Table 3: Cormatrix (Pearson's) of 3 mindset-scales ($n = 86$)

	(i)	(m)	(c)	B(i)	B(m)	B(p)	B(l)	B(s)	B(sp)
(i) r		.67	.57	.76	.44	.45	.28	.21	.11
p		<.01	<.01	<.01	<.01	<.01	<.01	.06	.3
(m) r	.66		.77	.55	.71	.57	.33	.27	.17
p	<.01		<.01	<.01	<.01	<.01	.03	.01	.1
(c) r	.57	.77		.49	.55	.61	.27	.32	.17
p	<.01	<.01		<.01	<.01	<.01	.01	<.01	.1

(i)=intelligence (m)=math intelligence (c) =computing intelligence
B(i)=intelligence (data B) B(m)=mathematics (data B) B(p) = programming (data B)
B(l)=languages (data B) B(s)=social skills (data B) B(sp)=sports

4.6 Group differences

Exam performance per students' mindset-class (Table 2) are given in Table 4. Exam scores from all students who scored more than zero points in the course exam of BAP ($n = 56$) were included in the analysis. On contrary to what could be expected based on previous research on self-theories, those with a fixed self-theory in regards of intelligence, mathematics intelligence or computing intelligence seemed to perform better. However, analysis of variance (ANOVA) did not confirm the differences as statistically significant. Mindset on intelligence was the closest to statistical significance ($p = .073$), and in this case a TukeyHSD was performed for pairwise-comparison between groups: differences between groups *Gro* and *Fix* were significant at $p = 0.068$ level. If growth-mindsetters are compared directly to fixed-mindsetters with Student's t-test, the results show significant differences at levels of $p = .02$ (intel), $p = .03$ (math), and $p = .01$ (computing). These results suggest that those with a fixed mindset performed better in the BAP course.

Table 4: Group differences in Exam Scores

ExamScore	*Gro*	*Mix*	*Fix*	ANOVA p	t-test (Gro-Fix) p
Intelligence	60.96	62.94	73.73	.073	.02
Math intelligence	62.61	63.59	74.2	.19	.03
Comp intelligence	63.27	62.59	78.0	.15	.01

4.7 Nonparametric statistics

If exam points are converted to grades, information is lost but the use of nonparametric statistics becomes available. Table 5 shows the categorisation of students per mindset and course grade in intelligence, mathematics intelligence and computing intelligence for those students who attended the BAP course ($n = 65$). In neither of the three cases are the differences statistically significant ($\chi^2 = 14, df = 10, p = .2$, intel), ($\chi^2 = 7.8, df = 10, p = .7$, math intel), ($\chi^2 = 10, df = 10, p = .4$, computing intel). Thus, nonparametric statistics did show significant group differences, which is possibly partly due to small n. More data in the future is needed. Also, a qualitative inspection of fixed and growth mindsetters who score low and high grades is needed. Non-parametric analysis revealed no significant differences between any of the self-theory scales and any of the variables of Data B, or between variables of data B, or between Data B and final grade in BAP. For example, in regards of concept of stable or dynamic nature of social skills and final grade in BAP, χ^2-test resulted in $p = .7, \chi^2 = 17, df = 20$.

	Gro	Mix	Fix		Gro	Mix	Fix		Gro	Mix	Fix
0	5	2	2	0	6	1	2	0	5	4	0
1	4	5	0	1	5	3	1	1	5	4	0
2	5	0	3	2	5	2	1	2	6	2	0
3	5	2	2	3	5	2	2	3	7	2	0
4	4	7	3	4	4	7	3	4	4	6	3
5	6	3	7	5	9	3	4	5	8	4	3
Intelligence				Math intelligence				Computing intelligence			

Table 5: Mindset per grade

4.8 Other observations

The mean total time in assignment submissions for growth mindsetters was 74149 seconds as compared to 64049 seconds for fixed mindsetters (no statistical significance: $p = .3$, Student's t-test). The total number of exercise submissions also differed with mean 571.7 submissions (growth mindset) and 495.7 (fixed mindset), no statistical significance ($p = .2$, Student's t-test). Total time used correlated with no. of submissions ($r = 0.61, p < .01$). Time used or number of submissions did not correlate with exam score.

5 QUALITATIVE RESULTS

Students' answers were coded in ATLAS.ti. In most ($n = 56$) cases, students' conceptualised intelligence as an *ability*, while only in few answers, intelligence was conceptualised as a *factor* ($n = 3$), *skill* ($n = 4$), or as *speed*, or *processing power* ($n = 3$). For those who defined intelligence as an ability, a total of 19 different verbs were used. The most common verbs were *apply, infer, internalize, learn, process, solve,* and *understand.* A total of 12 objects were used with the verbs, the most common ones being *information, knowledge, logical problems, new things, problems,* and *things.* In most cases, students equated intelligence directly with an ability, such as the ability to solve problems. For example, one student wrote: *"(Intelligence is) the ability to solve problems."* Most common conceptualisations of intelligence are summarised in Table 6.

In three cases, intelligence was defined as a "background factor", which influences things, such as learning, and the ability to solve problems. One student wrote: *"Intelligence is an inborn factor, which defines a person's ability in logical inference, thinking, and capacity to learn."* In a total of five cases, intelligence was defined as a combination of intelligencies. One student wrote: *"(Intelligence includes) logical problem solving ability and emotional intelligence. General intelligence is the sum of many things."*, while another respondent wrote *"Intelligence is a wide domain, which includes everything from social to emotional and language and mathematical intelligence."* Most responses did not discuss the origins of intelligence. Only in few cases (n=4) intelligence was perceived as "inborn", while in

Table 6: Code co-occurrence for "ability to"

	Information	Knowledge	Logical problems	New things	Problems	Things
Apply	1	3				1
Infer	1		1			
Internalize		1		1		1
Learn		1		4		1
Process	2					1
Solve			2		13	
Understand	1				1	6

Note: These numbers do not represent individual students, but conceptualisations.

three (n = 3) cases, it was perceived that intelligence can be developed through work or efforts. In a couple of student responses, intelligence was connected to *rationality*, *creativity*, or *collaboration*.

It is noteworthy that conceptualisation of intelligence as an ability differs from typical definitions of intelligence as a general cognitive factor that reflects on a number of abilities (eg. [44]). Students' perception of intelligence, in general, leaned towards general, cognitively oriented theories (g), while "modern" conceptualisations including multiple intelligencies [17], collective intelligence [44] or systems intelligence [21] were present, but on a lesser scale.

6 DISCUSSION

The first research question asked *"What are the 1st year CS and CE students' self-theories in intelligence, mathematics, and computing?"* The results show the following. First, growth mindset is more common than fixed mindset. In regards of three tested mindset-scales, intelligence is considered as the most stable, followed by mathematics intelligence. Computing intelligence is considered the most dynamic. The three scales overlap partly, but are different, confirming and adding to observations from previous research [34]. Mindset on computing is, according to these results, more general than just a mindset on programming.

Second, the questions in regards of the stable versus dynamic nature of various domains confirms that students perceive intelligence as the most stable, followed by mathematics. It was a bit surprising to find that social skills was considered almost as stable as mathematics intelligence, and as clearly more stable than performance in sports, languages, and programming. On the other hand, in general, students considered programming to be something that anyone can learn, but considered social skills to be something that is stable and can not be learned. This is a dire misconception, and research shows that it is a direct obstacle to personal development, judgment on others, and collective behaviour [10, 21, 32]. Perhaps this also means that the learning environment at university does not support learning of social skills? Most research on mindset has previously concentrated on intelligence and academic achievement, while social skills mindset has received perhaps too little attention. Thus, further research on this matter is of high priority.

The second research question asked *"What statistical associations can be found between students' self-theories and academic achievement in first CS courses?"* It was a small surprise that the results are opposite to much of the previous research. Those with a fixed mindset achieved better grades. However, the results are statistically speaking weak, and previous skills and knowledge might have played a part. On the other hand, some research suggest that mindset and especially mindset-interventions may be effective only in regards of academically high-risk students [38]. In any case, further research is needed to gain a longitudinal perspective, after the students complete more courses. Also, high achieving students with a fixed-mindset, according to research of Dweck [10] conceive high grades to be proof of their superior fixed ability, and do not develop themselves further, which is a serious problem. These results show that it is not clear if and what kind of intervention may be needed.

The third research question asked *"How do 1st year CS and CE students conceptualise intelligence?"* The qualitative results reveal several things. First, the students' conceptualisation, in general, differed from the typical conceptualisations of intelligence such as cognitively oriented g-theories, or theories of multiple intelligencies, but many students equated intelligence directly with ability to "solve problems." Second, the conceptualisations orient towards the cognitive domain of abilities. Third, a relatively small number of conceptualisations that lean towards multiple intelligencies were found. The results perhaps reflect a computing identity as a cognitive problem solver, confirming previous findings [27].

7 CONCLUSIONS

From the individual perspective, the most crucial psychological mechanisms are one's perceptions of intellectual capacities, which are directly related to effort in challenging tasks [20]. Extensive research [10, 11] shows that learners who consider intelligence as a stable construct avoid situations where they risk "looking stupid", leading to significantly less effort, and weaker learning outcomes.

The collective aspects of learning are being increasingly recognised by educational experts [8, 15, 20, 22, 24]. Experiments show that groups that contain only high-achieving students produce less interesting and creative outcomes that groups that contain students from diverse backgrounds [20]. In general, pedagogical experts agree that educational institutions should move to teach "the four C:s.", critical thinking, communication, collaboration and creativity (eg. [8, 24]). This is also well acknowledged in CSE [3, 23, 27, 29].

How to do this in practice is another thing, where the teachers' side to the matter is of utmost importance [3, 27, 29]. This can be challenged for example by a collective disrespect for "soft" topics [3], and mismatches between educational demands and students' preferences [27], and a narrow problem-solver identity, confirmed in this paper and also recognised in previous research [29].

Research on self-theories needs to go hand in hand with development and research on modern constructs such as grit [40], digital capital [43], multiple intelligencies [17], collective intelligence [44], and computing intelligence, introduced in this paper. Systemic and holistic positive development in CS identities are needed. These efforts must work in concert with efforts to develop courses and interventions to help students achieve their dreams and potential.

ACKNOWLEDGEMENTS

The research was supported by the Growing Mind-project[4], funded by the Strategic Research Council of the Academy of Finland.

[4]https://growingmind.fi

REFERENCES

[1] Joshua Aronson, Carrie B. Fried, and Catherine Good. 2002. Reducing the Effects of Stereotype Threat on African American College Students by Shaping Theories of Intelligence. *Journal of Experimental Social Psychology* 38, 2 (2002), 113–125.

[2] Lisa S. Blackwell, Kali H. Trzesniewski, and Carol Sorich Dweck. 2007. Implicit Theories of Intelligence Predict Achievement Across an Adolescent Transition: A Longitudinal Study and an Intervention. *Child Development* 78, 1 (2007), 246–263.

[3] Å. Cajander, M. Daniels, D. Golay, J. Moll, A. Nylén, A. Pears, A. Peters, and R. McDermott. 2017. Unexpected student behaviour and learning opportunities: Using the theory of planned behaviour to analyse a critical incident. In *2017 IEEE Frontiers in Education Conference (FIE)*. 1–8.

[4] Susana Claro, David Paunesku, and Carol S. Dweck. 2016. Growth mindset tempers the effects of poverty on academic achievement. *Proceedings of the National Academy of Sciences* 113, 31 (2016), 8664–8668.

[5] John W. Creswell. 2014. *Research Design: Qualitative, Quantitative, and Mixed Methods Approaches* (4th ed.). Sage Publications, California, USA.

[6] Quintin Cutts, Emily Cutts, Stephen Draper, Patrick O'Donnell, and Peter Saffrey. 2010. Manipulating Mindset to Positively Influence Introductory Programming Performance. In *Proceedings of the 41st ACM Technical Symposium on Computer Science Education (SIGCSE '10)*. ACM, New York, NY, USA, 431–435.

[7] Quintin Cutts and Peter Donaldson. 2018. Investigating Attitudes Towards Learning Computer Science. In *Computer Science Education: Perspectives on Teaching and Learning in School*, Sue Sentance, Erik Barendsen, and Carsten Schulte (Eds.). Bloomsbury, 39–55.

[8] Cathy N. Davidson. 2017. *The New Education: How to Revolutionize the University to Prepare Students for a World In Flux*. New York: Basic Books.

[9] Martyn Denscombe. 2010. *The Good Research Guide for Small-Scale Social Research Projects*. Open University Press.

[10] Carol S. Dweck. 1999. *Self-Theories: Their Role in Motivation, Personality, and Development*. Psychology Press (Taylor & Francis).

[11] Carol S. Dweck. 2006. *Mindset: How You Can Fulfill Your Potential*. Random House, New York, NY, USA.

[12] Carol S. Dweck. 2008. Mindsets and Math/Science Achievement. In *Carnegie Corporation of New York-Institute for Advanced Study Commission on Mathematics and Science Education*.

[13] Carol S. Dweck and David S. Yeager. 2019. Mindsets: A View From Two Eras. *Perspectives on Psychological Science* (2019), 1–16.

[14] Stephen Edwards and Zhiyi Li. 2016. Towards Progress Indicators for Measuring Student Programming Effort During Solution Development. In *Proceedings of the 16th Koli Calling International Conference on Computing Education Research (Koli Calling '16)*. ACM, New York, NY, USA, 31–40.

[15] Yrjö Engeström and Annalisa Sannino. 2010. Studies of expansive learning: Foundations, findings and future challenges. *Educational Research Review* 5, 1 (2010), 1–24.

[16] K. Anders Ericsson and Paul Ward. 2007. Capturing the Naturally Occurring Superior Performance of Experts in the Laboratory: Toward a Science of Expert and Exceptional Performance. *Current Directions in Psychological Science* 16, 6 (2007), 346–350.

[17] Howard Gardner. 2011. *Frames of Mind: The Theory of Multiple Intelligencies*. Basic Books.

[18] Helen Grant and Carol S. Dweck. 2003. Clarifying Achievement Goals and Their Impact. *Journal of Personality and Social Psychology* 85, 3 (2003), 541–553.

[19] Robert Greene. 2013. *Mastery*. Penguin Books.

[20] Kai Hakkarainen. 2017. Kollektiivinen luovuus, yhteisöllinen oppiminen ja itsensä ylittäminen (in Finnish). *Aikuiskasvatus* 27, 1 (2017), 47–56.

[21] Raimo P. Hämäläinen, Rachel Jones, and Esa Saarinen. 2014. Being Better Better – Living with Systems Intelligence. *Aalto University School of Science Publications* (2014).

[22] Yuval Noah Harari. 2018. *21 Lessons for the 21st Century*. Random House.

[23] Päivi Kinnunen, Matthew Butler, Michael Morgan, Aletta Nylen, Anne-Kathrin Peters, Jane Sinclair, Sara Kalvala, and Erkki Pesonen. 2018. Understanding initial undergraduate expectations and identity in computing studies. *European Journal of Engineering Education* 43, 2 (2018), 201–218.

[24] Charles Kivunja. 2015. Teaching Students to Learn and to Work Well with 21st Century Skills: Unpacking the Career and Life Skills Domain of the New Learning Paradigm. *International Journal of Higher Education* 4, 1 (2015).

[25] Clayton Lewis. 2007. Attitudes and Beliefs About Computer Science Among Students and Faculty. *SIGCSE Bull.* 39, 2 (June 2007), 37–41.

[26] Laurie Murphy and Lynda Thomas. 2008. Dangers of a Fixed Mindset: Implications of Self-theories Research for Computer Science Education. In *Proceedings of the 13th Annual Conference on Innovation and Technology in Computer Science Education (ITiCSE '08)*. ACM, New York, NY, USA, 271–275.

[27] A. Nylén, Å. Cajander, M. Daniels, A. Pears, and R. McDermott. 2017. Why are we here? Student perspectives on the goal of STEM higher education. In *2017 IEEE Frontiers in Education Conference (FIE)*. 1–7.

[28] David Paunesku, Gregory M. Walton, Carissa Romero, Eric N. Smith, David S. Yeager, and Carol S. Dweck. 2015. Mind-Set Interventions Are a Scalable Treatment for Academic Underachievement. *Psychological Science* 26, 6 (2015), 784–793.

[29] Anne-Kathrin Peters, Anders Berglund, Anna Eckerdal, and Arnold Pears. 2015. Second Year Computer Science and IT Students' Experience of Participation in the Discipline. In *Proceedings of the 15th Koli Calling Conference on Computing Education Research (Koli Calling '15)*. ACM, New York, NY, USA, 68–76.

[30] Carissa Romero, Allison Master, Dave Paunesku, Carol S. Dweck, and James J. Gross. 2014. Academic and Emotional Functioning in Middle School: The Role of Implicit Theories. *Emotion* 14, 2 (2014), 227–234.

[31] Esa Saarinen and Raimo Hämäläinen. 2010. The Originality of Systems Intelligence. In *Essays on Systems Intelligence*, Raimo P. Hämäläinen and Esa Saarinen (Eds.). Systems Analysis Laboratory, 9–26.

[32] Esa Saarinen and Raimo P. Hämäläinen. 2004. Systems Intelligence: Connecting Engineering Thinking with Human Sensitivity. In *Systems Intelligence – Discovering a Hidden Competence in Human Action and Organizational Life,*, Raimo P. Hämäläinen and Esa Saarinen (Eds.). Helsinki University of Technology: Systems Analysis Laboratory Research Reports, A88, October 2004.

[33] Mehran Sahami, Steve Roach, Ernesto Cuadros-Vargas, Elizabeth K. Hawthorne, Amruth Kumar, Richard LeBlanc, David Reed, and Remzi Seker. 2014. ACM/IEEE-CS Computer Science Curricula 2013: Implementing the Final Report. In *Proceedings of the 45th ACM Technical Symposium on Computer Science Education (SIGCSE '14)*. ACM, New York, NY, USA, 175–176.

[34] M. J. Scott and G. Ghinea. 2014. On the Domain-Specificity of Mindsets: The Relationship Between Aptitude Beliefs and Programming Practice. *IEEE Transactions on Education* 57, 3 (Aug 2014), 169–174.

[35] Martin E. P. Seligman. 2011. *Flourish: A Visionary New Understanding of Happiness and Well-being*. ATRIA Paperback, New York, NY, USA.

[36] Chen Shen, David B. Miele, and Marina Vasilyeva. 2016. The relation between college students' academic mindsets and their persistence during math problem solving. *Psychology in Russia. State of the Art* 9, 3 (2016), 38 – 56.

[37] Beth Simon, Brian Hanks, Laurie Murphy, Sue Fitzgerald, Renée McCauley, Lynda Thomas,,and Carol Zander. 2008. Saying Isn'T Necessarily Believing: Influencing Self-theories in Computing. In *Proceedings of the Fourth International Workshop on Computing Education Research (ICER '08)*. ACM, New York, NY, USA, 173–184.

[38] Victoria F. Sisk, Alexander P. Burgoyne, Jingze Sun, Jennifer L. Butler, and Brooke N. Macnamara. 2018. To What Extent and Under Which Circumstances Are Growth Mind-Sets Important to Academic Achievement? Two Meta-Analyses. *Psychological Science* 29, 4 (2018), 549–571.

[39] Robert J. Sternberg. 1999. Successful intelligence: Finding a Balance. *Trends in Cognitive Sciences* 3, 11 (1999), 436–442.

[40] Xin Tang, Ming-Te Wang, Jiesi Guo, and Jaana Katariina Salmela-Aro. 2019. Building Grit: The Longitudinal Pathways between Mindset, Commitment, Grit, and Academic Outcomes. *Journal of Youth and Adolescence* (5 2 2019).

[41] Juha Törmänen, Raimo P. Hämäläinen, and Esa Saarinen. 2016. Systems intelligence inventory. *The Learning Organization* 23, 4 (2016), 218–231.

[42] Ashok Kumar Veerasamy, Daryl D'Souza, Rolf Lindén, and Mikko-Jussi Laakso. 2018. The Impact of Prior Programming Knowledge on Lecture Attendance and Final Exam. *Journal of Educational Computing Research* 56, 2 (2018), 226–253.

[43] Tina Vrieler. 2017. Digital Capital: A Platform for Developing Computational Thinking. In *Proceedings of the 17th Koli Calling International Conference on Computing Education Research (Koli Calling '17)*. ACM, New York, NY, USA, 205–206.

[44] Anita Williams Woolley, Christopher F. Chabris, Alex Pentland, Nada Hashmi, and Thomas W. Malone. 2010. Evidence for a Collective Intelligence Factor in the Performance of Human Groups. *Science* 330, 6004 (2010), 686–688.

[45] David S. Yeager and Gregory M. Walton. 2011. Social-Psychological Interventions in Education: They're Not Magic. *Review of Educational Research* 81, 2 (2011), 267–301.

Identifying and Validating Java Misconceptions Toward a CS1 Concept Inventory

Ricardo Caceffo
State University of Campinas
Campinas, SP, Brasil
caceffo@ic.unicamp.br

Pablo Frank-Bolton
The George Washington University
Washington, D.C, USA
pfrank@email.gwu.edu

Renan Souza
State University of Campinas
Campinas, SP, Brasil
renan-plsouza@uol.com.br

Rodolfo Azevedo
State University of Campinas
Campinas, SP, Brasil
rodolfo@ic.unicamp.br

ABSTRACT

A misconception is a common misunderstanding that students may have about a specific topic. The identification, documentation, and validation of misconceptions is a long and time-consuming work, usually carried out using iterative cycles of students answering open-ended questionnaires, interviews with instructors and students, exam analysis, and discussion with experts. A comprehensive list of validated misconceptions in some subject can be used to build formal evaluation methods like the Concept Inventory (CI), a multiple-choice questionnaire that is usually performed as pre-post tests in order to assess any change in student understanding. In CS1, validated misconceptions were identified and documented in C and Python programming languages. Although there are studies related to misconceptions in the Java language, these misconceptions lack the formality, comprehensiveness, and robustness of their C and Python counterparts. On this work, we propose a methodology to adapt the validated misconceptions in C and Python to Java. Initially, through the analysis of an initial list of 33 misconceptions in C and 28 in Python, we identified and documented in an antipattern format 31 possible misconceptions in Java. We then developed a final term exam, composed of 7 open-ended questions, in which each question was designed to address some of the misconceptions covered in the course (N = 27). Through the analysis of the exams answers (N = 69 students), it was possible to validate 22 of the misconceptions (81%). Also, 6 new misconceptions were identified, leading to a total of 28 valid misconceptions in Java.

CCS CONCEPTS

• **Social and professional topics → CS1**; **Student assessment**; • **Software and its engineering → General programming languages**; *Patterns*.

KEYWORDS

CS1; Course; Misconception; Concept; Inventory; Java; Student; Assessment; Introductory; Programming; Multiple; Choice; Question

ACM Reference Format:
Ricardo Caceffo, Pablo Frank-Bolton, Renan Souza, and Rodolfo Azevedo. 2019. Identifying and Validating Java Misconceptions Toward a CS1 Concept Inventory. In *Innovation and Technology in Computer Science Education (ITiCSE '19), July 15–17, 2019, Aberdeen, Scotland Uk.* ACM, New York, NY, USA, 7 pages. https://doi.org/10.1145/3304221.3319771

ACM ISBN 978-1-4503-6301-3/19/07...$15.00
https://doi.org/10.1145/3304221.3319771

1 INTRODUCTION

Learning to program has increasingly become a required skill both in academic and professional [31] areas. However, as explained by Figueiredo & Garcia-Penalvo [15], the difficulties of teaching and learning programming are concerning enough to require the development of special pedagogical strategies.

For these reason, novel educational learning approaches are being developed, adapted and employed inside the classroom. Particularly, the adoption of Active Learning [1] techniques, like the Problem-based learning (PBL) and Peer-Instruction (PI), has been shown to be a positive factor on students' learning and motivation when compared to traditional lecture-based learning [7].

In order to formally measure the impact of these interventions, formal assessment methods are required. One typical example is the Concept Inventory (CI), a multiple-choice questionnaire in which each wrong choice is mapped to a common misconception among students. Usually performed as pre- and post-tests, it allows the assessment of the student's learning gains in a certain period of time.

For introductory programming courses (CS1), misconceptions were identified and documented in the C and Python programming languages with the purpose of supporting the design of CIs. Although there are studies related to misconceptions in the Java language, these misconceptions lack the formality, comprehensiveness, and robustness required to design a CI in this language. Also, the design process to identify and validate misconceptions to support the creation and assessment of a CI, is long and costly [3].

Therefore, on this study we propose to answer the following research questions:

- **RQ1:** Is it possible to map and document misconceptions in Java from other programming languages, thus making the process of CI creation less costly and more effective?
- **RQ2:** Is an open response test a proper way to validate the identified misconceptions?

This work is organized as follows: section 2 details the concepts presented in the introduction, also describing the **related works** and how this research is positioned with respect to the literature; section 3 presents the research **methodology**; section 4 the **outcomes**; section 5 presents a **discussion** of the outcomes and how the research questions were answered; and section 6 presents the conclusion and future work.

2 RELATED WORK

A **misconception** is an understanding issue students have when learning some subject. In the CS1 context, as explained by Kurvinen *et al.* [24], finding the most relevant misconceptions students have in relation to programming would help teachers and lecturers address the main obstacles faced by the students.

Studies related to the identification and use of misconceptions in CS1 courses can be classified into three groups: (1) real-time coding detection tools, that aim to identify student's misconceptions when programming, providing a reliable feedback; (2) identification of misconceptions for general purposes; and (3) identification of misconceptions to support the design of Concept Inventories.

The first group — real-time coding detection tools — is characterized by the identification of misconceptions closest to the program syntax and organization. For example, Bulmer [4] built a Java code visualizer that animates the programming process dynamically, summarizing error metrics in real time. The tool detects poor coding practices, which could lead to poorly structured programs. Examples of misconceptions identified by Bulmer *et al.* [4] are unclosed scanners, brackets and quotes miscounts or mismatches, misplaced semi-colons, and misaligned whitespaces.

Moreover, Hristova *et al.* [20] details a project conducted by faculty and advanced students in the creation of an educational tool for Java programming, called Expresso. The tool was created upon a list of 20 essential misconceptions, classified as syntax errors (*e.g* = versus == and == versus *.equals*), semantic errors (*e.g* invoking class method on object), and logic errors (*e.g.* incompatibility between the declared return type of a method and in its invocation).

For their part, Gusukuma *et al.* [17] propose a tool named Misconception Driven Feedback (MDF), which uses a cognitive student model and program analysis to detect mistakes and uncover underlying misconceptions in a Python course. The tool is aimed at detecting misconceptions in student code, and delivering appropriate and real-time feedback.

Similarly, Soltanpoor *et al.* [29] propose a framework to help individual students to overcome their misconceptions through personalized prescriptive quizzes, significantly improving the learning outcomes of novice programmers.

The second group — identification of misconceptions for general purposes — aims to identify and measure the frequency of misconceptions in CS1, supporting, for example, the adoption of new learning approaches and the design of tools to enhance CS1 learning. Studies in this context, associated with the Python programming language, include for example the work of Cherenkova *et al.* [11], which found that conditionals and loops proved particularly problematic when learning to program. Sirkia [28] analyzed the mistakes in over 24,000 student-submitted solutions to a Visual Programming Simulation tool. They identified 26 mistakes as the most frequent ones, requiring further discussion. Topics identified included variable assignment, control structures, booleans, and functions. Also, Miller *et al.* [12] identified misconceptions in advanced object-oriented concepts during a CS2 course in Python, with the most relevant ones being related to parameters and reference specifications.

Also in this category, but related to C programming, Kennedy & Kraemer [22] performed a questionnaire with 21 open-ended questions, identifying misconceptions mainly on parameter passing and scope. They also encouraged students to provide the reasoning behind each answer. The goal, as explained by the authors, was to *"give a more concrete understanding of not only misconceptions that students have in introductory computer science classes, but also why they are having them; and longer term, to develop and evaluate interventions to address these misconceptions"*.

On this category, a study related to Java programming is the work of Kurvinen *et al.* [24], which analyzed three open-ended questions to grasp a more comprehensive idea of students' knowledge. The answers were analyzed and categorized as syntax, indexing, return statement, comparison, try-catch structures, state, and execution.

Finally, the third group — identification of misconceptions to support the design of Concept Inventories — is aimed at the identification and documentation of misconceptions for the design of Concept Inventories (CIs). As explained by Herman *et al.* [18], Concept Inventories are standardized assessment tools that evaluate how well a student's conceptual framework matches the accepted conceptual framework of a discipline. In practice, a CI is a multiple-choice questionnaire, usually composed of around 30 questions to be answered in an interval of between 30 and 60 minutes, in which each wrong choice is mapped to a previously documented misconception. A CI is usually performed as a pre- and post-test, measuring students' learning gains in some courses [26] .

CIs exist in many learning areas. The first and most known CI is the Force Concept Inventory (FCI)[19], designed to cover misconceptions related to the Newton' laws. In Computer Science, misconceptions were identified and CIs designed for Digital Logic [18], Operating Systems [32] and the CS2 topic, like the analysis of algorithms [14], heaps and binary search trees [21].

Several studies in the literature propose methodologies to create CIs. For example, Porter *et al.* [27] propose an open collaboration system for the CI development. The system would mimic the principles common to open source software communities, which have regularly demonstrated their ability to produce high-quality results. The authors propose a basic framework for "open source" CI development, identifying the obstacles faced, and sketching the design-space and trade-offs necessary to make it viable. Although promising, such a system is yet to be deployed.

Another approach is the one proposed by Almstrum *et al.* [3], as shown in Figure 1.

Table 1: Summary of related work regarding: real-time coding detection tools; general misconceptions; misconceptions for Concept Inventories; and CS1 Concept Inventories, considering C, Python and Java programming languages.

Programming Language	Real-time coding detection tools	General Misconceptions	Misconceptions for Concept Inventories	Concept Inventory
C	-	Kennedy & Kraemer [22]	Caceffo *et al.* [5, 9, 10]	Caceffo *et al.* [8]
Python	Gusukuma *et al.* [17]	Cherenkova *et al.* [11] Sirkia *et al.* [28] Miller *et al.* [12] (CS2)	Gama *et al.* [16]	–
Java	Bulmer *et al.* [4] Hristova *et al.* [20] Soltanpoor *et al.* [29]	Kurvinen *et al.* [24] Paul & Vahrenhold [25]	This work	–

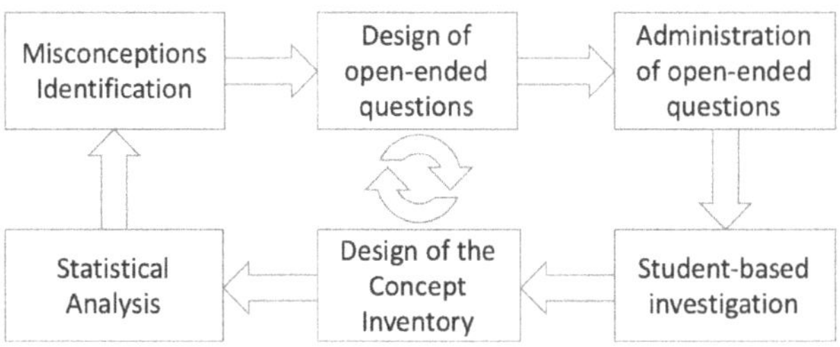

Figure 1: An adaptation of the Concept Inventory design and assessment approach as proposed by Almstrum *et al.* in [3]. Initially, a first version of the misconceptions is identified through interviews with experts and/or an analysis of the literature. Then, an open-ended exploratory questionnaire is designed and administered to students. Results are also analyzed through a student-based investigation, resulting in a revised list of misconceptions. Finally, the misconceptions identified support the design of a Concept Inventory (CI), which has its statistical reliability evaluated. The cycle is repeated many times as required to reach viable misconceptions, leading to a CI with statistical reliability.

Almstrum *et al.* [3] suggest a long and costly iterative process, in which the misconception's fundamental concepts are initially identified through interviews with experts and/or literature analysis; then, open-ended questions are designed and answered by students, supporting the validation of the previous and the identification of new misconceptions; and a student-based investigation, in which students and instructors are interviewed about the misconceptions found, resulting in a revised list of misconceptions. The cycle is repeated many times as required to reach viable misconceptions, leading to a CI with statistical reliability.

Also, the authors [3] highlight the need to deconstruct the misconceptions, which may lead to a much deeper level of detail than the one required by the misconception definitions usually found in the other categories. For example, one could document a misconception explaining the students' mental models related to that topic, when the referred misconception occurs, why it occurs, and how it could be avoided. In CS1, misconceptions were identified and deconstructed using the method proposed by Almstrum *et al.* [3], which permitted the design of CIs, in Python and C programming languages. The former relates to Gama *et al.* work [16], which performed a series of analyses of Python exams and interviews of Python instructors. These lead to the documentation of 28 misconceptions on that language, which were later organized into 8 topics. The latter relates to Caceffo *et al.*, which through the analysis of open-ended exams and interviews with instructors [10], and through the administration of an exploratory questionnaire [9], identified and documented 33 misconceptions in the C language [5]. These were organized into 7 topics. The misconceptions were then employed to support the design of a CI composed of 27 multiple-choice questions [8].

Overall, Table 1 classifies the CS1 related work into the three categories described on this section, also presenting the respective CIs when available. The current work aims to fill the gap in the identification and documentation of Java misconceptions to support the further design of Concept Inventories in such language.

3 METHODOLOGY

On this work, as illustrated by Figure 2, we employed an alternative methodology to the Almstrum *et al.* [3] iterative cycle for misconception identification.

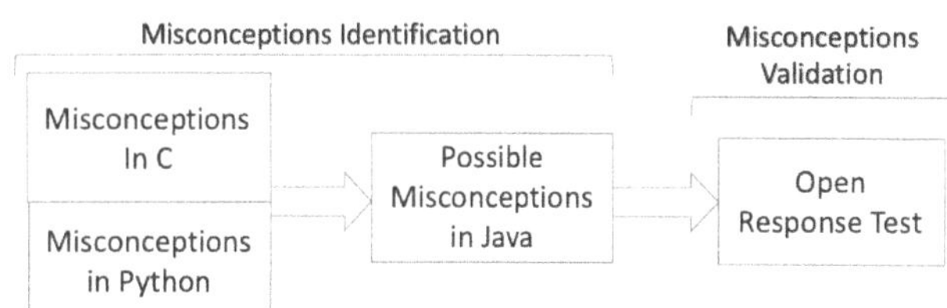

Figure 2: Methodology used in this work. Instead of the iterative cycle defined by Almstrum et. al [3], we propose the identification of possible misconceptions through the analysis of already identified misconceptions in C and Python, that were converted, if possible, to Java. An open response test, composed of open-ended questions, was created to validate the identified misconceptions and also identify new ones.

In our approach, we initially identified and documented possible Java misconceptions through the analysis of the previously defined misconceptions in C and Python, available respectively in [16] and [5]. This was carried out using exam analysis, and instructor and student interviews, as proposed by Almstrum *et al* [3]. Then followed the application of an open response test composed of open-ended questions, created to validate the previously identified misconceptions, and to allow the identification of new ones. The following subsections detail each part of the chosen methodology.

3.1 Identification of Possible Misconceptions in Java

Our hypothesis is that misconceptions are, at least up to a point, language independent. For example, both C and Python works [5, 16] have a misconception named "Parameter value set by external source". For this misconception, in the first line of a function/method that has a parameter, the student overwrites the parameter value with an external value – usually the input from the keyboard – thus losing the correct value passed by parameter. In the C language, a student with this misconception would include the command `scanf("%d", &param);` in Python the student would include `param = int(input());` the equivalent instruction in Java would be something akin to `int num = scan.nextInt()`. Therefore, although the syntax is different, the misconceptions would be equivalent.

However, while Python and Java are object-oriented, C is not. It is therefore expected that some misconceptions would be shared by Java and Python, while not present in C.

The methodology employed was: (1) build a table mapping the misconceptions in C [5] and Python [16]; (2) have experts discuss the presence of equivalent misconceptions in Java, based on experience; (3) transcribe the pertinent misconceptions to Java.

In total, 31 possible misconceptions were identified in the Java language, and organized into 7 topics: (A) Function Parameter Use and Scope (N=6); (B) Variables, Identifiers, and Scope (N=4); (C) Recursion (N=3); (D) Iteration (N=6); (E) Structures (N=3); (F) Pointers (N=1); (G) Boolean Expressions (N=4); and (H) Classes and objects (N=4). These misconceptions were mapped from C and Python equivalents (N=18), from C misconceptions only (N=10), and from Python misconceptions only (N=3).

Table 2 shows part of the mapping table. The complete mapping table was published as a Technical Report ([30] pp4-6). In the report [30], each one of the 31 misconceptions were also documented — following the deconstruction approach proposed by Almstrum *et al.* [3] — as an antipattern [13]. Table 3 shows, as an example, the misconception D.1 documented as an antipattern.

3.2 Validation of Misconceptions

The validation of the misconceptions was carried out using an open response test where students were asked to complete program templates to obtain specific outcomes. The questions were carefully crafted to allow the possible emergence of a certain group of misconceptions (*e.g.* those related to loops would need questions that address iteration). Overall, all previously detected Java misconceptions were covered, except the three related to topic C (recursion), and one related to *final* variables in topic H (classes and objects), as these topics were not covered in the classes. Therefore, a total of 27 misconceptions were employed to craft the open response test.

The test was taken by 69 students of a standard upper-level undergraduate introductory Java programming course and was scheduled at the end of the semester so that the students had the required experience. The tests were analyzed by a team of graders to find errors and catalog them as any of the known misconceptions, or as newly detected ones.

Questions where presented as incomplete starter code that provided enough information so that students could achieve the required goal while allowing the misconceptions to appear. The first question (Problem 1) of the response test, covering the misconceptions related to function parameter use and scope (topic A) was:

Problem 1: To complement the following main, write the function `subtractNumbers` that receives two integers and returns their subtraction.

```
public class Training {
  public static void main (String [] args) {
    int a = 5;
    int b = 15;
    int result = subtractNumbers (a, b);
    System.out.println ("a - b is " + result);

    result = subtractNumbers (b, a);
    System.out.println ("b - a is " + result );
  }
  // Your method would go after this point

}
```

The complete open response test is available as a complementary material [6].

4 RESULTS

Of the 27 misconceptions considered in the open response test, 22 were observed. In addition, 6 new possible misconception instances were identified, extending the possible range of Java misconceptions to 28.

Results are presented on Table 4. IDs were organized to maintain standardization and compatibility with misconceptions identified in C (Caceffo *et al.*[5]) and Python (Gama *et al.* [16]). We also published a complementary material [6] with the updated list of 28 misconceptions, documented in the antipattern format.

5 DISCUSSION

Research question **RQ1** was successfully answered as of the initial 33 misconceptions in C and 28 misconceptions in Python, it was possible to map, deconstruct and document 31 misconceptions in Java. Also, this corroborates our hypothesis that misconceptions identified for Concept Inventories are, at least up to a point, language independent.

An unexpected fact was, however, that more misconceptions were mapped solely from C to Java language (N=10, 32% of the total) than solely from Python to Java language (N=3, 10% of the total), although Python is an object-oriented language, and C is not.

This can be explained as C is considered to be a more difficult programming language and with more nuances than Python. Indeed, Python tops the list of most popular programming languages

Table 2: Part of the table ([30] pp4-6) that maps the C [5], Python [16] and our suggestion of equivalent Java misconceptions.

Misconc.	Description	C [5]	Python [16]	Possible Java Misc.
Parameter value set by external source	In the first line of a function/method that has a parameter, the student sets the parameter with an external value, thus losing its correct value.	`scanf("%d",&param)`	`param = int(input())`	`int num = scan.nextInt();`
Attempt to call class attribute through indices	An object is instantiated, and then one attempts to change the values of its attributes with bracket operators and indices, as if the object was a list or similar structure.	–	`c = Car("R",1)` `c[1] = 5`	`Car c = new Car("R",1);` `c[1] = 5;`
...	...	...	...	...
Total	–	**33**	**28**	**31**

Table 3: Misconception D.1 documented as an antipattern.

ID:	D.1
Name:	Improper update of a loop counter.
Description:	Wrong update of a loop counter, leading to an incorrect number of loop iterations.

Example:	`int i = 0;`
	`int sum = 0;`
	`while (i < 10) {`
	`    sum = sum + i;`
	`    i = 1;`
	`}`
	`System.out.println(sum);`

Rationale:	Students don't understand how the loop counter should be updated to reach the desired number of iterations.
Consequences:	Infinite loop or wrong results if the output uses values calculated inside the loop.
Where to detect:	In any loop structure.
How to detect:	The loop counter is incorrectly updated.
Improvement:	Students should be able to check (e.g. through the debug or a print) the counter value at each iteration.

taught in college-level introductory computer science courses [23]. Hence, our results point to a greater proximity between the misconceptions of C and Java, although additional studies would be needed to revisit this finding.

For **RQ2**, we wanted to investigate whether an open response test (*c.f.* section 3.2) is a proper way to validate the identified misconceptions. The test was crafted in order to potentially identify 27 of the 31 misconceptions previously documented in Java. Overall, 22 of the 27 misconceptions were detected (81%) (*i.e.* had at least one occurrence). Specifically, 6 had exactly one occurrence (0.9% of the total 111 misconceptions detected), 12 had between 2 and 5 occurrences (1.8% to 4.5% of the total), and 4 had between 5 and 12 occurrences (4.5% and 10.8% of the total). Also, 6 new possible misconceptions were identified in the process.

Although we consider **RQ2** was successfully answered, the adopted methodology presents some limitations. The presence or not of determined misconception among students depends on a number of factors, such as the way the instructor presents his/her classes, the topics covered, and also the order in which these topics were presented to students. Therefore, the fact that a misconception was not identified – or have a low rate – is not a proof that the misconception does not exist, but rather an indication that in that context it is not relevant.

Additional studies are required in other Java CS1 courses to identify whether the misconceptions identified in Java are present or not, including those that have not been verified in the test, such as the ones related to recursion. Also, the deconstruction of misconceptions requires validation through interviews with students and instructors, thus allowing the consideration of the student's mental models as proposed by Almstum *et al.* [3].

On the other hand, this study contributes significantly by presenting an initial – and validated – set of misconceptions identified for CIs in Java CS1 courses. The rate of each misconception is also important to serve as the basis for future studies in the area, as well as presenting the necessary resources for the creation of a first version of a Java CI.

6 CONCLUSION

A misconception is an understanding issue students have when learning some subject. We classified the studies related to misconceptions in CS1 courses into three groups: (1) real-time coding detection and feedback tools; (2) identification of misconceptions for general purposes; and (3) identification of misconceptions to support the design of Concept Inventories (CIs), multiple-choice questionnaires in which each wrong choice is mapped to a misconception.

This work contributes in the latter category as we propose a methodology to identify misconceptions in some programming language (in this case, Java) from previous misconceptions already identified in other languages (in this case, C and Python). The

Table 4: Open response test results (N=69 students). Overall, 111 misconceptions were identified during the test correction. Of the 27 misconceptions covered in the test design, 22 were detected in the student's answers; 6 new possible misconceptions were found. The complementary material [6] presents these 28 misconceptions documented in the antipattern format.

ID	Misconception	Number of Occurrences	Frequency
A.3	Attempt to access parameter from outside scope.	12	10.8%
A.4	Incorrect order of function parameters.	3	2.7%
A.5	Function return value not handled by caller function.	1	0.9%
A.6	Logic error related to parameters when calling function.	3	2.7%
A.7 (New)	No return value in a function that returns something.	21	18.9%
A.8 (New)	No parameters used when calling a method.	5	4.5%
B.1	Attempt to access local variables, except parameters, from outside scope.	5	4.5%
B.2	Global variables considered local in current scope.	3	2.7%
B.3	Parameter mistaken for same-name variable outside function	3	2.7%
B.4	Global variables assumed inaccessible from within function.	6	5.4%
B.7 (New)	Wrong order in logical or arithmetic operations.	5	4.5%
D.1	Improper update of loop counter.	1	0.9%
D.4	Loop iterates an incorrect number of times.	1	0.9%
D.5	Absence of loop (single iteration).	3	2.7%
D.6	Loop construction incoherent with remainder of code.	2	1.8%
E.2	Struct identifier compared to field.	2	1.8%
E.5	Use of "struct" keyword after declaration.	1	0.9%
E.6 (New)	Using Local variables as member variables of an object.	1	0.9%
E.7 (New)	Value assigned to class reference instead of its member variable.	1	0.9%
F.4	Void function returns value.	1	0.9%
G.1	Incorrect precedence for boolean operators.	3	2.7%
G.2	Nested if-statements instead of boolean expression.	4	3.6%
G.3	Arithmetic expression instead of boolean expression.	6	5.4%
G.4	Attempt to evaluate boolean expression through loops.	3	2.7%
G.5	Condition added after *else*.	1	0.9%
H.4	Class attribute invoked without being imported or with no class specified..	10	9.0%
H.7	Attempt to call class attribute through indices.	3	2.7%
H.9 (New)	New class constructed every time a method is needed instead of using an existing class' method.	1	0.9%
Total	28 misconceptions	111	100%

proposed methodology aims to complement the process currently adopted in the literature [3], presenting a more efficient and less costly way to identify an initial list of misconceptions for a determined language.

We gathered evidence that misconceptions for CIs are, at least up to a point, language independent, so it is possible to convert most of them from one language to another. In this work, from the C (N=33) and Python (N=28) misconceptions used as reference, it was possible to map, deconstruct and document 31 misconceptions in Java.

We then designed an open response test to potentially identify 27 of the 31 misconceptions identified — 4 were not considered, as their topics had not been covered in class. The answers were analyzed, allowing the detection of 22 of the previous misconceptions. Also, 6 new possible misconceptions were identified, leading to an updated list of 28 misconceptions. These new misconceptions were deconstructed (documented in the antipattern format, explaining of why/where/how the misconceptions happen), and the updated data published as a complementary material of this paper [6].

As future work we plan to follow the methodology proposed by Almstrum *et al.* [3], performing think-aloud [2] interviews with students and instructors, validating the documentation and also updating the misconceptions list. Finally, a first version of a Java CI will be designed and its internal statistical reliability assessed.

7 ACKNOWLEDGEMENTS

This research was supported by: Brazilian National Council for Scientific and Technological Development (CNPq), under grant 309794/2017-0; Brazilian Coordination for the Improvement of Higher Education Personnel (CAPES); State University of Campinas (Unicamp/FAEPEX); grant #2014/07502-4, São Paulo Research Foundation (FAPESP) and; grant #2013/08293-7, São Paulo Research Foundation (FAPESP), under the Research, Innovation and Dissemination Centers (REDIC).

REFERENCES

[1] 1991. *Active Learning: Creating Excitement in the Classroom (J-B ASHE Higher Education Report Series (AEHE))*. Jossey-Bass. http://www.amazon.com/exec/obidos/redirect?tag=citeulike07-20&path=ASIN/1878380087

[2] 2017. Critical Acclaim for Research Methods in Human Computer Interaction, Second Edition. In *Research Methods in Human Computer Interaction (Second Edition)* (second edition ed.), Jonathan Lazar, Jinjuan Heidi Feng, and Harry Hochheiser (Eds.). Morgan Kaufmann, Boston, v – viii. https://doi.org/10.1016/B978-0-12-805390-4.09986-6

[3] Vicki L. Almstrum, Peter B. Henderson, Valerie Harvey, Cinda Heeren, William Marion, Charles Riedesel, Leen-Kiat Soh, and Allison Elliott Tew. 2006. Concept Inventories in Computer Science for the Topic Discrete Mathematics. *SIGCSE Bull.* 38, 4 (June 2006), 132–145. https://doi.org/10.1145/1189136.1189182

[4] Jeff Bulmer, Angie Pinchbeck, and Bowen Hui. 2018. Visualizing Code Patterns in Novice Programmers. In *Proceedings of the 23rd Western Canadian Conference on Computing Education (WCCCE '18)*. ACM, New York, NY, USA, Article 7, 6 pages. https://doi.org/10.1145/3209635.3209652

[5] Ricardo Caceffo, Breno de França, Guilherme Gama, Raysa Benatti, Tales Aparecida, Tania Caldas, and Rodolfo Azevedo. 2017. *An Antipattern Documentation about Misconceptions related to an Introductory Programming Course in C.* Technical Report IC-17-15. Institute of Computing, University of Campinas. In English, 43 pages.

[6] Ricardo Caceffo, Pablo Frank-Bolton, Renan Souza, and Rodolfo Azevedo. 2019. *Identifying and Validating Java Misconceptions – Complementary Material.* Technical Report IC-19-05. Institute of Computing, University of Campinas. In English, 50 pages.

[7] Ricardo Caceffo, Guilherme Gama, and Rodolfo Azevedo. 2018. Exploring Active Learning Approaches to Computer Science Classes. In *Proceedings of the 49th ACM Technical Symposium on Computer Science Education (SIGCSE '18)*. ACM, New York, NY, USA, 922–927. https://doi.org/10.1145/3159450.3159585

[8] Ricardo Caceffo, Guilherme Gama, Raysa Benatti, Tales Aparecida, Tania Caldas, and Rodolfo Azevedo. 2018. *A Concept Inventory for CS1 Introductory Programming Courses in C.* Technical Report IC-18-06. Institute of Computing, University of Campinas.

[9] Ricardo Caceffo, Steve Wolfman, Kellogg Booth, Guilherme Gama, Islene Garcia, Tania Caldas, and Rodolfo Azevedo. 2018. *An Exploratory Questionnaire to Support the Identification and Assessment of Misconceptions in CS1 Courses Based on C Programming Language.* Technical Report IC-18-16. Institute of Computing, University of Campinas.

[10] Ricardo Caceffo, Steve Wolfman, Kellogg S. Booth, and Rodolfo Azevedo. 2016. Developing a Computer Science Concept Inventory for Introductory Programming. In *Proceedings of the 47th ACM Technical Symposium on Computing Science Education (SIGCSE '16)*. ACM, New York, NY, USA, 364–369. https://doi.org/10.1145/2839509.2844559

[11] Yuliya Cherenkova, Daniel Zingaro, and Andrew Petersen. 2014. Identifying Challenging CS1 Concepts in a Large Problem Dataset. In *Proceedings of the 45th ACM Technical Symposium on Computer Science Education (SIGCSE '14)*. ACM, New York, NY, USA, 695–700. https://doi.org/10.1145/2538862.2538966

[12] John Lalor Craig Miller, Amber Settle. 2015. *Learning Object-Oriented Programming in Python: Towards an Inventory of Difficulties and Testing Pitfalls.* Technical Report. DePaul University.

[13] M. El-Attar and J. Miller. 2006. Matching Antipatterns to Improve the Quality of Use Case Models. In *14th IEEE International Requirements Engineering Conference (RE'06)*. 99–108. https://doi.org/10.1109/RE.2006.42

[14] Mohammed F. Farghally, Kyu Han Koh, Jeremy V. Ernst, and Clifford A. Shaffer. 2017. Towards a Concept Inventory for Algorithm Analysis Topics. In *Proceedings of the 2017 ACM SIGCSE Technical Symposium on Computer Science Education (SIGCSE '17)*. ACM, New York, NY, USA, 207–212. https://doi.org/10.1145/3017680.3017756

[15] José Figueiredo and Francisco José García-Peñalvo. 2018. Building Skills in Introductory Programming. In *Proceedings of the Sixth International Conference on Technological Ecosystems for Enhancing Multiculturality (TEEM'18)*. ACM, New York, NY, USA, 46–50. https://doi.org/10.1145/3284179.3284190

[16] Guilherme Gama, Ricardo Caceffo, Renan Souza, Raysa Bennati, Tales Aparecida, Islene Garcia, and Rodolfo Azevedo. 2018. *An Antipattern Documentation about Misconceptions related to an Introductory Programming Course in Python.* Technical Report IC-18-18. Institute of Computing, University of Campinas.

[17] Luke Gusukuma, Austin Cory Bart, Dennis Kafura, and Jeremy Ernst. 2018. Misconception-Driven Feedback: Results from an Experimental Study. In *Proceedings of the 2018 ACM Conference on International Computing Education Research (ICER '18)*. ACM, New York, NY, USA, 160–168. https://doi.org/10.1145/3230977.3231002

[18] Geoffrey L. Herman, Michael C. Loui, and Craig Zilles. 2010. Creating the Digital Logic Concept Inventory. In *Proceedings of the 41st ACM Technical Symposium on Computer Science Education (SIGCSE '10)*. ACM, New York, NY, USA, 102–106. https://doi.org/10.1145/1734263.1734298

[19] David Hestenes, Malcolm Wells, and Gregg Swackhamer. 1992. Force concept inventory. *The Physics Teacher* 30, 3 (1992), 141–158. https://doi.org/10.1119/1.2343497 arXiv:https://doi.org/10.1119/1.2343497

[20] Maria Hristova, Ananya Misra, Megan Rutter, and Rebecca Mercuri. 2003. Identifying and Correcting Java Programming Errors for Introductory Computer Science Students. *SIGCSE Bull.* 35, 1 (Jan. 2003), 153–156. https://doi.org/10.1145/792548.611956

[21] Kuba Karpierz and Steven A. Wolfman. 2014. Misconceptions and Concept Inventory Questions for Binary Search Trees and Hash Tables. In *Proceedings of the 45th ACM Technical Symposium on Computer Science Education (SIGCSE '14)*. ACM, New York, NY, USA, 109–114. https://doi.org/10.1145/2538862.2538902

[22] Cazembe Kennedy and Eileen T. Kraemer. 2018. What Are They Thinking?: Eliciting Student Reasoning About Troublesome Concepts in Introductory Computer Science. In *Proceedings of the 18th Koli Calling International Conference on Computing Education Research (Koli Calling '18)*. ACM, New York, NY, USA, Article 7, 10 pages. https://doi.org/10.1145/3279720.3279728

[23] Nick Kolakowski. 2014. Python Tops Popular Languages for College Intro Courses. (jul 2014). https://insights.dice.com/2014/07/09/python-popular-languages-college-intro-courses/

[24] Einari Kurvinen, Niko Hellgren, Erkki Kaila, Mikko-Jussi Laakso, and Tapio Salakoski. 2016. Programming Misconceptions in an Introductory Level Programming Course Exam. In *Proceedings of the 2016 ACM Conference on Innovation and Technology in Computer Science Education (ITiCSE '16)*. ACM, New York, NY, USA, 308–313. https://doi.org/10.1145/2899415.2899447

[25] Wolfgang Paul and Jan Vahrenhold. 2013. Hunting High and Low: Instruments to Detect Misconceptions Related to Algorithms and Data Structures. In *Proceeding of the 44th ACM Technical Symposium on Computer Science Education (SIGCSE '13)*. ACM, New York, NY, USA, 29–34. https://doi.org/10.1145/2445196.2445212

[26] Steven Pollock and Noah Finkelstein. 2008. Sustaining Educational Reforms in Introductory Physics. *Physical Review Special Topics - Physics Education Research* 4 (05 2008). https://doi.org/10.1103/PhysRevSTPER.4.010110

[27] Leo Porter, Cynthia Taylor, and Kevin C. Webb. 2014. Leveraging Open Source Principles for Flexible Concept Inventory Development. In *Proceedings of the 2014 Conference on Innovation & Technology in Computer Science Education (ITiCSE '14)*. ACM, New York, NY, USA, 243–248. https://doi.org/10.1145/2591708.2591722

[28] Teemu Sirkiä and Juha Sorva. 2012. Exploring Programming Misconceptions: An Analysis of Student Mistakes in Visual Program Simulation Exercises. In *Proceedings of the 12th Koli Calling International Conference on Computing Education Research (Koli Calling '12)*. ACM, New York, NY, USA, 19–28. https://doi.org/10.1145/2401796.2401799

[29] Reza Soltanpoor, Charles Thevathayan, and Daryl DSouza. 2018. Adaptive Remediation for Novice Programmers Through Personalized Prescriptive Quizzes. In *Proceedings of the 23rd Annual ACM Conference on Innovation and Technology in Computer Science Education (ITiCSE 2018)*. ACM, New York, NY, USA, 51–56. https://doi.org/10.1145/3197091.3197097

[30] Renan Souza, Ricardo Caceffo, Pablo Frank-Bolton, and Rodolfo Azevedo. 2018. *An Antipattern Documentation about Possible Misconceptions related to Introductory Programming Courses (CS1) in JAVA.* Technical Report IC-18-20. Institute of Computing, University of Campinas. In English, 42 pages.

[31] Christopher Watson and Frederick W.B. Li. 2014. Failure Rates in Introductory Programming Revisited. In *Proceedings of the 2014 Conference on Innovation & Technology in Computer Science Education (ITiCSE '14)*. ACM, New York, NY, USA, 39–44. https://doi.org/10.1145/2591708.2591749

[32] Kevin C. Webb and Cynthia Taylor. 2014. Developing a Pre- and Post-course Concept Inventory to Gauge Operating Systems Learning. In *Proceedings of the 45th ACM Technical Symposium on Computer Science Education (SIGCSE '14)*. ACM, New York, NY, USA, 103–108. https://doi.org/10.1145/2538862.2538886

Explaining Novice Programmer's Struggles, in Two Parts

Revisiting the ITiCSE 2004 working group's study using dual process theory

Tony Lowe
School of Engineering Education, Purdue University
West Lafayette, IN USA
lowe46@purdue.edu

ABSTRACT

Identifying the cause of a problem is often much more difficult than identifying the problem. The ITiCSE 2004 working group, led by Raymond Lister, conducted a study following up on the McCracken group's finding that many novices struggled with presumedly easy coding tasks. Rather than a test of coding, Lister et al.'s participants completed multiple-choice questions to ascertain their level conceptual understanding of coding constructs. Lister and team reported that participants understood programming concepts yet lacked the consistent apply that knowledge to trace code. This paper revisits the analysis of two of twelve questions to reinterpret their data using dual process theory to explain novice inconsistencies better. Dual process theory describes cognition as two mechanisms: slow, focused, rational thinking versus quick, automatic, and effortless responses. The results suggest dual process theory changes the epistemological meaning of what is to 'know' how to program. Mature programmers utilize more than just knowledge of concepts, but also require speed and intuition obtained through practice. Dual process theory provides a new lens for assessing novice maturity and pedagogy in programming.

CCS CONCEPTS: • Social and professional topics → CS1

KEYWORDS: Computer Science, Programming, Education, Dual Process Theory, Tracing, Fragile Knowledge

ACM Reference format:
Tony Lowe. 2019. Explaining novice programmer's struggles, in two parts. In *Proceedings of 24th Annual ACM Conference on Innovation and Technology in Computer Science Education (ITiCSE'19), July 15-17, 2019, Aberdeen, Scotland, UK.* ACM, New York, NY, USA, 7 pages https://doi.org/101145/3304221.3319775

1 Redefining novice struggles in programming

The goal of this paper is to introduce a tiny piece of a broader theoretical framework aimed at describing the mind of the programmer.

 ACM ISBN 978-1-4503-6301-3/19/07...$15.00
https://doi.org/10.1145/3304221.3319775

Expert programmers seem to think differently than novices, so understanding how experts 'think about programming' can hopefully smooth path from fledgling to competence. The foundation of this new theory shifts how we conceive of cognition resulting in an epistemological shift in what it means to know how to program. Neuroscience and psychology show thinking consists of two mechanisms: the deliberate and logical side vital in programming, but also an intuitive side described in dual process theory [1], [2]. Studies of dual process theory provide evidence of how much of our 'purely rational' thinking is influenced by intuition and intuitive experience over reason and explicit knowledge.

Dual process theory provides greater explanatory power of novice struggles than past theoretical frameworks of learning. CS education literature utilizes various learning theories (e.g., di Sessa [3], Neo-Piagetian theory [4], [5], conceptual change theory [6]) but these theories miss *why* novices struggle and fail to adequately detail what pedagogical changes can help. Dual process theory provides a contrast between novice thinking in comparison to that of an expert, describes the gap and offers a strategy to bridge the gap. This paper revisits two of the questions utilized within the ITiCSE 2004 working group's study [7]. The first question demonstrates how fledgling intuition and a lack of automation distinguish levels of competence in novices. The second highlights how intuition drives reasoning as often as logic in programming. This paper is the first in a line of publications in exploring to the role of dual process theory but will provide an example of how a new view of cognition can improve research, assessment, and pedagogy within programming education.

1.1 Results: Inconsistent and Incompatible

The mind of novice programmers seem forgetful, irrational, and their performance paradoxical. They often appear to be on the right path only to make irrational mistakes. Novices show understanding of a language constructs, then fail to apply that knowledge appropriately. They will show promise by successfully tracing through code on one problem, only to fail to use that knowledge a few questions later. McCracken et al. [8] conducted an international study testing participants' ability to write code near the end of their CS1 experience. Their participants struggled to write code for 'simple' problems, sometimes being unable even to write compiling code. The researchers reported they believed the students struggled in problem-solving, though individuals reported they lacked understanding of the language.

A follow-up study investigated the student's level of conceptual understanding of programming constructs. Lister et al.

[7] asked if "students may simply not understand the programming constructs" (p. 120) or might understand the concept but have trouble consistently applying it, which they refer to as fragile knowledge. Perkins and Martin [9] first wrote about fragile knowledge in a study where they observed kids while writing code, offering assistance to varying degrees. When participants struggled, researchers prompted the participant hoping they would remember the concept. If the prompt failed to help, researchers would hint at an approach the student might follow, sometimes finally devolving to providing exact instructions to complete the code if the participant was unable to make progress on their own. Perkins and Martin showed researchers regularly needed to offer each type of intervention, even to remind students of similar concepts. They showed novices often knew facts about a language, but inconsistently applied that knowledge when the time came to write code. Lister et al., as discussed in the next section, show that fragile knowledge also applies to code tracing. While fragile knowledge names the phenomenon of inconsistent novice performance, it fails to shed light on the nature of novices' inconsistent performance.

1.2 Observations by Lister et al.

Lister et al. believe the woes of participants in the McCracken group's study are not entirely attributable to immature problem-solving abilities. They tested conceptual understanding using multiple-choice questions coming to the following observation on participant performance.

> One observation we make about the middle 50% of students is that, by virtue of the fact that they answered some questions correctly, they have demonstrated a conceptual grasp of loops and arrays. Therefore, the weakness of these students is not that they do not understand the language constructs. Their weakness is the inability to reliably work their way through the long chain of reasoning required to hand execute code, and/or an inability to reason reliably at a more abstract level to select the missing line of code. Based on the performance data, it is not possible to draw any firm conclusions as to the exact cause of this weakness [7, p. 128]

Lister et al. report their participant understood concepts, but this did not help them consistently trace code. They investigate the causes of weak tracing using qualitative data, some of which will later be reinterpreted using dual process theory to explain the nature of the inconsistent performance.

The participants in Lister et al.'s study better met expectations than those in McCracken et al.'s as they demonstrated knowledge but could not flexibly apply it in tracing. Lister et al. analyze the 'doodles' participants create while working on the test as a qualitative source of data. They created categories for the doodles used by participants and related the categories to participant success. Their coding scheme identifies the functional purpose of the doodles in answering the question, as perceived by the researcher. They ranked each category of doodles by the percentage of students who successfully answered each question. Doodle category data may provide correlation to the types of doodles successful students employ but does little to tell us *why* that chosen notation helps (or lack thereof fails to help) the novice. Many students answer questions successfully with doodling! Fragile knowledge cuts both ways: sometimes we expect participants to perform yet fail and sometimes participants succeed when without using successful "doodling strategies". Random luck could offer one explanation, but dual process theory provides a more robust model of knowledge in action.

1.3 Explaining Fragile Knowledge

To explain fragile knowledge, we must rethink the belief that novices, or any human, perfectly applies knowledge. Philosophers and economists have long based decision theories on the rationality of humans; as it seems many programming instructors and researchers do. They assume if people know information, they must apply that knowledge logically! Psychologists Daniel Kahneman and Amos Tversky disabused this notion in economics with their Nobel Prize work on Prospect theory [10]. Prospect theory changed how economists model decision-making for the average person. For centuries, economists assumed people made decisions based on self-interest, probable outcomes, and logical reasoning. Kahneman and Tversky showed that people, even highly trained ones, often forgo reason when making decisions. Kahneman tells a story of how he tricked "a sophisticated statistician and skeptic" [1, p. 149] into forgetting a fundamental principle of statistics. This expert was aware of the 'trick' being studied yet still made a simple mistake in reasoning despite being trained to do otherwise. Would you consider the expert's knowledge fragile? Should we be surprised when novices fail to use new information consistently? The work of Kahneman and Tversky contributes to a broader theory of cognition known as dual process theory [1], [2], which provides fascinating insights to fragile knowledge.

Dual process theory provides an alternative explanation for how we make decisions. Our brain is not exclusively a slow chugging engine for processing rules but integrates intuition. Even when our thinking seems rational, our (re)actions are inexplicable. Intuitive versus rational thinking is not new to CS education [11], but its implications are not typically fully explored. The next section introduces dual process theory and suggests how it applies to programming, before revisiting a narrow slice of the findings of Lister et al. [7] as an example of its use.

2 Dual Process Theory

2.1 Introducing the two Systems

Dual process theory separates mental processing into two mechanisms, named simply System 1 and System 2. Our brain contains a logical, focused, and reasoning side (System 2) paired with an intuitive, quick responding, automatic side (System 1). System 1 drives most of our daily activity, providing quick responses to the world around us. System 1 perpetually observes our environment, learning and tracking patterns, and choosing optimal responses. In familiar environments, System 1's choices are comfortable and accepted by our System 2, which is content to remain uninvolved until needed. Kahneman goes so far as to describe System 2 as "lazy". System 2 requires attention and effort which is energy better conserved for meaningful tasks when danger or opportunity strikes. System 1 employs the sum of our experiences to make good decisions quickly, where System 2 jumps in when we need to deal with the unknown or resolve conflicting impulses. Each system has its specialty, and it is the combination of the two that make up our thinking prowess.

System 1 excels at complex but mundane tasks. For example, System 1 translates the text you are reading now into meaning. System 1 recognizes faces and emotions on those faces. It automates well-practiced math problems, can literally take the wheel when driving down a familiar route with little traffic, or help a master chess player pick a strong move [1]. System 1 provides quick and reliable answers to well-trained problems. System 1 learns slowly and responds only as robustly as the variety of our trained experience. The study of artificial neural networks is the study of the mechanics of System 1 [12]. Machines learn through *many* repeated inputs and perform only well as the representativeness of the data set to real-world situations, in a simulated version of our intuitive thinking.

System 1 and 2 coordinate in our decision making. Just as artificial neural networks are only a part of traditional applications, the impressive results provided by System 1 are reviewed by our rational System 2, which balances quick reaction with logic. System 2 can evaluate the System 1 response to include other information, values, goals, or alternative needs altering our final response. The coordination of System 1 and 2 generally happens seamlessly, but one example quickly illustrates the behavior of your two Systems. Eagleman and Downar present a task where you speak aloud color of a printed word rather than reading the word, which is sometimes the name of a different color [13, p. 422]. This type of conflicting tasks induces the Stroop effect, a mental load occurring when our System 2 must suppress the automatic response of System 1; in this case, to say the name of the color rather than the word that automatically comes to mind and tongue. For most people and situations, our two Systems coordinate beautifully, but at times of conflict breaks down our ability to perform.

A breakdown in the interplay between System 1 and 2 is a common cause of fragile knowledge. To respond quickly to the world, System 1 jumpstarts System 2 with a possibly relevant context in a process known as priming. System 1 primes System 2 by preloading information that has been useful to past situations. For example, you might look down, see a snake, and jump away, only to see your new puppy dart away from you! System 1 incorrectly primed System 2 with color patterns of local poisonous snakes that match the color of the new leash you bought. Since the leash and dog are new, System 1 first recalls snakes, not leashes. Our instinct to flee from snakes might override the need to keep our new dog close. Immature priming can mislead otherwise rational System 2 to incorporating incorrect information. Knowledge can be fragile within System 2 if it is not yet fully learned. It can also become fragile if it is not yet familiar to System 1, or there is a breakdown between the two Systems. The next section looks to describe how dual process theory can be utilized to describe fragile knowledge in the mind of the programmer.

2.2 Dual process and Programming

The art of programming education traditionally focuses on maturing System 2, yet System 1's contribution often noted in CS education research. Soloway [14] promotes the need to teach "Tacit Knowledge", which experts "are not necessarily conscious of... [and] refer to 'intuition, gut feel, etc.' as the sources of their inspiration" (p. 851). Experts come to possess a source of information that transcends the classroom instruction provided to novices. Wiedenbeck [11] focused on the differences between novices and expert, which Lister et al. [7] summarize as "expert programmers carry out low-level programming-related activities faster than novices... expert programmers had 'automated' these processes" (p. 138). Both Soloway and Wiedenbeck indirectly describe System 1's role in programming. System 1 learning requires time and "continuous practice" [11, p. 389], yet when proficient performs quickly and effortlessly. What exact role(s) does System 1's play in the mind of a programmer?

Given enough practice, System 1 supports System 2 through priming and by automating basic tasks. Experienced programmers benefit from a well-trained System 1 in many ways, but we can generalize from a simple example. A competent programmer gains the same benefits from System 1 as a skilled reader: instant translation of symbols into meaning. A new reader might struggle to find meaning in each word slowly piecing together sentences, where the competent reader instantly and automatically transforms text to information. The Stroop effect [13] example from earlier demonstrates how impossible it avoids reading a familiar word; we can only hope to alter our response. Experienced programmers develop the same automaticity in reading code. They require zero effort to identify the language constructs or often the construct's patterns of use. System 1 might prompt 1) the code contains a loop, 2) it is looping over values within a data structure, and 3) the code is searching/sorting/summing/etc before we start to consider the details. System 1 priming aids System 2 by "chunking" language constructs the same way we "chunk" sentences. Novice programmers must utilize limited short-term memory to discern meaning from even simple constructs, where experienced programmers have moved on to problem-solving or other complex tasks.

The novice requires both conceptual understanding within System 2 but also proper automaticity and intuition in System 1. Lister et al. noted that participants' answers vary when presented with the same concept. This type of fragile knowledge may be due to System 1's ability to accurately prime System 2. The wrong prime would misdirect System 2 if the user is not sure of their conceptual knowledge. Participants may not have had an experience from which to prime, meaning System 2 must conduct a long and demanding search for the applicable knowledge. When we are forced to search our memory, it demands focus and effort which can drive away all other thoughts. As a novice programmer scans their mind for the more details on which construct does that syntax identify, how that construct work, how is it used in this algorithm, the details of the original problem are likely forgotten[1].

[1] This could be described as a typical problem addressed by Cognitive Load Theory (CLT) [24]. CLT is important to address, but outside the scope of this work.

Incomplete or inaccurate priming wastes effort and confuses the novice with similar but incorrect information. For example, native English speakers might be confused by "terms don't always mean the same in English as they do in programming" [15, p. 87]. Terms like *if* and *while* require specific use in programming different than what a novice's System 1 might use in priming System 2. Kahneman showed us an example where a mistake in priming caused a skeptical expert to fail, so what hope does a novice have? The Stroop effect not only is a functional phenomenon but one that causes emotional strain. The dissonance between the two Systems is strenuous and causes strife. Overloaded novices sometimes resort to starting from scratch or simply stop [16] as a result. Developing a mature System 1 response is perhaps more important for novice self-efficacy than forming a perfect understanding of programming concepts. The role of System 1 can be used to reinterpreting Lister et al.'s findings to identify the otherwise inexplicable outcomes.

2 Reinterpreting Lister et al.'s Findings

2.1 Question 1: Tracing

Lister et al.'s share an example of student tracing for Question 1 which provides insight into the mind of the participant, but under dual process theory, in expected ways. The student was able to derive the correct answer from their trace (shown with highlights added in Figure 1) showing they understand the concepts, but their 'doodles' hint they may still be maturing.

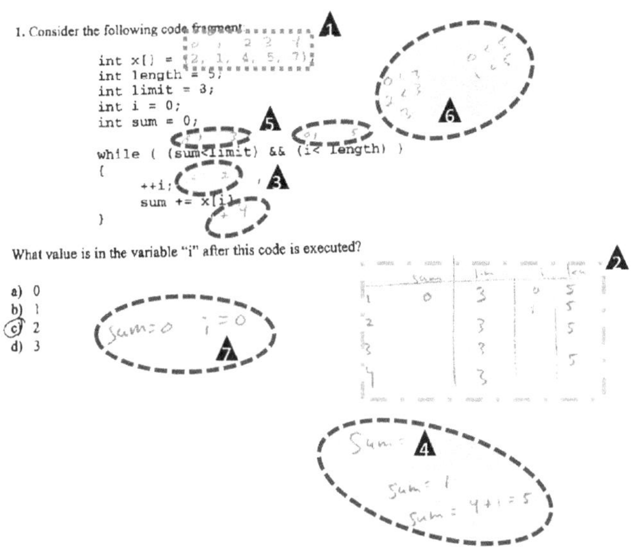

Figure 1: Annotated sample of participant trace [7, p. 130]

The participant captures information about the trace haphazardly. At the *triangle marked 1*, the participant annotates the index values for the elements in the array x. Lister et al. considered this doodle a sign of steady progress as the participant accurately captures the array index rule, a positive example of applied System 2 knowledge. Array indices should, however, be tacit knowledge in a competent programmer, who would not need to remind themselves explicitly. This doodle indicates the participant's System 1 might be unsure/unprepared enough to support System 2 and they think they are providing the quick access to the index values System 1 is not ready to contribute. Another possibility is they are following a procedure they were taught rather than tracing intuitively. While a protocol for tracing is helpful to scaffold early efforts, it adds another item to be practiced and remembered, and may not account for the unknowns that will later come.

The examples show additional evidence the participant is conducting a 'tracing ritual'. The assumed ritual might start with writing down known information: the indices (*triangle 1*), initial values of variables (*triangle 7*) and a trace table (*triangle 2*). Lister et al. consider the trace table a good sign of maturity yet fail to note that the table is incomplete and unused in actual tracing. The participant fills in the two variables (which are constant) and must be pre-filling the four rows since, even though the participant gets the right answer, the loop will only execute two times. The columns of numbers appear to perfectly align vertically, also implying they were all written all at once rather than through each iteration of the loop. The table seems to be unrelated to the rest of the trace. The participant doodles changes to variables in multiple other places (*triangles 3 & 4*) then the table. The table is unused for its most important purpose, managing change. The student seems to be fulfilling a step, rather than understanding the purpose of the table and integrating it into their thinking.

Dual process theory suggests doodles would be most evident in intermediary learners with experts and abject novices writing down little or nothing, like a bell curve. System 1 automation allows competent coders to trace simple snippets 'in their head' (and for complex code they use debuggers and log files!). Abject novices are unable to doodle because their System 2 is not ready, or they have yet to learn or imagine their own meaningful 'doodle'. Doodles give evidence of the quality of System 2 reasoning, but too many doodles, for too long, may imply a weak System 1 and may confuse novices with too many notations.

Specific doodle notations require training as much as the language. The participant in Figure 1 has adopted the trace table format yet has only mastered its creation, not its use. Using a structured tracing approach requires another notation structure that System 2 must remember and use. It is supplementary to code, but externally imposed, and equally artificial as coding syntax. The participant in Figure 1 spent good time to build the table but does not seem to understand the information at *triangle 4* could be in the table or find value in putting it there. Tracing notation might even be counterintuitive and distracting due to similar experiences. To a novice, code might look like algebra, an oft-used analogy. The trace table looks like a spreadsheet, a likely familiar representation of data, where the traces in *triangle 3* better show how the growing mental model of the underlying hardware behaves. The trace table may be more accessible to check work later but may not conflict with their maturing mental model of a computer. It is impossible to know the full motivation for the doodles in Figure 1, but it seems this student is still working through organizing the understanding and approach to coding and tracing.

Doodles can be used to compensate for an unsure System 1. Figure 1 includes true doodles alongside formal techniques. Notice how the participant copies values as they work through the trace:

1.) Captures how array indices work (*triangle 1*)
2.) Write down more of what I know (*triangle 7*)
3.) Complete the ritual of the 'trace table' (*triangle 2*)
4.) Now start focusing on the code (*triangles 3-6*)
    a. Capture the index update (*triangle 3*)
    b. Update the sum (*triangles 3 & 4*)
    c. Update the loop variables (*triangle 5*)
    d. Check the loop conditions (*triangle 6*)

The participant updates the value of 'sum' in 4 places (*triangle 3-6*). Why track 'sum' in so many places? The redundant doodles capture the value within each construct (addition/assignment, loop constraint, comparison). The participant can probably add simple numbers in their mind yet writes down the "4 + 1 = 5" (*triangle 4*). The unfamiliar "+=" operator may have instilled enough unsurety to prompt the additional reminder doodle. The value of 'sum' is captured again each time a new construct uses it. The participant felt the need even to capture "0<3" independently (*triangle 6*). Lister et al. use doodles as a sign of maturity, and indeed this participant is well along the path of learning to code. The doodles also provide evidence of an unsure, untrusted, or untrained System 1 supporting a fledgling, but not incompetent, System 2. Dual process theory suggests their next step in 'knowing' how to program is not in the knowledge within System 2, but coordination with System 1.

2.2 Question 8: Completion

Lister et al. found the participant work on Question 8 paradoxical. Question 8 asks the participants to fill in missing code (see Figure 2) and is proven 'harder' as more participants answered incorrectly *and* fewer doodled on Question 8 than an easier Question 2, as shown in Table 1.

Table 1: Comparing Questions 2 and 8

	% Correct	% Used Doodles
Question 2	65%	80%
Question 8	51%	55%
Difference	-14%	-25%

Lister et al. called this observation "counter-intuitive" referencing Davies [17] to make the case that participants used short-term memory over doodling to trace code where "experienced programmers habitually doodle when trying to understand a difficult piece of code" [7, p. 132]. Lister et al.'s argument means 25% more test takers decide to trace (through possibly to 4 answers) in their head on the 'harder' problem? The sudden reduction in any doodling seems counterintuitive given the previous discussion of Question 1, where one student 'over-traced'. Even tracing the chosen answer would help dramatically since only 2 of the answers, as shown in Figure 2, result in the answer 10. Answer d, however, is the second most chosen answer by participants. It seems more likely many participants did not trace at all, but why?

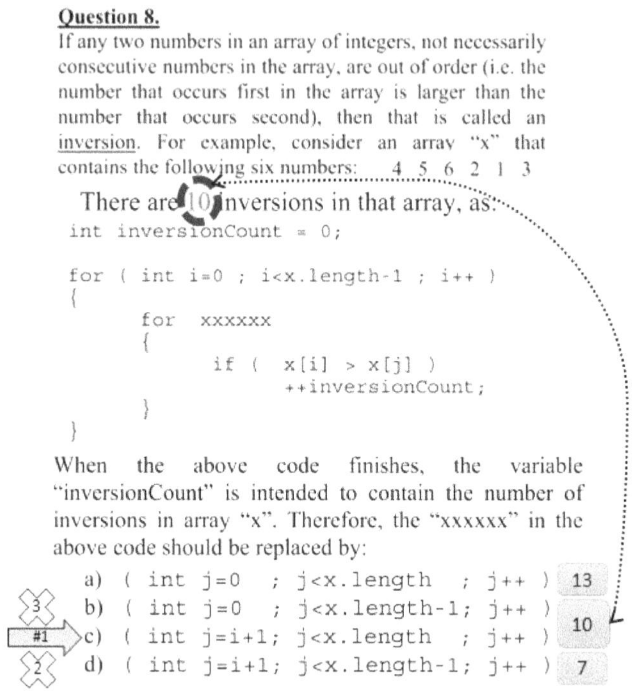

Question 8.
If any two numbers in an array of integers, not necessarily consecutive numbers in the array, are out of order (i.e. the number that occurs first in the array is larger than the number that occurs second), then that is called an inversion. For example, consider an array "x" that contains the following six numbers: 4 5 6 2 1 3

There are 10 inversions in that array, as:

```
int inversionCount = 0;

for ( int i=0 ; i<x.length-1 ; i++ )
{
      for  xxxxxx
      {
            if (  x[i] > x[j] )
                  ++inversionCount;
      }
}
```

When the above code finishes, the variable "inversionCount" is intended to contain the number of inversions in array "x". Therefore, the "xxxxxx" in the above code should be replaced by:

```
a) ( int j=0   ; j<x.length   ; j++ )   13
b) ( int j=0   ; j<x.length-1; j++ )
c) ( int j=i+1; j<x.length   ; j++ )   10
d) ( int j=i+1; j<x.length-1; j++ )   7
```


Figure 2: Question 8 [7, p. 143] **formatted for space**

Dual process theory provides a simpler and less paradoxical explanation for the participants' performance on Question 8. Question 8 appears to demand careful analysis and tracing but leans towards a quick, intuitive answer from System 1. Lister et al. [7] created their questions to be tricky: "A good distracter should be plausible enough to appeal to some students. It should be clearly incorrect, however, so that it does not mislead those students who really know the material" (p. 123). Question 8 seems to provide perfect distractors as participants used "heuristics for selecting a plausible answer without genuinely understanding the [question]" [7, p. 132]. The answer to Question 8 is most often delivered first by System 1 and while System 2 could catch a wrong answer through tracing it prefers to be "lazy".

Test takers with a well-trained System 1 or an entirely incompetent System 1 have the best shot at successfully answer Question 8. If System 1 provides no intuitive answer, then proper tracing would at least get a 50/50 chance at the answer. My experience with Question 8 provides an example of a successful System 1 response. I first read Question 8 at 3 AM, about four hours into my work that evening. I read the problem carefully, scanned the options and immediately chose the right answer. As a long-time coder, I recognized the nature of the problem: Nested loops typically stagger the range of the inner loop to start after the index of the outer loop and continue to the last element, while the outer loop usually stops short. The pattern identified in the previous sentence came with writing this paper, not in solving the problem. My lazy (sleep-deprived) System 2 was content with my

System 1 answer that held the logic I just described. I never looked at the array values, even after, and only briefly checked my selection mentally out of ego, not need. Expert intuition serves particularly well in even complex decisions about programming.

By reframing Question 8 from a 'fill-in-the-blank' question to a programmer writing new code, we write the loop statement then test it. We build code from our mental model of what it is doing, so jumping to one of the choices is more natural than processing through each in turn. The dramatic drop in tracing and outcome seems to indicate System 1 is driving the choice and System 2 is not engaging deeply enough to check wrong answers.

3 Impacts of Dual Process Theory

3.1 Implications from Lister et al.

Dual process theory explains the root causes for the fragile knowledge plaguing some novice programmers. Lister et al.'s use of multiple-choice question provides a simple example for the role of dual process theory in programming. Analyzing just two questions demonstrates how the inclusion of System 1 can radically alter how we understand novice failures. The doodles from Question 1 showed Lister et al. how well the student was progressing, yet dual process theory shows their current abilities are tenuous and provides an explanation of *what is needed to grow competence*. The haphazard doodles a show a disorganized and disconnected novice compared to a competent programmer who would quickly aggregate concepts. We would expect an expert to produce structured and less redundant doodles if any. Strong tracing skills require understanding language constructs and automation to speed up mental execution and other coding skills.

Question 8 shows how a single view of cognition may bias researchers and educators. Experts tend to underestimate the mental load demanded of novices who have not yet developed a strong System 1. It is not that students are lazy when they skip tracing; we all are subject to part of our brain that prefers to avoid (perceived) unnecessary work. By incorporating dual process theory, we can anticipate novice limitations caused by an underdeveloped System 1. Novices lack the intuition and automation an expert implicitly develops. By accounting for System 1 in pedagogy and assessment, we can improve expectations of novices on programming tasks. In Question 8, many novices needed to employ System 2 to double-check the intuitive System 1 answer. Requiring students to 'prove their answer' would force them to engage System 2. In problems like Question 1, System 2 benefits from automated mental tracing provided by a mature System 1. Tasks like Question 8 require an experienced System 1 that has seen diverse ways of solving problems, supported by follow-on analysis by System 2. Dual process theory presents a granular model for programming activities which identifies more clearly how the brain completes programming tasks.

3.2 Next Steps

Looking at the mind of a programmer through the dual process theory alters the epistemological definition of what it is to 'know' how to code. The plight of the novice programmer is well explored, giving us a rich set of data in which to apply dual process theory. Literature hints of the knowledge a novice must possess [6], [14], [18], [19], misconceptions they may hold [9], [20], [21], and methods of assessment [7], [8], but provide static models of knowledge, rather than showing how the mind uses knowledge. Lister and his former student Teague place tracing as an identifier of maturity for novices [4], [22]. They propose stages, where novices progress from: 1) unreliable to become 2) competent tracers, eventually 3) discerning lines of code into abstractions, before 4) finally being able to reason using abstractions. Lister and Teague's strong Neo-Piagetian model of development only provides a "theory of the direction of growth than of the causes of growth" [23, p. 66] as Bruner once said of Piaget. Dual process theory supports this trajectory with a means to explain learner struggles and supports new methods for improving pedagogy.

Dual process theory alone is not enough to explain or manage mental complexity in learning to code. This paper only looks (secondhand) at very novice programmers, and then only at their ability to read and trace basic code. System 1 plays a significant role in software development from design, code, testing, debugging, peer-reviews... basically every stage, but while intuition is hinted at it not often unaddressed in pedagogy. Future work must consider how dual process theory fits into more programming tasks, including other theories to account for the complex interplay between the two Systems and the challenging task of efficiently teaching System 1. Lister et al. [7] note that in their study "some institutions attract students with a greater innate talent for programming" (p. 125). Can dual process theory start to address the question of what 'talent' is and how to create it? What if we can explain 'talent', and thus manufacture it, as a by-product of a better exposed, practiced, and integrated System 1? By changing how we teach and assess progress in learning to program, we can offer students lasting progress and hopefully reach struggling novices with new approaches.

ACKNOWLEDGMENTS

This paper is an introduction to a piece of a broader theory of mind created within my dissertation. I thank my advisor (Dr. Sean Brophy) and committee (Drs. Ruth Streveler and Michael Loui) for a generous contribution of support of time and wisdom. I also want to thank my wife for patiently waiting for "five minutes" (three hours later) for me to finish the next section.

REFERENCES

[1] D. Kahneman, *Thinking, fast and slow.* Macmillan, 2011.
[2] J. S. B. T. Evans and K. E. Frankish, *In two minds: Dual processes and beyond.* Oxford University Press, 2009.
[3] A. A. diSessa, "Knowledge in pieces.," in *Constructivism in the Computer Age,* G. Forman and P. B. Pufall, Eds. Hillsdale, NJ, USA: Lawrence Erlbaum Associates, Inc, 1988, pp. 49–70.
[4] D. Teague, "Neo-Piagetian theory and the novice programmer," 2014.
[5] R. Lister, "Concrete and Other Neo-Piagetian Forms of Reasoning in the Novice Programmer," in *Proceedings of the Thirteenth Australian Computing Education Conference,* 2011, no. 114, pp. 9–18.
[6] J. Sorva, "Notional machines and introductory programming education," *ACM Trans. Comput. Educ.,* vol. 13, no. 2, pp. 1–31, 2013.
[7] R. Lister *et al., A multi-national study of reading and tracing skills in novice programmers,* vol. 36, no. 4. 2004.
[8] M. McCracken *et al.,* "A multi-national, multi-institutional study of assessment

of programming skills of first-year CS students," *ACM SIGCSE Bull.*, vol. 33, no. 4, p. 125, 2001.

[9] D. N. Perkins and F. Martin, "Fragile knowledge and neglected strategies in novice programmers," Washington, DC, 1985.

[10] A. Tversky and D. Kahneman, "Advances in Prospect Theory: Cumulative Representation of Uncertainty," *J. Risk Uncertain.*, vol. 323, pp. 297–323, 1992.

[11] S. Wiedenbeck, "Novice/expert differences in programming skills," *Int. J. Man. Mach. Stud.*, vol. 23, no. 4, pp. 383–390, 1985.

[12] R. Sun, "Learning, action and consciousness: A hybrid approach toward modelling consciousness," *Neural Networks*, vol. 10, no. 7, pp. 1317–1331, 1997.

[13] D. Eagleman and J. Downar, *Brain and behavior a cognitive neuroscience perspective*. New York; Oxford: Oxford University Press, 2016.

[14] E. Soloway, "Learning to program = Learning to construct mechanisms," *Commun. ACM*, vol. 29, no. 9, pp. 850–858, 1986.

[15] M. Clancy, "Misconceptions and attitudes that interfere with learning to program," *Comput. Sci. Educ. Res.*, pp. 85–100, 2004.

[16] D. N. Perkins, C. Hancock, R. Hobbs, F. Martin, and R. Simmons, "Conditions of Learning in Novice Programmers," *J. Educ. Comput. Res.*, vol. 2, no. 1, pp. 37–55, 1986.

[17] S. P. Davies, "Display-based problem solving strategies in computer programming," *Proc. Wkshp. Empir. Stud. Program.*, pp. 59–76, 1996.

[18] B. Du Boulay, T. O'Shea, and J. Monk, "The black box inside the glass box: presenting computing concepts to novices," *Int. J. Hum. Comput. Stud.*, vol. 51, no. 3, pp. 265–277, 1981.

[19] I. Milne and G. Rowe, "Difficulties in Learning and Teaching Programming—Views of Students and Tutors," *Educ. Inf. Technol.*, vol. 7, no. 1, pp. 55–66, 2002.

[20] B. Du Boulay, "Some Difficulties of Learning to Program," *J. Educ. Comput. Res.*, vol. 2, no. 1, pp. 57–73, 1986.

[21] R. D. Pea, "Language-Independent Conceptual 'Bugs' in Novice Programming," *J. Educ. Comput. Res.*, vol. 2, no. 1, pp. 25–36, 1986.

[22] R. Lister, "Toward a Developmental Epistemology of Computer Programming," *Proc. 11th Work. Prim. Second. Comput. Educ. ZZZ - WiPSCE '16*, pp. 5–16, 2016.

[23] J. S. Bruner, "Celebrating divergence: Piaget and Vygotsky," *Hum. Dev.*, vol. 40, no. 2, pp. 63–73, 1997.

[24] J. L. Plass, R. Moreno, and R. Brünken, "Cognitive Load Theory," *Americas (Engl. ed).*, vol. 32, pp. 10013–2473, 2010.

Novice Rationales for Sketching and Tracing, and How They Try to Avoid It

Kathryn Cunningham
University of Michigan
Ann Arbor, Michigan, USA
kicunn@umich.edu

Shannon Ke
Georgia Institute of Technology
Atlanta, Georgia, USA
shannonke@gatech.edu

Mark Guzdial, Barbara Ericson
University of Michigan
Ann Arbor, Michigan, USA
{mjguz,barbarer}@umich.edu

ABSTRACT

Prior research has shown that sketching out a code trace on paper is correlated with higher scores on code reading problems. Why do students sometimes choose not to draw out a code trace, or if they do, choose a different sketching technique than their instructor has demonstrated? In this study, we interviewed 13 CS1 students retrospectively about their decisions to sketch and draw on a recent programming exam. When students do sketch, we find that their sketching choices do not always align with a strict execution of the notional machine. Sketching choices are driven by a search for a program's patterns, an attempt to create organizational structure among intermediate values, and the tracking of prior steps and results. When novices don't sketch, they often report that they've identified the goal that the code achieves. In either case, novices are searching for the functionality of code, rather than merely tracing its behavior.

CCS CONCEPTS

• **Social and professional topics → Computing education**; *CS1*.

KEYWORDS

CS1, novice programmers, tracing, sketching, notional machine, external cognition, program visualization

ACM Reference Format:
Kathryn Cunningham, Shannon Ke, and Mark Guzdial, Barbara Ericson. 2019. Novice Rationales for Sketching and Tracing, and How They Try to Avoid It. In *Innovation and Technology in Computer Science Education (ITiCSE '19), July 15–17, 2019, Aberdeen, Scotland UK.* ACM, New York, NY, USA, 7 pages. https://doi.org/10.1145/3304221.3319788

1 INTRODUCTION

When novice programmers solve programming problems, they sometimes use pen and paper. They might draw out variable states, re-write code snippets, or work through calculations. Called sketching [2], annotations [12], or doodles [10], these drawings are an external representation that many students find useful. Research supports the utility of sketching. Sketching is correlated with greater success on code reading problems, with sketched traces being the most successful [2, 10].

Prior research on student sketching has involved qualitative and quantitative analysis of scratch sheets. However, the motivations of the sketchers remained a mystery. If sketching is associated with success, why do students only occasionally use it? Why do students sometimes stop part-way through a code trace, behavior that has been associated with particularly low success [2]? Student sketches differ in several ways from the more formal memory diagrams proposed by instructors [7], or the graphics in program visualization tools [19]. We have shown that students' sketches often have a different style than the ones used by their teachers [2]. Students' motivation for why and how they sketch is unclear.

If we knew more about the reasons students sketch and the approaches they favor, perhaps we could design sketching or other visualization techniques that students are more likely to understand, use, interact with, and learn from. In this study, we perform interviews with CS1 students to explore the following:

- Why do novice programmers choose to sketch or not sketch on different problems?
- What rationales do novice programmers provide for their sketching styles?
- Why do novice programmers choose a different sketching technique than their instructor?

2 BACKGROUND

2.1 Tracing and other ways novices read code

Tracing a piece of code involves tracking memory states over time as the execution of code is simulated. Tracers are running a mental model of the notional machine [17], acting as "human compilers".

We want students to trace code because it can lead to students' greater accuracy during problem-solving [24], and it may play a role in improving learning about the notional machine, a concept where students have many misconceptions [18]. But students do not necessarily trace because it is good for them, and they may take other approaches to solve problems. In this paper, we ask students why they trace code and why they trace the *way* that they do.

We do know that students voluntarily trace when faced with complex problems. The Leeds Working Group [10] asked students to read and predict the execution of programs that used loops and arrays. Students' scratch paper was collected and analyzed, finding that many students had sketched a code trace.

Fitzgerald et al. [4] performed cognitive walkthroughs with introductory CS students as they solved problems with the same problems used in the Leeds Working Group exam. Using grounded theory, the researchers identified 19 strategies students used while

ACM ISBN 978-1-4503-6301-3/19/07...$15.00
https://doi.org/10.1145/3304221.3319788

solving code reading problems, including close tracing (the most frequent) as well as various types of pattern recognition (e.g., recognizing that this program was like one seen before). However, the use of a certain strategy did not predict success.

Fitzgerald et al.'s interviews have also been analyzed with the SOLO taxonomy as a theoretical lens. Lister et al. found that students were more likely to describe using a multistructural approach, where they discussed the function of multiple pieces of code, rather than a relational approach, where they discussed the code as a whole [11]. Other literature has reported that novices focus on the pieces rather than the program purpose. For example, expert programmers are more likely to use abstract mental representations that focus on the goal the code achieves, while novices are more likely to focus on details of how the code executes [1].

Vainio and Sajaniemi identified factors that they felt inhibited novice code tracing [22]. Tracing requires attention to detail, which can lead to cognitive overload and mistakes (e.g., tracking and using variables) and poor use of external representations. Like Fitzgerald et al.'s pattern recognition, Vainio and Sajaniemi found that students assume functionality from a syntactic structure that matches a previously seen pattern.

2.2 When and why do students sketch?

We know that while solving code reading problems, sketching a code trace correlates with success [2, 10]. However, students are more likely to create these types of sketches on some types of code reading problems than others [12]. For questions that are not about code reading, like Parsons problems [14], students rarely sketch anything [2]. Also, students' sketches often does not use the types of diagrams that instructors teach [2, 23].

Analysis of the Leeds Working Group data showed that sketching varied widely from institution to institution, from as as low as 28% of problems sketched to as high as 92% [12]. Students consistently sketched more often on code prediction problems than on code completion problems.

Sketches have the potential to not only offload cognition, but also to better coordinate thought [9]. Certainly, sketching out variable states provides a persistent way to track information too complex to remember accurately. But also, in the unconstrained space of a sheet of paper a sketcher can re-arrange information to bring key referents closer together, or make certain information more explicit than it was in a prior form [9].

2.3 What external representations are common in novice programming?

The process of code execution, known as the action of the notional machine [3], is not self-evident from code syntax or program output. Systems that teach *code tracing* attempt to make this challenging, hidden process visible[6, 13, 24].

Software that displays program visualizations is a common approach in the effort to help students form accurate mental models of program execution. Systems like the Online Python Tutor [5] and UUhistle [20] demonstrate the action of the notional machine that a student can step through line by line (see Figure 1a,b). The

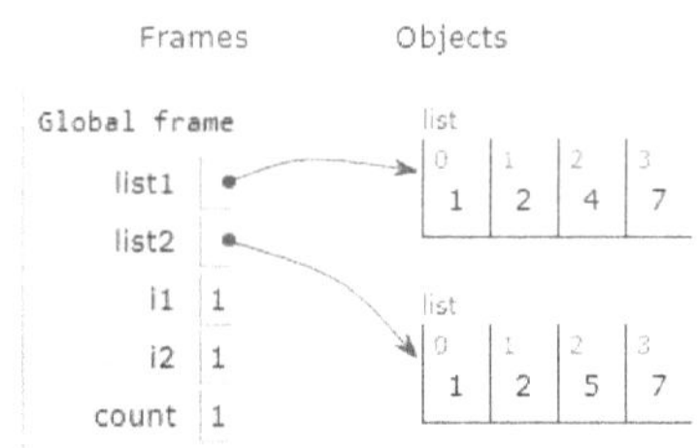

(a) Variables and lists illustrated in PythonTutor [5]

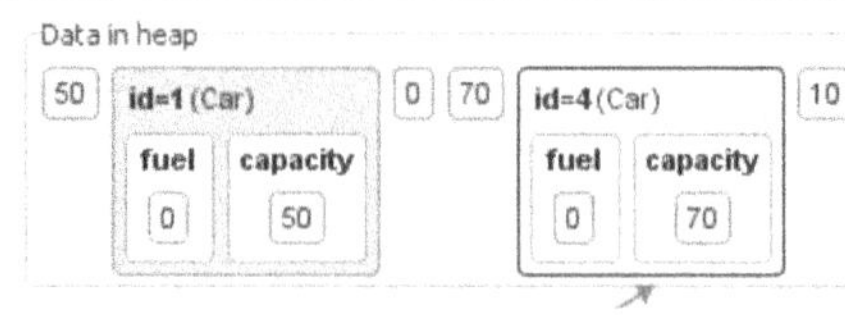

(b) Variables and instances illustrated in UUhistle [20]

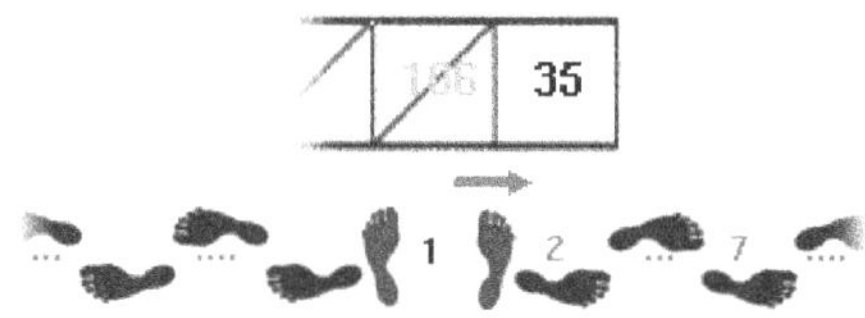

(c) A "most-recent-holder" and a "stepper" variable illustrated in PlanAni [15].

Figure 1: Variable visualizations in program animation tools

visualization style of the great majority of these systems is remarkably consistent in nearly all such systems [19]: variable values are encased in boxes, and prior values are erased and overwritten.

A notable exception is PlanAni [15], a visualization tool that illustrates variables based on their "roles" [16], or functionality. The "most-recent-holder" role and the "stepper" roles are both illustrated with previous values (see Figure 1c).

Empirical studies of visualization systems for use in introductory programming and in algorithms have had inconsistent results [8, 19]. Visualizations do not always help students, possibly because watching a visualization is a passive learning experience. An *interactive* process for visual program simulation is more likely to be effective [18]. This may involve an interactive GUI interface, like that of UUhistle [20], or potentially a sketching interface. To that end, viewing visualizations that students create for themselves may suggest new directions for the design of these tools.

3 METHOD

CS1 students from a large research university in North America participated in a computer-mediated experiment, using their own laptops in a supervised setting. The experiment took place during the 10th week of a 16 week semester.

The analysis presented here is from five multiple-choice code reading questions in the pre-test portion of this experiment. These questions were written in Python, and tested CS1 knowledge on lists, loops, and conditionals. In these questions, participants were asked to determine the result after the code had executed. Some questions were examples of common programming plans (see Table

Table 1: Code plans appearing in code reading questions.

#	Apparent code goal	Achieves goal?
1	Find minimum in a list subset	Yes
2	Find number of common list elements	No
3	Count appearances of target in a list subset	No
4	None (arbitrary arithmetic)	N/A
5	Find average of list subset	Yes

1), although the goal of the code was never specified. Students had 15 minutes to answer the five questions.

During the test, participants were instructed to use provided pens and blank scratch paper (labeled with their unique identification number) if they wished to draw. Participants were instructed to return their scratch paper to the experiment administrators after completion of the test.

3.1 Class observations

All participants had the same CS1 course instructor. The first author attended two class sessions during weeks 5 and 6, when lists were introduced. Field notes about instructional strategy were taken, and the sketches created by the instructor during these sessions were collected.

3.2 Interviews

Twenty-six of 167 test-takers consented to be contacted about a follow-up interview. A subset of those who consented were contacted, in order to maximize the variability the interviewees scores on the pre-test. Twenty-one students were contacted, and 13 agreed to participate in an interview. Of those 13, three got four questions right, six got three questions right, two got two questions right, one got one question right, and one got no questions right.

Interviews were semi-structured, lasted 30 minutes, and occurred in weeks 14, 15, and 16 of the semester.

During the interviews, interviewees' scratch paper from their pre-test was presented, along with the problems from the original exam. Interviewees were given time to re-familiarize themselves with their work, and then asked to describe their choices to sketch or not sketch on each problem. Then, the instructor's sketches were presented, and the students were asked to describe why they chose to sketch similarly or differently than their instructor.

Interviews were recorded and transcribed. They were coded thematically by two coders (the first and third authors), working individually.

4 WHY SKETCH (OR NOT)?

4.1 Goal and pattern recognition

4.1.1 Identifying a goal. Most questions matched or appeared to match familiar coding plans (see Table 1). For those problems, several students claimed to have identified the goal of the code, and didn't feel a need to sketch anything at all.

Said one interviewee about problem five: *"Once you look at the code and figure out what it's doing, then it's like, okay, I can compute an average without writing it down, especially if it's only two values."* Another non-sketcher agreed, with the following thoughts on problem one: *"To me, it's very clear that you're looking for a minimum value within a certain range, and so for that, I didn't feel a need to necessarily write down anything."*

The opposite was also true. Describing their process for solving problem two, an interviewee recalled how not identifying a goal for the code led to a tracing sketch: *"When I saw it I wasn't like 'Oh, I think I have a hunch that this code does this.' I'm going to need to work through it."*

4.1.2 Recognizing a pattern. In problems where an overall goal wasn't initially identified, sometimes tracing through a portion of the code execution was enough to identify a pattern and confidently predict the final result. This approach could lead to halting sketching halfway though, as this interviewee described on problem two: *"After I sort of got the hang of it, I just started to skip through writing it."* An interviewee who abandoned their trace on problem one said: *'You can also see the point where I realized like... and it clicked."*

4.1.3 Goal and pattern recognition was not reliable. Despite the confidence expressed by many interviewees in their ability to recognize goals and patterns, they were often wrong. Consistent with the conclusions of Fitzgerald et al. [4], there was significant variety in how well students used the pattern-matching strategy.

4.2 Anticipated cognitive load

The complexity of the problem corresponded with the amount of effort put into sketching a trace, with more complex problems sparking more organized tracing approaches. An interviewee recounted their choice to only sketch a few values in an unorganized way as they were solving problem one: *"I know it's a bit simpler, I immediately made like an assumption that it was easier, so I didn't put as much work into making a table or a chart."*

4.2.1 Complex variable interactions. How is complexity interpreted? Reflecting on their sketching choices for problem four, one interviewee felt that the amount of variable dependencies required a sketched trace: *"There were three [variables], I was like, "That's too many," and they're all related. I was like, 'I can't remember that,' and so I drew it out."*

4.2.2 Arithmetic or other math-like cues. Math-like cues within code syntax also prompted a move to close tracing: *"This [code in problem 4] looks like an equation. All the other ones don't look like equations. I guess when you don't have really long variable names also that might help."* Arithmetic was another factor that led to tracing: *"Instead of just reassigning values, I'm having to do some basic arithmetic, so keeping track of that through this method [a table] for me was the way to go about it."*

4.3 Problem-solving progression: From goal search to tracing (and re-tracing)

Rather than immediate use of a tracing technique, interviewees typically described an initial search for code's meaning, then a fall-back to tracing when no discernible goal or pattern was found.

Tracing was repeated two or more times, if an acceptable result was not found. Later tracing attempts were more organized, and more likely to take up a table-like format. In the words of one

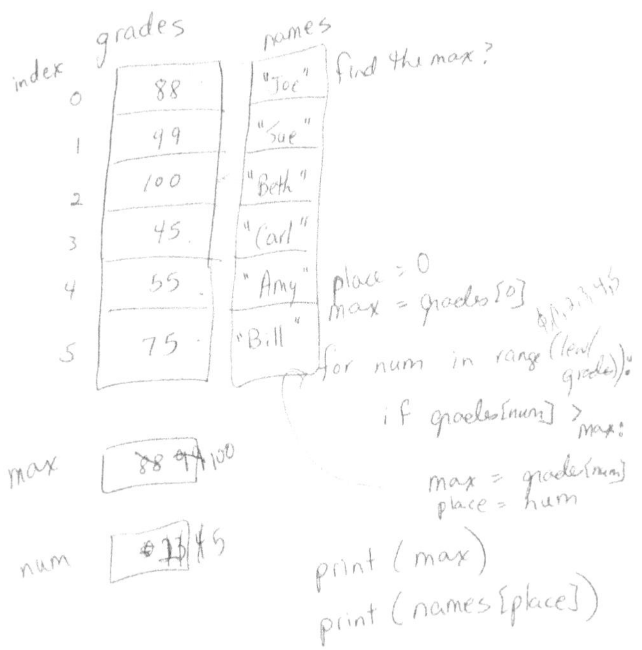

Figure 2: An in-class sketch by the instructor.

interviewee: *"When I do a problem, I usually just write stuff fast and try to get through to it. And then if I feel like that's becoming difficult to keep track of everything, I'll slow down and do something like this [a table], to make it easier to see."* More organization was often assumed to bring a greater chance of success: *"I was kind of annoyed that I didn't get the answer the first time so I was just like okay, putting down lines [creating a table to fill in]. I'm not going to get it wrong this time."*

5 WHY NOT SKETCH LIKE THE INSTRUCTOR?

The interviewees' instructor used sketched traces in class while teaching about lists and common list procedures, like finding a list's minimum value. One of her illustrations is shown in Figure 2. The instructor's choice to sketch boxes as representations of memory locations aligns with the design of the great majority of program animation software [19] (see Figure 1) as well as proposed designs for sketched memory diagrams (e.g. [6, 21]).

However, no participants re-created this sketching style while problem-solving. Instead, they opted for sketching techniques described in [10] and [2], where memory values are not bounded by boxes, but may be in rows, chunks, or tables. Why didn't students replicate the style repeatedly demonstrated by their instructor?

5.1 Seen as unnecessary and time-consuming

Interviewees described this sketching style as not worth the time and effort during exam conditions. *"Boxes take too long to draw, basically"*, said one participant. *"I'm always kind of hesitant to diagram things out to the max if I can save time by doing that." "It would take me longer to (draw) the boxes than to write the number, and probably, it will be a mess,"* said another interviewee.

An interviewee described the instructor's technique as overly detailed, and not prioritizing important values over unimportant ones: *"She's trying to illustrate everything as opposed to me just trying to illustrate specifically what I need to get through a problem....she literally writes out every single thing. Even really simple things like if it's a value and it's fixed, she'll write it. Like, it won't change."*

Others noted that they didn't see a functional difference in the tracing sketch they performed and what the instructor sketched: *"I just didn't circle the numbers, I guess."*

5.2 Visual details seem distant from code

Some students didn't feel that a box was the most appropriate representation for a variable. Said one interviewee who sketched traces using variable names and equals signs (e.g. `t = 1`): *"I think I just see it a little more clearly as saying that it's a variable that's equivalent to something, as opposed to maybe being a placeholder. I prefer to just write out what it actually is, in terms of a visualization."* This student appears hesitant to move away from representations that aren't similar to code syntax.

This prioritization of code was echoed by another participant: *"Because the high demand to put code in programming, I feel like, you don't have time to sit there and draw a picture most of the time for a simple list."*

5.3 Boxes are reserved for another purpose

For two interviewees, boxes had a clear meaning from their use in other subjects: identifying final results. Said one interviewee, *"If I cross them out, or box them then I end up getting very confused, because I use boxes and circles for other kinds of notation. I usually box my answers."* Pointing at variables in Figure 2, another interviewee said: *"I'm guessing those are the initial values but it kind of makes it look like they're the finals. Because from physics, like for homework, I always circle my finals....I saw the box first here and I'm like oh I don't like that."*

Boxing a key result, but not intermediate steps, is a technique students likely practiced across years of mathematics and physics courses. These participants didn't want to to change the meaning of this representation.

6 WHAT DO NOVICE SKETCHES INCLUDE?

While participants' sketches didn't closely match their instructor's sketches, or the style used in program animation tools, they did show a variety of consistent trends.

6.1 Organizing and structuring of traces

6.1.1 Organizing around loop iterations. Sketching out a trace was described as difficult without some sort of organizing structure. The index of the looping variable provided guidance during this cognitively challenging process. As one participant recalled: *"I think this one I had to actually do it a couple of times. The first time I went through I actually didn't put the zero, one, two, and three, because that really helped me count the range. Before when I didn't do that I really lost track of what my* `i` *value was so it got confusing, so I*

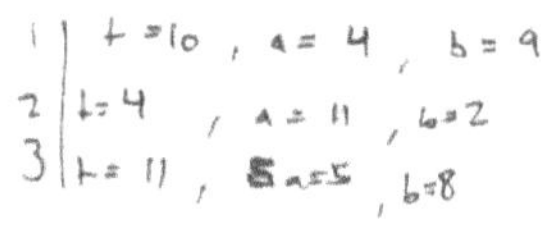

(a) Each row of variable values begins with a loop index

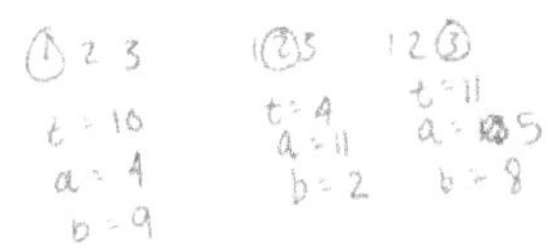

(b) Columns of variable values headed by loop indices

Figure 3: Tracing organized by loop indices

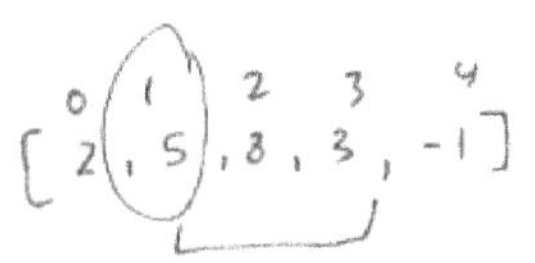

(a) Indice annotations, circling a key value, and demarcating a sub-list

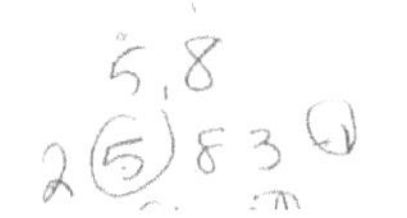

(b) Circling a key value and rewriting sub-list

Figure 4: Tracing organized around a list

erased it a couple of times. Then I put the i *values next to it, and it became much more clear."*

Describing their sketch (pictured in Figure 3a), another interviewee said: *"It's just for me to establish here's an iteration, here's an iteration, here's an iteration, just so I know what I'm dealing with and then not getting confused between iterations and numbers."* This participant's sketch indicates that loop indices are considered a distinct variable type. The loop variables aren't labeled by their variable name, and instead serve to separate parts of the sketched trace.

6.1.2 Organizing around annotated lists. Rather than jumping to a full sketched trace on the questions involving lists, participants used the list itself to organize an abbreviated trace. An interviewee described the creation of such as sketch (pictured in Figure 4): *"And then I guess I circled five to start with that. And then I also labeled each value that I knew was probably going to change."* Recognizing that the list is key to the question, the interviewee centered their problem-solving there, using the list to get an overview of what occured in the code.

6.2 Persistence of past values and calculations

Interviewees were cognizant of the possibility that their sketched trace may need to be re-used or modified. Keeping previous values of variables around for easy reference was a priority, as this interviewee described: *"if I mess up, I can go back and know that I either wrote a variable wrong or something like that."*

For one participant, this need was enough to dictate their writing utensil: *"I like to do coding in pen because if I make a mistake I can clearly see it because I have to cross it. I can't erase it, I have to cross it out."* For another, this goal led to careful tallying of the evaluation of conditionals as well as variable values, *"so if I ever had to go back through a problem and check my work, I'd be like that's why I did this."* Figure 5b shows this sketch.

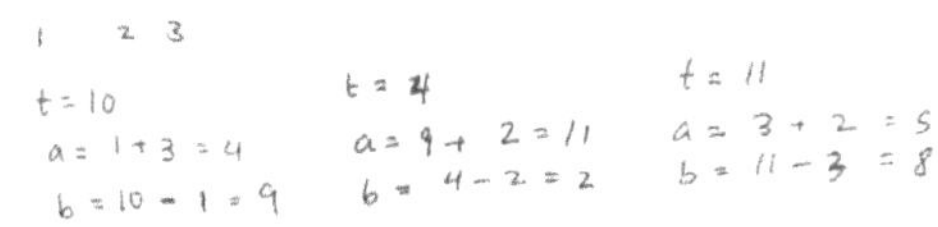

(a) Intermediate values in arithmetic expressions are preserved

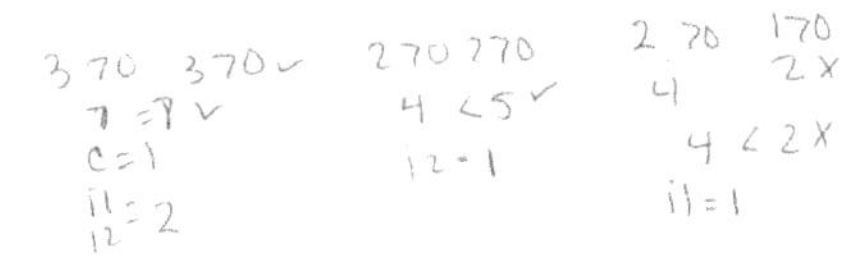

(b) Boolean expression values and variable values are preserved

Figure 5: Persistence of past values

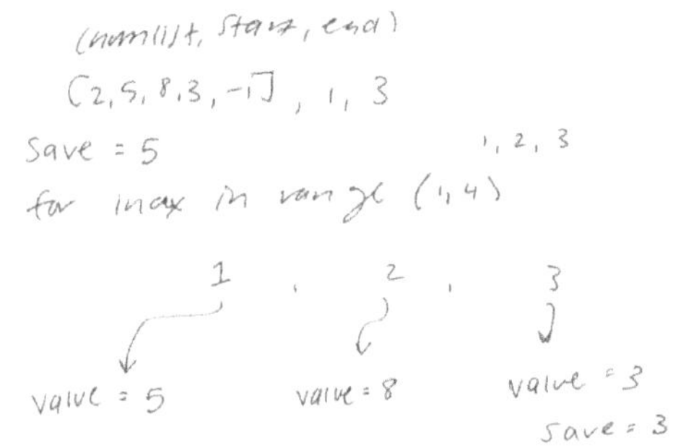

Figure 6: Organizing tracing around code structure

Keeping past values also allowed interviewees to better observe patterns over time. *"For me, I think it was just visual and then being able to see it laid out helped me also keep track of it. Because this is going back and forth and iterating it a bunch of times, so seeing the physical changes of the new variables was really helpful."*

6.3 Anchoring with visible values and structures

6.3.1 Re-writing initial values. Where should students start when faced with a complex code tracing problem? Students often started with initial values. As one interviewee explained: *"I always rewrite the first list. It's like for math. I always rewrite the original problem. I know some people don't do that. It takes up a lot of time."*

Despite the time commitment, several participants re-wrote starting values, like the arguments passed into the function, or initial variable values.

6.3.2 Using code structure to anchor tracing. Some students re-wrote code in a way that oriented their trace, most often for looping structures. In Figure 6, this participant combined the for loop syntax with a trace across three iterations.

7 DISCUSSION

Our results identify several problem-solving approaches of CS1 students that differ from the work of a strict "human compiler".

7.1 Search for goals and patterns is primary

These findings suggest that the first task of novice code readers is an attempt to find patterns and goals within code. Novices scan code in an effort to recognize its functionality, or perform an incomplete trace in the hopes of seeing a trend. In both cases, the cognitively demanding work of full, close tracing is avoided.

Such a strategy is understandable, considering the tedium of close tracing. If a student doesn't have a strong understanding of the notional machine, close tracing may be just as error-prone as looking for familiar code structures and divining the functionality from there.

Current visual program simulation approaches connect code structure (the syntax) to code behavior (the action of the notional machine). However, these approaches do not shed light on the function the code is trying to achieve. Can new approaches help learners not only better understand the notional machine, but also more accurately recognize patterns in code?

7.2 Variables are treated differently based on context

While a compiler doesn't treat loop variables differently than other variables, novice sketchers do. Loop variables are often used by novices to organize the tracing of other variables. Novices appear to have different classes of variables, based on semantic meaning.

Can visual program simulations treat loop variables differently than other variables? Or, can they use variable names to infer meaning, and emphasize or de-emphasize variable changes accordingly?

7.3 Past values are retained

Novice tracers show a preference for retaining previous values as they trace, in order to identify patterns or be able to re-trace their steps.

In program visualizations, the previous value is typically replaced as soon as a new value is assigned to the variable. However, maintaining past values may allow novices to better detect patterns. What effects might retaining some past values in program visualization have on learners?

7.4 Variables are un-boxed

Novices are unlikely to maintain a box representation in their own sketched visualizations. The use of boxing may interfere with sketching strategies learned in other courses (like boxing the final value in physics). Or, it may simply be irrelevant when creating a sketch, but still useful when teaching. Visualizing variables in a table-like form creates a more direct opportunity for transfer to a sketching environment.

8 LIMITATIONS AND THREATS TO VALIDITY

Our small number of participants allowed for a detailed, qualitative investigation of novice programmer rationales for sketching. However, due to the small sample, we cannot claim any generalizability of our findings. Qualitative research explores experiences or artifacts in rich detail, establishing the existence of phenomena. In order to determine whether these behaviors are replicated by many students, we would need to increase our sample size.

While our findings suggest new possibilities for sketching and visualization techniques, they do not translate into recommendations for classroom practice. We cannot claim that if instructors used the sketching approaches favored by students, better learning will result. Further research with more participants is needed to determine whether certain visualization techniques are typically associated with successful outcomes.

While our participants' sketches served to ground our interviews in past experience, our data ultimately depends on recall based on self-report. Additionally, in the weeks since the exam, participants likely improved their understanding of programming, creating additional challenges to accurate recall.

9 CONCLUSION

Sketching is a tangible trail of students' problem-solving process. However, pieces of paper alone can only tell us so much. By talking to novice programmers about their sketches, we identified their motivations for sketching differently than their instructor, for avoiding sketching and tracing, and for organizing their sketching in a variety of styles.

Visualization techniques in the computing education literature are designed by computing experts. Whether in program animation software or sketched by hand, these visualizations emphasize a high fidelity with the way the computer executes code "under the hood". The separation of memory values from code reflects the separation of instruction bytes from data bytes. The box analogy is consistent with parceling of only a certain number of bits per variable. The computer doesn't understand the semantic difference between a loop variable and a counter variable, so they are often illustrated identically.

Novice programmers aren't aware of the "reality" of the machines they are working with, and so while sketching and tracing they mix code and memory values, de-prioritize certain variables, and keep prior values around for reference. Each of these actions supports their ultimate end: the search for goals and patterns in the code they are trying to understand at a human level.

Humans are different than compilers. While a computer must parse and execute code token by token, human learners can infer patterns and identify goals.

Our current visualization techniques don't offer affordances for this type of action. With inspiration from the visualizations novices choose to create for themselves, we may be able to create visualization techniques that students are not only more likely to use, but that could also support their ability to generate meaning from the code they are reading and tracing.

ACKNOWLEDGMENTS

This material is based upon work supported by the National Science Foundation Graduate Research Fellowship under Grant No. DGC-1148903. We also thank the University of Michigan for financial support.

REFERENCES

[1] Beth Adelson. 1984. When novices surpass experts: The difficulty of a task may increase with expertise. *Journal of Experimental Psychology: Learning, Memory, and Cognition* 10, 3 (1984), 483.

[2] Kathryn Cunningham, Sarah Blanchard, Barbara Ericson, and Mark Guzdial. 2017. Using Tracing and Sketching to Solve Programming Problems: Replicating and Extending an Analysis of What Students Draw. In *Proceedings of the 2017 ACM Conference on International Computing Education Research (ICER '17)*. ACM, New York, NY, USA, 164–172. https://doi.org/10.1145/3105726.3106190

[3] Benedict Du Boulay. 1986. Some Difficulties of Learning to Program. *Journal of Educational Computing Research* 2, 1 (1986), 57–73. https://doi.org/10.2190/3LFX-9RRF-67T8-UVK9

[4] Sue Fitzgerald, Beth Simon, and Lynda Thomas. 2005. Strategies That Students Use to Trace Code: An Analysis Based in Grounded Theory. In *Proceedings of the First International Workshop on Computing Education Research (ICER '05)*. ACM, New York, NY, USA, 69–80. https://doi.org/10.1145/1089786.1089793

[5] Philip J. Guo. 2013. Online Python Tutor: Embeddable Web-based Program Visualization for Cs Education. In *Proceeding of the 44th ACM Technical Symposium on Computer Science Education (SIGCSE '13)*. ACM, New York, NY, USA, 579–584. https://doi.org/10.1145/2445196.2445368

[6] Matthew Hertz and Maria Jump. 2013. Trace-Based Teaching in Early Programming Courses. *Proceedings of the 44th ACM Technical Symposium on Computer Science Education* (2013), 561–566. https://doi.org/10.1145/2445196.2445364

[7] Mark A. Holliday and David Luginbuhl. 2004. CS1 assessment using memory diagrams. *ACM SIGCSE Bulletin* 36, 1 (2004), 200. https://doi.org/10.1145/1028174.971373

[8] Christopher D. Hundhausen, Sarah A. Douglas, and John T. Stasko. 2002. A Meta-Study of Algorithm Visualization Effectiveness. *Journal of Visual Languages and Computing* 13, 3 (2002), 259–290. https://doi.org/10.1006/S1045-926X(02)00028-9

[9] David Kirsh. 2010. Thinking with external representations. *Ai & Society* 25, 4 (2010), 441–454.

[10] Raymond Lister, Otto Seppälä, Beth Simon, Lynda Thomas, Elizabeth S. Adams, Sue Fitzgerald, William Fone, John Hamer, Morten Lindholm, Robert McCartney, Jan Erik Moström, and Kate Sanders. 2004. A multi-national study of reading and tracing skills in novice programmers. In *ACM SIGCSE Bulletin*, Vol. 36. 119–150. https://doi.org/10.1145/1041624.1041673

[11] Raymond Lister, Beth Simon, Errol Thompson, Jacqueline L Whalley, and Christine Prasad. 2006. Not seeing the forest for the trees: novice programmers and the SOLO taxonomy. *ACM SIGCSE Bulletin* 38, 3 (2006), 118–122.

[12] Robert McCartney, Jan Erik Moström, Kate Sanders, and Otto Seppälä. 2004. Questions, Annotations, and Institutions: observations from a study of novice programmers. In *the Fourth Finnish/Baltic Sea Conference on Computer Science Education, October 1–3, 2004 in Koli, Finland.* Helsinki University of Technology, Department of Computer Science and Engineering, Laboratory of Information Processing Science, FINLAND, 11–19.

[13] Greg L Nelson, Benjamin Xie, and Andrew J Ko. 2017. Comprehension first: evaluating a novel pedagogy and tutoring system for program tracing in CS1. In *Proceedings of the 2017 ACM Conference on International Computing Education Research*. ACM, 2–11.

[14] Dale Parsons and Patricia Haden. 2006. Parson's Programming Puzzles: A Fun and Effective Learning Tool for First Programming Courses. In *Proceedings of the 8th Australasian Conference on Computing Education - Volume 52 (ACE '06)*. Australian Computer Society, Inc., Darlinghurst, Australia, Australia, 157–163. http://dl.acm.org/citation.cfm?id=1151869.1151890

[15] Jorma Sajaniemi. 2002. *PlanAni-a System for Visualizing Roles of Variables to Novice Programmes*. University of Joensuu, Department of Computer Science.

[16] Jorma Sajaniemi and Marja Kuittinen. 2005. An experiment on using roles of variables in teaching introductory programming. *Computer Science Education* 15, 1 (2005), 59–82.

[17] Juha Sorva. 2013. Notional Machines and Introductory Programming Education. *Trans. Comput. Educ.* 13, 2, Article 8 (July 2013), 31 pages. https://doi.org/10.1145/2483710.2483713

[18] Juha Sorva et al. 2012. *Visual program simulation in introductory programming education*. Aalto University.

[19] Juha Sorva, Ville Karavirta, and Lauri Malmi. 2013. A Review of Generic Program Visualization Systems for Introductory Programming Education. *ACM Transactions on Computing Education* 13, 4 (2013), 15.1 – 15.64. https://doi.org/10.1145/2490822

[20] Juha Sorva and Teemu Sirkiä. 2010. UUhistle: A Software Tool for Visual Program Simulation. In *Proceedings of the 10th Koli Calling International Conference on Computing Education Research (Koli Calling '10)*. ACM, New York, NY, USA, 49–54. https://doi.org/10.1145/1930464.1930471

[21] Lynda Thomas, Mark Ratcliffe, and Benjy Thomasson. 2004. Scaffolding with Object Diagrams in First Year Programming Classes: Some Unexpected Results. In *Proceedings of the 35th SIGCSE Technical Symposium on Computer Science Education (SIGCSE '04)*. ACM, New York, NY, USA, 250–254. https://doi.org/10.1145/971300.971390

[22] Vesa Vainio and Jorma Sajaniemi. 2007. Factors in Novice Programmers' Poor Tracing Skills. *SIGCSE Bull.* 39, 3 (June 2007), 236–240. https://doi.org/10.1145/1269900.1268853

[23] Jacqueline Whalley, Christine Prasad, and P. K. Ajith Kumar. 2007. Decoding Doodles: Novice Programmers and Their Annotations. In *Proceedings of the Ninth Australasian Conference on Computing Education - Volume 66 (ACE '07)*. Australian Computer Society, Inc., Darlinghurst, Australia, Australia, 171–178. http://dl.acm.org/citation.cfm?id=1273672.1273693

[24] Benjamin Xie, Greg L Nelson, and Andrew J Ko. 2018. An explicit strategy to scaffold novice program tracing. In *Proceedings of the 49th ACM Technical Symposium on Computer Science Education*. ACM, 344–349.

Non-restricted Access to Model Solutions: A Good Idea?

Henrik Nygren
University of Helsinki
henrik.nygren@helsinki.fi

Juho Leinonen
University of Helsinki
juho.leinonen@helsinki.fi

Arto Hellas
University of Helsinki
arto.hellas@cs.helsinki.fi

ABSTRACT

In this article, we report an experiment where students in an introductory programming course were given the opportunity to view model solutions to programming assignments whenever they wished, without the need to complete the assignments beforehand or to wait for the deadline to pass. Our experiment was motivated by the observation that some students may spend hours stuck with an assignment, leading to non-productive study time. At the same time, we considered the possibility of students using the sample solutions as worked examples, which could help students to improve the design of their own programs. Our experiment suggests that many of the students use the model solutions sensibly, indicating that they can control their own work. At the same time, a minority of students used the model solutions as a way to proceed in the course, leading to poor exam performance.

CCS CONCEPTS

• **Social and professional topics → Computing education**.

KEYWORDS

model solutions, introductory programming, sample solutions, self-regulation

ACM Reference Format:

Henrik Nygren, Juho Leinonen, and Arto Hellas. 2019. Non-restricted Access to Model Solutions: A Good Idea?. In *Innovation and Technology in Computer Science Education (ITiCSE '19), July 15–17, 2019, Aberdeen, Scotland UK*. ACM, New York, NY, USA, 7 pages. https://doi.org/10.1145/3304221.3319768

1 INTRODUCTION

Students come to introductory programming courses with a wide variety of backgrounds. Some have programmed before, some have not, some have studied for years, and some are just starting their studies. In the same way as students' backgrounds differ, so do their approaches to studying. Some are driven to deeply understand what they are learning, while some put in the minimum effort needed to complete course work [17, 18]. Some may even avoid learning altogether through piggybacking or using solutions from others [1, 13, 22].

The difference between solutions from others and examples in course materials, in the end, is not vast – what matters is what students do with the content. Examples in course materials, demonstrations, and worked examples can all be beneficial for learning [8, 23]. Regardless of the source of the examples, for learning to be successful, the student is expected to work on their own solutions, often following the principles set out by the examples and the teachers [7]. We are interested in seeing what would happen if the use of "solutions from others" – here, model solutions to programming problems given by us – would be legitimized, and students could use the model solutions to support their learning.

Such knowledge is particularly interesting in programming, where learning – like when learning any complex cognitive skill – takes plenty of effort and practice [20]. One of the particular characteristics in programming is that programming languages are typically highly vulnerable to even small mistakes, and a simple typo can take a significant amount of time to fix [2, 9]. Furthermore, a single character may change the functionality of a program completely, or even stop the program from working at all.

In this article, we discuss an experiment where we changed the dynamics of our introductory programming course and allowed our students to freely access model solutions. Students could view the model solution of each course assignment without the need to complete the assignment or to wait until the deadline of the assignment passed. This closely resembles the approach taken in e.g. many primary and secondary education mathematics books, where students have access to solutions so that they can verify their work. In our case, however, as we are working with computer programs, students have the access to full source code which corresponds to one of the possible ways to solve each particular assignment.

Perhaps the closest match to our experiment is the work on intelligent tutoring systems [4], some of which allow students to ask for hints as they are working on problems. A tutoring system may suggest the next meaningful step, provide guidelines on how to proceed, or show source code to the student [3, 5, 19]. Intelligent tutoring systems do, however, often base showing hints or guiding the students on students' previous behavior, while in our experiment, students' behavior does not change whether they have access to the solutions or not. Moreover, intelligent tutoring systems often have a vast repository of problems that the student can work on.

This article is organized as follows. Next, in Section 2, we outline related research on model solutions, focusing on the use of examples in instruction. Then, in Section 3, we outline the overall design of our experiment, including the study context, data, and the research questions. This is followed by the methodology and the results of our experiment in Section 4. In Section 5, we discuss the results and implications of our experiment, and then in Section 6, we conclude the article and point possible future directions for the work.

ITiCSE '19, July 15–17, 2019, Aberdeen, Scotland UK

ACM ISBN 978-1-4503-6301-3/19/07...$15.00
https://doi.org/10.1145/3304221.3319768

2 BACKGROUND

A model solution, by definition, is a solution to a problem that a student can use to compare their own solution with. Model solutions are typically made available after the student has solved the problem or worked on the problem for a sufficient time, for example until the deadline of the problem has passed. The extent to which the model solution captures the process by which the outcome was achieved varies greatly. For example, some mathematics books outline only expected numeric outcomes, while in programming, model solutions may contain the whole expected source code.

Model solutions are beneficial for verifying results and the thought process and they can be used to increase reflection. Students may, for example, compare and contrast their own solution and the solution given by a teacher. Model solutions are different from students' own previous work in that, while students' own previous work can be similar to model solutions, students have constructed the solutions in their own work either by themselves, in collaboration with others, or by following an example. It is known that having a repository of previous self-constructed solutions can be beneficial [11], as they can then be referred to when facing new problems.

Model solutions can be distinguished from examples. Examples do not typically contain immediate answers to the problems that the students are working on but provide similar content that the student is expected to internalize and then use to solve the given problems. One should take care, however, as too challenging learning materials and examples may hinder students' progress [10], and the quality of the examples influences the quality of students' solutions [12]. Two particular types of examples used to support learning are worked examples [23], which are step-by-step examples showing how a problem should be solved, and modeling [6, 7], which means the process of a teacher showing how a particular task is accomplished. The effectiveness of these approaches is influenced by students' attention, effort, and previous knowledge – for example, guidance that is beneficial for novices may lead to negative outcomes if targeted to more advanced students [14].

Examples that students are given access to should be relevant to the task they are working on. Studying an example and completing an assignment related to the example can lead to better performance, and working on additional assignments helps learning over viewing examples [24]. Even if students are given examples of work that they are expected to do, however, students' differences influence how they work with the examples. For example, poorly performing students may copy content verbatim, while advanced students may try to solve the subsequent problems themselves but only refer to examples when stuck, wanting to check a step, or wanting to avoid a more complex task such as detailed calculation [25].

3 EXPERIMENT DESIGN

3.1 Context and data

Our experiment was conducted in a seven-week introductory programming course offered at the University of Helsinki. Students in the course learn the principles of procedural and object-oriented programming using Java. The course starts with basic input and output, conditional statements and loops, and continues with lists. This is followed by the construction of objects that are mostly used to represent data. Finally, students learn to use maps and learn about basic algorithms that are used to search and sort data. The course has a total of seven programming assignment sets with a total of 177 programming assignments. Each assignment set corresponds to a week in the course and has a deadline. At the end of the course, students attend an exam. Each assignment has a corresponding model solution that includes source code of a working solution to the assignment. The course uses an online course material with embedded videos, questionnaires, and programming assignment handouts. The programming assignments are worked on in a separate programming environment, from where they are submitted to an automated assessment system that grades the work and provides feedback to the students (see [28]). There are walk-in labs that students can attend simply to work on their own or to ask questions from course assistants and course teachers – the labs are available for at least 20 hours each week (for more details on the course organization, see e.g. [26, 27]).

In the previous course iterations, students have been able to view model solutions to programming assignments once they have either completed the programming assignment or once the assignment deadline has passed. In our experiment, we removed the restrictions that limited access to the programming assignment model solutions. Instead of students having to complete the assignment or to wait until the deadline of the assignment set passed, students could access the model solutions whenever they wished, even before starting to work on the actual assignment. Direct copy-pasting of solutions was strongly discouraged, and lectures also discussed the effort that learning to program requires.

In order to view the model solutions, students had to log in to the automated assessment system. Every time that a student viewed a model solution, the system stored the student's id, the programming assignment that was viewed, and the timestamp. Similarly, when students submit their work for grading, the automated assessment system stores students' information. In addition to the logs from the automated assessment system, we have access to the results of the course, and have conducted semi-formal interviews with 16 students and teaching assistants on the course.

When comparing this iteration of the course to previous iterations, students now were expected to complete 75% of the assignments each week in order to access the course exam and the course grade was fully based on the exam score, where 40% of the exam points corresponded to the worst passing grade, and 90% of the exam points corresponded to the best passing grade. In previous course iterations, the course grade has been based on a combination of completed programming assignments and the course exam. Moreover, in some previous course iterations, students have had multiple exams during the course, while this iteration had a single exam. Due to these differences, we discuss the differences between the grades of different course iterations only briefly.

3.2 Research questions

Studying the data collected during the experiment and the interviews, we answer the following research questions: **RQ1** How do students use the opportunity to view model solutions?; **RQ2** To what extent does students' use of model solutions correlate with course outcomes?; **RQ3** How do students and course assistants perceive the opportunity to see model solutions?

To answer RQ1, we study model solution access logs. We focus on whether students looked at the model solutions before or after completing assignments, and analyze whether student sub-populations differ in their use of model solutions. To answer RQ2, we study the correlation between model solution use and programming assignment completion as well as model solution use and exam outcomes. Furthermore, as some of the course participants drop out of the course, we also study the difference between the model solution usage of the population that stays in the course weekly as well as the population that does not stay in the course. Finally, to answer RQ3, we analyze the semi-structured interviews that were conducted with 16 course participants and teaching assistants and highlight the main themes from those interviews.

In the analysis, we consider a student having viewed a model solution before completing an assignment if the student has viewed a model solution before receiving full marks from the assignment. Similarly, we consider a student having viewed a model solution after completing an assignment if the student has viewed a model solution after receiving full marks from the assignment. The grading is done automatically by the automated assessment system. For our analysis, we count each view only once. That is, even if a student views a model solution to a particular assignment multiple times, it is still counted as a single view.

4 METHODOLOGY AND RESULTS

4.1 Descriptive statistics

In total, 342 students signed up to the course in our University course registration system. From the 342 students, 314 showed up and continued to the second week of the course. From the 314, who we count as having participated, 262 continued working on the course assignments until the end of the course, and 242 attended the course exam (77.1% of the participating students). It is possible that some of the students decided to attend an exam later, to which we do not have access at the present time.

At the beginning of the first week of the course, students were asked to provide consent for the use of their data for the analysis. From the course participants, 206 provided consent. Subsequently, the analysis focuses on the 206 students. From the 206 consenting students, 107 identified themselves as female, 92 male and 7 chose to not to disclose their gender. The median age of the students was 23, average age 25, and approximately 30% of the students had at least some programming background. From the 206 students, 167 attended the course exam (81.1% of the population who consented for the analysis).

4.2 Students' use of the opportunity to view model solutions

The course has 177 programming assignments distributed across seven weeks. The earlier weeks of the course have more assignments, but the assignments are smaller in size, while the later weeks of the course have fewer but larger assignments. This data in combination with model solution usage is summarized in Table 1.

Students use the model solutions less during the earlier weeks of the course than the latter weeks of the course. During the first week of the course with simple assignments, the average number of model solutions viewed before completing the assignment was 7.9, which corresponds to approximately 18.8% of the weekly assignments. During the last week of the course with more complex assignments, the average number of model solutions viewed before completing the assignment was 5.5, which corresponds to approximately 61.1% of the weekly assignments.

Table 1: Number of model solutions viewed before and after completing the programming assignment. Here, # corresponds to the number of programming assignments during the week and *std* corresponds to standard deviation.

		Before completion			After completion		
Week	#	median	mean	std	median	mean	std
1	42	4	7.9	9.9	1	1.9	3.3
2	33	6	10	10	1	2	3.3
3	34	11	12.6	11	1	2.3	3.9
4	28	8	9.7	8.5	0	1.4	2.9
5	17	8	7.7	6	0	0.8	2.2
6	14	9	8	4.8	0	0.7	1.7
7	9	6	5.5	2.9	0	0.3	0.8
All	177	47	56.6	46.6	5	9.1	14.6

Students viewed the model solutions significantly more before completing programming assignments than after completing programming assignments. During the first week of the course, the average number of model solutions viewed after completing the assignment was 1.9, which corresponds to less than 5% of the weekly assignments. Similarly, during the last week of the course, the average number of model solutions viewed after completing the assignment was almost zero.

When considering all the weeks combined (row "All" in Table 1), students on average viewed 56.6 model solutions before completing assignments, which corresponds to 32.0% of the total number of programming assignments in the course. The lower trend in the number of times that model solutions were viewed after completing programming assignments was visible here as well. On average, students viewed a model solution 9.1 times out of the 177 assignments, after completing the assignment, which corresponds to 5.1% of the total number of programming assignments in the course.

We also studied if the number of model solutions viewed before completing an assignment could be explained by (1) gender, (2) previous programming experience, or (3) major. Using Kolmogorov-Smirnov -test with Bonferroni correction to compare the use of model solutions before completing the assignment, we found no statistically significant difference in gender ($p = 0.07$). There was a statistically significant difference in the use of model solutions when comparing students with at least some programming experience to those with no programming experience ($p = 0.012$); students with some programming experience viewed less model solutions. When comparing students' major, we found a statistically significant difference in the use of model solutions between students who major in computer science and students who major in other subjects ($p < 0.001$). Computer science majors view fewer model solutions than students who major in other subjects – students in other subjects viewed 42% more model solutions before completing the assignments.

4.3 Model solution use and course outcomes

Next, we studied the model solution usage and course outcomes. We first study the connection between model solution usage and assignments completed in the course, and then model solution usage and dropping out of the course. Finally, we study model solution use and exam outcomes.

First, using Spearman's rank correlation with Bonferroni correction, we found no statistically significant correlation between the number of completed assignments and the number of model solution views before completing programming assignments ($r = 0.08, p = 0.25$). There was a moderate statistically significant correlation between viewing the model solutions after completing programming assignments and the number of completed programming assignments ($r = 0.41, p < 0.0001$).

Second, we analyzed whether dropping out of the course could be explained to some extent by viewing model solutions. For each course week from 1 to 6, we divided the students into two populations – those who completed assignments in the subsequent week and those who did not – both populations had completed a comparable number of course assignments in the current week. Then, for the populations each week, we studied their use of model solutions to determine if the model solution usage could explain students dropping out. The comparison of the populations was done using the Kolmogorov-Smirnov test with Bonferroni correction. No statistically significant difference in terms of model solution usage between the populations that dropped out of the course and the population that stayed in the course was observed ($week1 - week6, p > 0.05$). Here, however, the average number of students dropping out each week was 6, which biases the comparison due to the small number.

Finally, we analyzed students' use of model solutions and exam outcomes. Focusing on the 167 students in the exam with consent, we studied the correlation between the number of viewed model solutions before and after completing the assignments and the exam outcomes. Using Spearman's rank correlation with Bonferroni correction, we identified a strong negative correlation between the number of viewed model solutions before completing assignments and the course exam ($r = -0.71, p < 0.0001$). There was no correlation between the number of viewed model solutions after completing assignments and the course exam ($r = 0.01, p = 0.93$). Figure 1 illustrates students' exam points and model solution views before completing assignments.

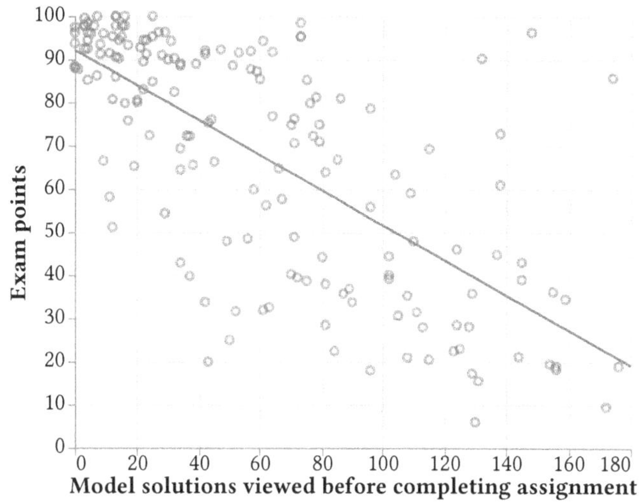

Figure 1: The number of model solution views before completing an assignment plotted with exam points. Note that a student may have viewed a model solution for a particular assignment multiple times, but our analysis calculates that as a single view event.

4.4 Students' and teaching assistants' views on the availability of model solutions

We then analyzed the 16 semi-structured interviews with the course participants and teaching assistants to study how the experiment was perceived. Overall, feelings were mixed, and the majority of the interviewed saw both benefits and downsides to the experiment. Here, we first outline the positive observations regarding the experiment and then discuss the negative observations.

4.4.1 Positive observations. Both students and teaching assistants felt that model solutions were highly beneficial if not abused – the importance of self-regulation and meta-cognition rose multiple times as themes in the interviews, albeit students did not use the actual terms. Some also pointed out that, when compared to other courses, they thought more about their learning process due to the availability of model solutions.

Several mentioned having been stuck for a while at a rather simple problem, for example due to a typo, which was then easily noticed and fixed when comparing their solution with the model solution. Issues with, for example, the expected formatting of the output could take plenty of time to fix without being able to use the model solutions. One student mentioned an assignment, where the program was expected to output `"The sum is: " + number` and the student had written `"The sum is " + number`. The student pointed out that figuring out the mistake was easy with the model solution, but that they had spent plenty of time trying to find bugs in the program logic.

A common theme was also the benefit of studying model solutions. Some pointed out that studying model solutions, either before or after completing the assignment, provided an opportunity for reflection. Moreover, model solutions were seen as a good source for learning and a good source for new approaches to solving a problem, especially if the students' own solution was different than the model solution.

There were also students who had attended the course previously or who had programmed previously. Some mentioned that the use of model solutions was a simple way to jump forward in the course – a student could copy the solution to "a boring problem" and focus on assignments that they felt were not trivial to them. This behavior, however, also requires insight into the students' own level of competence. Finally, some also pointed out that the availability of model solutions helped them stay on the course. There were those who had taken too many courses, and model solutions made it possible to handle the worst time conflicts. These students often, however, noted that they would then have to revisit the problems and do the actual studying afterward.

4.4.2 Negative observations. First, many considered the experiment very unorthodox and thought about the model solutions as "an easy way for others to cheat" and "an easy way to lie to yourself". Some simply pointed out that they thought that the whole experiment was "stupid", often pointing out that the approach was completely different to what they were used to. Some pointed out that the availability of model solutions opened a highway on which students could avoid learning but still proceed in the course, also obfuscating what was supposed to be learned.

Some noted that the model solutions themselves were not always helpful. They were highly helpful when fixing simple issues such as typos and formatting output, but "when the problem was bigger, the model solution was often of no use". This was especially evident in cases, where the student's own – not yet complete – solution was very different to the model solution. Here, students could become even more confused when viewing the model solution.

One unexpected observation came from the teaching assistants. When compared to the previous course iterations, the attendance in the walk-in labs had reduced significantly. Where previously the teaching assistants often had many students to help, the experiment made the labs feel redundant at times. Many of the students had replaced the walk-in labs and the teaching assistants with the model solutions, potentially also removing the possibility to discuss their solutions with others. Even with this observation, some teaching assistants pointed out that the availability of model solutions is not a bad thing by itself, but there should be some way to limit the access to them – for example, by limiting the number of times that model solutions could be accessed each week.

5 DISCUSSION

5.1 Model solutions were popular

Overall, the use of model solutions was popular and almost every student viewed a model solution at least once. On average, students viewed the model solution of over 50 programming assignments out of 177 before completing the programming assignment. Students were more likely to view the model solution of an assignment in the later weeks of the course than in the earlier weeks. It is possible that this was caused by the increasing complexity of the assignments.

We also observed that students were more likely to view model solutions before completing the programming assignment than after completing the programming assignment. Model solutions were viewed after completing the assignment significantly fewer times than before completing the assignment. One should note, however, that we did not study whether the students who viewed the model solutions before completing the assignment and the students who viewed the model solutions after completing the assignment were the same. That is, for some of the students who have viewed the model solution before completing the assignment, viewing the assignment afterward can be redundant. Similarly, there may be some students who complete the assignment but do not submit it for grading – instead, they may compare their completed but not submitted solution with the model solution before actually submitting the work; our current analysis which is based on the submission and model solution view timestamps cannot determine whether such behavior existed.

When looking at the differences in the use of model solutions between gender, previous programming experience, and major, we did not identify any significant difference in the use of model solutions that could be explained by gender. Our analysis, however, showed that there was a difference in the use of model solutions between students who have at least some previous programming experience and those who have no previous programming experience. Similar difference was identified in students' majors – students who major in Computer Science are less likely to view model solutions than students majoring in other subjects. Computer Science majors viewed considerably fewer model solutions than others, which may suggest that the students who major in the subject are more conscious of their learning, possibly due to knowing that the programming course is a prerequisite to many subsequent computer science courses, but it is possible also that they have more previous exposure to programming. In our case, the course had also some students for whom computer science is a mandatory minor – it is possible that some of these students have sought to put in the minimum effort to the course through the use of model solutions.

5.2 Model solutions and course outcomes

When analyzing the correlations between the number of assignments the students completed and the number of times the students viewed model solutions before assignments, no statistically significant correlation was identified. However, there was a statistically significant difference between viewing model solutions after the assignment and the number of completed assignments. This could be due to more meticulous students both viewing more model solutions after the assignment and completing more assignments. Interestingly, viewing model solutions after the assignment was, however, not correlated with exam scores.

When analyzing course exam outcomes and model solution usage, we observed a strong negative correlation between model solution usage before completing the assignment and overall exam points. This indicates that the more model solutions students used, the worse their exam outcome was. When looking at the Figure 1, we observe that there are also students who do well in the course even if they use large amounts of model solutions and that there are students who do poorly in the course even if they do not use many model solutions. It is possible that the negative correlation is caused e.g. by worse performing students requiring more help – and thus consulting the model solutions more. In any case, we suggest that others attempting a similar experiment should limit the number of times that model solutions can be viewed.

5.3 Model solutions and our community of learners

In our courses that are organized using the traditional model, the walk-in labs have been quite popular with students. Through the use of the walk-in labs, we have sought to build a community of learners – a particular type of community of practice [15, 27] where new students come to the campus as legitimate peripheral participants and work on the course assignments in collaboration with others. Having this type of community has also been important as a pool of potential teaching assistants, and typically active students have been recruited to be TAs on subsequent courses.

In the current experiment, where students were able to look at the model solutions whenever they wished, the use of the walk-in labs diminished noticeably. This made the teaching assistants feel their work as somewhat unnecessary and may have also influenced whether students come to the campus. It is also possible that some of the activity that has traditionally been conducted in a physical classroom has moved to online environments – we have observed the formation of online communities of learners in the course. The change in the number of walk-in labs attendants has, regardless, been so sudden that it is likely that the experiment was the cause.

5.4 A comparison with previous course iterations

As noted in 3.1, the course organization changed due to the experiment with making model solutions visible for all. Students no longer were given points towards their grade from completing course assignments and the students were expected to complete at least 75% of the weekly assignments to be allowed to attend the exam. Students have previously had more than one exam during the course, while in our experiment there was only a single exam at the end of the course. Also, due to students having just a single exam at the end of the course, the exam was more challenging as it covered more content.

When comparing the proportion of students who started the course and attended the exam, there is no noticeable difference between the course iterations. In the experiment reported in this article, 77.1% of the students participated in the course exam, while in the course version from last year, 77.9% of the students participated in the last exam. The students from the previous year fared better in their exam, but as the whole exam was different and somewhat easier than the current exam, a deeper analysis is not meaningful. The only somewhat comparable question in the (final) exam from last year and the (only) exam in our current experiment was a variant of the Rainfall problem [21]. In our experiment, students scored on average 88.1% in the problem, while the students in the previous year scored on average 91.8% in the problem.

Over the years, we have collected a set of "unofficial" solutions to the programming assignments offered in our course. These solutions come from a wide variety of sources ranging from Github and Pastebin-like services to solutions that students have admitted to having plagiarized from elsewhere. While in our typical courses a handful of students are found to have used these unofficial sources, in the current experiment we did not identify the use of these sources or plagiarism in the assignments. At the same time, quite a few of our students did use our official model solutions as a part of their work. That is, it seems that our experiment moved the source of the undesirable behavior to a controlled environment.

5.5 Limitations of work

There are limitations in this work, which we outline next. First, as we did not conduct a randomized controlled trial with the experiment, all of the course participants had the same material and activities. Thus, it is not possible to say which changes to the course affected the outcomes the most. We cannot, for example, say to what extent the model solutions, the different grading criteria, and the increased mandatory amount of weekly assignments contributed to students' behavior. As we recruited the interviewed students and teaching assistants from the course labs, there is a possible selection bias. It is possible that the interviewed students were more active students in the course. We do not, however, have their grade information and cannot explore this further. Finally, there is a population bias as the study was conducted in Finland, a country with a rather homogeneous population, which also tends to rank highly when examining trust between individuals and trust of authorities, which may influence the use of model solutions – it is not certain whether the results obtained here generalize to other contexts.

6 CONCLUSIONS AND FUTURE WORK

In this article, we described an experiment where students could view model solutions to programming assignments whenever they wished, regardless of whether they had completed the assignment. Our motivation was to give students the possibility to avoid unproductive time spent stuck on an assignment and to possibly facilitate learning. Additionally, having the option could give students more ownership of their learning, and being able to see an "official" solution can act as a worked example and reduce unwanted plagiarism.

Our results suggest that if model solutions are made available, students will use them. In our case, on average, students viewed the model solution of almost 30% of the course assignments before completing the assignment. There was no significant difference in the way how students with and without previous programming experience used the model solutions, nor was there any significant difference in gender. We did observe, however, that the students who are majoring in computer science use the model solutions less than others, which may suggest that students who know that they will need the knowledge in the future may control their learning better. Overall, our experiment also suggests that the more model solutions the students use before completing assignments the worse they will perform in the course exam on average.

To summarize, our answers to the research questions are as follows. **RQ1** How do students use the opportunity to view model solutions? **Answer:** *Many refer to the model solutions when completing programming assignments. At the same time, very few look at the model solutions after completing assignments.* **RQ2** To what extent does students' use of model solutions correlate with course outcomes? **Answer:** *Viewing model solutions before completing assignments correlates negatively with course outcomes, while viewing model solutions after completing assignments seems to not be connected with exam outcomes.* **RQ3** How do students and course assistants perceive the opportunity to see model solutions? **Answer:** *Many see benefit in making model solutions available, however, many also note that students can abuse model solutions.*

In our ongoing work, we have chosen not to continue with the experiment of giving unrestricted access to model solutions. The main reason for this decision was the observation that students who used a lot of model solutions performed worse in the course exam. We do still provide students access to model solutions, but instead of being able to use them without any constraint, students have access to a limited number of model solutions during the course – this may prevent students from abusing the availability of the model solutions as the limited number of model solutions can be seen as a scarce resource that students may wish to retain [16].

REFERENCES

[1] Cheryl L Aasheim, Paige S Rutner, Lixin Li, and Susan R Williams. 2012. Plagiarism and programming: A survey of student attitudes. *Journal of information systems education* 23, 3 (2012), 297.

[2] Amjad Altadmri and Neil CC Brown. 2015. 37 million compilations: Investigating novice programming mistakes in large-scale student data. In *Proceedings of the 46th ACM Technical Symposium on Computer Science Education*. ACM, 522–527.

[3] John R. Anderson and Edward Skwarecki. 1986. The automated tutoring of introductory computer programming. *Commun. ACM* 29, 9 (1986), 842–849.

[4] Ryan S Baker. 2016. Stupid tutoring systems, intelligent humans. *International Journal of Artificial Intelligence in Education* 26, 2 (2016), 600–614.

[5] Peter Brusilovsky and Gerhard Weber. 1996. Collaborative example selection in an intelligent example-based programming environment. In *Proceedings of the 1996 international conference on Learning sciences*. International Society of the Learning Sciences, 357–362.

[6] Allan Collins, John Seely Brown, and Ann Holum. 1991. Cognitive apprenticeship: Making thinking visible. *American educator* 15, 3 (1991), 6–11.

[7] Allan Collins, John Seely Brown, and Susan E Newman. 1989. Cognitive apprenticeship: Teaching the crafts of reading, writing, and mathematics. *Knowing, learning, and instruction: Essays in honor of Robert Glaser* 18 (1989), 32–42.

[8] Vanessa P Dennen and Kerry J Burner. 2008. The cognitive apprenticeship model in educational practice. *Handbook of research on educational communications and technology* 3 (2008), 425–439.

[9] Paul Denny, Andrew Luxton-Reilly, and Ewan Tempero. 2012. All Syntax Errors Are Not Equal. In *Proceedings of the 17th ACM Annual Conference on Innovation and Technology in Computer Science Education (ITiCSE '12)*. ACM, New York, NY, USA, 75–80. https://doi.org/10.1145/2325296.2325318

[10] Walter Doyle. 1983. Academic work. *Review of educational research* 53, 2 (1983), 159–199.

[11] Jeremiah M Faries and Brian J Reiser. 1988. *Access and use of previous solutions in a problem solving situation*. Technical Report. Princeton University Cognitive Science Laboratory.

[12] Katherine Fu, Jonathan Cagan, and Kenneth Kotovsky. 2010. Design team convergence: the influence of example solution quality. *Journal of Mechanical Design* 132, 11 (2010), 111005.

[13] Mike Joy and Michael Luck. 1999. Plagiarism in programming assignments. *IEEE Transactions on education* 42, 2 (1999), 129–133.

[14] Slava Kalyuga. 2009. The expertise reversal effect. In *Managing Cognitive Load in Adaptive Multimedia Learning*. IGI Global, 58–80.

[15] Jean Lave and Etienne Wenger. 1991. *Situated learning: Legitimate peripheral participation*. Cambridge university press.

[16] Michael Lynn. 1991. Scarcity effects on value: A quantitative review of the commodity theory literature. *Psychology & Marketing* 8, 1 (1991), 43–57.

[17] Ference Marton and Roger Säljö. 1976. On qualitative differences in learning: I—Outcome and process. *British journal of educational psychology* 46, 1 (1976), 4–11.

[18] Paul R Pintrich. 2000. The role of goal orientation in self-regulated learning. In *Handbook of self-regulation*. Elsevier, 451–502.

[19] Kelly Rivers and Kenneth R. Koedinger. 2017. Data-Driven Hint Generation in Vast Solution Spaces: a Self-Improving Python Programming Tutor. *International Journal of Artificial Intelligence in Education* 27, 1 (01 Mar 2017), 37–64. https://doi.org/10.1007/s40593-015-0070-z

[20] Anthony Robins, Janet Rountree, and Nathan Rountree. 2003. Learning and teaching programming: A review and discussion. *Computer science education* 13, 2 (2003), 137–172.

[21] Otto Seppälä, Petri Ihantola, Essi Isohanni, Juha Sorva, and Arto Vihavainen. 2015. Do We Know How Difficult the Rainfall Problem is?. In *Proceedings of the 15th Koli Calling Conference on Computing Education Research (Koli Calling '15)*. ACM, New York, NY, USA, 87–96. https://doi.org/10.1145/2828959.2828963

[22] Judy Sheard, Martin Dick, Selby Markham, Ian Macdonald, and Meaghan Walsh. 2002. Cheating and Plagiarism: Perceptions and Practices of First Year IT Students. In *Proceedings of the 7th Annual Conference on Innovation and Technology in Computer Science Education (ITiCSE '02)*. ACM, New York, NY, USA, 183–187. https://doi.org/10.1145/544414.544468

[23] John Sweller and Graham A Cooper. 1985. The use of worked examples as a substitute for problem solving in learning algebra. *Cognition and instruction* 2, 1 (1985), 59–89.

[24] J Gregory Trafton and Brian J Reiser. 1993. Studying examples and solving problems: Contributions to skill acquisition. In *Proceedings of the 15th conference of the Cognitive Science Society*. Citeseer, 1017–1022.

[25] Kurt VanLehn. 1998. Analogy events: How examples are used during problem solving. *Cognitive Science* 22, 3 (1998), 347–388.

[26] Arto Vihavainen, Matti Paksula, and Matti Luukkainen. 2011. Extreme apprenticeship method in teaching programming for beginners. In *Proceedings of the 42nd ACM technical symposium on Computer science education*. ACM, 93–98.

[27] Arto Vihavainen, Thomas Vikberg, Matti Luukkainen, and Jaakko Kurhila. 2013. Massive increase in eager TAs: Experiences from extreme apprenticeship-based CS1. In *Proceedings of the 18th ACM conference on Innovation and technology in computer science education*. ACM, 123–128.

[28] Arto Vihavainen, Thomas Vikberg, Matti Luukkainen, and Martin Pärtel. 2013. Scaffolding students' learning using test my code. In *Proceedings of the 18th ACM conference on Innovation and technology in computer science education*. ACM, 117–122.

Visual Portrayals of Data and Results at ITiCSE

Simon
University of Newcastle
Newcastle, Australia
simon@newcastle.edu.au

Brett A. Becker
University College Dublin
Dublin, Ireland
brett.becker@ucd.ie

Sally Hamouda
Rhode Island College
Providence, RI, USA
shamouda@ric.edu

Robert McCartney
University of Connecticut
Storrs, CT, USA
robert@engr.uconn.edu

Kate Sanders
Rhode Island College (Emerita)
Providence, RI, USA
ksanders@ric.edu

Judy Sheard
Monash University
Caulfield East, Victoria, Australia
judy.sheard@monash.edu

ABSTRACT

We present an analysis of the visual portrayals of data (including results) in the full papers and working group reports of ITiCSE from 2013 to 2018. We find that tables are the most common visual portrayal of data in these publications, but that a number of graphical forms are also widely used. We examine the quality of the data portrayals for tables, graphs, and images using visual quality indicators derived from the literature.

Overall, our findings are not positive. We find that many papers present data in such a way that it cannot be readily interpreted. The most common problem is captions that do not adequately describe the table, figure, or image. In tables, the main issues affecting readability of numeric data are poor alignment of numbers within a column, unnecessary notations, and unwarranted precision. In graphs and images, the prevalent problem is text that is too small to be read.

We conclude with guidelines for future authors to ITiCSE and other computing education venues, in the hope that we can contribute to an improvement in the quality of computing education publications.

CCS CONCEPTS

• **Social and professional topics → Computer science education.**

KEYWORDS

Visualisation; Data; Results; Graphics; Figures; Diagrams; Tables; Graphs

ACM Reference Format:
Simon, Brett A. Becker, Sally Hamouda, Robert McCartney, Kate Sanders, and Judy Sheard. 2019. Visual Portrayals of Data and Results at ITiCSE. In *Innovation and Technology in Computer Science Education (ITiCSE '19), July 15–17, 2019, Aberdeen, Scotland, UK.* ACM, New York, NY, USA, 7 pages. https://doi.org/10.1145/3304221.3319742

ITiCSE '19, July 15–17, 2019, Aberdeen, Scotland, UK

ACM ISBN 978-1-4503-6301-3/19/07...$15.00
https://doi.org/10.1145/3304221.3319742

1 INTRODUCTION AND MOTIVATION

In writing a computing education paper, the authors have many ways to communicate their message, including text, tables, graphs, diagrams, screenshots, and other visual representations. The authors must choose the most appropriate ways to effectively communicate their key points. Poor presentation can confuse, frustrate, and mislead the reader, and fail to communicate the intended message.

Having read many published computing education papers, we had observed effective portrayals that enhance the papers in which they appear, but also portrayals that are all but pointless: perhaps they cannot be read without magnification; perhaps they do not appear to illustrate the point that the authors are using them to illustrate; or perhaps they are simply confusing. These impressions led to the following research questions:

RQ1 What types of visual representation are used in computing education papers and what are their relative frequencies?
RQ2 How well do computing education papers use visual representations?

Problems with portrayals of data are by no means unique to computing education, so we begin with a discussion of the broader literature. We then present the results of an analysis of all the full papers and working group (WG) reports from several years of ITiCSE proceedings, in which we examine the portrayals used and evaluate them using criteria derived from the literature. We conclude with some recommendations for authors and reviewers and suggestions for future work in this area.

2 BACKGROUND AND RELATED WORK

A number of authors have analysed visual portrayals of data in different sets of publications, all focusing on graphical forms of presentation; we found none that focus on tables.

Cleveland [3] conducted two studies on the 377 graphs published in *Science* in 1980 (volume 207). In the first study he defined four error types: construction (mistakes in how the graph was drawn); degraded image (aspects missing due to poor reproduction); explanation (something in the graph not properly explained); and discrimination (items that cannot be visually distinguished). He then counted the number of errors illustrated by each graph. The results, inferred from a graph in that paper, are that around 23% of the figures had errors of one type, around 8% had errors of two types, and none had errors of more than two types. In a second study on the *Science* data he counted instances of each kind of graph, characterised by the dimensionality of the data: one-dimensional data (bar charts, histograms, point graphs, and others); two-dimensional data (x-y plots); and three-dimensional data (such as values at locations of a two-dimensional map). Two-dimensional graphs dominated the sample, accounting for over 80% of the data set.

Cooper et al. [4] analysed 128 graphics from *Annals of Emergency Medicine*, checking for three broad properties: internal characteristics (is the graphic clear, self-explanatory, and internally consistent?); external characteristics (is the graphic consistent with the text, is it redundant with information in text or tables, and does it adequately portray the nuances of the data?); and graphical efficiency (does the graphic maximise information and minimise extraneous noise?). Each of these broad properties comprises a number of items, such as 'graphic is not self-explanatory', 'internal contradictions', 'lack of visual clarity', and 'nonstandard graphing conventions'. The analysis found that 40% of the graphics had problems with internal characteristics, 33% had problems with external characteristics, and 32% had problems with graphical efficiency.

Chen et al. [2] conducted a similar analysis on a set of 342 graphs randomly selected from 20 medical journals, using completeness and visual clarity as their broad measures of quality. Their observed error rates were 54% for completeness and 59% for visual clarity.

In addition to these studies, some papers provide positive or negative evaluation criteria, often addressing presentation of both tables and figures. On the positive side, Franzblau and Chung [6] and Schriger and Cooper [10] provide indications, advantages, and disadvantages of the common graph types; Durbin [5], Franzblau and Chung [6], O'Shea [8], and UNECE [12] also provide these for tables and figures. Cleveland [3, p268] offers a set of general guidelines for authors, such as "Graphs must be visually clear and capable of withstanding reduction" and "Proofread graphs".

The above studies [2–4] also address negative criteria. Explicit short lists are also given by Slutsky [11] and Franzblau and Chung [6] for scientific papers; and more general criteria with examples from newspapers are given by Wainer [13]. A number of issues tend to recur on these lists – incomplete descriptions, visual clutter ('chart junk'), redundancy, numerical distortion, features that cannot be distinguished – but some are less common, such as shuffling ordered data [13] and excessive precision [6].

3 VISUAL QUALITY INDICATORS

In the literature we find a number of guidelines for the visual portrayal of data. For our analysis of quality in this study we decided to focus on portrayals of data in tabular, graphical, or diagram form. From a synthesis of the literature we formulated a set of quality indicators for these types of visualisation. Considering the three broad categories of Cooper et al. [4], we decided to focus mainly on internal characteristics, assessing each item on its visual clarity and the extent to which it was self-explanatory.

The resulting criteria are listed in Table 1. All but one of these criteria are internal. They assess whether an item is comprehensible without reference to the text and has a meaningful caption (self-explanatory); and whether it contains legible text and numbers, avoids excess notation, and, in the case of tables, has correct number alignment and precision (visual clarity).

The indicator 'consistent format' is external, as it assesses whether an item has the same format as other items of the same type (table, diagram, or particular type of graph) in a given publication. However, this addresses just the relationship of a portrayal to other portrayals; it is beyond the scope of our initial investigation to address the broader question of how portrayals relate to the text of the publication in which they appear.

4 METHOD

Our data set comprises the 321 full papers and 38 working group reports published in ITiCSE proceedings from 2013 to 2018, a total of 359 data items. Table 2 shows the numbers of each type of publication for each year in our data set. Our analysis had four phases: a pilot, a qualitative counting phase, a qualitative evaluation phase, and a quantitative phase.

Phase 1: pilot. In this phase, we examined all the publications from the proceedings of ITiCSE 2017 (the most recently published proceedings when we began this work). As well as full papers and working group reports, the proceedings include working group proposals, poster abstracts, keynote abstracts, panel abstracts, and tips, techniques, and coursework papers.

In a qualitative analysis, for each publication we noted the occurrence of each type of visual portrayal. Quantitative analysis then showed that the shorter papers contributed very few visual portrayals of data, the bulk of which were in the full papers and the working group reports. We then decided to narrow our scope to full papers and working group reports, counting the most frequently occurring items: tables, bar charts, histograms, scatter plots, box plots, other graphs (a miscellaneous category for rarely occurring graph types such as radar charts and pie charts), diagrams, screenshots, photos/pictures, code, and text other than code.

Phase 2: qualitative counting. In the next phase we expanded the data set to the years from 2013 to 2018 inclusive. Each paper and report was examined by one person, who noted the presence or absence of different visualisation types; it was then re-examined by another, who counted the occurrences of each type. Most cases were straightforward: a paper is seen to include five tables, two bar charts, and three screenshots. However, disparities sometimes arose regarding the nature of a particular item: for example, whether a particular figure was a bar chart or a histogram. These disparities were resolved by the two researchers, after consultation with the remainder of the team if required.

Phase 3: qualitative evaluation. In the evaluation phase, individuals or pairs looked more closely at tables, graphs, and diagrams to investigate their qualities according to the indicators specified in Section 3. For each paper and report, for each indicator, the assessor recorded whether a violation of that indicator was found.

Phase 4: quantitative. Finally, the quantitative analysis produced frequencies and other descriptive statistics based on the results of the qualitative counting and evaluation. The output of this phase is described in Section 5.

5 RESULTS

Our results comprise a quantitative overview of the types of portrayal used in recent ITiCSE publications, along with an evaluation of the quality of the portrayals that we found.

Table 1: Quality indicators for tables (T), graphs (G) and diagrams (D): descriptions and sources

Indicator	Applies to	Description	Sources
Consistent format	T, G, D	Should have the same format as other items of the same type in the paper	[4]
Comprehensible	T, G, D	Should be understandable without reference to the text	[2, 8–10]
Meaningful caption	T, G, D	The caption should make it clear what the graph, the diagram, or the values in the table represent	[7–9, 12]
Legible	T, G, D	All features should be visually discernible without magnification	[2, 11]
No excess notations	T, G, D	Contains no redundant information or 'chart junk'	[2, 5, 6, 12]
Number alignment	T	Within a table column, numbers should be aligned on the decimal point or right aligned in the absence of a decimal point	[6, 8, 12]
No unnecessary precision	T	Should include only the number of decimal places needed for the information presented – generally none for percentages	[6, 8, 12]

5.1 RQ1: Types and Frequencies

Table 3 shows the number of papers that include each type of portrayal that we counted and the number of instances we found of each type. We report counts for working group reports and full papers separately, as they are quite different (full papers being limited to six pages, while working group reports average $22\frac{1}{2}$ pages long and subsequently contain more tables, graphs, and diagrams). Since the full papers comprise 88% of the data set, their results would dominate.

For the purposes of this analysis, we considered tables to be displays of numbers and/or text in rows and columns. We consider graphs in the sense reported by Kelly et al. [7, p5], artefacts that "use spatial arrangement on the page or screen to convey numerical information".[1] A diagram, for our purposes, is defined as "a simple plan drawn to represent something ... usually to explain how it works or how it is put together" [1].

In our data set, tables are used mainly for presenting numeric data, but are also used for textual data such as descriptions or interview extracts. Graphs include bar charts, box plots, histograms, line graphs, scatter plots, and a few other infrequently occurring types such as statistical maps and radar charts (grouped together as 'other graphs'). Diagrams include some that are characteristic of computing, such as architecture diagrams, box-and-arrow diagrams, dependency graphs, entity-relationship diagrams, flowcharts, and UML; others, such as Venn diagrams, are more widely used. The diagrams portray, among other things, individual courses or modules, curriculums, software tools, and a robot racetrack.

Graphs with nodes and edges, due to their name, might be considered a borderline case between 'graph' and 'diagram'; but because they generally display structure and/or behaviour rather than numerical information, we classify them as diagrams.

[1] We generally use 'graph', but defer to 'plot' for phrases in which that is the more common term, such as scatter plots and box plots, and 'chart' in phrases where it is common, such as bar charts.

Table 2: Numbers of ITiCSE publications in our data set, by year and publication type

Type	2013	2014	2015	2016	2017	2018	Total
Full papers	51	53	52	53	56	56	321
WG reports	4	3	7	7	8	9	38
Total	55	56	59	60	64	65	359

As shown in Table 3, tables, graphs (taken as a group), and diagrams are all widely used. Tables in particular occur most frequently, and in the greatest number of publications, in both papers and WG reports. Many papers have five or more distinct tables, and two papers each have 12 tables; one WG report, 23 pages long, includes 33 tables. There are many instances of screenshots, which are found in almost a third of the papers.

5.2 RQ2: Quality of Portrayals

The papers and WG reports in the data set were analysed to check for violations of the quality indicators listed in Table 1. Due to space limitations, we present the results for papers only, summarised in Tables 4 and 5. The results for WG reports are similar.

The evaluation focuses on tables, graphs, and diagrams. Each of these portrayal types is widely used in our data set, and almost all of the full papers in our data set (294, 92%) contain at least one table, graph, or diagram.

As shown in Table 4, most of the papers (86%) in the data set fail to meet at least one of the quality criteria. The most frequent problem is the lack of a meaningful caption; the next most frequent are incomprehensibility and illegibility.

Table 3: Number of papers (n = 321) and working group reports (n = 38) that include each feature, and total instances of each feature

	Papers		WG Reports	
Feature	**Number**	**Instances**	**Number**	**Instances**
Tables	**222**	**667**	**35**	**284**
Graphs	**149**	**524**	**22**	**192**
Bar chart	97	272	15	127
Box plot	19	41	0	0
Histogram	12	30	6	15
Line graph	37	85	6	17
Scatter plot	22	43	2	6
other graph	25	53	7	27
Diagrams	**114**	**249**	**24**	**61**
Other images	**152**	**543**	**12**	**54**
Code	30	89	1	2
Photo/picture	31	73	6	9
Screenshot	106	335	5	20
Text	30	46	4	13

Table 4: Percentages of full papers (n = 321) that fail to meet quality criteria, by type of visualisation; 'All' is the percentage of full papers that fail to meet the specified quality criterion for any type of visualisation

Indicator	Tables	Graphs	Diagrams	All
Caption not meaningful	38	31	17	61
Excess notation	18	24	6	39
Illegible	9	31	24	50
Incomprehensible	27	19	17	51
Inconsistent format	11	7	7	23
Bad number alignment	30	n/a	n/a	30
Unnecessary precision	16	n/a	n/a	16
Other issues	7	9	n/a	16
At least one of the above	62	45	31	86

5.2.1 *Tables.* A high percentage (86%) of papers with tables include at least one violation. Almost a quarter of the papers (23%) and working group reports (19%) with more than one table fail to apply a consistent format across the tables. Sometimes there are just minor variations, perhaps in shading, but often there are very noticeable differences in the use of borders, vertical rules (lines) and horizontal rules.

We found many tables whose styles do not conform with current guidelines for drawing tables. These specify that vertical rules should be completely avoided and horizontal rules should be used sparingly, perhaps just to mark the beginning and end of the table and to separate the headings from the body. This is the style that is used in the ACM *sigconf* template, and is the style applied in the tables in this paper (with one notable exception). Many of the observed papers use far more rules than recommended, doubling them where something extra seems to be called for. However, as recently as 2015 some of the ACM templates used vertical rules in tables, so it would not be reasonable to expect all papers in our data set to comply with current guidelines.

The most common violation, occurring in more than half of the papers, is the absence of a meaningful caption for a table. Most often the captions do not adequately describe what is presented in the table. A small number of articles have tables that are not captioned at all, and a few have tables that are incorrectly labelled as figures, or number the tables non-sequentially. A related issue is comprehensibility, where an article contains at least one table that we could not easily interpret without reference to the text. This is found in more than a third of the papers (40%). Common errors are lack of information about the scale of measurement and units of measurement of the data in the table, and the presentation of statistics without any information about the test used.

We found the presentation of numeric data problematic. The most common issue is lack of alignment of numbers within a column, which affects the readability of the table. The guideline that numbers should be aligned on the decimal point, or integers aligned to the right, is breached by 79% of the papers. Another issue affecting readability is the excessive use of notations. The most common violation of this type is the use of the % symbol on numbers within tables where it is clear from the headings or caption that the numbers represent percentages. There are also many cases where the use of the % symbol could be reduced by specifying in the column

Table 5: Percentages of full papers with tables, graphs, or diagrams that fail to meet quality criteria; for each column, n is the number of papers in the data set that contain that type of portrayal

Indicator	Tables (n = 222)	Graphs (n = 149)	Diagrams (n = 114)
Caption not meaningful	55	66	46
Excess notation	27	50	18
Illegible	15	66	68
Incomprehensible	40	41	49
Inconsistent format*	16	15	19
Bad number alignment	67	n/a	n/a
Unnecessary precision	23	n/a	n/a
Other issues	11	20	n/a
At least one of the above	86	96	87

Note: the numbers in the row marked * understate the severity of this problem, as they show the proportions of all n papers with a consistency problem, whereas the notion of consistency is meaningful only for those <n papers that have more than one table, graph, or diagram.

header that the numbers are percentages. There are some cases where italics or highlighting are used for no apparent reason, distracting the reader from interpreting the data presented. Displaying numbers to an unnecessary degree of precision can also reduce the readability of data in a table. Integer percentages are perfectly adequate for most purposes, but we found many tables in which percentages are presented with one, two, or more decimal places. A common guideline for presenting statistical results is to use no more than two decimal places in general, no more than three decimal places for a p-value, and none for a percentage. The precision exceeds these recommendations in many papers.

The least common of the violations that we specifically tagged is the legibility of the text and numbers: most tables are presented in text of a readable size.

A few occurrences of other issues were found in the presentation of tables. For example, a few tables do not fit within the column, a couple split unnecessarily over a page break, and some have unnecessarily wide columns, making it difficult to read the data across a row. Some tables have text or numbers wrapped incorrectly, and some tables are overly complex and could be presented more simply by separating them into multiple tables.

5.2.2 *Graphs.* Four of the quality criteria are commonly violated in the papers with graphs: meaningful caption, legible, no excess notations, and comprehensible; the first three are each evident in more than half of the papers with graphs. Captions are often not meaningful because they fail to describe in sufficient detail what is being presented, or they use acronyms that are explained elsewhere in the paper. Legibility issues – usually text or features that are too small to distinguish – occur much more commonly than in tables. Excess notation also occurs in more than half of the papers, most commonly due to redundancy; for example, having a chart label on a graph that matches text in the caption, or having numbers on each bar of a bar chart. Other examples of excess involve using three-dimensional presentations for one- or two-dimensional data. The last of the most common violations is incomprehensibility: a graph that cannot be understood without reading the text of the paper. These include graphs that fail to explain the values on the axes, or graphs that show the levels of some undescribed variable or acronym. Incomprehensibility is sometimes the result of a poor caption, and sometimes of illegibly small features.

Many of the graph quality problems appear to emanate from the use of tools that produce graphs from data. Tools such as Excel allow the user to produce bar charts, pie charts, histograms, and so forth quite easily, but the graphs produced are often cluttered and not most efficiently laid out. 'Chart labels', large captions within the figure that are added by default, are particularly problematic in terms of redundancy. Another problem is that when graphs are added to a paper they are generally scaled down to fit, so something that is legible on a full screen becomes illegible when made to fit in a single column, or even across the full page. Appendix 1 of Kelly et al. [7], *Making Microsoft Excel default graphs suitable for scientific publication*, provides guidelines for cleaning up Excel graphs, with examples; the particular commands are somewhat out of date, but the approach is still valid.

5.2.3 Diagrams. The most frequent flaw that we found in papers with diagrams is illegibility arising from small font size. As a rule of thumb for diagrams, and for tables and graphs, we checked whether they contain any text or numbers that are smaller than the text in the paper's copyright notice. Some diagrams contain text or numbers that are only slightly too small, but many are very difficult or impossible to read when the paper is printed or displayed without magnification.

In addition, a substantial number of papers include at least one diagram that cannot be understood without reference to the text (incomprehensible) or that is not adequately explained in its caption. Diagrams and/or their captions often use acronyms that are specific to the paper. Even when these are explained somewhere in the text, this practice prevents diagrams from efficiently conveying the information. Another common practice that obstructs the efficient transmission of information is the inclusion of superfluous features. Many of the diagrams in our data set include text or numbers that are inconsequential to the main point of the diagram. The reader is then required to actively ignore these features in order to ascertain what the diagram is meant to present. Another less frequent but substantial issue is the placement of diagrams in the text with no figure number or caption. Finally, many diagrams use colour inconsistently, requiring undue attention from the reader, or use colour with no explanation, requiring effort from the reader to determine whether the colours have meaning or are simply decorative.

6 DISCUSSION

6.1 Comparisons with Other Studies

In Section 2 we discussed studies by Cleveland [3], Cooper et al. [4], and Chen et al. [2], who analysed graphs in papers. Some of our results can be directly compared with these studies. Table 6 shows the percentage of each graph type found in each study, where possible. Clear differences are observed in the large number of scatter plots in Cleveland, possibly correlated with the journal and time (*Science*, 1980); and the large number of survival curves reported in Chen et al., undoubtedly because they are sampled from medical journals. Our data show a very large percentage of bar charts, which are more than twice as common as in Cooper et al. It is possible that bar charts have become more popular over time: Chen et al. report the percentage of bar charts and simple point plots (which they combine) as 53%.

Table 6: Percentages of graphs by type in this study (full papers only), Cleveland 1984 [3], Cooper et al. 2001 [4], and Chen et al. 2017 [2]; for each column, n is the number of graphs in the data set

Graph type	This study (n = 524)	Cleveland (n = 377)	Cooper (n = 128)	Chen (n = 346)
Bar charts	52	6	24	-
Histograms	6	3	6	3
Box plots	8	-	3	5
Scatter plots	8	83	8	11
Survival curves	0	-	6	25

It is more difficult to compare the quality evaluations among the studies. The quality measures in this study are assessed on a per article basis, while in the other studies they are assessed per graph. Moreover, while the studies may consider the same things, such as legibility, redundancy, and chart junk, they are combined in different ways; for example, redundancy with chart junk in our study and Cooper et al., legibility with chart junk in Chen et al. However, all of the studies find recognisable flaws in more than half of the graphs presented.

6.2 Threats to Validity

The data set for this paper is drawn from only one conference. It is possible that our results would be somewhat different if we looked at journals or other conferences. However, the size of our data set suggests that these results are still worth taking into account, even if the frequency of errors might differ between venues.

It is also possible that our tagging is not transferable. Tagging is necessarily subjective, conditioned by the background and experience of the researchers. To compensate for this, we have aimed to provide a sufficiently detailed description of our work that others could replicate it, either on the same data set (which is publicly available in the 2013–2018 ITiCSE proceedings) or by applying our criteria to publications in other computing education conferences or journals.

6.3 Lessons Learned

Our quality analysis focuses on tables, graphs, and diagrams, which are the most common forms of visual portrayal in ITiCSE proceedings. It is somewhat concerning that 86% of the papers we analysed fail at least one of the seven quality criteria that we assessed, as listed in Table 1.

Here are a few guidelines suggested by our examination of the tables, graphs, and diagrams in these papers, and supported by other authors [3, 6].

(1) Write meaningful captions that describe the features of the portrayal, not a generic description such as 'Survey results'. Define any acronyms used.

(2) Make sure that tables, graphs, and diagrams are self-contained. It should be possible to understand them without having to refer back to the text.
(3) Make sure that everything is visually distinguishable when reduced to the size it will appear in the paper.
(4) If using colour without a clear meaning, consider whether it is necessary at all. If using colour with meaning, examine the paper in greyscale to be sure that there is a clear contrast between the colours used.
(5) Avoid redundancy in a portrayal. Having a chart title within a figure is almost always a bad idea; if that information is useful it should be in the caption.
(6) Only use a visual representation when it contributes to the paper. A small number of data points might better be presented in text than in a table, or in a table instead of a graph.
(7) Avoid extra clutter. Do not use 3-D effects on 2-D data in graphs; do not have extra rules (lines) in tables; do not use unnecessary fill patterns.
(8) Proofread all tables, graphs, and diagrams, and make sure that the numbers are consistent with the rest of the paper.

The best graphs and diagrams share a minimalist quality: they contain no distracting superfluous features, use fonts and features that are legible and appropriately sized, have meaningful, consistent, and succinct captions, and are comprehensible independently of the paper's text, efficiently communicating without clutter, distracting use of colour, or redundant information.

By way of illustration, we invite readers to consider Figure 1, Figure 2, and Table 7, and ponder how many such portrayals they have seen in computing education papers. These illustrations are not from any of the papers that we examined, but they are highly typical of the portrayals that we found. In Figure 1, readers who can make out the text might notice that the terminology is not entirely consistent with that in the body of the paper. In Table 7, keen readers might be able to work out the lowest possible number of students in each of the four groups GA, GB, FS, and FT; but few will be able to deduce what those column headings signify.

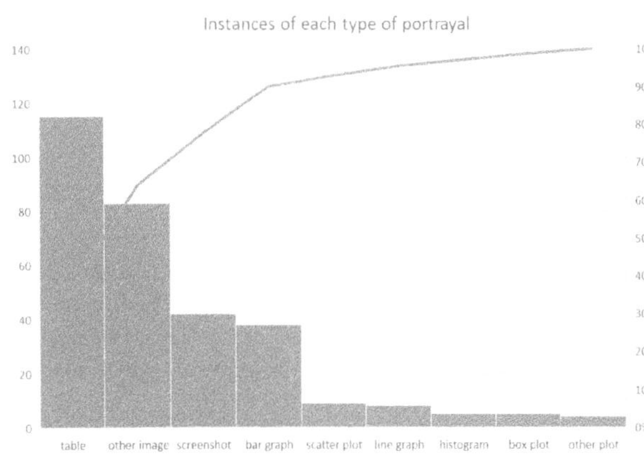

Figure 1: Example of a bad Pareto chart showing the number of instances of each type of portrayal

Figure 2: Example of a bad screenshot, including code too small to read

Table 7: Example of a bad table

	GA	GB	FS	FT
strongly agree	**29.41**	**30.77**	**14.292**	**10.00%**
agree	47.06	153.85	21.435	30.00%
neutral	**11.76**	**0.00**	**35.716**	**30.00%**
disagree	0.00	37.69	7.0	20.00%
strongly disagree	**11.76**	**3.09**	**21.438**	**10.00%**

7 CONCLUSIONS, IMPLICATIONS AND FUTURE WORK

We have examined the proceedings of the six most recent years of ITiCSE (2013–2018) to determine how portrayals of data are used in computing education publications. We present the results of an analysis of the portrayals in this data set, using criteria derived from related work in other fields. Clearly not all of the papers displayed flaws, but as a group, we can do better. We include some guidelines for authors, based on what we have found so far.

Unfortunately, our results might be overly positive, since we primarily examined only internal features, those that involve looking at a visualisation in isolation. We have not yet looked at external indicators other than whether all tables/graphs/diagrams in a given paper have a consistent format.

In particular, we did not look at the relationship between visual presentations and the text. Important questions to be investigated in future work include 'Is the portrayal consistent with the text of the paper?', 'Does the portrayal complement the text?', and 'Does the portrayal help to effectively communicate the central points of the text?'

ACKNOWLEDGMENTS

We thank the authors of ITiCSE's full papers and working group reports for providing the data for our study, and assure them that our intention is to guide future authors, not to criticise past authors.

REFERENCES

[1] Cambridge Dictionary (online). 2019. Definition of "diagram" - English Dictionary. (2019). https://dictionary.cambridge.org/us/dictionary/english/diagram Accessed 21 Jan 2019.

[2] Jennifer C Chen, Richelle J Cooper, Michael E McMullen, and David L Schriger. 2017. Graph Quality in Top Medical Journals. *Annals of Emergency Medicine* 69, 4 (April 2017), 453–461.e5. https://doi.org/10.1016/j.annemergmed.2016.08.463

[3] William S Cleveland. 1984. Graphs in Scientific Publications. *The American Statistician* 38 (November 1984), 261–269. https://www.jstor.org/stable/2683400

[4] Richelle J Cooper, David L Schriger, and David A Tashman. 2001. An Evaluation of the Graphical Literacy of Annals of Emergency Medicine. *Annals of Emergency Medicine* 37, 1 (January 2001), 13–19. https://doi.org/:10.1067/mem.2001.111569

[5] Charles G Durbin. 2004. Effective Use of Tables and Figures in Abstracts, Presentations, and Papers. *Respiratory Care* 49, 10 (2004), 1233. http://rc.rcjournal.com/content/49/10/1233.abstract

[6] Lauren E Franzblau and Kevin C Chung. 2012. Graphs, Tables, and Figures in Scientific Publications: The Good, the Bad, and How Not to Be the Latter. *Journal of Hand Surgery* 37 (March 2012), 591–596. https://doi.org/10.1016/j.jhsa.2011.12.041

[7] D Kelly, J Jasperse, and I Westbrooke. 2005. *Designing Science Graphs for Data Analysis and Presentation: the Bad, the Good and the Better.* Department of Conservation Technical Series 32. New Zealand Department of Conservation, Wellington.

[8] McKenzie O'Shea. 2012. *Writing for Psychology* (6th ed.). Cengage Learning Australia.

[9] Rodrigo Pereira Duquia, João Luiz Bastos, Renan Rangel Bonamigo, David Alejandro González-Chica, and Jeovany Martínez-Mesa. 2014. Presenting Data in Tables and Charts. *Anais Brasileiros de Dermatologia* 89, 2 (2014), 280–285.

[10] David L Schriger and Richelle J Cooper. 2001. Achieving Graphical Excellence: Suggestions and Methods for Creating High-Quality Visual Displays of Experimental Data. *Annals of Emergency Medicine* 37, 1 (January 2001), 75–87.

[11] David J Slutsky. 2014. The Effective Use of Graphs. *Journal of Wrist Surgery* 3, 2 (2014), 67–68. https://doi.org/10.1055/s-0034-1375704

[12] United Nations Economic Commission for Europe UNECE. 2009. Making Data Meaningful Part 2: a Guide to Presenting Statistics. (2009). http://www.unece.org/fileadmin/DAM/stats/documents/writing/MDM_Part2_English.pdf Accessed 7 Jan 2019.

[13] Howard Wainer. 1984. How to Display Data Badly. *The American Statistician* 38, 2 (May 1984), 137–147. https://www.jstor.org/stable/2683253

A Survey of Introductory Programming Courses in Ireland

Brett A. Becker
University College Dublin
Dublin, Ireland
brett.becker@ucd.ie

ABSTRACT

Between January and April of 2018, a comprehensive survey of introductory programming courses was undertaken across all sectors of Irish third-level institutions (universities, institutes of technology, and private colleges). The survey instrument was based on – and nearly identical to – recent surveys in the UK and Australasia. In total we report on 39 introductory programming courses at 25 third-level institutions. This includes 6 of 7 universities and 13 of 14 institutes of technology, representing 90% of all publicly funded institutions. We also report on 4 private colleges representing 80% of colleges in the Irish Higher Education Colleges Association that offer computing degrees.

In addition to general course structure and composition, we explore programming language use, the reasons for using them, and their impact on teaching and learning. We also gain first-hand insight from instructors through an analysis of their own course aims, and explore their viewpoints on teaching introductory programming. The results of this survey provide a unique insight into the CS1 courses of a single country that is currently introducing computer science at the K-12 level.

CCS CONCEPTS

• **Social and professional topics → Computing education; Computer science education; CS1.**

KEYWORDS

CS1; CS 1; CS-1; Instructors; Introductory Programming; Novice Programmers; Programming Languages; Survey; Teaching Languages; Australasia; Ireland; UK; United Kingdom

ACM Reference Format:

Brett A. Becker. 2019. A Survey of Introductory Programming Courses in Ireland. In *Innovation and Technology in Computer Science Education (ITiCSE '19), July 15–17, 2019, Aberdeen, Scotland UK.* ACM, New York, NY, USA, 7 pages. https://doi.org/10.1145/3304221.3319752

1 INTRODUCTION

Introductory Computer Programming is often called CS1 [11] when taken as part of a computing, computer science, or similar degree. These courses have been the subject of much study over the decades. A central focus of this course is typically the teaching and learning of a first programming language [26]. However, programming students continue to face numerous struggles in learning to program [2]. This fuels the idea that programming is 'hard to learn', a claim that regularly goes back to the 2001 ITiCSE 'McCracken working group', which found that "many students do not know how to program at the conclusion of their introductory courses" [20, p 125]. Another well-cited ITiCSE working group found that "three decades of active research on the teaching of introductory programming has had limited effect on classroom practice" [24, p 204]. The reasons for this are believed to be multifaceted, and that difficulties in learning to program contribute to low motivation and high dropout rates [4]. It has also been argued that what we expect of CS1 students is too much [14], and some work has gone into trying to gauge what exactly is expected of CS1 students [1].

CS1 has evolved over the past 50 years in terms of languages and paradigms used, topics, structure and ethos [5]. Even the approach of ACM/IEEE model curricula has changed markedly over the years. CC2001 provided three 'programming-first' implementations (imperative, objects-first, and functional) [23]. CS2008 noted that "The issue of programming languages and paradigms caused considerable debate at the time of the final public consultation" [7, p 18]. In CS2013, the knowledge unit *Fundamental Programming Concepts* in the Knowledge Area *Software Development Fundamentals* identified "only those concepts common to all paradigms" [12, p 167].

Successfully delivering a CS1 course in the present day is not straightforward. Increasingly, topics such as student motivation [31], diversity (in terms of prior knowledge as well as socioeconomic and demographic) [30], implicit and explicit expectations [15], the context provided with assessment [6], student sense of belonging [21], and a host of other factors put unique demands on the adoption of best practice when delivering these courses. For instance, it has been claimed that motivation does not play an equal role in the various subfields of programming education [27]. Also, the role that programming plays in computing degree dropout, and how that impacts majors and non-majors, is an important issue [3]. Today, perhaps more than ever, awareness of the decisions that others in similar contexts are making, the reasons behind these decisions, and if they lead to success, is important.

1.1 Higher Education in Ireland

The Republic of Ireland is a member of the European Union and a signatory to the Bologna Process. It has a population of approximately 4.8 million people and high third-level participation rates. 42% of the population have a third-level education[1] (43% female, 41% male). Third-level education is sponsored by the state for residents, but students are responsible for a registration fee of approximately

ITiCSE '19, July 15–17, 2019, Aberdeen, Scotland UK

ACM ISBN 978-1-4503-6301-3/19/07 $15.00
https://doi.org/10.1145/3304221.3319752

[1] www.cso.ie/en/releasesandpublications/ep/p-cp10esil/p10esil/tl/

€3,000 (≈$3,500) per year. Entry is coordinated by a Central Applications Office and is based on the results of the 'Leaving Certificate', which is a largely summative set of exams held at the end of the second-level school career, normally at age 17-18. Students typically take exams in English, Irish and mathematics, in addition to five other subjects. Since September 2018, computer science is being offered as an official leaving certificate subject [25].

At the time of this study there were seven universities and fourteen institutes of technology in Ireland, plus a handful of smaller private colleges in the Higher Education Colleges Association[2] awarding tertiary computing degrees. On January 1, 2018, three institutes of technology merged to form the eighth university, leaving the number of public institutions at eight universities and eleven institutes of technology.

Despite a relatively small population, Ireland is the world's second largest software exporter, and has been in first or second place for decades. Ireland is home to the EMEA headquarters of many multinational tech firms, and 16 of the 20 top global technology companies have strategic operations there including Apple, Facebook, Google and Microsoft.[3] Dell/EMC, Ericsson, HPE, IBM, Intel, Microsoft and Oracle have all been present in Ireland since before 1990 and still maintain significant operations there.[4]

A small population combined with a centralized third-level admissions system and a globally competitive technology industry creates a unique environment for computing students and institutions. For instance, the presence of corporations such as Intel have directly influenced the computing curricula of Ireland's third-level institutions [13]. For many years, Ericsson has had a similar influence. Recognizing the demands of this unique environment, the heads of computing departments along with government, industry and other stakeholders meet several times annually at the 'Third-level Computing Forum'.[5] It is acknowledged that the recent introduction of computer science as a Leaving Certificate subject (discussed in Section 2.1) brings the potential for significant changes to third-level computing programs in the near future. This made 2018 an important time to conduct a wide survey of third-level introductory programming offerings, before the new second-level curriculum has an impact on third-level student intakes.

2 RELATED WORK

In 2012 Siegfried et al. noted that "The choice of programming language and pedagogic approach used in teaching an introductory programming course for computing majors has been a subject of debate for the past forty years" [28, p 24]. Seven years later the current landscape is led by Java with a rising Python popularity, and the debates continue. In 2010, Stefik and Hananberg, in discussing the 'programming language wars' [29], encouraged educators to take up three responsibilities: *1. Conduct competitive analysis of programming languages with students at all levels of the academic pipeline, 2. Carefully map out language usage in academia,* and *3. Teach students about the language wars, providing evidence-based arguments on the debate.* Comments and recommendations such as these provide impetus to continue work on determining who is currently teaching what, and why. They could also be taken as evidence that there have not been enough recent surveys, meta-analysis and reviews on introductory programming literature or practice. Fortunately, there has been a flurry of activity very recently. A 2018 working group led by Luxton-Reilly and Simon produced a 52-page literature review of introductory programming research [16], processing over 5,000 papers, reduced to 1,844 after applying exclusion criteria, and citing 761. Another recent paper processed over 700 SIGCSE Technical Symposium papers focusing on Introductory Programming, noting several interesting trends in the first 49 years of the Symposium (1970-2018) [5]. One take-away from both of these studies is that CS1 courses are not only focused on programming and programming languages [5]. Nonetheless CS1 and programming languages remain inextricably linked.

On the surveying practice front, several recent studies have taken place. In 2017, Mason and Simon carried out a survey of introductory programming courses in Australasia [19]. Prior to this Mason and Cooper [17] carried out a similar survey in 2013, and in 2016 Murphy, Crick and Davenport [22] carried out a similar survey in the UK. Although there were other Australasian studies prior to the 2013 Mason and Cooper report (2001 [8], 2003 [9] and 2010 [18]), it was the 2013 survey whose questions made it to the UK [22] and then to Ireland for this study.

Another long-term initiative that provides important historical insight was Reid's list of first programming languages. This was started in the early 1990s, reported on US institutions, and was updated roughly twice per year (whenever 10% of the current list had changed). The list reported the first programming language used in introductory programming courses taken by computing majors, including the reasons these languages were chosen. The list was compiled and maintained largely by direct correspondence and grew to over 400 courses. Upon Reid's retirement in 1999, the initiative was continued by Frances Van Scoy, a former student of Reid, through the 25th "Reid List" published in 2006. In 2012, Siegfried et al. revived the concept and produced the 26th Reid List which contained data for 393 institutions [28]. Java was the most popular first language with 197 courses offering it, followed by C++ (82), Python (43), C (18) and Scheme or Racket (11). All other languages (or language combinations) were used in less than 10 courses. Siegfried maintains a repository of the available Reid's Lists, from list 6 (1992) through list 23 (2002) at home.adelphi.edu/~siegfried/ReidList/.

2.1 The Irish Context

There has been a flood of interest in introductory programming in Ireland in recent years and some of this has had global impact. For instance, the CoderDojo movement was started in Ireland in 2011 and is headquartered in Dublin. Ireland has also implemented a nationwide second-level (high school) computer science curricula which started being taught in September 2018 [25].

Only one large-scale survey in the area is known to have taken place in Ireland. In 2016, Strong et al. [30] conducted a survey of 321 students from 8 institutions, all studying programming in the first year of an undergraduate degree course, not limited to computing/computer science degrees. Their survey focused almost exclusively on the prior experience of these students, and the nature thereof. Of these respondents, 24% were female and 76% were

[2]www.heca.ie
[3]www.idaireland.com/doing-business-here/industry-sectors/software
[4]www.idaireland.com/newsroom/publications/ireland-for-software-q1-2018
[5]thirdlevelcomputingforum.ie

male. 76% were between the ages of 18-22, and 24% were aged 22 or more years. The authors note that the Irish Higher Education Authority reported 14.9% females undertaking computing degrees and 18.1% undertaking engineering degrees, and do not offer an explanation for the 24% they reported, although not limiting the survey to computing/engineering students seems to be a likely cause. Additionally, 66% of respondents reported having no prior programming experience. Of the 34% that did, 59% had experience with Java, followed by C/C++/C# (40%), Python (33%), HTML (28%), other languages (22%), JavaScript (17%), variants of Basic (14%), PHP (12%), and Scratch (1%). The authors posit that the low representation of Scratch was due to the open-question format, and students not reporting Scratch due to a perception of what constitutes a "real" programming language [30, p 9]. Arguably, similar could be said of HTML, although this represented 22% which brings this explanation for Scratch into question.

When questioned on the sources of prior programming experience, 27% reported school activities including summer courses, second-level curricula (international students), and informal learning. 13% reported club activities including CoderDojo (36%), other computing clubs (27%), third-level access and youth programs (19%) and adult education courses (18%). 42% reported online activities, 63% reported self-directed learning, and 30% reported other sources of experience including post second-level courses that were not diplomas or degrees (43%), previous third-level courses (23%), and previous employment (13%). Note that participants could choose multiple sources in the above figures.

3 METHOD

To recruit participants, an email was circulated to the Irish Third-Level Computing Forum (discussed in Section 1.1). Additionally, direct contact was made with the heads of computing departments in the small number of private colleges. Where known, CS1 lecturers were also directly contacted. Through personal correspondence, duplicates and other issues were directly addressed with the respondents. Recruitment and participation took place between January and April 2018. The survey used in the UK [22] was kindly provided by those authors as discussed in Section 2. We left the questions unchanged, only changing the "information for participants" section for the Irish context. A total of 41 questions were on the survey. In this paper we report on what we feel are the most significant findings.

4 RESULTS

We obtained valid responses from the instructors of 39 courses at 25 institutions, including 6 of 7 universities, 13 of 14 institutes of technology, and four private colleges. This represents 90% of all publicly funded institutions in Ireland and 80% (four out of five) of the private colleges recognized by the Higher Education Colleges Association offering computing degrees.

4.1 Overview

In this section we describe responses to questions on general course structure and composition. Using the responses from questions on prerequisites (Section 4.1.3) and major (Section 4.1.4), we conclude that 29/39 (74%) of the courses we report on fit the definition of CS1 utilized by Guo (the first programming course that has no-prerequisites and is required for computing majors) [10]. It should be noted however that there is no universally agreed upon definition of CS1, despite being used colloquially quite often [11].

4.1.1 Attendance. Of the 39 courses analyzed, the average academic year 2017/18 attendance was 123 (min 30, max 400).

4.1.2 Scheduling. 54% of courses were offered in semester 1 (Fall) and 13% in semester 2 (Spring). 33% were year-long courses, and two courses had different scheduling.

4.1.3 Prerequisites. 82% of courses had no prerequisites and 18% had prerequisites. Topics of prerequisite courses (where provided) include basic programming and problem solving skills.

4.1.4 Majors. 87% of courses were required for computing majors and 13% were not. 67% were restricted to computing majors, with 33% open to majors of other disciplines. Of these 33%, 10% were for non-computing majors only. These questions defined 'computing majors' as students majoring in computing-based degrees, such as computer science, software engineering, etc.

4.1.5 Experience of Instructors. Figure 1 shows the experience of Irish CS1 instructors in years. 32% of instructors have between 11 and 20 years of experience followed by 29% who have 2 to 5. 11% have between 20 and 30 years of experience followed by 5% with more than 30. Only 3% have less than 2 years of experience.

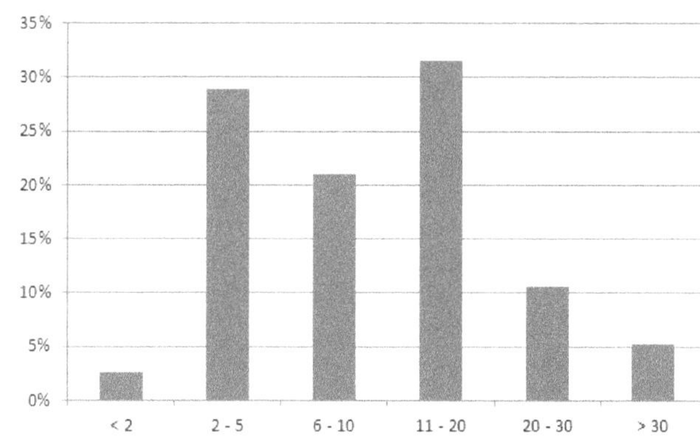

Figure 1: Experience of Irish introductory programming instructors in years.

4.1.6 External Delivery. All instructors were asked the following question: *Do you offer external delivery of your course? (i.e. do you have options for your course where students are not required to attend regular lectures, workshops, labs or tutorials?)* One respondent skipped this question. 95% of courses do not offer external delivery, with only two courses (5%) doing so.

4.2 Programming Languages

4.2.1 Paradigms Used. Table 1 shows the programming paradigms reported. 43% of courses utilize an object-oriented paradigm, followed by 23% procedural, 15% functional, 8% logical, 8% using other or mixed paradigms, and 5% using no particular paradigm.

Table 1: Paradigms used in Irish introductory programming courses. Percentages total to more than 100 due to rounding.

Paradigm	%
Object-Oriented	43
Procedural	23
Functional	15
Logical	8
Other / mixed	8
No particular paradigm	5

4.2.2 Languages Used. Figure 2 shows the languages reported. In total there are 13 languages represented. 49% of courses used Java, including one that starts with Scratch followed by Java. 28% use Python, 18% use JavaScript, and C and C# were used by 10% of courses (each). C++, PHP, Processing, and Ruby were used by less than 10% of courses. 13% used others: CSS 3% (1); HTML 3% (1); R 3% (1); and Scratch 8% (3).

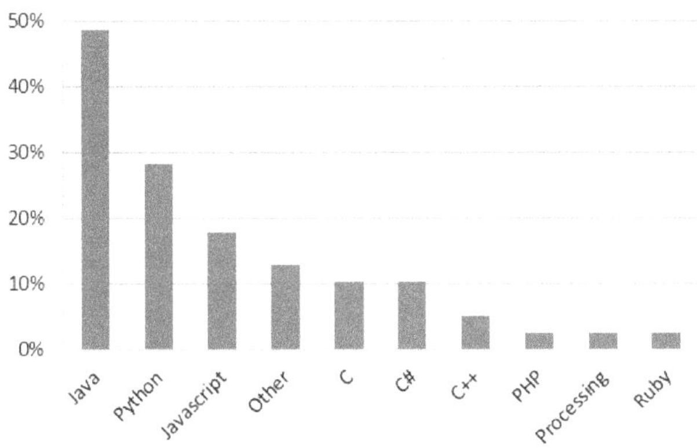

Figure 2: Programming languages used in Irish introductory programming courses. Respondents could select more than one.

4.2.3 Sole vs Multiple Languages. Figure 3 shows what languages are used for the whole course, for the first part of the course followed by another language, and after another language used in the first part of the course (for the top 5 languages). It is interesting to note that of the courses that use Python, 90% use it exclusively, and 10% for the first part of the course followed by another language, with none using it after another language. Of the courses that use Java, nearly 80% use it exclusively, none use it before another language, and just over 20% use it after another language. Of courses that use JavaScript and C, about half tend to use these languages first, while the other courses somewhat evenly divide using these languages for the first part of the course followed by another language and after another language. Of the courses that use C#, 50% use the language exclusively, and the other 50% use it after another language, with none using it first, before another language.

4.2.4 Reasons for Choosing a Language. Figure 4 shows the reasons provided for the choice of programming languages. Five reasons were selected by over 50% of courses: *Relevance to industry, Availability/Cost to students, Pedagogical benefits, Object-oriented language,* and *Easy to find appropriate texts.*

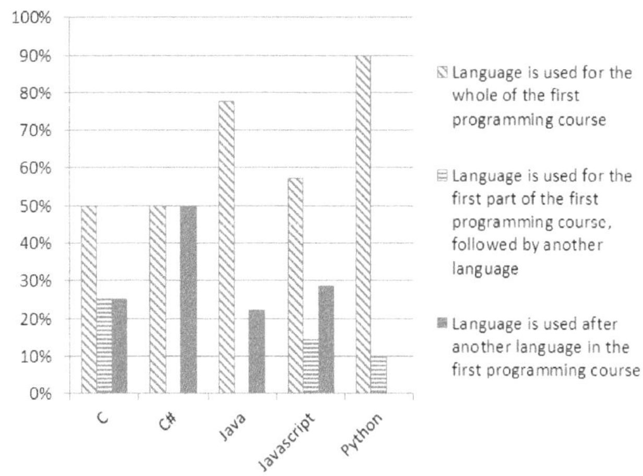

Figure 3: Use of the top 5 languages in Irish introductory programming courses: what languages are used for the whole course, for the first part of the course followed by another language, and after another language used in the first part of the course. It is important to note that, for instance, it is 90% *of the courses that use Python* that use Python for the whole course. It is not the case that 90% *of all courses* use Python for the whole course.

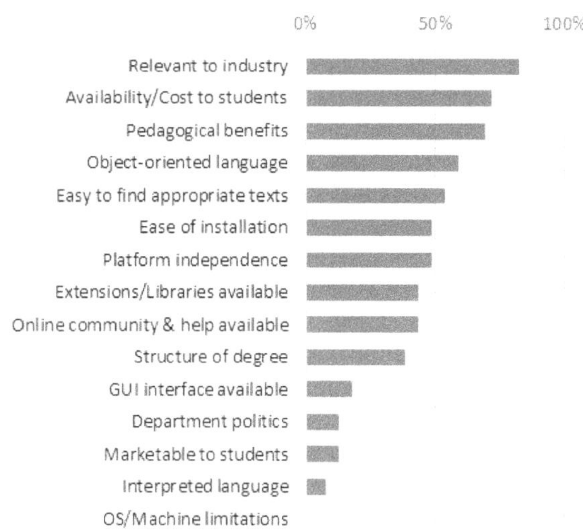

Figure 4: Reasons languages in Irish introductory programming courses were chosen.

4.2.5 Perceived Difficulty to Learn. Each respondent was asked the question *How difficult do you think each language is for students to learn?* Two respondents skipped this question. Choices ranged from extremely easy to extremely difficult on a 1-7 scale (1 ⟶ extremely easy, 7 ⟶ extremely difficult). Figure 5 shows the results for each language. C++ (5.5), Java (5.11) and C (5.0) were perceived as the most difficult to learn. Interestingly, the 'Other' languages collectively scored as the easiest (1.75). The Other languages were CSS, HTML, R (1 course each) and Scratch (3 courses).

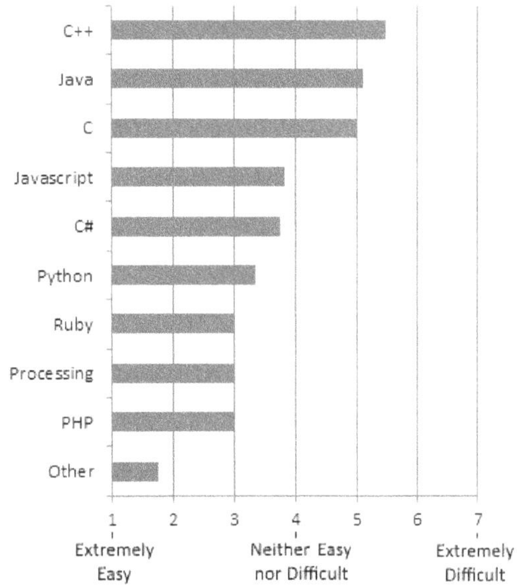

Figure 5: Perceived difficulty for learning of reported languages. 1 ⟶ Extremely easy, 7 ⟶ Extremely difficult. The actual question was: *How difficult do you think each language is for students to learn?*

4.2.6 Perceived Usefulness for Teaching. Each respondent was asked the question *How useful do you think each language is for teaching the fundamental concepts of programming?* Two respondents skipped this question. Choices ranged from extremely useless to extremely useful on a 1-7 scale (1 ⟶ extremely useless, 7 ⟶ extremely useful). Figure 6 shows that the perceived usefulness for teaching for all languages was relatively good (the maximum weighted average was 6.5, exactly halfway between moderately and extremely useful. The usefulness did not vary drastically across languages with a minimum weighted average of 5, corresponding to slightly useful.

4.2.7 The Relationship Between difficulty and Usefulness. The previous two subsections indicate that at least some of the languages perceived as more difficult for students to learn (Figure 5) are seen as some of the more useful for learning the fundamental concepts of programming (Figure 6). For instance, C++ is ranked as the most difficult language to learn, but is tied for first place as the most useful language for teaching. This could be a function of the fact that only two courses reported using C++. However, more difficult languages such as Java and C were mid-table in terms of usefulness for teaching. On the opposite end of the spectrum, languages ranked as easy to learn such as PHP and Ruby, were ranked as the least useful for teaching. Python and Processing both represent a very good ease of learning / usefulness for teaching balance. Both are ranked among the easier to learn languages, and are ranked as the second and third most useful for teaching (behind C# and C++ which are tied as the most useful).

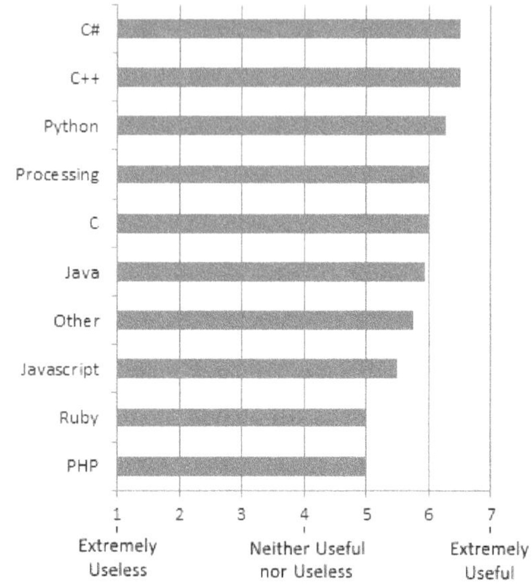

Figure 6: Perceived usefulness for teaching of reported languages. 1 ⟶ Extremely useless, 7 ⟶ Extremely useful. The actual question was: *How useful do you think each language is for teaching the fundamental concepts of programming?*

5 COURSE AIMS AND INSTRUCTOR VIEWPOINTS

5.1 Course Aims

Question 37 asked *What do you consider to be the 3 most important aims of an introductory programming course?* Respondents were able to enter up to three free-text answers. Upon inspection it appeared that despite being full-text responses, the majority might be covered by a relatively small number of categories. A total of 104 aims were collected out of a total possible of 117; four respondents did not complete this question and one only provided two aims. Nine of these 104 aims were difficult to categorize or at times, interpret as aims, leaving 95 aims, which were categorized into 21 categories. Figure 7 shows the 12 categories that were represented by more than 5% of courses. Figure 7 also shows the percentage of aims that were categorized into each category. For instance, the most popular category was *programming basics / concepts / principles.* 58% of courses had an aim that was put in this category, and this category contained 28 individual aims (representing 30% of all aims).

It is important to recognize that the question asked about the aims of "**an** introductory programming course", not necessarily the courses that the instructors were currently teaching and detailing in the other questions. Additionally, we acknowledge that our categorization of aims may have been done differently by other authors. To put a rough figure on the reliability of our categorization we asked a colleague not involved in this research to categorize each of the 104 aims into exactly one of our categories (as we did). This resulted in 93 aims being placed in the same category with 11 placed in different categories, roughly demonstrating 89% agreement.

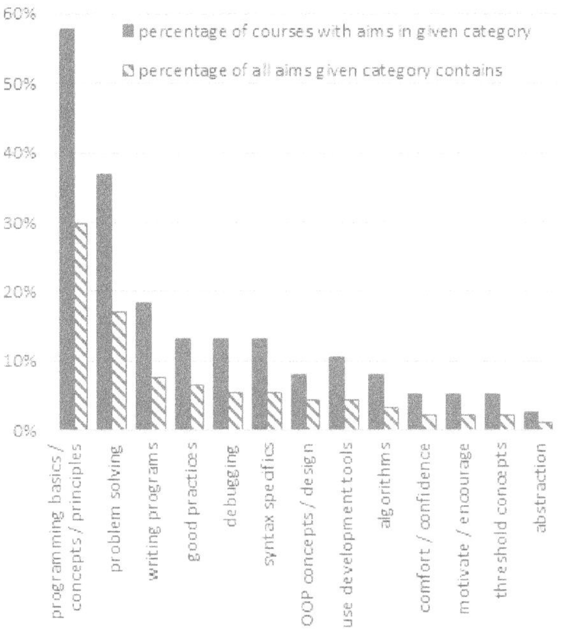

Figure 7: Course aims (by category) that were reported by 2 or more courses (≥ 5% of courses). Categories with aims from one course each were: *abstraction, awareness of the importance of programming, computational thinking, creativity / imagination / interests, dispelling myths, having fun, how computers work, web programming, moderately complex programming,* and *working in groups.*

5.2 Instructor Viewpoints

Question 39 stated: *If there are any other comments you would like to offer about the teaching of introductory programming, please use the space below.* Several instructors took the time to give us their thoughts and we felt that they were insightful enough to include here. The following comments are not verbatim; the wording has been paraphrased and condensed.

- Despite significant effort in trying different languages and development environments issues persist. Many students aren't willing to put in the effort required to learn how to program, with many not engaging sufficiently in assessments and coursework.
- Novices find learning to program difficult. Students' interests and experiences often don't match the typical context of programming.
- In large groups of students it can be difficult to find a middle ground. Some find programming easy, but others struggle and seem to have little interest. Trying to get these students interested while at the same time keeping the more advanced students challenged can be difficult.
- Teaching large classes to program is very challenging. Teaching needs to be properly resourced with capable and interested lecturers and teaching assistants in addition to good lab support and appropriate assessment modes.
- Lab-based exams are the best way to determine how well students have understood course material. When traditional theory-based exams are used, some students who knew the theory but not the practical aspects often got good grades despite not having good programming ability.

These viewpoints show that the following are problematic for Irish introductory programming instructors:

- language and environment choice
- student engagement and interest
- difficulty with programming, specifically with how students relate to the context of computer programming
- teaching to large numbers of students
- assessment (theory and paper-based exams vs lab-based practical ability)
- teaching resources including lab assistants

These difficulties do not make Ireland unique. In fact all of these issues are common at many other institutions in other countries. However, having first-hand feedback on the issues that the relatively few Irish CS1 instructors are currently facing in teaching introductory programming is important. For instance, such evidence can be taken into account as the roll-out of the new, nationwide second-level computing curriculum continues. Also, in the near future, the third-level student intake could change significantly as a result of the new second-level curriculum. Therefore the Irish third-level computing institutions and instructors should ensure that solutions to address today's problems will continue to be effective into the future as this landscape changes.

6 CONCLUSIONS AND FUTURE WORK

We presented the highlights of a comprehensive survey of Introductory Programming courses at Irish third-level institutions. In addition to general course structure and content, we explored programming languages, the reasons for using them, and their impact on teaching and learning. We also gained insight from instructors through an analysis of their most important course aims and their viewpoints on teaching introductory programming.

Ireland is currently rolling out a second-level (high school) computer science curriculum, and as this survey was conducted just prior to this, the timing proved opportune. We plan to repeat this survey in a few years, after the effects of the second-level curriculum on third-level intakes takes hold.

We have plans to complete further work comparing the results of this survey to those recently conducted in the UK and Australasia. In addition, with the authors of prior UK and Australasian surveys, we plan on conducting future surveys using a unified survey and method in Ireland, the UK and Australasia.

ACKNOWLEDGMENTS

The author would like to thank Ellen Murphy and James Davenport (University of Bath) and Tom Crick (Caridff Metropolitan University) for generously providing their survey questions. These were kindly provided to them by Raina Mason and Graham Cooper (Southern Cross University). I also would like to thank Simon (University of Newcastle) and Raina Mason again, for sharing some of their data and for providing insight.

REFERENCES

[1] Brett A. Becker and Thomas Fitzpatrick. 2019. What Do CS1 Syllabi Reveal About Our Expectations of Introductory Programming Students?. In *Proceedings of the 50th ACM Technical Symposium on Computer Science Education (SIGCSE '19)*. ACM, New York, NY, USA. https://doi.org/10.1145/3287324.3287485

[2] Brett A. Becker, Kyle Goslin, and Graham Glanville. 2018. The Effects of Enhanced Compiler Error Messages on a Syntax Error Debugging Test. In *Proceedings of the 49th ACM Technical Symposium on Computer Science Education (SIGCSE '18)*. ACM, New York, NY, USA, 640–645. https://doi.org/10.1145/3159450.3159461

[3] Brett A. Becker and Catherine Mooney. 2016. Categorizing compiler error messages with principal component analysis. In *12th China-Europe International Symposium on Software Engineering Education (CEISEE 2016), Shenyang, China, 28-29 May 2016*.

[4] Brett A. Becker, Cormac Murray, Tianyi Tao, Changheng Song, Robert McCartney, and Kate Sanders. 2018. Fix the First, Ignore the Rest: Dealing with Multiple Compiler Error Messages. In *Proceedings of the 49th ACM Technical Symposium on Computer Science Education (SIGCSE '18)*. ACM, New York, NY, USA, 634–639. https://doi.org/10.1145/3159450.3159453

[5] Brett A. Becker and Keith Quille. 2019. 50 Years of CS1 at SIGCSE: A Review of the Evolution of Introductory Programming Education Research. In *Proceedings of the 50th ACM Technical Symposium on Computer Science Education (SIGCSE '19)*. ACM, New York, NY, USA. https://doi.org/10.1145/3287324.3287432

[6] Dennis Bouvier, Ellie Lovellette, John Matta, Bedour Alshaigy, Brett A. Becker, Michelle Craig, Jana Jackova, Robert McCartney, Kate Sanders, and Mark Zarb. 2016. Novice Programmers and the Problem Description Effect. In *Proceedings of the 2016 ITiCSE Working Group Reports (ITiCSE '16)*. ACM, New York, NY, USA, 103–118. https://doi.org/10.1145/3024906.3024912

[7] Association for Computing Machinery (ACM) CS2008 Review Taskforce and IEEE Computer Society. 2008. *Computer Science Curriculum 2008: An Interim Revision of CS 2001*. Technical Report. New York, NY, USA. https://www.acm.org/education/curricula-recommendations

[8] Michael De Raadt, Richard Watson, and Mark Toleman. 2002. Language trends in introductory programming courses. In *Proceedings of the 2002 Informing Science+ Information Technology Education Joint Conference (InSITE 2002)*. Informing Science Institute, 229–337.

[9] Michael de Raadt, Richard Watson, and Mark Toleman. 2004. Introductory Programming: What's Happening Today and Will There Be Any Students to Teach Tomorrow?. In *Proceedings of the Sixth Australasian Conference on Computing Education - Volume 30 (ACE '04)*. Australian Computer Society, Inc., Darlinghurst, Australia, Australia, 277–282. http://dl.acm.org/citation.cfm?id=979968.980005

[10] Philip Guo. 2014. Python Is Now the Most Popular Introductory Teaching Language at Top U.S. Universities. https://cacm.acm.org/blogs/blog-cacm/176450-python-is-now-the-most-popular-introductory-teaching-language-at-top-u-s-universities/fulltext. (2014).

[11] Matthew Hertz. 2010. What Do "CS1" and "CS2" Mean?: Investigating Differences in the Early Courses. In *Proceedings of the 41st ACM Technical Symposium on Computer Science Education (SIGCSE '10)*. ACM, New York, NY, USA, 199–203. https://doi.org/10.1145/1734263.1734335

[12] Association for Computing Machinery (ACM) Joint Task Force on Computing Curricula and IEEE Computer Society. 2013. *Computer Science Curricula 2013: Curriculum Guidelines for Undergraduate Degree Programs in Computer Science*. Technical Report. New York, NY, USA. https://www.acm.org/education/curricula-recommendations 999133.

[13] Karlin Lillington. 2013. Intel turned Leixlip into Ireland's Silicon Valley. *The Irish Times* (Nov 2013). https://www.irishtimes.com/business/intel-turned-leixlip-into-ireland-s-silicon-valley-1.1593495

[14] Andrew Luxton-Reilly. 2016. Learning to Program is Easy. In *Proceedings of the 2016 ACM Conference on Innovation and Technology in Computer Science Education (ITiCSE '16)*. ACM, New York, NY, USA, 284–289. https://doi.org/10.1145/2899415.2899432

[15] Andrew Luxton-Reilly, Brett A. Becker, Yingjun Cao, Roger McDermott, Claudio Mirolo, Andreas Mühling, Andrew Petersen, Kate Sanders, Simon, and Jacqueline Whalley. 2017. Developing Assessments to Determine Mastery of Programming Fundamentals. In *Proceedings of the 2017 ACM Conference on Innovation and Technology in Computer Science Education (ITiCSE '17)*. ACM, New York, NY, USA, 388–388. https://doi.org/10.1145/3059009.3081327

[16] Andrew Luxton-Reilly, Simon, Ibrahim Albluwi, Brett A. Becker, Michail Giannakos, Amruth N. Kumar, Linda Ott, James Paterson, Michael James Scott, Judy Sheard, and Claudia Szabo. 2018. Introductory Programming: A Systematic Literature Review. In *Proceedings Companion of the 23rd Annual ACM Conference on Innovation and Technology in Computer Science Education (ITiCSE 2018 Companion)*. ACM, New York, NY, USA, 55–106. https://doi.org/10.1145/3293881.3295779

[17] Raina Mason and Graham Cooper. 2014. Introductory Programming Courses in Australia and New Zealand in 2013 - Trends and Reasons. In *Proceedings of the Sixteenth Australasian Computing Education Conference - Volume 148 (ACE '14)*. Australian Computer Society, Inc., Darlinghurst, Australia, Australia, 139–147. http://dl.acm.org/citation.cfm?id=2667490.2667507

[18] Raina Mason, Graham Cooper, and Michael de Raadt. 2012. Trends in Introductory Programming Courses in Australian Universities: Languages, Environments and Pedagogy. In *Proceedings of the Fourteenth Australasian Computing Education Conference - Volume 123 (ACE '12)*. Australian Computer Society, Inc., Darlinghurst, Australia, Australia, 33–42. http://dl.acm.org/citation.cfm?id=2483716.2483721

[19] Raina Mason and Simon. 2017. Introductory Programming Courses in Australasia in 2016. In *Proceedings of the Nineteenth Australasian Computing Education Conference (ACE '17)*. ACM, New York, NY, USA, 81–89. https://doi.org/10.1145/3013499.3013512

[20] Michael McCracken, Vicki Almstrum, Danny Diaz, Mark Guzdial, Dianne Hagan, Yifat Ben-David Kolikant, Cary Laxer, Lynda Thomas, Ian Utting, and Tadeusz Wilusz. 2001. A Multi-national, Multi-institutional Study of Assessment of Programming Skills of First-year CS Students. *SIGCSE Bull.* 33, 4 (Dec. 2001), 125–180. https://doi.org/10.1145/572139.572181

[21] Catherine Mooney, Brett A. Becker, Lana Salmon, and Eleni Mangina. 2018. Computer Science Identity and Sense of Belonging: A Case Study in Ireland. In *Proceedings of the 1st International Workshop on Gender Equality in Software Engineering (GE '18)*. ACM, New York, NY, USA, 1–4. https://doi.org/10.1145/3195570.3195575

[22] Ellen Murphy, Tom Crick, and James H Davenport. 2017. An Analysis of Introductory Programming Courses at UK Universities. *The Art, Science, and Engineering of Programming* 1, 2 (2017).

[23] The Joint Task Force on Computing Curricula IEEE Computer Society and Association for Computing Machinery. 2001. *Computing Curricula 2001, Computer Science*. Technical Report. New York, NY, USA. https://www.acm.org/education/curricula-recommendations

[24] Arnold Pears, Stephen Seidman, Lauri Malmi, Linda Mannila, Elizabeth Adams, Jens Bennedsen, Marie Devlin, and James Paterson. 2007. A Survey of Literature on the Teaching of Introductory Programming. In *Working Group Reports on ITiCSE on Innovation and Technology in Computer Science Education (ITiCSE-WGR '07)*. ACM, New York, NY, USA, 204–223. https://doi.org/10.1145/1345443.1345441

[25] Keith Quille, Roisin Faherty, Susan Bergin, and Brett A. Becker. 2018. Second Level Computer Science: The Irish K-12 Journey Begins. In *Proceedings of the 18th Koli Calling International Conference on Computing Education Research (Koli Calling '18)*. ACM, New York, NY, USA, Article 22, 5 pages. https://doi.org/10.1145/3279720.3279742

[26] Anthony Robins. 2010. Learning Edge Momentum: A New Account of Outcomes in CS1. *Computer Science Education* 20, 1 (2010), 37–71. https://doi.org/10.1080/08993401003612167

[27] Amber Settle, Arto Vihavainen, and Juha Sorva. 2014. Three Views on Motivation and Programming. In *Proceedings of the 2014 Conference on Innovation & Technology in Computer Science Education (ITiCSE '14)*. ACM, New York, NY, USA, 321–322. https://doi.org/10.1145/2591708.2591709

[28] Robert Michael Siegfried, Daniel Greco, Nicholas Miceli, and Jason Siegfried. 2012. Whatever happened to Richard Reid's list of first programming languages? *Information Systems Education Journal* 10, 4 (2012), 24.

[29] Andreas Stefik and Stefan Hanenberg. 2014. The Programming Language Wars: Questions and Responsibilities for the Programming Language Community. In *Proceedings of the 2014 ACM International Symposium on New Ideas, New Paradigms, and Reflections on Programming & Software (Onward! 2014)*. ACM, New York, NY, USA, 283–299. https://doi.org/10.1145/2661136.2661156

[30] Glenn Strong, Catherine Higgins, Nina Bresnihan, and Richard Millwood. 2017. A Survey of the Prior Programming Experience of Undergraduate Computing and Engineering Students in Ireland. In *IFIP World Conference on Computers in Education*. Springer, 473–483.

[31] Daniel Zingaro, Michelle Craig, Leo Porter, Brett A. Becker, Yingjun Cao, Phill Conrad, Diana Cukierman, Arto Hellas, Dastyni Loksa, and Neena Thota. 2018. Achievement Goals in CS1: Replication and Extension. In *Proceedings of the 49th ACM Technical Symposium on Computer Science Education (SIGCSE '18)*. ACM, New York, NY, USA, 687–692. https://doi.org/10.1145/3159450.3159452

Helping Students Solve Parsons Puzzles Better

Amruth N. Kumar
Computer Science
Ramapo College of New Jersey
Mahwah, NJ, USA
amruth@ramapo.edu

ABSTRACT

In a Parsons puzzle, the student must re-assemble the lines of a program that are provided in scrambled order, and eliminate any distracters included within the scrambled lines of code. We investigated two issues in terms of whether they helped students solve the puzzles better: 1) Would it be better to present distracters and the lines of code of which they are a variant paired together or randomly separated apart? 2) Would telling students that they would not be penalized for any mistakes they make before submitting a complete solution for the first time enable them to get closer to the correct solution when they first submit it? We conducted a controlled study over five semesters and used ANOVA to analyze the data collected from introductory programming students who solved Parsons puzzles on `if-else` statements. We found that when students were told that their puzzle-solving actions before the first submission would not be penalized, they took significantly more exploratory actions. But, their solution was not significantly closer to being correct. So, trial-and-error exploration was no better for solving Parsons puzzles than deliberate approach. Presenting distracters paired together with the original line of code was found to be beneficial only on the longer puzzle.

ACM Reference format:

Amruth Kumar, 2019. Helping Students Solve Parsons Puzzles Better. In *Proc. of the 24th Annual Conf. on Innovation & Technology in Computer Science Education (ITiCSE'19). July 15–17, 2019, Aberdeen, Scotland UK., ACM, New York, NY, USA, 6 pages.*
https://doi.org/10.1145/3304221.3319735

1 Introduction

In a Parsons puzzle [17], a problem statement and a program written for the problem are presented to the student. But, the lines in the program are presented scrambled. The student is tasked with rearranging the lines in their correct order. A few distracters, which are incorrect variants of lines of code in the program, are mixed in with the scrambled lines. The student must properly identify and eliminate these distracters. The puzzles were designed to be an engaging way to learn programming [17].

Parsons puzzles have gained popularity for use in exams [4], since they are easier to grade than code-writing exercises. Scores on Parsons puzzles were found to correlate with scores on code-writing exercises [4]. Solving Parsons puzzles was found to take significantly less time than fixing errors in code or writing equivalent code, but resulted in the same learning performance and retention [7]. In electronic books, students were found to prefer solving Parsons puzzles more than other low-cognitive-load activities such as answering multiple choice questions and high-cognitive-load activities such as writing code [6]. Researchers have placed Parsons puzzles in a hierarchy of programming skills alongside code-tracing [15]. Software to administer Parsons puzzles have been developed for Turbo Pascal [17], Python (e.g., [3,10]) and C++/Java/C# [12].

The focus in Parsons puzzles research is lately on how students solve them and what does/does not help students solve them better, e.g., the patterns in how students go about solving the puzzles [9,11]; that sub-goal labels help students solve puzzles significantly better [16]; adaptive practice of Parsons puzzles is more efficient while being just as effective as writing code [5]; but, motivational supports [13] and the use of mnemonic variable names [19] do not help students while solving puzzles.

In this vein, we investigated two issues in terms of whether they helped students solve Parsons puzzles better, i.e., with fewer corrective actions and/or less time:

1. A distracter is an incorrect variant of a line of code. Would distracters and the lines of code of which they are a variant be better presented paired together or separated randomly apart?
2. Students could be penalized for every mistake while solving a puzzle, or only those that they commit after submitting a complete solution for the first time. Would telling students that they would not be penalized for any mistakes they make before submitting a complete solution for the first time prompt them to explore the solution more before submitting it for the first time? Would this enable them to get closer to the correct solution when they first submit it?

ITiCSE '19, July 15–17, 2019, Aberdeen, Scotland UK.

ACM ISBN 978-1-4503-6301-3/19/07..$15.00
https://doi.org/10.1145/3304221.3319735

2 The Study

2.1 Distracters

A distracter (also spelled distractor in literature) is an incorrect variant of an existing line of code in the puzzle. It may be a syntactically incorrect variant (e.g., `5 = variable;` instead of `variable = 5;`), semantically incorrect (e.g., `variable += 2;` instead of `variable *= 2;`) or pragmatically inadvisable (e.g., `int x;` instead of `int months;`) [17]. Each distracter and the line of code of which it is a variant may be presented **paired together** in the scrambled code, or randomly **separated apart**. Presenting the two paired together reduces the cognitive load that is not relevant to problem-solving or programming [4]. So, we hypothesized that *students would be able to solve Parsons puzzles with fewer mistakes and hence, fewer actions when distracters were paired together rather than separated apart.*

2.2 Grading Schemes

The solution to a Parsons puzzle is **complete** when all the lines in the puzzle have been accounted for, i.e., they have either been placed in the solution space or have been discarded as distracters. The solution is also **correct** when all and only the distracters have been discarded and all the lines in the solution space have been placed in their correct order. A correct solution is necessarily complete, but the vice versa is not true.

If a puzzle contains n lines of code (including distracters), it can be solved completely and correctly with n actions, assuming each line is individually manipulable. The possible puzzle-solving actions include 1) moving a line of code from problem/puzzle space to (its correct location in) solution/program space; 2) discarding a distracter from problem space; 3) reordering a line of code within solution space. A student who is not sure of the correct solution typically takes many more than n actions to solve a puzzle, and all the actions beyond the first n are redundant. During grading, these redundant actions are penalized. We refer to this scheme of penalizing all the redundant actions as **aggressive** grading, the grading that was in effect early in our use of Parsons puzzles.

In response to feedback from students who thought that aggressive grading scheme was too unforgiving, later in our use of Parsons puzzles, we instituted a new grading scheme: a student would be allowed to take as many actions without any grading penalty until the student submitted a complete solution for the first time (henceforth referred to as **pre-completion actions**). The student would be penalized for only the actions taken after the submission of the first complete solution to fix any remaining errors in the solution (henceforth referred to as **post-completion actions**). We refer to this scheme of penalizing only post-completion actions as **lenient** grading.

A student must carry out at least n actions before submitting a complete solution for the first time. So, the following relations hold:

$$\text{pre-completion actions} \geq n$$

$$\text{post-completion actions} \geq 0$$

In aggressive grading scheme, all the actions beyond the first n are penalized, i.e., negatively graded when computing the student's grade on the puzzle. So, the grade penalty is applied to:

$$\text{pre-completion actions} + \text{post-completion actions} - n$$

In lenient grading scheme, negative penalty is applied only to post-completion actions.

Cognitive strategies used to solve Part-Complete Solution Method (PCSM), a variant of Parsons puzzles [20], have been categorized into five levels: unplanned and random at the bottom end, followed by low-level consideration, some level of consideration, high level of consideration with some strategy and finally, deliberate approach at the top end [20]. Given that students with aggressive grading would want to minimize *all* redundant actions, they had greater incentive to use deliberate approach during pre-completion actions than those with lenient grading scheme. In contrast, since they would not be penalized, students with lenient grading had the incentive to engage in trial-and-error exploration during pre-completion actions. We wanted to find out which of the two grading schemes led students closer to the correct solution when they first submitted their solution – *aggressive grading that incentivized deliberate approach or lenient grading that incentivized trial-and-error approach.*

So, our experimental hypotheses were two-fold:

1. Students with lenient grading would engage in more trial-and-error exploratory actions before submitting a complete solution for the first time, i.e., pre-completion actions would be significantly more with lenient grading than with aggressive grading;
2. Lenient grading that incentivizes trial-and-error exploration would result in a solution closer to being correct when first submitted than aggressive grading that incentivizes deliberate approach. (Null hypothesis would be to find no difference between the two grading schemes.) So, post-completion actions would be significantly less for lenient grading than aggressive grading.

3 The Experiment

3.1 The Instrument

For this study, we used a Parsons puzzle software tutor from a suite of tutors called epplets [12]. The tutor presents a series of Parsons puzzles, lets the student solve the puzzles, provides feedback to help the student correct the solutions, and grades each solution. Its user interface contains an Instruction Panel where the problem statement is presented, a Problem Panel where scrambled lines are listed, a Solution Panel where the student re-assembles the lines of code in their correct order, a Trash Panel to which the student drags distracters and a Feedback Panel where feedback is presented to the student [12] – this layout with drag-and-drop interface affords the puzzle-solving actions described in Section 2.2, It is accessible online (epplets.org) and can be used by students on their own time.

Students using the tutor cannot submit their solution to a puzzle until it is complete, i.e., they have accounted for all the lines in the puzzle. With the aid of the feedback provided by the tutor, students can fix errors in their solution and resubmit their solution as often as they want till the solution is correct. They are required to correctly solve a Parsons puzzle before moving on to the next puzzle.

The tutor is adaptive, i.e., if it determines that a student does not know how to solve a puzzle, it will present additional practice puzzles to the student. So, students had the incentive to solve each puzzle with the best grade possible, i.e., with the fewest redundant actions possible. The more mistakes students made on the initial puzzles, the more puzzles the tutor would have them solve.

The tutor used the grading schemes described earlier to determine whether a student knew how to solve a puzzle: it used aggressive grading scheme from Fall 2016 to Fall 2017 and lenient grading scheme in Spring 2018 and Fall 2018. Before each tutoring session, the grading scheme in effect was explained to the students and they were asked to aim for the best grade possible when solving puzzles:

3.2 The Puzzles

For this study, we had students solve Parsons puzzles on `if-else` statements. The first puzzle was on a single `if-else` statement and the second was on nested `if-else` statements. All the students solved these puzzles. The puzzles that they solved after the first two, if any, depended on how well they had solved these two puzzles. Therefore, for our study, we considered data from only the first two puzzles.

The first puzzle was on a program to read two numbers and print the smaller value among them. This program contained 16 lines that were provided scrambled, which included all the lines of code within `main` as well as 2 distracters. The shell of `main` and the comments within it were provided as context [20]. The largest number of lines of code students had to re-assemble under a single comment/context was 8. Following is the puzzle program in C++:

```
// The C++ program
#include <iostream>
using namespace std;
int main()
{
  // Declare firstInput
  short firstInput;
  // Declare secondNum
  short secondNum;
  // Read firstInput
  cout << "Enter the first value";
  cin >> firstInput;
  // Read secondNum
  cout << "Enter the second value";
  cin >> secondNum;
  // If firstInput is less than secondNum, print firstInput.
  // Otherwise, print secondNum
  if( firstInput < secondNum )
  {
    cout << firstInput;
  } // End of if-clause
  else
  {
    cout << secondNum;
  } // End of else-clause
} // End of function main
```

Following is a typical randomly scrambled puzzle based on this program that is presented to the student:

```
{
  cout << firstInput;
} // End of if-clause
cin >> firstInput;
cin << firstInput;
if( firstInput < secondNum )
cin >> secondNum;
cout << secondNum;
else
} // End of else-clause
short secondNum;
short firstInput;
cout << "Enter the second value";
cout < < "Enter the second value";
{
cout << "Enter the first value";
```

Note that the puzzle contains 16 lines. It includes two distracters that have been presented paired.

The second puzzle was on a program to read numerical grade, convert it to letter grade - A (90 and up), B (80-89), C (70-79), D (55-69) and F otherwise - and print it. This program contained 36 lines that were provided scrambled, which included all the lines of code within `main` as well as 2 distracters. Once again, the shell of `main` and the comments within it were provided as context. The largest number of lines of code students had to re-assemble under a single comment/context was 29. Following is the program in C++:

```
// The C++ program
#include <iostream>
using namespace std;
int main()
{
  // Declare number
  long number;
  // Declare letterGrade
  char letterGrade;
  // Read number
  cout << "Enter the numerical grade";
  cin >> number;
  // Compute letterGrade based on number
  if( number >= 90 )
```

```
{
  letterGrade = 'A';
} // End of if-clause
else
{
  if( number >= 80 )
  {
    letterGrade = 'B';
  } // End of if-clause
  else
  {
    if( number >= 70 )
    {
      letterGrade = 'C';
    } // End of if-clause
    else
    {
      if( number >= 55 )
      {
        letterGrade = 'D';
      } // End of if-clause
      else
      {
        letterGrade = 'F';
      } // End of else-clause
    } // End of else-clause
  } // End of else-clause
} // End of else-clause
// Print letterGrade
cout << letterGrade;
} // End of function main
```

4 Data Collection and Analysis

4.1 Variables

The dependent variables of the study were:

- **Pre-completion ratio:** calculated as pre-completion actions / n, i.e., the number of actions taken by the student before submitting it for the first time, divided by the number of lines in the puzzle. We considered pre-completion ratio instead of the number of pre-completion actions so that we could compare student performance across two puzzles with different number of scrambled lines.
- **Post-completion ratio:** calculated as post-completion actions / n, i.e., the number of steps, if any, taken by the student to correct the solution after submitting it for the first time, divided by the number of lines in the puzzle
- The time spent per line to solve the puzzle, in seconds
- The grade on the puzzle. In order to be able to compare aggressive and lenient grading schemes, we used lenient grading scheme to re-calculate the grades of all the students based on their post-completion actions only.

The independent variables of the study were:

- Grading scheme: the grading scheme that students were told was being used when they were solving the puzzles - aggressive or lenient.
- Pairing of distracters: whether each distracter was presented paired together or separated apart from the correct line of code of which it was a variant.
- The puzzle number: whether the data pertained to the first or the second puzzle presented to the student.

4.2 Data Collection

The subjects of the study were students in introductory programming courses, who were asked to solve the puzzles as after-class assignment, and who had given IRB permission for their data to be used in the study. We collected data over 5 semesters: Fall 2016 through Fall 2018. In each semester, students from multiple institutions used the tutor. The institutions were randomly assigned to control group (distracters separated apart) and experimental group (distracters paired together). The tutor used aggressive grading during the first three semesters (Fall 2016 – Fall 2017) and lenient grading in the last two semesters (Spring 2018, Fall 2018). The number of students in each of the four conditions (pairing of distracters X grading scheme) is listed in Table 1. Varying levels of retention and assignment submission rates explain the differences in the number of students in the four conditions.

Students could use the tutor as often as they wanted. If a student used the tutor more than once, data from only the first session wherein the student had solved the most number of puzzles was considered for the study.

Table 1: Number of students in each treatment

	Aggressive	Lenient
Separated apart	192	56
Paired together	101	162

4.3 Data Analysis

Pre-completion ratio: One-way ANOVA analysis of pre-completion ratio with grading policy, pairing of distracters and puzzle number as fixed factors found a significant main effect for grading policy: [F(1,828) = 10.732, p = 0.001]. Mean pre-completion ratio was 1.201 ± 0.032 with aggressive grading (at 95% confidence interval) and 1.288 ± 0.041 with lenient grading. In other words, with lenient grading, students took 28.8% more pre-completion actions than the number of lines in the puzzle whereas with aggressive grading, they took 20.1% more actions on average. This confirms the hypothesis that, *with lenient grading, students would carry out more trial-and-error exploratory actions before submitting the complete solution for the first time.*

The other significant main effect found was for the puzzle number [F(1,828) = 21.184, p < 0.001]: Mean pre-completion ratio was 1.306 ± 0.035 for the first puzzle which contained 16 scrambled lines and 1.184 ± 0.039 for the second puzzle which contained 36 scrambled lines. In other words, students took

30.6% (4.9) more pre-completion actions than the number of lines (16) on the first puzzle, but took 18.4% (6.6) more pre-completion actions on the second puzzle with 36 lines. So, *the number of exploratory pre-completion actions did not increase linearly with the number of lines in the puzzle.* One possible explanation is practice effect, i.e., students felt more confident at solving Parsons puzzles and therefore, took a smaller percentage of pre-completion actions on the second puzzle than on the first.

Post-completion ratio: Similar ANOVA analysis of post-completion ratio found a significant main effect for puzzle number [F(1,828) = 8.426, p = 0.004]: Mean post-completion ratio was 0.496 ± 0.081 for the first puzzle and 0.315 ± 0.091 for the second puzzle. In other words, the post-completion actions students took were 49.6% (7.9) of the number of lines (16) on the first puzzle, and 31.5% (11.3) of the number of lines (36) on the second puzzle. Just as in the case of pre-completion actions, *post-completion actions did not increase linearly with the number of lines in the puzzle either.*

Students were required to solve each puzzle correctly. Since neither pre-completion actions nor post-completion actions increased linearly with the number of lines in the puzzle, students took proportionately fewer unnecessary actions to solve the second puzzle with 36 lines of code than the first puzzle with 16 lines of code. Apart from practice effect, another possible explanation is that the level of difficulty of solving Parsons puzzles does not increase linearly with the number of lines in the puzzle, possibly because of more duplicated lines (e.g., `else`). This is a hypothesis worth exploring further with more data.

We did not find a main effect for grading policy, though. Post-completion ratio was statistically no different between students with lenient versus aggressive grading. So, the hypothesis that students with lenient grading would be closer to the correct solution than those with aggressive grading by the time they submitted a complete solution for the first time was not confirmed by the data. *Trial-and-error approach incentivized by lenient grading did not lead to a more correct solution than deliberate approach incentivized by aggressive grading.*

Time spent per line: ANOVA analysis of the time spent per line yielded a marginal main effect for grading scheme [F(1,827) = 3.318, p = 0.069]: students spent a mean of 18.741 ± 1.332 seconds per line with aggressive grading compared to 20.736 ± 1.687 seconds per line with lenient grading. So, students spent marginally more time per line with lenient grading than with aggressive grading. Lenient grading may have prompted students to think more before each action.

ANOVA analysis of the time spent per line yielded a significant main effect for puzzle number [F91,827) = 44.977, p < 0.001]: students took 23.411 ± 1.426 seconds per line on the first puzzle and 16.067 ± 1.608 seconds per line on the second puzzle. One explanation is practice effect – *students got faster at solving puzzles with practice.*

Grade: ANOVA analysis of the grade did not yield any significant main effect, but yielded a significant interaction between pairing of distracters and puzzle number [F(1,828) = 5.009, p = 0.025], as shown in Table 2. When distracters were separated apart, students scored more on the shorter first puzzle (16 lines) than on the longer second puzzle (36 lines), but this difference was not statistically significant. When distracters were paired together, students scored more on the longer second puzzle than on the shorter first puzzle, and this difference was statistically significant [F(1,438) = 6.076, p = 0.014]. *So, the hypothesis that puzzles with distracters paired together are easier to solve than those with distracters separated apart was found to be true only for the longer puzzle.*

Table 2: Interaction of Grade Between Pairing of Distracters and Puzzle Number

	Puzzle 1	Puzzle 2
Separated apart	0.761 ± 0.058	0.724 ± 0.066
Paired together	0.662 ± 0.047	0.753 ± 0.053

5 Discussion

We found that with lenient grading, students indeed carried out more exploratory actions to solve Parsons puzzles before submitting a complete solution for the first time. They also took marginally more time per line to solve the puzzle. In spite of these, they were no closer to the correct solution than students with aggressive grading because the post-completion actions they needed to correct their solution were no fewer than those needed by students with aggressive grading. In other words, students did not benefit from lenient grading. Trial-and-error exploration was no better for solving Parsons puzzles than deliberate approach.

Empirical research has consistently shown that anxiety negatively affects educational achievement [21]. With aggressive grading, pre-completion actions that are incorrect are irrecoverable in the sense that they will be penalized. In contrast, with lenient grading, they are recoverable, i.e., bear no penalty. So, a disadvantage of aggressive grading, and a reason why students might prefer lenient grading over it is that aggressive grading is likely to induce more anxiety during pre-completion actions. So, it is reasonable to expect that students would do better with lenient grading than with aggressive grading. But, our study did not support this hypothesis.

Anxiety can be task-directed, i.e., facilitating, or task-irrelevant, i.e., debilitating [22]. One explanation for why lenient grading was no different from aggressive grading might be that the stress induced by aggressive grading was task-directed or facilitating. So, unpleasant as the anxiety may have been to the students, it helped them focus on solving the puzzle with as few mistakes as possible.

Presenting distracters paired together reduces cognitive load not relevant to problem-solving or programming [4]. But, we found that pairing together distracters was beneficial only on the longer puzzle.

Parsons puzzles are rapidly gaining popularity in programming education. In this context, research is called for to answer questions such as what affects how efficiently students solve the puzzles and what affects the level of difficulty of solving the puzzles. In this study, we have attempted to answer some questions (Does aggressive grading lead to inefficient puzzle solutions? Does pairing together distracters make a puzzle easier to solve?) while raising another (Is the number of lines in a puzzle an accurate measure of the level of difficulty of solving the puzzle?) We see our study as adding another piece of evidence to the body of literature (e.g., [5,9,11,13,16,19]) on how to effectively use Parsons puzzles for programming education.

ACKNOWLEDGMENTS

Partial support for this work was provided by the National Science Foundation under grants DUE-1432190 and DUE-1502564.

REFERENCES

[1] Eran Avidan and Dror G. Feitelson. 2017. Effects of variable names on comprehension an empirical study. In *Proceedings of the 25th International Conference on Program Comprehension (ICPC '17)*. IEEE Press, Piscataway, NJ, USA, 55-65. DOI: https://doi.org/10.1109/ICPC.2017.27.

[2] Scott Blinman and Andy Cockburn. 2005. Program comprehension: investigating the effects of naming style and documentation. In Proceedings of the Sixth Australasian conference on User interface - Volume 40 (AUIC '05), Mark Billinghurst and Andy Cockburn (Eds.), Vol. 40. Australian Computer Society, Inc., Darlinghurst, Australia, Australia, 73-78.

[3] Nick Cheng and Brian Harrington. 2017. The Code Mangler: Evaluating Coding Ability Without Writing any Code. In *Proceedings of the 2017 ACM SIGCSE Technical Symposium on Computer Science Education (SIGCSE '17)*. ACM, New York, NY, USA, 123-128. DOI: https://doi.org/10.1145/3017680.3017704.

[4] Paul Denny, Andrew Luxton-Reilly, and Beth Simon. 2008. Evaluating a new exam question: Parsons problems. In *Proceedings of the Fourth International Workshop on Computing Education Research (ICER '08)*. ACM, New York, NY, USA, 113-124. DOI=http://dx.doi.org/10.1145/1404520.1404532.

[5] Barbara J. Ericson, James D. Foley, and Jochen Rick. 2018. Evaluating the Efficiency and Effectiveness of Adaptive Parsons Problems. In *Proceedings of the 2018 ACM Conference on International Computing Education Research (ICER '18)*. ACM, New York, NY, USA, 60-68. DOI: https://doi.org/10.1145/3230977.3231000

[6] Barbara J. Ericson, Mark J. Guzdial, and Briana B. Morrison. 2015. Analysis of Interactive Features Designed to Enhance Learning in an Ebook. In *Proceedings of the eleventh annual International Conference on International Computing Education Research (ICER '15)*. ACM, New York, NY, USA, 169-178. DOI: https://doi.org/10.1145/2787622.2787731.

[7] Barbara J. Ericson, Lauren E. Margulieux, and Jochen Rick. 2017. Solving Parsons problems versus fixing and writing code. In *Proceedings of the 17th Koli Calling International Conference on Computing Education Research (Koli Calling '17)*. ACM, New York, NY, USA, 20-29. DOI: https://doi.org/10.1145/3141880.3141895.

[8] G. W. Furnas, T. K. Landauer, L. M. Gomez, and S. T. Dumais. 1987. The vocabulary problem in human-system communication. Communications of the ACM 30, (November 1987), 964-971 DOI= https://doi.org/10.1145/32206.32212

[9] Juha Helminen, Petri Ihantola, Ville Karavirta, and Lauri Malmi. 2012. How do students solve parsons programming problems?: an analysis of interaction traces. In *Proceedings of the ninth annual international conference on International computing education research (ICER '12)*. ACM, New York, NY, USA, 119-126. DOI: https://doi.org/10.1145/2361276.2361300.

[10] Petri Ihantola and Ville Karavirta. 2010. Open source widget for parson's puzzles. In *Proceedings of the fifteenth annual conference on Innovation and technology in computer science education (ITiCSE '10)*. ACM, New York, NY, USA, 302-302. DOI: https://doi.org/10.1145/1822090.1822178

[11] Petri Ihantola and Ville Karavirta. 2011.Two-Dimensional Parson's Puzzles: The Concept, Tools, and First Observations. *Journal of Information Technology Education: Innovations in Practice*. Vol 10. 2011. 119-132. DOI= https://doi.org/10.28945/1394

[12] Amruth N. Kumar. 2018. Epplets: A Tool for Solving Parsons Puzzles. In *Proceedings of the 49th ACM Technical Symposium on Computer Science Education (SIGCSE '18)*. ACM, New York, NY, USA, 527-532. DOI: https://doi.org/10.1145/3159450.3159576.

[13] Amruth N. Kumar. 2017. The Effect of Providing Motivational Support in Parsons Puzzle Tutors. I*n Proceedings of Artificial Intelligence in Education. (AI-ED 2017)*, Wuhan, China, June 2017, 528-531. DOI= https://doi.org/10.1007/978-3-319-61425-0_56

[14] Dawn Lawrie, Christopher Morrell, Henry Feild, and David Binkley. 2006. What's in a Name? A Study of Identifiers. In Proceedings of the 14th IEEE International Conference on Program Comprehension (ICPC '06). IEEE Computer Society, Washington, DC, USA, 3-12. DOI: https://doi.org/10.1109/ICPC.2006.51

[15] Mike Lopez, Jacqueline Whalley, Phil Robbins, and Raymond Lister. 2008. Relationships between reading, tracing and writing skills in introductory programming. In *Proceedings of the Fourth International Workshop on Computing Education Research (ICER '08)*. ACM, New York, NY, USA, 101-112. DOI=http://dx.doi.org/10.1145/1404520.1404531.

[16] Briana B. Morrison, Lauren E. Margulieux, Barbara Ericson, and Mark Guzdial. 2016. Subgoals Help Students Solve Parsons Problems. In Proceedings of the 47th ACM Technical Symposium on Computing Science Education (SIGCSE '16). ACM, New York, NY, USA, 42-47. DOI: https://doi.org/10.1145/2839509.2844617.

[17] Dale Parsons and Patricia Haden. 2006. Parson's programming puzzles: a fun and effective learning tool for first programming courses. In Proceedings of the 8th Australasian Conference on Computing Education - Volume 52 (ACE '06), Denise Tolhurst and Samuel Mann (Eds.), Vol. 52. Australian Computer Society, Inc., Darlinghurst, Australia, Australia, 157-163.

[18] Felice Salviulo and Giuseppe Scanniello. 2014. Dealing with identifiers and comments in source code comprehension and maintenance: results from an ethnographically-informed study with students and professionals. In Proceedings of the 18th International Conference on Evaluation and Assessment in Software Engineering (EASE '14). ACM, New York, NY, USA, , Article 48 , 10 pages. DOI: http://dx.doi.org/10.1145/2601248.2601251

[19] Amruth N. Kumar. 2019. Mnemonic Variable Names in Parsons Puzzles. In *Proceedings of ACM Global Computing Education Conference (CompEd'19)*, Chengdu, China. ACM. New York, NY, USA.

[20] Stuart Garner. 2007. An Exploration of How a Technology-Facilitated Part-Complete Solution Method Supports the Learning of Computer Programming. *Issues in Informing Science and Information Technology*. Vol 4. 491-501.

[21] Gaudry, E. and C.D. Spielberger, Anxiety and educational Achievement 1971, New York: John Wiley.

[22] Alpert, R. and R. Haber, Anxiety in academic achievement situations. Journal of Abnormal and Social Psychology, 1960. 61: p. 207-215.

The Relationship Between Students' Engagement and the Development of Transactive Memory Systems in MUVE: An Experience Report

Louis Nisiotis†
Faculty of Science, Technology and Arts (STA)
Sheffield Hallam University
Sheffield, United Kingdom
l.nisiotis@shu.ac.uk

Styliani Kleanthous
Cyprus Center for Algorithmic Transparency
Open University of Cyprus
Nicosia, Cyprus
styliani.kleanthous@ouc.ac.cy

ABSTRACT

The use of educational Multi-User Virtual Environments that provide synchronous interaction, interactive and social learning experiences have the potential to increase student engagement. Due to increased social and cognitive presence, the use of such environments can result in greater student engagement when compared to traditional asynchronous learning environments. In this work, we hypothesized that students' engagement in collaborative learning activities will increase if Transactive Memory System constructs are present. Thus, we employed the theory of TMS that emphasizes the importance of Specialization, Coordination and Credibility between members in a team. The results show that there is a significant correlation between the development of TMS and students' engagement.

CCS CONCEPTS

•**Applied computing** → **Education**; *Collaborative Learning*; • **Human-centered computing** →Collaborative and social computing; *Computer supported cooperative work*

KEYWORDS

Engagement, Virtual Worlds, Transactive Memory, CSCL

ACM Reference format:

Louis Nisiotis, Styliani Kleanthous. 2019. The Relationship Between Students' Engagement and the Development of Transactive Memory Systems in MUVE: An Experience Report. In *Proceedings of Innovation and Technology in Computer Science Education (ITiCSE '19), ACM, Aberdeen, Scotland, UK, 7 pages.* https://doi.org/10.1145/3304221.3319743

ACM ISBN 978-1-4503-6301-3/19/07...$15.00
https://doi.org/10.1145/3304221.3319743

1. Introduction

The need for education to become more active, engaging and customized to the learners' individual needs is imperative [1]. One of the ways that higher education institutions are adapting to this change is through the adoption of technology to assist learning and teaching. While modern students are familiar with the use of the Internet, smartphones, high quality 3D graphical computer games, virtual reality and other technological affordances, in their everyday life, it is important to engage them in the learning process when in classroom. Student engagement in higher education is a topic that drew much international research and literature [2], and there are studies suggesting the positive effects of technology [3-5] towards student engagement. One of the many technologies that are being used to support students, is the use of Multi-User Virtual Environments (MUVEs). These are computer generated 3D virtual worlds, in which users can interact with and with each other using their Avatar [6]. Employing such environments in education, enables us to develop educational activities that promote collaboration, socialisation and engagement [4, 7, 8].

Effective communication and collaboration contribute to student learning and are integral parts of the development of Transactive Memory System (TMS). TMS development within working groups has been identified to be very beneficial. The TMS theory relates to the encoding, storage and retrieval of information, and can provide the option to recall previously visited areas of information, and to identify relevant knowledge [9]. It also enables to create awareness of 'who knows what' within a group, and this provides opportunities for effective collaboration. However, while there is a lot of knowledge around the phenomenon of TMS in the field of organisational psychology and behavioural sciences, little is known about the potential relation of TMS with students' engagement and especially, within a MUVE. To investigate this, we have designed a 10-week experimental study, implemented as part of a Computer Science module, delivered through a MUVE we designed. Section 2 presents the theoretical underpinnings of this investigation, and Section 3 describes the methods, instrumentations, and experimental procedures of this study.

The results of this investigation are presented in Section 4, and Section 5 provides a discussion and concludes the paper.

2. Theoretical Background

2.1 Students' Engagement in MUVE

Students' engagement is an important topic in higher education in general, and Computer Science education in particular. Initially, the concept of student involvement in education was defined as the amount of both physical and psychological energy a student commits on the educational experience [10], and there is a debate about the meaning of student engagement since then [4, 11]. Especially in Computer Science there are several ongoing discussions on how academics view the concept of engagement (e.g. [12, 13]), and how students' engagement in computer science classes can be improved [14]. This is even more important when we are dealing with first year students in introductory Computer Science modules [15, 16].

A number of researchers have defined engagement as the involvement, participation or commitment of the student in learning. Particularly, some suggest that students engagement refers to the extent to which students are involved and actively participate in learning activities [17]. Others indicate that engagement relates to the effort in time and energy the student commits to purposeful educational activities [18]. These definitions enable us to summarize and understand the close relationship between the student and the need to devote effort, time, involvement, active participation and commitment to the learning process. In this work we consider students' engagement by measuring three types of Student Engagement [19, 20] and adapting them to the topic of MUVEs:

- **Behavioral Engagement** – what is the student's behavior towards learning through an MUVE e.g. i) I follow the rules of the MUVE; ii) When I am in the MUVE, I just 'act' as if I am learning; iii) I am able to consistently pay attention when I am taking the online class in MUVE.
- **Emotional Engagement** – How the student is feeling when following the class in the MUVE e.g. i) I like taking the online class in MUVE; ii) I feel happy when taking online class in MUVE; iii) I feel bored by the online class in MUVE.
- **Cognitive Engagement** – whether the student is following the material he/she read within the MUVE to further develop his/her knowledge e.g. i) I study at home even when I do not have a test; ii) When I read the course materials, I ask myself questions to make sure I understand what it is about; iii) I talk with people outside of school about what I am learning in the MUVE.

The topic of student engagement through the use of technology mediated learning tools and online learning environments has been positively investigated in the literature, and one of the methods that can increase students' engagement is through the use of the educational MUVE [4].

A MUVE is a computer generated and persistent three-dimensional environment in which users can navigate and interact with the environment and others, using a virtual representation of themselves known as avatar [6]. MUVEs enable users to immerse in the virtual environment and communicate, interact and coexist in the same shared space at the same time. Over the past few years, the use of MUVEs gained a lot of popularity in education [21] especially in a mixed method teaching and learning scenarios. Educators who are interested to improve, differentiate and enhance their teaching and learning practices use these environments that offer a range of functionalities and possibilities that cannot be found in the traditional online learning systems [22]. MUVEs offer access and synchronous participation in learning activities that make learning more interesting [23], social [24] and engaging [25]. MUVEs allow teachers to develop immersive experiential and problem based learning activities to support and engage students in the learning process [8].

One of the most important attributes of a MUVE is the feeling of presence that the user is developing when interacting and participating in the environment. Presence is concerned with the extent to which the individual feels present in the virtual environment rather than the physical [26], experiencing the illusion of 'being there', regardless if 'there' actually exists in the real world [27]. It has been established that increasing presence also increases learning and performance [28] and it has been suggested that when managed properly, the sense of presence in a MUVE can increase student engagement and improve learning [29, 30]. It was also identified that presence is positively correlated with learning success, because it motivates and engages students in learning [31].

Furthermore, due to increased social and cognitive presence, the use of such environments can result in greater student engagement when compared to asynchronous learning environments [32]. Furthermore, the ability of a MUVE to bring students together in the same shared space helps to develop the feel of belonging to a community and this removes the lack of student engagement and isolation that occurs in traditional online environments [33].

Thus, while in traditional face-to-face delivery, instructors experience difficulties maintaining students' engagement and successfully promoting active learning [34], other methods (e.g. [16, 35]) including the use of technology as a mean to draw students interest with modern learning methods is a great asset in the toolbox of each academic. Robinson and Hullinger [36] mentions that one of the way educators can offer modules that promote student engagement, is through the use of online learning environments, as these tools are now used at most of the higher education institutions [37]. Such tools are usually used as repositories of information and to provide interactive and collaborative activities [38].

2.2 Transactive Memory Systems in MUVE

TMS is defined as a memory system of a group that comprises of the memory systems of individuals, and the processes involved for communicating the information within the group [9]. The processes involved in this procedure are what is needed so the group is able to encode, store and retrieve information held by its members. Following these processes members of a team can facilitate collaboration by utilizing the maximum of their knowledge and information resources [39] and in extend achieve team efficiency and satisfactory results. As a consequence, being part of a team that has developed and utilized TMS can be a positive and fulfilling experience at an individual level [40].

There is a substantial body of research that looked into the development of TMS in several contexts and using different parameters, and TMS proved to be very promising for the functioning of couples, teams and groups in face-to-face [9, 41] and online communication [42, 43].

A widely used and validated measure for TMS is the one by Lewis [44], where TMS is decomposed into three parameters: Specialization, Credibility, Coordination, and each one is measured by five items in a Likert scale. According to Lewis, specialization deals with unique information and knowledge that a member holds and can be shared or is valuable to the rest of the team as long as the knowledge available is known to, and accessible by others. Coordination is about the ability of the team to work together, coordinate task execution and manage misunderstanding. Finally, credibility is about trusting the knowledge others are sharing and decisions they make.

In addition, measuring TMS is not only a matter of the information and knowledge available, but it is also related to the willingness of the people to contribute and to the task at hand thus, *we argue that TMS should be positively related to students' engagement.* A successful collaboration should not only be judged by the final output of the team.

Many tools allow the researchers to collect log data of users' collaborative activities and provide the opportunity to mine this data for behavioral and interaction patterns related to collaboration (e.g. [45]). While the educational affordances of MUVE have been investigated thoroughly in the existing literature, little is known about the extent to which TMS and Student Engagement are related to each other within a MUVE, during collaborative learning activities. To ascertain this, building on previous work [7, 46, 47] that investigated how various tools in a MUVE relate to TMS building, we have devised the following research questions.

RQ1: What are the students' perceptions of their Behavioral, Emotional and Cognitive Engagement when participating in learning activities within the MUVE?

RQ2: Is there a correlation between Student Engagement and the development of TMS in a MUVE?

3. Methods and Instrumentation

3.1 The VirtualSHU

To conduct this investigation, the VirtualSHU MUVE has been used (Fig. 1). The environment is implemented using the Opensimulator MUVE platform, and its design is representing a common educational setting featuring different areas dedicated to each of the topics of the module. In particular, the environment has a main campus with lecture rooms, activity and recreational areas, and a courtyard for students to meet and set-up for activities. An orientation area is also provided for students to learn the basic navigation and features of the environment. The environment provides a fantasy and 'sandbox' areas in which students can build their own objects. Lastly, a quiet area is also provided for students who do not wanted to be distracted, or are 'away from keyboard' but do not want to disconnect from the environment. Information on how someone can visit the VirtualSHU can be found here [50]

Figure 1: The VirtualSHU Layout

3.2 Experimental Study

To conduct this investigation, we have setup an experiment for a period of 10 weeks to support the tutorial sessions of the Introduction to Information Communication Technology (ICT) module at our university. The module consisted of four tutorial classes with 16 to 20 students attending each class. Students were put in groups of 4 and 5 in the beginning of the academic year, and each session lasted for 60 minutes. During the period of the module, students were collaborating through the MUVE in completing module related tasks (Table 1). All tutorial tasks, for the duration of the experiment, took place within the virtual environment. To access the environment, students had a computer at their disposal, and they were accessing the visual aspect of the environment using their computer monitor, as well as their keyboard and mouse to interact with other users and the environment. The communication affordances of the environment (nearby chat, instant message, group message) were utilized to establish communication and information sharing among students and tutors. Each week's topic was taking place in different dedicated rooms, utilizing a range of in-world tools designed to provide access to PowerPoint slides, website loaders, YouTube videos and information boards.

To design the learning activities, we have used McGrath's typology of tasks [48]. This is a validated, and established taxonomy illustrating activities that need to be performed at each stage of the group's development. We have used this taxonomy when designing activities to keep them diverse and ensure that results would not be activity dependent, to develop and maintain the interest and motivation of students, and to allow them to develop different skills through each activity according to the learning goals of the module. The designed activities required students to generate ideas, perform action tasks, make decisions, solve problems, plan, and resolve conflicts of viewpoints. Furthermore, while having a range of activities, students had the chance to use multiple tools within MUVE for communication, task execution and information sharing, ensuring that results will not be dependent on a single communication tool, and to allow the dynamics of the team to be explored at the maximum possible.

Table 1: Activities conducted within the VirtualSHU

Description		Task Type
Orientation Session & Introduction to ICT		
Week 1 and 2: Account creation, orientation, avatar customization, team formation and icebreaking activity discussing the topic of ICT		
Topic 1: The Internet and the World Wide Web		
Week1	A virtual room was allocated to each team and had a topic of research assigned. Students had to brainstorm and create a 10 slides presentation in the virtual world	Generating ideas
Week2	Students reviewed the group notes from Activity 1, to improve their own and have presented their notes in class.	Perform action tasks
Topic 2: Communication Networks		
Week3	Questions were assigned to each group. Students reviewed in-world materials, and performed individual research to create notes and attempt to answer the questions.	Decision Making
Week4	Students were given an interactive quiz through the virtual world.	Solving problems
Topic 3: Cloud Computing		
Week5	Students were assigned a topic of research, and created a shared cloud document for notetaking, and preparing a presentation for the next session (Activity 6)	Planning
Week6	Students have spend some time finishing off their notes and present them in class..	Perform action tasks
Topic 4: The Internet of Things (IoT)		
Week7	Groups were assigned a topic, and students had to review in-world information, and prepare for a discussion (Activity 8).	Planning
Week8	An in-world and classroom discussion on the use of IoT in everyday life. Students presented their viewpoints on the topic.	Resolving Conflicts of Viewpoint

3.3 Data Collection Instruments

From the overall 71 students who were enrolled on the module, 48 students (34 male and 14 female), between 19 and 23 years old participated in the data collection.

The instruments used in this study were adapted from existing validated scales. To measure students' engagement in the MUVE and address RQ1, we have adapted the Engagement Scale initially developed by Fredricks et al. [20], and further edited by Sun and Rueda [19], measuring three types of Student Engagement: Behavioral, Emotional and Cognitive Engagement. Initially, the scale was designed to measure children's levels of school engagement, and Sun and Rueda [19] had modified some of the items to measure engagement of graduate and undergraduate students in distance education settings. To adopt the scale and ensure its fitness to the purpose of our investigation, we have further modified the scale by removing two items relating to homework and revisiting recorded lectures (BE5 and CE7 from the Sun and Rueda [19] scale), as these were not applicable to our case. Due to this change, it was imperative to ensure the reliability of the questionnaire, therefore we have calculated an internal consistency coefficient test (Cronbach's a) and the results indicated high internal consistency among the items comprising each scale.

Figure 2: Examples of Students Collaborating in the MUVE

To investigate the development of a TMS among groups working within the virtual world and address RQ2, we adopted the Transactive Memory System scale developed by Lewis [44]. The scale investigates the factors of Specialization, Credibility and Coordination and its interpretation suggests that when a TMS exists, it causes specialized knowledge, trust in each other's knowledge, and coordination in tasks processing.

While the reliability of the instruments used in this study was previously validated and reported, we have also performed reliability tests on the scales using the Cronbach's alpha coefficient. The results were consistent with the index reported by the original authors of each instrument; suggesting high reliability and internal consistencies among the items comprising each scale. All scales were measured using a 5-point Likert rating (5 = strongly agree, 4 = agree, 3 = neither agree nor disagree, 2 = disagree and 1 = strongly disagree). To collect the results, an online questionnaire was administered to students at the end of the experiment (available at [51]).

In addition to the quantitative data collected, we have employed observations and informal enquiries to collect additional data. This included classroom observations by tutors and informal discussions with students to better understand their behavior, performance, and environment use. The experiment was initiated with the assumption that the students had limited social interaction with each other, due to the fact that they were 1st year students who were only recently introduced to each other during the course induction week. The students were not expected to have specialization in any specific area, credibility, or any group coordination skills; attributes comprising the TMS phenomenon.

4. Results

Prior to conducting any statistical analyses, the data has been tested and verified for normality; therefore, parametric tests have been used. TMS results have first been investigated using descriptive statistics and are summarized in Table 2. It can be observed that the factors comprising TMS development have been perceived positively, suggesting that a TMS has been established among the working groups especially for Credibility and Coordination. These results are aligned with previous work [7, 46, 47, 49] validating the effectiveness of the MUVE we designed to support collaboration and TMS development.

Table 2: TMS Descriptive Statistics

Factor				
	M	SD	Min	Max
Specialization	3.34	.95	1	5
Credibility	4.1	.6	2.2	5
Coordination	4.03	.68	2.4	5
TMS	3.8	.6	2.33	5

The results indicate that there was overall medium to high Specialization among the students within the working groups, indicating that the students acknowledged and utilized the unique skills that different group members possessed. Mean Credibility is 4.1 out of 5 meaning that most of the students felt that the information shared, and actions taken during task execution by other members were credible and useful for the task at hand. Coordination construct measured how well the groups coordinate their actions, whether they needed to backtrack a lot and overall how well the coordination of activities achieved. Students in our sample thought that the coordination among their groups was good and that helped them achieve the output of each task. Thus, for us the above results confirm that the TMS was developed and the team members acknowledged the value of each member towards the achievement of the tasks' goals.

The Student Engagement results were then investigated, with respect to RQ1, to extract the students' perceptions of their Behavioral, Emotional and Cognitive Engagement when participating in learning activities within the MUVE and are summarized in Table 3. The results indicated that the students' Behavioral, Emotional and Cognitive Engagement were moderately high during activities. Students' indicated positive responses regarding their overall engagement with the course through the MUVE. For example, 75% of the students indicated that they constantly pay attention when they are taking the class in the MUVE; 58.3% mentioned they like taking the online class in the MUVE; 62.5% they feel excited by their work in the MUVE and 83.3% they mentioned they talk with people outside of school about what they are learning in the MUVE.

We understand that the environment itself might have affected how engaged students were with the material within the MUVE. A Pearson correlation test showed that the affordances, tools and design of the environment correlate significantly ($r=0.771$, $p=0.000$) with the student engagement scale. 66.7% rated the environment design was stimulating; 66.6%, thought that the object metaphors were intuitive; 75% mentioned that the amount of information displayed on the screen was adequate.

Table 3: Students' Engagement Descriptive Statistics

	M	SD	Min	Max
Behavioral Engagement	3.93	.89	1.50	5
Emotional Engagement	3.85	1.07	1.17	5
Cognitive Engagement	3.48	.82	2.00	5
Engagement Overall	3.75	.77	1.65	5

RQ2 of this study was set to investigate if there is correlation between Student Engagement and the development of TMS in a MUVE. Pearson correlation test was employed after all the assumptions met. The test revealed positive correlation ($r=.567$, $p=0.000$), between the two scales of TMS and Engagement. The relationship between the individual factors comprising TMS and Engagement were also assessed, revealing interesting correlations.

Table 4: Correlations Table

	Spec	Cred	Crd	BE	EE	CE
Spec	-	.34	.44	.24	.24	.56
Cred	.34	-	.69	.51	.42	.29
Crd	.44	.69	-	.53	.38	.32
BE	.24	.51	.53	-	.7	.39
EE	.24	.42	.38	.7	-	.42
CE	.56	.29	.32	.39	.42	-

**significant at the 0.05 level / ** significant at the 0.01 level. Spec=Specialization, Cred=Credibility, Crd=Coordination, BE=Behavioral, EE=Emotional, CE= Cognitive Engagement*

Specifically, the tests revealed positive correlation between Specialization and Cognitive Engagement ($r=.56$, $p=0.000$) indicating that the specialized knowledge and/or skills that members possessed relate to the cognitive engagement of the students. Credibility positively correlates to Behavioral ($r=.51$, $p=0.000$) and Emotional Engagement ($r=.42$, $p=0.003$) indicating that the development of credibility relates to how much involved is a student in terms of the behavior and emotional engagement to the course. Furthermore, positive correlation was also identified among Coordination with Behavioral ($r=.53$, $p=0.000$), and moderately positive correlation for Emotional ($r=.38$, $p=0.007$) and Cognitive Engagement ($r=.32$, $p=0.029$). This is an expected outcome since in order to coordinate actions within group activities students need to be highly engaged to the task.

4.1 Observations

One of the most interesting observations identified was that students were engaging in activities that required the team to delegate tasks in pairs or individuals. Tutors observed that activities requiring input from all students for a successful completion, was making students to contribute in order to make sure that they satisfy the rest of the team. This observation was later validated through the students' responses in the TMS questionnaire.

Another interesting behaviour observed by tutors was that the longer students were involved in the activity, the more they seemed to engage and be productive. It was also identified that students responded and delivered better and more complete results in less complicated tasks. Informal discussions between students and the teaching team, revealed that when a reward was offered upon task completion, students were engaging and persisting in trying to complete the activity. Tutors observed that the more the students were required to interact with each other during tasks, the more they kept engaged in the learning activities. This included not only knowledge transfer but also social interaction. Furthermore, since the student interactions established during task execution, active students appear to attract the attention of the disengaged students.

Some student groups were informally enquired about their group work at the end of each session, after the fourth week of the experiment. Students suggested that as time passed their collaboration evolved, they were becoming more confident in coordinating, communicating, delegating activities based on the skills of the individual team members, and trusted each other to complete their assigned tasks. These is in line the TMS results.

The students experience with the MUVE was also inquired and their responses were very positive towards the use of the environment to support the module. Students appreciated the immersive feeling of being in the virtual environment and the ability to collaborate and communicate with others in a technology enhanced learning setting. Students indicated that the environment was a useful addition to learning and that the learning experiences were enjoyable. The students also agreed that the use of the environment as an alternative method of learning and undertaking activities was very engaging, as it was different to the traditional sessions they are used to. Some students further discussed the ability of the environment to promote socialization by reducing awkwardness and shyness in social interactions.

However, some students indicated that the 3D graphical and 'gaming like' element of the environment was found as a distraction. Some students provided examples of students disengaging from the activity when finishing their assigned tasks early, and start editing their avatar, playing around or even disturbing other team members by virtually pushing, or spamming the chat room.

5. Discussion

The importance of promoting and accommodating for student engagement is crucial to ensure quality of learning. An effective modern classroom requires the use of technology, to establish effective collaboration among students, and utilization of learning activities that engage, stimulate and maintain the interest of students. The results of this study suggest that a MUVE can successfully engage students during collaborative learning tasks, through the building of TMS within groups. We have identified that when collaborative activities are designed within an MUVE, these can support Emotional, Behavioural, and Cognitive Engagement (RQ1), since Credibility, Specialisation and Coordination are achieved during the collaborative tasks. We have also determined that levels of Students' Engagement in a MUVE are significantly correlated with the factors that contribute to the development of a TMS within the environment (RQ2). In addition, as time passes, students are getting more familiar and develop better working relationships with their peers in the group and becoming more effective and productive.

Based on the results, observation, and lessons learned during this experimental project, some suggestions and considerations for the design of educational activities within a MUVE have been devised. Firstly, it is important to design activities that require equal input from all students, both in effort and time required for completion. This is necessary in order to ensure that all students are required to engage with the learning content for a successful outcome. Furthermore, it is important to ensure that the learning activities include elements that will involve all students of the group, to allow students time to focus and engage, as well as get to know their peers, each other abilities and capabilities. However, it is also important that these activities are intellectually stimulating and challenging to ensure that students are not losing interest.

Another aspect that an educator could consider is the social aspect of the activities which is essential in the learning process but also for the development of TMS. To promote social connections among students in the MUVE and in classroom, the activities design should aim to facilitate socialisation and let the students showcase their unique skills, knowledge and abilities so they can feel valuable to the group and valued by their peers. This can promote Cognitive and Emotional Engagement. This can be achieved by ensuring that a discussion, brainstorming, and/or information sharing is established within the group preferably at the beginning of the collaboration [7, 24]. Finally, the successful completion of activities should require students' attendance and participation in the MUVE, activities should require students to reflect on their learning in order to understand what they have been taught.

While this work has provided some very interesting insights on the topics under investigation, there are some limitations that may have impacted the results. One of the most important limitations of this research project is that students were also conducting activities offline as part of their normal university life, and this had an impact in their communication channels. However, this was a conscious decision as the module team wanted to ensure that the students would communicate and collaborate in real life as well as the virtual world, without being isolated during the semester. Future work will focus on collecting, further data in qualitative form that may help to develop a better understanding of the relationship between Engagement and TMS.

Acknowledgements

This project is partially funded by the European Union's Horizon 2020 research and innovation programme under grant agreements No. 739578 (RISE) and 810105 (CyCAT).

We would also like to thank the first year Business & Technology students at Sheffield Hallam University, for their participation in this research project.

REFERENCES

[1] Cardullo, V.M., Wilson, N.S., Zygouris-Coe, V.I. "Enhanced Student Engagement through Active Learning and Emerging Technologies". *Student Engagement and Participation: Concepts, Methodologies, Tools, and Applications: Concepts, Methodologies, Tools, and Applications*, Vol, 2017, pp. 399.

[2] Savin-Baden, M. "The Impact of Transdisciplinary Threshold Concepts on Student Engagement in Problem-Based Learning: A Conceptual Synthesis". *Interdisciplinary Journal of Problem-Based Learning*, Vol 10, (2), 2016, pp. 3.

[3] Chen, P.-S.D., Lambert, A.D., Guidry, K.R. "Engaging Online Learners: The Impact of Web-Based Learning Technology on College Student Engagement". *Computers & Education*, Vol 54, (4), 2010, pp. 1222-1232.

[4] Henrie, C.R., Halverson, L.R., Graham, C.R. "Measuring Student Engagement in Technology-Mediated Learning: A Review". *Computers & Education*, Vol 90, 2015, pp. 36-53.

[5] Junco, R., Elavsky, C.M., Heiberger, G. "Putting Twitter to the Test: Assessing Outcomes for Student Collaboration, Engagement and Success". *British Journal of Educational Technology*, Vol 44, (2), 2013, pp. 273-287.

[6] Boulos, M.N., Hetherington, L., Wheeler, S. "Second Life: An Overview of the Potential of 3-D Virtual Worlds in Medical and Health Education". *Health Information and Libraries Journal*, Vol 24, (4), 2007, pp. 233-45.

[7] Nisiotis, L., Kleanthous Loizou, S., Beer, M., Uruchurtu, E. 2017. The Development of Transactive Memory Systems in Collaborative Educational Virtual Worlds. In: D. Beck, C. Allison, L. Morgado, J. Pirker, F. Khosmood, J. Richter, and C. Gütl (eds.) Immersive Learning Research Network: Third International Conference, Ilrn 2017, Coimbra, Portugal, June 26–29, 2017. Proceedings. Cham: Springer International Publishing, 2017, 35-46

[8] Jarmon, L., Traphagan, T., Mayrath, M., Trivedi, A. "Virtual World Teaching, Experiential Learning, and Assessment: An Interdisciplinary Communication Course in Second Life". *Computers & Education*, Vol 53, (1), 2009, pp. 169-182.

[9] Wegner, D.M. 1987. Transactive Memory: A Contemporary Analysis of the Group Mind. Theories of Group Behavior. Springer, 1987, 185-208

[10] Astin, A.W. "Student Involvement: A Developmental Theory for Higher Education". *Journal of college student personnel*, Vol 25, (4), 1984, pp. 297-308.

[11] Trowler, V. "Student Engagement Literature Review. York: Higher Education Academy". *Trowler, V. and Trowler, P.(2010) Student Engagement Evidence Summary*, Vol, 2010, pp.

[12] Morgan, M., Sinclair, J., Butler, M., Thota, N., Fraser, J., Cross, G., Jackova, J. 2018. Understanding International Benchmarks on Student Engagement: Awareness and Research Alignment from a CS Perspective. Proceedings of the 2017 ITiCSE Conference on Working Group Reports. ACM, 1-24.

[13] Morgan, M., Butler, M., Thota, N., Sinclair, J. 2018. How Cs Academics View Student Engagement. Proceedings of the 23rd Annual ACM Conference on Innovation and Technology in Computer Science Education. ACM, 284-289.

[14] Gutica, M. 2018. Improving Students' Engagement with Large-Team Software Development Projects. Proceedings of the 23rd Annual ACM Conference on Innovation and Technology in Computer Science Education. ACM, 356-357.

[15] Butler, M., Morgan, M., Sheard, J., Falkner, K., Weerasinghe, A. 2015. Initiatives to Increase Engagement in First-Year Ict. Proceedings of the 2015 ACM Conference on Innovation and Technology in Computer Science Education. ACM, 308-313.

[16] Harrington, B., Chaudhry, A. 2017. Tracademic: Improving Participation and Engagement in Cs1/Cs2 with Gamified Practicals. Proceedings of the 2017 ACM Conference on Innovation and Technology in Computer Science Education. ACM, 347-352.

[17] Yang, Y.-F. "Engaging Students in an Online Situated Language Learning Environment". *Comp. Ass. Language Learning*, Vol 24, (2), 2011, pp. 181-198.

[18] Nakamaru, S. "Investment and Return: Wiki Engagement in a "Remedial" Esl Writing Course". *Journal of Research on Technology in Education*, Vol 44, (4), 2012, pp. 273-291.

[19] Sun, J.C.Y., Rueda, R. "Situational Interest, Computer Self-Efficacy and Self-Regulation: Their Impact on Student Engagement in Distance Education". *British Journal of Educational Technology*, Vol 43, (2), 2012, pp. 191-204.

[20] Fredricks, J.A., Blumenfeld, P., Friedel, J., Paris, A. 2005. School Engagement. In: K.A.M.L. Lippman (ed.) What Do Children Need to Flourish? : Springer, 2005, 305-321

[21] Cho, Y.H., Lim, K.Y. "Effectiveness of Collaborative Learning with 3d Virtual Worlds". *British Journal of Edu.Technology*, Vol 48, (1), 2017, pp. 202-211.

[22] Warburton, S., Garcia, M.P. "Analyzing Teaching Practices in Second Life". *Learning in Virtual Worlds: Research and Applications*, Vol, 2016, pp.

[23] Kamvisi, M., Kleanthous, S., Nisiotis, L. 2015. Experiences of Collaborating and Learning through Collab3dworld. In: M. Gardner, G. Christian, P. Johanna, and R. Jonathon, eds. Workshop, Short Paper and Poster Proceedings from the inaugural Immersive Learning Research Network Conference, Prague, CZ.

[24] Nisiotis, L., Beer, M., Uruchurtu, E. 2015. The Evaluation of a Cyber Campus to Support Distance Learning Activities. In: M. Gardner, G. Christian, P. Johanna, and R. Jonathon, eds. Workshop, Short Paper and Poster Proceedings from the inaugural ILRN Conference, Prague, CZ.

[25] Chou, C.C., Hart, R.K. "The Pedagogical Considerations in the Design of Virtual Worlds for Organization Learning". *Handbook of research on practices and outcomes in virtual worlds and environments*, Vol, 2012, pp. 551-569.

[26] Witmer, B.G., Singer, M.J. "Measuring Presence in Virtual Environments: A Presence Questionnaire". *Presence: Teleoperators and Virtual Environments*, Vol 7, (3), 1998, pp. 225-240.

[27] Steuer, J. "Defining Virtual Reality: Dimensions Determining Telepresence". *Journal of Communication*, Vol 42, (4), 1992, pp. 73-93.

[28] De Lucia, A., Francese, R., Passero, I., Tortora, G. "Development and Evaluation of a Virtual Campus on Second Life: The Case of Seconddmi". *Computers & Education*, Vol 52, (1), 2009, pp. 220-233.

[29] Dede, C., Salzman, M.C., Loftin, R.B., Sprague, D. 1999. Multisensory Immersion as a Modeling Environment for Learning Complex Scientific Concepts. Modeling and Simulation in Science and Mathematics Education. Springer, 1999, 282-319

[30] Winn, W., Windschitl, M., Hedly, N., Postner, L. 2001. Learning Science in an Immersive Virtual Environment. Annual Meeting of the American Educational Research Association, Seattle, WA.

[31] Schrader, C., Bastiaens, T.J. "The Influence of Virtual Presence: Effects on Experienced Cognitive Load and Learning Outcomes in Educational Computer Games". *Computers in Human Behavior*, Vol 28, (2), 2012, pp. 648-658.

[32] Claman, F.L. "The Impact of Multiuser Virtual Environments on Student Engagement". *Nurse education in practice*, Vol 15, (1), 2015, pp. 13-16.

[33] Gregory, S., Gregory, B., Wood, D., Grant, S., Nikolic, S., Hillier, M., Hearns, M., Jacka, L., Mcdonald, M., Reiners, T. "Me, Us and It: Insiders' Views of the Complex Technical, Organisational and Personal Elements in Using Virtual Worlds in Education". Vol, 2017, pp.

[34] Connor, E. "Perceptions and Uses of Clicker Technology". *Journal of Electronic Resources in Medical Libraries*, Vol 6, (1), 2009, pp. 19-32.

[35] Toth, D., Kayler, M. 2015. Integrating Role-Playing Games into Computer Science Courses as a Pedagogical Tool. Proceedings of the 46th ACM Technical Symposium on Computer Science Education. ACM, 386-391.

[36] Robinson, C.C., Hullinger, H. "New Benchmarks in Higher Education: Student Engagement in Online Learning". *Journal of Education for Business*, Vol 84, (2), 2008, pp. 101-109.

[37] Holmes, N. "Engaging with Assessment: Increasing Student Engagement through Continuous Assessment". *Active Learning in Higher Education*, Vol 19, (1), 2018, pp. 23-34.

[38] Blin, F., Munro, M. "Why Hasn't Technology Disrupted Academics' Teaching Practices? Understanding Resistance to Change through the Lens of Activity Theory". *Computers & Education*, Vol 50, (2), 2008, pp. 475-490.

[39] Theiner, G. "Transactive Memory Systems: A Mechanistic Analysis of Emergent Group Memory". *Review of Philosophy and Psychology*, Vol 4, (1), 2013, pp. 65-89.

[40] Michinov, E., Olivier-Chiron, E., Rusch, E., Chiron, B. "Influence of Transactive Memory on Perceived Performance, Job Satisfaction and Identification in Anaesthesia Teams". *British journal of anaesthesia*, Vol 100, (3), 2008, pp. 327-332.

[41] Hollingshead, A.B., Brandon, D.P. "Potential Benefits of Communication in Transactive Memory Systems". *Human communication research*, Vol 29, (4), 2003, pp. 607-615.

[42] Kotlarsky, J., van den Hooff, B., Houtman, L. "Are We on the Same Page? Knowledge Boundaries and Transactive Memory System Development in Cross-Functional Teams". *Comm. research*, Vol 42, (3), 2015, pp. 319-344.

[43] Kahn, A.S., Williams, D. "We're All in This (Game) Together: Transactive Memory Systems, Social Presence, and Team Structure in Multiplayer Online Battle Arenas". *Communication Research*, Vol 43, (4), 2016, pp. 487-517.

[44] Lewis, K. "Measuring Transactive Memory Systems in the Field: Scale Development and Validation". *J of App. Psy.*, Vol 88, (4), 2003, pp. 587-603.

[45] Loizou, S.K., Dimitrova, V. "Adaptive Notifications to Support Knowledge Sharing in Close-Knit Virtual Communities". *User Modeling and User-Adapted Interaction*, Vol 23, (2-3), 2013, pp. 287-343.

[46] Kleanthous, S., Michael, M., Samaras, G., Christodoulou, E. 2016. Transactive Memory in Task-Driven 3d Virtual World Teams. Proceedings of the 9th Nordic Conference on Human-Computer Interaction (ACM). 93.

[47] Nisiotis, L., Kleanthous, S. 2018. The Development and Evolution of Transactive Memory System over Time in Muves. 10th Computer Science and Electronic Engineering Conference. IEEE.

[48] McGrath, J.E., Hollingshead, A.B. "Putting the" Group" Back in Group Support Systems: Some Theoretical Issues About Dynamic Processes in Groups with Technological Enhancements". *Group support systems: New perspectives*, Vol, 1993, pp. 78-96.

[49] Kleanthous, S., Kapitsaki, G.M. 2018. Analyzing the Transactive Memory in Teaching Software Engineering. Proceedings of the 40th ICSE: Companion Proceeedings. ACM, 145-146.

[50] Instructions to Connect to VirtualSHU. Available From: http://virtualshu.com/instructions.html

[51] Data Collection Instruments Used in this Study. Available From: http://www.virtualshu.com/instruments.html

Are There Differences in Learning Gains When Programming a Tangible Object or a Simulation?

Grégoire Fessard
Institut Supérieur d'Électronique de Paris
Paris, France
gregoire.fessard@isep.fr

Patrick Wang
Institut Supérieur d'Électronique de Paris
Paris, France
patrick.wang@isep.fr

Ilaria Renna
Institut Supérieur d'Électronique de Paris
Paris, France
ilaria.renna@isep.fr

ABSTRACT

Physical computing is about programming and interacting with a tangible object to learn fundamental concepts of Computer Science (CS). This approach presents several benefits regarding motivation, creativity, and learning gains. Yet, these learning gains hardly are compared with those resulting from the programming of a simulation of a tangible object. In this article we present the results of a comparative study that has been conducted to explore this issue. With this study, we aimed to determine whether the programming of a tangible object or its digital simulation yields significantly different learning gains. In the experiment we conducted, participants (aged 14-17 with little or no prior programming knowledge) were divided into two groups: one programmed a tangible electronic board (the BBC micro:bit) while the other programmed a simulation of it. The results of this experiment suggest that, while each group significantly improved their understandings of fundamental CS concepts (i.e., variables, conditions, and loops), no significant difference was found when comparing the learning gains between the two groups.

CCS CONCEPTS

• **Human-centered computing → User studies**; • **Social and professional topics → Computing education**.

KEYWORDS

computer science education; comparative study; physical computing; digital computing; block-based programming

ACM Reference Format:
Grégoire Fessard, Patrick Wang, and Ilaria Renna. 2019. Are There Differences in Learning Gains When Programming a Tangible Object or a Simulation?. In *Innovation and Technology in Computer Science Education (ITiCSE '19), July 15–17, 2019, Aberdeen, Scotland UK*. ACM, New York, NY, USA, 7 pages. https://doi.org/10.1145/3304221.3319747

ITiCSE '19, July 15–17, 2019, Aberdeen, Scotland UK

ACM ISBN 978-1-4503-6301-3/19/07...$15.00
https://doi.org/10.1145/3304221.3319747

1 INTRODUCTION

Physical computing refers to the "design of tangible and interactive object using programmable hardware" [19]. Physical computing differentiates itself from a more traditional teaching approach that uses the command line as sole interface to the program execution. With the development of programmable robots and electronic boards, researchers took an interest in physical computing as a means to introduce computer science and programming to teenagers [9, 24]. However, and while focused on identifying the benefits of physical computing, these studies do not compare their results with what could be achieved with *digital* computing (i.e., the programming of a simulation of a tangible object).

In this article, we present a study designed to determine whether physical computing is more beneficial than digital computing (or vice-versa) to the learning and understanding of basic programming concepts (namely variables, conditional structures, and iterative structures). For this study, we have conducted an experiment which uses the BBC micro:bit. This electronic board can be programmed using a block-based programming language and was provided to our participants under either its tangible or simulated form.

In the following section, we provide a literature review of the use of physical computing to introduce programming to teenagers. In particular, we also look at block-based programming languages as they are often implemented in physical computing systems. In Sections 3 and 4, we describe the programming environment and the experimental protocol used in this study. Section 5 presents the results obtained in our experiment. Finally, the last two sections are dedicated to a discussion of our results and a description of future works that we plan on conducting.

2 LITERATURE REVIEW

The literature review on Computer Science Education has thoroughly investigated the learners' misconceptions and difficulties related to programming. For example, du Boulay [5] identifies three main difficulties. The first one concerns *notation* which refers to the difficulty of mastering the syntax and semantics of a programming language. The second difficulty relates to *structures* i.e., designing algorithms with the smallest units of programming instructions. The third difficulty is understanding the concept of *notional machine* which means realizing that the behavior of a machine is dictated by the programs being executed and the interactions the user has with this machine. Some more practical difficulties are also mentioned in the state of the art, and in particular regarding students' misconceptions of programming concepts [20, 26].

Visual programming languages, and especially block-based ones, are often used to alleviate the first two aforementioned difficulties. These programming languages are designed to allow learners to focus on the structure of an algorithm rather than on the syntax required to implement such algorithm. A comparative study between block-based and text-based programming languages showed that the use of a block-based programming language led to a better understanding of key programming notions [28]. This result explains the many studies benefiting from the use of block-based programming languages in introductory programming courses [17, 29].

Constructionism [18] is a theory often cited in Computer Science Education research which stipulates that "building knowledge structures [...] happen especially felicitously in a context where the learner is consciously engaged in constructing a public entity" [18, p. 1]. This theory is sometimes used to tackle the third difficulty we previously mentioned: there is a strong relation between designing a programmable object and seeing its behavior responds to changes in its program. As a result, constructionism paved the way to numerous studies using programmable objects in introductory programming courses. In the literature, such programmable objects could take two different shapes: they could either be tangible (e.g., LEGO Mindstorms [3], .NET Gadgeteer [9], or Thymio II [14]) or digital (e.g., Scratch [21] or Alice [4]).

Since physical computing concerns the design of tangible and programmable object, it is in a way inspired by constructionism. The literature review on physical computing highlights several advantages: increased learners' motivation and creativity [24], the inclusion of underrepresented minorities in Computer Science [23], and learning gains [3]. However, similar results can be also found when digital programmable objects are used to introduce Computer Science and programming [4, 15, 17].

Both situations (physical and digital computing) lead to learning gains, yet there is (to the best of our knowledge) no study trying to assess whether a situation is more beneficial than the other. The literature on Computer Science Education presents few studies using both a tangible programmable object and an equivalent simulation [2, 6, 8]. However, these articles do not compare learning gains but rather describe a system in which tangible and digital objects are complementary.

In this study, we wish to fill this gap in the literature by comparing the learning gains obtained from programming a tangible object or an identical simulation. Therefore, we ask the following research question: "are there differences in learning gains when programming a tangible object or an equivalent simulation of it?" In particular, we focused on the learning of three essential programming notions namely variables, conditional structures, and iterative structures. We thus re-formulate the previous question to focus on the learning of these three concepts.

To answer these three questions, we have developed a programming environment (described in the following section) with the objective of providing an identical user experience whether the user programs a tangible object or its simulation.

3 PROGRAMMING ENVIRONMENT

The programming environment used in our experiment consists of two components: the BBC micro:bit as the programmable object and the programming Web interface which implements a block-based programming language. Because we wish to compare the effects of physical and digital computing on students' learning gains, this programming environment comes in two versions: one for programming the tangible BBC micro:bit and the other for programming its simulation. These two versions provide an almost identical programming user experience as described in the following sections.

3.1 Programmable Object

The BBC micro:bit[1] is a programmable electronic board first released in 2016 in the United Kingdom. The objective of such an initiative was to make programming more accessible to teenagers by distributing these devices to middle school pupils aged 12-13 for free [1]. Since then, the BBC micro:bit has been used in several research projects related to introductory Computer Science courses, with positive results regarding the students' motivation, creativity, and basic knowledge of programming [22, 24, 25].

The micro:bit is a 4×5 cm pocket device that is equipped with a 256 kB flash memory and an ARM processor that controls all the components on the board. Some of these components are used to manage inputs and outputs. In particular, the micro:bit has an accelerometer, two push buttons, and a 5×5 grid of LEDs (see Figure 1). Because we target elementary programming notions, components that require at least a basic understanding of event-driven computing were not used in our experiment. As a consequence, we mainly took advantage of the LEDs to display information to the users. These LEDs can display alphanumeric characters or predefined shapes (see, for example, the heart in Figure 2, Zone 3). Longer texts can also be displayed on this grid thanks to a scrolling mechanism.

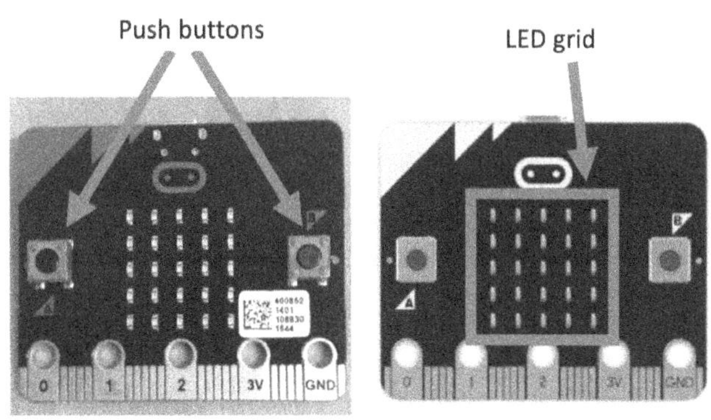

Figure 1: On the left, the tangible micro:bit card. On the right, a digital simulation.

To simulate the micro:bit, open source programs can be found on the Internet. For our experiment, we have exploited a program written in Javascript[2] which allowed us to easily implement the micro:bit simulation in our programming Web interface. This simulation was mainly used to display messages with the LEDs but it could also have replicated the effects of pressing the push buttons or activating the accelerometer if we wanted to use these components.

[1] https://microbit.org/
[2] https://github.com/Microsoft/pxt-microbit

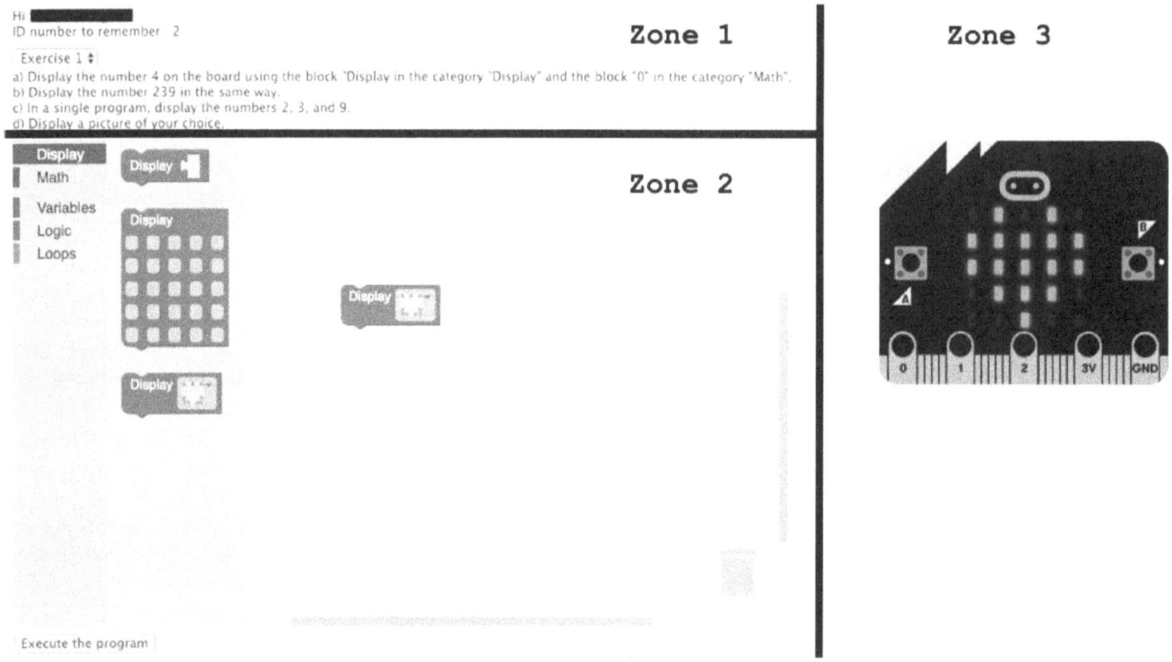

Figure 2: The block-based Web interface for programming the simulation of the micro:bit.

The execution of a program on the tangible micro:bit requires that it is connected to a computer via a USB cable. Its firmware can be updated by transferring a binary file to the flash memory of the micro:bit; this file actually contains the new program to be executed. The process of executing a program on the simulation is a little different: Javascript functions we have implemented are called to update the behavior of the simulation displayed on the screen. The internal process of executing a program on the tangible or simulated micro:bits might be different but, as explained in Section 3.2, it is invisible to the user: the simple action of pressing a button on the programming Web interface will let the user execute a program in both situations (with a tangible or a simulated micro:bit).

The two versions of the micro:bit can generate identical results for a same program. This was done to ensure an identical programming experience for the user regardless of the programmable object used. The only difference between the tangible and digital micro:bit lies in the space in which they can be manipulated. The interactions with the physical micro:bit can happen in a three-dimensional space: the board can be moved or flipped over. However, the digital micro:bit is statically represented in two dimensions on the computer screen: it cannot be moved nor rotated around any axis.

3.2 Programming Interface

We have developed a programming Web interface to program the micro:bit (see Figure 2). This interface implements Blockly[3], a library that allows users to write code using a block-based visual programming language. Two versions of this interface were also developed: one for programming the tangible micro:bit and one for programming its simulation. However these two interfaces differ in only a small part as described later in this section. Figure 2 illustrates the interface designed to program the micro:bit simulation. It can be divided in 3 main zones of interest.

Zone 1 displays some identification information related to the current user and a drop down menu which can be used to select a programming exercise out of all the proposed ones. The wording of the currently selected exercise is displayed beneath this drop down menu. These exercises are the same whether the user is programming the tangible or simulated micro:bit. The design of these exercises will be detailed in Section 4.2.

Zone 2 corresponds to the code edition area. The left-hand part in grey displays all the categories of blocks that can be used with this programming interface. For this experiment, we proposed five different categories: Display, Math, Variables, Logic, and Loops. Each category contains blocks that are specific to their theme. As an example, we will explain in details the "Display" category showed in Figure 2. This category contains three different blocks:

- the first one must be completed with another block in order to display a number on the micro:bit;
- the second block of this category allows the user to design a shape and to display it on the board;
- the last block can be used to display a pre-configured pictograph.

A user can build a program by dragging and dropping blocks from whichever category into the workspace (with the white background). A user can also create more complex programs by combining several different blocks like shown in Figure 3.

Zone 3 is the only zone of the programming interface that is different between the tangible and the simulation case. If the user programs the simulated micro:bit, Zone 3 displays the simulation

[3] https://developers.google.com/blockly/

which is updated each time the program is executed. If the user programs the tangible micro:bit, the simulation is replaced with instructions on how to execute a program on the tangible device.

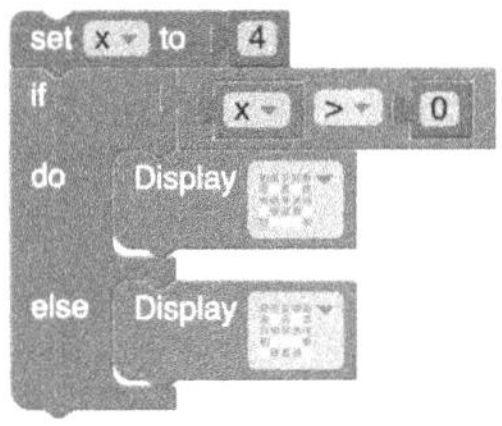

Figure 3: An example of a complex program written with multiple blocks.

We have made the process of executing the program on the micro:bit identical whether the user is programming the tangible or simulated device. Indeed, the user simply needs to click on the button located at the bottom of Zone 2. If programming the simulation, the program is directly executed on the display. If programming the tangible micro:bit, this leads to the block-based program being converted into a binary file and automatically transferred to the device. This results in an identical user experience whether the programmable object used is the tangible or simulated one.

4 EXPERIMENTAL PROTOCOL

To provide answers to our research questions, we have conducted an experimentation with teenagers aged 14-17 (n = 36, μ = 15.6 year old, with 9 girls and 27 boys). We asked the participants to assess their prior knowledge of programming before the experiment took place. Of the 36 participants, 23 declared having "no prior knoledge" and 13 affirmed having a "basic understanding" of programming. These participants were divided into two groups: one programming the tangible micro:bit and the other programming its simulation. The group composition has been defined prior to the experiment so as to balance both groups in terms of age, gender, and prior knowledge. This distribution was validated by a post-experiment analysis, which is presented in Section 5.1. The experimental protocol designed for this study is composed of a pre- and post-test questionnaire and a set of programming exercises (as seen in Figure 2, Zone 1). The questionnaire and exercises targeted the notions of variables, conditional structures, and iterative structures. Since we did not make any assumption, the hypothesis we wanted to test was that programming a tangible object or its simulation causes different learning gains for each of these concepts.

The experiment went through four phases. The first phase consisted in a presentation to our participants of the programming Web interface and its block-based programming language. During this phase, we did not introduce any concept of programming except for the display of information on the grid of LEDs. Indeed, this was necessary for the participants to understand the pre-test questionnaire, which was administered during the second phase of the experiment. The third phase consisted in working on the programming exercises. Finally, the fourth phase concerned the answering of the post-test questionnaire. During the whole duration of the experiment, participants were asked to work individually and we would intervene only to provide a technical support.

4.1 Pre-Test and Post-Test Questionnaire

The pre- and post-test questionnaire was composed of 14 multiple choice questions: five on the concept of variables, five on conditional structures, and four on iterative structures. For each notion, the questions were ordered in an increasing difficulty. We based this ordering and the design of the questionnaire on the revised Bloom's taxonomy [11].

Each question asked for the result of a small program written with blocks. The blocks used in this questionnaire actually were identical to the ones implemented in the programming Web interface. This design decision was made to suppress the risk of misunderstanding the programs written in each question.

These questions were also designed to require knowledge of a single and unique programming notion at a time. For example, we did not introduce questions using the notion of loop variable because it would necessitate to use knowledge related to both variables and iterative structures. This detail is important in the design of our study because it would have been much more difficult to identify separately the learning gains for each concept otherwise. Figure 4 illustrates three questions that we used, one for each concept (ie., variables, conditionals, and loops).

Each question only has a single correct answer. We based the design of the other wrong answers on the literature review on students' misconceptions [20, 26]. This makes for plausible answers that participants might be inclined to select.

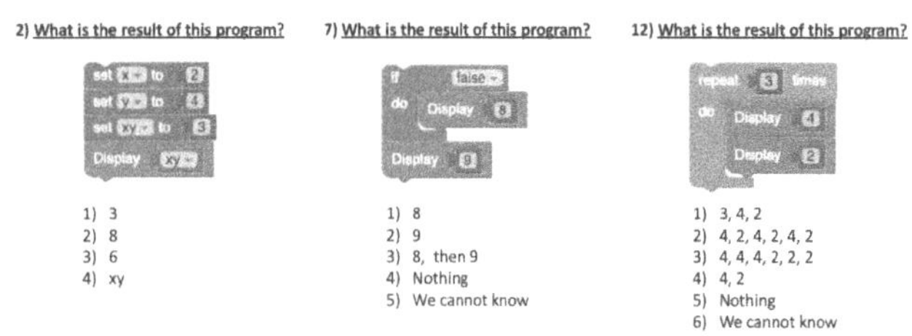

Figure 4: Three examples of questions used in the pre- and post-test questionnaire: left for variables, center for conditionals, right for loops.

4.2 Programming Exercises

During the third phase of the experiment, participants had 15 programming exercises to solve. Of these 15 exercises, four were on variables, three on conditional structures, and four on iterative structures. We also designed an exercise which was to be solved before all the others to familiarize our participants to the programming environment. We proposed another three exercises mixing concepts which were to be solved after all the others.

The design of the programming exercises used the same approach we have described in Section 4.1 for the pre- and post-test questionnaire. We used Qian and Lehman's literature review [20] to design exercises that could lead our participants into making mistakes and learning from them. The exercises were also proposed in an increasing level of difficulty; for each concept, the level of details provided in the wordings decreased while the number of blocks to manipulate increased from an exercise to the following one. Figure 5 illustrates this last point with two exercises of different levels of difficulties: Exercise 5 corresponds to the last exercise on variables and Exercise 6 is the first one on conditional structures. Exercise 6 explicitly tells the learner which blocks should be used to solve the exercise while the wording of Exercise 5 is less detailed.

Participants were asked to do the exercises in the order they were proposed. However, our interface did not implement any automated assessment tool and the participants were free to go to the next exercise as they pleased. They were also authorized to go back to any previous exercise to see or modify their solutions as they were displayed back in the editor in Zone 2 of the programming interface.

This last point implies that the states of the exercises are saved from an exercise to the other. We also have implemented functions to save all the participants' interactions with the programming interface. These logs are not detailed in this article as they will be used in a later stage of this research project.

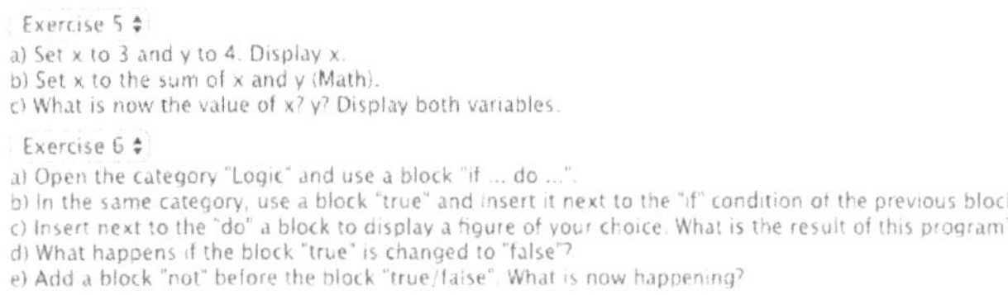

Figure 5: Two examples of questions with different levels of details in their wordings.

5 RESULTS

5.1 Validation of the Experimental Protocol

As mentioned in Section 4, the experiment gathered 36 participants aged 14-17. These participants were separated into two groups:

- The first group programmed the tangible micro:bit ($n = 18$, $\mu = 15.6$ year old). This group was composed of five girls and 13 boys. Eleven participants declared having no prior knowledge of programming and seven having an elementary understanding of programming.
- The second group programmed the simulation of the micro:bit ($n = 18$, $\mu = 14.8$ year old). This group was composed of four girls and 14 boys. In this group, 12 participants declared having no prior knowledge of programming and six having an elementary understanding of programming.

Because the participants were divided into groups before the start of the experiment, we wanted to verify that this distribution did not introduce a preliminary bias regarding the average initial programming knowledge of each group. Thus, we performed a two-tailed unpaired t-test to verify that the two groups were homogeneous in terms of initial programming knowledge. The results of this test ($t = 1.499$, $p = 0.145 > 0.05$) indicate that the mean scores obtained by each group for the pre-test were not significantly different. This first result confirms that the *a priori* group compositions did not introduce any initial bias in our experiment.

5.2 Learning Gains

Table 1 summarizes the scores obtained at the pre- and post-test.

5.2.1 Overall learning gains. We wanted to verify that participants to our experiment had significantly higher post-test scores, which would validate the design of our programming exercises. For this analysis, we performed two one-tailed paired t-tests: once for the group programming the tangible micro:bit and once for the group programming the simulated micro:bit. The results of the test ($t = 8.574$, $p = 7.014e\text{-}8 \ll 0.05$) suggest that the scores obtained at the post-test were significantly higher than those obtained at the pre-test for the participants programming the tangible micro:bit. A similar conclusion can be drawn for the participants programming the simulation of the micro:bit ($t = 5.242$, $p = 3.311e\text{-}5 \ll 0.05$). This aspect validates the design of our exercises to introduce elementary concepts to participants with little or no prior knowledge of programming.

We also wanted to compare the learning gains between each group by performing a two-tailed unpaired t-test. For each participant, the learning gain was calculated by subtracting the pre-test score to the post-test score. The results of this test ($t = 0.687$, $p = 0.497 > 0.05$) suggest that there was no significant difference between the average learning gains of each group.

5.2.2 Variables. We first evaluated the learning gains related to the concept of variables. We have used, for both groups, a one-tailed paired t-test to determine whether the results of the post-test were better than those of the pre-test. Regarding the group programming the tangible object, no significant increase could be found ($t = 0.325$, $p = 0.375 > 0.05$). The results concerning the group programming the simulation are similar ($t = 1.046$, $p = 0.155 > 0.05$).

Since both groups did not significantly improve their scores from pre-test to post-test, we did not pursue our analysis any further with a comparison of the learning gains between each group.

5.2.3 Conditional Structures. We have performed a similar analysis regarding the concept of conditional structures. For the group programming the tangible object, the results of the one-tailed paired t-test ($t = 6.556$, $p = 2.449e\text{-}6 \ll 0.05$) show that the scores have significantly improved from pre-test to post-test. A similar conclusion can be drawn for the group programming the simulation ($t = 6.761$, $p = 1.664e\text{-}6 \ll 0.05$). These results suggest that both groups have improved their understandings of conditional structures.

We have continued our analysis to highlight whether one group had higher learning gains than the other. Since we do not make any assumption as to which programming environment yields better results, we have performed a two-tailed unpaired t-test. The results ($t = 1.425$, $p = 0.163 > 0.05$) suggest that there is no significant difference in learning gains on conditional structures when a student programs a tangible object or a simulation.

5.2.4 Iterative Structures. Finally, we have run the same tests for the concept of iterative structures. The results of the one-tailed paired t-tests ($t = 6.174$ and $p = 5.099e\text{-}6 \ll 0.05$ for the group programming the tangible micro:bit, and $t = 3.915$ and $p = 5.579e\text{-}4 \ll 0.05$ for the group programming the simulated micro:bit) show that both groups significantly improved their scores from pre-test to post-test, indicating a better understanding of iterative structures.

However, and once again, the results of the two-tailed unpaired t-test ($t = 0.586$, $p = 0.562 > 0.05$) show that the two programming

Table 1: Results of the pre- and post-test for each group of participants.

Group	Variables (5 pts)		Conditional Structures (5 pts)		Iterative Structures (4 pts)	
	Pre-test	Post-test	Pre-test	Post-test	Pre-test	Post-test
Tangible micro:bit	$\mu = 4.167$	$\mu = 4.222$	$\mu = 1.667$	$\mu = 4.167$	$\mu = 2.389$	$\mu = 3.444$
	$\sigma^2 = 0.735$	$\sigma^2 = 0.889$	$\sigma^2 = 1.059$	$\sigma^2 = 1.441$	$\sigma^2 = 0.840$	$\sigma^2 = 0.497$
Simulated micro:bit	$\mu = 3.611$	$\mu = 4.000$	$\mu = 1.389$	$\mu = 3.222$	$\mu = 2.222$	$\mu = 3.111$
	$\sigma^2 = 2.605$	$\sigma^2 = 0.941$	$\sigma^2 = 0.605$	$\sigma^2 = 1.595$	$\sigma^2 = 0.771$	$\sigma^2 = 0.928$

environments seem to lead to equivalent learning gains regarding iterative structures.

6 DISCUSSION

The results of our study suggest that, while both groups significantly improved their scores at the post-test, there is no significant difference in learning gains when a student programs a tangible object or an exact equivalent simulation of it. A possible explanation for these results could be the fact that the experiment did not heavily rely on the manipulation of the tangible micro:bit. Indeed, the design of our exercises did not encourage participants to interact physically with the tangible device and the handling of the micro:bit had no impact on the program being executed. Still, these results question the benefits of using physical computing to learn elementary programming concepts as mentioned in the literature.

Our study involves participants that are older than the students usually initiated to programming with physical computing. The rationale behind this design decision is that we wanted to have participants that could progress in the activities without our assistance. Indeed, we did not teach any preliminary knowledge nor helped the participants during the experiment. Moreover, this let us have a really controlled set-up for this initial study about comparing learning gains using a tangible object or its simulation.

Regarding the concept of variable, results did not show any significant learning gain between the pre-test and the post-test. Indeed, both groups obtained good pre-test scores as shown in Table 1, which left little space for improvement in the post-test. We identified two possible reasons: the questions were too simple or the notion of variable is much easier to understand than the others. This last point can actually also be found in other studies [29].

Our experiment presents several possible points of improvement. Firstly, participants could interact with the programming environment only for half a day. Although our results show a significant learning gain for each group, it would be interesting to analyze data from a longer experiment conducted for example in an institutional context. Such an experiment would make it possible to comment on the interest of using programmable tangible objects in introductory programming courses.

Secondly, while our experiment involved a non-negligible sample size, it could be interesting to run a study with more participants. This would allow us to have a more representative sample from a statistical point of view. The results of such an experiment would complement those presented in this article and would also provide a stronger conclusion regarding the interest of using physical computing for the introduction and learning of programming.

7 CONCLUSION AND FUTURE WORK

In this article, we presented a study which compared the learning gains when a learner programs a tangible object or its simulation. The results indicate that, although a significant learning is observed in both cases, these situations appear to be broadly equivalent in terms of overall programming learning gains. More specifically, we could not observe a significant difference between these two situations regarding the learning of conditional and iterative structures. This conclusion questions us about the intrinsic benefits of physical programming sometimes mentioned in the literature. To further explore the potential benefits of physical and digital programming we plan to, in the future, improve our experimental set-up as follow.

The first area for future work concerns the study of learners' behaviors when they face a programming environment involving a tangible object or a simulation. During our experiment, learners had to answer a meta-cognitive [7, 13] questionnaire designed to evaluate how they situate themselves in the learning process [30]. In particular, we wish to evaluate if they experienced a flow [10] while learning programming and if this kind of exercise could improve their empowerment [12]. In this way, we hope to be able to provide additional answers about the extent of motivation and creativity when learners use physical and/or digital programming.

During the experiment, we also recorded the users interactions with the programming interfaces: all the participants' actions and mouse positions were logged. We are going to analyze this data to search for patterns or strategies used by learners to solve the programming exercises. Moreover, by looking at the participants' actions from one exercise to the other, we also aim to highlight the evolution of their understandings of a specific programming concept. Finally, this analysis will be coupled with the results of the pre- and post-tests to find possible correlations between learning strategies and learning gains.

Finally, we wish to conduct two new experiments. The first one will improve the study presented in this article by addressing the lack of physical interactions previously discussed. With a similar set-up (i.e., homogeneity of initial knowledge, same age group, balanced distribution between girls and boys), this new experiment will benefit from the push buttons and accelerometer present on the micro:bit and mentioned in Section 3.1 to engage participants in physically interacting with the tangible board. The second experiment will be designed to identify learning gains differences when physical computing is used in STEM (Science, Technology, Engineering, Mathematics). Some articles already present this type of practice [16, 27] and the idea is to conduct a similar comparative study with younger participants to highlight the benefits of physical computing in learning STEM notions.

REFERENCES

[1] Thomas Ball, Jonathan Protzenko, Judith Bishop, Michal Moskal, Jonathan de Halleux, Michael Braun, Steve Hodges, and Claire Riley. 2016. Microsoft Touch Develop and the BBC micro:bit. In *2016 IEEE/ACM 38th International Conference on Software Engineering Companion (ICSE-C)*. IEEE, Austin, TX, USA, 637–640.

[2] Philipp Brauner, Thiemo Leonhardt, Martina Ziefle, and Ulrik Schroeder. 2010. The Effect of Tangible Artifacts, Gender and Subjective Technical Competence on Teaching Programming to Seventh Graders. In *Teaching Fundamentals Concepts of Informatics*. Springer Berlin Heidelberg, Berlin, Heidelberg, 61–71.

[3] Daniel C. Cliburn. 2006. Experiences with the LEGO Mindstorms Throughout the Undergraduate Computer Science Curriculum. In *Proceedings. Frontiers in Education. 36th Annual Conference*. IEEE, San Diego, CA, USA, 1–6.

[4] Stephen Cooper, Wanda Dann, and Randy Pausch. 2000. Alice: a 3-D Tool for Introductory Programming Concepts. In *Proceedings of the Fifth Annual CCSC Northeastern Conference on The Journal of Computing in Small Colleges (CCSC '00)*. Consortium for Computing Sciences in Colleges, USA, 107–116. http://dl.acm.org/citation.cfm?id=364132.364161

[5] Benedict du Boulay. 1986. Some Difficulties of Learning to Program. *Journal of Educational Computing Research* 2, 1 (1986), 57–73.

[6] Barry Fagin. 2003. Ada/Mindstorms 3.0. *IEEE Robotics & Automation Magazine* 10, 2 (2003), 19–24.

[7] John H. Flavell. 1979. Metacognition and cognitive monitoring: a new area of cognitive-developmental inquiry. *American Psychologist* 34, 10 (1979), 906–911.

[8] Aaron Garrett and David Thornton. 2005. A Web-Based Programming Environment for LEGO Mindstorms Robots. In *Proceedings of the 43rd Annual Southeast Regional Conference - Volume 2 (ACM-SE 43)*. ACM, New York, NY, USA, 349–350. https://doi.org/10.1145/1167253.1167333

[9] Steve Hodges, James Scott, Sue Sentance, Colin Miller, Nicolas Villar, Scarlet Schwiderski-Grosche, Kerry Hammil, and Steven Johnston. 2013. .NET Gadgeteer: A New Platform for K-12 Computer Science Education. In *Proceeding of the 44th ACM Technical Symposium on Computer Science Education (SIGCSE '13)*. ACM, New York, NY, USA, 391–396. https://doi.org/10.1145/2445196.2445315

[10] Paolo Inghilleri, Giuseppe Riva, and Eleonora Riva. 2018. *Enabling Positive Change*. https://content.sciendo.com/view/title/506140

[11] David R. Krathwohl. 2002. A Revision of Bloom's Taxonomy: An Overview. *Theory Into Practice* 41, 4 (2002), 212–218.

[12] Creative Commons Attribution ShareAlike 4.0 International License. 2015. *Introduction to Physical Computing*. Technical Report. Maker Education Initiative.

[13] Jennifer Livingston. 2003. Metacognition: An Overview. (01 2003).

[14] Stéphane Magnenat, Fanny Riedo, Michael Bonani, and Francesco Mondada. 2012. A Programming Workshop Using the Robot "Thymio II": The Effect on the Understanding by Children. In *2012 IEEE Workshop on Advanced Robotics and its Social Impacts*. IEEE, Munich, Germany, 24–29.

[15] Louis Major, Theocharis Kyriacou, and Pearl Brereton. 2014. The Effectiveness of Simulated Robots for Supporting the Learning of Introductory Programming: a Multi-Case Case Study. *Computer Science Education* 24, 2-3 (2014), 193–228.

[16] Michela Maschietto and Sophie Soury-Lavergne. 2013. Designing a Duo of Material and Digital Artifacts: the Pascaline and Cabri Elem e-Books in Primary School Mathematics. *ZDM* 45, 7 (2013), 959–971.

[17] Orni Meerbaum-Salant, Michal Armoni, and Mordechai Ben-Ari. 2013. Learning Computer Science Concepts with Scratch. *Computer Science Education* 23, 3 (2013), 239–264.

[18] Seymour Papert and Idit Harel. 1991. Situating Constructionism. *Constructionism* 36, 2 (1991), 1–11.

[19] Mareen Przybylla and Ralf Romeike. 2014. Key Competences with Physical Computing. *KEYCIT 2014–Key Competencies in Informatics and ICT (Preliminary Proceedings)* (2014), 216.

[20] Yizhou Qian and James Lehman. 2017. Students' Misconceptions and Other Difficulties in Introductory Programming: A Literature Review. *ACM Trans. Comput. Educ.* 18, 1, Article 1 (Oct. 2017), 24 pages. https://doi.org/10.1145/3077618

[21] Mitchel Resnick, John Maloney, Andrés Monroy-Hernández, Natalie Rusk, Evelyn Eastmond, Karen Brennan, Amon Millner, Eric Rosenbaum, Jay Silver, Brian Silverman, et al. 2009. Scratch: Programming for All. *Commun. ACM* 52, 11 (2009), 60–67.

[22] Albrecht Schmidt. 2016. Increasing Computer Literacy with the BBC micro:bit. *IEEE Pervasive Computing* 15, 2 (2016), 5–7.

[23] Sue Sentance and Scarlet Schwiderski-Grosche. 2012. Challenge and Creativity: Using .NET Gadgeteer in Schools. In *Proceedings of the 7th Workshop in Primary and Secondary Computing Education (WiPSCE '12)*. ACM, New York, NY, USA, 90–100. https://doi.org/10.1145/2481449.2481473

[24] Sue Sentance, Jane Waite, Steve Hodges, Emily MacLeod, and Lucy Yeomans. 2017. Creating Cool Stuff: Pupils' Experience of the BBC micro:bit. In *Proceedings of the 2017 ACM SIGCSE Technical Symposium on Computer Science Education (SIGCSE '17)*. ACM, New York, NY, USA, 531–536. https://doi.org/10.1145/3017680.3017749

[25] Sue Sentance, Jane Waite, Lucy Yeomans, and Emily MacLeod. 2017. Teaching with Physical Computing Devices: the BBC micro:bit Initiative. In *Proceedings of the 12th Workshop on Primary and Secondary Computing Education (WiPSCE '17)*. ACM, New York, NY, USA, 87–96. https://doi.org/10.1145/3137065.3137083

[26] Juha Sorva. 2012. *Visual program simulation in introductory programming education*. Aalto University.

[27] Patrick Wang, Ilaria Renna, Frédéric Amiel, and Xun Zhang. 2018. Learning with Robots in CS and STEM Education: A Case Study with ISEP-R0B0. In *Proceedings of the 4th Workshop on Robots for Learning at ACM/IEEE HRI 2018*. 16–21.

[28] David Weintrop and Uri Wilensky. 2015. Using Commutative Assessments to Compare Conceptual Understanding in Blocks-based and Text-based Programs. In *Proceedings of the Eleventh Annual International Conference on International Computing Education Research (ICER '15)*. ACM, New York, NY, USA, 101–110. https://doi.org/10.1145/2787622.2787721

[29] David Weintrop and Uri Wilensky. 2017. Comparing Block-Based and Text-Based Programming in High School Computer Science Classrooms. *ACM Trans. Comput. Educ.* 18, 1, Article 3 (Oct. 2017), 25 pages. https://doi.org/10.1145/3089799

[30] Philip H. Winne. 2005. A perspective on state-of-the-art research on self-regulated learning. *Instructional Science* 33, 5–6 (2005), 559–565.

New Entrants' Expectations of the First Year Computer Science Experience in the Context of a New National High School Curriculum

Jyoti Bhardwaj
School of Computing
Edinburgh Napier University
Edinburgh, Scotland
j.bhardwaj@napier.ac.uk

ABSTRACT

Computer science (CS) has the highest first year dropout rate amongst UK undergraduates. In this context, understanding the expectations of new students is a first step to designing a CS curriculum that will improve their first year experience. The aim of this study was to present new entrants' reflections on their school CS, once they have started university and can compare teaching and learning in the different institutions.

The study is based on interviews with 84 Scottish-educated students in two cohorts that bridge the introduction of the Curriculum for Excellence (CfE) and new public examinations in Computing Science, intended to bring about significant change in students' attributes and attitudes to learning. The participants vary in level of computing qualifications, reflecting the heterogeneous background of CS entrants.

We asked both cohorts if they felt their learning in the senior years of high school had prepared them for university, and whether they felt they were taught or learned for themselves during school. The students were further asked whether they expected that the proportion of teaching to learning would differ at university.

The findings indicate that many students speak positively about high school CS, but many criticise the dominance of teacher-led instruction that ill-prepares them for self-regulated learning at university. Despite the intentions of CfE, the findings indicate little difference between the cohorts. However, students provide valuable perspective on the Scottish Computing Science experience and the role of Advanced Higher computing, which should prove interesting to those responsible for retention and curriculum design.

ACM ISBN 978-1-4503-6301-3/19/07...$15.00
https://doi.org/10.1145/3304221.3319770

CCS CONCEPTS

• **Social and professional topics** → **Computing education** • **Computing education programs** → **Computer science education** → CS1

KEYWORDS

computer science education; first year experience; self-regulated learning; computer science curriculum; non-progression

ACM Reference format:

Jyoti Bhardwaj. 2019. New Entrants' Expectations of the First Year Computer Science Experience in the Context of a New National High School Curriculum. In *Proceedings of 24th Annual ACM Conference on Innovation and Technology in Computer Science Education (ITiCSE'19), July 15-17, 2019, Aberdeen, Scotland, UK.* ACM, NY, NY, USA, 7 pages. https://doi.org/10.1145/3304221.3319770

1 INTRODUCTION

The purpose of this paper is to explore the expectations of new entrants to a Scottish university's Computer Science (CS) courses, and to discover whether the curriculum they studied and the teaching they received in the senior years of high school has any bearing on their attitude towards the teaching they will experience during their first year.

The context of this study is the fragility of numbers entering CS undergraduate degrees in the UK relative to the stubbornly high drop-out rate. Of all UK-domiciled young entrants to full-time first degree courses, those studying CS-related subjects are the least likely to be in their course in second year, regardless of the qualifications they entered with. The figures for 2015/16 show a 10.6% drop-out rate before second year [16] that at 17.0% is even higher for mature students [16]. The 11% increase in CS undergraduate numbers in Scotland during the years 2010/11 to 2015/6 has scarcely mitigated the high drop-out rate [28]. Indeed, the increase is unsteady, with a drop in actual numbers during 2015/16, before recovering the following session [14].

There's evidence that CS drop-out isn't a uniquely Scottish or British problem: neighbouring Ireland's 2015/16 figures for non-progression in CS after first year in universities, colleges and institutes of technology are similarly poor, at 15%, 23% and 29% respectively [20].

2 CURRICULUM CHANGE IN SCOTLAND

Curriculum change focusing on CS has taken place in recent years in New Zealand, Australia, Israel and Poland, as well as in England and Scotland [37]. The students in this study are drawn from two consecutive first year cohorts of CS students in a Scottish university.

Scottish education has recently experienced a radical and extensive change through the adoption of the Curriculum for Excellence (CfE) in all state schools. The purpose of CfE is encapsulated in the four capacities – "to enable each child or young person to be a successful learner, a confident individual, a responsible citizen and an effective contributor". The four capacities represent a move away from the curriculum prescribing what students can do or what they know, towards an attributes-capabilities model familiar to university practitioners involved in graduate employability [17].

Despite the relative homogeneity of the Scottish state education compared to England's, CfE was implemented on a highly devolved and phased basis, with individual schools, and therefore senior teachers, responsible for turning centrally issued guidelines into subject syllabuses and classroom activities. "Implementation [of CfE] is dependent upon the active engagement of professional and committed teachers" [24, p. 9].

In 2015, Education Scotland devised eight phrases describing their vision of "the successful CfE learner" [11] that universities could expect to receive once the senior phase (age 15-18) of the new curriculum had been rolled out. Of the eight descriptive phrases, two provided the basis for developing the interview questions in this study:

> He/she will be a confident, articulate, solution-focused learner.
>
> Finally and vitally, he/she will have high levels of attainment built on foundations that include real depth and personal involvement in learning. [11]

By questioning a sizeable sample of pre-CfE and post-CfE entrants about their own perceptions of their senior phase education, our aim was to explore whether the Curriculum for Excellence had deepened their personal involvement in learning, or at least given them the vocabulary to articulate it. We hoped also that, using van den Akker's typology of curriculum representations [35] as an underlying construct, we could examine whether the vision of the CfE learner could survive its implementation to make an impact on the learning experiences of the students.

Table 1: Typology of Curriculum Representations [35]

INTENDED	*Ideal*	Vision (rationale or basic philosophy underlying a curriculum)
	Formal/ Written	Intentions as specified in curriculum documents and/or materials
IMPLEMENT-ED	*Perceived*	Curriculum as interpreted by its users (especially teachers)
	Operational	Actual process of teaching and learning (also: curriculum in action)
ATTAINED	*Experiential*	Learning experiences as perceived by learners
	Learned	Resulting learning outcomes of learners

3 CS STUDENTS' EXPECTATIONS OF FIRST YEAR

A major challenge for CS course leaders and instructors is that they cannot assume, in the hope of meeting, their first year entrants' expectations of their course, because CS1 classes are large and the heterogeneity of students' background, experience and interest is most apparent in CS1 modules. Understanding first years' expectations is important if universities are to retain their hard-won entrants [36], given the assertion of Kinnunen, et al. in their longitudinal study on identity [18] that a mismatch between CS entrants' expectations of degree programme content and what they encounter contributes to low satisfaction, low engagement scores, and high rates of attrition.

3.1 Heterogeneity of CS Entrants' Educational Background and Experience

A contributory factor in the heterogeneity of entrants' experience is that, unlike many other degree courses, a post-16 qualification in computer science is not demanded by any UK university as a pre-requisite for undergraduate study, though many stipulate higher level maths.

Grover, Pea and Cooper [13] echo previous findings that unfamiliarity with CS causes school students to have misconceptions about CS; these misconceptions either hinder them from applying to study it at university, or, having enrolled, cause them to experience difficulties in completing introductory modules [31].

As Kinnunen, Marttila-Kontio & Pesonen discuss [19], many CS first years have had programming as a hobby. Such students may expect more self-regulated learning and challenge on their degree course, and need less support, than their less-experienced peers. Further, owing to massification of education [3], these first years typically experience introductory classes in which they may be learning alongside peers for whom programming is not a core subject [8]. A "hierarchy of ability" [29] develops that can discourage non-hobbyist and minority students [36]. Alvarado, Umbelino, & Minnes also propose that inexperienced students under-perform compared to their experienced peers when placed in the same introductory courses, and are more likely to drop out of the CS program [4].

However, Standl, Wetzinger, Futschek, & Guenther [34], in research into large classes containing entrants with highly varied prior experience analogous to the participants in our study, found that students' type of prior education, whether specialising in CS or not, has "no significant impact in their perception of teaching methods and teaching style", though those without computer science pre-education "required more time and effort to keep up with the lectures" [34].

3.2 Success and Independent Learning

Nelson, Shell, Husman, Fishman, & Soh propose that the presence of non-majors in CSI classes reinforces the need for instructors to adopt interventions or instructional changes that encourage more motivated and self-regulated learning in the classroom. They found that students undertaking CS1 as a non-major were more likely to adopt "maladaptive motivational and self-regulated learning profiles" and learn less than those considering a major in CS [23]. They define self-regulated learning inside the classroom as, for example, note taking and question asking, and outside of the classroom as studying; self-motivation is indicated by students persisting, even in the face of failure.

The requirement for self-motivation in CS may be greater because in CS knowledge can be conceptualised as more "absolute" than in softer disciplines [25]. It may be categorised as a hard, applied academic discipline according to Biglan's [7] model [32].

A consequence of this absolute nature of knowledge and problems is that, according to Zingaro [39], "one misstep along the way can prove fatal to a student's ability to write correct programs". For Gordon [12], this characterises CS as a discipline where "students who struggle to understand key concepts are not able to complete assignments to achieve a threshold pass", and are then vulnerable to withdrawal from the crucial first year through academic failure or loss of engagement.

The risk of first year CS failure can be mitigated by students' self-efficacy beliefs in their learning abilities arising from success in high school [27]. A recurring theme in our participants' responses was their belief that independent learning was the norm at university and experiencing it at school prepared them better for higher study.

3.3 High School CS Teaching Style

Webb et al. [37] found that professional development for teachers in computer science education is key to successful curriculum change, and yet presents a challenge in all the countries they studied. In their critique of high school teaching of programming, Alexandron, Armoni, Gordon, & Harel [1] propose that, in addition to knowledge enhancement, the educational objective of a course should include its contribution to learning fundamental ideas and forming useful habits of mind. Interestingly, Alhija [2] finds that students of what she terms "exact sciences" such as CS place significantly less importance on long-term student development as a feature of good teaching.

The large number of studies that advocate problem-based learning in high schools, for example, Smith & Hung [33], as preferable to more didactic teaching styles, would indicate a prevalence of transmissive instruction in high school computing. Bender, et al. [6] too favour a constructivist view [5] of learning and teaching in the classroom, but propose that some CS teachers have difficulty putting constructivist and other didactical concepts into practice in their classrooms, owing to insecurities about their own teaching abilities; yet their choice of teaching style greatly impacts students.

The pressure of implementing a new curriculum adds to the challenges experienced by CS teachers. Sentance & Csizmadia [30], in discussing the rollout of the new Computing curriculum in England to replace ICT, surveyed over 300 practising CS teachers. Their findings report teachers being challenged by lack of technology resources and the need to upskill in advance of the new curriculum, and students also having to adapt to new ways of teaching and different types of content.

4 CASE EXAMPLE OF TWO COHORTS OF CS ENTRANTS

We present a cross-sectional, two-year study, with the participants a purposive sample of first year undergraduates in a department of computer science in a relatively recently incorporated "post-1992" Scottish university. Students were interviewed during the first four weeks of their first semester. They were enrolled on bachelor's degrees in a broad spectrum of specialism: Business Information Systems; Information Technology Management; Computer Systems and Networks; Computer Security and Forensics; Computing; Software Engineering; Games Development; and Computer Science.

The first cohort of this study experienced the old curriculum aged 15 to 18 and entered university in 2015/16, and the second cohort was the first to be educated under the senior phase of CfE and entered university in 2016/7. The change in curriculum partly coincided with the introduction of new Higher qualifications, and together these aimed to "provide a solid basis for progression into higher education and [...] develop a new type of learner with a more mature approach and a wider range of higher-order skills" [26]. Disruption to learning caused by the new exams, particularly the maths Higher [10], was mentioned by nine students in the study.

4.1 Sampling

A total of 84 students were interviewed, 52 in Phase 1, giving a response rate of 49%, and 32 in Phase 2, giving a response rate of 39%. One interview in Phase 1 was truncated, resulting in these questions lacking a response from that individual. The final sample in both phases constitutes an acceptable size for fieldwork according to Charmaz [9], who advises 25 as "adequate for smaller projects". Wright [38] holds that there is an acceptably low risk of nonresponse bias, and further suggests that "if there is no relationship between the probability of response and the variable of interest, then a higher response rate will not lead to any decrease in bias".

Participants' CS background varied; we gathered information on their highest computing and highest maths qualification gained prior to university.

Table 2: Participants From Each Cohort

	Phase 1	Phase 2
Year cohort	159	175
Eligible students	106	82
Usable interviews	52	32
Response rate (of eligible students)	49%	39%

CS entrants ranged from eight with no computing qualifications at all, through 45 with Higher Computing, to 20 with next-level Advanced Higher, plus others with less usual CS backgrounds.

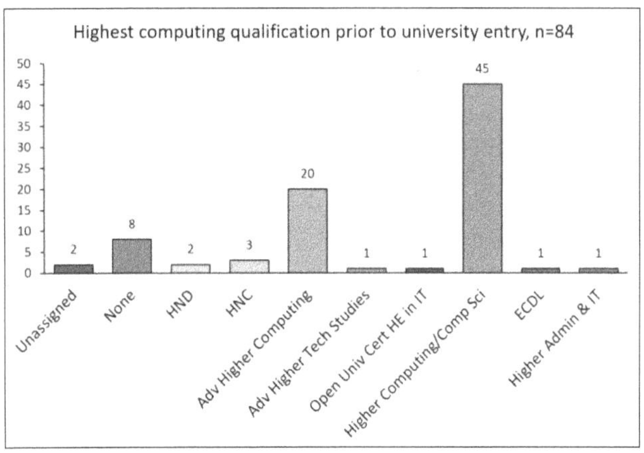

Figure 1: Participants' Highest Computer Science Qualification Prior to University Entry

Maths, on the other hand, was noticeably less varied, with fewer outliers and a large majority achieving Higher maths, seen as the requisite and typical university entry qualification for social science and STEM degree courses (see Figure 2).

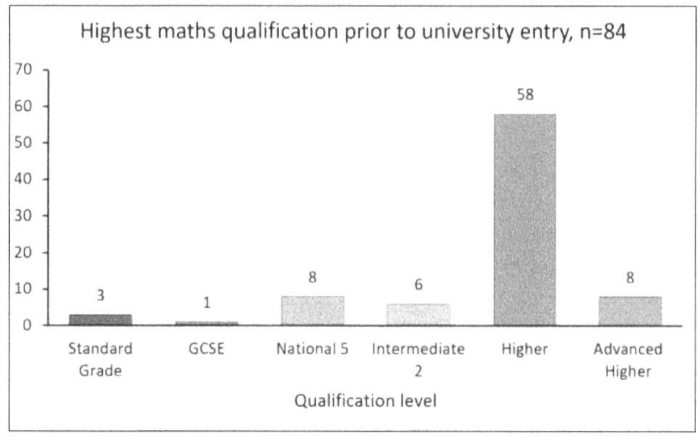

Figure 2: Participants' Highest Mathematics Qualification Prior to University Entry

4.2 Structured Interviews

Data collection was based on structured interviews with relatively little scope for extemporised questioning by the interviewer. This tight approach was influenced by modelling the questions closely on the wording of the well-delineated vision of the successful CfE learner. Apart from basic biographical information, the bulk of data gathered was participants' own assessment of their lived learning experience during the senior phases of high school. Headings indicating the full interview schedule can be found in Figure 3.

As part of the structured interview, participants were asked:

> How are you finding that your learning in school / college has prepared you for your course here, so far?
>
> How much do you think your higher studies at school were about you being taught (for example by teachers), and how much were about you learning?
>
> Do you think this will change at university? If so, in what way?

4.3 Coding in Nvivo 11

The main analytical method used in this study rests on condensation of the interviews through coding [21]. The interview data was coded using Nvivo 11 Pro by QSR. Figure 3 shows coding queries for the three main questions extracted and highlighted from Nvivo interview results. The number of individual responses, called 'references' in Nvivo, exceeds the number of participants because relevant responses from other questions were coded under these themes.

Thematic coding framework

Name	Sources	Reference
Confidence in learning	0	0
1.1 Ease of learning	83	92
1.2 Ease of learning example	83	103
1.3 Ease of learning respondent school or teacher	77	85
1.4 Positive experience while learning example	82	99
1.5 Negative experience while learning example	83	100
1.6 Preparation for course	83	106
Environmental awareness	0	0
Collaborative learning	0	0
Analytical, evaluative skills and working with criteria	0	0
Dialogue about learning	0	0
6.1 Being taught vs learning during highers	83	101
6.2 Being taught vs learning at university	83	122
Technology and knowledge sources	0	0
Emerging themes	0	0

Figure 3: Nvivo 11 Screen Showing Questions in Their Interview Context

5 RESULTS AND DISCUSSION

A number of themes emerged from the 84 participants' responses to the three questions. However, despite the formal intentions [35] of the Curriculum for Excellence, we could not find any indication from interviewees' responses of distinction between pre- and post-CfE students' attitudes.

5.1 How are you finding that your learning in school/college has prepared you for your course here, so far?

The responses were generally positive rather than critical of previous institutions, focusing on learning, in line with the question, rather than on style of teaching. Key themes that emerged from responses were: that taking the Advanced Higher course was beneficial; that some non-content learning could be useful preparation for university; there was an advantage to attending college between school and university.

Twenty of the 84 had an Advanced Higher (usually taken at age 18) in CS, and 45 had Higher CS (taken at usually at age 17), as their highest school CS qualification. Contrary to Standl et al's findings [34] that students' type of prior education has "no significant impact in their perception of teaching methods and teaching style", our participants commented unprompted on this:

> "I'd say my advanced Higher course was probably the best or most related to how I'm learning at university now. Because a lot of it is, you learn a bit of it in class and then you go and do your own research and do your own work at home."

Others valued Advanced Highers as good preparation for university in terms of content:

> "Well, the advanced Higher Computer course, there's been quite a lot of correlation within the content."

and as an opportunity to become more proficient at programming:

> "I think doing advanced Higher computing definitely helped as the programming experience."

Students, including who hadn't done Advanced Higher, commented favourably on study skills gained at school that prepared them for independent learning at university:

> "All of my teachers made us do the reading and finding research and stuff which I think is what I do a lot of here. More independent."

> "Time management. I was taught that. I know how to manage my time. To allocate study time and coursework and things like that."

Six students went to college from school, of whom several commented on this as beneficial preparation for university:

> "I think going from school to college to here was a lot better than from school to here. Because college seems like a sort of in-between the two."

Some students were self-critical in their reflection on preparation for their degree course:

> "It was more my mistakes in high school that prepared me for learning in university. Because I used to do a lot of cramming in high school and I really think that's not the way I learn. There was also a lot of trial and error with study techniques."

5.2 How much do you think your higher studies at school were about being taught (for example by teachers), and how much were about you learning?

More than a quarter of the 83 students who responded to this question, coming from both pre- and post-CfE cohorts, stated that teaching was transmissive or active depending on the subject, for example:

> "For maths it was all taught by the teachers and then you'd go over it. Computing would be very sort of maybe 30% taught, 60% do it yourself really [sic]. It was a lot of self-study, self-solve your own problems, teachers would only be in there for assistance."

Participants were able to distinguish between teachers who did and didn't adopt constructivist methods in the classroom [6]:

> "Sometimes it felt more like you were doing them to pass the exam [...] And other ones made it slightly more personal towards you. And sort of shaped it more around your learning and how it might help you more in the future."

Some students quantified the proportion of teaching against independent learning:

> "I'd say it's like 70% being taught, so it's more about the stuff being taught rather than us learning."

> "90% being taught. Yeah I'd say 90% taught and 10% learning."

Since the Advanced Higher is normally taken by the most proficient students, its teachers may also be more experienced and confident to employ a variety of teaching styles [6]. The more prevalent Higher qualification was often compared unfavourably:

> "Highers I feel are very teaching heavy. There wasn't anything that wasn't taught I don't think, it was all taught and then just revised."

Some were highly critical of the teaching at high school, using emotive language:

> "I felt that it was more of a memory game than learning. It was more 'remember lessons and regurgitate it' rather than understand it, really [...] I don't see any benefit to remembering lines and lines and lines of code..."

In contrast to Alhija's finding [2], many of these students were critical of learning which involves short-term, surface learning:

> "I know that I did a lot of passive learning, which I didn't remember half of even though I went through the notes several times afterwards."

> "I feel like school is more kind of spoon-fed."

Several issues might be leading to a perception of passive learning and spoon-feeding, including teachers needing professional development [37] that give them confidence in introducing a range of pedagogical approaches, especially where "technocentric" innovations that lend variety and novelty to learning are financially unrealizable [30].

5.3 Do you think this will change at university? And if so, how?

Having been at university for between a week and four weeks, all participants, bar two who were unsure, expected the proportion of learning to teaching to be greater at university, with many estimating how much in figures:

> "It's a different approach, I would say, from my experience so far. Some of it is the same but I would say that percentage would shift to maybe something like 70/30 [...] By that I mean taking teaching as being literal, like sitting in a classroom, having someone talking at you."

> "I would say yeah, I would say it's more like 20% teaching and 80% learning."

There was recognition of the different cognitive load at university, but also responses that welcomed the independence of self-regulated learning [23], despite the hard work:

> "Obviously the teachers or the lecturers aren't as demanding on you. It's sort of, you need to be demanding on yourself to make the effort to come in. And to pay attention, take notes and manage everything."

Several responses contrasted their expectation of learning at university with the passive style at school [33]:

> "I think it's going to be more actively learning, because I chose this subject based on the fact that I was very interested in it and I was good at it, so I will be actively learning, doing things by myself because I want to rather than because I have to."

Finally, several participants appeared to relish the difference between school and university, for example:

> "Oh yes definitely, more independent study. Yes. I'll actually enjoy learning it as well."

6 CONCLUSIONS

Our aim in this project was to explore whether the intended vision of Scotland's Curriculum for Excellence had made a discernable impression on the learning experience perceived by entrants to our CS courses [35]. Having asked students from the final pre-CfE cohort and the first CfE cohort identical questions regarding the proportion of didactic versus active learning during their pre-University course, we detected no difference in their responses across a number of themes that emerged. This could be because, despite several years' notice, the teachers responsible for turning curriculum guidelines into classroom activities had not yet succeeded in changing their didactic style. A further phase of data gathering, or delaying Phase 2 for another year or even two, could well yield a more obvious difference in entrants' reflections on their learning experience.

Although it is to be expected that questions setting up 'being taught' in opposition to 'learning' would elicit answers on teaching styles, we were surprised by the level of entrants' criticism of the way they were taught in high school, though the criticism did not extend to the content of the courses. Despite their heterogeneous background, and irrespective of curriculum cohort, our entrants were almost unanimous in their expectation that university would entail self-regulated learning, in contrast to their criticism of the transmissive style of their teachers as ill-preparing them for university.

Our findings should encourage course leaders and those teaching CS1 that, despite the hierarchy of ability [29] in their classrooms and labs, the new students relishing the prospect of independent learning at university will not necessarily be restricted to those who are most proficient and experienced.

ACKNOWLEDGMENTS

With thanks to Dr Ella Taylor-Smith for conducting the interviews used by this study.

REFERENCES

[1] G. Alexandron, M. Armoni, M. Gordon and D. Harel, "Teaching Scenario-Based Programming: An Additional Paradigm for the High School Computer Science Curriculum, Part 1," Computing in Science & Engineering, vol. 19, no. 5, pp. 58-67, 2017.

[2] F. N. A. Alhija, "Teaching in higher education: Good teaching through students' lens," Studies in Educational Evaluation, vol. 54, pp. 4-12, 2017.

[3] S. Allais, "A critical perspective on large class teaching: The political economy of massification and the sociology of knowledge," Higher Education, vol. 67, no. 6, pp. 721-734, 2014.

[4] C. Alvarado, G. Umbelino and M. Minnes, "The persistent effect of pre-college computing experience on college CS course grades," in Proceedings of the 49th ACM Technical Symposium on Computer Science Education, 2018.

[5] M. Ben-Ari, "Constructivism in computer science education," Journal of Computers in Mathematics and Science Teaching, vol. 20, no. 1, pp. 45-73, 2001.

[6] E. Bender, N. Schaper, M. E. Caspersen, M. Margaritis and P. Hubwieser, "Identifying and formulating teachers' beliefs and motivational orientations for computer science teacher education," Studies in Higher Education, vol. 41, no. 11, pp. 1958-1973, 2016.

[7] A. Biglan, "The Characteristics of Subject Matter," Journal of applied Psychology,, vol. 57, no. 3, pp. 195-203, 1973.

[8] T. Camp, A. Richards, B. Bizot, S. Davidson, M. Hall, S. Hambrusch, E. Walker and S. Zweben, "Generation CS: the growth of computer science," ACM Inroads, vol. 8, no. 2, pp. 44-50, 2017.

[9] K. Charmaz, Constructing grounded theory: A practical guide through qualitative analysis, Thousand Oaks, CA: Sage, 2006.

[10] A. Denholm, "Teachers issue warning after new Scottish exams hit by delays," The Herald, 22 March 2016.

[11] Education Scotland, "How Will Future University Entrants Differ As a Result of CfE?," 28 January 2015. [Online]. Available: https://web.archive.org/web/20160822194042/http:/www.educationscotland.gov.uk/learningandteaching/thecurriculum/whatiscurriculumforexcellence/learningthroughoutlife/highereducation/cfeschoolleaversuniversity.asp.

[12] N. A. Gordon, "Issues in retention and attainment in Computer Science," Higher Education Academy, York, 2016.

[13] S. Grover, R. Pea and S. Cooper, "Remedying misperceptions of computer science among middle school students," in Proceedings of the 45th ACM technical symposium on Computer science education, 2014.

[14] Higher Education Statistics Agency, "Higher Education Student Statistics: UK, 2016/17 - Subjects studied," 11 January 2018. [Online]. Available: https://www.hesa.ac.uk/news/11-01-2018/sfr247-higher-education-student-statistics/subjects.

[15] Higher Education Statistics Agency, "Higher Education Student Statistics: UK, 2016/17 - Summary," 11 January 2018. [Online]. Available: https://www.hesa.ac.uk/news/11-01-2018/sfr247-higher-education-student-statistics. [Accessed 20 July 2018].

[16] Higher Education Statistics Agency, "Non-continuation: UK Performance Indicators 2016/17," 8 March 2018. [Online]. Available: https://www.hesa.ac.uk/news/08-03-2018/non-continuation-tables. [Accessed 13 July 2018].

[17] T. Jorre de St Jorre and B. Oliver, "Want students to engage? Contextualise graduate learning outcomes and assess for employability," Higher Education Research & Development, vol. 37, no. 1, pp. 44-57, 2018.

[18] P. Kinnunen, M. Butler, M. Morgan, A. Nylen, A. K. Peters, J. K. S. Sinclair and E. Pesonen, "Understanding initial undergraduate expectations and identity in computing studies," European Journal of Engineering Education, vol. 43, no. 2, pp. 201-218, 2018.

[19] P. Kinnunen, M. Marttila-Kontio and E. Pesonen, "Getting to know computer science freshmen," in Proceedings of the 13th Koli Calling International Conference on Computing Education Research, Koli, 2013.

[20] M. Liston, Pigott, D. Frawley and D. Carroll, "A Study of Progression in Higher Education 2014/15 to 2015/16," Higher Education Authority, Dublin, 2018.

[21] M. Miles, A. Huberman and J. Saldaña, Qualitative data analysis : A methods sourcebook, 3rd ed., Thousand Oaks, Califorinia: SAGE Publications, 2014.

[22] M. Morgan, J. Sinclair, M. Butler, N. Thota, J. Fraser, G. Cross and J. Jackova, "Understanding International Benchmarks on Student Engagement: Awareness and Research Alignment from a Computer Science Perspective," in ITICSE-WGR'17: ITiCSE 2017 Working Group Reports, July 3–5, 2017, Bologna, Italy, 2017.

[23] K. Nelson, D. F. Shell, J. Husman, E. J. Fishman and L. K. Soh, "Motivational and self-regulated learning profiles of students taking a foundational engineering course," Journal of Engineering Education,, vol. 104, no. 1, pp. 74-100., 2015.

[24] M. Priestley and S. Minty, "Developing Curriculum for Excellence: Summary of findings from research undertaken in a Scottish local authority," University of Stirling, Stirling, 2012.

[25] T. Rosman, A. Mayer, M. Kerwer and G. Krampen, "The differential development of epistemic beliefs in psychology and computer science students: A four-wave longitudinal study," Learning and Instruction, vol. 49, pp. 166-177, 2017.

[26] SQA, "New qualifications – new opportunities," August 2015. [Online]. Available: https://www.sqa.org.uk/files_ccc/BD7045_CfE_Universities_guide.pdf.

[27] P. Schoeffel, R. Wazlawick and V. Ramos, "Impact of Pre-University Factors on the Motivation and Performance of Undergraduate Students in Software Engineering," in Software Engineering Education and Training (CSEE&T), 2017 IEEE 30th Conference, 2017.

[28] Scottish Government, "Science, Technology, Engineering and Mathematics (STEM) Evidence Base," October 2017. [Online]. Available: https://www.gov.scot/binaries/content/documents/govscot/publications/publication/2017/10/science-technology-engineering-mathematics-education-training-strategy-scotland/documents/00526537-pdf/00526537-pdf/govscot%3Adocument.

[29] S. Secules, A. Gupta, A. Elby and C. Turpen, "Zooming Out from the Struggling Individual Student: An Account of the Cultural Construction of Engineering Ability in an Undergraduate Programming Class," Journal of Engineering Education, vol. 107 , no. 1, pp. 56-8, 2018.

[30] S. Sentance and A. Csizmadia, "Computing in the curriculum: Challenges and strategies from a teacher's perspective," Education and Information Technologies, vol. 22, no. 2, pp. 469-495, 2017.

[31] S. Sentance, E. Barendsen and C. Schulte, Computer Science Education: Perspectives on Teaching and learning in school, London: Bloomsbury Academic, 2018.

[32] A. Simpson, "The surprising persistence of Biglan's classification scheme," Studies in Higher Education, vol. 42, no. 8, pp. 1520-1531, 2017.

[33] C. S. Smith and L. C. Hung, "Using problem-based learning to increase computer self-efficacy in Taiwanese students," Interactive Learning Environments, vol. 25, no. 3, pp. 329-342, 2017.

[34] B. Standl, E. Wetzinger, G. Futschek and E. A. Guenther, "First-year computer science students perception of lectures in relation to type of high-school education," in Global Engineering Education Conference (EDUCON), 2018.

[35] J. van den Akker, "Curriculum perspectives: An introduction," in Curriculum landscapes and trends, Dordrecht, Springer, 2004, pp. 1-10.

[36] E. Q. Villa, "ACM RETENTION COMMITTEE Minority voices: interrupting the social environment to retain undergraduates in computing," ACM Inroads, vol. 9, no. 3, pp. 31-33, 2018.

[37] M. Webb, N. Davis, T. Bell, Y. Katz, N. Reynolds, D. Chambers and M. & Sysło, "Computer science in K-12 school curricula of the 2lst century: Why, what and when?," Education and Information Technologies, vol. 22, no. 2, pp. 445-468, 2017.

[38] G. Wright, "An empirical examination of the relationship between nonresponse rate and nonresponse bias," Statistical Journal of the IAOS, vol. 31, no. 2, pp. 305-315, 2015.

[39] D. Zingaro, "Examining interest and grades in Computer Science 1: a study of pedagogy and achievement goals," ACM Transactions on Computing Education (TOCE), vol. 15, no. 3, p. 14, 2015.

Applying Gamification to Motivate Students to Write High-Quality Code in Programming Assignments

Remin Kasahara
Waseda University
Tokyo, Japan
remin@ruri.waseda.jp

Kazunori Sakamoto
Waseda University
Tokyo, Japan

Hironori Washizaki
Waseda University
Tokyo, Japan

Yoshiaki Fukazawa
Waseda University
Tokyo, Japan

ABSTRACT

Background: Traditional programming education focuses on training students' ability to write correct code that meets the specifications in programming assignments. In addition to correctness, software engineering studies argue that code quality is important. **Problem:** Nurturing students' ability to write high-quality code in programming assignments is difficult due to two main reasons. (1) Considering code quality while grading is undesirable because there are no objective and fair measurement metrics. (2) Grading assignments from multiple viewpoints (correctness and quality) is difficult and time-consuming. **Approach:** We propose applying gamification with code metrics to measure code quality in programming assignments. Our approach can motivate students to write code with good metric scores independent of grading. We implemented our approach and conducted a control experiment in a programming course at a university. **Result:** Our approach did not interfere with students' submissions but improved metric scores significantly. Hence, our approach can engage students to write high-quality code.

CCS CONCEPTS

• **Applied computing** → **Education**; • **Social and professional topics** → *Software engineering education*; • **Human-centered computing**;

KEYWORDS

programming education; code quality; code metrics; leaderboard; gamification; online judge

ACM Reference Format:
Remin Kasahara, Kazunori Sakamoto, Hironori Washizaki, and Yoshiaki Fukazawa. 2019. Applying Gamification to Motivate Students to Write High-Quality Code in Programming Assignments. In *Innovation and Technology in Computer Science Education (ITiCSE '19), July 15–17, 2019, Aberdeen, Scotland, UK*. ACM, New York, NY, USA, 7 pages. https://doi.org/10.1145/3304221.3319792

ITiCSE '19, July 15–17, 2019, Aberdeen, Scotland, UK

ACM ISBN 978-1-4503-6301-3/19/07.
https://doi.org/10.1145/3304221.3319792

1 INTRODUCTION

It is important to foster students' ability to write a program that meets specifications. In programming education, most assignments and examinations focus on writing programs that meet specifications (i.e., writing correct programs). For example, an online judge, which is an automatic programming assignment grading system [13, 15], judges whether the submitted program meets the specifications. Teachers usually motivate students to submit correct programs for assignments by grading them because meeting specifications is a clear and fair grading criterion.

It is also important to nurture students' ability to write high-quality source code because low-quality code leads to problems such as reduced productivity [6]. To develop ability, students need to be motivated to write high-quality code in programming assignments. Although grading is a good way to motivate students, it is difficult to grade assignments with regard to code quality for two main reasons. (1) Since objective and fair metrics do not exist, grading code quality is undesirable. (2) Grading assignments comprehensively from multiple viewpoints (correctness and quality) is difficult and time-consuming.

To overcome these problems, herein we propose a combination of gamification and code metrics, to motivate students to write high-quality code in assignments. Gamification can raise student motivation and stimulate certain actions [9]. Code metrics (e.g., lines of code (LOC) and cyclomatic complexity (CC) [17]) measure the quality of code and represent it as a score. Although a score does not necessarily indicate good code, code with a good score tends to be high-quality [6]. Since gamification does not require complete fairness, it can motivate students to improve metric scores, and may engage students to write high-quality code without grading.

Numerous studies have investigated how to successfully motivate students by gamification [4, 22], and several papers have reported the undesirable effects of gamification [27]. Herein, we focus on a leaderboard, one of the most major gamification elements to evaluate our approach systematically.

We set the following three research questions:

- **RQ1** Does an online judge with a leaderboard using the CC change the number of problems solved by each student?
- **RQ2** Does an online judge with a leaderboard using the CC change the CC of code written by students?
- **RQ3** Does an online judge with a leaderboard using the CC change the code quality?

Our research contributions include:

- We proposed a leaderboard using the CC in an online judge. This setup evaluates the quality of the submitted code and provides instant feedback about the correctness and code quality.
- We added a leaderboard to an existing online judge that students used in a programming course.
- We analyzed the results of multiple assignments in the experiment systematically by employing meta-analysis as well as the submitted code by hand.
- We found that the leaderboard improved with the CC scores with a statistical significance in the intervention (RQ2), and it did not interfere with students' submissions (RQ1).
- We found two cases where students improved code quality during the intervention and one case where a student stuck to reduce the CC scores without improving the code quality (RQ3).

2 BACKGROUND

The **online judge** is a web application that automatically grades programming assignments [15]. When students submit code to a programming problem to an online judge, it compiles the submitted code to generate and then test a program. The online judge tests the program by checking whether the program yields the expected outputs corresponding to the given inputs. Consequently, more than one program can be correct. The online judge not only helps students learn programming with its instant feedback but also assists teachers in monitoring students' learning. Several online judges have been proposed and developed for educational purposes [13, 21, 23]. Some organizations and companies use them today to manage online programming contests, e.g., Code Jam [1] and Codeforces [2].

In software engineering, several **code metrics** (e.g., LOC, CC, and Halstead Complexity [11]), and Chidamber and Kemerer metrics (CK metrics) [7] have been proposed to measure and evaluate code quality [18, 28]. Software developers use code metrics to improve code quality because extremely complicated code lowers productivity [6].

Deterding et al. defined **gamification** as the use of game design elements in non-game contexts [9]. They classified game design elements into five levels: game interface design patterns (e.g., points, badges, leaderboards, levels), game design patterns and mechanics (e.g., time constraints, limited resources, turns), game design principles and heuristics (e.g., enduring play, clear goals, variety of game styles), game models, and game design methods. The goal of gamification is to motivate users' activities.

3 PROPOSAL

To encourage students to write high-quality code, we employ gamification that shows code metrics as a score in an online judge. The target is students in an intermediate programming course.

3.1 Method

The following procedure was used in our online judge system, which was extended for gamification:

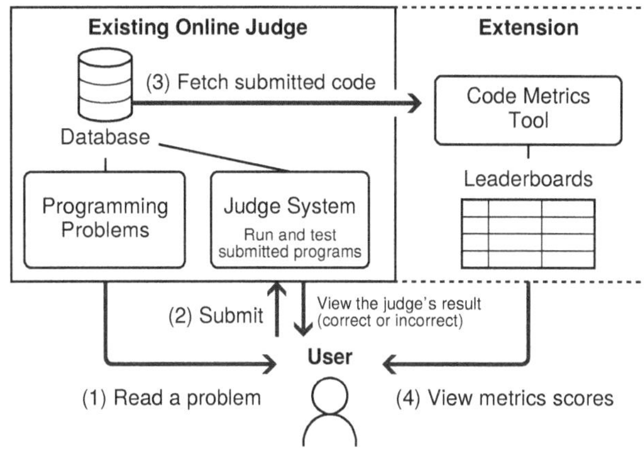

Figure 1: Implementation overview.

(1) A student answers a programming problem by submitting code to an online judge system.
(2) The system measures the CC of the submitted code.
(3) The system instantly shows the CC score with a leaderboard to the student.
(4) The student resubmits his/her code zero or more times, and the system updates the results. The system records the smallest CC score.

Step 1 is the same as the original system. The online judge asks students to solve competitive-programming-style tasks. For the second and third steps, the system provides the score to the students.

This paper selected CC as the score element due to its theoretical basis and usability [28]. The CC reflects the code complexity well compared to the file size or LOC. In addition, the concept of the CC is easy for students to comprehend and use. However, the system may use another metric and instructors can change the metrics according to their viewpoints.

The essential idea of this method is not the selection of code metrics but the competition by a leaderboard with code metrics measurement. We employed a leaderboard from gamification elements for two reasons. (i) Since it is difficult to select suitable threshold scores of code metrics to judge whether code is good or bad, students should be able to compare their score with others instead of a predetermined goal to evaluate their score. (ii) The leaderboard concept is familiar in competitive programming such as a contest. To ensure that this experiment is systematic and reproducible, we did not employ other gamification elements.

In step 4, we expect gamification to motivate students to write better code. Thus, neither the system nor the instructors forced the students to resubmit.

3.2 Implementation

Figure 1 overviews the implementation of the gamification system. We used the Waseda Online Judge (WOJ) as our online judging system. WOJ is a web application provided by the department of computer science at Waseda University. To implement gamification, we developed an extensional web application: WOJ Standings (WOJS). The WOJS shares a database with the online judge. When

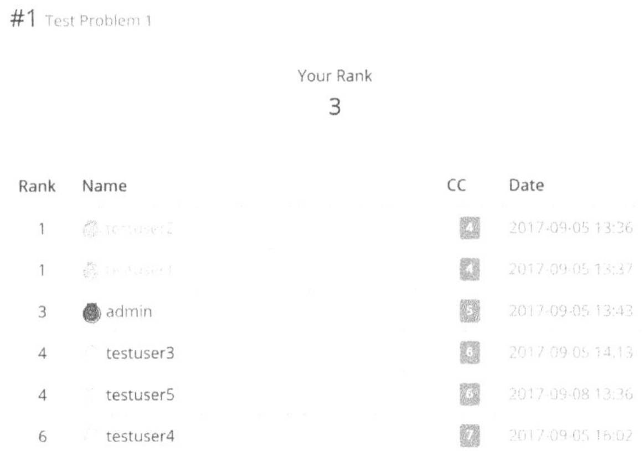

Figure 2: Screenshot of the leaderboard on the WOJS.

a student submits code to the online judge, the WOJS measures the CC and shows the student his or her score.

The CC is usually calculated for each module such as class and function. The code complexity analyzer we used in WOJS, Lizard [3], measures the CC for each function. In software development, code metrics tools monitor whether the CC exceeds the reference value. Developers are making efforts to avoid functions with a large CC. Thus WOJS used the largest CC of a program as the score.

Students can compare their scores to those of other students on the leaderboard (Fig. 2). The leaderboard shows ranks, user names, CC scores, and submission time. The leaderboard is generated for each programming problem because the CC values depend on the problem. Students can edit their own user name freely. The lower the CC score, the higher his/her rank. Users ranked from first to third are displayed in different colors.

4 EVALUATION

We conducted a six-week experiment using the WOJS in a C programming course to evaluate the effectiveness of our system.

4.1 Experiment

Participants were students taking a C programming course at Waseda University. Because all participants had completed an introductory programming course the previous year, they could solve primary programming problems independently. We provided students with an overview of the experiment and an explanation of CC during the first lecture. A total of 35 participants submitted a consent form. We randomly divided the participants into two groups: group A (17 students) and B (18 students). We also divided the course period into two halves: weeks 1 to 3 and weeks 4 to 6. For the control experiment, students in group A used the WOJS only in the first half, while group B used it only in the second half. Each week, all students in the course were asked to solve three programming problems, which were turned into the online judge. These problems had varying levels of difficulty. Problems 1 and 2 were appropriately difficult, whereas Problem 3 consisted of more challenging tasks from past international programming contests. According to the circumstances of the course, problem 1 was not set in weeks 3 and 6.

Table 1: Number of students in group A/B who submitted correct code by problem.

Problem	A	B	Problem	A	B
1-1	14	11	4-1	10	12
1-2	9	8	4-2	9	13
1-3	4	4	4-3	1	5
2-1	11	11	5-1	12	12
2-2	8	11	5-2	9	11
2-3	2	1	5-3	0	0
3-2	10	11	6-2	6	8
3-3	1	2	6-3	0	0

Note: A row (*W-P*) means the problem (*P*) in the week (*W*). Gray color shows the results for problem 3 of each week, which we excluded as noise.

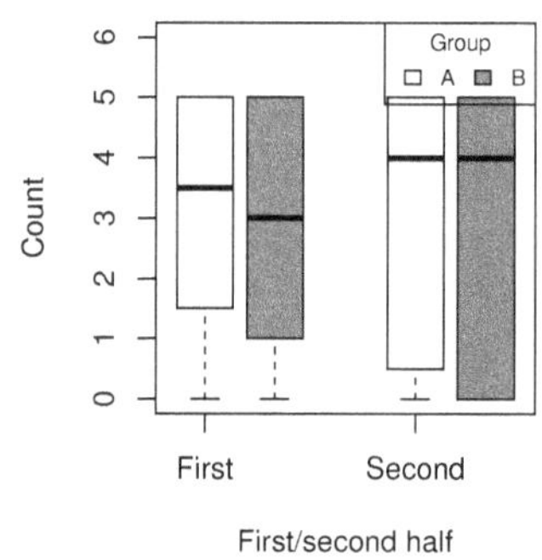

Figure 3: Number of problems solved by group in the first half (1-1 to 3-2) and the second half (4-1 to 6-2).

During the experiments, students were not provided with a reward such as prizes or bonus grades. In other words, participation in the experiment and use of the WOJS was voluntary. This point was emphasized in the first lecture. Note that submissions of answers to the problems, or assignments, were included in the teacher's grading of students, which is standard for the course.

After the experimental period, we collected all submitted code that passed the tests given by the online judge. Failed code was excluded from the data because its CC could not be compared with the CC of the correct code. We then analyzed the CC scores.

4.2 Results

Table 1 shows the number of students in each group who submitted correct code by problem. The problem column indicates the type of the problems in a given week. For example, 1-2 means the 2nd problem in the 1st week. The number of students who submitted correct code depended on the problem. Few students submitted correct answers to the 3rd group of problems because they were too difficult for the students to solve. Since the number of submitted answers for problem 3 each week was too small to analyze statistically, we excluded the results of problem 3.

Figure 3 summarizes the number of problems solved by the students in each half as a box plot. Since the number of problems in each half (except the one excluded as noted above) is 5, the plot falls ranges from 0 to 5. Group A and group B have similar submissions.

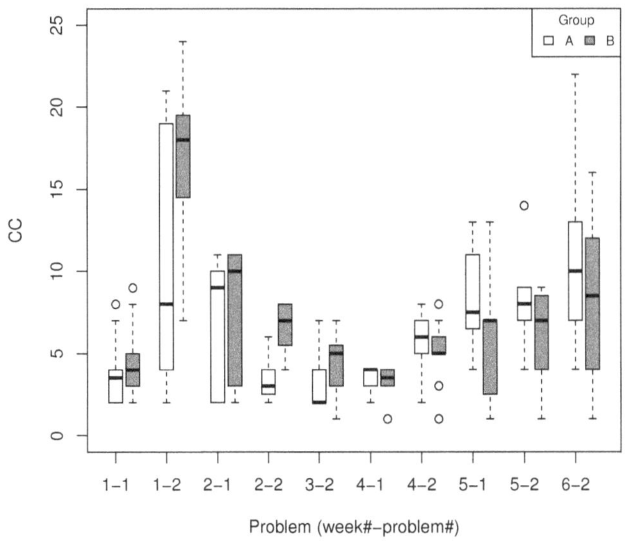

Figure 4: Summary of the CC score by group for each problem.

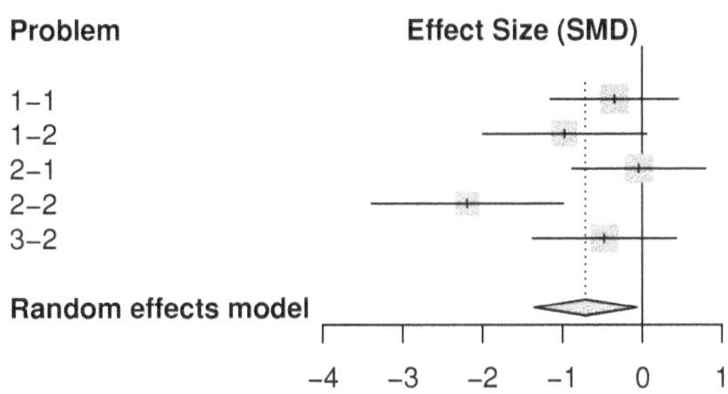

(a) First half of the course.
(Combined SMD is −0.71. Combined 95% CI is [−1.35, −0.07].)

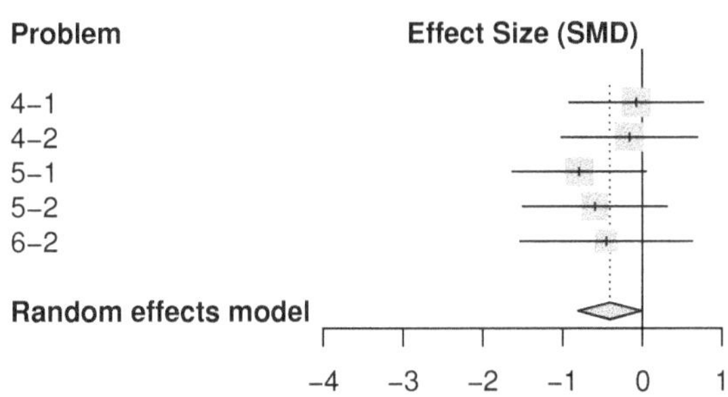

(b) Second half of the course.
(Combined SMD is −0.41. Combined 95% CI is [−0.81, −0.01].)

Figure 5: SMD of the CC score combined by meta-analysis.
Note: SMD = 0: no effect, SMD < 0: intervention lowered CC.

The p-value by the Wilcoxon-Mann-Whitney test is 0.5985 in first half and 0.7400 in second half. Therefore, we cannot find significant difference in the number of solved problems.

Figure 4 presents the CC scores associated with each problem as a box plot. During the first half of the course, the CC of group A tended to be smaller than that of group B. After changing the intervened group, the CC of group B became small. However, the CC varied depending on the problem. We could not compare the CC scores directly because the problems and the answers differed. Thus, we applied a statistical method from meta-analysis[1]and combined the results.

Figure 5 shows the forest plot for each half of the course where a line represents the outcome of each problem. The outcome was represented as the standardized mean difference (SMD), which is called the effect size of each problem. That is, each effect size shows the size of the CC of the intervention group compared to that of the control group. An effect size less than 0 means that the intervention lowered the CC of the group. Each plot shows the effect size, and the horizontal line segment shows the 95% confidence interval (CI) of the effect size. The size of a square mark indicates the weight for combined effect size. The rhombus shape at the bottom shows the 95% CI of the combined effect size. It takes into account both the within-problem variance and the inter-problem variance.

Figure 5a shows the analysis of the first half of the course. Only the students in group A used WOJS in the first half. The CC of code written by group A was smaller than that of group B. The combined 95% CI was also less than 0. In the second half of the course (Fig. 5b), only the students in group B used WOJS. The CC of code written by group B was significantly lower than that of group A during the second half of the course. Therefore, gamification intervention lowered the CC of code written by the students.

We compared typical a student in each group. The student from group A (Student A6) wrote a low-CC code under the intervention (Fig. 6a), but not after the intervention (Fig. 6b). In contrast, the typical student from group B (Student B4) did not written a low-CC code before the intervention (Fig. 6c) but did during the intervention (Fig. 6d). Both students reduced the CC by using arrays and functions only in the intervention period.

We also analyzed the code submitted by other students. We read the code and compared small-CC code with large-CC code produced for each problem. The students used several techniques to reduce the CC of their code:

- Reducing redundant `if` statements.
- Reducing redundant conditional expressions.
- Rewriting multiple `if` statements in fewer `if` statements with `for` statements.
- Creating new functions to remove duplicate code.
- Using an array of function pointers to branch.

We did not anticipate the function pointers method. One student in group B used this technique to lower the CC score to 1. This

[1] Meta-analysis is a method to combine the results of multiple studies on the same subject [10, 12]. After collecting results, meta-analysis calculates the effect size of each study. When the outcome is continuous data, the standardized mean difference (SMD) can be set as the effect size. SMD is calculated using the following formula:

$$d = \frac{\overline{X}_1 - \overline{X}_2}{\sigma_{\text{pooled}}}$$

where $\overline{X}_1 - \overline{X}_2$ is the difference in means and σ_{pooled} is the pooled standard deviation (SD). Then meta-analysis combines the effect sizes by a weighted mean. The multiplicative inverse of the variance in each study is used as the weight. We used a forest plot [16] to summarize the results of this meta-analysis.

```
void A(int x) {
  if (x == -1) exit(0);
}

int main(void) {
  int x;
  char a[8][3] = {"N", "NW", "W", "SW", "S", "SE", "E", "NE"};
  while (1) {
    scanf("%d", &x);
    A(x);
    x = x / 45;
    printf("%s\n", a[x]);
  }
  return 0;
}
```

(a) 2-1 by A6 (under the intervention).

```
int main(void) {
  while (1) {
    int d;
    scanf("%d", &d);
    if (d == 0) printf("N\n");
    if (d == 45) printf("NW\n");
    if (d == 90) printf("W\n");
    if (d == 135) printf("SW\n");
    if (d == 180) printf("S\n");
    if (d == 225) printf("SE\n");
    if (d == 270) printf("E\n");
    if (d == 315) printf("NE\n");
    if (d == -1) break;
  }
  return 0;
}
```

(c) 2-1 by B4.

```
int main(void) {
  int n, i, A, E;
  scanf("%d", &n);
  for (i = 0; i < n; i++) {
    scanf("%d %d", &A, &E);
    if (A + E == 0) {
      printf("G\n");
      continue;
    }
    switch ((A + E) / 10) {
      case 10:
        printf("A+\n");
        break;
      case 9:
        printf("A+\n");
        break;
      case 8:
        printf("A\n");
        break;
      case 7:
        printf("B\n");
        break;
      case 6:
        printf("C\n");
        break;
      default:
        printf("F\n");
        break;
    }
  }
  return 0;
}
```

(b) 5-1 by A6.

```
void grade(int point);

int main(void) {
  int N, i;
  int A, E;

  scanf("%d\n", &N);

  for (i = 0; i < N; i++) {
    scanf("%d %d\n", &A, &E);
    grade(A + E);
  }
  return 0;
}

void grade(int point) {
  char grade[12][4] = {"G\n", "F\n", "F\n", "F\n", "F\n", "F\n", "F\n", "C\n", "B\n", "A\n", "A+\n", "A+\n"};

  point = (point != 0) * (point + 10);
  point /= 10;
  printf("%s", grade[point]);
}
```

(d) 5-1 by B4 (under the intervention).

Figure 6: Code submitted for problem 2-1/5-1 by student A6/B4.

Note: `#include` directives are removed due to space limitations in the paper.

method can reduce the CC, but it does not improve the quality of the code because it just replaces all `if`, `for`, and `while` statements one by one. For example, the following C program calls the function `f2` only if `x` is `0` without an `if` statement.

```
void (*func[2])();
func[0] = f1;
func[1] = f2;
func[!x]();
```

5 DISCUSSION

We discuss the results in according with the research questions.

> **RQ1** Does an online judge with a leaderboard using the CC change the number of problems solved by each student?

We compared the number of problems solved by each student in group A and that in group B by the Wilcoxon-Mann-Whitney test. We could not find a statistically significant difference both in the first half and in the second half. Moreover, the difference in the actual values seems very small. Thus, our approach does not interfere with students' grades (i.e., the number of problems solved). However, we cannot confirm that there is no difference statistically.

> **RQ2** Does an online judge with a leaderboard using the CC change the CC of code written by students?

The CC of the code written by group A was lower than that of group B in the first half of the course. The difference was significant at the 5% level. The CC of the code written by group B was smaller than that of group A at a 5% significance level in the second half of the course. Therefore, the leaderboard using the CC can reduce the CC of code written during the intervention. Thus, the score and the leaderboard modify behavior in programming education without any additional rewards.

> **RQ3** Does an online judge with a leaderboard using the CC change the code quality?

After reading the submitted code, we found that students implemented several techniques to improve the CC scores. For example, in the intervention period, some students tried dividing the main function into multiple functions and avoiding duplicated code. The techniques found in the students' code would be the first step in learning code quality improvement.

However, we observed that one student stuck to reduce the CC without improving the code quality. The competitive environment of the leaderboard caused students to lower their CC greedily. Such a behavior may occur even when using other simple code metrics such as LOC. One solution is to choose advanced code metrics or a combination of metrics that students cannot improve simplistically. We plan to find suitable metrics to motivate students to write high-quality code in future.

6 THREATS TO VALIDITY

An internal threat to validity is the novelty effect. The novelty effect is a bias for new technology [8]. Although we confirmed that our approach works well in three weeks, it is possible that the effect of our approach will be reduced due to the novelty effect. We plan to conduct a longer experiment to assess the impact of the novelty effect.

The experiment was conducted in a single programming course, which is a threat to the external validity. We gathered participants from students in a programming course at our university. Moreover, not all the students in the course participated in the experiment because some students did not submit a consent form. However, the proposed method can be applied to other courses. In the future, we will evaluate the effectiveness of gamification elements in other groups of students.

Another threat to external validity is that the selection of the programming problem might have been biased. To minimize the bias among the problems, we used multiple problems in each half of the course and combined the outcomes. However, we could not analyze the results of the third-level problems due to the limited number of submissions. We plan to conduct an experiment with students who can solve more difficult problems.

7 RELATED WORK

Several researchers have mentioned code quality in programming education. Breuker et al. compared the static code quality of first year students to that of second year students [5]. They pointed out that programming courses do not emphasize code quality. Zhou et al. revealed the weak points of a previous online judge such as its inattention to code quality [29]. They designed a framework for a new online judge, with four new features: personalized feedback, code quality check, code similarity check, and teaching adjustment. We also improved an online judge by adding a leaderboard with a code metric measurement. Although Zhou et al. did not implement an online judge and did not conduct an experiment, we conducted an experiment to advance the research of code quality in programming education.

There are several practical publications on gamification in software engineering. Singer and Schneider proposed using gamification in a version control system [26]. They developed a web application using a leaderboard to motivate participating students to make more commits. Arai et al. created a gamification tool to motivate developers to remove warnings of static bug finders [4]. They gave points to developers who made commits that solve the warnings. Prause et al. conducted an experiment to evaluate gamification used to enforce coding conventions [22]. They used a score calculated from the number of violations, and developers improved their scores during an intervention. Pedreira et al. showed the systematic mapping of research on gamification in software engineering [20]. They claimed that most studies lack the methodological support to make their proposals reproducible in other settings.

Gamification has also been studied in programming education. Khaleel et al. stated that gamification encourages students to learn a programming language [14]. They designed a gamification application for programming education. Olsson et al. employed a gamification e-learning tool in programming course [19]. Their web application visualized the progress of learning with progress bars and badges. They pointed out that badges induced positive feeling for the course. Rojas et al. created a multiplayer game that teaches mutation testing [24, 25]. They employed point system, which gave scores to winner of each match.

These gamification studies in software engineering and programming education are related to our work. However, we did not find any study combining gamification with code metrics measurement for educational purposes as far as we investigated. Consequently, our paper should contribute to these research fields.

8 CONCLUSIONS

Students are usually motivated to write and submit correct programs by grades in programming courses. However, when a grade is not suitable to motivate a target behavior, gamification can provide another incentive. Here, we propose employing a leaderboard with code metric measurements to motivate students to improve code quality. We developed a web application, which measures the CC of code submitted to an online judge. We conducted a six-week experiment in an intermediate programming course to evaluate our approach.

We collected the submitted code, which passed the tests executed by the online judge through the experiment. We applied meta-analysis to the CC of submissions for each programming problem. Students wrote code with a lower CC under gamification conditions. Therefore, our approach motivates students to improve code metrics without additional rewards. The results also suggest that a leaderboard using the CC does not interfere with students' grades.

In the future, we will design another gamification experiment. To evaluate the effect of gamification (including the novelty effect) more accurately, long-term experiments with more control groups are necessary. In addition, code metrics to measure code quality precisely should be evaluated.

ACKNOWLEDGMENTS

This work was partially supported by JST Presto Grant Number JPMJPR14D4. I am deeply grateful to Prof. Kana Shimizu of Waseda University for the opportunity to conduct this experiment. Students' participation was also invaluable. Advice given by Prof. Ryo Okada of Kagawa University was of great help in the evaluation process.

REFERENCES

[1] 2003. Google Code Jam. https://code.google.com/codejam/

[2] 2010. Codeforces. http://codeforces.com/

[3] 2012. Lizard code complexity analyzer. http://www.lizard.ws/

[4] Satoshi Arai, Kazunori Sakamoto, Hironori Washizaki, and Yoshiaki Fukazawa. 2014. A Gamified Tool for Motivating Developers to Remove Warnings of Bug Pattern Tools. In *2014 6th International Workshop on Empirical Software Engineering in Practice*. IEEE, 37–42. https://doi.org/10.1109/IWESEP.2014.17

[5] Dennis M. Breuker, Jan Derriks, and Jacob Brunekreef. 2011. Measuring static quality of student code. In *Proceedings of the 16th annual joint conference on Innovation and technology in computer science education - ITiCSE '11*. ACM Press, New York, New York, USA, 13. https://doi.org/10.1145/1999747.1999754

[6] E. T. Chen. 1978. Program Complexity and Programmer Productivity. *IEEE Transactions on Software Engineering* SE-4, 3 (may 1978), 187–194. https://doi.org/10.1109/TSE.1978.231497

[7] S.R. Chidamber and C.F. Kemerer. 1994. A metrics suite for object oriented design. *IEEE Transactions on Software Engineering* 20, 6 (jun 1994), 476–493. https://doi.org/10.1109/32.295895

[8] Richard E Clark and Brenda M Sugrue. 1988. Research on Instructional Media, 1978-1988. In *Educational Media Yearbook 1987-88*. Littletown, CO: Libraries Unlimited, 327–343. https://www.gwern.net/docs/psychology/1991-clark.pdf

[9] Sebastian Deterding, Dan Dixon, Rilla Khaled, and Lennart Nacke. 2011. From game design elements to gamefulness: defining "gamification". In *Proceedings of the 15th International Academic MindTrek Conference on Envisioning Future Media Environments - MindTrek '11*. ACM Press, New York, New York, USA, 9. https://doi.org/10.1145/2181037.2181040

[10] Gene V. Glass. 1976. Primary, Secondary, and Meta-Analysis of Research. *Educational Researcher* 5, 10 (nov 1976), 3–8. https://doi.org/10.3102/0013189X005010003

[11] Maurice H. (Maurice Howard) Halstead and Maurice H. 1977. *Elements of software science*. Elsevier. 127 pages. https://dl.acm.org/citation.cfm?id=540137

[12] Larry V. Hedges and Ingram. Olkin. 1985. *Statistical methods for meta-analysis*. Academic Press. 369 pages. https://www.sciencedirect.com/science/book/9780080570655

[13] Petri Ihantola, Tuukka Ahoniemi, Ville Karavirta, and Otto Seppälä. 2010. Review of recent systems for automatic assessment of programming assignments. In *Proceedings of the 10th Koli Calling International Conference on Computing Education Research - Koli Calling '10*. ACM Press, New York, New York, USA, 86–93. https://doi.org/10.1145/1930464.1930480

[14] Firas Layth Khaleel, Noraidah Sahari@ Ashaari, Tengku Siti Meriam, Tengku Wook, and Amirah Ismail. 2015. The study of gamification application architecture for programming language course. In *Proceedings of the 9th International Conference on Ubiquitous Information Management and Communication - IMCOM '15*. ACM Press, New York, New York, USA, 1–5. https://doi.org/10.1145/2701126.2701222

[15] Andy Kurnia, Andrew Lim, and Brenda Cheang. 2001. Online Judge. *Computers & Education* 36, 4 (may 2001), 299–315. https://doi.org/10.1016/S0360-1315(01)00018-5

[16] S Lewis and M Clarke. 2001. Forest plots: trying to see the wood and the trees. *BMJ (Clinical research ed.)* 322, 7300 (jun 2001), 1479–80. http://www.ncbi.nlm.nih.gov/pubmed/11408310http://www.pubmedcentral.nih.gov/articlerender.fcgi?artid=PMC1120528

[17] T. J. McCabe. 1976. A Complexity Measure. *IEEE Transactions on Software Engineering* SE-2, 4 (dec 1976), 308–320. https://doi.org/10.1109/TSE.1976.233837

[18] Allan Mori, Gustavo Vale, Markos Viggiato, Johnatan Oliveira, Eduardo Figueiredo, Elder Cirilo, Pooyan Jamshidi, and Christian Kastner. 2018. Evaluating domain-specific metric thresholds. In *Proceedings of the 2018 International Conference on Technical Debt - TechDebt '18*. ACM Press, New York, New York, USA, 41–50. https://doi.org/10.1145/3194164.3194173

[19] Marie Olsson, Peter Mozelius, and Jonas Collin. 2015. Visualisation and Gamification of e-Learning and Programming Education. *Electronic Journal of e-Learning* 13, 6 (2015), 441–454. https://eric.ed.gov/?id=EJ1087309

[20] Oscar Pedreira, Félix Garcia, Nieves Brisaboa, and Mario Piattini. 2015. Gamification in software engineering âĂŞ A systematic mapping. *Information and Software Technology* 57 (jan 2015), 157–168. https://doi.org/10.1016/J.INFSOF.2014.08.007

[21] Jordi Petit, Omer Giménez, and Salvador Roura. 2012. Jutge.org: an educational programming judge. In *Proceedings of the 43rd ACM technical symposium on Computer Science Education - SIGCSE '12*. ACM Press, New York, New York, USA, 445. https://doi.org/10.1145/2157136.2157267

[22] Christian R. Prause and Matthias Jarke. 2015. Gamification for enforcing coding conventions. In *Proceedings of the 2015 10th Joint Meeting on Foundations of Software Engineering - ESEC/FSE 2015*. ACM Press, New York, New York, USA, 649–660. https://doi.org/10.1145/2786805.2786806

[23] Miguel A Revilla, Shahriar Manzoor, and Rujia Liu. 2008. Competitive Learning in Informatics: The UVa Online Judge Experience. *Olympiads in Informatics* 2 (2008), 131–148. https://ioinformatics.org/journal/INFOL035.pdf

[24] Jose Miguel Rojas and Gordon Fraser. 2016. Code Defenders: A Mutation Testing Game. In *2016 IEEE Ninth International Conference on Software Testing, Verification and Validation Workshops (ICSTW)*. IEEE, 162–167. https://doi.org/10.1109/ICSTW.2016.43

[25] José Miguel Rojas, Gordon Fraser, Thomas White, and Benjamin Clegg. 2016. Code Defenders. http://code-defenders.org/

[26] Leif Singer and Kurt Schneider. 2012. It was a bit of a race: Gamification of version control. In *2012 Second International Workshop on Games and Software Engineering: Realizing User Engagement with Game Engineering Techniques (GAS)*. IEEE, 5–8. https://doi.org/10.1109/GAS.2012.6225927

[27] Armando M Toda, Pedro H D Valle, and Seiji Isotani. 2018. The Dark Side of Gamification: An Overview of Negative Effects of Gamification in Education. In *Higher Education for All. From Challenges to Novel Technology-Enhanced Solutions*, Alexandra Ioana Cristea, Ig Ibert Bittencourt, and Fernanda Lima (Eds.). Springer International Publishing, Cham, 143–156.

[28] Sheng Yu and Shijie Zhou. 2010. A survey on metric of software complexity. In *2010 2nd IEEE International Conference on Information Management and Engineering*. IEEE, 352–356. https://doi.org/10.1109/ICIME.2010.5477581

[29] Wenju Zhou, Yigong Pan, Yinghua Zhou, and Guangzhong Sun. 2018. The framework of a new online judge system for programming education. In *Proceedings of ACM Turing Celebration Conference - China on - TURC '18*. ACM Press, New York, New York, USA, 9–14. https://doi.org/10.1145/3210713.3210721

Paper or Online? A Comparison of Exam Grading Techniques

Yingjun Cao, Leo Porter, Soohyun Nam Liao, Rick Ord
Department of Computer Science and Engineering
University of California, San Diego
La Jolla, CA, USA

ABSTRACT

As computer science enrollments continue to surge, exam grading requires significant instructional resources. Online grading platforms have been developed in recent years and have been adopted at a number of institutions; however, their effectiveness compared with traditional grading on paper is not fully known. This study is the first in CS to compare online and paper grading. Comparing overall time to grade, including all factors, online grading doesn't show a consistent advantage compared with paper grading. We observed that online grading is much faster during the actual grading phase, but some of this benefit is offset by the additional overhead prior to grading (e.g., scanning) for online grading. Examining student and grader preferences based on feedback, both groups show a strong preference for the online format, predominately due to the convenience of the online platform. Graders report being able to grade more accurately online with the ability to modify rubrics, but that grading on paper tends to result in more social interactions among graders.

CCS CONCEPTS

• **Social and professional topics → Computing Education.**

KEYWORDS

Assessment; Exam Grading; Online Grading System

ACM Reference Format:
Yingjun Cao, Leo Porter, Soohyun Nam Liao, Rick Ord. 2019. Paper or Online? A Comparison of Exam Grading Techniques. In *Innovation and Technology in Computer Science Education (ITiCSE '19), July 15–17, 2019, Aberdeen, Scotland Uk.* ACM, New York, NY, USA, 6 pages. https://doi.org/10.1145/3304221.3319739

1 INTRODUCTION

The importance of both formative and summative assessments is well established. Formative assessments inform students of where misconceptions lie, enabling future practice and study. In fact, students often focus on various skills or concepts when they believe they will need to use them on an exam. Furthermore, we know that students (and indeed people in general) will learn something better when they are tested on it, a phenomenon known as the "testing effect" [25]. Similarly valuable, summative assessments are the primary mechanism for instructors to measure how much each student has learned.

In computer science classes, summative (and often formative) assessments frequently take the form of written exams, particularly in lower-division courses [26]. Instructors often seek to make the experience valuable for the students by providing useful feedback for students by (and when) grading. In fact, feedback on exams and quizzes may lead to better knowledge retention [12, 21, 28].

As computer science enrollments surge [9], there is an increased need to scale all the components of the course. Recent work has examined how pedagogies scale [22], but here we focus on scaling assessments, specifically the grading of exams. For instructors of these large classes, they are finding that grading has become an increasingly time-consuming task [19]. If the exams are predominately multiple choice questions, there are automated tools to reduce this time demand (e.g., automatically grading using tools such as Scantron machines). However, multiple choice questions do not always meet instructors' assessment needs. To more authentically assess desired learning outcomes in a course, many computer science exams have short answer or coding questions which often do not have unique answers. These questions require instructional staff to grade manually.

In order to grade the large quantity of exams (and to provide timely feedback), a large number of graders are often needed to grade hundreds of papers in hours. This instructional staff often have limited hours of employment, so time spent grading reduces time spent helping students. As a result, CS educators are seeking means of improving grading efficiency without resorting to exams which are strictly multiple choice questions.

Software tools to improve grading have been proposed with a major goal to improve efficiency. For example, programming projects have been increasingly autograded and feedback automatically generated [17, 20]. Exam grading tools have also been proposed though not as abundant as programming projects [4, 26]. One such tool and the tool used in this study is Gradescope [26]. Gradescope allows instructors to scan student exams, upload them to an online system, and grade online.

Despite claims in support of these tools, there is no empirical evidence to support that exam grading systems offer superior grading over traditional paper grading. This study is designed to investigate this claim in three ways: 1) the comparison of grading time between exam grading systems and paper grading on real computer science exam papers containing coding questions, 2) students' concern on these two forms of grading, and 3) comparing grader experiences using grading tools and grading on paper.

2 BACKGROUND

The role of assessment in student learning is a broad area of inquiry [8, 11, 15]. Assessments strongly influence student learning

ITiCSE '19, July 15–17, 2019, Aberdeen, Scotland Uk

ACM ISBN 978-1-4503-6301-3/19/07...$15.00
https://doi.org/10.1145/3304221.3319739

activities [27]. The so-called hidden curriculum, i.e., what students perceive will appear in future assessments, dominates what topics students study and the time they invest in that studying. Students usually try to achieve high study efficiency by aligning their study as much as they can with perceived assessment requirements [2, 5].

Formative assessments are also valuable to students for identifying areas of weakness and for helping self-regulate their learning [24]. Summative assessment is a necessary component in the role of certifying a student's knowledge [6, 18]. Due to potential academic integrity issues with take-home exams, summative exams in CS classes are usually conducted on paper with proctors during designated time periods. Given the important role of assessments in computing, we focus here on the practical issue of how to grade given limited instructor resources.

With regard to grading, educators in computer science have designed systems to improve the grading process for a variety of assessments. One recent work on exam grading by Harrington et. al. [19] examined the quality of manual TA markings during marking parties, and recommended organized group exam marking sessions. Another area of work has been designing systems to improve grading for coding projects [23]. For example, Dewey et al. [10] used constraint logic from the programming language literature to develop test suites for autograding. We refer readers to this review article on project autograding [20]. However, on the automation of exam grading, most systems rely on Scantron to grade multiple choice questions. Exams in computer science usually involve coding and short answers which are not suitable for Scantron.

Though it is possible to take exams entirely on computers, nearly all online exam grading systems in CS start by scanning handwritten exam papers then grading can be done on computers [4, 26]. One newly developed system, SAFE [7] starts to use student's electronic devices to conduct exams directly. There is no empirical study on how efficient it is to grade scanned exams on computer, and what are potential differences between grading on computer and grading on paper. This study seeks to answer this practical question.

Gradescope [26] is the platform commonly used on our campus for online grading and was hence selected in this study to compare with grading on paper. The system requires that handwritten papers be scanned into PDF formats and uploaded into Gradescope server. It allows instructors to build templates based on where students will write their answers on the exam paper and allows graders to only focus on student answers in the scanned papers. Standard rubrics can be developed for every exam question, and the rubrics are easy to modify. To limit the amount of papers to be scanned, instructors can create answer sheets on which students will write their answers.

3 ONLINE GRADING

In this section, we aim to describe the process of online grading to provide context to those unfamiliar. Using Gradescope to grade an exam, as we did in this study, consists of the following steps:

1. Exam Creation. The exam is created as usual. In large classes,the instructor might create different versions of the exam to ensure no cheating occurs. If this is the case, the instructor should ensure version numbers are adjacent to each question for ease of grading. Questions on all exams should appear in the same location on the page. Creation of the solutions is similar to standard exams.

2. Giving the Exam. Exams are printed and given to students in the standard manner. Students are reminded that their answers should fall within the assigned question region on the exam.

3. Online Setup. The instructor uploads a copy of the exam as a template and delineates bounding boxes around each question (or sub-part of a question). The instructor can also denote how many points each question is worth.

4. Scanning. One of the drawbacks to online grading is this step, where exams are digitized. At our institution, there are two sets of paper cutters and high-speed scanners. Instructional staff take exams, cut off the staples for ease of scanning, and then scan the exams into large *PDF* files.

5. Uploading Exams. After scanning the exams, the exams can be uploaded onto the online platform. The platform automatically splits the uploaded PDFs based on the number of pages in the template. If multiple versions are used, uploading one version at a time makes grading easier.

6. Student Identification. Instructional staff have to manually match students to exams. This is a fast process as the tool shows the staff member only the name region and assists the staff with an auto-complete feature.

7. Rubric. This can be developed by the instructor, at least in part, prior to exam grading. The rubric can be changed at any time during grading, and any changes in points for rubric items are applied retroactively. For example, if a syntax error was deducted 2 points in the initial rubric, changing the rubric item to only deduct 1 point applies to all exams which have that rubric item marked. This feature is particularly helpful when graders decide to change rubric criteria.

8. Grading Process. The grading process has generally been streamlined on this platform. A grader can be assigned to grade a single question, and keyboard hot keys allow the grader to apply a rubric and to retrieve the next ungraded exam. This eliminates the need to pass around paper copies and set to the correct page.

9. Monitoring Progress. During paper exam grading, instructors can typically see (and often anticipate) bottlenecks in the grading. The online platform makes this easier by providing the percentage of answers graded per question to aid with load balancing efforts.

10. Totaling Exams. This is a major advantage for online grading as the exams are automatically totaled when grading completes, and because students are already matched to the exam, there is no need to enter grades into any system.

11. Returning Exams. The instructor can release the exam once it is graded and students will receive an e-mail notifying them it is available. They can then view the exam online and view the rubric items applied per question.

12. Regrade Requests. Regrade requests can also be submitted online and answered online. A positive benefit for Academic Integrity is that students cannot modify original exams.

4 METHOD

In this section, we first list the questions we seek to address with this work, then provide details on the setting for the work.

4.1 Research Questions

This study intends to answer three related research questions on exam grading techniques:

- **RQ1**: Are there significant time efficiency differences between online exam grading and grading on paper?
- **RQ2**: What are the differences, if any, on experiences from students between online and paper exam grading?
- **RQ3**: What experiences and preferences do exam graders have on the two forms of exam grading?

RQ1 is the primary question, as grading expediency is often cited as the reason for adopting online grading systems. As instructors, we recognize that time spent grading is only one factor we need to consider. As such, RQ2 and RQ3 offer more insights on the most relevant parties of exams, the students and graders. These questions focus on their experiences and preferences with these grading techniques.

4.2 Setting and Experimental Design

The study was carried out in a 10-week advanced data structure class at a large research institution in North America during the 2016-2017 academic year. The class had two sections (A and B), both meeting on MWF and the instructor of both sections is an author of this paper. The course is structured to have two midterms, each one month apart, and the two sections hold exams on the same day. Section A started with 205 students and section B has 200 students at the beginning of the term.

For all practical purposes relevant to this study, the two sections were essentially identical. The only key difference is how the exams were graded: section A's first midterm was graded and returned online while section B's first midterm was graded and returned on paper. For the second midterm, the technique was switched (section A on paper and section B online) to limit potential confounding due to possible differences in students in each section. This experimental design allows each student from both sections to be exposed to both exam grading formats.

Exams on both midterms and both sections were printed on paper, and the exams were graded in a large on-campus eatery either one or two days after the exam. The class had 24 graders for both sections, and most graders are familiar with Gradescope. About 10–15 staff participated in each exam grading, but they arrived and departed during grading at various times to accommodate their class schedules.

To compare the efficiency of the two grading techniques (RQ1), a detailed log of the grading process was recorded with respect to the number of people participating in grading over various time periods. Additionally, time spent before exams (e.g., exam design, answer sheet creation, preparation with online tools, etc.) were also recorded. We also kept track of events after the exam, including the number of students who collected (or viewed) their graded exam and the number of regrade requests received by course staff. To further investigate students' experience and preference with the grading techniques (RQ2), a customized survey with five questions was distributed via a Google form to students at the end of the term to collect their experience on both exam grading formats. The survey contains four Likert-scale questions and one open-ended question. A minimal extra credit was offered to students who completed the survey. To examine graders' experiences (RQ3), we provided graders with a survey with four open-ended questions.

Each midterm exam had four versions with similar questions but different numbers in those questions. The exam contents and question types are as follows:

Midterm 1. Write the outputs of 3 segments of code (fill in the blanks); write a method for a binary search tree (BST) (coding); draw a multiway trie (MWT) or a ternary search tree (TST) (graphical question); complete a hashtable and calculate probability of collision (short answer), and one runtime analysis question comparing BST with TST and MWT (short answer).

Midterm 2. Complete and analyze an example using the count-min sketch algorithm (short answer); fill in the blanks on a red-black tree insertion example; fill in the blanks for a Huffman encoding question; a code writing problem to perform bitwise operations, and fill in the blanks related to Dijkstra's algorithm. This exam also had two multiple choice questions for code efficiency analysis.

5 RESULTS

In this section, we will provide results for the research questions.

5.1 Grading Time Efficiency (RQ1)

5.1.1 Pre-grading Time. A log was recorded for each midterm including exam design phase and the grading phase. Table 1 includes the time for events that occurred before the grading phase.

Table 1: Logs for pre-grading events (Time unit: minutes)

Pre-grading Events	Exam 1		Exam 2	
	Online	Paper	Online	Paper
Exam question design	480	480	270	270
Answer key preparations and rubric design	48	48	34	34
Create answer sheet and enter rubrics on online system	48	0	42	0
Copy answer key for paper grading	0	11	0	14
Exam digitization (including sorting, cutting, scanning, uploading, and name matching)	230	0	420	0
Total Time	806	539	766	318

Exam and answer key preparations are the same for both grading formats. The difference is that online grading requires a rubric to be created on the platform with a certain format. For paper grading, answer keys need to be copied to distribute to graders during grading. The one big difference between the grading formats is the scanning time. To use the online platform, the answer sheet from each student will be sorted in page order and will be scanned using scanner(s). For midterm 1, one grader scanned all the answer sheets for section A and the total time was reported to be 200 minutes in total. For the second midterm, 4 graders worked together for 100 minutes to complete the scan process for section B. The total time is calculated as the number of graders multiplied by the time they spent. The reason for a longer exam 2 scanning time is the scanner being used had a very slow interface with old USB drives, and the scanning staff were unaware of this limitation. Note that only the section that is being graded online has its exam papers scanned. The digitization time also includes name matching by a single grader: 30 minutes total for midterm 1 and 20 minutes total for midterm 2.

5.1.2 Grading Time. The grading phase log is shown in Figure 1 and total times appear in Table 2.

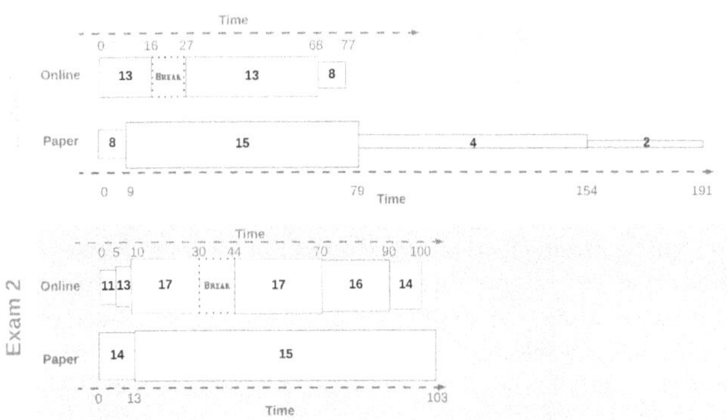

Figure 1: Time logs during grading for two midterms. Time unit is minute. The heights of boxes in the figure are proportional to the number of graders grading in a time period. For both midterms, we started with online grading then moved to grading on paper.

Table 2: Grading time in minutes.

Format	Exam 1			Exam 2		
	t_{total}	# exams	*average*	t_{total}	# exams	*average*
Online	861	195	4.42	1392	185	7.52
Paper	1526	197	7.75	1562	194	8.05

The metric we choose to compare grading techniques is the average time it takes to grade an exam paper by a single grader. To calculate this metric, the total amount of time for grading is obtained by weighing the time by the number of people grading. For example, for exam 1 online grading, the total time is calculated as 13 graders × 16 + 13 graders × (68 - 27) + 8 graders × (77 - 68) = 813 minutes. There were two extra delays in midterm 1 for online grading due to a misplaced answer sheet and more time spent grading that paper which are included in the table results. Table 2 also includes the time the instructor spent grading questions that existing rubrics do not fully apply for each grading technique in both exams (about 30 minutes). For grading on paper, the time to total exam scores and to enter exam grades to a spreadsheet is also included. We acknowledge that the metric is not the only choice though we believe it is one of the fairest for comparison purposes.

RQ1 is answered by Tables 1 and 2: while the online grading format has more overhead before grading, the total actual grading time as well as the average time per exam paper seems to be shorter with online grading. This pattern is true for both exams. However, if we combine both pre-grading and the actual grading time, and calculate the average time per grader per exam paper, there is no consistent pattern. For midterm 1, the average per paper is 12.51 minutes for paper grading, and for online, it is 8.55 per paper. For midterm 2, the trend reversed. It took 9.69 minutes to grade an exam on paper, and 11.66 minutes to grade an exam online.

5.2 Student Experience (RQ2)

An anonymous survey containing five questions was distributed to students near the end of the term. The survey results of the four Likert-scale questions are shown in Table 3. Results indicate that students overwhelmingly prefer to receive exams back from the online grading system and they report being more likely to "pick up" and review exams if they are returned via the online system. Regrade submissions follow a similar trend. The last question on a sense of being more "personally connected" is relatively more balanced: 50.2% of students prefer online compared with 31.9% preferring paper.

Table 3: Survey results on student experience with two grading techniques. Number of entries in the survey is 256. The annotation for ++ is strongly prefer and + is for prefer.

Question	Online ++	Online +	Neutral	Paper +	Paper ++
How do you prefer to receive your exams back?	49%	23.3%	8.9%	9.7%	8.9%
In which grading scenario are you likely to pick up/ review your graded exam?	47.5%	20.6%	12.8%	9.7%	9.3%
In which grading scenario do you feel comfortable submitting regrades?	43.6%	26.5%	17.5%	6.6%	5.8%
Which grading scenario do you feel personally connected to your exam results?	32.7%	17.5%	17.9%	14.4%	17.5%

5.3 Grader Experience (RQ3)

After the final exam, graders were asked to complete the following four-question online survey concerning the two grading formats: **Q1** - Convenience to grade exams; **Q2** - Speed to grade exams; **Q3** - Communication and team-bonding during grading; and
Q4 - Comment on the overall grading experience

Out of 24 graders, 13 responded and two of these responses were dropped as their responses indicated they misunderstood the questions. The remaining 11 responses show the following themes.
Q1. *Most graders feel that online grading is more convenient.* Arguments for using the online grading system include 1) ease of rubric adjustment, 2) ease of final score totaling, 3) ease of returning of exams, 4) the ability to easily skip hard-to-grade questions, 5) ease of splitting grading tasks into subparts for parallel grading, 6) support for grading remotely, and 7) ease of the regrading process. As for paper exams, graders' responses indicate that grading on paper seemed to be harder and less convenient.
Q2. *Most graders feel that online grading is faster than grading on paper* with one grader thinking that the speed is not that different between the two grading techniques. One grader commented that grading on paper is faster on coding problems while grading online seemed to work better for other types of questions.
Q3. Six graders commented that grading on paper seemed to encourage better communication among graders. Two graders believed there was no difference, one grader thought grading online in front of a machine facilitates better communications, and two graders

did not respond. For this question, grading on paper is a slight preference for graders.

Q4. We did not observe any consistent theme on Q4. Five graders stated that they like grading on paper for the fun factor and four graders preferred the online system because of speed and accuracy. Two expressed no preference.

6 DISCUSSION

6.1 Time Efficiency Comparison

Tables 1 and 2 show two distinctive patterns. Online grading has more initial overhead for scanning and answer sheet design. This is especially true for midterm 2 where the overhead is more than twice of that from paper grading. However, the availability and proper use of high-speed scanners may reduce this overhead. For the actual time grading the exams, the online platform was faster for both midterms. One benefit with paper grading is that it allows for grading immediately after the exam (no need to wait for scanning). We couldn't measure the grading accuracy of these two formats except counting the number of regrade requests. Though grading on paper seems to have fewer regrade requests, the difference may simply be due to the easiness of submitting regrades online.

6.2 Student Experience

As can be seen from Table 3, more than 70% of students preferred receiving graded exams electronically. In comparison, slightly less than 20% prefer to receive the paper exams back. More than 67% of students reported getting exams back online also made them more likely to review their exams. Again, about 20% of students reported they prefer retrieving physical exams for review.

These differences are large and to understand the reasons behind these preferences, we analyzed the open-ended question on the survey on students' opinions on receiving exams online and on paper. We coded the themes from the open survey question, and top themes are shown in Table 4.

Table 4: The list of top themes in the open-ended question on students' experience on the online exam grading system and paper. Number of valid responses is 256.

	Theme	%
ONLINE	Convenient and easily accessible	40.8
	Regrade is easy	21.2
	Detailed rubrics are helpful	12.6
	Online storage of exam is safe	7.7
	Online grading system works great for the final exam	7.1
	No cheating on regrades on the online system	4.0
	Some rubrics are vague	2.4
	Better privacy when "picking up" papers	1.8
	Too much technology already	1.2
	Answer sheets without exams are not convenient to review	1.2
PAPER	Getting exam paper back is time consuming and inconvenient	29.4
	Having paper exam back is better for review and study	24.8
	Paper feels better and embodies a personal touch	20.9
	Hand graded exams have more personal comments	5.2
	Grading rules are easy to understand on paper	4.6
	Writings on paper exams may not be clear	4.6
	Getting the paper by the end of class is nice	3.3
	Can write notes on paper exam	2.6
	Want to keep a hard copy	2.6
	Midterms on paper is good	2.0

The primary reason that students like the online grading format is its convenience. The availability of exams online allows students to review their exams remotely without worrying about losing their exam papers. Students stressed that being able to access the graded exam remotely was especially useful for the final exam as students often leave campus prior to exams being graded. Also convenient for students is the ability to submit a regrade request through the platform by only providing a brief justification. The grader who graded the problem is also conveniently notified that a request was submitted. Students also reported valuing the detailed rubrics provided online which are typically not provided for paper exams (but could be). There are also some side-benefits to support the use of online grading systems. For example, online systems have a scan of the original papers so students cannot modify their exam when they submit a regrade request.

The most important reason that students do not prefer paper exams back is surprisingly the inconvenience of getting it back. Most instructors try to hand back exams near the end of a class section but with hundreds of students, multiple assistants have to be on site and students will go to a specific assistant based on their last name or some other identifiers. If a student misses that class, she has to go to the instructor's office to collect the exam. Moreover, students reported being concerned about the privacy of their grade as when exams are returned in-class, grades are sometimes seen by other students.

Although nearly all students acknowledge the convenience of online grading systems, grading on paper exams has benefits as well. We suspect a large benefit of paper exams is in having more verbose and personalized feedback. Particularly on code-writing questions, it is easier to identify and mark errors on paper than online. (Note that the online platform allows for custom rubric items and for graders to write on exams using a tablet; in our experience, this feature has not been used heavily.) The next important reason is that having a hard copy is more tangible and may connect students more personally to the exam.

The ease of regrades may impact student preference. Our data shows that for midterm 1, there are 9 regrade requests from the online grading system, and 4 from exams graded on paper. For midterm 2, there were 48 regrade requests online while there were 14 from exams returned on paper. All but one online regrade request is frivolous. Therefore, the ease of regrades may make the grading process more fair by reducing the number of grading errors. We do note, however, that ease in submitting regrades may cause students to abuse the system. In our classes, we typically caution students that regrades are to be used to correct obvious grading errors, not to argue for more points.

As described for online grading systems, some students stated that getting midterm exams back on paper is better while receiving exams back online is better for the final exam. Students also like personal comments graders may put on the exam paper though the online system also provides similar functionalities. Last but not least, some students find grading rules on paper are easier to understand compared to the online system. Though they didn't elaborate, we hypothesize that these students probably refer to coding or complicated short answer questions. Graders can draw and write on the location where certain mistakes have occurred while it is not easy to do it on the online system, at least not efficiently.

6.3 Grader Experience

In general, graders reported preferring online grading as it reduced many of the administrative chores compared with grading on paper. However, paper grading might promote better communication among graders and, possibly, community building. With the current discussion on utilizing undergraduate students as teaching assistants to help scaling CS classes [13, 16], this feedback from graders might be valuable. The instructor of the class also observed that graders seem to enjoy the grading process and interact with each other more during grading sessions on paper. They more frequently share exams with each other to decide if a certain solution is worth some partial credit. Having the physical copy may have made this kind of sharing more convenient.

Graders also echoed some of the points raised by students regarding different types of questions may impact which system is preferred. For example, graders tended to remark that code-writing problems are easier to grade on paper as they can make marks on the paper. Multiple choice or short answer questions might be more easily graded on the online system without having to flip through pages on paper exams. Graders also discussed the convenience of changing grading rubrics on the online system. It is much more convenient to apply a change on the allocation of points on the online system than grading on papers. In particular, if rubrics have to be changed after an exam has been distributed, paper exams will involve a huge administrative cost to collect all distributed papers and regrade them. This can be done easily with the online system.

6.4 Quality of Feedback

Existing research has shown that quality feedback may have one of the most influential effects in student learning [3, 14]. Students indicated in the survey that having detailed rubrics from the online platform is helpful to them. However, they may sometimes focus on trying to determine how well their answer matches the rubric to argue for more points instead of trying to understand the concepts. Bennett et al. [1] shows that if feedback is provided together with the marks of assessment, students tend to over-focus on the exam scores instead of examining and reflecting on the feedback. Paper exams are more convenient for students to put notes on their mistakes and it might be easier for graders to provide customized comments, but paper exam return typically does not include providing detailed rubrics. Most of the time, students will only know the correct answer if it is written on their exam papers. Future research on the effect of rubrics on student learning might reveal more nuanced findings.

7 CONCLUSION

This work is the first to empirically compare online grading systems and paper grading in computing from three important perspectives: grading time efficiency, student preferences, and grader preferences. Results show online grading was faster during actual grading, but required scanning before grading. A more streamlined scanning process might be the key to achieve better overall time efficiency using online grading. Students, in general, prefer the online grading system because of its convenient accessibility, regrading system, and available detailed rubrics. Exams graded on paper tend to result in difficulties receiving the exam due to absence on days the exams are returned and time to return the exam in large classes. Exams graded on paper may ofter other advantages including students possibly feeling more connected to the physical exam. Graders tend to prefer online grading for convenience, yet paper grading may result in a better atmosphere among graders. For future studies, we plan to randomly sample exams from students and compare the accuracy of two grading formats on different types of problems.

REFERENCES

[1] R. E. Bennett. Formative assessment: a critical review. *Assessment in Education: Principles, Policy & Practice*, 18(1):5–25, 2011.
[2] J. Biggs. Enhancing teaching through constructive alignment. *Higher Education*, 32(3):347–364, 1996.
[3] P. Black. Formative assessment: raising standards inside the classroom. *School Science Review*, 80(291):39–46, 1998.
[4] A. Bloomfield and J. F. Groves. A tablet-based paper exam grading system. *SIGCSE Bull.*, 40(3):83–87, June 2008.
[5] A. Cain and M. A. Babar. Reflections on applying constructive alignment with formative feedback for teaching introductory programming and software architecture. In *ICSE 2016*.
[6] Y. Cao and L. Porter. Evaluating student learning from collaborative group tests in introductory computing. In *SIGCSE 2017*.
[7] K. Chebrolu, B. Raman, V. C. Dommeti, A. V. Boddu, K. Zacharia, A. Babu, and P. Chandan. Safe: Smart authenticated fast exams for student evaluation in classrooms. In *SIGCSE 2017*.
[8] N. R. Council et al. *How people learn: Brain, mind, experience, and school: Expanded edition*. National Academies Press, 2000.
[9] CRA. Computing Research Association, The Taulbee Survey. https://cra.org/wp-content/uploads/2018/05/2017-Taulbee-Survey-Report.pdf. Accessed Jan. 15, 2019.
[10] K. Dewey, P. Conrad, M. Craig, and E. Morozova. Evaluating test suite effectiveness and assessing student code via constraint logic programming. In *ITiCSE 2017*.
[11] F. Dochy, M. Segers, D. Gijbels, and K. Struyven. Assessment engineering. In *Rethinking assessment in higher education: learning for the longer term.*, pages 87–100. Oxford: Routledge, 2007.
[12] M. L. Epstein, A. D. Lazarus, T. B. Calvano, K. Matthews, R. A. Hendel, B. B. Epstein, and G. M. Brosvic. Immediate feedback assessment technique promotes learning and corrects inaccurate first responses. *The Psychological Record*, 52:187–201, 2002.
[13] J. Forbes, D. J. Malan, H. Pon-Barry, S. Reges, and M. Sahami. Scaling introductory courses using undergraduate teaching assistants. In *SIGCSE 2017*.
[14] B. J. Fraser, H. J. Walberg, W. W. Welch, and J. A. Hattie. Syntheses of educational productivity research. *International Journal of Educational Research*, 11(2):187–212, 1987.
[15] G. Gibbs, C. Simpson, P. Gravestock, and M. Hills. Conditions Under Which Assessment Supports Students' Learning. *Learning in Teaching in Higher Education*, 1(1):3–31, 2004.
[16] C. Gregg and C. M. Lewis. Working with undergraduate teaching assistants: Best practices and lessons learned. In *SIGCSE 2015*.
[17] S. Gulwani, I. Radiček, and F. Zuleger. Feedback generation for performance problems in introductory programming assignments. In *FSE 2014*.
[18] W. Harlen and M. James. Assessment and learning: differences and relationships between formative and summative assessment. *Assessment in Education: Principles, Policy & Practice*, 4(3):365–379, 1997.
[19] B. Harrington, M. Ahmadzadeh, N. Cheng, E. H. Wang, and V. Efimov. TA Marking Parties: Worth the Price of Pizza? ICER 2018.
[20] P. Ihantola, T. Ahoniemi, V. Karavirta, and O. Seppälä. Review of recent systems for automatic assessment of programming assignments. In *Koli Calling 2010*.
[21] H. Keuning, J. Jeuring, and B. Heeren. Towards a systematic review of automated feedback generation for programming exercises. In *ITiCSE 2016*.
[22] S. N. Liao, W. G. Griswold, and L. Porter. Impact of class size on student evaluations for traditional and peer instruction classrooms. In *SIGCSE 2017*.
[23] T. MacWilliam and D. J. Malan. Streamlining grading toward better feedback. In *ITiCSE 2013*.
[24] D. J. Nicol and D. Macfarlane-Dick. Formative assessment and self-regulated learning: A model and seven principles of good feedback practice. *Studies in higher education*, 31(2):199–218, 2006.
[25] H. L. Roediger and J. D. Karpicke. The power of testing memory: Basic research and implications for educational practice. *Perspectives on Psychological Science*, 1(3):181–210, 2006.
[26] A. Singh, S. Karayev, K. Gutowski, and P. Abbeel. Gradescope: A fast, flexible, and fair system for scalable assessment of handwritten work. In *L@S 2017*.
[27] B. R. Snyder. *The hidden curriculum*. New York: Knopf, 1970.
[28] J. A. Stone. Using reflective blogs for pedagogical feedback in CS1. In *SIGCSE 2012*.

Measuring Instruction Comprehension by Mining Memory Traces for Early Formative Feedback in Java Courses

Frank Höppner
Ostfalia University of Applied Sciences
Wolfenbüttel, Germany
f.hoeppner@ostfalia.de

ABSTRACT

To support students in a computer science programme in their first steps with programming in Java, we provide a tool for early formative feedback regarding the comprehension of the instruction types. The tool asks the students to enter memory traces for ordinary Java programs. To increase the effectiveness, we consider how to provide substantial hints to the students, where exactly they have to change their mental model of program execution. This requires the detection of co-occurring problems across multiple Java programs. We present a data mining approach that allows to automatically detect code fragments that cause systematic difficulties in the group of students. First results are promising and the desired effective feedback seems within reach.

CCS CONCEPTS

• **Social and professional topics → Student assessment**; • **Information systems → Association rules**.

KEYWORDS

introductory programming; instruction comprehension; formative feedback; memory trace; code pattern; data mining

ACM Reference Format:
Frank Höppner. 2019. Measuring Instruction Comprehension by Mining Memory Traces for Early Formative Feedback in Java Courses. In *Innovation and Technology in Computer Science Education (ITiCSE '19), July 15–17, 2019, Aberdeen, Scotland, UK*. ACM, New York, NY, USA, 7 pages. https://doi.org/10.1145/3304221.3325529

1 INTRODUCTION

Learning the very first programming language is not an easy endeavour. Many students start their studies without having any experience in computer programming. Typical foundation courses introduce the ideas of computational thinking, present the key elements of the programming language and require the students to practice as much as they can: weekly exercises have to be uploaded somewhere to get graded by some unit tests. The students thus face a wide spectrum of challenges: Apart from the obvious ones, the syntax and semantics of the programming language, they usually find the exercises difficult to understand and/or to solve, experience difficulties in transforming their idea of a solution into a structured representation, e.g. pseudo code, struggle with the peculiarities of the integrated development environment (IDE) and hardly understand the feedback of unit tests.

Some fraction of the students always gets along well with this setting, especially if they have some experience in programming already. This paper focusses mainly on helping the remainder of the course. For them the first explanation and example may not be sufficient to fully grasp the semantics of a new instruction. But as the next lecture covers yet another instruction type, there is not much room for repetition or adjustment. So their knowledge remains vague and, due to their uncertainty, their interpretation may switch spontaneously. Such an erratic behaviour has also been observed as problematic in the literature. A teacher may neither want to adopt the course speed to this group nor precautionary prepare additional material and repeatedly grade the students replies. Some students will thus keep making the same errors over and over again – possibly without noticing as they get no feedback. Later, if the course objective is in danger and the teacher observes these problems, it makes her no longer wonder why this student failed in simple programming exercises: without having understood the semantics of the instructions, a correct program is obtained by chance only. Understanding the mechanics of program execution earlier might have helped such students to master the course successfully.

In this paper we investigate whether it is possible to provide an autonomous tool that can help students to improve their understanding of the Java language semantics with as little involvement of the lecturer as possible. To achieve this, two questions have to be answered: How do we challenge the students perception of program execution to detect problems? And, secondly, is it possible to automatically analyse the problems to distinguish substantial problems from oversights/careless mistakes. The latter is the main research question of this paper because only a positive answer would enable us to address relevant problems autonomously and encourage students to correct their mental model of program execution.

The remainder of the paper is organized as follows: After discussing related work in the section 2, we introduce memory traces as our means to observe the instruction comprehension in section 3. The obtained data is far more complicated to evaluate than the answer to, say, multiple choice questions and will be discussed in section 4. Results on a first course will be presented in section 5.

2 RELATED WORK

Novices do not start studying without any prior knowledge, but connect what they learn to existing knowledge, may it be appropriate or not. Step by step they construct their mental model of

ITiCSE '19, July 15–17, 2019, Aberdeen, Scotland, UK

ACM ISBN 978-1-4503-6301-3/19/07...$15.00
https://doi.org/10.1145/3304221.3325529

how a programming language works. For simple concepts, such as assignments, test questions were developed and presented to students and the answers were matched against a broad variety of possible *mental models* such as right-to-left copy, left-to-right copy, equality, ... [5]. It is an interesting research question how mental models evolve, as such knowledge might be used to reveal how a learning processes should look like. In this line of argumentation the authors of [14] state that "the problem of helping students to *convert* this diverse and persistent range of non-viable mental models into viable ones presents a real challenge to computer science educators". Given the limited time, however, the lecturer does not want to spent her time on analyzing mental models of all students individually, but to *effectively teach all students a viable mental model.*

There are many efforts in the literature that may help shaping a viable mental model. One approach is to visualize what happens at execution time of some Java program, e.g. Jeliot [15], Java2Sequence [4], Jive [10], sometimes integrated into the IDE [11], more refs. in [13]. While watching an animation everything appears plausible – just like the convincing explanation of an experienced lecturer makes all students nodding. But that does not mean that all students actually adopted their models correctly. If methods provide no feedback, there is a lack of student involvement. Multiple-choice or constructed-response questions might be used instead, e.g. [3, 9, 17], but their construction is often time-consuming and are usually targeted to known misconceptions. In [3, 9] domain models are constructed to induce the misconception in the students model, however, it seems that many students do not behave consistently and analytically [5], which may also be one of the reasons why providing effective hints is difficult [16].

To support the students, new concepts are often illustrated using analogies, e.g. boxes for variables or arrows for pointers/references, to connect new concepts easily to existing knowledge. These analogies are almost never a perfect fit, but appear helpful from one perspective (boxes can store things) but also misleading from another (boxes do not care about data types and may store multiple things at the same time) [12]. Therefore the instructor guidelines of [12] advise not to use them: (1) Show behaviour, no analogy, e.g. do not use the analogy of boxes for variables. (2) Build concepts first, jargon last; analogies alone may provoke wrong presumptions. (3) Constant repetition. The last point seems very important, because reasoning by analogy connects to ideas that have been consolidated over the past, which is why we may find them easier to argue with. But constant repetition may be the only way to prevent non-viable concepts from infiltrating the students mental model of program execution and improve consistency.

Other studies confirm the importance of a viable model: For novices learning Prolog the study of [18] came to the conclusion that those who were successful had a mechanical understanding of the way the *language implementation* worked. A popular technique that points into the same direction, although there might not be so many publications about it, are memory traces which require students to write down the state of all variables throughout code execution. The use of such techniques has been reported to lead to a significant increase in student performance [6]. Hand-crafted tracing questions are also the basis for the analysis of misconceptions in the aforementioned approaches [3, 5, 9, 17].

3 MODEL ALIGNMENT BY MEMORY TRACES

Our setting is an introductory Java programming course in a computer science programme. We start with imperative programming and then extend to the object-oriented paradigm – rather than an objects first approach. The lecturer explains syntax and semantics of statements and provides examples, but cannot be sure how viable the students mental model is: *is the students prediction of program execution close enough to reality?* As an autonomous tool will never gain access or understand a students mental model, the best we can possibly hope for are means to validate its viability. We use memory traces as the vehicle to achieve this. The design of the traces is motivated by the following key factors, which connect to the discussion in the previous section: (1) Analogies are avoided. (2) Low question bias, all aspects of the language are covered. (3) Traces stick tightly to the true mechanics, switching to a debugger seems effortless. (4) A full trace allows to reproduce every single step, nothing is removed or replaced (in contrast to object diagrams, which become messy if constantly changed with every code line). (5) Repetition is important: The same misconception is tested in many different disguises in contrast to predefined questions which address a single misconception and may be memorized.

3.1 Memory Traces

In this section we elaborate on what we understand by memory trace, cf. example in Figs. 1 and 4. Bear in mind that the students do not face these details at once, but the complexity slowly increases week by week with new instruction types.

- Given a small piece of Java code, the students identify in which order the code lines are visited, starting with sequential execution only. Just before we switch to the next code line, the current content of all variables, the line number and a full memory snapshot is noted.
- The memory snapshot is subdivided into stack, heap and static area, starting with stack only. If the program execution reaches a local variable declaration, the students have to place its content on top of the stack. If the surrounding block ends, they have to release it from the stack.
- A (static) function call is noted in multiple stages: The function call is prepared by copying the values of all arguments on top of the stack (plus one extra space in case of a return value). Then we continue at the first code line of the function. Upon returning to the caller line, execute the remaining operations, such as assignment of the return value, and finally clean up the arguments and return value from the stack.
- An object is stored at a freely choosable address in heap memory. Unlike the stack area, we artificially enumerate the positions in the heap so that we can refer to specific positions using these *addresses*. A reference to an object simply stores this address.
- For a method call we follow the same procedure as with a function call. The object, for which the method is called, is treated just like an additional parameter named '*this*'.

The final level of detail is intentionally high (cf. (3)). The distinction between stack and heap becomes absolutely necessary once objects get involved, but we start the traces with a stack area only and introduce the heap later. The use of addresses to represent object

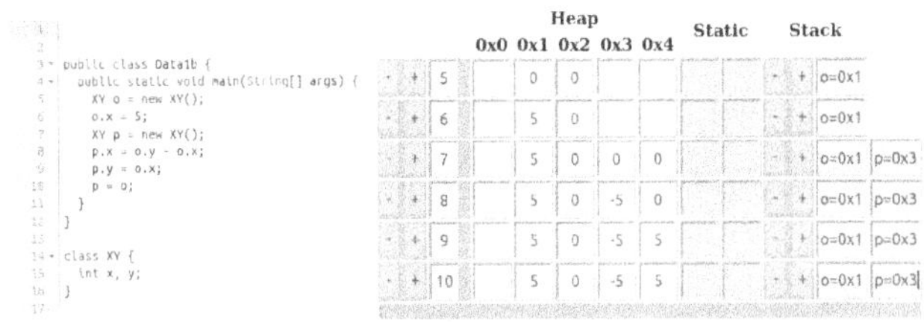

Figure 1: Screenshot of Java Memory Tracer.

references avoid analogies (cf. (1)) and allows to explain new situations as a natural consequence of what we have learnt earlier: e.g. the assignment or comparison of references (just compare the content of the memory cell, no matter whether it is of a primitive type or a reference) or the passing of an object to a function (we have placed copies of primitive types on the stack, so we do the same with references – no distinction between call by value and call by reference necessary). Other details are intentionally omitted, for instance, we do not distinguish the size of the primitive data types, neither on stack nor on heap. We do not introduce a new stack frame with every function call, hiding the variables of earlier calls, because now the students see that the very same local variable piles on the stack over and over again with every recursive function call and we tempt them to change the wrong one. Misconceptions can only be discovered if they get the chance of making errors.

3.2 Web Application for Formative Feedback

Filling out such a program execution trace on the blackboard is useful to introduce the notation of the trace and explain new instructions for the first time, but it is far more important to let *all students* fill out the traces themselves. To avoid a cumbersome manual grading, a web application has been developed that performs the evaluation automatically (cf. (5)). Lecturers may upload arbitrary Java code and the Java debugger is employed to construct the solution automatically (cf. (3)). Therefore examples 'invented' during the lectures are turned into a new exercise easily. In case of an error in the trace, only the wrong lines are indicated but not the exact position of the error. This is a design decision to prevent guessing values by hiding the exact position of the error in the trace line. A screenshot of the web application is shown in Fig. 1. The web application currently offers about 75 small exercises, grouped into multiple sections. Students can request an evaluation of the trace entered so far at any time, but exercises of the next level are only offered once they completed an exercise of the current level without too many errors. By means of the web application, the students receive feedback from the very first lectures, starting with variable declarations and expressions only.

4 MINING TRACES

To become an even more effective tool, the goal is to robustly detect *serious problems* automatically, but to ignore slips and oversights. The traces require quite a number of inputs, so slips eventually occur, and students may not realize that they repeat some mistakes consistently. With an automatic detection a later version of the tool may approach students like "You have faced a situation like this M times across N exercises, but entered consistently a wrong solution (P%). Chances are high that you did not understood statement X correctly. This is also a common problem for P% of your fellow students." We must be sure that we tackle serious problems such that students value the feedback and start to care. This is challenging as it requires the analysis of traces from different exercises.

4.1 Memory Traces as Interval Sequences

While a high error count at the same position of the same exercise likely indicates a difficulty, it is much harder to accumulate these counts across different exercises automatically: The exact source code varies from exercise to exercise, e.g. the content of the loop body, but some properties of the code remain the same, e.g. prefix-increment in for-statement. The goal is to identify characteristic properties that hint to a difficult situation that has not yet been adequately included in the students mental model. To identify such characteristic properties, we have to establish some means to generalize the error situation, that is, dropping irrelevant and focusing on important aspects of the source code. We have the correct memory trace, but from the trace alone we do not know which instructions occurred in a specific line of code. Therefore we use an abstract syntax tree (AST) as a second ingredient. The tree, however, may contain statements that never get executed during the exercise, e.g. an else case if the condition expression evaluates to true.

Usually a problem is not caused by a single statement, but it may be necessary to include e.g. the nesting of instructions ("an assignment within a block of an if-statement within a for-loop"). While an assignment is completed in a single trace line, the instructions of a block cover multiple steps in the trace, and multiple executions of the same block may be instances of the same for-loop body. The fusion of both information, instruction types and trace steps, into a sequence of labelled intervals is shown in Fig. 2: From the example code (top left) the memory trace (bottom left) and AST (middle) is generated automatically. The new representation is shown on the right, where the x-axis corresponds to the eight time steps of the memory trace. Each box represents the execution of a certain instruction type (label) over a certain time interval. We arrive at this representation by stepping through the lines of the trace and asking the AST which nodes cover this line (note the line numbers next to the AST nodes). For each node, a new labelled interval with the resp. AST-node as its label is created or an existing interval is extended. Labels are abbreviated to capital letters in Fig. 2, e.g. VDS for variable declaration statement. For instance, in time step $t = 3$ of the memory trace, we have just entered the body of the for-loop (lines 6-7) and face a variable declaration statement in code line 6. From the AST we find in code line 6 a node "Block" and a node "Variable Declaration Statement" (VDS) and thus insert intervals (starting at current time step $t = 3$) with the respective label. The next line of the memory trace refers to code line 7 and we learn from the AST that one of the intervals we have just introduced, namely "Block", persists from code line 6 to 7, so we extend the interval just introduced to $t = 4$, while the interval labelled VDS does not extend to $t = 3$. Having processed the full trace we arrive at the final representation (right). The full trace covers a single method declaration (main) with a variable declaration followed by a for loop (red), whose body is executed twice, hence two intervals "Block" (orange) from $t = 3..4$ and $t = 6..7$.

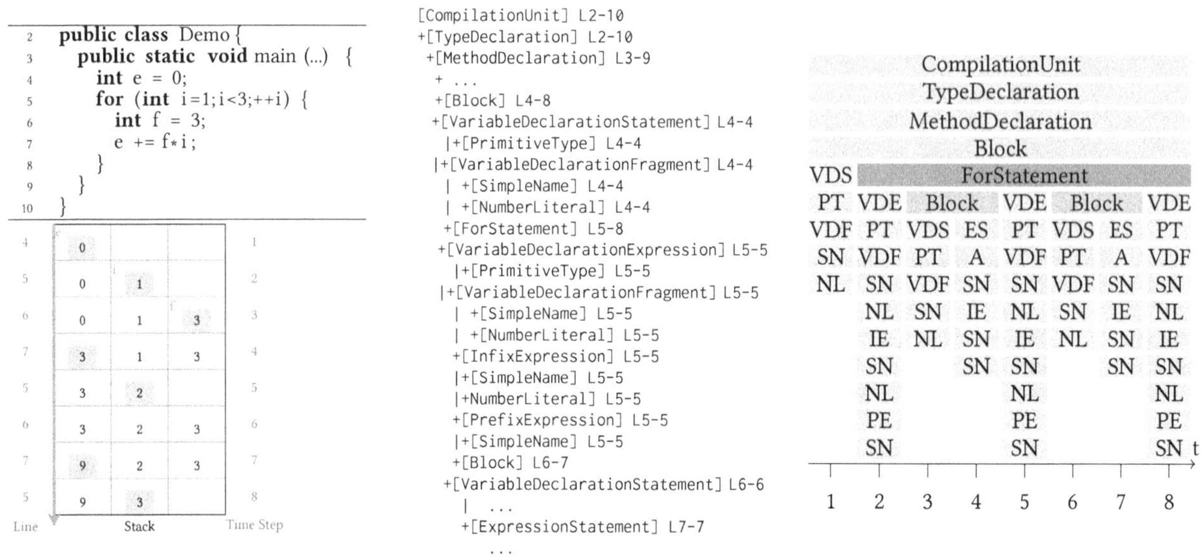

Figure 2: Data fusion: From the source code (top left) the memory trace (left bottom) and abstract syntax tree (middle) is generated automatically. The source code line numbers are used to connect elements from the memory trace to the respective node of the AST. The labels of the intervals shown on the right are derived from the AST and stretch over the associated time steps (x-axis) of the memory trace.

4.2 Construction of a Classified Data Set

Next we prepare a dataset that captures the problematic spots of the source code. For each submission we extend the interval sequence of the respective exercise by additional intervals indicating the type and position of the error. For instance, if a student forgot to introduce a new variable f in step $t_{\text{error}} = 3$, his trace was correct for time steps $t_{\text{error}} < 3$, but we recognize a missing element on the stack at $t = 3$. We thus introduce an interval "current position" and "missing stack element" at $t_{\text{error}} = 3$. To describe the circumstances of the error, we keep all intervals that cross t_{error} as well as a 2-3 lines before t_{error}, assuming that the few lines before the error may provide enough contextual information. Intervals beyond t_{error} cannot be helpful to diagnose the problem as they lie in the future (relative to the error position). In addition to those interval sequences describing error situations we construct a random subsample of situations where students entered a correct trace. We select a random position in the memory trace, add an interval labelled "current position", but no interval indicating an error.

4.3 Searching for Substantial Patterns

We want to identify patterns in the set of interval sequences that lead to an increased likelihood of an error at the "current position". There are many ways to define patterns in a stream of intervals [8], we settled at a representation that uses Allens interval relationships [2]: For any pair of intervals (labelled A and B in Fig. 3), there are 13 different interval relationships. A set of n intervals can be described by all pairwise relationships of participating intervals. For instance, the pattern in Fig. 5(a) can be described as 'If-Statement *is finished by* Block', 'VDS *starts* Block', 'Error *meets* Block'. The remaining relationships can then be determined unambiguously.

Next, in the fashion of association rule mining [1], we identify all patterns that occur in at least q% of the sequences (we used q=0.8). This is done levelwise: Starting from patterns of size 1, consisting of a single labelled interval, we successively increase the pattern size until none of the pattern reaches the support of q% any more. To efficiently enumerate these patterns we used the algorithms described in [7], but other approaches are possible (cf. refs. in [8]).

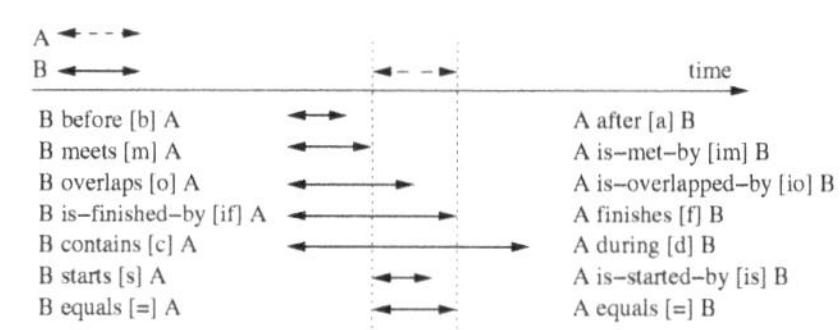

Figure 3: Allen's Interval Relationships.

In the obtained set of patterns we find interesting patterns p by inspecting the fraction f_p of sequences containing errors. To eliminate spurious patterns, we consider only those patterns p where the fraction f_p is significantly larger than f_q for all of its subpatterns q, that is, where one of the intervals in p was removed (χ^2 independence test). The accepted patterns p with the highest fraction f_p are most interesting in the sense that (a) an occurrence of this situation is a strong predictor for a challenging situation for the student and (b) the labelled intervals are specific to the error situations, otherwise one of the tests would have failed.

5 EMPIRICAL EVALUATION

The tool was used during the lecture and in weekly homework exercises, its use was recommended but optional. The usage statistics differ greatly among students. Some practised weekly as requested, others started late, some ignored the tool almost completely.

5.1 Usage Overview and Pre-Test

Table 1 shows a summary of all attempts to solve the exercises. For the subsequent analysis we had roughly 22000 evaluated traces out of which about 5300 were erroneous. The students may evaluate their traces multiple times, but if they switch to another exercise, we consider this attempt as closed. The data consists of 3132 attempts, so we have about 7 traces per attempt on average. When the attempt is closed the trace may be finished or incomplete. If a student did not succeed in the first attempt, he may return to it for a second trial later on. The sequence number of the attempt is shown on the top of the table. If an exercise has been solved on the first attempt, it is less likely that the student repeats this exercise but instead switches to a different one. The total number of traces for attempt $n + 1$ varies around 75% of the incomplete traces in trial n. Thus most students retry the exercises several times to get it completed. As the students were not obliged to do so, we take this as an indicator that they found the tool helpful. Table 2 shows results from a small experiment before the first introduction of the tool: a group of students was subdivided, half of them had to practice and discuss the traces paper-based (column p) and the other half used the tool (column t). The table shows how many students got the lifetime of variable right (row ok) or wrong in a manually graded test afterwards ($\chi^2 = 7.353, p < 1\%$).

attempt no.	1	2	3	4	≥ 5
finished	911	289	127	49	52
incomplete	953	421	172	85	73
total	1864	710	299	134	125

Table 1: Do students retry an uncompleted exercise?

	p.	t.
¬ok	11	3
ok	12	26
	23	29

Table 2: Paper vs tool practice

5.2 Evaluation of a Live Exercise

Although not in the main focus of this paper, we provide a brief example of evaluating a live exercise during the lecture, typically after having introduced a new concept or instruction. The live exercise is meant to replace the trace construction on the blackboard by all course members collectively, which also provides some feedback, but not individually to each student. Besides the feedback to the student (cf. Fig. 1), there is also feedback to the lecturer: Fig. 4 shows a summary of about 34 entered traces. The code is shown on the left, the correct solution to the right. The error frequency for each value is color-coded: the more errors were made the more the color changes from green to red. The most common wrong inputs may be inspected. The lecturer may then decide to elaborate on certain aspects of the instruction type once more.

5.3 Error Patterns across Exercises

In this section we return to the main question, whether it is possible to induce relevant error situations from the traces alone without any intervention from the lecturer. They shall be used in later versions of the tool to address the students directly. The extracted patterns were ordered by their error-probability and we discuss some of the top-ranked patterns in this list. At the top we found very simple patterns about array or class instance creation. They refer to the introduction of the heap when students had to distinguish between entering references and values.

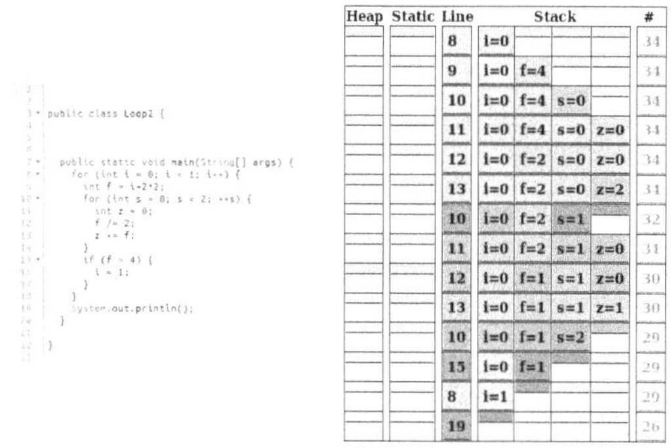

Figure 4: Live evaluation of traces entered in the lecture.

Pattern (a) in Fig. 5 is about the lifetime of a variable. It includes an if-statement with a block that starts with a variable declaration statement (VDS). The pattern occurs 196 times with an error rate of 73% (144 cases). Relative to the overall error rate of 24% in the whole dataset, an error is 3 times more likely than on average. The error occurs at the end of the if-statement. In 81% of the cases, the error consists of a wrong stack value, in 71% the code line in the trace is wrong, and in 54% the stack has too many elements. The latter case is most obvious: the lifetime of the variable declared within the block of the if-statement ends with the block but was not removed from the stack by the student. A wrong stack value may occur for the same reason if the error line itself includes a variable declaration (then the stack height is correct but the old value was not removed and is therefore wrong). A wrong code line may easily slip through because the block typically ends with a code line that is empty except the closing curly bracket – such lines do not get traced, so the auto-increment of the last code line by the GUI is wrong and double-checking is easily forgotten.

Pattern (b) indicates problems with interpreting the loop condition. It consist of a for-Statement with a one-liner block, which is also the error position. Again, the likelihood of an error is 3 times higher (244 instances, 175 errors). The most likely error types are wrong stack values and wrong line numbers. A wrong line number may occur if the student decided that the for-loop has ended, but actually it takes another iteration. Tracing a different code position by mistake may easily lead to wrong stack values, as well as wrong calculations in the block.

Pattern (c) refers to semantics of the for-statement. It describes an error in a code line with an Infix- and a Prefix-Operator embedded into a for-loop (2.95 times more likely than average, 221 instances, 158 errors). The operators refer to the update and loop condition of the for statement. If such an error occurs, we observe in 75% a wrong stack value (students are not fully aware of when the for-update statement is executed), in 53% an over-length stack (due to local variables that might have been declared in the for block which has just ended) and in 24% a wrong line number (after the final iteration they did not realize that we still have to go back to the for-loop declaration to check the loop-condition again).

Finally pattern (d) refers to an assignment which involves a function or method invocation (MI). Students are often not aware

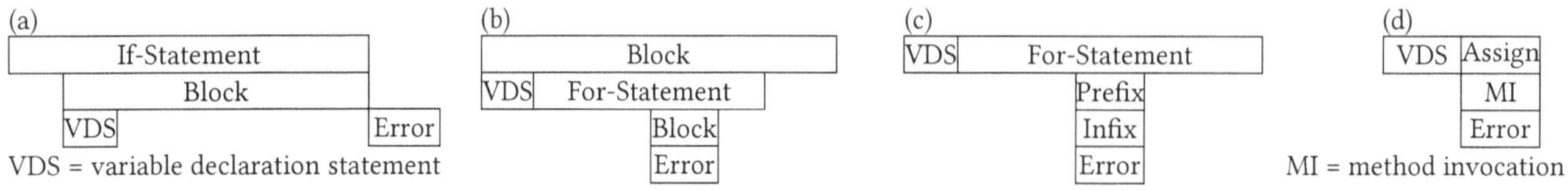

Figure 5: Discovered code fragments that frequently led to erroneous traces.

that the invocation requires to copy all parameters on the stack. The error likelihood is 2.91 times higher than normal (235 instances, 164 errors). In 53% the stack height is too small (no arguments copied on the stack) and in 23% it is too large (with methods '*this*' is often forgotten). In 35% the values and in 18% the variable names on the stack are wrong, which is due to an incorrect evaluation of the parameters or a wrong parameter order.

5.4 Discussion

In summary, the examples show that we successfully discovered code fragments across multiple exercises that led to a significantly increased error rate. The goal was to derive substantial patterns automatically, which hint at substantial misunderstandings. In that sense, the fact that the discussed patterns sound familiar to CS teachers underlines that this goal has been achieved. It increases the confidence that other (high-confidence) patterns refer to misconceptions, too.

There is quite a long list of other patterns that were not discussed here, partly because of space limits and partly because we have not (yet) an explanation for them. Several patterns have a high similarity to other patterns, so they may describe essentially the same problem and can be eliminated in a further post-processing step. For other cases it does not seem obvious, why they might have been evolved, for instance *an error at the end of a block which contained an assigment.* Observing the pattern alone does not tell us what kind of misconception might be the root cause. At this point we may decide to investigate this situation in detail to learn what kind of misconception or mental model turned this code fragment into a problem. This, however, has to be done manually together with the students. In this particular case we stumbled by chance over a possible explanation: Few students were surprised that changes made within the block are not revoked at the end of the block. They had the idea of blocks being like sandboxes and changes within the block do not reach outside the block or disappear when it ends.

Although interesting, our main concern is to *effectively teach all students a viable mental model* rather than understanding and collecting the misconceptions. Due to the trace comparison the students were able to identify an inconsistency in their beliefs. At this point we do not know how many other students share this vision or entered wrong traces for other reasons. But we do not need to know this to discover the constellation that systematically cause errors and face the students with their inconsistencies.

We have also checked the likelihood of certain errors over the course time. Many students behaved "as expected", they did certain errors a few times and then stopped repeating them. Others made long pauses (several weeks) and started to repeat the same errors again. A few seemed to be resistant against any positive effect, at least regarding the examined patterns. May be they were just playing around with the user interface and did not take the traces seriously – or they needed more constructive feedback what to do, which is what we are aiming at with the discovery of substantial patterns. Here, further research is required.

Upon starting the inspection of the patterns we had quite strong expectations what student would have been filled out wrongly. The variety of different error types (e.g. wrong line number, missing stack element, wrong stack value, etc.) within the very same code pattern was somewhat surprising. This may be due to the nature of the traces – or may also be evidence that students are not easily assoziated to a small set of prototypical misunderstandings. It seems likely that some mental models are inconsistent or even contradictory, they may be best described by a mixture of several prototypical misconceptions – which complicates their detection. Therefore we tend to take the identified patterns, even without annotating them with well-known misconceptions, and confront the students with their inconsistent behaviour. This hopefully encourages them to revise their mental model by studying the course material related to the instruction types that occur in the pattern – or, if still in doubt, approaching their teacher.

6 CONCLUSIONS

When learning a programming language for the first time, a few explanations and examples may not be enough to teach a viable mental model of program execution. Without understanding the instructions completely, programming becomes even more challenging. It requires a lot of effort and intuition on the lecturers side to correct such misconceptions. To support both we have presented a tool and methodology to let students verify their understanding by means of detailed memory traces that can be evaluated automatically. The comprehension of new instruction types can be evaluated live in class for a particular exercise, but we were particularly interested in the automatic discovery of code fragments repeating across multiple exercises that hint at substantial problems. First results with voluntary usage confirm that students are not fully aware of the instruction semantics and that students seem to value the provided opportunity: some filled out several hundreds of traces. A few of the top-ranked patterns were discussed in the paper and most CS teachers would probably agree that they represent typical problems with instruction semantics. We take this as evidence that other patterns, which are less easy to interpret, may also point to systematic problems. Exploring manually what mixture of misunderstandings may lead to which wrong answer is cumbersome, does not scale with large courses and does not help with the next group of students. Instead, we suggest to use these patterns to clearly point out inconsistent behaviour to individual students, such that they can make up their mind and improve their mental model.

REFERENCES

[1] Charu C Aggarwal and Jiawei Han. 2014. *Frequent pattern mining.* Springer.

[2] James F Allen, Henry A Kautz, Richard N Pelavin, and Josh D Tenenberg. 1991. *Reasoning about Plans.* Morgan Kaufman.

[3] Paul Baffes and Raymond Mooney. 1996. Refinement-based student modeling and automated bug library construction. *Journal of Artificial Intelligence in Education* 7, 1 (1996), 75–116.

[4] João Paulo Barros, Luís Biscaia, and Miguel Vitória. 2011. Java2Sequence: a tool for the visualization of object-oriented programs in introductory programming. In *Proceedings of the 16th annual joint conference on Innovation and technology in computer science education.* ACM, 369–369.

[5] Richard Bornat, Saeed Dehnadi, and Simon. 2008. Mental models, consistency and programming aptitude. *Conferences in Research and Practice in Information Technology Series* 78, 1986 (2008), 53–61. http://dl.acm.org/citation.cfm?id=1379253

[6] Matthew Hertz and Maria Jump. 2013. Trace-Based Teaching in Early Programming Courses. *Proceedings of the 44th ACM Technical Symposium on Computer Science Education* (2013), 561–566. https://doi.org/10.1145/2445196.2445364

[7] Frank Höppner and Frank Klawonn. 2002. Finding Informative Rules in Interval Sequences. *Intelligent Data Analysis* 6, 3 (2002), 237–256.

[8] Frank Höppner and Sebastian Peter. 2014. Temporal Interval Pattern Languages to Characterize Time Flow. *Wiley Interdisc. Rev.: Data Mining and Knowledge Discovery* 4, 3 (2014), 196–212.

[9] Amruth N Kumar. 2006. Explanation of step-by-step execution as feedback for problems on program analysis, and its generation in model-based problem-solving tutors. *Technology, Instruction, Cognition and Learning* 4, 1 (2006).

[10] Demian Lessa, Bharat Jayaraman, and Jeffrey K. Czyz. 2010. *JIVE: A pedagogic tool for visualizing the execution of Java programs.* Technical Report. University of New York at Buffalo. http://www.cse.buffalo.edu/jive/

[11] Stanislav Litvinov, Marat Mingazov, Vladislav Myachikov, Vladimir Ivanov, Yuliya Palamarchuk, Pavel Sozonov, and Giancarlo Succi. 2017. A tool for visualizing the execution of programs and stack traces especially suited for novice programmers. In *International Conference on Evaluation of Novel Approaches to Software Engineering.* 235–240.

[12] Andrew K Lui, Reggie Kwan, Maria Poon, and Yannie H Y Cheung. 2004. Saving weak programming students. *ACM SIGCSE Bulletin* 36, 2 (2004), 72. https://doi.org/10.1145/1024338.1024376

[13] Andrew Luxton-Reilly, Ibrahim Albluwi, Brett A Becker, Michail Giannakos, Amruth N Kumar, Linda Ott, James Paterson, Michael James Scott, Judy Sheard, Claudia Szabo, et al. 2018. A review of introductory programming research 2003–2017. In *Proceedings of the 23rd Annual ACM Conference on Innovation and Technology in Computer Science Education.* ACM, 342–343.

[14] Linxiao Ma, John Ferguson, Marc Roper, and Murray Wood. 2007. Investigating the viability of mental models held by novice programmers. *Proceedings of the 38th SIGCSE technical symposium on Computer science education - SIGCSE '07* (2007), 499. https://doi.org/10.1145/1227310.1227481

[15] Andrés Moreno, Niko Myller, Erkki Sutinen, and Mordechai Ben-Ari. 2004. Visualizing programs with Jeliot 3. *Proceedings of the working conference on Advanced visual interfaces - AVI '04* (2004), 373. https://doi.org/10.1145/989863.989928

[16] Kristin Stephens-Martinez and Armando Fox. 2018. Giving hints is complicated: understanding the challenges of an automated hint system based on frequent wrong answers. In *Proceedings of the 23rd Annual ACM Conference on Innovation and Technology in Computer Science Education.* ACM, 45–50.

[17] Kristin Stephens-Martinez, An Ju, Krishna Parashar, Regina Ongowarsito, Nikunj Jain, Sreesha Vekat, and Armando Fox. 2017. Taking Advantage of Scale by Analyzing Frequent Constructed-Response, Code Tracing Wrong Answers. In *Proceedings of the 2017 ACM Conference on International Computing Education Research.* ACM, 56–64.

[18] Maarten W. van Someren. 1990. What's wrong? Understanding beginners' problems with Prolog. *Instructional Science* 19, 4-5 (1990), 257–282.

Quantifying Activity and Collaboration Levels in Programming Assignments

James F. Power
Department of Computer Science
Maynooth University, Ireland
james.power@mu.ie

John Waldron
School of Computer Science & Statistics
Trinity College Dublin, Ireland
john.waldron@tcd.ie

ABSTRACT

This paper presents an experience report from a third-year undergraduate compiler design course that is taught as part of a four year computer science degree. We analyse data from a study of practical assignments, evaluated in the context of take-home formative assignments and a supervised summative examination. We implement metrics to quantify the degrees of similarity between submissions for programming assignments, as well as measuring the level of activity. We present the results of our study, and discuss the utility of these metrics for our teaching practice.

CCS CONCEPTS

• **Social and professional topics** → *Computer science education*;
• **Software and its engineering** → *Compilers*.

KEYWORDS

Programming assignments, program similarity, Jaccard index

ACM Reference Format:
James F. Power and John Waldron. 2019. Quantifying Activity and Collaboration Levels in Programming Assignments. In *Innovation and Technology in Computer Science Education (ITiCSE '19), July 15–17, 2019, Aberdeen, Scotland UK*. ACM, New York, NY, USA, 7 pages. https://doi.org/10.1145/3304221.3319769

1 INTRODUCTION

In this paper we present an experience report describing the deployment of an automated assessment and data collection system in a *Compiler Design* module given to Computer Science degree students in their third year of study. The module has a practical emphasis involving a series of six programming assignments using the *flex* and *bison* tools. With a class size of 96 during the twelve week module, over half a million lines of code were submitted. The only practical way to grade and provide timely feedback for this scale of work is automated assessment.

We present our analysis of the data extracted from electronic records of the student interaction with the learning technology used. We measure the frequency and quantity of interactions with the automated system and how this effects results. One important question with large class sizes and automated assessment is the degree of collaboration or plagiarism that may arise. We describe various different measures that can be used to compare code submissions and also algorithms and implementations to efficiently analyse approximately 12 Megabytes of source code.

ITiCSE '19, July 15–17, 2019, Aberdeen, Scotland UK

ACM ISBN 978 1 4503 6301 3/19/07...$15.00
https://doi.org/10.1145/3304221.3319769

In Section 2 of this paper we briefly review the background to our approach and the related work on automated assessment and similarity measures. In Section 3 we describe in more detail the compiler design module, the programming assignments and the technology we have developed to handle the large volume of submitted code. We elaborate on an algorithm to compare two different files in the context of compiler design, and its implementation. Here we also present a broad summary of the characteristics of our data. In Section 4 we reflect on our techniques and study how they relate to outcomes as measured by both formative and summative assessments. Section 5 describes dynamically generated graphical results which we believe best indicate instances of similarity between programs that merit further investigation and enable the instructor to provide relevant feedback.

2 BACKGROUND AND RELATED WORK

Issues related to assessment in Computer Science courses have received much attention in recent years, particularly in relation to automated assessment, and we only attempt a brief review of some of the main approaches here.

2.1 Automated assessment

A large number of different systems exist to assign marks to code, typically based on testing [6], but also potentially using quality metrics and other features [19, 21]. In addition to their use in standard introductory programming courses, automated assessment tools have recently been used for topics as diverse as databases [11], graphics [20] and functional programming [2].

A principal advantage of automated assessment is that it facilitates increased frequency of formative assessment, even for large class groups. This learning experience can be enhanced by providing more targeted automated feedback [10] and, as a side-effect, can provide a large body of data that can be used for learning analytics [8]. Even for summative assessment it has been argued that automated assessment for programming provides an environment that is closer to the code-and-test loop used in realistic programming scenarios [9].

Formative assessment typically occurs during a course and is directed at enhancing, rather than evaluating, student learning [3]. Often such assessment is awarded low marks and takes the form of take-home exams, as is the case for this paper. One of the challenges with such assessment, particularly in the context of automation,

Table 1: Summary of the programming assignments. There were six programming assignments over 11 weeks. The averages show the number of attempts per student and the average number of lines-of-code (LOC) per attempt.

	Assignment	Week	Kind	Total Students	Total Files	Avg. attempts	LOC in total	LOC per attempt
1	even	2	flex	95	857	9	17 867	21
2	comments	3	flex	91	2 640	29	63 266	24
3	plates	4	flex	91	3 848	42	178 663	46
4	roman	6	flex/bison	86	2 197	13	98 960	90
5	romcalc	9	flex/bison	84	1 911	12	161 526	170
6	calcwithvariables	11	flex/bison	71	972	7	48 081	98

is the possibility of plagiarism [4, 5] and the difficulty of ensuring academic integrity in the assessment process [15]. An alternative is to insist on supervised examinations, possibly also involving automated assessment [13].

In recent years, the use of automated assessment systems has also allowed instructors to collect a large amount of information, and some of this can be relevant in analysing student behaviour. For example, one study of students on an introductory Java course showed that the number of attempts at an exercise correlates better with performance on a final exam than the actual results of the exercise [1]. Another approach used start and end times for submissions, along with a similarity measure, as one element in identifying possible patterns of collaboration [7]. Recently, a study combined similarity measures and submission information to calculate a 'plagiarism probability' index for code [17].

One feature of many of these measures is that they are very fragile to the level of student knowledge of their use. For example, if students know the basic parameters of the algorithm being used to detect plagiarism, they can take measures to defeat it. Similarly, if students know that indices on the differences between first and final attempts are being calculated, it would be straightforward to ensure that this value is maximised.

2.2 Measuring similarity

There are many ways of measuring similarity between two documents and/or programs and the options have been extensively discussed in the literature [4, 14]. For our purposes, we were dealing with a relatively limited corpus of mixed-language submissions, and we wanted a simple and easy-to-interpret measure. We chose initially to use the Jaccard similarity index [16], later generalising this to an instance of the Tversky index.

The initial step is to represent a document as a set (of words, tokens, lines etc.). Given two programs represented by sets X and Y, their Jaccard similarity index is defined as:

$$J(X, Y) = \frac{|X \cap Y|}{|X \cup Y|}$$

The Jaccard index is symmetric, so $J(A, B) = J(B, A)$, which can be a problem when the sizes of the sets are not similar. For example, adding more lines to just one of the programs would decrease the similarity index for both. In order to compensate for this, we used an asymmetric index, where we normalised by the number of lines in the first program only.

That is we calculated the similarity between two sets as

$$S(X, Y) = \frac{|X \cap Y|}{|X|}$$

More formally, both of these are instances of the Tversky index [18], defined as:

$$S(X, Y) = \frac{|X \cap Y|}{|X \cap Y| + \alpha|X - Y| + \beta|Y - X|}$$

The index is defined by two parameters $\alpha, \beta \geq 0$. The Jaccard index puts $\alpha = \beta = 1$, whereas we put $\alpha = 1, \beta = 0$ so that additional (different) elements in set Y would not change the index for X.

3 CONTEXT

The module *Compiler Design* is a one-semester, 12 week, module taken by ninety-six students in the third year of a Computer Science degree at Trinity College Dublin. The module has a practical emphasis, and students study tools designed for writers of compilers and interpreters which are also useful for many other applications. The module is relevant for any application that looks for patterns in its input or has an input or command language.

The module is assessed using a summative invigilated written examination at the end of the semester worth 80%, along with six formative take-home programming assignments during the module, worth a total of 20%.

3.1 Automatic assessment system

A survey of attendees at SIGCSE 2015 showed that the majority of attendees that use automation often or extensively also use homegrown tools [19], and we use this approach as well. All the programming assignments are submitted and marked automatically using a virtual learning environment and course management system called CODEMARK which has been developed internally in Trinity College Dublin.

CODEMARK is written in a combination of PHP and HTML for the front end. The back end is a combination of the relevant programming tools, Unix utilities and shell scripts. It runs on a Citirix XenServer which is a hypervisor platform that enables the creation and management of virtualised server infrastructure.

CODEMARK allows students to submit programming assignments using PHP forms. Either code can be pasted directly into a web page form for smaller programs or uploaded in an archive file for larger tasks or those involving multiple files. It then uses the programming

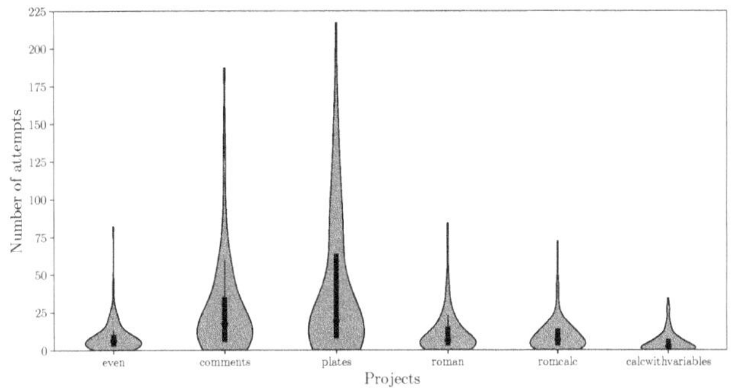

Figure 1: Activity per assignment, measured in terms of the number of attempts per student for each assignment.

tools to analyse the code for syntax errors and if none are found the resulting program is run against multiple test cases and a mark is automatically awarded based on the number of successful results.

3.2 The assignments

During the module the students study the use of the *flex* and *bison* tools [12]. Both these tools are code generators: *flex* takes as input a specification consisting of regular expressions and generates the source code for a lexical analyser, while *bison* takes as input a specification consisting of a context-free grammar and generates the source code for a parser. In both cases, the user may add snippets of C code interwoven with the specification, or whole segments of C code at the beginning or end of the file.

There are six formative programming assignments distributed throughout the module, and summarised in Table 1. There are three lexical analysis assignments (just using *flex*) and three lexical analysis/parsing assignments (using both *flex* and *bison* tools). In total the students submit six *flex* files and three *bison* files, and may make multiple submissions up to the assignment deadline.

Table 1 also list some basic metrics for each assignment to quantify the size of the data. For each assignment, Table 1 shows the number of students that attempted the assignment (a total of 96 students registered for the module) and the overall total number of files and lines of code (LOC) submitted for that assignment. Throughout this paper, we use 'code' to mean the flex/bison specifications (and embedded C code) submitted by the student, but not the code that is generated by these tools.

Table 1 also shows two averages for each assignment: the average number of attempts per student, and the average number of LOC per attempt. Overall, the CODEMARK system analysed 12,425 flex/bison source files submitted during the module, comprising 568,363 lines of code and totalling 11.8 Megabytes of data.

3.3 Processing the data

Each time a student submits an assignment for marking, the submission is logged and the files are stored by the CODEMARK system, allowing us to study the level of *activity* during the module. Figure 1 contains a violin plot for each assignment that shows the distribution of the level of activity. In Figure 1 each violin plot represents the level of activity measured in terms of the number of submissions for each student. The white dot shows the median and the black bar shows the inter-quartile range.

Figure 1 shows that the level of activity reached a peak for the third assignment, and decreased substantially thereafter. We speculate that the lower level of interactions in the first assignment was due to it being relatively easy, and the decrease after the third assignment was due to time pressures on the students as the semester proceeded. This is also reflected in the drop-off in the number of students doing each assignment from 95 to 71 as shown in Table 1.

We experimented with different algorithms to measure code similarity, essentially varying the Tversky index with different values of α and β. We did not compare submissions for different assignments and restricted ourselves to only the final submission for each assignment. Initially we developed a prototype implementation using the Unix *sort* and *comm* tools but this proved prohibitively computationally expensive, so we implemented the analyses in Python, giving a run-time in seconds. This made it feasible to perform many variations of the analysis.

In order to allow for trivial modifications to the code, we preprocessed it by removing blank lines and multiple white-space sequences, particularly in the middle of lines. We chose to split the programs based on lines (rather than words or characters) since both *flex* and *bison* lead naturally to line-oriented specifications. Because of the relative terseness of these specifications, as shown by the average LOC counts in Table 1, and the natural structuring due to using the same grammar, we felt that a word-oriented count would produce too many false positive matches. Since the variants of the Tversky index are based on comparing sets, duplicate lines in a program were automatically excluded.

Figure 2 presents a summary of the data analysed for three measures of similarity between programs: raw line counts, the Jaccard index, and the Tversky index. In each case we compare the final submission for each student for each of the 9 programs submitted, resulting in 63,814 pairwise comparisons (or 31,907 for the symmetric measures). The histograms in Figure 2 show that the Tversky index provides a greater degree of discrimination between programs for our data set.

We also analysed results with various Tversky index threshold settings and we heuristically decided on 75% to be a reasonable compromise between precision and recall. Due to the syntax of *flex* and *bison* programs we would expect a certain number of lines to be identical and not indicative of plagiarism.

As shown in the histogram in Figure 2 only a relatively small number of submissions showed a Tversky score above our threshold, suggesting that the vast majority of the students worked independently on the assignments.

4 ANALYSING THE DATA

In this section we present an analysis of the data collected during the module. This data included student marks in the assessment and final exam, student programs collected during the module, and the dates and times these files were submitted. To make the analysis manageable, we concentrate on four measures, calculated for each student and normalised as a percentage:

- **Formative**: the total marks for the *formative* assessment, comprised of the six take-home assignments described in

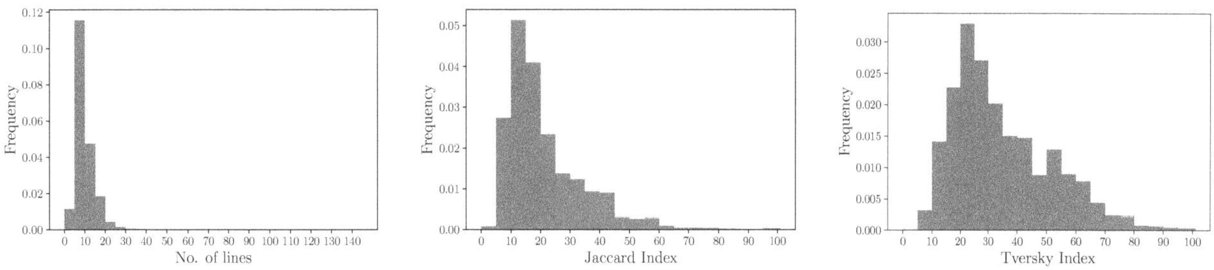

Figure 2: Distribution of similarity measures. These three histograms show the distribution of three similarity measures for the data set studied in this paper. Note that the vertical axis is on a different scale for each histogram.

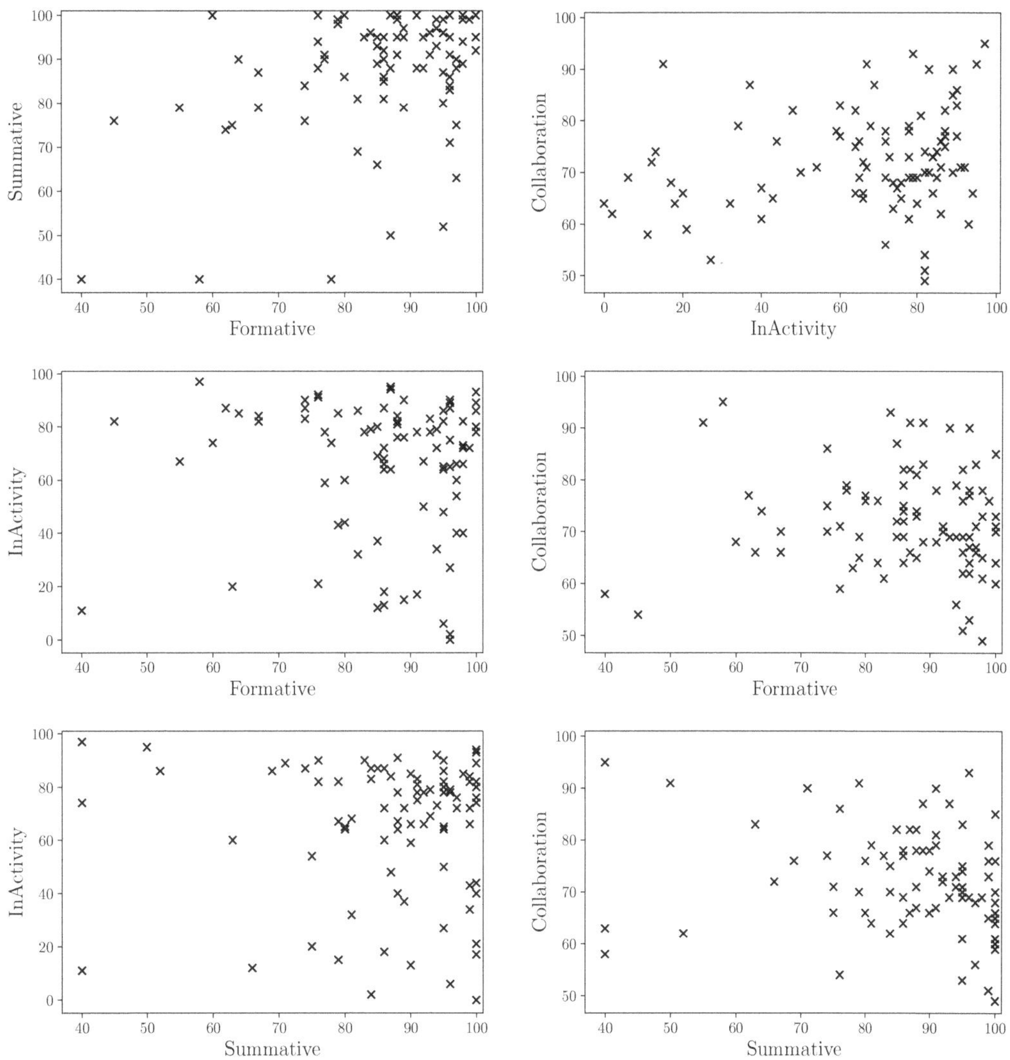

Figure 3: Six scatter-plots showing the relationships between the summative and formative marks, and the indices of inactivity and similarity. Each mark on the graph represents data for one student.

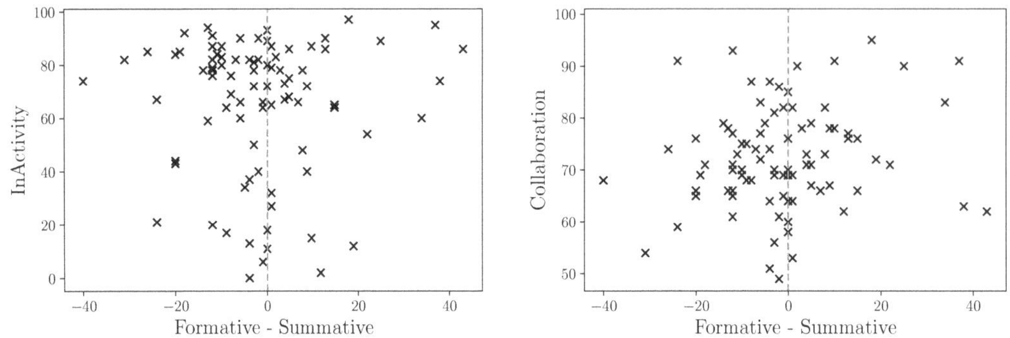

Figure 4: Two scatter-plots showing the relationship between the difference in the formative and summative marks, with the activity (left) and similarity indices (right).

Section 3. Each assignment was automatically assessed using the CODEMARK system, the mark awarded was their best mark for that assignment, and this was then averaged over the six assignments.

- **Summative**: the mark in the *summative* exam, an invigilated written examination given at the end of the module.
- **Collaboration**: a measure of the degree to which a student's code was similar that of other students. For each assignment, we took the maximum similarity measure between a student's code and that of other students, and averaged this over the number of assignments attempted by the student.
- **Activity**: We measured a student's activity by calculating the total number of submissions over the duration of the module. This was then normalised by dividing by the maximum number of submissions (407 in total for one student) and expressed as a percentage. When analysing the data we found it simpler to express this as an *in*activity measure, which is just the activity measure subtracted from 100.

Figure 3 contains six scatter-plots, showing the relationships between these four measures. Each mark on a plot represents the data for one student. Since relatively few students scored under 40% in the exam marks, we have minimised the formative and summative marks at 40% to better highlight the data. The minimum collaboration level reported for any student was 50%. By definition, the minimum activity level is 0%, the value for the most active student.

The two scatter-plots on the first row of Figure 3 depict the relationship between the exam and non-exam marks. The first plot shows the relationship between formative and summative marks. Both of these sets of marks were relatively high overall, since this is a third-year module taken by experienced students. We were particularly interested in those students who did well in the formative exams but then did poorly in the summative exam, those in the bottom-right of the first plot. We identified the 10 students nearest the bottom-right corner and examined their other measures manually, but could not distinguish any particular trend. The scatter-plot on the right of the first row of Figure 3 plots collaboration against inactivity. Again, examining those with collaboration levels over 75% did not show any identifiable trend in terms of activity.

The second and third rows of Figure 3 examine the relationships between the non-exam measures and the exam measures. We had speculated that students with high inactivity or high collaboration would exhibit poorer summative marks overall than formative marks, but a visual examination of the data in Figure 3 does not support this. While we examined individual cases, and experimented with modifications to our measures, we did not feel that more sophisticated statistical techniques were warranted on this data.

One other hypothesis we investigated was that students who exhibited a large difference between their formative and summative marks might also have distinctive patterns in their levels of activity or collaboration. To visualise this, Figure 4 has two scatter-plots, showing the relationship between the non-exam measures and the difference in the two exam measures. Students on the right of these two plots are those who increased their mark between formative and summative exams. Again, there is not a clear relationship between these students and either the inactivity or collaboration measures. We performed a one-sided Mann-Whitney U test using the difference ($<= 0$ and > 0) as a classifier for both activity and collaboration, and confirmed that this is not an informative classifier in this case.

5 COLLABORATION GRAPHS

The overall measures summarised in Section 4 did not allow us to make general statements regarding the predictive capabilities of the measures we used. However, the results are still interesting on an individual level, and could be used to provide information to the instructor during the course.

The CODEMARK system provides a large amount of data, and it can be difficult to pick out interesting features on a per-student basis. After experimenting with a number of possibilities, we have found it most useful to visualise the levels of collaboration using a *collaboration graph*, an example of which is shown in Figure 5. This graph is generated automatically from the data analysis elements of our code, and the visualisation is produced using the *Graphviz* graph visualisation software using the *circo* layout engine.[1]

[1]Graphviz version 2.38.0, available from https://graphviz.org/

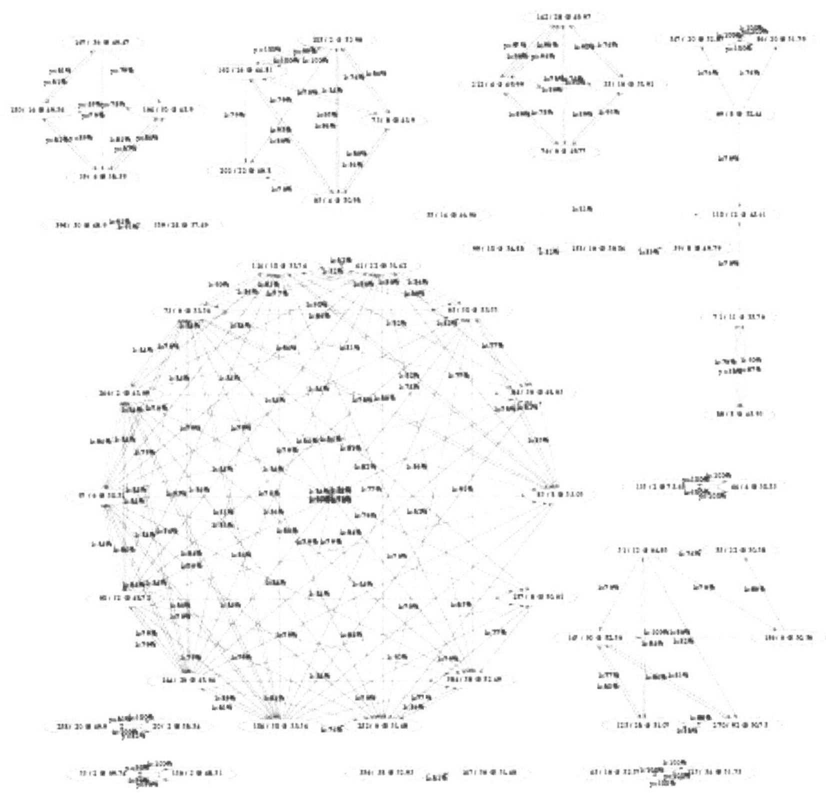

Figure 5: An example of a collaboration graph for the fifth assignment. Each node represents a student, and each (directed) edge represents the maximum similarity level from one student to the other, thresholded at 75%.

Figure 5 contains a directed graph, where the nodes represent students, and the edges represent a collaboration from one student to another, based on our collaboration measure. We have deleted identifying details from this example, but the student number would normally be included in each node. The collaboration has been thresholded at 75%, as discussed earlier in Section 3.3, but this can be changed, with a lower threshold producing more edges.

As can be seen from the overall structure of Figure 5, the collaboration graph quickly identifies groups of students who have high levels of similarity between their submissions, and the weighting on the edges gives an indication as to the level of collaboration. The graph in Figure 5 shows one large collaboration on the bottom-left, a heavily connected network of 14 students. A number of other smaller collaborative groups are also shown, as are collaborations between two students.

When analysing the collaboration networks we found it useful to have extra information available to help with identifying more likely instances of copying. Thus, in each node we print activity information, showing the overall level of activity, the level of activity for this assignment, and the time (in days since the start of the module) of the last submission. For example, the node in the bottom-left of the graph is labelled "356 / 38 @ 52.93", meaning that this student has 356 submissions overall, 38 in this project, and the last submission was toward the end of day 52 of the module.

In general we interpret high activity and early submission as more favourable indicators of a student's engagement, and are interested in situations where these metrics differ between collaborating students. We would not advocate using these metrics on their own, but rather as an indicator of situations that merit further investigation.

6 REFLECTION

In this paper we have described our use of an automated system, CODEMARK, to provide assessment and data analysis for a third-year *Compiler Design* module. As such, it contributes to a growing body of knowledge on the use of such systems, both in introductory programming courses and at more advanced levels [2, 11, 20].

It should be noted that these results are based on a single group of students, so generalising these results would require further studies using different groups. We hope to explore this issue in future work to provide a broader context for our analysis.

Our work demonstrates the feasibility of deploying such software for a large class group with an intensive assessment schedule. It also indicates the difficulty of choosing suitable metrics that can provide insight on the large body of data collected. Because of our analytical techniques and associated software implementation, it is now practical for the instructor to see this information in real time and to conduct appropriate interventions. It is our thesis that the best policy must be based on a well-informed personal intervention after manual inspection of the data, and our work here is intended to provide a foundation for that approach.

REFERENCES

[1] Alireza Ahadi, Raymond Lister, and Arto Vihavainen. 2016. On the Number of Attempts Students Made on Some Online Programming Exercises During Semester and their Subsequent Performance on Final Exam Questions. In *ACM Conference on Innovation and Technology in Computer Science Education*. Arequipa, Peru, 218–223.

[2] Luciana Benotti, Federico Aloi, Franco Bulgarelli, and Marcos J. Gomez. 2018. The Effect of a Web-based Coding Tool with Automatic Feedback on Students' Performance and Perceptions. In *49th ACM Technical Symposium on Computer Science Education*. Baltimore, MD, USA, 2–7.

[3] Benjamin S. Bloom, Thomas Hasting, and George Madaus. 1971. *Handbook of formative and summative evaluation of student learning*. McGraw-Hill, New York, USA.

[4] Paul Clough. 2003. *Old and new challenges in automatic plagiarism detection*. Technical Report. Department of Information Studies, University of Sheffield.

[5] Charlie Daly and Jane Horgan. 2005. A Technique for Detecting Plagiarism in Computer Code. *Comput. J.* 48, 6 (2005), 662–666.

[6] Charlie Daly and John Waldron. 2004. Assessing the Assessment of Programming Ability. *SIGCSE Bull.* 36, 1 (March 2004), 210–213.

[7] Arto Hellas, Juho Leinonen, and Petri Ihantola. 2017. Plagiarism in Take-home Exams: Help-seeking, Collaboration, and Systematic Cheating. In *ACM Conference on Innovation and Technology in Computer Science Education*. Bologna, Italy, 238–243.

[8] Petri Ihantola, Arto Vihavainen, Alireza Ahadi, Matthew Butler, Jürgen Börstler, Stephen H. Edwards, Essi Isohanni, Ari Korhonen, Andrew Petersen, Kelly Rivers, Miguel Ángel Rubio, Judy Sheard, Bronius Skupas, Jaime Spacco, Claudia Szabo, and Daniel Toll. 2015. Educational Data Mining and Learning Analytics in Programming: Literature Review and Case Studies. In *ITiCSE on Working Group Reports*. Vilnius, Lithuania, 41–63.

[9] An Ju, Ben Mehne, Andrew Halle, and Armando Fox. 2018. In-class coding-based summative assessments: tools, challenges, and experience. In *23rd Annual ACM Conference on Innovation and Technology in Computer Science Education*. Larnaca, Cyprus, 75–80.

[10] Hieke Keuning, Johan Jeuring, and Bastiaan Heeren. 2016. Towards a Systematic Review of Automated Feedback Generation for Programming Exercises. In *ACM Conference on Innovation and Technology in Computer Science Education*. Arequipa, Peru, 41–46.

[11] Anthony Kleerekoper and Andrew Schofield. 2018. SQL tester: an online SQL assessment tool and its impact. In *23rd Annual ACM Conference on Innovation and Technology in Computer Science Education*. Larnaca, Cyprus, 87–92.

[12] John Levine. 2009. *Flex & Bison*. O'Reilly Media, Sebastopol, CA, USA.

[13] Phil Maguire, Rebecca Maguire, and Robert Kelly. 2017. Using automatic machine assessment to teach computer programming. *Computer Science Education* 27, 3-4 (2017), 197–214.

[14] Chanchal Kumar Roy and James R. Cordy. 2007. *A Survey on Software Clone Detection Research*. Technical Report No. 2007-541. School of Computing, Queen's University at Kingston, , Ontario, Canada.

[15] Judy Sheard, Simon, Matthew Butler, Katrina Falkner, Michael Morgan, and Amali Weerasinghe. 2017. Strategies for Maintaining Academic Integrity in First-Year Computing Courses. In *ACM Conference on Innovation and Technology in Computer Science Education*. Bologna, Italy, 244–249.

[16] Kwangho Song, Jihong Min, Gayoung Lee, Sang Chul Shin, and Yoo-Sung Kim. 2015. An Improvement of Plagiarized Area Detection System Using Jaccard Correlation Coefficient Distance Algorithm. *Computer Science and Information Technology* 3, 3 (2015), 76–80.

[17] Narjes Tahaei and David C. Noelle. 2018. Automated Plagiarism Detection for Computer Programming Exercises Based on Patterns of Resubmission. In *ACM Conference on International Computing Education Research*. Espoo, Finland, 178–186.

[18] A. Tversky. 1977. Features of similarity. *Psychological Review* 84, 14 (1977), 327–352.

[19] Chris Wilcox. 2016. Testing Strategies for the Automated Grading of Student Programs. In *47th ACM Technical Symposium on Computing Science Education*. Memphis, Tennessee, USA, 437–442.

[20] Burkhard C. Wünsche, Zhen Chen, Lindsay Alexander Shaw, Thomas Suselo, Kai-Cheung Leung, Davis Dimalen, Wannes van der Mark, Andrew Luxton-Reilly, and Richard Lobb. 2018. Automatic assessment of OpenGL computer graphics assignments. In *23rd Annual ACM Conference on Innovation and Technology in Computer Science Education*. Larnaca, Cyprus, 81–86.

[21] Tao Xie, Nikolai Tillmann, Jonathan de Halleux, and Judith Bishop. 2015. Educational Software Engineering: Where Software Engineering, Education, and Gaming Meet. In *Computer Games and Software Engineering*. CRC Press, 113–133.

How Teachers Would Help Students to Improve Their Code

Hieke Keuning
Open University of the Netherlands and Windesheim University of Applied Sciences
hw.keuning@windesheim.nl

Bastiaan Heeren
Open University of the Netherlands
bastiaan.heeren@ou.nl

Johan Jeuring
Utrecht University and Open University of the Netherlands
j.t.jeuring@uu.nl

ABSTRACT

Code quality has been receiving less attention than program correctness in both the practice of and research into programming education. Writing poor quality code might be a sign of carelessness, or not fully understanding programming concepts and language constructs. Teachers play an important role in addressing quality issues, and encouraging students to write better code as early as possible.

In this paper we explore to what extent teachers address code quality in their teaching, which code quality issues they observe and how they would help novices to improve their code. We presented student code of low quality to 30 experienced teachers and asked them which hints they would give and how the student should improve the code step by step. We compare these hints to the output of professional code quality tools.

Although most teachers gave similar hints on reducing the algorithmic complexity and removing clutter, they gave varying subsets of hints on other topics. We found a large variety in how they would solve issues in code. We noticed that professional code quality tools do not point out the algorithmic complexity topics that teachers mention. Finally, we give some general guidelines on how to approach code improvement.

CCS CONCEPTS

• **Social and professional topics → Computer science education; Software engineering education**;

KEYWORDS

Programming education; code quality; refactoring

ACM Reference Format:
Hieke Keuning, Bastiaan Heeren, and Johan Jeuring. 2019. How Teachers Would Help Students to Improve Their Code. In *Innovation and Technology in Computer Science Education (ITiCSE '19), July 15–17, 2019, Aberdeen, Scotland UK*. ACM, New York, NY, USA, 7 pages. https://doi.org/10.1145/3304221.3319780

ITiCSE '19, July 15–17, 2019, Aberdeen, Scotland UK

ACM ISBN 978-1-4503-6301-3/19/07...$15.00
https://doi.org/10.1145/3304221.3319780

1 INTRODUCTION

An increasing number of studies have focused on the *quality* of programs written by novices, as opposed to the *correctness* of student programs, which has had quite some attention in research the past decades [7, 16]. These studies show that student programs contain a substantial amount of various quality issues, which often remain unsolved [8, 11, 15]. While there has not been much research into the reasons why quality issues remain unsolved, one can imagine that students are satisfied once their solutions pass all tests. They might not even be aware of quality aspects such as maintainability, performance and testability, or simply do not know how to satisfy them. Although a wealth of tools exists to analyse and refactor code, they are often not targeted at novices. Therefore, teachers play an important role in raising awareness of quality issues and encouraging students to improve functionally correct code.

There is little information on how to support students with improving the quality of their code, and what teachers consider to be a high-quality program. We conducted a study in which we collected this knowledge from experts. We asked 30 experienced educators who teach programming how they perceive the role of code quality in their courses. We showed them a number of functionally correct programs that have several issues related to quality, and asked them which hints they would give to help improve the program. We also asked them to describe the steps they would want the student to take to refactor the program into an improved version.

This paper (1) gives insight into how teachers assess the quality of novice programs, (2) shows how their hints compare to feedback generated by tools, (3) analyses how teachers would rewrite poor student code, and (4) describes how they would approach this rewriting in a stepwise way. These insights can be used to improve the development of courses and tools.

Section 2 gives some background and discusses related work. Section 3 describes the research questions, and how we collected and analysed the data. Section 4 shows the results for each research question, which are discussed in Section 5. Section 6 concludes and describes future work.

2 BACKGROUND AND RELATED WORK

This section establishes the meaning of central terms used in this paper and summarizes related work on code quality in education.

2.1 Code quality terms and definitions

Code quality deals with the directly observable properties of source code, such as algorithmic aspects (flow, expressions, language constructs) and structure (decomposition, modularization). Some examples of code quality issues are (1) duplicated code, (2) an expression that could be shortened, and (3) unnecessary conditional checks.

Although layout and commenting are certainly indicators of code quality, these aspects are beyond the scope of our study.

Fowler [10] uses the term *code smells* to describe characteristics in code that might indicate that something is wrong with the design of functionally correct code, which can have an impact on its quality. In the long term, low quality code may affect software quality attributes such as maintainability, performance and security. There are many tools available (e.g. PMD, SonarQube, Resharper, linters) to automatically detect quality issues and code smells in a program.

Code refactoring is improving code step by step while preserving its functionality. The well-known work by Fowler [10] describes a collection of refactorings, mainly focused on the structure of the code. Code Complete [13], a well-known handbook for software construction, describes refactorings on multiple levels: data-level (e.g. inline an expression), statement-level (e.g. use return instead of a loop control variable), routine-level (e.g. extract method), class implementation, class interface and system-level. Some IDEs offer support for refactorings, such as renaming variables and extracting methods. These IDEs execute a refactoring in a single step, which would not give novices much insight into how refactoring works.

An ITiCSE working group [5] investigated which quality aspects are considered important by teachers, students and developers. In our study we zoom in on how teachers assess the quality of student code, focussing on data-, statement- and routine-level refactorings, which are most relevant for the programs that beginners write.

2.2 Code quality in education

Multiple studies have investigated the quality of student programs. Pettit et al. [15] analysed submissions to an automated assessment system and found that several complexity metrics increased with every submission. Keuning et al. [11] detected many quality issues in over 2 million student programs, which were hardly ever fixed. Whether the student used a quality tool or not did not decrease the amount of issues. Breuker et al. [6] found no clear quality improvement between the code of first- and second-year students. De Ruvo et al. [8] investigated a set of 19.000 code submissions on 16 semantic style indicators, which address small issues such as unnecessary return statements, and too complex if-statements. They found instances in both code of novices and more experienced students. Luxton-Reilly et al. [12] investigated differences between correct solutions to programming exercises, identifying variation in structure, syntax and presentation. The authors found that even for simple exercises there are numerous variations in structure, and in some instances the teacher's solution was not the most popular one among students.

Although professional code quality analysers and refactoring tools are being used in education (e.g. [14]), there are also some tools designed specifically for education that give feedback on code quality, such as Style++ [2], FrenchPress [3], and AutoStyle [20]. AutoStyle gives stepwise feedback on how to improve the style of correct programs, based on historical student data.

Educators have designed several projects that teach students about refactoring, usually for more advanced students [1, 9, 17, 19]. Experienced educators studied the quality of object-oriented examples in Java textbooks [4]. They found several issues, in particular related to object-oriented thinking.

3 METHOD

The research questions this study addresses are:

RQ1 To what extent do teachers address code quality in their programming courses?

RQ2 What kind of hints related to code quality do teachers give to students, and how do these hints compare to the output of code quality tools?

RQ3 Which (stepwise) approach do teachers suggest to help students improve their programs, and what does the final improved program look like?

3.1 Study design

We designed a questionnaire[1] in which participants answer five questions about themselves and four short questions on the role of code quality. Next, we give our definition and scope of code quality and present three student programs of poor quality (see Section 3.1.1). We ask (1) how they would assess the program, (2) which hints they would give, and (3) how they would want the student to improve the program step by step, by typing the code after each step. We tested the questionnaire with a teacher who is not involved in this research, and adjusted the questionnaire according to his feedback.

We invited university teachers with at least two years of experience in teaching CS/programming-related courses to participate in our study. We did not ask professional programmers, because they do not necessarily have experience with teaching programming. We sent our invitation to 66 teachers from various institutes and countries, and asked them to forward the invitation to colleagues and other acquainted teachers.

3.1.1 Programs. The first exercise was taken from another study, including the most popular student solution (see Program 1) [12]. Its description is: 'Implement the sumValues method, which adds up all numbers from the array parameter, or only the positive numbers if the positivesOnly boolean parameter is set to true.'

We designed the second exercise ourselves: 'Write the code for the method unevenSum. This method should return the sum of the numbers at an uneven index in the array that is passed as a parameter, until the number -1 is seen at an uneven index.' We collected 78 solutions from an institution one of us works at. We composed the first solution (Program 2a) by mixing a number of actual student solutions. Program 2b is an actual correct student solution (with variable names translated into English).

We ran three well-known static analysis tools on the three programs: PMD with the full set of rules, Checkstyle, and SonarLint[2] with default checks and full checks. Because Checkstyle always reported a subset of the PMD and/or SonarLint messages (besides layout), we omit Checkstyle messages from this paper.

3.2 Data analysis

We analysed the answers to the open question on which hints a teacher would give both qualitatively and quantitatively. We labelled the hint topics using an open coding method, and categorized

[1] The questionnaire can be found at www.hkeuning.nl/ImproveCode

[2] pmd.github.io/pmd-6.9.0, checkstyle.sourceforge.net (version 8.14), www.sonarlint.org/eclipse (version 4)

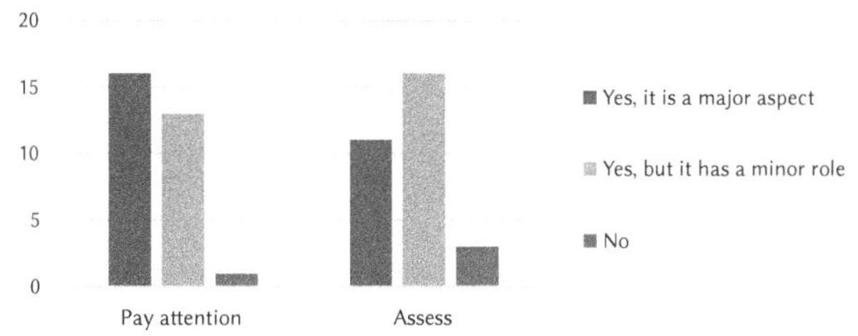

Figure 1: Responses to questions 'Do you pay attention to code quality while teaching programming to first- and second-year students?' and 'Do you explicitly assess/grade code quality aspects in programming assignments?'

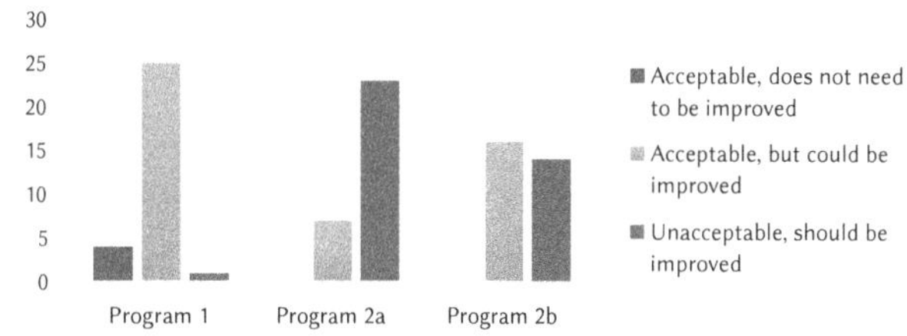

Figure 2: Responses to question 'How would you assess this solution in a formative situation (e.g. feedback during a lecture or lab)?' for all three programs.

them using the rubric by Stegeman et al. [18]. This rubric has been developed for assessing student code quality, based on a model with ten criteria. We assigned each topic to one of the four criteria that deal with algorithms and structure, which are *flow* (nesting, code duplication), *idiom* (choice of control structures, reusing library functions), *expressions* (complexity, suitability data types) and *decomposition*. The open coding was performed by one author. Another author checked the labelling of a randomly chosen 10% of the hints (with 89% agreement), and differences were discussed.

For the question on improving the program stepwise we performed a series of actions on the submitted programs. First, we removed steps in which the code was not changed (possibly a copy-paste issue). Next, because most participants probably did not use a compiler, we corrected syntax errors such as missing brackets and misspelled names, and converted to Java syntax (all given programs were written in Java, although we did not explicitly mention this). We also corrected some other small errors that were clearly unintentional. All programs were tested with a set of test cases. We assigned each program to a *cluster* based on the control flow of the program (loops, conditionals, branching and methods), because control flow shows the main structure and complexity of a method (the scope of the programs in our study). Clustering allows us to investigate similarities and differences without being distracted by details. We identified *transformations* as the add/edit/delete steps between two adjacent program *states* in a sequence.

4 RESULTS

4.1 Background of teachers

In total, 30 participants took part in our study. All participants teach programming and other CS-related courses in 3 different countries: The Netherlands (27), Sweden (3) and China (1). The 28 participants that reported their institute, teach at 15 different institutes: 10 in The Netherlands, 4 in Sweden and 1 in China, with between 1 and 5 teachers per institute. A few teach at more than one institute and country. The teachers have between 2 and 33 years of teaching experience, with an average of 11.4 years, and a median of 9 years. A total of 90% teach first year courses, 80% teach second year courses, and 70% teach courses for students in their third year or higher.

4.2 Role of code quality (RQ1)

We asked teachers if code quality appears in the learning goals of their first- and second-year programming courses, to which 23 replied with 'yes' and 7 with 'no'. Figure 1 shows to what extent teachers address and assess code quality aspects. Code quality clearly has a smaller role in assessment than in teaching.

A total of 11 out of 30 teachers do not advise or prescribe tools that deal with code quality/refactoring to their students. The 19 that do advise or prescribe tools, mostly mention static analysis tools (e.g. SonarQube, Checkstyle, linters) and IDE functionality or their plugins (e.g. Resharper). To a minor extent testing and code reviewing is mentioned. All tools mentioned are professional tools, and not explicitly intended for education.

4.3 Program hints and steps (RQ2 and RQ3)

4.3.1 Program 1. Running PMD on Program 1 reports that the for could be replaced by a foreach, and that unnecessary comparisons in boolean expressions should be avoided. SonarLint only reports on the equals true. Figure 2 shows how the teachers would assess this solution in a formative situation. Most teachers (25) answered 'acceptable, but could be improved'.

We asked the teachers to describe all hints they would give to a student to improve this program. Table 1 shows all hint topics and the number of mentions. For the issue that was pointed out the most, the flow inside the loop, some participants focussed more on the duplication, and others more on the complex if-structure.

Next, we asked the teachers how they would want the student to edit (refactor) the program step by step. In total 3 teachers did not provide any steps: 1 found the method specification itself problematic, the others did not give a reason. The remaining 27 teachers provided 2.8 steps on average, with a median of 3 (min 1, max 5) and a total of 76 program states, of which 11 were incorrect.

Regarding the type of loop, 10 teachers transformed the for into a foreach at various stages of the process, always as a single step in which nothing else was done. As a last step, 2 teachers replaced the loop by a functional style solution, calling a higher-level sum function on the array. Teachers mentioning this approach mostly said that they would only suggest it to more advanced students.

Regarding the flow in the loop, in 8 final programs the duplicated sum increment was still present. Removing the duplication by merging the ifs into a single statement, was often done as an early step, after removing the `==true`. In 2 cases a continue was used to skip a value that should not be added. However, we noticed merging the ifs was problematic: all 11 incorrect programs contained a merging mistake. Some of those mistakes were fixed in a next step.

We assigned each (intermediate) program to a cluster based on its control flow, identifying 13 clusters. The final programs were

Program 1: Most popular solution to exercise 1.

```
1  int sumValues(int [] values,
2                boolean positivesOnly) {
3      int sum = 0;
4      for (int i = 0;i < values.length;i++) {
5          if (positivesOnly == true) {
6              if (values[i] >= 0) {
7                  sum += values[i];
8              }
9          }
10         else {
11             sum += values[i];
12         }
13     }
14     return sum;
15 }
```

Table 1: Hint topics for program 1, as reported by 30 teachers. Indented topics are more specific.

Category	Description	Count
Expressions	Remove equals true (line 5)	20
	Do not add 0 to sum (line 6)	2
Flow	Improve flow in loop	1
	Improve nested ifs (line 5–12)	17
	Remove duplicated `sum +=` .. (line 7 and 11)	11
Idiom	Change type of loop (line 4)	11
	Use a higher-level function	3
Decomposition	Move common code to method	2
	`positivesOnly` check to method (line 5)	2
Other	General	2
	Misc. mentioned once (various categories)	5

Table 2: Correct end clusters for program 1.

Start:	12x:	3x:	2x:	6x:

`for`
`if`
`if`
`else`
`return`
	`for/foreach`
	`if`
	`return`
		`for/foreach`
		`if`
		`if`
		`else`
		`return`
			`for/foreach`
			`if`
			`continue`
			`return`
				Others

distributed over 10 clusters; excluding 4 incorrect final programs, we counted 9 clusters, as shown in Table 2.

4.3.2 Program 2a. PMD reports three 'dataflow anomalies' for the `total` and `stop` variables in Program 2a. PMD considers this a low-priority issue that might not be problematic. PMD also points out equals false and the self-assignment. SonarLint with default settings also reports on equals false and even gives two messages on the self-assignment. With full checks, it mentions that the if-else if (lines 7–11) should end with an else, and a constant should be used for magic number 2.

The program contains a functional error regarding the stop condition. We instructed participants to ignore this error when answering the questions. However, the first 10 participants did not see this note and read that it was a correct solution. Figure 2 shows the response to the question on formatively assessing the solution, to which most teachers (23) answered it was unacceptable. The fact that the solution was incorrect could have contributed to this score.

Table 3 shows the hint topics for this program. Teachers often mentioned improving the complex flow in the loop, exiting from the loop when the stop condition was met, changing the loop type and removing clutter in the expressions.

Looking at the edit steps, 28 teachers provided 3.0 steps on average (min 1, max 5), with a median of 3 steps and a total of 83 program states. Two teachers did not provide any steps (they did not know what to suggest or what a student would have to do). Of the 83 program states, 8 were not functionally correct according to either stop condition (-1 or negative). We excluded 1 of the 28 sequences from the analyses below because it had unclear steps.

Although we did not explicitly ask this, 15 teachers tried (sometimes unsuccessfully) to fix the functional error. Most of them (11) started fixing in the first step; 3 of the others first removed clutter. In general, almost all clutter (the else with self-assignment, the redundant if) was removed by everyone mostly in the first or second step. The `==false` was mostly removed as part of another step.

The loop type was changed into a while 8 times at various stages of the process, and 1 teacher replaced the loop by recursion. Almost all participants changed the program to exit from the loop when the stop condition was met: 5 used a break, 5 used a return, and a majority of 14 added a stop condition to the loop header. Exiting from the loop was also done at various stages. The `stop` variable was eliminated from 20 sequences, and 7 kept it.

In total 20 clusters were identified, and the final programs were in 12 clusters. Table 4 shows the 10 final clusters if we exclude the 5 incorrect final programs.

4.3.3 Program 2b. Running PMD on the body of Program 2b reports multiple dataflow anomalies, and reports that the variable `number` could be made 'final'. SonarLint with full checks mentions magic number 2 on line 7. Figure 2 shows the formative assessment.

The hint topics for this program are shown in Table 5. The main topics were exiting from the loop when the stop condition is met, improving the complex flow in the loop, removing the duplicated increment, and replacing the foreach by another type of loop.

For the steps, 26 teachers provided 2.9 steps on average (min 1, max 5), with a median of 3 steps and a total of 76 program states. Of the 4 teachers that did not provide steps, 2 teachers advised that the student should start over instead of rewriting the program. The other 2 did not give a reason.

Teachers made multiple mistakes rewriting this program: of the 76 program states, 21 functionally incorrect programs were created by 10 teachers. The majority of the mistakes were related to incorrect indexing (not looping through only the odd indices). This mistake was often made in a step that also transformed the foreach into a for. We excluded 2 sequences from the analyses below because they had unclear steps, leaving 24 valid sequences.

Although in 2a the for-loop was mostly kept, followed by a few while-loops, in 2b we only counted 9 for-loops and 2 while-loops. The foreach was kept 13 times. Transforming the foreach into a for was mostly done in the first step, transforming to while was always done after a transformation into a for. Of the 11 that used a for or while, 6 skipped the even indices by incrementing the index

Program 2a: Solution to exercise 2.

```
1  int unevenSum(int [] array) {
2      int total = 0;
3      boolean stop = false;
4
5      for (int i = 1;i < array.length;i = i + 2) {
6          if (stop == false) {
7              if (array[i] >= 0) {
8                  total += array[i];
9              } else if (array[i] < 0) {
10                 stop = true;
11             }
12         }
13         else {
14             total = total;
15         }
16     }
17     return total;
18 }
```

Table 3: Hint topics for program 2a.

Category	Description	Count
Expressions	Remove self assignment (line 14)	12
	Remove equals false (line 6)	7
	Use compound operator += (line 5)	2
Flow	Exit from loop when done	20
	Improve flow in loop	6
	Remove redundant if (line 9)	10
	Remove unnecessary else (line 13–15)	7
	Reverse if-else (line 6–15)	2
Idiom	Change type of loop (line 5)	8
Other	Fix functional error stop condition	13
	General hints	9
	Add tests	3
	Misc. mentioned once (various categories)	7

by 2. For the remaining, 14 kept the modulo check, 2 introduced a boolean that switched between true and false, and 2 made a mistake.

Exiting from the loop was solved rather differently than in program 2a: more teachers used a break (10 vs. 5) and fewer teachers (6 vs. 14) added a stop condition to the loop header. This step was usually done somewhat later in the sequence.

All but 1 teacher removed the duplicated increment, mostly in an early step. Sometimes this was done in 2 steps: first moving the increment outside the if-else, followed by reversing the if-else and removing the then empty else. Transforming the foreach into a for also eliminates the duplication by moving the increment to the loop header.

Variables were renamed in a few cases: 4 renamed `answer` to `sum` or `total`, and `value` was occasionally renamed to `done` or `stop` if it was still used. Renaming was done at various stages.

In total we identified 31 clusters, and the final programs were in 14 clusters. Excluding 8 buggy final programs, we counted 11 clusters, as shown in Table 4. We would expect that the final programs after improving 2a match those of 2b (the error from 2a does not have to affect the cluster). However, only 5 participants ended in the same cluster for program 2a and 2b.

Table 4: Correct end clusters for program 2a and 2b.

Program 2a (n=22)

Start:
```
for
  if
    if
    else
      if
  else
return
```

6x:
```
for/while
return
```

4x:
```
for/while
  if
  else
return
```

2x:
```
for
  if
  else
    break
return
```

2x:
```
for
  if
    return
  else
return
```

2x:
```
for
  if
  else
    return
return
```

2x:
```
for
  if
    break
return
```

4x: Others

Program 2b (n=16)

Start:
```
for
  if
  else
    if
    if
return
```

4x:
```
foreach/for
  if
    if
      break
return
```

2x:
```
foreach/for
  if
    if
    if
return
```

2x:
```
for/while
return
```

8x: Others

5 DISCUSSION

In this section we answer the research questions and discuss the results in more depth.

RQ1. The results of RQ1 show that while code quality is certainly an important topic for most teachers, its role is smaller in the summative assessment of student code.

RQ2. Based on teacher feedback on three low-quality implementations of simple methods, the hints that teachers would give deal with improving control flow, choosing representative names, using suitable language constructs, removing clutter, and optimising the algorithm. Although some hint topics are mentioned by a majority, other topics are only mentioned by much smaller subgroups, implying that teachers do not consider the same things important. This finding contradicts Nutbrown and Higgins' claim that their assessors were in agreement on assessment criteria [14].

Regarding the form of the feedback, we noticed several aspects. Hints were often formulated as a question, such as 'Is there any code duplication that you could remove?' The amount of detail considering *why* something should be improved varied: for transforming a for into a foreach, an example with more motivation is: 'If we are traversing all values in the array, couldn't we use another type of loop?' Other hints mention that the 'other type of loop' is a foreach, and some even provide the syntax of the foreach header.

When comparing teacher hints to what professional tools report, we see many differences. Tools do not give feedback with increasing detail as teachers would do. Issues related to control flow and algorithmic optimisations are not pointed out by tools. A main reason is that tools do not know what the code they analyse should do. Also, default tool settings usually have high thresholds, so minor issues such as small duplicated blocks are usually not reported. Our

Program 2b: Actual student solution to exercise 2.

```
1  int unevenSum(int[] array) {
2      int answer = 0;
3      int index = 0;
4      boolean value = true;
5
6      for(int number: array) {
7          if(index % 2 == 0) {
8              index++;
9          } else {
10             if(number == -1) {
11                 value = false;
12             }
13             if(value) {
14                 answer = answer + number;
15             }
16             index++;
17         }
18     }
19     return answer;
20 }
```

findings support and complement the finding of Nutbrown and Higgins that static analysis tools miss context-specific issues [14].

RQ3. While others have already shown the great diversity in student solutions (e.g. [12]), our study also shows this diversity in teacher solutions. Remarkable is the difference in final states for program 2a and 2b that solve the same problem. Program 2b was probably the most problematic, and this starting point could have influenced the final program. For example, about half of the teachers kept the foreach in 2b, but a foreach is never introduced in 2a. Perhaps there are simply multiple ways that are equally fine, however, not all hints seem to be addressed in the final programs for program 2b. Finally, some teachers could have lost their focus for the last program, which would also explain the number of mistakes.

The large variety in steps and final programs makes it difficult to give an approach on how to improve a problematic program. General guidelines we can extract from the data are: remove clutter first, fix errors early, keep testing along the way (even teachers make mistakes), rename to meaningful names, and do larger refactorings later one step at a time. Starting over could sometimes be advisable. However, learning *why* a program has flaws, and *how* to address those flaws step by step could be a valuable learning experience. We provide some examples of stepwise improvement sequences with hints for the programs discussed in this paper online.[3]

If educators want to assess code quality, there should be agreement on what a high-quality program is. Code quality should not be a teacher's personal preference. One could argue that quality is not that important for novices, however, we argue that several issues pointed out in the previous section are caused by misunderstanding certain language constructs. Improving a solution may be a valuable way of learning more about how a programming language works. Although the issues mentioned in this paper are of a low level, and the topic of 'refactoring' is mostly associated with restructuring complex object-oriented software, we advise to start refactoring early with the statement/method level, to the class level later in a study program.

[3]www.hkeuning.nl/ImproveCode

Table 5: Hint topics for program 2b.

Category	Description	Count
Flow	Exit from loop when done	14
	Improve flow in loop (line 7–16)	5
	Remove value variable	3
	Reorder conditionals (line 7–16)	3
	Improve flow in else (line 10–16)	2
	Duplicated increment (line 8 and 16)	9
	Skip even indices	6
Idiom	Change type of loop (line 6)	14
Other	General hints	9
	Rename variable	7
	Misc. mentioned once (various categories)	9

5.1 Threats to validity

Because we only discussed three programs, we cannot generalise to all novice programs. However, the programs cover a broad set of constructs, and in this study we particularly aimed to make code quality, a potentially vague topic, more concrete by working with actual code. Conducting interviews could give us higher-quality data, but would not have given us insight into the diversity of the responses. It would be an interesting next step to discuss the various responses with the teachers to arrive at a more general view of which hints to give and which steps to take.

This study does not consider the responses of students to hints. A teacher would possibly adapt and give a more concrete hint when a student does not understand the initial hint. This was even mentioned by some participants in their responses. There might also be some differences between the type of hints for absolute beginners and second-year students.

6 CONCLUSION AND FUTURE WORK

This paper describes a study in which we asked teachers for their opinion on the quality of student code and how they would help students to improve it. While teachers find the topic of code quality important, they have different views on how to improve code. Teachers mostly agree on issues related to reducing algorithmic complexity and removing clutter, but they give different subsets of hints. Professional code quality tools do not point out these algorithmic complexity topics that teachers mention. We also discussed the great diversity in the final programs, which is influenced by the initial state of the code, and derived some general guidelines in how to approach an improvement sequence.

In future work we intend to use our findings to build better tools that help students improve the quality of their code. This research also calls for more debate on what a high-quality solution would look like for a novice. Experiments in the classroom with students are required to further study how we should learn students to improve their code, to which this study contributes.

ACKNOWLEDGMENTS

This research is supported by the Netherlands Organisation for Scientific Research (NWO), grant number 023.005.063.

REFERENCES

[1] Shamsa Abid, Hamid Abdul Basit, and Naveed Arshad. 2015. Reflections on Teaching Refactoring: A Tale of Two Projects. In *Proceedings of ITiCSE*. 225–230. https://doi.org/10.1145/2729094.2742617

[2] Kirsti Ala-Mutka, Toni Uimonen, and Hannu-Matti Jarvinen. 2004. Supporting students in C++ programming courses with automatic program style assessment. *Journal of Information Technology Education: Research* 3 (2004), 245–262.

[3] Hannah Blau and J. Eliot B. Moss. 2015. FrenchPress Gives Students Automated Feedback on Java Program Flaws. In *Proceedings of ITiCSE*. 15–20. https://doi.org/10.1145/2729094.2742622

[4] Jürgen Börstler, Marie Nordström, and James H Paterson. 2011. On the quality of examples in introductory Java textbooks. *ACM Transactions on Computing Education (TOCE)* 11, 1 (2011), 1–21. https://doi.org/10.1145/1921607.1921610

[5] Jürgen Börstler, Harald Störrle, Daniel Toll, Jelle van Assema, Rodrigo Duran, Sara Hooshangi, Johan Jeuring, Hieke Keuning, Carsten Kleiner, and Bonnie MacKellar. 2017. "I know it when I see it" Perceptions of Code Quality. In *Proceedings of ITiCSE, Working Group Reports*. 70–85. https://doi.org/10.1145/3174781.3174785

[6] Dennis Breuker, Jan Derriks, and Jacob Brunekreef. 2011. Measuring Static Quality of Student Code. In *Proceedings of ITiCSE*. 13–17. https://doi.org/10.1145/1999747.1999754

[7] Neil CC Brown and Amjad Altadmri. 2017. Novice Java programming mistakes: large-scale data vs. educator beliefs. *ACM Transactions on Computing Education (TOCE)* 17, 2 (2017), 7. https://doi.org/10.1145/2994154

[8] Giuseppe De Ruvo, Ewan Tempero, Andrew Luxton-Reilly, Gerard B. Rowe, and Nasser Giacaman. 2018. Understanding Semantic Style by Analysing Student Code. In *Proceedings of the Australasian Computing Education Conference*. 73–82. https://doi.org/10.1145/3160489.3160500

[9] Serge Demeyer, Filip Van Rysselberghe, Tudor Girba, Jacek Ratzinger, Radu Marinescu, Tom Mens, Bart Du Bois, Dirk Janssens, Stéphane Ducasse, Michele Lanza, et al. 2005. The LAN-simulation: a refactoring teaching example. In *International Workshop on Principles of Software Evolution*. IEEE, 123–131. https://doi.org/10.1109/IWPSE.2005.30

[10] Martin Fowler. 1999. *Refactoring: improving the design of existing code*. Addison-Wesley Professional.

[11] Hieke Keuning, Bastiaan Heeren, and Johan Jeuring. 2017. Code Quality Issues in Student Programs. In *Proceedings of ITiCSE*. 110–115. https://doi.org/10.1145/3059009.3059061

[12] Andrew Luxton-Reilly, Paul Denny, Diana Kirk, Ewan Tempero, and Se-Young Yu. 2013. On the Differences Between Correct Student Solutions. In *Proceedings of ITiCSE*. 177–182. https://doi.org/10.1145/2462476.2462505

[13] Steve McConnell. 2004. *Code Complete: A Practical Handbook of Software Construction, Second Edition*. Microsoft Press.

[14] Stephen Nutbrown and Colin Higgins. 2016. Static analysis of programming exercises: Fairness, usefulness and a method for application. *Computer Science Education* 26, 2-3 (2016), 104–128. https://doi.org/10.1080/08993408.2016.1179865

[15] Raymond Pettit, John Homer, Roger Gee, Susan Mengel, and Adam Starbuck. 2015. An Empirical Study of Iterative Improvement in Programming Assignments. In *Proceedings of SIGCSE*. 410–415. https://doi.org/10.1145/2676723.2677279

[16] Yizhou Qian and James Lehman. 2017. Students' Misconceptions and Other Difficulties in Introductory Programming: A Literature Review. *ACM Transactions on Computing Education (TOCE)* 18, 1, Article 1 (2017), 1:1–1:24 pages. https://doi.org/10.1145/3077618

[17] Suzanne Smith, Sara Stoecklin, and Catharina Serino. 2006. An Innovative Approach to Teaching Refactoring. In *Proceedings of SIGCSE*. 349–353. https://doi.org/10.1145/1121341.1121451

[18] Martijn Stegeman, Erik Barendsen, and Sjaak Smetsers. 2016. Designing a rubric for feedback on code quality in programming courses. In *Proceedings of the Koli Calling International Conference on Computing Education Research*. ACM, 160–164. https://doi.org/10.1145/2999541.2999555

[19] Sara Stoecklin, Suzanne Smith, and Catharina Serino. 2007. Teaching Students to Build Well Formed Object-oriented Methods Through Refactoring. In *Proceedings of SIGCSE*. 145–149. https://doi.org/10.1145/1227310.1227364

[20] Eliane S. Wiese, Michael Yen, Antares Chen, Lucas A. Santos, and Armando Fox. 2017. Teaching Students to Recognize and Implement Good Coding Style. In *ACM Conference on Learning @ Scale*. 41–50. https://doi.org/10.1145/3051457.3051469

Bridging the Digital Skills Gap*

Are computing degree apprenticeships the answer?

Ella Taylor-Smith[†]
School of Computing
Edinburgh Napier University
Edinburgh, Scotland, UK
e.taylor-smith@napier.ac.uk

Sally Smith
School of Computing
Edinburgh Napier University
Edinburgh, Scotland, UK
s.smith@napier.ac.uk

Khristin Fabian
School of Computing
Edinburgh Napier University
Edinburgh, Scotland, UK
k.fabian@napier.ac.uk

Tessa Berg
School of Mathematical and Computer Sciences
Heriot-Watt University
Edinburgh, Scotland, UK
t.berg@hw.ac.uk

Debbie Meharg
School of Computing
Edinburgh Napier University
Edinburgh, Scotland, UK
d.meharg@napier.ac.uk

Alison Varey
School of Computing
Edinburgh Napier University
Edinburgh, Scotland, UK
a.varey@napier.ac.uk

ABSTRACT

This paper describes a study investigating whether apprenticeship computing degrees in Scotland are attracting additional entrants who will become IT professionals and fill a skills need. Government policy reports, from around the world, set out plans to address computing skills shortages by introducing additional education or training programmes [23]. In the UK, this is put forward as a key goal of the new higher level apprenticeships, including Graduate Apprenticeships in Scotland and Degree Apprenticeships in the rest of the UK. These are promoted as bridging the skills gap by involving employers in curriculum design and widening access to people who would not want to study towards a traditional degree, because of the financial burden or time out of employment. New graduate apprentices at three Scottish universities were encouraged to complete a short survey, asking about their route into the degree, including their aspirations, motivations, and previous experience. Most respondents had begun an IT career before they started the apprenticeship and were upskilling and gaining an internationally recognised qualification. A third could be considered new to IT, including those coming straight from school and those moving into IT mid-career. The apprentices' primary motivation was to gain skills. They chose the apprenticeship, rather than a traditional degree, because of the integration of work experience, followed by financial reasons: graduate apprentices earn salaries and can avoid student debt. These apprenticeships create a new route to a computing degree-level qualification. We consider their potential in addressing digital skills shortages.

*Bridging the Digital Skills Gap

ITiCSE '19, July 15–17, 2019, Aberdeen, Scotland UK

ACM ISBN 978-1-4503-6301-3/19/07...$15.00 https://doi.org/10.1145/3304221.3319744

CCS CONCEPTS

• Social and professional topics → Computing education

KEYWORDS: Graduate apprenticeship; degree apprenticeship; digital skills; work-based learning.

ACM Reference format:

Ella Taylor-Smith, Sally Smith, Khristin Fabian, Tessa Berg, and Debbie Meharg. 2019. Bridging the Digital Skills Gap: Are computing degree apprenticeships the answer? In *Proceedings of the 24th Annual Conference on Innovation and Technology in Computer Science Education (ITiCSE'19). ACM, NY, NY, USA, 7 pages.* https://doi.org/10.1145/3304221.3319744

1. Introduction

The digital skills discourse identifies a shortage of people with appropriate digital skills, mostly evidenced through consulting employers [6, 30, 25, 34], but also via labour market analytics [21]. The digital skills gap, explored in more detail below, is described in terms of both a deficit in the number of digitally-skilled workers and a lack of appropriate skills in those who are currently employed, including computing graduates entering the workplace [34]. Governments across the world are concerned [23]. European forecasts based on the number of students currently studying computing subjects in Higher Education Institutions (HEIs) indicate that a step-change is needed to fill vacancies in "top bottleneck occupations", which require professional IT skills [31]. In the UK, employers have repeatedly expressed their dissatisfaction with the skills of university graduates; specifically, they expect computer science graduates to have good computer science skills (such as programming languages and approaches), soft skills (including communication) and project management skills [30]. In parallel, the Wakeham review notes evidence that "employers are tending to devote fewer resources to 'on the job' training, increasingly relying on 'oven-ready' graduates to hit the ground running" [34, p18-19]. While acknowledging the range of digital skills needed by employees at all levels and in areas of life beyond the work context, here we are concerned, like Shadbolt and Wakeham, with the skills that computing graduates need for sustainable and successful careers.

To this end, the UK and Scottish governments updated models of apprenticeships to extend their coverage into higher education [14, 26]. Employers would decide the skills content of these higher level apprenticeships [11, 12, 22] and the apprentices would be paid employees. The scheme, including payment of university tuition fees, would be funded through the new apprenticeship levy, where, since April 2017, all large employers contribute 0.5% of their salary costs [20].

This study investigates the potential of Graduate Apprenticeships (GAs) in computing in Scotland to help to close the digital skills gap, bringing new talent into the IT profession and ensuring graduates are equipped with the necessary skills for sustainable employment. Graduate apprentices studying one of the four computing apprenticeship degrees at three universities were surveyed during their first trimester. Their responses to questions about their aspirations and motivations for choosing the programme and about their previous relevant experience are analysed to identify who is taking up these early apprenticeship opportunities. Are the apprentices new talent, attracted by the format and finance? Or are they students who were planning to study computing at university but have opted for this route? The apprentices' journey into their apprenticeship degrees also provides insights into the likely future take-up of the degrees. This study is an initial exploration into the extent to which higher apprenticeships might help to close the digital skills gap.

2. The digital skills gap

As expressed by industry and recruiters, the digital skills shortage or gap is not a new problem, but an issue that governments are focusing on, in order to address the changing industrial climate, including the threats and opportunities of automation, digitalisation, and big data [23, 33]. In the context of apprenticeships and higher education, the gap is discussed in terms of the skills needed in employment as digital technologies and data become increasingly central to more processes and industry evolves into new forms [33], sometimes described as Industry 4.0 [5]. This development requires technical skills, such as programming, managing networks and databases, and working with large datasets, plus soft skills, such as communication and project management [15, 30]. As this context is also characterised by continuous change, a third set of skills is necessary, often conceptualised as "learning to learn" [e.g., 9]. These skills are also discussed in terms of meta-skills [e.g., 5], higher-order skills which support other skills. The first two sets of skills (technical and soft skills) are those identified by employers as essential (and sometimes lacking in graduates) in their responses to government consultations [cf. 30, 34]. The third set of skills are discussed more by academics and professional bodies, especially in the context of work-based learning and the need for professionals to continue to develop their learning and skills after finishing courses [e.g., 8, 9]. This is essential in IT, where *specific* knowledge and skills learned at university are perceived by employers to go quickly "out of date" [1, 5]. The annual Scottish Technology Insights Survey consistently shows software and web application development skills in highest demand [e.g., 25], however the specific programming languages cited in recent reports are multiple and varying. Between 2010 and 2017, nine different programming languages are mentioned; five are mentioned only once. As such, it is not in universities' or graduates' best interests to structure a four year degree course around building very specific skills based on the shifting sands of industry demand.

Nonetheless, apprenticeship policy aims to address the digital skills shortage by increasing the numbers gaining digital skills; and increasing the numbers of those with higher-level digital skills to meet the evolving contexts of technology in their roles. Employers are given a central role in identifying the necessary skills, acknowledging their in situ need and awareness, as well as their previous dissatisfaction with the job-readiness of computing graduates. Universities need to provide the fundamental knowledge underpinning skills so that their graduates continue to seek out, contextualise, and apply new knowledge throughout their careers [3, 14].

Collaborating with employers could also help universities to address retention problems in Computing. Figures from HESA (the UK government's Higher Education Statistics Agency) indicate that 10.5% of UK-domiciled undergraduates who started their degrees in 2015/16 at UK universities have left higher education without achieving any awards, compared to 6.4% across all subjects [10]. Various studies have focused on computing students' conceptualisation of computing/IT at university as an indication of their likely progression [e.g., 2, 13, 18, 19]. A narrow focus on programming, within the human-computer dyad, suggests a difficult course and unattractive career; whereas students who see programming as creative, collaborative, and integrated with the outside world, enjoy the associated hard work. Kinnunen et al. specifically note the disparity between students' expectations of their course (mostly programming) and their career aspirations, including managing projects and companies, but also contributing to society and making a difference [13]. Dziallas and Fincher [7], asking computing graduates to look back over their degrees, which included a year in industry, found that their experience in the workplace could transform their understanding of themselves as programmers and increase their engagement in the final year of their course. Based in the workplace, apprentices have a major input into their understanding of computing as a practice and career, potentially providing the contextual and social elements which give their studies meaning [18].

To address the perceived disconnect between computing studied at university and digital skills needed by industry, as well as the need for more computing graduates, apprenticeships focusing on digital skills have been prioritised in Scotland [28]. The first graduate apprenticeships were established in 2017 as collaborations between employers and HEIs, facilitated by Skills Development Scotland, the executive public body of the Scottish Government tasked with managing Graduate Apprenticeships.

3. Graduate Apprenticeships

Ryan and Unwin [24] define contemporary apprenticeships as "a structured programme of vocational preparation, sponsored by an employer, juxtaposing part-time education with on-the-job training and work experience" (p. 100). In 2017, Scotland's first computing graduate apprentices began their degrees, including BScs in Software Development, Cyber Security, and Information Technology Management for Business. Data Science apprenticeships became available in 2018.

Graduate Apprenticeships are degree programmes in which the students are in full-time, salaried employment, while completing degree credits. The curricula are developed in each university running apprenticeship degrees to satisfy frameworks approved by industry-led technical expert groups. Undergraduate degrees are completed over four years, the same as for a traditional full-time degree in Scotland. Models vary between courses; for example, apprentices may study on campus one day per week, or in blocks, or online, combined with work-based learning, throughout the year. Their fees are paid, via Skills Development Scotland, from the UK Apprenticeship Levy and, initially, the European Social Fund. The degrees parallel Degree Apprenticeships in England, though there are important national differences in implementation.

The policy papers and promotional material around the Graduate Apprenticeships highlight their potential to address Scotland's digital skills shortage [e.g., 26, 28]. This also enables employers to frame their role in employing apprentices or supporting staff to study degrees as contributions to the national good, i.e. by helping to address the digital skills gap [e.g., 4, 16], rather than increasing their organisation's skill base or recouping their contributions to the Apprenticeship Levy. This study focuses on the individual level of the digital skills gap [23] by surveying apprentices. We explore their experience of moving into or forward in IT professional roles as they embark on their apprenticeships. Are there differences in the demographics or ambitions of apprentices according to whether they are upskilling or new to IT? Are the apprenticeships supporting the expansion of the pool of digitally-skilled graduates or just supplying a new route? The following sections describe the survey of new apprentices and contextualise findings according to the policy aims to address the digital skills gap.

4. Methodology

Graduate apprentices at three Scottish universities were invited to complete a short survey during their first trimester. New apprentices at one university completed the survey on paper in both 2017 and 2018; apprentices at the other two universities completed surveys online in 2018. A dataset was created from these surveys, using only responses from apprentices studying computing degrees: i.e., Cyber Security, Data Science, Information Technology Management for Business, or Software Development. The aim of the data analysis was to identify the apprentices' paths into their degree programmes, especially the extent to which they were moving into IT careers or moving forward within established IT careers.

5. Findings from the survey

5.1 Apprentices' backgrounds

The survey aimed to build a picture of the new graduate apprentices. Who was choosing this degree? Who was being put forward by their employer or recruited into it? We are particularly interested in whether new people are being attracted into IT careers by this innovative degree.

To discover more about routes in to these new apprenticeships, we analysed the survey responses to identify whether the apprentices were *new recruits into IT* (n=29) or *upskillers*, already employed in IT roles (n=53). New recruits were mostly recruited, by their employer, directly into their role as graduate apprentices (without previous IT qualifications or related experience of higher education); two were already working for their employer, but in a non-IT role (such as electrical engineer). Our upskillers were either already working for their employer when they started the Graduate Apprenticeship, in a more or less skilled *IT role* (e.g., testing, helpdesk, project management, developer) or were recruited into the Graduate Apprenticeship but had previous qualifications or experience in IT, such as a Modern Apprenticeship or previously starting a computing degree. These two groups were then compared, using survey data about their demographics and skills preferences.

Table 1: Survey respondents' demographic data

Demographic Data (N=82)		Count (Col %)	Upskillers (Col %)	New to IT (Col %)
Gender	Female	17 (21%)	12 (23%)	5 (17%)
	Male	63 (77%)	40 (75%)	23 (79%)
	NS	2 (2%)	1 (2%)	1 (3%)
Age	25 below	64 (78%)	36 (68%)	28 (97%)
	26 above	18 (22%)	17 (32%)	1 (3%)
Ethnicity	White UK	73 (89%)	44 (83%)	29 (100%)
	Other	9 (11%)	9 (17%)	0 (0%)
First in the family to uni	Yes	31 (38%)	22 (42%)	9 (31%)
	No	48 (59%)	30 (57%)	18 (62%)
	NS*	3 (4%)	1 (2%)	2 (7%)
SIMD**	20-40	15 (18%)	10 (19%)	5 (17%)
	40+	38 (46%)	20 (38%)	18 (62%)
	NS*	29 (35%)	23 (43%)	6 (21%)
Recruitment	Into GA	37 (45%)	9 (17%)	27 (93%)
	Existing employment	45 (55%)	43 (83%)	2 (7%)
		N = 82	n = 53	n = 29

*NS = not specified

**Scottish index of Multiple Deprivation

Table 1 summarises the characteristics of these two groups.The Scottish Index of Multiple Deprivation (SIMD) is used as an indication of the apprentices' socio-economic backgrounds. SIMD brings together a variety of indices that describe deprivation related to health, education, crime, and housing. SIMD categories are based on postcode data, with 20-40 indicating the two most deprived quintiles [27]. These figures provide a useful overview, but should be approached with caution as there are likely to be mismatches between people and their current residential location. Postcodes were not collected in the 2017 survey, hence the relatively high proportion of *Not Specified*). Apprentices were also asked whether they were the first in their family to attend university.

From the survey data, it appears employers are enabling existing employees to take advantage of the apprenticeship to gain a recognised award: 55% of respondents were with their current employer when they started the Graduate Apprenticeship, while 45% were recruited specifically as graduate apprentices. However, these two categories contain both upskillers and new recruits to IT: nine people who were recruited by their employer to do the Graduate Apprenticeship had previous IT experience (upskillers) and two people who were with their employer before the Graduate Apprenticeship were in non-IT roles (new to IT), while 83% of upskillers were with their current employer before starting the apprenticeship (Table 1).

The computing discipline in the UK is not gender-balanced: only 17% of on-campus students identify as female [HESA https://www.hesa.ac.uk/data-and-analysis/students/whos-in-he]. The gender balance of our new to IT group, reflects this imbalance at 17%, however 23% of our upskillers are female. This could indicate that women move into the IT profession at a later stage on their careers, which could be a useful steer for recruiters and for universities' marketing. The ethnicity data shows a worrying lack of diversity, especially as 7/9 of the *other* category are white non-UK—nearly 99% white, compared to Scotland's most recent (2011) census figure of 96% white [https://www.scotlandscensus.gov.uk/].

Not surprisingly, only one of our new entrants to IT is over 26, versus 32% of our upskillers, a statistically significant difference in proportion, as assessed by Fisher's exact test ($p<.001$) The data also shows that employers have chosen relatively young candidates to fill newly created apprenticeship roles. If we break down the age data according to whether the apprentices were recruited directly into the Graduate Apprenticeship, we see that only one of the directly-recruited apprentices is over 26 (under 3%), whereas 36% of those already employed are over 26. A further exploration of recruitment decisions and promotion of the apprenticeship opportunity would uncover whether this was intentional (and why). Were older potential candidates less likely to apply or less likely to be successful? For example, the salary for new Graduate Apprentices may be more attractive to school-leavers who are living with their parents or in student accommodation than to those living independently.

Apprentices with prior IT experience are more likely to be the first in their family to attend university (41% to 31%) and slightly more likely to come from an area of multiple deprivation (19% to 17%) than those entering IT. These *upskillers*' profiles suggest that, if successful, the IT industry will enjoy an increase in both number and diversity of highly qualified IT workers. Certainly, through completing the degree, the upskillers will acquire more widely recognised qualifications.

5.2 Apprentices' skills and motivations

Participants were asked about the skills they had gained prior to starting the apprenticeship. The free text responses were coded into the three areas: subject knowledge, project management, and soft skills (Table 2). These were the areas identified in the Shadbolt report [30, p.53].

Table 2: Existing skills

Relevant Skills	Upskillers (Row %)	New to IT (Row %)	Total
Subject Knowledge	36 (67%)	18 (33%)	54
Soft Skills	23 (62%)	14 (38%)	37
Project Management	8 (62%)	5 (38%)	13

Of the valid responses, 67% (54) declared some working knowledge of computing, 46% (37) identified having soft skills like problem solving and communication skills, and 16% (13) have skills in project management. As may be expected, a breakdown of these numbers indicates that those with prior experience in IT identified a wider range of relevant skills than the new recruits. Further research would be needed to identify the extent of these existing skills, especially compared to students starting on-campus undergraduate degrees. Understanding the apprentices' diverse baselines of experience is necessary for universities to pitch teaching at the appropriate level.

Table 3: Importance of new skills

Skills	N	Mean	Std. Deviation
(1) Technical skills I can apply at work	58	4.72	0.62
(2) Using technologies (e.g. Using specific business tools or software)	58	4.09	0.94
(3) Personal development (problem solving, critical thinking, self-management etc.)	58	4.02	1.03
(4) Theoretical knowledge (e.g. understanding relevant theory and models)	57	3.89	1.18
(5) Professional skills (e.g. Career development, understanding business processes)	58	3.84	1.25
(6) Management and project management.	58	3.33	1.55
(7) Interpersonal skills (e.g. working as a team, communications)	58	3.28	1.17
(8) Writing (e.g. technical writing, report writing)	55	2.71	1.46

Participants were asked about the skills they wanted to develop on the course. In 2017, this was a free-text option. Based on the responses gathered in 2017, the question was developed, specifying eight skills and asking apprentices to rate them on a scale of 0 to 5, where a score of 5 reflects high importance, and 0 low importance. Thus Table 3 contains responses from 2018 only. The ratings show that, for most apprentices, *technical skills they can apply at work* are the most relevant/important skills followed by the ability to *use specific tools and software* (mean = 4.09, sd = .94) and *soft skills related to personal development* (mean = 4.02, sd = 1.03). Apprentices, irrespective of their previous background, were most interested in learning skills that could be applied at work, which aligns with employers' requests for workers with immediately relevant skills [34].

An independent t-test of the skills-rating from those new into IT versus the upskillers (see Table 4) showed that those with previous IT experience scored *theoretical knowledge* and *writing skills* slightly higher than those new to the IT (with small effect sizes of .255 and .433). The skills categories *technical skills, using technologies, interpersonal skills* and *professional skills,* were scored slightly higher by those new into IT (effect sizes ranging between =.201 to .358). None of these differences were statistically significant. It is difficult to say whether this is due to the small sample size or indicates homogeneity between the groups. The exploration of apprentices' current and desired skills (including any meaningful difference according to their background) is important in creating flexible learning paths, one of the tenets of the Graduate Apprenticeship specification [29]. For example, skilled and experienced apprentices could benefit from the creation of different degree entry points, including entry to a later stage of the course when topics contain more theoretical concepts and less direct application of skills.

Table 4: Importance of new skills (Prior experience of IT, New to IT)

Skills	New to IT	N	Mean	SD	p-value	Effect Size
Technical skills	No	32	4.66	0.75	.329	0.25
	Yes	26	4.81	0.40		
Using technologies	No	32	4.00	0.95	.444	0.20
	Yes	26	4.19	0.94		
Personal Development	No	32	4.03	0.82	.910	0.03
	Yes	26	4.00	1.26		
Theoretical knowledge	No	31	4.03	1.14	.339	0.26
	Yes	26	3.73	1.22		
Professional Skills	No	32	3.72	1.30	.400	0.22
	Yes	26	4.00	1.20		
Project Management	No	32	3.34	1.60	.931	0.02
	Yes	26	3.31	1.52		
Interpersonal Skills	No	32	3.09	1.25	.190	0.36
	Yes	26	3.50	1.03		
Writing Skills	No	32	2.97	1.49	.121	0.43
	Yes	23	2.35	1.37		

In 2018 the apprentices were asked: "Were you considering other options? (e.g., part-time degree, GA in another subject, certificates)." Table 5 summarises the free text responses according to the two groups, indicating that those who were new to IT were much more likely to be considering studying a traditional degree (50%); About a quarter of the upskillers were also considering traditional study (27%), including part-time study options (12%). These alternative plans reflect the ages and employment status of the two groups: 58% of the new to IT group had left school in the last 18 months, compared to 9% of the Upskillers. This indicates that up to half of the new to IT group were not brought to IT by the apprenticeship opportunity, but were following their plans, established at school, to study computing.

Table 5: Other options

	Upskillers (n=34)	New to IT (n=26)
Full-time degree	5 (15%)	13 (50%)
Part-time degree/ other study	4 (12%)	0 (0%)
Another GA	3 (9%)	6 (23%)

However, responses to the question "Why did you choose this apprenticeship degree, rather than a traditional full-time degree?" indicate that many apprentices did not consider themselves in a position to take on a traditional degree. Common themes were identified in the free text responses to this question and the number of respondents mentioning each of six themes was counted (across all the respondents). The most common reason given for choosing the apprenticeship route was the integration with work experience: 41% (34) of respondents mentioned this. For example: "I like working and gaining experience while studying." The second most important factor was financial reasons, with 33% (27) of responses mentioning this. While Scottish-domiciled students' fees are paid by the government, they generally need to take on considerable loans and/or paid work to cover their living expenses, whereas graduate apprentices are paid a salary. Some apprentices felt they could not have afforded to do a traditional degree: for example, "I could not really afford to go to university and did not want to get in debt with student loans." As noted above, over half the apprentices were already with their employer when they started the degree; keeping their job was a solid reason to choose the apprenticeship: 22% (18) mentioned this; for example, "Mostly because I am already in my Dream Role but would like to further my career whilst working".

6. Discussion

The aims of the new degree apprenticeships in computing were to increase the number of IT workers with computing degrees and ensure that these computing graduates' skills matched the industry's needs (indicated by the employers' role in designing the degree frameworks). Our survey data found evidence of both of these aims being shared by the apprentices themselves: when asked about gaining skills, the apprentices rated all the suggested skills categories as relatively important and the skills most explicitly linked with work (in their given descriptions) as most important. The number of highly-skilled IT professionals is on the way to being increased on two fronts: apprentices new to IT and people with IT careers gaining higher level skills.

The GA frameworks have been approved by an industry-focused technical expert group. The framework development approach to ensure relevance of degree courses has been used elsewhere, e.g., through publication of specifications and accreditation activity by the ACM and the British Computer Society (BCS). None of these curriculum specifications (ACM, BCS or GA) list current products, such as specific programming languages, database systems, or cloud architectures. And yet, much of the criticism of computing graduates' skills centres on a lack of a specific products and languages, with employers each requesting their latest project toolsets, as evidenced by ScotlandIS [25]. The pragmatic framework approach of the apprenticeship degrees collates employers' needs. Combined with close involvement in the workplace delivery of these degrees, this will hopefully lead to a better shared understanding of the graduate profile—that graduates will know fundamental concepts, know specific skills, and know how to learn and apply new skills, throughout their careers. These apprenticeship degrees are an opportunity to re-frame the relationships between universities and employers and work together on skills development, rather than demand that graduates are proficient in the latest technologies, as industry surveys [e.g., 25] consistently show these to be short-lived.

As the funding is limited, these apprenticeship degrees will not entirely replace traditional computer science degrees. To develop all their computing courses, universities need to continue working together with bodies such as the BCS and ACM who continually refresh their curricular frameworks. However, at present, BCS accredit degree apprenticeships only to *Registered IT Technician*, rather than full chartered professional level [BCS https://www.bcs.org/media/1209/accreditation-guidelines.pdf]. For the Graduate Apprenticeships, the survey data suggests that apprentices have a good sense of what they want from their degree; plus, ongoing negotiation of workplace learning can be used to ensure university computing curricula increasingly align with local industry needs.

In terms of increasing the number of skilled IT workers, the survey provided some evidence of apprentices being drawn from currently under-represented groups, including a slightly higher percentage of women studying computing than for the three universities' on-campus courses: for example, 21% of our survey respondents identify as female, compared to 19% of undergraduate computing students in one of the universities and 12% in another. The current ethnicity figures are worrying, although the Scottish context should be noted: for example, in one of the survey universities, 92% of the undergraduate computing students identify as white. The collaborations may provide opportunities for employers and universities to share their approaches to increasing diversity and social mobility [e.g. see 17]. As apprentices' fees are paid throughout their course and they receive salary, they can avoid student debt and this may help to widen access to those from more debt-averse backgrounds. Survey respondents included people from areas of multiple deprivation and people who were the first in their family to attend university, though these proportions are still some way off reflecting the population.

While the majority of apprentices had some experience of the IT industry or computing higher education, the survey revealed how the number of new recruits jumped, as a proportion, between the 2017 and 2018 cohorts: in 2017, 17% of respondents had been recruited for the Graduate Apprenticeship; in 2018, 53% were recruited straight in. This is probably due to employers having a greater understanding of the degrees in their second year and more time available for employers to recruit and universities to market the degrees. This jump is evident in the data for the one university which surveyed apprentices in both years, so it is not due to a difference in marketing between the universities. However, the alternative plans of the new to IT group suggest that half would have studied computing at university anyway if the apprenticeship had not been available to them. In parallel, NCUB [17] try to uncover whether organisations employing graduate and degree apprentices are increasing their employees overall or replacing graduate recruitment with the apprenticeships. In NCUB's study of twelve employers, all twelve were planning to increase both the number of degree apprentices and the ratio of apprentices to graduate recruits.

Whether the Graduate Apprenticeship provides new pathways into the IT profession or new opportunities to gain skills (and internationally recognised qualifications) for current employees, it is a major investment in people that will benefit the IT industry. It has been suggested that the intensity of graduate and degree apprenticeships may make them more suitable for people with some experience of the IT profession, rather than young people straight from school who are likely to be less certain about their career goals [32]. Further work is required to follow these new apprentices through to degree completion, to explore the nature of work-based learning as the course is delivered and seek confirmation that the digital skills gap is being addressed in terms of quality. Repeating the survey in the coming years and involving more universities will reveal the extent to which the skills gap is being addressed in terms of quantity and diversity.

7. Conclusion

Degree apprenticeships in computing subjects present a new opportunity for universities to work with funders and employers to increase the numbers of graduates with the right skills. The new Apprenticeship Levy, funding these endeavors, enables new courses, with apprentices both embedded in the workplace and attending university. We report on an early study into the prior backgrounds and ambitions of the first cohorts of computing apprentices in three Scottish universities. The combined responses indicate that initial employer approaches to recruiting staff to these apprenticeships constitute a mix of direct recruitment of new staff and allocating places to existing staff. There is some indication from the survey data that the proportion of new recruits to upskilling may change over time, reflecting NCUB's account [17] of employers developing their understanding of how the apprenticeships fit in with their recruitment and training processes. Early indications about the opportunity to bridge the skills gap by this means look positive: new recruits will gain computing skills; existing staff will gain advanced skills and a recognised qualification. Computing apprenticeships look like they might be part of the answer, though limited by the restriction on funded apprenticeship places. It remains to be seen how this limit, or the intense nature of the apprenticeships, will impact on the diversity of people gaining computing degrees this way.

REFERENCES

[1]. Valerie Antcliff, Sue Baines, and Elizabeth Gorb. 2016. Developing your own graduate employees: employer perspectives on the value of a degree apprenticeship. *Higher Education, Skills and Work-Based Learning* 6, 4, 378-383. DOI: https://doi.org/10.1108/HESWBL-05-2016-0032

[2]. Maureen Biggers, Anne Brauer, and Tuba Yilmaz. 2008. Student Perceptions of Computer Science: A Retention Study Comparing Graduating Seniors with CS Leavers. *ACM SIGCSE Bulletin*, ACM 40, 1, 402–406.

[3]. Darryll Bravenboer. 2016. Why Co-design and Delivery Is 'A No Brainer' for Higher and Degree Apprenticeship Policy. *Higher Education, Skills and Work-based Learning* 6, 4, 384–400.

[4]. Hannah Burley. 2018. Solarwinds launches apprenticeship with Edinburgh-Napier. (November, 2018). The Scotsman. Retrieved December 4, 2018 from https://www.scotsman.com/business/companies/tech/solarwinds-launches-apprenticeship-with-edinburgh-napier-1-4835570

[5]. Centre for Work-Based Learning. 2018. *Skills 4.0 A skills model to drive Scotland's future.* Skills Development Scotland Retrieved January, 7, 2019 from https://www.centreforworkbasedlearning.co.uk/media/1542/skills-40_a-skills-model.pdf

[6]. Department for Business Energy and Industrial Strategy (DBEIS). 2017. *Industrial Strategy: building a Britain fit for the future (White paper).* UK Government. Retrieved November 29, 2018 from https://www.gov.uk/government/publications/industrial-strategy-building-a-britain-fit-for-the-future

[7]. Sebastian Dziallas and Sally Fincher. 2016. Aspects of Graduateness in Computing Students' Narratives. In *Proceedings of the 2016 ACM Conference on International Computing Education Research* (ICER '16). ACM. DOI: http://dx.doi.org/10.1145/2960310.2960317.

[8]. Alison Fuller and Lorna Unwin. 2003. Learning as Apprentices in the Contemporary UK Workplace: creating and managing expansive and restrictive participation. Journal of Education and Work 16, 4, 407-426. DOI: https://doi.org/10.1080/1363908032000093012

[9]. Ruth Helyer. 2015. Learning through reflection: the critical role of reflection in work-based learning (WBL). *Journal of Work-Applied Management* 7, 1, 15-27. DOI: https://doi.org/10.1108/JWAM-10-2015-003

[10]. HESA. 2018. Non-continuation: UK Performance Indicators 2016/17 (March 2018). Retrieved January 21st, 2019 from https://www.hesa.ac.uk/news/08-03-2018/non-continuation-tables

[11]. Ann Hodgson, Ken Spours, and David Smith, 2017. Future apprenticeships in England: the role of mediation in the new model. *Journal of Education and Work* 30, 6, 653-668. DOI: https://doi.org/10.1080/13639080.2017.1349299

[12]. Institute for Apprenticeships, 2017. *'How to' guide for trailblazers.* UK: Institute for Apprenticeships. Retrieved November 29, 2018 from https://www.instituteforapprenticeships.org/media/1033/how_to__guide_for_trailblazers_-_v2.pdf

[13]. Päivi Kinnunen, Matthew Butler, Michael Morgan, Aletta Nylen, Anne-Kathrin Peters, Jane Sinclair, Sara Kalvala, and Erkki Pesonen, 2018. Understanding initial undergraduate expectations and identity in computing studies. *European Journal of Engineering Education* 43, 2, 201-218, DOI: 10.1080/03043797.2016.1146233

[14]. Steve Lambert, 2016. Are current accountability frameworks appropriate for degree apprenticeships? *Higher Education, Skills and Work-Based Learning* 6, 4, 345–356. DOI: https://doi.org/10.1108/HESWBL-05-2016-0027

[15]. Simon O'Leary. 2016. Graduates' experiences of, and attitudes towards, the inclusion of employability-related support in undergraduate degree programmes; trends and variations by subject discipline and gender. *Journal of Education and Work* 30,1, 84-105. DOI: 10.1080/13639080.2015.1122181

[16]. Maggie Morrison. 2018. How Scotland's Technology Sector Can Bridge the Skills Gap. (October 2018). Digit. Retrieved December 4, 2018 from https://digit.fyi/how-scotlands-technology-sector-bridge-skills-gap/

[17]. NCUB. 2018. Degree Apprenticeships: impacts, challenges, future opportunities, National Centre for Universities and Business. Retrieved January 7, 2019 from http://www.ncub.co.uk/images/reports/NCUB-Degree-Apprenticeships-Report-Mar-18-WEB.pdf

[18]. Anne-Kathrin Peters, Anders Berglund, Anna Eckerdal, and Arnold Pears. 2014. First Year Computer Science and IT Students' Experience of Participation in the Discipline. In *proceedings of 2014 International Conference on teaching and learning in computing and engineering (LaTiCE), Kuching, April 11–13,* 1–8. IEEE.

[19]. Anne-Kathrin Peters, Anders Berglund, Anna Eckerdal, and Arnold Pears. 2015. Second Year Computer Science and IT Students' Experience of Participation in the Discipline. In *proceedings of the 15th Koli calling conference on computing education research, November 19–22,* ACM, 68–76.

[20]. Philip Powell and Anita Walsh, 2018. Whose curriculum is it anyway? Stakeholder salience in the context of Degree Apprenticeships. *Higher Education Quarterly* 72, 2, 90-106. DOI: https://doi.org/10.1111/hequ.12149

[21]. Dan Restuccia, Bledi Taska, and Scott Bittle. 2018. *Different Skills, Different Gaps; Measuring and Closing the Skills Gap.* Burning Glass Technologies for U.S. Chamber of Commerce Foundation. Retrieved November 29, 2018 from https://www.burning-glass.com/research-project/skills-gap-different-skills-different-gaps/

[22]. Doug Richard, 2012. *The Richard Review of Apprenticeships.* London: Department for Business, Innovation & Skills. Retrieved November 29, 2018 from https://assets.publishing.service.gov.uk/government/uploads/system/uploads/attachment_data/file/34708/richard-review-full.pdf

[23]. Lizzie Richardson and David Bissel. In press. Geographies of digital skill. *Geoforum.* DOI: https://doi.org/10.1016/j.geoforum.2017.09.014

[24]. Paul Ryan and Lorna Unwin. 2001. Apprenticeship in the British 'training market'. *National Institute Economic Review* 178, 1, 99–114.

[25]. ScotlandIS. 2018. *Scottish Technology Industry Survey.* ScotlandIS. Retrieved January 4, 2019 from https://www.scotlandis.com/resources/scottish-technology-industry-survey/

[26]. Scottish Government. 2016. *Scottish Government response to the UK Government apprenticeship levy.* The Scottish Government Retrieved November 29, 2018 from https://www.gov.scot/publications/scottish-government-response-uk-government-apprenticeship-levy/pages/4/

[27]. Scottish Government. 2016. *Introducing the Scottish Index of Multiple Deprivation 2016.* National Statistics. Retrieved January 7, 2019 from https://www2.gov.scot/Resource/0050/00504809.pdf

[28]. SDS. 2015. Degree-level apprenticeships address digital skills shortage. (November 2015). Skills Development Scotland .Retrieved December 4, 2018 from https://www.skillsdevelopmentscotland.co.uk/news-events/2015/november/degree-level-apprenticeships-address-digital-skills-shortage/

[29]. SDS. 2016. Graduate Level Apprenticeships at SCQF level 10: Technical Specification (June 2016). Skills Development Scotland.

[30]. Nigel Shadbolt. 2016. *Shadbolt Review of Computer Sciences Degree Accreditation and Graduate Employability.* London: Department for Business, Innovation & Skills. Retrieved November 29, 2018 from https://www.gov.uk/government/publications/computer-science-degree-accreditation-and-graduate-employability-shadbolt-review

[31]. Svetlana Tikhonenko and Cristina Pereira. 2018. *Informatics Education in Europe: Institutions, degrees, students, positions, salaries. Key Data 2012-2017.* Informatics Europe. Retrieved November 30, 2018 from http://www.informatics-europe.org/publications.html

[32]. UCAS. 2017. *Progression Pathways 2017: Pathways through higher education.* UCAS (Universities and Colleges Admissions Service). Retrieved January 7, 2019 from https://www.ucas.com/files/progression-pathways-2017-report

[33]. UKCES. 2015. *High level STEM skills requirements in the UK labour market. UK Commission for Employment and Skills (UKCES).* Retrieved November 29, 2018 from https://www.gov.uk/government/publications/high-level-stem-skills-requirements-in-the-uk-labour-market

[34]. William Wakeham. 2016. *Wakeham Review of STEM Degree Provision and Graduate Employability.* London: Department for Business, Innovation & Skills. Retrieved November 29, 2018 from https://www.gov.uk/government/uploads/system/uploads/attachment_data/file/518582/ind-16-6-wakeham-review-stem-graduate-employability.pdf

Programme Integrating Courses Fighting to Get Engineers to Reflect on Non-technical Topics

Emma Riese
Division of Theoretical Computer Science
KTH Royal Institute of Technology
Stockholm, Sweden
riese@kth.se

Olle Bälter
Division of Media Technology and Interaction Design
KTH Royal Institute of Technology
Stockholm, Sweden
ob1@kth.se

Björn Hedin
Division of Media Technology and Interaction Design
KTH Royal Institute of Technology
Stockholm, Sweden
bjornh@kth.se

Viggo Kann
Division of Theoretical Computer Science
KTH Royal Institute of Technology
Stockholm, Sweden
viggo@kth.se

ABSTRACT

Programme Integrating Courses (PICs) aim to tie students, teachers and courses in education programmes closer together. In this study, we investigate three PICs, as part of engineering programmes in computer science and media technology. The purpose of this study was to gain a deeper understanding of how students and mentors experience the PICs with a focus on the assessment and the relationship between students, and students and mentors. We used a mixed method approach, interviewed 22 students and 6 mentors, and sent out questionnaires to all 25 mentors and all students from two of the three courses (630+470 students). The results showed that the students and mentors appreciated the social aspects of the courses, getting to know each other and share experiences. However, some were uncomfortable reflecting upon the given non-technical topics. On a general level, the students stated that their mentors assessed their reflections correctly but they were sceptical towards being graded on a scale other than pass/fail.

CCS CONCEPTS

• **Social and professional topics → Computational science and engineering education**

KEYWORDS

Programme integrating course; assessment; engineering students; reflection; higher education

ACM Reference format:

Emma Riese, Olle Bälter, Björn Hedin and Viggo Kann. 2019. Programme Integrating Courses Fighting to Get Engineers to Reflect on Non-technical Topics. In *Proceedings of 24rd Annual ACM Conference on Innovation and Technology in Computer Science Education (ITiCSE'19), July 15-17, Aberdeen, Scotland, UK.* ACM, New York, NY, USA, 7 pages, https://doi.org/10.1145/3304221.3319754

ITiCSE '19, July 15-17, 2019, Aberdeen, Scotland, UK.

ACM ISBN 978-1-4503-6301-3/19/07. http://dx.doi.org/10.1145/3304221.3319754

INTRODUCTION

At universities that offer educational programmes where the courses are offered by different departments, with their own research and teaching traditions, students can perceive the programme as scattered and question the value of certain courses. This can lead to less motivated students with poorer results as a consequence. One way to include the students in a discussion about the programme and its content is in a Program Integrating Course (PIC). A PIC aims to tie courses in an education programme closer together by offering the programme's students time to reflect on taken courses and the relationship between them. This is carried out in smaller groups (10-18 students) together with a mentor, a teacher on the programme. In addition, the PICs would also include other topics to reflect upon, such as ways to handle procrastination and relation between the education, work and private life [11].

The PIC concept was developed ten years ago at KTH Royal Institute of Technology (KTH), Stockholm, Sweden [10] and has now spread to other universities [12] and Computer Science institutions in both the UK and US are planning to introduce similar courses. The PICs at KTH have been evaluated repeatedly [13, 14, 15] with positive results and have also been a vessel for the development of *walking seminars* [5]. These studies have shown that PICs can be a powerful instrument to improve what the students get out of their studies and also to get participating teachers more familiar with the students' study situation. However, we see that the PICs fail to reach some students. If we can better understand why, we can hopefully improve the design of the courses so that they become rewarding for virtually all participants. Previous studies of PICs have relied solely on questionnaires, but in this study, we have also included interviews in order to achieve a more nuanced picture both from the students and the mentors with a focus on three questions:

- Which is the perceived purpose with the course?

- How is the assessment in these programme integrating courses perceived?
- How is the relationship between students, and students and mentors perceived?

RELATED RESEARCH

Academic success is linked to students' use of self-regulating learning strategies, such as self-evaluation, organization, seeking social assistance (peers, teacher, or other adults) and planning [21]. However, just telling students about such strategies is not sufficient. "Educators can pave the way by placing learning about learning on the agenda of their educational programs" [16], which can be done using reflection tasks. In a study of alumni of engineering education programmes, engineers in work life have difficulties finding relevance of the actual learning and studies within the engineering educational programmes. Looking back, they "view their education as compartmentalized or fragmented, and they lack a main thread in the educational programme" [18]. PICs are designed to address this, help the students to use self-regulating learning strategies and make them aware of how the different courses, knowledge areas and skills are linked together. A recent study shows that the students of the PICs have the same view of the competences that their education programmes should develop as the programme coordinator has [7].

When designing a course, constructive alignment [2] is a concept where the learning *activities*, the *assessment* and the *learning outcomes* are aligned. That is, the learning activities are created in such a way that, if undertaken, they will lead to a passed assessment and thereby to a learning outcome matching the intended learning outcomes. Constructive alignment can be applied with varying granularity: from learning modules, over courses to entire programmes.

The teacher-students relationship has been well studied and recognized as an important factor for success in school settings, but not studied to the same extent in higher education [8]. This can be explained by the fact that interactions between teachers and students tend to be fragmented and that the students are expected to be independent adults when reaching this level [8]. However, already in 1975, a theoretical model of student retention was presented and argued that those students who are integrated both socially and academically will persist and be successful in their studies [20]. There is also empirical evidence that the social relationships, between students and between students and faculty, have an impact on the students' sense of belonging and retention rate [19]. How much the faculty should care about and interact with their students, has on the other hand, shown to cause some disagreement [8]. For example, while some faculty experienced being part of student integration as beneficial and important, others experienced is as being unnecessary [17]. How teachers treat their students is a factor in successful teaching, but attributed to mutual trust and engagement rather than personality of the teachers [1]. There are, however, few studies that have been conducted on how faculty experience their interactions with students [8], something that will be further explored in this paper.

RESEARCH SETTING

In this paper, we study three different PICs at KTH, each mandatory within an educational programme. The three PICs are described as they were structured during the academic year 2017/2018, see Table 1.

Table 1. Descriptions of the studied PICs

Course	PIC1	PIC2	PIC3
Years	3	3	2
Cycle	first	first	second
Part of Education programme	Media Technology	Computer Science and Engineering	Computer Science
Number of groups	20	39	24
Mentors	6	13	12
Number of students per group	10-12	12-14	16-18
Length of seminar	80 minutes	60-70 minutes	50 minutes
Grading of seminar activity	yes, point system	yes, two levels	no, pass/fail
Grading of reflection documents	yes, point system	yes, two levels	no, pass/fail
Peer comments	yes, within the group	no	yes, within the group

The students in each PIC are divided into seminars groups that consist of students from all years of the programme and one mentor, a teacher on the programme. All three courses are centered around four reflection seminars each year, with a dedicated topic, such as procrastination or ethics. Before each seminar, the students are asked to study the topic and write a reflection based on this and their own experiences. A 4-level reflection model developed by Kann and Magnell [15], based on Hatton and Smith [9], is used in PIC1 and PIC2. In all three PICS, the students also reflect upon recently taken courses. The reflection is shared to the group members including the mentor, who asynchronously discuss the texts online. The topic and the courses are then discussed further at a physical meeting, such as a *walking seminar* [5], where the group discusses the topic while walking in the woods behind campus.

In all three PICs the students' reflections and participation are assessed, but according to different systems. In PIC1, a point-based grading scheme is used, 7 points is given if everything is done as instructed and points are deducted, for example, if the assignment is handed in too late. In PIC2, the mentors grade both the submitted reflection and the seminar activity using a two level scale. In order to reach the highest grade for the reflection, the student has to submit a document fulfilling all stated criteria. For second and third year students, the criteria include reaching level 3 and 4 in the reflection model. To reach the highest grade for the seminar activity, the student has to be on time and be active during the seminar. In PIC3, the students are graded pass/fail on the reflection documents and on participation in the seminar.

METHODOLOGY

In this study, data was collected from late spring 2017 to early fall 2018, using both questionnaires and interviews with students and mentors. This mixed method [6] approach was chosen since we were interested in both the general perceptions and trends, but also getting a dataset that could further explain these experiences.

The interviews were conducted from spring to early fall 2018. Participation was voluntary and as a small token of appreciation, all interviewees were given a voucher for a cinema ticket. The interviews were conducted by the first author who had no previous experience from any of the studied courses, and is not a mentor nor course coordinator, to avoid conflict of interest. All interviewees agreed to have their interview recorded and to be part of the study. To protect the interviewees' privacy, names and another type of identifications are not presented in the results. The interviews were semi-structured, with a special focus on overall experience/attitude towards the courses, assessment and student-mentor relationship. To recruit students to interview, we asked mentors to list students that they thought had different opinions about the course; negative, positive or mixed/changed over time. Then we selected students, at least two from each year, from different mentor groups from each of the three courses, that was as heterogeneous as possible. For PIC3 students, we also took into account if they were international students, and if they enrolled in a PIC during their first cycle studies. In total, eight students from PIC1, seven students from PIC2, and seven students from PIC3 were interviewed. For the mentors, all mentors that answered the questionnaire were invited to also express their interest in participating in an interview. Two mentors from each course were chosen to be interviewed, six in total, none of them are authors of this paper. Each interview lasted approximately half an hour. The interviews were analyzed using thematic analysis [3] for each of the three questions studied. A thematic analysis is an inductive approach that is used to interpret data by identifying themes and was conducted according to six steps described by Braun and Clarke [4]. The thematic analysis has been carried out by the first author and the identified themes verified by the other authors.

In PIC2 and PIC3, anonymous course questionnaires are mandatory to answer for all students. The answers cannot be traced back to individual students and have no impact on the students' grades. Students could also choose to have their anonymous answers excluded from the research study. We used a 7 point Likert scale, ranging from *1. No, I strongly disagree with the statement* to 7. *Yes, I strongly agree with the statement.* The questionnaires were sent out at the end of the academic year, in both 2017 and 2018. In PIC1, the students are not required to participate in a course questionnaire, and therefore no PIC1 students were part of the questionnaire data collection. A questionnaire was also sent out to all mentors in each of the three courses, end of spring semester 2018, containing both 7 point Likert scale questions and open questions.

RESULTS

Out of the 25 mentors (out of which six are mentors in two of the courses), 22 answered the questionnaire (88%). Since the questionnaires for PIC2 and PIC3 are mandatory, all students that participated in these courses answered the questionnaires, however, 5 percent in 2017 and 7 percent in 2018 choose to not be part of the study and their answers were of course excluded. In total 950 remaining responses came in from the PIC2 questionnaires 2017 and 2018, but in that number most students that were in year 1 and 2 2017 also answered the questionnaire in 2018, possibly answering differently. The total unique students who took part in the questionnaires were 630. For PIC3, 590 responses were registered, and the unique students who took part in the questionnaires were 470. The thematic analysis of the interview data resulted in seven themes. The results from both interviews and questionnaires are presented under each of the three questions addressed, where the found themes from the thematic analysis are subheadings and some example quotes are presented.

1 Which Is the Perceived Purpose?

In general, the students stated that they are aware of the purposes of the seminars and the whole course. The third year students of PIC2 and all PIC3 students evaluated the statement *I know the purpose of the programme integrating course* in 2017 (n=446) and *I understand the aims of the seminars and activities of the programme integrating course* in 2018 (n=450), see Figure 1. The PIC2 questionnaire also confirms that PIC2 students think that *it has been interesting and fruitful to listen to students from other grades at the seminars* (n=947), also shown in Figure 1. The statement *Overall, the programme integrating course has been fruitful* was evaluated in the questionnaires of both PIC2 and PIC3 in 2017 and 2018. Figure 2 presents the result for each grade.

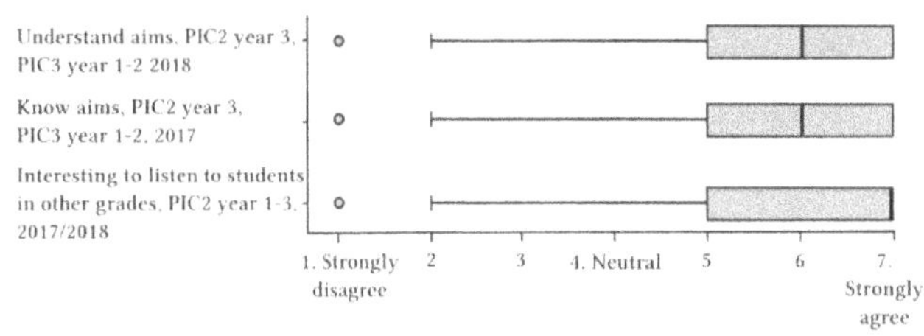

Figure 1: Questionnaire answers to the statement regarding aims and discussions across grades.

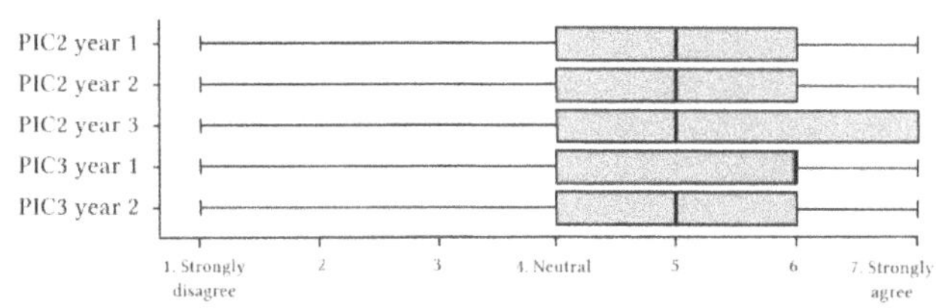

Figure 2: Questionnaire answers to the statement "*Overall, the PIC course has been fruitful*".

1.1 Sharing Experience – Evoking Change

All interviewed students, even those disliking the course, enjoyed getting to know other students and sharing their experiences. It was described as both creating a sense of not being alone in struggling with courses and also a way to get useful information from older students. This was particularly valuable for students who transferred and first year students enrolled in PIC1 or PIC2.

Discussing the programmes' courses and how they link to each other, was described to be an important part of the PICs, where the mentors were seen as gateways to change things, even though students and mentors felt like not all complaints were brought to the responsible person or dealt with. That this channel was somewhat missing was also stated as something that could be improved in the courses by several of the mentors in the open-ended question of their questionnaire. The mentors in PIC2 have an informal meeting in connection with each round of seminars, something PIC1's and PIC3's mentors described as missing.

"You get the opportunity to see what you should focus on during the education. Talking to people who are in the grades above, who know more. "– PIC1 student year 3

1.2 Not My Subject

Not all students saw value in discussing topics that were non-technical and experienced to be far from what they choose to study. This opinion was common among the interviewed CS-majors, but also found among some of PIC1's students. The mentors also describe that students' attitudes towards some topics could be disappointing. It could be frustrating for the mentors who experienced that they did not succeed in getting across the importance of these non-technical topics. Some mentor also expressed that discussing these topics could be out of their own comfort zone. The courses were, however, described to fill in gaps in the learning objectives of the programme, by both students and mentors. Some students did also see the course as an opportunity to reflect about questions they might not otherwise have time for and it could be a positive break from all the regular courses. The number of students who do not think a topic is fruitful, differs between the topics, but is always a clear minority, see Table 2, showing the proportion of the PIC2 students in year 1 2017 and year 2 2018 answering below 4 in the Likert scale on the statement *I think that the topic X was fruitful.*

Table 2. The proportion of students negative to the fruitfulness of the first 8 topics of PIC2

Topic	Percentage that scored below 4
Study motivation and study techniques	14%
Learning objectives, criteria and assessment	28%
Plagiarism and my own responsibility	22%
My future role as computer science engineer	13%
Masters programmes	8%
Study and work abroad	15%
Minorities and equal treatment	23%
Quality in education - what is that?	16%

"It's not so much about technology, but it's more about other things that aren't really so interesting. Like, how do you learn to program from this?"- PIC2 student year 1

2 How Is the Assessment Perceived?

In the questionnaires, five questions regarding the assessment were asked, showed in Figure 3. In general, the students from PIC2 and PIC3 agreed that assessment of the reflections was correctly done by their mentor. But, when asked about how the reflections were assessed in other groups, the answers were more neutral. PIC3 students were sceptical towards using a grading scale and the PIC2 students had different opinions regarding if their two-level scale was motivating, resulting in a natural median.

2.1 Easy to Pass, but What Are We Graded On?

All students seem to know that it is important to hand in the reflection documents on time, but other than that, the interviewed students did not know much about the grading systems used, what they were assessed on or based on which criteria. Some students felt a bit unsure if their mentor actually read their texts and expected full marks as long as they handed in their reflection document on time. The students from PIC1 and PIC3 had a hard time picturing how you could grade the reflection documents, since they are personal opinions. The interviewed PIC3 students that had enrolled in PIC2, did see that having the reflections graded in two levels had a point because they experience that they, themselves, and their peers were more serious about the assignments and therefore wrote better reflections. However, just grading the assignments pass/fail was thought to contribute to everyone actually expressing their opinion, rather than trying to write what they thought the mentor wanted to read.

"I think it is good that only pass/fail is used, because otherwise people would probably stress about it and try to write more formally, not what they actually think." –PIC1 student year 2

To the question *How do you experience the assessment of the students' reflections?*, the majority of the mentors were indifferent or stated it was more easy/clear than difficult/unclear, see Figure 4 (n=16, 6 declined to answer). The interviewed mentors did however, described the assessment as the trickiest part, not necessarily something they were used to do. The interviewed mentors did also confirm the students' picture that they do not always have the time to read through all the texts properly. In PIC1 and PIC3, the mentors should also assess the quality of the students' comments on each other's reflections (that comments were not just statements like "I agree"), which were sometimes overlooked.

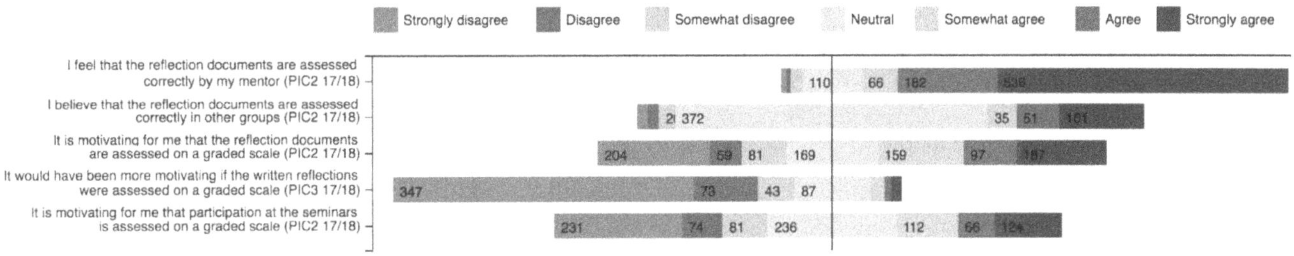

Figure 3: Questionnaire answers to statements regarding assessment in PIC2 and PIC3.

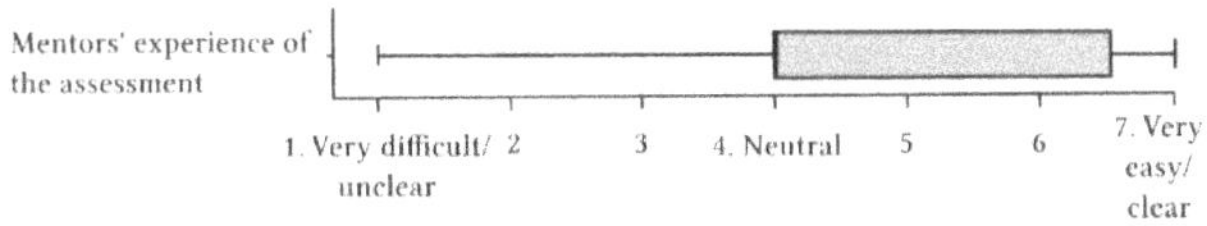

Figure 4: Mentors' questionnaire answers to how they experience the assessments.

2.2 Judged by Peers – Could Be Too Personal

The topics discussed were sometimes experienced as too personal, which made some students uncomfortable sharing their thoughts and opinions. Fearing their texts might be shared outside class. Some students expressed to be uncomfortable by the informal "judgments" and tried to adapt their texts towards the general opinion of the group. This peer-review system was also brought up by the mentors and thought to give the students more motivation to write better reflections. However, the mentors could also feel that they were intruding on their students' personal space by reading and commenting on their reflections.

"I didn't like PIC1 much at all. I had a hard time writing, reaching the word limit, because I didn't like to share personal information. Also, you post it, you give other people access to it. You do not know what will happen to that text." - PIC3 student year 2, that have also enrolled in PIC1

2.3 Bad Timing - Not Priority

In the interviews, some of students expressed that the timing of these reflections always was the worst possible; when all the other courses had assignments due. Students' from all courses described how that made them rush through these assignments, and they were not prioritized. The reason given for this prioritization was explained by the fact that it was not a high stake assessment and viewed as easy to pass/get full credit on. The mentors did also express that some students rushed their reflections, and did themselves also experience that timing could be far from perfect. Lack of time could, as mentioned above, result in not having the time to read through all documents, or having any time to write feedback. But not all mentors saw the grading or their involvement as something important, the more important part was thought to be that the students did reflect and attended the seminars.

"Everyone has lot of other courses they are doing, too many deadlines, too many assignments. So, we mostly concentrate on them and we usually forget about this." - PIC3 international student year 2

3 How Is the Relationships Perceived?

No specific question regarding the relationships between students, or students and mentors were asked in the questionnaires. The themes presented below are from the thematic analysis of the interviews, but also verified by mentors' answers to open questions on their questionnaire.

3.1 Knowing Each Other by Name

Experienced mentors expressed to be fortunate to follow the development of their students throughout the years. To be able to know their names, which might not be possible in other courses with large number of students. The mentors expressed to be proud of the students that expressed well-phrased opinions, but a bit disappointed by those students who showed that they would have preferred to not enroll in the course.

"Sometimes, the regular courses I teach has more than 250 students so there I often do not get the chance to get to know individuals. [...] It is nice to see how they develop and if I don't know who is who, then it's hard to." – mentor PIC 3

The students described their relationships to the mentor to be much depending on the mentor. If the mentor showed interest, listen and shared their own opinions, it was experienced as good relationship. It could then, extend to be a mentorship outside the course, a person to which you could turn to with any study related issues, almost like a mentor from high school. The students who felt their mentors did not seem to care so much or to be there only because they had to, would, understandably, not seek their mentors outside class. Some students even expressed a disappointment that they had not got to know the mentor, as they expected.

3.2 Personality and Engagement

Both mentors and students described the personality of the students to influence the seminars. Some students are talkative and some are shy. Both students and mentors described how they tried to get these shy members of the group to also participate, although that was not always possible. The level of engagement in the course, from both students and mentors, was also described to influence the experience of the course, and the students that felt their mentors or fellow group members did not seem to care were, understandably, not that interested in the course either. A couple of the mentors did also express as comments in the questionnaire, that they had been assign to be a mentor, not given the choice to become one. The student-student relationship, were, as stated in the theme "Sharing Experience – Evoking Change", viewed as an important part of the course and much appreciated.

"In PIC3, it has generally felt like all teachers and all students, thinks 'this is just something we have to do. We just have to get through this'"- PIC3 student year 1

DISCUSSION AND CONCLUSIONS

We have performed an interview and questionnaire study to gain a deeper understanding of how students and mentors experience PICs. The students are generally positive, stating to understand the aims and find it rewarding to hear the opinion of others. However, there is room for improvement as not all students experience the courses as "fruitful". We could also see a difference between the grades, where year 3 students ranked the "fruitfulness" higher than year 1 and year 2 students.

The interviewed students all expressed that sharing experience that could evoke change, was the main benefit of the course. The mentors, and some students, were however, not entirely satisfied with how this feedback given to the mentors was dealt with. The feedback channel could be further improved and, as suggested by the mentors, become more structured. After this study, changes have been implemented in PIC1, so that all unfiltered reflections regarding courses are also sent to the responsible teacher, if permitted by the student.

Writing a reflection and discussing a given topic, received mixed reviews by the interviewees and was perceived as unnecessary by some. The results from the interviews could point towards that these more sceptical students fail to see how these assignments aligns with what they perceived to be the purpose of the course, the sharing of experiences. However, the learning objectives are an integrated part of the topics in the PICs. It is therefore more likely that these students simply do not agree with all learning objectives and do not see a point in fulfilling them. Hence, this particular group of students, could be put in contrast with previous findings [7], that showed that the students collectively have the same view as the programme coordinator of which competences the education programme should develop. Reflecting on non-technical topics seems to be out of some of the students' comfort zone and the level of engagement differs. A (better) motivation *why* these topics are important, beyond the learning outcomes, might assist this. In some cases, the topics are personal, which of course adds to the discomfort. One way to reduce this could be to formulate topic-related alternatives in such a way that the students are not required to share personal information.

The students felt that the assessment of the reflections was correctly done by their mentor. But interestingly, when asked about the assessment in other groups, the answers were quite different. The main difference was that instead of answering *"strongly agree"*, the students either answered *"neutral"* or declined to answer. An explanation could be that the students are not aware of the quality of the assessment in other groups, which we did not anticipate, but in retrospect it seems natural. We could also see a similar trend in the mentors' questionnaire answers (large number declined to answer this question), indicating that not all mentors have reflected about the assessment.

The question regarding if the present grading scale in PIC2 (pass/pass with distinction) is motivating, divides the students: about the same number of students are negative and positive - the median is "neutral". The students from PIC3 that only have one passing grade do, however, unite in the opinion that more levels would be negative. Perhaps information on why each scale is used could increase the understanding and reminders on how the grading is done could possibly reduce the uncertainty about what is graded for students and mentors.

The mentor-student relation, growing over the years, are appreciated by both sides, but not all mentors seem to be engaged to the same extent in the course and engagement is important [1]. For the PICs it might be even more important to recruit mentors who are interested in these kinds of social relationships with the students. Further strengthening of the collaboration and discussion among the mentors, described as somewhat missing in PIC1 and PIC3, could possibly make the mentors a bit more engaged.

Since these seminars occur only four times per year, they appear as a regular surprise, always with a bad timing for some. Considering the workload of the students, it is doubtful whether there are any good time slots. One remedy could be to add a weekly time slot in the schedule for the students to work on their reflection, or at least as a reminder that they ought to do that.

From these results, it is apparent that the mentors are engaging in different ways, with varying results among the students. Future research of PICs should aim at identifying and spreading best practices among the mentors.

REFERENCES

[1] K. Bain. *What the Best College Teachers Do.* Cambridge: Harvard University Press. 2011.

[2] J. Biggs. Teaching for Quality Learning at University – What the Student Does 2nd Edition SRHE / Open University Press, Buckingham, 2003.

[3] R.E. Boyatzis. Transforming qualitative information: thematic analysis and code development. CA: SAGE publications, 1998.

[4] V. Braun and V. Clarke. Using thematic analysis in psychology. Qualitative Research in Psychology, vol. 3, no. 2, pp. 77–101, 2006.

[5] O. Bälter, B. Hedin, T. Helena, & S. Toivanen. Walking Outdoors during Seminars Improved Perceived Seminar Quality and Sense of Well-Being among Participants. International Journal of Environmental Research and Public Health, 15(303), 2018.

[6] C. Conrad and R. Serlin. The Sage handbook for research in education: Pursuing ideas as the keystone of exemplary inquiry (2nd ed.). Thousand Oaks, Calif.: SAGE Publications. 2011.

[7] S. Frezza et al. Modelling competencies for computing education beyond 2020: a research based approach to defining competencies in the computing disciplines. ITiCSE 2018 Companion Proceedings Companion of the 23rd Annual ACM Conference on Innovation and Technology in Computer Science Education. Pages 148-174, 2018.

[8] G. Hagenauer and S. Volet. Teacher-student relationship at university: An important yet under-researched field. *Oxford Review of Education, 40*(3), 370-388, 2014.

[9] N. Hatton and D. Smith. Reflection in teacher education: Towards definition and implementation. Teaching and teacher education, 11(1):33–49, 1995.

[10] B. Hedin. Program integrating course: A tool for reflection and quality management. In Proc. 2:nd Development Conference for Sweden's Engineering Programs, 2009.

[11] B. Hedin and V. Kann, Improving Study Skills by Combining a Study Skill Module and Repeated Reflection Seminars, *Education Research International*, vol. 2019, Article ID 9739854, 8 pages, 2019. https://doi.org/10.1155/2019/9739854.

[12] F. Heintz, A. Berglund, B. Hedin, V. Kann. A comparison between program integrating courses at KTH and Linköping University (in Swedish). In *Proceedings of 5:th Development Conference for Sweden's Engineering Programs*, 2015.

[13] V. Kann. A program integrating course with many functions (in Swedish). In *Proceedings of the 3:rd Development Conference for Sweden's Engineering Programs*, pages 153–156, 2011.
[14] V. Kann and A.-K. Högfeldt. Effects of a Program Integrating Course for Students of Computer Science and Engineering. In *Proceedings of the 47th ACM Technical Symposium on Computing Science Education (SIGCSE '16)*. ACM, Memphis, Tennessee, USA, 510–515, 2016.
[15] V. Kann and M. Magnell. Reflektionsseminarier som håller ihop och utvecklar programmet (in Swedish). In *Proceedings of the 4:th Development Conference for Sweden's Engineering Programs*, Umeå University. 2013.
[16] A. Y. Kolb and D. A. Kolb. The learning way meta-cognitive aspects of experiential learning. Simulation & Gaming, 40(3):297–327, 2009.
[17] S. Lähteenoja and A.-M. Pirttilä Backman. Cultivation or coddling? University teachers' views on student integration. Studies in Higher Education, 30, 641–661, 2005.
[18] S. Nilsson. On the meaning of higher education in professional practice: the case of physicians and engineers. Journal of Education and Work, 23(3):255–274, 2010.
[19] L. Strauss and J. Volkwein. Predictors of Student Commitment at Two-Year and Four-Year Institutions. The Journal of Higher Education, *75*(2), 203-227, 2004.
[20] V. Tinto. Dropout from higher education: a theoretical synthesis of recent research. Review of Higher Education, 45, 89–125, 1975.
[21] B. J. Zimmerman. Self-regulated learning and academic achievement: An overview. Educational psychologist, 25(1):3–17, 1990.

Digital Storytelling and Group Work:

Integrating the Narrative Approach into a Higher Education Computer Science Course

Ari Korhonen
Aalto University
ari.korhonen@aalto.fi

Marianna Vivitsou
University of Helsinki
marianna.vivitsou@helsinki.fi

ABSTRACT

This study discusses the integration of digital storytelling and the narrative approach into a University level Computer Science course. The pedagogical intervention took place on a project basis. The plan involved student work in groups for the production of digital stories in three phases, including an abstract, a manuscript and a final story. The overall instructional design included workshops and lectures, online tutorials, and group work. The students were assigned to explore the topic of recursion. Face-to-face meetings for the coordination of group work were emphasized during lectures, workshops and project instructions.

The study uses qualitative research methods and the findings indicate two main patterns of group work. The first pattern follows from loose coordination and division of tasks among group members at the initial stages of the project. This results in documentary-like and program-based video stories. The second pattern involves tighter collaboration with face-to-face meetings for common task completion, video recording and editing, and manuscript improvement. This mode of work results in short-film style stories where recursion is well-represented. In both patterns, however, the videos present external rather than internal examples of recursion. As a result, the digital stories represent what the code does instead of how it does it.

CCS CONCEPTS

• **Social and professional topics → Computing literacy**;

KEYWORDS

Digital Storytelling; Narrative; Group Work; Critical Thinking; Higher Education; Computer Science; Data Structures; Algorithms

ACM Reference Format:

Ari Korhonen and Marianna Vivitsou. 2019. Digital Storytelling and Group Work:: Integrating the Narrative Approach into a Higher Education Computer Science Course. In *Innovation and Technology in Computer Science Education (ITiCSE '19), July 15–17, 2019, Aberdeen, Scotland Uk.* ACM, New York, NY, USA, 7 pages. https://doi.org/10.1145/3304221.3325528

ACM ISBN 978-1-4503-6301-3/19/07...$15.00
https://doi.org/10.1145/3304221.3325528

1 INTRODUCTION

While curricula open up to make room for Computer Science (CS) nowadays, computer scientists and theorists (e.g. [2, 6, 12, 26]) point out the need to include both social and technical aspects in the way we think about the field. As, for example, software-based technologies increasingly shape our social, political and economic lives, the need becomes more and more pressing to view CS elements, such as algorithms, not only technically, but also embedded culturally, contextually and ethically [12].

This perspective would require an interdisciplinary approach in the CS curricula. The integration of digital storytelling (DST) as a pedagogical method informed by the principles of narrative approach would fit well with the need for interdisciplinarity. The narrative approach focuses on the development of plot and character for telling stories with digital technologies that can be shared with peers and other interested audiences. Concerning implementation, this view raises questions about what methods and techniques would best fit with the principles of narrative DST in combination with a socio-technically grounded CS education.

Earlier studies on DST in schools [10, 15, 18, 19, 21, 23, 24, 27–30] have shown the potential of the method to open up spaces for student involvement in group work to tell and share video stories with peers online. As the process requires to deal with heterogeneous elements for the synthesis of stories with a beginning, a middle and an end [11, 22], the students enter a process of resignification and, thus, develop a deeper understanding of the object of study in a contextualized way [27, 29]. In addition, previous research has shown that the process allows storytellers to structure their personal narratives in time [8, 32] through the accounts of events and the building of characters that DST entails. Based on these considerations, we assumed that the DST pedagogy would open up the opportunity for students with CS as part of their major and minor studies to work together, set shared purposes and use digital technologies to tell stories based on CS concepts and content. As CS concepts are abstract, our hypothesis was that the task to build stories and characters for coherent and clear representations would lead students to more concrete configurations. Thus, the students were asked to look for manifestations of recursion in real life and in nature. In this way, the approach to recursion would be contextualized and, thus, more practical than theoretical.

Although there have been studies on DST in Higher Education [9], to our knowledge, its pedagogical integration in CS courses has not been studied to the point of writing. In addition, in the case of [20]'s study with university students, storytelling is scripted and concerns the development of a specific software rather than the narrative structure. Our study, however, focuses on student's own work with story lines and characters authored and developed in groups. It would be interesting, therefore, to examine how narrative

DST works for students who select the course for their major or minor studies and get involved in the project on a voluntary basis.

As this is an initial study, the overall goal is to explore DST integration by raising questions and making hypotheses concerning content, group work and narrative development. Thus, rather than giving definitive answers, the study aims to set the ground in terms of methods and frameworks of analysis to be further tested and enriched in future interventions.

2 THEORETICAL BACKGROUND

Digital storytelling (DST) is a 21st century metaphorical adjective-noun phrase that signifies mapping of two domain areas in the meaning making process. In this mapping, 'digital' signals the comparison between the domain of technology and that of telling stories [28, 29]. Here, storytelling involves multiple modes of expression through language and other symbols and media. Contrary to traditional visual and cinematic storytelling, digital technologies nowadays offer the possibility for interactive ways of telling stories online through the use of web-based platforms and internet services (e.g., [16]). In terms of language and communication, this means that sometimes the adjective of the metaphorical phrase is more marked (i.e., more important, thus, capitalized here, DIGITAL), when the storytellers are more interested in the technologies used. Other times, storytellers pay more attention to the development of the narrative, the story line and the characters. In these cases, the noun is more marked (i.e., STORYTELLING).

Group work. Group work has been extensively researched in CSEd with encouraging results concerning students' motivation, creativity, critical thinking etc. [3, 31] Based on previous research experience in the field, in this study we look into group work as an inherent element of narrative DST. Narrative DST is a process of multiple story lines. It is actually about stories within stories and, therefore, in group work students synthesize the stories of their own development. When students take up a project voluntarily, they do so to earn credits to contribute to the overall grading of the course. The starting point therefore is mainly utilitarian. Group work however is more than the sum of required outputs per group. More importantly, it is about developing a sense of belonging, or being part of a whole (i.e., the group, the class, the university). Group work therefore is not only about content knowledge production; it is about identification as well. Based on insights of group theorists in social psychology and psychoanalysis (e.g. [5, 14, 17]), high levels of identification can increase leadership in the group. This, in turn, generates more possibilities for innovative/creative thinking.

Based on these, another research interest of the study is to investigate how group work relates to the development of the narrative and the representation of the central concept in the students' digital stories. For this purpose, we will define levels of identification on the basis of time spent on common tasks and in face-to-face meetings and the types of leadership developed in the groups. To do so, we will draw from data resulting from student manuscripts, interviews and digital stories.

Topic: recursion. In this study, we depart to examine how the elaboration of the plot (i.e., story line) and character development relate to the representation of the central concept (i.e., recursion), when the students work in DST groups. In other words, we look into whether and to what degree deliverables such as abstracts, manuscripts and final stories result in a balanced version of the metaphor, where both parts of the phrase are marked (i.e., DIGITAL STORYTELLING). Our selection of recursion as the central theme of DST was based on the fact that the concept is fundamental for the Data Structures and Algorithms course. Although other themes are possible, many notions are related to or are dependent on recursion. In addition, our previous experience of integrating DST into the course ([29]) showed that it was challenging for students to deal with both selecting from a long list of topics and the complexity of the DST process itself. Narrowing down the options reduced the overall complexity. Moreover, assigning only one topic served the research purposes. In this way, it was possible to compare students' digital stories in terms of character and narrative development.

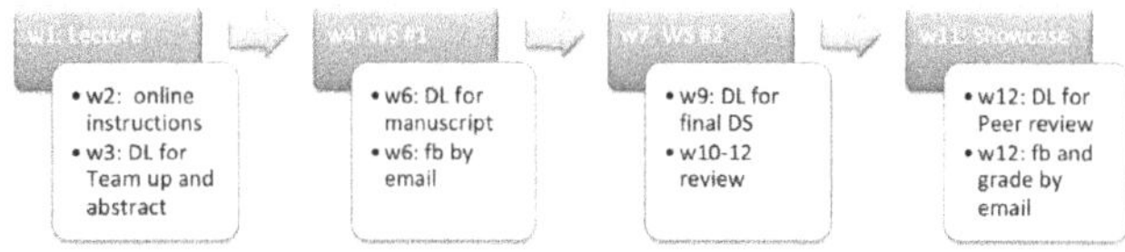

Figure 1: The first lecture in week 1 (w1) introduced the project briefly. Workshops (WS) introduced the project and DST in a more detailed level. Deadlines (DL) and feedback (fb) were planned according to the face-to-face meetings.

3 AIMS AND METHODS

This study aims to discuss and analyze the implementation of a digital storytelling (DST) project within a narrative framework and group work. To do so, we will focus on the organization of student group purposes and patterns of work, and the development of plot and character in video stories aiming to explain recursion to peers and other audiences. The study aims to seek responses to the following research questions:

(1) In what ways do students develop the plot and the main character(s) in their digital stories?
(2) What role does student group work play in the development of digital stories?
(3) In what ways does student group work and narrative development relate with representations of recursion?

Course context and participants. This study draws from the Data Structures and Algorithms course targeting 2nd year CS minor students in Aalto University, Finland. The prerequisite for this course is at least one programming course (typically taught in Python). Many students enroll in this course even though it is not compulsory in their study program. However, not all registered students complete the course. For the Fall term 2018, the total enrollment was 289 students. About half of the students (140) passed the course. The low percentage is due to the fact that the course is not compulsory for most of the students.

Figure 1 shows the course time line and events. During the 12 week semester, the course had 6 lectures, 2 workshops, and weekly lab sessions (students divided to 6 lab groups). The focus of one of the 6 lectures was on the basics of DST, building the narrative structure and developing the story-line/plot and the characters.

The workshops aimed to give time to the groups to present their ideas and plans and receive feedback from peers and the instructors for revisions and improvements. During the first workshop, the groups presented draft ideas, while the plans were more concrete in the second workshop. In addition, group formations became more stable in the second workshop. As some group members withdrew their participation in the project, members who decided to stay had to be integrated into other groups to meet the threshold for participation (i.e., 3-5 students/group).

For other activities than group work, the course had lab sessions. The lab sessions were targeted to students seeking help for the weekly assignments, most of which were automatically graded. The course has a long history of using automatically graded assignments, which also has changed the student behavior during the years. Many students take the course almost completely on-line, which makes unnecessary to travel to campus or meet other students. Especially, automatic assessment [1, 13] is very well received by the students, and it has shaped the course participation a lot.

In addition to automatically graded assignments, the course had a range of voluntary extra exercises, assignments, and a project for those aiming to best grades (i.e., above 3/5). Although, almost all the assignments were supposed to be individual work, DST was utilized to produce a framework for the project done in small groups. However, it was not the only voluntary exercise, and students needed to consider which options to take in case they wanted to pursue the best grade 5/5. Thus, we assume the project attracted especially those students more willing to participate in team work compared with those who might prefer individual work.

During the course period (October-December 2018), 64 unique students (22 %) participated in closed labs at least once. In addition, as blended learning methods were applied ([4]), the students had the option to ask for guidance in an on-line discussion forum integrated into the learning management system. 184 students enrolled into the discussion forum during the course (64 %). Thus, the preferred mode to study and ask for support for individual work was on-line.

Demographics. The students were mainly minor students from the School of Business (BIZ), School of Chemical Engineering (CHE), School of Electrical Engineering (ELE), School of Engineering (ENG), and School of Science (SCI). Twelve groups (44 out of 289 students, which is 15 % of the students) started the DST project and submitted an abstract (First Draft). Each of the 12 groups consisted of 3-5 students. 8 out of 12 groups submitted a manuscript that included a draft plan of DST tasks. 7 groups out of 8 completed their project by submitting a video. These 7 groups also submitted an improved version of their text-based manuscript along with the digital story. In addition, each student reviewed other groups' manuscript and digital story after submitting their own.

Our study focuses on the 28 students in these 7 groups (appr. 10 % of the whole course). The overall male–female ratio was not significantly different in project groups compared to the whole course (about 79 % compared with 21 % in both). All groups had male members, and 4 groups had 1–2 female members. The average age was 25 years. The ages varied between 20 and 39 years. The two oldest students were in the same group. In the rest of the groups, the ages varied between 20 and 27 years. The average age is quite high. This is natural as the course is typically took in the second year, and many students drop it and try again. 5 out of the 28 students that took the project were in this course the second or third time.

16 out of 44 did not complete the project, which is 36 %. This is rather high percentage, but it is explained by the fact that the project was not a compulsory part of the course. In addition, the course included other tasks that could be taken in order to achieve the desirable grade. Students had the chance to compare work load in different tasks and make the final decision to take the project or not. Some students felt that the work load for the project was too high compared to other alternatives.

The estimated work load was based on European Credit Transfer and Accumulation System (ECTS). The course was 5 credit point course, and one credit point—that is approximately 25–30 hours of work—was allocated to the project. Thus, a group having 4 members should have invested all together some 100–120 hours to the project. This was monitored in each phase as the groups were expected to report time-on-task in each submission. In the team up phase, they needed to plan their timings in the abstract. In the manuscript and the final submission, they needed to report on the time-on-task for each member.

Data analysis. The study aims to offer an analysis of content of data resulting from students' interviews, manuscripts and digital stories. There were 7 manuscripts (i.e., abstracts and reports) and 7 digital stories in video format, resulting from the work of 7 groups. Out of these, 4 groups and 11 students participated in 4 interviews. Each interview lasted approximately 40-45 minutes. For research purposes, the interviews were transcribed and anonymized. The transcriptions were sent to the participants to check and comment. The participants made it explicit under what copyright and licensing they shared their digital/video stories on the Web, with teachers and peers, and other audiences.

For the analysis, we moved inductively from more concrete to more abstract codes, themes and categories [7, 25]. With regard to the frameworks of analysis, we used thematic analysis to code and categorize interview data. Following transcription, excerpts from the interview data set were highlighted and coded manually. Then the coded excerpts were transferred to an Excel worksheet and set into larger categories and themes. A similar process was used for manuscript data. Then categories from interview and manuscript data were compared. In addition, discourse analysis was applied to the manuscripts in order to get a better insight into attributes of categories. When, for instance, the focus was on character development, we looked into the structure of student written expression in the manuscripts. Some manuscripts hardly mentioned the characters. Some others used complex main sentences and subordinate clauses with action verbs to elaborate on character development. To cross-examine findings we moved abductively back and forth from manuscripts to video stories to student interviews.

For reliability, both authors/researchers went through all the data sets. One researcher coded for group work and narrative development, then discussed emergent themes and categories with the other researcher. The same process was repeated for the analysis of representations of recursion where the other researcher took the lead. It was a joint decision what data to include and what to exclude from this paper. Although, the process was performed inductively, the description and discussion of results follows a deductive logic.

4 FINDINGS

In the following Subsections 4.1-4.3, we describe our observations from three different point of views. These correspond to the three research questions we have. The results are combined in Table 1.

4.1 The narrative in digital storytelling

Types of digital stories. The analysis shows that group work had different orientations in planning and decision making about character development and story elaboration, and resulted in three types of digital/video stories. (1) Short films (G4 and G7). Two groups describe their story as short film aiming to educate and inspire audiences by combining unfamiliar (i.e., recursion) with familiar (e.g., Koch snowflake) elements into brief and fun videos. In addition to educating audiences, the short films aim to increase group's own awareness and knowledge of the topic through the articulation of definitions, properties and features in easily understandable language and format. To this end, the students use real-world examples in such ways that no prior knowledge of the concepts is required. (2) Documentary-style stories (G1 and G2). Two groups came up with videos that give emphasis rather on a 'fact-based' representation of recursion than a character-plot interaction. The narrative is linear and built on alternating still images. The storytelling is done through voice over (G1), and with a student-actor who provides the account of events (G2). (3) Program-based stories (G3, G5 and G6). The narrative here is based on selection, which means that it is built on if–then–else (i.e., conditional) basis. When a character meets an issue, for instance, possible solutions are not presented or elaborated in detail. Instead, the narrative moves forward into the next character or the next event based on a programmed condition. Typically the submissions of this type of story was not a manuscript (PDF) including a link to the video, but a zip file including also the software to execute the story (e.g., an interactive game).

Character development. For character development, we looked into language use in student manuscripts. For instance, G7 use action verbs and complex grammatical structures and adverbials to describe how characters develop: *The story deals with Essi, who is a student who always leaves preparing for an exam to the very last minute... Having heard of recursion she panics and leaves her room to find assistance...* In a similar way, G4 develop their characters through action verbs and elaborate structure. The narrative in these stories indicates a change in the characters' thinking and action and, therefore, the development is visible and clear. However, other groups' (e.g., G2) characters remain floating between a presenter's and a narrator's role. In this story, the character's role to plot development is not clear, although there is alternation from one event to the next. However, the story is a linear account of facts rather than a reconfiguration of the storytellers' ideas.

In stories where characters are not well-developed, an account of actions is missing or the need for a character is not explicit, e.g., in G3 story. This might relate to the fact that G3 work was more independent and based on a clear task division. This organization, although based on a well-articulated rationale, came up with unclear character whose relation to the events of the story was loose. Following a similar pattern, G5 work results in a mythical character whose purposes and actions remain undefined. Contrary to the way the narrative develops in G3 story, which is also based on the logic of conditional branching, the plot in the former is rather linear and closed-ended. Overall, in conditional-based stories, the main character is male and, instead of developing a 'life of his own', revolves around a right/wrong decision before moving on to the next choice.

The plot. To understand how plot was elaborated, we looked into event descriptions in the manuscripts. The plots in short films were well-articulated with complex structure. Also, the program-based story of G3 uses complex sentences and dependent clauses. However, despite the elaborate expression, the background of this story is made available only in the manuscript, which might lead the audience to a partial understanding of what is going on, unless the written text is available. For G3, getting the concepts straight meant the process would be smooth enough not to not have to go back and start all over again. This plot elaboration seems to have happened on a random basis at the expense of concept representation. The students in G7 expressed similar views in the interview about the narrative-concept relation. Despite this overlap, their short story balanced character development and plot elaboration, and resulted in clear representations of central concepts.

Another indication of a well-elaborated plot is the element of surprise. Some groups recognized the need to include elements of surprise through accounts of unexpected events leading to different configurations of the story. Adversities, however, remain underdeveloped in the G5 programmed story and mainly concern the obstacles the character falls over when running the maze. Groups 4 and 7 also use adversities, only in a more elaborate way. For instance, G4 write, *However, Admin ends up in the trouble as there is no safely way to get back down. Admin's travel partner Network Specialist offers to help ...*

4.2 Group work in narrative digital storytelling

Joint planning and decisions involved dividing the work into more concrete tasks. As G1 write in their manuscripts: *As a group, we quickly decided that the work packages for the project involved voice acting, script writing, research, video editing and organizational tasks. As a group it was determined that this division of work packages covered everything related to the project.* Splitting the tasks led to different tactics among the groups similar to those described by Waite et al. [31] as: Sequential segmentation (SS, "I work on it for a while, then pass it along to you."); Parallel segmentation (PS, "We break it up and everyone does a piece."); Natural selection (NS, "We each carry it out and then choose the best result, or we choose the best person and let them do it."); and, Collaboration (Co, "We interact closely during the task.").

As Waite et al. [31] put it: "In each of the first three cases, the members of the group are effectively working alone. Working alone is our students' preference [...] and therefore whenever they are given a task they actively employ one or more of those three tactics regardless of the intent of the professor." However, we can see real collaboration as well, for example, in G7. As the members of this group said in their interviews: I-ee 3: *I've done quite a few groupworks during my studies and this one was different... In these you just divide the tasks, everyone does their own part and then you just put things together. In that sense, this was a nice change...*

Table 1: Narrative development, group work (GW) and representations of recursion.

Type of story	Character	Plot	Tactics	GW	Recursion in video	R. in manuscript
Short film (G4, G7)	well-developed	well-elaborated	Co	CP, MR	clear	clear
Documentary (G2)	not clear	linear	Co	CP, MR	clear	not defined
Documentary (G1)	not clear	linear	PS	CF	explicit misconception	not defined
Program (G5)	not well-developed	well-elaborated	Co, NS	CP, Am	no misconceptions	no misconceptions
Program (G6)	not well-developed	well-elaborated	Co, NS	CP, Am	no misconceptions	not defined
Program (G3)	not well-developed	random	PS, NS	CP, FL	no misconceptions	no misconceptions

Overall, the way tasks were allocated and the time students spent together on face to face (f2f) group work resulted in different types of group leadership and identification, i.e., an individual's sense of belonging to the group. See Table 1. We denote the leadership centripetal (CP) in case we see distributed type of leadership in collaboration, or centrifugal leadership (CF) that typically occur in case the tactics is sequential segmentation (SS), parallel segmentation (PS), or natural selection (NS). For identification, we have analyzed the group work in order to observe mutual recognition (MR) among group members.

Group work and leadership. Most groups (G4-G7) both shared and divided into distinct tasks. Two groups (G2 & G3) had only shared tasks, while G1 split the work into completely distinct tasks, which they coordinated through different Web platforms and software (e.g., telegram, google docs, WhatsApp). This allocation led to a centrifugal leadership (CF), in the sense that, although the overall purpose was met (i.e., the digital story was completed and submitted), evidence for a common purpose is scant. The fact that the members of G1 hardly met f2f kept identification at low level.

On the other hand, the groups that shared or both shared and divided tasks, developed a centripetal (CP) type of leadership. This means that leadership was distributed among the group members. More particularly, in addition to attending lectures and workshops, G2 and G7 spent more than 2 and 4 hours in face-to-face (F2f) meetings, respectively. F2f time allows to grow this something in common that makes group identification between group members possible [14]. Spending time together, therefore, seems to have led to more concrete sets of common purposes. As a result, mutual recognition (MR) among group members has also grown. Mutual recognition became evident in groups 2, 3 and 7 interviews, where the members acknowledged one another's work and contributions. This means that the degree of identification is higher in these cases.

Also, in the case of G3, where the group looked up to the peer with more working hours on programming, leadership is more focused (FL) than distributed. It seems that a kind of transference has occurred in this case, in the sense that the students recognize a certain binding quality in their peer. Although this is a different enactment from the case of G7, where all the members are poles of leadership, both G3 and G7 are evidences of student interest in – at least– as much in the object of study as in the grading points. It is therefore the object of study (i.e., programming) that constitutes an element of unification as well. Finally, in the cases where time spent together remains unconfirmed (i.e., in interviews or manuscripts, G5 and G6), mutual recognition is ambiguous (Am), despite the fact that group leadership seems to be centripetal.

4.3 Representations of recursion and code

None of the digital stories covered or visualized stack frames or some other representation for how to implement recursion in computing. This was partially due to the assignment: we explicitly asked examples of recursion in nature. Thus, the projects show more external examples of recursion than internal implementation details even though many projects included also source code. Thus, the digital projects focused on showing what the code does rather than how it does it. Another reason for this might be in the fact that the students were minor CS students. Major students might have different approach to technical representations.

One of the challenges in representing recursion is that its outer behavior does not differ from iteration, i.e. for- and while-loops in algorithms. This seems to be very hard to grasp for the students, but even harder to express in their digital stories. In addition, some of the stories included explicit function calls, but it was unclear if they were recursive or just a function calling another function, calling another function, etc. This shows up in some projects which hold explicit misconceptions about recursion even though they got feedback during the project. For some reason, they did not pay attention to the critic received.

We also evaluated the manuscripts and videos according to the accuracy of the terminology as well as representation in Table 1. In some videos and manuscripts we can see (explicit) misconceptions such as missing base case (or cases) or the recursive steps do not reach the base case(s). Some representations had possible misconceptions related to the fact that neither the manuscript nor the video made it clear whether the story actually represents recursive or iterative process. This is kind of implicit misconceptions as the task was to represent recursion. The groups did not make adequate distinction between these two. The third category includes the rest of the stories that were considered correct. They cannot be misinterpreted to be iterative processes even though there is no actual recursive algorithm represented in the manuscript. However, most of this type of stories included also recursive code fragments to illustrate recursion.

5 DISCUSSION AND CONCLUSIONS

Table 1 combines the results and it is sorted according to the type of story. The groups that produced short films developed a centripetal (CP), distributed type of leadership, while mutual recognition (MR) among group members was high. More particularly, in relation to types of stories, digital stories that were categorized as short films displayed well-elaborated characters and well-developed plots. In addition, the representations of recursion were very clear both in

Table 2: Types of DST. There seems to be correlation among emphasis of DST, types and accuracy of digital stories.

Emphasis	Type of story	Identification	Narrative	Representation/recursion
DIGITAL STORYTELLING	Short film	high	well-elaborated	well-represented
digital STORYTELLING	Documentary	high	fact-based but linear and unclear	no explicit misconception
	Documentary	low	fact-based but linear and unclear	explicit misconception
DIGITAL storytelling	Programmed	high/NS	well-thought plot but loose characters	possible misconceptions

the manuscript and video. In documentary-like stories, the plot was fact-based and linear with ambiguous characters whose development remained unclear. The groups that produced this story genre displayed two types of leadership. When the leadership was moving outside the group and was, therefore, centrifugal (CF), the level of identification was low. This group work resulted in an explicit misconception of recursion. On the contrary, the documentary-like story of the group with tighter coordination of activities and face-to-face meetings displayed no explicit misconception. It seems, therefore, that face-to-face collaboration influences the group narrative, which, in turn, influences the grasp of the central concept.

Group work and narrative development in programmed stories overall confirm this finding. It seems, however, that the stories were in the middle of the way. Although the characters were better defined than in documentaries, they were not as well-developed as in short films. Although, the plots were well-elaborated, they were conditional with binary alterations of a 'yes/no' type. Moreover, the type of leadership seems to have been centripetal. There was scant evidence concerning time spent together or how common tasks were dealt with or if common tasks existed at all. Thus, mutual recognition remains questionable for two out of the three groups of this category. Contrary to this, the third group's interview provided evidence of mutual recognition. Moreover, this group is an example of Natural Selection type of tactics. However, this group work resulted misconceptions in the description of recursion in the manuscript. A possible explanation could be that misconception went unnoticed, as, along with leadership, the 'responsibility' for successful task completion was transferred to a single peer/leader.

Overall, the students who were interviewed described the multilayered task of representing recursion by using digital technologies and telling stories as a positive learning experience. During interviews, the participating students expressed the belief that they had grasped a better understanding of recursion through the process of documenting ideas in narrative form (i.e., abstracts, manuscripts and video stories). Developing the story line seemed to be more important than characters at first; however, three groups mentioned that the role of the character became clearer to them during the second workshop. Then they made changes by further elaborating the stories. As this was an initial study, measurement of the learning outcomes mainly took place through the interviews. Nevertheless, as we see the digital stories themselves as documentation of learning, we will use insights from the representations of recursion to build our future endeavors. Besides, this was one first step to better understand differences between automated assessment and qualitative evaluation (e.g., through peer feedback). Future interventions, then, could include control and experimental groups to compare the two types of evaluation of learning a common concept. Considering the above, three versions of DST have resulted in relation to types of stories, group narratives and representations of recursion (See Table 2) :

DIGITAL STORYTELLING. Group work that displays recursion in short films relates to a high level of identification and a narrative of mutual recognition. Leadership is distributed among group members and the development of characters and plot are of equal importance. In this approach, the representation of recursion is both clear and accurate.

digital STORYTELLING. These emerge out of documentary-style stories, with a fact-based representation of recursion, alternating still images and an elaborated, but linear, plot. In this case, the use of digital technologies was narrow in the production and/or the editing process. Technology overall seems to have played a minor role, as there was no code in the groups' manuscripts. This result correlates with two distinct types of leadership. Centrifugal leadership keeps the level of group identification low and comes up with a misconception in the representation of recursion. Centripetal leadership leads to an accurate representation of recursion.

DIGITAL storytelling. This version emerges out of programmed stories, where a lot of attention was given on programming and code development. In these stories, the use of technology played an important role. However, character development was unclear and loose, although the plot well-elaborated. In addition, identification with the group leader and natural selection of leadership seems to relate with misconceptions in the way recursion was represented in the video story.

5.1 Validity issues

The project was not the only voluntary exercise to achieve the best grade 5/5, thus many students considered carefully which options to use. As a voluntary exercise, this brings certain bias to the population. This is evident if we look at the final results. 23 out of 28 students (82 %) have passed the course at the time of writing. The rest 5 have not taken the final exam or re-exam, which is required to pass the course. Thus, the percentage is going to be even higher after the last re-exam in September. This is significantly different from the overall passing rate that is around 50 %. Thus, we can conclude that those students taking part in the project were not only more motivated to achieve a good grade, but also more motivated to pass the course compared with students that did not choose the project. Moreover, due to the low number of groups, our findings are more hypotheses than definitive results. It would be good to see replication studies in the future to confirm or falsify our findings. This would help us to figure out how to introduce this kind of project work in HE including continuous orientation and motivation, support for group work (e.g., workshops), encouragement to attend campus events, etc. At least we can say that DST is a promising approach to allure some students back to campus.

REFERENCES

[1] T. Auvinen and A. Korhonen. 2014. Rubyric Assessment and Annotation Tool. In *EdMedia: World Conference on Educational Media and Technology*. Association for the Advancement of Computing in Education (AACE), Waynesville, NC, 1087–1091.

[2] P. Dourish. 2016. Algorithms and their others: Algorithmic culture in context. In *Big Data & Society*. SAGE Publications, open access, 1–11. https://doi.org/10.1177/2053951716665128

[3] H. Drury, J. Kay, and W. Losberg. 2003. Student satisfaction with groupwork in undergraduate computer science: do things get better?. In *Australasian Computing Education Conference (ACE2003)*, T. Greening and R. Lister (Eds.). Conferences in Research and Practice in Information Technology, Adelaide, Australia, 9 pages.

[4] C. Dziuban, C. Graham, P. Moskal, A. Norberg, and N. Sicilia. 2018. Blended learning: the new normal and emerging technologies. *International Journal of Educational Technology in Higher Education* 15, 3 (2018). https://doi.org/10.1186/s41239--017--0087--5

[5] S. Freud. 2001. Group Psychology and the Analysis of the Ego (1921). In *The Standard Edition of the Psychological Works of Sigmund Freud*, J. Strachey (Ed.). Vol. XVIII. Vintage, London, UK.

[6] T. Gillespie. 2016. Algorithms, clickworkers, and the befuddled fury around Facebook Trends. https://socialmediacollective.org/2016/05/18/facebook--trends/.

[7] B. G. Glaser and A. L. Strauss. 1995. *The Discovery of Grounded Theory: Strategies for Qualitative Research*. Aldine Publishing Co, NY, USA.

[8] G. Hull and M. Katz. 2006. Crafting an agentive self: case studies of digital storytelling. *Research in the Teaching of English* 41, 1 (2006), 43–81.

[9] G. Jamissen, P. Hardy, Y. Nordkvelle, and Pleasants H. (Eds.). 2017. *Digital Storytelling in Higher Education - International Perspectives*. Springer International Publishing AG, Switzerland.

[10] H. Jenkins, M. Ito, and D. Boyd. 2016. *Participatory Culture in a Networked Era, A Conversation on Youth, Learning, Commerce & Politics*. SAGE, Cambridge, UK.

[11] D. M. Kaplan. 2003. *Ricoeur's Critical Theory*. SUNY, N.Y., USA.

[12] R. Kitchin. 2017. Thinking critically about and researching algorithms. *Information, Communication & Society* 20, 1 (2017), 14–29. http://dx.doi.org/10.1080/1369118X.2016.1154087

[13] A. Korhonen and L. Malmi. 2000. Algorithm simulation with automatic assessment. *ACM SIGCSE Bulletin* 32, 3 (2000), 160–163. DOI10.1145/353519.343157

[14] E. Laclau. 2005. *On Populist Reason*. Verso, London, UK.

[15] J. Lambert. 2013. *Digital storytelling: Capturing lives, creating community*. Routledge, NY, USA.

[16] A. Marwick and D. Boyd. 2014. Networked privacy: how teenagers negotiate context in social media. *New Media & Society* 16, 7 (2014), 1051–1067.

[17] W. McDougall. 1920. *The Group Mind*. Cambridge University Press, Cambridge, UK.

[18] P. McGee. 2015. *The instructional value of digital storytelling: Higher education, professional, and adult learning settings*. Routledge, NY, USA.

[19] H. Niemi, V. Harju, M. Vivitsou, K. Viitanen, J. Multisilta, and A. Kuokkanen. 2014. Digital storytelling for 21st-century skills in virtual learning environments. *Creative Education* 5, 9 (2014), 657–671.

[20] J. Nuutinen. 2009. *Nucleus Model for Designing Social Mindtools: Woven Stories*. Ph.D. Dissertation. Faculty of Science, University of Joensuu, Joensuu, Finland.

[21] J. Penttila, V. Kallunki, H. M. Niemi, and J. Multisilta. 2016. A Structured Inquiry into a Digital Story: Primary School Students Report the Making of a Superball. *International Journal of Mobile and Blended Learning* 8, 3 (2016), 19–34.

[22] P. Ricoeur. 1992. *Oneself as Another*. University of Chicago Press, Chicago, USA.

[23] B. Robin. 2008. Digital storytelling: A powerful technology tool for the 21st century classroom. *Theory into practice* 47 (2008), 220–228.

[24] A. Sadik. 2008. Digital storytelling: A meaningful technology-integrated approach for engaged student learning. *Educational Technology Research & Development*, 56 (2008), 487–506.

[25] J. Saldana. 2009. *The Coding Manual for Qualitative Researchers*. SAGE, London, UK.

[26] Z. Tufekci. 2016. Technology in Global Activism, Uprisings & Social Movements. https://shorensteincenter.org/zeynep-tufekci/.

[27] M. Vivitsou. 2019. Constructing Identities in Online Encounters – A Study on Finnish & Greek Young Students' Digital Storytelling Practices. *International Journal of Teacher Education and Professional Development (IJTEPD)* 2 (2019).

[28] M. Vivitsou. 2019. Digital storytelling in teaching & research. In *Encyclopaedia of Education & Information Technologies*, A. Tatnall & J. Multisilta (Ed.). Springer, Springer Nature Switzerland AG.

[29] M. Vivitsou and A. Korhonen. 2018. Digital Storytelling for Socio-Technical Literacies: Participatory Methods in a Computer Science Higher Education Course. https://ssrn.com/abstract=3175925.

[30] M. Vivitsou, H. Niemi, G. Wei, V. Kallunki, and R. Miao. 2017. Teachers' practices to support student work in digital storytelling: A study on Finnish and Chinese school teachers' experiences. *Seminar.net International Journal of Media, technology and Lifelong Learning* 13, 2 (2017), 14–29. https://journals.hioa.no/index.php/seminar/article/view/2306

[31] W. M. Waite, M. H. Jackson, A. Diwan, and P. M. Leonardi. 2004. Student Culture vs Group Work in Computer Science. *SIGCSE Bull.* 36, 1 (March 2004), 12–16. https://doi.org/10.1145/1028174.971308

[32] J. Woodhouse. 2008. Storytelling: A telling approach in healthcare education. In *The Narrative Practitioner international conference*. open access, Wrexham, England, UK, 1–6. https://www.researchgate.net/publication/30067784_Story-telling_a_telling_approach_in_healthcare_education

Does Studying CS Automatically Foster a Growth Mindset?

Michael Lodi*
University of Bologna & INRIA
Department of Computer Science and Engineering (DISI)
Bologna, Italy
michael.lodi@unibo.it

ABSTRACT

Many arguments are used to advocate for the introduction of Computer Science (CS) / Computational Thinking / "coding" in K-12 education. Growth mindset theory (GM) is also becoming very popular among educators and researchers. Some claims stating that studying CS can foster a GM have emerged. However, educational research shows that transfer of competences is hard. Very little research has been conducted on the relationship between GM and CS learning, with conflicting results. We measured some indicators (e.g., mindset, computer science mindset) at the beginning and the end of a high school year in five different classes: three CS oriented, one Chemistry oriented, and one Transportation&Logistics oriented. In one of the CS oriented classes, we did a very brief GM intervention. At the end of the school year, none of the classes showed a statistically significant change in their mindset. Interestingly, non-CS oriented classes showed a significant decrease in their computer science growth mindset. In the intervention class, students suggested, to stimulate a GM, the need for activities that are more creative, engaging, and related to the real world and their interests.

CCS CONCEPTS

• **Social and professional topics** → **Computing education**; **K-12 education**; *Computational thinking*.

KEYWORDS

computer science mindset, growth mindset, high school, transfer

ACM Reference Format:

Michael Lodi. 2019. Does Studying CS Automatically Foster a Growth Mindset?. In *Innovation and Technology in Computer Science Education (ITiCSE '19), July 15–17, 2019, Aberdeen, Scotland, UK.* ACM, New York, NY, USA, 7 pages. https://doi.org/10.1145/3304221.3319750

*Part of this research was conducted while the author was visiting Prof. Tim Bell and the Computer Science Education Research Group at the Department of Computer Science and Software Engineering, University of Canterbury, Christchurch, New Zealand.

ITiCSE '19, July 15–17, 2019, Aberdeen, Scotland, UK

ACM ISBN 978-1-4503-6301-3/19/07...$15.00
https://doi.org/10.1145/3304221.3319750

1 INTRODUCTION

Recently the introduction of Computer Science (CS) / Computational Thinking (CT) / "coding" in K-12 education has gained massive attention from researchers, educators, and media. Many arguments are used to advocate this introduction, e.g., understanding our digital world, being active and creative digital citizens, learning skills for digital jobs, and learning to "think better." However, some of them seem not to be based on sound educational research (see the recent [18] for a good review).

At the same time, mindset theory [10] (as it is widely known today, more formally called "implicit theories about intelligence" [7]) is becoming very popular among educators and researchers. People hold personal ideas (*implicit theories*) about their intellectual abilities. These ideas lay on a continuous spectrum, but two main groups can be identified. Some people have a *fixed mindset* (an *entity theory of intelligence*): they think their intelligence is a fixed aspect, and they cannot do much to change it. By contrast, other people have a *growth mindset* (an *incremental theory of intelligence*): they think intelligence is malleable and can be developed with study and effort. Some studies show that students' mindset can influence their achievement [4]. Moreover, Dweck showed that a growth mindset could be fostered with brief specific interventions [4] or specific teaching strategies (e.g., giving growth mindset feedback [9]). Dweck acknowledges that one can have different mindsets with respect to different disciplines [10]: in this paper, we will refer to the *mindset with respect to CS* as *Computer Science mindset*.

Some claims stating that studying CS/CT/programming/"coding" can foster a GM have emerged: partially because of the popularity in educational contexts, partly because some characteristics of Computer Science - and in particular of programming (e.g., collaboration, iterative development, continually finding and correcting errors) - fit well in the mindset theory. The thesis that learning computing can foster a growth mindset is exemplified by some quotes from online educational blogs. "*Not only can the process of learning to code be used to help develop a growth mindset, there are aspects of coding that help reinforce this mindset*" [34]. "*[...] its contribution to a growth mindset, is one of the reasons why debugging is such an important part of computing education*" [3]. "*But did you know that by learning to code, you can simultaneously grow your growth mindset in the process?*" [36][1]. "*Over three years of helping kids teach themselves computer programming, I have decided that youth coding programs are the best way to instill a growth mindset in another human being*" [32]. "*Posing challenging tasks such as basic*

[1] Another blog post on Mindsetworks also seems to acknowledge the opposite direction of the implication: Having a Growth Mindset helps learning to code [35].

coding even at the elementary level pays great dividends and fosters a Growth Mindset among even the youngest students" [13].

Other CS Ed. researchers seem to acknowledge the problem. For example, Lewis states, talking about growth mindset and grit, that "*programming has been speculated to be uniquely qualified to help normalize failure and thus encourage productive learning strategies*" [18]. As Lewis herself recognizes, research in education tells us that transfer is difficult and unlikely to happen, especially between knowledge domains far from one another [2]. Research has shown that it is possible to teach transfer, if the activities are explicitly designed to do so: for example, in the 1980s, in the context of LOGO programming, some researchers were able to explicitly teach debugging and to transfer it to "buggy" situations outside programming (e.g. in wrong road directions or furniture arrangement in a room) [17]. Note however that these contexts are much more similar to the original programming one than perseverance or growth mindset are. Research about transfer in Computer Science education (also regarding transversal competencies/skills) is recognized to be contradictory and outdated [27].

To better understand the relationship between studying or not studying Computer Science and mindset (and other related constructs, especially CS mindset), we decided to conduct a study in a high school with different tracks. One track is Computer Science oriented, while others are oriented to different technical skills (e.g., Chemistry, Logistics and Transportation). With our experiment, we tried to address the following research questions:

RQ1 Does studying or not studying Computer Science in high school automatically influence students' mindset, Computer Science mindset, and other related constructs?

RQ2 Can a small explicit intervention alter students' mindset?

RQ3 After being taught about mindset theory, what are students' recommendations to foster it?

2 COMPUTER SCIENCE AND GROWTH MINDSET

2.1 Growth Mindset

Students[2] with a growth mindset show **learning-oriented goals** (not afraid to ask and make errors, in order to learn) and **mastery-oriented responses** (greater effort and new strategies) to challenges and setbacks, while students with a fixed mindset show **performance goals** ("appear intelligent", so avoiding difficult tasks) and **helpless responses** to challenges (e.g. giving up or blaming the teacher for their failure).

In many studies, Dweck and colleagues showed that students' mindset could predict their achievement, in particular in Math and Science, and their ability to cope with challenges [4, 9]. Moreover, female students with a growth mindset showed less susceptibility to the adverse effects of stereotypes about women and math [12].

Some interventions [9] can positively stimulate a growth mindset: explicitly teaching students about mindsets, brain plasticity and the idea that intelligence can be trained with effort; portraying challenges, effort and mistakes as highly valued; praising process and effort (e.g., "You worked so hard and did an excellent job!") rather than person or talent ("Good! You must be very smart!"), and giving constructive feedback rather than praising the person or being judgmental.

[2]Part of this section is an expansion of those in [19, 20].

2.2 Growth Mindset in Computer Science

In [22] it is argued that a growth mindset can be particularly important in CS education. For example, in programming, students are continually facing errors and challenges; female enrollment in CS is low, possibly due to fixed views about who can and who cannot succeed in CS; collaboration is fundamental in CS and is fostered by growth mindset students whose goal is to learn rather than to appear smart, and so on. Factors like repeated exposure to errors and stereotypes are recognized to potentially foster a fixed mindset, as has been suggested for math [5]. In [6] is stated that Carol Dweck herself describes CS as a discipline that requires a growth mindset.

Very few studies assessed students' mindset before and after a CS course (at a college level). In [11] the authors observed changes in CS1 students (CS-majors, other STEM-Majors, but also Arts and Business Majors) across the semester, finding a significant increase in a fixed mindset and a significant decrease in a growth mindset. Moreover, in [28] it was found that beliefs about intelligence and programming aptitude form two distinct constructs in undergraduate software engineering students. The mindset for programming aptitude had greater utility in predicting software development practice, and a follow-up survey showed that it became more fixed after a programming module. In [15], third-year bachelor students' mindset was assessed, finding no correlations between their mindset and their grades.

Even fewer studies have tried to alter students' mindset, and these have found conflicting results. The authors in [30] tried a small intervention on CS Majors and Minors, finding a shift toward fixed mindset despite the intervention. In contrast, the authors in [6] performed three structured interventions into an introductory programming course, gaining significant improvement in growth mindset level of students and also a positive correlation in their test scores.

We could not find any studies about Computer Science and growth mindset at the high school level.

3 THE STUDY

3.1 Context

In Italy, high school (formally "upper secondary school") lasts five years (usually students start when they are 14 y.o. and finish when they are 19 y.o.). Students can choose between **lyceums**, which give a theoretical basis in classical, scientific or artistic areas and naturally lead to university studies; **technical institutes**, which give both theoretical basis and a high qualified specialization in a specific area (divided in: *economic institutes*, preparing for economics, management and business-oriented computer programming, and *technological institutes*, preparing for areas such as mechanics, electronics, computer science, chemistry), leading to a job or to university studies; or **professional institutes**, preparing students with practical skills to enter the job market immediately.

After choosing the kind of school, students select a specific track offered by the school (e.g., "IT and telecommunications," "fashion"),

Table 1: Descriptive statistics of the sample

Class	N	Males	Females	Prev. exp
INF1	16	16	0	7
INF2	14	11	3	1
INF3	7	7	0	7
TRAN	6	6	0	3
CHEM	23	16	7	12
ALL	*66*	*56*	*10*	*30*

whose curriculum is decided at national level. Almost every curriculum includes Italian, English, History, Math, Natural Sciences, Sports, and the subjects of the chosen track.

3.2 Participants

We conducted the experiment in four classes (third year, 16-year-old students) of a large technological institute (in brackets we give a short code we will use to identify the classes): 2 classes of "IT and telecommunications" (INF1, INF2); 1 class mixed "IT and telecommunications" (INF3) and "transport and logistics" (TRAN) (students follow intersecting subjects together and split when following specific subjects); and 1 class of "chemistry, materials and biotechnology" (CHEM).

During the first two years (usually very similar, to allow pupils to change track), all students of a technological institute should have followed some introductory computing lessons (no more than 2-3 hours a week for one or two years), but the content varies a lot: from the use of office suites to visual programming in Scratch to web development. We asked students if they had already programmed, to check for potential effects.

During the third year, students in "IT and telecommunications" follow three courses related to Computer Science and programming (Network systems, IT project management, Computer science) for a total of 13 hours a week. Students in "transport and logistics" and "chemistry, materials and biotechnology" do not follow any CS-related course.

We asked for an informed consent from students' parents, and only those who gave us back the approved informed consent participated in the study. As the study involved a pre and a post questionnaire, students were anonymously identified with a secret code (the name of a color) they had to remember. We report, in Table 1, number, gender and previous programming experience of only students that completed both the pre and the post-questionnaire. Most of the students are males, and the females are almost all from the CHEM class. This is not surprising since technological tracks, especially those related to mechanics, electronics and computer science, are usually chosen mainly by males in Italy.

3.3 Methods

We decided to measure some constructs (some belonging to general mindset theory, e.g., performance vs. mastery orientation - see subsection 2.1 - and some specifically related to CS mindset) at the beginning and at the end of the third year (school year 2017/2018). Moreover, we decided to implement a small mindset intervention in the INF1 class, halfway through the year, to see if we could alter students' mindset.

3.3.1 Questionnaire. Research on mindsets is usually conducted by asking students to rate how much they agree (on a Likert scale, e.g., 1-6) on some statements like "*You have a certain amount of intelligence, and you can't really do much to change it.*" and then calculating a score representing students' mindset. In the online appendix of this paper [21], the full questionnaire is reported, with details on how the scores are calculated.

For traditional mindset constructs, robust and validated scales are available. We used the wording in [8], an Italian translation of Dweck's book [7], to measure:

- **Mindset**, obtaining a value from 1 (fixed mindset) to 6 (growth mindset);
- **Confidence in one's intelligence**, obtaining a value from 1 (low confidence) to 12 (high confidence);
- **Goal choice**, obtaining a value from 1 (performance orientation) to 6 (mastery orientation).

To measure belief constructs related to CS, we adapted and translated in Italian some scales from [33], a Ph.D. thesis studying specifically Mathematical Mindsets, changing the word "Math" to "Computer Science" in the questionnaire proposed by the author. In particular, we measured:

- **Computer Science Mindset**, obtaining a value from 1 (fixed CS mindset) to 6 (growth CS mindset);
- **Beliefs about the nature of CS**, obtaining a value from 1 (CS as a fixed discipline, where you have to learn facts, rules, give quickly the *only* right solution to problems) to 6 (CS as a creative discipline, where you can learn from your errors and have many solutions to problems);
- **Identification with CS**, obtaining a value from 1 ("not a CS person", bad at CS) to 5 ("a CS person", good at CS);
- **Mastery orientation in CS**, obtaining a value from 1 (performance orientation in CS) to 5 (mastery orientation in CS).

The school was unable to authorize access to students' grades. However, we asked CS-oriented students if their grades in CS-related disciplines decreased, increased or remained the same.

The questionnaire was administered to all classes in two days, one at the beginning and one at the end of the school year, in school laboratories, through Google Forms, by the author (who has no relationships with the school, and presented himself as an entirely external subject, to avoid the tendency to socially desirable answers given by students to their teachers).

3.3.2 Intervention. In class INF1, halfway through the year, we performed a mindset intervention, attempting to alter students' beliefs by explicitly teaching them about growth mindset (analogously to what Dweck and colleagues did in many experiments: see for example [4]). The intervention (a 2 hours lesson conducted by the author, who is a computer scientist with a background in education) was inspired by material prepared by Khan Academy and PERTS [16]. The lesson included, in order: a discussion on what students think intelligence is, and if it could be changed; a discussion about a situation where they learned to do something they were not able to do yet; a presentation of the Mindset theory

Table 2: Internal consistency (Cronbach's alphas)

Measure		INF1	INF2	INF3	CHEM	TRAN	ALL
GM	pre	0.86	0.90	0.66	0.70	0.89	0.83
	post	0.94	0.97	0.93	0.82	0.26	0.89
CONF	pre	0.62	0.87	-0.34	0.81	0.49	0.67
	post	0.71	0.79	0.17	0.60	0.07	0.65
GOAL	pre	0.62	0.50	-0.21	0.46	-0.19	0.46
	post	0.35	0.29	-0.39	0.37	0.59	0.30
CSM	pre	0.60	0.80	0.57	0.71	0.52	0.72
	post	0.53	0.79	0.82	0.77	0.80	0.75
NAT	pre	-0.43	-0.21	0.13	-0.56	0.05	-0.08
	post	0.30	0.27	0.73	-0.52	0.51	-0.01
IDCS	pre	0.88	0.84	0.70	0.87	0.60	0.86
	post	0.91	0.77	0.76	0.83	0.74	0.85
MAST	pre	-0.43	0.69	0.81	0.35	0.49	0.40
	post	0.21	0.60	0.75	0.66	0.31	0.57

through a table translating a diagram from Nigel Holmes [14]; a short video [29] on neuroplasticity (with Italian subtitles); and a description by the researcher of "a situation where he overcame a struggle in learning and learned to solve a problem" [16].

In the last part of the lesson, three open questions were administered through a Google Form. Students were asked to think of a time when they overcame a struggle to learn something and then to:

- OQ1 Advise future students on how to overcome an obstacle when learning something new (translation of question in [16])
- OQ2 Suggest what a teacher could do to stimulate a growth mindset in students (proposed by us)
- OQ3 Suggest some concrete strategies to a future CS student to succeed and not be discouraged when facing difficulties in learning to program (inspired by [30])

The full wording of the questions is available in the online appendix of this paper [21].

4 RESULTS

4.1 Quantitative analysis

Responses were analyzed through the statistical programming language R [25], with the packages *Hmisc, pastecs, lsr, psych, dplyr.*

Internal consistency was measured through Cronbach's alpha [23] for questions about mindset (GM), confidence in one's own intelligence (CONF), goal choice (GOAL), Computer Science mindset (CSM), beliefs about nature of CS (NAT), identification with CS (IDCS), mastery orientation in CS (MAST) for pre- and post-questionnaire responses, for each class and for the whole sample of students. Values are reported in Table 2.

For many measures the internal reliability is very low: it could be due to the relatively small sample size, or to the translation/adaptation to CS of some questions, or other factors. An in-depth analysis of the reasons is out of the scope of this work. We decided to explore further with the analysis of GM, CSM and IDCS, that have acceptable (> 0.70) Cronbach's alphas [23] for both pre and post test for combined samples.

4.1.1 Difference between beginning and end of the year. To check if studying or not studying CS had an impact, we performed statistical tests on the difference between pre and post scores for each class and each of the three measures. Moreover, we also performed the test for all the samples combined.

Paired samples t-test works if the differences between pre and post scores are normally distributed. We checked that with the Shapiro-Wilk normality test and, since often it gives false positive results for small samples, also checked normality graphically through QQ-plots. Whenever we were unsure about the normality of data, we performed a non-parametric version of the test, in particular, the Wilcoxon signed rank test with continuity correction, that does not require a normality assumption. When we found significant results, we also measured the effect size through Cohen's d for paired samples. Results are reported in Table 3.

Mindset decreased in INF1, INF3, CHEM and increased in INF2 and TRAN, but in no case was the change statistically significant. Regarding the combined samples, mindset decreased for both CS and non-CS students, but not significantly.

Identification with CS decreased in INF classes, and increased in CHEM and TRAN, but not significantly in any case. This reflects on the fact that it decreases for CS students combined, and increases for non-CS students (not significantly, but with $p = 0.10$).

Computer Science mindset decreased, but not significantly, in INF1 and INF2, remained stable in INF3, but decreased significantly ($p = 0.02$) in CHEM (with a medium effect size $d = 0.52$) and decreased ($p = 0.09$, with a large effect size $d = 0.87$) in TRAN. In the combined samples, CSM decreased, but not significantly, in CS students, and significantly in non CS students ($p < 0.01$, with a medium/large effect size $d = 0.59$).

4.1.2 Difference between different subgroups. To check if there were significant differences between some subgroups, we performed many independent samples tests. In particular, we checked for differences in GM and CSM (at the beginning, at the end, and their difference) between males and females, between students with and without previous programming experience, and between students of CS and non-CS classes.

To perform an independent samples t-test, both subgroups must be normally distributed and have the same variance. All normal subgroups were checked with the F-test to compare the two variances and were found to have the same variance. Groups that were not normally distributed were analyzed with Wilcoxon rank sum test with continuity correction, which does not require normality assumption. Results are shown in Table 4.

We found no statistically significant differences in mindset between any of the subgroups. By contrast, we see significant differences in the difference between final and initial CS growth mindset. In particular, it decreased in females more than in males ($p = 0.16$), decreased much more in novices than in those with previous experience ($p = 0.06$) and, confirming previous observations, decreased statistically significantly more in non-CS students than in CS students ($p = 0.03$).

4.1.3 Correlation with grades. To see if mindset influences CS grades, we calculated Pearson's r between GM/CSM (pre, post, diff) and the reported variation in grades, but didn't find significant correlations, as shown in Table 5.

Table 3: Paired samples tests

Sample	Measure	n	normal	pre		post		t-test			Cohen's d	Wilcoxon-test	
				mean	sd	mean	sd	t	df	p		V	p
INF1	GM	16	yes	4.02	1.28	3.33	1.39	1.56	15	0.14			
	CSM	16	not sure	4.50	0.84	4.20	0.97					38.00	0.31
	IDCS	16	yes	3.28	0.96	3.07	0.94	1.02	15	0.32			
INF2	GM	14	yes	4.05	1.54	4.17	1.69	-0.36	13	0.72			
	CSM	14	not sure	4.68	1.02	4.38	1.12					58.50	0.38
	IDCS	14	not sure	3.71	0.65	3.68	0.83					47.00	0.94
INF3	GM	7	yes	4.29	1.15	4.05	1.46	0.35	6	0.74			
	CSM	7	not sure	3.50	0.80	3.50	1.14					8.50	0.89
	IDCS	7	not sure	3.83	0.46	3.75	0.55					10.00	0.59
CHEM	GM	23	yes	4.22	1.07	3.99	1.22	0.98	22	0.34			
	CSM	23	yes	4.21	1.11	3.71	1.12	2.51	22	0.02*	0.52		
	IDCS	23	yes	2.79	0.83	2.91	0.88	-0.83	22	0.42			
TRAN	GM	6	no	2.89	1.34	3.22	0.78					2.00	0.79
	CSM	6	yes	5.04	0.62	4.33	0.90	2.14	5	0.09	0.87		
	IDCS	6	not sure	2.59	0.45	3.20	0.44					1.00	0.06
ALL CS	GM	37	yes	4.08	1.33	3.78	1.53	1.14	36	0.26			
	CSM	37	no	4.38	0.98	4.14	1.08					259.50	0.20
	IDCS	37	yes	3.54	0.79	3.43	0.88	1.18	36	0.25			
ALL NON-CS	GM	29	yes	3.94	1.23	3.83	1.17	0.55	28	0.59			
	CSM	29	yes	4.38	1.07	3.84	1.10	3.18	28	0.00*	0.59		
	IDCS	29	yes	2.75	0.76	2.97	0.81	-1.71	28	0.10			

4.2 Qualitative analysis

We analyzed the responses to open questions from the students in INF1. Although the questions asked them to write a letter or to give suggestions in at least five sentences, all responses were brief and schematic. This, however, made the coding procedure straightforward: we identified categories of advice and could easily fit answers in those categories.

We analyzed the responses (see sec. 3.3.2) of the 16 students of INF1 that also completed both the pre and the post questionnaires.

Categories and the number of suggestions fitting in that category are reported here. Note that many answers contained more than one piece of advice, so fit in more than one category.

OQ1 Categories: put effort (4); do not discourage (2); practice a lot (2); be convinced before choosing CS (1); take private / extra lessons (2); ask teacher (1); decompose problems (1); ask online (1); (in the context of video-game programming) find and remember errors early to avoid them later (1).

OQ2 Categories: make students have fun (3); repeat things often (3); link to student interest/passion (3); limit boring explanation/theory (2); encourage group work (2); involve students in logic reasoning (2); deliver interactive lessons (1); avoid numeric grades (1); propose creative exercises (1); link subject to real life (1); teach value of effort and training (1); personalize teaching (1).

OQ3 Categories: program on your own at home constantly (9); watch online video tutorials/examples (6); constantly study (5); have objectives/interest/motivation regarding CS (4); believe in yourself/ do not discourage (4); ask questions (4); pay attention during lessons (3); study the programming language (syntax) (3); understand fundamentals (2); take notes (2); not remain behind: concepts builds on previous ones (2); you can do everything with programming (1); study theory (1); there are many ways to solve a problem (1); reflect on errors (1); understand instead of learning by hearth (1); break down the problem in sub-problems (1); read compiler error messages (1); try to engage yourself by programming video games (1).

5 DISCUSSION, CONCLUSIONS AND FURTHER WORK

We found (RQ1) no statistical evidence that studying (or not studying) CS for one year automatically fosters growth mindset in high school students. Moreover, we did not find significant differences between males and females, students with or without previous programming experiences, CS or non-CS students.

We see these results neither as surprising nor as negative, since they are in line with educational research, stating that transfer is difficult between distant domains and does not happen automatically [2]. Our results support warnings about enthusiastic claims around CS fostering GM.

We still think some characteristics of CS can help to develop a GM, but only if teaching interventions are explicitly designed to

Table 4: Independent samples tests

	M		F		t/Wilcocxon			
n	56		10					
	m	sd	m	sd	t	W	p	d
GM pre	3.99	1.27	4.17	1.36	-0.39		0.70	
GM pos	3.70	1.40	4.40	1.12		194	0.12	
GM diff	-0.30	1.40	0.23	1.37	-1.11		0.27	
CSM pre	4.36	0.96	4.47	1.36		236	0.43	
CSM pos	4.06	1.04	3.70	1.33	0.96		0.34	
CSM diff	-0.30	0.96	-0.78	0.88		359	0.16	
	EXP		NO EXP		t/Wilcocxon			
n	30		36					
	m	sd	m	sd	t	W	p	d
GM pre	4.07	1.21	3.98	1.35		512	0.72	
GM pos	3.94	1.20	3.69	1.51	-0.76		0.45	
GM diff	-0.12	1.36	-0.30	1.44	-0.50		0.62	
CSM pre	4.28	0.99	4.46	1.04		593	0.50	
CSM pos	4.21	1.02	3.83	1.13	-1.41		0.16	
CSM diff	-0.08	0.91	-0.63	0.94		395	0.06	0.6
	CS		NO CS		t/Wilcocxon			
n	37		29					
	m	sd	m	sd	t	W	p	d
GM pre	4.08	1.33	3.94	1.23		496	0.60	
GM pos	3.78	1.53	3.83	1.17		544	0.93	
GM diff	-0.30	1.59	-0.12	1.12	0.52		0.60	
CSM pre	4.38	0.98	4.38	1.07	0.00		1.00	
CSM pos	4.14	1.08	3.84	1.10	-1.11		0.27	
CSM diff	-0.24	0.98	-0.54	0.92		371	0.03*	0.3

Table 5: Correlation between grades and mindsets

Grades					
GM	r	sig.	CSM	r	sig.
pre	0.04	0.80	pre	0.07	0.70
post	0.27	0.11	post	0.16	0.33
diff	0.22	0.19	diff	0.11	0.50

do so (and if they leverage, for example, on the creative and iterative nature of CS, as we have successfully shown in a preliminary study [20]).

CSEd research should also focus on the opposite implication: CS is a challenging subject, therefore a growth mindset can be particularly important to succeed in it [18, 22].

The intervention where we explicitly taught about Growth Mindset in one of the CS classes (INF1) was not effective (RQ2): the average mindset of INF1 students decreased (although not significantly) from 4.02 out of 6 to 3.33 out of 6. One of our possible explanations is the fact that the initial discussion during the lesson really engaged students and took much more time than scheduled, forcing the researcher to rush through the subsequent points. Furthermore, a shift towards a more fixed mindset was also found after a similar intervention in CS1 courses [30]. Finally, the efficacy of this kind of intervention is debated [31].

However, INF1 students, after receiving the intervention, gave to hypothetical colleagues coherent GM suggestions (RQ3) to overcome difficulties (put effort, ask questions, practice regularly and so on). Surprisingly, when asked what a teacher should do to stimulate a growth mindset, almost no one answered with typical GM teaching suggestions (e.g., teach explicitly about brain growth, praise effort): the vast majority advocated more creativity, engagement, fun, connection with the real world or student passions. This is interesting because in other fields, for example, engineering, the suggested approaches proved to be effective: during the first year of University, students usually move towards a fixed mindset. However, introducing open-ended, socially relevant engineering design projects into the curriculum helps to lessen or eliminate the shift toward fixed mindset [26]. Our preliminary results on Primary Education students seem to agree with that [20].

We found (RQ1) a statistically significant decrease in "Computer Science mindset" only in students not studying CS. The decrease was higher for girls and students without any previous programming experience. This is not desirable: if we think CS has a universal social value, reinforcing stereotypes about a "geek gene" [1, 24] will be harmful and lead to a problem similar to those many students are experiencing in Math, as international tests reveal. This adds to the evidence on the importance of introducing CS principles for all K-12 students.

Identification with CS decreased (RQ1) in CS students, confirming what was already observed for Math [37]. Its (small) increase in non-CS students is worth further analysis.

This research was conducted in a high school in Italy, with 16-year-old students. To generalize the results, it should be reproduced with different samples (different kind of schools, different geographic areas, different age and previous experience, different teaching methodologies, and so on). Items on CS beliefs were translated into Italian and adapted from recent Math research: thus, we need validation studies and better calibration to assess CS beliefs effectively.

ACKNOWLEDGMENTS

Thanks to the students involved and to their teachers, especially to N.A. for believing in the study. Thanks to Alle Serra for creating the link with the school. Thanks to my supervisor Simone Martini for the support; to Tim Bell for hosting me; and to both for providing useful suggestions.

REFERENCES

[1] Alireza Ahadi and Raymond Lister. 2013. Geek genes, prior knowledge, stumbling points and learning edge momentum. *Proceedings of the ninth annual international ACM conference on International computing education research - ICER '13* (2013). https://doi.org/10.1145/2493394.2493416

[2] Susan A. Ambrose, Michael W. Bridges, Michele DiPietro, Marsha C. Lovett, and Marie K. Norman. 2010. *How learning works: Seven research-based principles for smart teaching.* John Wiley & Sons.

[3] Miles Berry. 2015. Teaching computing. Retrieved January 20, 2019 from http://milesberry.net/2015/02/teaching-computing/

[4] Lisa S. Blackwell, Kali H. Trzesniewski, and Carol S. Dweck. 2007. Implicit Theories of Intelligence Predict Achievement Across an Adolescent Transition: A Longitudinal Study and an Intervention. *Child Development* 78, 1 (Jan 2007), 246–263. https://doi.org/10.1111/j.1467-8624.2007.00995.x

[5] Jo Boaler. 2013. Ability and mathematics: the mindset revolution that is reshaping education. In *Forum*, Vol. 55. Symposium Journals, 143–152.

[6] Quintin Cutts, Emily Cutts, Stephen Draper, Patrick O'Donnell, and Peter Saffrey. 2010. Manipulating mindset to positively influence introductory programming performance. *Proceedings of the 41st ACM technical symposium on Computer science education - SIGCSE '10* (2010). https://doi.org/10.1145/1734263.1734409

[7] Carol S. Dweck. 2000. *Self-theories: Their role in motivation, personality, and development.* Psychology Press.

[8] Carol S. Dweck. 2003. *Teorie del Sé. Intelligenza, motivazione, personalità e sviluppo.* Erickson.

[9] Carol S. Dweck. 2008. Mindsets and Math/Science Achievement. *The Opportunity Equation* (2008).

[10] Carol S. Dweck. 2017. *Mindset (Updated Edition).* Robinson.

[11] Abraham E. Flanigan, Markeya S. Peteranetz, Duane F. Shell, and Leen-Kiat Soh. 2015. Exploring Changes in Computer Science Students' Implicit Theories of Intelligence Across the Semester. *Proceedings of the eleventh annual International Conference on International Computing Education Research - ICER '15* (2015). https://doi.org/10.1145/2787622.2787722

[12] Catherine Good, Aneeta Rattan, and Carol S. Dweck. 2012. Why do women opt out? Sense of belonging and women's representation in mathematics. *Journal of Personality and Social Psychology* 102, 4 (2012), 700–717. https://doi.org/10.1037/a0026659

[13] Karin Schreier Hallett. 2016. Building Growth Mindset Through Coding. Retrieved January 20, 2019 from https://liquidliteracy.com/2016/12/28/building-growth-mindset-through-coding/

[14] Nigel Holmes. 2016. Two mindsets. Retrieved January 20, 2019 from http://www.nigelholmes.com/site/wp-content/uploads/2016/09/two$_m$indsets.png

[15] Antti-Juhani Kaijanaho and Ville Tirronen. 2018. Fixed Versus Growth Mindset Does Not Seem to Matter Much: A Prospective Observational Study in Two Late Bachelor Level Computer Science Courses. In *Proceedings of the 2018 ACM Conference on International Computing Education Research (ICER '18).* ACM, New York, NY, USA, 11–20. https://doi.org/10.1145/3230977.3230982

[16] Khan Academy and PERTS. 2014. Growth Mindset Lesson Plan. Retrieved January 20, 2019 from https://cdn.kastatic.org/KA-share/Toolkit-photos/FINAL+Growth+Mindset+Lesson+Plan.pdf

[17] David Klahr and Sharon McCoy Carver. 1988. Cognitive objectives in a LOGO debugging curriculum: Instruction, learning, and transfer. *Cognitive Psychology* 20, 3 (1988), 362 – 404. https://doi.org/10.1016/0010-0285(88)90004-7

[18] Colleen M. Lewis. 2017. *Good (and Bad) Reasons to Teach All Students Computer Science.* Springer International Publishing, Cham, 15–34. https://doi.org/10.1007/978-3-319-54226-3_2

[19] Michael Lodi. 2017. Growth Mindset in Computational Thinking Teaching and Teacher Training. In *Proceedings of the 2017 ACM Conference on International Computing Education Research (ICER '17).* ACM, New York, NY, USA, 281–282. https://doi.org/10.1145/3105726.3105736

[20] Michael Lodi. 2018. Can Creative Computing Foster Growth Mindset?. In *Joint Proceedings of the 1st Co-Creation in the Design, Development and Implementation of Technology-Enhanced Learning workshop (CC-TEL 2018) and Systems of Assessments for Computational Thinking Learning workshop (TACKLE 2018) co-located with 13th European Conference on Technology Enhanced Learning (ECTEL 2018), Leeds, United Kingdom, September 3rd, 2018. (CEUR Workshop Proceedings)*, Alicja Piotrkowicz, Rosie Dent-Spargo, Sebastian Dennerlein, István Koren, Panagiotis Antoniou, Paul Bailey, Tamsin Treasure-Jones, Ilenia Fronza, and Claus Pahl (Eds.), Vol. 2190. CEUR-WS.org. http://ceur-ws.org/Vol-2190/TACKLE$_2$018$_p$aper$_3$.pdf

[21] Michael Lodi. 2019. Appendix to "Does Studying CS Automatically Foster a Growth Mindset?". Retrieved April 6, 2019 from https://lodi.ml/appendix-mindset-iticse19

[22] Laurie Murphy and Lynda Thomas. 2008. Dangers of a fixed mindset. *ACM SIGCSE Bulletin* 40, 3 (Aug 2008), 271. https://doi.org/10.1145/1597849.1384344

[23] Jum C Nunnally. 1978. *Psychometric Theory: 2d Ed.* McGraw-Hill.

[24] Elizabeth Patitsas, Jesse Berlin, Michelle Craig, and Steve Easterbrook. 2016. Evidence That Computer Science Grades Are Not Bimodal. In *Proceedings of the 2016 ACM Conference on International Computing Education Research (ICER '16).* ACM, New York, NY, USA, 113–121. https://doi.org/10.1145/2960310.2960312

[25] R Core Team. 2013. *R: A Language and Environment for Statistical Computing.* R Foundation for Statistical Computing, Vienna, Austria. http://www.R-project.org/

[26] Kenneth J. Reid and Daniel M. Ferguson. 2014. Do design experiences in engineering build a growth mindset in students?. In *2014 IEEE Integrated STEM Education Conference.* 1–5. https://doi.org/10.1109/ISECon.2014.6891046

[27] Ronny Scherer. 2016. Learning from the Past–The Need for Empirical Evidence on the Transfer Effects of Computer Programming Skills. *Frontiers in Psychology* 7 (2016), 1390. https://doi.org/10.3389/fpsyg.2016.01390

[28] Michael J. Scott and Gheorghita Ghinea. 2014. On the Domain-Specificity of Mindsets: The Relationship Between Aptitude Beliefs and Programming Practice. *IEEE Transactions on Education* 57, 3 (Aug 2014), 169–174. https://doi.org/10.1109/TE.2013.2288700

[29] Sentis. 2012. Neuroplasticity. Retrieved January 20, 2019 from https://www.youtube.com/watch?v=ELpfYCZa87g

[30] Beth Simon, Brian Hanks, Laurie Murphy, Sue Fitzgerald, Renée McCauley, Lynda Thomas, and Carol Zander. 2008. Saying isn't necessarily believing. *Proceeding of the fourth international workshop on Computing education research - ICER '08* (2008). https://doi.org/10.1145/1404520.1404537

[31] Victoria F. Sisk, Alexander P. Burgoyne, Jingze Sun, Jennifer L. Butler, and Brooke N. Macnamara. 2018. To What Extent and Under Which Circumstances Are Growth Mind-Sets Important to Academic Achievement? Two Meta-Analyses. *Psychological Science* 29, 4 (2018), 549–571. https://doi.org/10.1177/0956797617739704 arXiv:https://doi.org/10.1177/0956797617739704 PMID: 29505339.

[32] Kelly Smith. 2016. Why code club is the best way to develop a growth mindset. Retrieved January 20, 2019 from https://medium.com/coding-at-the-library/why-code-club-is-the-best-way-to-develop-a-growth-mindset-2ac354ab7322

[33] Katherine L. Sun. 2015. *There's no limit: mathematics teaching for a growth mindset.* Ph.D. Dissertation. Graduate School of Education, Stanford University. http://purl.stanford.edu/xf479cc2194

[34] Arjun Venkataswamy. 2016. How Learning to Code Can Help Develop a Growth Mindset. Retrieved January 20, 2019 from https://www.digitaladventures.com/news/2016/5/2/how-learning-to-code-can-help-develop-a-growth-mindset

[35] Kristin Villanueva. 2018. How Having a Growth Mindset Can Help You Learn to Code. Retrieved January 20, 2019 from http://blog.mindsetworks.com/entry/how-having-a-growth-mindset-can-help-you-learn-to-code

[36] Kristin Villanueva. 2018. How Learning to Code Can Help You Develop a Growth Mindset. Retrieved January 20, 2019 from http://blog.mindsetworks.com/entry/how-learning-to-code-can-help-you-develop-a-growth-mindset

[37] Allan Wigfield, Jacquelynne S. Eccles, Douglas Mac Iver, David A. Reuman, and Carol Midgley. 1991. Transitions during early adolescence: Changes in children's domain-specific self-perceptions and general self-esteem across the transition to junior high school. *Developmental psychology* 27, 4 (1991), 552.

Understanding How Work Habits influence Student Performance

Seth Copen Goldstein
*Carnegie Mellon University
Pittsburgh, PA
seth@cmu.edu

Hongyi Zhang
Peking University
Beijing, China
hongyizhang@pku.edu.cn

Majd Sakr*
msakr@cs.cmu.edu

Haokang An*
haokanga@andrew.cmu.edu

Cameron Dashti*
cdashti1@andrew.cmu.edu

ABSTRACT

Understanding the relationship between a student's broader work habits and their performance, particularly on open-ended programming assignments, is key towards being able to guide students towards success. In spite of this, most evidence of student behavior and its relationship to performance is anecdotal. The advent of large-scale courses which use online tools for delivering course content, monitoring the programming environment, and providing automatic feedback as well as grading now makes it possible to dive into the data and develop data-driven methods for understanding how a student's approach to an assignment—from their first exposure to the description of the problem to their final submission of their completed assignment—influences their final performance.

This study is a first look at a subset of the data collected from a project-based, online, upper-level course on cloud computing. We examine three raw data streams which include information on the time students spend on reading the project write-up, the timing, grades, and number of submissions they make, and the cloud resources used (both time and cost) in solving the assignment. Using these and several synthetic metrics we were surprised to find that there are few behaviors that are highly correlated to student success. Instead, we find that there is a strong correlation between students who continually apply consistent behaviors over the course of the semester to good final performance in the course. From this we use LASSO to create a predictor (adjusted $R^2 = .48$) of final performance based on two kinds of consistency measures across 15 metrics.

KEYWORDS

Online education; student performance; educational data mining; learning analytics; project-based learning; work habits

ACM Reference Format:

Seth Copen Goldstein, Hongyi Zhang, Majd Sakr, Haokang An, and Cameron Dashti. 2019. Understanding How Work Habits influence Student Performance. In *Innovation and Technology in Computer Science Education (ITiCSE '19), July 15–17, 2019, Aberdeen, Scotland Uk.* ACM, New York, NY, USA, 7 pages. https://doi.org/10.1145/3304221.3319757

ITiCSE '19, July 15–17, 2019, Aberdeen, Scotland Uk

ACM ISBN 978-1-4503-6301-3/19/07...$15.00
https://doi.org/10.1145/3304221.3319757

1 INTRODUCTION

There is a significant literature on how students work and the impact it has on their performance; sometimes even on how they learn. Until recently most of these studies were limited to small populations and/or survey based approaches because students did most of their work in an unobservable way. While there are numerous studies, they often come to conflicting conclusions, e.g., more effort is either positively or negatively correlated with performance. With the advent of online courses, more data can be collected. However, even studies based on this new source of data yield conflicting results. All of these conflicting studies exist against a backdrop of teachers making well meaning suggestions to students to help them do well: start your project early, read the entire write-up before doing any coding, take lots of short breaks, spread your work over a few days, don't pull all-nighters, etc. Unfortunately, there is no real data to suggest these suggestions are useful.

This study is a first look at data that covers how students work on projects from the moment they get the write-up on a Learning Management System (LMS) to the time of their final submission on an auto grading system. We collect 15 data streams from 11 different one-week projects over the course of a single semester of an online upper-division project-based course.

While our ultimate goal is to identify which work habits are correlated with the most learning; we instead use grades as a proxy for learning and look at which work habits are correlated with the best performance. We had hoped to identify which habits are best; to support (or refute) the common wisdom often given to students. However, we soon found that few habits are good for all students. As we discuss in Section 3, we find that there is little evidence that any one work habit is best for all students. In retrospect, this is not surprising as it is well known that different people have different work styles [4, 8]. Further investigation suggests that there is a significant and strong positive correlation between the consistency in how they tackle each project and their final performance.

We describe our infrastructure and how we collect the data in Section 2. We present our main results which lead to a useful predictor of performance which explains more than 40% of the variance in our data in Section 3. We briefly outline related work in Section 4 and conclude with some ideas for future work in Section 5.

2 METHODOLOGY AND DATA COLLECTION

We investigate whether specific student behavior leads to improved performance in a project-based upper-level CS course. We attempt to find a correlation between direct and synthetic student behavior metrics (see Table 1) and performance. We analyze whether the temporal consistency of student behavior and performance are correlated. Finally, we propose a model for performance prediction.

Metric	Description	Data Sources
Starting Early	The negative of the number of hours into the week they start seriously reading the write-up.	pLMS
Finishing Early	The number of hours before the project deadline that they make their the last submission.	AGS
Write-up Completion	The percentage of the handout that was read before the first submission was made.	pLMS + AGS
Wall-Clock Time	Total wall-clock time between when they first start reading the write-up and when they make their final submission.	pLMS + AGS
Short Breaks	The number of short breaks a student takes. A break is a period of less than 1 hour of no activity bordering work activity of at least 1 hour.	pLMS, AGS, CSP
Work Periods	The number of periods of contiguous activity broken up by periods of inactivity of more than 5 hours.	pLMS, AGS, CSP
Total Active Time	The total amount of time the student is working on the project; derived from reading the write-up, using cloud resources, and making submissions.	pLMS, AGS, CSP
Pre-submission Time	The time between when the student starts seriously reading the write-up and their first submission. We measure this both for wall-clock time and active time.	pLMS + AGS
Number of Submissions	The total number of submissions made to the autograder, both per project and per task.	AGS
ECR Cycle Time	Median time between submissions of the same task.	AGS
Submission Grade Delta	The median difference in the scores between two submissions.	AGS
Cloud time	The total time that cloud resources are instantiated for the project.	CSP
Cost	The percentage of the allocated budget that the student uses to complete the project.	CSP

Table 1: *Metrics, how we calculate them, and what their source is.*

Metric	Correlation
Starting Early	0.198*
Finishing Early	0.444***
Write-up Completion	−0.130
Wall-Clock Time	−0.043
Short Breaks	0.093
Work Periods	0.124
Total Active Time	0.105
Pre-submission Activity Time	−0.279***
Pre-submission Wall-clock Time	−0.385***
Number of Submissions	0.221**
Number of Submissions/Task	0.074
ECR Cycle Time	−0.135
Submission Grade Delta	−0.004
Cloud Time	−0.097
Cost	0.013

Significance levels: * $p < .05$; ** $p < .01$; *** $p < .001$

Table 2: *Correlation between metrics as described in Table 1 and final performance.*

The data was collected from a semester-long online project-based course offered to students at Carnegie Mellon University's four global campuses in Spring 2018. The course, cross-listed as an undergraduate and graduate course, requires students to complete 11 individual projects and (for the graduate students) to participate in a team project. Since this is an online course, there are no lectures to attend. Students in this online course complete conceptual topics and assessments on an LMS platform and use another homegrown platform, TheProject.Zone, to access and submit solutions to the programming projects. Students in the course interact with the teaching staff and with other students on Piazza, a question and answer forum. The course has been offered 10 times before in the same format. The data collected and reported on in this paper are from undergraduate and graduate students working on the individual projects only.

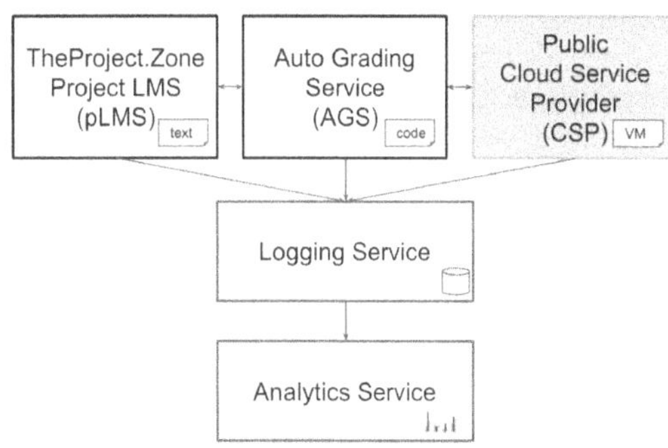

Figure 1: *We use three data sources to infer behavior, logs from: the pLMS where students access the project write-up, the AGS where students submit their solutions and get automated and contextualized feedback, and from the CSP which indicate when students provision cloud resources as well as their cost.*

Data were collected from 154 students enrolled in our course in the Spring 2018 semester. The data sources (see Fig. 1) include TheProject.Zone, a project LMS (pLMS), the Auto Grading Service (AGS) and student logs from provisioning resources on a public Cloud Service Provider (CSP). From the pLMS, we collected their heartbeat time and their scoreboard data. Heartbeat is an indicator that students are currently interacting with the project write-up. It is recorded every 5 minutes to capture student online behavior continuously, and we can trace down to the specific write-up section the student is reading. Scoreboard data presents students' score for each task and each project, and it is visible to both the instructor and the students. From AGS, we collected their submission information and the corresponding feedback, from which we can see how the student score increases over time as they go through the whole project. From CSP, we collected their cloud resource running time and the corresponding cost. Every project is associated with a particular budget, and the students should monitor and manage their cloud resources so that they do not go over the budget or their score is reduced.

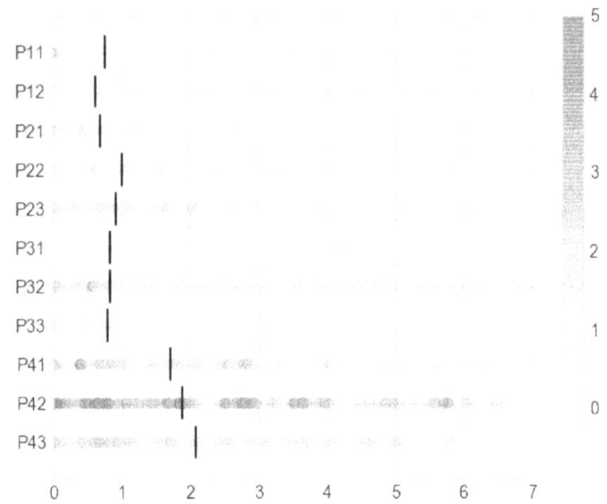

Figure 2: *The time students start reading the project write-up. (Vertical bars in this and future figures indicate the median value.)*

While most of the metrics we discuss come directly from the data sources described here, we do have to estimate the time that students are actually working on the project. We call it the *Total Active Time* in Table 1, to account for the time that the students are working offline or on their local computer. We use the heartbeat from the pLMS as the basis for their active time. Submission activity from the AGS is included as an hour worth of work if there is no heartbeat within an hour of the submission, or we consider the student as working during the interval between the closest heartbeat and the time of submission. Finally, we include from the CSP the time that cloud resources are running as long as those resources are running for less than 12 hours. (If they are running for more than that, we assume the student forgot to turn them off.) The total active time is the union of the heartbeat time, the merged submissions, and the cloud resource running periods.

While we cannot capture all student behavior—i.e., some of their work may happen off-line when they are not engaged with the data sources—we are capturing most of it as indicated by comparing the self-reported time spent on each project (from post-project survey data) and the estimated active time. Of the eleven individual projects, three projects have students reporting (in aggregate) that they spend between 1.2x and 1.7x our estimate while all the projects have student reported times which are ±10% of our estimate.

3 EXPERIMENTS

The ultimate goal of this research is to understand how students learn and then to develop interventions which aid their learning. Here we present a preliminary evaluation of some of the data we have collected with the caveat that measuring learning, particularly in the case of a single course, is difficult at best. Thus, we look at how student behavior relates to final performance (i.e., grades) as a poor, but measurable, proxy for learning. We hope that understanding how student behavior is related to student performance will shed some light on how students succeed and indirectly lead us to understand the best way to enable student learning in future work. Table 1 describes the data sources that we examine, how we gather them, and when appropriate how we calculate them.

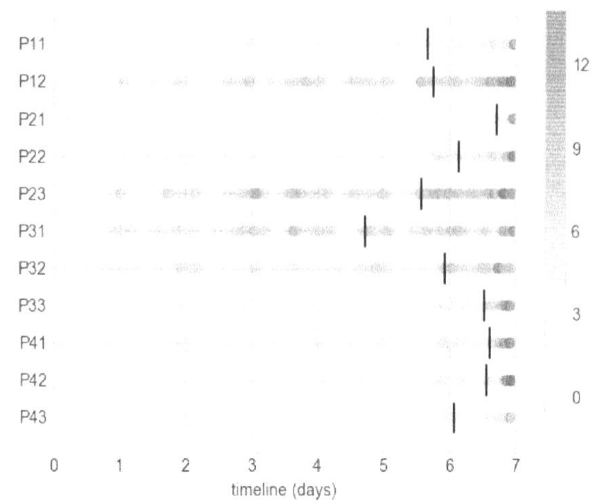

Figure 3: *The time at which students finish the project.*

3.1 Direct Work Habits

Here we look at different work habits and their relationship to performance. The correlation and significance between each metric and the final performance of the student can be found in Table 2.

One work style, often praised by faculty, is starting a project early. Because the write-up for each project is delivered online we can measure when students begin the project by recording when a student begins seriously reading[1] the write-up. As Fig. 2 shows, students generally start reading the project quite early in the week, but starting times can vary quite a bit. Surprisingly, the correlation between starting early and doing well on a project is only slightly significant. (See the first row, labeled *Start Early,* of Table 2.)

We do, however, find a strong and significant correlation ($r = 0.444^{***}$) [2] between how early a student finishes the project (measured in how many hours before the deadline they make their final submission) and their performance on the project. (See row two, labeled *Finishing Early,* Table 2.) Fig. 3 shows the distribution of end times for our 11 projects. Interestingly, the correlation is not strictly an artifact of students stopping when they get a perfect score. Depending on the project, less than half the students who finish early have a perfect score. While we cannot be sure what work habit this is linked to, our hypothesis is that busy students who are good at managing their time are likely to realize that it is not worth the extra time to get only a marginally better score. Alternatively, finishing early may be a sign that the students are not procrastinating; which is significantly correlated with performance [3, 6, 12].

Generally, we advise students to read the entire write-up before beginning work on the project. The percentage of the write-up read by students before they make their first submission varies significantly. Contrary to our intuition, there is no evidence that this impacts performance either positively or negatively. (See row labeled *Write-up Completion* of Table 2.)

The next four rows of Table 2 deal with how students allocate their time on a project. *Wall-Clock Time* refers to the total amount of time between when they first start reading the write-up until

[1] By "seriously reading," we mean more than just glancing at the write-up. I.e., they must be interacting with the write-up for more than 5 minutes to count as "seriously reading" it.

[2] Whenever we include correlation numbers we also include their significance level: * $p < .05$; ** $p < .01$; *** $p < .001$.

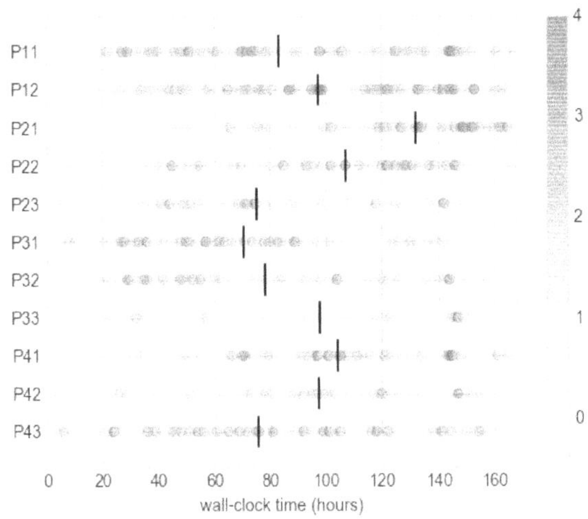

Figure 4: *The wall clock time from the start to the end of the project.*

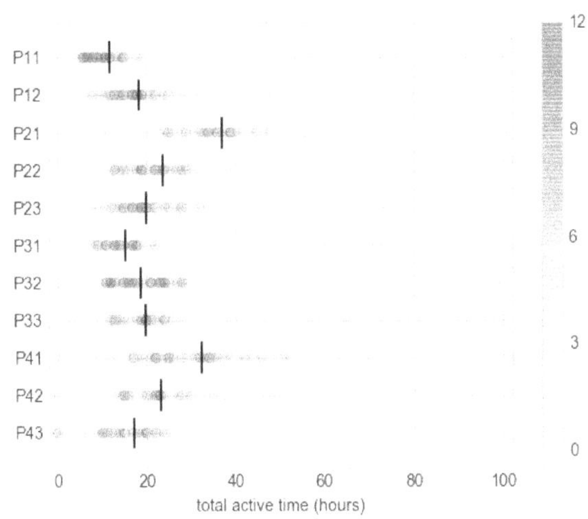

Figure 5: *The total amount of time (derived) that students spend on a project.*

their final submission. In other words, do they spread out their work over the week (a long wall-clock time), or strongly focus on this project alone (a shorter start to end period). As Fig. 4 shows, students vary significantly in how they focus on the project. *Short Breaks* is an indication of how many short breaks the student takes during the course of working on the project. And, *Work Periods* (see different distribution of work periods in Fig. 7.) refers to how many long sessions the student takes to complete the project. Contrary to standard intuition none of these work habits significantly correlate with final performance. It is no surprise then, that the *Total Active Time* spent on the project (which varies significantly as shown in Fig. 5.) is also not correlated with final performance.

We can determine not only how long students work, but also when they work. The day-night cycles are clearly evident in Fig. 6, as is the fact that students tend to pull an all-nighter for the harder projects, e.g., P21 and P33. Other artifacts from the course are also evident, E.g., P41, P42, and P43 run coincidentally with the team project and many students seem to focus on the team project, delaying work on the individual projects to the end of the week.

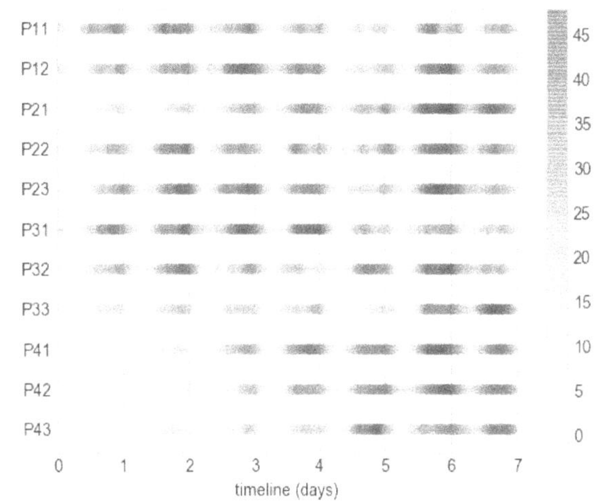

Figure 6: *A depiction of when students work on each project.*

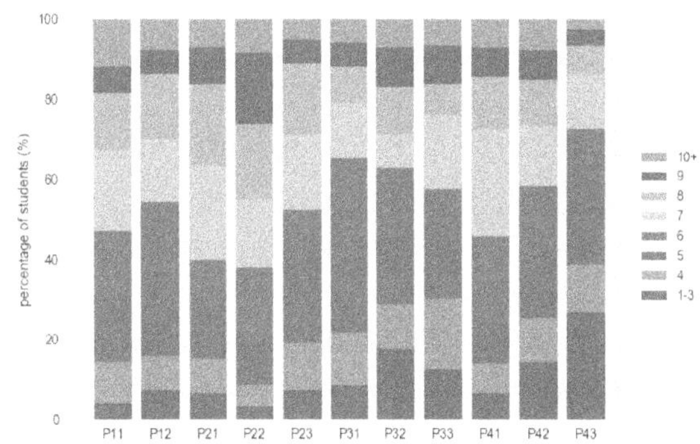

Figure 7: *Number of periods students take to finish a project.*

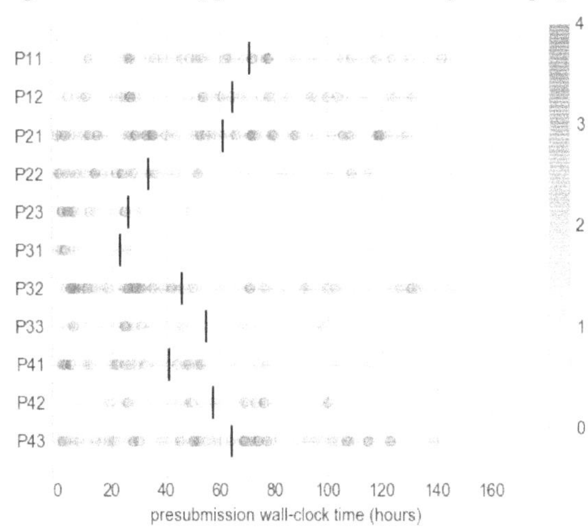

Figure 8: *The wall-clock time a student spends working on the project before their first submission.*

The aforementioned metrics are easy to collect and directly reflect a work habit. We now look at metrics collected from the AGS, the times and scores of project submissions, from which we infer student behaviors. *Pre-submission Time* is the time students spend before submitting their first solution. We look at both the wall-clock time (See Fig. 8) and active time (See Fig. 9). Since we do not have data that reflects when they actually start coding, we use this as

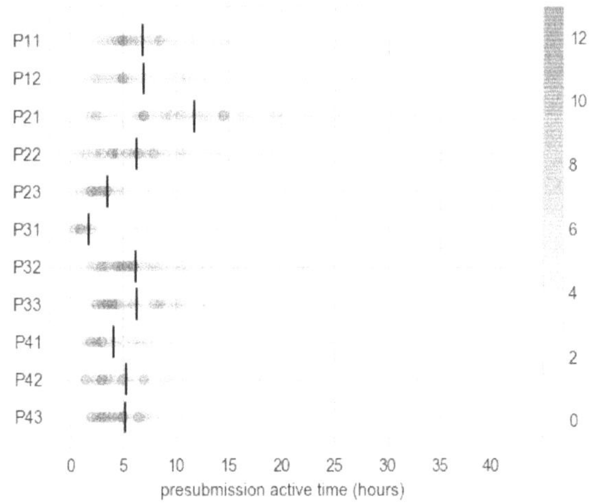

Figure 9: *The active time a student spends working on the project before their first submission.*

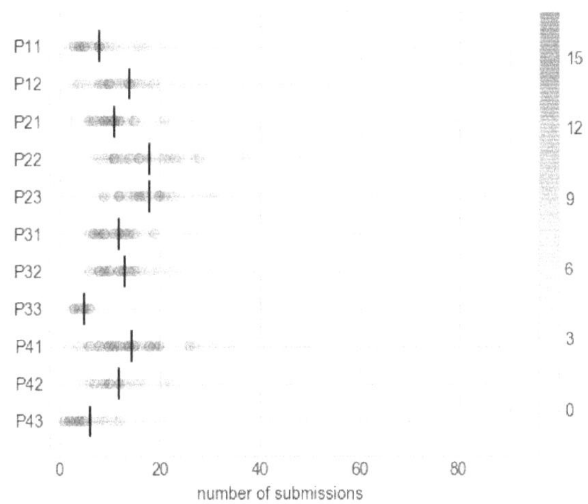

Figure 10: *Number of submissions made per student per project.*

a proxy for how much time (and thought) the students are giving to the project before they dive into coding. Surprisingly, there is a strong and significant negative correlation between how much time is spent before they make their first submissions ($r = -0.385^{***}$ for wall-clock time and $r = -0.279^{***}$ for active time). Possibly this metric is not a proxy for thinking time, but a proxy for procrastination; possibly supported by the fact that wall-clock time is more negatively correlated with their final performance than active time.

Students almost always need to make more than one submission to reach their final grade. The time between submissions and the change in scores of these submissions could be proxies for how the students approach development and debugging. Are they thinking hard between each edit-compile-run (ECR) cycle? Are they practicing test-driven development? Or, are they using the AGS as a debugging tool? Except for the total number of submissions, for which we find a moderately significant positive correlation ($r = 0.221^{**}$), none of these behaviors have any significant relationship to final performance. The strong correlation between the number of submissions and final performance is a perfect example of how hard it is to untangle performance and learning. One possible interpretation of students who submit often is that they are using

Metric	Absolute	Relative (By Rank)
Starting Early	0.004	0.290***
Finishing Early	0.514***	0.235**
Write-up Completion	0.009	0.047
Wall-Clock Time	0.162*	0.222**
Short Breaks	0.188*	0.252**
Work Periods	0.216**	0.077
Total Active Time	0.235**	0.374***
Pre-submission Activity Time	0.011	−0.005
Pre-submission Wall-clock Time	−0.161*	0.227**
Number of Submissions	0.454***	0.337***
Number of Submissions/Task	0.249**	0.337***
ECR Cycle Time	−0.048	−0.012
Submission Grade Delta	0.015	0.093
Cloud Time	0.292**	0.332***
Cost	0.480***	0.390***

Significance levels: * $p < .05$; ** $p < .01$; *** $p < .001$

Table 3: *Correlation between the consistency of each metric (as described in Table 1) over all projects and final performance.*

the AGS as a debugging tool—something that is probably hindering their learning, but is an effective way to get a good grade. In the future, we hope to design a submission mechanism that will allow us to determine if this is true and encourage students to engage more deeply in the debugging of their code.

The last two metrics we analyze are specific to the cloud computing course from which we collected this data. Each project requires that the students use cloud resources and that they do so with a fixed dollar budget. We expect that the total amount of time that they have resources spun up (the row labeled *Cloud Time*) to reflect the students' intentionality; less time being related to more intentionality. Likewise, since they have a budget requirement (labeled *Cost* in Table 2), the less they spend to complete the project the more likely they are to have exhibited intentionality in their work habits. Notice how both of these metrics have a correlation of close to zero and furthermore are insignificant.

Overall we find that the amount of time they spend (on the clock or actively working) and how early they finish to be the only significant metrics with respect to their final performance. (This remains true on a per-project basis as well, though we don't present the data here for lack of space.) At first glance this is surprising, but on reflection, we think this is reasonable—no one work habit or work style is best for everyone, so no one work habit is likely to be significantly correlated with good performance.

3.2 Consistent Work Habits

In pursuit of our goal of understanding how to help students improve their learning and overall performance we hoped to discover some underlying "truths," i.e., habits that promote success. The data, however, suggests that there is no one size fits all approach. This begs the question: are there any habits that are useful for individual students? To explore this we looked to see if students who consistently applied the same behaviors over the course of the semester performed well. We used two different consistency measures. We measured absolute consistency following [15] as the negative of the coefficient of variation (CoV) over the metric (to compare on the same scale) over the course of the semester, i.e., the ratio of the negative of the standard deviation σ to the mean μ[3]. This is in column two of Table 3. We also look at the relative consistency, defined as the standard deviation of the percentile rank for each metric of each student among the entire class. See the last column of Table 3. We developed the relative consistency measure because it is invariant under linear transformations and thus more robust than the absolute CoV measure. For example, depending on whether we use "x hours before the deadline" or "$7 \times 24 - x$ hours into the project" as the finish time will dramatically change the CoV metric from σ/μ to $\sigma/(7 \times 24 - \mu)$, but leaves relative consistency unchanged.

By looking at Table 3 we can immediately see that students who perform consistently during the semester do better than those who do not. The CoV measure has seven highly significant and positive correlations and the relative measure has 10 positive and significant correlations. In other words, students who have found a habit that works for them and stick to it do well. This does not mean that the student was consistently using the "best" method, but rather that they were using a method that worked for them. So, students who consistently spent almost the entire budget along with students who were consistently parsimonious both performed well.

The three most important metrics, in terms of consistent behavior, are being consistent about finishing at the same time each week, using the same method of development (as measured by consistency of submission count), and about spending the same proportion of their budget. The only metrics with negative correlations (which would suggest that being consistent is harmful) are not significant.

Variables	adjusted R^2
Direct metrics (from Table 2)	0.260
Absolute Consistency (column 2 of Table 3)	0.459
Relative Consistency (column 3 of Table 3)	0.310
Absolute + Relative Consistency	0.483

Table 4: *Adjusted R^2 of different predictors created with LASSO using 5-fold cross validation.*

3.3 Predicting Performance

The information presented sheds light on student behavior and begins to explain how it influences their final performance. To test out whether this is useful in predicting importance we develop a prediction model using LASSO to perform model selection with k-fold cross validation ($k = 5$)[4] to determine the best-fit model. Table 4 shows the different predictors and their adjusted R^2. We see that the consistency measures produce a better predictor than the direct measures. The best predictor is produced when we use both the absolute and relative measures together, yielding a predictor which explains more than 40% of the variance in our data.

4 RELATED WORK

Several studies investigate how student behavior, in particular time spent, is related to their final performance. Some studies [2, 11, 20] report, as one would intuitively expect, a positive correlation between time spent and final performance. Yet others [16, 18, 21], suggest that effort is a weak predictor of student performance. Finally, [10], finds that the relationship between effort and performance is complicated and depends on the course considered.

Few studies consider the longitudinal aspect of individual students and the issue of dynamic change in student behavior remains under-explored. Some studies [1, 19] found that the most visited part of the course website viewed by all students can change over time, and gradual transitions from one part to another can be observed. From the perspective of individual students, Kinnebrew et al. [7] focused on the delta of certain behavior patterns over time. Other studies investigated the stability of students' learning profile for those enrolled twice in the same course [5, 9]. All these findings, however, have not related temporal evolution to student performance. Nevertheless, some studies [14] take performance into account, and suggest increased student activity may lead to better performance.

Unfortunately, there is no standard definition of "consistency." Studies in face-to-face course settings [17] suggest that consistent attendance leads to better performance. Employing a quantitative approach, Patron and Lopez [15] defined behavior consistency as the coefficient of variation of the amount of time spent on the course each day, and suggested that consistency is more predictive of the final performance than the effort students put into the course. Alternatively, Mojarad et al. [13], proposed consistency to be the average time between two actions, and showed students with higher consistency (in their sense) and effort tend to have better performance. It has also been pointed out that inconsistency may be due to students' procrastination or laziness [22]. This is partly verified by the negative correlation between the level of procrastination and performance for online students as reported in [3, 6, 12].

5 CONCLUSIONS

This study investigates whether student behavior or the temporal consistency of behavior can predict performance in a project-based, online, upper-level course on cloud computing. Using direct and synthetic metrics we find that few behaviors are highly correlated to student performance, but that there is a strong and significant correlation between temporally consistent behaviors over the course of the semester and final performance. This strongly suggests that when analyzing learning data or designing interventions, personal habits and behaviors must be taken into account. Using our findings we create a good predictor (adjusted $R^2 = .48$) of final performance based on two measures of student consistency across 15 metrics.

We hope to expand our study by increasing the granularity for certain metrics, e.g., the pLMS heartbeat, and incorporating other data sources, e.g., when and what questions students ask. With the improved data we hope to identify behavior inconsistency earlier in the semester and trigger possible interventions. Furthermore, we plan to include an assessment of pre- and post-project skills so we can more directly tie our study to actual learning.

ACKNOWLEDGMENTS

This work is supported in part by an AWS Educate grant, Microsoft Azure Educator Grant Award and a Google Cloud Platform grant.

[3]We flip the sign on CoV so our measure is more intuitive, i.e., more positive numbers indicate more consistency

[4]We partition the dataset into five equal-sized sub-samples and use one sample for validation and the rest for training. We perform LASSO five times, using a different sub-sample for validation each time. The five results are then averaged to evaluate the model and choose the best regularization parameter.

REFERENCES

[1] Hercy NH Cheng, Zhi Liu, Jianwen Sun, Sanya Liu, and Zongkai Yang. 2017. Unfolding online learning behavioral patterns and their temporal changes of college students in SPOCs. *Interactive Learning Environments* 25, 2 (2017), 176–188.

[2] Damian S Damianov, Lori Kupczynski, Pablo Calafiore, Ekaterina P Damianova, Gökçe Soydemir, and Edgar Gonzalez. 2009. Time spent online and student performance in online business courses: A multinomial logit analysis. *Journal of Economics and Finance Education* 8, 2 (2009), 11–22.

[3] Greg C Elvers, Donald J Polzella, and Ken Graetz. 2003. Procrastination in online courses: Performance and attitudinal differences. *Teaching of Psychology* 30, 2 (2003), 159–162.

[4] Richard M Felder, Linda K Silverman, et al. 1988. Learning and teaching styles in engineering education. *Engineering education* 78, 7 (1988), 674–681.

[5] Rebecca Ferguson and Doug Clow. 2015. Consistent Commitment: Patterns of Engagement across Time in Massive Open Online Courses (MOOCs). *Journal of Learning Analytics* 2, 3 (2015), 55–80.

[6] Kyung Ryung Kim and Eun Hee Seo. 2015. The relationship between procrastination and academic performance: A meta-analysis. *Personality and Individual Differences* 82 (2015), 26–33.

[7] John S Kinnebrew, James R Segedy, and Gautam Biswas. 2014. Analyzing the temporal evolution of studentsâĂŹ behaviors in open-ended learning environments. *Metacognition and learning* 9, 2 (2014), 187–215.

[8] Alice Y Kolb and David A Kolb. 2005. Learning styles and learning spaces: Enhancing experiential learning in higher education. *Academy of management learning & education* 4, 2 (2005), 193–212.

[9] Vitomir Kovanović, Srećko Joksimović, Dragan Gašević, James Owers, Anne-Marie Scott, and Amy Woodgate. 2016. Profiling MOOC course returners: how does student behavior change between two course enrollments?. In *Proceedings of the Third (2016) ACM Conference on Learning@ Scale*. ACM, New York, NY, USA, 269–272.

[10] Chris Masui, Jan Broeckmans, Sarah Doumen, Anne Groenen, and Geert Molenberghs. 2014. Do diligent students perform better? Complex relations between student and course characteristics, study time, and academic performance in higher education. *Studies in Higher Education* 39, 4 (2014), 621–643.

[11] James W Michaels and Terance D Miethe. 1989. Academic effort and college grades. *Social Forces* 68, 1 (1989), 309–319.

[12] Nicolas Michinov, Sophie Brunot, Olivier Le Bohec, Jacques Juhel, and Marine Delaval. 2011. Procrastination, participation, and performance in online learning environments. *Computers & Education* 56, 1 (2011), 243–252.

[13] Shirin Mojarad, Alfred Essa, Shahin Mojarad, and Ryan S Baker. 2018. Data-driven learner profiling based on clustering student behaviors: learning consistency, pace and effort. In *International Conference on Intelligent Tutoring Systems*. Springer, New York, NY, USA, 130–139.

[14] Jihyun Park, Kameryn Denaro, Fernando Rodriguez, Padhraic Smyth, and Mark Warschauer. 2017. Detecting changes in student behavior from clickstream data. In *Proceedings of the Seventh International Learning Analytics & Knowledge Conference*. ACM, New York, NY, USA, 21–30.

[15] Hilde Patron and Salvador Lopez. 2011. Student effort, consistency, and online performance. *Journal of Educators Online* 8, 2 (2011), n2.

[16] E Ashby Plant, K Anders Ericsson, Len Hill, and Kia Asberg. 2005. Why study time does not predict grade point average across college students: Implications of deliberate practice for academic performance. *Contemporary Educational Psychology* 30, 1 (2005), 96–116.

[17] David Romer. 1993. Do students go to class? Should they? *Journal of Economic Perspectives* 7, 3 (1993), 167–174.

[18] Howard Schuman, Edward Walsh, Camille Olson, and Barbara Etheridge. 1985. Effort and reward: The assumption that college grades are affected by quantity of study. *Social Forces* 63, 4 (1985), 945–966.

[19] Daniel T Seaton, Yoav Bergner, Isaac Chuang, Piotr Mitros, and David E Pritchard. 2014. Who does what in a massive open online course? *Commun. ACM* 57, 4 (2014), 58–65.

[20] Kuang-Cheng Tseng and Shan-Ying Chu. 2010. Traditional versus online courses, efforts, and learning performance. *The Journal of Human Resource and Adult Learning* 6, 1 (2010), 115.

[21] MM Van den Hurk, HAP Wolfhagen, DHJM Dolmans, and CPM Van der Vleuten. 1998. The relation between time spent on individual study and academic achievement in a problem-based curriculum. *Advances in Health Sciences Education* 3, 1 (1998), 43–49.

[22] Wei-Kang Wong. 2008. How much time-inconsistency is there and does it matter? Evidence on self-awareness, size, and effects. *Journal of Economic Behavior & Organization* 68, 3-4 (2008), 645–656.

Making CS Learning Visible

Case Studies on How Visibility of Student Work Supports a Community of Learners in CS Classrooms

Amber Solomon[1], Vanessa Oguamanam[1], Mark Guzdial[2], Betsy DiSalvo[1]
[1]Georgia Institute of Technology, [2]Univerity of Michigan
{asolomon30,vanogu,bdisalvo}@gatech.edu,mjguz@umich.edu

ABSTRACT

Modern learning theories emphasize the critical social aspect of learning. Computer science (CS) classrooms often have "defensive climates" that inhibit social learning and prevent the development of a community of learners. We believe that we can improve the social context of computer science learning by expanding CS learning beyond the single student in front of a display screen. Our theory is that the single student and single display inhibits collaboration and collaborative awareness of student work. In this paper, we present two case studies where we explored ways to make student work visible to peers. The first case study involved using a studio model for learning enabled by projection-based Augmented Reality (AR), and the second case study involves using a maker-oriented curriculum to make student work visible. Findings suggest the visibility of student work in CS classrooms helped support a community of learners: students collaborated, used each other as sources of inspiration, and felt more comfortable asking for help.

CCS CONCEPTS

• **Social and professional topics → Computing education.**

KEYWORDS

visibility; community of learners; defensive climates; design studio; learning environments

ACM Reference Format:
Amber Solomon[1], Vanessa Oguamanam[1], Mark Guzdial[2], Betsy DiSalvo[1]. 2019. Making CS Learning Visible: Case Studies on How Visibility of Student Work Supports a Community of Learners in CS Classrooms. In *Innovation and Technology in Computer Science Education (ITiCSE '19), July 15–17, 2019, Aberdeen, Scotland Uk.* ACM, New York, NY, USA, 7 pages. https://doi.org/10.1145/3304221.3319791

1 INTRODUCTION

Modern theories of learning emphasize that effective learning is often a social process. Individuals learn because there is social value in learning, and they are supported in learning through peers and mentors [22, 24]. Ideally, a computer science (CS) classroom would have a learning environment that supports a community of learners (CoL). Students and teachers would actively engage in learning with one another, build on each other's ideas, avoid passing judgment, and be empathetic, cooperative and supportive [22]. This supported engagement would motivate students to persist when they are challenged, and help teachers be aware of their students' progress.

However, most CS classrooms have a learning environment that is considered a defensive climate [2, 11]. Students and teachers are often judgmental and fail to show concern for other people in the classroom [11]. Students are competitive rather than cooperative with each other. We argue that the ways that CS is taught is part of what contributes to a defensive climate. In CS classrooms, the opportunities for cooperation and visibility are limited to those who can see the computer's display; this causes a focus on individual work, rather than group work [8]. In contrast, pair programming puts two students at the same display, and we see benefits in both learning and attitudes towards computing [20]. When there is a lack of visibility, students tend to be less empathetic to their peers and present themselves in ways that reinforce a social hierarchy that values hostility and unhealthy competitiveness, and reinforces stereotypes. In this work, we explore one approach to making CS learning visible — make students' work visible similar to a design studio — to support a CoL.

We were inspired by design studio environments to help create a CoL in CS classrooms. In design studios, students can see each other's work, which encourages creativity, innovation, cooperation, and helps build strong peer learning environments [8]. In this work, we wanted to know whether it is possible to create a non-defensive classroom environment by making student's work visible. We define visibility of student work as students working "in the open" so that everyone else can consistently see each other's work and see each other's entire making process. Specifically, we ask the following research questions: What effects does making student work visible have on CS classroom culture? More specifically, how does making student work visible effect the way students interact and behave with each other? We found that the CS classroom culture can be reoriented from a defensive climate to a culture that supports a CoL when students' work is made visible.

There are a number of efforts to improve CS classroom culture, including those that seek to implement aspects of studio pedagogy [13]. They have either focused on the instructors using project-based learning approaches and public critiques of studio art courses, or have been co-taught with studio arts or design courses and CS courses [5]. These approaches have had some success, but adapting the CS classroom to studio pedagogy has a number of content and infrastructure issues which makes it very difficult in many institutions [3, 6]. We sought to understand how this small change, making student work visible, might change the CS classroom culture.

While we have seen a focus on increasing diversity of students in CS classrooms [18, 19], there has been less research exploring how

ITiCSE '19, July 15–17, 2019, Aberdeen, Scotland Uk

ACM ISBN 978-1-4503-6301-3/19/07...$15.00
https://doi.org/10.1145/3304221.3319791

best to prepare the CS classrooms for this diverse group of students. Indications from our findings suggest that making student work visible may be the small change needed in the infrastructure of the CS classroom to engage them to be partners in learning rather than competitors. This suggests that by changing the infrastructure, we can create affordances to increase the diversity.

Making learning visible, or making student work visible, is not a new notion; it has been part of larger approaches to learning, such as work by Giudici et al., Making Learning Visible at Project Zero [12]. Researchers, such as Dohn [9], have discussed advantages, challenges, and tensions that are outcomes of making student work visible in online and in-person classrooms. Furthermore, pedagogical techniques to promote collaboration and that use studio pedagogy, like POGIL [16], help make students more aware of other students work. However, in our approach the emphasis is about making work visible similar to studio environments, where the work is present, and not called to attention or shared between a pair or small group. The visibility of the work becomes a passive part of the environment, not something required for students to view or comment on, in which students can chose to comment on.

In this paper we present two case studies that describe the learning environments of interventions that explored ways to make student work visible in CS classrooms and what we gain from making student work visible in CS classrooms. In the first case study, we describe using a maker-oriented learning approach in two CS classes to change the classroom culture. In the second case study, we used augmented reality to project student's work onto the walls around them. We noticed three emerging patterns across these two different case studies: students cooperatively learning, students gaining inspiration from one another, and students exhibiting help-seeking behavior.

This research makes two main contributions. First, we provide evidence that the approaches described can produce a classroom environment that is less judgmental and more supportive. Specifically, making student work visible to other students seems to be a key element that contributes to a positive environment. Second, finding ways to promote positive and constructive classroom environments is an important area to study, especially as our CS classrooms become, hopefully, more diverse. This research provides some tools for instructors to help create such environments.

2 LITERATURE REVIEW

In this section, we first discuss what creates defensive climates in CS classrooms, then describe CoL. We provide a discussion and description to rationalize why the notion of "visibility of student work" from design studios can transform the CS classroom culture from competitive and defensive to cooperative and personable.

2.1 How Defensive Climates form

Barker et al. spent over 250 hours in 10 CS courses to immerse themselves in CS classroom culture [2]. They found that CS classrooms have a unique culture that they defined as a *defensive climate*. The CS classroom is more a place to demonstrate one's acumen and expertise, and a less a place to develop expertise through collaboration. Defensive climates are a result of two categories of interactions: (1) informal student hierarchies, and (2) impersonal environments and guarded behaviors.

2.1.1 *Informal Student Hierarchies.*

CS classrooms have social hierarchies characterized as competitive and evaluative — students quickly find out if they belong and fight to gain status to move to the top of the hierarchy [2]. These hierarchies result from communication that "emphasizes superiority rather than equality" [11]. Students typically don't ask questions for clarification, but to "show-off" [11] what they know. Students who don't feel like they belong, remain silent, "avoiding notice by peers"[2].

2.1.2 *Impersonal Environments and Guarded Behaviors.*

Depersonalized environments, characterized by "neutral, as opposed to empathetic" [11] communication, cause impersonal environments and guarded behaviors. A social environment is impersonal and guarded when it is easy for someone, " to remain relatively anonymous and socially distant" [11]. Barker et al. state there is little talk amongst students, students typically sit in isolation, and students rarely discuss anything other than work with peers. The guarded and impersonal nature in CS courses unintentionally communicates rejection rather than acceptance, "and therefore support of the value of the individual" [2].

2.2 Community of Learners

A CoL is a learning environment where, "people participate in shared endeavors with others, with all playing active but often asymmetrical roles in a sociocultural activity" [22]. All members share responsibility for each other's learning and members cooperate and offer help when needed. Students involved in the classroom share experiences and inspire each other, which helps them be empathetic towards each other and treat each other as resources and collaborators rather than competitors [22].

2.3 Design Studios Make Products Visible

Although there are many aspects of studio-based pedagogy that can be beneficial for learning environments, our focus is on making student work visible. In design studios, students typically work in the open, allowing the entire making process to be visible to each student [17]. Studio walls might be covered in "pin ups," where students' drawings are pinned to the wall, to make both the artifacts and design process visible [7]. When products are on display, they can be referenced by the students for extended periods of time. By not just showing work as a "final product", students can iteratively analyze, deconstruct, and reimagine their artifacts [23].

The idea of making student work visible in CS classrooms is promising for three reasons. First, visibility of student work raises awareness of peer's work promoting cooperation and interactions [7], making students' less guarded. Second, because visibility promotes cooperation and opportunities for interactions, students share experiences and understandings [17]. Shared experiences and understandings help students have empathy. When students are empathetic, they show concern for peers and offer help, making the environment less impersonal [22]. Third, because students are making artifacts that will be seen by peers, students begin to take more responsibility and ownership of their work and feel like they can contribute to the space [10]. When they feel like they can contribute and when they take ownership, students begin to feel like they belong, challenging preconceived notions of "who belongs."

3 CASE STUDIES

We present two case studies where we evaluated different learning environments that made CS learning visible; we show ways that we made student work visible. In the first case study, we describe a maker-oriented learning approach. In the second case study, we take advantage of augmented reality technology to project student work on the surrounding walls. During data analysis, we found the same three themes emerge in both case studies that indicate a reorientation from a culture that's defensive to a culture that supports a CoL: (1) cooperative learning, (2) students gaining inspiration from each other, and (3) students proactively seeking help. We organize our findings in each case study by these emerging themes.

3.1 Case Study 1: Maker-Oriented Learning Approach

The Maker Movement, a do-it-yourself trend that relies on physical prototyping and electronic crafting, has increasingly found its way into classrooms. Between August 2015 and May 2017, we engaged in an ongoing effort to develop a maker-oriented curriculum, inspired by constructionism [21] and project-based learning [4], in courses at a university in the United States to study the impact that making activities had on students, instruction, and culture in computer science classrooms.

3.1.1 The Study. To evaluate the maker-oriented curriculum, we conducted a qualitative study that followed two upper-level CS undergraduate courses: Human-Computer Interaction (HCI) and Mobile-Ubiquitous Computing (MUC). In the HCI course, students design, implement, and evaluate user interfaces. In the MUC course, students design and implement a mobile and ubiquitous technology. Both courses typically attract third- and fourth-year students majoring in CS, industrial engineering, electrical and computer engineering, and computational media. This study lasted two academic years, or four semesters. The intervention involved 2 instructors, 4 teaching assistants (TAs), and 207 students.

3.1.2 The Maker-Oriented Curriculum. Typically, both courses are taught lecture style to roughly 60 students. Students complete group-based, open-ended projects outside of class. The projects were mostly focused on creating interfaces for screens rather than physical prototyping. Students rarely interacted with peers outside of their groups for two reasons: work was done outside of class and groups were only aware of other groups' projects when they presented their final projects to the class.

The maker-oriented curriculum shifted the classrooms from lecture-centered to student activity-centered, in-class interactions. The purpose of the curriculum was to create and implement hands-on activities, that produce visible artifacts to create unique opportunities for learning, increasing creativity and participation. The curriculum included six modules: rapid paper prototyping, 2D design and fabrication, 3D design and fabrication, wearable technology prototyping, interactive prototyping with Arduino, and deconstruction of technology. Because of the class sizes, students still had open-ended group projects, but, now, students made physical objects that have interactivity instead of software-based projects.

The in-class activities were structured so that first, the conceptual knowledge and appropriate tools were presented, then students in groups engaged in a prototyping activity. An example of a prototyping activity was the interactive lamp activity where students brainstormed, sketched, and fabricated an interactive lamp, and then use Arduinos to program the interactivity.

To ensure students in different groups were aware of students' work outside of their group, we implemented weekly critique sessions. Students critically evaluated the design of technology, communicated their design intentions and choices, and gained design inspirations and ideas from others' work. Students were given critique cards that had prompts, e.g, point out one strength of the design, to help students think critically about other students work. Because of the class sizes, instead of having one group present to the other 70 students, a member of each group would present five or so separate times to the other groups.

3.1.3 Data Collection and Analysis. At the end of each semester, we conducted hour-long semi-structured interviews with 8-15 students (a total of 44) and all the two different instructors and some TAs (a total of 4), to understand their overall experience of participating in the curriculum and their understanding for challenges that emerged from this learning environment. Semi-structured interviews were recorded and transcribed using a third-party vendor. Transcripts were analyzed using thematic analysis looking for patterns of collaboration and help-seeking behavior. One researcher independently coded a set of the data to make a codebook of emergent themes. That same researcher then used that codebook to code the remaining transcripts. Three researchers independently read through and coded the data based on the codebook. Then they compared themes and reanalyzed themes based on discussions and past literature.

3.1.4 Study Limitations. There are two main limitations of this study. First, this is not a comparative study in that we did not conduct interviews with students and faculty previous to the interventions. While faculty and TAs have experience with both approaches to teaching these courses, the maker approach and the traditional lecture-based approach with hands-on project work taking place outside of the classroom, they were only interviewed after the intervention. Second, the sample size (N=44) represents only about 20% of the students who participated in the courses.

3.1.5 Findings. The maker-oriented curriculum was designed with the goal to create a CoL, in part through the visibility afforded by the curriculum. Because students could see each other's physical artifacts, rather than working solely on the computer screen, and the maker activities were in-class, rather than outside work assigned, the students' visibility of each other's work was increased.

Cooperative Learning. We define cooperative learning as students working on their own but helping each other when necessary. Critiques proved to be difficult to implement inside of the CS Classroom because of the defensive environment, including students who dominated the conversation at the expense of their peers participating. To encourage a shift toward more balanced contributions, instructors used a scaffolding technique for critiques, handing out critique cards. Students were given three cards and asked to turn them in to the instructor with their names written on the back after they followed the directions at one of the pin up stations. The cards elicited the kinds of critique responses that we wanted. Instructors told us that an unanticipated benefit of the cards is that they disrupted the way that CS classrooms operate, and the most talkative students often saw that others still had cards in their hand and held off their comments until everyone had a chance to talk. Therefore, the visual evidence of who had a chance to participate created a more cooperative learning environment.

Critique sessions and students' physical work also created opportunities for cooperation. In one example a group was developing an interactive "shoe of types," and another group was developing an interactive backpack. As they were presenting to each other, they realized that they were largely trying to create the same type of interaction, just in a different medium. Members of both groups actually talked to each other after class to try to consolidate some of the knowledge that each of them had, and then went back to their respective groups and to try to implement those ideas into their projects.

Inspiration. Many students told us that they got ideas from the regular and informal critique sessions that inspired them to try new things or to learn new skills: "I know one team did like a toilet paper roll and they used Blender [15]... So, seeing theirs, I've gone home and read a lot more about Blender. It's almost like it kick-started I guess an interesting, different thing."

Many times conversations continued outside of the critique session. After class, instructors said it was common for members to walk up to other class members who weren't in the same group and continue those conversations: "They'll actually go on for maybe 15-20 minutes after class has ended trying to push forward on those ideas and kind of make them even better."

This inspiration from peers is a benefit in that it encourages learning new skills and sets a precedent where students understand that they can learn from students as well as teachers.

Help-Seeking Behavior. Students working on something physical made it easy for them to "lean over", see what other students were struggling with, and help them. Instructors said this could not happen in the previous versions of the courses:"No, because they could never see each other's stuff. They were all making stuff, but it was on their computers."

Making students work visible also helped students understand when they "just aren't getting it", helping them track their progress and know when to ask for help. In the Interactive Prototyping with Arduino module, students worked in small groups with a kit consisting of an Arduino microcontroller, a breadboard, resistors, LED, and various sensors. They were asked to create a circuit to make the LED blink and control the rate of blinking and then to make a circuit with three LEDs blink where they could control the rate and order of blinking. We saw students regularly looking over at other groups work and interacting with other groups. Some groups who had less experience would look around at the progress of other groups and note to each other that they were "behind" and needed to "focus." Sometimes one group member would seek help from a group that was further ahead, and sometimes when one group would see another falling behind, they would offer to help.

3.2 Case Study 2: AR Visible Classroom

In this project, we sought to provide the advantages of a studio learning experience in an introductory programming CS class by using AR to project images of students' work-in-progress on the room around them. Our goal was to enable students to see each other's work so that they could learn from others' projects, provide critiques, and share techniques.

3.2.1 The Study. We conducted a pilot study with an introductory CS course called Introduction to Media Computation (Media Comp) at a university in the United States. Media Comp is intended for first-year non-technical undergraduate majors with little experience in programming courses [14]. This course was selected for the study because the projects which students work on have visual components. Students use Python to manipulate digital images and to learn basic CS concepts. Our goal with a shared visibility version of Media Comp was to allow students to continually project their projects to the class as soon as any code that had a visual output ran.

The Media Comp course is taught lecture style to roughly 100 students. There is a complimentary recitation, or workshop, where students can interact with other students and Teaching Assistants (TAs) and practice programming. During the recitation, the TAs briefly lecture on a topic, then have students work on a short, ten minute, in-class assignment about that topic. Students work from their laptops. After the allotted time, the TAs go over the solution to the assignment. For example, the TA might first introduce if-statements, then have the students work on an assignment like the following: "Use an if-statement to change the hue of an image. If the pixel is red add 255 or if the pixel is blue subtract 255." TAs do not instruct students to work together, but students are free to work with other students.

Recitations meet weekly and last for 80 minutes. Students are not required to attend, and work done in recitations is not graded. The study looked at two recitation sections, one taught in a typical manner and one using AR.

3.2.2 The typical recitation. The typical recitation had 50 students and two TAs who were undergraduate students who previously had taken the class. This particular class met in a lecture hall where students worked on tables that were bolted to the floor in an arc on tiered platforms with movable chairs. The TAs were stationed in front of the class and used the projector and computer already in the room.

3.2.3 The AR Visibility Classroom. The AR visibility classroom had 12 students, one instructor that was a full professor, and an undergrad TA who had taken the class previously. Students in the AR Visibility Class signed up for the class not knowing it was different. We then sent those students an email warning them what the section would be like and gave students the option to switch out. Some students did switch courses; however, it is unclear if it was due to the AR Visibility, or general schedule shuffling that occurs at the beginning of the semester. Students received no extra credit for being in the course. Tables in this course were arranged to form an open circle. Due to the constraints of the technology, the instructor was placed in one corner of the room where some students had to physically turn around in order to see the instructor.

The AR Technology. The AR technology allowed us to make visible work that typically can only be seen by the person directly in front of a computer. AR allowed us to use one projector to project several students' digital pin ups. Each student had their own pin up, which included their image output from generated code, and their pseudonym to protect their anonymity in the study. To allow pin ups, we modified and applied the RoomAlive software to map the room structure and project students' work on the walls [1].

3.2.4 Data Collection and Analysis. The goal of our data collection was to understand how students interacted in both classes. Observations and interviews were conducted. The lead author conducted observations in six sessions, three typical recitations and three AR recitations. Observation data consisted of notes taken using a two-column approach, with observations in one column and corresponding reflections added after the session. Informal observations were also reported by the full professor who acted as an instructor in the course.

We conducted semi-structured interviews with students in both recitation sections. Six students from the AR recitation (five females and one male) and five students (all females) from the typical recitation were interviewed. Students volunteered to participate; no compensation was given for participating. Students were asked about collaboration in the classroom, techniques for seeking help during class, and interactions in the classroom. Semi-structured interviews were recorded and transcribed by hand. We analyzed transcripts using thematic analysis looking for patterns of collaboration and help-seeking behavior. One researcher independently coded a set of the data to make a codebook of emergent themes.

Study Limitations. This study does not provide a rigorous comparison between the two recitations. Rather, we offer them as a contrast. Much was in common between the two sections, e.g., same curriculum and same programming environment and language. We saw a different behavior in the classroom with AR visibility, which was in marked contrast to both the traditional recitation and to what we know about the defensive climate in CS classrooms.

Another limitation comes from the course selected to study. Media Comp is typically more than 40% female, with females often succeeding at a higher rate than males [14]. Our interview data was biased in favor of females, and the sex makeup of both recitations was primarily female. In future work, there needs to be a better distribution of sexes in the data. Moreover, as we mentioned, the work done in recitations for Media Comp is not graded and we chose not to project students' code for privacy and plagiarism considerations. Both of these choices could or could not have an effect on our findings. We need further investigation in different CS courses, e.g. algorithms, where output is not visual and where work is graded.

3.2.5 Findings. Making student work visible had an effect on the CS classroom culture, which helped support a CoL. We see saw evidence of a defensive climate in the typical recitation, with students "showing-off" or working in isolation. We changed the names of participants to protect their identities.

Cooperative Learning. In the typical recitation, students rarely worked with each other for two reasons. First, students rarely cooperated because visibility of student work was limited to who could see each other's computer screen, so there were few opportunities for cooperation. In an interview, Geri from the typical recitation said the following when asked if she worked with other students: "Not really unless I was sitting directly next to them... I wouldn't generally look at other people's screens." Second, students rarely cooperated because they typically isolated themselves, choosing not to work with other students. Even when TAs would suggest students to "pair off", the majority of the class still chose to work by themselves.

Unlike the typical CS recitation, in the AR visibility classroom cooperation was fluid and part of the culture. During interviews, every student said they felt comfortable talking with their peers in the class, and we observed students noticing and commenting on their peers' work during every observation session. Kelley, from the AR classroom, said the following about cooperation in the classroom: "If you got it and someone around you didn't, it would be pretty easy for them to notice and be like, hey, how did you do this?" In one instance while students were working on an in-class example, two students were struggling with their code and noticed another student's pin up was correct. They were never observed to have spoken to that student previously, but after seeing their successful pin up they asked that student for help on the example.

Inspiration. Our observations in the AR visibility classroom indicated that students wanted to create interesting visuals and were motivated by their classmates to "do something interesting." Claire said the following: "It was cool to look at what other people were doing. I'd be like, oh how'd they do that? Let me try this. And usually I wouldn't get what they did, but I would get something else that I like."

Students would frequently engage in reflective dialogue with their peers and TAs about how they accomplished an effect. Seeing another student get an interesting effect on their work made some students want to attempt a similar effect. The following exchange was typical in the AR recitation but rarely possible in typical CS classrooms: Jessie pointed to another student's pin up and asked the following question: "So, your image came out green because you divided the pixels by 5... so, if I want to get a red image, I need to multiply the pixels. Right?"

Help-Seeking Behavior. Interviews with the students in the typical recitation were more like what we read in the literature on defensive climate. Students didn't tell us that they were inspired by other students' work in the typical recitation, and students "showed off" by asking questions about topics that were never discussed. Every interview with students from the typical recitation suggested they preferred to figure out issues by themselves: "Uhmmm but yeah for the most part I just tried to figure out myself." Students did not feel comfortable asking questions to or in front of their peers. Sometimes, students would ask a TA for help after recitation ended, using the TAs as a resource outside of the community setting.

The AR classroom promoted student agency shown by students' willingness to receive help when dealing with issues. Sam said the following about the pin ups: "It was easier to tell when you didn't get something, like if you were the only one who your code wasn't showing up like everyone else's. That was helpful, because, then, you know that you're doing something wrong." The pin ups also forced students to get help. Students frequently asked other students for help if they noticed their pin displayed the wrong image: "... but like if I was the only one that didn't have it then I felt like more like self-conscious... but it helps force you to get help." Students were also more willing to help one another: "...so you could see who had understood... people who are struggling you can help them."

4 DISCUSSION

Typical CS classrooms use teaching practices that limit students' opportunities to cooperate and share perspectives. We argue that this contributes to a defensive climate. The narrow focus on one's own work encourages the "superiority rather than equality" perspective. In contrast, when we made student work visible, we saw evidence of students cooperating, gaining inspiration and new perspectives, and seeking help. These are characteristics of a CoL.

Visibility fostered awareness of student work, which brought about chances for reflection, anchors for further discussion, understanding of how work should progress, and opportunities to motivate or be motivated. Students physically seeing each other's work (e.g. through pin ups and working with physical computing objects) provided them something tangible to reflect on, which helped students understand what they were and were not understanding. For example, pin ups served as a formative assessment for each student. The visibility of product and transparency around process gave them the opportunity and permission to seek help. By seeking help, the students may be developing a greater sense of agency, i.e., giving students more control in their own learning.

Awareness of other students' work created new opportunities for cooperation and learning [5]. The seen objects, e.g. pin ups and physical computing objects in a room, served as anchors to center discussions and encouraged cooperation. These unique perspectives and experiences combined to create more diverse plans which in turn led to better final products.

The visuals of progress (e.g. critique cards and pin ups) made process transparent, and made all students aware of how well other students were progressing. The awareness is a direct counter to the defensive climate, because everyone could see what the average pace was. The awareness of progress enabled students to facilitate their peers' learning, (e.g. stepping back when others still had critique cards or offering help when the products appearing on the classroom walls showed a student lagging). We argue that this awareness made these students into a CoL.

Students learned from each other by either motivating or being motivated by one another in ways not possible in a typical CS classroom. Our learning interventions moved away personal screens, allowing people to see everyone's work. Students could see process and product that they only imagined before, and many students imagined themselves as being far behind [19]. Being able to transparently see what was happening and what progress was possible broadened the students' perspective on problem solving in more concrete ways than a single instructor could provide. Seeing product and process gave students the opportunity to expand on their work and to try new techniques, which led to producing more complex and interesting work.

We were concerned that making student work visible could have an adverse effect by reinforcing a defensive climate. Students might feel anxious having to display their work since it invites critiques. However, we did not observe this in the two classroom settings. Instead, we found that students became empathetic towards each other and took ownership of their learning, instead of maintaining competitive and evaluative behavior.

Students become empathetic when they can imagine themselves in the situation of another, usually from some shared experience. In interviews students said they were initially uncomfortable having their work on display out of fear of judgment for making a mistake. Being wrong is typically (and unjustly) stigmatized as unacceptable and often associated with shame and embarrassment. However, this fear went away. The visibility of product and transparency of process gave students the chance to compare their work to others and realize that they either (1) knew more than they thought or (2) it helped them identify what they did not understand. Students showed responsibility for their peers' learning. They demonstrated their concern for peers by their willingness to seek out and help students who needed it.

Because students' work was showcased for those around them, students became invested in their work in a way different from when the work is only visible to themselves. They felt some sense of ownership. As a result, they developed their own questions and began inquiries to answer those questions. They used their peers as resources, and knew from the visibility of the class who could best answer those questions. When students take ownership of their work, a community forms, where they believe they "belong" and are active participants.

We do not propose that our findings from our qualitative studies are necessarily true for other CS courses. The selected CS courses for study were suited for the interventions. We recognize that our research focused on a small number of students in rarefied contexts, and the danger of shame rather than empowerment is still real. Our work also focused on student-student interactions rather than capturing instruction-student interactions. However, we offer new perspectives on ways to encourage supportive and cooperative learning environments in CS classrooms.

5 CONCLUSION

We argued that the logistics and infrastructure of many CS classrooms are contributors to a defensive computing culture and are not productive for learning. We presented case studies that demonstrate how making CS learning visible can disrupt the defensive computing culture by making the products visible and making the process transparent. When we make CS learning visible, the classroom culture change and students take more control of their learning. While the AR Visibility Classroom (and similar approaches) may be effective, the high cost and infrastructure may make it difficult to implement. In contrast, the use of maker or other physical activities and scaffolding critiques are approaches that all instructors can implement with little overhead. The critical over-arching point is that these case studies suggest that a focus on visibility in the CS classroom is promising. Perhaps we do not need complex social interventions to change the culture of the CS classroom, but instead we need to change the physical and logistical structure of the CS classroom. By making student learning and work visible, students can see each other and themselves as part of a learning community.

REFERENCES

[1] [n. d.]. anonymous for review.

[2] Lecia Jane Barker, Kathy Garvin-Doxas, and Michele Jackson. 2002. Defensive climate in the computer science classroom. *ACM SIGCSE Bulletin* 34, 1 (2002), 43–47.

[3] Lecia J Barker, Kathy Garvin-Doxas, and Eric Roberts. 2005. What can computer science learn from a fine arts approach to teaching?. In *ACM SIGCSE Bulletin*, Vol. 37. ACM, 421–425.

[4] Brigid JS Barron, Daniel L Schwartz, Nancy J Vye, Allison Moore, Anthony Petrosino, Linda Zech, and John D Bransford. 1998. Doing with understanding: Lessons from research on problem-and project-based learning. *Journal of the learning sciences* 7, 3-4 (1998), 271–311.

[5] Erik Brunvand and Paul Stout. 2011. Kinetic art and embedded systems: a natural collaboration. In *Proceedings of the 42nd ACM technical symposium on Computer science education*. ACM, 323–328.

[6] Adam S Carter and Christopher D Hundhausen. 2011. A review of studio-based learning in computer science. *Journal of Computing Sciences in Colleges* 27, 1 (2011), 105–111.

[7] Katherine Cennamo and Carol Brandt. 2012. The âĂIJright kind of tellingâĂİ: Knowledge building in the academic design studio. *Educational Technology Research and Development* 60, 5 (2012), 839–858.

[8] Katherine Cennamo, Sarah A Douglas, Mitzi Vernon, Carol Brandt, Brigitte Scott, Yolanda Reimer, and Margarita McGrath. 2011. Promoting creativity in the computer science design studio. In *Proceedings of the 42nd ACM technical symposium on Computer science education*. ACM, 649–654.

[9] Nina Bonderup Dohn. 2009. Web 2.0: Inherent tensions and evident challenges for education. *International journal of computer-supported collaborative learning* 4, 3 (2009), 343–363.

[10] Thomas A Dutton. 1987. Design and studio pedagogy. *Journal of architectural education* 41, 1 (1987), 16–25.

[11] Kathy Garvin-Doxas and Lecia J Barker. 2004. Communication in computer science classrooms: understanding defensive climates as a means of creating supportive behaviors. *Journal on Educational Resources in Computing (JERIC)* 4, 1 (2004), 2.

[12] Claudia Giudici, Carla Rinaldi, and Mara Krechevsky. 2001. *Making learning visible: Children as individual and group learners.* Project Zero, Harvard Graduate School of Education Cambridge, MA.

[13] Saul Greenberg. 2009. Embedding a design studio course in a conventional computer science program. In *Creativity and HCI: From experience to design in education*. Springer, 23–41.

[14] Mark Guzdial. 2003. A media computation course for non-majors. In *ACM SIGCSE Bulletin*, Vol. 35. ACM, 104–108.

[15] Roland Hess. 2007. *The essential Blender: guide to 3D creation with the open source suite Blender.* No Starch Press.

[16] Helen H Hu and Tricia D Shepherd. 2013. Using POGIL to help students learn to program. *ACM Transactions on Computing Education (TOCE)* 13, 3 (2013), 13.

[17] Sarah Kuhn. 2001. Learning from the architecture studio: Implications for project-based pedagogy. *International Journal of Engineering Education* 17, 4/5 (2001), 349–352.

[18] Jane Margolis. 2010. *Stuck in the shallow end: Education, race, and computing.* MIT Press.

[19] Jane Margolis and Allan Fisher. 2003. *Unlocking the clubhouse: Women in computing.* MIT press.

[20] Charlie McDowell, Linda Werner, Heather Bullock, and Julian Fernald. 2002. The effects of pair-programming on performance in an introductory programming course. *ACM SIGCSE Bulletin* 34, 1 (2002), 38–42.

[21] Seymour Papert and Idit Harel. 1991. Situating constructionism. *Constructionism* 36, 2 (1991), 1–11.

[22] Barbara Rogoff. 1994. Developing understanding of the idea of communities of learners. *Mind, culture, and activity* 1, 4 (1994), 209–229.

[23] Dhaval Vyas, Gerrit van der Veer, and Anton Nijholt. 2013. Creative practices in the design studio culture: collaboration and communication. *Cognition, Technology & Work* 15, 4 (2013), 415–443.

[24] Etienne Wenger. 2000. Communities of practice and social learning systems. *Organization* 7, 2 (2000), 225–246.

Perspectives on the Student Transition into CS1

Angela A. Siegel †
Faculty of Computer Science
Dalhousie University
Halifax, NS, Canada
siegel@dal.ca

Mark Zarb
School of Computing Science and Digital Media
Robert Gordon University
Aberdeen, UK
m.zarb@rgu.ac.uk

Richard Glassey
KTH Royal Institute of - Technology
Stockholm, Sweden
glassey@kth.se

Janet Hughes
School of Computing and Communications
The Open University
Edinburgh, UK
janet.hughes@open.ac.uk

ABSTRACT

As students transition into higher education, their experience can be quite new and foreign to them. This experience, while an individual one, consists of many concerns that are shared amongst these transitioning students. Partly as a result of these concerns, retention rates of first year Computer Science students suffer. Members of this panel have been involved in multi-year studies across Scotland [2, 5] as well as an international study [3] looking at the student experience as they transition into undergraduate Computer Science.

This panel hopes to discuss the transition into CS1 and implications for Computer Science retention rates from varied international perspectives as well as through the lens of online learning. It further hopes to discuss new ways that we might be able to better support first year CS student retention in light of collected transition data, as well as the current state of any implemented recommendations in previous work (you may want to rephrase this).

CCS CONCEPTS: • Applied computing → Education • Social and professional topics → CS1.

KEYWORDS: Concerns; Transition; CS1; Applicants; Retention; Higher Education

ACM Reference format:

Angela A. Siegel, Mark Zarb, Richard Glassey and Janet Hughes. 2019. Perspectives on the Student Transition into CS1. In *Proceedings of 24th Annual ACM Conference on Innovation and Technology in Computer Science Education (ITiCSE'19), July 15-17, 2019, Aberdeen, Scotland, UK.* ACM, NY, NY, USA, 2 pages. https://doi.org/10.1145/3304221.3325540

†Moderator

ACM ISBN 978-1-4503-6301-3/19/07.
https://doi.org/10.1145/3304221.3325540

1 SUMMARY

As students transition into higher education computer science, their experience can be quite new to them (especially for students who are first in their family to attend higher education), with some viewing the prospect of higher education as a foreign entity [1]. This experience, while an individual one, consists of many concerns that are shared amongst these transitioning CS1 (first year Computer Science) students irrespective of background, culture or institution. Partly as a result of these concerns, retention rates of first year Computer Science students suffer.

Members of this panel have been involved in multi-year studies across Scotland [2, 5] as well as an international study [3] looking at the student experience and self-reported concern as they transition into undergraduate Computer Science. Following three years of data collection across Scotland, where over 700 prospective CS1 students were surveyed [2, 5], an international investigation was launched via a Working Group at ITiCSE 2018. While differences exist, the collected data revealed several consistencies between relative areas of concern across nations, gender and delivery methods [3].

The internationally-collected data showed that topics such as concern regarding failing, and those such as time management, workload expectation, being good at the course and choosing the right degree were amongst the top concerns [3]. These were followed by concerns regarding housing costs, securing good employment, and the availability of academic staff [3].

The panel will look at how these concerns are addressed within the Computer Science departments across the three countries represented within the panel as well as within the distance learning environment. Traditionally, higher education institutions put in an effort to target concerns such as applying for scholarships, homesickness, finding roommates and finding part-time jobs through dedicated careers services. However, year after year, those topics were all in the bottom half of the rankings in the survey conducted [3].

Analysis of the gathered data from the ITiCSE Working Group will help us understand which concerns appear to be the most pressing when students are transitioning into CS1. The panel will hope to bring together international educators to discuss how to best support and retain our first year Computer Science undergraduates.

In this panel, each member will discuss how the student transition experience is supported within their own university, how the collected data has shaped the ways in which they view student support for CS1 students differently and suggest ways in which we might rethink student support moving forward. The goal of this panel will be to help identify ways in which we can help tackle these concerns and allow us to improve and enhance the student experience through better understanding of the transition experience of CS1 students.

2 PANEL STRUCTURE

The moderator will first give a brief background to the topic, highlighting the key research into student transition into CS1. Each panelist will then be given 10 minutes to present their respective positions as well as an overview of data collected from their home institution, including those from three countries (Canada, the United Kingdom and Sweden) as well as from the perspective of online learning. Following the presentation, the moderator will facilitate the audience discussion. We anticipate questions about how student retention efforts could be improved in light of collected data and how this and ongoing research might redirect our focus when it comes to better supporting our CS1 students.

3 PANELISTS

The panel is comprised of the following four members:

3.1 Angela Siegel (Moderator)

As the CS Undergraduate Chair in a large Canadian University, I help support roughly 400 incoming undergraduate CS1 students each semester. My primary focus is on instructional support and development within the Faculty of Computer Science at Dalhousie University. I am currently in the process of supporting a complete review of all first-year offerings within our Computer Science and Applied Computer Science programs. My interest in successful transitions has led me to consider how we can better incorporate student concerns into our curriculum and teaching practice. Work in this area includes helping set student expectations early in their undergraduate career through the use of autograding softwares and the utilization of smaller problems of the day to emphasize time management and the importance of practicing ones craft.

Mark Zarb and I were awarded a Higher Education Academy grant in 2015 to explore transitions to higher education CS within Scotland. After this initial project, we surveyed and spoke to over 700 applicants about their concerns, resulting in the organization of a national workshop [5], a number of invited talks at national conferences and international publications [2, 3]. After these initial investigations of student transitions in Scotland, I have enjoyed continuing this work within Nova Scotia, Canada.

3.2 Mark Zarb

I am a Senior Lecturer and Course Leader within the School of Computing Science and Digital Media at the Robert Gordon University (RGU) in Aberdeen, Scotland. My main research area is in computing education, looking at ways to improve the student experience throughout their time in higher education, from application to graduation. In addition to the work that Siegel and I have completed together, I led a Working Group at ITiCSE 2018, bringing together an international team of educators to consider student transition concerns from this international perspective with two of the other panelists [3].

3.3 Richard Glassey

I am a lecturer at KTH Royal Institute of Technology in Stockholm, Sweden. My main responsibility is to welcome and support the first year cohort to their exciting journey into Computer Science. Despite an intake of 200 students, I endeavour to make the first year experience feel cosy, connected and involved. Despite all our differences, each student at KTH should feel equal, respected and empowered to be the best they can in their education. My research focus aims at moving computer science education forward by lifting the standards of what we can achieve with our first year experience. Also, I have investigated the concerns of students in their transition to first year in Swedish context, and how this compares with other countries [3].

3.4 Janet Hughes

As a Staff Tutor with the Open University based out of Edinburgh in the United Kingdom, I am concerned about the experience of part-time learners studying in a supported distance learning environment. Student concerns in this realm can differ slightly from those in the classroom, particularly for those studying whilst working full-time and for different groups of non-traditional learners. Not only do we need to support similar needs of students as in a traditional classroom education, but we must also consider additional factors, such as self-efficacy and time management, that can be particularly important in a distance learning environment.

REFERENCES

[1] P. Askham. (2008) Context and identity: exploring adult learners' experiences of higher education. *Journal of Further and Higher Education.*

[2] A.A. Siegel and M. Zarb. (2016) Student concerns regarding transition into higher education CS. *Annual Conference on Innovation and Technology in Computer Science Education, ITiCSE* (Arequipa, Peru, 2016).

[3] M. Zarb, B. Alshaigy, D. Bouvier, R. Glassey, J. Hughes, and C. Riedesel. (2018) An International Investigation into Student Concerns regarding Transition into Higher Education. In *Proceedings of 23rd Annual ACM Conference on Innovation and Technology in Computer Science Education* (ITiCSE'18). ACM, New York, NY, USA, 20 pages. https://doi.org/10.1145/3197091.3205842

[4] M. Zarb, and A.A. Siegel. (2016) SICSA Education Workshop http://www.sicsa.ac.uk/events/sicsa-education-workshop-student- transitions-within-computing/

[5] M. Zarb and A.A. Siegel. (2018) An Analysis of Pupil Concerns regarding Transition into Higher Education. In *Higher Education for All*, (HEFA 2017, Maceió, Brazil, March 20–24, 2017). A. I. Cristea et al. (Eds.), CCIS 832, Springer, 3–16. https://doi.org/10.1007/978-3-319-97934-2

How Prior Programming Experience Affects Students' Pair Programming Experiences and Outcomes

Nicholas A. Bowman
nick-bowman@uiowa.edu
Educational Policy & Leadership Studies
The University of Iowa
Iowa City, Iowa

Lindsay Jarratt
lindsay-jarratt@uiowa.edu
Educational Policy & Leadership Studies
The University of Iowa
Iowa City, Iowa

KC Culver
kc-culver@uiowa.edu
Educational Policy & Leadership Studies
The University of Iowa
Iowa City, Iowa

Alberto Maria Segre
alberto-segre@uiowa.edu
Computer Science
The University of Iowa
Iowa City, Iowa

ABSTRACT

Pair programming is a collaborative learning approach in computer science in which students (or employees) work closely with a partner on the same programming task. A long-standing question within pair programming is whether certain combinations of students lead to greater learning, effort, and/or performance. Earlier studies have explored the role of prior programming experience, including the discrepancy between partners' experience, as a potentially important factor in shaping these outcomes. However, the previous findings are highly inconsistent, which may result from divergent (and often suboptimal) ways of defining previous experience or skill, problems with self-selection into pairs, and small sample sizes that often yield nonsignificant results. The present study sought to improve on all of these limitations through an examination of 587 undergraduates who each participated in three different randomly assigned pairings. Not surprisingly, students' own programming experience was positively related to understanding concepts from lab, confidence in the finished product, and overall interest in computer science. However, students who worked with a more experienced partner actually had poorer outcomes, including lower effort exerted on the assignment, perceptions that their partner gave more effort than they did, less time in the driving role (i.e., typing out the assignment), lower understanding of concepts from lab, and less interest in computer science overall. The partner's experience is unrelated to other outcomes, including confidence in the finished assignment, feeling productive during lab session, and average grades received during the pairing. These results provide important considerations for the assignment of students to pairs.

CCS CONCEPTS

• **Social and professional topics → CS1.**

KEYWORDS

Pair programming; pair characteristics; pair incompatibility; programming experience; computer science; collaborative learning; college students; university students; student outcomes; experimental research; randomized controlled trial.

ACM Reference Format:
Nicholas A. Bowman, Lindsay Jarratt, KC Culver, and Alberto Maria Segre. 2019. How Prior Programming Experience Affects Students' Pair Programming Experiences and Outcomes. In *Innovation and Technology in Computer Science Education (ITiCSE '19), July 15–17, 2019, Aberdeen, Scotland UK*. ACM, New York, NY, USA, 6 pages. https://doi.org/10.1145/3304221.3319781

ACM ISBN 978-1-4503-6301-3/19/07...$15.00
https://doi.org/10.1145/3304221.3319781

1 INTRODUCTION

Popularized by proponents of agile programming methods [2], pair programming has become increasingly prevalent in both industry and classroom settings as an efficient, effective, and enjoyable method for producing code (for reviews, see [11, 12, 15, 32, 35]). Scholarship has often found that the implementation of pair programming leads to increased coding output, improved product quality, reduction of errors, and greater programmer enjoyment [3, 15, 16, 18, 24, 26, 27, 37, 38, 40]. However, despite the wealth of evidence suggesting the benefits of pair programming, it can also sometimes lead to ineffective, irritating, and exhausting interactions if partners are not compatible [7].

This large-scale experimental study explores the effects of individual programming experience and pair composition on students' confidence, lab attendance, understanding of concepts, effort, and productivity, as well as perceptions of a partner's effort. Results of previous studies on this topic have been mixed; while scholars generally agree that prior experience matters for pair compatibility and outcomes of pair programming, there is minimal agreement on how it matters and under what conditions. This study supports recommendations that students with similar skill levels be matched together, and it adds nuance by illustrating the negative effects of pairing less experienced students with more experienced partners.

The remainder of this paper is organized as follows: Section 2 provides a summary of literature on the relationship between student experience and pair programming outcomes and satisfaction. Section 3 introduces our study and describes our research methods and analysis procedures. In Section 4, we share our results, followed by a discussion of our findings in Section 5 and possibilities for future research in Section 6.

2 PREVIOUS RESEARCH

The existing literature has explored how students' prior experience and ability might influence their perceptions of pair programming, but the findings are highly inconsistent. For example, some scholars have found that stronger or more confident coders are more likely to enjoy pair programming [14], while others have found the opposite to be true [21, 34], and still others have found no relationship [23]. This disagreement may be due to wide variation in how skill and confidence are measured as well as divergent protocols for matching students.

More tangibly, the observed behaviors of veteran and novice programmers differ in pair programming situations. For example, more expert programmers average fewer interactions per hour, while novice programmers spend twice as much time suggesting and counter-suggesting [5]. Additionally, less-skilled programmers are more likely to have or perceive increased efficiency with pair programming, while more skilled programmers are more likely to become frustrated by challenges that arise in pair programming situations [7]. Plonka et al. [29] observed that novice programmers are at risk of disengagement, particularly when serving in the navigator role. Building on this observation, a subsequent study examining knowledge transfer in pair programming observed more expert partners struggling to balance the cognitive load of simultaneously thinking through code and explaining concepts to more novice partners [30].

Although personality mismatch is often cited as a reason for poor pair programming experiences and outcomes, it has only modest predictive power when compared with expertise and task complexity [17]. Differences in the relative skill of partners is one of the most consistently offered explanations for poor pair outcomes, but there is little agreement on how best to pair programmers. Some researchers have asserted that instructors should avoid pairing programmers with a wide disparity in ability and experience [4, 6, 7, 10, 20, 33, 36, 39], but how much variation in skills is desirable or acceptable is less clear. Oya and Uchida [28] found that the best pairs had a small difference in academic ability but a large difference in experience with computers, and Van Toll et al. [36] observed the most positive learning environments when one partner had slightly more experience than the other without letting the gap be too large. Another large-scale study found that pairing by skill level was important for graduate students, but that first-year students developed compatibility by partnering with a different personality type [20]. Still others have found that pair performance is uncorrelated with the skill match of pairs [25].

Perhaps guided by fears of the "Go make me a cup of tea" syndrome forewarned by Stephens and Rosenberg [33], where expert programmers do all the work, several studies that found overall positive effects for pair programming began with a process of matching students by skill level or grades (e.g., [9, 41]). However, student feedback from another pair programming experiment indicated that pairing two experts together would not enhance their experience [7], a result that was partially mirrored in an industry experiment [1]. In addition, questions about the viability of pairing two novices together complicate this pair matching process. While some scholars have suggested that instructors should avoid pairing weak programmers together [7, 8], other studies contradict this advice, suggesting that pairs of novice programmers actually yield the greatest gains [1, 22]. Lack of resolution in this area is likely due in some part to the wide variation in how skill and experience have been operationalized. Taken together, it seems that instructors wishing to implement pair programming effectively in their classrooms have much to consider but no consensus to guide their planning.

The current study explored data from a large sample of undergraduate students enrolled in introductory CS coursework to better understand how, if at all, student programming experience matters within pairs. By doing so, it sought to address several problems with the previous literature. First, pairings were randomly assigned, which means that strong causal conclusions about pair composition can be drawn. Previous research has used a wide variety of pair matching approaches, many of which may contain problems with self-selection into pairs. Second, the large sample in this study provides the necessary statistical power for identifying significant differences if they exist. Many earlier findings did not rise to the level of statistical significance due, at least in part, to small sample sizes. Third, previous studies have faced challenges in identifying appropriate measures of skill and experience; this problem is exacerbated by a tendency for more expert programmers to underestimate their ability, while more novice programmers tend to overestimate their ability [5]. In particular, earlier research has often asked students to rate their previous experience on a 0-100 scale or a Likert scale with vague response options. As an alternative, the present study used a more concrete approach by asking participants to separately rate their experience with website design, mobile apps, and several programming languages.

3 METHOD

3.1 Research Design and Participants

Participants took an introductory computer science class at the University of Iowa during the academic year from Fall

2016 to Spring 2018. Three different introductory courses are available at the institution; the most technical is designed for computer science and statistics majors, the least technical is for humanities majors, and an intermediate course is intended for social and information science majors. The analytic sample included students who (a) were enrolled in one of the two most technical courses (virtually all students in the least technical course had little or no prior programming experience), (b) were enrolled after the fourth week of the semester (some students dropped the class in the first few weeks), and (c) had not participated in the study in a previous semester (some students took the same class multiple times or took multiple classes). Participants engaged in three different pairings throughout the course; each of these randomly assigned pairings lasted for approximately 1/3 of the semester.

Students were occasionally assigned to a group of three if there was an odd number of students in the first lab section of the pairing. Only two-person pairings were included in the analyses so that a single level of partner experience could be examined. The full sample consisted of 587 undergraduates; 36% of these participants were computer science majors, 28% were female, 25% were international students, and 18% were domestic students of color.

3.2 Measures

Students often participated in multiple surveys and multiple paired assignments during each pairing, and the exact number and timing of these assessments varied somewhat across courses, semesters, and pairings. Therefore, to create outcome variables with the same timeframe as partner characteristics, students' responses within each pairing were averaged to create the dependent variables. As a result, students had three different measures of each outcome: one that represented the average across surveys or assignments for the first pairing, one for the second pairing, and one for the third pairing.

These outcomes included whether the student attended the lab section (0 = no, 1 = yes), the percentage of the assignment completed (1 = 0-10%, to 10 = 91-100%), how productive they felt within this pairing (1 = not at all productive, to 5 = very productive), and how interested they were generally in computer science (1 = not at all interested, to 5 = very interested). Participants also rated their level of agreement with several items (1 = strongly disagree, to 5 = strongly agree): understanding all concepts relevant to the assignment, putting a good amount of effort into the assignment, and being confident in the finished product. Participants also compared their own effort with that of their partner (1 = my partner invested more effort in this assignment, to 3 = my partner invested less effort in this assignment) and provided the percentage of time in which they took the driving role, which involved sitting at the keyboard and typing out the assignment (0-100). All grades earned for lab work and homework completed during a particular pairing were averaged to indicate the level of academic performance on submitted assignments.

Computer programming experience was measured via the average of nine items that asked about prior experience with website design; programming mobile apps; and using BASIC, C/C++, Java, Javascript, Perl, Python, and Ruby. All items used a four-point scale (1 = none, to 4 = a lot), and the Cronbach's alpha for this index was .76. Given the right skew of the resulting distribution, the natural log of the original measure was used. A corresponding variable was created to indicate the programming experience of the partner within each pairing. Both of these measures were then standardized with a mean of zero and a standard deviation of one, and an interaction term was created by multiplying the two standardized variables. An important benefit of this recoding is that the inclusion of the interaction term did not affect the results or interpretation of the main effects (see [19]). Dummy variables were used to indicate the order of the pairing within the semester (second and third, with the initial pairing as the referent group) and the level of the introductory course (0 = intermediate, and 1 = most technical).

3.3 Analyses

The primary outcome consisted of students' responses within a pairing, which were nested within two higher-order levels: participants (since each participant engaged in three pairings) and partners (since the partner worked on the assignment and therefore shaped the outcomes). However, participants and partners are not hierarchical to each other, since they are both students in the same class. To analyze this complex sample appropriately, cross-classified multilevel models were examined, with participants and partners crossed with each other (see [13, 31]). The key predictors were the participant's prior computer programming experience, the partner's prior experience, and the interaction between the two. Timing during the semester and course level served as control variables. Given the experimental design of this study, we used a lenient threshold for determining statistical significance ($p < .10$); we also provide significance values at several significance cutoffs so that readers can make sense of these findings.

4 RESULTS

The results for all outcomes are provided in Table 1. Participants' own prior programming experience was positively and significantly associated with several outcomes: understanding concepts from the lab section, confidence in the finished assignment, feeling productive during the lab section, perceiving that their partner gave less effort than they did, and overall interest in computer science. No significant relationships were observed for the other five outcomes.

In contrast, the partner's programming experience was significantly, but negatively, related to five of the ten participant outcomes: exerting effort on the assignment, perceiving that the partner gave less effort, time spent in the driving role of pair programming, understanding concepts from the lab, and overall interest in computer science. The other five relationships were non-significant. Two of the interaction terms were

Table 1: Results for cross-classified models predicting student outcomes in introductory computer science courses.[†]

Predictor	Exerted Effort on Assignment	Partner Gave Less Effort	Time in Driving Role	Attended Lab Sections	Percent Assignment Completed	Productive during Lab Section	Understand Concepts from Lab	Confident in Finished Assignment	Average Assignment Grade	Interest in Computer Science
Participant's experience	.048	.041+	1.276	-.008	.143	.097*	.320***	.203***	.004	.467***
	(.036)	(.023)	(.823)	(.007)	(.126)	(.038)	(.045)	(.042)	(.009)	(.049)
Partner's experience	-.050+	-.074***	-1.373+	-.006	.097	-.009	-.061+	.010	-.007	-.088**
	(.029)	(.022)	(.754)	(.006)	(.070)	(.029)	(.005)	(.035)	(.006)	(.031)
Participant × partner	-.052+	.010	.618	-.017**	-.045	-.017	-.005	-.048	-.004	-.000
	(.030)	(.022)	(.773)	(.006)	(.087)	(.033)	(.037)	(.038)	(.006)	(.032)
Second pairing	-.127*	.083+	1.551	-.002	-.049	.017	-.061	-.149+	-.017	-.176**
	(.059)	(.048)	(1.485)	(.013)	(.156)	(.062)	(.055)	(.078)	(.014)	(.059)
Third pairing	-.213**	.098*	3.305*	-.040**	.192	.070	.055	-.101	-.087***	-.277***
	(.065)	(.047)	(1.605)	(.013)	(.165)	(.065)	(.083)	(.085)	(.014)	(.059)
Most technical CS course	-.134+	-.008	1.336	-.012	.715**	-.145+	.397***	-.161+	-.090***	-.127
	(.079)	(.050)	(1.754)	(.015)	(.273)	(.084)	(.098)	(.096)	(.019)	(.105)

[†] $+p < .10$ $*p < .05$ $**p < .01$ $***p < .001$

also significant, such that high levels of programming experience for both the participant and partner predicted lower participant effort on the assignment and less attendance of lab sections above and beyond the main effects. None of the prior experience variables was significantly related to average assignment grade or percent of the assignment completed.

Regarding the control variables, several outcomes declined during the third and final pairing. Specifically, students' effort on assignments, perception of effort relative to their partner, lab section attendance, average assignment grade, and interest in computer science were all lower within the third pairing than the first pairing (i.e., the referent group for the analyses). These declines over time may result from fatigue several months into the semester. The overall means for the outcomes differed across the two introductory courses in an inconsistent manner, which may be the product of receiving somewhat different pair programming assignments in those courses. Finally, supplemental analyses (not reported here) examined potential interactions between introductory course type (intermediate versus most technical) and the prior programming experience of participants and partners; these found that the primary relationships of interest did not differ significantly across the two computer science courses.

5 DISCUSSION

The various negative results for partners' prior experience are quite noteworthy, especially since the random assignment of pairings means that these patterns represent causal effects. Most of the significant findings pertain to the amount or allocation of effort; participants with more experienced partners generally perceive that they exerted less effort, that their partner exerted more effort than they did, and that they spent less time in the driving role. These findings are consistent with an interpretation that students may let experienced partners take the lead on the pair programming assignments and/or the experienced partner assumes the lead regardless of how involved the other partner wants to be. In some ways, this effort allocation serves a useful short-term functional role, since students with prior experience may be better equipped to complete the assignment successfully, so distributing effort accordingly may lead to a higher grade on that pair programming assignment.

However, this lower effort may not be helpful—and can sometimes backfire—in terms of other relevant outcomes. Partners' prior experience is actually unrelated to perceived productivity during the lab section, percent of the assignment completed, and confidence in the finished assignment. In fact, perhaps because of this deference within the group work, partners' experience contributes to reductions in not only participants' understanding of concepts from the lab section, but also their overall interest in computer science. Another explanation for these two patterns is that having a more experienced partner leads to reduced self-confidence among students who may perceive that they are not as well-prepared or knowledgeable as their peers. Regardless of the mechanism, these negative effects stand in stark contrast to an ideal vision of collaborative learning, in which more experienced and knowledgeable students help mentor and promote the development of other team members.

The finding that more experienced participants perceived exerting more effort than their partner provides further evidence for the explanation that effort tends to be associated with prior experience. Additional findings based on participants' prior experience likely provide further insight into this relationship. Almost by definition, students with more programming experience should have a better understanding of relevant course concepts. It follows logically that experienced students would then be more confident in their assignment by employing this prior knowledge, which may also be useful for enhancing productivity during the class period. The fact that experienced students have already engaged in relevant activities also suggests that they should generally enter the course with—and likely maintain—a greater overall interest in computer science.

The interaction terms between participant and partner experience were generally unrelated to student outcomes after accounting for the main effects discussed above; the two exceptions were significant, negative relationships for attending lab sections and exerting effort on the assignment. In both cases, pairings that consisted of two highly experienced members may not have needed to work as hard in order to complete the assignment successfully. Overall, the frequency of significant results for the main effects of partner experience, coupled with the rare significant findings for the interactions, suggest that partners' prior experience may be more important than pair similarity in determining student outcomes.

6 CONCLUSION AND FUTURE WORK

This large-scale study improves our understanding of the relationships between prior experience and pair programming outcomes through implementation of a true experimental design and use of more concrete measures of programming experience than in previous research. For instructors using pair programming, the findings presented here support recommendations that pairs be formed by matching similar skill or experience levels rather than making random assignments. The negative effects of being matched with a more experienced partner may reflect a learning environment that is less collaborative than intended. That said, more work is needed to explore the effects of novice-novice pairings and whether instructors should ethically pair students by experiential similarity, which could create disparities in short-term performance. Additionally, we hope that future research will build on the work of scholars such as Bryant [5] and [29] by using observational qualitative methods to better understand how and when experience shapes pair programming dynamics.

ACKNOWLEDGMENTS

This material is based upon work supported by the National Science Foundation under Grant No. 1611908 (AMS and NAB, CoPIs). Any opinions, findings, and conclusions or recommendations expressed in this material are those of the authors and do not necessarily reflect the views of the National Science Foundation. The authors wish to thank Professors James Cremer, Ines Curto, and Denise Szecsei as well as graduate teaching assistants Abhijeet Kharkar and Sai Kalyan Moguloju from the University of Iowa Computer Science Department for their support and assistance during the data collection portion of this study.

REFERENCES

[1] E. Arisholm, H. Gallis, T. Dyba, and D.I.K. Sjoberg. 2007. Evaluating pair programming with respect to system complexity and programmer expertise. *IEEE Transactions on Software Engineering* 33, 2 (Feb. 2007), 65–86. https://doi.org/10.1109/TSE.2007.17

[2] K. Beck, M. Beedle, A. van Bennekum, A. Cockburn, W. Cunningham, M. Fowler, J. Grenning, J Highsmith, A. Hunt, R. Jeffries, J. Kern, B. Marick, R.C. Martin, S. Mellor, K. Schwaber, J. Sutherland, and D. Thomas. 2001. Manifesto for agile software development. http://www.agilemanifesto.org

[3] A. Begel and N. Nagappan. 2008. Pair programming: What's in it for me?. In *Proceedings of the second ACM-IEEE international symposium on empirical software engineering and measurement ESEM08.* ACM Press, Kaiserslautern, Germany, 120–128. https://doi.org/10.1145/1414004.1414026

[4] J. Bevan, L. Werner, and C. McDowell. 2002. Guidelines for the use of pair programming in a freshman programming class. In *Proceedings 15th conference on software engineering education and training (CSEE&T02).* IEEE Comput. Soc, Covington, KY, 100–107. https://doi.org/10.1109/CSEE.2002.995202

[5] S. Bryant. 2004. Double trouble: Mixing qualitative and quantitative methods in the study of eXtreme programmers. In *2004 IEEE symposium on visual languages - Human centric computing.* IEEE, Rome, 55–61. https://doi.org/10.1109/VLHCC.2004.20

[6] L. Cao and P. Xu. 2005. Activity patterns of pair programming. In *Proceedings of the 38th Hawaii International Conference on System Sciences HICSS05.* IEEE, Big Island, HI, 88a–88a.

[7] E.A. Chaparro, A. Yuksel, P. Romero, and S. Bryant. 2005. Factors affecting the perceived effectiveness of pair programming in higher education. In *Proceedings of the Psychology of Programming Interest Group* (Brighton, UH). 5–18.

[8] W. Chigona and M. Pollock. 2008. Pair programming for information systems students new to programming: Students' experiences and teachers' challenges. In *PICMET '08 - 2008 Portland International Conference on Management of Engineering & Technology.* IEEE, Cape Town, South Africa, 1587–1594. https://doi.org/10.1109/PICMET.2008.4599777

[9] K.S. Choi, F.P. Deek, and I. Im. 2008. Exploring the underlying aspects of pair programming: The impact of personality. *Information and Software Technology* 50, 11 (Oct. 2008), 1114–1126. https://doi.org/10.1016/j.infsof.2007.11.002

[10] D.C Cliburn. 2003. Experiences with pair programming at a small college. *Journal of computing sciences in colleges* 19, 1 (2003), 20–29.

[11] T. Dyba, E. Arisholm, D.I.K. Sjoberg, J.E. Hannay, and F. Shull. 2007. Are two heads better than one? On the effectiveness of pair programming. *IEEE Software* 24, 6 (Nov. 2007), 12–15. https://doi.org/10.1109/MS.2007.158

[12] S. Faja. 2011. Pair programming as a team based learning activity: A review of research. *Issues in information systems* 12, 2 (2011), 207–216. http://iacis.org/iis/2011/207-216_AL2011_1700.pdf

[13] A. Fielding and H. Goldstein. 2006. *Cross-classified and multiple membership structures in multilevel models: An introduction and review.* Technical Report Research Report no. 791. University of Birmingham, Birmingham, UK.

[14] B. Hanks. 2006. Student attitudes toward pair programming. *ACM SIGCSE Bulletin* 38, 3, 113–117.

[15] B. Hanks, S. Fitzgerald, R. McCauley, L. Murphy, and C. Zander. 2011. Pair programming in education: A literature review. *Computer Science Education* 21, 2 (2011), 135–173.

[16] B. Hanks, C. McDowell, D. Draper, and M. Krnjajic. 2004. Program quality with pair programming in CS. In *Proceedings of the 9th annual SIGCSE conference on innovation and technology computer science education.* Leeds, UK, 176–180.

[17] J.E. Hannay, E. Arisholm, H. Engvik, and D.I.K. Sjoberg. 2010. Effects of personality on pair programming. *IEEE Transactions on Software Engineering* 36, 1 (Jan. 2010), 61–80. https://doi.org/10.1109/TSE.2009.41

[18] E.V. Howard. 2006. Attitudes on using pair-programming. *Journal of Educational Technology Systems* 35, 1 (Sept. 2006), 89–103. https://doi.org/10.2190/5K87-58W8-G07M-2811

[19] J. Jaccard and R. Turrisi. 2003. *Interaction effects in multiple regression* (2nd ed.). Sage Publications, Thousand Oaks, CA.

[20] N. Katira, L. Williams, E. Wiebe, C. Miller, S. Balik, and E. Gehringer. 2004. On understanding compatibility of student pair programmers. In *Proceedings of the 35th SIGCSE technical symposium on computer science education.* Norfolk, VA, 7–11.

[21] L. Layman. 2006. Changing students' perceptions: An analysis of the supplementary benefits of collaborative software development. In *Proceedings of the 19th Conference Software Engineering Education and Training.* IEEE, Turtle Bay, HI, 159–166. https://doi.org/10.1109/cseet.2006.10

[22] K.M. Lui and K.C.C. Chan. 2006. Pair programming productivity: Novice–novice vs. expert–expert. *International Journal of Human-Computer Studies* 64, 9 (Sept. 2006), 915–925. https://doi.org/10.1016/j.ijhcs.2006.04.010

[23] G. Melnik and F. Maurer. 2005. A cross-program investigation of students' perceptions of agile methods. In *Proceedings of the 27th International Conference on Software Engineering ICSE05.* IEEE, St. Louis, MO, 481–488.

[24] E. Mendes, L. Al-Fakhri, and A. Luxton-Reilly. 2006. A replicated experiment of pair-programming in a 2nd-year software development and design computer science course. *ACM SIGCSE Bulletin* 38, 3 (2006), 108–112.

[25] M.M. Muller and F. Padberg. 2004. An empirical study about the feelgood factor in pair programming. In *10th International Symposium on Software Metrics, 2004. Proceedings.* IEEE, Chicago, IL, 151–158. https://doi.org/10.1109/METRIC.2004.1357899

[26] N. Nagappan, L. Williams, M. Ferzli, E. Wiebe, K. Yang, C. Miller, and S. Balik. 2003. Improving the CS1 experience with pair programming. *ACM SIGCSE Bulletin* 35, 1 (2003), 359–362.

[27] J.T. Nosek. 1998. The case for collaborative programming. *Commun. ACM* 41, 3 (March 1998), 105–108. https://doi.org/10.1145/272287.272333

[28] Y. Oya and K. Uchida. 2013. Practical consideration of pair problem solving in computer literacy education. *IAFOR Journal of Education* 1, 1 (May 2013), 103–120. https://doi.org/10.22492/ije.1.1.04

[29] L. Plonka, H. Sharp, and J. van der Linden. 2012. Disengagement in pair programming: Does it matter?. In *2012 34th International Conference on Software Engineering (ICSE).* IEEE, Zurich, 496–506. https://doi.org/10.1109/ICSE.2012.6227166

[30] L. Plonka, H. Sharp, J. van der Linden, and Y. Dittrich. 2015. Knowledge transfer in pair programming: An in-depth analysis. *International Journal of Human-Computer Studies* 73 (Jan. 2015), 66–78. https://doi.org/10.1016/j.ijhcs.2014.09.001

[31] S.W. Raudenbush and A.S. Bryk. 2002. *Hierarchical linear models: Applications and data analysis methods* (2nd ed.). Sage Publications, Thousand Oaks, CA.

[32] N. Salleh, E. Mendes, and J. Grundy. 2011. Empirical studies of pair programming for CS/SE teaching in higher education: A systematic literature review. *IEEE Transactions on Software Engineering* 37, 4 (July 2011), 509–525. https://doi.org/10.1109/TSE.2010.59

[33] M. Stephens and D. Rosenberg. 2003. *Extreme programming refactored: The case against XP.* Apress, Berkeley, CA.

[34] L. Thomas, M. Ratcliffe, and A. Robertson. 2003. Code warriors and code-a-phobes: A study in attitude and pair programming. *ACM SIGCSE Bulletin* 35, 1 (2003), 363–367.

[35] K. Umapathy and A.D. Ritzhaupt. 2017. A meta-analysis of pair-programming in computer programming courses: Implications for educational practice. *ACM Transactions on Computing Education* 17, 4 (Aug. 2017), 1–13. https://doi.org/10.1145/2996201

[36] T. Van Toll III, R. Lee, and T. Ahlswede. 2007. Evaluating the usefulness of pair programming in a classroom setting. In *6th IEEE/ACIS International Conference on Computer and Information Science (ICIS 2007).* IEEE, Melbourne, Australia, 302–308. https://doi.org/10.1109/ICIS.2007.96

[37] E.N. Wiebe, L. Williams, J. Petlick, N. Nagappan, S. Balik, C. Miller, and M. Ferzli. 2003. Pair programming in introductory programming labs. In *Proceedings Submitted to the American Society for Engineering Education Annual Conference and Exposition* (Washington, DC).

[38] L. Williams and R. Kessler. 2002. *Pair programming illuminated.* Addison-Wesley, Boston, MA.

[39] L. Williams, L. Layman, J. Osborne, and N. Katira. 2006. Examining the compatibility of student pair programmers. In *AGILE 2006 (AGILE'06).* IEEE, Minneapolis, MN, 411–420. https://doi.org/10.1109/AGILE.2006.25

[40] L. Williams, C. McDowell, N. Nagappan, J. Fernald, and L. Werner. 2003. Building pair programming knowledge through a family of experiments. In *2003 International Symposium on Empirical Software Engineering, 2003. ISESE 2003. Proceedings.* IEEE Comput. Soc, Rome, Italy, 143–152. https://doi.org/10.1109/ISESE.2003.1237973

[41] N.Z. Zacharis. 2011. Measuring the effects of virtual pair programming in an introductory programming java course. *IEEE Transactions on Education* 54, 1 (Feb. 2011), 168–170. https://doi.org/10.1109/TE.2010.2048328

A Large-Scale Experimental Study of Gender and Pair Composition in Pair Programming

Lindsay Jarratt
lindsay-jarratt@uiowa.edu
Educational Policy & Leadership Studies
The University of Iowa
Iowa City, Iowa

Nicholas A. Bowman
nick-bowman@uiowa.edu
Educational Policy & Leadership Studies
The University of Iowa
Iowa City, Iowa

KC Culver
kc-culver@uiowa.edu
Educational Policy & Leadership Studies
The University of Iowa
Iowa City, Iowa

Alberto Maria Segre
alberto-segre@uiowa.edu
Computer Science
The University of Iowa
Iowa City, Iowa

ABSTRACT

The proportion of women in computer science majors is currently lower than in any other STEM major. Various studies have sought to explain—and ultimately find ways to reduce—gender disparities in computer science participation and persistence. Pair programming has been proposed as a practice that may not only promote outcomes overall within college and workplace environments, but also help diminish isolation and boost the confidence of women in computer science. Some promising results have been obtained for women in pair programming, but the findings are not consistent across studies, and the limitations of previous research make it difficult to draw strong conclusions. The present study examined 969 undergraduates in several introductory computer science courses who engaged in three different pairings throughout the semester. All pairings were randomly assigned, so the findings reflect the causal influence of the gender pair characteristics on a variety of student outcomes. Overall, having a female partner led to several positive outcomes relative to having a male partner; these included greater lab section attendance as well as greater confidence in the finished product and confidence in the solution for the pair programming assignment. The advantages of having a female partner were occasionally greater for female students than for male students. Overall, the significant findings were most pronounced in the course intended for computer science majors. These results offer evidence for the educational benefits of pair programming for promoting women's participation in computer science, as well as the need for careful consideration of pair composition.

CCS CONCEPTS

• **Social and professional topics** → **CS1**.

KEYWORDS

Pair programming; pair characteristics; pair incompatibility; gender; women in computing; computer science; collaborative learning; college students; university students; student outcomes; experimental research; randomized controlled trial.

ACM Reference Format:
Lindsay Jarratt, Nicholas A. Bowman, KC Culver, and Alberto Maria Segre. 2019. A Large-Scale Experimental Study of Gender and Pair Composition in Pair Programming. In *Innovation and Technology in Computer Science Education (ITiCSE '19), July 15–17, 2019, Aberdeen, Scotland UK*. ACM, New York, NY, USA, 6 pages. https://doi.org/10.1145/3304221.3319782

1 INTRODUCTION

The participation of women in computer science is lower than in any other STEM field [10]. The computer science gender gap has also increased notably over time. In fact, 44% of computer science majors were women in 1980, which then plummeted to 12% in the mid-2000s and 15% in 2011 [31]. Despite a broad and intense research program that seeks to address the disparity, this problem has persisted in various Western cultures [36].

Pair programming has been championed as a promising practice that may reduce gender disparities by ending isolation and boosting confidence [3, 26, 37]. and some evidence suggests that the gender composition of pairs may affect outcomes [11, 12, 22, 32]. The present large-scale experimental study explores the effects of pair composition on confidence, attendance, understanding of concepts, effort, and productivity. The results demonstrate that gender composition matters, but the results are not entirely consistent with previous literature. Our findings add nuance to an ongoing conversation about the benefits of pair programming, especially how to

ITiCSE '19, July 15–17, 2019, Aberdeen, Scotland UK

ACM ISBN 978-1-4503-6301-3/19/07...$15.00
https://doi.org/10.1145/3304221.3319782

best design and implement pair programming to benefit both male and female students.

The remainder of this paper is organized as follows: Section 2 provides a summary of literature on computer science and pair programming experiences and outcomes through the lens of gender, and Section 3 describes our research methods and analytic procedures. In Section 4, we share our results, followed by a discussion of our findings in Section 5 and possibilities for future research in Section 6.

2 PREVIOUS RESEARCH

Many of the explanations for women's underrepresentation in CS focus on possible gendered differences in experience, behavior, and interest. One study found that women and men differed in their "tinkering" behavior and understanding [24], and several studies have pointed to a lack of experience and early exposure to computing (e.g., [4, 10, 24, 33]). Other research has emphasized women's stronger interpersonal orientation [4, 20, 31]. Generally, studies have found no gender differences in quantitative or academic ability (e.g., [5, 11, 33]). One national analysis found that academic ability of men and women in CS did sometimes differ, but not in a consistent direction [25]. Despite this similarity in ability, both men and women persistently perceive women's math and computing abilities as being lower than men's [5, 31]. Relatedly, a consistent finding is that women in CS report lower confidence or self-efficacy in their computing skills—sometimes even less than men who are not CS majors [4, 5, 10, 25]. This dynamic may be why women in early CS coursework are less likely to express an identity as a computer scientist [15] and are more likely to be undecided in their career plans [25].

Other explanations focus on the learning environment in CS programs, pointing to a pervasive masculine culture [10]. Beyer [4] found that classroom environment and instruction are powerful predictors for students' decisions to continue in a CS major. There is evidence that pedagogy matters; in a review of findings from published studies from computer-supported collaborative learning, researchers observed that gender differences were less pronounced or non-existent in classrooms where participation and inclusion were explicitly promoted [29].

Toward this end, perhaps the most studied pedagogical intervention in CS is pair programming, popularized by proponents of agile programming methods [1]. In the idealized definition of pair programming, two programmers sit side-by-side, sharing one screen and one keyboard to program collaboratively, swapping roles between "driving" or typing code and "navigating" or offering suggestions. A host of studies proclaim the wide benefits of pair programming in terms of coding output, quality of product, reduction in errors, and enjoyment and satisfaction of programmers, to name just a few [2, 14, 18, 21, 27, 28, 38–40]. However, the results have not always been consistent [8, 19], perhaps because the idealized version of pair programming is often not actualized in practice [7, 13, 38]. Particular attention has been paid to the role of pair compatibility in disparate outcomes of pair programming [9, 22, 23, 34].

While pair programming has shown promising results for all students, the outcomes for women may be more pronounced. Studies show that pair programming boosted confidence of all students with partners (when compared to solo programmers), but that the effects may be larger for women [3, 26, 37]. In interviews, women programmers expressed their appreciation for pair programming, saying that it was useful for time management because they felt responsible to their partners [20].

The gender composition of pairs may also play a moderating role in the success of pair programming as a pedagogical intervention. Several studies have found that same-gender pairs out-perform, are more compatible, and express greater satisfaction than mixed-gender pairs, particularly for women [11, 12, 22, 32]. Qualitative responses from women differ after pair-programming experiences based on the gender of their partner: Those in same-gender pairs talk about how the experience increased their comfort, while those in mixed-gender pairs talk about difficulties in communication [11]. Similar studies with children working on computer-based problem-solving have observed less cooperation and verbal interaction in mixed-gender pairs [35] and more divergent learning elaboration among mixed-gender pairs, indicating the dominance of one partner [16].

Although the existing scholarship paints pair programming as a promising practice for women, many previous findings did not rise to the level of statistical significance due to small sample sizes. In addition to the lack of statistical power, frequent problems with self-selection have also made it difficult to assess the validity of the results. The current study explores data from a large sample of undergraduate students enrolled in introductory CS coursework to better understand how, if at all, gender composition matters in predicting the outcomes of pair programming.

3 METHOD

3.1 Research Design and Participants

Participants were undergraduates who took an introductory computer science course at a large, Midwestern research university from Fall 2016 to Spring 2018. The institution has three different introductory courses; the most technical is designed for computer science and statistics majors, the least technical is for humanities majors, and an intermediate course is intended for social and information science majors. Students were included in the sample if they participated in pair programming, were enrolled after the fourth week of the semester (i.e., they had not dropped the class), and were in their first semester in an introductory CS course (some students enrolled in multiple introductory courses or multiple times in the same course). Students engaged in three different pairings during the lab section throughout the course; each pairing lasted for approximately 1/3 of the semester.

Pairings were randomly assigned, but an adjustment was made to increase the likelihood of female-female pairings in the most technical class, which had a low representation of female students. Students were assigned to a trio (rather than a pair) if there was an odd number of students in the first lab section of the pairing. Given the presence of multiple partners (and resulting difficulties with measuring partner characteristics), these trios were not included in the analyses. The total analytic sample consisted of 969 undergraduates (41% female, 24% computer science majors). The primary unit of analysis was participants' survey responses within a particular pairing. Across all two-person pairings, 40% were male-male, 34% were female-male, and 26% were female-female.

3.2 Measures

Students frequently participated in multiple surveys and multiple paired assignments during each pairing, but the exact number and timing of these assessments differed as a function of courses, semesters, and pairings. Therefore, in order to create outcome variables with timeframes that corresponded to partner characteristics, students' responses were averaged within each pairing to create the dependent variables. As a result, each student had three different measures of each outcome: one that represented the average across surveys or assignments within the first pairing, one for the second pairing, and one for the third pairing.

The dependent variables included weekly attendance ("Did you attend your discussion section this week?" 0 = no, 1 = yes), work accomplished during lab ("What percentage of the assignment were you able to complete during the discussion section?" 1 = 0-10%, to 10 = 91-100%), and perceptions of productivity ("How productive did you feel during discussion section?" 1 = not at all productive, to 5 = very productive). Participants were also asked about their general interest in computer science in each survey ("How interested are you in computer science overall?" 1 = not at all interested, to 5 = very interested). Additionally, participants indicated their level of agreement (1 = strongly disagree, to 5 = strongly agree) with the following statements: "I understand all of the concepts used in this assignment"; "I put a good amount of effort into completing this assignment"; "This assignment is error free or has just one or two errors"; "I am confident in the finished product"; and "I enjoyed completing this assignment." Students also rated their own skill relative to their partner (1 = my partner has more technical competency, to 3 = my partner has less technical competency) and their effort (1 = my partner invested more effort in this assignment, to 3 = my partner invested less effort in this assignment).

The primary independent variables were the gender of the participant and the partner (for both items, 0 = male, 1 = female). Technically, this item measured sex, not gender, but we believed that any differences by sex would have occurred as a result of social dynamics pertaining to gender (rather than biological differences by sex). As a result, consistent with previous research, we use "gender" to describe the findings in this study. In addition, an interaction term was created by multiplying the variables for participant gender and partner gender by each other. Dummy variables were also used to indicate for the level of the introductory course (most technical and intermediate, with least technical as the referent group) and the order of the pairing within the semester (second and third, with the initial pairing as the referent group).

3.3 Analyses

Students' responses within a pairing, which constituted the primary measurement of the outcome, were nested within two higher-order levels: participants (since each participant engaged in three pairings) and partners (since the partner also worked on the assignment and therefore shaped the outcome). However, neither participants nor partners are hierarchical to each other, since these both occur at the student level. As a result, cross-classified multilevel models were conducted to analyze this complex sample appropriately, with participants and partners crossed with each other (for more information, see [17, 30]. The key predictors were the participant's gender, partner's gender, and the interaction between the two. Variables for the course level and timing during the semester were also included. Because pairings were randomly assigned, the results for partner's gender can be interpreted as causal effects.

Analyses were conducted within the entire sample and separately for each course. The results were more pronounced for the most technical course than for the other two courses, so subgroup analyses for the most technical course are also presented here. The analyses predicting perceptions of the partner's relative effort in the full sample did not converge successfully, perhaps as the combined result of the complexity of the multilevel model and the relatively modest range of the outcome measure. Therefore, the results for this outcome are only presented for the subgroup analyses.

Supplemental analyses (not reported here) indicate that the results described here are generally consistent when including additional control variables, such as students' interest in computer science. Therefore, it appears that the present findings are largely attributable to gender dynamics rather than other student characteristics. That said, partners' prior experience with computer programming, which varies by gender, does have a notable and unique impact on student outcomes in pair programming [6].

4 RESULTS

The results for the full sample are provided in Table 1. Students who were randomly assigned a female partner (rather than a male partner) attended class more often, were more confident that the solution was correct, and more confident in the finished product that they created. However, being assigned a female partner was also associated with completing a smaller percentage of the assignment.

In this same set of analyses, female participants were significantly less likely than male participants to agree that they understood all of the lab concepts, were less confident in the finished assignment, were less interested in computer science, and were more likely to feel that their partner was

Table 1: Results for cross-classified models predicting student outcomes across all introductory computer science courses.†

Predictor	Attended lab sections	Understand concepts from lab	Confident solution is correct	Confident in finished product	Percent assignment completed	Productive during lab section	Exerted effort on assignment	Interest in computer science	Partner is less competent
Partner is female	.045*	.018	.227**	.191**	-.309+	.020	-.013	.001	.080
	(.018)	(.079)	(.070)	(.070)	(.167)	(.063)	(.059)	(.066)	(.053)
Participant is female	.033	-.276**	-.111	-.135+	-.273	-.087	-.012	-.658***	-.124*
	(.020)	(.090)	(.080)	(.080)	(.223)	(.076)	(.069)	(.094)	(.057)
Partner × participant	-.026	-.077	-.131	-.132	.438+	.003	.120	-.032	.005
	(.026)	(.112)	(.100)	(.102)	(.258)	(.094)	(.084)	(.090)	(.072)

†Analyses controlled for the timing of the pairing; $+p < .10$ $*p < .05$ $**p < .01$ $***p < .001$

more competent than them. Only one of the relationships exhibited a significant moderation effect: The combination of female participant and female partner led to completing a greater portion of the assignment in class.

Table 2 contains the results for analyses that only examined the most technical course, yielding similar results to the full sample. Relative to students who worked with a male partner, students who worked with a female partner were more confident that their solution was correct, more confident in the finished product, and more likely to attend lab section at all. However, having a female partner instead of a male partner was also associated with completing a smaller proportion of the assignment in class.

In this more technical course, female participants were significantly less likely than male participants to agree that they understood all concepts for the assignment, were less confident in the finished product, were less likely to report that they exerted good effort on completing the assignment, and were less interested in computer science overall. Female participants did attend class more often, but they were also more likely to perceive that their partner was more competent and gave more effort than they did. The interaction of a female participant having a female partner was positively associated with agreeing that they exerted good effort on the assignment as well as feeling that their partner was less competent and exerted less effort than they did.

5 DISCUSSION

This randomized controlled trial provides strong evidence that pair composition affects some student outcomes. In particular, students are more confident about their work—and even more likely to attend the lab section in the first place—when they are randomly assigned a female partner rather than a male partner. These patterns are consistent among all introductory computer science courses and specifically within the course designed for majors, which serves a particularly important function for shaping the demographics of computer science professionals. For the most part, the positive effects for female partners are apparent regardless of the participant's own gender. Thus, the present findings support an additional argument for promoting the representation of female students within computer science: Working with female students in pair programming may bolster the academic outcomes of all students. These results in a higher education context run contrary to previous studies of children that suggest male students benefit from interacting with a male partner [16, 35].

As shown in the interaction analyses, female students sometimes benefit even more than male students as a result of being assigned a female partner. The particular results differ across analyses; when examining all courses, having a female partner yielded a significantly greater gain in the percentage of the assignment completed among female students than among male students. Within the course designed for majors, working with a female partner had more favorable effects for female students in terms of exerting more effort on the assignment and perceiving themselves as having greater competence and effort than their partner. Taken as a whole, it appears that facilitating female-female pairings may be an especially effective approach.

However, the interpretation for the competence and effort findings may be complicated. These items specifically asked participants whether their competency and effort were lower than, similar to, or higher than that their partner's attributes. As one interpretation of the positive relationships for these variables, this same-gender pairing may lead to improvements in self-perceptions, which then lead to greater ratings in comparison with the partner. The positive finding for the female × female interaction and exerting effort appears to support this explanation for effort, whereas the lack of significant results for other outcomes (such as confidence in the solution and the finished product) does not. It is worth noting that prior research has also yielded some favorable results for female-female pairings [11, 12, 22, 32].

Finally, the differences between female and male students were consistent with previous research (e.g., [4, 5, 25]). Among all courses and within the most technical course, female students were less likely to feel that they understood concepts from lab, were less confident in their finished product, had lower perceptions of their competence relative to their partner, and had less interest in computer science overall. Unfortunately, although pair programming may help to reduce gender disparities, this pedagogical approach does not completely remedy this issue.

Table 2: Results for cross-classified models predicting student outcomes in the most technical introductory computer science course.‡

Predictor	Attended lab sections	Understand concepts from lab	Confident solution is correct	Confident in finished product	Percent assignment completed	Productive during lab section	Exerted effort on assignment	Interest in computer science	Partner is less competent	Partner gave less effort
Partner is female	.043*	.104	.243*	.253*	-.384+	.094	.077	.130	.069	-.069
	(.022)	(.119)	(.112)	(.111)	(.200)	(.090)	(.093)	(.094)	(.084)	(.069)
Participant is female	.046+	-.454**	-.207	-.235+	.021	-.113	-.228*	-.486**	-.243*	-.171*
	(.025)	(.140)	(.138)	(.135)	(.412)	(.122)	(.115)	(.153)	(.095)	(.073)
Partner × participant	-.024	.081	-.246	-.171	.401	-.037	.312+	-.006	.406**	.288*
	(.039)	(.214)	(.214)	(.213)	(.401)	(.169)	(.171)	(.171)	(.147)	(.120)

‡Analyses controlled for the timing of the pairing; $+p < .10$ $*p < .05$ $**p < .01$ $***p < .001$

6 CONCLUSION AND FUTURE WORK

Our study corroborates claims that the gender composition of pairs moderates the effects of pair programming. However, unlike previous results on the apparent benefits of same-gender pairs, our findings suggest that having a female partner seems to benefit both male and female students, adding further urgency to the need to recruit more women into CS. Given the increased benefits for female students and their stark underrepresentation, instructors utilizing pair programming should consider overrepresenting female-female pairings relative to random chance.

It is not entirely clear why such a discrepancy exists between our findings and the previous literature. It may be a result of the differences in context or from using random assignment for establishing pair groups instead of allowing students to select their own partners. Additionally, the more pronounced effects in the most technically difficult course may suggest that experience and/or commitment to computer science moderates the role of gender compatibility in pair programming, but more work is necessary to understand these relationships. Finally, these findings may simply be idiosyncratic to our particular implementation of pair programming (although we are unsure about what those idiosyncratic attributes might be).

Future research should examine the effects of gender composition when pairs are assigned by instructors versus chosen by students. The present results may not hold if, for instance, female-female pairings were a result of male students only choosing each other. In this vein, scholarship should begin turning to the ideal conditions under which pair programming should be implemented and where it is most successful. How do classroom climate and environmental cues affect the dynamics of gender in paired relationships? Which instructor practices encourage equitable and productive relationships? Finally, more work is needed that explores the effects of pair composition on longer-term outcomes, such as taking subsequent computer science courses and persisting with computer science majors.

ACKNOWLEDGMENTS

This material is based upon work supported by the National Science Foundation under Grant No. 1611908 (AMS and NAB, CoPIs). Any opinions, findings, and conclusions or recommendations expressed in this material are those of the authors and do not necessarily reflect the views of the National Science Foundation. The authors wish to thank Professors James Cremer, Ines Curto, and Denise Szecsei as well as graduate teaching assistants Abhijeet Kharkar and Sai Kalyan Moguloju from the University of Iowa Computer Science Department for their support and assistance during the data collection portion of this study.

REFERENCES

[1] K. Beck, M. Beedle, A. van Bennekum, A. Cockburn, W. Cunningham, M. Fowler, J. Grenning, J Highsmith, A. Hunt, R. Jeffries, J. Kern, B. Marick, R.C. Martin, S. Mellor, K. Schwaber, J. Sutherland, and D. Thomas. 2001. Manifesto for agile software development. http://www.agilemanifesto.org

[2] A. Begel and N. Nagappan. 2008. Pair programming: What's in it for me?. In *Proceedings of the second ACM-IEEE international symposium on empirical software engineering and measurement ESEM08*. ACM Press, Kaiserslautern, Germany, 120–128. https://doi.org/10.1145/1414004.1414026

[3] S.B. Berenson, K.M. Slaten, L. Williams, and C-W. Ho. 2004. Voices of women in a software engineering course: Reflections on collaboration. *Journal on Educational Resources in Computing (JERIC)* 4, 1 (2004), 3. https://doi.org/10.1145/1060071.1060074

[4] S. Beyer. 2014. Why are women underrepresented in computer science? Gender differences in stereotypes, self-efficacy, values, and interests and predictors of future CS course-taking and grades. *Computer Science Education* 24, 2-3 (July 2014), 153–192. https://doi.org/10.1080/08993408.2014.963363

[5] S. Beyer, K. Rynes, J. Perrault, K. Hay, and S. Haller. 2003. Gender differences in computer science students. *ACM SIGCSE Bulletin* 35, 1 (2003), 49–53.

[6] N.A. Bowman, L. Jarratt, K.C. Culver, and A.M. Segre. 2019. How Prior Programming Experience Affects Students' Pair Programming Experiences and Outcomes. In *ACM Conference on Innovation and Technology in Computer Science Education (ITiCSE19)*. ACM, New York, NY.

[7] S. Bryant, P. Romero, and B. du Boulay. 2008. Pair programming and the mysterious role of the navigator. *International journal of human-computer studies* 66, 7 (July 2008), 519–529. https://doi.org/10.1016/j.ijhcs.2007.03.005

[8] G. Canfora, A. Cimitile, G.A. Di Lucca, and C.A. Visaggio. 2006. How distribution affects the success of pair programming. *International Journal of Software Engineering and Knowledge Engineering* 16, 02 (April 2006), 293–313. https://doi.org/10.1142/S0218194006002756

[9] E.A. Chaparro, A. Yuksel, P. Romero, and S. Bryant. 2005. Factors affecting the perceived effectiveness of pair programming in higher education. In *Proceedings of the Psychology of Programming Interest Group* (Brighton, UH). 5–18.

[10] S. Cheryan, S.A. Ziegler, A.K. Montoya, and L. Jiang. 2017. Why are some STEM fields more gender balanced than others? *Psychological Bulletin* 143, 1 (Jan. 2017), 1–35. https://doi.org/10.1037/bul0000052

[11] K.S. Choi. 2015. A comparative analysis of different gender pair combinations in pair programming. *Behaviour & Information Technology* 34, 8 (Aug. 2015), 825–837. https://doi.org/10.1080/0144929X.2014.937460

[12] K.S. Choi, F.P. Deek, and I. Im. 2009. Pair dynamics in team collaboration. *Computers in Human Behavior* 25, 4 (July 2009), 844–852. https://doi.org/10.1016/j.chb.2008.09.005

[13] J. Chong and T. Hurlbutt. 2007. The social dynamics of pair programming. In *29th International Conference on Software Engineering (ICSE'07)*. IEEE, Minneapolis, MN, 354–363. https://doi.org/10.1109/ICSE.2007.87

[14] T.H. DeClue. 2003. Pair programming and pair trading: Effects on learning and motivation in a CS2 course. *Journal of computing sciences in colleges* 18, 5 (May 2003), 49–56. http://dl.acm.org/citation.cfm?id=771832.771843

[15] J. Dempsey, R.T. Snodgrass, I. Kishi, and A. Titcomb. 2015. The emerging role of self-perception in student intentions. In *Proceedings of the 46th ACM technical symposium on computer science education - SIGCSE15*. ACM Press, Kansas City, MO, 108–113. https://doi.org/10.1145/2676723.2677305

[16] N. Ding, R.J. Bosker, and E.G. Harskamp. 2011. Exploring gender and gender pairing in the knowledge elaboration processes of students using computer-supported collaborative learning. *Computers & Education* 56, 2 (Feb. 2011), 325–336. https://doi.org/10.1016/j.compedu.2010.06.004

[17] A. Fielding and H. Goldstein. 2006. *Cross-classified and multiple membership structures in multilevel models: An introduction and review.* Technical Report Research Report no. 791. University of Birmingham, Birmingham, UK.

[18] B. Hanks, C. McDowell, D. Draper, and M. Krnjajic. 2004. Program quality with pair programming in CS. In *Proceedings of the 9th annual SIGCSE conference on innovation and technology computer science education*. Leeds, UK, 176–180.

[19] S. Heiberg, U. Puus, P. Salumaa, and A. Seeba. 2003. Pair-programming effect on developers productivity. In *Extreme programming and agile processes in software engineering.*, M Marchesi and G Succi (Eds.). XP 2003. Lecture notes in computer science, Vol. 2675. Springer, Berlin, Heidelberg, 215–224.

[20] C-W. Ho, K. Slaten, L. Williams, and S. Berenson. 2004. *Examining the impact of pair programming on female students.* Technical Report NCSU CSC Technical Report 2004-20. North Carolina State University.

[21] E.V. Howard. 2006. Attitudes on using pair-programming. *Journal of Educational Technology Systems* 35, 1 (Sept. 2006), 89–103. https://doi.org/10.2190/5K87-58W8-G07M-2811

[22] N. Katira, L. Williams, and J. Osborne. 2005. Towards increasing the compatibility of student pair programmers. In *Proceedings of the 27th international conference on software engineering*. IEEE, St. Louis, MO, 625–626.

[23] N. Katira, L. Williams, E. Wiebe, C. Miller, S. Balik, and E. Gehringer. 2004. On understanding compatibility of student pair programmers. In *Proceedings of the 35th SIGCSE technical symposium on computer science education*. Norfolk, VA, 7–11.

[24] S. Krieger, M. Allen, and C. Rawn. 2015. Are females disinclined to tinker in computer science?. In *Proceedings of the 46th ACM Technical Symposium on Computer Science Education - SIGCSE '15*. ACM Press, Kansas City, MO, 102–107. https://doi.org/10.1145/2676723.2677296

[25] K.J. Lehman, L.J. Sax, and H.B. Zimmerman. 2016. Women planning to major in computer science: Who are they and what makes them unique? *Computer Science Education* 26, 4 (Dec. 2016), 277–298. https://doi.org/10.1080/08993408.2016.1271536

[26] C. McDowell, L. Werner, H.E. Bullock, and J. Fernald. 2006. Pair programming improves student retention, confidence, and program quality. *Commun. ACM* 49, 8 (Aug. 2006), 90–95. https://doi.org/10.1145/1145287.1145293

[27] E. Mendes, L. Al-Fakhri, and A. Luxton-Reilly. 2006. A replicated experiment of pair-programming in a 2nd–year software development and design computer science course. *ACM SIGCSE Bulletin* 38, 3 (2006), 108–112.

[28] N. Nagappan, L. Williams, M. Ferzli, E. Wiebe, K. Yang, C. Miller, and S. Balik. 2003. Improving the CS1 experience with pair programming. *ACM SIGCSE Bulletin* 35, 1 (2003), 359–362.

[29] F.R. Prinsen, M.L.L. Volman, and J. Terwel. 2007. Gender-related differences in computer-mediated communication and computer-supported collaborative learning: Gender-related differences in CMC and CSCL. *Journal of Computer Assisted Learning* 23, 5 (Feb. 2007), 393–409. https://doi.org/10.1111/j.1365-2729.2007.00224.x

[30] S.W. Raudenbush and A.S. Bryk. 2002. *Hierarchical linear models: Applications and data analysis methods* (2nd ed.). Sage Publications, Thousand Oaks, CA.

[31] L.J. Sax, K.J. Lehman, J.A. Jacobs, M.A. Kanny, G. Lim, L. Monje-Paulson, and H.B. Zimmerman. 2017. Anatomy of an enduring gender gap: The evolution of women's participation in computer science. *The Journal of Higher Education* 88, 2 (March 2017), 258–293. https://doi.org/10.1080/00221546.2016.1257306

[32] S. Schiller, F. Nah, B. Mennecke, and K. Siau. 2011. Gender differences in virtual collaboration on a creative design task. In *ICIS 2011 Proceedings*.

[33] J. Sinclair and S. Kalvala. 2015. Exploring societal factors affecting the experience and engagement of first year female computer science undergraduates. In *Proceedings of the 15th Koli Calling Conference on Computing Education Research - Koli Calling '15*. ACM Press, Koli, Finland, 107–116. https://doi.org/10.1145/2828959.2828979

[34] L. Thomas, M. Ratcliffe, and A. Robertson. 2003. Code warriors and code-a-phobes: A study in attitude and pair programming. *ACM SIGCSE Bulletin* 35, 1 (2003), 363–367.

[35] J. Underwood, G. Underwood, and D. Wood. 2000. When does gender matter? Interactions during computer-based problem solving. *Learning and Instruction* 10, 5 (2000), 447–462.

[36] A. Vitores and A. Gil-Juarez. 2016. The trouble with 'women in computing': A critical examination of the deployment of research on the gender gap in computer science. *Journal of Gender Studies* 25, 6 (Nov. 2016), 666–680. https://doi.org/10.1080/09589236.2015.1087309

[37] L.L. Werner, B. Hanks, and C. McDowell. 2004. Pair-programming helps female computer science students. *Journal on Educational Resources in Computing* 4, 1 (March 2004), 1–8. https://doi.org/10.1145/1060071.1060075

[38] E.N. Wiebe, L. Williams, J. Petlick, N. Nagappan, S. Balik, C. Miller, and M. Ferzli. 2003. Pair programming in introductory programming labs. In *Proceedings Submitted to the American Society for Engineering Education Annual Conference and Exposition* (Washington, DC).

[39] L. Williams and R. Kessler. 2002. *Pair programming illuminated.* Addison-Wesley, Boston, MA.

[40] L. Williams, C. McDowell, N. Nagappan, J. Fernald, and L. Werner. 2003. Building pair programming knowledge through a family of experiments. In *2003 International Symposium on Empirical Software Engineering, 2003. ISESE 2003. Proceedings*. IEEE Comput. Soc, Rome, Italy, 143–152. https://doi.org/10.1109/ISESE.2003.1237973

More Effective Contextualization of CS Education Research: A Pair-Programming Example

Briana Bettin
Michigan Technological University
Houghton, MI, USA
bcbettin@mtu.edu

Linda Ott
Michigan Technological University
Houghton, MI, USA
linda@mtu.edu

Leo Ureel
Michigan Technological University
Houghton, MI, USA
ureel@mtu.edu

ABSTRACT

This position paper discusses the need for greater inclusion of context in papers describing computer science education research. This inspiration arose from our efforts to compare our experiences with pair programming in an introductory computer science course with experiences described in the literature. We quickly observed that the behaviors associated with the term "pair programming" and the contexts can differ greatly between universities and yet the phrase pair programming is often used with no further explanation.

A brief literature survey is used to demonstrate differences in the implementation of pair programming and the context that might impact the results. We identify attributes that are likely appropriate for much CS education research, as well as specifically consider relevant attributes for research involving pair programming. This anchors our paper and demonstrates specific attributes that require consideration beyond the general computer science classroom.

Our goal is to foster conversations on providing appropriate context in computer science education research. We argue that by providing such context, studies can be more easily replicated or distinguished, a greater understanding of attributes influencing the research can be gained, and other educators can more easily determine the relevance of the research to their classroom environment.

CCS CONCEPTS

• **Social and professional topics → Computer science education**;

KEYWORDS

Computer science education research, CS1, pair programming, student perception, context, attributes

ACM Reference Format:
Briana Bettin, Linda Ott, and Leo Ureel. 2019. More Effective Contextualization of CS Education Research: A Pair-Programming Example. In *Innovation and Technology in Computer Science Education (ITiCSE '19), July 15–17, 2019, Aberdeen, Scotland Uk.* ACM, New York, NY, USA, 7 pages. https://doi.org/10.1145/3304221.3319790

ACM ISBN 978-1-4503-6301-3/19/07...$15.00
https://doi.org/10.1145/3304221.3319790

1 INTRODUCTION

As computer science educators, we have often seen a line similar to "our CS1 course uses pair programming" in papers we have read. This can feel sufficient at first, but this is because of our own interpretations of what that means. We may visualize our own classrooms that use pair programming. We may assume an ideal lab for pair programming, such as those described in well-known papers. Or perhaps we expect something else entirely - perhaps based on a lab seen in visits to industry.

The words "pair programming" appear to convey a complete concept, but there is much context missing. By providing more implementation detail, we can better reflect on the experiences we create for our students. Our readers can also better conceptualize the environment surrounding our work. This can help us to find research that is similar to our context, to recognize differences in implementations when we work to replicate research, or to understand what may appear on the surface to be contradictory findings.

There is need for context in any academic writing, and examining what is meant by "our classroom uses pair programming" is a start in the computing science education space. There are many aspects to what we mean by context. Some may be more critical than others for specific studies, and far too many exist to include them all. Our position here explores initial ideas for what may be useful in computing education papers. Specifically, we explore what additional information would aid in understanding the pair programming context, much of which overlaps with the larger context of computing education. Our hope is that this motivates discussion on what context is needed in computing education research.

2 MOTIVATIONS

When describing our own courses, we have used the phrase "our course uses pair programming". As we've explored the literature on pair programming, we realized the need for greater clarity in what we and others mean by that phrase. For example, the computer lab we use is not optimized for pair programming. When our students do not follow the pair programming practices we've taught, a source of difficulty may be our lab set-up. Our lab has 40 computers each with an individual keyboard and mouse. The computers are on tables grouped in pairs. Each student could have a computer and often students become frustrated when told to share one computer shoulder-to-shoulder in classic pair programming style. Many of their complaints are valid: "It's easier to have the problem set open on this screen so we can see our objectives quickly!" and "If we switch roles but simply swap the working computer, we aren't tripping over each others' backpacks!". Allowing these reasonable behaviors often results in students sliding into habits that are inconsistent with sharing context on a single computer.

In discussions with colleagues elsewhere [2], it became apparent that the classic definition of pair programming is not always what individuals mean when they say "pair programming". Indeed the discussions made clear that student behaviors we were considering as divergent, others believed to fall under the definition of pair programming. Given that pair programming behaviors are not standard across our classrooms - but as a community, we often write as though they are - we felt compelled to begin this discussion.

A lack of sufficient description of context in computing education research is not restricted solely to research on pair programming. A 2018 ITiCSE working group [9] conducted a major systemic literature review on introductory programming in tertiary institutions. One finding was that many of the 735 papers analyzed did not provide adequate context for other educators to assess the relevance of the research findings to their institution and/or to replicate the research study. Suggested context included demographic details and syllabus. We attempt to further this discussion here by recommending details to be considered in adding context. The focus on pair programming research is meant to demonstrate that additional context may be needed in specific research areas.

3 BACKGROUND

In order to identify potential attributes that may be valuable in creating context, we examined papers describing pair programming studies with background context in mind. The collection of papers is not meant to be comprehensive, but to provide insight into what is reported as contextual information and what may be missing.

Papers selected focused on pair programming, with many using pair programming as the primary tool to answer a research question - such as "does pair programming affect X?". Each paper chosen described the methodology with detail beyond simply stating pair programming occurred. Several were also chosen for their appearance as citations in numerous other pair programming works - highlighting the papers' influence. The papers we discuss presented interesting and often unique contextual information. Also highlighted in our discussion are questions that lingered after reading - such as information that was presented in other papers, or largely appeared to be missing but may be of value.

Work in pair programming has already explored several unique factors - personality types, skill levels, and confidence are just a few. By adding context to work such as this, data trends that may not have been visible previously can surface. It may also yield more new hypotheses: the traditional results may hold true, but perhaps certain contexts benefit more from specific modifications. Indeed, in other disciplines [3, 17, 20, 22] reviewing the similarities and differences in fidelity of implementation for classroom interventions has proven valuable in assessing what core aspects are critical to an implementation, and what may change among contexts. Without first establishing this context in our papers however, we cannot begin to design such reviews, which allow us to better understand and implement our interventions.

3.1 Lab Design

In a reflection of pair programming work by Williams [24], background is provided on their university lab setup, including a diagram of the table layout. The lab is noted to have been designed for pair programming - with each computer having two monitors, two keyboards, and two mice. This allows the reader to visualize the space in which these studies are occurring and immediately recognize differences from their own space. The pair programming space may impact student perception or success of the activity. Williams [24] has noted that students should not need to "get up" to switch roles. In other works by Williams [25, 26] however, this context is not fully specified. If one reviews only specific papers by the author, this valuable lab design information may be missing. When working with collaborators at different universities [25], distinctions between the universities were also not presented.

Chong and Hurlbutt [5] conduct their research in an industry setting, but also provide valuable insight into the setup of the pair programming work-space. Their study is conducted between two separate "teams", and the difference in team spaces, from both layout of desks to setup of machines, is documented.

Beck [1] describes "one computer, one mouse, one keyboard" as ideal. Clearly the lab Beck describes and the lab Williams [24] describes differ, even if this distinction might be considered slight. Both make strong arguments for lab design playing a role. Both argue for pair programming's effectiveness in proximity and shared context of programmers - yet their well-documented designs differ.

Questions about lab design become apparent in further studies [11, 16, 19]. Each of these studies provides great context in other areas, but misses discussion on the actual design of their space. In Thomas et al. [19], Beck's proposed space design is referenced in describing pair programming, but the actual space used is not described. One might assume their lab is designed in a similar manner to Beck's, but this is speculative. Simon and Hanks [16] review pair programming attitudes at two different institutions, but do not describe similarities and difference in lab setup. McDowell et al. [11] describe time spent in the lab space and expectations, but do not detail the layout of the space.

If a lab is not built for pair programming, it is likely that there is a computer for each chair. While students may be encouraged to work at one computer, this setup is distinct from those of Williams and Beck. Instructors are likely to monitor and encourage expected behavior, but the space itself allows for behavioral differences. These differences in lab design may reveal new questions or insights based on the different setups. The layout of the space may impact research results, but we can only determine this if the space is clearly described.

3.2 Pairing Methodology

Several papers center discussions on methods for choosing effective student pairs. Even papers for which this is not a focus often provide some insight into this space.

In some papers, students are paired by personality traits [14, 28]. In others, students are paired based on confidence or skill levels [19, 27]. Williams et al. [24, 26] note several possible approaches that have been studied in their labs. They find that some of the best compatibility options may be midterm scores, pairing together a Myers-Briggs sensor and intuitor, or similar work ethic. Pairings of these kinds can be created through data collection and compatibility assessments, and the use of these tools can greatly aid in pairing consistency for instructors.

McDowell et al., as well as Williams and Kessler [11, 25], describe processes in which students are able to have some choice in their partner selection. This approach appears to align with work suggesting that comfort between group members and self selection of groups can best motivate confidence, responsibility, and success in all members [12, 18].

Pairing methodology appears to be one of the most widely covered topics in the pair programming literature. Much of the pair programming research includes the pairing methodology as an attribute. Even when the pairing methodology is not the focus of the study, the value of it in describing context seems to be widely accepted based on the frequency of its reporting. Novel methods of pairing are likely to impact results, and as there are many potential methods for pairing, it would be difficult for a reader to assume a given scenario without one being explicitly described.

3.3 Demographics

As stated, many papers describe in detail their pairing methodologies. Goals may often refer to a specific demographic, such as the encouragement of women in computing. Details on the student population of the institution and even the classroom itself, however, are often omitted.

The omissions of such details may be due to an assumption that the demographic of the university is not relevant. However, research shows that sense of belonging is highly critical to student retention and perceptions of computing [18, 21]. Diversity efforts in pair programming papers have focused largely on positive impacts for women, such as Werner et al.'s work [23], but other underrepresented groups are often not noted unless they are the study's primary focus.

These details may not appear relevant to non-focused studies, but understanding class composition can impact understanding the role sense of belonging may play in the pair. When working in closely knit groups, students of underrepresented groups may feel an amplified disconnect, which may affect belonging and performance [6]. Observed interventions, such as those by Scott et al. [15] with underrepresented groups, have shown positive correlations with their persistence and performance in computing despite initial marginalization. Focused studies showcase that demographic factors can greatly impact students. Thus, a better understanding - even at a high level - of demographics may increase our understanding of pair programming research.

Even when not being observed in pairing research, personality differences may be valuable demographic information. Layman [8] finds introverted, reflective learners who are confident in their skills are more likely to be reluctant to pair. This is not to say they will not benefit, but that they may not warm up to the idea of pairing easily, which may decrease a partner's sense of belonging. This result was also noted by Thomas et al. [19] when observing pairs, where students are coined as "Code Warriors" who are highly confident, and are noted to have more frustration with pairing. A classroom largely comprised of students exhibiting these traits may result in different observations than one that differs - such as being full of extroverted learners who are not as confident in their skills. This indicates that not only is pairing methodology relevant, but that additional details are valuable in illustrating sense of belonging and willingness to participate.

Primary student year and non-major enrollment may affect the classroom population as well. McDowell et al., as well as Williams and Kessler [10, 25], make note not just of the course but the year students enroll in it. This is valuable - a CS1 course with a significantly high number of third-year non-major students may be distinct from a CS1 course that is almost exclusively first-year major students. For example, students in later years likely have developed stronger study habits and more effective collaborative skills, even if they lack confidence in programming. First-year students, on the other hand, are primarily relying on collaborative skills learned doing projects in K-12 and so may exhibit different behaviors. Non-majors may also have unique motivations for pursuing a computing course, which may affect their perception or performance. Without making clear not just what course we are teaching, but what type of students are enrolled, we cannot parse appropriate observations.

Details of demographics may be valuable not only at a classroom level, but at a departmental and university level. If the course's composition differs from the overall department, this may have relevance to observations on retention or motivation. If the university differs from the department or course, students may feel a heightened or lessened sense of belonging in the computing space.

Location and size of the university or department may also be relevant. A large university in an urban setting and a small rural university have quite different contexts for numerous reasons, and it is likely students choosing to attend each have different motivations, experiences, and perceptions. Location may also relate to other demographic attributes that may be of interest. Some universities may have greater populations of non-native speakers, nontraditional students, or students needing accommodations. Having this information allows educators to aggregate and review in order to determine what might affect the student experience in their classrooms.

The lack of a discussion about demographics may be because we largely expect that our contexts do not differ. However, not stating this information also means we do not challenge this assumption. Clearly all academic environments are not the same. When made concrete we are better able to view a more comprehensive picture of our teaching practices.

3.4 Pairing Behavior

Largely the original catalyst behind this paper was actual pairing behaviors. These are often difficult to discuss or observe, but may be vital for greater understanding. Although we may provide students with a definition of pair programming that we expect them to follow, we know students do not always perform as anticipated.

Pair programming is described by Williams [24] as two programmers working at one computer on the same problem. Two roles are expected to exist: the driver, who implements the design, and the navigator, who plans and oversees the design implementation. It is widely acknowledged that pair programming as a practice is effective in student learning [13]. But to fully understand what really is effective when students are pairing, any changes in their behavior from our assumptions needs to be described.

Chong and Hurlbutt [5] note shifts in expected pairing behaviors quite clearly. In particular, they highlight that while "driver" and "navigator" roles are widely acknowledged, groups often do not perform these roles as anticipated. Bryant's [4] role analysis shows the behaviors are traded off somewhat erratically. Chong and Hurlbutt [5] also found that the language is so deeply pervasive, asking qualitative questions will often not be enough to distinguish if role divergence has occurred. The "driver" and "navigator" terminology were utilized despite deviation - respondents believed they had behaved in these roles as expected. Simon and Hanks [16] note that students may describe these roles, but not actually use the driver/navigator terms.

One of pair programming's assumed benefits is context sharing [5, 16]. Both students viewing the same code at the same point have a grounded basis of operation. The benefit is improved debugging and collaborative problem solving to increase code quality and production. Students may sometimes remove themselves from this shared context by altering the assumed roles. For instance, a navigator may take on the role of researcher. In this role, the navigator searches for helpful materials while the driver continues to test different ideas while waiting for the navigator's feedback.

In labs with a computer to each student, this researcher role may result in the two students on separate machines [2]. Students are working the same problem and likely the same aspect of the problem - but the navigator is no longer guiding the driver and assisting in debugging. Instead, they are working to solve the problem in separate contexts. In labs with only a single machine to a pair, this may still occur with the navigator using a separate device such as a cell phone or simply reviewing a textbook.

This behavior is not inherently negative. When students are stuck, reviewing materials or identifying code patterns to replicate and modify can be an extremely useful learning tool. However, this is not the behavior described in the definition we often assume for pair programming, which emphasizes the benefits of a consistent shared context. While students may largely share the context together, divergence can certainly exist. Acknowledging this behavior may yield new research questions, such as what causes students to separate from sharing context and at what point do they return. This may provide greater understanding of what we mean by pair programming as well - perhaps we may discover benefits to this behavior and thus feel comfortable allowing it in our classrooms.

In our own observations [2], we noted not only the researcher role exhibited, but a "leader and follower" role, in which the driver is leading the coding efforts with the navigator building identical code alongside on their own machine. As an anecdote, some students showing this behavior felt they were not "getting enough of a chance to practice writing code" when their time was halved between driver and navigator. This variant of the roles was their solution that still encompassed sharing the same problem context and discussing/debugging as they built, but working on distinct machines. Students also exhibited what could be called "race and regroup", in which both worked on the same problem separately, reconvening to share ideas for the best method of moving past obstacles. Both students would agree upon the optimal solution for submission, but developed separately and collaborated primarily at critical points. This particular behavior was described to some degree by Williams and Kessler [25] as partners doing simple coding and testing separately. We also observed groups that would begin their work as pairs but over time be seen working entirely separately. These groups may even be observed attempting to "divide and conquer", with both students working on entirely separate problems, thus sharing no context.

In our case we frequently intervened to remind students of the "optimal" pairing strategies, but students often fall back to the observed collaborative habits. Perhaps these behaviors are not negative, as Chong and Hurlbutt [5] suggest. There may indeed be multiple forms of effective pairing behaviors, as we often see teams behave differently and yet achieve similar success. Indeed, Williams and Kessler [25] note that students may recognize that certain parts of their process may benefit more from a combined effort. This may be so persistent that for some researchers, certain behaviors may be completely expected during pair programming, without it being recognized that it is a variation. Without acknowledging observed variations in behavior, we cannot begin to understand the positive or negative effects these behaviors may have.

Pairing behavior also encompasses areas such as partner dynamics. Domination in the partnership can result in the non-dominant student suffering both in confidence and performance [19, 26, 27]. This research shows the importance of recognizing divergent behaviors - to distinguish the beneficial from the harmful and find ways to motivate positive practices for all students.

It can be difficult without a focused study to clearly assess pairing behavior. However, simply beginning to discuss these behaviors starts providing context and uncovering further research questions. Perhaps students pair program as expected at the beginning of the course, but toward the end changes in behavior can be seen. Perhaps the pair programming expectations of the course allow for students to exhibit differing behaviors. Stating this information allows readers to not assume the theoretically perfect pair programming behaviors when that may not be the reality.

3.5 Course Structure

Course structure may impact student perceptions, performance and how they work with their partner. Course design concerns of particular interest to pairing include how much pair programming students are assigned, where they are observed pairing, and the portion of their grade influenced by the pair programming activities.

In some courses such as Williams's [24], students primarily do individual work with a subset of their work (such as lab work) being done with pair programming. In other courses such as McDowell et al.'s [11], nearly all work, except for exams, is done using pair programming. There are certainly many more variations beyond these, but these pairing expectations may impact the research results.

Further, the space in which pairing is observed (if at all) is important. A general assumption may often be a supervised lab space working on specific problem sets such as what Williams [24] describes, but this is of course speculative if not stated. If pairing behavior occurs in unsupervised contexts, in non-required labs such as McDowell et al. [11], or remotely such as Hanks [7], the results may be affected.

Languages taught, material covered, and tools utilized provide greater understanding of the course and allow for exploration of potential interactions. Some papers describe the content covered [10, 25, 27]. The degree of detail varies, but all note aspects of course content and expectations. Others describe the type of course, but not the material presented to students [11, 16, 19]. Perhaps a collaboration tool assists students in knowing when to switch roles, or a unique topic is taught. Noting this allows an understanding of uniqueness between seemingly similar contexts, where "a CS1 course" does not. Without it, assumptions are likely made - perhaps such as that what is left unsaid mimics our own context.

How students are taught about pair programming may impact their understanding and implementation of the process. Students may be taught through a short presentation/lecture [25, 27] or by reading a paper [11, 25].

Students partnership may stay the same through a course, or may rotate several times through the semester as Williams [24] describes. Some, such as Wood et al. [27] change as frequently as every session. This can change the formation and expectations of teaming behaviors. There may also be expectations of when students swap roles - such as after set time periods, or after specific problems. These choices all may alter the environment and perceptions surrounding pairing in a course.

4 CONTEXT ATTRIBUTES

Our review of the literature suggested context that is likely broadly relevant to computer science education research along with context specific to pair programming. Below is suggested context attributes for consideration. Many include example attribute values for clarification.

4.1 Context for CS Education Research

University Attributes

(1) The student population consists of students who are:
    ([specify ethnicity and race]; [specify gender]; Commuter/Residential/Remote; Non-traditional; Non-native language speakers; Extroverted/Introverted; Neurotypical/Neurodiverse; First generation ...)
(2) The university has: ( ) students
(3) The university location is largely: (Urban; Rural)
(4) The faculty population of the university when compared to students: (Largely matches; Varies in terms of...)

Department Attributes

(1) The department's student population when compared to the university: (Largely matches; Varies in terms of...)
(2) The students who persist in computing to graduation when compared to the department: (Largely matches; Varies in terms of...)
(3) The department's faculty population when compared to the university: (Largely matches; Varies in terms of...)

Course Attributes

(1) The student population that enrolls in this course when compared to the department: (Largely matches; Varies in terms of...)
(2) Non-major enrollment in this course is approximately: ()%
(3) Non-major enrollment in this course may be influenced by the fact that it:
    (Can fulfill a general education requirement by taking the course if they are non-majors; Is required for a large portion of non-majors in their chosen major)
(4) The course is: (CS0; CS1; CS2; ...)
(5) Most students are (first, second, ...) year students:
(6) The course content consists of:
    ([specify languages used]; [specify topics covered])
(7) Tools used in the course include:
    ([specify Programming environment], [specify submission system/classroom management tools], [specify any course tie-ins such as polling software], [specify any collaboration tools]; [specify any visualization tools])
(8) Student work is:
    (Entirely individual; Entirely pair work; Entirely in teams; Mostly individual, with pair programming in some projects; Mostly collaborative, with individual assessments)
(9) Research related to this course is being used:
    ([To change curriculum for a specified purpose], [To observe habits for a specified purpose])
(10) Additional resources available to students for this course include:
    (Scheduled time with a tutor; A learning center with walk-in hours; Discussion forums with other students; Retry or mastery based grade systems)

4.2 Context for Specific Research

Pair Programming Attributes

(1) The room in which students pair program is set up such that:
    (Each student has their own computer; There are two keyboards controlling one computer; There is one computer and keyboard for a pair of students)
(2) When students pair program, they are expected to work:
    (In a supervised lab section on specific problems; In a supervised lab on any assigned work; Collocated, but are unsupervised; Remotely)
(3) Students are taught the following about pair programming:
    (It is an industry standard; Communicating code ideas is a marketable job skill; There are expected driver and navigator roles; Only one computer should be used; Roles should switch often)
(4) Students are taught about pair programming practices by:
    (Reading a publication; Watching an instructional video; Listening to an explanation or lecture; Observing a skit; Diving in to work together with interventions as needed
(5) Students pairing decisions are made by:
    (Allows students to choose their own partner; Matches them with a partner whose personality is [similar/different]; Matches them with a partner whose skill level is [similar/different]; Matches them based on another assessed trait [specify]; Partners are chosen at random by instructor; Partners are based upon where students first sit)

(6) Student partners change: (Never; Each week; Every other week; After major assignments; Halfway through the course; If changes are requested or voted on)
(7) Students are expected to swap driver and navigator roles: (After each problem; After a set time interval; Whenever the pair decides but non-swapping is intervened upon; Whenever the pair decides with no interventions)

4.3 Example Context Statement

Below is an example using a fictional university to illustrate how this seemingly large addition of context can be approached. This information might be included in a paper's background section, or broken apart with relevant information in specific sections.

Our university has 23,000 students and is located in a rural area of the United States. The majority of the student body are white males who live on campus. Approximately 20% of our students are indigenous females who commute and 5% are non-native language speaking students who take courses remotely. The students in our department differ from the campus as a whole, being primarily remote non-native language students. The faculty on our campus are primarily white females, and our department matches this trend as well.

In our CS1 course, students more closely resemble the university as a whole, with non-major enrollment being approximately 60% as many non-majors are required to take CS1. Students are typically in their second year. We cover introductory concepts in Python using PyCharms, and assign work via Blackboard. Our students collaborate using pair programming on all assignments, except for assessments. A tutor is available for students to schedule help sessions. The investigators for this research are not the instructors of the course. The goal of this research is to observe student habits of communication while pair programming.

In our classroom, there is one computer to each pair of students, who work in a supervised one-hour lab on assigned coursework. Pair programming is introduced to students with an instructional video, which discusses the driver and navigator roles and teaches them that they should switch roles often. Students are paired based on similar personality types, which are assessed using OCEAN. Partners change halfway through the course. Students are encouraged to swap roles whenever they complete a problem, but are not forced to.

4.4 Considerations

We listed a broad range of attributes and have attempted to suggest values without judgment. For instance, in describing pair programming behaviors, a range of behaviors are described. Some may be considered positive, while others negative. Noting both without judgment allows for ultimately arriving at a better understanding of which behaviors do actually matter.

In addition to the context attributes we've noted, we identified several behavioral observations that can be made to help understand and contextualize research findings on student pair programming. In papers that are focused on the topic, these may likely be of similar importance to the above attributes. These include:

(1) Generally, student perceptions of pair programming in the course are:
(Enjoy it throughout; Enjoy despite initial hesitations; Begin enjoying but become frustrated as the course continues; Dislike it, despite initial optimism; Dislike it throughout; Seem to have no strong feelings)
(2) When observed pairing, students are often seen:
(Pointing to code on screen; Switching roles frequently; Drawing diagrams or gesturing to visualize; Discussing the same problem; Explaining an idea to their partner; Asking questions unrelated to a shared context; Becoming distracted; Researching online for resources; Working on the same problem [with the navigator researching separately / with one following along / independently]; Working on separate problems)
(3) When students change their behavior, it is often:
([specify common time periods in class or semester changes occur]; [specify how the behavior shifts])

5 EXPLORING ADDITIONAL CONTEXTS

This paper makes the case for context through an exploration of pair programming practices that may be critical to study designs in which pair programming is a focus. However, many more contexts exist within the computer science education space which require deeper exploration and context as well. One such example may be flipped classroom practices, which are also commonly cited in the field. We might recommend a similar approach be taken in exploring flipped classroom's context, but with a focus on relevant questions in that area. Such questions may include how often flipped activities occur, what types of flipped activities are used, what portion of the student grade/assessment is based on flipped activity outcomes, how large group sizes are for flipped activities, and how collaborative grouping is determined and structured in the class. Obviously a thorough discussion of this context would warrant its own review and deeper consideration which is out of the scope of this paper. However, this shows the capability of this approach for developing context in areas beyond simply pair programming.

6 CONCLUSIONS AND FUTURE WORK

In this position paper, we have presented the beginning of what we hope is a continued discussion on contextualizing computing education research. This is certainly not a complete representation of context. It is meant as a basis for discussion, but obviously does not and cannot contain all the attributes of a given environment that may be noted in computing education research. As more researchers think about presenting more context for their work, additional significant attributes will likely become apparent, and some presented here may become irrelevant.

Further, the hope is that this work can lead into fidelity of implementation studies like those explored in other disciplines [3, 17, 20, 22] in order to better assess the most critical components of our interventions. In adding context to our papers, we allow for fidelity of implementation to be better assessed in future work.

ACKNOWLEDGMENTS

We thank the students in our CS1 course, for their efforts in pair programming that have motivated our research. We also thank the instructors and assistants in our CS1 course, for their insights and observations regarding pair programming that contributed to our understanding and investigation.

REFERENCES

[1] Kent Beck. 2000. *Extreme Programming Explained: Embrace Change.* Addison-Wesley Longman Publishing Co., Inc., Boston, MA, USA.

[2] Briana. Bettin, Jamie L. Berger, Sarah. Larkin, and Leo. Ureel. 2018. Enforcing Positive Pair Programming by Shattering Student Perceptions. Poster presentation at the 2018 Grace Hopper Celebration for Women in Computing.

[3] Maura Borrego, Stephanie Cutler, Michael Prince, Charles Henderson, and Jeffrey E. Froyd. 2013. Fidelity of Implementation of Research-Based Instructional Strategies (RBIS) in Engineering Science Courses. *Journal of Engineering Education* 102, 3 (2013), 394–425. https://doi.org/10.1002/jee.20020

[4] Sallyann Bryant. 2005. Rating expertise in collaborative software development. In *in Proc. PPIG.* PPIG, University of Sussex, Brighton, 19–29.

[5] Jan Chong and Tom Hurlbutt. 2007. The Social Dynamics of Pair Programming. In *Proceedings of the 29th International Conference on Software Engineering (ICSE '07).* IEEE Computer Society, Washington, DC, USA, 354–363. https://doi.org/10.1109/ICSE.2007.87

[6] Katelyn M. Cooper and Sara E. Brownell. 2016. Coming Out in Class: Challenges and Benefits of Active Learning in a Biology Classroom for LGBTQIA Students. *CBE-Life Sciences Education* 15, 3 (2016), ar37. https://doi.org/10.1187/cbe.16-01-0074 PMID: 27543636.

[7] Brian Hanks. 2005. Student Performance in CS1 with Distributed Pair Programming. *SIGCSE Bull.* 37, 3 (June 2005), 316–320. https://doi.org/10.1145/1151954.1067532

[8] Lucas Layman. 2006. Changing Students' Perceptions: An Analysis of the Supplementary Benefits of Collaborative Software Development. In *Proceedings of the 19th Conference on Software Engineering Education & Training (CSEET '06).* IEEE Computer Society, Washington, DC, USA, 159–166. https://doi.org/10.1109/CSEET.2006.10

[9] Andrew Luxton-Reilly, Simon, Ibrahim Albluwi, Brett A. Becker, Michail Giannakos, Amruth N. Kumar, Linda Ott, James Paterson, Michael James Scott, Judy Sheard, and Claudia Szabo. 2018. A Review of Introductory Programming Research 2003–2017. In *Proceedings of the 23rd Annual ACM Conference on Innovation and Technology in Computer Science Education (ITiCSE 2018).* ACM, New York, NY, USA, 342–343. https://doi.org/10.1145/3197091.3205841

[10] Ian McChesney. 2016. Three Years of Student Pair Programming: Action Research Insights and Outcomes. In *Proceedings of the 47th ACM Technical Symposium on Computing Science Education (SIGCSE '16).* ACM, New York, NY, USA, 84–89. https://doi.org/10.1145/2839509.2844565

[11] Charlie McDowell, Linda Werner, Heather E. Bullock, and Julian Fernald. 2006. Pair Programming Improves Student Retention, Confidence, and Program Quality. *Commun. ACM* 49, 8 (Aug. 2006), 90–95. https://doi.org/10.1145/1145287.1145293

[12] Scott A. Myers. 2012. Students' Perceptions of Classroom Group Work as a Function of Group Member Selection. *Communication Teacher* 26, 1 (2012), 50–64. https://doi.org/10.1080/17404622.2011.625368

[13] Leo Porter, Mark Guzdial, Charlie McDowell, and Beth Simon. 2013. Success in Introductory Programming: What Works? *Commun. ACM* 56, 8 (Aug. 2013), 34–36. https://doi.org/10.1145/2492007.2492020

[14] N. Salleh, E. Mendes, J. Grundy, and G. S. J. Burch. 2009. An empirical study of the effects of personality in pair programming using the five-factor model. In *2009 3rd International Symposium on Empirical Software Engineering and Measurement.* IEEE Computer Society, Washington, DC, USA, 214–225. https://doi.org/10.1109/ESEM.2009.5315997

[15] Allison Scott, Alexis Martin, Frieda McAlear, and Sonia Koshy. 2017. Broadening Participation in Computing: Examining Experiences of Girls of Color. *ACM Inroads* 8, 4 (Oct. 2017), 48–52. https://doi.org/10.1145/3149921

[16] Beth Simon and Brian Hanks. 2008. First-year Students' Impressions of Pair Programming in CS1. *J. Educ. Resour. Comput.* 7, 4, Article 5 (Jan. 2008), 28 pages. https://doi.org/10.1145/1316450.1316455

[17] Marilyne Stains and Trisha Vickrey. 2017. Fidelity of Implementation: An Overlooked Yet Critical Construct to Establish Effectiveness of Evidence-Based Instructional Practices. *CBE life sciences education* 16 (02 2017), rm1. https://doi.org/10.1187/cbe.16-03-0113

[18] Elli J. Theobald, Sarah L. Eddy, Daniel Z. Grunspan, Benjamin L. Wiggins, and Alison J. Crowe. 2017. Student perception of group dynamics predicts individual performance: Comfort and equity matter. *PLOS ONE* 12, 7 (07 2017), 1–16. https://doi.org/10.1371/journal.pone.0181336

[19] Lynda Thomas, Mark Ratcliffe, and Ann Robertson. 2003. Code Warriors and Code-a-phobes: A Study in Attitude and Pair Programming. In *Proceedings of the 34th SIGCSE Technical Symposium on Computer Science Education (SIGCSE '03).* ACM, New York, NY, USA, 363–367. https://doi.org/10.1145/611892.612007

[20] Chandra Turpen, Melissa Dancy, and Charles Henderson. 2016. Perceived affordances and constraints regarding instructors' use of Peer Instruction: Implications for promoting instructional change. *Physical Review Physics Education Research* 12 (02 2016). https://doi.org/10.1103/PhysRevPhysEducRes.12.010116

[21] Nanette Veilleux, Rebecca Bates, Cheryl Allendoerfer, Diane Jones, Joyous Crawford, and Tamara Floyd Smith. 2013. The Relationship Between Belonging and Ability in Computer Science. In *Proceeding of the 44th ACM Technical Symposium on Computer Science Education (SIGCSE '13).* ACM, New York, NY, USA, 65–70. https://doi.org/10.1145/2445196.2445220

[22] Emily M. Walter, Charles R. Henderson, Andrea L. Beach, and Cody T. Williams. 2016. Introducing the Postsecondary Instructional Practices Survey (PIPS): A Concise, Interdisciplinary, and Easy-to-Score Survey. *CBE-Life Sciences Education* 15, 4 (2016), ar53. https://doi.org/10.1187/cbe.15-09-0193 arXiv:https://doi.org/10.1187/cbe.15-09-0193 PMID: 27810868.

[23] Linda L. Werner, Brian Hanks, and Charlie McDowell. 2004. Pair-programming Helps Female Computer Science Students. *J. Educ. Resour. Comput.* 4, 1, Article 4 (March 2004), 8 pages. https://doi.org/10.1145/1060071.1060075

[24] Laurie Williams. 2007. Lessons Learned from Seven Years of Pair Programming at North Carolina State University. *SIGCSE Bull.* 39, 4 (Dec. 2007), 79–83. https://doi.org/10.1145/1345375.1345420

[25] Laurie Williams and Robert Kessler. 2000. Experiments with Industry's "Pair-Programming" Model in the Computer Science Classroom. *IEEE Software - SOFTWARE* 11 (01 2000), 11. https://doi.org/10.1076/csed.11.1.7.3846

[26] Laurie Williams, Lucas Layman, Jason Osborne, and Neha Katira. 2006. Examining the Compatibility of Student Pair Programmers. In *Proceedings of the Conference on AGILE 2006 (AGILE '06).* IEEE Computer Society, Washington, DC, USA, 411–420. https://doi.org/10.1109/AGILE.2006.25

[27] Krissi Wood, Dale Parsons, Joy Gasson, and Patricia Haden. 2013. It's Never Too Early: Pair Programming in CS1. In *Proceedings of the Fifteenth Australasian Computing Education Conference - Volume 136 (ACE '13).* Australian Computer Society, Inc., Darlinghurst, Australia, Australia, 13–21. http://dl.acm.org/citation.cfm?id=2667199.2667201

[28] Murat Yilmaz, Rory V. OConnor, Ricardo Colomo-Palacios, and Paul Clarke. 2017. An Examination of Personality Traits and How They Impact on Software Development Teams. *Inf. Softw. Technol.* 86, C (June 2017), 101–122. https://doi.org/10.1016/j.infsof.2017.01.005

Instructional Framework for CS1 Question Activities

Rita Garcia, Katrina Falkner, Rebecca Vivian
University of Adelaide
Adelaide, Australia
{firstname.lastname}@adelaide.edu.au

ABSTRACT

Questioning is a learning activity that can promote the use of critical thinking skills, where thinking processes are required to answer a posed question. In this paper, we map instructional question types to Bloom's Taxonomy–a classification of critical thinking skills required for cognition–to form a framework for educators to construct learning activities through questioning. The preliminary instructional framework is applied to a question activity within a blended CS1 learning environment to support students in better understanding on how to solve a programming assignment. Our results show students meeting the desired Bloom's cognitive level when answering the question activity. Future research opportunities are presented to test the framework for upper-division CS courses and further explore the framework as an intervention for programming assignments.

CCS CONCEPTS

• **Social and professional topics → Computer science education**; *CS1*;

KEYWORDS

Bloom's; questions; critical thinking skills; teaching activity

ACM Reference Format:
Rita Garcia, Katrina Falkner, Rebecca Vivian. 2019. Instructional Framework for CS1 Question Activities. In *Innovation and Technology in Computer Science Education (ITiCSE '19), July 15–17, 2019, Aberdeen, Scotland Uk.* ACM, New York, NY, USA, 7 pages. https://doi.org/10.1145/3304221.3319732

1 INTRODUCTION

Instructional question types (IQTs) are classifications of questions that can be used to ascertain students' understanding of learning materials [11]. Instructional questions can reduce students' misconceptions [24] and identify misunderstandings [9] about a problem. IQTs can encourage self-explanation [6] and higher learning gains [17], and have been classified for CS questioning, to help improve teaching practices [4].

In this paper, we present an Instructional Framework developed through mapping IQTs to Bloom's Taxonomy, to diversify learning activities that could help students utilise the appropriate cognitive level in their CS1 learning. Student-initiated questions have been previously classified [11] to Bloom's, but to the best of our knowledge, this is the first attempt to map instructor-initiated CS question categories.

We illustrate the framework in a blended learning environment by developing a question activity as an intervention for a programming assignment. The activity is designed to encourage students to answer using the cognitive level appropriate in their learning. A mixed-methods approach of qualitative and quantitative data collection and analysis identified students answering the activity at the appropriate cognitive level. Additional research is needed to explore the framework as an intervention for programming assignments. The paper concludes with future plans for the framework.

2 BACKGROUND

Questioning is a learning activity that can encourage students to use critical thinking skills that require cognitive processes to reflect on a problem prior to answering [3]. Question taxonomies have been developed to generate questions for applications [14], target problem solving using the scientific method [8], and help improve teachers' question-asking skills [11]. Posed questions can help reduce 'monotonous ineffective tutoring dialogs' [14], encourage positive learning behaviours [24], and promote higher-order thinking skills that require internal reflection, domain knowledge, and opinions to form an answer [3]. Students can independently practice higher-order thinking skills in online learning environments by constructing artefacts within digital activities [7].

IQTs classification for CS questioning was performed by Boyer et al. [4], involving dialogues between 78 upper-division CS students and 17 tutors. Table 1 displays the 23 IQTs and example questions from the study. The IQTs were collated to assist CS teachers in asking effective questions to encourage students to use both lower and higher-order thinking skills.

Lower-order thinking skills help to recall, memorise, and understand learning materials [23] and are predominantly used by educators in classroom-based environments as short-answer questions to assess students' domain knowledge [10]. Questions promoting higher-order thinking skills are deep-reasoning [3] and knowledge inference [6] questions, which are not commonly used by educators in learning environments [8].

The cognitive processes required for lower and higher-order thinking skills have been previously defined in the Structure of the Observed Learning Outcome (SOLO) [2] and Bloom's [3] educational objective taxonomies. SOLO examines students' solutions to measure their mastery of the domain, while Bloom's addresses the depth of learning. Table 1 shows the Bloom's levels and definitions, ordered from lower to higher-order cognitive levels. Prior work using SOLO has classified CS reading problems [13] and exam

ITiCSE '19, July 15–17, 2019, Aberdeen, Scotland Uk

ACM ISBN 978-1-4503-6301-3/19/07...$15.00
https://doi.org/10.1145/3304221.3319732

Level	Bloom's Definition	Instructional Question Types [4]	
		Category	Example
Uncategorised		Backchannel*	Right?
		Focus*	See where the array is declared?
		Hints*	We didn't declare it; should we do it now?
Recall	"Involves the recall of specifics and universals, the recall of methods and processes, or the recall of a pattern, structure, or setting." [3]	Definition	What does that mean?
		Knowledge*	Have you ever learned about arrays?
Comprehension	"Refers to a type of understanding or apprehension such that the individual knows what is being communicated and can make use of the material or idea being communicated without necessarily relating it to other material or seeing its fullest implications." [3]	Calculation	What is 13 % 10?
		Casual Consequence	What if the digit is 10?
		Clarification*	What do you mean?
		Confirmation*	Does that make sense?
		Enablement	How are the digits represented as bar code?
		Procedural	How do we get the ith element?
		Quantification	How many times will this loop repeat?
Application	"Use of abstractions in particular and concrete situations." [3]	Free Creation	What shall we call it?
		Goal Orientation	Did you intend to declare a variable there?
Analysis	"Breakdown of a communication into its constituent elements or parts such that the relative hierarchy of ideas is made clear and/or the relations between ideas expressed are made explicit." [3]	Casual Antecedent	Why are we getting that error?
		Feature/Concept Completion	What do we want to put in digits[0]?
		Free Option	Should the array be in this method or should it be declared up with the other private variables?
		Judgment	Would you prefer to use math or strings?
		Justification	Why are we getting the error?
		Plan	What should we do next?
Synthesis	"Putting together of elements and parts so as to form a whole." [3]	Improvement	Can you see what we could do to fix that?
Evaluation	"Judgments about the value of material and methods for given purposes." [3]	Assessment*	Do you think we're done?
		Status*	Do you have any questions?

Table 1: Instructional Framework (* denotes emerging question category [4])

questions [16, 25]. Bloom's has been used to develop CS classroom exercises [18], analyse assessments [12], develop assessment requirements [22], and identify the cognitive level for testing [19]. Frameworks using Bloom's have been developed for programming knowledge [5] and higher order problem-solving questions [26].

3 MOTIVATION

This study was motivated to inform the design of evidence-based materials for new CS instructors and support them in designing learning activities. The work attempts to answer the following research questions:

- ***RQ1:*** *How do the 23 CS-focused instructional question types align with Bloom's Taxonomy cognitive levels?*
- ***RQ2:*** *Does eliciting the questions in an online CS1 learning environment promote the expected cognitive level?*

The study was conducted in two parts. First, the framework was constructed using methods described in Section 4. Section 5 describes the study's second part, illustrating how the framework can assist CS1 students to use the appropriate cognitive level in their learning.

Illustrating the question activity was performed in a 12-week CS1 course, with teaching sessions occurring in a classroom environment. Instructional materials were provided in Canvas, a Learning Management System (LMS) that students, teachers, and lab supervisors used to communicate and submit assignments.

4 INSTRUCTIONAL FRAMEWORK

This section describes constructing the framework as an instructional instrument and the results when mapping the IQTs to Bloom's.

4.1 Instrument Development

To align the 23 IQTs to Bloom's Taxonomy, we evaluated the question categories within the context of a CS1 learning environment, a different context than the discourse approach applied by Boyer et al. [4]. To better understand the cognitive requirements for answering questions, we examined previous question taxonomies [4, 9, 14]. For eight emerging IQT categories, denoted with asterisks in Table 1, we performed additional research to better understand these categories. This included evaluating definitions for the categories and evaluating a model for detecting dialogue acts [21] that included the *Backchannel*, *Knowledge*, and *Clarify* categories.

After collecting the background materials, the primary author classified the 23 IQTs within Bloom's. The classification process was similar to the task assessments constructed by Thompson et al. [22], where assessments were first constructed by the researchers individually and later discussed as a group, to identify discrepancies and form a classification for each cognitive level. A pilot project was created to evaluate the coding criteria applied to students' answers. Table 2 shows example answers from the pilot that the authors discussed. The authors agreed on the coding from a subset of student answers before coding the remaining answers. The construction of the instructional framework involved the primary author validating the placement of the IQTs in the Bloom's level by generating questions for the programming assignment used in this study. Difficult question generation suggested the IQT was in the wrong cognitive level, prompting placement reassessment in another level until question generation became easier.

4.2 Results

Table 1 is the Instructional Framework, showing Bloom's levels and definitions. The table includes the IQTs and example questions from Boyer et al. [4] study organised within the cognitive levels.

Validating the IQTs using question generation resulted in the reassessment for three categories. Both *Feature/Concept Completion* and *Plan* IQTs were initially categorised in the *Application* cognitive level, but the questions generated were focusing on how tasks were related to solve the problem, which is more aligned to the *Analysis* level. Subsequent generated questions for these categories were easier to construct when moved to *Analysis*. The third category, *Focus*, was initially categorised in *Comprehension*, but like *Backchannel* and *Hints*, mapping became difficult due to the context, with generated *Focus* questions being applicable to different cognitive levels. Therefore, for the preliminary framework, the three IQTs (*Backchannel*, *Focus*, and *Hints*) remain uncategorised.

5 ILLUSTRATION

When using the framework as an instructional instrument, we selected question types for the activity that engage lower-order thinking skills to reflect on previously learned language constructs, and higher-order thinking skills to promote the application of programming knowledge to the assignment's problem domain. By practising both thinking skills, students might develop a cross-referencing comprehension strategy, where the program and problem domain layers are utilised for a solution, resulting in a higher level of understanding about the problem [15].

Figure 1 shows the question activity used in the experiment that followed the description of the programming assignment. The question activity is designed using the cognitive levels aligned with the context of the programming assignment, giving students the context for answering the activity. The first question is from the *Knowledge* IQT and is mapped to Bloom's *Recall* level. This question is designed to help students reflect and apply their internal knowledge to solve the problem. The second question is a *Plan* IQT mapped to the *Analysis* level, designed to encourage students to deconstruct the problem's tasks. The questions are designed to compliment each other, layering what students already know on their problem-solving skills.

- *Q1: What do you already know about collecting and organising data for products sold that might help you complete this assignment? (open-text)*
- *Q2: Breaking down the problem into smaller tasks will help you complete the assignment. How would you go about breaking down this problem into smaller tasks? (open-text)*

Figure 1: Applied Instructional Question Types

5.1 Participants

The experiment included three groups of students new to software development and design concepts. The control group (C1) was the August 2017 course with 134 students and was given a week to complete the Rainfall Problem [20] without the question activity.

The remaining two groups were enrolled in the March 2018 course, and were given an isomorphic version of the Rainfall Problem and the non-compulsory question activity. The first experiment group (E2.1) contained 129 students that did not participate in the question activity, while the second experiment group (E2.2) contained 120 students that did participate in the activity.

5.2 Data Collection and Analysis

Figure 1 shows the open-text questions in the activity that allowed students to respond in their own words. Answers were collected anonymously in a Google spreadsheet and analysed using a mixed methods approach of qualitative and quantitative data analysis. Analysis was performed against the six Bloom's cognitive levels and the four revised Bloom's knowledge dimensions [1]: factual, conceptual, procedural, and metacognitive knowledge. Qualitative analysis involved coding segments of the answers into the appropriate Bloom's cognitive levels and knowledge dimensions. Frequencies of the content analysis, against the Bloom's cognitive levels and knowledge dimensions, were extracted using a matrix table in NVivo and imported into SPSS for statistical analysis.

Qualitative analysis was performed by the primary author using the NVivo software tool. To ensure coding reliability, a co-author coded 25% of the students' answers, and negotiated the partial coding with the primary author. To strengthen the coding validity, due to the software limitation in inter-rater reliability, alternate coding reliability was performed.

Negotiation on a coding criteria was agreed upon by the authors and influenced by Thompson et al. interpretation of Bloom's knowledge dimensions for CS programming assessments [22]. Table 2 shows an excerpt of the pilot coding criteria described in Section 4.1. The table includes sample answers by the students for each cognitive level. When evaluating the answers during negotiation, the authors discussed the delineation between the *Application* and *Analysis* cognitive levels. The authors decided answers in *Analysis* identify relationships between tasks as part of the problem-solving process, while answers that map tasks or constructs to parts of the problem-solving process were coded as *Application*.

Level	Coding Criteria	Example Student Answers
Recall	• When student provides the name of the schema or language construct. • When the student provides the definition for the language construct.	• Arrays are used • if and else • you can use arrays to store the data
Comprehension	• When the student incorporates part of the current problem description into their answer, along with basic description of the schema or language construct.	• An array with n elements (representing n days) can be created, and filed with the number of elements sold for each day. • use if and else to decide the number is positive or negative and distinguish between -789 and other numbers
Application	• Student maps tasks or constructs to a part of the problem-solving process.	• First generate the random numbers of products sold. • Setting something to read out how many things are in the array before -789.
Analysis	• Student connects constructs to form parts of the problem-solving process. • Student identifies the relationship between tasks to solve the problem.	• Create an array of products sold, program goes through array and calculates how many days (how many elements in array) until reach value -789 (end loop), calculate average of products sold (loop from array (0 to N-1)
Synthesis	• Student describes how all of the tasks or constructs work collectively to solve the problem.	• shopkeeper who can simply enter the products sold in chronological order. • Next, to find the average, all the elements of the array (now with no negatives)
Evaluation	• The student expresses judgment or assessment of the suitability or quality of an approach.	• The former because sales aren't always consistent and the later because of holidays, unforeseen events, etc • make sure that works before testing edge tests

Table 2: Excerpt of the Coding Criteria for Students' Answers

5.3 Results

We evaluated the results from the question activity using directed context analysis to determine the cognitive levels students used when answering. The overall average of the programming assignment was also examined to determine if the question activity might have impacted the students' programmed solution.

We evaluated the overall class average for the three groups' programming assignments. Group C1 with no exposure to the question activity had an overall average of 83%. Group E2.1 who received but did not participate in the activity had an overall average of 86.6%, and group E2.2 that answered the activity had an overall average of 86.9%. Comparing the results showed no significant differences when students participated in the question activity. We also analysed the results using t-tests, the control group $t(211)_{C1}$ = -1.194, p=0.861, and the experiment groups E2.1 and E2.2, $t(247)_{E2.1}$ = -0.140, p=0.889 and $t(242.241)_{E2.2}$ = -0.140, p=0.889, with the results showing no significant differences.

Words in the answers were analysed, where *array* (f=202) was the most frequently used, followed by *number* (f=162), and *products* (f=157). Though *array* focused on language constructs, the second and third commonly used word relate to the problem's context. We observed the language construct *loop* was the next most commonly used term, ranking 12th (f=80) in the frequency list.

The remainder of this section analyses 141 unique responses to the question activity from group E2.2. Table 3 represents the coded answers aligned with Bloom's cognitive levels, while Table 4 shows the coded answers against the knowledge dimensions. Both tables provide the percentages of the coded answers, representing the frequency of lexical items used to answer each question.

A bivariate correlation was performed across both Q1 and Q2 for more substantial data analysis. We report on high correlations between the Bloom's cognitive levels and knowledge dimensions, shown in Tables 3 and 4. The analysis shows a high correlation between *Recall* and the *Factual* (r=0.515) and *Conceptual* (r=0.399) knowledge dimensions, while *Analysis* has a high correlation with *Conceptual* (r=0.430) and *Procedural* (r=0.418) knowledge dimensions. Further discussion on notable correlations is in Section 6.

5.3.1 Analysis of Activity Question 1. The first question, Q1, targets the Bloom's *Recall* cognitive level, to engage the students' internal knowledgebase. Of the 120 participates in group E2.2, 12.8% (n=18) did not answer Q1. Table 3 shows answers predominately residing in the *Recall* 13.31% (n=54) and *Comprehension* 14.43% (n=58) levels. Answers in *Recall* include the definitions of language constructs, such as 'For loops can be used to check elements', 'arrays are useful for storing and organising data', and 'Data is best stored and organised in an array'. The *Comprehension* level show students answering in more detail, such as 'An array with n elements (representing n days) can be created, and filled with the number of elements sold for each day' and 'Number of products sold and the number of days that they are sold on can vary'.

Evaluating Q1 against the Bloom's knowledge dimensions, shown in Table 4, shows most answers residing in *Principles and Generalisations* 8.51% (n=42) and *Determine Procedures* 6.93% (n=39). Answers for *Principles and Generalisations* were about the use of the array to 'create an array to store data', and data manipulation, where 'collecting and organising data will help to sort the data out.' Some answers go into greater detail on selecting the procedures and criteria for using the array. For example, 'Your program processes each day from the array until your program encounters the value -789 in the array', 'more efficient to use arrays when several values of the same variable are used', and 'the program reads data in array. Each element which is collected in this array represents the number of products sold for one day.'

5.3.2 Analysis of Activity Question 2. The second question, Q2, targeted the *Analysis* level, to encourage the use of strategic knowledge and to promote the identification of tasks prior to implementation. Of the 120 students that submitted answers, 12% (n=12) did not answer Q2. Within the Bloom's cognitive levels, shown in Table 3, answers mainly resided in the *Analysis* 23.07% (n=77) and *Application* 10.91% (n=38) levels. Answers residing in the *Application* layer identified parts of tasks, for example, 'That the program needs to be written so that it's able to read the data that is inputted and then sorted in some way to produce the desired outcome', 'breaking down the multiple conditions in the correct orders allows coding easier', and 'figure out which parts of the code would be repetitive and decide on a way to do them easier.'

Determine Procedures 6.82% (n=41) and *Principles and Generalisation* 4.44 % (n=35), shown in Table 4, were the predominately used knowledge dimensions. In *Determine Procedures*, students described procedures in detail, for example 'using if loops. Make it such that any negative number will be set to zero and such that if -789 is found, the products sold will stop', 'make program processes each day from the array until it encounters the value -789 in the array', and 'checking for the -789 value, otherwise the value would be changed to zero and the stop requirement wouldn't be met until the whole array was checked.' The last example demonstrates the student's ability to describe the algorithm by identifying tasks, such as the sentinel marker (-789). Answers within *Principles and Generalisation* contained fewer task details, for example 'finally did the calculation and displaying of data', 'calculating the average value of array elements', and 'determining the number of days and the number of products sold each day.'

6 DISCUSSION

The goal of this paper was to align instructional question types to the Bloom's cognitive levels and the revised knowledge dimensions to form a framework that could help CS1 students answer questions that engage cognitive levels appropriate to their learning. To illustrate the framework, a question activity was developed as an intervention for a programming assignment, giving students the opportunity to practice lower and higher-order thinking skills in a blended learning environment. The illustration also demonstrates to educators that layering questions can help promote the use of critical thinking skills by students.

Bloom's Taxonomy	Q1	Q2
Recall	54 (13.31%)	8 (1.96%)
Comprehension	58 (14.43%)	25 (5.07%)
Application	32 (6.5%)	38 (10.91%)
Analysis	7 (1.51%)	77 (23.07%)
Synthesis	3 (0.45%)	4 (0.55%)
Evaluation	3 (0.63%)	4 (0.21%)

Table 3: Group E2.2 Results for Bloom's Cognitive Levels

Knowledge Dimensions	Q1	Q2
Factual Knowledge		
Terminology	25 (4.69%)	10 (1.61%)
Details & elements	30 (5.84%)	30 (3.83%)
Conceptual Knowledge		
Classifications & categories	3 (0.64%)	0 (0%)
Principles & generalisations	42 (8.51%)	35 (4.44%)
Theories, models & structures	8 (1.54%)	13 (3.26%)
Procedural Knowledge		
Skills & algorithms	18 (2.61%)	21 (4.32%)
Techniques & methods	8 (1.65%)	24 (4.83%
Determine procedures	39 (6.93%)	41 (6.82%)
Metacognitive Knowledge		
Strategic knowledge	9 (1.89%)	28 (5.11%)
Cognitive tasks	1 (0.35%)	10 (1.79%)
Self-knowledge	5 (0.93%)	1 (0.09%)
Other		
Does not understand	5 (1.27%)	3 (1.06%)
Unrelated	1 (0.35%)	1 (0.35%)

Table 4: Group E2.2 Results for Knowledge Dimensions

The first research question (RQ1) evaluates how the 23 IQTs align with Bloom's. We were successful in mapping most of the IQTs, except for *Backchannel, Focus,* and *Hints.* We found these IQTs could span multiple cognitive levels based on the question's context. Results from Boyer et al. show *Hints* as the most frequently posed question type, perhaps due to student-teacher discourse generating hints within multiple contexts and cognitive levels. Our inability to classify these categories might be how the questions are applied in the two studies. Boyer et al. used questioning in a student-teacher discourse, while this study utilises questioning as an intervention to a programming assignment.

We observed the *Comprehension* level containing the most instructional question types. These findings support educators frequent use of comprehension-based questions in classroom environments [11]. Perhaps in the Boyer et al. study, educators used familiar question-asking strategies they employed in the classroom. Results also demonstrate students predominately using *Procedural Knowledge* that referenced language constructs to answer the questions. The predominate use of *Procedural Knowledge* correlating to Bloom's *Analysis* level might be a unique behaviour for CS over other disciplines, since students might draw on algorithms and programming techniques when analysing problems.

Answering the question might require different cognitive levels, depending on the students' domain knowledge and abilities. A previous study [5] observed students using lower than the intended cognitive levels to complete CS assessments, showing students' prior experience and domain knowledge influenced their cognitive level. When using the framework to construct the question activity, educators might observe students answering with different or unexpected levels. If answers fall into unexpected cognitive levels, this might indicate students are struggling with concepts, might not understand the questions, neglectful in forming satisfactory answers, or the question does not elicit the desired cognitive or knowledge levels, which may require question revision by the educator.

The second research question (RQ2) considers whether the expected cognitive level was achieved when answering the question activity. The results show students achieving the desired cognitive levels, using both lower and higher-order thinking skills. Students predominately engaged the *Recall* and *Comprehension* levels for lower-order thinking skills, while *Analysis* was prevalent for higher-order thinking skills. These results are aligned with the design of the first question in the activity, encouraging students to reflect on what they know for solving the problem. The encouragement can be seen influencing the answers with the *Recall* level correlating to *Factual* and *Conceptual* knowledge dimensions, where a student took a critical approach to answering the question by drawing on what they already know (*Factual*) and bringing the factual knowledge together to solve the problem or parts of the problem (*Conceptual*).

Through the lense of comprehension strategy, the most frequently used words, *array*, *number*, and *sold*, demonstrate knowledge usage from the program and domain layers. If the word count predominately resided in the program layer, students' comprehension of the problem might be lower, but concepts in both program and domain layers show a higher degree of comprehension [15].

6.1 Threats to Validity

There are limitations to this study. The control and experiment groups are from different semesters, potentially affecting the overall grades. Additional measurements are needed to determine the impact of the question activity as a problem-solving intervention, since the results showed no significant gains in the overall class average. The results showed students in group E2.1 and E2.2 having similar results in the programming assignment. E2.1 might have benefited from receiving the activity without providing answers, but additional analysis is needed for confirmation. Additional analysis of the students' approach to implementing their solution could determine whether the question activity helped reduce the completion time and students' mistakes. When approaching the deadline, we notice a trend that students were generating shorter answers coded to the *Recall* level. We can further investigate whether these students benefited from the question activity using shorter answers. Another limitation was the presentation as a non-compulsory activity. Embedding the questions as a graded activity might produce answers from expected or higher cognitive levels and knowledge dimensions, potentially giving educators a better view into any misconceptions the students might have in the assignment description.

7 CONCLUSION

We hope that educators use this Instructional Framework to explore ways in which they can specifically target cognitive levels in instructional questioning. During the development of the framework, we identified future research opportunities, such as the classification of *Backchannel*, *Focus*, and *Hints* into Bloom's Taxonomy, and establish guidelines for educators to achieve the intended cognitive level when posing questions from these categories. Though the presented framework is based on Bloom's, the process of question classification could be performed using SOLO, with future research comparing and contrasting the results between the taxonomies. While the initial study is promising, further work is required on the framework to better assess as an intervention.

We are currently providing the CS1 educators at the University of Adelaide with the framework to use within their courses to construct learning activities and investigating how different IQTs from the framework could help students build metacognitive skills for solving programming problems. We also intend on expanding the framework's instructional context for adoption by upper-division CS courses.

REFERENCES

[1] L. Anderson and D. Krathwohl. *Taxonomy for Learning, Teaching and Assessing: A Revision of Bloom's Taxonomy of Educational Objectives.* Longman, New York, 2001.

[2] J. B. Biggs and K. F. Collis. The SOLO taxonomy (structure of the observed learning outcome). In A. J. Edward, editor, *Evaluating the Quality of Learning*, New York, New York, 1982.

[3] B. S. Bloom. *Taxonomy of Educational Objectives: The Classification of Educational Goals.* Longmans, Green, New York, 1956.

[4] K. E. Boyer, W. Lahti, R. Phillips, M. D. Wallis, M. A. Vouk, and J. C. Lester. Principles of asking effective questions during student problem solving. *Proceedings of the 41st ACM Technical Symposium on Computer Science Education*, pages 460–464, 2010.

[5] J. Buckley and C. Exton. Blooms' taxonomy: A framework for assessing programmers' knowledge of software systems. *Proceedings of the 11th IEEE International Workshop on Program Comprehension*, pages 165–174, 2003.

[6] M. T. H. Chi, N. de Leeuw, M. Chiu, and C. LaVancher. Eliciting self-explanations improves understanding. *Cognitive Science*, 18:439–477, 1994.

[7] A. Churches. Bloom's taxonomy blooms digitally. *Educators' eZine*, 2008.

[8] A. Collins. Teaching reasoning skills. In . R. G. S. Chipman, J. Segal, editor, *Thinking and Learning Skills, Vol 2*, Hillsdale, NJ, 1985. Lawrence Erlbaum Associates.

[9] A. Collins and A. Stevens. A cognitive theory of inquiry teaching. In C. Reigeluth, editor, *Instructional-design theories and models*, pages 203–230, Norwood, NJ, 1983. Lawrence Erlbaum Associates.

[10] J. Dillon. The classification of research questions. *Review of Educational Research*, 54:327–361, 1984.

[11] A. Graesser and N. Person. Question asking during tutoring. *American Educational Research Journal*, 31(1):104–137, 1994.

[12] R. Howard, C. Carver, and W. Lane. Felder's learning styles, Bloom's taxonomy, and the Kolb learning cycle: Tying it all together in the CS2 course. *Proceedings of the Twenty-Fifth SICSE Technical Symposium in Computer Science Education*, 1996.

[13] R. Lister, B. Simon, E. Thompson, J. L. Whalley, and C. Prasad. Not seeing the forest for the trees: Novice programmers and the SOLO taxonomy. *ITiCSE '06 11th Annual Conference on Innovation and Technology in Computer Science Education*, pages 118–122, 2006.

[14] R. D. Nielsen, J. Buckingham, G. Knoll, B. Marsh, and L. Palen. A taxonomy of questions for question generation. *Proceedings of the 1st Workshop on Question Generation*, 2008.

[15] N. Pennington. Comprehension strategies in programming. *Second Workshop on Empirical Studies of Programmers*, pages 100–113, 1987.

[16] A. Petersen, M. Craig, and D. Zingaro. Reviewing cs1 exam question content. *SIGCSE '11*, pages 631–636, 2011.

[17] M. Roy and M. T. H. Chi. The self-explanation principle in multimedia learning. In R. Mayer, editor, *The Cambridge Handbook of Multimedia Learning*, pages 271–286. Cambridge University Press, 2005.

[18] I. Sanders and C. Mueller. A fundamentals-based curriculum for first year computer science. *Proceedings Thirty-First SIGCSE Technical Symposium on Computer Science Education*, pages 227–231, 2000.

[19] T. Scott. Bloom's taxonomy applied to testing in computer science. *Proceedings of the 12th Annual CCSC Rocky Mountain Conference, Consortium for Computing Sciences in Colleges*, pages 267–274, 2003.

[20] E. Soloway, J. Bonar, and K. Ehrlich. Cognitive strategies and looping constructs: an empirical study. *Communications of the ACM*, 26(11):853–860, 1983.

[21] A. Stolcke, K. Ries, N. Coccaro, E. Shriberg, R. Bates, D. Jurafsky, P. Taylor, R. Martin, C. V. Ess-Dykema, and M. Meteer. Dialogue act modeling for automatic tagging and recognition of conversational speech. *Computational Linguistics*,

26(3):339–373, 2000.

[22] E. Thompson, A. Luxton-Reilly, J. L. Whalley, M. Hu, and P. Robbins. Bloom's taxonomy for CS assessment. *ACE '08 Tenth Australasian Computing Education Conference*, pages 155–161, 2008.

[23] E. Tikhonova and N. Kudinova. Sophisticated thinking: higher order thinking skills. *Journal of Language and Education*, 1:12–23, 2015.

[24] B. K. A. Weusijana, C. K. Reisbeck, and J. T. W. Jr. Fostering reflection with socratic tutoring software: Results of using inquiry teaching strategies with web-based HCI techniques. *ICLS '04 Proceedings of the 6th International Conference on Learning Sciences*, pages 561–567, 2004.

[25] J. L. Whalley, R. Lister, E. Thompson, T. Clear, P. Robbins, P. A. Kumar, and C. Prasad. An Australasian study of reading and comprehension skills in novice programmers, using the Bloom and SOLO taxonomies. *Eighth Australasian Computing Education Conference (ACE2006)*, pages 353–382, 2006.

[26] A. Zohar and A. B. David. Explicit teaching of meta-strategic knowledge in authentic classroom situations. *Metacognition and Learning*, 3(1):59–82, 2008.

Behaviors of Higher and Lower Performing Students in CS1

Soohyun Nam Liao[1], Sander Valstar[1], Kevin Thai[1], Christine Alvarado[1],
Daniel Zingaro[2], William G. Griswold[1], Leo Porter[1]
[1]University of California, San Diego
[2]University of Toronto, Mississauga

ABSTRACT

Although recent work in computing has discovered multiple techniques to identify low-performing students in a course, it is unclear what factors contribute to those students' difficulties. If we were able to better understand the characteristics of such students, we may be better able to help those students. This work examines the characteristics of low- and high-performing students through interviews with students from an introductory computing class. We identify a number of relevant areas of student behavior including how they approach their exam studies, how they approach completing programming assignments, whether they sought help after identifying misunderstandings, how and from whom they sought help, and how they reflected on assignments after submitting them. Particular behaviors within each area are coded and differences between groups of students are identified.

CCS CONCEPTS

• **Social and professional topics → Computing education; CS1;**

KEYWORDS

student performance, student behaviors, student interviews, CS1

ACM Reference Format:

Soohyun Nam Liao, Sander Valstar, Kevin Thai, Christine Alvarado, Daniel Zingaro, William G. Griswold, Leo Porter. 2019. Behaviors of Higher and Lower Performing Students in CS1. In *Innovation and Technology in Computer Science Education (ITiCSE '19), July 15–17, 2019, Aberdeen, Scotland, UK.* ACM, New York, NY, USA, 7 pages. https://doi.org/10.1145/3304221.3319740

1 INTRODUCTION

Pass rates in introductory computing courses have been historically low with an average of 67.7% worldwide, and they have not improved significantly over the years [33]. At the same time, skyrocketing CS enrollments [7] make it more difficult for instructors to identify and support struggling students, as per-student resources are spread thinner.

Recent work has focused on building more accurate automated models for early identification of students who are likely to struggle to pass introductory courses. These models use a variety of naturally-occurring data sources, including programming behaviors and clicker data, and are capable of identifying potentially struggling students at increasing levels of accuracy [2, 5, 18, 24, 31, 34].

Yet, identifying which students are likely to struggle is only half the battle: we must also endeavor to help these students. Unfortunately, designing effective interventions is challenging, and the literature on interventions has yielded few successes [6, 9]. Interventions that require extra work, such as supplemental help sessions or the opportunity to redo prior work, usually fail to reach struggling students, who have too much on their plate already [16, 23]; more general "learning how to learn" interventions are too far removed from the specific course material to be effective [9]. Moreover, one-size-fits-all interventions may fail in CS because we have reason to suspect that students in CS classes may succeed for different reasons than those in other disciplines [36].

A deeper understanding of the behaviors employed by successful and unsuccessful students in introductory computing would aid in developing effective interventions. To gain a broad understanding of the gamut of student behaviors, we conducted a series of semi-structured interviews with students in an introductory CS course at a large public university and qualitatively analyzed interview transcripts. Our choice of qualitative research methods is informed by our goal of exploring students' individual contexts and identifying new variables of interest [8].

In these interviews, we inquired about student behaviors in the course, including how they prepare for exams and solve programming assignments. To analyze these interviews, we used an open-coding approach [12, 22] to identify and categorize student behaviors. A natural division appeared between behaviors associated with preparing for exams and behaviors associated with completing programming assignments. We believe some of the behaviors within these two categories are specific to learning computer science, whereas others fall under general study skills.

At the end of the course, with the knowledge of which students ultimately performed poorly or well, we analyzed the codes from interview transcripts and found that for some categories of behavior, the behaviors of unsuccessful and successful students varied in distinctive ways. This distinction lays the foundation for future work to study the prevalence of these behaviours. Moreover, researchers may be able to experiment with interventions geared at encouraging positive behaviors common to higher-performing students and/or discouraging behaviors common to lower-performing students.

2 BACKGROUND

Researchers have qualitatively studied the factors that motivate students to persist or drop out of introductory computing courses. Those studies found that time constraints, low prioritization of CS courses, ineffective study skills, difficulty, and motivation were characteristics often associated with students who drop CS1 [26, 32].

ITiCSE '19, July 15–17, 2019, Aberdeen, Scotland, UK

ACM ISBN 978-1-4503-6301-3/19/07...$15.00
https://doi.org/10.1145/3304221.3319740

Table 1: Components of the Studied Course

Component	Description
Lecture	Class with clickers and Peer Instruction. [27]
Podcast	Recording of class, posted online.
Discussion	Extra weekly lecture run by graduate student TAs. Attendance optional.
Office Hours	Held by undergraduate tutors, graduate TAs, or the instructor.
Piazza	Online question board and discussion forum.
Reading Assignment	Weekly textbook-reading assignment for lecture preparation.
Lab	Weekly programming practice session led by tutors.
Lab Quiz	Online quiz given at the end of each lab.
Review Quiz	Weekly online quiz for the week's material.
PSA	Weekly programming assignment.
Star Points	Optional extra credit assignments for each PSA.
Practice Midterm	Midterm exam questions from a previous term, provided by the instructor.
Midterm	50 minute In-class exams; held in week 4 and 7.
Final	Summative Assessment in Week 11.

These prior studies uncover some of the same behaviors that we identify, but they focus only on those students who drop CS1 or leave computer science. In addition, there is a strong quantitative tradition that investigates student persistence and progress in introductory CS courses, focusing on factors such as motivation [29], achievement goals [36], measures of programming behavior [4, 10, 15, 35], and measures of students' social behaviors [3]. While these studies have informed techniques for identifying at-risk students, they do not give insight into the particular antecedents of these behaviours.

Finally, there are numerous qualitative studies that report on student behaviours and attitudes, such as study strategies of students when they are stuck [21], debugging or problem-solving strategies during programming [14, 25], students' perceptions of their ability [17], and students' perceptions of their behaviors [30]. That work, however, focuses on class-level data, not the particular experiences of individual students.

3 METHOD

Our goal was to discover behaviors that might be associated with higher or lower student performance in introductory computing courses. We chose an open-coding technique, which iteratively groups and regroups related fragments of interview transcripts in order to identify themes and uncover patterns in the data [12, 22]. Below, we describe our data collection procedure, interview structure, and analysis and coding process.

3.1 Course Context

We selected an introductory CS course ("CS1") at a large North American research-focused university as the context for our study. Students from two terms (fall and winter) participated in the study. This 10-week CS1 course is designed for CS majors, intended CS majors, and non-majors alike. It uses a media computation curriculum to teach students basic programming in Java [13]. Table 1 lists the main components of the course; we refer to these components throughout the paper.

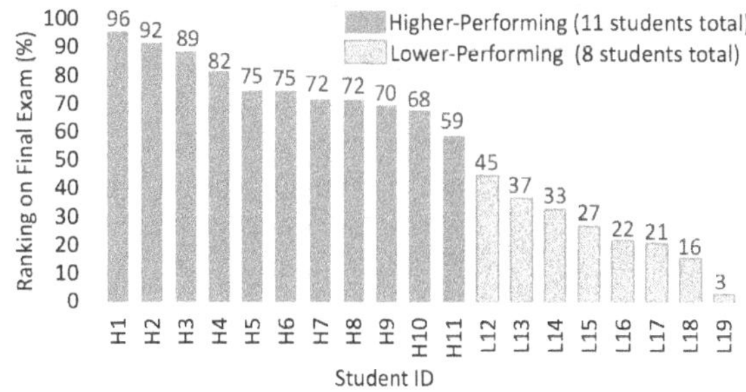

Figure 1: Interviewee Performance on Final Exam

3.2 Interview Participants

Students were recruited to participate in interviews, as approved by our institution's Human Subjects Review Board. Students were compensated for their time with gift cards. During the first term, we interviewed 8 students. We then used the data from these interviews to refine the interview process, and interviewed 19 students in the second term.

3.2.1 ***First Term.*** The first round of our study began in the middle of the term. The students had by that time completed their first midterm and received grades and feedback on it. The course instructor provided the midterm exam rankings of the 441 consenting students to a research colleague, who then helped us invite students (124) to participate. These 124 students were selected such that at least some portion were in the bottom 40% of midterm grades. Eight of these students agreed to participate in the interviews. To avoid unintentionally influencing the interviews, the interviewers were unaware of which students did poorly on the midterm.

3.2.2 ***Second Term.*** In the second round of the study, we began recruiting for the interviews before students took the first midterm, so we needed a different way of selecting a representative sample group. When recruiting students to participate in the study, we asked those interested to apply via an online survey. Part of that survey asked students to report the grade they were aiming to get in the course. 45 out of approximately 400 students responded to the survey. Because most students reported aiming for an "A" in the course, we first selected all students that aimed for a grade less than "A" (5 out of 45). One of those students did not respond to our request to schedule an interview. Students were then selected randomly until our participant pool reached 20 confirmed students (though one student dropped the class prior to the interview). Again, the interviewers did not inquire about actual student grades directly (though students sometimes volunteered the information) until after interviews were completed.

Although the grade a student is aiming for does not necessarily reflect their performance in the course, we felt that it would help us diversify the achievement levels of students in our pool. Indeed, as shown in Figure 1, the approach seemed successful.

3.3 Categorizing Performance

We used final exam grades to divide students from the second term into two categories after the interviews: Higher-Performing (HP) and Lower-Performing (LP). Students who received final exam scores in the top 50% of the class were considered high performers, while those in the bottom 50% of the class were considered lower performers. This threshold reflects the way that Ahadi et al. defined at-risk and not-at-risk students [1]. We recognize that performance in a course is on a continuum; though we have used a binary classification in our analysis, we also include the rank of each student (among our interviewees) to help provide readers with a more nuanced perspective of performance.

3.4 Interviews

3.4.1 ***First Term.*** During the first term, we conducted interviews shortly after the first midterm and follow-up interviews after the second midterm. Starting one week before the second midterm, students were asked to keep a timetable. In this table they recorded the date, start time, finish time, what they studied, and the difficulty of the studied material (1-5, where 1 is very easy and 5 is very hard). Additionally, students were asked to take a picture of their work environment every time they filled in the table. During interviews, we used the timetable and pictures to help the students recall what exactly they were studying at a specific point in time, similar to Fincher et al.'s My Programming Week [11]. Finally, students were asked to bring all their study materials (e.g., laptop, notes, textbook) to the interview. Two authors interviewed the students; these authors were not associated with the course in any way.

3.4.2 ***Second Term.*** Three interviews were conducted for each student: after the first midterm, after the second midterm, and shortly before final exams. The main focus of our analysis is the first interview, as this interview captures student behaviors early in the term. To prepare for the first interview, students were asked to keep a timetable during the week prior to the first midterm. Students were again asked to take pictures of their study area and bring all their study materials to the interview. The interviews were semi-structured, with some prompts originating from our interview experience in the first term. Examples of these prepared questions include *"How is your term going so far?"*, *"How did you prepare for the midterm?"*, *"Do you usually begin your programming assignments on this day?"*, *"How did you fix this bug here in your code?"*, and *"Can you explain this method?"*. The same two authors from the first term interviewed the students and again were not associated with the course.

3.5 Interview Analysis

Analysis was performed by two of the authors. We first transcribed the interviews. Next, we chose two student interviews from the first term, segmenting their transcripts into topical components. We printed these snippets and worked together to assign codes to them. After this session we began coding the rest of the interviews. We iteratively improved our coding rubric and validated each iteration by having the two authors independently code at least 10% of our data (two interviews) and subsequently measuring the inter-coder reliability. After 3 total iterations of independently coding interviews and further refining the coding rubric, we had reduced our initial rubric from 111 codes to 41 codes and achieved an inter-coder reliability of 87% agreement.

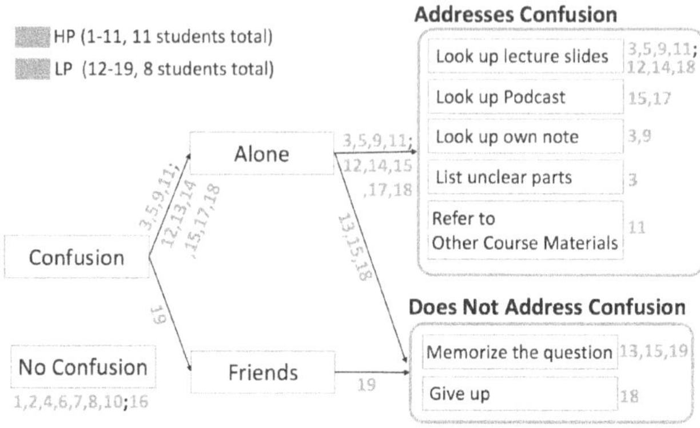

Figure 2: How Students Address Confusions Encountered on Practice Midterm (numbers represent student identifiers)

4 RESULTS

In this section, we describe our observations of how students prepare for the first midterm and work on programming assignments, including their particular study practices, help-seeking behaviors, willingness to correct identified gaps and confusion, and whether they continue to seek out answers to questions even after deadlines. We refer to students as "H" (Higher-Performing) or "L" (Lower-Performing) along with their final exam rank relative to other interviewees (e.g., 11 out of 19).

4.1 Midterm Preparation

All but four students started midterm preparation by working on the practice midterm. Two of those four students did not recall how they started their preparation. The third of the four, H11, used the practice midterm after reviewing other materials to assess whether they were prepared for the actual midterm. However, H11 identified some difficulties from the practice midterm, so they followed the same study pattern as the rest of the participants after taking the practice test: *"...I just got mistakes on, referencing [from the practice midterm], which showed I needed to study more on referencing" [H11].*

Figure 2 shows our codes for how students addressed concerns on the practice midterm while studying for the actual midterm. Seven HPs and one LP (L16) identified no significant difficulty on the practice midterm. Although they did not necessarily get every question entirely correct, they said they made only simple mistakes. For example: *"But they were just like ... dumb in my mind. I think one of them was uh, it asks 'What file is the, turtle class in?' And then I was like, 'Oh, isn't that dumb? It's in the turtle class.' But no, it's in the turtle.java, so I was like ...'Oh, of course' " [H6].*

Of the remaining 11 students, seven students reported resolving all of the difficulties that they identified (H3,5,9,11; L12,14,17), while the other four (L13,15,18,19) did not. All HPs who identified challenges succeeded in overcoming those challenges, while less than half of the LPs succeeded.

The following provides details on the four categories we identified in which HP and LP behavior differed.

4.1.1 ***Memorize or Give Up.*** The 11 students who identified confusion using the practice midterm worked to resolve it in different ways. As seen in Figure 2, the LPs who did not address their confusion either memorized the solution to relevant practice midterm questions (L13, 15, 19) or gave up, hoping it would not be on the exam (L18): *"I just redid the practice exam properly to try and see how much of it I actually did remember how to do. That's kinda just standard procedure with me when I'm given a practice test" [L13]. "...the eight different kinds of primitives was actually on the midterm but...I didn't memorize them because I thought we didn't have to...[when studying them]" [L18].* Moreover, L15 mentioned making note cards for memorization: *"'Okay, I understand this problem,' and then just save that note card for in the future, for hypothetical case if I forgot how to do a certain problem..." [L15].*

L19 also exhibited a behavior of focusing excessively on getting the right answer, as opposed to gaining understanding (L19 was in the bottom 3% on the final exam): *"I would just sit there for a while trying to figure it out. And whenever I thought I finished, I'll get my friend to check it, and then he would tell me yes or no. And if he said no, then I would go erase it and do it again." [L19].*

4.1.2 ***Resources Used.*** As shown in the Addresses Confusion box in Figure 2, students used different resources when studying for the midterm and attempting to address their confusion. It was common for students to refer to lecture materials, with most examining the lecture slides. Only two students (L15,17), both LPs, watched the video podcasts of the lectures. One of those (L17) went so far as to watch multiple lectures back-to-back: *"I just sat on my bed, and put on the TV and then I sped them up a little and just listened to them...I skipped the first beginning ones because they were pretty straightforward, and then I picked some of the middle ones...then went up to whichever one before the midterm" [L17].*

Beyond lecture material, HPs availed themselves of additional resources such as their own notes, the textbook, quiz questions, and the Internet: *"...I look at how some functions the textbook asks us to do, or...in the slides, [but] some idea that I want to understand is not covered in the slides, I'm trying to refer to my notes to get the extra information" [H9].* H3 also took the time to list the things they were not sure about and reviewed it right before the midterm exam: *"If I missed something, like I didn't know this, sometimes I write it down...It was all just like, random notes...[and I read it in] like the morning before the midterm" [H3].* H11 generated and practiced their own questions to strengthen their understanding: *"So after finishing the test in, like, 30 minutes, I think I did, or 20 minutes. I just went back and studied references again...I went onto the Internet, and I learned it a little bit...And then I used the textbook. [Also] I just keep on trying to make new questions and see if it was right or not" [H11].*

4.1.3 ***Friends Involved.*** While all HPs and most LPs worked on the practice midterm on their own, two LPs (L14, 19) worked together with a friend (Friends box in Figure 2). However, both reported that their friend did not end up being helpful. L14 reviewed alone after the meeting with the friend to resolve confusion, and L19 did not resolve their confusion. L19 acknowledged that tutors would explain an answer in more detail, but ended up not going to tutor hours for the practice midterm because they were working on it at the last minute: *"one of my suite mates is also a CSE major. And I will just ask him. I mean, but the thing is that...he will just tell me how to do it. He doesn't teach me, just says...'This is how you do it.' I'm like, 'Okay.' But I don't know what this means. And that's why I'll go to the tutoring ... to be like, 'Uh, what does this mean? I don't get it'" [L19].*

4.1.4 ***After-exam Behavior.*** H1, whose final exam score was in the 96th percentile, worked to resolve a confusion after the midterm exam. No other students described such behavior: *"...I believe it's a problem about reference. I asked different tutors and they give me different answers. I just feel confused so I double-check it with my professor yesterday, even after the midterm" [H1].*

4.2 Programming Assignments

Figure 3 illustrates student behaviors when overcoming challenges during programming assignments. Every student except for H9 reported encountering challenges while working on programming assignments. The following subsections discuss each of the constitutive boxes of the figure, specifically the challenge they faced and whether they were successful in addressing the challenge.

4.2.1 ***Planning.*** Two HPs and three LPs started programming assignments quite late, a day or less before the deadlines. However, the HPs who reported starting late were the two strongest-performing HPs (H1,2), did not show any concern about starting late, and were able to complete the assignments successfully. On the other hand, two of the three LPs were the bottom-ranked LPs and bemoaned the lack of help available at the last minute. One of those two, L19, started assignments on the due date or the day before the due date. As such, the student had no choice but to work on the assignment until late at night: *"when I'm programming and there's an error, um, usually...it's late at night, so I have no one really to contact. So I just sit there for a long period sometimes trying to figure it out" [L19]. "Yes because I couldn't get my program to work properly, so...and there was no tutors, any help, because it was like almost last minute..." [L18].*

These two LPs also mentioned that they thought of posting questions on the Piazza discussion board, but did not feel that they had enough time to wait for a tutor's response. Therefore, they felt they had to either go back to campus to ask questions to a random classmate or just give up on the problem: *"... once I asked the question but didn't respond till the next day. But...I can't wait that long. So I just went to the lab...asked someone, sitting there, 'Do you know how to do this?'" [L19]. "considering like the time that I was working on it, I didn't ask on Piazza because I didn't expect a response by then... I worked on it too late so that was kind of the setback on being able to finish this" [L18].*

However, contrary to the rest of the LP students, L12 did not seem to worry about starting programming assignments late. Later, we noticed that L12 had a classmate who worked on the programming assignments with them, and L12 thought the classmate was much smarter than them. Based on L12's comments, it seemed likely that they were overdependent on their programming partner: *"... a lot of the times, I start on Saturday [the day before the due date] 'cause if I don't understand it the first day, I'll take a step back and come back the due date. And try and just do it because the assignments usually don't take that long."* After a long pause they continued, *"He's a lot smarter than me, 'Cause he has prior experience, but... I didn't really know what he was saying. So then, he wasn't that far into it, so we just started working together. He explained to me this part, and then, we just kind of did the rest of it together..." [L12].*

4.2.2 ***Debugging Challenges.*** All except H4, 6, and 9 brought up debugging experiences (i.e., fixing errors in the code) that were

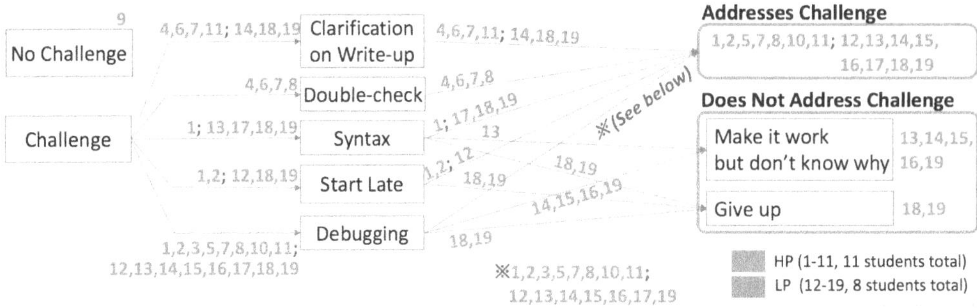

Figure 3: How Students Respond to Challenges during Programming Assignments (numbers represent student identifiers)

challenging to them. The majority of the LPs (L13,14, 15,16,18,19) were unable to resolve all of their debugging challenges. Once they were able to get their code to work, sometimes with help from tutors, they reported moving on without understanding why it worked. In some cases, the code was deemed to work because it appeared to have the desired effect or it passed test cases provided by the instructor: *"I don't know why it's going negative but my tests are passing. The whole time I was just trying to make my test pass. And when I finally got them passed, I was like, 'I shouldn't change anything.' 'Cause I feel like it's all gonna go down...the drain if I do. So I just left it as is...I turned it in" [L19].* When L14 was asked whether the friend's advice helped, they answered *"Yes. I think it did...We were able to somehow change it to make it actually display these values" [L14].*

Moreover, when we asked the LPs to explain a part of the code that they debugged with help from tutors or friends, some of them were not able to explain it at all. When L15 was asked about a return statement in their code, they replied *"Why I need that line? Um... It's similar to using the System.out.println()... is like the way I remember it... Okay, this was kind of confusing..." [L15].*

4.2.3 ***Syntax Challenges***. H1 and four LPs (L13,17,18,19) revealed challenges on the correct usage of the Java language and methods. H1 had some initial difficulty with boolean operators, because the instructor had not covered that material yet. However, H1 figured it out by reading a web page: *"...at that time, we didn't learn this operator like || ...So I just look it up online, so I feel like, we need to use some concepts we never learned before...That's a challenge, I think" [H1].*

On the other hand, most LP students struggled with what they had already been taught in class. They either went to tutor hours to ask for help, or did not try to understand the problematic material: *"It was mostly questions that I was confused about. Like...arrays at the time. I knew what an array was... but I didn't understand how to code it" [L19]. "I wasn't sure why and how it [array indexing] is formatted that way...I was just a little lazy looking through the book so I didn't really understand it...it was probably part of the starter code, or I just looked at the book and just copied off it" [L13].*

4.2.4 ***Double-check Answers***. Only HP students (H4,6,7,8) confirmed their answers with others—knowledgeable classmates or tutors—before they submitted their code: *"I talk with them...they're pretty knowledgeable in CS, too...It's more of just like, 'Hey, what did you do? Okay, I did this, too'... Like we both did it, we're just going over like, how we did it. Or if we're even doing it right...to make sure" [H6]. "I asked the TA, 'Oh, is this good?' But she told me, 'You gotta change it,'...so I had to re-change it...when the deadline comes up, I go to the lab. So, you know, just to make sure" [H7].*

4.2.5 ***Post-deadline Behavior***. H2 did the Star Point assignment on their own: *"For PSA 2, um, it [the Star Point assignment] was a research into other object-oriented programming. That one, um, I didn't have enough time to actually start it, so I didn't do that one, either. Though, I did, like, afterwards [after the PSA deadline], when I had more time...I wouldn't be able to, like, uh, submit anything like that, but it was interesting to read on like, Python with how they do object-orientating" [H2].* On the other hand, L16 knew that they lost points from a submitted programming assignment and remembered the tutor's comments, but they did not understand why and did not try to address it: *"they said 'Even though you called the Math.abs(), you should put it in the while condition.' ... Eh, um, can I just say 'I don't know'?" [L16].*

5 DISCUSSION

5.1 Implications

Table 2 serves to summarize our findings from Section 4, focusing on the trends that emerged from our analysis. For each trend in the table, we refer back to the appropriate subsection in Section 4 for more details. Some of the observed trends may relate to more general (non-CS specific) study skills (e.g., HP students tend to seek out extra resources to help clarify material and resolve challenges). Similarly, some of these trends are tied to general student metacognition [28] (e.g., LP students may perform untargeted reviews of course materials before exams because they are unclear about where their conceptual weaknesses lie). Lastly, there are behaviors that clearly relate to student self-regulation [19] (e.g., HP continuing to work on assignments even after deadlines to ensure they fully understand course concepts, and the role of procrastination on each group). These trends may be encouraging to the computing education community insofar as we may be able to leverage literature outside of computer science to improve the ways that students study.

Some concerning behaviors do appear to be more computing-specific: assembling a programming assignment solution from bits contributed by friends and instructional staff, stopping work when the right answer is in hand before understanding why it is correct, or emphasizing memorization of code before an exam. These behaviors may be due to students' unfamiliarity with the field of computer science. They may simply be unaware that some behaviors, such as memorization of prior code solutions, may not be effective study strategies. Here, the computing education community can seek

Table 2: Summary of Differences Encountered Between Student Groups

	Higher-Performing	Lower-Performing
Exam study strategy	• execute targeted review of areas of perceived weakness (4.1.2) • create new questions to solve (4.1.2) • review course notes	• execute untargeted review (reviewing everything) (4.1.2) • memorize existing code (4.1.1)
Getting help	• solicit help, successfully addressing their challenges (4.2.3, 4.2.4)	• solicit help, only sometimes addressing challenges (ask friends for help, 4.1.3)
Addressing confusion	• refer back to their own course notes for answers (4.1.2) • seek out extra resources (4.1.2) • double-check solutions with others (4.2.4) • keep notes on areas of confusion (4.1.2)	• give up if cannot find answer (4.1.1, 4.2.1) • get correct answers from others, but do not seek to understand why the answers are correct (4.1.1) • through debugging, can get the code to work but may not understand why (4.2.2, 4.2.3)
Post-deadline behaviors	• will continue working on assignments (4.1.4, 4.2.5)	–
Procrastination	• when they do, it does not impact them significantly as they can still complete assignments (4.2.1)	• when they do, they are unable to find help when they need it to overcome problems (4.2.1)

ways to better inform students of productive and unproductive behaviors specific to computer science.

We also note that although some of these behaviors may result from lack of prior experience, we believe that many of the student struggles are tied to CS-specific and general study strategies. As such, we are encouraged that possible interventions might be successful without necessarily relying on background knowledge.

5.2 Next Steps and Possible Interventions

An ongoing next step to this work is to determine how common these behaviors are among students. This would allow us to craft interventions that target the most common (or most problematic) behaviors.

In the meantime, based on the results from Section 4, we argue for two features of interventions designed to help LPs that we believe may be most effective when applied in concert. First, help students to focus on achieving conceptual understanding rather than understanding particular solutions. While HPs tend to invest effort in clarifying and confirming their understanding (H3,9,11 in Section 4.1.2), LPs did not do so (L13,15,18,19 in Section 4.1.1), simply memorizing solutions without understanding the underlying concepts (Section 4.1.1 and the last two quotes of Section 4.2.2). Thus, the instructional team should keep in mind that there may be a mismatch between perceived and actual student understanding. We therefore argue for the importance of confirming conceptual understanding with students, rather than relying on student self-report.

Second, and perhaps more obviously, help students to be aware of deadlines and plan accordingly. Prior literature suggests that procrastination leads to lower grades on programming assignments [20]. We similarly find that effects of poor study practices appear to be amplified when students procrastinate. For instance, L19 could not ask for help to understand the concepts behind the practice midterm because they started working on it at the last minute. Thus, the instructional team might consider an intermediate deadline to encourage students to start earlier, or use email reminders to encourage early participation [20]. Similarly, exam review sessions might be scheduled well before the exam, rather than the day before. Ultimately, we believe these recommendations will be most effective when combined, as starting earlier will likely be ineffective unless one also abandons poor study strategies like code memorization.

5.3 Threats to Validity

Our interview participants were all from a single CS1 course, and our sample size is small, so findings may not generalize to students in this or other CS1 courses. For instance, if another CS1 course does not offer practice midterm questions, the observations we found might not be applicable. In addition, we are relying here on self-reported data, though we did ask students to log their behavior and take pictures of their work environment to increase reliability. Furthermore, we moved on to the next topic if we noticed, or students themselves mentioned, that they could not accurately reply to our prompt. Lastly, even though we sought not to impact student behaviors, students might have behaved differently during the term as a result of any reflection hatched by participation in our study.

6 CONCLUSION

This paper presents an analysis of CS1 interviews in an effort to understand the range of behaviors demonstrated by students. We distinguish between the behaviors of higher- and lower-performing students to investigate whether there are any notable trends in behaviors within or between groups. Our interviews revealed differing behavioral characteristics of higher- and lower-performing students that may be valuable in crafting potential interventions. Refining and deploying the intervention strategies suggested in this paper in a real classroom setting is an important next step for this work. The CS education research community has invested considerable effort in high-accuracy identification of at-risk students [1, 5, 18]. While that work remains important, we argue for a corresponding focus on using those identifications to intervene and help these students. We hope that our qualitative investigation here, along with our initial suggestions stemming from that work, will further this important research agenda.

7 ACKNOWLEDGEMENTS

We greatly appreciate the reviewers for their helpful feedback. This work was supported in part by NSF award 1712508.

REFERENCES

[1] A. Ahadi, R. Lister, H. Haapala, and A. Vihavainen. Exploring machine learning methods to automatically identify students in need of assistance. In *Proceedings of the 11th International Conference on Computing Education Research*, pages 121–130, 2015.

[2] S. Bergin, A. Mooney, J. Ghent, and K. Quille. Using machine learning techniques to predict introductory programming performance. *International Journal of Computer Science and Software*, 4(12):323–328, 2015.

[3] A. S. Carter and C. D. Hundhausen. With a little help from my friends: An empirical study of the interplay of students' social activities, programming activities, and course success. In *Proceedings of the 12th International Conference on Computing Education Research*, pages 201–209, 2016.

[4] A. S. Carter, C. D. Hundhausen, and O. Adesope. The normalized programming state model: Predicting student performance in computing courses based on programming behavior. In *Proceedings of the eleventh International Conference on Computing Education Research*, pages 141–150, 2015.

[5] K. Castro-Wunsch, A. Ahadi, and A. Petersen. Evaluating neural networks as a method for identifying students in need of assistance. In *Proceedings of the 48th Technical Symposium on Computer Science Education*, pages 111–116, 2017.

[6] S. P. M. Choi, S. Lam, K. C. Li, and B. T. M. Wong. Learning analytics at low cost: At-risk student prediction with clicker data and systematic proactive interventions. *Journal of Educational Technology & Society*, 21(2):273–290, 2018.

[7] CRA Enrollment Committee Institution Subgroup. Generation CS: Computer science undergraduate enrollments surge since 2006. Computing Research Association, 2017.

[8] J. W. Creswell and C. N. Poth. *Qualitative Inquiry and Research Design, Fourth Edition.* Sage Publications, Inc, 2017.

[9] L. Deslauriers, S. E. Harris, E. Lane, and C. E. Wieman. Transforming the lowest-performing students: an intervention that worked. *Journal of College Science Teaching*, 41:80–88, 2012.

[10] S. H. Edwards, J. Snyder, M. A. Pérez-Quiñones, A. Allevato, D. Kim, and B. Tretola. Comparing effective and ineffective behaviors of student programmers. In *Proceedings of the fifth international Conference on Computing education research*, pages 3–14, 2009.

[11] S. Fincher, J. Tenenberg, and A. Robins. Research design: necessary bricolage. In *Proceedings of the seventh international conference on Computing education research*, pages 27–32, 2011.

[12] B. G. Glaser and A. L. Strauss. The discovery of grounded theory: Strategies for qualitative research. *Transaction Publishers*, 1967.

[13] M. Guzdial. A media computation course for non-majors. *SIGCSE Bulletin*, 35(3):104–108, 2003.

[14] B. Hanks and M. Brandt. Successful and unsuccessful problem solving approaches of novice programmers. In *Proceedings of the 40th Technical Symposium on Computer Science Education*, pages 24–28, 2009.

[15] M. Jadud. Methods and tools for exploring novice compilation behaviour. In *Proceedings of the 10th International Conference on Computing Education Research*, pages 73–84, 2006.

[16] P. Jensen and R. Moore. What do help sessions accomplish in introductory science courses? *Journal of College Science Teaching*, 38(5):60, 2009.

[17] C. M. Lewis, K. Yasuhara, and R. E. Anderson. Deciding to major in computer science: A grounded theory of students' self-assessment of ability. In *Proceedings of the Seventh International Conference on Computing Education Research*, pages 3–10, 2011.

[18] S. N. Liao, D. Zingaro, M. A. Laurenzano, W. G. Griswold, and L. Porter. Lightweight, early identification of at-risk CS1 students. In *Proceedings of the 12th International Conference on Computing Education Research*, pages 123–131, 2016.

[19] D. Loksa and A. J. Ko. The role of self-regulation in programming problem solving process and success. In *Proceedings of the 12th Conference on International Computing Education Research*, pages 83–91, 2016.

[20] J. Martin, S. H. Edwards, and C. A. Shaffer. The effects of procrastination interventions on programming project success. In *Proceedings of the Eleventh International Conference on Computing Education Research*, pages 3–11, 2015.

[21] R. McCartney, A. Eckerdal, J. E. Mostrom, K. Sanders, and C. Zander. Successful students' strategies for getting unstuck. In *Proceedings of the 12th Conference on Innovation and Technology in Computer Science Education*, pages 156–160, 2007.

[22] A. J. Mills, G. Durepos, and E. Wiebe. Coding: Open coding. In *Encyclopedia of case study research*, 2010.

[23] R. Moore. Who does extra-credit work in introductory science courses? *Journal of College Science Teaching*, pages 12–15, 2005.

[24] J. P. Munson and J. P. Zitovsky. Models for early identification of struggling novice programmers. In *Proceedings of the 49th Technical Symposium on Computer Science Education*, pages 699–704, 2018.

[25] L. Murphy, G. Lewandowski, R. McCauley, B. Simon, L. Thomas, and C. Zander. Debugging: The good, the bad, and the quirky – a qualitative analysis of novices' strategies. In *Proceedings of the 39th Technical Symposium on Computer Science Education*, pages 163–167, 2008.

[26] A. Petersen, M. Craig, J. Campbell, and A. Tafliovich. Revisiting why students drop CS1. In *Proceedings of the 16th Koli Calling International Conference on Computing Education Research*, pages 71–80, 2016.

[27] L. Porter, D. Bouvier, Q. Cutts, S. Grissom, C. Lee, R. McCartney, D. Zingaro, and B. Simon. A multi-institutional study of peer instruction in introductory computing. *ACM Inroads*, 7(2):76–81, 2016.

[28] G. Schraw, K. J. Crippen, and K. Hartley. Promoting self-regulation in science education: Metacognition as part of a broader perspective on learning. *Research in Science Education*, 36(1):111–139, Mar 2006.

[29] D. F. Shell, L.-K. Soh, A. E. Flanigan, and M. S. Peteranetz. Students' initial course motivation and their achievement and retention in college CS1 courses. In *Proceedings of the 47th Technical Symposium on Computer Science Education*, pages 639–644, 2016.

[30] B. Simon, S. Esper, L. Porter, and Q. Cutts. Student experience in a student-centered peer instruction classroom. In *Proceedings of the Ninth International Conference on Computing Education Research*, pages 129–136, 2013.

[31] A. Vihavainen. Predicting students' performance in an introductory programming course using data from students' own programming process. In *IEEE 13th International Conference on Advanced Learning Technologies*, pages 498–499, 2013.

[32] R. Vivian, K. Falkner, and N. Falkner. Computer science students' causal attributions for successful and unsuccessful outcomes in programming assignments. In *Proceedings of the 13th Koli Calling International Conference on Computing Education Research*, pages 125–134, 2013.

[33] C. Watson and F. W. Li. Failure rates in introductory programming revisited. In *Proceedings of the 19th Conference on Innovation and Technology in Computer Science Education*, pages 39–44, 2014.

[34] C. Watson, F. W. Li, and J. L. Godwin. No tests required: Comparing traditional and dynamic predictors of programming success. In *Proceedings of the 45th Technical Symposium on Computer Science Education*, pages 469–474, 2014.

[35] C. Watson, F. W. B. Li, and J. L. Godwin. Predicting performance in an introductory programming course by logging and analyzing student programming behavior. In *International Conference on Advanced Learning Technologies*, pages 319–323, 2013.

[36] D. Zingaro, M. Craig, L. Porter, B. A. Becker, Y. Cao, P. Conrad, D. Cukierman, A. Hellas, D. Loksa, and N. Thota. Achievement goals in CS1: Replication and extension. In *Proceedings of the 49th Technical Symposium on Computer Science Education*, pages 687–692, 2018.

Experience Report: Thinkathon - Countering an "I Got It Working" Mentality with Pencil-And-Paper Exercises

Quintin Cutts
quintin.cutts@glasgow.ac.uk
University of Glasgow

Matthew Barr
matthew.barr@glasgow.ac.uk
University of Glasgow

Mireilla Bikanga Ada
mireilla.bikangaada@glasgow.ac.uk
University of Glasgow

Peter Donaldson
peter.donaldson.2@glasgow.ac.uk
University of Glasgow

Steve Draper
steve.draper@glasgow.ac.uk
University of Glasgow

Jack Parkinson
jack.parkinson@glasgow.ac.uk
University of Glasgow

Jeremy Singer
jeremy.singer@glasgow.ac.uk
University of Glasgow

Lovisa Sundin
lovisa.sundin@glasgow.ac.uk
University of Glasgow

ABSTRACT

Goal-directed problem-solving labs can lead a student to believe that the most important achievement in a first programming course is to get programs working. This is counter to research indicating that code comprehension is an important developmental step for novice programmers. We observed this in our own CS-0 introductory programming course, and furthermore, that students weren't making the connection between code comprehension in labs and a final examination that required solutions to pencil-and-paper comprehension and writing exercises, where sound understanding of programming concepts is essential. Realising these deficiencies late in our course, we put on three 3-hour optional revision evenings just days before the exam. Based on a mastery learning philosophy, students were expected to work through a bank of around 200 pencil-and-paper exercises. By comparison with a machine-based hackathon, we called this a Thinkathon. Students completed a pre and post questionnaire about their experience of the Thinkathon. While we find that Thinkathon attendance positively influences final grades, we believe our reflection on the overall experience is of greater value. We report that: respected methods for developing code comprehension may not be enough on their own; novices must exercise their developing skills away from machines; and there are *social* learning outcomes in programming courses, currently implicit, that we should make explicit.

CCS CONCEPTS

• **Social and professional topics** → **Computer science education**; Computational thinking; Student assessment.

ACM ISBN 978-1-4503-6301-3/19/07...$15.00
https://doi.org/10.1145/3304221.3319785

KEYWORDS

mastery learning, introductory programming, program comprehension, goal-directed problem solving

ACM Reference Format:
Quintin Cutts, Matthew Barr, Mireilla Bikanga Ada, Peter Donaldson, Steve Draper, Jack Parkinson, Jeremy Singer, and Lovisa Sundin. 2019. Experience Report: Thinkathon - Countering an "I Got It Working" Mentality with Pencil-And-Paper Exercises. In *Innovation and Technology in Computer Science Education (ITiCSE '19), July 15–17, 2019, Aberdeen, Scotland UK.* ACM, New York, NY, USA, 7 pages. https://doi.org/10.1145/3304221.3319785

1 INTRODUCTION

In a meeting of our CS-0 programming course team, around four-fifths of the way through the semester, we were discussing a wide range of misconceptions evident among the students. The common thread across all the comments was the students' conviction that *getting the program working* was the most important consideration. Understanding either the process they'd gone through to get the program working, or the programming language constructs and patterns they'd used, was of secondary value, if any. This might not have been important if the students were going to be assessed in a lab with the support system of teaching assistants (TAs), friends and the internet all around. Instead, in just four weeks, they would face a written programming exam requiring good conceptual understanding for both code comprehension and code writing questions with nothing more than their brain and a pen in their hand.

We considered remediation. How could we enable weaker students to attempt enough exam-like questions in exam-like circumstances to give them a hope of succeeding in the final examination; in essence, to give them a flavour of Mastery Learning [2]? We discounted added traditional exercises in the last two weeks' class sessions due to insufficient preparation time for the course team. Someone suggested an all-night crash session for students "like a hackathon", with another team member extending this idea with "but for these kinds of exercises, surely it's a *Think*-athon" - and so a new concept was born. Over the next three weeks, we constructed over 200 paper-based exercises and just a few days before the exam, ran three evening Thinkathon sessions for our students.

This paper is fully an experience report. We had a course that we thought was rather well designed; as we reflected on our students' learning journey, we realised that they were insufficiently prepared for the terminal exam and so designed a remediation, the Thinkathon; as we reflected on student and staff evaluations of the Thinkathon combined with student exam performance, we developed new insights into the incorporation of code comprehension within a programming course. In particular, we find that:

- respected methods for developing code comprehension may not be enough on their own;
- students and staff who experienced the Thinkathon now recognise how important it is for novices to think and work away from machines;
- there are a number of *social* intended learning outcomes on a programming course which the instructor should incorporate and broadcast to students.

The next two sections introduce the overall course design and that of the Thinkathon respectively, making reference to the literature supporting the design choices as necessary. Section 4 outlines the evaluation methodology, with the following two sections detailing the quantitative and qualitative results of the evaluation. Section 7 discusses the whole experience, drawing out our learning, and Section 8 concludes with next steps.

2 COURSE DESIGN

To provide context, our course is now described; one aim in doing this is to show that the development of code comprehension and conceptual understanding was not ignored in the course design. Our course, a CS-0 introductory programming course, runs over 11 weeks, with two 2-hour large class sessions and one 2-hour lab session each week. The large class sessions are based on Peer Instruction (PI) [15, 27], requiring students to complete reading and on-line tasks prior to every class, take a short quiz on that work at the start of the class, and then answer/discuss PI questions for the rest of the class.

The course design incorporates a strong code comprehension element, in line with a number of researchers' recommendations: pre-class activities encourage students to practice their code-reading ability [18]; PI questions foster understanding and analysis of programs at a range of levels of detail [4, 24]; the concept of the notional machine is introduced to learners during class, and they are shown how the activities they have been undertaking should help to develop their own notional machine understanding [6, 7, 29]; labs encourage the development of a number of smaller programs rather than just one large one [10]; some lab sessions encourage students to explore complete programs and draw out re-usable patterns [19]; the staff-student ratio in the labs is high to provide sufficient time for students to talk to staff about their programs, displaying their understanding. These discussions are intended to emphasise the importance of understanding over simply getting programs working. TAs are expected to quiz the students about their programs, for example, pointing at a piece of code and asking the student to explain how it works and why they used it, and award an advisory progress grade depending on the students' responses.

In line with other courses [9, 26], this course introduces students to two languages: for the first 5 weeks, students learn a block-based language, in this case Alice; for the remaining 6 weeks, they learn Python. To give a sense of the scope of the course, the most complicated problems explored will require reading in data from a text file, storing it in a data structure requiring some combination of lists and dictionaries, processing the data structure in some way usually according to user input, and finally writing results either to screen or back into a file.

While the course does have a practical assessment for credit, the primary assessment is a written final examination. The questions in this exam require students to display both code comprehension and code writing skills, with no access to notes or a machine. The course designers believe that the questions are simple enough that a competent hard-working student should be able to internalise the programming concepts, syntax and patterns during the course, and therefore should not require recourse to external aids. The exam contains the following four question types:

- Evaluation of expressions involving simple types and lists and dictionaries
- Hand/desk execution
- Identifying and correcting errors in code, given a problem statement
- Problem-solving: given a problem statement, write a solution in programming language code

3 THINKATHON DESIGN

The Thinkathon idea was born from the realisation that students were not developing sound conceptual understanding, and we aimed to provide an extended immersive experience - not unlike a "boot camp" [30] - to correct this. The Thinkathon design was iterative, involving discussion among our 17-strong CS education group, including PhD students and academic staff, mainly CS but with some members from other schools, with widely varying breadths of experience. Our overall goals were to:

- enable the students to succeed in the upcoming exam and be well-prepared for follow-on programming courses;
- help them to develop appropriate attitudes and approaches to learning programming, for example, to have the confidence to know whether or not they've correctly solved a problem, tackled a bug, or written a fragment of code.

The issues with the students' learning that arose in our discussions and that we were aiming to address were perceived to be as follows:

- The operation of programming language constructs is not well-enough understood by students, as evidenced by the poor quality of discussions between TAs and students in labs. The use of PI in CS is typically expected to address this [27], but we are not the only ones to find that PI does not ensure all students succeed [12]. We suspect that while the preparation and discussion aspects of PI do ensure students understand concepts *in the moment*, there is not enough repetition for these understandings to become permanent.
- The number of larger problems/tasks and solutions developed or studied by students is not enough. PI cannot easily handle this issue, as PI questions typically deal with small code fragments. This results in the students not developing

a sufficiently advanced pattern memory, without which they are unable to quickly break down a new problem into known chunks with known solutions.

- The students are too dependent on outside sources of help, preventing them from developing their own understanding and confidence. For example, the programming environment is used as a crutch to tell them whether what they've developed is correct; the internet can be used to find fragments of code to solve problems, a practice rarely appropriate in an introductory programming lab, unless the student knows that he/she has to thoroughly understand such fragments; and, help from friends or TAs may simply solve a student's programming problem, rather than helping them learn how to solve their own problem, a more useful long-term goal.

Our task was to develop exercises for the students to tackle on the Thinkathon evenings, completion of which would help to meet the goals and address the issues identified above. We came up with five objectives for the Thinkathon exercises:

- All the exercises should be paper-based to break the dependence on a machine. Such "unplugged" computing activities [1] are generally deployed for younger learners and not at university level.
- There should be sufficient exercises of every type, along with model solutions, to support Mastery Learning, identified as an under-used but highly desirable learning practice for programming education in [14, 25]. Under such a practice, a student should be able to find out if their solution attempt is correct; if it is not, to work out why, and then to try again on another similar exercise; if it is correct, and the student has now completed a number of similar exercises correctly, then they can move on to exercises at the next level of difficulty.
- Students should be able to work at their own pace, essential for independent learning and in a subject where students are at so many different levels.
- Students should not get stuck often. This requires the exercises to follow a developmental sequence, where each incremental step is small. The development of such sequences is not regarded to be straight-forward in CS [21].
- Students should be able to gain assistance from other students, but not to be dependent on it. A student's peers are a strong support mechanism, and it is important to develop those connections, but also to make sure that students are aware of more and less constructive ways of supporting their peers.

We struggled with the complexity of large numbers of each type of exercise for Mastery Learning, combined with the two dimensions associated with developing a developmental sequence. First, there is a progression from code comprehension to code writing – e.g. it is easier to trace code than it is to write from scratch [13]; second there is a progression through examples that make use of steadily more complex, and more complex combinations of, programming language constructs and programming patterns.

We judged there to be no perfect progression that we could readily develop, and so made a compromise. We created 5 packs of exercises, sequenced on the comprehension/writing dimension, containing several kinds of exercises, which largely match the style of exam questions for the course. The exercise styles, described with reference to what aspect of Schulte's Block Model for code comprehension [24] must be understood to complete them, are:

(1) Describing, evaluating and creating expressions and simple statements – an extension of our exam practice to ensure that students thoroughly understand primitives. Structure section of the Block Model, at the Atom level only.
(2) Hand/desk execution. Block Model's complete Structure section.
(3) Parsons Puzzles [20]. These code rearrangement exercises represent a developmental stepping-stone from code reading to writing. All parts of the Block Model, both Structure and Function.
(4) Validating/debugging code. These exercises have the problem statement and some incorrect code, and the instruction to find and fix the errors. All parts of the Block Model.
(5) Problem-solving from scratch

Broadly, the exercises in each pack were ordered to follow a typical sequence for introducing programming language concepts and patterns. Novice programmers value exposure to example programs [22]. Our packs provided sequences of such programs in a scaffolded setting. 'Learning by doing' is considered by novices to be effective; they report exercises to be more useful than lectures [11]. Here, students started with code completion activities [17], moving through the recognition of plans and patterns [28] and finishing with coding *ex nihilo* problems [16].

Students were alerted via email and lecture to the Thinkathon sessions, which occurred immediately prior to exams. The sessions ran from 4-7pm, with pizza and soft drinks provided half-way through, initially on two consecutive evenings. The students encouraged us to run a third session. At each session, around 8 TAs/instructors were on hand to check student work and answer queries. The packs were only available on paper. Students were directed to use the materials as follows: start at the first exercise pack; dip in at any point; if the questions seemed easy, jump ahead, if hard, then drop back; once the exercises are complete, take them to a TA to be checked, and if they're correct, move on to the next pack.

In the interests of fairness, all the exercises and their answers were uploaded to the course VLE (Moodle) after the third session. This enabled access to those students who didn't attend, citing pressure of revision for exams scheduled earlier than the CS exam, and students who hadn't completed all packs by the end of the three sessions.

The materials can be found at: http://ccse.ac.uk/thinkathon.

4 EVALUATION METHODOLOGY

As part of the Thinkathon, we developed and implemented an evaluation to establish whether students' academic performance improved after the introduction of the new practice, and to determine student and staff views.

The intervention, which sought to deepen the understanding of programming among learners in line with code comprehension ideals and to explore the impact of a change in practice, used action research as a means of enquiry. Action research involves "practitioners studying their own professional practice and framing their own questions. This style of research has the immediate goal to assess, develop or improve practice" [31].

We were interested in the following questions:

(1) What are the students' perceptions of the Thinkathon exercises?
(2) Is there a difference in performance in the final exam between Thinkathon participants and those who did not attend, possibly taking into consideration mid-term exam performance.
(3) Do those who attended the Thinkathon perform better than those who only accessed the questions and answers online.
(4) Does the Thinkathon highlight deficiencies in the current course design and if so how?

The qualitative evaluation was designed to address the first and fourth questions, with the quantitative evaluation addressing the second and third.

The study participants were students enrolled in our CS-0 course. There was a total of 114 students. However, only 108 took the final exam. Ethical approval was obtained before the study. To compare the group who attended the Thinkathon to those who did not participate, the study used their mid-term and final exam scores. To analyse student perception of the Thinkathon exercises, a survey was sent to students before and after they had attended the Thinkathon. Finally, a round-table meeting of all staff involved in the Thinkathon was held where we collected staff viewpoints, sometimes recording verbatim quotes and sometimes a summary of particular views.

Descriptive and statistical analyses of means and standard deviation were calculated to provide quantitative results. A comparative examination of participants' confidence level before and after the Thinkathon was also performed. Qualitative data from student Thinkathon participants was collected using four open-ended questions in the post-test survey.

- Reflecting on the Thinkathon exercises, what programming concepts or types of problem did you initially find difficult?
- In what ways do you feel the Thinkathon sessions helped you better understand these concepts or problem types?
- What else - not covered above - was good about the Thinkathon session(s) you attended? What other realisations or learning or gains about programming have you made as a result of attending?
- What could we have done better at the Thinkathon session(s) you attended?

In the initial coding pass, an inductive analysis of individual student responses to survey questions was carried out independently by two of the paper's authors. However, during comparison and discussion of these initial results it became apparent that a simultaneous coding approach [23] using a hierarchical coding scheme [23] that grouped all responses by student would be more appropriate; the same issue could appear across several of their answers, with distinct aspects of interest like the instructional design and their own level of understanding blended together. This was supplemented by a simpler inductive descriptive coding [23] of a summary of the Thinkathon staff debriefing meeting.

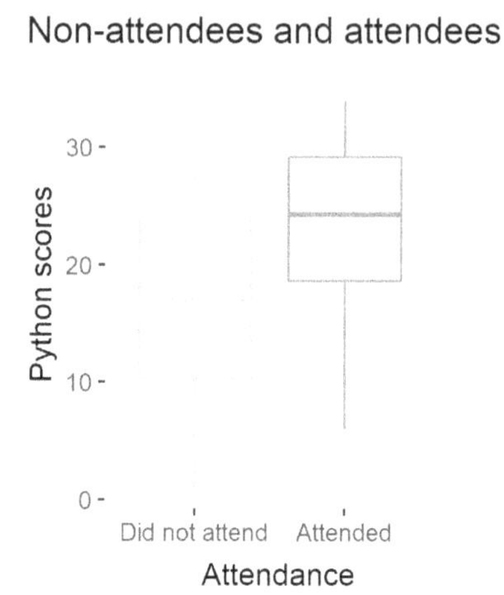

Figure 1: Final exam scores as boxplot

5 QUANTITATIVE RESULTS

For an understanding into the Thinkathon's effect on the students' Python skills, attendees' survey data was analysed in combination with their final exam performance.

Out of the 108 students who took the final exam, 37 took the pre-test survey, and 34 took the post-test survey. From the union of these responses, it can be estimated that 44 students participated in the Thinkathon event while 64 didn't.

First, we looked into whether there was a group difference among attendees and non-attendees for the first two Python exam questions, since they were concerned with the first set of Thinkathon exercises, which attendees were most likely to have completed, namely hand execution. Descriptive statistics indicated no such differentiating ability. The full set of Python questions did, however, reveal that attendees on average scored higher (see the Figure 1). Attendees had a mean of 23.42 (SD = 7.5) while non-attendees had a mean of 17.37 (SD = 8.31), with a maximum score of 37.

This inference had to be qualified by the lack of random allocation of students to attend/non-attend groups. Those that chose to attend may already have had greater experience, academic conscientiousness or test-taking ability. We reasoned that students' mid-term performance could be used as a proxy for these, since this shows a linear association with the final exam (see Figure 2); yet, looking into the ranks in the mid-term versus final exam, Thinkathon attendees had a median improvement of 7.5 places while non-attendees on average ranked 6.5 places *lower*.

Thus, a one-way analysis of covariance (ANCOVA) was conducted. Even after controlling for mid-term performance, there was a statistical difference on performance by attendance [$F(2, 104) = 29.76$, $p<.05$]. This suggests that the Thinkathon contributed causally to an improvement in Python programming ability.

This is a conservative analysis: while attendance was based on completion of the on-line surveys and not on a session register, we counted over 50 attendees on the first evening, and so some students must have not completed the survey; also, 32 people downloaded the packs after the event without attending. These aspects would tend to flatten any correlation. Descriptive analysis suggested that

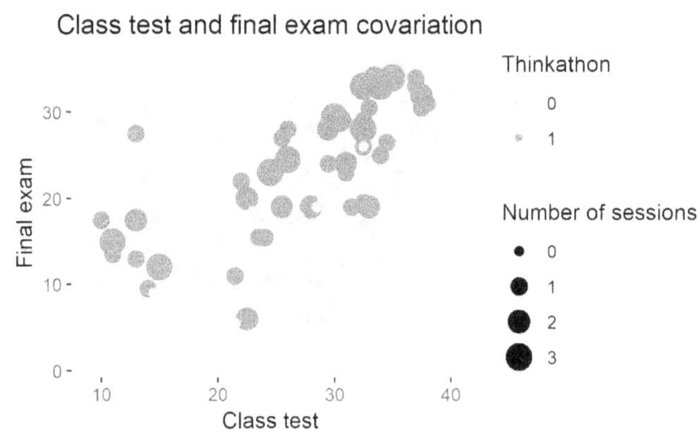

Figure 2: Relationship between mid-term result and final exam

"downloading only" led to no discernible improvement compared with doing neither - only the group that also attended improved.

In an analysis of the 23 participants who completed both the pre and post survey we found there was a modest increase in confidence about the exam from a mean of 2.91 (SD = 0.95) to a mean of 3.30 (SD = 0.63). When comparing all pre or post survey participants (n=42) who had made final grade estimates to their actual grades we discovered that the upper-quartile of final exam performers most frequently underestimated their final exam grade and the lower-quartile most frequently overestimated their final grade.

6 QUALITATIVE RESULTS

6.1 Student Experience

Two overarching themes emerged from qualitative analysis of the post-Thinkathon survey data: *instructional design* and *student learning*. Most of the discussion relating to the instructional design either highlighted benefits or improvements that could be made either to the course or future Thinkathon events. Student learning comments mostly related to either perceived benefits of taking part or particular difficulties that they realised they had.

Reflecting on the instructional design of the Thinkathon, student responses related primarily to the support afforded by tutors and peers, the nature of the presented exercises, and the opportunity to practice solving problems. Tutors were variously described as being "super engaged", "helpful and supportive", and "very encouraging", while peers were thought to provide a useful alternative perspective: "Having not just tutors but other students helped, as we could discuss problems and by seeing things slightly differently helped me to understand different problems and how to solve them". The literature tells us novices benefit from interaction with their peers[5]. They also maintain high motivation to succeed when they receive personal tutoring from expert humans[3]. The informal Thinkathon environment fostered both these kinds of interactions.

The way the exercises were presented proved more divisive, with some students appreciating that the high number of similar exercises provided an opportunity to "practice them over and over", while others felt the exercises to be "repetitive". One student summarised this tension as follows: "whilst it was good there was so many questions in each booklet, it gave a lot of practice, at the same time I think it's very easy to get bogged down in them". Students also suggested that a greater sense of variety might be achieved by enforcing some system of rotation, whereby groups of students would be tasked with completing one kind of exercise before being asked to move to another.

The value of practice was frequently expressed in terms of the upcoming examination, with comments relating to "writing code on paper" or how the exercises "helped me see how exam questions would be laid out".

Student participants described their learning experience primarily in computing science-related terms, commenting on how the exercises enhanced their ability to comprehend and write code. The experience also appeared to facilitate learning that might be described as affective (improving confidence), cognitive (enhancing problem-solving skills), or meta-cognitive (facilitating self-assessment).

Improvements to code comprehension were described in terms of understanding the code at hand ("trying to solve or execute a code without a computer helps for deeper understanding"), including the attendant concepts, and being able to describe it ("describing code showed me what terminology I need to revise in order to talk freely about code").

References to the Thinkathon experience leading to improved code writing ability were abundant, and the challenge of being asked to write programs "from scratch" was highlighted by many as being most significant: "It [Thinkathon] has helped me really think about a program before writing it. Before I'd just write anything that came to mind and fix it until it worked but now I tend to get correct solutions the first or second attempt at a problem."

In terms of self-assessment, the following comment proved particularly illuminating: "I didn't know what to expect on the exam. In a way, I didn't know what I didn't know." This echos findings that students with low or partial knowledge find it difficult to accurately assess their own level of competence and tend to overestimate their ability [8].

6.2 Staff Experience

The one-and-a-half-hour discussion among the 17 TAs and staff who had been involved in either or both of the Thinkathon design and the sessions themselves elicited a number of interesting topics.

Those present at the sessions could tell how much the students enjoyed them, and were surprised at the high level of interaction between students – they were helping each other a lot. The first two packs clearly got the students thinking: a TA said "hand execution forces you to think through code, to think about every line – e.g. mental models of variables. Can get lazy in front of a machine – try, try, try until it works." Indeed, the first pack which included expression evaluation, naming constructs and describing how they operated, as well as expression writing, took most students the whole of the first session. This was a great surprise to staff. When queried, students were keen to stress that they did not want to miss out on anything and to make sure they had a firm foundation. Staff described seeing real 'light-bulb moments' for the students, e.g. that a single element slice of a list is still a list, and understanding fully about the identity of data structures and their mutability – aspects discussed in class but perhaps not followed up enough.

The high level of interaction was somewhat at odds with our intention to help the students develop the confidence to be able to answer questions on their own. In discussion with staff, the students felt the peer interaction was essential, and repeatedly stressing our goal for them to answer confidently on their own did not change their behaviour. Students noted how confronting it could be "to talk to folk I don't know well about what I don't know", indicating their nervousness in approaching instructors and even TAs. The implication here is that the Thinkathon questions highlighted for the students that there was a lot they didn't know; and that for most students, not just a few, there was real learning even at the simpler levels. This was not just a revision session.

Considering self-direction in the students' study, we discussed the relationship between the Thinkathon exercise packs and a text-book in, say, mathematics that has a very large number of questions, with answers, presented in a well-tried developmental sequence. While staff remembered using such text-books in a self-study Mastery Learning manner in mathematics and other subjects, they also recognised that larger programming problems did not have the kind of direct right/wrong answers as had the math questions.

Those in our group from other disciplines commented on how labs are quite disconnected from lectures in the other sciences, and exam preparation is based around reading of notes, hand-outs and a text-book. In computing, the labs look real, authentic. By comparison, neither the Thinkathon nor the exam look realistic. A non-CS colleague commented "getting them to do stuff on paper exams is the wrong thing", a prevalent attitude among computer scientists too, but another responded "the exam is doing exactly the right thing, getting the student to articulate what they do and don't know, which is not required or effectively evidenced in the lab." This highlights the challenges we have in effectively signposting to students the learning outcomes of a programming course.

7 DISCUSSION

While we have been excited and motivated by the Thinkathon experience, attendance appearing to raise final course grade, it has also delivered a salutary lesson. We started off acting on a clear misunderstanding in students' minds between lab activities and the written exam, but we have realised that the problem lies somewhere in the learning design between the PI-based lectures and the lab sessions. Furthermore, the students really don't know what it is they should be learning. Unpacking this, we note the following.

We have depended on PI to satisfy the code comprehension side of our curriculum. The pre-lecture work should help to embed concepts; the discussion in class should induct novices into a programmers' community of practice. Coupling this with relatively traditional lab-based practical code writing activities has proven to be wanting, however. The evaluation tells us that students, including good students, don't know even what we might consider the basics: naming of constructs, explanation of how they work, evaluation of expressions, simple desk execution. They spent an entire evening on this material. Fundamentally, we have forgotten how much there is to know, taking it for granted. Why should a novice be expected to pick up a new vocabulary for a new kind of language and the grammatical terms required to be able to talk about it, without explicit instruction? PI does try to address this, but we suspect it does it in too inefficient a manner.

On reflection, both staff and students now realise the huge value of thinking and working on programming exercises *away from machines*. We will re-introduce tutorial sessions in rooms away from our labs, in which students work on Thinkathon style problems, and possibly with regular hand-ins and grading. We moved away from these in years past, for logistical reasons and also to maximise programming time – but that was before we understood about the importance of building the foundations soundly.

Tutorials bring with them the notion of discussion, and this brings to mind Francis Bacon's instruction from the 1600s that a good education required both reading and writing, and also "conference" – the ability to speak and argue one's case. We have writing in abundance in our programming courses, and code comprehension indicates that we should have reading, but what of conference? If we can't talk and argue about our practice, what kind of practitioner are we? PI again can support this, but are we doing enough to foster fruitful discussion, and have we identified good ways of putting it to use? Our own labs have included limited elements of discussion, but we could add code reviews or set up discussions on the benefits of different programs solving the same problem.

The overall experience suggests to us a number of "social" learning outcomes for a programming course that currently lie hidden:

- The students need to know the full range of what matters to us – explaining code using the correct language, hand-execution, developing solutions away from machines (and we need to adjust our instructional designs accordingly)
- Students must be able do all this *on their own*, and do it exactly. Furthermore, with practice, we expect them to be able to complete these activities correctly *first-time*. It is no good for their peers or the TA to show them the answer.
- A resource like the Thinkathon packs are *for individuals*, not a group thing. It is a self-learning resource at best, enabling students to find out what they know and what they don't.

The Thinkathon succeeded on the first of these points, but even with our encouragement to the students during the sessions, it was less effective on the second two points.

8 CONCLUSION

Realising late in our CS-0 course that our students were not prepared for the upcoming written exam, we developed an evening revision session format we dubbed *Thinkathon*, that proved effective in raising students' grades. Evaluating the exercise has led us to identify a number of important short-comings in our PI-based course design, and consequent adjustments. In particular, we note: the need to learn language vocabulary and grammatical terms thoroughly; the value of working away from machines; the importance of discussion; and the explicit presentation of *social* learning outcomes for a programming course.

ACKNOWLEDGMENTS

Many thanks to those who spent hours in discussion, developing the Thinkathon exercises and supporting students during the sessions: Niall Barr, Elizabeth Cole, Sarah Honeychurch, Fionnuala Johnson, Derek Somerville and Ethel Tshukudu.

REFERENCES

[1] Timothy C. Bell, Mike Fellows, and Ian H. Witten. 1998. *Computer Science Unplugged: Off-line Activities and Games for All Ages.* Computer Science Unplugged.

[2] Benjamin S Bloom. 1968. Learning for Mastery. Instruction and Curriculum. Regional Education Laboratory for the Carolinas and Virginia, Topical Papers and Reprints, Number 1. *Evaluation Comment* 1, 2 (1968).

[3] Kristy Elizabeth Boyer, Robert Phillips, Michael D. Wallis, Mladen A. Vouk, and James C. Lester. 2009. Investigating the role of student motivation in computer science education through one-on-one tutoring. *Computer Science Education* 19, 2 (Jun 2009), 111–135. https://doi.org/10.1080/08993400902937584

[4] Quintin Cutts, Sarah Esper, Marlena Fecho, Stephen R. Foster, and Beth Simon. 2012. The Abstraction Transition Taxonomy: Developing Desired Learning Outcomes Through the Lens of Situated Cognition. In *Proceedings of the Ninth Annual International Conference on International Computing Education Research (ICER '12).* ACM, New York, NY, USA, 63–70. https://doi.org/10.1145/2361276.2361290

[5] Adrian Devey and Angela Carbone. 2011. Helping First Year Novice Programming Students PASS. In *Proceedings of the Thirteenth Australasian Computing Education Conference - Volume 114 (ACE '11).* Australian Computer Society, Inc., 135–144. http://dl.acm.org/citation.cfm?id=2459936.2459953

[6] Benedict du Boulay. 1986. Some Difficulties of Learning to Program. *Journal of Educational Computing Research* 2, 1 (1986), 57–73.

[7] Benedict du Boulay, Tim O'Shea, and John Monk. 1981. The black box inside the glass box: presenting computing concepts to novices. *International Journal of Man-Machine Studies* 14, 3 (1981), 237–249. https://doi.org/ttps://doi.org/10.1016/S0020-7373(81)80056-9

[8] David Dunning, Kerri Johnson, Joyce Ehrlinger, and Justin Kruger. 2003. Why People Fail to Recognize Their Own Incompetence. *Current Directions in Psychological Science* 12, 3 (2003), 83–87. https://doi.org/10.1111/1467-8721.01235 arXiv:https://doi.org/10.1111/1467-8721.01235

[9] Dan Garcia, Brian Harvey, and Tiffany Barnes. 2015. The Beauty and Joy of Computing. *ACM Inroads* 6, 4 (Nov. 2015), 71–79. https://doi.org/10.1145/2835184

[10] Kelly Downey Joe Michael Allen, Frank Vahid and Alex Daniel Edgcomb. 2018. Weekly Programs in a CS1 Class: Experiences with Auto-graded Many-small Programs (MSP). In *2018 ASEE Annual Conference & Exposition.* ASEE Conferences, Salt Lake City, Utah.

[11] Essi Lahtinen, Kirsti Ala-Mutka, and Hannu-Matti Jarvinen. 2005. A Study of the Difficulties of Novice Programmers. In *Proceedings of the 10th Annual SIGCSE Conference on Innovation and Technology in Computer Science Education (ITiCSE '05).* ACM, 14–18. https://doi.org/10.1145/1067445.1067453

[12] Soohyun Nam Liao, Daniel Zingaro, Kevin Thai, Christine Alvarado, William G. Griswold, and Leo Porter. 2019. A Robust Machine Learning Technique to Predict Low-performing Students. *ACM Trans. Comput. Educ.* 19, 3, Article 18 (Jan. 2019), 19 pages. https://doi.org/10.1145/3277569

[13] Mike Lopez, Jacqueline Whalley, Phil Robbins, and Raymond Lister. 2008. Relationships between reading, tracing and writing skills in introductory programming. In *Proceedings of the fourth international workshop on computing education research.* ACM, 101–112.

[14] Andrew Luxton-Reilly, Simon, Ibrahim Albluwi, Brett A. Becker, Michail Giannakos, Amruth N. Kumar, Linda Ott, James Paterson, Michael James Scott, Judy Sheard, and Claudia Szabo. 2018. Introductory Programming: A Systematic Literature Review. In *Proceedings Companion of the 23rd Annual ACM Conference on Innovation and Technology in Computer Science Education (ITiCSE 2018 Companion).* ACM, New York, NY, USA, 55–106. https://doi.org/10.1145/3293881.3295779

[15] Eric Mazur. 2017. *Peer Instruction.* Springer Berlin Heidelberg, Berlin, Heidelberg, 9–19. https://doi.org/10.1007/978-3-662-54377-1_2

[16] Michael McCracken, Vicki Almstrum, Danny Diaz, Mark Guzdial, Dianne Hagan, Yifat Ben-David Kolikant, Cary Laxer, Lynda Thomas, Ian Utting, and Tadeusz Wilusz. 2001. A Multi-national, Multi-institutional Study of Assessment of Programming Skills of First-year CS Students. In *Working Group Reports from ITiCSE on Innovation and Technology in Computer Science Education (ITiCSE-WGR '01).* ACM, 125–180. https://doi.org/10.1145/572133.572137 Canterbury, UK.

[17] J. J. G. van Merrienboer and H. P. M. Krammer. 1990. The "completion strategy" in programming instruction: theoretical and empirical support. *Research on instructional design and effects / eds. S. Dijkstra, B.H.A.M. van Hout Wolters, P.C. van der Sijde* (1990), 45–61.

[18] Heng Ngee Mok. 2014. Teaching tip: The flipped classroom. *Journal of Information Systems Education* 25, 1 (2014), 7.

[19] Orna Muller, David Ginat, and Bruria Haberman. 2007. Pattern-oriented Instruction and Its Influence on Problem Decomposition and Solution Construction. In *Proceedings of the 12th Annual SIGCSE Conference on Innovation and Technology in Computer Science Education (ITiCSE '07).* ACM, New York, NY, USA, 151–155. https://doi.org/10.1145/1268784.1268830

[20] Dale Parsons and Patricia Haden. 2006. Parson's programming puzzles: a fun and effective learning tool for first programming courses. In *Proceedings of the 8th Australasian Conference on Computing Education-Volume 52.* Australian Computer Society, Inc., 157–163.

[21] Anthony Robins. 2010. Learning edge momentum: A new account of outcomes in CS1. *Computer Science Education* 20, 1 (2010), 37–71. https://doi.org/10.1080/08993401003612167

[22] Anthony Robins, Janet Rountree, and Nathan Rountree. 2003. Learning and Teaching Programming: A Review and Discussion. *Computer Science Education* 13, 2 (Jun 2003), 137–172. https://doi.org/10.1076/csed.13.2.137.14200

[23] Johnny Saldaña. 2015. *The coding manual for qualitative researchers.* Sage.

[24] Carsten Schulte. 2008. Block Model: An Educational Model of Program Comprehension As a Tool for a Scholarly Approach to Teaching. In *Proceedings of the Fourth International Workshop on Computing Education Research (ICER '08).* ACM, New York, NY, USA, 149–160. https://doi.org/10.1145/1404520.1404535

[25] P. Seeling. 2016. Switching to blend-Ed: Effects of replacing the textbook with the browser in an introductory computer programming course. In *2016 IEEE Frontiers in Education Conference (FIE).* 1–5. https://doi.org/10.1109/FIE.2016.7757620

[26] Beth Simon and Quintin Cutts. 2012. How to Implement a Peer Instruction-designed CS Principles Course. *ACM Inroads* 3, 2 (June 2012), 72–74. https://doi.org/10.1145/2189835.2189858

[27] B. Simon, M. Kohanfars, J. Lee, K. Tamayo, and Q. Cutts. 2010. Experience report: peer instruction in introductory computing. , 341–345 pages. https://doi.org/10.1145/1734263.1734381

[28] Elliot Soloway and Kate Ehrlich. 1984. Empirical Studies of Programming Knowledge. *IEEE Trans. Softw. Eng.* 10, 5 (Sep 1984), 595–609. https://doi.org/10.1109/TSE.1984.5010283

[29] Juha Sorva. 2013. Notional Machines and Introductory Programming Education. *Trans. Comput. Educ.* 13, 2, Article 8 (July 2013), 31 pages. https://doi.org/10.1145/2483710.2483713

[30] John Stamey and Steve Sheel. 2010. A Boot Camp Approach to Learning Programming in a CS0 Course. *J. Comput. Sci. Coll.* 25, 5 (May 2010), 34–40.

[31] Jane Zeni. 1998. A guide to ethical issues and action research [1]. *Educational action research* 6, 1 (1998), 9–19. https://doi.org/10.1080/09650799800200053

A Multi-Level Study of Undergraduate Computer Science Reasoning about Concurrency

Aubrey Lawson, Eileen T. Kraemer, S. Megan Che, Cazembe Kennedy
[aubreyl,etkraem,sche,cazembk]@clemson.edu
Clemson University

ABSTRACT

In computing, concurrency relates to the situation in which different processes or threads may execute at the same time or in an interleaved manner. Many real-world computing systems utilize concurrency, but concurrency-related concepts have proven difficult for students. With an informed understanding of student reasoning in this context, instructors will be better able to create appropriate pedagogical materials and aid student learning. The research questions we seek to address are: *What is the nature of undergraduate computer science students' conceptions of concurrency?* and *How does student reasoning about concurrency differ across the levels of the undergraduate computing program?* To study student conceptions of concurrency, we used Lewandowski et al.'s "Concert Tickets" problem, in which multiple vendors sell tickets to a concert and students are asked to provide a natural language response that identifies problems that may occur and to provide possible solutions. We present an analysis of sixty student responses drawn from all four years of the undergraduate CS program at a large, public university in the United States. The analysis utilizes a qualitative open coding approach to uncover common features in student solutions. Most students identified the concurrency related problem of double-booking and did so uniformly across student year. We performed a thematic analysis of student responses about double-booking and found emerging clusters around language for access control, speed, visualization, human protocols, and added states. Knowledge of these student conceptions can help instructors to construct pedagogical materials that build on the strengths and prior knowledge that students bring with them at each level and to address troublesome aspects of these concepts.

CCS CONCEPTS

• **Social and professional topics → Computing education**; • **Theory of computation → Concurrency**; • **Computing methodologies → Concurrent computing methodologies**.

KEYWORDS

concurrency, undergraduate education, pedagogical content knowledge

ACM ISBN 978-1-4503-6301-3/19/07...$15.00
https://doi.org/10.1145/3304221.3319763

ACM Reference Format:
Aubrey Lawson, Eileen T. Kraemer, S. Megan Che, Cazembe Kennedy. 2019. A Multi-Level Study of Undergraduate Computer Science Reasoning about Concurrency. In *Innovation and Technology in Computer Science Education (ITiCSE '19), July 15–17, 2019, Aberdeen, Scotland UK.* ACM, New York, NY, USA, 7 pages. https://doi.org/10.1145/3304221.3319763

1 INTRODUCTION

To effectively engage students in thinking and learning, instructors must possess both subject matter knowledge and pedagogical content knowledge (PCK). Shulman states that pedagogical content knowledge is not merely domain knowledge plus a generic set of teaching strategies[14]. Rather, expert instructors know where students in their discipline struggle, have a ready collection of good examples to address those struggles, and know "how to tap into students' existing knowledge in order to make new information meaningful"[1].

However, PCK for computer science education (CS-PCK) is underdeveloped compared to other disciplines and little research exists on PCK related to the study of concurrency in computing [5, 18]. In our work, we seek to explore students' existing knowledge of and reasoning about concurrency concepts, with the goal that instructors can then build on this knowledge in their teaching.

In computing, concurrency relates to the situation in which different processes or threads may execute at the same time or in an interleaved manner. Such simultaneous or interleaved use of shared resources can lead to memory consistency errors or the inability to progress. A correct program for concurrent systems must maintain liveness by ensuring that a state is never reached in which progress is not possible (e.g. deadlock, livelock, or starvation). Thus, the design of concurrent systems involves finding reliable techniques for decomposing programs into subprograms and coordinating the execution and data sharing of the subprograms in a way that maintains correctness (the final outcome is unaffected by the order in which they execute) and provides good performance.

Concurrency has proven difficult for students[8]. Its concepts have typically been presented in upper-level undergraduate courses and deeply embedded in the technical context of operating system programming. However, as described in[11], the NSF/TCPP curriculum initiative and the ACM/IEEE curriculum guidelines are focused on integrating such concepts throughout the undergraduate curriculum. In seeking to understand students' difficulties in reasoning about concurrency concepts, we explore their preconceptions and approaches to solving concurrency-related problems, across the four years of the undergraduate computing curriculum. The research questions we seek to address are: *What is the nature of undergraduate computer science students' conceptions of concurrency?* and *How does student reasoning about concurrency differ across the levels of the undergraduate computing program?*

2 BACKGROUND AND RELATED WORK

Given the increasing prevalence of hyperthreading and multicore architectures[16, 17], concurrency is at the forefront of computing as it scales to meet ever-growing, real-world demands [2], and computing curricula are adapting to include concurrency[11]. Students who engage in the study of concurrency bring preconceptions from both their real-world experience and their prior computing education. Previous work has explored how students interact with concurrency topics. Resnick spearheaded pedagogically motivated research into common bugs in concurrent programming assignments using MultiLogo [12]. He categorized the bugs as relating to program decomposition, synchronization, or object-oriented design. Program decomposition bugs demonstrated the "sequentialist thinking" students had acquired. He suggests real-world examples to remind students of naturally occurring concurrency. Synchronization bugs occur when students inappropriately apply parallelism excessively without full consideration of all courses of action, so Resnick suggests pedagogical activities that play out the actors' roles. Object-oriented design bugs, though paradigm specific, occur due to the generalized nature of the objects acting as agents. Thus, he recommends an implementation-based approach with specialized objects in multiple scenarios to contextualize knowledge.

Concurrency is traditionally presented as an advanced topic reserved for higher level classes. Kolikant and Ben-Ari found that novice programmers who have not been exposed to formal concurrency topics can leverage real-life experiences to reason about concurrency related problems [7]. They also found that students struggle to adapt their computational model to multiprocessing. Students often reduce a problem's complexity by applying an inappropriate computational model. For example, the assumption that multiple processors or threads proceed at a constant rate of execution was prominent in student solutions [7].

Further studies showed that concurrency offers the opportunity to enculturate students into the role of programmer [8]. An end-user based perspective is insufficient for concurrency related problems, as it abstracts away the handling of independent processors and access control of shared data. The complexity of concurrency challenges students to adopt the more refined mental models of computers used by practitioners to reason logically about what occurs "under the hood" of modern, real-world systems.

Lewandowski et al. developed the Concert Tickets problem assessment to gather student conceptions about concurrency at a more conversational level. The Concert Tickets problem presents a concurrency-related problem, multiple sellers selling concert tickets, in a natural language assessment in which students discuss possible problems and solutions [9]. They found that students preferred centralized solutions, which they considered easier to predict and control, and often changed the problem space to simplify the problem. Though students leveraged their real-world experiences with buying tickets online, they did not always apply the correct computational models [9].

2.1 Theoretical Background

Several theories and concepts relate to the development of pedagogical content knowledge for computer science, including constructivism and the misconceptions literature. Our understanding of learning is informed by a constructivist epistemology that asserts that students actively engage with their environments as they seek to make sense[3]. Further, they construct and refine personalized knowledge frameworks that represent their prior knowledge. Instructors should be aware of this prior knowledge and develop methods that stimulate students to modify and expand those frameworks to incorporate concurrency concepts.

In the context of constructivist theory, learning happens as students extend and refine their knowledge frameworks. Students bring a rich set of experiences and preconceptions that they utilize in the learning process. Some struggles that arise as students adapt their cognitive structures to new experiences and information may be due to the "overloading of language, mathematical symbols and previous programming experience" and from "taking information from one context and using it in another"[4].

Prior research has shown how the knowledge of common student misconceptions aids in the development of effective, pedagogical materials[6, 15]. In a recent study of science teachers, Sadler found that the teachers need to know science, but also that the most effective science teachers are able to predict how their students will respond to questions about particular topics, the difficulties they will encounter and how those difficulties may manifest[13]. Our work seeks to help provide such knowledge for computer science instructors.

We seek to explore students' existing knowledge of topics in concurrency–to give insight into aspects of their knowledge frameworks, and to identify and understand the difficulties they encounter in modifying and refining their knowledge frameworks to include concurrency concepts.

3 MATERIALS AND METHODS

To study student conceptions of concurrency, we employed an assessment that included a natural language problem that explores student thinking on concurrency. We used a natural language problem because it is accessible for students at any level. We sought a single problem space for students that presents a concurrency-related problem, a race condition due to interleaving, and allows students to explore a key aspect of concurrency, access control. We used Lewandowski et al.'s Concert Tickets problem, in which multiple vendors sell tickets to a concert, and asked students to provide a natural language response that identifies problems that may occur and provide possible solutions[9]. The problem statement is seen in figure 1.

While students identified a number of problems, we focus on the problem of double booking: that even for a single seat, two sellers (e.g., SellerA and SellerB) could simultaneously query the status of a given seat (e.g., 17A), see that it is available and both sellers mark it as unavailable and sell a ticket for seat 17A, unaware that the seat had been sold twice. We chose to focus on double booking, as it presents a real-world example of a race condition. This allows students to explore their preconceptions of interleaving and shared

Suppose we sell concert tickets over the telephone in the following way: when a customer calls in and asks for a number (n) of seats, the seller:

(1) finds the n best seats that are available
(2) marks those n seats as unavailable
(3) deals with payment options for the customer (e.g. getting credit or debit card number, or sending the tickets to the Will Call window for pickup).

Suppose we have more than one seller working at the same time. What problems might we see, and how might we avoid those problems?

Figure 1: Concert Tickets problem statement

resource management to provide a solution that ensures access control of tickets for sale.

To preclude double booking, the system must guarantee that the sequence of steps: [check status; update status] must not be interrupted, i.e., the composite action must be executed atomically. Thus, the Concert Tickets problem challenges students to regulate access to seat tickets (access control) while managing the independent and sometimes overlapping seller actors (synchronization).

The study was administered to undergraduate students at a large, public university in the United States in Spring 2018. Four courses were selected to capture data from the four years (referred to as Y1, Y2, Y3, Y4) of undergraduate study in computer science: Year 1: Introduction to Computing, Year 2: Software Development Foundations, Year 3: Introduction to Software Engineering, and Year 4: Seminar in Professional Issues. These courses are all part of the required curriculum for computer science students. Responses from fifteen students at each level were studied for a total of sixty responses.

The study received approval from the university's Institutional Review Board . Students were offered extra credit or lab credit or completed the survey as part of a non-credit laboratory assignment. Students had the option to complete an alternative, non-research-related assignment to receive the same credit. Those who agreed to participate remained in the room for the 50 minutes allotted to the survey. All responses were then anonymized for analysis, with each response randomly assigned a three digit identifier. The student's class number (year) was retained but intentionally not included in the identifier to avoid bias during initial analyses.

4 RESULTS

We utilized a qualitative open coding approach to uncover common features in student solutions (see figure 3). We removed class identification markers and did not apply *a priori* hypotheses. Data were iteratively and incrementally analyzed to derive emergent trends. Through multiple iterations of thematic analysis with three raters, we developed ten main codes to classify the responses according to features related to the concurrency problem of double booking.

Problem features:

- double-booking: acknowledges sellers may sell same ticket to multiple people
- non-responsive: participant does not engage with the problem.

Solution features:

- **automation**: an over-reliance on automation without sufficient explanation, e.g. "an application handles it", "the system knows / decides"
- **split inventory**: distributing seats among sellers to avoid conflict.
- **added state**: addition of another label to a resource, e.g. a "reserved" ticket.
- **access control**: the ability to restrict modification of shared resources, whether through locking or otherwise. This may also be at the seller/system level with "one-at-a-time" access to the entire system or to a block of seats.
- **test-and-set**: more advanced (though possibly still naive) access control. This indicates explicit description of testing and modifying a value atomically.
- **human protocols**: defining communication protocols for sellers, e.g. best practices for sellers, sellers checking who is accessing the system
- **visualization**: visual language; the use of images to reduce conflict among sellers
- **speed**: a focus on speed as a way to avoid the possibility of interleaving (indicating a focus on outrunning potential race conditions/issues), e.g. "at the same time", "live-updating system"

Intercoder agreement was reached through discussion for all sixty responses. An independent coder processed a quarter of the dataset using the resulting rubric leading to 98.3 % inter-rater reliability.

4.1 Problem Features

Students at all levels were able to identify the critical concurrency related problem of double booking and did so relatively uniformly across class levels (Y1=10, Y2=11, Y3=12, Y4=9). Many of the students stated that it is the "biggest" or "most important" problem in the scenario. This lack of difference across years may be surprising given that roughly half of the year 3 students and all of the year 4 students had studied such issues in detail in their Operating Systems course. Only one student, a first year student, did not respond to the prompt.

4.2 Solution Features

The solution feature codes are not mutually exclusive, and each response is represented by multiple codes. Students interacted with the problem in productive ways, applying their preconceptions and experiences. **Automation** (Y1=3, Y2=1, Y3=0, Y4=0) was represented with students in lower levels. Solutions with this feature referred to things happening "automatically" or suggested the use of highly specific components of computing systems, such as a bus topography, without appropriately defining them or describing their role. For example, year 1 student 029 recognized double booking then states "A way we avoid that is by setting up an automatic distributor. Making payments and availability of seats known to the customer."

Human Protocols (Y1=0, Y2=2, Y3=0, Y4=1) and **Visualization** (Y1=4, Y2=3, Y3=0, Y4=1) represent solutions that focus on sellers' behavior and their awareness of data through the artifacts they interact with. Year 2 student 031 focused on sellers and their

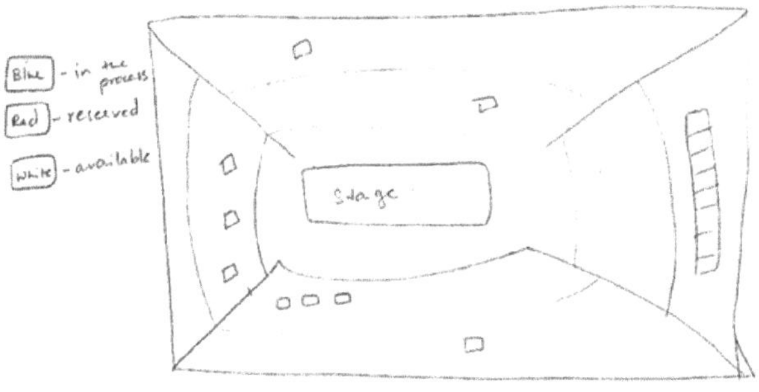

Figure 2: Student 163 drawing

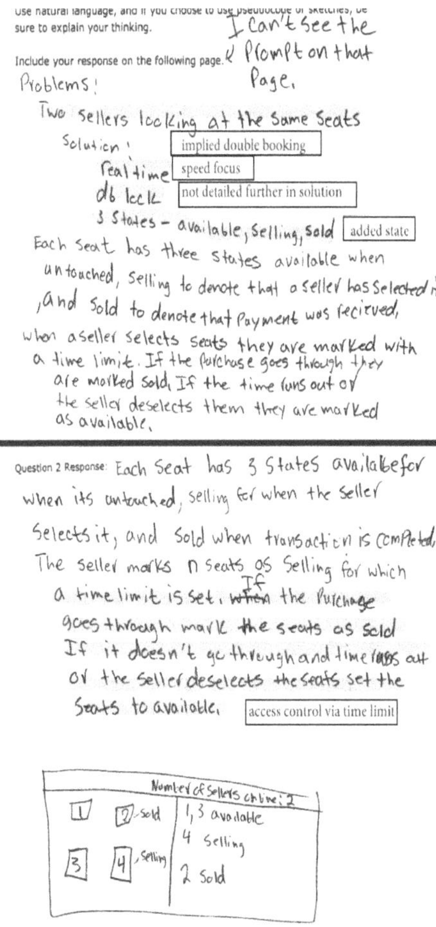

Figure 3: Year 2 student 122 response annotated by coder

communication so that "the seller can speak with another seller in an adjacent section to get additional seats". Some student solutions addressed issues around block seating, though the crucial solution component of controlling access to tickets remains the same.

Year 1 student 086 shared a focus on sellers with their concise, visualization-based solution: "have an active screen for sellers to show seats that are available and unavailable in order to lessen conflict." Year 4 student 163 provided a more detailed solution with a system in which "one seller will know if the other sellers are dealing with customers through graphical indicators on the system" (see figure 2 for student drawing).

Solutions that feature **Speed** (Y1=6, Y2=5, Y3=3, Y4=5) may also reflect the end user perspective of faster-is-better. Students at all levels provided solutions based on increasing computational speed. Some students focused on minimizing lag on seller screens. Year 3 student 301 suggested "updating the application at least every 15 seconds should help." Other solutions treated lag as practically removable. Year 2 student 083 said "sellers, ideally, should have access to a live-updating web application that displays a visual layout of the seats". This avoidant strategy attempted to outrun undesirable outcomes (i.e. unregulated interleaving), and was well represented across each level.

Students that **split inventory** (Y1=0, Y2=3, Y3=1, Y4=1) divided the seats among sellers to parallelize the problem and eliminate overlap. Year 2 student 031 states, "I would have different sellers working with different parts of the venue. Then only one seller would have access to a certain section of seats, and they wouldn't be able to double book them." Year 4 student 333 describes the same approach to avoid the problem, "assign each salesperson a 'zone' they are responsible to sell to avoid overlap." While these are practical solutions for avoiding double booking, they fail to meet the "best seats" criterion of the problem statement.

Added states (Y1=2, Y2=6, Y3=5, Y4=10) were well represented across student responses, especially with upper level students. Solutions with added ticket states were often explicit such as year 2 student 122's solution which defined "3 states–available, selling, sold". Year 4 student 183 even provided integer values "representing status. 1=available, 0=on hold, -1=sold". These solutions shift the race condition from changing the ticket state to "reserved" or "selling" rather than "sold", not realizing that two sellers might both mark the same seat "reserved" as easily as they both might mark it "sold". Added state based solutions add unnecessary complexity to push the point of concurrency, and this has been found in prior work [9]. We find that this behavior is more prominent with higher level students.

Access control (Y1=1, Y2=7, Y3=6, Y4=4) was exhibited in student solutions in many different ways only some of which led to a correct solution. One approach was to bottleneck seller access to all seats, like year 1 student 078–"Solution: Let only 1 seller in at a time". Year 2 student 011 assigned time sensitive confirmation codes to callers to allow exclusive access for a limited time. Year 3 student 658 queued requests and assigned seats "using a FIFO call" to restrict access to seats fairly but did not designate any control over access to the queue. Year 4 student 349 stated the seat access problem "can be fixed with mutexes to allow only one seller to change a seat status at a time".

The **test-and-set** (Y1=0, Y2=1, Y3=1, Y4=0) feature was only explicitly represented in a few responses. Year 2 student 007 suggested "having the protocol that marks seats unavailable return whether or not the seats have already been marked unavailable". Though implementation details were not provided, the solution provides a promising conception of access control from a second year computer science student.

A correct student solution to the double booking issue in the Concert Tickets problem requires a clear form of access control. Though students were not required to include implementable code, they needed to enforce mutual exclusion for ticket access by sellers. Year 4 student 067's solution stated "You would need an access control scheme to prevent [double booking]. One way of fixing the problem is locking read write capabilities to one user at a time. This way a second sales person would never be shown seats that another employee was in the process of selling." Year 4 student 349 stated double booking "can be fixed with mutexes to allow only one seller to change a seat status at a time." Year 3 student 952 also proposed a correct solution with a shared database and "the function marking seats as unavailable an atomic function".

5 DISCUSSION

The key to the Concert Tickets problem lies in defining an access control scheme for seat tickets. The application of an access control scheme is predicated on concepts of data management and machine architecture:

- Data access can be shared and parallelized to speedup update operations
- Shared data requires logical structure to prevent undesirable outcomes (high-level, abstracted interleaving)
- Source code is decomposed into multiple machine instructions (low-level, machine level interleaving)
- Rates of execution are not constant across threads/processes.

Student responses reflect varying combinations of these concepts as shown through the emergent features. In this section we discuss how student responses to the Concert Tickets problem reveal the concept-rich preconceptions and growing computational models they bring to concurrent environments.

Fifty-nine out of sixty students were willing to interact with the problem space, and the majority of them discussed concurrency explicitly by acknowledging that sellers were sharing seat data. This agrees with prior findings that novices can reason about concurrent computing problems by leveraging preconceptions developed through real-world experiences [7].

Students who understand the benefits of shared data may choose a user perspective that focuses on actors and their interactions with a system rather than the system itself. Both human protocol and visualization features focus on this readily available information, and often assume users will adhere to a social contract of best practices. Concurrency provides a rich opportunity to explore how these solutions are insufficient, as even well-intentioned users can produce undesirable interleaving. For the Concert Tickets problem, a required conversation between two sellers would not scale to 1000 sellers for an in-demand concert. Though these best practice rules may not form a suitable solution, instructors can guide students towards logic-based rules for computing objects that will always adhere to their prescribed contract.

Students who do focus on a computational perspective may have fragile knowledge of interleaving and its modeling, which affects the logic they choose to structure data access. This uncertainty emerged in student responses. Year 4 student 183 said "These problems cannot be fully avoided, but the damage done can be

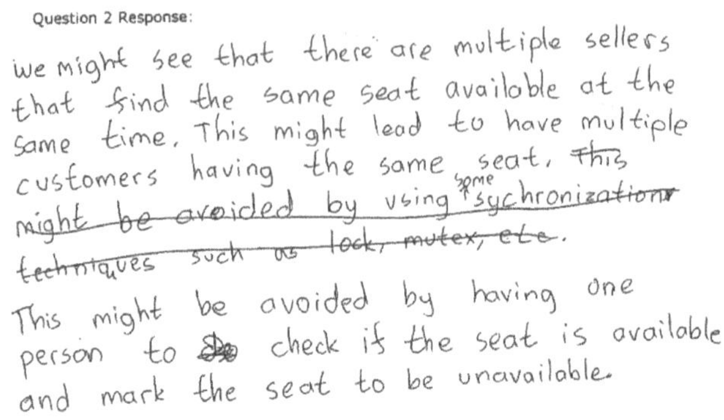

Figure 4: Student 108 response with avoidant behavior

reduced"–indicating the belief that concurrency-related problems are unsolvable. Year 2 student 108's response demonstrates fragile knowledge (see figure 4). Though they provided a list of terms they crossed them all out and chose instead a sequential solution to avoid concurrency. Interleaving avoidance emerged as a trend in student responses that was represented differently at each level.

Lower level student responses featuring access control bottlenecked the system such that only one seller could access all of the data at a time. Instructors can use contrasting cases to showing runtime examples of systems with processes that overlap and those that don't, revealing motivating performance and architecture factors for managing rather than avoiding interleaving. By understanding when and why concurrency should be used, students will be prepared to conditionalize the machine level knowledge they acquire about interleaving.

High level student responses that avoided interleaving featured added states. This proved an interesting trend as the additional complexity expands the problem space unnecessarily. Instruction to mitigate this should provide scenarios exposing how pushing the point of concurrency does not resolve it.

Students at all levels also avoided interleaving completely by restricting the problem space or relying on ill-defined automation. Problem space restriction is shown in the split inventory responses that parallelize sellers but don't allow their overlap. Though this prevents them from selling the best seats, the split inventory solution is a step towards multiprocessing sellers that applies structure to their access of the seat data. Automation-based responses demonstrate an over-reliance on computer systems to avoid addressing the requirements of the problem space. In both situations, instructors can encourage students to apply a programmer perspective to adhere to problem requirements and explore the inner workings of automation. Such experiences can help transition students into a programming community of practice [8].

Those who understand the abstract concept of interleaving may still struggle with how it is applied at the machine level. Many students who featured access control utilized a queue in their solution. Year 3 student 658 queued caller requests and "using a FIFO call guarantees the first to request and pay gets the seats". The queue solution was found in students who had taken at least one computer science course and was especially prominent in those who had just taken a data structures course. It connotes a focus on fairness and organizing requests among multiple processes which is productive. Instructors can leverage the focus on data structures to explore how modifying the value of a shared variable, whether representing the state of a ticket or a position in a queue, is subject to interleaving.

Another difficulty with low level interleaving was demonstrated with students who applied atomicity inappropriately. This was demonstrated by year 3 student 155 who proposed to "check before marking a seat as taken every time (like if(seat.available==false)then reserve)." This response shows a third year student who found the double booking problem, developed a supposed atomic solution, and applied it with a conditional logic structure they are confident in at the source code level. Students with these solutions have nearly reached an appropriate solution, but lack a computational model of machine level instructions. Source code is decomposed into machine level instructions that can be interleaved even though they are derived from a single code statement. This level of interleaving should be demonstrated clearly to students to support robust models of atomicity.

As students develop computational models to accommodate concurrency, they must adopt the notion of multiple rates of execution. Some responses featured speed to assume a constant, cooperative rate of execution. Year 3 student 155's response reflected a model in which "any seller who is working at the same time would not be able to reserve a seat at exactly the same time". Many responses reflected an illusory correlation between lag and undesirable interleaving, and thus their solutions focused on eliminating latency. As previously mentioned, year 4 student 163's first solution rule is to "actively refresh servers continuously". Year 4 student 139 also relies on "a live-update software". A faulty model of execution can lead to solutions that attempt to outrun concurrency issues. Instructors should be aware that students who have been formally introduced to concurrency in the classroom may still hold these models. As concurrency is traditionally introduced in an operating systems context, students may not apply the same computational models to a problem situated in a different context. A problem like the Concert Tickets problem relates to "real-world experiences" more than to operating systems programming which may explain why students apply their experienced-based perceptions of speed and response time to their solutions.

A few solutions (students 067 and 349), mentioned in the previous section, propose correct solutions but also include the added complexity of additional states. These responses highlight the ongoing developmental process in which students are constantly refactoring their preconceptions to accommodate newly acquired knowledge.

Of note, the students who proposed correct solutions used concurrency specific terminology to denote the required level of access control at the machine level to prevent undesired interleaving. Prior work has shown that students who have taken courses with concurrency topics still possess fragile knowledge around the vocabulary [10]. Terms such as atomic and mutual exclusion are closely coupled with the crucial understanding of machine instruction sequencing. We suggest that these terms be used more frequently, including in examples at the abstract level (such as the Concert Tickets problem), to name and demystify the low level machine knowledge required to understand concurrent systems.

5.1 Limitations

This study was conducted at the beginning of the spring semester. Y1 students were beginning CS1 and thus may have had no prior programming experience, Y2 students had completed CS1 and CS2, and Y3 and Y4 students had completed the associated, higher level prerequisites. We found this helped us capture a broad array of experiences and include the preconceptions about concurrency that computing students bring to the program prior to formal instruction. For some sections this assessment was designated an optional lab assignment, so these students opted to participate. In other sections, the instructor assigned the assessment as the first lab assignment, so these students had higher incentives to complete the assessment. Student completion was sufficient to collect the desired amount of responses from each level even though the incentive models varied.

6 CONCLUSION AND FUTURE WORK

Concurrency is inherent in natural processes, and modern computer systems are expected to handle multiple requests and actions simultaneously. Students are commonly introduced to concurrency within very technical contexts, such as operating systems courses. Thus student difficulties in reasoning are commonly attributed to misunderstanding at the implementation level [10]. This work builds upon prior research to show that students struggle with concurrency even at an abstracted, conceptual level, and here we find that students of all levels of an undergraduate program demonstrate these difficulties.

Encouragingly, we found that most students of all levels discovered the key concurrency-related problem of double booking in the scenario. Thus their difficulties lie in the pathways from problem discovery to solution. We found that students possess strong prior knowledge about concurrency that they utilize either alongside or in place of content knowledge received in the classroom.

Many students applied their preconceptions to a level of sophistication representative of their developing mental models of computation. Lower level students presented a more black box approach to the system, choosing to control seller access to the entire system, one at a time. Though bottlenecked, this solution displays a clear focus on the concurrency related conflict and the need for access control. Farther along the pathway of the program, upper level students presented solutions with finer granularity, with some attempting to ensure mutual exclusion with user level code. Though these solutions may not have appropriately addressed interleaving at the level of machine instructions, their expression shows insight into key ideas and provides instructors the opportunity to refine their understanding by introducing the associated machine level instructions at this point in student development. Students also applied preconceptions to "fill in the gaps" of their solution designs. This was especially notable in solutions that pushed the point of concurrency or avoided complexity by mentioning concurrency terminology but not applying it.

We have identified a number of key conceptions that students hold about solution approaches, Awareness of these student conceptions can help instructors to construct pedagogical materials that build on the strengths and prior knowledge that students bring with them and to address troublesome aspects of these concepts.

REFERENCES

[1] "National Research Council". 2000. *How people learn: Brain, mind, experience, and school: Expanded edition.* National Academies Press.

[2] National Research Council et al. 2011. *The Future of Computing Performance: Game Over or Next Level?* National Academies Press.

[3] Peter E Doolittle. 2014. Complex constructivism: A theoretical model of complexity and cognition. *International Journal of teaching and learning in higher education* 26, 3 (2014), 485–498.

[4] Anna Eckerdal, Robert McCartney, Jan Erik Moström, Mark Ratcliffe, Kate Sanders, and Carol Zander. 2006. Putting threshold concepts into context in computer science education. In *ACM SIGCSE Bulletin*, Vol. 38. ACM, 103–107.

[5] Peter Hubwieser, Johannes Magenheim, Andreas Mühling, and Alexander Ruf. 2013. Towards a conceptualization of pedagogical content knowledge for computer science. In *Proceedings of the ninth annual international ACM conference on International computing education research.* ACM, 1–8.

[6] Cazembe Kennedy and Eileen T Kraemer. 2018. What Are They Thinking?: Eliciting Student Reasoning About Troublesome Concepts in Introductory Computer Science. In *Proceedings of the 18th Koli Calling International Conference on Computing Education Research.* ACM, 7.

[7] Yifat Ben-David Kolikant. 2001. Gardeners and cinema tickets: High school students' preconceptions of concurrency. *Computer Science Education* 11, 3 (2001), 221–245.

[8] Yifat Ben-David Kolikant. 2004. Learning concurrency as an entry point to the community of computer science practitioners. *Journal of Computers in Mathematics and Science Teaching* 23, 1 (2004), 21–46.

[9] Gary Lewandowski, Dennis J Bouvier, Robert McCartney, Kate Sanders, and Beth Simon. 2007. Commonsense computing (episode 3): concurrency and concert tickets. In *Proceedings of the third international workshop on Computing education research.* ACM, 133–144.

[10] Zhen Li. 2013. *Programming with concurrency; barriers to learning and explorations in teaching.* Ph.D. Dissertation. University of Georgia, Athens, GA, USA. http://hdl.handle.net/10724/29101

[11] Sushil K Prasad, Anshul Gupta, Arnold Rosenberg, Alan L Sussman, Charles Weems, and Chip Weems. 2018. *Topics in Parallel and Distributed Computing: Enhancing the Undergraduate Curriculum: Performance, Concurrency, and Programming on Modern Platforms.* Springer.

[12] Mitchel Resnick. 1990. MultiLogo: A study of children and concurrent programming. *Interactive learning environments* 1, 3 (1990), 153–170.

[13] Philip M Sadler, Gerhard Sonnert, Harold P Coyle, Nancy Cook-Smith, and Jaimie L Miller. 2013. The influence of teachersâĂŹ knowledge on student learning in middle school physical science classrooms. *American Educational Research Journal* 50, 5 (2013), 1020–1049.

[14] Lee S Shulman. 1986. Those who understand: Knowledge growth in teaching. *Educational researcher* 15, 2 (1986), 4–14.

[15] John P Smith III, Andrea A DiSessa, and Jeremy Roschelle. 1994. Misconceptions reconceived: A constructivist analysis of knowledge in transition. *The journal of the learning sciences* 3, 2 (1994), 115–163.

[16] Herb Sutter. 2005. The free lunch is over: A fundamental turn toward concurrency in software. *Dr. DobbâĂŹs journal* 30, 3 (2005), 202–210.

[17] Herb Sutter and James Larus. 2005. Software and the concurrency revolution. *Queue* 3, 7 (2005), 54–62.

[18] Aman Yadav, Marc Berges, Phil Sands, and Jon Good. 2016. Measuring computer science pedagogical content knowledge: An exploratory analysis of teaching vignettes to measure teacher knowledge. In *Proceedings of the 11th Workshop in Primary and Secondary Computing Education.* ACM, 92–95.

Final Year Students' Approaches to Implementing Complex Distributed Systems

Claudia Szabo
The University of Adelaide
Adelaide, Australia
claudia.szabo@adelaide.edu.au

Michael Scott Pointon
The University of Adelaide
Adelaide, Australia
michael.pointon@adelaide.edu.au

ABSTRACT

Understanding how final year students build complex software systems is critical for determining whether desired graduate outcomes have been met, for identifying curriculum gaps, and for designing scaffolding and support structures. A large body of work focuses on the programming strategies employed by novice programmers, with few existing research in understanding programming strategies and development focus of final year students, in particular with respect to non-functional requirements. In this paper, we analyse consecutive revisions of 77 students across two cohorts that implemented a large and complex Distributed Systems assignment with several non-functional requirements. To obtain a qualitative overview of the students' approach to software development, we manually read and tagged all sourcefiles in all assignment revisions with specific development focus categories. Our analysis identifies how the students' development focus evolves throughout the assignment timeline. We visualise the software development process and identify several areas that require further support.

CCS CONCEPTS

• **Social and professional topics** → **Computing education**;

KEYWORDS

introductory programming; novice programming; error fixing; compile behavior

ACM Reference Format:
Claudia Szabo and Michael Scott Pointon. 2019. Final Year Students' Approaches to Implementing Complex Distributed Systems. In *Innovation and Technology in Computer Science Education (ITiCSE '19), July 15–17, 2019, Aberdeen, Scotland Uk.* ACM, New York, NY, USA, 7 pages. https://doi.org/10.1145/3304221.3319774

1 INTRODUCTION

First year students enrolled in CS0-CS2 courses have been the focus of a large body of work that analyses how they create small programs, trace code, compile, and run their code among others [13, 20]. Few works have looked at the programming strategies and software development processes used by final year students, and in particular at how they build larger, more complex programs.

ACM ISBN 978-1-4503-6301-3/19/07.
https://doi.org/10.1145/3304221.3319774

Existing work has shown that software development strategies mature as students progress through their degrees, specifically with respect to the presence of testing, while design paradigms and prototyping are not frequently used [9]. Final year students have been shown to be able to maintain and debug significantly large codebases (up to 11,000 LOC) by using processes such as reverse engineering, the creation of UML diagrams, and pen and paper debugging [24]. There is still a need to understand how final year students develop their code, in particular large, complex software programs, in order to provide support for specific tasks or assignments.

Beyond how students build software to address functional requirements, it is important for educators to understand if and how students address non-functional requirements in their design and code, since the development of quality software is a frequent graduate outcome [27]. Non-functional requirements such as usability, flexibility, performance, security, scalability, maintainability and interoperability are equally important as functional requirements in determining the quality of a software [5]. However, partially due to the need to have software deliverables against tight deadlines, non-functional requirements tend to be overlooked and can eventually cause significant and costly failures. Failing to fulfill one or more of the above non-functional requirements can cause economic losses [1], exposure of sensitive information [4] or, in extreme cases, loss of life [28] with reports showing that the cost of downtime in industry can range from $100K to $540K per hour on average [10]. Teaching students about non-functional requirements requires that they engage with large, complex systems as non-functional requirements could become trivial in the context of simple toy programs. However, with the development of a complex software system comes the risk that students will focus even more on the functional aspects of the code and disregard non-functional aspects altogether.

In this paper, we aim to understand the software development process of final year students solving a Distributed Systems assignment. The assignment requires the implementation of non-functional requirements such as fault tolerance, scalability, and maintainability. By looking at the students' revisions throughout the assignment timeline, we aim to understand the aspects of software development that students focus on as the assignment deadline approaches, as well as the students' software development process, in the hope of identifying the need for additional scaffolding or support for specific tasks. The contributions of this paper are twofold. Firstly, we introduce a qualitative approach for analysing and visualising student code that identifies the evolution of the software development focus as well as the software development process employed. Secondly, we identify several areas where graduating students require additional support, highlighting the need for introducing several concepts such as software development approaches, testing and refactoring earlier in the degree or course.

2 RELATED WORK

A large body of existing work focuses on the teaching of software development models, using traditional lecture-based formats [7], capstone projects [15], games [7] or using the Personal Software Process [12]. Several systematic mapping studies present a comprehensive picture of the field [15, 19]. Significant research is focused on learning analytics, but is mostly trageted at first year students [13] without presenting a qualitative view of the software development process. Bareiss et al. [2] analysed the evolution of software engineering knowledge of 16 master students across their entire degree, and found that their mental models of requirements analysis and process management improved significantly as they approached the end of their degree. They also found that more in-depth analysis of the software development process is needed. Falkner et al. [9] compared the software development processes of first year students with those of final year students and found that while software development strategies were significantly more advanced for final year students, in particular with respect to testing, several areas, specifically related to prototyping and design, were still immature in final year students' processes.

The development of larger assignments, especially in advanced courses typically follows a software development process. Moskal and Wass [18] propose the Interpersonal Process Recall to encourage students to think more about their software development processes, through an added element of reflection. Focusing on collaborative activities, Mittal and Sureka [17] propose to employ repository commit metrics to understand contributions to a collaborative software development project. Commit history was unable to reveal a software development process, however it did highlight that the frequency of commits for all teams increases significantly as the deadline approaches. Through the mining of specific bug reports as reported to a in-house bug tracking tool, and the use of Disco [11], a process mining tool, Mittal and Sureka were able to visualise the bug fixing process employed by the entire student cohort (n=99 students). Our work is similar to this in that we attempt to understand and visualise the student software development process using revision history, however we expand on this by using a manual tagging process that allows us to focus on a more qualitative understanding of what students are focused on in their development.

A significant area of research focuses on understanding the software development process of professional software developers in order to ensure quality and facilitate maintenance, with many automated approaches proposed in the literature [6, 16, 22, 29]. Roehm and Maalej [21] propose to identify the current development activity of professional software developers and whether they are facing a problem. Their approach uses the TeamWeaver instrumentation framework [26] to determine, using a Hidden Markov Model, whether the developer is searching for a solution, searching for the cause of a found problem, or testing a solution.

With respect to non-functional requirements such as maintainability, reliability and testability, Mäntylä and Lassenius [14] discuss the importance of code commenting to reduce student code development and debugging times. An analysis of over 20 million Stack Overflow posts with over 32 million comments made from July 2008 to September 2014 focuses on understanding the non-functional requirements that developers focus on [30]. The study identifies that developers mostly discuss usability and reliability (with 'failure' and 'fault tolerance' included in reliability) and that maintainability (includes testing) and efficiency (includes scalability) are the least discussed. The most unresolved problems were related to usability and reliability.

3 PROPOSED APPROACH

In this work, we attempt to provide a qualitative overview of the software development process employed by final year students when developing large, complex assignments. In particular, we focus on how students approach the development and subsequent testing of non-functional requirements. Our research questions are:

- **RQ1** What functional and non-functional aspects do students focus on in their software development process?
- **RQ2** Are scalability, fault tolerance, and code quality a consistent focus throughout the assignment development?
- **RQ3** What testing strategies do students employ?

3.1 Distributed Systems Assignment

The assignment under study is a final year assignment in the topic area of Distributed Systems given to students at the University of xxx, in 2014 and 2015. Distributed Systems concepts are delivered through a Level 3 face-to-face course in a single semester that is taken mostly by students who are close to graduation or in the final year of study. The assignment was offered across both years and requires students to implement a news aggregation system comprising of a news aggregation server, news generation servers and news requesting clients. Communication between entities happens over sockets, with XML being used as the standard for transfer. The focus of the assignment is on implementing and testing a realistic distributed system, with frequent failures and mechanisms to address and recover from failures. Students were given a detailed specification of how the system should work but were asked to design the class structure themselves and to design and implement solutions for fault tolerance, synchronisation and persistence. Students were explicitly directed to resources on XML parsing and asked to use template code already provided. Students prepared for the assignment with teaching materials that extensively discussed the relevant topics in the form of lectures, tutorials, and collaborative discussion sessions.

The assignment was part of summative assessment, although it contained formative elements, and was worth 10% of the final mark for the course in each offering. The assessment components were:

- **Functionality** - XML parsing, server-client connections, GET/PUT operations, multiple content servers - 24%
- **Fault tolerance** - Lamport clocks, heartbeat, server restart - 30%
- **Testing** - 30%
- **Design** - 10%
- **Code quality** - 6%

of the assignment mark.

The assignment took place over a period of six weeks, with two major checkpoints along the way. Firstly, the students were asked to produce a design drawing, due in the first week, with feedback received in the second week. Secondly, around the fourth week mark the lecturer checked each students' repository and sent individual emails to all students to check-in and discuss any issues. Addressing the multiple content servers requirement implies the use of multi-threading to ensure scalability. The implementation of fault tolerance requires the use of Lamport clocks, checking for regular status updates from other servers (heartbeat) and having mechanisms in place to allow for the restart of the server, such as saving the server data in local files. The average mark across both cohorts is 54, with no significant differences across the two cohorts. In both years, the assignment was manually marked by an external marker following a rubric provided by the course lecturers. The assignment was the same across both years, and code analyzers checked for collusion (no collusion across years found).

For the purpose of this research, the assessment components of the assignment can be categorised in the following groups:

- **Functional requirements**: 20% (average mark: 70)
- **Non-functional requirements**: 50% (average mark: 59)
  - **fault tolerance**: 30%
  - **scalability**: 4% (multiple content servers)
  - **maintainability**: 16% (design & code quality)
- **Testing**: 30% (average mark: 35)

3.2 Data Analysis

We analysed SVN submission code from students across the two cohorts from each of their revisions. We only included students who had more than three revisions. For each revision, we looked at all changes made to the source code from the previous revision. In the initial stages of the coding process, the changes were classified into thirteen categories (Table 1) iteratively refined as the researchers read the sourcefiles. After an initial reading to determine the thirteen categories, to ensure inter-rater reliability the researchers initially coded the submissions of two of the students with the most revisions (70 and 50 respectively) and the submissions of two of the students with the least revisions (3 and 3 respectively) across both years. Discussions about the coding and category refinement followed iteratively until inter-rater reliability reached 100%. Another random student submission was coded by each researcher (inter-rater reliability 100%) before the submissions were split equally among researchers. Weekly meetings were held where any uncertainties were discussed.

Table 1: Categories of Development Focus

Category	Values
Code removal	Code removal
Comments	Comments
Cosmetic	Cosmetic
Fault tolerance	Lamport clocks, heartbeat, server restart
File modification	Reading/writing of local files
Operations	Connection, data management
Refactoring	Refactoring
Requests	Request creation, request analysis, parsing, request response, response creation, response analysis, file sending
Scalability	Multi-threading
Stubs	Stubs
Testing	Unit testing, complex scenarios
TODO	TODO
XML Parsing	XML parsing/writing

4 ANALYSIS

We analysed the submissions of a total of 97 students across 2014 (n=40) and 2015 (n=57). 77 students had more than three revisions, with 38 students in 2014 and 39 students in 2015, with an average of 15.13 revisions per student (11.87 std deviation), and a median of 12.0 revisions (no significant differences between cohorts). Figure 1 shows the spread of revision counts, with students ordered based on the number of revisions.

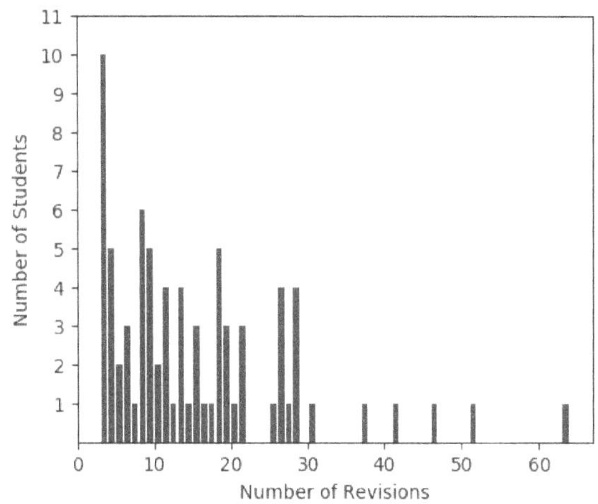

Figure 1: Spread of Revision Counts (N=77)

As students had variable revision counts we normalised the revisions to a range between zero and one to compare trends as the assignment progressed and the deadline approached. This was achieved by modifying each revision number to subtract the minimum number (necessary to achieve a data point at zero) and dividing by the range of revision values. With all the data in the same range, data from each student is then interpolated to create 100 evenly-spaced data points for creating averages and trend lines.

4.1 Overview of Development Focus

We counted the total number of unique change contents per revision per student and normalised the values as discussed above. Specifically, if a student worked on 'scalability' in more than one file during one revision, this was counted as a single occurrence of 'scalability'.

Figure 2 shows the normalised, averaged results, showing that the focus of development work seems to be on `Requests` and `Operations` for most of the assignment timeline. We can see a decreasing trend towards the end of the assignment for both. `Fault tolerance` shows an upward trend, peaking in the middle of the assignment and decreasing towards the end. The initial focus on requests and operations is as expected, as these form the functional

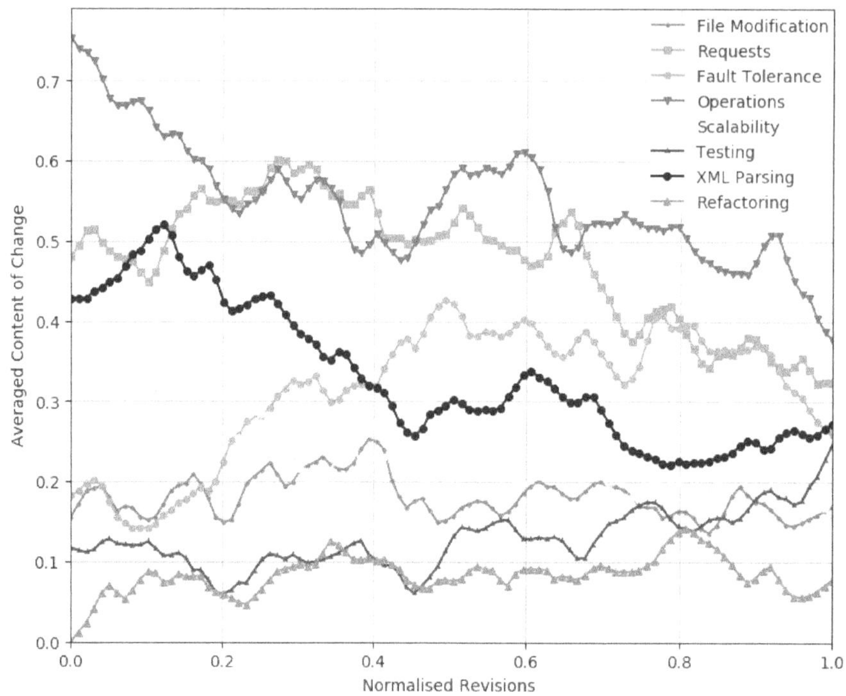

Figure 2: Normalised Development Focus Across Revisions

core of the assignment. To better understand the specific aspects of the assignment that students focused on, we present average student totals across revisions in Figure 3.

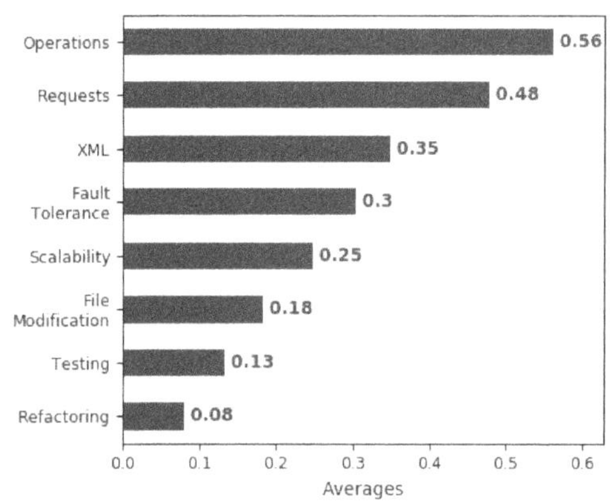

Figure 3: Average Change Content per Student per Revision

We can see that on average, students worked on operations 56% of the revisions, and on requests 48% of the time. Students worked on testing and refactoring only 13% and 8% of the time respectively.

The plot in Figure 4 identifies when students first started working on a particular aspect of the assignment. As expected, we see that the majority of students focused on `Operations`, `Requests`, `File modifications` and `XML parsing` in the first part (0-20%) of the assignment timeline.

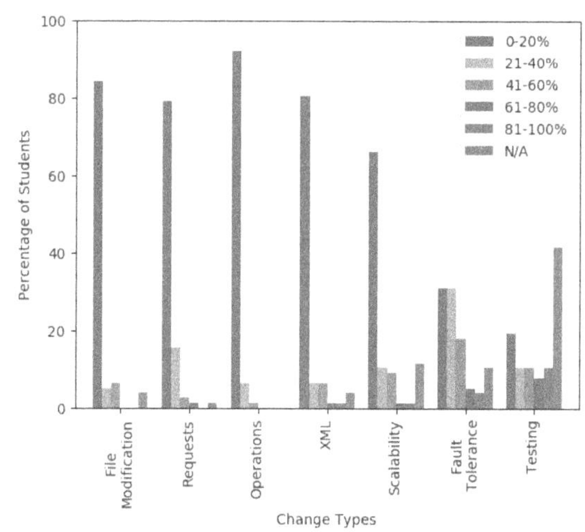

Figure 4: First Occurrence of Development Focus

4.2 Focus on Non-functional Aspects

Although non-functional requirements and testing represented 80% of the assignment mark, students received poor marks on all, as discussed above. One commonly encountered anecdote suggests that students underperform in addressing non-functional requirements because these are not part of the software design from the beginning and/or students start working on non-functional requirements too late in the assignment. Our results in Table 2 and Figure 4 and 6 attempt to test this.

4.2.1 Scalability and Fault tolerance. Table 2 shows that almost 90% of students used a thread-based structure to allow multiple clients to

Table 2: Percentage of Students' First Focus on a Category Against Assignment Timeline (N=77)

Completion	**0-20%**	**21-40%**	**41-60%**	**61-80%**	**81-100%**	**N/A**
File Modification	84.4%	5.2%	6.5%	0%	0%	3.9%
Requests	79.2%	15.6%	2.6%	1.3%	0%	1.3%
Operations	92.2%	6.5%	1.3%	0%	0%	0%
XML	80.5%	6.5%	6.5%	1.3%	1.3%	3.9%
Scalability	66.2%	10.4%	9.1%	1.3%	1.3%	11.7%
Fault Tolerance						
Lamport clocks	22.1%	26.0%	10.4%	9.1%	7.8%	24.7%
Heartbeat	9.1%	16.9%	20.8%	15.6%	9.1%	28.6%
Server restart	6.5%	11.7%	11.7%	13.0%	14.3%	**42.9%**
Testing	19.5%	10.4%	10.4%	7.8%	10.4%	**41.6%**
Refactoring	15.6%	20.8%	5.2%	10.4%	2.6%	**45.5%**

connect to the server, with over 65% of students focusing on multi-threading in the first part (0-20%) of their assignment timeline. However, an analysis of the marks and assignment feedback shows that 72% of the students did not have a working multi-threading solution. Thus while scalability is an area of early development focus, and potentially students had a lot of time to implement solutions, the produced solutions are immature and/or incomplete.

A large percentage of students did not focus on mature `Fault tolerance` solutions in their assignment, with most implementing simple fault tolerant mechanisms such as Lamport clocks and heartbeats. `Server restart` was implemented by 57.1% of students, towards the end of their assignment. In contrast, students who implemented Lamport clocks (75.3%) did so early.

4.2.2 Testing. Figure 2 shows a steady growth in the implementation of testing, with a slight spike towards the assignment deadline. Table 2 shows that 58.4% of students included `Testing` in their implementation and that nearly 30% started implementing some basic testing infrastructure early in their assignment. Of the 45 students that did do testing, 35 did unit testing, with ten students testing additional extensive scenarios, with multiple clients connecting to the server as well as various failures.

4.2.3 Design & Code quality. Figure 5 analyses comments, stubs and refactoring across the normalised revisions. As can be seen, the use of stubs is very low across the assignment timeline, and, as expected, decreases towards zero as the assignment progresses. This is to be expected given that the use of stubs is normally expected in the first stages of a top-down design, with the stubs being filled with functional code as the implemented system matures. However, only half (49%) of the students use stubs, with 36% of students using stubs in the first 0-20% of their assignment. An overview of this is presented in Figure 6. This suggests a bottom-up design approach, favored by the majority (51%) of students who never use stubs. We can also observe a dramatic increase in the use of comments towards the end of the assignment.

`Refactoring` seems to be ignored by a large percentage of students (45.5%), although students who do refactor code do so more as the assignment progresses, potentially in an attempt to address the code quality aspect of the assessment. A similar trend can be

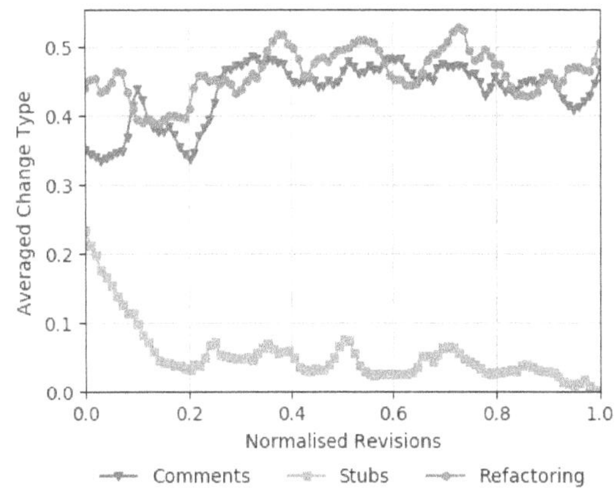

Figure 5: Average Code Quality Focus

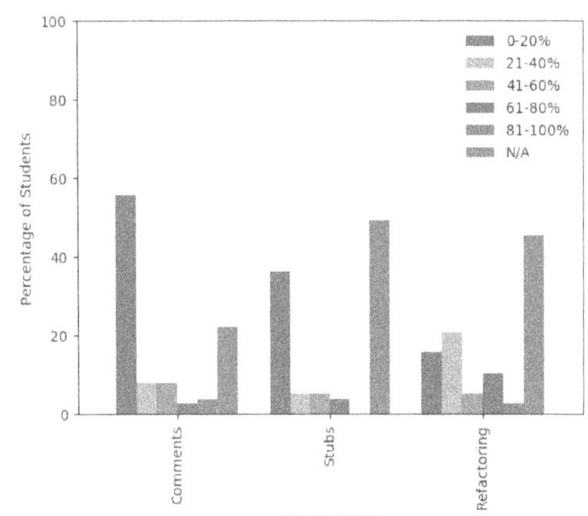

Figure 6: First Occurrence of Code Quality Focus

observed in Figure 5 for `Comments`, however the majority of students start including comments in the first part of their assignment. Surprisingly, nearly 20% of students never commented their code.

4.3 Software Process Overview

A better overview of the software development process is given through a process diagram, which can be obtained individually for each student, or, through the use of process mining tools such as

Disco [11], for the entire cohort. Disco [11] is a process visualisation tool that discovers the overall process employed by a cohort by interpreting the sequences of activities in the submitted log file. We use the revision number and file modification descriptors to determine timestamps and the order of changes. We imported our data into Disco and generated a software development process diagram for the entire cohort as shown in Figure 7. For simplicity,

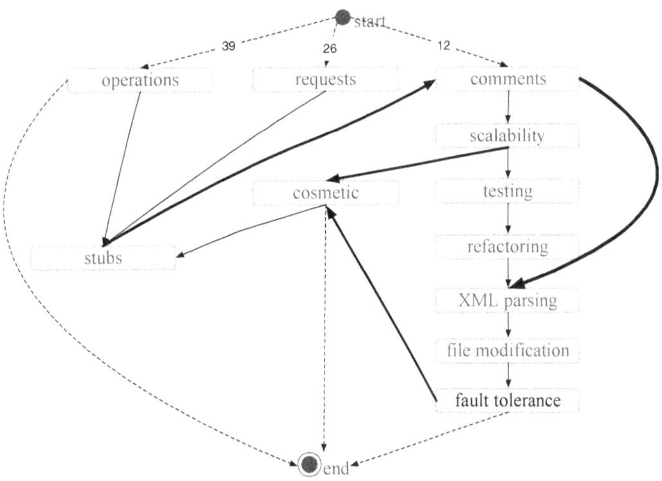

Figure 7: Overview of Software Development Process

we show the most used paths through the process in a stronger line. We can see that students start their software development process by working on functional requirements such as `operations`, focused on the connection between entities and `requests`, focused on the reply-response cycle. Students then aim to address other requirements either using stubs or directly by attempting to implement `scalability` solutions (multi-threading) and by parsing the request-response messages (`XML parsing`). Testing and refactoring follow in the process, with around half of the students implementing this path. After working on `XML parsing`, students in general work on file modification, followed by fault tolerance.

4.4 Discussion

4.4.1 Development focus throughout the assignment. The mined software development process as well as our change analysis shows that the main development focus of students is on operations, requests and XML parsing. This focus on functional requirements in the beginning of the assignment is to be expected, however the plot in Figure 2 shows a consistent focus on functional requirements throughout the assignment, with around 50% of changes still focused on functional requirements as the assignment is due.

4.4.2 Non-functional requirements. We find that while students focused on scalability from the beginning of the assignment, their multi-threading solutions tended to not function. Similarly, students tended to provide solutions for simple fault tolerance issues and avoided implementing backups for more serious scenarios, such as a server restart. Due to time constraints, in the distributed systems course, multi-threading and fault tolerance are only taught using simple examples. Our analysis suggests that there is a critical need to allow students to practice with more complex multi-threading and fault tolerance scenarios in a formative setting, either in lectures or during the course's collaborative sessions.

Nearly half of the students did not do any code refactoring or use stubs when building their code. This could suggest a bottom up approach, however further analysis is needed as this is influenced by the time when the first revision was submitted, e.g., students may have built a nearly complete solution and only then commit to SVN. A quick analysis of the first submissions suggests that this is not the case, but nevertheless further work is needed.

Around 40% of students did not do any testing despite it being assigned a high percentage of the assignment mark (30%). 45% of all students employed only unit testing, and nearly 13% of students tested extensive connection and fault tolerance scenarios. However, nearly 20% of the students focused on testing starting with the first part of their assignment development, suggesting a more mature approach to testing a large system. This could be rectified through the introduction of test-driven development [3, 8] in a practical setting beyond the toy examples usually employed in the software engineering course [23]. For example, in addition to the design sketch they provide as the first hurdle, students could also define their first tests and implement the architecture necessary to run them [23]. This would also allow students to further explore the use of stubs and better understand top-down software design [25].

Figure 2 shows the development focus of both functional and non-functional requirements as the assignment progresses towards its deadline. Our expectation was that a scissors plot, showing a decrease in functional requirements changes and an increase in non-functional requirements would become apparent, however the only non-functional requirement that appears to fit this profile is `Fault tolerance`. This suggests that testing, code quality and scalability need to be explicitly included in teaching, perhaps by allowing students to experiment with real-life codebases [24].

5 CONCLUSION

Understanding the software development process of final year students and the evolution of development focus from functional to non-functional requirements is critical both to determine whether graduate attributes have been met but also to aid in course re-design. Our analysis of final year students' evolving implementations of a complex distributed systems assignment shows a consistent focus on functional requirements such as connections between entities and request/response processing. In contrast, and despite representing 80% of the assignment marks, non-functional requirements and testing never become the principal development focus as the assignment progresses towards its deadline. We find that students focus on scalability in the beginning of their assignment development, but the focus decreases significantly as the assignment progresses, and the provided solutions tend not to work. The focus on fault tolerance increases steadily as the assignment progresses, however a large percentage of the solutions (42.9%) only consider simple failure scenarios. We also find that around 40% of students never test their code, 45% of students do not do any code refactoring, 51% of students never use stubs, and around 20% never comment their code. This suggests a critical need to allow students more practice with non-functional requirements both in simple and complex scenarios.

REFERENCES

[1] [n. d.]. The Cost of Downtime. http://blogs.gartner.com/andrew-lerner/2014/07/16/the-cost-of-downtime/.

[2] Ray Bareiss, Todd Sedano, and Edward Katz. 2012. Changes in transferable knowledge resulting from study in a graduate software engineering curriculum. In Software Engineering Education and Training (CSEE&T), 2012 IEEE 25th Conference on. IEEE, 3–12.

[3] Kent Beck. 2003. Test-driven development: by example. Addison-Wesley Professional.

[4] Christian Cachin and Matthias Schunter. 2011. A Cloud You Can Trust. IEEE Spectrum 48, 12 (2011), 28–51.

[5] Lawrence Chung and Julio Cesar Sampaio do Prado Leite. 2009. On non-functional requirements in software engineering. In Conceptual modeling: Foundations and applications. Springer, 363–379.

[6] Irina Diana Coman and Alberto Sillitti. 2008. Automated identification of tasks in development sessions. In Program Comprehension, 2008. ICPC 2008. The 16th IEEE International Conference on. IEEE, 212–217.

[7] Alan J Dutson, Robert H Todd, Spencer P Magleby, and Carl D Sorensen. 1997. A review of literature on teaching engineering design through project-oriented capstone courses. Journal of Engineering Education 86, 1 (1997), 17–28.

[8] Stephen H Edwards. 2003. Using test-driven development in the classroom: Providing students with automatic, concrete feedback on performance. In Proceedings of the international conference on education and information systems: technologies and applications EISTA, Vol. 3. Citeseer.

[9] Katrina Falkner, Claudia Szabo, Rebecca Vivian, and Nickolas Falkner. 2015. Evolution of software development strategies. In Software Engineering (ICSE), 2015 IEEE/ACM 37th IEEE International Conference on, Vol. 2. IEEE, 243–252.

[10] Mostafa Farshchi, Jean-Guy Schneider, Ingo Weber, and John Grundy. 2015. Experience Report: Anomaly Detection of Cloud Application Operations Using Log and Cloud Metric Correlation Analysis. In Proceedings of the 26th International Symposium on Software Reliability Engineering. 24–34.

[11] Fluxicon. 2018. Process Mining for Professionals. $http://fluxicon.com/disco/$.

[12] Susan K Lisack. 2000. The personal software process in the classroom: Student reactions (an experience report). In Software Engineering Education & Training, 2000. Proceedings. 13th Conference on. IEEE, 169–175.

[13] Andrew Luxton-Reilly, Ibrahim Albluwi, Brett A Becker, Michail Giannakos, Amruth N Kumar, Linda Ott, James Paterson, Michael James Scott, Judy Sheard, Claudia Szabo, et al. 2018. Introductory programming: a systematic literature review. In Proceedings Companion of the 23rd Annual ACM Conference on Innovation and Technology in Computer Science Education. ACM, 55–106.

[14] Mika V Mäntylä and Casper Lassenius. 2009. What types of defects are really discovered in code reviews? IEEE Transactions on Software Engineering 35, 3 (2009), 430–448.

[15] Maíra R Marques, Alcides Quispe, and Sergio F Ochoa. 2014. A systematic mapping study on practical approaches to teaching software engineering. In Frontiers in Education Conference (FIE), 2014 IEEE. IEEE, 1–8.

[16] Roberto Minelli, Andrea Mocci, and Michele Lanza. 2015. I know what you did last summer: an investigation of how developers spend their time. In Proceedings of the 2015 IEEE 23rd International Conference on Program Comprehension. IEEE Press, 25–35.

[17] Megha Mittal and Ashish Sureka. 2014. Process mining software repositories from student projects in an undergraduate software engineering course. In Companion Proceedings of the 36th International Conference on Software Engineering. ACM, 344–353.

[18] Adon Christian Michael Moskal and Rob Wass. 2018. Interpersonal process recall: a novel approach to illuminating studentsâĂŹ software development processes. Computer Science Education (2018), 1–18.

[19] Sofia Ouhbi, Ali Idri, José Luis Fernández-Alemán, and Ambrosio Toval. 2015. Requirements engineering education: a systematic mapping study. Requirements Engineering 20, 2 (2015), 119–138.

[20] Ihantola. P. and A. et al. Vihavainen. 2015. Educational Data Mining and Learning Analytics in Programming: Literature Review and Case Studies. In Proceedings of the 2015 ITiCSE Working Group Reports. 41–63.

[21] Tobias Roehm and Walid Maalej. 2012. Automatically detecting developer activities and problems in software development work. In Software Engineering (ICSE), 2012 34th International Conference on. IEEE, 1261–1264.

[22] Jianqiang Shen, Jed Irvine, Xinlong Bao, Michael Goodman, Stephen Kolibaba, Anh Tran, Fredric Carl, Brenton Kirschner, Simone Stumpf, and Thomas G Dietterich. 2009. Detecting and correcting user activity switches: algorithms and interfaces. In Proceedings of the 14th international conference on Intelligent user interfaces. ACM, 117–126.

[23] Jaime Spacco and William Pugh. 2006. Helping students appreciate test-driven development (TDD). In Companion to the 21st ACM SIGPLAN symposium on Object-oriented programming systems, languages, and applications. ACM, 907–913.

[24] Claudia Szabo. 2014. Student Projects Are Not Throwaways: Teaching Practical Software Maintenance in a Software Engineering Course. In Proceedings of the 45th ACM Technical Symposium on Computer Science Education (SIGCSE '14). ACM, New York, NY, USA, 55–60. https://doi.org/10.1145/2538862.2538965

[25] Willemien Visser and Jean-Michel Hoc. 1990. Expert software design strategies. In Psychology of programming. Elsevier, 235–249.

[26] Team Weaver. [n. d.].

[27] Claes Wohlin and Björn Regnell. 1999. Achieving industrial relevance in software engineering education. In Software Engineering Education and Training, 1999. Proceedings. 12th Conference on. IEEE, 16–25.

[28] W. Eric Wong, Debroy Vidroha, Adithya Surampudi, HyeonJeong Kim, and Michael F. Siok. 2010. Recent Catastrophic Accidents: Investigating How Software Was Responsible. In Proceedings of the 4th International Conference on Secure Software Integration and Reliability Improvement. 14–22.

[29] YoungSeok Yoon and Brad A Myers. 2011. Capturing and analyzing low-level events from the code editor. In Proceedings of the 3rd ACM SIGPLAN workshop on Evaluation and usability of programming languages and tools. ACM, 25–30.

[30] Jie Zou, Ling Xu, Mengning Yang, Xiaohong Zhang, and Dan Yang. 2017. Towards comprehending the non-functional requirements through DevelopersâĂŹ eyes: An exploration of Stack Overflow using topic analysis. Information and Software Technology 84 (2017), 19–32.

Qualitative Observations of Student Reasoning: Coding in the Wild

Cazembe Kennedy and Eileen Kraemer
Clemson University

ABSTRACT

Understanding student thinking and identifying student misconceptions are important precursors to developing high quality pedagogical materials and approaches. Prior work has used conceptual assessment surveys and task-based interviews to pursue this knowledge, typically having students evaluate existing code or predict or explain code behavior. However, features of student thinking captured under these conditions may differ from features of student thinking that occurs "in the wild." We present the results of a study conducted with 10 introductory CS students at a large, engineering-focused US university. In this work, students were asked to "Please, think aloud" as they interacted in a development environment, attempting to reverse engineer a solution to a defined task based on a provided executable. We captured and analyzed video recordings of the screen and audio recordings of their utterances to characterize their actions, current task, the relevant CS concept involved, current problem-solving phase, and expressed level of certainty. We also took note of the nature of their uncertainties and if and how these uncertainties were resolved. We found that students showed uncertainty regardless of success at task completion. Students who were successful at the task engaged in live experimentation to address these uncertainties in their thinking and coding. However, the ability to produce a program that behaved correctly did not guarantee that the students fully grasped the underlying concepts: some students submitted erroneous code that coincidentally worked, while expressing doubts about the correctness of their implementation.

CCS CONCEPTS

• **Social and professional topics → Student assessment**;

KEYWORDS

Computing education, pedagogical content knowledge, misconceptions

ACM Reference format:
Cazembe Kennedy and Eileen Kraemer. 2019. Qualitative Observations of Student Reasoning: Coding in the Wild. In *Proceedings of Innovation and Technology in Computer Science Education, Aberdeen, Scotland UK, July 15–17, 2019 (ITiCSE '19)*, 7 pages.
https://doi.org/10.1145/3304221.3319751

ACM ISBN 978-1-4503-6301-3/19/07...$15.00
https://doi.org/10.1145/3304221.3319751

1 INTRODUCTION

To obtain knowledge about what students are thinking and which concepts they find difficult, some researchers have developed concept inventories [2, 12, 19, 20], conceptual assessments [15–17], and others have utilized task-based interviews to gain insight into student reasoning about programming [10, 13, 15]. Concept inventories typically provide short code examples and gauge student reasoning based on their answers to multiple choice questions. Other assessments look at the outcomes of student efforts to create programs that solve particular problems, but do not follow their thought processes as they engage in the problem-solving task.

In this work, we seek to answer the research question: *How do intro CS students reason about the design and implementation of simple programs* ***in the wild****?* By "in the wild" we refer to coding that occurs without any initial skeleton or detailed instruction on how to approach the programming task. We seek to study how students reason as they are engaged in reverse engineering a solution from scratch, which may differ from their reasoning processes under the conditions associated with the administration of concept inventories. In the context of our study, students were not provided with any "starter" code but rather with an executable and were asked to recreate the functionality of this executable from scratch. We did provide them with two simple constraints, described in section 3, designed to force parameter passing. Thus, the coding sessions may be more precisely described as "in the semi-wild."

We conducted a think aloud study[8, 18] of introductory CS students in a course using the C programming language at a large, public US institution. The student programming session was captured on video, and their timestamped actions and utterances coded using thematic analysis, a method for identifying, analyzing, and reporting patterns or themes in qualitative data[1].

We report on the students' approach to implementation, the CS concepts they find troublesome, their uncertainties and resolutions (or lack thereof) to those uncertainties.

2 BACKGROUND AND RELATED WORK

Prior work observed student reasoning by having students analyze code or attempted to gauge misconceptions based on student responses to conceptual questions. This work includes concept inventories, criterion-referenced tests designed to help determine a student's knowledge of a specific set of concepts and to expose misconceptions. For example, Tew and Guzdial[20] developed the FCS1, a validated concept inventory that uses pseudocode in its questions, and Parker et al.[19] replicated the inventory as the SCS1 to enable broader distribution of the tool.

Other researchers developed assessments of programming ability and knowledge of CS concepts [5, 15, 17]. McCracken et al. [17] identified learning objectives for novice programmers and found that first year students perform significantly worse than expected when considering these objectives. We consider these objectives in our thematic analysis. Drachova [5] developed an inventory to measure principles for reasoning about correctness of software.

In a previous study, we developed a CS conceptual assessment that probed further than concept inventories by asking students to "Please explain your reasoning" after each question[15]. This assessment was meant to gauge misconceptions on concepts that Goldman et al.[9] had identified as "important and difficult." We categorized these misconceptions and found that students struggled with pass-by-reference versus pass-by-value semantics, "false sharing" of variables with the same name but in different scopes, and the semantics of access to global variables[15]. To further support these claims, we followed up with one-on-one task-based interviews requiring students to explain code snippets and allowing them to clarify their thoughts in a way not always possible through researchers retroactively reviewing responses to assessment questions.

In this work, we seek to analyze students' thoughts and actions as they try to complete a programming task. This method of obtaining student reasoning is similar to that of Craig [4] and Cherenkova [3], who both analyzed student code samples to gauge student reasoning. Cherenkova [3] did this by gathering over 250,000 student responses to weekly code-writing problems with the goal of identifying concepts that students found challenging. Her work showed that students have significant difficulties with conditionals and loops that persist through the duration of a course.

Craig's [4] work looked specifically at the concept of pointers. The data collected and analyzed were a mix of responses to multiple-choice questions and submissions of coding exercises based on pointers. Over 300 students submitted artifacts and results showed that students "confuse an address with a pointer," have trouble understanding the relationship between pointers and arrays, do not have a robust mental model of assignment statements even in their second year, and might apply operators blindly in an attempt to make the types consistent in their code. Craig goes on to say "while our analysis suggests that students misapply specific structures, a different type of study, one featuring think-aloud solutions to problems, for example, will be required to determine what mental models students are using in these situations." This motivating quote is precisely what our study aims to accomplish.

3 MATERIALS AND METHODS

We developed a simple calculator program designed to exercise selected concepts from CS1. The output of one iteration of the program is seen in figure 1, and an abridged version of an example correct implementation in figure 2. The process shown in figure 1 repeats until the user enters an exit code at this prompt (number that is not 1), and the final output gives the total number of operations performed.

3.1 Study

We solicited participants from the CS1 classes near the end of the semester and from CS2 classes at the beginning of the semester. The researchers followed all policies and procedures of the university's Institutional Review Board and appropriate approvals were obtained for the study. Participants were incentivized to participate with $10 Amazon gift cards. One researcher met individually with participants, briefly explained procedures and provided participants with an instruction sheet containing two rules for successfully completing the task: 1) The three operations (addition, subtraction, and flipping the signs) must be implemented in separate functions. 2) The statements that print out the results of the operations must be in the main function. These rules were meant to ensure that their solutions did not avoid the usage of key topics such as functions, return values, and pass by value/reference semantics.

Figure 1: The example calculator program

```
Please select an operation to perform:
1 = addition
2 = subtraction
3 = flipping the signs
2

Please enter an integer:
7
Please enter another integer:
16

The difference between 7 and 16 is -9.
```

Figure 2: An example solution, abridged

```
static int count = 0;
int add (int x, int y) { return x + y; }
int subtract (int x, int y) {return x - y;}
void flipsign (int num[2]) {
num[0] = num[0] * -1;
num[1] = num[1] * -1;
}

int main() {
int go, one, two, operation, answer, array[2];
go = 1;
.... display menu and obtain initial operation code

while (go == 1) {
... solicit and obtain input for each operand
if (operation == 1) { answer = add(one, two); ... and print result }
if (operation == 2) { answer = subtract(one, two); .. and print result
}
if (operation == 3) {
array[0] = one; array[1] = two; ... display original values
flipsign(array); ... display updated values in array[0] and array[1]);
}
count++;

// ... get another operation code or stop code
if (go != 1) { // ... print number ops performed }
}
else { ... again display menu and get operation code }
}
```

The participants completed a demographic survey online before beginning the coding task. All of the participants were confident or very confident in their CS course materials (Agree or Strongly Agree on Likert-Scale questions). We used the think-aloud method[8, 18] with the goal of obtaining a deeper understanding of what students are thinking as they reason about problem solving and software development in this context. The think-aloud method has been widely used in Human Computer Interaction research [18]. As recommended, we periodically remind participants to "Please keep talking." [7]. We used a time period of 120 seconds before prompting. Participants were given 60 minutes to complete the task.

3.2 Demographics

The ten participants ranged in age from 18 to 25; eight were male and two were female. Although CS1/2 are introductory level courses for computing majors, they are also taken by non-majors. Eight of the ten were working toward a BS/BA in Computer Science or a BS in Computer Information Systems, one was working toward a CS minor and one was a Mathematical Sciences BS student. Three classified themselves as freshmen, four as sophomores, two as juniors, and one as a senior.

3.3 Preparing the Data

The researchers reviewed the videos and transcribed the audio into timestamped, segmented "utterances" in a spreadsheet. Interesting phenomena were noted and researchers compared their notes across participants to develop an initial coding scheme that captured their observations.

After further discussion including a third researcher, it became apparent that the coding scheme could usefully employ codes associated with well-defined concepts in the literature. The authors both coded each of the remaining transcripts individually using this scheme, and came together to discuss and come to consensus on the coding, with a few additional sub-codes emerging from this process. A third researcher reviewed a subset of the videos, providing cross validation for the work. The final categories for which we recorded data were: **Time**, **Utterance**, **Action Code**, **Current Task**, **Problem Solving Phase**, **CS Concept**, and **Proposed Certainty Level**. Those with specialized codes are described below:

Action Code: The potential actions were Compile, Save, Edit, Execute Own, Check Executable, View, Review, Tools, or Comment.
Current Task: The potential current tasks were Main (Menu), Main (Loop), Main (Counting Operations), Addition function, Subtraction function, or Flipping Signs function.
Problem Solving Phase: Based on McCracken's[17] framework for the learning objectives of novice programmers, we used the phases Understanding the Problem, Breaking Into Subproblems, Implementing Solution (Subproblem), and Implementing Solution (Combine).
CS Concept: The codes we used for this work were based on Goldman[9] and included Parameters/Arguments I/II/III (PA1/2/3), Procedures/Functions/Methods (PROC), Control Flow (CF), Types (TYP), Boolean Logic (BL), Syntax vs. Semantics, Operator Precedence, Assignment Statements (SVS), Scope (SCO), Abstraction / Pattern Recognition and Use (APR), Iterations/Loops 0/2 (IT0/2), Arrays I/II/III (AR1/2/3), Memory Model, References, or Pointers (MMR), Design and Problem Solving I/II (DPS1/2), Debugging / Exception Handling (DEH), and Other (OTH). The Iterations/Loops 0 category was created by the authors using the same description as Iterations/Loop I, but replacing "nested loops" with "non-nested loops."
Proposed Certainty Level: The codes for this column were No Knowledge, Uncertain, Muddled, Certain (Correct), and Certain (Incorrect). These were used to categorize our view of participants' confidence in what they did/said.

4 RESULTS

As described above, each of the authors individually reviewed all 10 videos and then engaged in a discussion to reach consensus on any points of difference in their coding.

Evaluating Success. The overall results of the study with respect to success at recreating the functionality are: **Successful**: Seven participants (4 CS1, 3 CS2) and **Not Successful**: Three participants (1 CS1, 2 CS2). Our definition of success did not hinge on having exact wording or spacing for the output prompts or results. Rather, we defined a successful implementation as one that showed the menu, accepted a menu choice and two integers and printed the result, all in a loop that continued until the user chose to exit, and then finally displayed the total number of calculations performed.

Qualitative Analysis. Our primary results are qualitative in nature. This section reports on the observations we made about students' solution approaches, issues and resolutions, and their perceived self-efficacy. Solution approach captures the order in which the students worked, the order of elements in the program, any observable guiding principles to their workflow, when and how often they compiled and executed, whether they stopped to review and reflect on their code or engage in any refactoring or code cleanup, as well as any indications of planning, avoidance or delay. They typically implemented the elements of the program in the order in which they encountered the functionality in the provided executable, beginning with the initial menu prompts in the main method, and adding variables needed to store operation codes, operands and results.

The issues and resolution sections capture aspects of the program about which participants were uncertain or exhibited misconceptions and describes if and how they were able to resolve the issue. In terms of self-efficacy, most students exhibited some form of self-talk, often critical, which we capture and provide evidence below in the following sections.

Due to space limitations, we report in detail on only five of the ten total participants of the study, chosen because their results taken together provide coverage of the key insights gained from the study. However, we included our summary of all 10 participants in the discussion section.

4.1 Participant 0049 (CS2)

4.1.1 Solution Approach. Participant 0049 followed the common solution approach described above and it was clear that his development process was driven by the behavior of the provided executable. The factors guiding his progress feedback from the editor, from the compiler, and from the example executable and he was ultimately successful.

4.1.2 Issues and Resolution. Participant 0049 encountered a variety of interesting issues, many of which he was able to resolve and some that he remained uncertain about and decided to ignore.

Issue: Omissions and typographical errors; **Resolution:** Editor feedback, compiler messages and code review. This participant noted that changes in the color of text in the editor indicated some syntax errors.

Issue: function parameters (PROC); **Resolution:** code review, recall. The participant implemented the addition function but was uncertain if he needed to actually name the formal paramters or if could just use the types. He later reviewed his code and realized that he needed to use names as well as types.

Issue: call-by-reference, parameters, return values (PROC); **Resolution:** compiler messages, testing, not completely resolved. In implementing the flipping method, his thinking was muddled. He realized that something different was needed here, saying "when flipping a sign, you're going to need to return two values, so ... there are a few ways you could do it: declare a "regular pointer" and then return that pointer ... returning an integer array that will hold 2 values." His interesting solution was to create a flipping function with three input parameters: an integer intended to hold a copy of the first element of the array, an integer to hold a copy of the second element of the array, and then the array itself. The function attempted to return the array, although the function return type was simply an integer.

His series of edits were largely guided by compiler error messages: he was "99% certain" that he should not have to place a '*' in front of the array name to return the array, but he did so anyway based on compiler messages (he was returning an integer array but had declared a return type of int). This version compiled and his output was correct because he assigned the flipped values to the array elements before his return statement "return *newVals," which actually returned a copy of the value of the first element of the array. However, his simple tests passed and he was satisfied with the final product, despite his unease with dereferencing the array name in the return statement .

Issue: function prototypes (TYP); **Resolution:** compiler errors. Compiler errors revealed that his placement of the addition, subtraction, and flipping function after the main method meant that he had to declare prototypes prior to the main method.

4.1.3 Self-efficacy. Participant 0049 was confident and appeared quite comfortable with the assigned task and exhibited little to no self-critical talk. Rather, he exhibited curiosity, with statements such as "Let's just see" and "I'm pretty sure that ...".

4.2 Participant 0048 (CS2)

4.2.1 Solution Approach. Participant 0048 took the standard approach of running the executable and then breaking the task into parts, tackling them in the order in which they appeared in the menu of the provided executable. His programming decisions were driven by classroom experience, having learned from mistakes or feedback received from previous classes. He worked through trial-and-error in multiple instances to solve problems, and expressed that he was aware of the fact that this method helped with and was part of the learning process. He compiled throughout the task and used the compiler errors to resolve issues. He also showed signs of planning ahead when programming, speaking of "wondering also how to flip these signs" while working on earlier parts of the program. These approaches allowed him to successfully complete the task in the allotted time.

4.2.2 Issues and Resolutions. Participant 0048 was able to successfully interact with the compiler feedback to resolve many problems. **Issue:** Function prototypes and return values (PROC); **Resolution:** Compiler messages, recall. On one compiling instance, he notes "Oh, cause I don't have function prototypes...And then I need to make sure I return 0 because that did throw me a warning." In instances where the participant isn't clear on the compiler error given, he has ideas of potential resolutions to problems. A great example of this are the utterances "I'm just not incredibly sure what all of that means, but I'll figure it out." "Should I use...is it like star or am I gonna have to do the &? I'll find out in a bit." This particular grouping of utterances was dealing with pointer functionality (Pointers). **Issue:** Pointers (MMR); **Resolution:** Compiler messages, trial-and-error. The concept of pointers were where participant 0048 had the most issues. He implemented the flip signs function using them, but he spent time going between compiler errors and trying to fix the syntax of the function. Although the participant had enough knowledge of how to implement pointers that he was successful, he still exhibited muddled thinking regarding the semantics of referencing and dereferencing pointers, such as when to use "&" versus "*."

Something that stood out about this participant was his explicit mention of learning occurring through working on problems and getting feedback. He says "That's why I don't do good on exams because I like to test my programs. I guess a lot of how I do it is throwing things at it and seeing if it works..just because it helps me learn what I should do and what I shouldn't." This speaks to the use of written assessments in computer science, noting that students who may not be able to give a correct exam answer about a concept may be able to demonstrate correct use of that concept when asked to implement it. Another example of this learning-focused language occurs when he says "So I'm actually going to see if that will even compile. Cause that's where I fix a lot of my stuff." These utterances show evidence of the benefits that can be gained in CS from working at problem solving and constructing knowledge using a combination of classroom experiences and information with hands-on practice.

4.2.3 Self-efficacy. Participant 0048 had multiple occurrences of using self-deprecating language in a light-hearted manner, once stating "Oh...I'm *dumb*..almost didn't catch myself" when referring to declaring a variable without giving it a type (TYP) and once stating "So I've been wondering also how to flip these signs and maybe that's *dumb* that it took me this long but, if I just multiply the values by -1 then they'll flip...obviously." The other example of self-efficacy directly speaks towards confidence, with him saying "Great. I'm confident that I can" referring to being able to successfully complete the task.

4.3 Participant 0043 (CS1)

4.3.1 Solution Approach. Participant 0043 followed the standard approach of running the executable and then working on tasks in the order seen in the executable. He resolved problems through either reviewing his code or deciphering compiler feedback to successfully complete the task. He did not compile many times (5), but did check the executable many times to clarify formatting and functionality, allowing him to successfully complete the task.

4.3.2 Issues and Resolutions. **Issue:** Array declaration (AR3 + TYP); **Resolution:** Compiler messages, code review. Participant 0043 encountered an error with variable declaration. Alerted to the issue via a compiler message, he commented "Conflicting types..Oh. Probably just because you can't do the logic while you're declaring it," but he soon realized, "Ah! I declared it twice" after going back to look at the code. He was able to resolve those issues through compiler feedback. **Issue:** call-by-reference, passing array as argument (PA1 + AR2); **Resolution:** avoidance. While working with the flip signs function, he originally attempted to declare and return an array. He received a compiler message, and said "Invalid initializer. Did I declare up here? Nope! That'll do it," showing the ability to understand the compiler error message and remedy the mistake. He remarks that "they told us how to do it but I can't remember" with respect to returning two variables in a function but then "maybe that's not how they told us to do it" after running into compiler errors with implementation. The resolution eventually comes in a problem solving epiphany of just calling the flip signs function twice, allowing it to just return one value. This workaround allows him to "avoid the problem entirely."

4.3.3 Self-efficacy. Participant 0043 used language that might imply low self-efficacy, but said it in a light-hearted manner that made it apparent that he did not actually lack confidence. When catching a minor syntax error, he remarks "Whoops. I'm *stupid*." Also, when implementing addition function, he says "So sum's gonna equal num1 + num2. Easy!" showing confidence in working through the task.

4.4 Participant 0564 (CS2)

4.4.1 Solution Approach. Participant 0564 followed the common approach of running the executable and then working on tasks in the order seen in the executable. He did not compile for the first time until about 44 minutes into the study. This led to an overwhelming number of errors and issues to fix within the allotted time. He eventually attempted to avoid the issues faced when too many errors arose. An interesting facet of his solution approach is that he did check for extra input validation by the executable, stating "Well I tested this to see if it would produce an error message if I used a number that wasn't 1, 2, or 3." This participant was not successful at completing the task in the allotted time.

4.4.2 Issues and Resolutions. **Issue:** call-by-value vs. call-by-reference (PA1); **Resolution:** not resolved. This participant encountered difficulty with parameter passing. However, his decision to delay compiling until quite late in the session prevented him locating the error. He attempted to resolve multiple errors from the feedback of the compiler one at a time, noting "End of non-void function..." "z undeclared...Ok. e undeclared." "Expected before..e and z...Line 56."

Issue: Scope (SCO); **Resolution:** not resolved. This participant encountered scope (SCO) issues in which he attempted to access a variable local to a function while in the main function. He then decided to work on other parts after encountering some errors, such as when stating "Error label at end of..Line 63..? Why am I getting this error?" referring to the switch statement he had attempted to implement. Scope issues were prevalent. He spent 44 minutes editing his code and running the provided executable before attempting to verify the logic of the three functions, and mostly understood how to successfully do it. He used an interesting algorithm for flipping signs (x = x - 2x). However, not being able to resolve the issue of capturing the return value from the function, he was never able to successfully compile or execute his code.

4.4.3 Self-efficacy. 0564 used the word "tripping" multiple times to refer to making a mistake during the task. After seeing a compiler error, he remarked "Dang. I'm tripping." Another error led him to say "Why am I getting this error? I'm tripping. What am I doing?" These utterances indicate uncertainty, but the participant seems to feel the issues should not be occurring.

4.5 Participant 0044 (CS1)

4.5.1 Solution Approach. Participant 0044 followed the common approach described above of running the executable and then working on sub-tasks in the order encountered when running the executable. She showed signs of avoiding issues and moving to work on other parts if resolutions could not be found. She compiled early and and frequently (16 times), but was unable to resolve her issues and ran out of time before she was able to display the result of either of those functions and was ultimately unsuccessful.

4.5.2 Issues and Resolutions. This participant was able to resolve syntax issues through the help of compiler feedback. Commenting things such as "Oh! I didn't put the function header. Yeah. That would do it" or "Parameter names..without types. Awww. I forgot that. Yeah. I would." After implementing the addition function below the main method with the function prototype in the main method, compiling and receiving errors, she was able to resolve this issue. **Issue: Parameter passing (PROC)** ; Participant 0044 encountered issues with function prototypes returning values from a function and with receiving the result of function call in the calling context (PROC). She attempted many variations of the code but was unable to resolve the issue of the combined action of returning a value from the function and capturing that returned value in order to print it (PROC). **Issue: Scope (SCO)** ; **Resolution: not resolved** . She was confused about scoping rules (SCO) and seemed to believe that having variables in the function with the same names as in the main method would result in a transfer of the values. Her combined confusion about scope and return values led to consternation on her part and prevented her from successfully completing the assignment. She tried multiple ways, but continued to get values of 0 regardless of the integers input when executing the program. "So it's still 0. Hmmm. Why is it?...I guess I should just try it a different way." Eventually, the participant moved on and attempted to work on other parts of the task, uttering things such as "Wait. Work on something else and then come back to the.." and "Ok. Let's move on...Try something else."

4.5.3 *Self-Efficacy.* This participant showed multiple instances of low self-efficacy, doubting her own skills and abilities. One common theme was the feeling of "Ugh. I'm making this really complicated.," She this or a slight variation of this seven times. Participant 0044 also felt that the struggle was unnecessary, remarking "I feel like this is really easy and I'm overthinking it" and "Ugh. This should not be this hard."

5 DISCUSSION

We observed student uncertainty about scope, pointers, arrays, function prototypes, parameters and parameter passing, and return values. These students exhibited fragile knowledge, a result that was found in our previous work looking at conceptual assessments [15]. Students were able to resolve their uncertainties in various ways: editor feedback, compiler error messages, reflection/recall, code review, and testing, but these resolutions did not always equate to a full understanding of the concepts. Although students relied on compiler error messages to resolve uncertainties and to uncover issues, they had difficulty interpreting compiler error messages, a problem Gusukuma [11] noticed and worked towards remedying through the use of misconception-driven feedback.

We also observed that the ability to create a program with correct output did not equate to full comprehension of the programming language concepts and features employed. For example, we saw students who could not properly implement call-by-reference succeed in creating a "correct" program output but only through trial-and-error and workarounds that they were certain were incorrect. Such workarounds and trial-and-error were previously reported by Hundhausen [14] and the goal of moving away from trial-and-error in student programming is discussed by Edwards [6].

We found pointer-related evidence to support the result of Craig's [4] work claiming that students apply operators blindly in an attempt to get their code working. From a design perspective, we note trends of students' decisions with respect to implementation order. Most participants attempted to implement the program in the order that the executable was presented, starting with the main method (menu) and then working on the addition, subtraction, and flip sign functions in that order, and lastly implementing the loop and counter functionalities. This caused some students to run into errors as they did not originally include function prototypes before the main method. Multiple students mentioned working on the flip signs function last because it seemed trickier. We would be interested to explore the effect of changing the order of the functions in the executable, placing the flip signs first, to see if students would follow the observed order or first tackle the easier functions to avoid. Students showed signs of avoiding complexity, sometimes devising innovative solutions to solve a problem. For the flipSign function, we saw solutions such as having the function return one value but calling it twice in main (0045), attempting to "put a dash in front" of the number to flip the sign (0045), and using number line thinking for the algorithm to flip the sign as opposed to multiplying by -1 (0042, 0043, 0045, 0564, 0045).

This work allowed us to view unexplored features of student reasoning such as the self-efficacy of the students, which gave insights into level of certainty; their problem solving approaches; and how they resolve issues. Students show evolved reasoning about the semantics of programming language constructs as they interacted with the edit-review-compile-test cycle. Practice such as this helps students to learn. However, we saw that these feedback mechanisms alone may be insufficient to uncover student misconceptions about such semantics, or worse yet to induce flawed mental models of the actual semantics, which means that evaluating student knowledge based on correct output alone may lead to the introduction and/or "hardening" of misconceptions (0049). In summary, intro CS students while coding "in the wild" seem to follow a few trends: focus on the order of the specification provided; avoid complexities through workarounds or innovative solutions that sometimes work but may not address the intended concept instructors would like students to learn; and use compiler feedback combined with the fragile knowledge of concepts to address problems through trial-and-error.

This work suggests several pedagogical techniques: carefully crafting programming assignments to force correct usage; evaluating code and not just correct output for programming assignments as suggested by Edwards [6]; mining studies like this one and student submissions to find dysfunctional code that "works" but embodies misconceptions and using these as instructional tools in which students are asked what the code does or why it coincidentally works; and incorporating the knowledge gained into CS pedagogical content knowledge, allowing instructors to create assignments and assessments that probe for these uncertainties and misconceptions in the local context.

We also observed problem-solving approaches that promoted student success, such as intermittent code review and incremental development. When students encountered uncertainty, they either delayed implementation of the problematic feature (0044), avoided it entirely (0564) or engineered a solution through trial-and-error that worked, but that they did not understand (0565, 0049, 0048).

Limitations of the work may include generalizing from our context: our participants came from a CS1 course at a large, public university in the United States. Some of the participants were just finished CS1 in December. Others were just beginning CS2 but in August, so they had a summer during which to "ripen," though they had no additional formal instruction. Different phenomena may be observed in students at other stages of their CS educations or with more or less prior preparation. Reaching out to classrooms and offering incentives for participation is not uncommon as a methodology, but it is dependent on students' willingness to provide their time, especially in a one-on-one research setting. Thus, the students in this study may be representative of those who are willing to volunteer their time for outside of class CS work. Students also were programming in an editor not of their choosing. To ensure consistency, we had all students use the same editor for the study, though it turned out that this was not the preferred editor for any of the students. In the future, we would like to study students at different levels of their CS education, engaged in implementing programs that exercise a wider variety of CS concepts.

6 ACKNOWLEDGEMENTS

The authors of this paper acknowledge Aubrey Lawson for her contributions to the coding scheme and data analysis, suggestions for related work, and insights included in the discussion section.

REFERENCES

[1] Virginia Braun and Victoria Clarke. 2006. Using thematic analysis in psychology. *Qualitative research in psychology* 3, 2 (2006), 77–101.

[2] Ricardo Caceffo, Steve Wolfman, Kellogg S Booth, and Rodolfo Azevedo. 2016. Developing a computer science concept inventory for introductory programming. In *Proceedings of the 47th ACM Technical Symposium on Computing Science Education*. ACM, 364–369.

[3] Yuliya Cherenkova, Daniel Zingaro, and Andrew Petersen. 2014. Identifying challenging CS1 concepts in a large problem dataset. In *Proceedings of the 45th ACM technical symposium on Computer science education*. ACM, 695–700.

[4] Michelle Craig and Andrew Petersen. 2016. Student difficulties with pointer concepts in C. In *Proceedings of the Australasian Computer Science Week Multiconference*. ACM, 8.

[5] Svetlana V Drachova-Strang. 2013. *Teaching and assessment of mathematical principles for software correctness using a reasoning concept inventory*. Clemson University.

[6] Stephen H Edwards. 2004. Using software testing to move students from trial-and-error to reflection-in-action. *ACM SIGCSE Bulletin* 36, 1 (2004), 26–30.

[7] KA Ericsson. 6. 8: Simon, HA (1984). Protocol analysis: Verbal reports as data. (6).

[8] Karl Anders Ericsson and Herbert Alexander Simon. 1993. *Protocol analysis: Verbal reports as data, Rev.* the MIT Press.

[9] Ken Goldman, Paul Gross, Cinda Heeren, Geoffrey Herman, Lisa Kaczmarczyk, Michael C Loui, and Craig Zilles. 2008. Identifying important and difficult concepts in introductory computing courses using a delphi process. *ACM SIGCSE Bulletin* 40, 1 (2008), 256–260.

[10] T. C. Nicholas Graham, Catherine A. Morton, and Tore Urnes. 1996. ClockWorks: Visual programming of component-based software architectures. *Journal of Visual Languages and Computing* 7, 2 (1996), 175–196.

[11] Luke Gusukuma, Austin Cory Bart, Dennis Kafura, and Jeremy Ernst. 2018. Misconception-Driven Feedback: Results from an Experimental Study. In *Proceedings of the 2018 ACM Conference on International Computing Education Research*. ACM, 160–168.

[12] Geoffrey L. Herman, Lisa Kaczmarczyk, Michael C. Loui, and Craig Zilles. 2008. Proof by Incomplete Enumeration and Other Logical Misconceptions. In *Proceedings of the Fourth International Workshop on Computing Education Research (ICER '08)*. ACM, New York, NY, USA, 59–70. https://doi.org/10.1145/1404520.1404527

[13] Celia Hoyles, Richard Noss, Ross Adamson, and Sarah Lowe. 2001. Programming rules: what do children understand?. In *PME conference*, Vol. 3. 3–169.

[14] Christopher D Hundhausen, Jonathan L Brown, Sean Farley, and Daniel Skarpas. 2006. A methodology for analyzing the temporal evolution of novice programs based on semantic components. In *Proceedings of the second international workshop on Computing education research*. ACM, 59–71.

[15] Cazembe Kennedy and Eileen T Kraemer. 2018. What Are They Thinking?: Eliciting Student Reasoning About Troublesome Concepts in Introductory Computer Science. In *Proceedings of the 18th Koli Calling International Conference on Computing Education Research*. ACM, 7.

[16] Raymond Lister, Elizabeth S Adams, Sue Fitzgerald, William Fone, John Hamer, Morten Lindholm, Robert McCartney, Jan Erik Moström, Kate Sanders, Otto Seppälä, et al. 2004. A multi-national study of reading and tracing skills in novice programmers. In *ACM SIGCSE Bulletin*, Vol. 36. ACM, 119–150.

[17] Michael McCracken, Vicki Almstrum, Danny Diaz, Mark Guzdial, Dianne Hagan, Yifat Ben-David Kolikant, Cary Laxer, Lynda Thomas, Ian Utting, and Tadeusz Wilusz. 2001. A multi-national, multi-institutional study of assessment of programming skills of first-year CS students. In *Working group reports from ITiCSE on Innovation and technology in computer science education*. ACM, 125–180.

[18] Janni Nielsen, Torkil Clemmensen, and Carsten Yssing. 2002. Getting access to what goes on in people's heads?: reflections on the think-aloud technique. In *Proceedings of the second Nordic conference on Human-computer interaction*. ACM, 101–110.

[19] Miranda C Parker, Mark Guzdial, and Shelly Engleman. 2016. Replication, validation, and use of a language independent CS1 knowledge assessment. In *Proceedings of the 2016 ACM conference on international computing education research*. ACM, 93–101.

[20] Allison Elliott Tew and Mark Guzdial. 2011. The FCS1: a language independent assessment of CS1 knowledge. In *Proceedings of the 42nd ACM technical symposium on Computer science education*. ACM, 111–116.

Resources for Researching and Teaching Computing Education in Primary and Secondary Schools: What Exists and What is Still Needed

Monica M. McGill (Moderator)
Knox College
Galesburg, IL, USA
mmmcgill@knox.com

Miles Berry
University of Roehampton
London, England, UK
m.berry@roehampton.ac.uk

Leigh Ann DeLyser
CSforAll Consortium
New York, NY, USA
leighann@csnyc.org

Briana Morrison
University of Nebraska at Omaha
Omaha, NE, USA
bbmorrison@unomaha.edu

CCS CONCEPTS

• **Social and professional topics → Computing education; Computing education programs; Computer science education.**

KEYWORDS

Educational research, CSforAll, repository, evaluation, assessment, constructs, K-12, teaching tips, primary, secondary, resources

ACM Reference Format:

Monica M. McGill (Moderator), Miles Berry, Leigh Ann DeLyser, and Briana Morrison. 2019. Resources for Researching and Teaching Computing Education in Primary and Secondary Schools: What Exists and What is Still Needed. In *Innovation and Technology in Computer Science Education (ITiCSE '19), July 15–17, 2019, Aberdeen, Scotland, UK*. ACM, New York, NY, USA, 2 pages. https://doi.org/10.1145/3304221.3325541

1 SUMMARY

In this panel presentation, we will present an overview and discussion of several recent and complementary resources geared towards primary and secondary computing education. The moderator will present a brief introduction to the purpose of this panel and provide the format for the session. Each panelist will have 5 minutes to present the purpose of their resource followed by a demonstration of its content. Each panelist will share with the audience the resource, its content, its intended target demographic, and how it can be and has been used. Following the initial presentations, several minutes will be allotted for immediate questions and answers pertaining to the resource just presented.

Immediately after the presentation of all of the resources, the moderator will ask the panelists questions about future plans for each site in an effort to address resources still needed for the primary and secondary computing education community (including researchers). We will also engage with the audience to discuss these resources and discuss what types of resources are still needed to improve the quality of primary and secondary education. Attendees will be encouraged to ask questions and provide suggestions for improving and enhancing the resources if they are currently using one or more of them.

The intended audience for this panel is anyone in the computing education community who may find these resources useful in their classroom or scholarship, particularly those researching, teaching, designing curriculum, or providing oversight of or input into primary and secondary school computing education. Given the varied nature of these resources, there is something for many different types of faculty scholars who may be attending ITiCSE.

By the end of the panel, the audience will have learned enough about these resources to begin to formulate ways in which they can use their content in their research, evaluation, teaching, or curriculum design initiatives.

1.1 csedresearch.org (McGill)

The K-12 Computer Science Education Research (csedresearch.org) resource contains a database of program element data derived from relevant peer-reviewed articles that report on K-12 computing activities and curriculum, evaluation instruments that can be used in computing education studies, and resources for conducting and reviewing research [5]. Targeted users for this resource are researchers, educators, and evaluators. Data has been curated from over 500 articles from ten ACM/IEEE venues and other journals and conference proceedings that focus on computing education or a closely related field for the years 2012-2018.

In addition, the evaluation instruments page includes a list of over 100 instruments searchable on such items as content knowledge, noncognitive factors (self-efficacy, interest, beliefs, etc.), year published, and more. The site also contains several resources for designing, as well as writing and reviewing articles on studies. Users can also submit their own articles and evaluation instruments for inclusion in the database. Although many articles are from studies conducted in the U.S., we welcome and encourage articles from other countries to make the set of data collected more robust. You can also follow csedresearch.org on twitter (@csedresearch), where posts related to csedresearch are shared, including article summaries and evaluation instruments as they are added to the site.

ACM ISBN 978-1-4503-6301-3/19/07.
https://doi.org/10.1145/3304221.3325541

1.2 Project Quantum (Berry)

In the UK, Computing At School, working with Cambridge Assessment and Durham University's Centre for Evaluation and Monitoring, has crowd sourced over 9,000 multiple choice questions on computing for use by primary and secondary school teachers (see Project Quantum at http://bit.ly/projectquantum) [1]. The corpus of questions provides a shared interpretation of England's computing programmes of study, a way to drive lesson content, an easy way to check understanding within the lesson and a tool for summative assessment over a term or longer. The questions are freely available to all at http://bit.ly/quantumquestions and are released under a Creative Commons licence. Rasch analysis provides measures into the difficulty and quality of individual items, and responses to items provide some insights into progression within computing and common misconceptions.

1.3 CSforAll (DeLyser)

CSforALL is a central resource for individuals and organizations interested in K-12 computer science education in the United States [2]. The organization connects curriculum and program providers, schools and districts, funders, and researchers working towards the goal of providing quality computer science education to every child in the United States. CSforALL maintains a website, www.csforall.org, with a listing of all of its members that is searchable and filterable, helping website visitors identify curriculum, local programs, or research regarding CS education.

The CSforALL website is constantly growing, not only with new members, but also new features. In the panel, Dr. DeLyser will present the current state of the member page, and discuss planned expansions and thier implications for the CS Education research community. CSforALL also is the co-principal investigator in the RPPforCS project, a National Science Foundation funded project that is committed to providing a connected community of practice for research practice partnerships exploring K-12 CS in the US. The project currently has over 50 member projects featured on the site and is producing resources for the larger community about RPPs and CS Education research in general.

1.4 NCWIT's EngageCSEdu (Morrison)

The National Center for Women & Information Technology (NCWIT) developed EngageCSEdu with Google because both organizations recognize the importance of introductory undergraduate courses in attracting and keeping women in computing [3]. Research suggests that having high quality assignments, projects, and labs that are meaningful and relevant to a student's life, building inclusive student community, and providing high quality student support can increase the recruitment and retention of women in our field. One outcome of the initial project was the NCWIT Engagement Practices Framework that consists of research-based teaching practices for broadening participation in computing through excellent pedagogy and curriculum.

The other outcome was the EngageCSEdu (http://www.engagecsedu.org) website that is a living, open-source collection of computer science instructional materials submitted by and designed for use by high school teachers and instructors of introductory-level college courses. All instructional materials submitted to EngageCSEdu undergo a peer-review process like an academic journal with both computer science and social science reviewers. In addition, all materials in the collection make use of at least one NCWIT Engagement Practice. Currently, the collection contains over 800 items and is highly searchable and well integrated with the Engagement Practices Framework. Since launch, EngageCSEdu has had over a quarter million pageviews and has hosted over 66,000 sessions. About twenty percent of the registered users are high school teachers.

1.5 CS Teaching Tips (DeLyser)

The CS Teaching Tips site (http://csteachingtips.org/) is a repository of over 1,300 teaching tips for those teaching computing in primary, secondary, and post-secondary education. These tips are derived from best practices rooted in empirical evidence from research in computing education and interviews with over 150 CS educators. Teaching tips are categorized and searchable [4] and these brief, but important, tips are also shared on twitter (@CSTeachingTips). The site also provides quick-reference 1-page tip sheets and short videos with advice for topics such as lecturing, pair programming, encouraging students to seek help, and reducing bias.

2 AUDIENCE

The intended audience for this special session is anyone in the computing community who would find these resources useful in their classroom or in their scholarship. Given the varied nature of the content of these repositories, there is something for many different types of faculty scholars presented here. At the end of the session, we hope that the audience has learned enough about these repositories to begin to formulate ways in which they can use the content of these repositories in their scholarship or teaching.

3 ACKNOWLEDGEMENTS

Project Quantum has received funding from Microsoft, Google and ARM. EngageCSEdu was originally funded by a gift from Google and is currently funded by NCWIT.

CSforALL is supported by grants number 1645894 and 1745199 from the National Science Foundation. csedresearch.org is based upon work supported by the U.S. National Science Foundation under Grant Nos. 1625005, 1625335, 1757402, and 1745199. csteachingtips.org is based upon work supported by the U.S. National Science Foundation under Grant No. 1339404. Any opinions, findings, and conclusions or recommendations expressed in this material are those of the authors and do not necessarily reflect the views of the National Science Foundation.

REFERENCES

[1] Computing at School. 2016. Project Quantum. https://community.computingatschool.org.uk/resources/4382/single
[2] Computer Science for ALL Students. 2016. CSforALL. https://csforall.org
[3] National Center for Women & Information Technology. 2015. NCWIT EngageCSedu. http://www.engagecsedu.org
[4] Colleen M. Lewis. 2014. CS Teaching Tips. https://csteachingtips.org
[5] Monica M. McGill and Adrienne Decker. 2017. Computer Science Education Repository. https://csedresearch.org

Teaching AVR Assembly by Building an Arduino Arcade Machine

Michael Black[†]
Computer Science
Bridgewater State University
Bridgewater, MA
m1black@bridgew.edu

Joseph Matta
Computer Science
Bridgewater State University
Bridgewater, MA
j1matta@student.bridgew.edu

ABSTRACT

This paper describes a series of homework assignments, labs, and a project developed to teach AVR assembly language as part of a sophomore-level Computer Organization course. At the culmination of this module, students built a handheld arcade machine out of an Arduino Uno and programmed it, in assembly language, to play the classic game of Breakout on an LED matrix display. While completing this project students learned most of the fundamentals of low-level programming, including registers, bit operators, control flow, stack handling, subroutine calls, hardware interrupts, delay loops and instruction timing, and communicating with I/O. This project was assigned to three classes of students in the Fall 2018 and Spring 2019.

CCS CONCEPTS

• Computers and education → General

KEYWORDS

computer organization; assembly language; AVR; Arduino

1 INTRODUCTION

The classic arcade game of Breakout consists of a paddle, ball, and hovering blocks, with the objective of knocking the ball so that it hits all the blocks without falling to the ground. Video games are a good way of teaching low-level programming because they are I/O-heavy, require precise timing, and most students can relate to them [1].

The author previously assigned Breakout as an assembly project to be done in x86 assembly on a PC [2]. As much as students enjoyed the project, most chose to write the project in an emulator rather than directly on their computer. On a microcontroller, however, students must wire the hardware themselves and cannot rely on system calls for I/O. The Arduino has several advantages over the PC. It, and Atmel microcontroller inside it, are ubiquitous in industry and the Maker hobby movement. It has a relatively simple assembly language (AVR) and an easy-to-install development environment. Moreover, because of its slow clock speed and extremely limited memory, using the assembly language is rather beneficial on that platform. There are challenges, however. An Arduino does not include a keyboard and display, apart from a serial port. "Hello World" is not an easy starting point. Furthermore, compared with x86, there is a relative scarcity of resources and tutorials on assembly for the Arduino.

ACM ISBN 978-1-4503-6301-3/19/07.

1.1 Materials and Equipment

At the beginning of the semester, in lieu of a textbook, students were asked to buy a $30 starter kit that includes an Arduino Uno, a breadboard, pushbuttons, LEDs, a speaker, and wires. They were additionally provided with a 788BS 8x8 LED matrix. Students downloaded the Atmel Studio 7 development environment, which includes a hardware emulator. As the Atmel software is only available for Windows, students using other operating systems were asked to partner with a student using Windows [3].

1.2 Labs, Homeworks, and Class Exercises

About two weeks of class time were spent on labs and class exercises leading up to the project. The first lab introduced students to breadboards and wiring. This was a one hour lab held in class that nearly every student was able to complete. The final step was to build a NAND gate using two transistors, two push buttons, and an LED. Besides exposing them to gates, this taught them how to how to wire pushbuttons with pullup resistors.

A homework assignment required students to connect a 7-segment display to seven Arduino pins and have it count down from 9 to 0 in one second intervals. Students first wrote this in C but were then required to redo it in assembly. This taught students how to write to I/O pins in assembly and how to make a one-second delay using the assembly equivalent of three nested for-loops.

Figure 1: Homework submission

Finally, over a two-day exercise, the class wrote a program, in assembly, that would beep "Mary Had a Little Lamb". Students started by making tones on a buzzer, using delay loops to set the pitch. This taught students to use clock speed and instruction cycle time to calculate the exact delay for each note. Next the class put this into a subroutine and learned how to set up the call stack. Finally musical notes were read from an array in memory to show the class how indirect addressing works.

2 BREAKOUT

The Breakout project consisted of seven steps, as shown in Table 1, and covered all the assembly-language learning outcomes for the course. The figure shows a finished project: an Arduino Uno connected directly to an 8x8 LED display that shows ball, blocks, and paddle, and two pushbuttons for moving the paddle left or right. The game plays continuously until the ball hits the bottom row.

Students were given some template assembly code for the project. Because of the limited pins, LED display must be scanned very quickly row-by-row (like a CRT). The template code uses an internal timer to interrupt the program every millisecond and draw a row from a "video RAM" table stored in memory. Consequently, students need only store a 1 or a 0 to a designated memory location to turn on and off a pixel.

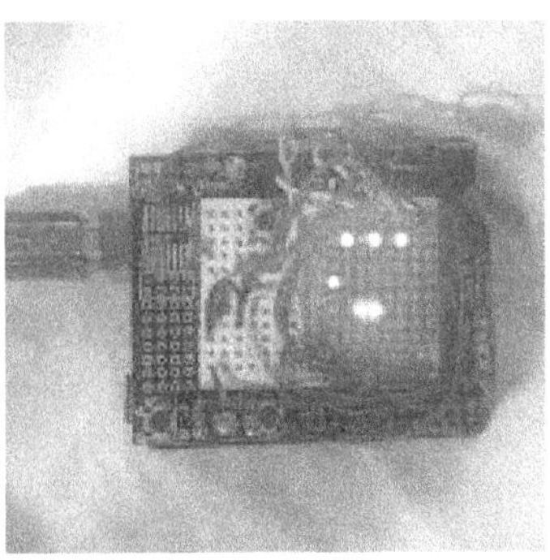

Figure 2: Completed Breakout project

3 STUDENT EXPERIENCE

The AVR Breakout project was first tested in a smaller evening class section in the Fall, 2018. Six students attempted the project. All six completed the wiring correctly and displayed the ball, paddle, and blocks. Five made the paddle move in response to button pushes, but only one student made the ball move and bounce. Student feedback suggested that the main sticking points were implementing a delay loop within the ball movement, followed by the difficulty finding resources on the language.

The count-down counter homework and music class exercise were developed for the Spring semester to make sure students thoroughly understand delay loops before starting the project. Of the twenty counter submissions, thirteen were correctly written in assembly, while two more showed numbers but did not include a delay loop. The remaining five did not attempt the assembly.

Table 1: Breakout project steps and corresponding learning outcomes

Step	Learning outcome
1. Connect the display to the Arduino	Wire a digital circuit on a breadboard
2. Draw a paddle, ball, and blocks on the display	Stores register to memory
3. Create variables for paddle and ball position	Loads and stores
4. Make the ball move	Writing a delay loop, subroutine calls
5. Make the ball bounce off of walls	Conditional branches
6. Move the paddle	Handling hardware interrupts
7. End the game if the ball touches the ground	Conditional branches

REFERENCES

[1] John Aycock. 2015. Applied Computer History: Experience Teaching Systems Topics through Retrogames. In Proceedings of the 2015 ACM Conference on Innovation and Technology in Computer Science Education (ITiCSE '15). ACM, New York, NY, USA, 105-110.

[2] Michael Black, Christian Brady, and Tyler Goulski. 2017. Breakout from x86 assembly to a breadboard: a lab for introductory computer organization. J. Comput. Sci. Coll. 33, 1 (October 2017), 131-138.

[3] Microchip Technology Inc., Atmel Studio 7 (Downloads), https://www.microchip.com/mplab/avr-support/atmel-studio-7

Connecting Majors/Non-Majors Courses Via Tabular Data

Ali Erkan
Ithaca College
Ithaca, NY, USA
aerkan@ithaca.edu

Adam Lee
Ithaca College
Ithaca, NY, USA
alee@ithaca.edu

ABSTRACT

As is the case with many Computer Science departments, we offer one set of courses for our majors and another (smaller) set for non-majors. Historically, the divide between these sets has been fairly visible, an academic reality that may be typical for many institutions. Initially triggered by a desire to improve and advance our most heavily enrolled non-majors course, we have been working for the past several years to dovetail courses across this "great divide" by focusing on tabular data. This report is an outline of our progress (in general) and this one course that experienced most change (in particular); we believe the direction we are headed and the gains we hope to see might be valuable for other institutions as well.

CCS CONCEPTS

• **Information systems** → **Relational database model**; **Database views**; **Structured Query Language**; • **Social and professional topics** → **Computer science education**; *Information systems education*; • **Applied computing** → **Spreadsheets**.

KEYWORDS

Google Sheets, Sqlite, Tables

ACM Reference Format:
Ali Erkan and Adam Lee. 2019. Connecting Majors/Non-Majors Courses Via Tabular Data. In *Innovation and Technology in Computer Science Education (ITiCSE '19), July 15–17, 2019, Aberdeen, Scotland Uk.* ACM, New York, NY, USA, 2 pages. https://doi.org/10.1145/3304221.3325551

1 OUR EVOLVING ACADEMIC CONTEXT

With 25-30 students per section and four to six sections per semester, COMPUTERS AND INFORMATION TECHNOLOGIES (referred more succinctly as INFORMATION TECHNOLOGIES) had historically been our most heavily enrolled course. Originally designed to teach Microsoft Excel and Access, it had been serving students who simply wanted to list these two programs in their resumes. Given the discrepancy between the somewhat stagnant form it had taken and the greater potential institutional impact it held, we decided in 2014 to improve and advance this course. The incremental changes we have done since then have led to a set of courses to collectively improve and to connect across our majors/non-majors divide in a meaningful way. Figure 1 shows a portion of our majors as well as non-majors courses as of the beginning of this period:

ITiCSE '19, July 15–17, 2019, Aberdeen, Scotland Uk

ACM ISBN 978-1-4503-6301-3/19/07.
https://doi.org/10.1145/3304221.3325551

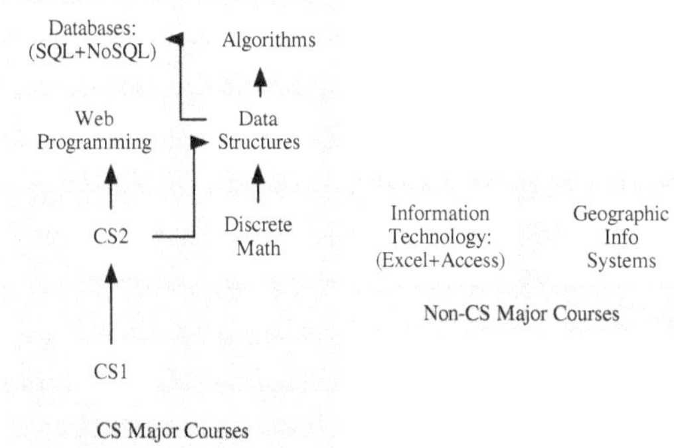

Figure 1: Old curricular setup... For simplicity, we only show the courses that are relevant to this report. The terms in parentheses represent the focus of the associated course.

- CS1 → CS2 → DATA STRUCTURES → ALGORITHMS is the familiar four-course sequence for CS majors with Discrete Math playing the necessary mathematical supporting role.
- WEB PROGRAMMING focuses on the server side of web-dev.
- DATABASE SYSTEMS focuses on SQL, relational algebra, normalization theory, query optimization, etc.
- GEOGRAPHIC INFO SYSTEMS is a new course for the spatial data processing needs of our institution.

Guided by the over-arching principles of (i) making our majors-courses better understood by non-majors, (ii) making our non-majors courses be of higher value for our majors, and (iii) dovetailing the listed courses by an emphasis on tabular data, our configuration has evolved into the arrangement shown in figure 2:

- TABULAR DATA[1] is a substantially evolved version of INFORMATION TECHNOLOGIES that aims to serve as an unofficial introduction to computational problem solving; as a side-effect of tackling problems defined on real-world data-sets, our goal is to have our students become well-versed in the use of spreadsheets and the view-generation aspects of SQL. This course also carries the "Quantitative Literacy" designation which satisfies an all-college graduation requirement.
- GEOGRAPHIC INFO SYSTEMS now requires TABULAR DATA so that incoming students easily filter, modify, enhance conventional non-spatial table-oriented data sources to focus on spatial aspects of data; with 200-300 students taking TABULAR DATA per academic year, this is a high-bandwidth prerequisite. This course also carries the "Writing Intensive" designation which satisfies

[1] This is not yet an official name as there still are many moving pieces.

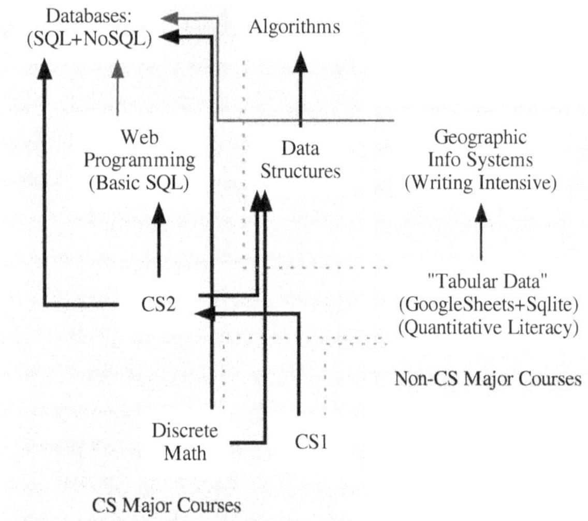

Figure 2: Targeted curricular setup... The black lines are prerequisites, the blue/dashed lines are anticipated student flows, and the red/dotted lines are explicit course-to-course connections.

another all-college graduation requirement and (more importantly) show our students the importance of the narrative in presenting computational results.

- Web Programming has consistently grown its coverage of basic SQL and, like Tabular Data, has come to provide a time-saving prelude to our Database Systems course.
- With an in-stream of students who are semi-proficient in SQL (shown with blue/dashed arrows in figure 2), Database Systems now completes SQL in a shorter time and thus allocates five to six weeks to cover two NoSQL databases (typically MongoDB and Neo4J), providing a structured-data[2] closure to a path that had started with tabular-data.

2 A COURSE ON TABULAR DATA

Since Tabular Data is a critical part of the arrangement outlined in the previous section and since we aim to make it an alternative introduction to computation (particularly for members of underrepresented communities), it is important for us to highlight its most important qualities:

- While Information Technologies was based on Excel and Access, Tabular Data uses Google Sheets and Sqlite/SqliteStudio, simpler tools that afford us time to focus on problem solving.
- Many aspects of spreadsheets are associated with typical concepts of a CS1/CS2 course. For example, the operation of the '`=sum()`' function is first covered as a running sum placed in a '`for`'-loop and then in a more recursive form of "*The sum in cell B10 is the sum in cell B9 plus the value in A10*".
- Each big idea is presented in two steps: first with a dataset that fits a single screen and then with a second one of identical structure but with many more rows and columns. We have observed that having a visual reference to the entirety of a dataset is a significant scaffolding factor for non-trivial aspects of spreadsheets (such as '`=vlookup`'), especially for students who have not had a chance to engage in any computational course.
- As a stepping stone between spreadsheets and databases, we use the recently added '`=filter()`' and '`=query()`' functions of Google Sheets which allow students to understand the basics of database operations in the context of spreadsheets.
- The document sharing feature of Google Sheets simplifies collaboration for our students as they engage in group-based inquiries on large data-sets.
- We occasionally engage in "replication of interesting results" exercises based on introductory challenges we encounter on data-sites such as https://www.kaggle.com.

While we do not anticipate Tabular Data to be a hard prerequisite for our majors courses, we do expect a non-trivial number of students to subsequently take at least one more CS course, one that would likely count towards a degree; in fact, in the trial offering of this course, six of the 17 students had done just that. Therefore, we now have well-defined connections between Tabular Data and our core courses, as shown with the red/dotted lines in figure 2:

- As mentioned earlier, the connection with CS1 is to offer concrete examples of programming constructs before students encounter them in CS1. This is a particularly important goal for us, one whose effectiveness has to be assessed in terms of how much abstract ideas become more real for students who have never engaged any form of programming in their high-school education. In the near future, we also hope to make use of the scripting language that comes with Google Sheets to create exercises to give a flavor of actual coding in Tabular Data.
- The connection with Discrete Math has to do with spreadsheets being used as a hands-on lab component in our Discrete Math course (for a survey of hands-on components used in discrete math, please see [1]). Once again, since mathematics is associated with a steep learning curve for a constituent of our students, we hope that having them exposed to a tool to facilitate their learning of abstract ideas will help their success in Computer Science.
- The connection with Algorithms has to do with pivot tables (present in Google Sheets) being used as almost a game-changer tool in assessing the efficiency of competing data structures and competing algorithms via empirically collected data, for students to have a more concrete understanding of asymptotic complexity.

As we approach the end of our design/refine phase, we plan to assess the degree to which we are reaching our goals such as (i) faster comprehension of topics in CS1 by those students who have taken Tabular Data, (ii) completion of more advanced projects in Geographic Info Systems, and (iii) thorough comprehension of NoSQL systems in Database Systems.

REFERENCES

[1] James F. Power, Thomas Whelan, and Susan Bergin. 2011. Teaching Discrete Structures: A Systematic Review of the Literature. In *Proceedings of the 42nd ACM Technical Symposium on Computer Science Education (SIGCSE '11)*. ACM, New York, NY, USA, 275–280. https://doi.org/10.1145/1953163.1953247

[2] We use the phrase "structured data" to distinguish the datasets we use from large and unstructured "big-data" on which AI/ML techniques are typically applied.

Automatic Evaluation of the Quality of Solutions for an Open Programming Task

Stephan Euler
TH Mittelhessen University of Applied Sciences
61169 Friedberg, Germany
Stephan.Euler@mnd.thm.de

ABSTRACT

This paper describes a tool for analysis of solutions to programming tasks. The analysis addresses both the code and the generated graphical output. First results on the correlation between quality of code and complexity of the output are reported.

CCS CONCEPTS

• **Applied computing** → *Interactive learning environments*; • **Human-centered computing** → Visualization toolkits;

KEYWORDS

learning environments, programming, automatic code evaluation

ACM Reference Format:

Stephan Euler. 2019. Automatic Evaluation of the Quality of Solutions for an Open Programming Task. In *Innovation and Technology in Computer Science Education (ITiCSE '19), July 15–17, 2019, Aberdeen, Scotland Uk.* ACM, New York, NY, USA, 2 pages. https://doi.org/10.1145/3304221.3325546

1 INTRODUCTION AND MOTIVATION

In several programming courses we use the *Board of Symbols* (BoS) environment. With BoS programmers can place symbols of different form, color and size on a rectangular board [1]. In this way even beginners can create graphical output. The courses start with an introductory exercise: write code to draw a letter. The resulting letters show a wide range in complexity, both within a course and between different courses. Therefore the question arises as to what extent the solutions provide information about the students motivation and programming experiences. One possible benefit of identifying students strength is shown in [3]. More specific, the analysis could provide insight into:

- range of solutions within group and compared to other groups
- correlation between previous knowledge and complexity of solution

Using BoS a solution consists of two components: the program code and the pattern. For the sake of simplicity we consider only static patterns. In BoS it is fairly simple to animate the patterns. This is used later in some courses to visualise algorithms such as sorting. So far, however, no student has included animation in the letter task we examine in this paper. Figure 1 shows as an example code and the resulting picture for a simple letter *L*.

```
size( 10, 10 );
for( int x=2; x<6; x++ ) {
    color2( x, 2, BLUE );
    form2( x, 2, "s" ); }
for( int y=2; y<8; y++ ) {
    color2( 2, y, BLUE );
    form2( 2, y, "s" ); }
color2( 5,3, BLUE);
form2( 5,3, "b");
symbolSize2( 5, 3, 0.2 );
```

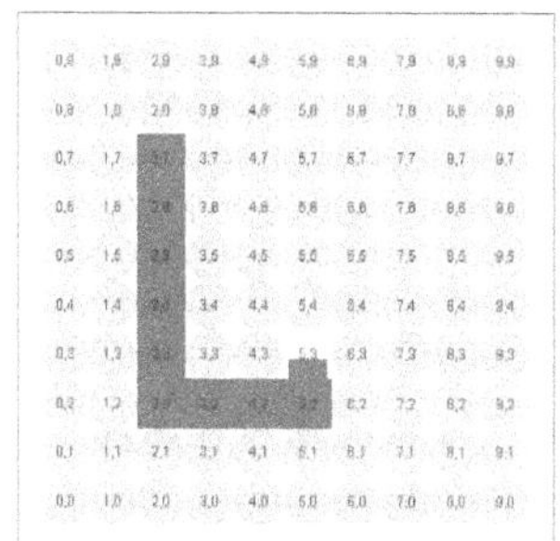

Figure 1: Example code and resulting pattern

Each method such as `color2` sends a command in the BoS language (BoSL) to the board. The board keeps a history of received commands.

2 EVALUATOR

We developed a tool *Evaluator* to automatically analyse code snippets. Basically, this tool reads the snippets from all files in a given directory structure. Filters both for the snippet names and text strings in the code can be applied to select only a subset of the snippets. The tool executes each code and performs the analysis described below. The resulting pictures are stored as files (jpeg) and the analysis results are written in a XML file. Finally, the XML result is transformed to HTML including links to the images. In this way the result can be viewed conveniently in a browser.

3 PATTERN COMPLEXITY

The Kolmogorov complexity or algorithmic information is defined as the length of the shortest program that computes or outputs x. Using this general idea we have implemented two methods to assess the pattern complexity: the size of the compressed representation and the number of required BoSL commands. In the first approach we generate a serialized form of the pattern (XML String), compress this string and use the size Z (number of bytes) of the compressed string as criteria.

As an alternative we consider the minimal number C of BoS method calls (or equivalently the number of BoSL commands) required to generate a given pattern. Each symbol has up to 5 attributes. Therefore for a given board with N symbols a maximum

ACM ISBN 978-1-4503-6301-3/19/07.
https://doi.org/10.1145/3304221.3325546

of $5N$ calls is sufficient to generate any pattern. In general, however, many symbols do not have a non-standard size, background color or text content. Then the corresponding calls can be saved. Furthermore C can be reduced by using global commands for color and form. E. g. the call `colors(BLUE)` changes the color of all symbols simultaneously. Then the following strategy is implemented

(1) find the most frequent color (form) in the pattern
(2) set all symbols to this color (form)
(3) change color (form) as required for individual symbols

As an example the pattern in Figure 1 has a compressed size of $Z = 487$ Bytes and requires $C = 22$ calls.

4 CODE QUALITY

The students submit running program code. Their code has no compiler errors and produces the letter. Nevertheless the code is in general not perfect. Often the code is poorly formatted or the names for variables are not appropriate. Furthermore in some cases the code may contain unnecessary BoSL commands. In the following we introduce measures for these two levels of quality.

4.1 Syntactic quality

Well written program code adheres to coding standards. This can be very specific guide lines or more general considerations such as described e. g. in [2]. A number of tools are available for automatic checking of code. We use the tool *Checkstyle*[1] and the rules from the *Google Java Style Guide*[2] to check the provided code snippets. Then the number of generated warnings are considered as an indicator for the code quality. The example code yields two warnings: the curly braces } should be in new lines.

A pattern can be generated in BoS by simply chaining the method calls. Students with programming experience will however avoid the tedious work and use control structures. Therefore the presence of such programming features in a code snippet suggests some experience – or the motivation to get the information ahead of the course schedule. Currently we consider {}-blocks, comments and method calls. We count the number of blocks and comments and calculate a weighted sum from these values and the maximum nesting depth. Then we add a bonus for using methods to obtain a measure for what we call *code maturity M*. The example code has $nb = 2$ blocks with a maximum nesting depth of $max = 1$ resulting in

$$M = 2 * nb + 3 * max = 2 * 2 + 3 * 1 = 7$$

4.2 Semantic quality

Finally we consider the effectiveness of a code in terms of used method calls. As described above the tool calculates the minimum number of calls required for a given pattern. We compare this with the actual number of calls. A snippet may contain the following types of gratuitous calls:

- unnecessary calls: setting the color of a symbol and later overwriting the color with another color
- duplicate calls: setting the same color to a symbol twice
- out of bounds: addressing symbols that are not within the given board

Currently we do not distinguish the first two types. We count the number of such calls and add the number of range errors as an additional penalty.

[1] http://checkstyle.sourceforge.net/
[2] https://google.github.io/styleguide/javaguide.html

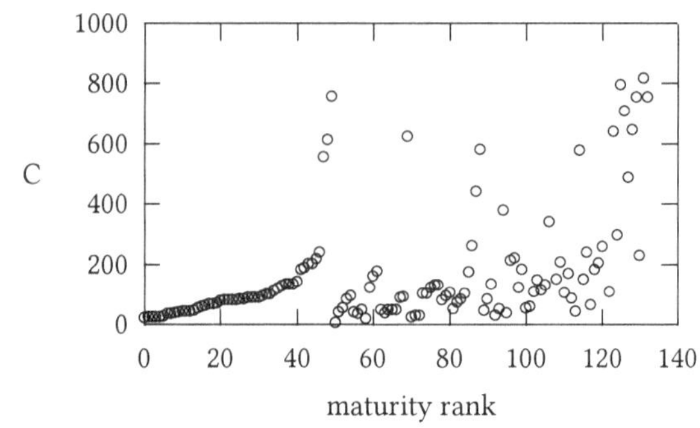

Figure 2: Number C of BoSL commands in solutions ordered by code maturity

5 FIRST TEST

We tested the approach in a course for programming beginners (first semester bachelor *media and computing*). After a short introduction in Java and BoS the students were given the letter task. The task was formulated very general without constraints regarding board size or complexity. The students knew, however, that their image later will be included in a gallery on the BoS web site.

In total 134 students submitted a code snippet. We found a wide range of board sizes from 1 to 20000 symbols. But most solutions had the default board size of 10×10. We sorted all solutions using the code maturity M as first key and the number C of BoSL commands as second. The result is shown in Figure 2. Approximately 50 solutions have maturity 0. We assume that these students do not have any programming experience. Nevertheless some of them wrote many lines of code to produce a more complex letter.

6 FURTHER WORK

We have already collected snippets from tasks in one course. As next step we plan to gather snippets from other courses so that we can apply our approach to a larger dataset. In particular, we will examine more systematically the usefulness of the proposed criteria. This probably will also lead to a refinement of the evaluation procedure.

REFERENCES

[1] Stephan Euler. 2018. Board of Symbols: A Tool for Teaching Programming. In *Proceedings of the 23rd Annual ACM Conference on Innovation and Technology in Computer Science Education (ITiCSE 2018)*. ACM, New York, NY, USA, 352–353. https://doi.org/10.1145/3197091.3205833

[2] Robert C. Martin and James O. Coplien. 2009. *Clean code: a handbook of agile software craftsmanship*. Prentice Hall, Upper Saddle River, NJ [etc.].

[3] Linda Ott, Briana Bettin, and Leo Ureel. 2018. The Impact of Placement in Introductory Computer Science Courses on Student Persistence in a Computing Major. In *Proceedings of the 23rd Annual ACM Conference on Innovation and Technology in Computer Science Education (ITiCSE 2018)*. ACM, New York, NY, USA, 296–301. https://doi.org/10.1145/3197091.3197139

csedresearch.org: Resources for Primary and Secondary Computer Science Education Research

Monica M. McGill
Knox College
Galesburg, IL, USA
mmmcgill@knox.com

Adrienne Decker
University at Buffalo
Buffalo, NY, USA
adrienne@buffalo.edu

ABSTRACT

In this Tips, Techniques, and Courseware talk, we will provide an overview of csedresearch.org, a site designed to provide resources for primary and secondary computer science (CS) education researchers. This resource center has three primary functions: 1) to provide a quick and easy way to search and access manually-curated data from over 500 articles from ten targeted venues (currently 2012-2018), 2) to provide a centralized location for evaluation instruments, many of which are focused on computing, and 3) to provide resources for computer science education research (checklists for studies, how to design a study, how to write a research question, etc.). Users can search for articles by filtering at a granular level on various curriculum and activity components, including student demographics, instructor demographics, and program components. Users can also search for evaluation instruments on criteria such as type, year published, constructs measured in the instrument, and whether the instrument has been validated or tested for reliability. We will provide a brief summary of the rationale for the site, the current state of the site, and how educators and researchers are using the site to date. We will also discuss future plans for the site and enable the audience to provide feedback that may help us shape the site to better meet the needs of the community.

CCS CONCEPTS

• **Social and professional topics → Computing education; Computing education programs; Computer science education; K-12 education.**

KEYWORDS

Educational research, resources, evaluation, assessment, constructs, K-12, primary, secondary, cognitive, noncognitive

ACM Reference Format:
Monica M. McGill and Adrienne Decker. 2019. csedresearch.org: Resources for Primary and Secondary Computer Science Education Research. In *Innovation and Technology in Computer Science Education (ITiCSE '19), July 15–17, 2019, Aberdeen, Scotland, UK.* ACM, New York, NY, USA, 2 pages. https://doi.org/10.1145/3304221.3325545

ACM ISBN 978-1-4503-6301-3/19/07.
https://doi.org/10.1145/3304221.3325545

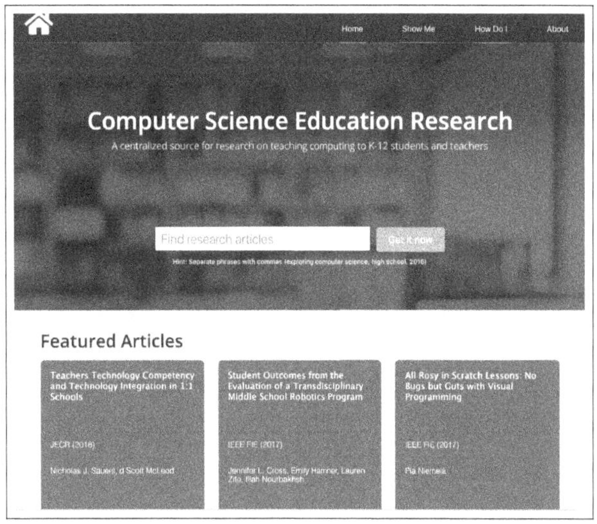

Figure 1: csedresearch.org

1 OVERVIEW

It is often challenging to find articles that provide sufficient data to evaluate for effectiveness and for replicating the study or the activity/curriculum being evaluated [4]. csedresearch.org was originally conceived in order to collect data needed to discover empirically-based best practices for teaching K-12 computing across the demographic spectrum, with an eye towards improving the efficacy of outreach activities and curriculum for underrepresented groups [1–3] (Figure 1). As part of a five-year U.S. National Science Foundation (NSF) research project, the site now houses manually curated data from over 500 articles across ten targeted venues and over 150 evaluation instruments, with nearly half of these focused on computing. The goals of this research project include:

- Provide resources for the K-12 CS education research community in order to promote better reporting of the activity and/or curriculum and
- Improve data analysis in order to gauge the impact of the intervention on its participants.

By housing data from our intensive literature review across multiple years and journals on one free, publicly accessible site, we have made it easier for those in the K-12 community to find previously published works in their areas of interest.

1.1 Research Articles

We seeded the collection of article data by curating data from articles related to K-12 CS education from each of the following ten journals (2012-2018) across five different publishers:

- ACM International Computing Education Research (ICER)
- ACM Innovation and Technology in Computer Science Education (ITiCSE)
- ACM Technical Symposium on Computer Science Education (SIGCSE)
- ACM Transactions on Computing Education (TOCE)
- Frontiers in Education (FIE)
- IEEE Global Engineering Education Conference (Educon)
- IEEE Transactions on Education
- Journal of Educational Computing Research (JECR)
- Koli Calling (Koli)
- Taylor & Francis Computer Science Education (CSE)

The article curation process includes organizing, evaluating, and parsing articles using a formal methodology [4]. The articles come from a variety of venues, and each article has been analyzed to identify its primary research questions, data that was collected as part of the study, the activities that were evaluated, and more. A team of ten people have been involved in identifying and analyzing articles. Each article undergoes two reviews.

1.2 Evaluation Instruments

In an effort to provide a centralized location for evaluation instruments related to computing education, we have curated over 150 evaluation instruments [1]. Over half of these instruments evaluate cognitive and noncognitive constructs related to computing [5].

By sharing a set of instruments that have been validated and tested for reliability in previous studies, researchers can easily find them and use or adapt them for use in their own studies. Not only does this save researchers valuable time, but if researchers start to use existing instruments when applicable, it may also provide better data for comparison across multiple studies and different demographic groups.

1.3 Research Resources

In addition to the above, the site continues to add resources for authors and those who review articles for publications. Included in this are how to write a research question and other guides currently under review. We provide two checklists on the site: a list of questions for ensuring that articles reporting on research in general and a list of program elements to include in the article.

2 THE PRESENTATION

In this talk, we will demonstrate several ways that primary and secondary educators, researchers, and evaluators interested in primary and secondary computer science education can use the csedresearch.org resources. We will highlight and demonstrate how easy it is to engage in this as both a contributor to and as an end-user of this site and encourage collaboration and feedback from those in attendance as the site continues to evolve. We will show:

- how to perform article searches by filtering on relevant demographics,
- how to contribute relevant articles to the site,
- how to search for useful evaluation instruments based on type of study being performed or constructs being measured,
- how to contribute new evaluation instruments to the site,
- how to request a copy of the data for further research,
- how to find tips on conducting research, and
- as the site evolves and becomes more adopted by the community, we will show attendees the best mechanism for providing feedback and ideas on how to improve the site for individuals performing research.

3 AUDIENCE APPEAL

csedresearch.org is designed for researchers, educators, and evaluators engaged in primary and secondary education. We expect that given the nature of topics addressed at ITiCSE, those falling in all three categories will be in the audience, with researchers and educators comprising the bulk of the attendees.

We have had considerable feedback on the website to date. Feedback from the community includes:

- I totally love the site, use it *all* the time and recommend it to others all the time. Thanks for the great work!
- The collection of evaluation instruments will be appreciated by graduate students for many years to come.
- Very useful and informative. Thanks for putting this together.

In addition to sharing this resource with those in attendance, we will actively seek their feedback so we can improve the site to make it even more meaningful for those in the CS education community working in this space.

4 CONCLUSION

We have designed and developed the site with input from researchers, educators, and evaluators, including primary and secondary teachers. Based on the feedback so far, this site is becoming an important resource for many in the community. Sharing this site with the ITiCSE community may help additional researchers save time and resources finding relevant articles or evaluation instruments.

ACKNOWLEDGMENTS

This material is based upon work supported by the U.S. National Science Foundation under Grant Nos. 1625335, 1649671, 1745199, and 1757402.

REFERENCES

[1] Adrienne Decker and Monica M. McGill. 2019. A Topical Review of Evaluation Instruments for Computing Education. In *Proceedings of the 50th ACM Technical Symposium on Computer Science Education*. ACM.

[2] Monica M. McGill and Adrienne Decker. 2017. Computer Science Education Repository. https://csedresearch.org

[3] Monica M McGill and Adrienne Decker. 2018. Defining Requirements for a Repository to Meet the Needs of K-12 Computer Science Educators, Researchers, and Evaluators. In *Frontiers in Education Conference (FIE)*. IEEE.

[4] Monica M McGill, Adrienne Decker, and Zachary Abbott. 2018. Improving Research and Experience Reports of Pre-College Computing Activities: A Gap Analysis. In *Proceedings of the 49th ACM Technical Symposium on Computer Science Education*. ACM, 964–969.

[5] Monica M McGill, Adrienne Decker, Tom McKlin, and Kathy Haynie. 2019. A Gap Analysis of Noncognitive Constructs in Evaluation Instruments Designed for Computing Education. In *Proceedings of the 50th ACM Technical Symposium on Computer Science Education*. ACM, 706–712.

If Memory Serves: A Game to Supplement the Instruction of Concepts Related to Pointers

Monica M. McGill
Knox College
Galesburg, Illinois, USA
mmmcgill@knox.com

Ian Pollock
California State University, East Bay
Hayward, California, USA
ian.pollock@csueastbay.edu

ABSTRACT

In this Tips, Techniques, and Courseware presentation, we will provide an overview of If Memory Serves, a game designed to complement the instruction of pointers in computer science courses. The game was first designed during a working group in ITiCSE 2017 as a tool to enable deeper understanding of pointers due to the difficulties students often face when learning about them. Over the last two years, the game has continued to evolve and has moved from a concept of the game to near-alpha. During this talk, we will demonstrate the game, provide insight into why it was developed, and discuss how it can be used to teach pointers. We will also briefly discuss our concept behind this open-source game and invite feedback from the audience as well as invite others to remix, test, and engage in research on testing the game's effectiveness.

Figure 1: Title screen for If Memory Serves

CCS CONCEPTS

• **Social and professional topics → Computing education**; **Computer science education**; • **Applied computing** → *Interactive learning environments*.

KEYWORDS

Educational research, computing education, games for education, games, learning, pointers

ACM Reference Format:
Monica M. McGill and Ian Pollock. 2019. If Memory Serves: A Game to Supplement the Instruction of Concepts Related to Pointers. In *Innovation and Technology in Computer Science Education (ITiCSE '19), July 15–17, 2019, Aberdeen, Scotland, UK*. ACM, New York, NY, USA, 2 pages. https://doi.org/10.1145/3304221.3325550

1 INTRODUCTION

At ITiCSE 2016, the first of a two-sequence working group was convened to explore games in computer science education. The Game Development for Computer Science Education working group explored over 120+ games for computer science education, classifying these games in terms of the ACM/IEEE 2013 Computing Curricula Knowledge Areas [5]. This working group found, among other descriptive data, that the heaviest concentration of existing games addressed learning in the Software Development Fundamentals (SDF) area, with the majority of games focused on early programming concepts.

This followed with the second working group at ITiCSE 2017, where that knowledge was taken and explored further, with the intention of designing and developing a game for teaching concepts in computer science. Based on the results of the previous years' study, the team decided to choose an area for which no known games existed. Given the previous research, we discovered that pointers were a particularly challenging area for students. In fact, research by Boustedt et al [3] found that pointers were "...commonly identified as a candidate threshold concept in surveys of computer science educators." [6] Further research confirms this, including work by Craig and Peterson, Adcock, et al, and Allevato, et al [1, 2, 4].

After the area of focus was selected, the team began the ideation process, considering what might be culturally relevant for students as well as how the concepts of pointers could be incorporated into the game. The initial mechanics were created, and we released the game as a concept build soon after ITiCSE 2017.

Since then, work on the player experience, including the user interface, art, and sound, as well as game flow have been slowly but steadily ongoing. In the next sections, we highlight the learning objectives we established and built into the game, provide an overview of the game, and define the audience for this presentation.

2 GAME OVERVIEW

If Memory Serves (https://ifmemoryserves.org) was designed for a target audience of 18- to 24-year-old students, since pointers are a concept often taught in more advanced computer science courses. We chose to make the game a two-player collaborative experience, in order to benefit from many research studies that show the benefits and effectiveness of pair programming.

ACM ISBN 978-1-4503-6301-3/19/07.
https://doi.org/10.1145/3304221.3325550

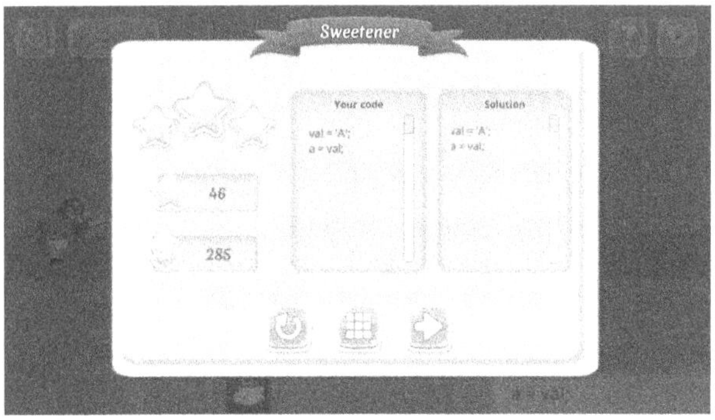

Figure 2: Level complete screen.

In addition, we have created the game as an open-source project so the community can further build upon this work. Available on github.com, the game can be remixed, extended, and modified by others.

2.1 Learning Objectives

We identified eight learning objectives to be included in the game and identified assessment criteria for each. The learning objectives include:

(1) Copying values (no pointers)
(2) Create pointer, assign value, retrieve value, and dereferencing
(3) Swap values using pointers
(4) Value versus pointers
(5) Pointer arithmetic
(6) Double pointers
(7) Malloc/Free
(8) Data Structure

As the design of the game continued, we were able to create fifteen levels across five worlds to address the first five learning objectives. We also created a concept inventory to cover what is being taught in the game. This inventory will be used to measure effectiveness in a experimental-control type study.

2.2 Design

The game features two sisters, Addy and Val, from the Pointers family–yes, the Pointers Sisters–with Addy representing the address and Val representing the value. Add and Val are sloths who have recently opened a cafe. We situated each world within a theme within the cafe narrative to make the game more engaging and interesting. We purposefully chose a theme that would be familiar to students.

Addy and Val can swap beverages and food, create new beverages and food from existing ones using special magic, and much more, in order to quickly get food to the customers.

To solidify the correlation between in-game actions and pointers, each movement the player takes is associated with a line of code. Players can turn this code panel on to see the code appear during gameplay. The code also appears at the end of each level and players can compare the code they generated through their actions with the code of the ideal gameplay for that level.

3 CONCLUSION

The intended audience for this Tips, Techniques and Courseware talk is anyone in the computing education community who teaches the concepts of pointers or who is interested in different ways games can be created to teach or help teach concepts throughout computing education. During the presentation, we will play through several levels of the game explaining the concepts behind each of these levels.

Given the nature of this open-source game, we invite the community to add to the game, test the game by using and/or revising resources we have already provided (including the concept inventory for pointers), and use the game in their courses.

REFERENCES

[1] Bruce Adcock, Paolo Bucci, Wayne D. Heym, Joseph E. Hollingsworth, Timothy Long, and Bruce W. Weide. 2007. Which Pointer Errors Do Students Make?. In *Proceedings of the 38th SIGCSE Technical Symposium on Computer Science Education (SIGCSE '07)*. ACM, New York, NY, USA, 9–13. https://doi.org/10.1145/1227310.1227317

[2] Anthony Allevato, Stephen H. Edwards, and Manuel A. Pérez-Quiñones. 2009. Dereferee: Exploring Pointer Mismanagement in Student Code. In *Proceedings of the 40th ACM Technical Symposium on Computer Science Education (SIGCSE '09)*. ACM, New York, NY, USA, 173–177. https://doi.org/10.1145/1508865.1508928

[3] Jonas Boustedt, Anna Eckerdal, Robert McCartney, Jan Erik Moström, Mark Ratcliffe, Kate Sanders, and Carol Zander. 2007. Threshold Concepts in Computer Science: Do They Exist and Are They Useful?. In *Proceedings of the 38th SIGCSE Technical Symposium on Computer Science Education (SIGCSE '07)*. ACM, New York, NY, USA, 504–508. https://doi.org/10.1145/1227310.1227482

[4] Michelle Craig and Andrew Petersen. 2016. Student Difficulties with Pointer Concepts in C. In *Proceedings of the Australasian Computer Science Week Multiconference (ACSW '16)*. ACM, New York, NY, USA, Article 8, 10 pages. https://doi.org/10.1145/2843043.2843348

[5] Chris Johnson, Monica McGill, Durell Bouchard, Michael K Bradshaw, Víctor A Bucheli, Laurence D Merkle, Michael James Scott, Z Sweedyk, J Ángel, Zhiping Xiao, et al. 2016. Game development for computer science education. In *Proceedings of the 2016 ITiCSE Working Group Reports*. ACM, 23–44.

[6] Monica M. McGill, Chris Johnson, James Atlas, Durell Bouchard, Chris Messom, Ian Pollock, and Michael James Scott. 2017. If Memory Serves: Towards Designing and Evaluating a Game for Teaching Pointers to Undergraduate Students. In *Proceedings of the 2017 ITiCSE Conference on Working Group Reports (ITiCSE-WGR '17)*. ACM, New York, NY, USA, 25–46. https://doi.org/10.1145/3174781.3174783

In-Depth Feedback on Programming Assignments Using Pattern Recognition and Real-Time Hints

Amir Rubinstein
Blavatnik School of CS
Tel-Aviv University
Tel-Aviv, Israel
amirr@tau.ac.il

Noam Parzanchevski
Blavatnik School of CS
Tel-Aviv University
Tel-Aviv, Israel
parzan@gmail.com

Yossi Tamarov
Blavatnik School of CS
Tel-Aviv University
Tel-Aviv, Israel
yossi.tamarov@gmail.com

ABSTRACT
Automatic grading of students' programs is a challenge in computer science (CS) education. In the last two years we have been using a machine learning tool called 'Sense Education' in our 'Intro to CS' course. The tool provides real-time pedagogical hints while students work on solutions, and in-depth feedback on submissions. It also provides a "bird's eye" view of the class's current capabilities, misconceptions, and biases in approaches to solutions. We describe this effort and several test cases. Our goal is to provide teachers with tips on how to effectively use such tools.

CCS CONCEPTS
Social and professional topics~Computer science education

KEYWORDS
Clustering; Automated Grading; Feedback; Pattern Recognition

ACM Reference format:

Amir Rubinstein, Noam Parzanchevski, Yossi Tamarov. In-Depth Feedback on Programming Assignments Using Pattern Recognition and Real-Time Hints. In *Proceedings of 24rd Annual ACM Conference on Innovation and Technology in Computer Science Education (ITiCSE'19), July 2019, UK.* ACM, New York, NY. 2 pages. https://doi.org/10.1145/3304221.3325552

1 Introduction
A major challenge in CS education is providing students with in-depth feedback on their programs in terms of algorithmic approach, efficiency, solution style and choice of language constructs. Merely testing output correctness will not expose misconceptions in underlying programming principles. In-depth feedback is especially important in introductory CS courses, where habits are formed. In reality, even in medium sized classes, not to mention large scale MOOCS, it is not feasible for educators to give personalized attention, feedback and advice. In recent years several tools have been proposed to solve this issue[1,2].

2 Clustering using 'Sense'
'Sense Education'[1] is a novel machine learning tool for semi-automated assessment and pedagogical feedback. It is based on unsupervised pattern recognition techniques, using methods from computational biology (DNA motif discovery). This tool provides personal feedback to students and a view of the class for teachers. The tool has two main usage modes: **(1)** Clustering mode, used to group students' solutions into clusters according to combinations of patterns. A pattern is a meaningful piece of the solution, contained in several solutions, although the exact code implemented in each instance of the pattern (by each student) may differ. Once constructed, feedback is composed for each cluster by a teacher, and delivered to each student within the cluster. **(2)** Instant feedback, or "hints mode", provides interactive feedback and pedagogical hints while students compose a solution, allowing for multiple resubmissions. This mode uses existing clusters from previous submissions (*e.g.*, past semesters), and classifies each new solution to the closest cluster. The students gradually improve their code according to hints given after every attempt, until they decide to submit for grading. Teachers can track students' improvements, both at the single student level and across assignments and classes.

ACM ISBN 978-1-4503-6301-3/19/07. https://doi.org/10.1145/3304221.3325552

3 Usage Examples
We have been using Sense since 2016 in our 'Intro to CS' course [3]. This course is taken by students in the CS major tracks, with ~450 participants each year (split into two semesters). It is a topic-based course, offering a wide cover of key CS subjects, accompanied by implementations in Python. In a typical instance, students are given 6 homework assignments, each including several programming tasks. As well as standard input-output correctness grading (unit test), we choose a subset of these exercises and apply Sense in both modes mentioned above. Next, we describe concrete examples and show how Sense revealed misconceptions and identified bias of some solutions over others. This information is valuable, as we can use it to improve the course - both in real time during the semester and in retrospect.

3.1 Clustering Mode
We presented students with the following example for an "accumulating computation": the sum of $x_0, x_1, \ldots x_k$ can be computed as $(\cdots((0+x_0)+x_1)+\cdots+x_k)$, where in each step x_i is added to $\Sigma_{j=0}^{i-1} x_j$. We asked students to generalize this example and write a recursive accumulating function `acc`. The parameters for this function are a function `f(x,y)`, an initial value `v`, and a list of values `lst`. We intentionally neither formally specified what `acc` should return, nor made any assumptions on `f`, but only gave the following example for list summation:

```
def my_sum(lst):
    return acc((lambda x,y: x+y), 0, lst)
```

The solution we aimed for calls `acc` directly and does not assume that `f` is either associative or commutative:

```
def acc(f, v, lst):
    if len(lst) == 0:
        return v
    else:
        return acc(f, f(v,lst[0]), lst[1:])
```

The results of the clustering mode helped us reveal the generalization process students had done, as well as the (perhaps unaware) assumptions they made on `f`. Out of 219 solutions, 89 gave some version of the above perfect solution. 84 students used an indirect recursive call, first applying `f` and only then `acc`:

```
return f(v, acc(f, lst[0], lst[1:]))
```

This solution does not work if `f` is not associative. More importantly, this hints at a misunderstanding of the fundamental requirement of the assignment, i.e., treating `acc` as the recursive function and `f` as a black-box object. In two additional clusters, students recursed on `acc` directly but failed on non-associative (18 solutions, (a)) or non-commutative (4 solutions, (b)) `f`'s:

```
(a) return acc(f, f(lst[-1],v) ,lst[:-1])
(b) return acc(f, f(lst[0],v), lst[1:])
```

Detecting the above-mentioned misconceptions and understanding the underlying faults in flawed submissions was aided by the use of the system's clustering mode, as mere input-output tests and visual examinations of submissions fail to shed light on recurring thought patterns. The rest of the solutions were either non-recursive (6) or did not fit in any of the above clusters (18). Being classified among the latter, somewhat unique solutions, does not necessarily imply a problem. Students whose solutions were unclassified in any cluster were advised to carefully compare their solutions to the exemplars we published from each of the other clusters.

In another assignment students were asked to identify, given two integers n, k, the longest sequence of digits in n that are divisible by k. For example, if $k = 2$, the output should be the longest sequence of even digits. Most students (361 out of 472) first converted n into a string in order to more easily iterate over its digits. 30 students used floor division ($n\%10$ and $n//10$) to directly iterate over n's digits as an integer. In class we show students both ways to iterate over a number, so it was surprising to see this large bias. We used this opportunity to expose students to other approaches and discuss the pros and cons of each (*e.g.*, memory usage). Additional clusters contained 41 students using a list to store all the relevant subsequences and at the end computed the maximal one; 6 students used a nested loop, a solution whose running time is quadratic; 34 students remained outside these clusters due to significantly different solutions.

3.2 Instant Feedback ("hints mode")

We showed students in class how to implement a hash table based on chaining, assuming keys are unique. As a homework assignment they had to implement a version in which keys may repeat. We already had existing clusters of the hash table's search method from previous semesters, so we could classify each of the new 112 solutions in real-time. We graded the clusters, according to correctness, efficiency, and style. Students could submit their solutions multiple times, until they decided to submit them for final grading. Each submission was given immediate pedagogical feedback and in some cases an improvement hint.

Out of 112 students, 68 (61%) submitted the assignment more than once, and 5 students submitted 8 times. 60 students achieved the ideal solution, 33 of them did so only by resubmitting. The Alluvian diagram in Fig. 1 depicts the trends of students' trajectories across the clusters' quality. For example, one cluster (3 students) contained solutions that unnecessarily scanned all the chains in the hash table, instead of the single chain mapped by the hash function. This is a major conceptual error, which cannot be captured by unit tests. Those students got this hint: "Recall the O() notation for runtime efficiency. What's your program's efficiency?". All 3 students fixed this issue and resubmitted.

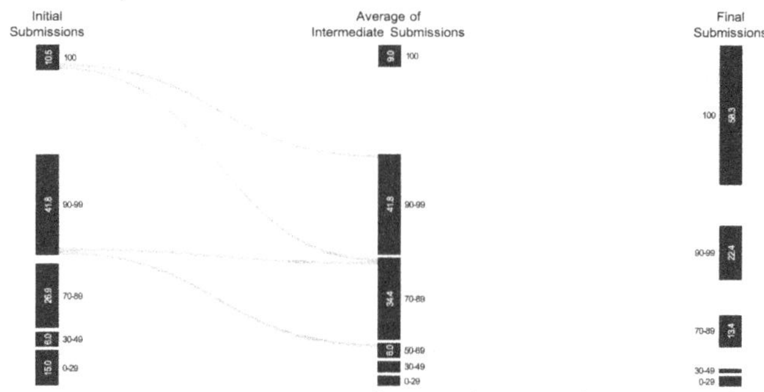

Figure 1: Improvement in student grades over three stages: first submission, average of intermediate submissions and last submission. Grades are grouped in bins: 0-29, 30-49, 50-69, 70-89, 90-99 and 100, and the percentage of students in each bin appears in the grey rectangles. Green denotes increase in grade, Red denotes decrease in grade and Yellow denotes no change between submissions.

4 Conclusion

Clustering and classification of students' programs provides valuable and incremental feedback to students at large scale, in addition to pedagogical insights to teachers. These tools can aid teachers in detecting conceptual trends that are hard to notice when using manual examination tools alone. Furthermore, in the advent of MOOCs, automatic instant feedback systems are a necessity.

REFERENCES

[1] Joyner, David, et al. "From Clusters to Content: Using Code Clustering for Course Improvement." Proceedings of the 50th ACM Technical Symposium on Computer Science Education. ACM, 2019.

[2] Glassman, Elena L., et al. "OverCode: Visualizing variation in student solutions to programming problems at scale." ACM Transactions on Computer-Human Interaction (TOCHI) 22.2 (2015): 7.

[3] Chor, Benny, and Rani Hod. "CS1001. py: a topic-based introduction to computer science." Proceedings of the 17th ACM annual conference on Innovation and technology in computer science education. ACM, 2012.

Teaching Self-Balancing Trees Using a Beauty Contest

Samah Senbel
School of Computer Science & Engineering
Sacred Heart University
Fairfield CT USA
senbels@sacredheart.edu

ABSTRACT

Trees data structures and their performance is one of the main topics to teach in a data structures course. Appreciating the importance of tree structure and tree height in software performance is an important concept to teach. In this paper, a simple and amusing activity is presented. It demonstrates to students the importance of a well-balanced tree by comparing the height of a binary search tree to a balanced (AVL) tree build upon some personal data to find the "prettiest" tree (minimum height). The activity highlights the fact that, irrelevant of your data sequence, a balanced tree guarantees a height of O(log n) and everyone "wins" the beauty contest.

CCS CONCEPTS

• Social and Professional topics → Computing education programs

KEYWORDS: Self-balancing trees; AVL trees; Binary Search Trees; Tree Height; Search Complexity

ACM Reference format:
Samah Senbel. 2019. Teaching Self-Balancing Trees Using a Beauty Contest. In *Proceedings of the 24th Annual Conference on Innovation and Technology in Computer Science Education (ITiCSE'19), 15-17/July, 2019, Aberdeen, Scotland, United Kingdom.* ACM, New York, NY, USA, 2 pages. https://doi.org/10.1145/3304221.3325544

1 INTRODUCTION

Data structures is a significant part of the foundation of computer science for computer programming students. It introduces students to the different data structures and their uses, properties and implementation. This is a core part of software design and development [5]. At Sacred Heart University, the data structures course is taught in the second semester of the freshman year for all computer science and engineering students. It starts by covering the simpler linear data structures: arrays, linked lists, stacks, queues, and hashing, then trees of all types; binary search trees (BST), AVL trees [1] or red-black trees, heaps, and B-trees, and finally graphs are introduced towards the end of the course.

ITiCSE '19, July 15-17, 2019, Aberdeen, Scotland UK

ACM ISBN 978-1-4503-6301-3/19/07.
https://doi.org/10.1145/3304221.3325544

Students often have no problem understanding the concepts and uses of the different data structures, but struggle with the analysis, comparison, and implementation of the different structures. Therefore, it is important to introduce as many demonstrations, examples, memorable activities and interesting assignments as possible [4].

An important concept to teach in a data structures course is the different types of trees and their applications and performance measures. After studying the main concept of each tree type and its uses, we analyze and compare its performance to the others before starting on its implementation. The importance of the tree height in tree processing and performance cannot be understated [3].

Typically, the binary search tree and its implementation is covered first in its own lecture followed by a self-balancing tree: AVL trees and/or Red-Black trees. We introduce an exercise to be done at the beginning and middle of the self-balancing tree lecture.

2 ACTIVITY DESCRIPTION

The goal of this activity is to demonstrate the efficiency of AVL trees. Students build a BST from a set of personalized integers, check the height, and the student with the lowest height "wins". Then, an AVL tree is built from the same data, and now everyone has the same tree height and are all "winners" of the tree beauty contest.

The first issue is how big to make the data set to make sure all students get an AVL tree of the same height and "win". Figure 1 charts the eight range for both BST and AVL trees, as given in the following equations [2]:

BST tree height: $\log_2(n+1) \leq h < n$ (1)

AVL tree height: $\log_2(n+1) \leq h < 1.44 \log_2(n+2) - 0.328$ (2)

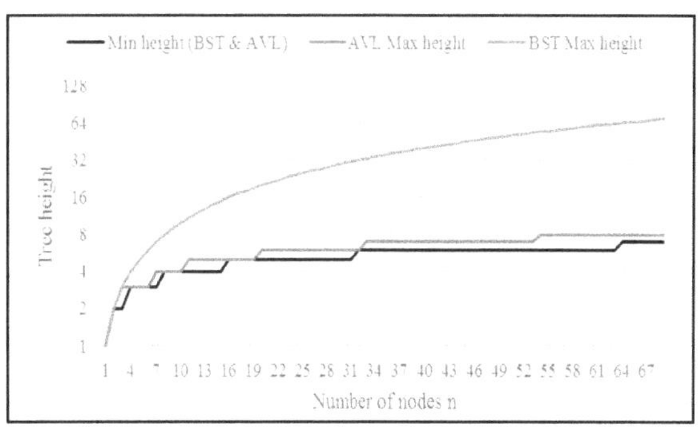

Figure 1: Height range of a BST and AVL tree

Based on figure 1, only 11 values of n give a fixed value of the AVL height: 4, 5, 6, 8, 9, 10, 16, 17, 18, 19, and 32. Any of these can be used in this activity, 16 was chosen as it is large enough to need a few rotations hopefully, and can be done in a short time.

Activity 1: (2 minutes) Each student is given a sheet with 16 questions that need to be answered with integer replies, such as "How many siblings do you have?" and "What is your dorm room/ home number?". The students are allowed to answer with wrong answers to protect their privacy. In case of a repeated number, they should change it to a new number.

Activity 2: (3 minutes) Using the exact sequence of answers, they draw a BST of their personal data. The resulting tree would have height of 5 to 16, depending on their answers.

Activity 3, Group discussion: (5-10 minutes) Students are asked for their BST height, and the student(s) with the shortest heights are declared the winner(s) and given a small reward (Sticker & Candy). Figure 2 shows a sample answer.

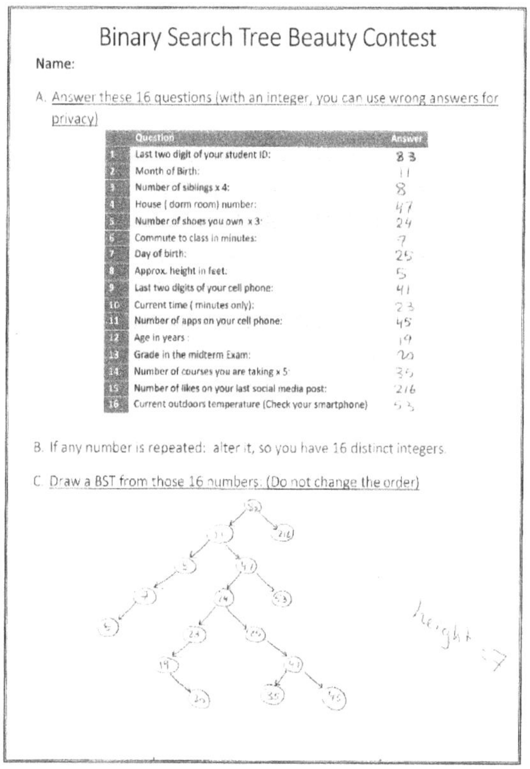

Figure 2: Sample BST answer for the contest

Having done these activities, the concept of self-balancing trees is explained and how the AVL trees does that by performing single and double rotations as needed. Several examples are solved to demonstrate the technique. Tree operations are briefly explained, as well as tree height (figure 1) and how it affects performance. This takes about 45-50 minutes. Before going into the details of actually coding the AVL tree, the following activities are performed:

Activity 4: (5 minutes) Using the same data set, the students build up their individual AVL tree. A sample is shown in figure 3.

Activity 5: (5 minutes): Students are asked for their AVL tree height, and as expected, all the students get a height of 5, and are all "winners" now. The same small reward is given to the entire class as they show their trees, and any errors found are fixed.

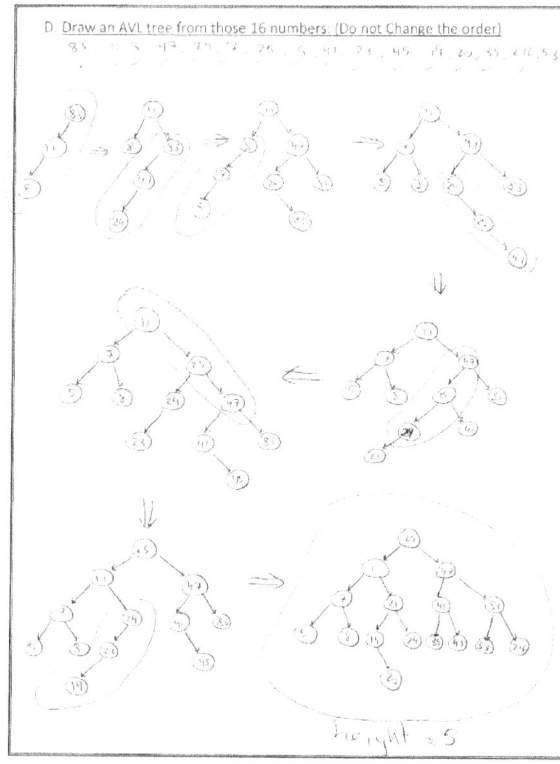

Figure 3: Sample AVL tree answer

Having set the mood of the class into a more positive mood, the students get a 15-minute break, and then we start on the intricacies of the actual coding of the AVL tree and its operations (about 75 minutes). Total class time is 2 hours and 45 minutes. This exercise has been practiced with freshman students over the past four years and proved to be an effective way to teach tree performance.

REFERENCES

[1] Adelson-Velsky, G. and Landis, E. 1962. An algorithm for the organization of information. In *Proceedings of the USSR Academy of Sciences (in Russian). Vol 146: pp. 263–266.* English translation by Myron Ricci in *Soviet Mathematics.* Doklady, vol 3: pp.1259–1263.

[2] Donald Knuth. 2000. Sorting and searching. Addison-Wesley, Boston, Massachusetts, USA. ISBN 0-201-89685-0.

[3] Koffman, E. and Wolfgang, P. 2015. Data Structures abstraction and design. Chapter 9, John Wiley Publishers, Hoboken, New Jersey, USA. ISBN-10: 1119355214.

[4] Lawrence, R. 2004. Teaching Data Structures Using Competitive Games. In *IEEE Transactions on Education, Vol. 47, no. 4.* IEEE.

[5] Liu, X., Wang, X. and Wang, R. 2013. Application of Blended Learning in Data Structures and Algorithms Course Teaching, In *Proceedings of the International Conference on Education Technology and Information System (ICETIS '13).* Atlantis Press, Paris, France.

Exploring the Potential of Social Annotations for Predictive and Descriptive Analytics

Shaveen Singh
Faculty of Information Technology
Monash University
Melbourne, VIC, Australia
shaveen.singh@monash.edu

ABSTRACT

In this paper, we illustrate the successful implementation of a social annotation tool within a content authoring platform that allows students to discuss learning material with their fellow classmates. The tool also allows students to self-report on their cognitive, metacognitive and affective states by self-coding their annotations as they journey through the learning material. We explore the predictive potential of such self-reports against the students completion rate and assessment scores and examine how the visualisation of these annotation classifications can help instructors easily identify issues and better support their students and improve learning material.

CCS CONCEPTS

• **Applied computing → Interactive learning environments**; *Distance learning*; *E-learning*; Collaborative learning.

KEYWORDS

annotations, self-report, e-learning, prediction, learning analytics

ACM Reference Format:

Shaveen Singh. 2019. Exploring the Potential of Social Annotations for Predictive and Descriptive Analytics. In *Innovation and Technology in Computer Science Education (ITiCSE '19), July 15–17, 2019, Aberdeen, Scotland UK.* ACM, New York, NY, USA, 2 pages. https://doi.org/10.1145/3304221.3325547

1 INTRODUCTION

Many large courses today use online discussion forums to allow educators and students help one another understand the teaching material [6]. However, in a large course, it can be difficult for instructors to find the student and the comments that need the most assistance, especially if they do not have the capacity to read or respond to every comment. The use of automatic identification or machine learning approaches also struggle when the comments in the forum are not rich, has misspellings or use poor vocabulary—making it difficult for the classifier to distinguish between more nuanced affective states, such as confusion, curiosity and so on [4]. Determining these nuanced affective states and experiences have ramifications for instructors aiming to provide interventions for their students, as an instructor would likely have different response for different types of reported encounters. Another related problem is the *overload of disparate discussions* that are all lumped into the same place with little context of what the conversation is about [6].

To mitigate these challenges, our work presents a practical strategy for collecting nuanced affective states and experiences in learning material. We developed an annotation interface that supports self-coding of student posts using predefined annotation categories. We choose this method as student authors may be one of the best sources regarding their own affective state and the approach provides us an easy and accurate way to acquire labeled and contextual dataset. The subsequent sections discuss the features of the annotation tool and some preliminary results on the predictive potential of the self-coded annotations as well as the value of annotation data in helping educators improve the teaching material and instructions.

2 THE ANNOTATION TOOL

Numerous studies [3] [5] cite annotation as useful for learners but there is lack of investigation on how it could be used to inform teaching changes. The annotation tool we adopted for this study has been extended from Hypothes.is [1]. It allows students to asynchronously annotate learning material in a chat-like fashion.

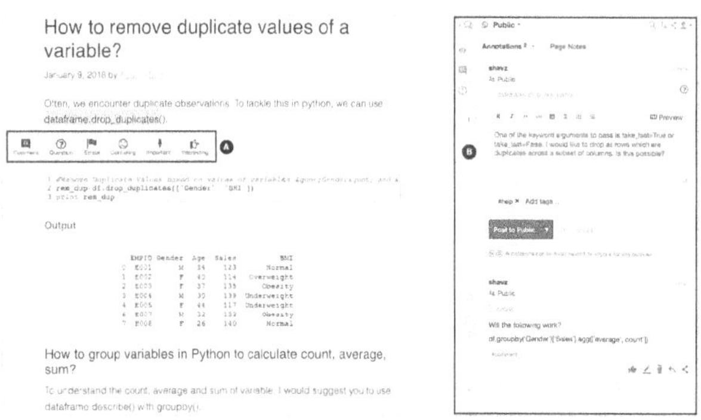

Figure 1: The annotation tool showing (A) the popup dialog when a user selects the text and (B) the annotations in the right hand pane

Figure 1 shows what the student sees after accessing the reading material and highlighting a specific passage on a page. The six pre-defined annotation options available to the students are *Comment, Question, Errata, Important, Confusing, and Interesting.* Upon selecting one of the options, a conversation window opens in the right hand pane where the student can pose a question or post a comment. The annotation categories and custom tags are searchable and can be used to connect with others working on the same topic or to follow a group's annotation activity across the material. Annotations are public by default but can be made private.

ITiCSE '19, July 15–17, 2019, Aberdeen, Scotland UK

ACM ISBN 978-1-4503-6301-3/19/07.
https://doi.org/10.1145/3304221.3325547

3 PRELIMINARY RESULTS

We trialed the annotation tool in a Python programming workshop, which was conducted over two weeks. A total of 37 students enrolled in the workshop. Students were given a 20 page preparatory reading to complete in their own time (online) before attending a 3 hour face-to-face (F2F) workshop in the second week. The annotation platform was integrated with the content authoring platform. The choice to annotate was completely voluntary and no marks were awarded for making annotations, however, students were informed that the annotations made would be used to adapt the teaching focus in the F2F workshop session. Fine-grained data regarding annotations, author and posting timestamp was captured.

3.1 Students use of the annotation tool

A total of 307 annotations were made by 36 out of the 37 students in the 20 page document. The average annotations made per page was 15.3 ($SD = 2.2$) and the average annotation posts per student at 8.57($SD = 3.1$). The average interactions with an annotation by a student (up-vote/view/read) stood at 24.6 ($SD = 4.3$).

3.2 Predictive Ability of Annotation Data

The next step was to investigate whether annotations had an effect on completion rate and student performance in the course. This was carried out by considering the degree of linear relationship (strength and direction) between the annotation variables using the Pearson's correlation coefficient, *r*. Looking at the correlation matrix, there was a strong positive correlation between the total annotations made and the completion rate, $r = 0.536, n = 36, p < 0.001$. Total number annotations made also had a strong positive correlation with quiz performance, $r = 0.503, n = 36, p < 0.001$.

By categorising annotations by their classifications, we saw that *Help* and *Confusing* annotations had strong negative correlation ($r = -0.6, n = 36, p < 0.001$) and ($r = -0.584, n = 36, p < 0.001$) with the completion rate. Similarly, *Help* and *Confusing* annotations also had negative correlation with quiz performance with $r = -0.463$ ($p < 0.005$) and $r = -0.435$ ($p < 0.005$) respectively. Having seen the correlations between the predictors and the outcome variables, we built linear regression models to study the relationship between the annotating behaviour with completion rate and quiz performance. We found that students who had a significant percentage of their annotations created using the help or confusing label were the ones who have incomplete readings and lower quiz performance. Our model for course completion rate showed that we could predict 26.7% of the variability in students completion rate by taking into account the number of annotations they make during pre-reading. When we add the percentage breakdown of these annotations (categories), we found that we could predict almost 46% more of the variability in student completion (adjusted $R^2 = 72.7\%$). In term of quiz performance, we found that including the proportion of each annotation category and total annotations made predicted 56.1% of the variability in student performance.

3.3 Descriptive Insights from Annotation Data

One of the benefits we foresee from using annotation data is that it provides contextual and qualitative feedback to instructors for actioning interventions—something that is much needed in programming courses to understand students' difficulties with content and concepts. Using the annotation data, we built a simple dashboard (Fig. 2) to provide instructors with a birds-eye view of annotation hotspots in the course material (Fig. 2). The colour of the bubble corresponds to the category of annotation and the size corresponds to the frequency of annotations made on that module. Clicking on the bubble leads the instructor to an itemized list of all annotations that were made on that page corresponding to their classification.

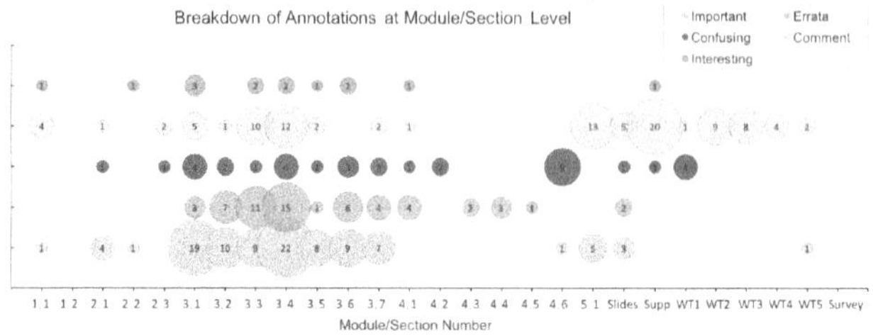

Figure 2: The annotation breakdown report

The philosophy behind the Annotation Breakdown Report is based on Just-in-Time-Teaching [2], which uses feedback from students to immediately inform teachers on where students are routinely grappling with difficult concepts. In this instance, by inspecting the dashboard, the instructor of the workshop was able to easily spot high occurrence of confusion in Module 4.6 and intervened by creating a guided tutorial on the confusing concept. Additionally, the instructor was able to tailor his teaching strategy and time allocation for topics in the face-to-face session based on the distribution of help and confusing annotations posted in various modules.

4 CONCLUSION

Whilst the main limitation of this study is that—it is based on small number of students, the fact that there is strong correlation between the nature of annotations with performance and completion rate is encouraging. The novel use of tagged pre-reading data can be very promising—as by referring to annotations as feedback of students' learning, instructors can make decisions and intervene instantly. We showed that the categorisation of annotations is a good predictor of the completion rate and performance. Percentage (%) of confusing and help annotations seem to be the dominant predictor in both the models. We also showed the potential use of descriptive analytics from annotation data to improve teaching material and approaches. Our next step is to further explore the data and to also take this experiment to the next level, that is from the small scale pilot workshops to larger university offerings to validate the findings.

REFERENCES

[1] Hypothes.is. 2018. Hypothesis - The Internet, peer reviewed. https://web.hypothes.is/
[2] GM Novak, ET Patterson, AD Gavrin, and Wolfgang Christian. 1999. Just-In-Time Teaching: Blending Active Learning with Web Technology Prentice Hall. *New Jersey* (1999).
[3] Alexander Thayer, Charlotte P Lee, Linda H Hwang, Heidi Sales, Pausali Sen, and Ninad Dalal. 2011. The imposition and superimposition of digital reading technology: the academic potential of e-readers. In *Proceedings of the SIGCHI Conference on Human Factors in Computing Systems*. ACM, 2917–2926.
[4] Diyi Yang, Miaomiao Wen, Iris Howley, Robert Kraut, and Carolyn Rose. 2015. Exploring the effect of confusion in discussion forums of massive open online courses. In *Proceedings of the second (2015) ACM conference on learning@ scale*. ACM, 121–130.
[5] Jeffrey R Young. 2009. 6 Lessons One Campus Learned about E-Textbooks. *Chronicle of Higher Education* 55, 39 (2009).
[6] Amy X Zhang. 2017. Systems for improving online discussion. In *Adjunct Publication of the 30th Annual ACM Symposium on User Interface Software and Technology*. ACM, 111–114.

Laughter over Dread: Early Collaborative Problem Solving through an Extended Induction using Robots

Mark Zarb
School of Computing Science and Digital Media
Robert Gordon University
Aberdeen, United Kingdom
m.zarb@rgu.ac.uk

Michael Scott
Games Academy
Falmouth University
Cornwall, United Kingdom
michael.scott@falmouth.ac.uk

ABSTRACT

Software development companies want new hires with strong interpersonal and problem solving skills. To ensure the development of such skills, they must be embedded throughout the curriculum. However, many students struggle to collaborate with peers and in self-regulated practice during the early stages of their course. Explicit scaffolding can, however, motivate such engagement. This tips and techniques session shows how an ice-breaker using LEGO EV3 robots at two UK institutions enhanced peer interaction and increased self-regulated practice over the first four weeks of 2016-17 and 2017-18.

CCS CONCEPTS

• **Social and professional topics** → **CS1**; Computational thinking; Model curricula.

KEYWORDS

Interpersonal Skills, Teamwork, Problem Solving, Induction, Communities of Practice, Robots

ACM Reference Format:

Mark Zarb and Michael Scott. 2019. Laughter over Dread: Early Collaborative Problem Solving through an Extended Induction using Robots. In *Innovation and Technology in Computer Science Education (ITiCSE '19), July 15–17, 2019, Aberdeen, Scotland Uk.* ACM, New York, NY, USA, 2 pages. https://doi.org/10.1145/3304221.3325548

1 INTRODUCTION

The development of human capital in order to drive economic well-being has become a prominent focus of higher education. In recent years this has led to employability skills becoming central to definitions of student success. Employers in the technology sector often raise concerns about graduate employability, highlighting needs for interpersonal and problem solving skills [5]. The Shadbolt Review [9] echoes these concerns, illustrating that computing graduates have lower rates of employment compared to other STEM disciplines. This is despite reports of skills gaps and huge growth in the sector [11]. Furthermore, some computing graduates cite their university experience "could have better prepared them for '*the world of work*' in terms of developing their employability skills and knowledge" [3].

According to Ericsson's theory of deliberate practice, such skills require significant dedication and a sound strategy to develop [2]. Therefore, encouraging students to practice their interpersonal and problem solving skills early in the curriculum, such as the CS1 context, would afford greater time for students to develop them. Especially if it encourages subsequent self-regulated learning that is constructively aligned with employers' expectations.

However, challenges do arise. Firstly, establishing a context which inspires self-regulated practice. First-year students struggle to sustain their engagement without ongoing encouragement [4]. There is, therefore, a need to frame problem solving activities using approaches that encourage self-regulation (e.g. [15]). Secondly, when navigating the transition into higher education, many struggle to form a community of practice and engage with their peers [10, 12, 14]. Thus, they tend not to practice their interpersonal skills in a problem-centric manner early enough in their course.

Falmouth University and Robert Gordon University, together, have been exploring solutions to these challenges. While conducting previous research [7, 8, 13], the authors observed that students seemed to engage in peer support more readily, and were less intimidated by logic errors, when programming robots. Such activity seemed to evoke a sense of mastery, belonging, and agency, in line with building motivation according to self-determination theory [1]. To this end, the authors put together a series of induction activities centered upon notions of collaboratively building and programming robots.

2 INDUCTION DESIGN

Each team needs to have enough components to be able to build a basic Mindstorms robot (Figure 1), although this activity could be tweaked depending on available materials.

The LEGO Space Challenge using Mindstorms EV3 robots forms the thrust of the induction, organized into four key stages:

Introduction. A general introduction is given to the class, where students are divided into teams. Each team is handed a box containing all the components required to build a basic Mindstorms robot, a step-by-step handbook for construction, and an introduction to the coding interface.

Challenges. Once all teams have built the basic robot (or after a set time period), a document containing all the challenge briefs are handed to the teams. This can be supplemented with videos showcasing each challenge, to give teams a general consideration of the solution.

ITiCSE '19, July 15–17, 2019, Aberdeen, Scotland UK

ACM ISBN 978-1-4503-6301-3/19/07.
https://doi.org/10.1145/3304221.3325548

Figure 1: LEGO Mindstorms Robot

Development Time. Teams then being to solve the given challenges. The challenges themselves are set out so that teams can test their robot, so they can devise solutions using an iterative approach.

Competitive Play. At the end of the timescale, teams are asked to participate in the challenge event, where they are required to solve all challenges within a set time period. Each team's time taken can be used to populate a leader-board and announce the winning team.

The instruction given to students is fairly minimal: students are placed into teams, asked to build a basic robot from a number of parts as a common starting point, and then given a set time period to build and program the robot to solve a number of predetermined challenges. This forces them to work in multidisciplinary teams from the start, and learn to approach problem solving in an explicitly collaborative context.

3 FINDINGS

Variations of these sessions have been run annually since 2015 at Robert Gordon University, and since 2016 at Falmouth University. Extending already known benefits of educational robots in the programming context [6], qualitative data from observations and an end-of-task survey at both sites support hypotheses of improved collaboration and problem solving. Notably, students reported that it was fun to solve problems with the robots and that this activity was a great ice-breaker to make them interact with each other to build these robots and discuss out-of-the-box solutions. Further to this, many students successfully completed the space challenge, demonstrating key computational thinking skills.

This approach allows students to start working with each other without the expectation and pressure of grades, reaping the benefits of an informal experience. It was observed that students were successful in learning the foundations of computational thinking using LEGO robots, and that feedback from these challenges often resulted in "laughter rather than dread", encouraging the students to continue problem solving. This was deemed an excellent ice-breaker that opened up dialogue between newly-met peers. Furthermore, staff reported that these sessions allowed students to form small communities of practice early in the academic year, and that students tended to refer to these communities for support throughout the semester, even after the induction had ended.

REFERENCES

[1] Edward L Deci and Richard M Ryan. 2008. Self-determination theory: A macrotheory of human motivation, development, and health. *Canadian psychology/Psychologie canadienne* 49, 3 (2008), 182.

[2] K Anders Ericsson, Ralf T Krampe, and Clemens Tesch-Römer. 1993. The role of deliberate practice in the acquisition of expert performance. *Psychological review* 100, 3 (1993), 363.

[3] Innovation Great Britain. Department for Business and Skills (BIS). 2016. Computer science graduate employability: qualitative interviews with graduates. (2016).

[4] Tony Jenkins. 2001. Teaching programming–A journey from teacher to motivator. In *The 2nd Annual Conference of the LSTN Center for Information and Computer Science.*

[5] Ian Livingstone and Alex Hope. 2011. Next Gen: Transforming the UK into the world's leading talent hub for the video games and visual effects industries. *National Endowment for Science, Technology and the Arts (NESTA), London, UK* (2011).

[6] Louis Major, Theocharis Kyriacou, and O Pearl Brereton. 2012. Systematic literature review: Teaching novices programming using robots. *IET software* 6, 6 (2012), 502–513.

[7] Michael James Scott, Steve Counsell, Stanislao Lauria, Stephen Swift, Allan Tucker, Martin Shepperd, and Gheorghita Ghinea. 2015. Enhancing practice and achievement in introductory programming with a robot olympics. *IEEE Transactions on Education* 58, 4 (2015), 249–254.

[8] Michael James Scott, Alcwyn Parker, Brian McDonald, Gareth Lewis, and Edward J Powley. 2019. Nurturing Collaboration in an Undergraduate Computing Course with Robot-themed Team Training and Team Building. In *Proceedings of the 3rd Conference on Computing Education Practice.* ACM, 5.

[9] Nigel Shadbolt. 2016. Shadbolt review of computer sciences degree accreditation and graduate employability: April 2016. (2016).

[10] Angela A Siegel and Mark Zarb. 2016. Student Concerns Regarding Transition into Higher Education CS. In *Proceedings of the 2016 ACM Conference on Innovation and Technology in Computer Science Education.* ACM, 23–28.

[11] UK Tech City. 2016. Tech Nation 2016: Transforming UK industries (pp. 1-65, Rep.). *Tech City UK* (2016).

[12] Mark Zarb, Bedour Alshaigy, Dennis Bouvier, Richard Glassey, Janet Hughes, and Charles Riedesel. 2018. An international investigation into student concerns regarding transition into higher education computing. In *Proceedings Companion of the 23rd Annual ACM Conference on Innovation and Technology in Computer Science Education.* ACM, 107–129.

[13] Mark Zarb, Janet Hughes, and John Richards. 2015. Further Evaluations of Industry-Inspired Pair Programming Communication Guidelines with Undergraduate Students. In *Proceedings of the 46th ACM Technical Symposium on Computer Science Education.* ACM, 314–319.

[14] Mark Zarb and Angela A Siegel. 2017. An Analysis of Pupil Concerns Regarding Transition into Higher Education. In *Researcher Links Workshop: Higher Education for All.* Springer, 3–16.

[15] Barry J Zimmerman. 1998. Academic studing and the development of personal skill: A self-regulatory perspective. *Educational psychologist* 33, 2-3 (1998), 73–86.

Securing the Human: Broadening Diversity in Cybersecurity

Mohammad Azhar
Borough Of Manhattan Community College
United States
MAZHAR@bmcc.cuny.edu

Sajal Bhatia
Sacred Heart University
United States
bhatias@sacredheart.edu

Greg Gagne
Westminster College
United States
ggagne@westminstercollege.edu

Chadi Kari*
University of the Pacific
United States
celkari@pacific.edu

Joseph Maguire
University of Glasgow
United Kingdom
Joseph.Maguire@glasgow.ac.uk

Xenia Mountrouidou†
College of Charleston
United States
mountrouidoux@cofc.edu

Liviana Tudor
Politehnica University of Bucharest,
Petroleum-Gas University of Ploiesti
Romania
liviana.tudor@cs.pub.ro

David Vosen‡
College of St. Scholastica
United States
DVosen@css.edu

Timothy T. Yuen
The University of Texas at San Antonio
United States
Timothy.Yuen@utsa.edu

ABSTRACT

Recent global demand for cybersecurity professionals is promising, with the U.S. job growth rate at 28%, three times the national average [1]. Lacking qualified applicants, many organizations struggle to fill open positions [2]. In a global survey, 2,300 security managers reported that 59% of their security positions were unfilled, although 82% anticipated cyberattacks to their systems [3]. At the same time, the cybersecurity field is broadening, not only in technical concepts but also in human factors, business processes, and international law. The field has not become culturally diversified, however. Professionals hired in 2018 included only 24.9% women, 12.3% African Americans, and 6.8% Latinos [4]. These facts create an opportunity for higher education: diversify the profession while increasing the numbers of skilled computer scientists. New and integrated methods of attracting student populations in the field of cybersecurity are needed. The working group goal is to evaluate the effectiveness of approaches used in higher education to diversify the cybersecurity field through literature review, analysis of the findings, and a survey on techniques used for diversification of the cybersecurity field.

*Working Group co-leader.
†Working Group leader.
‡Working Group co-leader.

ITiCSE '19, July 15–17, 2019, Aberdeen, Scotland, UK

ACM ISBN 978-1-4503-6301-3/19/07.
https://doi.org/10.1145/3304221.3325537

CCS CONCEPTS

• **Security and privacy → Human and societal aspects of security and privacy; Social aspects of security and privacy;** • **Social and professional topics → Computing education;**

KEYWORDS

Cybersecurity; Diversification; Education

ACM Reference format:
Mohammad Azhar, Sajal Bhatia, Greg Gagne, Chadi Kari, Joseph Maguire, Xenia Mountrouidou, Liviana Tudor, David Vosen, and Timothy T. Yuen. 2019. Securing the Human: Broadening Diversity in Cybersecurity. In *Proceedings of Innovation and Technology in Computer Science Education, Aberdeen, Scotland, UK, July 15–17, 2019 (ITiCSE '19)*, 2 pages.
https://doi.org/10.1145/3304221.3325537

1 INTRODUCTION

Data breaches, social engineering, and cybercrime are continuously escalating [5]. Furthermore, pervasive adoption of the Internet of Things (IoT) smart devices, cloud storage, and mobile technologies expand into every economic sector and compound these security flaws by increasing the attack surface [6]. Thus, cybersecurity is no longer just about data and technology; it is about life and property with the the annual cost of global cybercrime is now estimated to be 600 billion USD, up more than a 100 billion from four years ago [5].

Global job demands for cybersecurity professionals reveals a long term workforce gap with a 3.5 million deficit of workers predicted by 2021 [2]. However, current Computer Science (CS) and Cybersecurity education programs neither are able to meet the demand nor provide the modern empirical training techniques needed especially in information technology security areas of social engineering, spear phishing, and ransomware attacks. Several questions arise for CS educators, industry, and governmental sectors: how effective is cybersecurity education if the knowledge is siloed or only expanded to CS majors? How effective are the solutions that are given by a non-diverse population of CS students that constitute the majority of cybersecurity professionals? Diversification of global security threats demands a diversification in the student population and educational approaches in computer science education. Our working group will address these issues regarding diversification of the cybersecurity field through analysis and evaluation of existing techniques.

2 WORKING GROUP OBJECTIVES

This working group will build upon ITiCSE cybersecurity endeavors from 2010, 2011, and 2018 [7, 8, 9] in expanding cybersecurity development to engage diverse undergraduate programs and interest. The goals of this working group are to:

(1) A detailed literature review of current methods used to attract additional students in the field, such as general education, gamification, active learning, pre-college education, conferences, summer camps, and peer instruction.
(2) An analysis of outcomes of these active learning techniques.
(3) A survey for educators that explores their formal and informal methods for diversifying the field of cybersecurity.
(4) An exploratory analysis of the interdisciplinary cybersecurity studies and the connection to the Internet of Things (IoT) systems. Smart devices are of interest regarding privacy implications and education opportunities that they may offer, such as hands on projects and experimentation [10].

The group will explore these issues in cybersecurity through a global perspective, investigating the approaches to, challenges of, and issues in broadening diversity around the world.

3 ACKNOWLEDGMENTS

The team acknowledges support provided by the US National Science Foundation under Award No. DUE-1700254. The team also acknowledges the support of ACM.

REFERENCES

[1] Bureau of Labor Statistics. 2019. *Occupational Outlook Handbook, Bureau of Labor Statistics.* https://www.bls.gov/ooh/computer-and-information-technology/information-security-analysts.htm.

[2] Steve Morgan. 2017. *Cybersecurity jobs report 2018-2021.* https://cybersecurityventures.com/jobs/.

[3] ISACA. 2018. *State Of Cybersecurity Study: Security Budgets Increasing, But Qualified Cybertalent Remains Hard To Find.* http://www.isaca.org/About-ISACA/Press-room/News-Releases/2018/Pages/State-of-Cybersecurity-Study-Security-Budgets-Increasing-But-Qualified-Cybertalent-Remains-Hard-to-Find.aspx.

[4] Bureau of Labor Statistics. 2019. *Labor Force Statistics from the current population survey, Bureau of Labor Statistics.* https://www.bls.gov/cps/cpsaat11.htm.

[5] James Lewis. 2018. *Economic Impact of Cybercrime, No Slowing Down.* McAfee. https://www.mcafee.com/content/dam/enterprise/en-us/assets/reports/restricted/economic-impact-cybercrime.pdf.

[6] Michael J Covington and Rush Carskadden. 2013. Threat implications of the internet of things. In *2013 5th International Conference on Cyber Conflict (CYCON 2013).* IEEE, 1–12.

[7] Stephen Cooper, Christine Nickell, Lance C. Pérez, Brenda Oldfield, Joel Brynielsson, As Gencer Gökce, Elizabeth K. Hawthorne, Karl J. Klee, Andrea Lawrence, and Susanne Wetzel. 2010. Towards information assurance (ia) curricular guidelines. In *Proceedings of the 2010 ITiCSE Working Group Reports* (ITiCSE-WGR '10). ACM, Ankara, Turkey, 49–64. ISBN: 978-1-4503-0677-5. DOI: 10.1145/1971681.1971686. http://doi.acm.org/10.1145/1971681.1971686.

[8] Lance C. Pérez, Stephen Cooper, Elizabeth K. Hawthorne, Susanne Wetzel, Joel Brynielsson, Asim Gencer Gökce, John Impagliazzo, Youry Khmelevsky, Karl Klee, Margaret Leary, Amelia Philips, Norbert Pohlmann, Blair Taylor, and Shambhu Upadhyaya. 2011. Information assurance education in two- and four-year institutions. In *Proceedings of the 16th Annual Conference Reports on Innovation and Technology in Computer Science Education - Working Group Reports* (ITiCSE-WGR '11). ACM, Darmstadt, Germany, 39–53. ISBN: 978-1-4503-1122-9. DOI: 10.1145/2078856.2078860. http://doi.acm.org/10.1145/2078856.2078860.

[9] Allen Parrish, John Impagliazzo, Rajendra K. Raj, Henrique Santos, Muhammad Rizwan Asghar, Audun Jøsang, Teresa Pereira, and Eliana Stavrou. 2018. Global perspectives on cybersecurity education for 2030: a case for a meta-discipline. In *Proceedings Companion of the 23rd Annual ACM Conference on Innovation and Technology in Computer Science Education* (ITiCSE 2018 Companion). ACM, Larnaca, Cyprus, 36–54. ISBN: 978-1-4503-6223-8. DOI: 10.1145/3293881.3295778. http://doi.acm.org/10.1145/3293881.3295778.

[10] Barry Burd, Lecia Barker, Felix Armando Fermin Perez, Ingrid Russell, Bill Siever, Nicoleta Tudor, Michael McCarthy, and Ian Pollock. 2018. The internet of things in undergraduate computer and information science education: exploring curricula and pedagogy. In *2018 ITiCSE Working Group Reports.* ACM. (November 2018).

Unexpected Tokens: A Review of Programming Error Messages and Design Guidelines for the Future

Brett A Becker*
University College Dublin
Dublin, Ireland
brett.becker@ucd.ie

Paul Denny*
University of Auckland
Auckland, New Zealand
paul@cs.auckland.ac.nz

Raymond Pettit*
University of Virginia
Charlottesville, Virginia, USA
raymond.pettit@virginia.edu

Durell Bouchard
Roanoke College
Roanoke, Virgina, USA
bouchard@roanoke.edu

Dennis J Bouvier
Southern Illinois University Edwardsville
Edwardsville, Illinois, USA
djb@acm.org

Brian Harrington
University of Toronto Scarborough
Scarborough, Ontario, Canada
brian.harrington@utsc.utoronto.ca

Amir Kamil
University of Michigan
Ann Arbor, Michigan, USA
akamil@umich.edu

Amey Karkare
Indian Institute of Technology Kanpur
Kanpur, India
karkare@cse.iitk.ac.in

Chris McDonald
University of Western Australia
Perth, Australia
chris.mcdonald@uwa.edu.au

Peter-Michael Osera
Grinnell College
Grinnell, Iowa, USA
osera@cs.grinnell.edu

Janice L Pearce
Berea College
Berea, Kentucky, USA
pearcej@berea.edu

James Prather
Abilene Christian University
Abilene, Texas, USA
james.prather@acu.edu

ABSTRACT

Diagnostic messages generated by compilers and interpreters such as syntax error messages have been researched for decades. Unfortunately these messages which include error, warning, and runtime messages, present substantial difficulty and could be more effective, particularly for novices. Recent years have seen increased number of papers in the area including studies on the effectiveness of these messages, improving or enhancing them, and their usefulness as a part of programming process data that can be used to predict student performance. Despite this increased interest, the long history of literature is quite scattered and has not been brought together in any digestible form.

We argue that in order to help the community proceed with more work on diagnostic messages, the literature needs to be presented in a state-of-the-art report. In addition we will synthesize and present the existing evidence for these messages including the difficulties they present and their effectiveness. We will also formulate a set of guidelines based on this evidence that can be used when designing or enhancing diagnostic messages. This work can serve as a starting point for those who wish to conduct research on such messages, those who wish to design better messages or those that aim to measure their effectiveness, more effectively.

*co-leader

ITiCSE '19, July 15–17, 2019, Aberdeen, Scotland UK

ACM ISBN 978-1-4503-6301-3/19/07.
https://doi.org/10.1145/3304221.3325539

CCS CONCEPTS

• **General and reference** → **Surveys and overviews**; • **Human-centered computing** → **Human computer interaction (HCI)**; • **Social and professional topics** → **Computing education**; **Computer science education**; *CS1*; • **Applied computing** → **Education**; • **Software and its engineering** → *General programming languages*; *Syntax*; *Compilers*; *Interpreters*; Semantics;

KEYWORDS

compiler error messages; CS1; design guidelines; diagnostic error messages; human computer interaction; HCI; introduction to programming; novice programmers; programming error messsages; review; runtime errors; survey; syntax errors

ACM Reference Format:
Brett A Becker, Paul Denny, Raymond Pettit, Durell Bouchard, Dennis J Bouvier, Brian Harrington, Amir Kamil, Amey Karkare, Chris McDonald, Peter-Michael Osera, Janice L Pearce, and James Prather. 2019. Unexpected Tokens: A Review of Programming Error Messages and Design Guidelines for the Future. In *Innovation and Technology in Computer Science Education (ITiCSE '19), July 15–17, 2019, Aberdeen, Scotland UK*. ACM, New York, NY, USA, 2 pages. https://doi.org/10.1145/3304221.3325539

1 BACKGROUND

Diagnostic error messages generated by compilers and interpreters, including error, warning, and runtime messages, have been researched for over 40 years with one obvious consensus: they present substantial difficulty and could be more effective [2, 12]. They are often vague, imprecise, confusing and at times seemingly incorrect [6], in particular for novices. Research has also shown that these messages can be a source of frustration for students [3, 8]. Unfortunately, drawing any more specific conclusions from this history of research is difficult. In 1983 Brown stated "There should be a deliberate and sustained effort to focus attention on the quality of error messages, both in compilers and other systems, so that the current appalling state-of-the-art can be improved" [6, p.249]. In 1984 Du Boulay and Matthew asked "Why cannot these messages be made clearer, less confusing and more accurate?" [5, p.109]. We argue that Du Boulay and Matthew's question is still valid, and Brown's call for action has not been fully met. We also note that educators strive for their feedback to students to be accurate [9], and we should expect the same from the tools we have students use.

Although there has been increased interest in programming errors (faults committed by students) and the diagnostic messages they generate [4, 10] the literature on these messages is quite scattered and has not been brought together in an easily digestible form. This is despite the fact that the presentation of empirical evidence on the effects of these messages has advanced recently [13]. Various studies have analyzed the types and frequency of diagnostic messages that students generate; others have explored how 'standard' messages can be enhanced to make them more usable; and others still have sought to determine how the effectiveness of these messages can best be measured. Yet the difficulties these messages present, and evidence for their effectiveness have not been comprehensively analyzed.

This is exacerbated by the fact that although some works have presented evidence on diagnostic message effectiveness [1] (or lack thereof [7]), this evidence seems to be conflicting [11]. Additionally, some message design guidelines (explicit and implicit) exist but they span several decades and many of them are also conflicting, leaving the way forward unclear. We argue that to help the community proceed with more work on such messages, a clear picture of the state-of-the-art in compiler/interpreter diagnostic message design and effectiveness is required. In addition, a synthesis of the evidence on these messages including the difficulties they present and their usefulness would be helpful. A literature- and evidence-backed set of guidelines for the design of diagnostic programming messages would also be a valuable resource for the community.

2 OBJECTIVES

There are two broad objectives for this working group. The first is to present a state-of-the-art report encompassing the difficulties that diagnostic messages present (particularly for novices), the design of these messages, and evidence of their effectiveness. This will bring together the literature and evidence on diagnostic programming messages from the disciplines of Computing Education, Human Computer Interaction, Programming Languages, and more. The second objective is to present a unified set of guidelines for the design (or improvement) of these messages. Some studies over the last few decades have provided concrete design guidelines—for instance, see [14]. However not all are backed by empirical evidence, and some are conflicting. We aim to present a unified set of guidelines based on the literature that can be used as a starting point for designing or improving diagnostic messages.

We intend the resulting report to be useful for researchers in several sub-disciplines and hope that our efforts can contribute to more progress in the research of diagnostic programming messages.

3 CONCLUSION

This working group report will provide a digestible presentation of what research has been done on diagnostic messages generated by compilers, interpreters, etc., how this work is related to other work, and what gaps in the research exist. In doing so it will present a synthesis of the evidence on these diagnostic messages including evidence of the difficulties they present and their effectiveness. Finally, it will provide a unified set of guidelines for designing or improving these messages. This report will lay an important foundation for future work on diagnostic programming error messages, and can serve as a starting point for those who wish to design better messages or measure their effectiveness, more effectively.

REFERENCES

[1] Brett A. Becker. 2016. An Effective Approach to Enhancing Compiler Error Messages. In *Proceedings of the 47th ACM Technical Symposium on Computing Science Education (SIGCSE '16)*. ACM, New York, NY, USA, 126–131. https://doi.org/10.1145/2839509.2844584

[2] Brett A. Becker, Kyle Goslin, and Graham Glanville. 2018. The Effects of Enhanced Compiler Error Messages on a Syntax Error Debugging Test. In *Proceedings of the 49th ACM Technical Symposium on Computer Science Education (SIGCSE '18)*. ACM, New York, NY, USA, 640–645. https://doi.org/10.1145/3159450.3159461

[3] Brett A. Becker, Cormac Murray, Tianyi Tao, Changheng Song, Robert McCartney, and Kate Sanders. 2018. Fix the First, Ignore the Rest: Dealing with Multiple Compiler Error Messages. In *Proceedings of the 49th ACM Technical Symposium on Computer Science Education (SIGCSE '18)*. ACM, New York, NY, USA, 634–639. https://doi.org/10.1145/3159450.3159453

[4] Brett A. Becker and Keith Quille. 2019. 50 Years of CS1 at SIGCSE: A Review of the Evolution of Introductory Programming Education Research. In *Proceedings of the 50th ACM Technical Symposium on Computer Science Education (SIGCSE '19)*. ACM, New York, NY, USA, 338–344. https://doi.org/10.1145/3287324.3287432

[5] Benedict du Boulay and Ian Matthew. 1984. Fatal error in pass zero: How not to confuse novices. *Behaviour & Information Technology* 3, 2 (1984), 109–118.

[6] PJ Brown. 1983. Error messages: the neglected area of the man/machine interface. *Commun. ACM* 26, 4 (1983), 246–249.

[7] Paul Denny, Andrew Luxton-Reilly, and Dave Carpenter. 2014. Enhancing Syntax Error Messages Appears Ineffectual. In *Proceedings of the 2014 Conference on Innovation & Technology in Computer Science Education (ITiCSE '14)*. ACM, New York, NY, USA, 273–278. https://doi.org/10.1145/2591708.2591748

[8] Paul Denny, Andrew Luxton-Reilly, and Ewan Tempero. 2012. All Syntax Errors Are Not Equal. In *Proceedings of the 17th ACM Annual Conference on Innovation and Technology in Computer Science Education (ITiCSE '12)*. ACM, New York, NY, USA, 75–80. https://doi.org/10.1145/2325296.2325318

[9] Andrew Luxton-Reilly, Brett A. Becker, Yingjun Cao, Roger McDermott, Claudio Mirolo, Andreas Mühling, Andrew Petersen, Kate Sanders, Simon, and Jacqueline Whalley. 2017. Developing Assessments to Determine Mastery of Programming Fundamentals. In *Proceedings of the 2017 ACM Conference on Innovation and Technology in Computer Science Education (ITiCSE '17)*. ACM, New York, NY, USA, 388–388. https://doi.org/10.1145/3059009.3081327

[10] Andrew Luxton-Reilly, Simon, Ibrahim Albluwi, Brett A. Becker, Michail Giannakos, Amruth N. Kumar, Linda Ott, James Paterson, Michael James Scott, Judy Sheard, and Claudia Szabo. 2018. Introductory Programming: A Systematic Literature Review. In *Proceedings Companion of the 23rd Annual ACM Conference on Innovation and Technology in Computer Science Education (ITiCSE 2018 Companion)*. ACM, New York, NY, USA, 55–106. https://doi.org/10.1145/3293881.3295779

[11] Raymond S. Pettit, John Homer, and Roger Gee. 2017. Do Enhanced Compiler Error Messages Help Students?: Results Inconclusive.. In *Proceedings of the 2017 ACM SIGCSE Technical Symposium on Computer Science Education (SIGCSE '17)*. ACM, New York, NY, USA, 465–470. https://doi.org/10.1145/3017680.3017768

[12] James Prather, Raymond Pettit, Kayla Holcomb McMurry, Alani Peters, John Homer, Nevan Simone, and Maxine Cohen. 2017. On Novices' Interaction with Compiler Error Messages: A Human Factors Approach. In *Proceedings of the 2017 ACM Conference on International Computing Education Research (ICER '17)*. ACM, New York, NY, USA, 74–82. https://doi.org/10.1145/3105726.3106169

[13] Andreas Stefik, Bonita Sharif, Brad Myers, Stefan Hanenberg, et al. 2018. Evidence About Programmers for Programming Language Design (Dagstuhl Seminar 18061). Schloss Dagstuhl-Leibniz-Zentrum fuer Informatik.

[14] V. Javier Traver. 2010. On Compiler Error Messages: What They Say and What They Mean. *Adv. in Hum.-Comp. Int.* 2010, Article 3 (Jan. 2010), 26 pages. https://doi.org/10.1155/2010/602570

Toward Developing a Cloud Computing Model Curriculum

D. Cenk Erdil*
School of Computer Science & Engineering
Sacred Heart University
Fairfield, CT, USA
erdild@sacredheart.edu

Laurie White*
Google
Washington, USA
lauriewhite@google.com

Derek Foster*
School of Computer Science
University of Lincoln
Lincoln, UK
defoster@lincoln.ac.uk

Joshua Adams
Donald R. Tapia College of Business, CS Department
Saint Leo University
Saint Leo, Florida, USA
joshua.adams03@saintleo.edu

Amadeo Jose Arguelles Cruz
Instituto Politecnico Nacional
Mexico
jamadeo@cic.ipn.mx

Brian Hainey
Glasgow Caledonian University
Glasgow, Scotland, UK
b.hainey@gcu.ac.uk

Harvey Hyman
College of Business, ISDS Department
University of South Florida
Tampa, Florida, USA
hhyman@usf.edu

Gareth Lewis
Falmouth University
Falmouth, England, UK
gareth.lewis@falmouth.ac.uk

Sajid Nazir
Glasgow Caledonian University
Glasgow, Scotland, UK
sajid.nazir@gcu.ac.uk

Manh Van Nguyen
Donald R. Tapia College of Business, CS Department
Saint Leo University
Saint Leo, Florida, USA
van.nguyen@saintleo.edu

Majd Sakr
School of Computer Science, Computer Science Department
Carnegie Mellon University
Pittsburgh, PA, USA
msakr@cs.cmu.edu

Lee Stott
Microsoft
London, UK
leestott@microsoft.com

ABSTRACT

Cloud Computing is a rapidly evolving field that is triggering a wave of innovations in various domains such as machine learning and artificial intelligence. Cloud skills are becoming essential for any technology-related profession. Furthermore, the accelerated adoption of cloud technologies by industry is increasing the demand for cloud-trained professionals. Thus, higher education institutions are offering training opportunities and programs in cloud computing, however, the lack of well-rounded and high-quality curricular materials continues to be a challenge for educators.

A 2018 Working Group (WG) created a report that –among other artifacts– described fourteen Knowledge Areas (KAs), with numerous Learning Objectives (LOs) for each KA, to teach cloud concepts. Expanding on that work, this WG will focus on providing a collection of resources that would eventually constitute a model cloud curriculum.

By relying on two particular surveys: one that looks at the existing curricular offerings, and another one that maps knowledge areas to job titles in cloud computing, we plan to provide a dynamic and configurable curricular exemplars repository for the cloud community-at-large, following the popularity of hands-on, project-based learning methodologies as our primary focus.

*Working Group Leader

ITiCSE '19, July 15–17, 2019, Aberdeen, Scotland, UK

ACM ISBN 978-1-4503-6301-3/19/07.
https://doi.org/10.1145/3304221.3325536

CCS CONCEPTS

• **Applied computing** → **Education**; • **Computer systems organization** → *Cloud computing*;

KEYWORDS

Cloud computing, education, computer science, curriculum development, project-based learning

ACM Reference Format:
D. Cenk Erdil, Laurie White, Derek Foster, Joshua Adams, Amadeo Jose Arguelles Cruz, Brian Hainey, Harvey Hyman, Gareth Lewis, Sajid Nazir, Manh Van Nguyen, Majd Sakr, and Lee Stott. 2019. Toward Developing a Cloud Computing Model Curriculum. In *Innovation and Technology in Computer Science Education (ITiCSE '19), July 15–17, 2019, Aberdeen, Scotland, UK.* ACM, New York, NY, USA, 2 pages. https://doi.org/10.1145/3304221.3325536

1 WORKING GROUP OBJECTIVES

To help create a better response to the needs of the cloud education community, following on our model from previous WG [2], we will design relevant survey instruments and reach out to the community, seeking their feedback. Based on the results of these surveys, we will prioritize subsequent tasks for each of the objectives of our working group, and provide practical solutions. In particular, we will focus on the following.

1.1 Survey Existing Curricular Resources

We will survey existing curricular resources to find course exemplars using the KAs, much as is done in Appendix C of [3]. These resources will allow the community to understand what is out there, and will provide a state-of-the-art view of existing cloud curricula. We will systematically categorize this content based on multiple different factors of potential importance for educators, such as vendors, operating system platforms, programming languages, datasets, storage requirements, and so on.

To ensure covering a larger footprint in administering the surveys, we will utilize our existing relationships with different constituents of cloud community-at-large, such as interest groups in professional organizations, vendor-specific groups and communications lists, as well as general-purpose announcements lists of industry and professional organizations.

1.2 Provide a List of Curricular Exemplars

This WG's primary objective is to enable an educator to teach relevant KAs in their content. To achieve this objective, we plan to compose a list of existing high-quality curricular resources as exemplars, so that educators can adopt them based on their needs, plug-and-play style. Based on survey results, we will group resources into subcategories, for each KA, while focusing on underlying LOs, to allow educators to adopt or implement certain modules of interest. For each module, relevant lesson plans, hands-on exercises, and (when applicable) pointers to datasets will be provided.

This repository will be designed to be maintained by the cloud community in a straightforward fashion, so any community member interested in providing additional content, or make updates to existing content can do so, with minimal administrative overhead. To achieve this goal, we plan to use an accessible, easy to use version control system, such as GitHub, with contemporary web-based browsing interface, as well as functional APIs for directly interacting with the content.

1.3 A Mapping of Knowledge Areas to Job Titles

In addition to the curricular content, we will also survey the current job market, and create a mapping of KAs to cloud job titles. Primary reason for surveying the current job market is to inform educators about the need for particular cloud-skills and help them make better informed decisions on how to adopt cloud modules for particular courses they design.

This mapping of KAs to job titles will also help students understand the importance of cloud-related skills in relevant fields such as cybersecurity (cloud security), data analytics, machine learning, and artificial intelligence.

2 SUMMARY

We envision this work will ultimately provide a framework similar to those done for (i) Cybersecurity Education in the NICE Cybersecurity Workforce Framework [4], (ii) Parallel and Distributed Computing in NSF/IEEE-TCPP Curriculum Initiative on Parallel and Distributed Computing-Core Topics for Undergraduates [6], or (iii) CSinParallel, Parallel Computing in the Computer Science Curriculum [1].

We will also implement a community website for hands-on modules that can be easily integrated into curricula, together with a repository of assignments following the recent nifty/peachy assignments model [5, 6]; both of which will be made available to the cloud community-at-large.

REFERENCES

[1] Richard Brown, Libby Shoop, and Joel Adams. 2016. CSinParallel: Parallel Computing in the Computer Science Curriculum. https://csinparallel.org.

[2] Derek Foster, Laurie White, Joshua Adams, D. Cenk Erdil, Harvey Hyman, Stan Kurkovsky, Majd Sakr, and Lee Stott. 2018. Cloud computing: developing contemporary computer science curriculum for a cloud-first future. In *Proceedings Companion of the 23rd Annual ACM Conference on Innovation and Technology in Computer Science Education, ITiCSE 2018, Larnaca, Cyprus, July 02-04, 2018.* 130–147. https://doi.org/10.1145/3293881.3295781

[3] Association for Computing Machinery (ACM) Joint Task Force on Computing Curricula and IEEE Computer Society. 2013. *Computer Science Curricula 2013: Curriculum Guidelines for Undergraduate Degree Programs in Computer Science.* ACM, New York, NY, USA. 999133.

[4] William Newhouse, Stephanie Keith, Benjamin Scribner, and Greg Witte. August 2017. National Initiative for Cybersecurity Education (NICE), Cybersecurity Workforce Framework. https://doi.org/10.6028/NIST.SP.800-181

[5] Nick Parlante, Julie Zelenski, Baker Franke, Arvind Bhusnurmath, Karen Her, Kristen Gee, Eric Manley, Timothy Urness, Marvin Zhang, Brian Hou, John DeNero, Josh Hug, and Kevin Wayne. 2016. Nifty Assignments. In *Proceedings of the 47th ACM Technical Symposium on Computing Science Education (SIGCSE'16). ACM, New York, NY, USA.* 588–589. https://doi.org/10.1145/2839509.2844678

[6] Sushil K. Prasad, Almadena Chtchelkanova, Frank Dehne, Mohamed Gouda, Joseph Jaja, Krishna Kant, Anita La Salle, Richard LeBlanc, Andrew Lumsdaine, David Padua, Manish Parashar, Viktor Prasanna, Yves Robert, Arnold Rosenberg, Sartaj Sahni, Behrooz Shirazi, Alan Sussman, Chip Weems, and Jie Wu. 2012. NSF/IEEE-TCPP Curriculum Initiative on Parallel and Distributed Computing - Core Topics for Undergraduates, Version I. http://www.cs.gsu.edu/~tcpp/curriculum.

An International Benchmark Study of K-12 Computer Science Education in Schools

Katrina Falkner*
School of Computer Science
The University of Adelaide
Adelaide, South Australia, Australia
katrina.falkner@adelaide.edu.au

Sue Sentance*
Raspberry Pi Foundation
Cambridge, England, UK
sue@raspberrypi.org

Rebecca Vivian*
School of Computer Science
The University of Adelaide
Adelaide, South Australia, Australia
rebecca.vivian@adelaide.edu.au

Sarah Barksdale
Department of Curriculum and Instruction
University of Minnesota
Minneapolis, Minnesota, USA
barks016@umn.edu

Leonard Busuttil
Department of Technology and Entrepreneurship Education
University of Malta
Msida, Malta
leonard.busuttil@um.edu.mt

Elizabeth Cole
School of Computer Science
University of Glasgow
Glasgow, UK
e.cole.2@research.gla.ac.uk

Christine Liebe
Lotus Education Institute
Parker, Colorado, USA
clynnliebe@gmail.com

Francesco Maiorana
Department of Education
University of Catania
Catania, Italy
fmaioran@gmail.com

Monica M. McGill
Faculty of Computer Science
Knox College
Galesburg, Illinois , USA
mmmcgill@knox.edu

Keith Quille
Department of Computing
Technological University Dublin
Tallaght, Dublin, Ireland
Keith.Quille@it-tallaght.ie

ABSTRACT

There has been a growing interest and increase in work shared about national K-12 Computer Science Education (CSED) curriculum and implementation efforts around the world. Much of this work focuses on curriculum analysis, country reports, experience reports and case studies.

The K-12 CSED community would benefit from an international strategic effort to compare, contrast and monitor K-12 CSED over time, across multiple countries and regions, to understand pedagogy, practice, resources and experiences from the perspective of teachers working in classrooms. Furthermore, there is a need for validated and robust instruments that can support comparable investigations into the current state of K-12 CSED in schools around the world.

Through a collaborative effort, this Working Group will develop a validated teacher survey instrument and collect data about CSED implementation and practice in K-12 classrooms. The authors will pilot the survey with K-12 teacher cohorts and analyse, compare and contrast survey findings across countries.

*Co-Leader

ITiCSE '19, July 15–17, 2019, Aberdeen, Scotland Uk

ACM ISBN 978-1-4503-6301-3/19/07.
https://doi.org/10.1145/3304221.3325535

CCS CONCEPTS

• **Social and professional topics → Computing education**; *K-12 education*; *Adult education*;

KEYWORDS

ITiCSE Working Group, K-12, Computer Science Education, Informatics Education, Schools, Survey

ACM Reference Format:

Katrina Falkner, Sue Sentance*, Rebecca Vivian*, Sarah Barksdale, Leonard Busuttil, Elizabeth Cole, Christine Liebe, Francesco Maiorana, Monica M. McGill, and Keith Quille. 2019. An International Benchmark Study of K-12 Computer Science Education in Schools. In *Innovation and Technology in Computer Science Education (ITiCSE '19), July 15–17, 2019, Aberdeen, Scotland Uk.* ACM, New York, NY, USA, 2 pages. https://doi.org/10.1145/3304221.3325535

1 RELATED WORK

A number of country and regional reports have been produced, detailing K-12 CSED curriculum and initiatives across Europe [1, 7] and the UK [15, 16]. The International Conference on Informatics in Schools (ISSEP) have also welcomed country reports, resulting in publications about the state of K-12 CSED in the Unites States (US)

[8], Wales [12] and Poland [14], among others. The ACM Transactions on Computing Education (TOCE) dedicated two volumes for a special issue that covered a range of countries as case studies in K-12 CSED (see Vol. 14, no. 2, 2014) [9] and increasingly researchers have published works about their country curricula and/or initiatives, including in France [5], the Netherlands [2], Australia [6] and England [4], to name a few. Researchers have also performed comprehensive curriculum analysis across countries and resources to identify the emergence of common K-12 CSED topics and concepts to inform future curriculum developments and research [3, 17].

Related to this Working Group topic, in 2011 a Group [11] undertook the process of collecting and evaluating research findings about secondary CSED from different countries, and in the process developed a category system (Darmstadt Model) to support future research activities and comparison of results across regional and national boundaries. Expanding this work, a Working Group applied the Darmstadt Model to analyse, compare and extract insights from the articles published within two K-12 CSED special issues for TOCE [10]. This work sought to understand CSED topics taught in schools, goals and competencies, programming languages and tools adopted, assessment practices and teacher training, however, the authors acknowledged that a limitation of the study was that it was restricted to the analysis of selected journal publications.

In 2013, a Working Group formed to investigate trends of CS as a subject in schools by inviting CSED and teaching professionals worldwide to complete an online questionnaire about the current state of K-12 CSED in their country [13]. Experts from 22 countries responded, addressing CSED topics and goals covered across K-12 as well as teaching methods, however, a limitation being that results were based on a small group of experts.

Prior work has set a strong foundation for understanding the state of K-12 CSED curriculum and implementation efforts, however, there is an opportunity to further expand this work to focus on what K-12 teachers are doing in classrooms. There is also a need to develop instruments that are robust and reliable for use in longitudinal, multinational studies for comparisons across countries.

2 OBJECTIVES

The broad objectives of the Working Group are:

- To build an international research collaboration and strategy for investigating K-12 CSED in schools.
- To initiate a scalable, collective effort for a deeper investigation into what is happening in schools, based on the experiences of educators in classrooms.
- To develop an open source teacher survey instrument that can be implemented across countries.

This Working Group will build on prior work to a develop a validated instrument for surveying K-12 teachers about their experiences and approaches to CSED implementation in the classroom, including demographics, self-efficacy, teaching methods, experiences, use of resources and curriculum topics implemented.

The Group will review and draw on earlier work to guide the development of a validated and reliable instrument that can transcend boundaries and be used for consistent, ongoing data collection. The authors will pilot the survey with K-12 teacher cohorts in their locations and the group will collectively analyse, compare and contrast the survey findings. The report will describe the survey instrument and present the survey findings. The group will make the survey instrument available as open-source.

REFERENCES

[1] Anja Balanskat and Katja Engelhardt. 2014. *Computing our future Computer programming and coding - Priorities, school curricula and initiatives across Europe.* Technical Report. https://doi.org/10.1111/j.1465-7295.200

[2] Erik Barendsen, NataÅąa Grgurina, and Jos Tolboom. 2016. A new informatics curriculum for secondary education in The Netherlands. In *Lecture Notes in Computer Science (including subseries Lecture Notes in Artificial Intelligence and Lecture Notes in Bioinformatics).* https://doi.org/10.1007/978-3-319-46747-4{_}9

[3] Erik Barendsen, Linda Mannila, Barbara Demo, NataÅąa Grgurina, Cruz Izu, Claudio Mirolo, Sue Sentance, Amber Settle, and GabrielÄŪ Stupurienė. 2015. Concepts in K-9 Computer Science Education. In *Proceedings of the 2015 ITiCSE on Working Group Reports - ITICSE-WGR '15.* https://doi.org/10.1145/2858796.2858800

[4] N Brown, M Kölling, T Crick, S Peyton Jones, S Humphreys, and S Sentance. 2013. Bringing computer science back into schools: lessons from the UK. In *44th ACM technical symposium on Computer Science education.* ACM, Denver, Colorado, USA, 269–274.

[5] Vanea Chiprianov and Laurent Gallon. 2016. Introducing Computational Thinking to K-5 in a French Context. In *Proceedings of the 2016 ACM Conference on Innovation and Technology in Computer Science Education - ITiCSE '16.* https://doi.org/10.1145/2899415.2899439

[6] Katrina Falkner and Rebecca Vivian. 2015. A review of Computer Science resources for learning and teaching with K-12 computing curricula: an Australian case study. *Computer Science Education* 25, 4 (2015), 390–429. https://doi.org/10.1080/08993408.2016.1140410

[7] W Gander, A Petit, G Berry, B Demo, J Vahrenhold, A McGettrick, R Boyle, M Drechsler, A Mendelson, C Stephenson, C Ghezzi, and B Meyer. 2013. *Informatics Education: Europe Cannot Afford to Miss the Boat.* Technical Report. Association for Computing Machinery &, Joint Informatics Europe ACM Europe Working Group on Informatics Education, New York. 1–21 pages.

[8] Hai Hong, Jennifer Wang, and Sepehr Hejazi Moghadam. 2016. K-12 computer science education across the U.S.. In *Lecture Notes in Computer Science (including subseries Lecture Notes in Artificial Intelligence and Lecture Notes in Bioinformatics).* https://doi.org/10.1007/978-3-319-46747-4{_}12

[9] Peter Hubwieser, Michal Armoni, and Michail N. Giannakos. 2015. How to Implement Rigorous Computer Science Education in K-12 Schools? Some Answers and Many Questions. *ACM Transactions on Computing Education* (2015). https://doi.org/10.1145/2729983

[10] Peter Hubwieser, Michail N. Giannakos, Marc Berges, Torsten Brinda, Ira Diethelm, Johannes Magenheim, Yogendra Pal, Jana Jackova, and Egle Jasute. 2015. A Global Snapshot of Computer Science Education in K-12 Schools. In *ITiCSE Working Group Reports.* ACM, Vilnius, Lithuani, 65–83. https://doi.org/10.1145/2858796.2858799

[11] Peter Hubwieser, Sigrid Schubert, Michal Armoni, Torsten Brinda, Valentina Dagiene, Ira Diethelm, Michail N. Giannakos, Maria Knobelsdorf, Johannes Magenheim, and Roland Mittermeir. 2011. Computer science/informatics in secondary education. In *Proceedings of the 16th annual conference reports on Innovation and technology in computer science education - working group reports - ITiCSE-WGR '11.* https://doi.org/10.1145/2078856.2078859

[12] F. Moller and T. Crick. 2016. A National Engagement Model for Developing Computer Science Education in Wales. In *The 9th International Conference on Informatics in Schools,.* Munster, Germany, 1–13.

[13] Carsten Schulte, Malte Hornung, Sue Sentance, Valentina Dagiene, Tatjana Jevsikova, Neena Thota, Anna Eckerdal, and Anne-Kathrin Peters. 2012. Computer science at school/CS teacher education - Koli working-group report on CS at school. In *International Conference on Computing Education Research, Koli Calling 2012.* https://doi.org/10.1145/2401796.2401800

[14] Maciej M. Sysło and Anna Beata Kwiatkowska. 2015. Introducing a new computer science curriculum for all school levels in Poland. In *Lecture Notes in Computer Science (including subseries Lecture Notes in Artificial Intelligence and Lecture Notes in Bioinformatics).* https://doi.org/10.1007/978-3-319-25396-1{_}13

[15] The Royal Society. 2012. *Shut down or restart? The way forward for computing in UK schools.* Technical Report. London. https://royalsociety.org/~/media/education/computing-in-schools/2012-01-12-computing-in-schools.pdf

[16] The Royal Society. 2017. *After the reboot: Computing education in UK schools.* Technical Report. The Royal Society, London, United Kingdom. 1–116 pages. royalsociety.org/computing-education

[17] Mary Webb, Niki Davis, Tim Bell, Yaacov J Katz, Nicholas Reynolds, Dianne P Chambers, and Maciej M Sysło. 2017. Computer science in K-12 school curricula of the 2lst century: Why, what and when? *Education and Information Technologies* 22, 2 (3 2017), 445–468. https://doi.org/10.1007/s10639-016-9493-x

Towards an Ability to Direct College Students to an Appropriately Paced Introductory Computer Science Course

James Heliotis
jeh@cs.rit.edu
Rochester Institute of Technology

Leo C. Ureel II
ureel@mtu.edu
Michigan Technological University

Mireilla Bikanga Ada
Mireilla.BikangaAda@glasgow.ac.uk
University of Glasgow

Mohsen Dorodchi
Mohsen.Dorodchi@uncc.edu
University of North Carolina

Victoria Eisele
Victoria.eisele@frontrange.edu
Front Range Community College

Megan E. Lutz
mlutz@uga.edu
University of Georgia

Ethel Tshukudu
2371984T@student.gla.ac.uk
University of Glasgow

ABSTRACT

We propose a working group to investigate methods of proper placement of university entrance-level students into introductory computer science courses. The main issues are the following.

(1) The ability to predict skill in the absence of prior experience
(2) The value of programming language neutrality in an assessment instrument
(3) Stigma and other perception issues associated with students' performance, especially among groups underrepresented in computer science
(4) The impact or potential impact on underrepresented populations (minorities, those with lower socioeconomic status)
(5) The outcomes/satisfaction/retention metrics in the major of the paced/tracked students compared to those in one-size-fits-all introductory classes

We perceive the current advanced placement exams offered by organizations such as The College Board to be inadequate for our purposes because they are language specific and they test the results of taking a standardized course. Their exams are not intended to determine whether or not a student who has not been exposed to computing or who has been exposed to a different computing paradigm or language would be able to grasp completely new concepts quickly.

Members of the group will collect evidence-based research on freshman college student readiness, the utility of so-called "placement" and "entrance" exams, and actual exams employed by universities.

Admission to the group has been determined largely by the documented ability of the applicant to collect such information and/or to be able to contribute to the anticipated intense debates that will be part of the work.

ITiCSE '19, July 15–17, 2019, Aberdeen, Scotland Uk

ACM ISBN 978-1-4503-6301-3/19/07.
https://doi.org/10.1145/3304221.3325538

CCS CONCEPTS

• **Social and professional topics → Computer science education; CS1; Student assessment.**

KEYWORDS

Assessment, placement, introductory courses

ACM Reference Format:
James Heliotis, Leo C. Ureel II, Mireilla Bikanga Ada, Mohsen Dorodchi, Victoria Eisele, Megan E. Lutz, and Ethel Tshukudu. 2019. Towards an Ability to Direct College Students to an Appropriately Paced Introductory Computer Science Course. In *Innovation and Technology in Computer Science Education (ITiCSE '19), July 15–17, 2019, Aberdeen, Scotland Uk.* ACM, New York, NY, USA, 2 pages. https://doi.org/10.1145/3304221.3325538

1 INTRODUCTION

Worldwide, computer science (CS) as a discipline is in a transition period as far as education is concerned. In adult life, in personal pursuits, but especially in careers, some level of familiarity with computational thinking and the ability to apply computer-based methods to analytical problems is becoming very widespread. But in the educational sphere, computer science and its related disciplines are still not universally considered as a pillar of educational systems, as are the humanities, the arts, mathematics, and the natural sciences.

As a result, there are still many students who have not been exposed to computing by the time they finish their secondary education. This causes two problems. The first is that unfamiliarity makes it difficult for an individual to make an experience-informed decision on a career path. The second problem is that, unlike in most other fields, the student and the higher educational institution have no data with which an initial course plan can be constructed.

This working group will be mostly concerned with the second problem. While some find evidence to support the notion that different students may need different forms of instruction [1][4][5], it should be noted that there is an opposing claim, also backed by evidence, that there is no need to start students of different abilities in different courses; that there are ways to design and deliver CS course material in such a way as to neutralize those differences and help everyone succeed. [2] [3] But given the pace at which some institutions prefer that their introductory CS courses proceed, and that placement exam results, offered by organizations such as The College Board and by individual institutions, are a completely normal part of course planning, this working group will be looking for an alternative placement approach for CS that also uses assessment.

2 ACTIVITIES AND EXPECTATIONS

Our working group approach is organized around four activities.

2.1 Capture a variety of perspectives on placement issues in introductory CS.

Participants will develop position papers describing their own perspectives of incoming student readiness, factors that affect student performance, and approaches to placement into introductory computer science courses. These papers will be synthesized by the workshop organizers prior to the working group meeting.

2.2 Collect evidence-based research on freshman college student readiness.

Participants will all be asked to contribute to the body of knowledge with which the group will work. Contributions should be in the form of published papers about well-run studies, plus other forms of preliminary data such as grades collected as various approaches were tried. The data can come from the participants' own work or from literature searches they perform. Publications contributed may very well include contrary positions, wherein researchers have recommended against assessment and any resulting classification of an incoming student cohort.

We perceive the current advanced placement exams offered by organizations such as The College Board to be inadequate for our purposes because they are either language specific, or intended to introduce computing in a general sense, and they test the results of taking a standardized course. Their exams are not intended to determine whether or not a student who has not been exposed to computing or has been exposed to a different computing paradigm or language would be able to grasp completely new concepts quickly. Furthermore, the AP CS Principles test is only two years old and too new for us to adequately predict how students will perform at the college level.

2.3 Classify

During the working group meeting, participants will attempt to categorize approaches along different dimensions. Although these dimensions will be firmed up later, here are some examples.

- Assessment instrument content: is it a previous experience questionnaire, a test of certain mathematical skills, the understanding of algorithms in pseudo code, or problems expressed in a programming language designed for the test?
- Demographics: is there anything about the student population involved that should be noted?
- Delivery method: distance, in-person handwritten, or in-person but still on-line and perhaps auto-graded? And when? (well before / before / after arrival on campus)
- Strength of results: how convincing are the results in terms of conventional experimental standards and statistical analysis?

2.4 Construct a reference model that relates the various approaches along various dimensions; conclusions if possible.

A reference model will be developed during the working group meeting that will attempt to collect information from the classification exercise into a matrix-like form that will help others who are considering assessment for this purpose. In addition, we will have separate discussions focusing on the studies which discuss the relationship of proper placements with more successful students as far as time to graduation, readiness for industry, and overall degree satisfaction by students.

2.5 Report

Besides a concluding single report, the goal will be to create an easily navigable web site with the work products of the above activities that will also enable for post-conference work.

3 GROUP LEADERS

James Heliotis – James E. Heliotis is a professor in the Computer Science Department at Rochester Institute of Technology where he has taught for over 35 years. Dr. Heliotis has been a steady instructor and frequent coordinator of the first-year courses for the approximately 500 CS, SE, and other majors who take the courses each year. In this capacity he has been involved in several internally and externally funded projects to improve and re-invent the introductory CS curriculum over the years.

Leo Ureel – Leo C. Ureel II is a lecturer in Computer Science at Michigan Technological University. Mr. Ureel teaches CS1 and CS2 courses, primarily to first year students. In these courses, he works to broaden the students' views of computing, ground them in a programming language, and teach them problem solving skills.

ACKNOWLEDGMENTS

This work is partly supported by the National Science Foundation under Grant No. 1820862. Mohsen Dorodchi is the corresponding author.

REFERENCES

[1] Glen Archer, Leonard Bohmann, Allison Carter, Christopher Cischke, Linda M Ott, and Leo Ureel. 2016. Understanding similarities and differences in students across first-year computing majors. In *Frontiers in Education Conference (FIE), 2016 IEEE*. IEEE, 1–8.

[2] Ivona Bezakova, James Heliotis, and Sean Strout. 2014. On the efficacy of board game strategy development as a first-year CS project. In *Proceedings of the 45th ACM technical symposium on Computer science education*. ACM, Atlanta, GA, USA, 283–288.

[3] Michael E Caspersen, Kasper Dalgaard Larsen, and Jens Bennedsen. 2007. Mental models and programming aptitude. *ACM SIGCSE Bulletin* 39, 3 (2007), 206–210.

[4] Lisa L Lacher, Albert Jiang, Yu Zhang, and Mark C Lewis. 2017. Aptitude and previous experience in cs1 classes. In *Proceedings of the International Conference on Frontiers in Education: Computer Science and Computer Engineering (FECS)*. The Steering Committee of The World Congress in Computer Science, Computer Engineering and Applied Computing (WorldComp), 87–95.

[5] Linda Ott, Briana Bettin, and Leo Ureel. 2018. The impact of placement in introductory computer science courses on student persistence in a computing major. In *Proceedings of the 23rd Annual ACM Conference on Innovation and Technology in Computer Science Education*. ACM, 296–301.

Program Comprehension: Identifying Learning Trajectories for Novice Programmers

Cruz Izu
The University of Adelaide
Adelaide, Australia
cruz.izu@adelaide.edu.au

Carsten Schulte
Paderborn University
Paderborn, Germany
carsten.schulte@uni-paderborn.de

Ashish Aggarwal
University of Florida
Florida, USA
ashishjuit@ufl.edu

Quintin Cutts
University of Glasgow
Glasgow, UK
quintin.cutts@glasgow.ac.uk

Rodrigo Duran
Aalto University
Helsinki, Finland
rodrigo.duran@aalto.fi

Mirela Gutica
British Columbia Institute of Technology
Burnaby, Canada
mirela_gutica@bcit.ca

Birte Heinemann
Paderborn University
Paderborn, Germany
birte.heinemann@uni-paderborn.de

Eileen Kraemer
Clemson University
Clemson, USA
etkraem@clemson.edu

Violetta Lonati
University of Milan
Milan, Italy
lonati@di.unimi.it

Claudio Mirolo
University of Udine
Udine, Italy
claudio.mirolo@uniud.it

Renske Weeda
Radboud University
Nijmegen, Netherlands
renske.smetsers@science.ru.nl

ABSTRACT

This working group asserts that Program Comprehension (PC) plays a critical part in the writing process. For example, this abstract is written from a basic draft that we have edited and revised until it clearly presents our idea. Similarly, a program is written in an incremental manner, with each step being tested, debugged and extended until the program achieves its goal.

Novice programmers should develop their program comprehension as they learn to code, so that they are able to read and reason about code while they are writing it. To foster such competencies our group has identified two main goals: (1) to collect and define learning activities that explicitly cover key components of program comprehension and (2) to define possible learning trajectories that will guide teachers using those learning activities in their CS0/CS1 or K-12 courses.

We plan to achieve these goals as follows:

Step 1 – Review the current state of research and development by analyzing literature on classroom activities that improve program comprehension.

Step 2 – Concurrently, survey lecturers at various institutions on their use of workshop activities to foster PC.

Step 3 – Use the outputs from both activities to define and conceptualize what is meant by PC in the context of novice programmers.

Step 4 – Catalog learning activities with regard to their prerequisites, intended learning outcomes and additional special characteristics.

Step 5 – Catalog learning activities with regard to their prerequisites, intended learning outcomes and additional special characteristics.

Step 6 – Develop a map of learning activities and thereby also models of probable learning trajectories.

KEYWORDS

program comprehension; learning trajectories; CS1;

ACM Reference Format:
Cruz Izu, Carsten Schulte, Ashish Aggarwal, Quintin Cutts, Rodrigo Duran, Mirela Gutica, Birte Heinemann, Eileen Kraemer, Violetta Lonati, Claudio Mirolo, and Renske Weeda. 2019. Program Comprehension: Identifying Learning Trajectories for Novice Programmers. In *Innovation and Technology in Computer Science Education (ITiCSE '19), July 15–17, 2019, Aberdeen, Scotland UK.* ACM, New York, NY, USA, 2 pages. https://doi.org/10.1145/3304221.3325531

ACM ISBN 978-1-4503-6301-3/19/07...$15.00
https://doi.org/10.1145/3304221.3325531

Related Work

Learning to program is not just about mastering the syntax and semantics of each construct of a programming language. From the outset, Soloway identified two key issues for learning to program: the ability to identify *chunks* (he renamed them plans) and the understanding of the way "the computer turns a static program written on a piece of paper into a dynamic entity that exists over time. In this dynamic representation, notions such as the causal relationship between the statements become very important and must be used in describing how a program works"[13, p. 854]. The latter issue is usually referred to in the literature as the notional machine [2].

Comprehension is usually conceptualized as a process in which an individual constructs his or her own mental representation of the program. Most novice programmer's misconceptions and logical errors are caused by poor understanding of that notional machine. Multiple models of program comprehension have been proposed in the literature [8, 16]. The 2010 WG report [11] compared and contrasted the way in which those models conceptualize program comprehension. Although this comparison was the main focus of the report, it also provided some insights into learning concepts and obstacles, effective learning tasks and teaching methods. Thus, this working group is picking up the baton by planning to collect and organize learning tasks that will develop program comprehension.

In the last ten years there has been a rising awareness and focus on program comprehension as part of learning to program. Assessment components have been proposed to include or target some aspects of program comprehension like reading [1], tracing [7], explaining [6], or reversing [3, 15]. Sudol et al. [14] vindicates using code comprehension questions as learning events instead of as assessment items. On a similar line, [12] selected 14 program comprehension tasks and survey practitioners to rank them in terms of perceived effectiveness in developing the novices' program comprehension.

Learning trajectories (LT) have garnered the attention of math and science educators [4], because their ability to model how the student's thinking about a specific topic evolves over time, and hence supporting (in the end) research based curriculum development. This is possible due to increased empirical knowledge about this progression - a knowledge currently lacking in computer science education. One reason is that there are seldom efforts to collect and systematize about such progressions in a domain; Rich et al [9] is an example of such approach in K-6 education.

The WG aims to extend our practical knowledge in the domain of program comprehension by collecting instructors' views of learning PC. We are therefore building on what Lobato and Walters have named the *hypothetical learning trajectory*, because the trajectory is seen through the eyes of the instructor [4, p. 84]:

> the starting point in teacher planning is the creation of conjectures regarding what students understand initially and what they may be able to learn next. Instructional tasks are selected, not only on the basis of generic task features, such as high cognitive demand or student interest, but also because of an inferred quality of being able to engender the next level of sophistication of student thinking.

The focus on how different tasks organize the thinking process of learners, and how tasks can and should be ordered to allow effective learning progressions is what distinguishes our WG from other approaches that have aimed at collecting useful examples and tasks (e.g. [10], [5]). In other words, we are not focusing on how to assess but looking at how to develop program comprehension. As mentioned before, assessment questions that target program comprehension can be extended to become learning activities. Thus, those previous collections of tasks will be analyzed to identify both tasks that require program comprehension and assessments that evaluate it.

REFERENCES

[1] Teresa Busjahn and Carsten Schulte. 2013. The Use of Code Reading in Teaching Programming. In *Proceedings of the 13th Koli Calling International Conference on Computing Education Research (Koli Calling '13)*. ACM, New York, NY, USA, 3–11. https://doi.org/10.1145/2526968.2526969

[2] Benedict du Boulay. 1986. Some Difficulties of Learning to Program. *J. of Educational Comput. Research* 2, 1 (1986), 57–73.

[3] Cruz Izu, Claudio Mirolo, and Amali Weerasinghe. 2018. Novice Programmers' Reasoning About Reversing Conditional Statements. In *Proceedings of the 49th ACM Technical Symposium on Computer Science Education (SIGCSE '18)*. ACM, New York, NY, USA, 646–651. https://doi.org/10.1145/3159450.3159499

[4] Joanne Lobato and C David Walters. 2017. *A Taxonomy of Approaches to Learning Trajectories and Progressions*. NCTM, 74–101.

[5] Andrew Luxton-Reilly, Brett A. Becker, Yingjun Cao, Roger McDermott, Claudio Mirolo, Andreas Mühling, Andrew Petersen, Kate Sanders, Simon, and Jacqueline Whalley. 2017. Developing Assessments to Determine Mastery of Programming Fundamentals. In *Proceedings of the 2017 ITiCSE Conference on Working Group Reports (ITiCSE-WGR '17)*. ACM, New York, NY, USA, 47–69. https://doi.org/10.1145/3174781.3174784

[6] Laurie Murphy, Renée McCauley, and Sue Fitzgerald. 2012. 'Explain in Plain English' Questions: Implications for Teaching. In *Proceedings of the 43rd ACM Technical Symposium on Computer Science Education (SIGCSE '12)*. ACM, New York, USA, 385–390. https://doi.org/10.1145/2157136.2157249

[7] Greg L. Nelson, Benjamin Xie, and Andrew J. Ko. 2017. Comprehension First: Evaluating a Novel Pedagogy and Tutoring System for Program Tracing in CS1. In *Proceedings of the 2017 ACM Conference on International Computing Education Research (ICER '17)*. ACM, New York, NY, USA, 2–11. https://doi.org/10.1145/3105726.3106178

[8] Nancy Pennington. 1987. Comprehension Strategies in Programming. In *Empirical Studies of Programmers: Second Workshop*, Gary M. Olson, Sylvia Sheppard, and Elliot Soloway (Eds.). Ablex Publishing Corp., Norwood, NJ, USA, 100–113.

[9] Kathryn M. Rich, Carla Strickland, T. Andrew Binkowski, Cheryl Moran, and Diana Franklin. 2017. K-8 Learning Trajectories Derived from Research Literature: Sequence, Repetition, Conditionals. In *Proceedings of the 2017 ACM Conference on International Computing Education Research (ICER '17)*. ACM, New York, NY, USA, 182–190. https://doi.org/10.1145/3105726.3106166

[10] Kate Sanders, Marzieh Ahmadzadeh, Tony Clear, Stephen H. Edwards, Mikey Goldweber, Chris Johnson, Raymond Lister, Robert McCartney, Elizabeth Patitsas, and Jaime Spacco. 2013. The Canterbury QuestionBank: Building a Repository of Multiple-choice CS1 and CS2 Questions. In *Proceedings of the ITiCSE Working Group Reports Conference on Innovation and Technology in Computer Science Education-working Group Reports (ITiCSE -WGR '13)*. ACM, New York, NY, USA, 33–52. https://doi.org/10.1145/2543882.2543885

[11] Carsten Schulte, Tony Clear, Ahmad Taherkhani, Teresa Busjahn, and James H. Paterson. 2010. An Introduction to Program Comprehension for Computer Science Educators. In *Proceedings of the 2010 ITiCSE Working Group Reports (ITiCSE-WGR '10)*. ACM, New York, NY, USA, 65–86. https://doi.org/10.1145/1971681.1971687

[12] A. Shargabi, S. A. Aljunid, M. Annamalai, S. M. Shuhidan, and A. M. Zin. 2015. Tasks that can improve novices' program comprehension. In *2015 IEEE Conference on e-Learning, e-Management and e-Services (IC3e)*. 32–37. https://doi.org/10.1109/IC3e.2015.7403482

[13] E. Soloway. 1986. Learning to Program = Learning to Construct Mechanisms and Explanations. *Commun. ACM* 29, 9 (Sept. 1986), 850–858. https://doi.org/10.1145/6592.6594

[14] Leigh Ann Sudol-DeLyser, Mark Stehlik, and Sharon Carver. 2012. Code Comprehension Problems As Learning Events. In *Proceedings of the 17th ACM Annual Conference on Innovation and Technology in Computer Science Education (ITiCSE '12)*. ACM, New York, NY, USA, 81–86. https://doi.org/10.1145/2325296.2325319

[15] Donna Teague and Raymond Lister. 2014. Programming: Reading, Writing and Reversing. In *Proceedings of the 2014 Conference on Innovation and Technology in Computer Science Education (ITiCSE '14)*. ACM, New York, USA, 285–290. https://doi.org/10.1145/2591708.2591712

[16] Susan Wiedenbeck and Vennila Ramaligan. 1999. Novice comprehension of small programs written in the procedural and object-oriented styles. *International Journal of Human-Computer Studies* 51, 1 (1999), 71 – 87. https://doi.org/10.1006/ijhc.1999.0269

1.5 Degrees of Separation: Computer Science Education in the Age of the Anthropocene

Ian Pollock*
California State University East Bay
Hayward, USA
ian.pollock@csueastbay.edu

Bedour Alshaigy*
Oxford Brookes University
Oxford, UK
b.alshaigy@brookes.ac.uk

Andrew Bradley
Oxford Brookes University
Oxford, UK
abradley@brookes.ac.uk

Birgit R. Krogstie
Norwegian University of Science and Technology
Trondheim, Norway
birgit.r.krogstie@ntnu.no

Viraj Kumar
Indian Institute of Science
Bengaluru, India
viraj@iisc.ac.in

Linda Ott
Michigan Technological University
Michigan, USA
linda@mtu.edu

Anne-Kathrin Peters
Uppsala University
Uppsala, Sweden
linda@mtu.edu

Charles Riedesel
University of Nebraska - Lincoln
Nebraska, USA
chuckr@unl.edu

Charles Wallace
Michigan Technological University
Michigan, USA
wallace@mtu.edu

ABSTRACT

Climate change is the defining environmental challenge now facing our planet. Babies born today will be 22 when global warming reaches 1.5 C, according to the latest IPCC report and forecasts. What will life be like in 2040? How do we as educators respond today, to the challenges that lie ahead for the next generation?

How do our practices evolve to take global climate change into account? How do we as educators respond when we see the impact our products have on climate change and the environment? Is it enough to relegate sustainability and climate change to a required course or can we begin to imagine sustainability as a conversation across the entire curriculum?

In this working group, we will collaboratively review the literature, and gather, assemble and compile sample syllabi, case studies, and assignments that address climate change in the context of computer science education. We will work together to think through how best to equip our students with the tools needed to adapt to a world shaped by climate change.

CCS CONCEPTS

• **Social and professional topics → Sustainability**; **Computing education**; **Model curricula**; • **Applied computing → Collaborative learning**.

KEYWORDS

anthropocene, sustainability, climate change, model curricula

*Leaders

ITiCSE '19, July 15–17, 2019, Aberdeen, Scotland Uk

ACM ISBN 978-1-4503-6301-3/19/07.
https://doi.org/10.1145/3304221.3325530

ACM Reference Format:
Ian Pollock, Bedour Alshaigy, Andrew Bradley, Birgit R. Krogstie, Viraj Kumar, Linda Ott, Anne-Kathrin Peters, Charles Riedesel, and Charles Wallace. 2019. 1.5 Degrees of Separation: Computer Science Education in the Age of the Anthropocene. In *Innovation and Technology in Computer Science Education (ITiCSE '19), July 15–17, 2019, Aberdeen, Scotland Uk.* ACM, New York, NY, USA, 2 pages. https://doi.org/10.1145/3304221.3325530

1 INTRODUCTION

Whether it is an increase in the frequency or intensity of hurricanes, rising sea levels, droughts, floods, or extreme temperatures and severe weather, the social, economic, and environmental consequences of climate change are great as the resource-stressed planet nears 9 billion inhabitants by mid-century [7].

The rapid technological advancements in software development and microchip production, coupled with cheap manufacturing costs, has contributed towards the reduction of a product's life cycle. This exploitation of a product's lifespan has manipulated consumers' purchasing practices which shifted towards buying electrical goods to follow the latest digital trends, or as a status symbol, rather than investing in a device, as is the case with the iPhone for example [2]. Others are left with no choice as constant software upgrades led to incompatibility issues that in many cases renders devices obsolete [3].

A report by the United Nations researchers [1] revealed that electronic goods, including laptops and mobile phones, are the "world's fastest growing waste problem". The majority of non recycled e-waste ends up in landfills which, if left untreated, has serious environmental and health consequences.

In recent years, there has been a growing global demand for sustainable electronics made with recyclable parts that are free from hazardous chemicals in order to reduce greenhouse effect [4]. Can innovations like Rebuild by Design[1] and Fairphone 2[2] shape the way we should think about the education of computer science

[1] http://www.rebuildbydesign.org/
[2] https://www.fairphone.com/en/

students? How do we consider blockchain as a way to better track energy use in contrast to bitcoin's ravaging appetite for power? In a world that is increasingly embedding circuits in all aspects of our lives, how does IoT evolve to address the cataclysmic changes that are coming?

2 METHODOLOGY

The IPCC 2018 report [5] has precipitated the need for a fundamental change in the conversation around sustainability. Unlike previous reports we can no longer expect that sustainable development will return us to the state of equilibrium. The implication of this new report is that no matter what we do we will be facing climate change. This climate change means that our models of responding have to begin to shift from a conversation of sustainable development to a conversation of sustainable adaptation. Similar to a previous paper on computing and sustainability [6], we seek to evaluate and recommend resources for educators.

Sustainability is a topic many educators understand to be pressing in need, yet there may be real barriers keeping these educators from incorporating these issues in their courses. According to Mann et al. (2009) they might include the limited knowledge about sustainability on the part of the faculty, the feeling that computing may not play significant role in the social and/or environmental sustainability, or the lack or poor accessibility of resources for the integration of sustainability in the computing curriculum [6]. For this working group paper we want to pursue the following strategies for an updated set of recommendations:

(1) We will examine some key pieces of literature for recommendations of how sustainability related topics might be introduced into a computer science curriculum.
(2) We will reach out to computer science education faculty via surveys and interviews to gather information with respect to sustainability and climate change in terms of: understanding of terminology, place in discipline, personal responsibility of incorporating them in the courses taught, and their institutions' position regarding climate change.
(3) We want to examine to what extent institutions of higher education are beginning to address the need for education and sustainability across all disciplines and institutional learning outcomes.
(4) Lastly, we want to see what sort of recommendations we can make of projects, and resources that would help educators address sustainability.

3 FUTURE WORK

The objective of this research is to address climate change in the context of computer science education on an international level. Members of this group are from different geographical regions (North America, Europe, and India) giving us a better understanding of experiences, concerns, and efforts in place to combat its mounting effects. We will also be targeting researchers from other countries to examine shared challenges, location-specific problems, in addition to successful efforts of incorporating climate change into the computing curriculum to determine whether the recommendations of this group are applicable globally.

4 LEADERS

Ian Pollock is an Assistant Professor at California State University, East Bay. He holds a Master of Fine Art degree in New Media Art Practice from the University of California, Berkeley, and a Bachelor in Fine Art in New Genres from the San Francisco Art Institute. Ian is involved in transdisciplinary research and collaborations into game jams, computer science and afro-futurism across traditional academic boundaries. He reviews academic and scholarly articles for SIGSCE and ITiCSE conferences.

Bedour Alshaigy is a recent doctoral graduate in Computing and Mathematical Sciences from Oxford Brookes University, UK. Her research interests include Computer Science Education and Human Computer Interaction. Bedour also holds a Postgraduate Certificate in Teaching in Higher Education and has several publication in the field; three of which are ITiCSE working group reports.

REFERENCES

[1] Cornelis P Balde, Vanessa Forti, Vanessa Gray, Ruediger Kuehr, and Paul Stegmann. 2017. *The global e-waste monitor 2017: Quantities, flows and resources.* United Nations University, International Telecommunication Union, and International Solid Waste Association.
[2] Marianne Bertrand and Emir Kamenica. 2018. *Coming apart? Cultural distances in the United States over time.* Technical Report. National Bureau of Economic Research.
[3] Brian X. Chen. 2017. A New Phone Comes Out. Yours Slows Down. A Conspiracy? No. Retrieved January 24, 2019 from https://www.nytimes.com/2017/11/15/technology/personaltech/new-iphones-slow-tech-myth.html
[4] PLATE Consortium. 2019. Product Lifetime and the Environment. Retrieved January 24, 2019 from https://www.plateconference.org/
[5] IPCC. 2018. Special Report Global Warming of 1.5 C. Retrieved January 26, 2019 from https://www.ipcc.ch/sr15/
[6] Samuel Mann, Logan Muller, Janet Davis, Claudia Roda, and Alison Young. 2009. Computing and Sustainability: Evaluating Resources for Educators. *ACM SIGCSE Bulletin* 41, 4 (2009), 144–155.
[7] University of Minnesota. 2012. Expeditions in Computing: Understanding Climate Change. A Data Driven Approach. Retrieved January 20, 2019 from http://climatechange.cs.umn.edu/highlights.php

Data Science Education: Global Perspectives and Convergence

Rajendra K. Raj*
Rochester Institute of Technology
USA
rkr@cs.rit.edu

Allen Parrish†
Mississippi State University
USA
aparrish@research.msstate.edu

John Impagliazzo†
Hofstra University
USA
john.impagliazzo@hofstra.edu

Carol J. Romanowski†
Rochester Institute of Technology
USA
cjr@cs.rit.edu

Sherif Aly Ahmed
The American University in Cairo
Egypt
sgamal@aucegypt.edu

Casey C. Bennett
DePaul University
USA
cbenne33@depaul.edu

Karen C. Davis
Miami University
USA
davisk4@miamioh.edu

Andrew McGettrick
Strathclyde University
UK
andrew.mcgettrick@strath.ac.uk

Teresa Susana Mendes Pereira
Instituto Politécnico de Viana do Castelo
Portugal
tpereira@esce.ipvc.pt

Lovisa Sundin
University of Glasgow
UK
2092502S@student.gla.ac.uk

ABSTRACT

Over the past two decades, data science or data analytics degree programs have begun to emerge, reflecting the world's demand for data specialists to make sense of the vast amounts of collected data in the sciences, engineering, business, and other domains. As degree creation has occurred mainly due to demand, ACM and other professional bodies have recently stepped in to provide curricular guidance. However, no *shared global framework* for data science as an academic discipline exists, making growth unfocused and driven by employer demands. More recently, the growth of artificial intelligence has also impacted data science programs.

This working group builds on prior efforts and participant experiences to develop a global taxonomy of approaches to data science education and expectations for graduates of data science programs to *think like data scientists*.

CCS CONCEPTS

• **Social and professional topics → Model curricula; Computing education; Computing education programs;**

*Working Group Leader
†Working Group Co-Leader

ACM ISBN 978-1-4503-6301-3/19/07.
https://doi.org/10.1145/3304221.3325533

KEYWORDS

ITiCSE working group, data science education, computing education, multidisciplinary education, global standards, accreditation.

ACM Reference Format:
Rajendra K. Raj, Allen Parrish, John Impagliazzo, Carol J. Romanowski, Sherif Aly Ahmed, Casey C. Bennett, Karen C. Davis, Andrew McGettrick, Teresa Susana Mendes Pereira, and Lovisa Sundin. 2019. Data Science Education: Global Perspectives and Convergence. In *Innovation and Technology in Computer Science Education (ITiCSE '19), July 15–17, 2019, Aberdeen, Scotland Uk.* ACM, New York, NY, USA, 2 pages. https://doi.org/10.1145/3304221.3325533

1 BACKGROUND

Degree programs in data sciences have been proliferating across the world for almost two decades. To distinguish themselves from traditional computing programs such as computer science or information systems, several of these programs emphasize the three pillars required for the field of data science: computing foundations, mathematical/statistical foundations, and finally domain expertise [2]. At the same time, principles of engineering are also crucial in defining a discipline and practice of data science. Overlaps with the field of artificial intelligence have also been observed [9].

Several US-based organizations have attempted to define the data science discipline and profession. These attempts include a workshop sponsored by the National Science Foundation [1], the Park City Math Institute data science effort [3], the National Academies of Sciences, Engineering, and Medicine report [7], and the Data Science Leadership Summit [10]. More recently, the ACM Data

Science Task Force has been working on a draft report to summarize the curricular efforts to date in this field, including an initial examination of data science competencies [2].

Beyond the US, the two-year European EDISON project (2015–17) attempted to accelerate data science as a profession [4] and identify various degree programs in the data science space [5]. Another major push in the data world came from Jim Gray's vision of data-intensive science as the fourth paradigm for 21st century science, following the first three: empiricism, theory, and computation [6].

This working group builds on earlier data science education efforts to examine global perspectives and to promote possible convergence. It plans to define expectations for graduates of data science programs to *think like data scientists* and to prepare a global framework for relating different curricular materials in this field.

2 WORKING GROUP OBJECTIVES

Building on the framework defined by Tukey [8], this working group has the following objectives:

(1) Capture a worldwide set of perspectives on data science education at the baccalaureate level.
(2) Construct a reference model to relate different approaches to data science education.
(3) Catalog existing skillsets, curricular and knowledge materials for data science.
(4) Develop and disseminate recommendations for moving forward with global curricular standards for data science.
(5) Provide specific feedback to the ACM Data Science Task Force and general feedback to CC2020.

3 WORKING GROUP MEMBERSHIP

Provided below are brief bios of the working group members.

Rajendra K. Raj, a professor of computer science at Rochester Institute of Technology, focuses his research and teaching on the nexus of data science and cybersecurity. He helped to create RIT's data science cluster within computer science in 2003. Raj's industry experience includes the development of worldwide private-cloud data infrastructures for financial applications and analytics.

Allen Parrish is associate vice president for research, and professor of computer science and engineering at Mississippi State University. Among other distinctions, he chaired ABET's Computing Accreditation Commission and serves as CSAB President. Parrish coauthored the Cybersecurity 2017 curricular report, and currently co-chairs the Computing Curricula 2020 (CC2020) project sponsored by ACM, IEEE-CS, AIS and AITP.

John Impagliazzo is professor emeritus at Hofstra University and serves on the CC2020 steering committee. His many contributions to computing include the curricular reports on computer engineering (CE2004 and CE2016) and information technology (IT2017). Impagliazzo is an IEEE Fellow, an ACM Distinguished Educator, and a CSAB Fellow.

Carol J. Romanowski is a professor of computer science at Rochester Institute of Technolog. She focuses on data science issues in critical infrastructure protection, cyberanalytics, data privacy, and knowledge management. At RIT, Romanowski helped to create the popular Big Data Analytics graduate certificate in 2013 and created the initial version of the MS Data Science degree.

Sherif Aly Ahmed is a professor of computer science and engineering at the American University in Cairo. Among other contributions, he helped to design and steer multiple academic programs including undergraduate programs in Data Science and Computer Engineering, and a graduate program in Business Analytics.

Casey C. Bennett currently is a senior data scientist at Cigna, and an adjunct professor of data science at DePaul University. He holds a PhD from Indiana University, and has been a practicing data scientist in healthcare for over 15 years.

Karen C. Davis is an associate professor in Computer Science and Software Engineering at Miami University. She focuses on data modeling and query optimization for traditional and emerging NoSQL database systems.

Andrew McGettrick, professor emeritus of computer and information sciences at The University of Strathclyde, serves on the ACM Data Science Task Force. Among other distinctions, he is the recipient of the 2017 ACM Presidential Award for his "commitment to computer science education–particularly in terms of its quality, breadth, and access–for generations of students worldwide."

Teresa Susana Mendes Pereira is adjunct professor at Instituto Politécnico de Viana do Castelo, Portugal for ICT and information security. She focuses on the use of ontologies, metadata, taxonomies and classification systems for rapid search and access.

Lovisa Sundin, a doctoral student at University of Glasgow, focuses on visual templates for acquiring common data scientific programming schemas. Interested in curricular commonalities and differences between data science, computer science and statistics, she is developing data science curriculum for high school teachers.

REFERENCES

[1] Boots Cassel and Heikki Topi. 2015. Strengthening Data Science Education Through Collaboration. Workshop on Data Science Education, October 2015, Workshop Report. https://goo.gl/F5xEkj
[2] Andrea Danyluk, Paul Leidig, Lillian Cassel, and Christian Servin. 2019. ACM Task Force on Data Science: Draft Report and Opportunity for Feedback. In *Proceedings of the 50th ACM Technical Symposium on Computer Science Education (SIGCSE '19)*. ACM, New York, NY, USA, 2.
[3] Richard D. De Veaux, Mahesh Agarwal, Maia Averett, Benjamin S. Baumer, Andrew Bray, Thomas C. Bressoud, Lance Bryant, Lei Z. Cheng, Amanda Francis, Robert Gould, Albert Y. Kim, Matt Kretchmar, Qin Lu, Ann Moskol, Deborah Nolan, Roberto Pelayo, Sean Raleigh, Ricky J. Sethi, Mutiara Sondjaja, Neelesh Tiruviluamala, Paul X. Uhlig, Talitha M. Washington, Curtis L. Wesley, David White, and Ping Ye. 2017. Curriculum Guidelines for Undergraduate Programs in Data Science. *Annual Review of Statistics and Its Application* 4, 1 (2017), 15–30. https://doi.org/10.1146/annurev-statistics-060116-053930
[4] EDISON Consortium. 2017. *EDISON Data Science Framework (EDSF)*. Technical Report. EDISON Initiative, Europe. http://edison-project.eu/book/export/html/488
[5] EDISON Consortium. 2017. *EDISON University Programs List*. Technical Report. EDISON Initiative, Europe. http://edison-project.eu/university-programs-list
[6] Tony Hey, Stewart Tansley, and Kristin M. Tolle (Eds.). 2009. *The Fourth Paradigm: Data-Intensive Scientific Discovery*. Microsoft Research, Redmond, Washington. http://research.microsoft.com/en-us/collaboration/fourthparadigm/
[7] National Academies of Sciences, Engineering, and Medicine. 2018. *Data Science for Undergraduates: Opportunities and Options*. The National Academies Press, Washington, DC. https://doi.org/10.17226/25104
[8] John W. Tukey. 1962. The Future of Data Analysis. *The Annals of Mathematical Statistics* 33, 1 (03 1962), 1–67. https://doi.org/10.1214/aoms/1177704711
[9] Nanyang Technological University. 2018. Bachelor of Science in Data Science and Artificial Intelligence. Brochure. http://scse.ntu.edu.sg/Programmes/CurrentStudents/Undergraduate/Documents/2018/DSAIbrochure.pdf
[10] Jeannette M. Wing, Vandana P. Janeja, Tyler Kloefkorn, and Lucy C. Erickson. 2018. *Data Science Leadership Summit: Summary Report*. Technical Report. Data Science Institute, USA. https://dl.acm.org/citation.cfm?id=3293458

Pass Rates in STEM Disciplines Including Computing

Simon*
University of Newcastle
Australia
simon@newcastle.edu.au

Andrew Luxton-Reilly*
University of Auckland
New Zealand
andrew@cs.auckland.ac.nz

Vangel Ajanovski
Ss Cyril and Methodius University
Republic of North Macedonia
vangel.ajanovski@finki.ukim.mk

Eric Fouh
University of Pennsylvania
USA
efouh@seas.upenn.edu

Chris Gonsalvez
Monash University
Australia
chris.gonsalvez@monash.edu

Juho Leinonen
University of Helsinki
Finland
juho.leinonen@helsinki.fi

Jack Parkinson
University of Glasgow
UK
jack.parkinson@glasgow.ac.uk

Matthew Poole
University of Portsmouth
UK
matthew.poole@port.ac.uk

Neena Thota
University of Massachusetts Amherst
USA
nthota@cs.umass.edu

ABSTRACT

Vast numbers of publications in computing education begin with the premise that programming is hard to learn and hard to teach. Many papers note that failure rates in computing courses, and particularly in introductory programming courses, are higher than their institutions would like. Two highly distinct research projects have established that average success rates in introductory programming courses world-wide are in the region of 67%.

However, there is little published work comparing pass rates in computing courses with those in other STEM disciplines. As institutions continually ask computing educators to justify the atypical failure rates in their courses, a thoroughly researched comparison of this sort could prove useful in demonstrating whether the phenomenon is real, and, if so, whether it extends somewhat beyond the boundaries of individual institutions.

This working group will gather information on pass rates in computing courses, particularly introductory programming courses, and in courses at comparable levels in other STEM disciplines. Members of the group will be required to gather the information from their own institutions, and further data will be gathered by way of a broad survey. The data will be analysed to see whether global patterns can be established, and the group will survey the literature to gather and summarise postulated explanations for any difference between pass rates in computing and in other STEM disciplines.

CCS CONCEPTS

• **Social and professional topics → Computing education.**

*Working group co-leader

ITiCSE '19, July 15–17, 2019, Aberdeen, Scotland, UK

ACM ISBN 978-1-4503-6301-3/19/07.
https://doi.org/10.1145/3304221.3325532

KEYWORDS

ITiCSE working group; CS1; introductory programming; pass rate; failure rate; STEM disciplines

ACM Reference Format:
Simon, Andrew Luxton-Reilly, Vangel Ajanovski, Eric Fouh, Chris Gonsalvez, Juho Leinonen, Jack Parkinson, Matthew Poole, and Neena Thota. 2019. Pass Rates in STEM Disciplines Including Computing. In *Innovation and Technology in Computer Science Education (ITiCSE '19), July 15–17, 2019, Aberdeen, Scotland, UK.* ACM, New York, NY, USA, 2 pages. https://doi.org/10.1145/3304221.3325532

1 BACKGROUND

The leaders of this working group were co-leaders of a 2018 ITiCSE working group [6] that conducted a broad-ranging review of the literature pertaining to the introductory programming course. At times it seemed that almost every one of the 1666 papers that they considered had words in its introduction to the effect of 'programming is hard to learn' or 'programming is hard to teach'.

The literature of computing education appears to recognise almost universally that learning to program computers is difficult, and therefore by extension that teaching computer programming is difficult. Most teachers of computing courses accept this, and understand that the pass rates in their courses are typically among the lowest rates at their institution. However, they are often subjected to pressure from their institutions to improve the pass rates, and when that happens they sometimes need to explain that this is a world-wide phenomenon, not specific to the one institution, and it would help if they could point to published research to back up that explanation.

In 2007, using a survey of computing academics worldwide, Bennedsen and Caspersen [1] established an average pass rate of 67% in introductory programming courses. Ten years later, Watson and Li [8] established almost exactly the same pass rate by means of a search of the computing education literature. These rates are not disastrous, but neither are they pleasing to university administrators.

There have been suggestions [2, 3] that some governments are considering tying university funding to pass rates in courses. This option clearly has the potential to pressure educators into passing students who are inadequately prepared for subsequent courses.

The literature has also seen a number of suggestions as to why pass rates are low in introductory programming courses. For example, Luxton-Reilly [5] suggests that "we make our introductory courses difficult by establishing unrealistic expectations for novice programming students"; Hoda and Andreae [4] suggest that the high level of attrition and failure are due not so much to incapable students as to inadequate teaching; and Parsons et al. [7] suggest that "the methods of assessment ... do not reflect the knowledge and skills that a real programmer needs to write real code".

The first purpose of this working group is to gather data from computing educators worldwide about pass rates in their own introductory courses and pass rates in introductory courses in other STEM disciplines at their own institutions. This will provide an update to the two prior studies of pass rates in introductory computing courses, but additionally it will help to establish whether pass rates in computing courses really are substantially lower than in other STEM courses, and whether this is a universal phenomenon.

The second purpose is to examine the literature for plausible hypotheses about the purported lower pass rates, and, if possible, to synthesise those hypotheses into a viable explanation.

2 METHOD

The working group will conduct a thorough survey of the computing education literature, gathering and summarising plausible explanations of the perceived poor pass rates in introductory programming courses.

Each member of the working group will gather data on pass rates in introductory courses from their own institution, both in computing and in other STEM disciplines. It is expected that each member will gather five years' data. Analysis of this data will give a picture of pass rates at a small number of institutions, and will help to establish whether any trends are discernible over the past five years.

The working group will also conduct a survey in which it asks respondents to provide the same data for just the most recent year at their own institutions. Analysis of that data will strengthen the findings from the institutions of the working group members, giving a clear snapshot of the current relationship between pass rates in introductory programming courses and those in other introductory STEM courses.

Finally, the working group will seek out publicly accessible data on pass rates reported at a state or national level. However, early indications are that such data is not sufficiently detailed to be of any assistance in the working group's endeavours.

REFERENCES

[1] Jens Bennedsen and Michael E Caspersen. 2007. Failure rates in introductory programming. *SIGCSE Bulletin* 39, 2 (June 2007), 32–36. https://doi.org/10.1145/1272848.1272879

[2] Alison Clear, Janet Carter, Amruth Kumar, Cary Laxer, Simon, and Ernesto Cuadros-Vargas. 2015. Global perspectives on assessing educational performance and quality. In *2015 ACM Conference on Innovation and Technology in Computer Science Education (ITiCSE 2015)*. ACM, New York, NY, USA, 326–327. https://doi.org/10.1145/2729094.2754843

[3] Alison Clear and Tony Clear. 2014. Introductory programming and educational performance indicators – a mismatch. In *2014 ITx Conference (ITx 2014)*. CITRENZ, New Zealand, 123–128.

[4] Rashina Hoda and Peter Andreae. 2014. It's not them, it's us! Why computer science fails to impress many first years. In *16th Australasian Computing Education Conference (ACE 2014)*. Australian Computer Society, Inc., Darlinghurst, Australia, 159–162. http://dl.acm.org/citation.cfm?id=2667490.2667509

[5] Andrew Luxton-Reilly. 2016. Learning to program is easy. In *2016 ACM Conference on Innovation and Technology in Computer Science Education (ITiCSE 2016)*. ACM, New York, NY, USA, 284–289. https://doi.org/10.1145/2899415.2899432

[6] Andrew Luxton-Reilly, Simon, Ibrahim Albluwi, Brett A Becker, Michail Giannakos, Amruth N Kumar, Linda Ott, James Paterson, Michael James Scott, Judy Sheard, and Claudia Szabo. 2018. Introductory programming: a systematic literature review. In *ITiCSE 2018 Working Group Reports (ITiCSE-WGR 2018)*. ACM, New York, NY, USA, 55–106. https://doi.org/10.1145/3293881.3295779

[7] Dale Parsons, Krissi Wood, and Patricia Haden. 2015. What are we doing when we assess programming?. In *17th Australasian Computing Education Conference (ACE 2015)*. ACS, Sydney, Australia, 119–127. http://crpit.com/confpapers/CRPITV160Parsons.pdf

[8] Christopher Watson and Frederick WB Li. 2014. Failure rates in introductory programming revisited. In *2014 Conference on Innovation & Technology in Computer Science Education (ITiCSE 2014)*. ACM, New York, NY, USA, 39–44. https://doi.org/10.1145/2591708.2591749

A Periodic Table of Computing Education Learning Theories

Claudia Szabo*
claudia.szabo@adelaide.edu.au
University of Adelaide
Adelaide, Australia

Nickolas Falkner*
nickolas.falkner@adelaide.edu.au
University of Adelaide
Adelaide, Australia

Andrew Petersen*
andrew.petersen@utoronto.ca
University of Toronto Mississauga
Mississauga, Canada

Heather Bort
heather.bort@marquette.edu
Marquette University
Milwaukee, Wisconsin, USA

Cornelia Connolly
cornelia.connolly@nuigalway.ie
NUI Galway
Galway, Ireland

Kathryn Cunningham
kicunn@umich.edu
University of Michigan
Ann Arbor, Michigan, USA

Peter Donaldson
peter.donaldson.2@glasgow.ac.uk
University of Glasgow
Glasgow, Scotland

Arto Hellas
arto.hellas@cs.helsinki.fi
University of Helsinki
Helsinki, Finland

James Robinson
james.robinson@raspberrypi.org
Raspberry PI Foundation
United Kingdom

Judy Sheard
judy.sheard@monash.edu
Monash University
Melbourne, Australia

ABSTRACT

Computing education research is built on the use of suitable methods within appropriate theoretical frameworks to provide guidance and solutions for our discipline, in a way that is rigorous and repeatable. However, the scale of theory covered extends well beyond the CS discipline and includes educational theory, behavioural psychology, statistics, economics, and game theory, among others. A computing education researcher's journey towards appropriate and discipline relevant theory can be challenging and, when a researcher has learned one area of theory, it can be easy to return to familiar theory, as it may not be clear what the next step could be. The periodic table is a visual arrangement of the elements to group like with like, providing insight into how families of elements will react. Could we do the same with learning theories located in the domain of computer science education, and would it be useful? The working group will identify and survey existing literature on relationships between key areas of theory in computing education, identify ways of organising these research areas to show how knowledge of one could assist another, and produce initial graphical representations of theory and their relationship groupings to assist researchers in understanding how computing theory is currently used in the discipline and what theories might become of interest.

*Working group co-leaders

ITiCSE '19, July 15–17, 2019, Aberdeen, Scotland Uk

ACM ISBN 978-1-4503-6301-3/19/07.
https://doi.org/10.1145/3304221.3325534

CCS CONCEPTS

• **Social and professional topics** → *Computer science education.*

KEYWORDS

learning theory, computing education, epistemology

ACM Reference Format:
Claudia Szabo, Nickolas Falkner, Andrew Petersen, Heather Bort, Cornelia Connolly, Kathryn Cunningham, Peter Donaldson, Arto Hellas, James Robinson, and Judy Sheard. 2019. A Periodic Table of Computing Education Learning Theories. In *Innovation and Technology in Computer Science Education (ITiCSE '19), July 15–17, 2019, Aberdeen, Scotland Uk.* ACM, New York, NY, USA, 2 pages. https://doi.org/10.1145/3304221.3325534

1 INTRODUCTION

Computing education research is built upon theoretical frameworks, both specific to computing education and situated more broadly in education, psychology, and other fields. Twenty years ago, Ben-Ari argued for the introduction of *constructivism*, a major learning theory, to computing education [1]. Just ten years later, Simon, in collaboration with various groups of colleagues [6–8], classified papers from a number of prominent computing education venues by topic, theme, and scope, and found a significant number (26% at ICER) that could be considered to focus on learning theories or models. Even more recently, Malmi et al. [3] demonstrated that computing education has begun to develop and extend its own, discipline-specific theories of learning. The field is maturing quickly.

However, recent work has also found that the use of theory is inconsistent across the discipline [3] and that the field may be held back by misunderstanding and mis-use of theory by both authors and reviewers [4]. The discipline needs a guide to help researchers understand how and where theory is currently being used, where gaps in theory exist, and where theories not yet utilized in computing education may be useful. Like Pears et al. [5], who sought to create a resource by developing a core corpus of computing education literature [5], or Kinnunen and Malmi, who investigated how specific methods have been utilized in computing education [2], this working group aims to create a resource for researchers in computing education. Our goal is to produce visual representations of the use of theory in the field to advance our understanding of how theory can be utilized.

REFERENCES

[1] Mordechai Ben-Ari. 1998. Constructivism in Computer Science Education. *SIGCSE Bull.* 30, 1 (March 1998), 257–261. https://doi.org/10.1145/274790.274308

[2] Päivi Kinnunen and Beth Simon. 2012. Phenomenography and grounded theory as research methods in computing education research field. *Computer Science Education* 22, 2 (2012), 199–218.

[3] Lauri Malmi, Judy Sheard, Simon, Roman Bednarik, Juha Helminen, Päivi Kinnunen, Ari Korhonen, Niko Myller, Juha Sorva, and Ahmad Taherkhani. 2014. Theoretical Underpinnings of Computing Education Research: What is the Evidence?. In *Proceedings of the Tenth Annual Conference on International Computing Education Research (ICER '14).* ACM, New York, NY, USA, 27–34. https://doi.org/10.1145/2632320.2632358

[4] Greg L. Nelson and Andrew J. Ko. 2018. On Use of Theory in Computing Education Research. In *Proceedings of the 2018 ACM Conference on International Computing Education Research (ICER '18).* ACM, New York, NY, USA, 31–39. https://doi.org/10.1145/3230977.3230992

[5] Arnold Pears, Stephen Seidman, Crystal Eney, Päivi Kinnunen, and Lauri Malmi. 2005. Constructing a Core Literature for Computing Education Research. *SIGCSE Bull.* 37, 4 (Dec. 2005), 152–161. https://doi.org/10.1145/1113847.1113893

[6] Simon. 2007. Koli Calling Comes of Age: An Analysis. In *Proceedings of the Seventh Baltic Sea Conference on Computing Education Research - Volume 88 (Koli Calling '07).* Australian Computer Society, Inc., Darlinghurst, Australia, Australia, 119–126. http://dl.acm.org/citation.cfm?id=2449323.2449336

[7] Simon. 2009. Ten Years of the Australasian Computing Education Conference. In *Proceedings of the Eleventh Australasian Conference on Computing Education - Volume 95 (ACE '09).* Australian Computer Society, Inc., Darlinghurst, Australia, Australia, 157–164. http://dl.acm.org/citation.cfm?id=1862712.1862735

[8] Simon, Angela Carbone, Michael de Raadt, Raymond Lister, Margaret Hamilton, and Judy Sheard. 2008. Classifying Computing Education Papers: Process and Results. In *Proceedings of the Fourth International Workshop on Computing Education Research (ICER '08).* ACM, New York, NY, USA, 161–172. https://doi.org/10.1145/1404520.1404536

Effective Computer Science Teacher Professional Development: Beauty and Joy of Computing 2018

Alexandra Milliken
Computer Science Department
North Carolina State University
Raleigh, North Carolina
aamillik@ncsu.edu

Christa Cody
Veronica Cateté
cncodyl@ncsu.edu
vmcatete@ncsu.edu
Computer Science Department
North Carolina State University
Raleigh, North Carolina

Tiffany Barnes
Computer Science Department
North Carolina State University
Raleigh, North Carolina
tmbarnes@ncsu.edu

ABSTRACT

The Advanced Placement Computer Science Principles (AP CSP) course has been fully active for 2 years, garnering a large group of diverse students [2], and flaming the need for highly trained CSP teachers, especially in effective practices for diversity and equity. We have conducted summer professional development (PD) workshops from 2012-2018 which have prepared 748 teachers to teach AP CSP using the Beauty and Joy of Computing (BJC) curriculum. To improve equity and readiness for teaching, we have refined our PD by: shortening the PD from 6 weeks to 1 week; developing new, highly scaffolded pre-PD work; and modifying the in-person schedule to incorporate more pedagogy and teaching experiences, while continuing to provide in-depth, hands-on support for teachers to learn the basics of programming. The most recent revisions to our PD schedule resulted in improved post-PD survey results, with teachers from the 2018 cohort planning to adopt more of the BJC curriculum than in past years. From 2017 to 2018, planned adoption rates increased by 13%, resulting in 73% of the 2018 PD participants planning to adopt more than 60% of the BJC curriculum and 58% planning to adopt 80-100% of the BJC curriculum in their classrooms in 2018-2019. In this paper, we discuss the most recent BJC PD implementation and provide evidence of increased teacher self-efficacy in areas including fostering interest in computing for underrepresented populations.

CCS CONCEPTS

• **Social and professional topics** → **Model curricula**; **K-12 education**;

KEYWORDS

Computer Science Principles, Professional Development, K12 Education

ACM ISBN 978-1-4503-6301-3/19/07...$15.00
https://doi.org/10.1145/3304221.3319779

ACM Reference Format:
Alexandra Milliken, Christa Cody, Veronica Cateté, and Tiffany Barnes. 2019. Effective Computer Science Teacher Professional Development: Beauty and Joy of Computing 2018. In *Innovation and Technology in Computer Science Education (ITiCSE '19), July 15–17, 2019, Aberdeen, Scotland UK.* ACM, New York, NY, USA, 7 pages. https://doi.org/10.1145/3304221.3319779

1 INTRODUCTION

In the United States, Computer Science education for K-12 is a revived concept, meaning that most teachers and schools are unequipped to handle computer science coursework and exams. In data collected on the "State of Computer Science Education", only 35% percent of secondary schools in the US teach computer science and only 22 states have K-12 computer science standards[3]. Furthermore, only 33 states have computer science teacher certification and most concerning, only 13 states have state-approved pre-service teacher preparation at institutions of higher education[3]. Meaning, the majority of teachers stepping up to the role have little to no experience in programming or computer science but are willing and passionate to learn how to teach these new topics so we can address the need for Computer Science in K-12. With computing occupations making up 58% of all projected new jobs in Science, Technology, Engineering and Mathematics fields[10], preparing in-service teachers to not only handle teaching a topic very new to them, but also giving them tools and resources to learn with their students is critical.

The National Science Foundation and the Collegeboard's Advanced Placement (AP) program worked together with educators to develop an AP Computer Science Principles (CSP) course. This rigorous, college-credit, course familiarizes high school students with the main concepts of computer science and explores how computing affects our world. By exploring computing innovations and impacts on society, students learn about how expansive computer science is as a field of study and work. The course requires students to create and write about two computational artifacts (e.g. programs) as a part of the exam. Since this course does not have a designated programming language, teachers have the flexibility to choose the programming language for their classroom [1].

The Beauty and Joy of Computing (BJC) is a curriculum endorsed by the Collegeboard for the AP CSP course and introduces teachers and students to 7 Big Ideas of computer science: creativity, abstraction, algorithms, programming, data, the internet, and global impacts, using 6 Computational Thinking Practices: connecting computing, programming, abstracting, analyzing problems and artifacts, communicating, and collaborating [5]. BJC was developed to appeal to a wide range of students, with the goal of providing computing education opportunities to groups that have been underrepresented in computer science. In order to help prepare teachers to teach Computer Science in K-12 schools, we, along with other CSP providers, host professional development (PD) programs [4, 9].

This paper discusses how refinements to our BJC professional development workshops align with Penuel's effective PD characteristics [12], and the results of our teacher PD surveys for summers 2016-2018.

2 THE BEAUTY AND JOY OF COMPUTING: PROFESSIONAL DEVELOPMENT

As part of the national CS10K effort, we have been coordinating regional AP CSP PD workshops to help teachers prepare to offer rigorous high school computer science courses. Since most in-service high school teachers have little programming experience or computer science knowledge, the PD typically has a primary focus on programming and teaching methods to support it. Our BJC PD workshops are led by current BJC teachers who use our curriculum and who have attended both a BJC PD and a facilitator PD. Each year, new and experienced facilitators attend the facilitator PD to prepare for the upcoming BJC PDs, and learn about new updates to the BJC curriculum and national AP requirements. Typically, two experienced facilitators, accompanied with one or two new facilitators, lead a BJC PD.

3 PROFESSIONAL DEVELOPMENT DESIGN RATIONALE

Our PD is developed through a design-based implementation research (DBIR) approach of iteratively designing, testing, and refining our model with frequent feedback loops and participatory design [11]. Each year the BJC PD is reevaluated and updated to provide the most effective PD experience for teachers. We also attempt to align our PD with known effective PD practices. In recent years, we designed the PD more around professional responsibility by adding an adapted version of the Teacher Learner Observer practice [2, 6] and the Lead Learner mindset [8] to our PD schedule. Our most recent schedule, which we will go into detail in Section 4, aligns with other effective PD characteristics [9, 12].

According to Penuel et al., effective professional development should be designed to (1) focus on content, (2) promote active learning, and (3) foster coherence [12]. Two of five of Mobile CSP's recommended core features for CS PDs include focus on content knowledge and active learning [14]. Focusing on content is critical, especially during the initial PD [12], when teachers focus on developing their knowledge and comfort with the material. Promoting active learning involves hands-on activities during the PD, opening up the floor to teacher inquiry and discussion, which can lead to higher student achievement outcomes [12]. Providing teachers time to explore and understand the curriculum by planning, enacting, and revising lessons during the PD, is a concrete example of a relevant hands-on activity. A core design feature of the "Exploring CS" teacher PD is the Teacher Learner Observer (TLO) practice, where teachers role play three different roles, practicing their teacher responsibilities, acting as students (learners), and reflecting on teaching and learning as observers [6]. Fostering coherence during PD allows time for teachers to compare their responsibilities and their district's goals to the curriculum's goals; if the goals and responsibilities align, teachers are more likely to adopt or adapt the curriculum [12].

4 BJC PROFESSIONAL DEVELOPMENT

In this section, we will describe our 2012-2015 CSP PD model and changes made to the model from 2016-2018.

4.1 2012 - 2015 BJC PDs

From 2012-2015, we held 2, 6-week PD workshops each year preparing a total of 133 high school teachers. During the 6-week PDs, teachers spent one week face-to-face, four weeks completing the BJC course online, and a final face-to-face week to prepare to teach. Price, et al. found that the 2012-2015 BJC PDs improved participants' confidence and listed several lessons learned over the years [13]. They determined one of the important aspects of high-quality PD is to address participants' needs and to adjust the PD for the participants [13]. For example, in 2012 and 2013, the six-week long BJC PD was taught by university faculty, but feedback quickly suggested that teachers would learn better from other teachers. Therefore, in 2014 and 2015, the PD was taught by experienced teachers who took the training and had taught the course. Another important takeaway from his paper was the need to model teaching and explicitly discuss pedagogy in the PD [13]. Many participants did not have a computer science background, and therefore needed to be taught both content and pedagogy. Lastly, teachers reported that experience with pair programming and team assignments helped build a community for support throughout the academic year [13].

4.2 Recent BJC PD Commonalities

In the next two sections we will discuss the 2016, 2017, and 2018 BJC PDs focusing on the major changes and the reasons behind the changes. The common elements in the face-to-face BJC PD schedule since 2016 include introductions to: (1) the BJC curriculum, (2) programming labs, (3) the programming language/environment, (4) growth mindset, (5) pair programming, (6) computing in the news, (7) course readings, and (8) The AP CSP Explore and Create Performance Tasks. Each year, teachers also complete a Create Task, where teachers create their own programs, demonstrate them to others, and answer the AP Create Task prompts based on their programs.

Each day of the 5-day PD week, teachers completed short Daily Feedback surveys asking 3 questions: (1) "What went well today," (2) "What can be improved," and (3) "Any other comments," which we review the following morning to discuss the changes for the day based on the previous day's suggestions to maximize the teacher's satisfaction and tailor to each specific group's needs. Each year, participants take a pre-PD survey, revealing their expectations and needs, and a post-PD survey, revealing their satisfaction with the PD and their expected use of the curriculum. We used online forums as a discussion platform to enable the teachers to connect before, during, and after the PD.

Table 1 compares the amount of pedagogy, programming and reflection from 2016 to 2018. Time was spent on other activities during the PD week which is not mentioned in the table.

4.2.1 2016 PD. During the 2016 PD, 104 teachers participated in 12 regional BJC PD workshops. We expanded the number of available PDs to make it more convenient for teachers to attend. We shortened the length of our PD experience from the 6-week model to a 3-week model because many teachers prior expressed that they could not commit to a 6-week PD, with many struggling to complete the online course on their own without pay. In the 2016 three-week model, the first week comprised preparatory online assignments, the second week was face-to-face, and the third week was online, comprising two assignments and office hours.

4.2.2 2017 PD. During the 2017 PD, 141 teachers participated in 7 regional BJC PD workshops. We used a 2-week model, continuing to shorten the PD to make it more feasible for more teachers. In the 2-week model, the first week comprised a smaller set of online preparatory assignments and the second week was the face-to-face week. We eliminated the third week by incorporating the assignments into the face-to-face week, and instead focused on engaging teachers in academic year online mentoring. We also lessened the amount of preparatory work, as noted in Table 1 since many teachers were unable to complete the preparatory work on their own due to time constraints and/or lack of prior knowledge.

We adjusted the 2017 BJC PD components which correlated with three of Penuel's recommendations to focus on **content**, to incorporate **active learning** into the PD, and to encourage **coherence** [12], which is networking with their peers. To improve the BJC PD content, we focused on helping teachers reflect on how students learn the BJC material by implementing the Lead Learner mindset [8]. In this mindset, teachers are encouraged to think of themselves as lead learners, helping students by showing them what an exemplary learner of CS content will do when facing problems [15]. Furthermore, we integrated more active learning into the PD in multiple ways, including reviewing student work and having teachers practice teaching labs and leading discussions. For reviewing student work, the teachers spent an hour reviewing and discussing past student submissions for the AP CSP Explore Performance Task. Teachers, assisted by BJC leaders, also led short discussions about computing in the news. During the computing in the news discussions, one teacher presents a current news article about new or interesting topics in computing and discuss the topic as a group, such as the social implications or how the topic affects them.

We also increased coherence at the PD by adding more time for networking during a teacher panel with experienced BJC teachers and from recent AP readers for the AP CSP course. These discussions helped teachers better understand the AP requirements and how the curriculum supports those requirements.

After the PD, teachers were encouraged to join online small groups facilitated by PD facilitator, and are added to our online CSP and BJC support forum that is monitored by project staff.

4.3 2018 BJC PD

When designing the 2018 PD, we kept our 2017 PD additions and incorporated more of Penuel's recommendations to continue increasing the efficacy of the BJC PD [12]. We kept the the Lead Learner mindset to help teachers think of themselves as models for their students, enabling them to learn alongside the students and demonstrate effective learning strategies [8]. We increased the number of active learning activities by incorporating an adapted version of the Teacher Learner Observer (TLO) practice [6] [2], giving teachers the chance to practice teaching, added more reflection and discussion time, having teachers complete the written components of the Create Task earlier, and adding a grading component to the PD.

To implement the TLO practice, we divided the teachers into three groups who would prepare and lead lessons (teachers) on three BJC programming labs, while other teachers would act as students (learners), and the facilitators would lead a discussion, prompting all participants to reflect on their observations (observers) of what worked from the teacher, student, and classroom perspectives [2, 6]. Initially, we followed the TLO model closely where some teacher participants should act solely as observers, but we quickly revised this directive as participant observers were upset that they could not learn the content being presented, therefore we developed Teach Learn Then Reflect (TLTR), adapted from the TLO practice. This practice integrates many of Penuel's suggestions for incorporating more active learning into the PD and helps align our PD content to the teacher's professional responsibilities, which Penuel suggests increases adoption rates [12]. We also increased coherence by adding 15 minutes of reflection and discussion time to the end of each teaching session of 60-90 minutes, where teachers take a few minutes to reflect on the activity, and then discuss what went well, what could have been improved, and how they would implement the content in their own classrooms. The remainder of this section will break down each day of the 2018 BJC PD.

Before attending the PD face-to-face week, participants are asked to complete a few short, and well-specified lab exercises from the first unit of the BJC curriculum as preparatory work. We dramatically reduced the amount of preparatory work in hopes that more participants would complete the work. Participants in prior years reported being dissatisfied with having to repeat preparatory content during the face-to-face week since other teachers did not complete it beforehand.

Day One. In the first morning, we introduce the programming environment, the BJC curriculum, and resources we will use during the remainder of the week. To set the tone for the week, we explain and discuss growth mindset. People with a "growth mindset believe that they can develop their intelligence over time" suggesting people's minds are not fixed [7]. We review the pre-PD work and then complete a programming exercise and reflection. After lunch, we complete another programming exercise and reflection, discuss some AP materials for the course, and review the expectations and schedule for the remainder of the week.

During each programming exercise, the PD leader introduces the goal of the programming activity and any new blocks or computer science concepts. Then teachers complete the programming activity in pairs to introduce them to pair programming. After completing the exercise, the class participates in a reflection, discussing what they learned and sharing how they would teach the lab in their own classroom.

Day Two. In the second morning, one teacher presents a recent article for computing in the news. Then we complete a programming exercise in pairs. After the reflection, we divide participants into 3 groups to learn and plan to teach 3 programming labs for the Teach Learn Then Reflect (TLTR) practice. In the afternoon, one of the three groups teaches their programming activity and the PD facilitators lead a TLO reflection discussion. We close the day by exploring classroom environments and social impacts, discuss the challenges with teaching and recruiting a diverse classroom, and introduce the AP Explore Task with past students' projects as demonstrations.

A core part of the BJC focus is on providing teachers with the skill to not only teach students CS but students with diversity, such as different races, socioeconomic backgrounds, and genders. We encourage teachers to recruit students from all kinds of groups to join the AP CSP class by introducing growth mindset on day 1 and by discussing recruitment and diversity in the PD on day 2.

Day Three. In the third morning, the other two groups teach their programming labs for the TLTR, each concluded with a facilitated discussion. As a whole class, we discuss the benefits of the TLTR practice and teachers point out any pedagogy techniques they plan to bring back to their classroom. In the afternoon, we complete a programming exercise focused on the CS concept of *lists* and reflect on the activity. Then, teachers complete another programming exercise focused on the CS concepts of *algorithms* and *abstractions*, afterwards reflecting on the activity and how it completes all of the requirements for the AP Create Task. To end the day, we introduce the teachers to the Create Task, which will be their project for next day.

The CSP Create Task is a required component for the AP CSP exam. Teachers pair up with a partner of their choice and decide a project which would complete all of the requirements for the AP Create Task. The teachers work on their Create Task all of day four and part of day five. After teachers have finished programming their projects, they create a short video demo of their program, and write a report to answer the Create Task questions, both of which are things their students would have to complete for the actual exam.

Day Four. On the fourth morning, we practice a computing in the news discussion. Then, we present the AP Create Task requirements and demonstrate student work samples. The teachers spend the majority of the day developing and programming their own Create Task with their partner. At the end of the day, we have a teacher panel where our participants are able to ask any questions they have about BJC, teaching BJC, the AP exams, or anything else to the experienced PD leaders who have taught the class.

Day Five. The last day contains overviews of the remaining BJC units we did not cover in depth during the PD week. In the morning, we introduce teacher-created BJC materials, and share AP Reader teacher insights and tips. Teachers finish their Create Task and grade another team's work using the AP Create Task rubric. After lunch, we reflect on the PD week, answer any remaining questions, discuss how teachers sign up to teach an AP course, and the teachers take the Post-PD survey, telling us how our BJC PD prepared them to teach the AP CSP course.

Table 1: Time spent on varying activities in the BJC PD schedule for 2018.

Time in hours spent on..	2016	2017	2018
Pedagogy	1.75	7.00	9.75
Programming	14.50	12.75	11.75
Reflection	3.50	3.75	4.50

5 METHODS

In order to evaluate and compare the effectiveness of the PD from 2016 to 2018, we collected data on (1) participant satisfaction with the PD, (2) participant's perception on their preparedness to teach the AP CSP course, and (3) the number of teachers who plan to adopt the BJC curriculum. We also collected supporting demographic information in the PD application to understand their contexts and prior CS/programming experience. The number of teachers who participated in research for the 2016, 2017 and 2018 PDs were 36, 72 and 67, respectively.

Demographic information collected on the PD application includes questions about teacher gender, school type (public/private/charter), school demographics by gender, race, and free/reduced lunch, and teacher experience level in programming (None, A Little, Moderate, and A Lot) as noted in Table 2.

Table 2: This table shows the teacher demographic for the 2016, 2017, and 2018 PD years.

Year	*N*	*Coding Experience*	*Gender*	*School Type*
2016	34	None 12% A Little 53% Moderate 32% A Lot 6%	56% F 43% M	91% Public 2% Private 5% Other
2017	54	None 15% A Little 44% Moderate 35% A Lot 6%	65% F 35% M	83% Public 14% Private 1% Other
2018	67	None 7% A Little 43% Moderate 36% A Lot 15%	60% F 40% M	73% Public 17% Private 8% Other

On the post-PD survey, participants answered 18 five-point Likert scale questions to rate their assessment of the utility, efficiency, and organization of the PD, as well as the appropriateness of the teaching environment provided. The questions, shown in Table 3, are asked to assess how well the PD met participant needs. Teachers read the questions, such as "I can use this training to positively impact the achievement of my students" and respond with one of the following: Strongly Disagree, Disagree, Neither Disagree or Agree, Agree, or Strongly Agree.

Table 3: This table shows the average survey responses to questions intended to assess the PD.

Assessing the PD Questions	2016 Avg	2017 Avg	2018 Avg
N=	*34*	*54*	*67*
1. I can use this training to positively impact the achievement of my students	4.35	4.64	4.49
2. The content of the pd is relevant to my professional responsibilities	4.35	4.45	4.51
3. The facilitators helped me understand how to implement my learning	4.38	4.48	4.49
4. This pd will extend my knowledge, skills, and performances	4.44	4.44	4.58
5. This pd was tailored to meet my needs as a learner	4.23	4.18	4.21
6. The pd was supported by effective and appropriate use of technology	4.47	4.46	4.55
7. New practices were modeled and thoroughly explained	4.26	4.21	4.37
8. Sufficient time was provided for guided practice and tasks	4.15	3.83	4.13
9. The instructional techniques used facilitated my learning	4.35	4.19	4.40
10. The material used were accessible and enhanced my learning	4.50	4.25	4.51
11. The pd activities were carefully planned and well organized	4.38	4.14	4.36
12. The pd goals and objectives were clearly specified	4.38	4.24	4.37
13. The pd included a variety of learning activities relevant to the topic	4.38	4.41	4.51
14. Time was used efficiently and effectively.	4.15	3.97	4.31

Furthermore, the post-PD survey asked participants about their planned BJC curriculum adoption, and 37 questions rating their self-perceived preparedness in the following areas: **Content** (level of fluency on CS concepts), **Inquiry/Engagement** (level of fluency when fostering varying CS teaching techniques in the classroom), **Equity** (level of comfort with engaging their students to consider equity-based practices and **Preparation** (level of comfort with managing different types of situations that arise in the classroom). Teachers rated themselves on questions like "What is your level of fluency in fostering self-directed learning with your students" on a 5-point Likert scale: Don't know, No experience, Somewhat fluent, Fluent, and Expert.

To determine if the changes to the PD from 2016 to 2018 had an affect on teacher responses, we used the Kruskal-Wallis test. Then, we further analyzed the significant differences using the Mann-Whitney U test to determine which years have differences between them.

6 RESULTS AND DISCUSSION

In the following sections, we share results about how our participants rated the BJC PD, their self-perceived ability to teach BJC, and their planned adoption rates from 2016 to 2018.

6.1 Teachers' Assessment of the PD

To evaluate the significance of the differences between the teachers assessment of the PD from 2016 to 2018, we used the Kruskal-Wallis test and Mann-Whitney U test as appropriate. Though we did not discover many significant differences between the years for the questions, the average rating for nearly all of the teacher assessment questions was above a 4.0, meaning on average teachers agreed with the questions, as shown on Table 3. That table also shows no harm has been done by between the years. Considering the reduction of time in the 2018 schedule, this can be viewed as a positive indication of the changes made.

6.1.1 Time Spent during PD. Two of the statements found on Table 3 asked about time spent during the PD: *Sufficient time was provided for guided practice and tasks* and *Time was used efficiently and effectively.* For these statements, we expected the average to show a downward trend from 2016, a 3-week PD, to 2018, a 1-week PD because we reduced the length of the PD; however, this is not the case. Although there were no significant differences in the teachers' assessments of the PD, we eliminated 2 weeks from the PD and our participants felt there was high-quality content and instruction, and that their time was used effectively.

6.1.2 Professional Responsibility and Teaching Techniques. Statements 2, 7, 9 and 13, found on Table 3, are related to teachers' responsibilities and instructional teaching techniques. From 2016 to 2018, the average response to these statements increased, which corresponds with the increase in the PD time spent on pedagogy from 3.75 hours to 9.75 hours as shown in Table 3. We also believe that our explicit focus on the Lead Learner mindeset and TLTR practice helped participants connect the PD to their professional responsibilities as a teacher. Teachers also got a chance to grade programming projects, which is another task these teachers will have to do regularly.

6.2 Teacher Perception on Teaching BJC

To evaluate the significance of the differences between the teachers' perceptions on teaching BJC on post-PD survey responses for each area (Content, Inquiry/Engagement, Equity, and Preparation as described in the Methods section) from 2016 to 2018, we used the Kruskal-Wallis test and Mann-Whitney U test as appropriate. Of the 37 questions, 9 have significant p-values.

Table 4 shows the 9 questions with significant differences. Each of the questions, except the last question, have a significant difference between years 2016 and 2017, and between years 2016 and 2018. The last question on the table only has a significant difference between years 2016 and 2017. This reflects the emphasis in PD on teaching for diversity, although social justice is a topic we need to continue to improve and reiterate upon.

6.2.1 Interest and Enjoyment. During 2017 and 2018, teachers self-reported a higher comfort level of fostering enjoyment and interest

Table 4: These teacher perception question were in the Post-PD survey comparing responses from 2016, 2017 and 2018.

Teacher's Perception on Teaching CSP	2016 (avg)	2017 (avg)	2018 (avg)	*p*
What is your level of fluency in fostering ... with your students				
self-directed learning	3.53	3.90	3.94	0.020
interest in cs activities	3.23	3.76	3.72	0.016
concentration of cs activities	3.26	3.68	3.64	0.031
enjoyment of cs activities	3.26	3.70	3.73	0.008
How well prepared do you feel to teach...				
cs to female students	3.35	3.96	3.97	0.000
cs to racial or ethnic students	3.32	3.80	3.81	0.008
cs to students of low socioeconomic backgrounds	3.26	3.83	3.78	0.002
students the relevance of cs in their daily lives	3.50	3.93	3.91	0.012
What is your level of fluency with integrating...into your instruction				
principles of social justice	3.29	3.72	3.58	0.033

with CS activities in their classroom. One possible reason is teachers at the 2017 and 2018 PD received more insight from a student's viewpoint with the Lead Learner mindset and TLTR practice than the 2016 teachers. In addition, our group of facilitators expanded over these three years from 8 to 36 leaders, bringing varied viewpoints and growing a larger community of practice rooted by the master teachers.

Another possible reason is more reflection time allowed for teachers to discuss each activity and determine how they would integrate them into their classrooms. In Penuel's paper, he concluded that teachers who have more time to think about the PD content, and ask questions to experienced teachers, would feel more prepared to teach their students [12].

6.2.2 Prepared for a diverse classroom. During 2017 and 2018, teachers self-reported a significantly higher preparedness level to teach Computer Science to female students, racial or ethnic students, and students of low socioeconomic backgrounds. We believe this is reinforced by the larger number of PD facilitators, and our improved facilitator training over the years that helped facilitators present a more consistent and research-based focus on helping diverse students succeed.

6.3 CSP Adoption Rate

Figure 1 demonstrates that many participating teachers planned to adopt or integrate some percentage of the BJC curriculum into their classroom. The 2016 data is more skewed towards the right. This may be explained by a difference in the project funding between 2016 and other years; in 2016 all participants were required to apply for crowd funding online, and this was a long and complex process that could only be completed by the most persistent and determined of teachers. Crowd-funded teachers had also publicly posted that they would teach the course, perhaps a higher bar than simply submitting an administrator support letter with their online application as required in 2017-2018. A higher percentage of teachers from the 2018 PD (73%) planned to adopt a larger amount of the BJC curriculum (81-100%) than teachers in the 2017 PD teachers (60%). We believe this is because of our adjustment to focus the PD more on the professional preparation needed to lead, facilitate, and grade programming assignments.

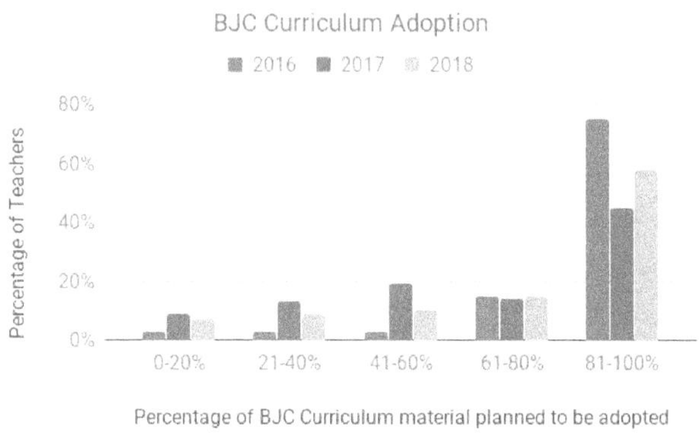

Figure 1: BJC Curriculum Adoption Rate Comparison 2016, 2017 and 2018

7 CONCLUSION

To conclude, the major contribution of this work is to show that careful refinement of the BJC teacher professional development can reduce the time teachers must spend preparing in the summer while maintaining perceived levels of quality and preparedness to teach. Specifically, we recommend that CSP or introduction to Computer Science courses PDs should (1) limit preparatory work to small, well-specified tasks that do not require prior CS or programming knowledge, (2) include reflection and discussion time after each activity, (3) provide teachers with experience facilitating, grading, and learning to program, (4) facilitate discussion with experienced teachers, (5) require collaborative work, and (6) explicitly discuss strategies for supporting diverse students and classrooms. These design principles help keep the PD focused on teachers' professional responsibilities, giving teachers a chance to determine if the curriculum is a good fit for their classroom and students, which could increase adoption rates. Our results suggest that these principles have been beneficial in maintaining high-quality instruction and resulted in high teacher satisfaction and self-perceived preparedness.

8 ACKNOWLEDGEMENTS

This material is based upon work supported by the National Science Foundation under grant numbers 1542922, 1138588, and 1346922. Any opinions, findings, and conclusions or recommendations expressed in this material are those of the author(s) and do not necessarily reflect the views of the National Science Foundation.

REFERENCES

[1] The College Board. 2017. *AP Computer Science Principles: Course and Exam Description.* College Board, New York, NY. https://apcentral.collegeboard.org/pdf/ap-computer-science-principles-course-and-exam-description.pdf
[2] Code.org. 2019. Promote Computer Science. https://code.org/promote

[3] Code.org Advocacy Coalition. 2018. State of Computer Science Education Policy and Implementation. Report. https://code.org/files/2018_state_of_cs.pdf
[4] Jan Cuny, Diane A Baxter, Daniel D Garcia, Jeff Gray, and Ralph Morelli. 2014. CS principles professional development: only 9,500 to go!. In *Proceedings of the 45th ACM technical symposium on Computer science education*. ACM, ACM, New York, NY, 543–544.
[5] Dan Garcia, Brian Harvey, and Tiffany Barnes. 2015. The beauty and joy of computing. *ACM Inroads* 6, 4 (2015), 71–79.
[6] Joanna Goode, Jane Margolis, and Gail Chapman. 2014. Curriculum is not enough: the educational theory and research foundation of the exploring computer science professional development model. In *Proceedings of the 45th ACM technical symposium on Computer science education*. ACM, ACM, New York, NY, 493–498.
[7] Aaron Hochanadel and Dora Finamore. 2015. Fixed and growth mindset In education and how grit helps students persist in the face of adversity. *Journal of International Education Research* 11, 1 (2015), 47–50.
[8] John Laughran, Kathy Smith, and Amanda Berry. 2011. *Scientific Literacy Under the Microscope: A Whole School Approach to Science Teaching and Learning*. Sense Publishers, The Netherlands. 42–99 pages.
[9] Ralph A Morelli, David Wolber, Jennifer Rosato, Chinma Uche, and Pauline Lake. 2014. Mobile computer science principles: a professional development sampler for teachers. In *Proceedings of the 45th ACM technical symposium on Computer science education*. ACM, ACM, New York, NY, 750–750.
[10] U.S. Bureau of Labor Statistics. 2018. Employment by detailed occupation. https://www.bls.gov/emp/tables/emp-by-detailed-occupation.htm
[11] William R Penuel, Barry J Fishman, Britte Haugan Cheng, and Nora Sabelli. 2011. Organizing research and development at the intersection of learning, implementation, and design. *Educational researcher* 40, 7 (2011), 331–337.
[12] William R. Penuel, Barry J. Fishman, Ryoko Yamaguchi, and Lawrence P. Gallagher. 2007. What Makes Professional Development Effective? Strategies That Foster Curriculum Implementation. *American Educational Research Journal* 44, 4 (2007), 921–958. https://doi.org/10.3102/0002831207308221
[13] Thomas W. Price, Veronica Cateté, Jennifer Albert, Barnes, and Daniel D. Garcia. 2016. Lessons Learned from "BJC" CS Principles Professional Development. In *Proceedings of the 47th ACM Technical Symposium on Computing Science Education (SIGCSE '16)*. ACM, New York, NY, 467–472. https://doi.org/10.1145/2839509.2844625
[14] Jennifer Rosato, Chery Lucarelli, Cassandra Beckworth, and Ralph Morelli. 2017. A Comparison of Online and Hybrid Professional Development for CS Principles Teachers. In *Proceedings of the 2017 ACM Conference on Innovation and Technology in Computer Science Education*. ACM, ACM, New York, NY, 140–145.
[15] Pat Thomson. 2018. Thinking about the school most of the time: studio as generative metaphor for critical reflection. *Journal of Educational Administration and History* 51, 2 (2018), 1–16.

Infusing Computing: Analyzing Teacher Programming Products in K-12 Computational Thinking Professional Development

Yihuan Dong, Veronica Cateté, Nicholas Lytle, Amy Isvik, Tiffany Barnes
Robin Jocius, Jennifer Albert, Deepti Joshi, Richard Robinson, Ashley Andrews
North Carolina State University, Raleigh, North Carolina
The Citadel, Charleston, South Carolina
{ydong2,vmcatete,nalytle,aaisvik,tmbarnes}@ncsu.edu,{rjocius,jalbert,djoshi,rjmr,ashley.andrews}@citadel.edu

ABSTRACT

In summer 2018, we conducted two week-long professional development workshops for 116 middle and high school teachers interested in infusing computational thinking (CT) into their classrooms. Teachers learned to program in Snap!, connect CT to their disciplines, and create infused CT learning segments for their classes. This paper investigates the extent to which teachers were able to successfully infuse CT skills of pattern recognition, abstraction, decomposition, and algorithms into their learning products.

In this work, we analyzed 58 teacher-designed programming products to look for common characteristics, such as project type, intended coding requirements for their students, and code features/functionality. Teacher-created products were classified into five types: animation, interactive story, quiz, intended game, and simulation/exploration tools. Coding requirements varied from using and/or explaining provided code, modifying existing code, programming with starter code, to building entire programs. Products were classified according to the extent to which they involved sprite manipulation, questions/answers, event handling, drawing, and control blocks. We found that teachers from different disciplines created products that vary in type, coding requirements, and features to suit their specific needs. Moreover, we found relationships between discipline, project type, and the required coding teachers expected students to do.

Our results inform future Infusing Computing Professional Development (PD) to provide more targeted training to support different teacher needs.

CCS CONCEPTS

• **Social and professional topics → Computational thinking**; *K-12 education.*

KEYWORDS

Professional Development; Computational Thinking; Programming; K-12

ITiCSE '19, July 15–17, 2019, Aberdeen, Scotland Uk

ACM ISBN 978-1-4503-6301-3/19/07...$15.00
https://doi.org/10.1145/3304221.3319772

ACM Reference Format:
Yihuan Dong, Veronica Cateté, Nicholas Lytle, Amy Isvik, Tiffany Barnes and Robin Jocius, Jennifer Albert, Deepti Joshi, Richard Robinson, Ashley Andrews. 2019. Infusing Computing: Analyzing Teacher Programming Products in K-12 Computational Thinking Professional Development. In *Innovation and Technology in Computer Science Education (ITiCSE '19), July 15–17, 2019, Aberdeen, Scotland Uk.* ACM, New York, NY, USA, 7 pages. https://doi.org/10.1145/3304221.3319772

1 INTRODUCTION

As computers have become an integral part of our life and work, it is widely agreed that helping students master computer science (CS) and computational thinking (CT) skills at an early age may help them become more competitive in the future workforce [8]. One way to broaden participation in computer science is to infuse computational thinking into daily K-12 classroom teaching [17]. However, since the majority of K-12 teachers have no prior training in computer science or computational thinking practices and skills [10], they need to be properly trained in order to design and teach CT-rich curricula.

Researchers have designed a number of professional development (PD) workshops and initiatives to equip teachers with the skills and tools to teach their students computer science and computational thinking [11, 13]. Programming has played an important role in many of these professional development workshops, because even though computational thinking can be taught without programming [4], learning to program can be a powerful tool to help elaborate computational thinking concepts, such as abstraction and algorithms, in a situated context. Programming can also enable teachers to create or modify existing programming artifacts in order to design curricular materials that infuse computational thinking with content-specific practices and skills.

To successfully infuse programming into K-12 classrooms, it is important to help teachers align programming with their subject learning goals [10]. This requires developing knowledge of what types of projects the teachers could use to align CT-infused activities with existing standards and curricula and to identify the kinds of coding activities the teachers design to support student learning. However, little is known about how teachers intend to infuse programming activities into their existing curricula.

In this work, we analyzed the teacher programming products collected from two computational thinking themed professional workshops for middle and high school teachers, guided by the following research questions:

- What project types were found in the teacher products?
- How much coding was designed for the students to do?

- What were the common features the teachers used to create their programs?
- How did the teachers connect coding activities to the CT elements?

We wish to help researchers understand middle and high school teachers' needs regarding the use of programming to teach CT in their domain. In addition, our findings can inform the improvement of programming elements in professional development training to become more targeted based on the teachers' varied needs.

2 LITERATURE REVIEW

Research shows that teacher professional development is critical to any successful change in educational practice [14], including changes related to computational thinking integration into K-12 schools [2, 3, 18]. Specifically, Barr and Stevenson (2011) identified two major areas of need in relation to teacher PD in CT: (1) a clear definition of what CT is and how it applies to students and content, and (2) explicit, ongoing training and support for K-12 teachers.

In order to realize CT as an essential component of the curriculum across disciplinary areas, teachers must integrate "activities that make visible the inherent overlap of CT ideas and practices with subject area concepts" that allow students to engage in hands-on concepts and learning [17]. However, teachers must first understand what CT is, how it connects to their curricula, and how it might support students' understandings of content.

We used the simplified PRADA framework [9] to help teachers understand computing concepts and recognize the CT elements that already exist in their curriculum. In PRADA, the focus is on Pattern Recognition, Abstraction, Decomposition, and Algorithms, we use these keywords to connect key CT elements to teachers' disciplines (e.g. a function in math is very similar to an algorithm). Additionally, we engage teachers in hands-on coding sessions to learn basic CT and programming skills, helping teachers to create their own Snap! projects.

Based on this design, we seek to discover ways that teacher programs reflect their understanding of CT and how their students might learn CT when doing the created activities. There have been attempts to evaluate student block-based programming projects to measure CT learning and programming outcomes for students. These studies categorizes student programming projects into types (e.g. games, music videos, storytelling, etc) and compare how these types of projects motivate students to use desired programming concepts, such as loops, conditionals, and variables [1, 5, 7]. Other research connects programming concepts with CT elements to measure how much CT is present in student projects. For example, Dr. Scratch[12] performs static analysis on Scratch projects to identify the presence or absence of key CT competencies such as parallelism, abstraction, and flow control.

Analyzing student programming artifacts helps identify what CT and programming concepts students can demonstrate. While the teachers participating in CT themed PD are similar to the students in terms of programming skill and prior knowledge, teacher-created projects may have a different focus than student projects, because teachers have purposefully designed their projects to serve as a tool for teaching both the subject knowledge and the CT concepts. Thus, analyzing teacher projects can provide insight into what CT and programming concepts the teachers value and how they relate them to their disciplines.

3 METHOD

We collected data from two intensive, five-day Infusing Computing PD workshops [1] in North and South Carolina in Summer 2018, during which we engaged 116 middle and high school teachers in designing plans to infuse computational thinking into their classrooms. According to our survey result prior to the PD, 48% of the participating teachers never had any programming experience, 22% had their students do hour of code activities, 28% had some but not extensive prior programming experience(e.g. HTML, JavaScript, Scratch, or code.org), and 2% claimed to be proficient in at least one programming language. We designed a 3C (Code, Connect, Create) model to structure the PD and designed each day to include sessions for each of these three elements. The Code sessions introduced basic concepts and operations in the Snap! programming environment [6] (e.g. sprites, blocks, drag and drop operations), control structures (e.g. loops, conditionals, variables), and lists using simple programming examples and finally culminating in practice with a simulation developed to integrate CT into science classes. In the discipline-specific Connect sessions, we introduced the PRADA elements and helped teachers identify the CT concepts that already exist or can be easily infused into their own content areas. The Create session allowed the teachers to work individually or to collaborate in teams to develop their CT-infused learning segments along with a Snap! program for use in their classrooms.

Table 1: The number of teacher products and project files by content area

	Science	Math	Inter-disciplinary	Humani-ties	Total
Products	18	11	4	7	40
Proj. Files	25	13	7	13	58

The teacher product analyzed in this work includes a learning segment document and a Snap! project file that teachers submitted at the end of the PD. Analysis of the learning segments allows us to understand teachers' intentions for their CT-infused lessons. Some of the items in the learning segments include: the disciplinary learning goal, the CT learning goal, the PRADA elements involved, the activities planned (with and/or without programming) for the students, and the end-product and evaluation criteria for grading. We required the teachers to do some programming and submit a Snap! project file so that they had experience with the types of programming concepts and practices their students could use in their classrooms. The Snap! project can either be a model for the type of project students would be expected to create themselves or a project that teachers created for the students to play with and explore. Teachers who worked in groups were asked to submit at least one Snap! project file per group, but they could submit more than one program if appropriate for their learning segment. Before analysis, we removed one product from our analysis for failing to submit their learning segment document, leaving us no way to

[1] For more information about the PD, visit https://www.infusingcomputing.com/

know how the teachers planned to use their Snap*!* project file in the class. In addition, we removed 4 project files for being starter code (that was repetitive with the corresponding complete project) and removed one duplicate project file. In total, we analyzed 40 teacher product submissions comprised of 40 learning segments and 58 Snap*!* project files, as is shown in Table 1.

We analyzed the teacher products at two levels: a high-level content analysis and a low-level automated programming concept analysis. Four of the authors performed a two-phase content analysis to identify the type of products, the programming features in the project files, and the coding activities designed for students. These raters were all CS education graduate students with experience designing, implementing, and evaluating CT curriculum for middle school classrooms. In the first phase, each rater looked through all the learning segments and the Snap*!* project files and took notes on the type, features, and the student coding requirements for each teacher project. The raters were given instructions on what to look for in general but were also encouraged to include anything that seemed relevant and/or uncertain for later discussion. In the second phase, the first author formed an initial categorization of the teacher products based on all the rater notes. Then, all four raters discussed each category definition until they reached full agreement. Since the type categories were more ambiguous, the four raters collaboratively determined the final type category for each project. For the other more straightforward characteristics, all the teacher projects were re-coded by the first author based on the final definition. Due to the design of our data collection instrument – it only provided small text boxes to indicate which PRADA elements related to their products – many teachers did not explain the relationship between their coding activity and their plans for teaching computational thinking. Thus, to identify how the teachers related the coding activities to their plans for teaching computational thinking, the raters manually read through the learning segments and extracted excerpts that suggest teachers' understanding of the connection between coding and CT.

The second analysis is a programming concept analysis. We created an *analysis program* that takes in the Snap*!* project files and counts if and how many times some blocks appeared, which may indicate teachers' level of understanding and ability to use certain programming concepts. The output of the analysis program includes the number of times each default or imported block is used, the number of variables (both local and global) created and used, and the number of custom (teacher-created) blocks created and used. This analysis can give us a general glimpse of how well the teachers were able to apply what they learned from the coding session to their project. The statistics also shed light on some findings in the content analysis as discussed below.

4 RESULTS

4.1 Content Analysis

4.1.1 Project Type. The raters identified five different project types in the teacher created project files:

(1) **Animation**: A non-interactive instructive, introductive, or model video
(2) **Interactive Storyboard**: A linear or non-linear animation with non-consequential interactions and a connected series of scenes
(3) **Quiz**: A project that asks students a series of questions with the sole intent to test students' knowledge about a subject
(4) **Intended Game**: A project intended to be made into a game by the teachers, even though the project may be non-game-like on submission
(5) **Exploration/Simulation Tools**: A project that provides a tool for the students to interactively explore and experiment with a concept

Figure 1 shows the number of teacher products of each type. Looking at the total number, we can see that more than a third of the products are Simulation/Exploration Tools. Animation and Interactive Storyboards together make up half of the teacher products. There are fewer Quizzes and Intended Games than the other types. Looking at the content area of each type, we find that the humanities and interdisciplinary projects are mostly Animation and Interactive Stories, whereas the Math products are mostly Intended Game and Simulation Tools. Science has about half of its projects in Simulation/Exploration Tools category while the rest of its projects were distributed roughly evenly among Animation, Interactive Storyboard, and Quiz, suggesting that science teachers may have more diverse uses for programs in their lessons.

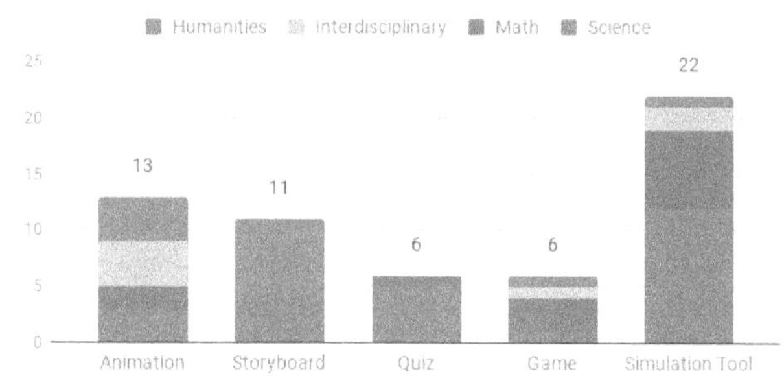

Figure 1: Number of projects in each project type

4.1.2 Student Coding Requirements. Many learning segments described the coding students would do to complete the activity. Some learning segments did not describe the coding requirement explicitly, but it could be inferred from the description of the activities. For example, a team of middle school science teachers first said "the students will be required to write their own code..." and then said "once they have created an account [in Netsblox], we will share the program with them... for themselves and their partners to manipulate", indicating the students need to write a program using a starter code. Six learning segments did not mention student coding activities at all, thus were given the 'unspecified' tag.

Raters identified four categories of student coding requirements from the teacher products. These coding requirements varied from using and/or explaining provided code, modifying existing code, programming with starter code, to building entire programs. For using and/or explaining provided code, the teachers planned to give the students a completed program for them to play and explore, sometimes accompanied by activities that require explaining the code in the program, without hands-on coding. Modifying existing code requires the students to play and make changes to the program to adapt to new information. For programming with starter code, the teachers would provide students with a starter project file that already has some code created and require students to either finish it or extend its functionalities. Building entire programs would require students to learn the requirements of the full project, usually through playing with a completed program, and then creating their own project from scratch.

The coding requirements discovered seem consistent with the popular Use-Modify-Create practice for teaching youth CT concepts [10], indicating that the teachers are familiar with the practice of having students use a working program to become familiar with an idea, then modify one, and then create their own.

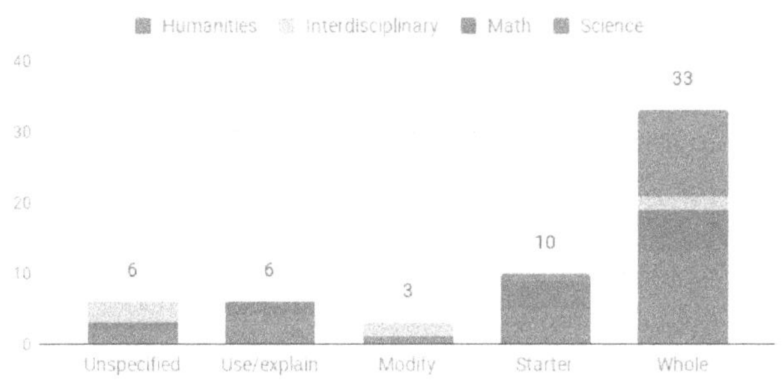

Figure 2: Number of projects with each coding requirement

Figure 2 shows the number of projects with each coding requirement. The result shows that more than half of the teacher projects tasked students with making the whole project from scratch.

4.1.3 Feature Analysis. The raters identified five common features (Sprite manipulation, QA, Event handling, Control, and Drawing) in the teacher projects. Figure 3 shows the percentage of the projects having each feature by project type. As expected, all 58 projects had some sort of Sprite Manipulation feature, which is the core mechanic and a major strength of the Snap*!* environment. Twenty-seven projects used Questions/Answers (QA), asking a question and checking answers. While QA was not present in the (non-interactive) animations, it was identified in all 6 of the quiz projects, and in over 50% of the interactive stories, games, and simulations, indicating that QA serves as an important type of interaction in the teacher-created Snap*!* projects. Two-thirds (40/58) of the projects involve Event Handling to synchronize behaviors between sprites. The most popular synchronization method (28/40) was by broadcasting a message to signal the next event. Three-quarters of projects (44/58) included basic programming control structures, such as if-then conditions, game loops, and randomized events. Animation having the lowest proportion using control structures, which makes sense given that most of the animations have a single, chronological plot that does not repeat or deviate based off of input conditions. Those animations with control structures usually used loops to draw shapes, corresponding to the DrawSquare and RowOfHouses programs introduced in the PD's Code session. Finally, 20 of the 58 projects used Drawing features.

Interestingly, we found that some teachers used the doWait block instead of message broadcasting for synchronization purposes. These teachers asked a sprite to wait a pre-set number of seconds for other sprites to complete their actions before continuing to the next action. This discovery is consistent with another research that studied creative products from elementary school students [16]. While using doWait block is one way to achieve synchronization, it is not a preferred method in many cases because of its static nature – one has to manually adjust the wait time for every sprite in the program to adapt to new information. This finding is one of the many examples that suggests problems that the Code session could easily address to help the teachers make certain features more efficiently.

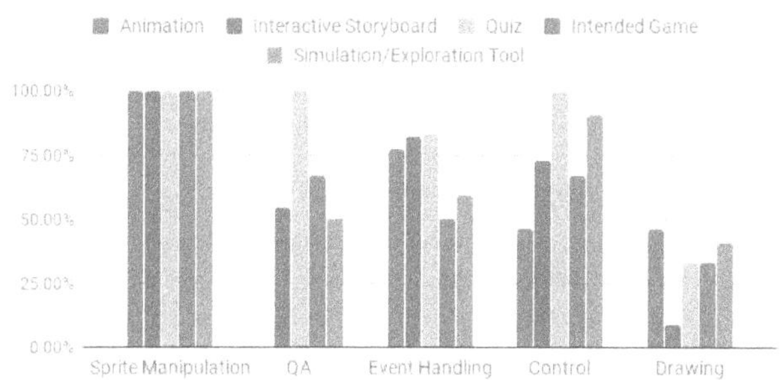

Figure 3: The percentage of the projects that have each feature by project type

4.1.4 CT in Coding Activities. We analyzed how teachers connected the coding activities to each element in PRADA by discussing what connection the teachers made with an excerpt from the learning segment that demonstrates the connection.

Pattern recognition does not seem to be a difficult element for the teachers to understand and relate to, as the teachers who identified pattern recognition in the coding activity generally made the correct connection. Teachers were able to recognize patterns in the code from two aspects. One aspect is having repeated code in a piece of script, linking it to a repeat block ("Using a repeat in the code to be able to use the 4 nitrogenous bases of DNA limitlessly"). The other aspect is having duplicate code between sprites ("6 regions that have the same code, and repetition within the code itself").

Decomposition in coding activities happens mostly when explaining and understanding existing code, often accompanied by making abstractions of decomposed code chunks ("Break down plot diagram into subcategories and look further into what blocks go into a specific abstraction"). Some teachers discussed decomposition in a more subtle way by considering the conditionals and loops as means to decompose an algorithm ("if" and 'repeat' blocks are used in the code to show a breakdown of the parts of the algorithm").

Many science and math teachers were able to identify different kinds of abstraction in the code. Many teachers were able to link the definition of custom blocks to abstraction (e.g. "Name these repeated steps [of calculating the roots and the vertex of a binary equation] by calling the process Find Roots and Find Vertex"). Some teachers recognized that the use of variables is also a kind of abstraction ("Variables have been created for specific [geological] values"). In contrast, abstraction seemed to be a more challenging concept for the interdisciplinary groups and humanities teachers to apply to their projects, as none of them mentioned abstraction in their coding activities. This finding suggests that more support is needed for the non-STEM teachers to conceptualize and apply abstraction in programming to their subject-specific context.

Similar to abstraction, algorithms were discussed only by science and math teachers. Some science and math teachers were able to relate algorithms to the "the code used in the script". These learning segments would require the students to "use an algorithm to create a block of code that will ask a question and respond to the answer as to whether correct or incorrect". A group of math teachers took a step further and noted the generalizability of an algorithm, stating that "Transcription is a step by step process and the code that is created demonstrating transcription can be used with any sequence of DNA nitrogenous bases to create an mRNA transcript." None of the interdisciplinary/humanities teachers mentioned how algorithms connect to coding in their learning segments.

4.2 Programming Concept Analysis

Table 2 shows the results of the programming concept analysis. In general, around two-thirds of the projects used loops and conditionals (If), but the percentage of projects having loops and conditionals varies greatly by type. This corroborates the finding in the content analysis where few Animation projects have Control features. Both Custom blocks and Variables appeared in about half of the projects, suggesting that these concepts are still hard for many teachers to apply. In addition, even though being a very useful data structure, lists may be difficult for the teachers to learn as it only appeared in 1/3 of the projects. Even fewer projects (13.79%) used advanced list operations like insertion or deletion.

Table 2: The number of projects that have each programming concepts by project type

	Loop	If	Custom	Var	List
Anim (13)	7(51%)	2(15%)	5(38%)	5(38%)	6(46%)
Story (11)	7(64%)	10(91%)	7(64%)	4(36%)	0(0%)
Quiz (6)	6(100%)	5(83%)	2(33%)	3(50%)	2(33%)
Game (6)	3(50%)	4(67%)	3(50%)	4(67%)	0(0%)
Sim (22)	15(68%)	20(91%)	14(64%)	18(82%)	11(50%)
Total	38(66%)	41(71%)	31(53%)	34(59%)	19(33%)

The programming concept analysis helps expose some potential issues in the teachers' understanding of programming concepts. For example, as experienced programmers we can see that the QA feature could be easily abstracted into a custom block that uses lists to manage questions and their corresponding solutions. However, only two out of six Quiz projects used custom blocks and lists. This could suggest that the teachers may have failed to recognize this abstraction or that they're simply not comfortable with using custom blocks and/or lists. Moreover, programming concept analysis helped identify the nature of the types. Animation and Interactive Storyboard projects had lower percentages of variable usage, which is most likely due to the fact that neither project type typically requires storing information for later use.

The Intended Game type scored a relatively low percentage on all programming concepts. This is also consistent with the result in the Feature analysis shown in Figure 3. Upon close inspection, we find that this could be due to the different mechanics of the games. The games that rely on mouse click-and-drag events tend to use fewer desired CT/programming concepts than others since their logic is often simply responding to cursor events. This suggests that teachers who want to make games should think about how their game mechanics relate to the programming/CT concepts they want students to learn.

5 DISCUSSION

To further investigate the coding activities in the teacher projects, we plotted the project type vs. coding requirements as shown in Figure 4. We arranged the project types according to CT/programming difficulty and the coding requirements according to how much coding students would do. Project types are arranged from left to right from least difficult to most difficult to infuse CT/programming concepts into if implemented correctly. Coding requirements range from the least (no coding) at the bottom to the most (whole project) at the top. Figure 4 shows the distribution of project types versus coding requirements for each content area with the size of the dot mapping to the number of projects at that spot.

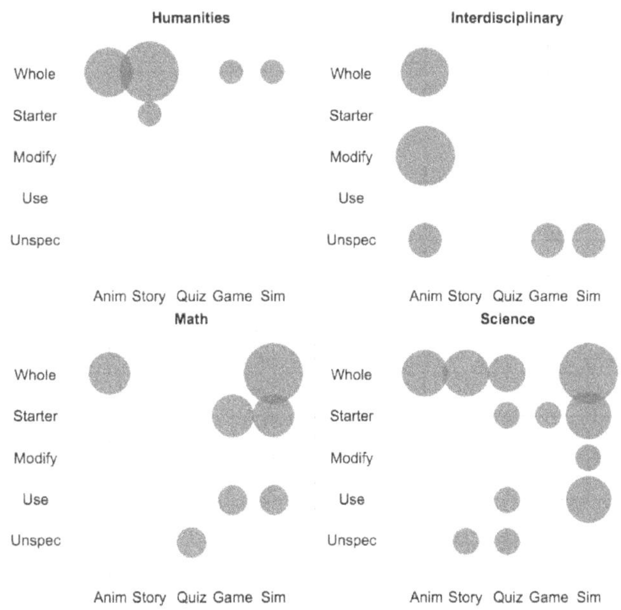

Figure 4: The relationship between project type and coding requirement by content area

These plots reveal tendencies for the teacher-created projects affiliated with each discipline. Specifically, the humanities projects lean more towards building animations and require students to do more coding. We think this is possibly due to the fact that humanities classrooms often require students to write or create content. In addition, as suggested by our product analysis, animations and interactive storyboards tend to have less complex logic and are relatively easy to make, so these teachers may feel more confident in their students' ability to make the whole project.

Math projects tend to be simulation/exploration based and expect students to do more coding. This could be because that many mathematical concepts, norms, practices, and vocabulary terms are in parallel with programming concepts [15]. For instance, the steps taken to solve a math problem can be easily transformed into an algorithm. By turning math problems like finding the best rates and exploring transformations into making simulation/exploration tools, students gain the opportunity to develop a deeper understanding of the concepts through hands-on programming.

Science projects are more varied in terms of project type and coding requirement, which may indicate that the science teachers have a larger variety of needs for their projects. For example, a group of science teachers created a curriculum to teach the Energy Pyramid. Their product included four project files: one project file is an interactive storyboard that introduces the food chain, one project file is a simulation that explores the population dynamics between the predator and the prey, and the other two project files are quizzes, one testing students' knowledge of the energy transformation in the energy pyramid, and one testing on the food chain. These varied needs are also reflected in the coding activities designed for students. For simpler concepts or phenomena, the teacher may want the students to create the whole program to increase understanding of the underlying mechanic. However, for more complex concepts, the teacher may simply want the students to use the project as a tool for the students to explore the pattern behind the phenomena.

By showing the disciplinary differences in terms of project type and coding requirements, we're not trying to argue which type or how much coding is good or bad. Rather, using the findings from the teacher product analysis, we hope to better understand the needs of the teachers from different disciplines in order to help them find better, more tailored ways to infuse programming and computational thinking into their curricula. For example, our findings show that humanities teachers are fond of using animation and interactive storyboards in their lessons but are having trouble identifying and infusing some CT elements and programming concepts into their products. A potential solution would be introducing simple modeling concepts to the teachers that transform their animations from heavily relying on the wait blocks to using variables and event handling to govern the chronological progression of the story. Other solutions may include showing the teachers diverse examples and types of coding activities that could potentially be used to teach the same knowledge.

In addition, the feature analysis and programming concept analysis not only tell us how much programming the teachers have learned, but also suggest places where we can provide more scaffolding to help the teachers be more successful in project development. For example, by better understanding what features teachers often need in their projects, we can provide more targeted scaffolding by creating pre-made features and example projects that the teachers can easily adapt and use in their projects, such as a QA block. It's important to understand and remember that these teachers are not learning programming to become professional programmers. Rather, they only need to concentrate on the elements of programming that afford CT and connect to their domain, standards, and curriculum. Thus, by giving the teachers pre-made features and examples during the Code sessions, we are not only giving them the chance to practice explaining code and examining how the features are made in the desired ways, but also relieving the teachers from the struggle of creating certain features so they can spend time on designing learning experiences for their lessons.

One limitation of this work is that the project files submitted weren't necessarily refined products ready to be used, but were mostly prototypes to showcase what the teachers intended for their students to do in their classrooms. Thus, certain features that could demonstrate teachers' understanding of programming concepts and CT elements may not have been completed. However, while the prototype characteristics were a limitation, they also afford insight into what the teachers were able to learn and make in a week of training, which might shed light on how much programming they feel comfortable teaching after a short-term training and how much they believe their students are able to learn in these lessons. Another limitation might be the fact that the coding sessions were taught mostly with create activities, which might affect the choice of the coding requirement teachers designed in their learning segments.

6 CONCLUSION

In this paper, we analyzed 58 middle and high school teacher-designed programming projects from two computational thinking PD workshops to help us understand how the K-12 teachers intend to use programming to teach CT in their classrooms.

From our analysis, we identified five project types in the teacher programming projects: animation, interactive storyboard, quiz, intended game, and simulation/exploration tool. The teachers generally have four kinds of coding requirements in their lesson plans: using and/or explaining provided code, modifying existing code, programming with starter code, and building entire programs. The common features in the teacher programming projects can be classified into five categories: sprite manipulation, QA, event handling, control, and drawing. Humanities and interdisciplinary products were mostly animations and interactive storyboards and required the students to code the whole project. The majority of the math projects were simulation/exploration tools and intended games that required students to either code the whole project from scratch or with starter code. The classification of the science products varied in project type and coding requirements, depending on the purpose of the project. Regarding connecting coding activities to computational thinking, many science and math teachers were able to make reasonable connections. However, humanities and interdisciplinary teachers appeared to have trouble identifying abstraction and algorithms in their planned coding activities.

Our work provides insights on how the teachers intend to use programming to teach computational thinking in their own content area lessons. These insights can help us provide more scaffolding for the teachers by making relevant example programs and pre-made custom blocks to help the teachers develop their projects more efficiently. We will use these pre-made examples in the Code sessions, modeling content that suits teachers' needs while also better conveying CT concepts that can be integrated and learned by students in their classrooms.

ACKNOWLEDGMENTS

This material is based upon work supported by the National Science Foundation under grant numbers 1742351 and 1742332.

REFERENCES

[1] Joel C Adams and Andrew R Webster. 2012. What do students learn about programming from game, music video, and storytelling projects?. In *Proceedings of the 43rd ACM technical symposium on Computer Science Education*. ACM, 643–648.

[2] Charoula Angeli, Joke Voogt, Andrew Fluck, Mary Webb, Margaret Cox, Joyce Malyn-Smith, and Jason Zagami. 2016. A K-6 computational thinking curriculum framework: Implications for teacher knowledge. *Journal of Educational Technology & Society* 19, 3 (2016).

[3] Valerie Barr and Chris Stephenson. 2011. Bringing computational thinking to K-12: what is Involved and what is the role of the computer science education community? *Acm Inroads* 2, 1 (2011), 48–54.

[4] Tim Bell, Jason Alexander, Isaac Freeman, and Mick Grimley. 2009. Computer science unplugged: School students doing real computing without computers. *The New Zealand Journal of Applied Computing and Information Technology* 13, 1 (2009), 20–29.

[5] Alexandra Funke, Katharina Geldreich, and Peter Hubwieser. 2017. Analysis of scratch projects of an introductory programming course for primary school students. In *Global Engineering Education Conference (EDUCON), 2017 IEEE*. IEEE, 1229–1236.

[6] Dan Garcia, Brian Harvey, and Tiffany Barnes. 2015. The beauty and joy of computing. *ACM Inroads* 6, 4 (2015), 71–79.

[7] Shuchi Grover, Satabdi Basu, and Patricia Schank. 2018. What We Can Learn About Student Learning From Open-Ended Programming Projects in Middle School Computer Science. In *Proceedings of the 49th ACM Technical Symposium on Computer Science Education*. ACM, 999–1004.

[8] Shuchi Grover and Roy Pea. 2013. Computational thinking in K–12: A review of the state of the field. *Educational Researcher* 42, 1 (2013), 38–43.

[9] Author Hidden. XXXX. Hidden Paper. In *Anonymous*.

[10] Irene Lee, Fred Martin, Jill Denner, Bob Coulter, Walter Allan, Jeri Erickson, Joyce Malyn-Smith, and Linda Werner. 2011. Computational thinking for youth in practice. *Acm Inroads* 2, 1 (2011), 32–37.

[11] María Cecilia Martinez, Marcos J. Gomez, Marco Moresi, and Luciana Benotti. 2016. Lessons Learned on Computer Science Teachers Professional Development. In *Proceedings of the 2016 ACM Conference on Innovation and Technology in Computer Science Education (ITiCSE '16)*. ACM, New York, NY, USA, 77–82. https://doi.org/10.1145/2899415.2899460

[12] Jesús Moreno-León and Gregorio Robles. 2015. Dr. Scratch: A web tool to automatically evaluate Scratch projects. In *Proceedings of the workshop in primary and secondary computing education*. ACM, 132–133.

[13] Jennifer Rosato, Chery Lucarelli, Cassandra Beckworth, and Ralph Morelli. 2017. A Comparison of Online and Hybrid Professional Development for CS Principles Teachers. In *Proceedings of the 2017 ACM Conference on Innovation and Technology in Computer Science Education (ITiCSE '17)*. ACM, New York, NY, USA, 140–145. https://doi.org/10.1145/3059009.3059060

[14] Lee S Shulman and Judith H Shulman. 2004. How and what teachers learn: A shifting perspective. *Journal of curriculum studies* 36, 2 (2004), 257–271.

[15] David Weintrop, Elham Beheshti, Michael Horn, Kai Orton, Kemi Jona, Laura Trouille, and Uri Wilensky. 2016. Defining computational thinking for mathematics and science classrooms. *Journal of Science Education and Technology* 25, 1 (2016), 127–147.

[16] David Weintrop, Alexandria K Hansen, Danielle B Harlow, and Diana Franklin. 2018. Starting from Scratch: Outcomes of early computer science learning experiences and implications for what comes next. In *Proceedings of the 2018 ACM Conference on International Computing Education Research*. ACM, 142–150.

[17] Aman Yadav, Hai Hong, and Chris Stephenson. 2016. Computational thinking for all: pedagogical approaches to embedding 21st century problem solving in K-12 classrooms. *TechTrends* 60, 6 (2016), 565–568.

[18] Aman Yadav, Chris Mayfield, Ninger Zhou, Susanne Hambrusch, and John T Korb. 2014. Computational thinking in elementary and secondary teacher education. *ACM Transactions on Computing Education (TOCE)* 14, 1 (2014), 5.

Impact of HFOSS Education on Instructors

Lori Postner, Darci Burdge
Nassau Community College
Garden City, NY, USA
lori.postner@ncc.edu
darci.burdge@ncc.edu

Heidi J. C. Ellis, Stoney Jackson
Western New England University
Springfield, MA, USA
ellis@wne.edu
stoney.jackson@wne.edu

Gregory W. Hislop
Drexel University
Philadelphia, PA, USA
hislop@drexel.edu

ABSTRACT

Student involvement in Humanitarian Free and Open Source Software (HFOSS) increases student self-reported learning while providing the motivation of "doing good" [11]. Supporting this type of student participation also impacts the instructors. This effect includes modifying one's teaching approach, providing a different perspective on the subject matter, and changing how instructors perceive their roles. This paper explores the impact on instructors that result from supporting student participation in HFOSS, including consideration of pedagogical practices, self-perceptions of teaching, and exposure to open source culture and technologies. The paper also examines resources that instructors consider important for HFOSS education. The analysis presented here is based upon a qualitative analysis of semi-structured interviews with 24 faculty members. Results indicate that exploring HFOSS education changes instructors' pedagogical approaches, broadens instructors' perspectives on the connections between academic content and professional practice, and has impact on instructors' attitudes and motivations when teaching.

CCS CONCEPTS

• **Social and professional topics → Computer science education.**

KEYWORDS

HFOSS, Humanitarian Computing, Computing Education

ACM Reference Format:

Lori Postner, Darci Burdge, Heidi J. C. Ellis, Stoney Jackson, and Gregory W. Hislop. 2019. Impact of HFOSS Education on Instructors. In *Proceedings of Innovation and Technology in Computer Science Education (ITiCSE '19).* ACM, New York, NY, USA, 7 pages. https://doi.org/10.1145/3304221.3319765

1 INTRODUCTION

Participation in Humanitarian Free and Open Source Software (HFOSS) projects has a positive impact on student attitude towards computing [7, 11], perceived learning of software engineering knowledge [5], technical knowledge and professional skills [7], and understanding how to plan, develop and maintain a software project [6]. In addition, female students report a greater understanding of project management aspects of HFOSS than do male students [6].

Given the benefits students reap from involvement in an HFOSS project, adoption of student participation in HFOSS is an attractive way to provide real-world experience to computing students. However, this participation is accompanied by a learning curve for both students and instructors [18, 22]. In addition, finding an appropriate project for a particular classroom context is challenging since the instructor must consider the language and technologies used by the project, the size of the project, and the culture of the community as well as any domain knowledge potentially needed in order to successfully contribute to it. After identifying an appropriate project, locating a mentor or contact person within the project smooths the start-up, but the right contact person may not be easy to find. Downloading and installing the project as well as learning the project work flow and processes may involve troubleshooting and investing time to learn new tools and technologies.

Although all of this may sound daunting and deter instructors from trying to incorporate HFOSS, the effort has benefits for the instructor too. Going through this process provides instructors, some of whom lack industry experience, exposure to professional practice in the open source world as well as the work environments their students will encounter upon graduation. This is a valuable experience for many instructors and helps them to keep current in the area of software development as well as to model for their students the importance of being a life long learner.

In order for student participation in HFOSS to be widely adopted, the impact on instructors of such participation must be examined in terms of both costs and benefits. An understanding of instructor experiences, specifically what it takes to successfully support student learning within HFOSS projects, will provide a solid basis for creating the right community infrastructure and instructor professional development to support expansion of student learning within HFOSS communities.

2 RELATED WORK

Free and Open Source Software (FOSS) projects are becoming more widely used to provide students with hands-on, real-world experience with software projects [3]. Frequently, student involvement in a FOSS project happens in Software Engineering courses [13, 19], and may also occur in lower level courses such as Data Structures [27], throughout the curriculum, [1, 2], and outside of the classroom via clubs or other extra-curricular activities [4].

HFOSS education can be viewed as one thread within the extensive body of computing education research that constitutes a shift from traditional lecture methods to forms of active learning including pair programming [26], flipped classrooms [10], blended learning [12], peer-instruction [23], problem-based learning [15]

ITiCSE '19, July 15–17, 2019, Aberdeen, Scotland UK

ACM ISBN 978-1-4503-6301-3/19/07...$15.00
https://doi.org/10.1145/3304221.3319765

and others. Many of these efforts share considerations related to the goals of HFOSS education. In this broad push to improve computing education, there is general recognition that the role of the instructor changes, but there has been relatively little investigation into how this shift affects instructors' perspectives on teaching. In addition, given the rapid rate of change in technology, computing instructors have relatively high burdens to keep current in their field, which also impacts their role as instructors.

Several studies are related to the current work in that they have addressed aspects of instructor perspectives on the instructor's role, and on issues of keeping up with technology or reflecting professional practice in teaching. A few studies have provided a comparison of student and instructor beliefs and attitudes about Computer Science. Perrenet [21] and Lewis [14] studied the enculturation of undergraduate CS students by comparing how their attitudes and beliefs transform as they progress through their degree program. Both works surveyed instructors about their belief about the CS discipline, although they did not survey instructors about what and how the instructors learned as computing advances.

Porter [24] reports on an instructor boot camp that has the goals of supporting classroom practices that have been shown by evidence to be successful and to change instructor perceptions of teaching so that they view it as a scholarly effort. Porter mentions that changing teaching practices may be difficult. Simon [28] reports on instructor development workshops to increase active learning in the classroom. They report a 44% adoption rate for active learning techniques, and the influences that positively impacted instructor adoption included sufficient technology support and a community of instructors working together.

Ni [20] used semi-structured interviews to determine barriers and helpers for instructors to adopt curriculum changes. Eight instructors from different academic institutions were interviewed and factors that influenced curriculum change included a sense that the traditional computer science curriculum was not effective, perceived benefits for students resulting from the curriculum change, and evidence that demonstrated that the adopted curriculum was more effective than the traditional one.

Zheng [30] reports on a grounded theory investigation into the perspectives of 14 MOOC instructors. Instructors were interviewed about their experiences in teaching MOOCs, particularly the motivations and challenges that occur when teaching MOOCs. Results identified four motivating factors that inspired instructors teaching MOOCs including professional growth, research opportunities, world-wide impact on students, and enhanced name recognition.

There has been little work done in the area of professors' perspectives on teaching open source. One effort [22] investigated the benefits, challenges, and opportunities of supporting student involvement in a FOSS project. Interviews were performed with seven Software Engineering professors from a variety of counties who included FOSS in their courses. The focus of these interviews was on how the FOSS projects were used within the course and did not cover instructor opinions on their own learning or impact on their teaching. Results indicated that instructors utilized FOSS projects in a variety of manners with a range of student learning activities. Benefits to students included improved student learning, both technical and professional, and barriers included the learning curve faced by both student and instructor. These results corroborate earlier research into student experiences with HFOSS [5–7].

3 METHODS

This paper focuses on the impact on instructors of supporting student participation in an HFOSS project. In particular, the following research questions motivate the analysis reported here:

- Q1: How did HFOSS education change the instructors' approaches and perspectives toward computing instruction?
- Q2: What resources did instructors believe were most important to their success in HFOSS education?

3.1 Study Design

The effort to expand student participation in HFOSS projects has included instructor professional development in the form of NSF-funded instructor workshops for instructors interested in incorporating HFOSS education into their courses. These Professors' Open Source Software Experience (POSSE) workshops have been held once or twice a year since 2013. Over 140 instructors from over 110 different institutions have completed the workshop. This community served as the population for this study.

The study involved an online survey followed by a semi-structured interview. The survey was intended to:

- Gather demographic information about the participants
- Construct a list of courses in which instructors successfully incorporated HFOSS
- Determine whether instructor background influenced success in HFOSS education
- Explore the hurdles instructors encountered as they incorporated HFOSS education into their courses

An analysis of survey results is reported in [25].

3.2 Data Collection

The goal of the semi-structured interview portion of the study was to obtain observations about the impact of supporting student involvement in HFOSS on the individual instructor. The participants were selected from instructors who had participated in a POSSE workshop and had at least one academic year after the workshop date to incorporate HFOSS into their classroom. At the start of the study, there were 77 eligible POSSE alumni who had attended a POSSE workshop at least one year in the past. This group was narrowed to include only one participant per institution, and to focus on instructors who had little or no experience with HFOSS education prior to attending the POSSE workshop, but had actively participated in the online and in-person parts of POSSE. This resulted in 41 potential participants who were contacted via email and invited to participate in the study by completing the initial survey [25]. This group included both instructors who had been successful in supporting student involvement in HFOSS and instructors who had not been successful yet. Twenty-six instructors completed the survey, a 66% response rate. Of these 26, 24 agreed to be interviewed and participated in a semi-structured interview. The interviewees consisted of 11 women and 13 men, a more gender balanced population than the general population of computing instructors [31]. This gender ratio is comparable to the larger POSSE alumni community.

The instructors in the study came from institutions located in 16 different U.S. states. Two institutions were 2-year and the remaining 22 were 4-year institutions. Eleven were private not-for-profit and 13 were public. There were five small institutions, eleven medium sized institutions, seven large institutions and one very large institution according to the Carnegie Classifications of Institutions of Higher Education [8]. Also according to the Carnegie Classifications, the selectivity of the institutions varied with 11 institutions being "more selective", eight being "selective", and two being "inclusive". The two 2-year schools and one of the 4-year schools were not rated based on selectivity.

As for the instructors, one was black, 21 were white and two declined to answer. Five were Assistant Professors, 11 were Associate Professors, four were full Professors and two were Professors and Chairs. In addition, there was an Associate Teaching Professor and a Clinical Assistant Professor. Table 1 shows the number of years of experience as a computing educator for the study sample. It is interesting to note that 83% of instructors had six or more years of computing education experience and over half had more than 10 years of experience. Table 2 shows the number of years of both industry and open source experience of the participating instructors.

Years	# Faculty
2-5	4
6-10	5
>10	15

Table 1: Years Experience as a Computing Educator

Years	# w/ Industry	# w/ Open Source
0	7	5
1-4	9	12
5-10	4	4
>10	4	3

Table 2: Industry and Open Source Experience

Faculty incorporated HFOSS into a wide range of courses at the 100, 200, 300 and 400 levels including: Object Oriented Program Design, Data Structures, Algorithms, Software Engineering, Computer Security, Senior Seminar and Mobile Development. There is some evidence that instructors teaching project courses such as Software Engineering or a capstone course find it easier to incorporate HFOSS into the classroom. The semi-structured interview focused on the instructor's experiences in the classes where they supported student involvement in HFOSS. There were four questions for instructors who had not involved students in HFOSS including *"Tell us a bit more about why you haven't involved students in HFOSS."* and *"What could the research project team do that might help you involve students in HFOSS?"* The interview for instructors who had involved students in HFOSS consisted of nine open-ended questions and included questions such as *"How did your use of HFOSS work in your class?"* and *"What have you learned from interacting with HFOSS communities?"* Interviews were conducted either face-to-face or over the phone. Interviews took between 30-60 minutes. For the face-to-face interviews, two researchers were present with one researcher asking the questions and the second taking notes.

3.3 Data Analysis

The data was analyzed using a grounded theory process of inductive coding [16, 29] using the CATMA textual analysis tool [17]. The raw data were the notes taken during the instructor interview. An initial set of categories and codes were derived from the interview questions. Two researchers then independently went through all of the interviews, coding the data and adding codes as needed. Once all of the data was coded, axial coding was used to relate codes and categories. The codes were reviewed, common codes identified, and a hierarchy of categories was created within code sets. One researcher created the initial category and code organization and a second researcher reviewed and suggested revisions. The interview data for 24 instructors provided a large corpus for a qualitative study, where the focus is on developing understanding and insight into the questions rather than the typical goals of statistical significance sought in quantitative studies.

4 RESULTS

The qualitative approach outlined above identified a series of themes in the data that help provide answers to the two research questions. These themes are discussed in the sub-sections below for each research question.

4.1 Impact on Instructors' Approach and Perspective

This section presents emergent themes that help to answer research question 1: How did HFOSS education change the instructors' approaches and perspectives toward computing instruction? The data for these themes comes from the interviews of the 19 instructors (seven women, 12 men) who incorporated HFOSS into their courses. The remaining five participants (four women, one man) had not been successful with HFOSS education at the time of the interview. When asked why they were not able to incorporate HFOSS into courses yet, these five cited not teaching an appropriate course and not having enough time to prepare HFOSS materials as the main reasons. Faculty described involvement in a number of HFOSS projects including: Ushahidi, Mifos, OpenMRS, GNOME Mousetrap, Mozilla, and SugarLabs.

4.1.1 Instructors as Participants in HFOSS Communities. HFOSS education often requires a level of participation by the instructor that is distinctive. Five of the interviewees (26%) mentioned their own connection to the HFOSS community in their interviews as having impacted their approach to teaching. Table 3 shows an example code and coded data for this theme. Additional codes included *Impact of FOSS, Community culture/politics rate of change, Participate in community,* and *Persistence (with regard to interacting with the community).*

Five interviewees made 12 observations about some aspect of HFOSS community participation in their interviews and one specifically stated that s/he did not interact with the HFOSS community. One of the most common discussion points related to the impact of the

Code	Raw Data
Importance of community	"You have to interact with the community as a professor."

Table 3: Example Coding for Instructors as Participants

FOSS community on learning. Finding an appropriate FOSS project community was identified as important as evidenced by statements such as *"It is important to find the right community, some are more welcoming, some less"*. Finding the right HFOSS community can be a challenge for a number of reasons. As another participant pointed out, the project politics may make it difficult: *"their [the project's] internal politics and dynamics changes a lot over time ... they were in a midst of a leadership meltdown of sorts"*. Another participant stated how important it is for the professor to interact so that s/he can understand the communications that occur and focus on working with community members who are positive *"Having some people that I know that I can rely on. Some interactions have been positive and some negative. ... Don't drop a project just because one person in the project isn't positive."* It seems likely that community interactions are key to successful student participation in HFOSS and instructor observations provide evidence of this.

Interviewees also talked about how their participation helped them learn about the real-world aspect of open source culture. One participant stated: *"I didn't have any concept of what it meant for anyone around the world to be involved in co-creating something at the same time ... if they could get that understanding to students, even if they don't create open source, that would be a good thing ... raising awareness about what open source is and open principles."*

4.1.2 Professional Practice as a Context for Computing Education. A second theme that emerged is that HFOSS education positions professional practice as a context for computing education. Some instructors don't have industry experience and therefore lack experience with collaborative, large scale projects. Involvement in HFOSS allows instructors to participate in current projects, using cutting-edge technologies, and model for their students how they approach new problems as they learn alongside their students.

There were 31 separate observations about professional practice and technical topics made by 12 (63%) of the interviewees (four women, eight men). Four had no industry experience, four had 1-4 years of industry experience, two had 5-10 years of experience and two had >10 years of experience. The fact that half of the interviewees mentioned learning a new technology provides evidence that HFOSS is a rich learning environment as even those with extensive industry experience commented on learning a new technology. Simply learning a new tool is unsurprising for computing faculty. The insight in this theme is that HFOSS Education puts technology in a context of professional practice, and instructors can use that context to enhance learning. Table 4 shows an example code and coded data for the Professional Practice as a Context for Computing Education theme. Additional codes included *Security, Tool knowledge, Open source workflow* and *Information literacy within a project.*

When instructors spoke about professional practice in HFOSS education, two main sub-themes emerged: process and tools/ technologies. Instructors spoke about how incorporating H/FOSS into their courses gave them a better understanding of the work flow used in software engineering/development. One instructor noted

Code	Raw Data
Software development process	"I wasn't aware of how extensive and distributed the software development base is and how sophisticated the tools used are to coordinate the software development process"

Table 4: Example Coding for Professional Practice as a Context

"I've gone from being kind of tersely familiar with open source software as a development area to being more involved in different ways of how people do software engineering, so now I feel better qualified to tell my students about best practices in this area." Another commented *"I learned a lot about work flow, particularly in open source project[s], because I've never done professional software development."* As academics, this was enlightening for several participants as they had no industry experience. By working in an HFOSS project they could see how the concepts they have taught play out in an open source project thus allowing them to provide real-world learning to students.

Several instructors commented that learning about software tools increased their ability to include those tools in their classroom. One instructor commented: *"I've learned more tools and ways to incorporate them into my classes."* and another stated when asked about what they learned *"...hearing how others used tools (slack). How they use it."* Comments like these reinforce the perception that HFOSS education provided a professional practice context that enabled instructors to enrich their teaching.

4.1.3 Instructors as Co-learners and Mentors. Perhaps the most interesting theme involved instructor reflections on themselves as an instructor, their transformation as an instructor, and their observations on the change of the instructor's role as a result of supporting student participation in HFOSS. Nine instructors (47%) made 20 self-observations related to their growth as an instructor. Table 5 shows an example code and coded data for this theme.

Code	Raw Data
More able to release control	"... you're letting go of setting the end point for students. I'm less sure of exactly where we're going and where we'll end up."

Table 5: Example Coding for Instructor as Co-Learner

The codes used for instructors as co-learners and mentors span topics that might be expected when employing a new instructional approach such as *Instructor Learning Curve* and *Increase in Confidence.* However, some interesting observations occurred under codes such as *More Comfortable with Things not Going as Planned, More able to Release Control, Able to Admit not Knowing Something"* and *Better at Taking Risks.* Additional tags included *More Open to new Technologies, More Enthusiastic having Students Work in the Open, Real-World Impact,* and *More Willing to Expose Students to Real-World Complexity.*

In analyzing these codes, five sub-themes emerged including confidence, ability to handle risk in the classroom, real-world applicability, understanding of teaching and/or learning, and motivation.

Four instructors commented on an increase in confidence or being more able to release control in the classroom. Some instructors also noted that they were more comfortable admitting to not knowing answers to student questions. One instructor commented that they were *"... more willing to cede authority and admit that I don't know something."* This provides some evidence that instructors are shifting from the "sage on the stage" to the "guide on the side" due to supporting student involvement in HFOSS.

Four instructors also remarked on an increased ability to handle risk in the classroom. One instructor commented that they were *"...better at trying something, taking a risk,..."* and another commented *"I've gotten more comfortable with things not going as planned..."* Another instructor indicated that they were more open to trying new technologies. These attitudes are often contrary to how instructors are used to teaching as many instructors have a fixed plan for a semester. The possibility of change is also contrary to the expectations that students have of their courses. However, this more fluid educational experience parallels the experiences students will have once they enter the workforce and therefore is valuable.

A third sub-theme that emerged was the real-world impact which included exposing students to code used in existing projects (not just academic examples), providing instructors with more than just the academic theory of software development, and working on a team to further develop a product already in use. One instructor indicated that it has given her/him that real-world context, not just the academic side. Another commented that s/he had *"... gotten much more explicit with students that my learning goal for them is to learn how to work through mucky problems."*

Four instructors provided evidence of greater understanding of teaching and/or learning with one instructor commenting on the learning curve by stating *"It is such a learning process as a professor, it took me a while to get to the point to getting students to contribute."* Another indicated that s/he felt *"...we're at the very early stage of learning how software development should be taught - working on a team to develop product we can trust ..."* One instructor commented on student capacity to learn stating *"What I learned is how far students could go on their own if you mentor them well; when they graduated, they could write code better than the profs by far."*

Perhaps the most interesting instructor comments were related to instructor motivation. Three instructors commented on how student participation in HFOSS transformed their teaching and was inspiring, with one instructor with more than 10 years experience as a computing educator stating that their teaching was *"transformed"*. Another instructor, also with more than 10 years experience as a computing educator, commented about how proud s/he was at their own learning stating *"... I learned a lot and was proud that I learned about it."* It is also interesting to note that there were no negative comments related to instructor motivation.

4.2 Resources for HFOSS Education

This section presents emergent themes that help to answer research question 2: What resources did instructors believe were most important to their effort in HFOSS education? As discussed earlier, there is considerable evidence of the value of HFOSS education for students. In addition, the prior section indicates that there are interesting positive impacts of HFOSS education for the instructors. At the same time, it has been clear for some time that there is a significant learning curve for instructors as well as students pursuing HFOSS participation. The interviews provided several insights related to the resources instructors found helpful in navigating that learning curve and getting started in HFOSS education.

4.2.1 Working with Other Faculty. - The learning curve for HFOSS education is partly technical, with faculty needing to learn HFOSS culture, tools, and processes. At the same time, many of the challenges in HFOSS education relate to pedagogy and curriculum issues. Given the changes in teaching method and perspective discussed earlier, it seems reasonable that instructors would turn to other instructors as they get started in HFOSS education. Table 6 shows an example code and coded data for this theme.

Code	Raw Data
Faculty at own institution	"... I did have another POSSE member here on campus so I felt lucky for that; we did talk about what we could do..."

Table 6: Example Coding for Working with Other Faculty

Collaborations among faculty members involved both experienced and new HFOSS educators, and also groups of new educators working together to problem solve and to co-develop HFOSS learning activities. While these collaborations were described as useful, they did not seem to be sustained. As one instructor noted, *"once we got busy during the fall semester, active collaboration stopped with that group of four or five."*

4.2.2 Community Gatherings. - Even though long-term collaboration on a regular basis seems difficult to maintain, many of the faculty interviewed have found periodic re-connection with the HFOSS education community to be of value. The faculty interviewed had all attended an initial POSSE workshop and so had some contacts within the community. Many of them have supplemented this initial experience by attending follow-up workshops often held in conjunction with other conferences related to computing education. These gatherings have created a community of HFOSS educators, one of the success factors for adopting new teaching approaches reported by Simon [28]. Table 7 shows an example code and coded data for this theme.

Code	Raw Data
Materials sprints	".... hard but useful work."

Table 7: Example Coding for Community Gatherings

Faculty also valued the ability to reach out to the community on an ad-hoc basis. One instructor noted the value of a *"community of experts that are easy to contact which is already in place."* Several of the instructors seemed to find this faculty community important to their success with HFOSS education. As one noted: *"If I was on my own, I probably would have given up."*

4.2.3 Shared Learning Materials. - Instructors always seem to struggle to find enough time to develop learning materials. The HFOSS education community has put considerable effort into applying open source principles to ease this struggle and promote sharing of learning materials. Materials are located at http:foss2serve.org and http:teachingopensource.org. Table 8 shows an example code and coded data for this theme.

Code	Raw Data
POSSE materials	"Learning activities were helpful."

Table 8: Example Coding for Shared Learning Materials

One instructor commented on teaching an HFOSS course that the shared learning materials provided *"a lot of material I used in this course."* Another instructor thought that the learning materials *"were helpful"* although s/he didn't use them directly but rather reported that they *"influenced and inspired"* creation of custom versions.

5 DISCUSSION

The results presented in the previous section demonstrate that incorporating HFOSS into the classroom is not just about what the students learn, it also has great impact on the instructors. Three themes related to the impact on instructors' approaches and perspectives that emerge from the qualitative analysis show striking aspects of that impact on instructors. HFOSS education motivates instructors to become HFOSS community participants and provides a richer context for framing computing education, particularly with regard to software development. Perhaps most interestingly, instructors find HFOSS education changing their role to co-learning and mentoring rather than more traditional lecturing. Instructors report that HFOSS education has helped them learn to be more flexible in the classroom and more comfortable with non-traditional classroom management. This release of control is necessary to provide students with real-world experiences that are frequently complex, unbounded, and have no easily identified answers. As a result of HFOSS use in classes, the instructors feel that they are better able to handle risk and unexpected developments while teaching. This evolution of instructor role in HFOSS education has similarity to results reported for other active learning approaches.

The interviews for this study were conducted with instructors who were one to several years into their HFOSS education efforts. Many of the instructors had little or no prior open source experience before incorporating it into their course. As discussed above, the comments from these faculty centered on instructors as HFOSS community participants. It is interesting to note that the research team has also observed cases where instructors guide learning for students without direct participation by the instructor in the HFOSS project. One area for future investigation is that these differing levels of instructor participation represent two points on the instructor learning curve. Initially, instructor participation is more important while the instructor is developing expertise in HFOSS. Later on, with more HFOSS expertise, the instructor's level of HFOSS community participation may be more variable while still allowing instructors to guide and support student learning within the complexities of an HFOSS project. This may imply that, with development of expertise, instructors can become more efficient at HFOSS education, which would help with sustainability of the approach.

In addition to instructor learning, it was interesting to note that instructors found the experience to be motivating and in at least some cases, transformed their teaching. This provides an encouraging indicator for widespread adoption of HFOSS education. Given that instructors have considerable control over teaching methods used in their classroom, this consideration of instructor motivation is important for any approach that changes the instructor role.

In considering the results based on the resources used by instructors to support HFOSS education and the manner in which they employed them, it is interesting to note that the mind set of open source appears to be influencing how instructors teach. One instructor mentioned *"a big thing is now that when I'm thinking about a course, I ask is there some way that open source would be a good contribution to the course"*. In addition, instructors appear to be reflecting on what they see in HFOSS communities and integrating some of that culture into their teaching. For instance, remarks by faculty members appear to indicate that they are more inclined to develop a course within a community of HFOSS educators, rather than a more typical approach where an instructor develops and delivers a course on his or her own. As one instructor indicated *"Also, when working with other people in POSSE, a lot of them have a lot more teaching experience than I have, so to see how they handle activities has opened up new possibilities for me..."*

These positive experiences for instructors come with a learning curve. As the themes related to the second research question show, connection with other faculty, access to learning materials, and periodic HFOSS education community events help with this learning curve. Even so, the required effort remains an inhibitor to adoption, and an area of future effort for the HFOSS education community.

5.1 Limitations

By definition, the instructors in this study had participated in the Professors' Open Source Software Experience (POSSE) [9] workshop. The results of this study are descriptive of that population, and may not be representative of the wider academic community, but the study does demonstrate the potential benefits gained not just by the students but also the instructors.

The process of identifying themes that emerge from the volume of data generated by 24 instructor interviews is inherently subjective. To mitigate this issue, best practices ensuring the rigor of qualitative research [16] were followed including using pairs of researchers to code with frequent meetings to resolve differences.

6 CONCLUSION AND FUTURE WORKS

The emphasis of much of the work in HFOSS education, and related pedagogical approaches, is what the students learn. This study provides some interesting and encouraging insights from investigating the impact on instructors of the process of supporting their students' involvement in an HFOSS project. Despite the learning curve, instructors who have been successful are enthusiastic about the opportunities HFOSS education provides for them. Future areas of study include an analysis of instructor expectations and student successes, and further examination of ways to reduce the learning curve for instructors interested in HFOSS education.

ACKNOWLEDGMENTS

This material is based on work supported by the National Science Foundation under Grant Nos. DUE-1525039, DUE-1524877, and DUE-1524898. Any opinions, findings and conclusions or recommendations expressed in this material are those of the author(s) and do not necessarily reflect the views of the National Science Foundation (NSF).

REFERENCES

[1] Judith Bishop, Carlos Jensen, Walt Scacchi, and Arfon Smith. 2016. How to Use Open Source Software in Education. In *Proceedings of the 47th ACM Technical Symposium on Computing Science Education (SIGCSE '16)*. ACM, New York, NY, USA, 321–322. DOI: http://dx.doi.org/10.1145/2839509.2844665

[2] Grant Braught, John Maccormick, James Bowring, Quinn Burke, Barbara Cutler, David Goldschmidt, Mukkai Krishnamoorthy, Wesley Turner, Steven Huss-Lederman, Bonnie Mackellar, and Allen Tucker. 2018. A Multi-Institutional Perspective on H/FOSS Projects in the Computing Curriculum. *ACM Trans. Comput. Educ.* 18, 2, Article 7 (July 2018), 31 pages. DOI: http://dx.doi.org/10.1145/3145476

[3] Moara Sousa Brito, Fernanda Gomes Silva, Christina von Flach G. Chavez, Debora C. Nascimento, and Roberto A Bittencourt. 2018. FLOSS in Software Engineering Education An Update of a Systematic Mapping Study. *SBES '2018, Brazilian Symposium on Software Engineering - Education Track* (2018).

[4] Darci Burdge, Gregory W. Hislop, and Joanna Klukowska. 2018. Open Source Student Clubs: (Abstract Only). In *Proceedings of the 49th ACM Technical Symposium on Computer Science Education (SIGCSE '18)*. ACM, New York, NY, USA, 1070–1070. DOI: http://dx.doi.org/10.1145/3159450.3162186

[5] Heidi J.C. Ellis, Gregory W. Hislop, Monisha S. Pulimood, Becka Morgan, and Ben Coleman. 2015. Software Engineering Learning in HFOSS: A Multi-Institutional Study. *122nd Association for Engineering Education Annual Conference and Exposition* (2015).

[6] Heidi J.C. Ellis, Gregory W. Hislop, Josephine Rodriguez, and Ralph A. Morelli. 2012. Student Software Engineering Learning via Participation in Humanitarian FOSS Projects. *119th Annual ASEE Conference and Exhibition* (2012).

[7] Heidi J. C. Ellis, Gregory W. Hislop, Stoney Jackson, and Lori Postner. 2015. Team Project Experiences in Humanitarian Free and Open Source Software (HFOSS). *Trans. Comput. Educ.* 15, 4, Article 18 (Dec. 2015), 23 pages. DOI: http://dx.doi.org/10.1145/2684812

[8] Carnegie Foundation. 2010. The Carnegie Classification of Institutions of Higher Education (n.d.). About Carnegie Classification. (2010). http://carnegieclassifications.iu.edu/2010/

[9] Red Hat. 2017. Open Source in Education. (2017). https://www.redhat.com/en/about/open-source-education/educators

[10] Antti Herala, Erno Vanhala, Antti Knutas, and Jouni Ikonen. 2015. Teaching Programming with Flipped Classroom Method: A Study from Two Programming Courses. In *Proceedings of the 15th Koli Calling Conference on Computing Education Research (Koli Calling '15)*. ACM, New York, NY, USA, 165–166. DOI: http://dx.doi.org/10.1145/2828959.2828983

[11] Gregory W. Hislop, Heidi J.C. Ellis, S. Monisha Pulimood, Becka Morgan, Suzanne Mello-Stark, Ben Coleman, and Cam Macdonell. 2015. A Multi-Institutional Study of Learning via Student Involvement in Humanitarian Free and Open Source Software Projects. In *Proceedings of the Eleventh Annual International Conference on International Computing Education Research (ICER '15)*. ACM, New York, NY, USA, 199–206. DOI: http://dx.doi.org/10.1145/2787622.2787726

[12] Yanli Hu, Liang Bai, and Bin Ge. 2018. Online Behavior Analysis-based Blended Learning Model. In *Proceedings of ACM Turing Celebration Conference - China (TURC '18)*. ACM, New York, NY, USA, 136–137. DOI: http://dx.doi.org/10.1145/3210713.3210748

[13] Zhewei Hu, Yang Song, and Edward F. Gehringer. 2018. Open-source Software in Class: Students' Common Mistakes. In *Proceedings of the 40th International Conference on Software Engineering: Software Engineering Education and Training (ICSE-SEET '18)*. ACM, New York, NY, USA, 40–48. DOI: http://dx.doi.org/10.1145/3183377.3183394

[14] Clayton Lewis. 2007. Attitudes and Beliefs About Computer Science Among Students and Faculty. *SIGCSE Bull.* 39, 2 (June 2007), 37–41. DOI: http://dx.doi.org/10.1145/1272848.1272880

[15] Hanna Mäenpää, Sasu Tarkoma, Samu Varjonen, and Arto Vihavainen. 2015. Blending Problem- and Project-Based Learning in Internet of Things Education: Case Greenhouse Maintenance. In *Proceedings of the 46th ACM Technical Symposium on Computer Science Education (SIGCSE '15)*. ACM, New York, NY, USA, 398–403. DOI: http://dx.doi.org/10.1145/2676723.2677262

[16] Nicholas Mays and Catherine Pope. 1995. Qualitative Research: Rigour and qualitative research. *BMJ* 311, 6997 (1995), 109–112. DOI: http://dx.doi.org/10.1136/bmj.311.6997.109 arXiv:https://www.bmj.com/content

[17] M.; Gius E.; Jacke J. Meister, J.C.; Petris. 2016. CATMA 5.0 [software for text annotation and analysis]. (2016). http://www.catma.de

[18] Becka Morgan and Carlos Jensen. 2014. Lessons Learned from Teaching Open Source Software Development. In *Open Source Software: Mobile Open Source Technologies*, Luis Corral, Alberto Sillitti, Giancarlo Succi, Jelena Vlasenko, and Anthony I. Wasserman (Eds.). Springer Berlin Heidelberg, Berlin, Heidelberg, 133–142.

[19] Debora M. C. Nascimento, Roberto Almeida Bittencourt, and Christina Chavez. 2015. Open source projects in software engineering education: a mapping study. *Computer Science Education* 25, 1 (2015), 67–114. DOI: http://dx.doi.org/10.1080/08993408.2015.1033159 arXiv:https://doi.org/10.1080/08993408.2015.1033159

[20] Lijun Ni, Tom McKlin, and Mark Guzdial. 2010. How Do Computing Faculty Adopt Curriculum Innovations?: The Story from Instructors. In *Proceedings of the 41st ACM Technical Symposium on Computer Science Education (SIGCSE '10)*. ACM, New York, NY, USA, 544–548. DOI: http://dx.doi.org/10.1145/1734263.1734444

[21] Jacob Perrenet. 2009. Differences in Beliefs and Attitudes About Computer Science Among Students and Faculty of the Bachelor Program. In *Proceedings of the 14th Annual ACM SIGCSE Conference on Innovation and Technology in Computer Science Education (ITiCSE '09)*. ACM, New York, NY, USA, 129–133. DOI: http://dx.doi.org/10.1145/1562877.1562920

[22] G. H. L. Pinto, F. F. Filho, I. Steinmacher, and M. A. Gerosa. 2017. Training Software Engineers Using Open-Source Software: The Professors' Perspective. In *2017 IEEE 30th Conference on Software Engineering Education and Training (CSEE T)*. 117–121. DOI: http://dx.doi.org/10.1109/CSEET.2017.27

[23] Leo Porter, Dennis Bouvier, Quintin Cutts, Scott Grissom, Cynthia Lee, Robert McCartney, Daniel Zingaro, and Beth Simon. 2016. A Multi-institutional Study of Peer Instruction in Introductory Computing. In *Proceedings of the 47th ACM Technical Symposium on Computing Science Education (SIGCSE '16)*. ACM, New York, NY, USA, 358–363. DOI: http://dx.doi.org/10.1145/2839509.2844642

[24] Leo Porter, Cynthia Lee, Beth Simon, and Mark Guzdial. 2017. Preparing Tomorrow's Faculty to Address Challenges in Teaching Computer Science. *Commun. ACM* 60, 5 (April 2017), 25–27. DOI: http://dx.doi.org/10.1145/3068791

[25] Lori Postner, Heidi J.C. Ellis, and Gregory W. Hislop. 2018. A Survey of Instructors' Experiences Supporting StudentLearning Using HFOSS Projects. In *Proceedings of the 49th ACM Technical Symposium on Computer Science Education (SIGCSE '18)*. ACM, New York, NY, USA, 203–208. DOI: http://dx.doi.org/10.1145/3159450.3159524

[26] Alex D. Radermacher and Gursimran S. Walia. 2011. Investigating the Effective Implementation of Pair Programming: An Empirical Investigation. In *Proceedings of the 42Nd ACM Technical Symposium on Computer Science Education (SIGCSE '11)*. ACM, New York, NY, USA, 655–660. DOI: http://dx.doi.org/10.1145/1953163.1953346

[27] Samuel A. Rebelsky. 2015. HFOSS-Lite in CS2: Incorporating the Ushahidi Crowdmapping Program in a Data Structures and Algorithms Course (Abstract Only). In *Proceedings of the 46th ACM Technical Symposium on Computer Science Education (SIGCSE '15)*. ACM, New York, NY, USA, 514–514. DOI: http://dx.doi.org/10.1145/2676723.2691885

[28] Beth Simon, Elizabeth Bales, William G. Griswold, and Stephen Cooper. 2011. Case Study: Faculty Professional Development Workshops for Innovation Diffusion. In *Proceedings of the 42Nd ACM Technical Symposium on Computer Science Education (SIGCSE '11)*. ACM, New York, NY, USA, 673–678. DOI: http://dx.doi.org/10.1145/1953163.1953350

[29] Steven J Taylor, Robert Bogdan, and Marjorie DeVault. 2015. *Introduction to Qualitative Research Methods: A Guidebook and Resource.* John Wiley & Sons.

[30] Saijing Zheng, Pamela Wisniewski, Mary Beth Rosson, and John M. Carroll. 2016. Ask the Instructors: Motivations and Challenges of Teaching Massive Open Online Courses. In *Proceedings of the 19th ACM Conference on Computer-Supported Cooperative Work & Social Computing (CSCW '16)*. ACM, New York, NY, USA, 206–221. DOI: http://dx.doi.org/10.1145/2818048.2820082

[31] Bizot B. zweben, S. 2017. 2017 CRA Taulbee Survey. (2017). https://cra.org/wp-content/uploads/2018/05/2017-Taulbee-Survey-Report.pdf

Evaluating the Effectiveness of Explicit Instruction in Reducing Program Reasoning Fallacies in Elementary Level Students

Ashish Aggarwal
University of Florida
Gainesville, FL 32611, U.S.A
ashishjuit@ufl.edu

Christina Gardner-McCune
University of Florida
Gainesville, FL 32611, U.S.A
gmccune@ufl.edu

David S. Touretzky
Carnegie Mellon University
Pittsburgh, PA 15213, U.S.A
dst@cs.cmu.edu

ABSTRACT

Previous research in K-5 CS education has focused on improving students' engagement in programming using visual block-based environments like Scratch. However, little is known about how elementary school students' reason about programs. We define computational reasoning as the ability to read, write, trace and debug programs and predict program behavior. Recently, computing education researchers have become interested in exploring how elementary school students build their computational reasoning abilities. This poster presents results from a study which analyzed the role of explicit instruction in the form of 'laws of computation' in cultivating elementary school (4th and 5th graders) students' ability to reason about programs using Microsoft Kodu Game Lab. We used pre-tests to record students' default models of reasoning about programs and then used post-tests to measure the effectiveness of intervention by noting students' reasoning responses on a similar program. Our findings indicate that by default students reason sequentially about program execution which can be incorrect in situations like parallel rule execution. We also found that the use of explicit instruction in the form of 'laws' is helpful for students to refine their understanding of program execution and to improve their reasoning ability.

CCS CONCEPTS

• **Social and professional topics~K-12 education**

KEYWORDS

Computational Reasoning, Explicit Instruction, Kodu, Elementary School Students, Analogical Reasoning, Program Comprehension.

ACM Reference format:

Ashish Aggarwal, Christina Gardner-McCune, and David S. Touretzky. 2019. Evaluating the Effectiveness of Explicit Instruction in Reducing Program Reasoning Fallacies in Elementary Level Students. In *Proceedings of ACM Conference on Innovation and Technology in Computer Science Education (ITiCSE'19). ACM, New York, NY, USA, 1 page.*
https://doi.org/10.1145/3304221.3325588

ACM ISBN 978-1-4503-6301-3/19/07.
https://doi.org/10.1145/3304221.3325588

1 EXTENDED ABSTRACT

As the demand to include computing activities into K-12 curriculum increases [4], it is important to focus on evaluating and assessing how students develop correct mental models [1]. In the past, there has been extensive work on the use of analogies in helping students learn about computers. While the use of analogies may be helpful, incorrect use of analogy may inhibit students from developing correct mental models of reasoning [2].

The study presented in this poster consisted of 18 elementary school students (4th and 5th grade) who were asked to predict the program behavior of similar programs before and after an intervention. In this intervention, the study staff explicitly taught the students to reason about programs using the 'laws of Kodu' [3]. The pre-test was used to observe students' default reasoning on program execution and the post-test was used to understand the effectiveness of intervention in guiding students' reasoning about program execution. We found that a majority of students were sequentially reasoning about the execution of programs which was incorrect, and their reasoning significantly improved after the intervention.

The research presented in this poster highlights two contributions: (1) students actively apply analogical reasoning models accumulated through their day-to-day experience in reasoning about programs; and (2) while students cannot be prevented from using analogical reasoning, the use of explicit instruction can help in molding a student's reasoning wherever analogies do not hold true. We can thus help students to develop correct mental models of how program statements are evaluated. These models will improve students' ability to read and understand programs and predict program behavior, which is essential for their success as computational thinkers.

REFERENCES

[1] Ashish Aggarwal, David S. Touretzky, and Christina Gardner-McCune. 2018. Demonstrating the Ability of Elementary School Students to Reason About Programs. In Proceedings of the 49th ACM Technical Symposium on Computer Science Education (SIGCSE '18). ACM, New York, NY, USA, 735-740. DOI: https://doi.org/10.1145/3159450.3159488

[2] Michael Clancy. 2004. Misconceptions and attitudes that interfere with learning to program. In Computer Science Education Research. London: Taylor & Francis Group, 85–100

[3] David S. Touretzky, Christina Gardner-McCune, and Ashish Aggarwal. 2017. Semantic Reasoning in Young Programmers. In Proceedings of the 2017 ACM SIGCSE Technical Symposium on Computer Science Education (SIGCSE '17). ACM, New York, NY, USA, 585-590.
DOI: https://doi.org/10.1145/3017680.3017787

[4] Allen Tucker. 2003. A Model Curriculum for K--12 Computer Science: Final Report of the ACM K--12 Task Force Curriculum Committee. Technical Report. ACM, New York, NY, USA. ACM Order No.: 104043.

A Conceptual Framework for Identifying Emotional Factors Leading to Student Disengagement in VLEs

Lubna Alharbi
lubna@liverpool.ac.uk
Department of Computer Science
University of Liverpool
Liverpool, UK

Floriana Grasso
floriana@liverpool.ac.uk
Department of Computer Science
University of Liverpool
Liverpool, UK

Phil Jimmieson
phil@liverpool.ac.uk
Department of Computer Science
University of Liverpool
Liverpool, UK

ABSTRACT

Higher Education is witnessing a mental health crisis without precedents. Learning analytics offer powerful tools to monitor students engagement, but would instructors in Virtual Learning Environments (VLEs) benefit from being able to monitor mental well-being as well? And how can this be implemented in a way that is not disruptive to education? We have devised a conceptual framework addressing this issue, which incorporate the role of the online tutor into an environment "observing" student communicative acts. The conceptual framework is evaluated in a series of experiments and case studies, aimed at assessing the feasibility and appreciate the usefulness of single potential components, and on the basis of expert commentaries.

CCS CONCEPTS

• **Social and professional topics → Computing education**.

KEYWORDS

Student mental health, Emotional analytics, VLEs

ACM Reference Format:
Lubna Alharbi, Floriana Grasso, and Phil Jimmieson. 2019. A Conceptual Framework for Identifying Emotional Factors Leading to Student Disengagement in VLEs. In *Innovation and Technology in Computer Science Education (ITiCSE '19), July 15–17, 2019, Aberdeen, Scotland Uk.* ACM, New York, NY, USA, 1 page. https://doi.org/10.1145/3304221.3325570

1 BACKGROUND

We are witnessing a mental health crisis in higher education without precedents. Recent statistics by the institute for Public Policy Research showed that 15,000 first year students in UK Universities reported a mental health issue in 2015/2016, a staggering fivefold increase from a decade ago, with 94% of HE institutions reporting an increase in mental health services requests [2]. Educational research increasingly use various learning analytics, students' educational history and demographic information in order to predict their performance, however, few studies have paid sufficient attention to the use of emotion and/or sentiment analysis, for a better understanding and prediction of student engagement.

ITiCSE '19, July 15–17, 2019, Aberdeen, Scotland Uk

ACM ISBN 978-1-4503-6301-3/19/07.
https://doi.org/10.1145/3304221.3325570

2 FRAMEWORK

The work presented in this paper constitutes a step towards addressing the issue of mental health in HE, as we seek to understand whether emotional factors could be identified from the analysis of online conversations in VLEs, and how this identification could best support the educators. We have devised a conceptual framework in which the role of the online tutor or facilitator is incorporated into an environment that coordinates together information coming from the various communicative acts happening during learning, from tasks in the classrooms, to question to the teachers to discussion among peers. The communicative acts are all "observed" through the lens of the "emotional loaded" prediction system, which can decide to intervene, or simply flag, when some communication needs to be looked at more carefully (Fig. 1).

3 EVALUATION

We are evaluating the various theoretical components of the conceptual framework in a series of experiments and case studies, aimed at both assessing the feasibility of single potential components, using datasets such as the Stanford MOOCs [1], and at appreciating the usefulness of the framework, by means of expert commentaries.

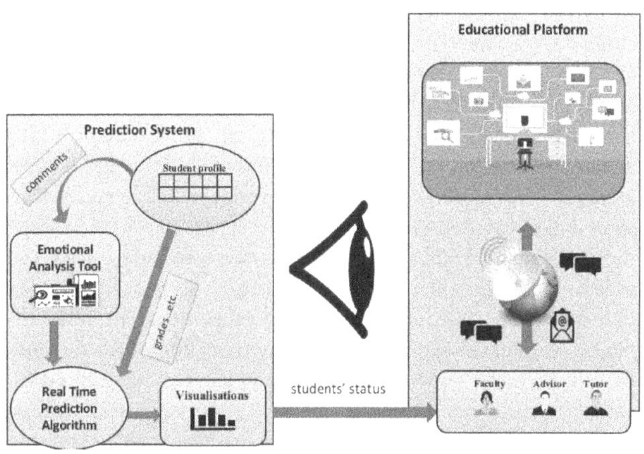

Figure 1: Conceptual Framework

REFERENCES

[1] Advanced Research On Learning. (Online). CAROL Learner MOOC Data Set. https://datastage.stanford.edu/#appB Accessed 28/03/2018.
[2] Institute for Public Policy Research. 2017. Not by degrees: improving student mental health in the UK's universities. https://www.ippr.org/research/publications/not-by-degrees

A Framework for Improving the Sharing of Teaching Practices among Computer Science Instructors

Nouf Almujally
University of Warwick
Coventry, UK
n.almujally@warwick.ac.uk

Mike Joy
University of Warwick
Coventry, UK
m.s.joy@warwick.ac.uk

ABSTRACT

In this poster we present a novel conceptual framework for enhancing the sharing of best teaching practices among academics. The proposed framework is constructed based upon the understanding and mapping of the [1] knowledge creation theory.

CCS CONCEPTS

• **Human-centered computing → Collaborative and social computing systems and tools.**

KEYWORDS

Knowledge Management System, Teaching Practices

ACM Reference Format:
Nouf Almujally and Mike Joy. 2019. A Framework for Improving the Sharing of Teaching Practices among Computer Science Instructors. In *Innovation and Technology in Computer Science Education (ITiCSE '19), July 15–17, 2019, Aberdeen, Scotland Uk.* ACM, New York, NY, USA, 1 page. https://doi.org/10.1145/3304221.3325590

1 INTRODUCTION

Computer Science instructors are involved in many responsibilities and tasks that prevent them from finding enough time for sharing their accumulated teaching-related knowledge with other instructors. Additionally, many years of valuable teaching experience could be lost due to academic retirement without being recorded in a proper knowledge management system. Consequently, novice teachers are facing a critical challenge in teaching and delivering subject knowledge that relates to algorithms, programming and the development of computational thinking skills. It would be more valuable if know-how knowledge were recorded, organized, and shared in a way that encourages new teachers to reuse it. Despite the availability of different educational resource repositories, such as learning management systems, these tools have been developed to facilitate the transmission of course-related content to learners but do not enable instructors to share their know-how teaching practices. In our view, know-how knowledge is considered as a valuable asset for achieving competitive advantage for educational institutions [2]. Therefore, the authors have developed the teaching practices management framework (TPMF), as shown in Figure 1, which aims to provide a collaborative environment for instructors to manage both know-what and know-how teaching practices by establishing a virtual community to enhance social interactions among its members. The proposed framework has been developed to address the following features:

- **Structured Knowledge**: Teaching practices have to be stored in a central repository and represented in a structured format to be easily read, retrieved and shared by instructors.
- **Motivation**: The framework implements an extrinsic motivator for scoring teaching practices through implicit feedback (e.g., downloads, views, and bookmarks) or explicit feedback (e.g., ratings). Earning reputation points and feedback can encourage an individual to share knowledge when they recognize this acknowledgement by others.

ITiCSE '19, July 15–17, 2019, Aberdeen, Scotland Uk

ACM ISBN 978-1-4503-6301-3/19/07.
https://doi.org/10.1145/3304221.3325590

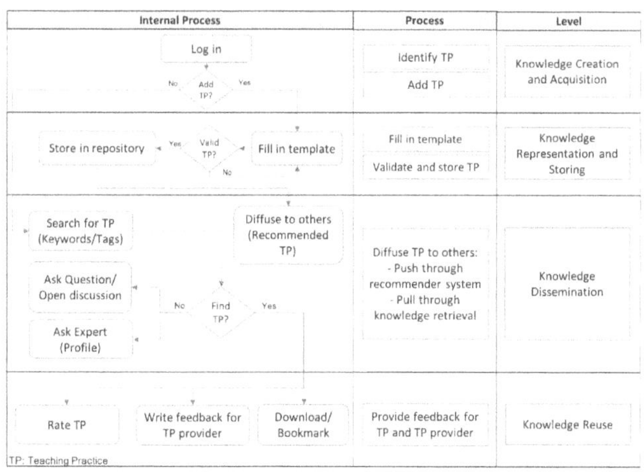

Figure 1: Teaching Practices Management Framework (TPMF).

2 FUTURE WORK

A teaching practices management system will be developed based on the TPMF; then an experiment will be conducted with the help of 40 computer science instructors to ensure that the proposed features would allow them to manage their teaching practices efficiently and effectively.

REFERENCES

[1] Ikujiro Nonaka. 2008. *The knowledge-creating company.* Harvard Business Review Press.
[2] Michael Polanyi. 2009. *The tacit dimension.* University of Chicago Press.

A Reflective Writing Framework for Computing Education

Huda Alrashidi
h.alrashidi@warwick.ac.uk
Computer Science Department,
University of Warwick
Coventry, UK

Mike Joy
m.s.joy@warwick.ac.uk
Computer Science Department,
University of Warwick
Coventry, UK

Thomas Daniel Ullmann
t.ullmann@open.ac.uk
Institute of Educational Technology,
The Open University
Milton Keynes, UK

ABSTRACT

Many disciplines already embed reflective practice in their curriculum as it is important for the professional development of their students. Many frameworks have been developed to capture reflective practice, but there is a lack of knowledge about what constitutes it in computer science education (CSE). This poster introduces a reflective writing framework (RWF) in CSE. This poster makes two contributions: (1) it outlines the construction process of the RWF for CSE, and (2) it discusses the proposed validation of the RWF with a panel of experts.

CCS CONCEPTS

• **Social and professional topics → Computing education.**

KEYWORDS

Reflection, Reflective Writing, Computer Science

ACM Reference Format:

Huda Alrashidi, Mike Joy, and Thomas Daniel Ullmann. 2019. A Reflective Writing Framework for Computing Education. In *Innovation and Technology in Computer Science Education (ITiCSE '19), July 15–17, 2019, Aberdeen, Scotland UK*. ACM, New York, NY, USA, 1 page. https://doi.org/10.1145/3304221.3325580

1 REFLECTIVE WRITING FRAMEWORK

Many reflection theories and frameworks have been developed to assess students' level of reflection especially in education, social science and nursing. However, to the best of our knowledge, no framework is targeting computing education. The overall aim of this research is to: 1) investigate the indicators that can be used to assess reflective writing in computing education based on the thinking activities that can be presented in the computer science writing, 2) validate the RWF with a survey of experts who will provide their suggestions and comments on the following items: the formulation of the language used in the description, and the relevance of these levels and the involved indicators, and 3) build an automatic tool to assess students' level of reflection in CSE based on the developed RWF. The focus of this poster is the first step investigating the indicators that can be used to build the RWF and assess reflective writing in computing education. The reflective writing framework (RWF) assess the levels of reflection in CSE. From the characteristics of computer science writing that involves unique elements such as: problem-solving, data structure, algorithms and software systems and based on the theoretical and empirical work about reflection [1, 3], we derived the RWF consisting of eight indicators and three levels (see Table 1) [2]. The non-technical aspect in the following example *"Ultimately this was content that is covered in any basic parallel algorithms book and I did not believe adding it all to my report would have been worthwhile"* for the suggested indicators that are associated with the reflective level, such as understanding, feelings, and reasoning. The following example illustrates, *"If I were to do this project again, I would have examined the Quasi-NC algorithm given for bipartite perfect matching instead of Kulkarni not algorithm as I feel this is more relevant and important result"*, shows evidence of reflective plus critical reflective levels' indicators, these are: understanding, feeling, reasoning, perspectives, new learning, and future action.

Table 1: Indicators of the RWF

Levels	Indicators
Descriptive	Reports a fact from experience and/or material.
Reflective	Understanding: understands and analyses the experience.
	Feeling: identifies and analyses their thoughts and feelings.
	Reasoning: explains the experience by reasons.
	Comparison: links the experience to another.
Critical-Reflective	Perspective: shows awareness of alternatives.
	New learning: describes a new learning.
	Future action: intends or plans to do something.

2 FUTURE WORK

The future work involves analysing the annotation provided by the raters to evaluate the RWF, updating the suggest indicators based on the results of the analysis and build automatic reflective writing analysis for CSE.

ITiCSE '19, July 15–17, 2019, Aberdeen, Scotland UK

ACM ISBN 978-1-4503-6301-3/19/07.
https://doi.org/10.1145/3304221.3325580

REFERENCES

[1] John D Bain, Colleen Mills, Roy Ballantyne, and Jan Packer. 2002. Developing reflection on practice through journal writing: Impacts of variations in the focus and level of feedback. *Teachers and Teaching* 8, 2 (2002), 171–196.

[2] Thomas Daniel Ullmann. 2019. Automated Analysis of Reflection in Writing: Validating Machine Learning Approaches. *International Journal of Artificial Intelligence in Education* (2019), 1–41.

[3] Frances KY Wong, David Kember, Loretta YF Chung, and Louisa Yan CertEd. 1995. Assessing the level of student reflection from reflective journals. *Journal of advanced nursing* 22, 1 (1995), 48–57.

Eye Tracking to Evaluate Comprehension of Computational Thinking

Abdurrahman Arslanyilmaz
Computer Science & Information Systems
Youngstown State University
Youngstown, OH, United States
aarslanyilmaz@ysu.edu

Kendra Corpier
Computer Science & Information Systems
Youngstown State University
Youngstown, OH, United States
kdcorpier@student.ysu.edu

ABSTRACT

Assessing comprehension of computational thinking (CT) concepts (CTCs), specifically in block-based programming environments like Scratch, has been challenging, and assessment instruments developed and presented in prior studies either do not provide a complete picture about students' cognitive processes or they are not easy-to-administer, subjective, or requires lengthy analysis of qualitative data. Eye-tracking has become one of the most popular methods to study what individuals view, in what order, for how long, and how often, and it is a technology that could give us a window into students' cognitive processes and could be used as an assessment tool for comprehension of CTCs [1].

This study presents eye-tracking technology as an objective, non-intrusive, and easy-to-administer assessment instrument to measure students' comprehension of core CTCs including sequences, loops, events, parallelism, conditionals, operators, data, motion, looks, sound, pen, and sensing. It explores gradual changes in students' comprehension of CTCs as reflected on three eye-gaze data as a proxy; FD (Fixation Duration), SA (Saccade Amplitudes), and RF (Regression Frequency).

CCS CONCEPTS

• Social and professional topics • Computational Thinking

KEYWORDS

Eye tracking; Assessment; Computational Thinking

ACM Reference format:
Abdurrahman Arslanyilmaz and Kendra Corpier. 2019. Eye Tracking to Evaluate Comprehension of Computational Thinking. In *Proceedings of 24th Annual ACM Conference on Innovation and Technology in Computer Science Education Research (ITiCSE' 19), July 15-17, 2019, Aberdeen, Scotland, UK.* ACM, New York, NY, USA, 1 page. https://doi.org/10.1145/3304221.3325555

1 EXPERIMENTAL STUDY

Fifteen middle school students participated in this preliminary experimental study for one session a week for 3 sessions in total. Low-cost Tobii 4C eye trackers were used to produce three eye gaze data (FD, SA, and RF) while fifteen students were involved in CT activities in three weekly sessions. As the sessions progressed, students were exposed gradually more complicated tasks (depth) involving more CTCs (breadth). An in-house software collected eye-gaze data and another one recorded the screens, both of which were synchronized to analyze the three eye gaze data over eleven CTCs throughout the sessions. Pearson Product Moment Correlation analyses between eye-gaze data and sessions were conducted to analyze progressive improvements over all CTCs comprehensively and on each CTC individually.

ACM ISBN 978-1-4503-6301-3/19/07.
https://doi.org/10.1145/3304221.3325555

2 RESULTS

When CTCs are considered altogether, there was no significant correlations between sessions and FD ($r = .054$, $p = .01$), SA ($r = -.005$, $p = .01$), or RF ($r = -.003$, $p = .01$). This result indicated that students' eye-gaze data in FD, SA, or RF did not improve gradually from first to the third session showing increased attention and improvement in comprehension of CTCs. On the contrary, a positive correlation, not statistically significant, between FD and sessions indicated more difficulty comprehending CTCs as sessions progressed.

In terms of individual CTCs, students' FD, SA, or RF scores neither improved nor declined significantly on any specific CTC with the exception of "Conditionals" for RF ($r = .825$, $p = .01$) with a significant positive correlation indicating that students revisited "Conditionals" type of CTC more frequently as sessions progressed because of difficulty in its comprehension. However, they did not have any problem in understanding the remaining CTCs (i.e., sequences, loops, events, parallelism, operators, data, motion, looks, sound, pen, and sensing).

3 CONCLUSIONS

This study revealed that eye-gaze data (FD, SA, and RF) recorded by eye-trackers may provide an objective, non-obstructive, and easy-to administer assessment instrument to be utilized as a proxy to evaluate students' comprehension of CTCs.

REFERENCES

[1] F Shic (2009). Computational methods for eye-tracking analysis: Applications to autism. Ph.D. Dissertation, Yale University, New Haven, CT, USA, 2009.

The Use of Gamification to Support the Process of Teaching Scrum

Luiz Ricardo Begosso
Informatics Research Center
FEMA
Assis, SP, Brazil
begosso@femanet.com.br

Luis Henrique Buzzo Franco
Informatics Research Center
FEMA
Assis, SP, Brazil
luishbfranco@gmail.com

Douglas Sanches da Cunha
Informatics Research Center
FEMA
Assis, SP, Brazil
dscunha2007@gmail.com

Luiz Carlos Begosso
FATEC
FEMA
Assis, SP, Brazil
begosso@gmail.com

ABSTRACT

This poster presents our work in progress using gamification principles to create a game for supporting the process of teaching Project Management concepts. We created the Scrum Simulator, a game that is focused on promoting the engagement of students in the learning process of agile concepts and the Scrum methodology. This game is based on CRPG – Computer Role-Playing game, where the student controls the actions of a character immersed in a well-defined world. Our game simulates different circumstances where the student can "live" the different Scrum phases and roles. We will describe the details of the implementation of the project and how students can experience real situations in software development.

CCS Concepts

Software and its engineering~Agile software development • Applied computing~Distance learning

KEYWORDS

Agile, Scrum, Gamification, Project Management, Simulator

ACM Reference format:

Luiz Ricardo Begosso, Luis Henrique Buzzo Franco, Douglas Sanches da Cunha and Luiz Carlos Begosso. 2019. The Use of Gamification to Support the Process of Teaching Scrum. In *Proceedings of 24th Annual ACM Conference on Innovation and Technology in Computer Science Education (ITiCSE'19), July 15-17, 2019, Aberdeen, Scotland, UK.* ACM, New York, NY, 1 page. https://doi.org/10.1145/3304221.3325583

1 Introduction

The teaching of Software Engineering concepts must be focused on improving students' technical skills in order to adapt them to the current demands of the software industry. The fundamental concepts of Software Engineering and project management must be approached taking into account the students' needs to go through a stage of practical application of the concepts and evaluation of the experiments performed. As the new generations have great affinity with technology, it has been motivating for the adoption of several experiences with the use of digital games and simulation environments to increase students' knowledge [1].

ACM ISBN 978-1-4503-6301-3/19/07.
DOI: https://doi.org/10.1145/3304221.3325583

2 Implementation of the Project

In this work-in-progress we developed a multi-language game focused on promoting engagement of students in the learning process of agile concepts and the Scrum methodology. Students can play online and in-game interaction allows other students to see the profile of all players online through ranking as a way to stimulate player competitiveness.

Scrum is composed of some roles, events and artifacts that ensure the proper functioning and administration of the project [2]. There are three key roles that make up the Scrum Team: Product Owner, Scrum Master, and the Development Team.

The idea behind our game is to support the teaching of Scrum methodology, by inserting the student into a virtual environment that simulates the steps of developing a software product in a team, starting with the initial communication with the client for getting knowledge about the requirements of the software that will be developed (product backlog), going through the phases of defining the "sprints", assuming the role of Scrum Master to ensure that all team members understood what needs to be done, and delivering the final product to the client.

As student progress through the phases of the game, he/she can reach the knowledge base, with the information acquired during the game and can unlock conquests and earn more experience points.

REFERENCES

[1] BEGOSSO, L. R.et al. "The Use of Gamification for Teaching Algorithms". In: 2018 Federated Conference on Computer Science and Information Systems, 2018, Poznan. Poznan, Poland: M. Ganzha, L. Maciaszek, M. Paprzycki (eds), 2018. v. 17. p. 225-231. http://dx.doi.org/10.15439/2018F165

[2] A. Gkritsi, "Scrum Game: An Agile Software Management Game", M.S. thesis, School of Electronics and Computer Science, Univ. of Southampton, Southampton, UK, 2011.

OurKidsCode: A National Programme to get Families Involved in CS Education

Nina Bresnihan
Trinity College
Dublin
Ireland
Nina.Bresnihan@tcd.ie

Glenn Strong
Trinity College
Dublin
Ireland
Glenn.Strong@tcd.ie

Lorraine Fisher
Trinity College
Dublin
Ireland
fisherl@tcd.ie

Richard Millwood
Trinity College
Dublin
Ireland
Richard.Millwood@tcd.ie

Áine Lynch
National Parents
Council Primary
Ireland
alynch@npc.ie

ABSTRACT

Across Europe, primary age children are being encouraged to learn computing. OurKidsCode is a joint project between the National Parents' Council (Primary) and Trinity College Dublin. The project's needs analysis found that families play an important role in supporting children's learning, indicating the opportunity for innovative computing workshops throughout Ireland. In response, OurKidsCode has designed family-friendly, mixed age workshops to help parents and children work together and build the confidence and competence to engage with computing. Challenges addressed through the design included widening recruitment, increasing engagement and sustaining involvement. Evaluation of the pilot workshops showed a significant increase in the computing confidence of the participants and an increased readiness to take part in future computing activites.

CCS CONCEPTS

• **Social and professional topics → Computing education**; *Informal education*.

KEYWORDS

Families, Computing, Primary education, Confidence

ACM Reference Format:

Nina Bresnihan, Glenn Strong, Lorraine Fisher, Richard Millwood, and Áine Lynch. 2019. OurKidsCode: a National Programme to get Families Involved in CS Education. In *Innovation and Technology in Computer Science Education (ITiCSE '19), July 15–17, 2019, Aberdeen, Scotland UK.* ACM, New York, NY, USA, 1 page. https://doi.org/10.1145/3304221.3325574

1 INTRODUCTION

The European Commission[1] argue that coding is a universal language which enhances creativity. In Ireland, including coding in the primary school curriculum is currently being explored by the National Council for Curriculum and Assessment. The National Parents' Council (Primary) has long argued that parents play a core role in supporting children's learning, but due to a lack of confidence and competence they need support if they wish to engage their children in CS activities. A needs analysis exploring parents' perceptions of computing, and their children's experience of using technology confirmed that the majority of parents wanted their children to learn computing and wanted to be involved in that.

In response, OurKidsCode has designed workshops for families to build the confidence and competence to sustain learning, following a 'co-creation' and 'Maker' ethos. Activities are scaffolded to promote parents' engagement with their children as 'computational co-creators'. In 2018, OurKidsCode piloted three such workshops (n=53) using Scratch with the Makey-Makey, and MakeCode with the BBC micro:bit. Workshops conclude with sharing and group reflection to discuss learning and explore further project ideas.

Three design challenges: widening recruitment, increasing engagement, and sustaining activity were identified through consultation with experts, needs analysis and literature review. The first challenge, of widening recruitment, was addressed by targeting families rather than parents and arranging workshops at times to suit family involvement. Existing networks including the National Parents Council and CoderDojo were leveraged and their existing facilitators (n=38) trained in the delivery of the workshops. The second challenge of increasing engagement was addressed by designing coding activities that also included making and decorating guided by step-by-step cards. This catered for different interests and ages. The cards also worked to address the third challenge of sustaining involvement by including advice on technical matters and facilitating workshops. The goal of sustained involvement will be further met in 2019 through the design of a 4-session workshop aimed at increasing independence and supported by a website for the organisation of local groups.

The pilot workshops were evaluated and overall findings included a significant rise in self-reported confidence levels of parent participants and more parents feeling both willing and able to organise similar activities at home in the future.

This project is interesting due to its national scale, focus on family-oriented creative computing and workshop design aimed for sustainability.

ACKNOWLEDGMENTS

OurKidsCode is funded by Science Foundation Ireland and supported by Microsoft Ireland.

REFERENCES

[1] European Commission. 2018. Coding - the 21st Century Skill. https://ec.europa.eu/digital-single-market/en/coding-21st-century-skill.

ITiCSE '19, July 15–17, 2019, Aberdeen, Scotland UK

ACM ISBN 978-1-4503-6301-3/19/07.
https://doi.org/10.1145/3304221.3325574

Student Motivation and Engagement in STEM Courses: Exploring the Potential Impact of Gamification

Lillian Cassel
Villanova University
Villanova PA 19085, USA
Lillian.Cassel@villanova.edu

Darina Dicheva
Winston Salem State University
Winston Salem, NC 271110, USA
dichevad@wssu.edu

Christo Dichev
Winston Salem State University
Winston Salem, NC 271110, USA
dichevc@wssu.edu

Breonte Guy
Winston Salem State University
Winston Salem, NC 271110, USA
guybs@wssu.edu

Keith Irwin
Winston Salem State University
Winston Salem, NC 271110, USA
irwink@wssu.edu

ABSTRACT

Gamification in education still lacks systematic studies assessing its impact on learning. This poster will present the design of our empirical studies on the effect of various combination of game elements on student motivation and engagement in CS courses.

CCS CONCEPTS

• **Applied computing** → *Learning management systems.*

KEYWORDS

Computing Education, Gamification, Student Engagement

ACM Reference Format:

Lillian Cassel, Darina Dicheva, Christo Dichev, Breonte Guy, and Keith Irwin. 2019. Student Motivation and Engagement in STEM Courses: Exploring the Potential Impact of Gamification. In *Innovation and Technology in Computer Science Education (ITiCSE '19), July 15–17, 2019, Aberdeen, Scotland, UK.* ACM, New York, NY, USA, 1 page. https://doi.org/10.1145/33044221.3325578

1 EXTENDED ABSTRACT

Although we are witnessing an increasing use of gamification in educational contexts, there is insufficient clarity on whether and how gamified learning increases student motivation and engagement. The majority of empirical studies on educational gamification have found more positive than negative effects on motivation, but its effectiveness for learning remains inconclusive due to limitations of the study design and analysis strategies [1].

The need of a more systematic study to validate existing evidence and provide guidance for further exploration motivated our research on understanding if and how gamification can deliver its promise in the context of STEM learning, and specifically, for computer science learning. This poster will describe our approach, which includes a set of empirical studies targeting the effects of individual game elements and combinations thereof on student motivation and engagement in the context of two Computer Science courses (Data Structures and Data Science).

The studies are based on the use of OneUp, a course gamification platform previously developed by the authors. OneUp supports game elements including avatars, XPs, progress bars, badges, leaderboards, virtual currency, unlocking content, and learning dashboards. Being highly configurable, it enables previously impossible research on the efficacy of not only individual game elements but also various combinations of elements on student engagement and motivation.

An important feature of our research design is that it is guided by Self Determination Theory [2], a well-validated psychological theory for understanding motivation and behavior change. This enables better understanding of the reasons for the success or failure of different gamification interventions in certain contexts.

The OneUp platform has been developed and applied in computer science classes over the past three years. Data collected has shown promise for increased interest and engagement of students using OneUp. An example from a Spring 2018 Data Structures course showed students responding very positively to a set of statements including "I felt more effective in learning using OneUp" and "Using OneUp helped me prepare for tests."

The poster will present, in addition to the approach used, specific results obtained to date. The strength of the OneUp platform is its configurability. Thus, the same platform can be used for many topics in a course and for topics in a variety of courses. An important factor in the use of OneUp is the development of a large set of challenges (questions or problems). Materials for use in the Data Structures course have been developed, and materials for Discrete Structures and for Data Science are in development. The poster will also describe our plans for collecting large sets of questions for use in these courses and for preparing computer science faculty to build suitable sets for outher courses.

ITiCSE '19, July 15–17, 2019, Aberdeen, Scotland, UK

ACM ISBN 978-1-4503-6301-3/19/07.
https://doi.org/10.1145/33044221.3325578

REFERENCES

[1] C. Dichev and D. Dicheva. 2017. Gamifying education: what is known, what is believed and what remains uncertain: a critical review. *International Journal of Technology in Higher Education* 14, 9 (2017).

[2] R. Ryan and E. Deci. 2000. Intrinsic and extrinsic motivations: classic definitions and new directions. *Contemporary Educational Psychology* 25 (2000), 54–67.

Computing: Ipsative Assessment. Improving the Student Experience in Higher Education Using Personalised Assessment and Feedback

Ryan Crosby
r.crosby@newcastle.ac.uk
Newcastle University
Newcastle Upon Tyne, England

Dr Marie Devlin
marie.devlin@newcasle.ac.uk
Newcastle University
Newcastle Upon Tyne, England

Dr Lindsay Marshall
lindsay.marshall@newcastle.ac.uk
Newcastle University
Newcastle Upon Tyne, England

ABSTRACT

Computing: Ipsative Assessment (C:IA) is a tool developed to help ameliorate the issues potentially causing student dissatisfaction regarding assessment and feedback within UK higher education. Using Newcastle University as a case study the system was given to a small group of students as a trial. This poster discusses some of the causes of the dissatisfaction that our students faced with their assessment and feedback, and how using the system we attempt to reduce the impact of these issues.

CCS CONCEPTS

• **Applied computing → Education.**

KEYWORDS

feedback; assessment; education

ACM Reference Format:

Ryan Crosby, Dr Marie Devlin, and Dr Lindsay Marshall. 2019. Computing: Ipsative Assessment. Improving the Student Experience in Higher Education Using Personalised Assessment and Feedback. In *Innovation and Technology in Computer Science Education (ITiCSE '19), July 15–17, 2019, Aberdeen, Scotland Uk.* ACM, New York, NY, USA, 1 page. https://doi.org/10.1145/3304221.3325565

1 SIGNIFICANCE AND RELEVANCE OF THE TOPIC

The National Student Survey within the UK shows that for the topic "Assessment and Feedback" students are reporting that they are dissatisfied with their experience [1]. Assessment and feedback are however among the most important aspects of the higher education experience; it is therefore crucial to identify the potential causes of this dissatisfaction. Across the UK the number of undergraduate students taking their first degree at a higher education institute is increasing. In the academic year 2015/2016 there were 1,563,900 student enrolments within higher education institutes, whereas in the 2016/2017 academic year there were 1,597,615 student enrolments [2]. This increase in student numbers could cause the issues regarding assessment and feedback to be amplified. This research aims to use a system called "Computing: Ipsative Assessment", to attempt to reduce the impact of these issues and improve student satisfaction.

ITiCSE '19, July 15–17, 2019, Aberdeen, Scotland Uk

ACM ISBN 978-1-4503-6301-3/19/07.
https://doi.org/10.1145/3304221.3325565

2 "COMPUTING: IPSATIVE ASSESSMENT" THE TOOL

The system itself was a web based system that put a focus on student goal setting and progress tracking. The content of the system was delivered in small bite sized chunks with quizzes at the end of the section. The system was given a small prototype trial with volunteer students from a second semester programming module, five students agreed to take part in the experiment. The response from the system was largely positive, with the personalised aspects gaining positive feedback. There were however some suggested improvements, the general opinion was that the difficult questions were too difficult and off putting. It was also suggested that the tool be turned into a mobile application for easy access when travelling.

3 CONTENT: A DESCRIPTION OF THE EXPECTED CONTENT OF THE POSTER

The poster has content on the following topics: "The Problem", the problem section focuses on why it is important rectify student dissatisfaction with regards to assessment and feedback in higher education. This section brings attention to the low satisfaction results within the Nation Student Survey. "Methodology", the methodology section discusses how the potential causes of dissatisfaction within our institution was gathered. "Results", this section discusses the opinions of the students with regards to assessment and feedback within our institution and the potential causes for the dissatisfaction. C:IA, this section explores the design of the system and how it was deployed with the trial group. "Conclusions and Future work", discusses the opinions of students regarding C:IA and the mentioned improvements from the students.

REFERENCES

[1] HEFCE. 2017. National Student Survey. http://www.hefce.ac.uk/lt/nss/results/. Accessed: 2019-03-16.
[2] Universities UK. 2019. Patterns and trends in higher education 2018. http://www.universitiesuk.ac.uk/facts-and-stats/data-and-analysis/Documents/patterns-and-. Accessed: 2019-03-16.

Development of a Checklist Tool for Teaching Problem-Solving Skills

Hillary Dawkins
University of Guelph
Guelph, Ontario, Canada
hdawkins@uoguelph.ca

Grant Douglas
University of Guelph
Guelph, Ontario, Canada
gdouglas@uoguelph.ca

Kevin Glover-Netherton
University of Guelph
Guelph, Ontario, Canada
kglovern@uoguelph.ca

David Hudec
University of Guelph
Guelph, Ontario, Canada
dhudec@uoguelph.ca

Sean Lunt
University of Guelph
Guelph, Ontario, Canada
slunt@uoguelph.ca

Dalton Polhill
University of Guelph
Guelph, Ontario, Canada
dpolhill@uoguelph.ca

Mostafa Rashed
University of Guelph
Guelph, Ontario, Canada
mrashed@uoguelph.ca

Matthew Sampson
University of Guelph
Guelph, Ontario, Canada
msamps01@uoguelph.ca

Alliyya Mohammed
University of Guelph
Guelph, Ontario, Canada
alliyya@uoguelph.ca

James Mosley
University of Guelph
Guelph, Ontario, Canada
mosleyj@uoguelph.ca

Rhys Young
University of Guelph
Guelph, Ontario, Canada
ryoung08@uoguelph.ca

Judi McCuaig
University of Guelph
Guelph, Ontario, Canada
judi@uoguelph.ca

ABSTRACT

Problem solving is a critical skill for computer science. However, the complexity and overhead of most programming tasks make problem solving difficult to explicitly teach. Previous studies describe explicit instruction of problem-solving strategies, but provide few details about how the strategies have been developed. We describe the development of a checklist tool that guides students in solving general programming tasks. The tool was developed by observing problem-solving strategies used by advanced computer science students in practice. We believe that the tool will provide a basis for explicit problem-solving instruction for novice programmers.

CCS CONCEPTS

• **Social and professional topics → Computing education.**

KEYWORDS

Problem solving; teaching aid development

ACM Reference Format:
Hillary Dawkins, Grant Douglas, Kevin Glover-Netherton, David Hudec, Sean Lunt, Dalton Polhill, Mostafa Rashed, Matthew Sampson, Alliyya Mohammed, James Mosley, Rhys Young, and Judi McCuaig. 2019. Development of a Checklist Tool for Teaching Problem-Solving Skills. In *Innovation and Technology in Computer Science Education (ITiCSE '19), July 15–17, 2019, Aberdeen, Scotland Uk.* ACM, New York, NY, USA, 1 page. https://doi.org/10.1145/3304221.3325560

ITiCSE '19, July 15–17, 2019, Aberdeen, Scotland Uk

ACM ISBN 978-1-4503-6301-3/19/07.
https://doi.org/10.1145/3304221.3325560

1 METHODOLOGY

Ten senior undergraduate students created individual problem-solving checklists through iterative task completion and evaluation. As each programming task was completed, students examined their own process, kept careful notes, and created a personalized checklist. The individual checklists were refined until they represented a robust description of the steps to problem solving in various programming contexts. The individual checklists were aggregated into a final version through consideration of common features and known processes from the literature. The resulting checklist describes the general stages of problem solving motivated by theory, further divided into computer-science specific steps motivated by observation. The final checklist tool also provides an explanation of each step at a level appropriate for novices. The result is freely available at www.cs.ubc.ca/wccce/Nifty/2019/ProblemSolving/.

2 PRELIMINARY USE AND FUTURE WORK

Novice programmers were instructed in the use of the checklist tool through a one-day workshop at the University of Guelph. All workshop materials are freely available at the above URL. Approximately 20 computer science undergraduates participated in the workshop, and many expressed their intentions to continue using the checklist tool in coursework. Anonymous feedback included comments such as "I wish I had a checklist like this sooner" and "I focused less on actually coding and more on planning and understanding how to attack the problem". We intend to conduct formalized workshops with the goal of measuring the effectiveness of our approach on student attitudes and self-efficacy.

Infusing Data Science Across Disciplines

Debzani Deb
Department of Computer Science
Winston-Salem State University
Winston-Salem, NC, USA
debd@wssu.edu

Russell M. Smith
Department of History, Politics & Social Justice
Winston-Salem State University
Winston-Salem, NC, USA
smithrm@wssu.edu

Muztaba Fuad
Department of Computer Science
Winston-Salem State University
Winston-Salem, NC, USA
fuadmo@wssu.edu

ABSTRACT

In this poster, we describe our effort to develop, pilot, and evaluate a model for infusing data literacy into undergraduate curricula across a variety of disciplines using a modular approach. Our pilot implementation achieved reasonable success in attaining student learning outcomes, enhanced engagement, and interests.

KEYWORDS: Data Science; CS+X; Computer Science Education

ACM Reference format:

Debzani Deb, Russell Smith and Muztaba Fuad. 2019. Infusing Data Science Across Disciplines. In *Proceedings of 24th Annual ACM Conference on Innovation and Technology in Computer Science Education (ITiCSE'19), July 15–17, 2019, Aberdeen, Scotland UK* ACM, New York, NY, USA, 1 page.. https://doi.org/10.1145/3304221.3325579

INTRODUCTION

Data Analytics is an essential skill for twenty-first century workforce and as a result the need to help all students acquire such skill has recently gained increased attention. CS+X is one such approach of integrating data literacy into discipline-specific undergraduate courses through faculty partnerships. However, in most such initiatives, X is typically a STEM or engineering field and there are very few approaches that focus on enhancing the skills of social science or humanities students. Also, almost all CS+X courses focus exclusively on teaching students to program and therefore has a chance of isolating data literacy from disciplinary content and propagating the conception that "Data Literacy = Programming". This may prevent social science faculties from forming a partnership with CS faculties in order to persistently and meaningfully infuse data literacy into their curriculum.

In this poster, we describe our effort to develop, pilot, and evaluate a model for infusing data literacy into undergraduate curricula across a variety of disciplines using a modular approach that does not rely entirely on programming. Rather than developing new discipline specific data science flavored courses, our approach integrates data literacy into existing courses through offering a week-long context-sensitive module and associated hands-on activities. We believe that the modular approach is rather straightforward and easier to adopt than designing a special topic course and adopting it in a densely-packed curricula. Also, by adopting the data science modules in discipline specific core courses, there is a greater chance to reach a broader audience of students. The proposed modules are designed to be short and autonomous for easier adoption and as a result, each of them spans two 75-minute classes and includes specific learning goals, lecture notes, and assessment resources. The assessment resources contain quiz questions, tutorials, input dataset, and hands-on projects etc. The modules are expected to be taught in a lecture-lab setting, where the basics of data science are covered on the context of the target discipline and students are introduced to the hands-on project along with the necessary tools and resources, that they will require to complete the project. The take home project contains multiple tasks and usually has two weeks of deadline.

During the Fall of 2018, one such module is designed and piloted to a general education course titled as "Environmental Justice and Sustainability" at Winston-Salem state university. The course is mostly attended by social science majors (N: 24, Male:11, Female:13) and examines critical perspectives on social justice and geography. The learning outcomes of the module are as follows: 1) to understand how advances in technology enable the field of data science, 2) to be familiar with the sources of data relevant to the discipline, 3) to analyze a data set using spreadsheet and pivot table, and 4) to convey meaningful insights from a data analysis through visualizations. The take home project requires the students to explore the census and environmental data of Forsyth county (available at https://www.epa.gov), to use their spreadsheet and pivot table manipulation skills to answer ten questions such as "What is the average cancer risk for the East vs. West Forsyth?", "What is the average respiratory hazard index for the older part of the city (more than 50% houses are built before 1960)?" and to provide necessary visualizations. Additionally, students are asked to complete a short six questions survey with some interesting results. While students overwhelmingly found data science to be interesting and could see the value of it for societal good, they remain mostly neutral about their desire to explore more of it in their future courses. The module and associated resources are available at http://ibigcloud.altl.org.

ACKNOWLEDGEMENT

This research was supported by NSF Award # 1600864.

ACM ISBN 978-1-4503-6301-3/19/07. https://doi.org/10.1145/3304221.3325579

Idempotent Factorizations: A New Addition to the Cryptography Classroom

Barry Fagin
US Air Force Academy
USAFA, CO
barry.fagin@usafa.edu

ABSTRACT

While it is commonly believed RSA requires two primes p and q, that is incorrect. Infinite examples of RSA encryption moduli $n = pq$ exist with p and/or q composite that generate correct RSA keys. This can be explained in the undergraduate cryptography classroom with support from public domain technologies like the python numbthy library [4] and the Gephi graph processor [3].

KEYWORDS

computer science education, cryptography, RSA, abstract algebra

ACM Reference Format:
Barry Fagin. 2019. Idempotent Factorizations: A New Addition to the Cryptography Classroom. In *Innovation and Technology in Computer Science Education (ITiCSE '19), July 15–17, 2019, Aberdeen, Scotland, UK.* ACM, New York, NY, USA, 2 pages. https://doi.org/10.1145/3304221.3325557

1 INTRODUCTION

The RSA cryptosystem [1] ostensibly requires two primes p, q with $pq = n$ and two integers e, d chosen such that $ed \underset{\phi(n)=(p-1)(q-1)}{\equiv} 1$, where ϕ denotes Euler's Totient function . Its security is based on the time required to factor $n = pq$ without knowing p or q, since no polynomial-time factoring algorithms are known.

Since large primes are tested probabalistically, students may ask what happens if one or both of p, q is composite. In fact, there are infinite examples of $n = pq$ with p and/or q composite where RSA continues to function correctly.

2 IDEMPOTENT FACTORIZATIONS AND CLASSROOM EXAMPLES

A factorization of n into pq is *idempotent* if $\lambda(n) \mid (p-1)(q-1)$, where λ is the Carmichael lambda function. Note p or q may be composite. The p and q of an idempotent factorization generate correctly functioning RSA keys [2].

There are infinite n with idempotent factorizations. A list of all such $n < 2^{26}$ is available at [5]. Rather surprisingly, integers exist for which all of their bipartite factorizations are idempotent. We call these integers *maximally idempotent* [2]. Examples of these are also available at [5].

ITiCSE '19, July 15–17, 2019, Aberdeen, Scotland, UK

ACM ISBN 978-1-4503-6301-3/19/07.
https://doi.org/10.1145/3304221.3325557

Maximally idempotent integers can be constructed by choosing a prime p, identifying all divisors a_i of $\lambda = p-1$ such that $p_i = a_i + 1$ is prime, and constructing the *divisor graph* for λ. A divisor graph has nodes for all a_i, with edges from a_i to a_j if $\lambda/a_i \mid a_j$. A f-clique corresponds to an f-factor maximally idempotent integer [2].

Divisor graphs can be visualized with Gephi [3]. The divisor graph for $\lambda = 36$ is shown in Figure 1. It has 6 3-cliques and one 4-clique, corresponding to 7 maximally idempotent integers from 2109 to 63973. Choosing $n = 2109, p = 57, q = 37$ or $p = 111, q = 19$ will generate valid RSA keys, even though p is composite.

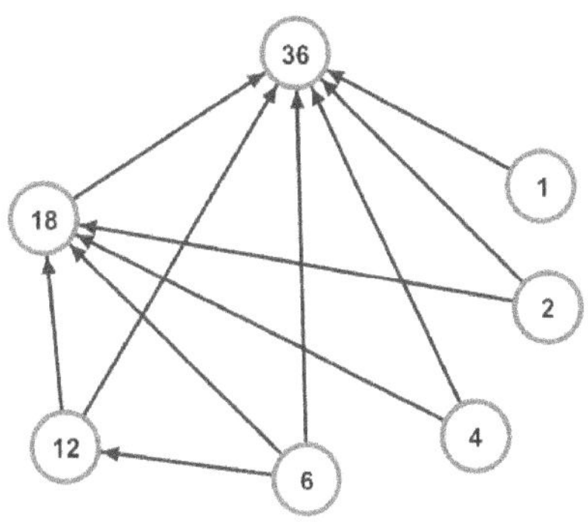

Figure 1: Divisor graph for $\lambda = 36$

3 CONCLUSIONS

Although it is common to tell students two primes are required for RSA to work, that is not strictly true. Any p, q for which $\lambda(pq) \mid (p-1)(q-1)$ will generate working RSA keys.

Knowledge of number theory is not required to present this material. For students and instructors in a more applied setting, the examples in [5] can be presented directly to demonstrate that primality is not required for RSA to function. Python code is also available at [6]. Teachers in a more theoretical setting can use the analysis here and in [2] to present these concepts in more detail.

REFERENCES

[1] Rivest, R.; Shamir, A.; Adleman, L. A Method for Obtaining Digital Signatures and Public-Key Cryptosystem. *Commun. ACM* **1978**, *21*, 120–126.
[2] Fagin, B. Idempotent Factorizations of Square-free Integers, *Mathematics of Computation*, under review. Contact barry.fagin@usafa.edu.
[3] https://gephi.org
[4] Campbell, R. https://github.com/Robert-Campbell-256/Number-Theory-Python/blob/master/numbthy.py, Number Theory functions in Python
[5] Fagin, B. Sequences A306330 and A306812 in *The On-Line Encyclopedia of Integer Sequences* 2019, https://oeis.org
[6] https://github.com/barryfagin/idempotency.py/archive/v1.0.zip

Improving Functional Programming Understanding through Student-Created Instructional Videos

Pedro G. Feijóo-García[1,2], Christina Gardner-McCune[1]
University of Florida, Gainesville, FL, United States of America[1]
Universidad El Bosque, Bogotá D.C., Colombia[2]
{pfeijoogarcia, gmccune}@ufl.edu

ABSTRACT

This poster presents findings on a pedagogical approach we designed to enhance undergraduate computing students' understanding of functional programming (FP) through student-created video-tutorials. Students created two video tutorials. The first video-tutorial assignment asked the students to develop explanations of FP concepts (theoretical understanding of FP). The second video-tutorial required students to explain their solutions to programming exercises using Haskell (application of FP). Our findings suggest that the use of student-created video-tutorial can be effective for increasing students' understanding and application of functional programming.

KEYWORDS

Student-created artifacts, Computing Education

ACM Reference format:

Pedro G. Feijóo-García and Christina Gardner-McCune. 2019. Improving Functional Programming Understanding through Student-Created Instructional Videos. In *Proceedings of 24rd Annual ACM Conference on Innovation and Technology in Computer Science Education (ITiCSE'19), July 15–17, 2019, Aberdeen, Scotland UK.* ACM, New York, NY. 1 page. https://doi.org/10.1145/3304221.3325587

1 INTRODUCTION

For decades, the Computer Science Education (CS Ed) community has been interested in how students learn to program [1]. A large focus has been on the first-year Computer Science (CS) curricula, with a considerable amount on CS0, CS1, and CS2. However, upper division CS classes have not been studied as extensively.

Based on the challenges we have observed while instructing a senior-level Functional Programming (FP) course, we designed a learning activity to enhance students' performance using student-created video tutorials. We present insights on the effectiveness of student-created artifacts, and impact on the use of active-learning activities on students' learning, motivation, and performance on CS-related assessments.

ACM ISBN 978-1-4503-6301-3/19/07.
https://doi.org/10.1145/3304221.3325587

2 INTERVENTION

This experience report is based on an undergraduate senior-level Functional Programming (FP) course at Universidad El Bosque, Colombia. We had sixteen senior CS students, both traditional (N=9) and non-traditional (N=7), between the ages of 18 to 35 years.

We assessed students' theoretical and practical knowledge of FP using two pre-assessments (PrAs) and a final post-assessment (PoA). First, students completed two PrAs on FP concepts and coding exercises using Haskell. Then, the students were asked to create two video-tutorials, one per PrAs. Each video-tutorial required the students to explain in detail their solutions to the exercises they encountered on the pre-assessment. Finally, students completed a theoretical-practical PoA, which used the same format as the PrAs. Following the PoA, students shared with us their experience with a survey.

Performance improved significantly for those students who created the video tutorials (N=14), based on a paired-samples Student's t-test comparing PrAs and PoA grades ($t(14) = 5.8$, $p = 1.8e^{-5}$). This, considering that the grades of the PoA ($\mu = 3.76, \sigma = 0.53$) were descriptively higher than PrAs grades ($\mu = 2.10, \sigma = 0.97$). Additionally, 86% of participants (N=16) reported they enjoyed the activity.

3 FINDINGS

Our findings suggest that using student-created video tutorials in a Functional Programming (FP) class can effectively enhance students' learning of programming concepts and skills. Additionally, we found that students perceived student-created video tutorials as helpful for increasing their learning and improving their performance.

REFERENCES

[1] Mark Guzdial. 2016. *Learner-Centered Design for Computing Education: Research on Computing for Everyone* (1st. ed.). Morgan& Claypool, Pennsylvania, U.S.A. Chapter 1.

We Need to Talk!! – A Chatroom Application Using a Student-Designed Protocol

Greg Gagne
ggagne@westminstercollege.edu
Westminster College
Salt Lake City, Utah, USA

ABSTRACT

This poster describes an assignment for a computer networks class in which students design and implement an application-layer protocol for a chatroom using a client-server architecture running over TCP-IP. Working collaboratively, students design a single protocol that will be implemented by all class members. The protocol is written in a style based on that used in a Request for Comments (RFC), the international standard for describing networking protocols. Students work in pairs to implement the protocol using a programming technology of their choice. This experience helps students to understand that different applications can communicate when they are all designed according to the same RFC specification.

CCS CONCEPTS

• **Networks** → **Network protocol design**; *Application layer protocols.*

KEYWORDS

computer networks; protocols; tcp-ip; client–server; computer science education

ACM Reference Format:

Greg Gagne. 2019. We Need to Talk!! – A Chatroom Application Using a Student-Designed Protocol. In *Innovation and Technology in Computer Science Education (ITiCSE '19), July 15–17, 2019, Aberdeen, Scotland, UK.* ACM, New York, NY, USA, 1 page. https://doi.org/10.1145/3304221.3325575

1 OVERVIEW

Chatroom design is a common programming assignment in computer networks classes. However, rather than providing students with a protocol, we have students design their own application-layer protocol for the chatroom, which they subsequently implement. The protocol specification includes the port number, character encoding, how a member joins and exits the chatroom, how broadcast and private messages are transmitted, and any necessary error handling. The protocol is then written up using a style similar to RFC's, and all students implement the same protocol, allowing the entire class to communicate across the same chatroom.

This assignment addresses many topics in the Networking and Communication Knowledge Area (KA) in the 2013 ACM curricula recommendations [1], including understanding application layer protocols, socket APIs, and writing networked software. It also intersects other KAs including Platform-Based Development, Parallel and Distributed Computing, Software Development Fundamentals, and System Fundamentals.

ITiCSE '19, July 15–17, 2019, Aberdeen, Scotland, UK

ACM ISBN 978-1-4503-6301-3/19/07.
https://doi.org/10.1145/3304221.3325575

2 EVALUATION

The process of designing and writing a protocol is a valuable experience for students. It requires them to review existing RFC documents, and it reinforces the importance of a thorough and unambiguous protocol that provides a specific format for communication exchange. Students work in pairs implementing the protocol and must address many different technical issues, including TCP-IP sockets, threading/concurrency, choice of data structures, and user interfaces. Students are free to choose any programming technology to implement the protocol – we feel this is important, because it allows them to better understand the distinction between the *specification* and *implementation* of a protocol – and have used various technologies, including Java, C#, JavaScript, python, Ruby, C++, and Swift. It is rewarding when, on demonstration day, students using disparate technologies can communicate over the same chatroom.

Student feedback has been favorable, identifying the chatroom as the single most important mechanism for helping them understand the role of protocols, network communication over sockets, and the value of being able to read existing RFCs. Students also say they better understand the usefulness of concurrency mechanisms such as threading, as well as the choice of data structures for delivering and storing messages. Over the past three years, 67% of graduating students have included their chatroom as one of five artifacts for their senior capstone portfolios, citing it as an example of some of their best work.

REFERENCES

[1] Association for Computing Machinery (ACM) Joint Task Force on Computing Curricula and IEEE Computer Society. 2013. *Computer Science Curricula 2013: Curriculum Guidelines for Undergraduate Degree Programs in Computer Science.* ACM, New York, NY, USA. 999133.

The Peanut Butter and Jelly Sandwich Challenge as an Approach to Improve Students Abilities in Test Case Writing

Kiev Gama
Universidade Federal de Pernambuco (UFPE)
Recife, Brazil

Andrew Diniz, Ricardo Almeida, Hendi Coelho
Pontificial Catholic University of Rio de Janeiro (PUC-Rio)
Rio de Janeiro, Brazil

ABSTRACT

Test cases are a set of test inputs, execution conditions, and expected results developed for a particular objective, such as to exercise a particular program path or to verify compliance with a specific requirement. Test cases that are written by students typically have recurring errors that make difficult to find hidden bugs or lack essential details about the data to be used and the instructions that must be followed. As an attempt to improve the quality of students test cases, we used a "Peanut butter and jelly sandwich challenge", typically used to teach algorithmic thinking, to show students the difficulties one may have repeating a simple set of instructions when they are not precisely described. That activity was adapted to cover contents focused on test case writing.

CCS CONCEPTS

• **Software and its engineering → Software testing and debugging;**

KEYWORDS

Software testing, Test cases, Blackbox testing

ACM Reference Format:
Kiev Gama and Andrew Diniz, Ricardo Almeida, Hendi Coelho. 2019. The Peanut Butter and Jelly Sandwich Challenge as an Approach to Improve Students Abilities in Test Case Writing. In *Innovation and Technology in Computer Science Education (ITiCSE '19), July 15–17, 2019, Aberdeen, Scotland UK*. ACM, New York, NY, USA, Article 4, 1 page. https://doi.org/10.1145/3304221.3325582

1 INTRODUCTION

Software Testing is the process of executing a program with the intent of finding errors [6]. One testing activity that is key to find errors is that of test scripting: documenting test cases in manual test scripts or automated test code [5]. A well-designed test case needs to have at least three important parts: inputs, outputs and order of execution [1]. Test cases written by students typically have recurring errors that make difficult to find hidden bugs [3] or lack details about the instructions that must be followed [4].

As an attempt to improve the quality of test cases produced by students we used a playful approach based on instructions for making a Peanut Butter and Jelly (PB&J) Sandwiches [2]. For instance, when executing a written instruction saying "open the bag of bread", the teacher rips open the bag sending pieces flying, passing the idea of the algorithm not being precise. This approach is often used when teaching algorithmic thinking but we found no attempt focused on software testing reported in literature. We performed the activity in a Software Engineering course but adapting it and exploring test cases concepts (e.g., inputs expected outcomes, order of execution). To verify the impact on the quality of the students test cases, we compared the test cases of a group of 14 students participating in the PB&J activity against students who did not participate, which worked as control groups: a group of 20 students from the same class; two groups from previous semesters (31 and 32 students, respectively). The analysis focused on five variables (input data, expected outputs, step-by-step description, variation of test case, number of steps) used in a study on test case quality [4].

ACM ISBN 978-1-4503-6301-3/19/07.
https://doi.org/10.1145/3304221.3325582

2 RESULTS

According to our analysis, the PB&J activity positively influenced the quality of students test cases. Test cases written by students who participated in the activity had a significantly higher level of detail and less ambiguity than the other groups. They were more explicit about the inputs and expected outcomes and also had the average number of steps higher than the other groups. However, it did not influence the creation of non-obvious test cases —those that make easier to find errors —since it was just equivalent to the control group that scored better in that characteristic. According to the feedback that was given, students enjoyed very much the activity and had the perception that playful activities help to learn new concepts without distracting from the primary purpose.

As some improvements in the activity, we suggest finding a way to explore variations of test cases, which would end up with non-obvious test more capable of finding errors. Also, emphasize to students that the important thing is not having too many steps but rather having detailed and unambiguous instructions.

REFERENCES

[1] Lee Copeland. 2004. *A practitioner's guide to software test design.* Artech House.
[2] Janet Davis and Samuel A Rebelsky. 2007. Food-first computer science: starting the first course right with PB&J. *ACM SIGCSE Bulletin* 39, 1 (2007), 372–376.
[3] Stephen H Edwards and Zalia Shams. 2014. Do student programmers all tend to write the same software tests?. In *Proceedings of the 2014 conference on Innovation & technology in computer science education.* ACM, 171–176.
[4] Sigrid Eldh, Hans Hansson, and Sasikumar Punnekkat. 2011. Analysis of mistakes as a method to improve test case design. In *2011 Fourth IEEE International Conference on Software Testing, Verification and Validation.* IEEE, 70–79.
[5] Vahid Garousi and Mika V Mäntylä. 2016. When and what to automate in software testing? A multi-vocal literature review. *Information and Software Technology* 76 (2016), 92–117.
[6] Glenford J Myers, Corey Sandler, and Tom Badgett. 2011. *The art of software testing.* John Wiley & Sons.

Teaching Logic with Iltis: an Interactive, Web-Based System

Gaetano Geck, Artur Ljulin, Jonas Haldimann, Johannes May, Jonas Schmidt,
Marko Schmellenkamp*, Daniel Sonnabend, Felix Tschirbs, Fabian Vehlken, Thomas Zeume*
{gaetano.geck | artur.ljulin | jonas.haldimann | johannes.may | jonas2.schmidt | marko.schmellenkamp |
daniel.sonnabend | felix.tschirbs | fabian.vehlken | thomas.zeume}@tu-dortmund.de
TU Dortmund
Dortmund, Germany

ABSTRACT

Iltis is an interactive, web-based system for teaching logic. It is designed to provide immediate and comprehensive feedback for exercises covering various aspects of the reasoning workflow. This poster presentation reports on new exercises and feedback mechanisms for modal and first-order logic.

CCS CONCEPTS

• **Theory of computation → Logic**; • **Applied computing → Interactive learning environments**.

KEYWORDS

logic; interactive learning environments

ACM Reference Format:

Gaetano Geck, Artur Ljulin, Jonas Haldimann, Johannes May, Jonas Schmidt, Marko Schmellenkamp, Daniel Sonnabend, Felix Tschirbs, Fabian Vehlken, and Thomas Zeume. 2019. Teaching Logic with Iltis: an Interactive, Web-Based System. In *Innovation and Technology in Computer Science Education (ITiCSE '19), July 15–17, 2019, Aberdeen, Scotland, UK*. ACM, New York, NY, USA, 1 page. https://doi.org/10.1145/3304221.3325571

1 MOTIVATION AND RELATED WORK

Logical concepts play an important role in many areas of computer science including artificial intelligence, formal software and hardware verification, and modern database query languages. Thus, learning the workflow for automated logical reasoning – how to model scenarios with logical formulae, how to transform formulae into normal forms, and how to infer new knowledge – is essential for prospective computer scientists. However, many students in introductory classes struggle with logical methods. At the same time, individual, human tutoring for these students becomes more and more difficult due to an increasing number of students enrolled in computer science courses [2].

A large variety of educational tools for parts of the logical modelling and reasoning workflow exist [1], yet many of them are not web-based. The few existing web-based tools (see e.g. [4]) only cover parts of this workflow.

The Iltis project provides a web-based framework for logic exercises with a uniform user interface for the whole reasoning workflow. In [3] we reported on a prototypical implementation of the framework and of exercises for the propositional workflow.

2 SUPPORTED EXERCISES: AN UPDATE

This poster presentation provides an update on the system's functionality, summarized in Table 1. The system now includes exercises for the reasoning pipeline for modal and first-order logic. Exercises for resolution and for modelling Kripke structures use a new flexible, easy-to-use graph widget. For propositional and modal logic, exercises for evaluating formulae have been added.

A key feature of Iltis is its comprehensive feedback. The feedback for propositional and modal logic modelling uses an error-rule-based mechanism introduced in [3]. Providing feedback for first-order modelling is more challenging due to undecidability of equivalence. Iltis supports first-order logic modelling for graph properties with graphical feedback. We plan to study theoretical properties of fragments of first-order logic usually used in didactic contexts for providing innovative, deeper feedback in the future.

We encourage readers to try Iltis themselves [5]. The system has been used for offering web-based exercises for a second year course on logic in computer science, and was well-received by students.

Task/Logic type	propositional	modal	first-order
Modelling	supported	supported	basic support
Transformation	supported	supported	no support$^\triangle$
Reasoning	supported	no support$^\triangle$	supported
Evaluation	supported	supported	no support$^\triangle$

Table 1: Overview of currently supported exercises in Iltis. Entries marked by $^\triangle$ are scheduled for implementation.

ACKNOWLEDGMENTS

This project is supported by a Fellowship for Innovation in Digital University Education by the state of North Rhine-Westphalia and the Stifterverband.

REFERENCES

[1] María Antonia and Huertas Sánchez. 2011. A classification of tools for learning logic. http://hdl.handle.net/10609/6501
[2] Computing Research Association. 2017. Generation CS: Computer Science Undergraduate Enrollments Surge Since 2006. http://cra.org/data/generation-cs
[3] Gaetano Geck, Artur Ljulin, Sebastian Peter, Jonas Schmidt, Fabian Vehlken, and Thomas Zeume. 2018. Introduction to Iltis: an interactive, web-based system for teaching logic. In *ITiCSE 2018*. 141–146. https://doi.org/10.1145/3197091.3197095
[4] Josje Lodder and Bastiaan Heeren. 2011. A Teaching Tool for Proving Equivalences between Logical Formulae. In *Tools for Teaching Logic*. 154–161. https://doi.org/10.1007/978-3-642-21350-2_18
[5] The Iltis project. March 2019. https://iltis.cs.tu-dortmund.de

*Corresponding author.

ITiCSE '19, July 15–17, 2019, Aberdeen, Scotland, UK

ACM ISBN 978-1-4503-6301-3/19/07.
https://doi.org/10.1145/3304221.3325571

Adapting the IT2017 Curricula for Two-Year Transfer Programs

Determining Appropriate Competencies for the First Two Years of a Baccalaureate IT Program

Markus Geissler
Computer Information Science
Cosumnes River College
Sacramento, CA, USA
markus.geissler@crc.losrios.edu

Cindy S. Tucker
Computer & Information Technologies
Bluegrass Community
& Technical College
Lexington, KY, USA
cindy.tucker@kctcs.edu

Christian Servin
Computer Science
El Paso Community College
El Paso, TX, USA cservin1@epcc.edu

Cara Tang
Computer Information Systems
Portland Community College
Portland, OR, USA
cara.tang@pcc.edu

Melissa Stange
Computer Science
Lord Fairfax Community College
Middletown, VA, USA
mstange@lfcc.edu

ABSTRACT

After the Association for Computing Machinery (ACM) and the IEEE Computer Society endorsed the recently completed Information Technology Curricula 2017 Curriculum Guidelines (IT2017) for Baccalaureate Degree Programs in Information Technology (IT) [1], the ACM Committee for Computing Education in Community Colleges (CCECC) at the direction of the ACM Education Board joined with the chair of the IT2017 task group to create corresponding guidance for two-year colleges offering IT transfer programs. In some countries, students can complete the first two years of a Bachelor's degree at a two-year school (which may be known as a community college, technical college, or junior college), and then transfer to a university to complete the remaining two years of their course of study [3]. The CCECC formed the IT Transfer Task Force (ITTTF), consisting of educators from both two-year colleges and four-year universities, to provide guidance for IT programs in such two-year schools. The guidance includes the competencies students should achieve during the first two years of an IT Bachelor's degree. The ITTTF is currently seeking public feedback from educators and IT industry representatives on an initial set of competencies to guide how the ITTTF should proceed to build IT Transfer Curriculum Guidelines. This poster will outline the initial selection of competencies to solicit feedback and input on the guidelines, including best practices for communication between two-year IT Transfer programs and their four-year university partners.

CCS CONCEPTS: • Social and professional topics → Professional topics →Computing education → Model curricula.

ACM ISBN: 978-1-4503-6301-3/19/07.
https://doi.org/10.1145/3304221.3325584

KEYWORDS: IT2017, Curricula, Transfer, Two-Year Colleges

ACM Reference format:

Markus Geissler, Cara Tang, Melissa Stange, Christian Servin, and Cindy S. Tucker. 2019. Adapting the IT2017 Curricula for Two-Year Transfer Programs: Determining Appropriate Competencies for the First Two Years of a Baccalaureate IT Program. In *Proceedings of 24th Annual ACM Conference on Innovation and Technology in Computer Science Education (ITiCSE'19), July 15-17, 2019, Aberdeen, Scotland, UK.* ACM, New York, NY, 1 page. https://doi.org/10.1145/3304221.3325584

1 INTRODUCTION

The Information Technology discipline has been growing and evolving as technology advances. To help address a predicted worldwide shortfall of 4.3 million technology, media, and telecommunications workers by 2030 [2], curriculum guidance will allow IT departments at two-year colleges to more easily define essential and supplemental transfer student competencies, to develop and maintain transfer programs with four-year universities, and to grow their capacity.

The ACM CCECC and its IT Transfer Task Force expect to release an IT Transfer curriculum guidance document just prior to the SIGITE 2019 Conference and look forward to receiving valuable feedback from the international Computing community at ITiCSE 2019.

REFERENCES

[1] Task Group on Information Technology Curricula, "Information Technology Curricula 2017," Association for Computing Machinery (ACM) and IEEE Computer Society (IEEE-CS), New York, NY, 2017.

[2] S. McLaren, "These Industries Will Face the Biggest Talent Shortages by 2030," LinkedIn Corporation, Sunnyvale, CA, 2018.

[3] C. Tang, E. Hawthorne, C. Tucker, E. Cuadros-Vargas, D. Cukierman, Simon, and M. Zhang. 2016. Global Perspectives on the Role of Two-Year/Technical/Junior Colleges in Computing Education. In ITiSCE '16. ACM, 204-205.

Unplugged Activities to Introduce Parallel Computing in Introductory Programming Classes: an Experience Report

Sheikh K. Ghafoor
sghafoor@tntech.edu
Tennessee Tech University

David W. Brown
dwbrown@tntech.edu
Tennessee Tech University

Mike Rogers
mrogers@tntech.edu
Tennessee Tech University

Thomas Hines
tmhines42@students.tntech.edu
Tennessee Tech University

ABSTRACT

Learning programming in early introductory classes is challenging for first year university students, and introducing parallel programming (PDC) in early classes along with traditional sequential programming is even more challenging. Unplugged activities may help alleviate some of the difficulties for students. Unplugged activities have been shown to increase student interest, and to enhance student understanding of CS programming concepts [1]. We have used unplugged activities to teach PDC concepts before introducing parallel programming. Our experiences show that using unplugged activities to introduce the PDC concepts reduce the barrier to learn parallel programming.

CCS CONCEPTS

• **Social and professional topics** → *CS1*; • **Computing methodologies**;

KEYWORDS

Unplugged Activities, Parallel and Distributed Computing, Introductory Programming

1 INTRODUCTION

Parallel and Distributed Computing (PDC) has become ubiquitous as modern computing devices from high-end servers to cell phones arrive with multiple cores as well as GPU capabilities. The changing landscape points to the need for every programmer to understand how parallelism and distributed computing affect problem solving. Early programming courses present complex concepts to novice students, and additionally they include added complexity with syntax, structures, and semantics of particular programming languages. Therefore, learning programming is challenging for early CS/CE students, as reported in the literature [2]. ACM has recommended Parallel and Distributed Computing as a required Knowledge Area for undergraduate Computer Science curricula because of the proliferation of computing devices with parallel capabilities and the need for students to be able to program these devices. Unfortunately, introducing PDC concepts and associated programming skills add more complexity and is more challenging for many students. Unplugged activities, which are activities done without writing programs or using computers and which usually have physical activity with visual components, have been shown to engage students and convey complex concepts in a way that enhances student learning [3].

ITiCSE '19, July 15–17, 2019, Aberdeen, Scotland Uk

ACM ISBN 978-1-4503-6301-3/19/07.
https://doi.org/10.1145/3304221.3325573

2 PRELIMINARY OBSERVATIONS

At Tennessee Tech University we have introduced PDC concepts in CS1 and CS2 classes using both unplugged and plugged activities. We have used two unplugged activities in CS1 and CS2 to help explain several PDC concepts before introducing hands-on programming exercises using OpenMP. One such unplugged activity is sorting colored candy, according to the color, first by one student and then by three students to illustrate the concept of concurrency, speedup, and sequential dependency. Another such activity was to find the youngest person in class, to illustrate the concept of multi-core, inter-process communication, and synchronization. Details of many such activities is available on our website[4]. We evaluated the impact of using unplugged activities on ease of learning, through pre-post surveys and also looking at the grades on PDC related exams and lab assignments. Our evaluation indicates that using unplugged activities makes it easier to learn PDC concepts. We have seen a gain of 1.55 points on a 5 point scale when using unplugged exercises in addition to plugged laboratories compared to a gain of .88 points when using the plugged activities alone.

3 FUTURE WORK

We plan to develop more hands-on exercises that are applicable to upper level classes and additional evaluations to comprehensively study the impact of the activities on learning PDC concepts.

REFERENCES

[1] B. Rodriguez, C. Rader, and T. Camp, "Using Student Performance to Assess CS Unplugged Activities in a Classroom Environment," in *Proceedings of the 2016 ACM Conference on Innovation and Technology in Computer Science Education - ITiCSE 16*, 2016, pp. 95 – 100

[2] C. Watson and F. W. B. Li, "Failure rates in introductory programming revisited," in *Proceedings of the 2014 conference on Innovation & technology in computer science education - ITiCSE 14, 2014*, pp. 39 – 44.

[3] T. Bell, J. Alexander, I. Freeman, and M. Grimley, "Computer science unplugged: School students doing real computing without computers," *New Zeal. J. Appl. Comput. Inf. Technol., vol. 13, no. 1*, pp. 20 – 29, 2009.

[4] "iPDC Modules", https://www.csc.tntech.edu/pdcincs/index.php/ipdc-modules/

From Data to Insights in CS1

Ananda Gunawardena
Department of Computer Science
Princeton University† | Rutgers University
Princeton, NJ
andyguna@gmail.com

ABSTRACT

In this poster, we present some insights from student interaction data based on a year-long study on how to rethink the instructional model of a large CS1 (n=800) course. A key goal of the study was to address the increasing academic diversity in large introductory courses. The redesigned curriculum uses a combination of automation, real-time data and a better utilization of teaching staff to deliver an enhanced learning experience. The new measures demonstrated significant improvements in student engagement and over 90% course satisfaction.

CCS CONCEPTS

• Information system • introductory computer science • Cross-computing tools

KEYWORDS

Introductory CS, video-based instruction, analytics

1 Introduction

Nearly 70% of all undergraduates at our institution take CS1 course. Our objective was to rethink how to utilize the content created for online learners to improve the experience and outcomes of students enrolled in a campus setting. This required complete redesign of the curriculum content and delivery including redefining staff roles, integration of video lectures, recitations for novices/advanced students, among other measures. Although the weekly meetings were optional, over 80% of the students attended the lecture.

2 Technology and Curriculum

Building on our prior experiences [1], we developed a new interactive video platform a-curate [2], to deliver videos in a more active learning setting. The videos were enhanced by *synchronized and searchable transcripts (created using machine learning based methods)* and allowed students to search and interact with any segment of the video from the collection. We gained following insights from over 5GB of text data.

ACM ISBN 978-1-4503-6301-3/19/07. https://doi.org/10.1145/3304221.3325586

3 Insights from Data

We analyzed 2.9 million records of 5 seconds each (4039 total hours). Here are some insights that helped us design a better curriculum and learning experiences for all students.

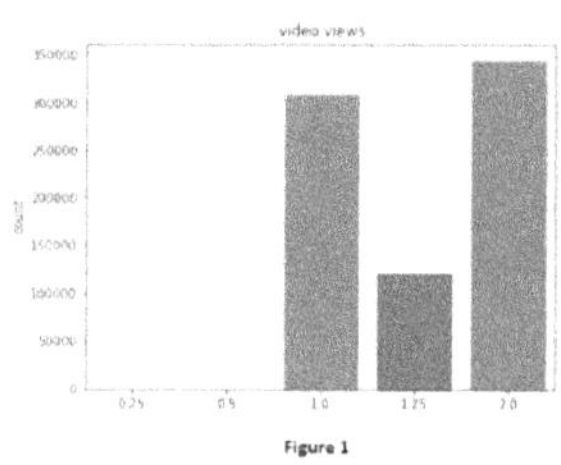

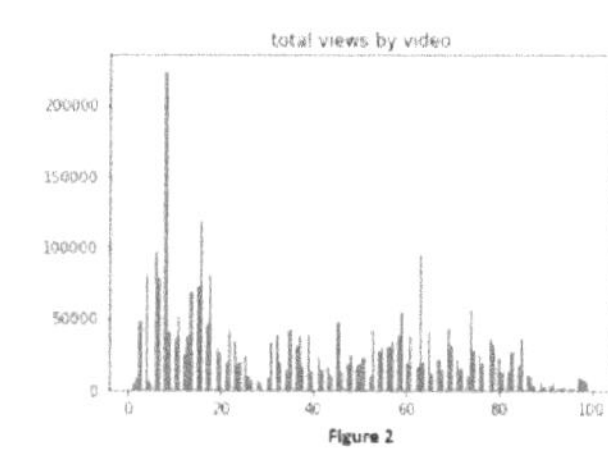

Figure 1: video playback speed is correlated to prior experience.
Figure 2: Higher counts (y-axis) were indicative of difficulty in specific concepts (x-axis is video ID).

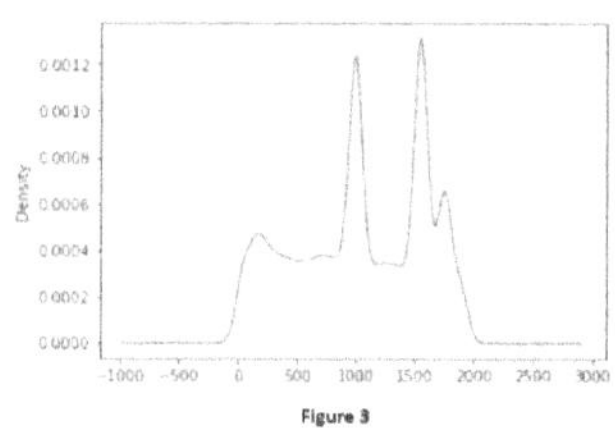

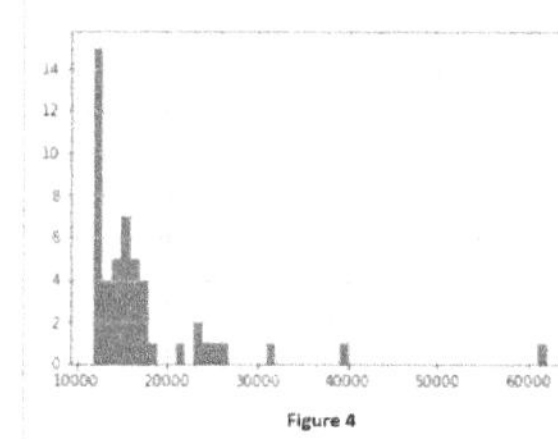

Figure 3: A kernel density estimator shows locations of high focus within videos to help design more location interactions.
Figure 4: Design custom experiences related to high view counts (y-axis) and video usage hours (x-axis).

ACKNOWLEDGMENTS

This research was supported by 250th innovation grant from Princeton University. We also thank Ibrahim Albluwi, Alan Kaplan, Dan Leyzberg, Jeremie Lumbroso, Bob Sedgewick and Kevin Wayne for their support.

REFERENCES

[1] A.D. Gunawardena, J. Barr (2010). Encouraging Reading and Collaboration using Classroom Salon. ITiCSE'10 Proceedings of the fifteenth annual conference on Innovation and technology in computer science education, ACM New York, USA ISBN: 978-1-60558-820-9.
[2] Acurate, an online platform for curated interactive videos, http://acurate.io

Motivating High School Girls to Study Computer Science

Mirela Gutica
British Columbia Institute of Technology
Burnaby, British Columbia, Canada
Mirela_Gutica@bcit.ca

ABSTRACT

This research study aims to identify design strategies, instructional models and technological tools (e.g., educational games) that can be used to motivate high school girls to pursue computer science (CS) education. Part of this study, an educational game *CodeBlock* intended to teach basic programming, was designed and implemented for HoloLens devices. This study evaluates to what extent participating in a coding workshop consisting of a set of coding exercises and the *CodeBlock* game play could increase the interest of high school girls in CS. The workshop is conducted by undergraduate students who were involved in the design and implementation of the game, which has an additional benefit of exposing young girls to technologies implemented by post-secondary students, thus increasing the chances they will pursue post-secondary education in CS related fields.

CCS CONCEPTS

• **Social and professional topics → CS1; K-12 education.**

KEYWORDS

computer science; motivation; girls; gender gap; role models

ACM Reference Format:

Mirela Gutica. 2019. Motivating High School Girls to Study Computer Science. In *Innovation and Technology in Computer Science Education (ITiCSE '19), July 15–17, 2019, Aberdeen, Scotland UK.* ACM, New York, NY, USA, 1 page. https://doi.org/10.1145/3304221.3325589

1 INTRODUCTION

Even though in some STEM disciplines gender distribution is more balanced, computer science and technology are still male dominated. At British Columbia Institute of Technology (BCIT), the number of female students enrolled in CS and technology undergraduate programs is below 15%. Efforts are being made to increase young girls' engagement with STEM and programming; however, as related literature [5] and my research suggests, the gender gap in STEM and CS education and careers has deep roots in broader sociocultural factors.

2 STUDY DESIGN

The study design was based on literature review and on an empirical investigation of factors that influence students' motivation to study and persist in CS undergraduate programs. According to findings resulting from interviews with twenty one undergraduate students (thirteen women from which two identified themselves as transgender, and eight men), aspects that influence the attainment value (perception of success, role models, self-confidence and stereotypes) as well as the level of exposure to this field of study during elementary and high school education present significant gender differences. The choice to implement a HoloLens educational game, besides exposing the girls to a cutting-edge technology, has additional pedagogical benefits related to visualization and spatial skills as video games can be useful in equalizing these differences associated with gender [4]. Problem solving and social play modes were included in the game design as these design characteristics are gender neutral [3]. Eight BCIT students contributed to the design and implementation of the game and coding activities, and four high school girls provided ideas and feedback in three pilot studies. Having students and not professionals involved in design is beneficial from a constructionist perspective [2]. As a person's interest is a powerful motivator to learn, this study is intended provide an opportunity for high school girls to experience a triggered situational interest event, which is a first phase in the process of interest development [1]. The study has a pre-questionnaire/intervention/post-questionnaire design. Participants report on aspects of attainment, challenge, enjoyment, engagement, and interest.

3 DISCUSSION

This study is currently in the stage of data collection. Preliminary results indicate a high level of engagement, enjoyment and interest, and perceived positive learning gains. I intend to refine and expand the coding activities and the *CodeBlock* game. Although this workshop could trigger girls' interest in CS, more should be done to maintain their interest over time. My final goal is to conduct a longitudinal study aimed to facilitate girls' achievement of well-developed individual interest in CS [1].

REFERENCES

[1] Suzanne Hidi and K. Ann Renninger. 2006. The Four-Phase Model of Interest Development. *Educational Psychologist* 41, 2 (June 2006), 111–127. https://doi.org/10.1207/s15326985ep4102_4

[2] Yasmin B. Kafai and Quinn Burke. 2015. Constructionist Gaming: Understanding the Benefits of Making Games for Learning. *Educational Psychologist* 50, 4 (Oct. 2015), 313–334. https://doi.org/10.1080/00461520.2015.1124022

[3] Mable B. Kinzie and Dolly R. D. Joseph. 2008. Gender differences in game activity preferences of middle school children: Implications for educational game design. *Educational Technology Research and Development* 56, 5-6 (2008), 643–663. https://doi.org/10.1007/s11423-007-9076-z

[4] Kaveri Subrahmanyam and Patricia M. Greenfield. 1994. Effect of video game practice on spatial skills in girls and boys. *Journal of Applied Developmental Psychology* 15, 1 (Jan. 1994), 13–32. https://doi.org/10.1016/0193-3973(94)90004-3

[5] Ming-Te Wang and Jessica L. Degol. 2017. Gender Gap in Science, Technology, Engineering, and Mathematics (STEM): Current Knowledge, Implications for Practice, Policy, and Future Directions. *Educational Psychology Review* 29, 1 (March 2017), 119–140. https://doi.org/10.1007/s10648-015-9355-x

ITiCSE '19, July 15–17, 2019, Aberdeen, Scotland UK

ACM ISBN 978-1-4503-6301-3/19/07...$15.00
https://doi.org/10.1145/3304221.3325589

Findings from a Multi-year Study of CT in K-2 Students in Formal and Informal Settings

Tony Lowe
School of Engineering Education
Purdue University
West Lafayette, IN USA
lowe46@purdue.edu

Sean Brophy
School of Engineering Education
Purdue University
West Lafayette, IN USA
sbrophy@purdue.edu

Monica Cardella
School of Engineering Education
Purdue University
West Lafayette, IN USA
mcardell@purdue.edu

ABSTRACT

For the past four years, our research group has conducted a series of NSF funded studies on Computational Thinking (CT) involving elementary school students, parents, and teachers. We developed curriculum, trained teachers, observed classrooms, created museum exhibits, followed students and families, explored theory, and utilized the diverse skills of a large multi-disciplinary research group to understand the intersection of STEM, literacy, and CT. As we close out this grant, we are looking to disseminate our findings, share lessons learned about research methods and data collection, and build collaborations for future research.

CCS CONCEPTS

- Social and professional topics → Computational thinking
- Social and professional topics → Computer science education

KEYWORDS

Computational Thinking, P-12, Formal and Informal Instruction, Professional Development

ACM Reference format:

Tony Lowe, Sean Brophy, Monica Cardella. 2019. Findings from a Multi-year Study of CT in K-2 Students in Formal and Informal Settings. In *Proceedings of Innovation and Technology in Computer Science Education (ITiCSE'119), July 14-17, 2019, Aberdeen, Scotland UK.* ACM, New York, NY, USA, 1 page. https://doi.org/10.1145/3304221.3325585

1 Introduction

The INSPIRE research institute received NSF grant No. DRL 1543175 and ECC 1442416 to investigate the development of CT in very young learners from grades K-2. Early efforts built upon an established engineering design curriculum to enhance elements that introduce CT and allowed for a better understanding of the capabilities for this very young age group [1]. In-service teachers learned about CT through professional development activities. Researchers followed the learning progress of children in the classroom [2], homeschooling [3], and through informal play activities including a newly designed museum exhibit on CT [4], [5].

ACM ISBN 978-1-4503-6301-3/19/07.
https://doi.org/10.1145/3304221.3325585

2 Lessons on CT Research

In addition to the findings of CT development in children, parents, and teachers we also captured experiences about the process of conducting CT research. The research protocols involved hundreds of hours of observations and video data across scores of classrooms, homes, and informal learning environments. Defining effective processes in which to collect, store, and organize this data became critical [6]. Through the project, we worked on evolving and codifying the moving target that is CT. We analyzed the various ways CT is defined in the literature and attempted to create working definitions [7] and provide data [8].

3 Future Research

This summer brings an end to our grant cycle of research but starts the next phase of our investigations into CT. We hope to share some of these ideas and find partners who are also motivated to understand how CT develops in learners.

REFERENCES

[1] M. M. Hynes *et al.*, "Inspiring computational thinking in young children's engineering design activities," 2016.

[2] E. M. Haluschak, K. M. Tank, T. J. Moore, and A. C. Johnston, "Actions and Approaches of Teachers Communicating Computational Thinking and Engineering Design to First Grade Students," in *ASEE Annual Conference and Exposition*, 2019.

[3] H. Ehsan, A. Rehmat, H. Osman, I. H. Yeter, and M. Cardella, "Examining the role of parents in promoting computational thinking in children: A focus on homeschool families," in *Proceeding of American Society for Engineering Education (ASEE) Conference & Exposition*, 2019.

[4] H. Ehsan, C. Ohland, T. Dandridge, and M. Cardella, "Computing for the Critters: Exploring Computational Thinking of Children in an Informal Learning Setting," in *2018 IEEE Frontiers in Education Conference (FIE)*, 2018, pp. 1–5.

[5] H. Ehsan and M. E. Cardella, "Capturing the Computational Thinking of Families with Young Children in Out-of-School Environments," in *124th ASEE Annual Conference and Exposition*, 2017.

[6] I. H. Yeter *et al.*, "Design and implementation of data collection in a large-scale, multi-year pre-college engineering study: A retrospective," in *ASEE Annual Conference and Exposition*, 2019.

[7] T. Lowe and S. Brophy, "An operationalized model for defining computational thinking," in *Frontiers in Education*, 2017.

[8] T. Lowe and S. Brophy, "Identifying Computational Thinking in Storytelling Literacy Activities with Scratch Jr.," in *ASEE Annual Conference Proceedings*, 2019, p. 10.

Devising Work-based Learning Curricula with Apprentice Research Software Engineers

Joseph Maguire
University of Glasgow
Glasgow, United Kingdom
joseph.maguire@glasgow.ac.uk

Quintin Cutts
University of Glasgow
Glasgow, United Kingdom
quintin.cutts@glasgow.ac.uk

Jack Parkinson
University of Glasgow
Glasgow, United Kingdom
jack.parkinson@glasgow.ac.uk

Matthew Barr
University of Glasgow
Glasgow, United Kingdom
matthew.barr@glasgow.ac.uk

Derek Somerville
University of Glasgow
Glasgow, United Kingdom
derek.somerville@glasgow.ac.uk

ABSTRACT

Work-based learning (WBL) is a delivery model that attempts to address the isolation of theory and practice by integrating them into a single programme. The concern is that through lack of experience and understanding, both universities and industry may devise 'Frankenstein' curricula, harming individuals rather than helping them. This poster introduces a small project to support curricula development by proposing universities act as both the learning provider and workplace for apprentice Research Software Engineers (RSEs).

CCS CONCEPTS

• **Social and professional topics** → *Computing education.*

KEYWORDS

work-based learning, research software engineers

ACM Reference Format:
Joseph Maguire, Quintin Cutts, Jack Parkinson, Matthew Barr, and Derek Somerville. 2019. Devising Work-based Learning Curricula with Apprentice Research Software Engineers. In *Innovation and Technology in Computer Science Education (ITiCSE '19), July 15–17, 2019, Aberdeen, Scotland UK.* ACM, New York, NY, USA, 1 page. https://doi.org/10.1145/3304221.3325576

1 INTRODUCTION

There are many different approaches to exposing industry to students, but Work-based Learning (WBL) is one delivery model that attempts to integrate academic theory in university with practical application in the workplace [3]. Devising WBL curricula is challenging and a significant concern is that universities will be 'reverse-colonised' by industry [2]. An alternative approach is for some universities to gain experience in the development of such programmes by acting as both the academic provider *and* workplace partner through apprentice Research Software Engineers (RSEs) [1].

ITiCSE '19, July 15–17, 2019, Aberdeen, Scotland UK

ACM ISBN 978-1-4503-6301-3/19/07.
https://doi.org/10.1145/3304221.3325576

2 POSSIBILITIES AND PITFALLS

There are many potential benefits from universities appointing apprenticeship RSEs for the purposes of curricula development:

- *Reliable authentic assessment.* The concern with some assessments is that while reliable, they are not valid as they are not informed by context [4]. Devising material with RSEs has the potential to increase validity while ensuring reliability.
- *Relevant curriculum coverage and staging.* The expectation is that apprentices should begin with legitimate peripheral participation, but this will require the academic partner to deliver valuable knowledge and skills as soon as possible. The expectation is that by working closely with research groups, lecturers gain experience in how to devise valid but relevant curriculum coverage and staging.

While there are potential benefits to the approach there are some concerns:

- *Curriculum with limited scope.* The scope and focus of the curriculum is a major concern when a university is essentially only 'talking to itself'. The shape of a RSE curriculum will be dependent on the breadth of disciplines and capabilities of research teams.
- *Limited awareness of software engineering.* The lack of exposure of generic industrial software engineering practices may result in a software engineer that has limited career progression outside of research.

3 FUTURE WORK

The initial project work has been investigating expectations of RSEs for a range of disciplines and plan for initial recruitment. The next stage is to devise appropriate structures to ensure curricula can be improved inline with the needs of the role.

REFERENCES

[1] Rob Baxter, N Chue Hong, Dirk Gorissen, James Hetherington, and Ilian Todorov. 2012. The Research Software Engineer. In *Digital Research Conference, Oxford.* 1–3.
[2] Paul Gibbs. 2013. Work-based quality: a collusion waiting to happen? *Quality in Higher Education* 19, 1 (2013), 1–6. https://doi.org/10.1080/13538322.2013.777520
[3] Joseph A Raelin. 1997. A Model of Work-based Learning. *Organization Science* 8, 6 (1997), 563–578. https://doi.org/10.1287/orsc.8.6.563
[4] Geoffrey Scheurman and Fred M Newmann. 1998. Authentic intellectual work in social studies: Putting performance before pedagogy. *Social Education* 62 (1998), 23–26.

Insights from using Supplemental Instruction (SI) in Data Structures Course to Increase Retention

Aparna Mahadev
Department of Computer Science
Worcester State University
Worcester, Massachusetts, USA
Aparna.Mahadev@worcester.edu

ABSTRACT

Data Structures (CS 242) ranks as one of the most challenging courses in our core curriculum. It has the steepest learning curve for our students and has the lowest retention rate. Students find it challenging to master the mathematical concepts, learn the data structures and apply them in large programs. Three years ago, the department decided to offer Supplemental Instruction (SI) in CS 242 and in Discrete Structures (CS 225), a co-requisite for CS 242, in the hope of increasing retention in CS 242. In this poster, the author shares experiences with the SI approach, and the results of a student survey to assess the efficacy of SI in both these courses.

KEYWORDS

Student engagement; Student Retention; Curriculum Issues; Pedagogy; Instruction; Data Structures.

1 INTRODUCTION

There has been a significant amount of educational research on the benefits of peer mentoring to both recipients and peer leaders [1] [3]. There are many models for peer mentoring and on our campus, we use the Supplemental Instruction model [2]. SI leaders engage students in CS- related lessons and mentoring activities in a collaborative setting to provide an alternative approach to student learning [2] [4]. These out-of-class study sessions are designed to guide SI attendees through course content and to provide unique learning opportunities. SI learning sessions are typically used in gateway courses to increase student retention beyond the introductory level [4]. In recent years, the enrollment in our introductory course has increased significantly but the retention rate in our sophomore-level data structures course has remained the same. Through our periodic program reviews and program assessment, we realized that CS 242 is a major stumbling block for our students.

ITiCSE '19, July 15-17, 2019, Aberdeen, Scotland, UK

ACM ISBN 978-1-4503-6301-3/19/07.
https://doi.org/10.1145/3304221.3325553

2 METHODOLOGY

To address retention in CS 242, the department linked CS 225 and CS 242 by reordering the coverage of topics in both courses. Additionally, three years ago, we started offering SI sessions in both courses. SI leaders are carefully chosen by our faculty for their demonstrated competence in the subject and their facilitation skills. SI leaders attend all class meetings and conduct two one-hour sessions per week. Leaders are given training on topics such as how students learn; strategies to strengthen student academic performance; how to manage sessions; and data collection. SI sessions are open to all students in the course, free of charge, with no added incentive such as extra credit, and attendance is anonymous to the instructor and voluntary. Leaders meet with the instructor weekly to plan the activities. Leaders are paid a modest amount for their work and the program is funded through our Aisiku STEM center. SI leaders also benefit from better understanding of the course material and find the mentoring experience enriching. The SI supervisor, who is not the course instructor, monitors the quality of SI sessions and evaluates the program at the end of each semester.

3 CONCLUSIONS

As corroborated by a student survey, students benefit from this initiative and there is a perceived grade improvement by the attendees. Anecdotal evidence also shows that SI attendees gain confidence in the subject matter and build a sense of community. We hope that by providing an alternative learning experience, we can improve the retention rate in CS 242.

REFERENCES

[1] S. Loos, S. Menzel and M. Poparad, (2005), Three Perspectives on peer tutoring for CS1, Proceedings of the Midwest Celebration of Women in Computing Conference, https://cgi.sice.indiana.edu/~midwic/papers/uploads/loos.pdf
[2] https://info.umkc.edu/si/
[3] C. Murphy, R. Powell, K, Parton and A. Cannon (2011), Lessons Learned from a PLTL-CS Program, SIGCSE'11, March 9-12, Dallas, Texas, USA, pp 207-212
[4] J. Cottam, S. Menzel, and J. Greenblatt, (2011) Tutoring for Retention, SIGCSE'11, March 9-12, Dallas, Texas, USA, pp 213-218

Exploring the Correlation Between Teacher Pedagogical Content Knowledge and Content Knowledge in Computer Science Classrooms

Tom McKlin
The Findings Group
Decatur, Georgia USA
tom@thefindingsgroup.org

Taneisha Lee
The Findings Group
Decatur, Georgia USA
taneisha@thefindingsgroup.org

Dana Wanzer
The Findings Group
Decatur, Georgia USA
dana@thefindingsgroup.org

Brian Magerko
Digital Media Program
Georgia Institute of Technology
Atlanta, Georgia USA
magerko@gatech.edu

Doug Edwards
Center for Education Integrating Science Mathematics and Computing
Georgia Institute of Technology
Atlanta, Georgia USA
doug.edwards@ceismc.gatech.edu

Sabrina Grossman
Center for Education Integrating Science Mathematics and Computing
Georgia Institute of Technology
Atlanta, Georgia USA
sabrina.grossman@ceismc.gatech.edu

Emily Bryans
The Findings Group
Decatur, Georgia USA
emily@thefindingsgroup.org

Jason Freeman
Center for Music Technology
Georgia Institute of Technology
Atlanta, Georgia USA
jason.freeman@gatech.edu

ABSTRACT

Educators have long claimed that pedagogical content knowledge (PCK), ways of presenting a subject that make it comprehensible to others, is a critical element of student academic success. This poster presents findings from a preliminary study of Computer Science Principles teachers that demonstrate a significant correlation between teacher PCK and student content knowledge. The study describes the measures used to assess PCK, operationalizes the mechanisms for measuring teacher pedagogical content knowledge, shares the results from a multi-level modeling analysis, and identifies methodological improvements for follow-up research. The findings from this initial study show correlations of teacher PCK with student content knowledge while accounting for other teacher- and student-level variables across multiple schools.

KEYWORDS

Computer science education, pedagogical content knowledge, teacher professional development, STEAM, music, broadening participation

ITiCSE '19, July 15-17, 2010, Aberdeen, Scotland Uk

ACM ISBN 978-1-4503-6301-3/19/07.
https://doi.org/10.1145/3304221.3325556

ACM Reference format:

Tom McKlin, Taneisha Lee, Dana Wanzer, Brian Magerko, Doug Edwards, Sabrina Grossman, Emily Bryans, and Jason Freeman. 2019. Exploring the Correlation Between Teacher Pedagogical Content Knowledge and Content Knowledge in Computer Science Classrooms. In *Proceedings of 24th Annual ACM Conference on Innovation and Technology in Computer Science Education (ITiCSE '19). ACM, New York, NY, USA, 1 page.* https://doi.org/10.1145/3304221.3325556

1 CONTEXT AND PRELIMINARY FINDINGS

Our preliminary study of 18 teachers and 473 consenting students reveals how teachers identify and address student misconceptions. A multi-level modeling analysis shows a significant relationship between teacher pedagogical content knowledge and student content knowledge. These findings, coupled with the growth in high school computer science and with Hubbard's research on PCK among computer science teachers [1], suggest that professional learning focus on how CS content is understood and misunderstood by students.

ACKNOWLEDGMENTS

The EarSketch project receives funding from the National Science Foundation (1417835 and 1612644). EarSketch is available online at earsketch.gatech.edu.

REFERENCES

[1] Hubbard, A. K. (2017). Learning to Teach Computer Science: Qualitative Insights into Secondary Teachers' Pedagogical Content Knowledge. Ph.D Dissertation. Northwestern University.

A Proposal for Recognizing Skills in Data Science Using Open Badges

Ernestina Menasalvas
Universidad Politécnica de Madrid
Madrid, Spain
emenasalvas@fi.upm.es

Ana M. Moreno
Universidad Politécnica de Madrid
Madrid, Spain
ammoreno@fi.upm.es

Nik Swoboda
Universidad Politécnica de Madrid
Madrid, Spain
nswoboda@fi.upm.es

ABSTRACT

The growing demand for data scientists and their importance in industrial trends has resulted in a number of recent initiatives to promote skills in data science. One of these initiatives is a badge based scheme for the recognition of skills in data science developed as part of the BDVe project with the collaboration of the BDVA. This initiative is based upon a committee of experts, from both academia and industry, which will define and maintain a list of skills required to play key roles in the data science ecosystem.

CCS CONCEPTS

• **Social and professional topics → Accreditation**; *Model curricula.*

KEYWORDS

Data Science Badges; Data Science Credentials; Open Badges

ACM Reference Format:
Ernestina Menasalvas, Ana M. Moreno, and Nik Swoboda. 2019. A Proposal for Recognizing Skills in Data Science Using Open Badges. In *Innovation and Technology in Computer Science Education (ITiCSE '19), July 15–17, 2019, Aberdeen, Scotland UK.* ACM, New York, NY, USA, 1 page. https://doi.org/10.1145/3304221.3325561

1 INTRODUCTION

Data scientists need, for example, widely recognized and verifiable credentials; employers need, among others, tools to compare candidates and a way to verify the authenticity of credentials; while educators need, for example, feedback from industry regarding their programs and the added value of an externally branded recognition. To meet those needs, a scheme for the recognition of data science skills is being developed as part of the BDVe project [2]. This recognition system involves the use of a hybrid approach, drawing upon aspects of traditional badge and certificate recognitions, in the form of Open Badges. Badges can be useful tools for recognizing learning and for motivating students [4]. Their use as alternatives to traditional credentials has also been discussed [1].

ITiCSE '19, July 15–17, 2019, Aberdeen, Scotland Uk

ACM ISBN 978-1-4503-6301-3/19/07.
https://doi.org/10.1145/3304221.3325561

2 BADGES FOR DATA SCIENCE SKILLS

The EDSF of the EDISON project [3] with modifications based upon feedback from industry and academia, is being used as the basis of the required skills for the program. Five badges (Data Science Analytics, Data Engineering, Data Science Management, Business Process Management, and Data Science Research Methods) at two levels (academic and professional) will be offered. As an example, the required skills for the Data Science Analytics Badge are currently as follows:

- DSA.1 Identify existing requirements to choose and execute the most appropriate data discovery techniques to solve a problem depending on the nature of the data and the goals to be achieved.
- DSA.2 Select the most appropriate techniques to understand and prepare data prior to modeling to deliver insights.
- DSA.3 Assess, adapt, and combine data sources to improve analytics.
- DSA.4 Use the most appropriate metrics to evaluate and validate results, proposing new metrics for new applications if required.
- DSA.5 Design and evaluate analysis tools to discover new relations in order to improve decision-making.
- DSA.6 Use visualization techniques to improve the presentation of the results of a data science project in any of its phases.

Experts from both industry and academia will periodically review the required skills for the badges and modify them to meet current needs. Programs which issue badges will thereby be encouraged to update their training. The work-flow of issuing badges at the academic level is as follows: (1) An educational program applies to issue a badge providing evidence regarding how the badge's skills are taught and evaluated; (2) Experts from industry and academia evaluate the application; (3) The program trains data science students and evaluates their skills; (4) Once students demonstrate that they meet the requirements of a badge, the program issues them a badge; and (5) Student display their badges online and in job applications. A pilot of the academic level of the Data Science Analytics Badge will be run in the spring of 2019.

REFERENCES

[1] June Ahn, Anthony Pellicone, and Brian Butler. 2014. Open badges for education: what are the implications at the intersection of open systems and badging? *Research in Learning Technology* 22 (Aug. 2014), 13.
[2] BDVe. 2019. The BDVe Project Skills Recognition Program. http://www.big-data-value.eu/skills/skills-recognition-program/
[3] EDISON. 2017. The EDISON Project. http://edison-project.eu/
[4] L. Facey-Shaw, M. Specht, P. van Rosmalen, D. Brner, and J. Bartley-Bryan. 2018. Educational Functions and Design of Badge Systems: A Conceptual Literature Review. *IEEE Transactions on Learning Technologies* 11, 4 (Oct 2018), 536–544.

A Gamification Pathway for Computer Science Student Success

Patricia Morreale
School of Computer Science
Kean University
Union, NJ USA
pmorreal@kean.edu

Nohelia Diplan
School of Computer Science
Kean University
Union, NJ USA
diplann@kean.edu

Dustin York
Department of Communication
Maryville University
St. Louis, MO USA
dyork1@maryville.edu

ABSTRACT

Surging enrollments in computer science programs have necessitated the scaling-up of many programs, resulting in more curriculum offerings and larger courses enrollments to meet increasing student demand. To ensure that all students are receiving equitable information and mentoring, a pathway for computer science student success has been designed as a game, offering concrete steps for students to take in each of their four undergraduate years. Incentives are offered to students as they complete each step, culminating in badges. The use of program-wide gamification has been well-received by students, with student engagement and retention positively impacted. Lessons learned from this pilot include the importance of early introduction to the students, faculty reinforcement in the classroom, and the use of experience rewards over material rewards.

KEYWORDS

Computer science education; Engagement; Retention; Mobile Application; Gamification

ACM Reference format:

Patricia Morreale, Nohelia Diplan, and Dustin York. 2019. A Gamification Pathway for Computer Science Student Success. In *Proceedings of the 24th Annual ACM Conference on Innovation and Technology in Computer Science Education (ITiCSE'19). July 15-17, 2019, Aberdeen, Scotland, UK.* ACM, New York, NY, USA, 1 page. https://doi.org/10.1145/3304221.3325577

1 INTRODUCTION

For both research-oriented and teaching colleges and universities, surging CS/IT enrollments have the potential to adversely impact student outcomes. Faculty and programs which had previously offered high-touch interactions to students are now faced with maintaining the quality of their teaching, research and advisement interaction with students in a larger environment, which does not allow as much one-to-one student-faculty engagement as before.

To clearly define and share the steps needed for academic and professional success in computing careers, a pilot program identifying a pathway for computer science success was defined at a teaching university. This program uses gamification techniques to incentivize the students to engage in activities which will develop academic and professional skills needed for success.

2 GAMIFICATION PATHWAY

A game board was developed, depicting discrete tasks to be accomplished each academic year, moving students towards their goals of academic success, development of a professional portfolio, landing a paid internship and, after graduation, beginning a graduate or professional career. The tasks correspond to three badges, developed to provide intermediate feedback to students as they moved along towards their goal. The three badges are the Ready to Succeed badge, Road to Graduate School badge, and Academic Mage badge. Badges can be earned by completing tasks on the pathway to success. Students play the game by downloading the mobile application supporting the game onto their phones.

3 RESULTS AND FUTURE WORK

More than 50% of the eligible students registered for the pathway for student success game the first semester it was available. Completion of tasks in support of professional success is high, and student internships and first destination job placements have increased over prior years when gamification was not used. Student and faculty feedback has been positive and encouraging.

Plans for future work include providing more rewards, such as inviting students to alumni events, where they can interact with recent graduates and learn about necessary professional preparation. Gamification provided by the pathway for success has increased both student understanding of what is needed for success and provided them with measurable steps and feedback. This has increased the number of students receiving specific, detailed information about their progress in and out of the classroom towards their professional goals.

ACM ISBN 978-1-4503-6301-3/19/07.
https://doi.org/10.1145/3304221.3325577

Impact of Part-Time CS Engineering Internships on Workload

Juan J. Olarte, César Domínguez, Arturo Jaime, Francisco J. García-Izquierdo
University of La Rioja
Logroño, Spain
{jjolarte, cesar.dominguez, arturo.jaime, francisco.garcia}@unirioja.es

ABSTRACT

This study evaluates the impact of part-time internships (PTI) on concurrent subjects and students' satisfaction, in a Computer Science (CS) Engineering degree program. PTI offer some advantages: the technologies learned have a very positive influence on the quality of subsequent capstone projects (CP), students maintain in contact with the university, and synergies can be generated. Nevertheless, there are some challenges as well: maintaining a reasonable workload for students and achieving optimal coordination among different subjects.

CCS CONCEPTS

• Social and professional topics ~ Computer Science Education

KEYWORDS

Internships, workload, coordination across subjects

ACM Reference format:

Juan J. Olarte, César Domínguez, Arturo Jaime and Francisco J. García-Izquierdo. 2019. Impact of Part-Time CS Engineering Internships on Workload. In *Proceedings of ACM Conference on Innovation and Technology in Computer Science Education (ITiCSE'19). ACM, New York, NY, USA, 1 page.* https://doi.org/10.1145/3304221.3325554

1 INTRODUCTION

Internships in CS Engineering degree programs present advantages for students, the participating companies and universities, as has been broadly reflected in the literature [1]. On the other hand, these types of internships also pose some challenges [1] in terms of design, finding collaborating companies, and company-university coordination. Internships can be full-time or part-time. This study analyzes how PTI affect students' workload in concurrent subjects, student satisfaction, and the internship's impact on CP.

2 RESULTS AND CONCLUSIONS

Organization. At our university, internships last for four months during the first semester (September-December) of the fourth year of the program (which is the last one). Internships occur simultaneously with three other subjects related to professional, cross-curricular and security topics. After the internship is completed, during their final semester, students complete their CP, which in 80% of the cases is done at the same company where the student did their internship. This arrangement maximizes the benefits of industrial CP and has been widely studied in the literature [2]. Students have a better opinion of their own skills and projects than academics do, and it seems that industrial CP attract more highly-skilled students [2].

Workload. During the internships, 35 fourth-year students declare a mean workload of 50 hours per week on a questionnaire (25 hours for internships, 15 for lectures, 10 for studying). After completing the internship, the workload decreased to 41.2 hours. Students in the first three years of the program (116) declare a mean of 38.7 hours at the beginning of the semester and 45.8 at the end. In addition, study time per lecture hour shows behavioral differences among students of the first three years of the degree program and those in the fourth and final year. During the first three years, the workload started out 0.8 hours, and then reached 1.3 in January. However, fourth-year students dedicated 0.5 hours during the internship, which increased to 0.8 after the internship was completed, which does not match the level of effort of past years. This could be because other subjects adapt their demands to students' availability. These facts prove a challenge of PTI: planning in the simultaneous subjects must consider workload of internships.

Satisfaction. Despite students' heavy workload during internships, students declared a high level of satisfaction with the organization of the program (4 points out of 5).

Conclusions. PTI share some of the benefits of full-time internships, and add other advantages: (1) The ICT technologies learned during PTI are then used in CP, thereby notably improving their quality, (2) students maintain contact with the university, and (3) synergies can be generated with simultaneous subjects. However, certain challenges must be addressed by the other subjects: (1) adapt their workload so that it is lower at the beginning of the semester and greater at the end; and (2) select subjects with more professional, cross-curricular or practical topics in order to facilitate synergies. Despite the benefits of internships, their integration into CS degree programs seems less evolved than in other areas such as health or education (at least in the case of Spain).

Acknowledgments. Partially supported by EDU2016-79838-P.

ACM ISBN 978-1-4503-6301-3/19/07.
https://doi.org/10.1145/3304221.3325554

REFERENCES

[1] Shin, Y. S., Lee, K. W., Ahn, J. S., & Jung, J. W. (2013). Development of internship & capstone design integrated program for university-industry collaboration. Procedia-Social and Behavioral Sciences, 102, 386-391.

[2] Olarte, J. J., Domínguez, C., Jaime, A., & García-Izquierdo, F. J. (2016). Student and Staff Perceptions of Key Aspects of Computer Science Engineering capstone projects. IEEE Transactions on Education, 59(1), 45-51.

Instructional Pseudocode Guide to Teach Problem-Solving

Svetlana Peltsverger
College of Computing and Software Engineering
Kennesaw State University
Kennesaw, Georgia USA
speltsve@kenncsaw.cdu

Sourav Debnath
College of Computing and Software Engineering
Kennesaw State University
Kennesaw, Georgia USA
sdebnath@students.kennesaw.edu

ABSTRACT

Teaching students problem-solving skills is the biggest challenge for many computing programs. Students often do not consider what questions they need to ask while designing a solution. This paper introduces how technical writing techniques and problem-solving strategies can be combined to help students find those questions and develop programming code through writing instructions and documenting their design process. Preliminary results indicate that this approach helps developing problem-solving skills and improves the student success rate in the first programming course.

CCS CONCEPTS

• Social and professional topics ~ Computing education • Social and professional topics~CS1

KEYWORDS

Computer Science Education; Programming; Success; CS1.

ACM Reference format:

Svetlana Peltsverger and Sourav Debnath. 2019. Instructional Pseudocode Guide to Teach Problem-Solving. In *Proceedings of the 24th Annual ACM Conference on Innovation and Technology in Computer Science Education (ITiCSE'19). uly 15-17, 2019, Aberdeen, Scotland, UK.* ACM, New York, NY, USA, 1 page. https://doi.org/10.1145/3304221.3325581

1. INTRODUCTION

Problem-solving is one of the first skills computing students need to master. This skill is usually taught in the first programming course CS1. Before Fall 2018, our college offered major specific CS1 courses in Java, C#, and Python. The average DFW (grades D/fail/withdraw) rate was 36% and did not depend on the programming language. We found that emphasis on the programming language distracts students from designing their solution. They may know the syntax and semantics of individual statements, but they do not know how to combine these features into valid programs [1]. A large body of literature shows that using pseudocode can help students accrue problem-solving skills [2,3]. The new CS1 course has been created: the lectures use pseudocode and emphasize the importance of logic and problem-solving, and the labs use C#, Java, and Python and require two deliverables for each assignment: design in pseudocode and code implementation. However, students treated pseudocode as another programming language and did not think about what questions they need to ask when designing the solution. They were coding the programs first either through trial and error or by searching the answers and then reverse engineering them to get the pseudocode.

ACM ISBN 978-1-4503-6301-3/19/07.
https://doi.org/10.1145/3304221.3325581

2. METHODOLOGY

Instructional Pseudocode: To help students develop a problem-solving plan and test it without using a compiler, we adopted the best practices from other disciplines: mathematical reasoning from Mathematics and instruction writing from Technical Writing. We created an instructional pseudocode guide to help students understand this new method. In this approach, the students are asked to write each step as an action a reader must follow to solve the problem. Each step must be numbered and start with an action word. All branch or loop statements must direct the reader to its referenced step numbers. A set of questions should be included between iterations to show why the next iteration is necessary.

Problem-solving submission template. To capture the students' thinking process and to reinforce problem-solving strategies we created an assignment submission template which explicitly asks students to document their thought process. The template was inspired by George Polya's [4] with modification of the look back plan to include a list of questions to test the solution. The template requires submission of all intermediate steps.

3. RESULTS AND DISCUSSION

Comparison of the posttest and pretest scores of the experimental group (n=60) and the control group who did not use the Problem-Solving Guide (n=399) showed 4% improvement in the posttest in the experimental group and 7% drop in the control group (effect size ~ 0.4). We also observed a small reduction in DFW rate from the previous semesters (~2%). Based on the observed results, we speculate that this approach by requiring documentation of self-assessment improves problem-solving skills, prevents reverse engineering of code and as the result reduces cheating. The guide and the submission template were included in the future offerings of the CS1 course for further observations and improvements.

REFERENCES

[1] L. Winslow. 1996. Programming pedagogy—a psychological overview. *ACM Sigcse Bulletin, 28*(3), 17-22.
[2]. S. Tasneem. 2012. Critical thinking in an introductory programming course. *Journal of Computing Sciences in Colleges, 27*(6), 81-83.
[3]. A. L. Olsen. 2005. Using pseudocode to teach problem-solving. *Journal of Computing Sciences in Colleges, 21*(2), 231-236.
[4] G. Pólya, J. H. Conway. 2005. *How to solve it: A new aspect of mathematical method.* Princeton, NJ: Princeton University Press.

Supporting Abstraction Skills Using Augmented Reality?

Rebecca Reuter
rebecca.reuter@oth-regensburg.de
OTH Regensburg
Regensburg, Germany

Marco Knietzsch
marco3.knietzsch@oth-regensburg.de
OTH Regensburg
Regensburg, Germany

Florian Hauser
florian.hauser@oth-regensburg.de
OTH Regensburg
Regensburg, Germany

Jürgen Mottok
juergen.mottok@oth-regensburg.de
OTH Regensburg
Regensburg, Germany

ABSTRACT

We investigated the potential of augmented reality (AR) to enable visualization of abstract concepts and present the first iteration of a teaching experiment that evaluates the use of AR as support for abstraction skills. Students were confronted with the task to present and explain information to different groups of stakeholders at the example of a coffee machine. Results show that students find it helpful to have a visual app-prototype and especially one that can be disassembled in different levels. The main goal was to sensitize students for the need to think about and to abstract information for certain roles and perspectives.

CCS CONCEPTS

• **Social and professional topics → Software engineering education.**

KEYWORDS

augmented reality, software engineering education, abstraction skills

ACM Reference Format:

Rebecca Reuter, Marco Knietzsch, Florian Hauser, and Jürgen Mottok. 2019. Supporting Abstraction Skills Using Augmented Reality?. In *Innovation and Technology in Computer Science Education (ITiCSE '19), July 15–17, 2019, Aberdeen, Scotland Uk.* ACM, New York, NY, USA, 1 page. https://doi.org/10.1145/3304221.3325562

EXTENDED ABSTRACT

Ever since AR became broadly available, research evaluating use-cases for this technology have been on the rise. Existing literature shows that AR has been recognized as a promising technology with the potential to improve the quality of education. In particular, different researchers found AR to enable visualization of otherwise invisible and abstract concepts and events to further explore the topic at hand [1]. Coming from this proposition, we intend to verify the potential of AR as a support for abstract thinking (AT). So the underlying research question is: Can we support AT using AR? In our opinion AT is one of the most important skills not solely in software engineering (SE) but also in higher education. Due out the course, the students learn requirements engineering and software design. Students need to understand the different perspectives regarding to object oriented design, namely the object, a functional, and a dynamic view (similar to Rumbaugh[3]). We developed a teaching scenario in which students have to design a coffee machine. The scenario is assisted by an AR application[1] which enables the students to retrieve an interactive view of the system in question (the coffee machine) on the different abstraction layers as suggested by Rumbaugh. The AR application should sensitize the students for the significance of different perspectives (the three layers) for software development.

The study was designed as a cross-sectional, within groups, controlled lab experiment using audio records. Our task setting has a three partite structure and is similiar to the one suggested by Kramer [2]: Students (N=9), individually, had to take the role of a coffee machine inventor. First, they had to explain the coffee machine to a developer based on a feature list. Second, they had to explain it to a technically unexperienced customer. Finally, the students were provided with the application. After making themselves familiar with the application and the MS Hololens, the students were asked what changes in their explanations they would make. We evaluated the experiment with leading questions [1] regarding to usability and applicability for teaching. A qualitative evaluation of the interview results[1] shows that the students recognize the necessity and importance of different perspectives. Students find it good to be able to step between the abstraction levels and have the possibility to disassemble the machine. The collected data allows us to deduce the first indications of students' abstraction skills. All in all, the students approved of the use of the exercise.

REFERENCES

[1] Murat Akcayir and Gökce Akcayir. 2016. Advantages and challenges associated with augmented reality for education: A systematic review of the literature. *Educational Research Review* 20 (2016), 1–11.

[2] Jeff Kramer and Orit Hazzan. 2006. Introduction to The Role of Abstraction in Software Engineering. *Proceedings of the 2006 international workshop on Role of abstraction in software engineering (ROA '06)* (2006), 1–2.

[3] James Rumbaugh, Michael Blaha, William Premerlani, Frederick Eddy, and William Lorenson. 1991. *Object-Oriented Modeling and Design.* Prentice Hall, Englewood Cliffs, N.J.

ITiCSE '19, July 15–17, 2019, Aberdeen, Scotland Uk

ACM ISBN 978-1-4503-6301-3/19/07.
https://doi.org/10.1145/3304221.3325562

[1] see:https://www.dropbox.com/s/nncykw80pe7stz4/AbstractWithPic.pdf

COOL: Cooperative Open Learning for Beginning Programmers

Barbara Sabitzer
Johannes Kepler University
Linz, Austria
barbara.sabitzer@jku.at

Iris Groher
Johannes Kepler University
Linz, Austria
iris.groher@jku.at

Johannes Sametinger
Johannes Kepler University
Linz, Austria
johannes.sametinger@jku.at

ABSTRACT

COOL Informatics (COOL stands for Cooperative Open Learning) is a teaching concept for beginning programmers that is based on brain-supporting teaching methods and materials. It includes several forms of cooperative learning like peer tutoring, pair programming, and talents exchange. We introduced the concept in a Java programming course of our Business Informatics bachelor program in 2018 and have been able to improve the learning outcomes (exam results) and to reduce drop-out rates compared to previous years and to reference groups of 2018.

CCS CONCEPTS

• **Social and professional topics → Computer science education**; • **Software and its engineering → Pair programming**.

KEYWORDS

brain-based learning, cooperative learning, discovery learning, CS1

ACM Reference Format:
Barbara Sabitzer, Iris Groher, and Johannes Sametinger. 2019. COOL: Cooperative Open Learning for Beginning Programmers. In *Innovation and Technology in Computer Science Education (ITiCSE '19), July 15–17, 2019, Aberdeen, Scotland, UK.* ACM, New York, NY, USA, 1 page. https://doi.org/10.1145/3304221.3325569

1 INTRODUCTION

Learning to code is difficult, be it at school or at university level. High drop-out rates in programming courses, hence, are a common problem all over the world that everyone tries to solve in different ways [2, 4]. The first author has already made positive experiences with a neurodidactical teaching approach tested in a Computer Science bachelor program at another university [3]. Based on the results and experiences gained in these first groups, the brain-based teaching approach had been adapted and extended to a more flexible and generic concept for different levels of education: *COOL Informatics.*

2 COOL INFORMATICS AT WORK

COOL Informatics applies principles of cooperation and discovery as well as individuality and activity in both lesson and task design. We considered several neurodidactical principles as basis for our teaching concept. The given tasks are designed especially for discovery learning, e.g. worked examples, which can improve problem-solving performance [1]. Individuality is achieved by giving students a certain freedom of choice regarding type, number, and context of exercises. The programming course consists of a weekly 90-minutes lecture and weekly 90-minutes exercises with groups of 30 students. The lecture consists of a slides presentation with many practical examples. A text book with one chapter for each lecture is provided. Grading is based on homework results and two exams during the semester. The exercises in the COOL groups are divided into three parts: (1) *questioning* (students ask the teacher or experienced students whatever they had not understood in the lecture), (2) *discovering* (students explore provided sample solutions to extract code structures and programming rules and to identify best practices), and (3) *pair-programming* (students work together on their homework assignments and ask their partner, the teacher, or other experienced students whenever necessary).

ITiCSE '19, July 15–17, 2019, Aberdeen, Scotland, UK

ACM ISBN 978-1-4503-6301-3/19/07.
https://doi.org/10.1145/3304221.3325569

3 METHODS AND RESULTS

In the Business Informatics bachelor program at the Johannes Kepler University Linz, we have compared the exam results and drop-out rates of three semesters, one traditional semester and two semesters with both COOL groups and non-COOL groups. In general, the drop-out rate decreased for the COOL-groups compared to the traditional ones. In the comparison groups, the drop-out was 8-20% higher than in the COOL-groups. The rate of students attending the exams is much higher in the COOL-groups (about 30% for the first and 20% for the second exam). Especially, COOL-females were longer in classes than all male students. Success rates are also higher in the COOL-groups. In addition, COOL students handed in more homeworks (especially COOL-females) and got better grades. Student feedback in the COOL-groups was very positive and their satisfaction with the course was much higher than in the comparison groups. Hence, the use of the COOL approach is worth being applied and investigated in other subjects, too.

BIBLIOGRAPHY

[1] Ouhao Chen, Slava Kalyuga, and John Sweller. 2015. The worked example effect, the generation effect, and element interactivity. *Journal of Educational Psychology* 107, 3 (2015), 689.
[2] Külli Kori, Margus Pedaste, Eno Tõnisson, Tauno Palts, Heilo Altin, Ramon Rantsus, Raivo Sell, Kristina Murtazin, and Tiia Rüütmann. 2015. First-year dropout in ICT studies. In *2015 IEEE Global Engineering Education Conference (EDUCON)*. IEEE, 437–445.
[3] Barbara Sabitzer and Stefan Pasterk. 2014. Brain-based programming continued: Effective teaching in programming courses. In *2014 IEEE Frontiers in Education Conference (FIE) Proceedings*. 1–6. https://doi.org/10.1109/FIE.2014.7044233
[4] Aharon Yadin. 2011. Reducing the dropout rate in an introductory programming course. *ACM inroads* 2, 4 (2011), 71–76.

Designing Engaging Learning Experiences

Raghav V. Sampangi
Faculty of Computer Science
Dalhousie University
Halifax, NS, Canada
raghav@cs.dal.ca

Angela A. Siegel
Faculty of Computer Science
Dalhousie University
Halifax, NS, Canada
siegel@dal.ca

ABSTRACT

A *learning experience* comprises several factors and understanding them becomes a crucial first step in developing engaging learning experiences, considering how learning is no longer always a passive "absorb what is told/what you read" exercise. Drawing lessons from designing user experiences, we present a structured and holistic approach to design engaging learning experiences and cater to both learners and teachers, by considering the factors and unique attributes of a learning experience. We explore the role of technology in augmenting learning experiences. Our work attempts to *understand* the factors/attributes that constitute *engaging learning experiences* and develop strategies/tools to help design such experiences.

CCS CONCEPTS

• **Social and professional topics~Computing education**

KEYWORDS

Learning experience; learning outcomes; human-centric learning

ACM Reference format:

Raghav V. Sampangi and Angela A. Siegel. 2019. Designing Engaging Learning Experiences. In *Proceedings of 24th Annual ACM Conference on Innovation and Technology in Computer Science Education (ITiCSE'19), July 15-17, 2019, Aberdeen, Scotland, UK.* ACM, New York, NY, 1 page. https://doi.org/10.1145/3304221.3325563

1 Overview

We believe that designing computer science (CS) learning experiences must begin with an understanding of the unique factors that constitute an experience; the same way web/mobile app design begins with user experience design. A learner-centric perspective helps design meaningful learning experiences [2], but a teacher [1] and other factors such as learning outcomes, assessments, etc., all contribute to the overall learning experience. The attributes of various factors often interact with and influence each other, and we believe that understanding them (Figure 1) helps design meaningful connections between them and paves the way to create engaging learning experiences to address the unique needs of teaching CS. Figure 1 is an evolving representation of factors of a learning experience and we recognize that there may be factors we may not have considered and/or perhaps one of the factors serves best as an attribute of another factor instead.

Through this work, we hope to address the following question—*with several factors impacting the overall learning (and teaching) experience, how do we create and offer engaging learning experiences?* The contributions of our work will benefit (a) teachers/instructional designers by guiding the design/update of learning experiences, and (b) learners by supporting their self-directed learning activities. Currently, we are designing an exploratory survey to better understand attributes of learners/teachers and stressors in present-day post-secondary CS education and their impact on the overall learning experience. We plan to use content analysis to analyze the survey results. We have also begun designing a tool that connects learner and teacher motivations/goals with outcomes and experiences. We hope to share initial results at the poster session and use the discussions/feedback to help guide our ongoing work.

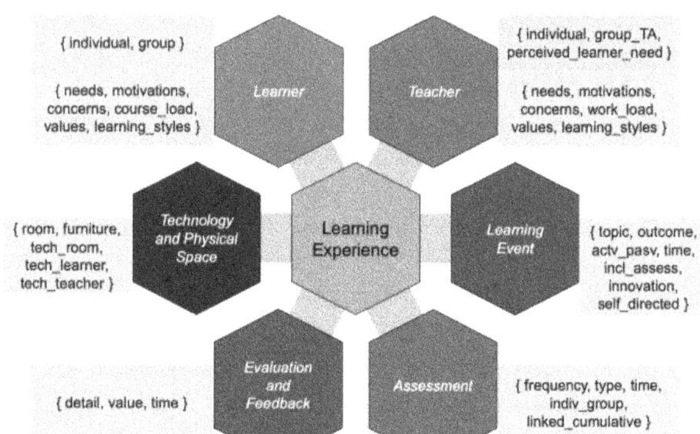

Figure 1: Factors and attributes of a *learning experience*. The six peripheral hexagonal blocks represent factors and the rectangular boxes list attributes for each factor.

REFERENCES

[1] Christopher Lynnly Hovey, Lecia Barker, and Margaret Luebs. 2019. Frequency of Instructor- and Student-Centered Teaching Practices in Introductory CS Courses. In *Proceedings of SIGCSE '19.* ACM, New York, NY, USA, 599-605. DOI: https://doi.org/10.1145/3287324.3287363.

[2] Learning Experience Design - The Most Valuable Lessons. *Interaction Design Foundation*, 2019. https://www.interaction-design.org/literature/article/learning-experience-design-the-most- valuable-lessons.

ACM ISBN 978-1-4503-6301-3/19/07. https://doi.org/10.1145/3304221.3325563

Shaping Curricular Guidelines for Associate-Degree Cybersecurity Programs

Melissa Stange
Lord Fairfax Community College
Middletown, VA, United States
mstange@lfcc.edu

Cara Tang
Portland Community College
Portland, OR, United States
cara.tang@pcc.edu

Christian Servin
El Paso Community College
El Paso, TX, United States
cservin1@epcc.edu

Cindy Tucker
Bluegrass Community & Technical College
Lexington, KY, United States
cindy.tucker@kctcs.edu

Markus Geissler
Cosumnes River College
Sacramento, CA, United States
geisslm@CRC.losrios.edu

ABSTRACT

As projections of the shortage of cybersecurity workers grow, the spotlight is on cybersecurity education. In December of 2017, the Joint Task Force on Cybersecurity Education published Cybersecurity Curricula 2017: Curriculum Guidelines for Post-Secondary Degree Programs in Cybersecurity (CSEC2017), representing a new discipline in ACM's Computing Curricula Series. Now the ACM CCECC (Committee for Computing Education in Community Colleges) is leading creation of a similar set of guidelines for two-year cybersecurity programs at the associate-degree level, called CSEC2Y. The CSEC2Y task force of community college educators presented and released the initial draft, called StrawDog at a special session at SIGCSE 2019. A survey seeking public feedback from educators, professionals, and global advisors collected feedback and input on the StrawDog draft. A second draft, called IronDog, will be available by mid-July. In this poster, survey results from the first draft, and the most recent draft will be presented for feedback and critique by the international community.

KEYWORDS

junior college, community college, technical college, two-year college, cybersecurity, curriculum

ACM Reference format:

Melissa Stange, Cara Tang, Christian Servin, Cindy Tucker, and Markus Geissler. 2019. Shaping Curricular Guidelines for Associate-Degree Cybersecurity Programs. In *Proceedings of Innovation and Technology in Computer Science Education (ITiCSE'119), July 14-17, 2019, Aberdeen, Scotland UK.* ACM, New York, NY, USA, 1 page. https://doi.org/10.1145/3304221.3325568

1 Background

Several driving factors motivated the ACM CCECC to create CSEC2Y: 1) worldwide security spending will hit $96.3 billion in 2018 [3], 2) 58% of business owners with up to 299 employees had been victims of a cyber-attack [4], 3) job predictions that information security analysts will grow by 28% between 2016 and 2026 [2], and 4) the creation of CSEC2017 guidelines for four-year cybersecurity programs [1]. CSEC2Y also includes mappings to cybersecurity frameworks such as the NICE Cybersecurity Workforce Framework and NSA CAE knowledge units along with professional codes of ethics.

ACM ISBN 978-1-4503-6301-3/19/07. https://doi.org/10.1145/3304221.3325568

2 Current Work

This poster provides an overview of CSEC2Y, including the following information: 1) Public input on StrawDog, 2) Percentage of CSEC2017 Knowledge Areas (KUs) that are appropriate in the first two years, and 3) Sample learning outcomes and rubrics.

3 Follow-on Opportunities

The IronDog draft of CSEC2Y is available for public review and critique by the global computing education community. Feedback from this review and the poster presentation will be collected and used to create the final curriculum guide. If you are interested in reviewing CSEC2Y or providing an exemplar for the curricular guide, send a message to acm.ccecc@ccecc.acm.org or visit ccecc.acm.org. The final updated guidelines for cybersecurity associate-degree curriculum are anticipated for release by 2020.

REFERENCES

[1] ACM, IEEE, AIS, and IFIP (2017) Cybersecurity Curricula 2017. https://cybered.hosting.acm.org/wp/.
[2] Bureau of Labor Statistics. (2016). Information Security Analyst. https://www.bls.gov/ooh/computer-and-information-technology/information-security-analysts.htm#tab-1.
[3] Gartner, Inc. (2018). Global security spending to reach $96.3bn in 2018. https://www.gigabitmagazine.com/big-data/global-security-spending-reach-963bn-2018-gartner.
[4] Nationwide Mutual Insurance Company. (2017). Nearly Half of Business Owners Have Been Victims of Cyberattacks – But Didn't Know It. https://www.nationwide.com/personal/about-us/newsroom/press-release?title=100917-cyber-security

Computing Opportunities for Students of Color

Gloria Townsend
DePauw University
Greencastle IN USA
gct@depauw.edu

Khadija Stewart
DePauw University
Greencastle IN USA
khadijastewart@depauw.edu

ABSTRACT

In fall 2018, the authors established a new student organization at DePauw University to address the severe underrepresentation of students of color (SoC) in computing. The organization, Computing Opportunities for Students of Color (COSOC), aims to create a community for SoC and to establish a sense of belonging through role modeling, mentoring, tutoring, and a series of academic and community events. This poster describes the need for such an organization, goals and objectives, pilot study, main components of COSOC, positive preliminary impact on SoC (including enrollment data), and additional planned assessment. Finally, the poster lists future plans for COSOC.

KEYWORDS

Underrepresentation in computer science; diversity; students of color; retention; mentoring; community; sense of belonging

ACM Reference Format:

Gloria Townsend and Khadija Stewart. 2019. Computing Opportunities for Students of Color. In *Innovation and Technology in Computer Science Education (ITiCSE '19), July 15–17, 2019, Aberdeen, Scotland Uk.* ACM, New York, NY, USA, 1 page. https://doi.org/10.1145/3304221.3325564

1 SIGNIFICANCE AND RELEVANCE

COSOC addresses two issues: (1) the underrepresentation of SoC in computing and (2) the predicted shortage of future skilled information technology (IT) workers. African-American students received only 10.7% of U. S. bachelor's degrees awarded in computer and information sciences, during academic year 2013-14; Hispanic students, 9.2% [1]. The National Center for Women & IT predicts a shortage (39%) of United States IT workers in the coming decade [2]. The shortage creates a pressing need for higher computer science graduation rates. Increasing the number of SoC (and women) in the IT workers' pool will help to alleviate job candidate shortages and to create a more appropriately diverse workforce.

2 POSTER CONTENT

- Purpose and goals of COSOC.
- Summary of pilot 2017–2018: The authors received a $1000 internal grant to create a prototype for COSOC. During spring 2018, the authors arranged an anonymous focus group and several successful activities that COSOC adopted in fall 2018. These activities included an industry trip, a graduate school visit, and two lunches with alumni of color.
- Description of additional 2018–19 COSOC components: role modeling videos, mentoring, and a revised tutoring program – all funded by a Ball Venture Fund grant.
- Enrolment numbers for SoC in DePauw's two introductory courses during spring 2018, fall 2018, spring 2019, and an analysis of these numbers which shows increasing enrolments (impact of both the pilot and COSOC itself) (Table 1). The authors highlight both Computer Science I (CS1) and Data Structures because their preliminary research indicated that dramatic attrition among SoC at DePauw University occurs in thesefi rst two courses.
- Results of spring 2018 baseline surveys concerning feelings of belonging among SoC.
- Subsequent 2019 survey results from SoC regarding feelings of belonging and participation in COSOC events and activities.
- Description of the authors' future plans for COSOC.

Table 1: Enrolment and percentages of SoC for all sections of CS1 (first course) and Data Structures (second course)

Semester	African-American	Latinx	Total
Spring 2019	13	16	29/140 (21%)
Fall 2018	11	14	25/127 (20%)
Spring 2018	12	8	20/116 (17%)

ACKNOWLEDGMENTS

The authors thank DePauw University President McCoy for COSOC pilot funding and recognise the Ball Brothers Foundation for its $25,000 grant that created COSOC.

REFERENCES

[1] NCES. 2019. National Center for Educational Statistics. https://nces.ed.gov/programs/digest/d16/tables/dt16_318.20
[2] NCWIT. 2018. National Center for Women & IT. http://www.poker-edge.com/stats.php

ITiCSE '19, July 15–17, 2019, Aberdeen, Scotland Uk

ACM ISBN 978-1-4503-6301-3/19/07.
https://doi.org/10.1145/3304221.3325564

A Prototype MATLAB Code Critiquer

Marissa Walther
mlwalthe@mtu.edu
Michigan Technological University
Houghton, MI, USA

Leo C. Ureel II
ureel@mtu.edu
Michigan Technological University
Houghton, MI, USA

Charles Wallace
wallace@mtu.edu
Michigan Technological University
Houghton, MI, USA

ABSTRACT

This poster presents MATLAB Critiquer, a system that examines code submissions and provides feedback to first year engineering students who are learning to program in MATLAB. Code Critiquers act as substitute mentors, when instructors are not available, and give students experience with interactive, test-driven development. [5] Students using our critiquer are engaged in communication by proxy with the instructor. This communication does not replace instructor feedback; rather, it codifies common feedback scenarios to assist the instructor in reaching students just when the student is engaged in problem solving and learning.

Our critiquer uses the MATLAB Java API; connecting to the MATLAB Engine that parses and executes student code submissions. [4] We process error messages that are returned using regular expressions, then use these results to craft feedback for the students. Static code analysis is used to provide feedback on style. The critique covers code structure, shakedown test results, and programming style in a manner appropriate for novice coders.

CCS CONCEPTS

• **Social and professional topics** → **Computer science education**; **Computer engineering education**; *Student assessment*; • **Applied computing** → *Interactive learning environments*; • **Software and its engineering** → Agile software development.

KEYWORDS

Code Critiquer, Autograder, MATLAB, Engineering Fundamentals

ACM Reference Format:

Marissa Walther, Leo C. Ureel II, and Charles Wallace. 2019. A Prototype MATLAB Code Critiquer. In *Innovation and Technology in Computer Science Education (ITiCSE '19), July 15–17, 2019, Aberdeen, Scotland Uk.* ACM, New York, NY, USA, 1 page. https://doi.org/10.1145/3304221.3325591

1 SIGNIFICANCE OF THE TOPIC

Increasingly, students across campus are required to learn some form of programming. Students with little or no programming experience can be easily confused or intimidated, so the feedback they get (both human and automated) must be carefully designed and targeted to novices. We believe that professional grade tools (*e.g.*, development environments, style checkers, unit test frameworks), designed for experts, provide feedback that is inappropriate and even counterproductive for novices.

Furthermore, not only are non-CS majors learning to program, but many non-CS faculty find themselves teaching programming courses and relying on professional tools to help provide feedback to their students. Besides large-scale initiatives in High Performance Computing, Big Data, and basic Computer Science Research, more and more computation-centric degrees are being offered by universities. Many students in non-computing majors must take programming courses to develop the required computational background for their field. For instance, the *MATLAB* language for numerical computing is commonly introduced to engineering students of all disciplines.

Through an automated MATLAB Critiquer, we can give engineering students early experience with interactive, test-driven software development. This exposure will prepare them better for today's computer-centric workplace. It will also reduce the frustration that students often experience in early programming projects, mitigating the risk of student burnout and helping with retention in computing-related majors.

2 CONTENT

In this poster we present a code critique for MATLAB. We provide examples of MATLAB code submitted by students and the feedback reported by our MATLAB Critiquer. We discuss the different kinds of feedback provided to students: code structure, shakedown test results, and programming style. A one-page handout will be available that describes our critiquer.

REFERENCES

[1] Stephen H. Edwards and Manuel A. Perez-Quinones. 2008. Web-CAT: Automatically grading programming assignments. *Proceedings of the 13th annual conference on Innovation and technology in computer science education - ITiCSE '08* (2008).

[2] Marios Fokaefs, Nikolaos Tsantalis, Eleni Stroulia, and Alexander Chatzigeorgiou. 2011. JDeodorant: Identification and Application of Extract Class Refactorings. *Proceeding of the 33rd international conference on Software engineering - ICSE '11* (2011).

[3] Mike Joy, Nathan Griffiths, and Russell Boyatt. 2005. The boss online submission and assessment system. *Journal on Educational Resources in Computing (JERIC)* 5, 3 (2005), 2.

[4] Inc. Mathworks. [n.d.]. MATLAB. https://www.mathworks.com/products/matlab.html

[5] Lin Qiu and Christopher Riesbeck. 2008. An incremental model for developing educational critiquing systems: experiences with the Java Critiquer. *Journal of Interactive Learning Research* 19, 1 (2008), 119–145.

[6] Jaime Spacco, David Hovemeyer, William Pugh, Fawzi Emad, Jeffrey K. Hollingsworth, and Nelson Padua-Perez. 2006. Experiences with marmoset: designing and using an advanced submission and testing system for programming courses. *Proceedings of the 11th annual SIGCSE conference on Innovation and technology in computer science education - ITiCSE '06* (2006).

[7] Arto Vihavainen, Matti Luukkainen, and Martin Pärtel. 2013. Test my code: An automatic assessment service for the extreme apprenticeship method. In *2nd International Workshop on Evidence-based Technology Enhanced Learning*. Springer, 109–116.

ITiCSE '19, July 15–17, 2019, Aberdeen, Scotland Uk

ACM ISBN 978-1-4503-6301-3/19/07.
https://doi.org/10.1145/3304221.3325591

How Can Children Express Their Intentions Through Coding? – Analysis of Viscuit Programs in Kindergarten–

Takeshi Watanabe
The University of Electro-Communications &
Digitalpocket LLC.
Tokyo, Japan

Yuriko Nakayama
Kagawa-fujimigaoka Kindergarten
Kanagawa, Japan

Yasunori Harada
Digitalpocket LLC.
Kanagawa, Japan

Yasushi Kuno
The University of Electro-Communications
Tokyo, Japan

ABSTRACT

Viscuit is a programming language developed by one of the authors. With Viscuit, you can move and change multiple pictures on the screen using eyeglasses, which make a sequence from left to right, following from-to (picture rewriting) rules. Its distinguishing feature is that the program is expressed solely with pictures and their layouts. No letters are necessary at all. Therefore, Viscuit is perfectly suitable for pre-school children. We have been carrying out regular programming lessons in a kindergarten in Japan since 2015. We have recorded and analysed almost all of the programs made by 56 children aged 5-6 years in a series of 13 lessons held during the school year 2017. In this poster we report how the children could express their intentions through coding.

CCS CONCEPTS

• **Social and professional topics → K-12 education.**

KEYWORDS

pre-school programming, Viscuit, expression of intention

ACM Reference Format:
Takeshi Watanabe, Yuriko Nakayama, Yasunori Harada, and Yasushi Kuno. 2019. How Can Children Express Their Intentions Through Coding? – Analysis of Viscuit Programs in Kindergarten– . . In *Innovation and Technology in Computer Science Education (ITiCSE '19), July 15–17, 2019, Aberdeen, Scotland Uk.* ACM, New York, NY, USA, 1 page. https://doi.org/10.1145/3304221.3325558

1 WHAT IS VISCUIT

Figure 1-left shows how Viscuit programs are created: (1) pre-supplied or originally drawn pictures are placed on the stage (blue area), (2) empty eyeglasses are placed on the middle area, (3) pictures are dragged into both circles of the glasses, and (4) this instantly moves the pictures on the stage. The rule is that pictures matching the left circle of the eyeglasses are changed to the properties of the right circle. In the case of Figure 1-left, triangles move toward the bottom left because the layout of the pictures in each eyeglass commands this to happen. Note that the sizes of the circles can be enlarged when necessary. How the pictures are shifted in the circle reflects the speed of the movement. If eyeglasses change picture A to picture B and another set of eyeglasses changes B to A, then a repeating pattern of A-B-A-B appears. This technique is used in the program of Figure 1-right.

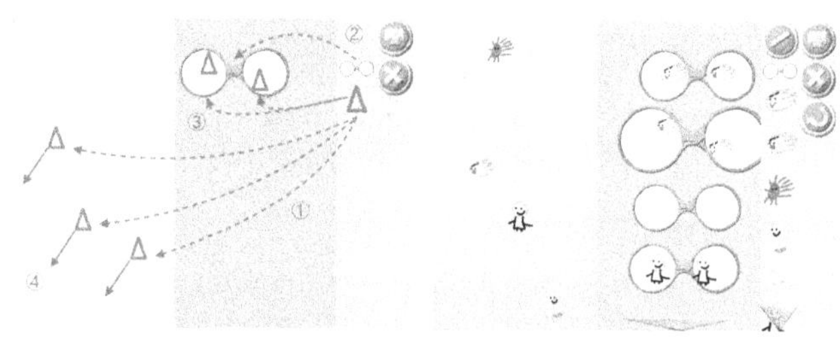

Figure 1: The Screen of Viscuit (left) and a Program Made by One Child (right)

2 OUR FINDINGS

We carried out a series of Viscuit lessons at the kindergarten [1]. Childrens' programs created during the lessons were automatically saved within the Viscuit system, and we analysed these programs. As a result, we have discovered the following situations in the programs of a majority of the children: when using Viscuit, they can understand and control (1) movement toward four directions (up, down, left, right), and (2) repeating constructs like A-B-A-B.

Figure 1-right shows one of the programs and pictures made by one child. The first and second pairs of eyeglasses create an animation of a breathing cloud. The third and fourth pairs of eyeglasses move raindrops downward and human figures leftward, correspondingly. We can ascertain whether they can make programs successfully according to their intentions by observing the relationship between their drawings and their programs.

REFERENCES

[1] T. Watanabe and Y. Kuno Y. Nakayama, Y. Harada. 2018. Programming Lessons for Kindergarten Children in Japan. In *Constructionism2018*. 741–744. http://www.constructionism2018.fsf.vu.lt/file/repository/Proceeding_2018_Constructionism.pdf

ACM ISBN 978-1-4503-6301-3/19/07
https://doi.org/10.1145/3304221.3325558

Challenges of Delivering a Graduate Apprenticeship

Tiffany Young
School of Computing Science and Digital Media
Robert Gordon University
Aberdeen, United Kingdom
t.young3@rgu.ac.uk

Mark Zarb
School of Computing Science and Digital Media
Robert Gordon University
Aberdeen, United Kingdom
m.zarb@rgu.ac.uk

ABSTRACT

Graduate Apprenticeship degree programmes look to overcome the segregation of learning and working, by integrating traditional education into the context of the work environment. This poster showcases a number of actions that were put into place to mitigate challenges that arose during the first run of these programmes.

CCS CONCEPTS

• **Social and professional topics → Computing education.**

KEYWORDS

Graduate Apprenticeship, Work-Based Learning, Support Student Success, Online Distance Learning

ACM Reference Format:
Tiffany Young and Mark Zarb. 2019. Challenges of Delivering a Graduate Apprenticeship. In *Proceedings of ACM Conference on Innovation and Technology in Computer Science Education (ITiCSE'19).* ACM, New York, NY, USA, Article 4, 1 page. https://doi.org/10.475/123_4

1 INTRODUCTION

Graduate Apprenticeships (GA) look to combine academic knowledge and qualification recognition along with practical skills development. Robert Gordon University (RGU) ran its first GA in 2017. This has now expanded to seven frameworks across RGU with the collaboration of seventy-seven industry partners. The primary drive behind the GA is to support employers to develop the skills of their workforce [2].

The School of Computing Science and Digital Media (CSDM) within RGU have adopted a blended approach to content delivery due to the large catchment area of employers and apprentices. This resulted in online distance learning as the primary delivery mode. Interactions were primarily through the Virtual Learning Environment with pre-recorded lectures and interactive video sessions using *Blackboard Collaborate ULTRA* being the main points of contact with students. Due to the structure of these degrees, students are expected to be work-based learners (WBL). The challenges of integrating work-based learning within higher education are well-documented [1], and these expected issues framed part of the curriculum development undertaken within the School of Computing Science and Digital Media at RGU. The mitigations outlined in *Table 1* were put in place.

Table 1: Work-Based Learning Challenges and Mitigations

Expected Challenges	Mitigations
Students' access to additional support	On-Campus Days Twilight Study Skills Appointments
Students' connection to tutors and peers	Use of Microsoft Teams Interactive Weekly Sessions on the VLE Academic Visits to the Workplace
Engagement with the taught content	On-Campus Days Peer Review Variety of Assessment Styles Interactive Weekly Sessions on the VLE
Students' prioritisation of work commitments over studying	Learning Plans

Learning plans are currently being used by students, mentors and academics to ensure that the module content better aligns with the professional content. This allows students to better integrate their studies within the WBL environment, with appropriate assessments that fit this context. On-campus days were introduced in the second year of the programme to supplement the online delivery style and encourage student engagement and access to additional support.

2 FUTURE WORK

The CSDM GA programmes are now in the middle of their second year, and it seems as if the initial challenges expected and encountered have been successfully mitigated against. There are now multiple avenues to allow staff and students to communicate, allowing a more collaborative approach to resolving any new challenges. With on-campus days being a new addition in 2018, RGU are discussing the potential benefits to the integration of more on-campus days in future years.

REFERENCES

[1] Belinda McLennan and Shay Keating. 2008. Work-integrated learning (WIL) in Australian universities: The challenges of mainstreaming WIL. In *ALTC NAGCAS National Symposium.* Citeseer, 2–14.
[2] Skills Development Scotland. 2019. Graduate Apprenticeships. https://www.skillsdevelopmentscotland.co.uk/what-we-do/apprenticeships/graduate-apprenticeships

ACM ISBN 123-4567-24-567/08/06.
https://doi.org/10.475/123_4

Incorporating On-Campus Days in a Graduate Apprenticeship

Tiffany Young
School of Computing Science and Digital Media
Robert Gordon University
Aberdeen, United Kingdom
t.young3@rgu.ac.uk

Mark Zarb
School of Computing Science and Digital Media
Robert Gordon University
Aberdeen, United Kingdom
m.zarb@rgu.ac.uk

ABSTRACT

Graduate Apprenticeships look to overcome the segregation of learning and working by integrating traditional education into the context of the work environment. This poster looks to highlight the importance of peer interactions, specifically for Online Distance Learners and how Robert Gordon University has implemented this within its GA programmes through on-campus days.

CCS CONCEPTS

• **Social and professional topics → Computing education.**

KEYWORDS

Graduate Apprenticeship, Work-Based Learning, Support Student Success, Online Distance Learning, On-Campus Days, Community of Practice

ACM Reference Format:
Tiffany Young and Mark Zarb. 2019. Incorporating On-Campus Days in a Graduate Apprenticeship. In *Proceedings of ACM Conference on Innovation and Technology in Computer Science Education (ITiCSE'19)*. ACM, New York, NY, USA, Article 4, 1 page. https://doi.org/10.475/123_4

1 INTRODUCTION

Graduate Apprenticeships (GA) look to combine academic knowledge and qualification recognition along with practical skills development. Scotland's inaugural year for GAs started in 2017 which saw Robert Gordon University (RGU), along with other Scottish institutions, partake in the industry-led delivery. The apprentices are full-time work-based learners (WBL) supported by their employers, whilst also studying full-time in an academic distance learning environment. This collaborative approach looked to more closely align graduates skills and knowledge with industry needs.

Previous research [1] shows that WBL are likely to be a member of a work-based Community of Practice within their workplace prior to becoming a Graduate Apprentice. Community of Practices (CoP) are "groups of people who share a concern or a passion for something they do and learn how to do it better as they interact regularly" [2]. Building an additional CoP within RGU was recognised as an important objective to allow these apprentices to benefit from peer interactions with others working towards the same qualification.

ACM ISBN 123-4567-24-567/08/06.
https://doi.org/10.475/123_4

Whilst the apprentices were given the option of communicating through weekly online interactive sessions and through collaborative tools such as *Microsoft Teams*, to further promote engagement and facilitate access to additional support, the course team felt that face-to-face interactions were required. Informal peer discussions tend to occur naturally when students are physically located on-campus, as traditional students usually are, but for these distance learning apprentices, this is something that requires more planning and coordination. To promote peer discussions between apprentices, the addition of on-campus contact sessions with students was organised.

In 2018, the second year of Graduate Apprenticeships for RGU, face-to-face sessions were developed to supplement the Online Distance Learning (ODL) delivery. These on-campus days facilitated peer interactions and encouraged the development of a supportive learning environment which proved beneficial to encourage engagement and promote support whilst allowing the students to build meaningful relationships with one another. As Vygotsky theorises, the creation of a supportive learning community would further enhance the students learning experience and provide access to more experienced and capable learners [2].

2 STRUCTURE OF ON-CAMPUS DAYS

Each academic year within the GA, as run by The School of Computing Science and Digital Media (CSDM), consists of four ten-week-long modules, each of which runs one on-campus day. Each module runs sequentially and the on-campus days are located in the middle of the delivery. This was to allow academic staff to meet with the apprentices face-to-face and highlight any potential difficulties encountered and implement any measures to mitigate these.

3 INITIAL RESULTS AND FUTURE WORK

As a result of these on-campus days, it is clear that apprentices are more engaged with their modules and have developed a familiarity with each other which was lacking in the previous run of the course. Apprentices found that these sessions helped them to connect with the student body and felt more involved with the student experience as a whole. RGU are in discussion to determine if the addition of more on-campus days would be beneficial to apprentices going forward.

REFERENCES

[1] Ruth Helyer. 2016. Editorial. *Higher Education, Skills and Work-Based Learning* 6, 3 (2016). https://doi.org/10.1108/heswbl-06-2016-0044
[2] Jean Lave and Etienne Wenger. 1991. Legitimate Peripheral Participation. *Situated Learning* (1991), 27âĂŞ44. https://doi.org/10.1017/cbo9780511815355.003

Integrating Real-World Clients in a Project Management Module

Mark Zarb
School of Computing Science and Digital Media
Robert Gordon University
Aberdeen, United Kingdom
m.zarb@rgu.ac.uk

Tiffany Young
School of Computing Science and Digital Media
Robert Gordon University
Aberdeen, United Kingdom
t.young3@rgu.ac.uk

William Ballew
James Fisher Digital
Barrow-in-Furness
Cumbria, United Kingdom
w.ballew@james-fisher.co.uk

ABSTRACT

Graduates in CS are required to have a background in project management, but often this is taught as a theoretical module, with little "real-world" relevance. A Project Management module has been redeveloped around the idea of having a real client interact with the class throughout the module, to positive comments from staff and students alike.

CCS CONCEPTS

• **Social and professional topics → Computing education; Student assessment.**

KEYWORDS

project management, client, agile

ACM Reference Format:
Mark Zarb, Tiffany Young, and William Ballew. 2019. Integrating Real-World Clients in a Project Management Module. In *Innovation and Technology in Computer Science Education (ITiCSE '19), July 15–17, 2019, Aberdeen, Scotland Uk.* ACM, New York, NY, USA, 1 page. https://doi.org/10.1145/3304221.3325559

1 INTRODUCTION

Traditionally, teaching within Higher Education Institutes happens within the confines of the classroom, lecture hall or laboratory. This separates the students' learning from the context and application of work-based activities. Having these as distinct entities disadvantages students from applying their learnings within a "real-world" context [1], specifically within more theoretical subjects, such as project management.

A curriculum redesign within the School of Computing Science and Digital Media at the Robert Gordon University provided the opportunity for a project management module to be refreshed.

Project Management and Software Engineering is a module taught to students within the School in their third year (in a four-year degree programme). Historically, this was paired with a partner module to distinguish between development and project management. Whilst this method had its advantages, it was not allowing students to properly experience complete software development lifecycles in a "real world" context, as students would often treat the two modules separately, choosing to complete the bulk of the project management and accompanying documentation after the code was completed. Furthermore, the project "client" was typically a lecturer with whom they had had previous interactions, thus diluting this very important experience and learning opportunity.

ITiCSE '19, July 15–17, 2019, Aberdeen, Scotland Uk

ACM ISBN 978-1-4503-6301-3/19/07.
https://doi.org/10.1145/3304221.3325559

The module was revamped as part of a curriculum redesign in 2017 and redeveloped to be a stand-alone module with its own project client. Whilst software development is a required component of this module, the summative assessment is based solely on the team's interactions with the client, and their produced documentation (e.g. Gantt charts, sprint backlogs, meeting minutes, class diagrams, etc.). The "new" version of the module has been taught three times, each with a different client - but always following the same format:

The client is asked to devote a number of meeting points (a minimum of four over a ten-week teaching period) where they interact with the students throughout the semester in an agile manner - this time is always restricted, thus being more representative of a "real world" situation. The meeting points, during which the client and module lecturers are available to give formative feedback, are typically as follows:

- First meeting: client gives a description and background of the real world problem to the entire class
- Second meeting: client meets with individual teams to sign off on their proposed solution
- A number of agile sprints follow, depending on client availability
- Final meeting: client signs off on student progress

The students, self-sorted in small groups, therefore inherit several responsibilities in the spirit of agile project management:

(1) To work in sprints around the client's available time;
(2) To learn to speak in a non-technical language (recent clients were located outside the technology sector);
(3) respect the time the client could give them (typically 10 minutes a fortnight) and learn to maximize this time.

2 REFLECTION

The introduction of a client-facing approach has been part of the module for the past three iterations and has been met with positive feedback from the students, who suggest that this module is no longer viewed as a theoretical/detached module, but one in which they are gaining important and relevant employability skills.

REFERENCES

[1] Hugh McCabe. 2016. Integrating Work Experience into the Digital Media Curriculum: A Case Study. (2016).

Lessons from Experts: Software Design Dialogues

Marian Petre
The Open University
m.petre@open.ac.uk

ABSTRACT

This talk will reflect on decades of empirical research on software design in high-performing teams and by experts. The talk will present three broad perspectives:

(1) It will identify some of the particular challenges of designing software and the practices that experts use to address them.
(2) It will characterise expert software design in terms of a complex of design dialogues.
(3) It will consider how expert practice can inform how we teach software design.

CCS CONCEPTS

• **Human-centered computing**; • **Social and professional topics → Computing education**; • **Software and its engineering → Software creation and management**; **Designing software**; **Software development techniques**; **Collaboration in software development**;

KEYWORDS

Software design; empirical studies of software development; expert software design practice; software design education

ACM Reference Format:
Marian Petre. 2019. Lessons from Experts: Software Design Dialogues. In *Innovation and Technology in Computer Science Education (ITiCSE '19), July 15–17, 2019, Aberdeen, Scotland Uk.* ACM, New York, NY, USA, 1 page. https://doi.org/10.1145/3304221.3325602

BIOGRAPHY

Marian Petre is a Professor of Computing at the Open University in the UK. She held a Royal Society Wolfson Research Merit Award, in recognition of her research on the nature of expertise in software design.

Marian's interdisciplinary research draws on cognitive theory and qualitative research methods to analyze how expert software designers behave and reason when solving design problems and is grounded in empirical studies of actual professional practice in industry. Her recent book with Andre van der Hoek, *Software Design Decoded*, is a succinct summary of insights from this research.

She is an Associate Editor of IEEE *Software* and of *ACM Transactions on Computing Education*. She has also conducted substantial empirical research in Computer Science Education, co-authoring *Computer Science Education Research* and *Principles and Pragmatics of Computer Science Projectwork*. She has a PhD in Computer Science from University College London and a BA in Psycholinguistics from Swarthmore College.

ITiCSE '19, July 15–17, 2019, Aberdeen, Scotland Uk

ACM ISBN 978-1-4503-6301-3/19/07.
https://doi.org/10.1145/3304221.3325602

Interdisciplinary Computer Science Pre-service Teacher Preparation

Francesco Maiorana [†].
University of Catania
Catania, Italy
fmaioran@gmail.com

Gretchen Richards
Jacksonville State University
United States
grichards@jsu.edu

Chery Lucarelli
The College of St. Scholastica
United States
clucarelli@css.edu

Miles Berry
University of Roehampton
United Kingdom
m.berry@roehampton.ac.uk

Barbara Ericson
University of Michigan
United States
barbarer@umich.edu

SUMMARY

Many researchers [1] recognize that great Computer Science (CS) teaching demands great pedagogy, technology, and subject knowledge. It is believed that without a focus on teachers, which are the connection between schools, universities, and work, and their preparation the gap in CS knowledge will be difficult to close [2] and the support to curricular indications, as the national curriculum for computing in England, Computer Science Principles, CS 10K, CS for All, CSTA, Scientix, will not sustainable. World-spread projects as Computing At School, Mobile Computer Science Principles or Initial Teacher Education Lab emphasize the role of teachers in reaching students, sustaining their daily practice. International initiatives as code.org, CoderDojo, Code Club are great examples of well propagated curricular, pedagogical and technological innovations in education. Beside this the research effort has produced many block-based programming languages, tools, and technologies "Low floor and high ceiling". With this deluge of content, pedagogical and technological innovations there is the necessity to involve and sustain teachers in getting confidence with CS. Ways to accomplish this will be discussed.

CCS CONCEPTS

• Computing education programs • Computational thinking
• Model curricula

KEYWORDS

Teacher preparation; Learning platform; Subject Knowledge standards; Interactive ebook; Parsons problems

†IISS G.B Vaccarini, Scientix ambassador, CoderDojo Champion

ITiCSE '19, July 15--17, 2019, Aberdeen, Scotland, UK.

ACM ISBN 978-1-4503-6301 3/19/07.
https://doi.org/10.1145/3304221.3325543

ACM Reference format:
Francesco Maiorana, Gretchen Richards, Chery Lucarelli, Miles Berry, and Barbara Ericson. 2019. Interdisciplinary Computer Science Pre-service Teacher Preparatio. In *Proceedings of Innovation and Technology in Computer Science Education (ITiCSE'119), July 14-17, 2019, Aberdeen, Scotland UK.* ACM, New York, NY, USA, 2 pages.
https://doi.org/10.1145/3304221.3325543

1 PANELIST POSITION STATEMENTS

Gretchen Richards, Ph.D

The infusion of technology into all levels and courses in P-12 and higher education has created two issues according to [2]: (a) what CS content to teach across different educational levels, and (b) what body of knowledge do teachers need to have to be able to teach the CS curriculum. Therefore, JSU has developed through research and observation, Expanding Computational Integration in Teacher Education (ExCITE) professional learning platform to with 5-to-10-minute videos that provide teachers content, pedagogy, and application of various digital literacy, computational thinking and CS information as it relates to cross-referenced standards and subject matter thus producing short, concise, subject-related content teachers can integrate easily into their existing courses.

Chery Lucarelli, Ph.D

The TeachCS@CSS is a teacher preparation model at The College of St. Scholastica that supports the United States "CSforAll" national movement that espouses the idea that computational thinking is a new literacy that all K12 students should have the opportunity to learn. To support these efforts, the computer science and Education faculty have collaborated in preparing preservice teachers across all licensure areas to provide CS conceptual understanding (theory) and experiences with students (practice), with an emphasis on computational thinking. With support from a grant from Google, the faculty have created a curriculum strand that provides CS content knowledge and methods for ***all*** pre-service teachers. Equally important to the curriculum is a focus on equity and broadening CS participation. The teacher preparation program has been revised to infuse computational thinking across a number of courses and includes an optional minor in CS education that will be offered beginning in the Fall of 2019. Ultimately, all of the new teachers at The College of St. Scholastica will have a basic computational thinking competency and awareness and an opportunity to serve as CS advocates in their future schools. In order to address the K12 computer science "CSforAll" national movement, there needs to be an equal focus on "CSforAll" teachers. By working with preservice teachers first, they may enter the teaching profession better prepared to address computer science concepts.

Miles Berry, University of Roehampton

Even before England introduced computing as a subject in its national curriculum (2014), it had developed a set of subject knowledge standards for new teachers of CS at both primary and secondary level. Generous, tax-free, training scholarships and bursaries have been made available. However, initial teacher training for computing has consistently under-recruited, and the recruitment and retention of teachers is an ongoing challenge in England. The University of Roehampton provides initial teacher training for both primary and secondary computing. In the former case, the students are generalists, preparing to teach all the subjects of the primary curriculum: few of these will have studied CS when at school themselves, and thus the university's modules must address this subject knowledge gap. The modules adopt a learner-centric approach, emphasizing how computational thinking and programming can be applied to other subjects in the primary curriculum, and to teachers wider professional responsibilities. Secondary trainees typically have some academic background in CS or software engineering, and thus modules can focus on the technical and pedagogic skills needed for a beginning teacher of computing.

Barbara Ericson, University of Michigan

Many countries want to provide computing education to all secondary students, but this will require training tens of thousands of secondary teachers to teach a subject that most have no prior experience with. Teachers don't need to learn to be software engineers, so we shouldn't train them as if they were CS majors. They do need to be able to read and fix programs. Teachers also need to be able to fit their learning into their busy schedules. Most introductory computing science classes require students to learn by writing lots of programs, which can take lots of frustrating hours. Teachers need different types of practice that help them learn in 20 minute sessions, which is the amount of time that teachers have told us that they have available. I have been creating, over several years, two free interactive ebooks [6] for the two Advanced Placement (AP) CS (CS) courses: Principles and A. Advanced Placement courses are courses that are offered in secondary schools that are intended to be equivalent to college-level courses. The ebooks use a worked examples plus low cognitive load practice approach. Teachers work through its chapters before attending face to face professional development (PD) and then are encouraged to continue working through the ebooks after the PD. Teachers have enjoyed the interactive features in the ebooks and report an increase in confidence in their ability to teach the material after completing the chapters [3]. I have been researching one type of low cognitive load practice problem, called a Parsons problem. In a Parsons problem the user is given the correct code to solve a problem, but the code is broken into blocks of mixed up code that has to be placed in the correct order. Parsons problems can also contain incorrect code blocks, called distractors. I have provided evidence that learners can solve Parsons problems significantly more quickly than fixing code with errors or than writing the equivalent code, with no significant difference in learning gains [4-5]. I also invented adaptive Parsons problems, which means that the difficulty of the problem is dynamically modified based on the learner's performance. Free interactive ebooks with low cognitive load practice problems, like adaptive Parsons problems, can help prepare the thousands of teachers needed to truly provide CS education for all students in a cost effective and efficient manner.

ACKNOWLEDGMENTS

This work was partially supported by Google K12 Education Outreach Fund TRF 16-04030.

REFERENCES

[1] Maiorana, F., Berry, M., Nelson, M., Lucarelli, C., Phillipps, M., Mishra, S., & Benassi, A. (2017, June). International Perspectives on CS Teacher Formation and Professional Development. In Proceedings of the 2017 ACM Conference on Innovation and Technology in Computer Science Education (pp. 236-237). ACM.

[2] Charoula, A., Voogt, J, Fluck, A., Webb, M., Cox, M., Malyn-Smith, J., Zagami, J. (2016). A K-6 computational thinking curriculum framework: Implications for teacher knowledge. Educational Technology & Society. 19(3), 47-57.

[3] Barbara Ericson, Steven Moore, Briana Morrison, and Mark Guzdial. 2015. Usability and Usage of Interactive Features in an Online Ebook for CS Teachers. In Proceedings of the Workshop in Primary and Secondary Computing Education (WiPSCE'15). ACM, New York, NY, USA, 111-120. DOI: https://doi.org/10.1145/2818314.2818335

[4] Barbara J. Ericson, James D. Foley, and Jochen Rick. 2018. Evaluating the Efficiency and Effectiveness of Adaptive Parsons Problems. In Proceedings of the 2018 ACM Conference on Int'l Computing Education Research (ICER'18). ACM, NY, NY, USA, 60-68. DOI: https://doi.org/10.1145/3230977.3231000.

[5] Barbara J. Ericson, Lauren E. Margulieux, and Jochen Rick. 2017. Solving parsons problems versus fixing and writing code. In Proceedings of the 17th Koli. [6] Barbara J. Ericson. CS Principles: Big Ideas in programming https://runestone.academy/runestone/static/StudentCSP/index.html

[7] Barbara J. Ericson. Java Review for the AP CS A Exam Assignments https://runestone.academy/runestone/static/JavaReview/index.html

A Grounded Theory of Computing Professional Identity Formation

Amanpreet Kapoor
Computer & Info. Science & Engineering
University of Florida, Gainesville, FL 32611, USA
kapooramanpreet@ufl.edu

ABSTRACT

Computing professional identity formation is critical for curriculum decision-making, workforce development, and retaining students in computing degree programs. However, we have limited knowledge of how computing professional identity develops. My research focuses on filling this gap by empirically understanding how undergraduate computing students form their professional identity through their negotiations in formal and informal learning environments. The end goal is to generate and test a theory, grounded in data, which can help Computer Science departments to design interventions for fostering computing professional identity formation.

CCS CONCEPTS

- **Social and professional topics** → Computing education

KEYWORDS

Identity; Grounded theory; Computing professional identity

ACM Reference format:

Amanpreet Kapoor. 2019. A Grounded Theory of Computing Professional Identity Formation. In *Proceedings of 24th Annual ACM Conference on Innovation and Technology in Computer Science Education (ITiCSE'19)*. ACM, New York, NY, USA, 2 pages. https://doi.org/10.1145/3304221.3325598

1 CONTEXT AND MOTIVATION

Research has shown that professional identity enables a person to be technically competent, self-confident, and experience a sense of belongingness to the profession [9,14]. Thus, as academic institutions, our role is to create pathways for professional identity development through our degree programs to ensure students' have a solidified computing professional identity before they graduate. However, we have a limited knowledge of how computing professional identity develops in undergraduate students. With regard to these limitations, CS Education researchers have expressed the need for a theory on computing identity [13] and argued for domain-specific theories in computing [10]. My research focuses on one facet of computing identity formation: *computing professional identity*.

ITiCSE '19, July 15–17, 2019, Aberdeen, Scotland UK.

ACM ISBN 978-1-4503-6301-3/19/07.
https://doi.org/10.1145/3304221.3325598

2 BACKGROUND

2.1 Identity. The operational definition of identity put forth in the Handbook of Identity Development by Schwartz, Luyckx, and Vignoles frames personal identity as "*the confluence of the person's self-chosen or ascribed commitments, personal characteristics, and beliefs about themself; roles and positions in relation to significant others; and their membership in social groups and categories (including both their status within the group and the group's status within the larger context)*" [14]. Theories of personal identity tend to focus especially on individual-level processes and often emphasize the agentic role of the individual in creating or discovering his or her own identity [6]. Socio-cultural identity theories suggest that identity is constructed through the interactions an individual has with a community [7]. Further, Marcia's Identity Theory suggests that commitment and exploration of careers is important when studying professional identity formation. These two factors are related to agency and social interaction [8]. Therefore, my dissertation research will focus on understanding CS students' *agency* and *social interactions* in CS degree programs and contribute a theory on the formation of computing professional identity.

2.2 Computing identity and professional identity. Computing identity is defined as the extent to which a student sees themselves as a computer scientist [12]. Research on formation of computing identity is limited [13] and includes Peter's longitudinal study at Uppsala University [12] which drew on social identity theory and found seven ways in which students experience CS/IT: creating, using, learning about technology, problem solving, problem solving for others, creating new knowledge, and contributing to society. She also found that students begin computing programs with broader interests but end with strict technical identities, rejecting their broader personal identities. Research on professional identity in CS includes McCartney and Sanders' case study which found peer interactions, courses, internships, interviews, and jobs influencing students' professional identity [9]. Parker also did a study to investigate professional identity formation for software engineering students and devise instruments for operationalizing identity [11]. Thus, prior work provides a foundation for my research and highlights an overall lack of research focused on understanding the formation of computing professional identity when CS students' consider careers in different computing sub-disciplines. My dissertation research will focus on the broader computing professional identities including specialized identities such as data scientists, web developers, user experience (UX) professionals, etc. and fill this gap by generating a theory of computing professional identity formation.

3 PROBLEM STATEMENT

We define computing professional identity *as the transformation of a person's interest in computing into a person's self-identification as someone who engages in computing professionally through one or more computing sub-disciplines and career paths* [3]. Evidence of computing professional identity development is demonstrated by a commitment to develop technical competencies and skills and to engage in continued professional development within one or more computing fields, or an interest in using technical skills and knowledge to solve problems and/or generate new knowledge with computing approaches, techniques, and tools [3]. My research focuses on answering the following research questions:

RQ1. How do CS undergraduate students' form their computing professional identity?

RQ1a. What role do CS degree programs play in supporting CS students' computing professional identity formation?

RQ1b. What roles do social interactions in informal learning environments play in supporting CS students' computing professional identity formation?

RQ1c. What role does agency play in students' computing professional identity formation?

4 RESEARCH GOALS & METHODS

Previously computing identity has been explored using qualitative methods including narratives [2], case studies [9], and phenomenology [12]. The end goal of my research is to generate and test a theory, grounded in data about students building their professional identities. This research can help CS departments to design interventions for fostering students' computing professional identity formation. To achieve this goal, I will use the grounded theory methodology [15], an iterative and inductive approach for forming theories. I will design a cross-sectional study consisting of a survey and interviews. The survey will be used to recruit interview participants equally representing gender and academic standing and gather information-rich cases through purposeful sampling. The interviews will be semi-structured and guided by the research questions but unstructured enough to allow the discovery of new information [15]. I will analyze the data using inductive coding and ensure the reliability of the coded data, by performing inter-rater reliability and member checks [1].

5 CURRENT & EXPECTED CONTRIBUTIONS

I am a second-year doctoral student, and my advisor, Dr. Christina Gardner-McCune and I conducted a pilot study in Spring 2016 at the University of Florida to understand the formation of computing professional identity. We found that CS undergraduate students professionally identify themselves as software engineers and with several specialized computing professions such as Web developers, UX Professionals, etc. [3,4]. We also found that students explore computing professions through their involvement in professional development activities, informal activities, coursework and negotiations with people in the broader community [5]. During this exploration process, they self-evaluate taking into account both intrinsic factors such as ability and enjoyment and discipline-specific factors such as utility to either continue exploring the discipline or committing to a specific computing profession. Their commitment subsequently leads to focused exploration to attain competence in their chosen profession [5]. We are currently in the process of running a multi-institutional study to understand the formation of computing professional identity across the United States. Through my dissertation research, I expect to contribute to the computing education literature:

1. A theory of computing professional identity formation,
2. A list of avenues that foster the formation of computing professional identity,
3. Degree/program-level opportunities for supporting the formation of computing professional identity,
4. Course-level opportunities that foster CS students' professional development.

REFERENCES

[1] John W. Creswell and J. David Creswell. 2017. *Research Design: Qualitative, Quantitative, and Mixed Methods Approaches.*

[2] Sebastian Dziallas. 2018. Characterising Graduateness in Computing Education: A Narrative Approach. (2018). Retrieved January 27, 2019 from https://kar.kent.ac.uk/69292/

[3] Amanpreet Kapoor and Christina Gardner-McCune. 2018. Understanding Professional Identities and Goals of Computer Science Undergraduate Students. In *Proceedings of the 49th ACM Technical Symposium on Computer Science Education - SIGCSE '18*, 191–196. DOI: https://doi.org/10.1145/3159450.3159474

[4] Amanpreet Kapoor and Christina Gardner-McCune. 2018. Understanding How Computer Science Undergraduate Students are Developing their Professional Identities. In *Proceedings of the 49th ACM Technical Symposium on Computer Science Education - SIGCSE '18*, 1080–1080. DOI: https://doi.org/10.1145/3159450.3162322

[5] Amanpreet Kapoor and Christina Gardner-McCune. 2019. Understanding CS Undergraduate Students' Professional Identity through the lens of their Professional Development. In *Proceedings of the 24th Annual ACM Conference on Innovation and Technology in Computer Science Education (ITiCSE'19).* DOI: https://doi.org/10.1145/3304221.3319764

[6] Jane Kroger and Kathy E. Green. 1996. Events associated with identity status change. *J. Adolesc.* 19, (1996), 359–380. DOI: https://doi.org/10.1006/jado.1996.0045

[7] Jean Lave and Etienne Wenger. 1991. *Situated learning: legitimate peripheral participation.* Cambridge University Press.

[8] James E. Marcia. 1966. Development and validation of ego-identity status. *J. Pers. Soc. Psychol.* 3, 5 (1966), 551–558. DOI: https://doi.org/10.1037/h0023281

[9] Robert McCartney and Kate Sanders. 2015. School/Work: Development of Computing Students' Professional Identity at University. In *Proceedings of the eleventh annual International Conference on International Computing Education Research - ICER '15*, 151–159. DOI: https://doi.org/10.1145/2787622.2787732

[10] Greg L. Nelson and Andrew J. Ko. 2018. On Use of Theory in Computing Education Research. In *Proceedings of the 2018 ACM Conference on International Computing Education Research - ICER '18*, 31–39. DOI: https://doi.org/10.1145/3230977.3230992

[11] Rick Parker. 2017. Studying Professional Identity in Software Engineering. In *Proceedings of the 2017 ACM Conference on International Computing Education Research - ICER '17*, 283–284. DOI: https://doi.org/10.1145/3105726.3105737

[12] Anne-Kathrin Peters. 2018. Students' Experience of Participation in a Discipline—A Longitudinal Study of Computer Science and IT Engineering Students. *ACM Trans. Comput. Educ.* 19, 1 (September 2018), 1–28. DOI: https://doi.org/10.1145/3230011

[13] Sarah L. Rodriguez and Kathleen Lehman. 2017. Developing the next generation of diverse computer scientists: the need for enhanced, intersectional computing identity theory. *Comput. Sci. Educ.* 27, 3–4 (October 2017), 229–247. DOI:https://doi.org/10.1080/08993408.2018.1457899

[14] Seth J. Schwartz, Koen Luyckx, and Vivian L. Vignoles. 2011. *Handbook of Identity Theory and Research.* Springer Science & Business Media.

[15] Anselm Strauss and Juliet Corbin. 2008. *Basics of Qualitative Research.* SAGE Publications, Inc.

Investigating Novice Programmers' Interaction with Programming Environments

Ioannis Karvelas
ioannis.karvelas@ucdconnect.ie
University College Dublin
Dublin, Ireland

ABSTRACT

Learning computer programming can be challenging for novices. Students have to deal with theoretical aspects of programming and problem solving in general, as well as mastering the syntax of a programming language. However, the feedback students receive from programming environments such as compiler error messages can be problematic. This work is aimed at better understanding the impact of these feedback mechanisms and working towards designing improved "novice-friendly" programming feedback to inform the development of pedagogical environments.

CCS CONCEPTS

• **Social and professional topics** → **Computer science education**; **CS1**; • **Human-centered computing** → *Human computer interaction (HCI)*; • **Applied computing** → *Interactive learning environments*.

KEYWORDS

compiler error messages; CS1; educational data mining; novice programmers; programming; programming process data

ACM Reference Format:

Ioannis Karvelas. 2019. Investigating Novice Programmers' Interaction with Programming Environments. In *Innovation and Technology in Computer Science Education (ITiCSE '19), July 15–17, 2019, Aberdeen, Scotland UK.* ACM, New York, NY, USA, 2 pages. https://doi.org/10.1145/3304221.3325596

1 CONTEXT AND MOTIVATION

Learning how to program can be a challenging aspect of studying computing. High dropout rates in introductory programming courses are concerning for educational researchers and many studies focus on addressing the reasons behind these rates and on improving introductory teaching by including unexplored practices in the course materials [13]. There is an urgency for educators to identify potential struggles that students face and tailor their learning accordingly.

While learning to program, students are not only required to learn the fundamental concepts of programming itself, but also to grasp the syntax of a programming language and implement their solutions using a programming environment. Modern IDEs feature various ways of displaying compilation error messages, a mechanism that should help programmers understand the nature of their mistakes and how to correct them.

Compilers analyse code and notify developers about potential problems that violate the specification of the programming language. Rather than implementing a solution and testing it in the end, developers can do partial testing during building a solution, and identify mistakes in their code. With experience, not only do programmers learn to manipulate a programming language more effectively, but also to interact with an IDE faster, and debug and test their programs with more efficiency. But this experience comes with a price: countless hours spent on debugging and figuring out mistakes through the frustrating task of dealing with compiler error messages [4]. Even modern compilers are often misleading, possibly inaccurate from the nocice programmer's point of view, and all too often the messages that are used to diagnose errors are described as cryptic amongst other undesirable adjectives [1].

It is beyond any doubt that students (in their early stages at least), should not have to deal with such complexity. For that reason, it is crucial that pedagogical IDEs are tailored to provide meaningful information about compilation events and help students focus more on developing solutions and less on deciphering error messages.

2 RELATED WORK

In a multi-national, multi-institutional study, McCracken et al. [9] provided convincing evidence that first-year university students were not nearly as proficient at programming as their tutors expected. This conclusion was based on students' assignment scores, designed to challenge their programming efficacy. A later single-institution study by McCartney et al. [8] partially replicated the McCracken experiment, reporting considerably improved student results. This difference was attributed to (a) a familiar environment (lab, resources, etc.), (b) extensive conceptual information provided for the task, and (c) the fact that some pieces of code that were not related to the purpose of the actual task were already provided, and that students had access to the programming language's documentation and an IDE, thus reducing their cognitive load. In 2013, Utting et al. [12] designed another multi-national, multi-institutional study to further explore these issues. Some groups of students used a test harness that provided feedback on whether their code components were functioning as they should, while other groups did not. Overall, results showed higher student scores and efficiency, especially in the test harness groups.

The specifics of these studies vary, but the results indicate that reducing the amount of information that students must process enables them to focus ore on important tasks, progress more efficiently, and ultimately can improve programming efficacy.

ITiCSE '19, July 15–17, 2019, Aberdeen, Scotland UK

ACM ISBN 978-1-4503-6301-3/19/07.
https://doi.org/10.1145/3304221.3325596

3 PROBLEM STATEMENT

Programming is a multi-dimensional process. Efficient programmers usually can "parse" a problem and understand what the solution should produce, are fully accustomed to modern programming concepts and efficient code-related architectural designs, and are experts in a programming language and its syntax.

IIowever, interpreting error messages can prove to be a cumbersome and time-consuming task, even for experienced programmers [11]. Improper, misleading, and generally confusing error messages can cause frustration [3], discouragement [2], and have effects contrary to their intended purpose . Instead of being designed from a user-perspective, commercial compilers are often designed based on other priorities, such as performance. It seems that compiler development teams do not have the luxury of investing their time in usability principles and their incorporation in to the design of their products [11]. It is unfortunate that the amount of research on compiler development and optimization outweighs the amount of research on compilers that are "programmer friendly", considering the potential benefits for novice programmers.

4 RESEARCH GOALS

The primary goal of this PhD thesis is to investigate the impact that different IDEs and compiler feedback mechanisms have on novice programmers and provide guidance related to the design of more novice-friendly programming environments by answering the following questions:

- How do different programming environment feedback mechanisms affect novices in terms of their programming behaviour and learning?
- What impact do IDEs that include "programmer friendly" features have on novices and their learning?

5 RESEARCH METHODS

The first stage of this research is to investigate how a major change in the popular BlueJ introductory IDE [7] may have affected novice programming behaviour. In 2017, BlueJ 4.0.0 was released and the environment's compilation mechanism changed from a standard "click to compile" to automatic "background compilation". In BlueJ 3.x, only the user could trigger a compilation, while in BlueJ 4.x, in addition to manual compilation, the compiler is triggered when the user moves the cursor from a modified code line (and in some other rare instances). A major change between versions is the manner in which users are presented with error messages. In BlueJ 3.x, only the first error is displayed by highlighting the background of the code line in red, regardless of how many errors the source contains. In BlueJ 4.x, if there are multiple errors present in the source code, all corresponding lines are underlined in red (both in manual and automatic compilations). However, users are not shown an error message until they use their keyboard or mouse to hover over a highlighted error or if they compile manually, in which case the error messages are shown sequentially from first to last (and possibly over again in round-robin style).

The investigation will be conducted by analysing data collected by the Blackbox project [6]. Since 2013, Blackbox has collected a substantial amount of data, and only 19 studies have made primary use of this: 18 reported in Brown et al. [5], and one [10] published since. These focus mostly on general statistics about the most common errors, the amount of time users spend on fixing them, and the nature of these fixes.

6 CONTRIBUTIONS

The near-term contributions of this work include (a) a clear picture of the differences between "click to compile" and automatic error checking mechanisms in terms of novices' programming behaviour. Future work will provide (b) an extensive investigation on the impact that modern feedback mechanisms have on novice programmers (including error message phrasing, highlighting, hints, tooltips, etc.), and (c) a framework for designing feedback mechanisms for use in pedagogical environments that incorporates the findings from (a) and (b).

REFERENCES

[1] Titus Barik. 2018. *Error Messages as Rational Reconstructions.* Ph.D. Dissertation. North Carolina State University, Raleigh, NC, USA.

[2] Brett A. Becker. 2016. An Effective Approach to Enhancing Compiler Error Messages. In *Proceedings of the 47th ACM Technical Symposium on Computing Science Education (SIGCSE '16).* ACM, New York, NY, USA, 126–131. https://doi.org/10.1145/2839509.2844584

[3] Brett A. Becker, Kyle Goslin, and Graham Glanville. 2018. The Effects of Enhanced Compiler Error Messages on a Syntax Error Debugging Test. In *Proceedings of the 49th ACM Technical Symposium on Computer Science Education (SIGCSE '18).* ACM, New York, NY, USA, 640–645. https://doi.org/10.1145/3159450.3159461

[4] Brett A. Becker, Cormac Murray, Tianyi Tao, Changheng Song, Robert McCartney, and Kate Sanders. 2018. Fix the First, Ignore the Rest: Dealing with Multiple Compiler Error Messages. In *Proceedings of the 49th ACM Technical Symposium on Computer Science Education (SIGCSE '18).* ACM, New York, NY, USA, 634–639. https://doi.org/10.1145/3159450.3159453

[5] Neil C. C. Brown, Amjad Altadmri, Sue Sentance, and Michael Kölling. 2018. Blackbox, Five Years On: An Evaluation of a Large-scale Programming Data Collection Project. In *Proceedings of the 2018 ACM Conference on International Computing Education Research (ICER '18).* ACM, New York, NY, USA, 196–204. https://doi.org/10.1145/3230977.3230991

[6] Neil C. C. Brown, Michael Kölling, Davin McCall, and Ian Utting. 2014. Blackbox: A Large Scale Repository of Novice Programmers' Activity. In *Proceedings of the 45th ACM Technical Symposium on Computer Science Education (SIGCSE '14).* ACM, New York, NY, USA, 223–228. https://doi.org/10.1145/2538862.2538924

[7] Michael Kölling, Bruce Quig, Andrew Patterson, and John Rosenberg. 2003. The BlueJ System and its Pedagogy. *Computer Science Education* 13, 4 (2003), 249–268. https://doi.org/10.1076/csed.13.4.249.17496 arXiv:https://doi.org/10.1076/csed.13.4.249.17496

[8] Robert McCartney, Jonas Boustedt, Anna Eckerdal, Kate Sanders, and Carol Zander. 2013. Can First-year Students Program Yet?: A Study Revisited. In *Proceedings of the Ninth Annual International ACM Conference on International Computing Education Research (ICER '13).* ACM, New York, NY, USA, 91–98. https://doi.org/10.1145/2493394.2493412

[9] Michael McCracken, Vicki Almstrum, Danny Diaz, Mark Guzdial, Dianne Hagan, Yifat Ben-David Kolikant, Cary Laxer, Lynda Thomas, Ian Utting, and Tadeusz Wilusz. 2001. A Multi-national, Multi-institutional Study of Assessment of Programming Skills of First-year CS Students. *SIGCSE Bull.* 33, 4 (Dec. 2001), 125–180. https://doi.org/10.1145/572139.572181

[10] Brad Richards and Ayse Hunt. 2018. Investigating the Applicability of the Normalized Programming State Model to BlueJ Programmers. In *Proceedings of the 18th Koli Calling International Conference on Computing Education Research (Koli Calling '18).* ACM, New York, NY, USA, Article 10, 10 pages. https://doi.org/10.1145/3279720.3279731

[11] V. Javier Traver. 2010. On Compiler Error Messages: What They Say and What They Mean. *Advances in Human-Computer Interaction* 2010 (2010), 1–26. https://doi.org/10.1155/2010/602570

[12] Ian Utting, Allison Elliott Tew, Mike McCracken, Lynda Thomas, Dennis Bouvier, Roger Frye, James Paterson, Michael Caspersen, Yifat Ben-David Kolikant, Juha Sorva, and Tadeusz Wilusz. 2013. A Fresh Look at Novice Programmers' Performance and Their Teachers' Expectations. In *Proceedings of the ITiCSE Working Group Reports (ITiCSE -WGR '13).* ACM, New York, NY, USA, 15–32. https://doi.org/10.1145/2543882.2543884

[13] Aharon Yadin. 2011. Reducing the Dropout Rate in an Introductory Programming Course. *ACM Inroads* 2, 4 (Dec. 2011), 71–76. https://doi.org/10.1145/2038876.2038894

From Studying to Learning Computer Science

A study of the first-year experience of computer science education at university

Madeleine Lorås
Norwegian University of Science and Technology
Trondheim, Norway

ABSTRACT

Ensuring that computer science students graduate and learn the desired curriculum is important in order to meet future demands. However, educational institutions have limited room for action as the number of students increases, without additional teaching and structural resources. The research presented here aims to combine knowledge about how computer science students' study and the effects of educational design to maximize the pedagogical potential within the room for action at universities today.

CCS CONCEPTS

• **Social and professional topics → Computer science education; Information technology education**; *CS1*.

KEYWORDS

Computer Science Education; First Year Experience; Study Behavior

ACM Reference Format:
Madeleine Lorås. 2019. From Studying to Learning Computer Science: A study of the first-year experience of computer science education at university. In *Innovation and Technology in Computer Science Education (ITiCSE '19), July 15–17, 2019, Aberdeen, Scotland Uk.* ACM, New York, NY, USA, 2 pages. https://doi.org/10.1145/3304221.3325595

1 CONTEXT AND MOTIVATION

The need for computer science (CS) skills and knowledge in society is increasing. With the current student enrollment and graduation rates there will be a gap between supply and demand in the future [12]. Simultaneously, both in Norway and the rest of the world computer science education (CSE) is experiencing an increasing number of students [11]. In other words, the even though the number of CS students is increasing, the demand for CS professionals is not met. This puts a pressure on educational institutions to lower drop-out rates and increase throughput. Research has shown that the first-year experience is essential for retention [3, 13]. Institutions need to develop new educational designs in the first year and innovative ways to keep up with high enrollment numbers.

The research presented here is based at the Norwegian University of Science and Technology (NTNU), which has 11 CS programs with approximately 650 new students every year. These programs are all designed and organized in various ways, which makes NTNU an interesting case. Furthermore, the research is focused on the two largest programs, computer science and computer science engineering, with 150 students each. These students are organized into courses with students from the whole university, which means they are taking a CS1 course with over 2000 students. This causes some challenges to the educational design, especially when it comes to the academic learning environment, sense of belonging and ensuring that the learning outcomes are met. In other words, the need for improvement is large, but the room for action is limited. This research aims to investigate this room for action in an attempt to meet these challenges. Accordingly, the problem statement for this research project is divided into the following three research questions (RQs):

- RQ1: What are different ways the first year of computer science education is designed?
- RQ2: How are students' study behavior effected by the educational design of the first year?
- RQ3: In what ways can the effect of educational design on learning be measured and researched?

ITiCSE '19, July 15–17, 2019, Aberdeen, Scotland Uk

ACM ISBN 978-1-4503-6301-3/19/07
https://doi.org/10.1145/3304221.3325595

2 BACKGROUND

The research questions for this project concern educational design, learning and study behavior in CSE, focusing on the first year. On the topic of educational design and learning the underlying theory used is constructivism. Ben Ari's paper describing constructivism in CSE states that the students create cognitive structures when learning and emphasizes that each individual will perform the construction differently, depending on preexisting knowledge, learning style and personality [1]. In other words, the design of a CS course or a program may to a varying degree enable the students to build such cognitive structures. Correspondingly, the way students' study within this design is important. When investigating learning and study behavior, Biggs' work the study process and Entwistle's work on learning and learning environments is used as a theoretical framework. Study behavior has been found to be strongly related to academic performance, and good study behavior is mostly developed early in the student's studies [5]. Study behavior includes both the study habits, skills and strategies of the students, as well as their attitudes and motivation towards studying [2, 8].

Lastly, the importance of the first year experience is based on Tintos research which discusses student departure as several stages; separation (from a known home environment), transition (into a new social and physical structure) and incorporation (into a community and culture) [13] argues that the students' first year experience lays important groundwork, even though students may drop out later in their study.

Table 1: Overview of research sub-projects and methods

Project	Data and analysis	Research question
Case study of a CS program	In-depth interviews with first year students	RQ2
	Analysis of first year student survey about perceptions and expectations (N=200)	RQ1
Systematic mapping and categorization	Mapping studies of Norwegian and Scandinavian CS programs	RQ1
	Analysis of data from a Norwegian student survey about educational quality (N=1200)	RQ3
Interventions and experiments	Implementation and evaluation of a study day for first year CS students	RQ2
	Quasi-experimental studies on study behavior and educational design	RQ3

3 RESEARCH GOALS

As the research conducted is part of a larger center dedicated to excellence in CS education in Norway, the overall goal of the project is to enhance the learning in NTNU's study programs through increased student engagement and co-reflection among students and staff. My focus is on the first-year experience, where the number of students is high and the distance between academic staff end students large. Firstly, the goal of the research is to increase the knowledge about how first year CSE is designed and implemented. Secondly, the goal is to take on the challenge of designing courses and programs for large student groups within the room for action at institutions today. The room for action is often limited by academic staff, access to appropriate learning areas, scheduling, financial resources and political guidelines.

4 RESEARCH METHODS

The research in this project has a mixed method design with a pragmatic approach. [9]. The project consists of three sub-projects as summarized in Table 1, which build on each other in an iterative manner. The first project, a case study of a CS study program, has an exploratory sequential design, meant to give insight into what challenges the students face and potential areas for improvement [6]. The second project, a systematic mapping of CS study programs in Norway and Scandinavia, has an explanatory sequential design, meant to act as a baseline, as well as help contextualize the research. Lastly, interventions and experiments will be designed and evaluated empirically based on the first two projects.

As seen in Table 1, the data gathered in this project is both qualitative and quantitative. For the qualitative data, a grounded theory approach as described by Corbin and Strauss is used for analysis [4]. For the quantitative data analysis, various statistical methods are used. Following the mixed method methodology, the results need to be combined, which is done iteratively as described my Creswell [7].

5 CONTRIBUTIONS

As of March 2019, a case study of a first year CS study program has been done, which involved following six students through their first year and a survey of first year students at various programs. The results from these inquiries have shown that students' priorities, strategies, habits, skills and attitudes are constrained by the educational design, which furthermore may lead to different learning outcomes than desired [?].

Concurrently, the first iteration of a systematic mapping survey of CS programs which was to look at all CS programs in Norway [10]. Based on this work, I am expanding the mapping to investigate selected programs in Nordic countries. The goal of this project is both to increase knowledge about how first year CS education is organized, as well as identify trends and areas for further research.

In the future, the goal is to use both these data sets as a basis for designing quasi-experimental studies for the next two academic years. In addition, some educational interventions are already in place and will be evaluated and analyzed consecutively. Although, this project already has contributed to knowledge about CSE in Norway, a limitation in my research is the generalizability and transferability to an international context.

REFERENCES

[1] Mordechai Ben-Ari. 2001. Constructivism in computer science education. *Journal of Computers in Mathematics and Science Teaching* 20, 1 (2001), 45–73.

[2] John Biggs. 1979. Individual differences in study processes and the Quality of Learning Outcomes. 8, 4 (1979), 381–394. https://doi.org/10.1007/BF01680526

[3] John M. Braxton, Jeffrey F. Milem, and Anna Shaw Sullivan. 2000. The Influence of Active Learning on the College Student Departure Process: Toward a Revision of Tinto's Theory. 71, 5 (2000), 569–590. https://doi.org/10.2307/2649260

[4] Juliet Corbin and Anselm Strauss. 2014. *Basics of Qualitative Research: Techniques and Procedures for Developing Grounded Theory* (4 ed.). SAGE Publications, Inc.

[5] Marcus Credé and Nathan R. Kuncel. 2008. Study Habits, Skills, and Attitudes: The Third Pillar Supporting Collegiate Academic Performance. 3, 6 (2008), 425–453. https://doi.org/10.1111/j.1745-6924.2008.00089.x

[6] John W. Creswell. 2011-03-10. *Educational Research: Planning, Conducting, and Evaluating Quantitative and Qualitative Research* (4 edition ed.). Pearson.

[7] John W. Creswell and Vicki L. Plano Clark. 2017-08-31. *Designing and Conducting Mixed Methods Research.* SAGE Publications. Google-Books-ID: eTwmDwAAQBAJ.

[8] N. J. Entwistle. 1991. Approaches to Learning and Perceptions of the Learning Environment: Introduction to the Special Issue. 22, 3 (1991), 201–4.

[9] Burke Johnson and Larry Christensen. 2012. *Educational Research: Quantitative, Qualitative, and Mixed Approaches* (4 ed.). SAGE. Google-Books-ID: 8qoaXPh6E4UC.

[10] Madeleine Lorås, Guttorm Sindre, and Trond Aalberg. 2018. First year computer science education in Norway. In *Proceedings from the annual NOKOBIT conference 2018*, Vol. 26.

[11] Engineering National Academies of Sciences. 2017. *Assessing and Responding to the Growth of Computer Science Undergraduate Enrollments.* The National Academies Press. https://doi.org/10.17226/24926

[12] Ministry of Local Government and Modernization. 2014. Dimensjonering av avansert IKT-kompetanse. https://www.regjeringen.no/no/dokumenter/Dimensjonering-av-avansert-IKT-kompetanse/id762445/

[13] Vincent Tinto. 1988. Stages of Student Departure: Reflections on the Longitudinal Character of Student Leaving. 59, 4 (1988), 438–455. https://doi.org/10.1080/00221546.1988.11780199

A Theory of Applied Mind of Programming

Understanding the challenges in learning to program

Tony Lowe
Purdue University
West Lafayette, IN USA
lowe46@purdue.edu

ABSTRACT

Computer Science teaching and education research often struggles to explain a novice programmer's struggles. This dissertation creates a theoretical framework utilizing cognitive psychology, neuroscience, and learning theory to describe the mind of the programmer and the gap novices must bridge. The resulting theory of applied mind for programming can provide greater explanatory power in research and guide assessment and pedagogical approaches.

CCS CONCEPTS

• Social and professional topics→CS1

• Social and professional topics→Computational science and engineering education

KEYWORDS: Computer Science, Programming, Education, Dual Process Theory, Neuroscience, Education Theory, Bruner

ACM Reference format:

Tony Lowe. 2019. A Theory of Applied Mind of Programming. In *Proceedings of 24th Annual ACM Conference on Innovation and Technology in Computer Science Education (ITiCSE'19), July 15–17, 2019, Aberdeen, Scotland UK.* ACM, New York, NY, USA, 2 pages. DOI: https://doi.org/10.1145/3304221.3325600

1 Context and Motivation

Nearly a half century of educational research on novice programmers tells us that learning to program was and continues to be a big challenge for novices. Computer Science (CS) education research attempts to leverage various theories of learning and cognition to improve education and investigate the learning process, but the performance of novices often confounds explanation and shows only marginal gains in student performance. Where most students in mathematics or physics education start the subject at a young age, first-time programmers bring a broad spectrum of prior learning, often none or worse, problematic, so the initial capabilities of students vary drastically.

ACM ISBN 978-1-4503-6301-3/19/07. https://doi.org/10.1145/3304221.3325600

Instructors must accommodate a classroom containing students unfamiliar with computers next to those who have passed advanced tests on the subject. Solving problems with computing is complex and multidisciplinary. Thus learners also differ in how interested they are in the subject, what they expect to do with their knowledge now and in the future. Teaching novices to program is a messy, but exciting challenge which can benefit from applying what we know about cognition to teaching and learning.

This dissertation looks to create a theoretical framework for learning to program leveraging a growing understanding of cognition. Human cognition is complex and enigmatic, yet models of learning too often presume rationality in learners. Neuroscience and cognitive psychology offer alternative models that include implicit knowledge and intuition as part of the way we think and learn [1], [2]. CS education research has noted the role of intuition [3], [4], yet much of the literature focuses on reason and logic as the core path to programming. By better explaining how experts use intuition and experience as part of programming, we can create new aids for novices who otherwise are failing in the existing educational pathways.

2 Background

An alternative view of cognition that has provided a powerful tool for reconsidering the way humans think and learn is dual process theory. Dual process theory describes the two systems of thinking, rational and intuitive, the brain utilizes in decision making and learning [1], [5]. Kahneman and Tversky revolutionized economic prediction through the introduction of prospect theory [6]. Prospect theory describes the role of intuition in decision making as an alternative to historical economic models which treated people as exclusively rational beings. Modeling the uncertain decision-making programmers utilize while coding using the dual process theory approach may guide what it takes to learn to code. Dual process theory may refine how we consider programming cognition, but more is required to improve learning.

Learning models typically focus on knowledge acquisition, but in programming knowledge must be applied to problem-solving. Jerome Bruner focused much of his learning theory around not just abstract learning but applying knowledge to problem-solving [7]. Bruner blended the works of Piaget and Vygotsky to create a model of learning that involves combining action, imagery, and systems of symbols [8], [9]. Programming is an artificial construct driven by many symbols, the programming language, but often with an invisible result that makes developing mental models of action and abstract images challenging. Describing, assessing, and maturing these invisible patterns of thinking in novices is essential to creating competence. Bruner's theory guides the formation of mental representations required to describe the mind of the programmer, both novice and expert.

CS education research provides a rich repository of findings and tough questions within those findings to offer fodder for applying the theory and testing its merit. Early work has utilized studies by Perkins [10], [11], McCracken [12], and Lister [13] to revisit the gaps they found in student performance. One of my goals at this consortium would be to find additional literature, challenges, and data to tackle with this theory and interesting problems to attempt to explain.

3 Hypothesis

Building a competent programmer is like making a solid stool. Each contains several 'legs' which must be strong and built in coordination. It is not enough to teach concepts, a language, or how to solve problems; they must learn and most importantly integrate each with the next. Dual process theory helps to separate declarative knowledge from implicit. Bruner's theory provides the necessary language to describe the complex interplay between logic and intuition, and enlighten learning strategies. Together these provide a foundation for a theory of mind applied to programming which can provide a theoretical framework for research and education.

4 Research Goals

The goal of this dissertation is to create a theoretical framework of cognition and learning customized to the applied task of programming. The dissertation will dually be providing a reasoned argument in constructing the theory while simultaneously educating the reader in the required cognitive and learning theories. The process will include 1) describe dual process theory and its presence in programming 2) revisit common learning theories (e.g., Piaget/Neo-Piagetian, Vygotsky) focusing on Bruner to describe mental representations of programmers at all levels 3) define a combined theory of mind utilizing 1 and 2 and finally 4) describe future research for validating the theory, creating pedagogy, and new avenues of study utilizing the theory.

5 Research Methods

This study utilizes existing theory and research. The proposed theoretical framework combines existing theories, applied to programming, formulated via logical argument and tested using past research as a counter-point. Reanalyzing past studies holds a change in theoretical framework as the only variable, removing nuisance variables and providing a built-in counter-example for comparison. Newly collected data introduces variances in population, methodology, and chance. Existing studies provide the author(s) data and original interpretation, plus point to gaps in understanding and allows the theory to be tested within a wider variety programming education contexts than would be feasible in a single new study.

6 Contributions

A theoretical framework should guide research and pedagogy [14]. An improved theory of mind directed at the activity of programming has the potential to explain enigmatic novice struggles research and hint at improved pedagogical approaches. This dissertation will investigate many of the gaps in identifying novice struggles and postulate they are rooted in an archaic view of monolithic, rational cognition in programmers. Incorporation intuition and tacit knowledge into student learning explain when knowledge is misapplied or fragile. Identifying the required mental representations of competent programmers can help to assess student progress and build instructional methods that foster novice mental development. The proposed theoretical framework can become a resource for future research and teaching in CS education. The theory provides alternative models for explaining student learning and interpreting assessment results. It suggests an alternative epistemology for programming which unpacks 'problem-solving' and 'coding' into separate but interrelated packages.

7 Biography

Tony Lowe is a graduate student at Purdue's School of Engineering Education after several decades in industry.

REFERENCES

[1] D. Kahneman, *Thinking, fast and slow.* Macmillan, 2011.

[2] L. R. Squire and E. R. Kandel, *Memory: From mind to molecules,* vol. 69. Macmillan, 2003.

[3] S. Wiedenbeck, "Novice/expert differences in programming skills," *Int. J. Man. Mach. Stud.,* vol. 23, no. 4, pp. 383–390, 1985.

[4] B. L. Sherin, "A comparison of programming languages and algebraic notation as expressive languages for physics," *Int. J. Comput. Math. Learn.,* vol. 6, no. 1, pp. 1–61, 2001.

[5] J. S. B. T. Evans and K. E. Frankish, *In two minds: Dual processes and beyond.* Oxford University Press, 2009.

[6] A. Tversky and D. Kahneman, "Advances in Prospect Theory: Cumulative Representation of Uncertainty," *J. Risk Uncertain.,* vol. 323, pp. 297–323, 1992.

[7] J. S. Bruner, *Toward a theory of instruction,* vol. 59. Harvard University Press, 1966.

[8] J. S. Bruner, "On cognitive growth II," in *Studies in cognitive growth: A collaboration at the center for cognitive studies,* Wiley and Sons, 1966, pp. 30–67.

[9] J. S. Bruner, "On cognitive growth," in *Studies in cognitive growth: A collaboration at the center for cognitive studies,* Wiley and Sons, 1966, pp. 1–29.

[10] D. N. Perkins, C. Hancock, R. Hobbs, F. Martin, and R. Simmons, "Conditions of Learning in Novice Programmers," *J. Educ. Comput. Res.,* vol. 2, no. 1, pp. 37–55, 1986.

[11] D. N. Perkins and F. Martin, "Fragile knowledge and neglected strategies in novice programmers," Washington, DC, 1985.

[12] M. McCracken *et al.,* "A multi-national, multi-institutional study of assessment of programming skills of first-year CS students," *ACM SIGCSE Bull.,* vol. 33, no. 4, p. 125, 2001.

[13] R. Lister *et al., A multi-national study of reading and tracing skills in novice programmers,* vol. 36, no. 4. 2004.

[14] E. Dubinsky, "Using a Theory of Learning in College Mathematics Courses," *MSOR Connect.,* 2013.

Gamification and Collaboration to Evaluate and Improve the Security Mindset of Developers

Léon McGregor
lm356@hw.ac.uk
Heriot-Watt University
Edinburgh, United Kingdom

ABSTRACT

My research involves investigating gamification and serious games in relation to secure programming. Current research has shown the effectiveness of serious games in other contexts, and I aim to discover what kinds of game or gameplay work most effectively and develop a more reusable system for designing serious games or gamifications for programming contexts.

CCS CONCEPTS

• **Security and privacy → Software and application security**; **Usability in security and privacy**; • **Social and professional topics** → *Software engineering education*; • **Software and its engineering** → *Interactive games*;

KEYWORDS

serious games, secure programming, developer centred security, gamification, usable security

ACM Reference Format:

Léon McGregor. 2019. Gamification and Collaboration to Evaluate and Improve the Security Mindset of Developers. In *Innovation and Technology in Computer Science Education (ITiCSE '19), July 15–17, 2019, Aberdeen, Scotland, UK*. ACM, New York, NY, USA, 2 pages. https://doi.org/10.1145/3304221.3325593

1 CONTEXT AND MOTIVATION

Improving the security mindset of developers is important as with an increase in the prevalence of not just software but myriad devices running software in the Internet of Things it is more important than ever to ensure that developers are considering security impacts as they develop and write code. My research is focused on using games to help educate software developers on the importance of secure development.

2 LITERATURE REVIEW

There are two primary areas of research related to my work. Research into issues developers encounter which introduces security flaws into software, and game design, and how games and gamification can be used as a tool for education.

ITiCSE '19, July 15–17, 2019, Aberdeen, Scotland, UK

ACM ISBN 978-1-4503-6301-3/19/07.
https://doi.org/10.1145/3304221.3325593

Some of the issues that developers face that can result in bugs being introduced include:

Motivation - Many of the people involved in the development of software may lack motivation to produce secure software. This issue of motivation can come from developers acting in a non-professional context (hobbyist programmers), or not understanding why it is important to consider security, even when it isn't a primary issue in a software project. A research project investigating these issues - "Motivating Jenny" [1] has recently been started.

API Usability - Often when programmers are producing code they will make use of APIs in languages or libraries that offer security controls or primitives this way they don't have to worry about implementation details themselves. This should be a good thing, however many security APIs (like `openssl` [7] and `Java SSE` [10]) lack decent usability which results in developers misunderstanding or misusing them, which introduces bugs into software instead of preventing it.

Information Sources - Developers can turn to many sources to get information relating to problems they encounter. However, not all sources are as useful as each other. Some sources, such as API documentation can lack sufficient or easily understood explanation of proper use [10], and Q&A sites like StackOverflow can give advice which is unsuitable or plain wrong, which can end up directly impacting the security of published applications [2].

Research topics relating to the use of games as an education tool include:

Serious Games - These are games with a purpose of educating on a particular topic. Many such games have been created before on cyber security topics and focused on teaching software development concepts. One serious game [4] was created to elicit cyber security awareness around social engineering. Another game "Code Defenders" was designed to teach the concept of mutation testing [8]. "Code Hunt" [11] gets players to implement a working solution by getting test cases to pass.

Gamification - Gamification is where game elements are integrated into non-game contexts [6]. It can be used as a way of encouraging developers to adopt desirable behaviours. One such example is the use of a points system [3] to encourage developers to fix compiler warnings and avoid creating new ones.

Contests - In programming contests a common theme is to "Capture the flag" - that is to break an opponents solution. There are parallels to secure programming, as this encourages developers to harden their implementation against any bug. Such contests include "Build-it Break-it Fix-it" [9] and the serious game "Code Hunt" has been used in a contest environment [5].

3 PROBLEM STATEMENT

I hypothesise that there will be some game elements or designs that are more (or less) effective at helping to encourage secure programming. Discovering what these are, or what patterns to avoid, will help more games designed in the future which will provide more help to developers to encourage more secure development.

4 RESEARCH GOALS

There are two primary goals that make up my research:

Motivational Game Design - I want to investigate the different kinds of designs that are used in games, and see how they affect the players who encounter them. With this, I plan to develop a framework for designing games in the future that will be effective at teaching security concepts for programming, or motivating players and programmers to consider more security when they write code.

Game Engine - A large part of the concept of a game relating to security will be that it may interact with code, tests or some other facet of software engineering and development. I want to investigate this to see if there are certain integrations that are common to many games and from this design a sort of meta-language for designing such games, potentially offering game engine plugins to make it easier to develop such games in the future.

5 RESEARCH METHODS

I have 3 main methodologies to my research that I plan to make us of:

Research Security Issues - This forms the first part of the background research / literature review that I have conducted so far. It involves reviewing the literature relating to major issues that developers encounter that result in insecure code being produced.

Research Existing Games - This forms the second part of my literature review. Many games have been created in the past that relate to the topic of developers, programming and security, and researching this will provide a good base to build off of.

Develop & Analyse Games - I plan to develop some small prototype games that aim to motivate developers to think about security when they are programming, so that I can then evaluate them by getting developers to play them. I can then compare and contrast the outcome of developers playing different games, and relate to existing games from the literature review.

This will reveal the effectiveness of game elements and across multiple games there may be common overarching themes that are effective for the game's purposes. It will also reveal if there are certain design aspects which have a negative effect to be avoided in future.

6 CONTRIBUTIONS

I have previously collaborated with members of the Glasgow School of Art to make a game that aims to help educate developers about security concerns relating to python programming APIs. As part of my goal to produce more games to analyse, I aim to do more collaboration with them.

I expect to produce a design for a game engine, with a framework for which concepts are most useful, which will empower more developers to develop useful interventions in the future.

ACKNOWLEDGMENTS

My study is funded by EPSRC. Thanks also to my supervisor, Manuel Maarek.

REFERENCES

[1] 2018. The Jenny Project. https://motivatingjenny.org/

[2] Y. Acar, M. Backes, S. Fahl, D. Kim, M. L. Mazurek, and C. Stransky. 2016. You Get Where You're Looking for: The Impact of Information Sources on Code Security. In *2016 IEEE Symposium on Security and Privacy (SP)*. 289–305. https://doi.org/10.1109/SP.2016.25

[3] Satoshi Arai, Kazunori Sakamoto, Hironori Washizaki, and Yoshiaki Fukazawa. 2014. A Gamified Tool for Motivating Developers to Remove Warnings of Bug Pattern Tools. In *Proceedings of the 2014 6th International Workshop on Empirical Software Engineering in Practice (IWESEP '14)*. IEEE Computer Society, Washington, DC, USA, 37–42. https://doi.org/10.1109/IWESEP.2014.17

[4] K. Beckers and S. Pape. 2016. A Serious Game for Eliciting Social Engineering Security Requirements. In *2016 IEEE 24th International Requirements Engineering Conference (RE)*. 16–25. https://doi.org/10.1109/RE.2016.39

[5] Judith Bishop, R. Nigel Horspool, Tao Xie, Nikolai Tillmann, and Jonathan De Halleux. 2015. Code Hunt: Experience with Coding Contests at Scale. In *2015 IEEE/ACM 37th IEEE International Conference on Software Engineering*, Vol. 2. 398–407. https://doi.org/10.1109/ICSE.2015.172

[6] Sebastian Deterding, Dan Dixon, Rilla Khaled, and Lennart Nacke. 2011. From Game Design Elements to Gamefulness: Defining "Gamification". In *Proceedings of the 15th International Academic MindTrek Conference: Envisioning Future Media Environments (MindTrek '11)*. ACM, New York, NY, USA, 9–15. https://doi.org/10.1145/2181037.2181040

[7] Martin Georgiev, Subodh Iyengar, Suman Jana, Rishita Anubhai, Dan Boneh, and Vitaly Shmatikov. 2012. The Most Dangerous Code in the World: Validating SSL Certificates in Non-browser Software. In *Proceedings of the 2012 ACM Conference on Computer and Communications Security (CCS '12)*. ACM, New York, NY, USA, 38–49. https://doi.org/10.1145/2382196.2382204

[8] J. M. Rojas and G. Fraser. 2016. Code Defenders: A Mutation Testing Game. In *2016 IEEE Ninth International Conference on Software Testing, Verification and Validation Workshops (ICSTW)*. 162–167. https://doi.org/10.1109/ICSTW.2016.43

[9] Andrew Ruef, Michael Hicks, James Parker, Dave Levin, Michelle L. Mazurek, and Piotr Mardziel. 2016. Build It, Break It, Fix It: Contesting Secure Development. In *Proceedings of the 2016 ACM SIGSAC Conference on Computer and Communications Security (CCS '16)*. ACM, New York, NY, USA, 690–703. https://doi.org/10.1145/2976749.2978382

[10] Chamila Wijayarathna and Nalin Asanka Gamagedara Arachchilage. 2019. Why Johnny can't develop a secure application? A usability analysis of Java Secure Socket Extension API. *Computers & Security* 80 (Jan. 2019), 54–73. https://doi.org/10.1016/j.cose.2018.09.007

[11] Tao Xie, Judith Bishop, Nikolai Tillmann, and Jonathan de Halleux. 2015. Gamifying Software Security Education and Training via Secure Coding Duels in Code Hunt. In *Proceedings of the 2015 Symposium and Bootcamp on the Science of Security (HotSoS '15)*. ACM, New York, NY, USA, 26:1–26:2. https://doi.org/10.1145/2746194.2746220

Computational Thinking At Primary School: Didactical and Psychological Aspects

Marialaura Moschella
mmoschella@unibz.it
Free University of Bolzano
Bressanone, Italy

ABSTRACT

The research project aims to identify the cognitive processes underlying the Computational Thinking (CT) skills of primary school pupils. Moreover, it investigates which didactical strategies are most effective for implementing CT in the curriculum. A mixed methods research was designed: qualitative data gathered from interviews and observations are combined with quantitative data collected through pre- and post-test measures with respect to the intervention.

KEYWORDS

Computational Thinking, Cognitive Skills, Agile Methodology

ACM Reference Format:
Marialaura Moschella. 2019. Computational Thinking At Primary School: Didactical and Psychological Aspects. In *Innovation and Technology in Computer Science Education (ITiCSE '19), July 15–17, 2019, Aberdeen, Scotland Uk.* ACM, New York, NY, USA, 2 pages. https://doi.org/10.1145/3304221.3325599

1 CONTEST AND MOTIVATION

Preparing students for society in the digital age is a challenge for educators and institutions. Large amounts of data are everywhere available, and data and information are produced increasingly and continuously. For this reason, Computational Thinking (CT) is deemed on of the most important 21st century skills. Even if many countries implemented principles of Informatics (or Computer Science) starting from the early elementary school, the challenge to teach this subject, in order develop the CT skills, is still under the magnifying glass. For instance,the argument on how to teach it in a cross-curricular way; whether it would be more appropriate to apply it among the subject curricula than to adopt a new Informatics curriculum; if a respectful development of the curriculum according to the psychological and pedagogical principles exists already. These topics are dealing with the discussion for both theoretical and practical aspects as well as for the pedagogical and didactic perspectives.

2 LITERATURE REVIEW

Computational Thinking is a set of cognitive skills, which allows thinking like a computer scientist. Three decades ago, Seymour Papert had insight into the need for intentional education to active computer use [6]. Consequently, he developed software and tools with the aim of critical use of computers in the formal and informal context. A decade ago Jeanette Wing [10] theorised the principles and components of CT skill and its crucial role in the modern digital society. Then, in the last years, the number of publications has been growing exponentially [8] [2] [4] [9]. But, only a few studies reported which CT skills could be learned at a certain age. According to the constructivism hypotheses, children could achieve a different level of abilities at a different stage during their growth. Early primary school children are generally considered to be between the pre-operational stage and the concrete operational stage, while their thoughts move from being symbolic to being concrete, and finally, abstract (in the last formal operational stage) [7]. With his studies, Seymour Papert developed the constructionism approach, when theorising the need for learners to construct an object-to-think-with and to experience situated learning. According to PiagetâĂŹs writings, a child is more likely to be able to manage abstract thoughts after the age of ten. At the same time, Papert developed an approach based on abstracting and algorithmic thinking for younger children. Successively in [?] and [3] the authors differentiated the dimensions of CT in Abstraction, Generalization, Decomposition, Algorithms (Sequencing, Flow of control), Debugging. In order to develop a K-6 curriculum, they then described each skill, from the age of six to eight and from grade K-2 to K-6. In a very recent publication Ainley [1] highlights how complicated is to conceptualise Computer literacy, since there are many strands of definitions and each country developed its curriculum. Starting from the statement that understanding some principles of computing has educational benefits [1], a challenge could be to demonstrate how computational thinking relates empirically with computer literacy and digital literacy, as until now conceptualized. Owing to the didactic aspects, from a literature review it emerged that the most used tools are Scratch, Computer Science Unplugged, Kodu Game Lab and Python. The best-known methodological strategies are quasi-experiment, with pre and post-test design. Surveys, questionnaires and content analysis were often used in the quantitative part of a mixed methods research design.

3 PROBLEM STATEMENT

Several countries adopted and implemented Computer Science curriculum starting from primary school level. From a brief analysis of the more recent reports emerged that even if in many countries curricular and pedagogical aspects have been developed, a lack on teacher training courses and teaching/learning strategies is still observable. Furthermore, the cross-curricular aspect is often not deemed as crucial. Generally, computer science and programming

ITiCSE '19, July 15–17, 2019, Aberdeen, Scotland Uk

ACM ISBN 978-1-4503-6301-3/19/07.
https://doi.org/10.1145/3304221.3325599

courses are not included in the study plan of university courses in education, but teachers should deal with this subject. For example, they are expected to plan cross-curricular computer science activities, starting from the primary school classes, or even earlier. In addition, they should diversify the activities, to consider the individual differences and the special education needs. In many countries, a compulsory computer science curriculum has been introduced for years [4], and whilst the theoretical issues are much investigated, empirical research is lacking, above all related to the primary school. For this reason, this project aims to contribute to filling the methodological and empirical gap by presenting two possible tools (ArtecBlocks and Computational Tinkering) while exploring the possibility to adopt Agile Methodologies for didactic purposes in primary schools (K-6).

4 RESEARCH GOALS

The research project has three main goals. The first is to determine how it is possible to encourage primary school pupils to achieve Computational Thinking skills in a cross-curricular way. For this purpose, a current investigation is pursued to determine if the development of these skills can enrich the school curriculum in an interdisciplinary way and whether a gradual and progressive curricular version for compulsory school exists. Determine the relationship between CT skills and other cognitive processes is the second objective of the research. It would be investigated whether a correlation between logic skills, orientation, abstraction, divergent thinking and computational thinking skills is recognizable. The third objective aims to describe the skill(s) of Computational Thinking for each grade of school and to develop appropriate forms of evaluation. Furthermore, strategies and tools, such as ArtecBlocks and Computational Tinkering, and methods (e.g., Cooperative Thinking [5]) will be implemented to observe if pupils can become creative and active, reflecting on tools and concepts, through a meta-cognitive approach.

5 RESEARCH METHODS

In order to gather data and analyze them, a mixed-methods research design will be pursued. The ecological study is structured in respect of the action research scheme. In the first part, a selected series of tests for measuring cognitive skills are performed by children. Then, researchers and teachers carry out the intervention, choosing stories and activities that could be adapted and transformed using programming, developing algorithms, managing construction of bricks and blocks. Then, they begin with the experimentation of the digital part. This part involves the following phases: the introduction to the new learning object, discovery moments, and problem-solving activities. Afterwards, creative activities are planned, in which children should develop a storyboard and build the objects they need for the story (Tools like ArtecBlocks and Computational Tinkering will be used in this phase). The third part involves code writing, in order to program the robots and make the objects "alive". In this session, children will experience the fundamental principles of Informatics, such as managing procedures and writing algorithms, reformulating problems, restructuring processes, solving problems and abstracting. Summarizing and reflecting moments are proposed to observe the evolution of thoughts and behaviours. Contextual observations and remarks will be carried out throughout the projects. After the conclusion, in order to comprehend whether and how CT skills are related to other critical cognitive processes, the series of test will be repeated. The data analysis will be pursued comparing the first results with the second, and findings will also be interpreted qualitatively and comparatively. An examination of strengths and weaknesses will be pursued with focus group. According to the perspective of action research, a plan for a new intervention will be included and carried out.

6 CURRENT AND EXPECTED CONTRIBUTIONS

Until now, the project has been implemented for the first time, and both qualitative and quantitative data were collected. The analysis is ongoing, and it will be finished in time for a second implementation at the beginning of the next school year. Two systematic literature reviews were conducted, and one has been accepted and presented in the form of full paper at the INTED 2019 [?]. The second one is under revision for the EER Journal. They are based on an analysis of tools and methodologies used in primary schools to teach computational thinking and on a mapping of three dimensions of computational thinking (Algorithmic Thinking, Abstraction, Decomposition) related to the most used tools. Future work will aim at the mapping of the other dimensions (Generalization, Pattern recognition, Debugging) of CT related to tools and strategies and at the literature review of Agile Methodologies in K-6 level. Then, the empirical research based on the PhD project will be reported in order to prove if there is a significance between cognitive skills and CT skills and whether specific strategies and tools are more effective than others.

REFERENCES

[1] Jack Ainley. 2018. Students and Their Computer Literacy: Evidence and Curriculum Implications. In *Second Handbook of Information Technology in Primary and Secondary Education*. Springer, 69–88.

[2] Ana Liz Souto de Araujo, L. Wilkerson, Andrade, and Dalton D Serey Guerrero. 2016. A systematic mapping study on assessing computational thinking abilities. In *2016 IEEE frontiers in education conference (FIE)*. IEEE, 1–9.

[3] Andrew Fluck, Mary Webb, Margaret Cox, Charoula Angeli, Joyce Malyn-Smith, Joke Voogt, and Jason Zagami. 2016. Arguing for computer science in the school curriculum. *Educational Technology Society* 19, 3 (2016), 38–46.

[4] Varvara Garneli, Michail Giannakos, and Konstantinos Chorianopoulos. 2015. Computing education in K-12 schools: A review of the literature. In *2015 IEEE Global Engineering Education Conference (EDUCON)*. IEEE, 543–551.

[5] Marcello Missiroli, Daniel Russo, and Paolo Ciancarini. 2017. Cooperative Thinking, or: Computational Thinking meets Agile. In *2017 IEEE 30th Conference on Software Engineering Education and Training (CSEE&T)*. IEEE, 187–191.

[6] Seymour Papert. 1980. *Mindstorms: Children, computers, and powerful ideas*. Basic Books, Inc.

[7] Jean Piaget. 1953. How children form mathematical concepts. *Scientific American* 189, 5 (1953), 74–79.

[8] Kathryn Rich, Carla Strickland, and Diana Franklin. 2017. A literature review through the lens of computer science learning goals theorized and explored in research. In *Proceedings of the 2017 ACM SIGCSE Technical Symposium on Computer Science Education*. ACM, 495–500.

[9] Joke Voogt, Petra Fisser, Jon Good, Punya Mishra, and Aman Yadav. 2015. Computational thinking in compulsory education: Towards an agenda for research and practice. *Education and Information Technologies* 20, 4 (2015), 715–728.

[10] Jeannette M Wing. 2008. Computational thinking and thinking about computing. *Philosophical Transactions of the Royal Society A: Mathematical, Physical and Engineering Sciences* 366, 1881 (2008), 3717–3725.

Pattern-Oriented Instruction and its Influence on Meaningful Learning of Algorithmic Patterns and Acquiring Fundamental Skills in Computer Science

Liat Nakar
Science Teaching
Weizmann Institute of Science
Rehovot, Israel
Liat.Nakar@Weizmann.ac.il

ABSTRACT

Pattern-oriented instruction (POI) is an instructional computer science (CS) approach that relies on algorithmic patterns (APs). Teaching through APs has been shown to help students acknowledge APs and incorporate them into their solutions, thus demonstrating abstraction skills, and particularly analogical reasoning and problem decomposition. However, further research is required to examine the influence of POI in a wider context, for example, examining the influence of POI on creativity in problem solving and specifically on the diversity of the employed problem-solving strategies.

CCS CONCEPTS

• Social and professional topics→K-12 education • Social and professional topics→Computer science education

KEYWORDS

Pattern-oriented instruction; algorithmic patterns; introduction to computer science; abstraction; meaningful learning; K-12

ACM Reference format:

Liat Nakar. 2019. Pattern-Oriented Instruction and its Influence on Meaningful Learning of Algorithmic Patterns and Acquiring Fundamental Skills in Computer Science. In *Proceedings of 24th Annual ACM Conference on Innovation and Technology in Computer Science Education (ITiCSE'19).* ACM, New York, NY, USA, *2 pages.* https://doi.org/10.1145/3304221.3325601

1 CONTEXT AND MOTIVATION

Pattern-oriented instruction (POI) [10] is an instructional approach for teaching algorithmic design, usually in the context of an introductory computer science (CS) course. In POI, students are introduced to algorithmic patterns (APs) [2], which are abstractions of solutions to common algorithmic problems, such as finding the maximal value in a given sequence of values. A POI-based curriculum is arranged by APs rather than by lower algorithmic structures (such as conditional or repeated execution). This emphasizes algorithmic thinking at a high level of abstraction, knowledge organization, and problem-solving strategies [13,4]. POI has been shown to improve abstraction skills [9], analogical reasoning [6], and problem decomposition [8]. However, the research tools that were used in these studies mainly included questions that were designed to fit the APs taught to the students, thus examining only a limited sphere of potential influence.

Besides the advantages mentioned above, a problem-solving strategy that relies on patterns may also have some negative effects, rooted in the habit of constructing an algorithmic solution based on known components taken from a certain set of patterns. Can patterns also limit the learners' thinking process, interfere with trying new types of solutions and new problem-solving strategies, and make it harder for the learners to find their own abstraction approaches, which may foster new and creative solutions? In addition, I am interested in examining whether students who were taught using POI can achieve meaningful learning of APs, and in particular, whether they can transfer their knowledge to other contexts. Furthermore, I am interested in examining whether these students rely only on APs to solve their problems, or whether they develop their own algorithmic ideas when appropriate.

2 LITEATURE REVIEW

APs are a problem-solving tool. Using them to solve a problem requires recognizing the relevant patterns, adjusting them to the problem at hand, and (when necessary) integrating several patterns into one solution. APs can be integrated sequentially or by combining several APs through nesting or merging [6]. APs are cognitive schemas [12] that organize pieces of information or experience regarding a specific algorithmic problem, and make it easier to retrieve knowledge that is relevant to that problem and thus, reduce cognitive load.

Students usually find it difficult to approach a problem, analyze it, and reach a strategy for solving it [7]. POI was designed to help students with their main difficulties, such as deciding "where to start", recognizing similarities between old and new problems, and thinking of a problem at different levels of abstraction [6].

ITiCSE '19, July 15-17, 2019, Aberdeen, Scotland UK

ACM ISBN 978-1-4503-6301-3/19/07.
https://doi.org/10.1145/3304221.3325601

A pattern-based perspective for problem solving was advocated by Schoenfeld [15], who viewed mathematics as a "science of patterns". Schoenfeld emphasized the aspect of identifying and developing patterns, using observation, study, and experimentation, whereas POI emphasizes the use of known patterns. In the context of CS, Reed [14] recommended teaching problem-solving patterns such as divide-and-conquer, but these represent algorithmic approaches rather than algorithmic solutions.

3 PROBLEM STATEMENT AND RESEARCH GOALS

In this research, I will examine the outcomes of POI in a broad context, beyond the immediate use of known APs for solving problems. Specifically, I will study three aspects: 1) **Meaningful learning of algorithmic patterns**: I will focus on two facets of meaningful learning: *understanding* (in terms of Perkins [11]) AP-based problem solving, and *transferring* [1] knowledge gained by the AP-based learning process to problem solving in other contexts. 2) **Acquirement of fundamental skills of CS**: Specifically, I will examine the effects of POI regarding acquiring *abstraction* and the use of *diverse problem-solving strategies*. 3) **The effect of POI by academic level:** POI may benefit some students more than others. I intend to examine this regarding students' academic level (high- and low-CS-achieving students).

4 RESEARCH METHODS

The educational context of the research is the two introductory units of the Israeli high-school CS curriculum. These units are taught for about 180 teaching hours, divided between frontal lessons and hands-on lab lessons. Data are collected during two school years, before, during, and at the end of the learning process.

The research population consists of CS teachers and their students. The teachers are divided into three groups: 1) **POI teachers**: Teachers who already use the POI approach and have sufficient relevant pedagogical knowledge. 2) **Non-POI teachers**: Teachers who do not use APs at all, either because they are not familiar with this approach or because they chose not to adopt it. 3) **Partial-POI teachers**: Teachers who use APs partially, without any solid rationale or structured guidelines. They may present APs occasionally, but they do not systematically use them as the main tool for instruction or problem solving. Teachers in this group may differ from one another regarding their tendency to use patterns.

This is a mixed method research [3], including both qualitative and quantitative components. The data collected at the beginning of the learning process, using a CS background questionnaire and a problem-solving ability test, serves to establish a common baseline for all the classes studied. Throughout the school year, routine exams, homework, and observations will be used for data collection. Students will be interviewed about twice a year. The final exam will be used to collect post-teaching data regarding students' understanding and transfer abilities. It will include problems that are at varying distances (in terms of problem context) from the problems that the students have encountered during the learning process. Teachers will be interviewed about their teaching experience and their students' achievements, based on their own assessment.

6 RESEARCH CONTRIBUTION

This research will enhance our understanding of the effects of POI on the students' learning of algorithmic problem solving. It will expand the current body of knowledge, employing a broader perspective, regarding both the problem-solving process and the acquired CS skills. Specifically, rather than assessing outcomes using only AP-oriented problems, I will use a variety of problems, which call for a diversity of strategies and skills. In particular, I expect that the results of this study will enable refining the guidelines for employing POI that were recommended by the developers of POI [10].

The analysis process will utilize several tools that I intend to develop, which will constitute a substantial contribution. The first tool will address students' understanding. It will be based on the framework presented in [5], which combines the SOLO and Bloom's taxonomies. This combined taxonomy will be augmented to incorporate Perkins' framework of *performance of understanding* [11]. Another tool will address the aspect of transfer from the familiar context to other contexts. It will utilize a transfer scale, for measuring the distance between the contexts of problems.

REFERENCES

[1] David P. Ausubel. 1963. *The Psychology of Meaningful Verbal Learning*. Grune & Stratton. New York, NY, USA.

[2] David Ginat. 2004. Algorithmic patterns and the case of the sliding delta. *ACM SIGCSE Bulletin, 36*(2), 29-33.

[3] Burke Johnson, and Larry Christensen, 2010. *Educational Research. Quantitative, Qualitative, and Mixed Approaches*. SAGE publications. Thousand Oaks, CA, USA.

[4] Dalit Levy, and Tamar Paz. 2005. The principle of pattern-oriented curriculum and its implementation in a computer science module for high school students. In *Proceedings of the 2005 IEEE Symposium on Visual Languages and Human-Centric Computing*, 321-322.

[5] Orni Meerbaum-Salant, Michal Armoni, and Mordechai Ben-Ari. 2010. Learning computer science concepts with scratch. *Computer Science Education, 23*(3), 239-264.

[6] Orna Muller. 2005. Pattern oriented instruction and the enhancement of analogical reasoning. In *Proceedings of the first International Workshop on Computing Education Research*. 57-67.

[7] Orna Muller. 2007. The Effect of Pattern-Oriented Instruction in Computer Science on Algorithmic Problem-Solving Skills. *Unpublished doctoral dissertation, Tel Aviv University, Israel (in Hebrew)*.

[8] Orna Muller, David Ginat, and Bruria Haberman. 2007. Pattern-oriented instruction and its influence on problem decomposition and solution construction. *ACM SIGCSE Bulletin, 39*(3), 151-155.

[9] Orna Muller, and Bruria Haberman. 2008. Supporting abstraction processes in problem solving through pattern-oriented instruction. *Computer Science Education, 18*(3), 187-212.

[10] Orna Muller, Bruria Haberman, and Haim Averbuch. 2004. (An almost) pedagogical pattern for pattern-based problem-solving instruction. *ACM SIGCSE Bulletin, 36*(3), 102-106.

[11] David Perkins. 1998. What is understanding? In *Teaching for Understanding*, Martha Stone Wiske (Ed.). Jossey-Bass. New York, NY, USA, 39-57.

[12] Jean Piaget. 1964. Part I: Cognitive development in children: Piaget development and learning. *Journal of Research in Science Teaching, 2*(3), 176-186.

[13] Noa Ragonis. 2012. Integrating the teaching of algorithmic patterns into computer science teacher preparation programs. In *Proceedings of the 17th ACM Annual Conference on Innovation and Technology in Computer Science Education*. 339-344.

[14] David Reed. 1998. Incorporating problem-solving patterns in CS1. *ACM SIGCSE Bulletin, 30*(1), 6-9.

[15] Alan Schoenfeld. 2009. Learning to think mathematically: Problem solving, metacognition, and sense-making in mathematics. *Colección Digital Eudoxus*, (7).

Learning through Construction's Influence on IT Students' Identity Formation

Justyna Szynkiewicz
justyna.szynkiewicz@nord.no
NORD University
Steinkjer, Norway

ABSTRACT

This PhD work aims to understand how Learning through Construction (LtC) affects the formation of IT identity in students. A thematic qualitative study using the principles of constructivist Grounded Theory investigates what students experience in the context of LtC and how they are affected by these experiences.

CCS CONCEPTS

• **Social and professional topics → Computer science education.**

KEYWORDS

Learning through Construction, Active Learning, IT Identity, Computer Science Education

ACM Reference Format:
Justyna Szynkiewicz. 2019. Learning through Construction's Influence on IT Students' Identity Formation. In *Innovation and Technology in Computer Science Education (ITiCSE '19), July 15–17, 2019, Aberdeen, Scotland Uk.* ACM, New York, NY, USA, 2 pages. https://doi.org/10.1145/3304221.3325597

1 CONTEXT AND MOTIVATION

In recent years, there has been significant investment in the incorporation of innovative practices into higher education curricula. The center for Excellent IT Education (ExcITEd) [4] aims to strengthen the quality of higher IT education in Norway in order to increase graduates and attract better candidates through higher student engagement. ExcITEd is involved in 17 study programs at the Norwegian University of Science and Technology (NTNU) and 2 programs at NORD University. The center focuses on methods such as project-based learning (PjBL), early involvement of students in research and development activities, self-assessment, peer-assessment, and reflection for both students and teachers. This work is done as part of ExcITEd and focuses on PjBL and its influence on students' identity. Although there are studies that have provided some insights into IT students' identity development, it is still necessary to get a better understanding of how it can be influenced by project practices.

ITiCSE '19, July 15–17, 2019, Aberdeen, Scotland Uk

ACM ISBN 978-1-4503-6301-3/19/07.
https://doi.org/10.1145/3304221.3325597

2 LITERATURE REVIEW

Learning through Construction (LtC) is a recently developed concept based on PjBL and Problem Based Learning (PBL) where students often work in a group to create artifacts. In the IT discipline students often create digital artifacts like apps, websites, and digital games [11]. By creating an interesting student experience, LtC courses increase engagement and motivation for the majority of students [12].

Identity is a complex concept and there are many identity conceptualizations [6, 15, 16] as well whole books written on the subject [1, 9, 17].

Problems such as dropouts, low female recruitment and low engagement in STEM particularly in the CS discipline, have recently been investigated from the perspective of IT identity. Previous work in the field [10, 13, 14] has examined students' identity development in higher education in Computing. Identity plays a key role in the process of defining a career path as well engagement in university-related activities. The major reason for student's dropping out of CS was shown to be a "loss of interest in the computing field and career" [10] followed by "feelings of not belonging and a notion that a non-CS career would be more fulfilling" [10].

Low diversity in CS education is caused by the exclusionary nature of computing culture, not a lack of interest or inability amoung diverse learners [5]. Students expect engineering to be hands-on learning, the ones that struggle to find their place in the field experience project work as interesting and their contribution as valuable [8].

3 PROBLEM STATEMENT

Problem Statement	Research Questions
How is university students' IT-identity formed through innovative learning in IT courses?	RQ1: What is IT identity for students?
	RQ2: What influences students to pursue a higher education in IT?
	RQ3: How is the process of IT identity formation shaped by group dynamics in LtC settings?
	RQ4: How do LtC classroom settings, including stakeholder and client involvement, influence students' identity formation?

Figure 1: Problem statement and research questions

The purpose of this project is to explore the process of students' IT identity development in the context of Learning through Construction at University. The investigation is guided by the research questions presented in Figure 1.

4 RESEARCH GOALS

The goal of this exploratory work is to present students' experiences in the context of LtC and their perception of how these experiences influence their IT identity development.

The researcher intends to interpret the process of identity formation from the participants' perspective. Rather than starting with a theory, inquirers will inductively develop a theory or pattern of meaning. Presented knowledge will be co-constructed by the researcher, not discovered in the world [3].

The exploratory fashion of this research allows theory to be included at the later stages of the analysis. The author will consider analyzing the data using two different identity conceptualizations: possessive and negotiated, as suggested by Pozzer and Jackson [15].

To communicate with the CS Education community, one article per research question will be published. In Article I author aim to present the variety of students' perception about IT identity. Article II will investigate what attracts students to become part of an IT culture and students' aspirations to become IT professionals. The goal of Article III is to understand how different roles in LtC teams affect the development of IT student's identity. The author hopes to gain an understanding of the characteristics of group dynamics in LtC courses. In Article IV the author will present how the involvement of external stakeholders and clients in LtC courses influences students' identity.

The author aims to present the complexity of students' views on their IT identity with the awareness that the author's own background (personal and cultural experiences) shapes interpretation.

5 RESEARCH METHODS

This thematic qualitative study use the principles of Grounded Theory (GT) to explore the process of IT identity development as it is viewed by the participants.

Grounded Theory (GT) is a qualitative systematic research approach with the aim of developing theory in social settings. GT is based on empirical data, and it aims to present findings from participants' perspective [7]. Kathy Charmaz's [2] constructivist version of the GT approach, which guides this research, acknowledges subjectivity, researcher participation in co-construction, and interpretation of the data.

The exploratory manner of GT studies allows the author to begin research with the goal of understanding certain questions: what do the students in this context experience and how are they affected by these experiences. The author has chosen the GT methodology to allow students to express their views and experiences of LtC methods and to begin developing theories about IT identity from these data.

In-depth interviews with students, using open-ended questions, as well as course observation are the main data collection methods. Data gathering is carried out at two Norwegian public universities, NORD University and the Norwegian University of Science and Technology (NTNU). The analysis builds on interviews and observations of students from two university courses: GameLab at NORD University and Concurrent Design at NTNU.

Key elements of grounded theory will be used to analyze data. The research process will be the spiral of cycles of data collection, coding, analysis, design and theoretical categorization.

6 CONTRIBUTION

This study seeks to contribute a theory on IT students' identity formation in the context of LtC and is intended to build a framework for future research.

The research aims to inspire IT educators to include well designed PjBL practices into university courses. The author hopes that LtC practices will broaden access to restrictive computing community for diverse students who can engage in computing in an unique ways.

Hopefully participation in PjBL courses will increase student engagement and students' sense of belonging to the computing discipline at the same time as recognizing their contributions as legitimate and valued.

REFERENCES

[1] Zygmunt Bauman and Benedetto Vecchi. 2013. *Identity: Coversations With Benedetto Vecchi.* Wiley, Oxford.

[2] Kathy Charmaz. 2006. *Constructing Grounded Theory: A Practical Guide through Qualitative Analysis.* SAGE Publications.

[3] John W. Creswell and Vicki L. Plano Clark. 2017. *Designing and Conducting Mixed Methods Research.* SAGE Publications.

[4] Excited. 2019. Center for Excellent IT Education. https://www.ntnu.edu/excited

[5] Allan Fisher and Jane Margolis. 2002. Unlocking the clubhouse: the Carnegie Mellon experience. *ACM SIGCSE Bulletin* 34, 2 (2002), 79. https://doi.org/10.1145/543812.543836

[6] James Paul Gee. 2000. Identity as an Analytic Lens for Research in Education. *Review of Research in Education* 25 (2000), 99–125. https://doi.org/10.2307/1167322

[7] Barney G. Glaser and Anselm L. Strauss. 2017. *Discovery of Grounded Theory : Strategies for Qualitative Research.* Routledge. https://doi.org/10.4324/9780203793206

[8] Henriette Tolstrup Holmegaard, Lene Møller Madsen, and Lars Ulriksen. 2016. Where is the engineering I applied for? A longitudinal study of students' transition into higher education engineering, and their considerations of staying or leaving. *European Journal of Engineering Education* 41, 2 (March 2016), 154–171. https://doi.org/10.1080/03043797.2015.1056094

[9] Richard Jenkins. 1996. *Social identity.* Routledge, London ; New York.

[10] Päivi Kinnunen, Matthew Butler, Michael Morgan, Aletta Nylen, Anne-Kathrin Peters, Jane Sinclair, Sara Kalvala, and Erkki Pesonen. 2018. Understanding initial undergraduate expectations and identity in computing studies. *European Journal of Engineering Education* 43, 2 (March 2018), 201–218. https://doi.org/10.1080/03043797.2016.1146233

[11] Line Kolås, Robin Isfold Munkvold, and Ståle André Nygård. 2017. Learning through construction in IT courses. *NOKOBIT – Norsk konferanse for organisasjoners bruk av informasjonsteknologi* (2017).

[12] Robin Isfold Munkvold. 2017. Game lab: A Practical Learning Approach for Game Development. Academic Conferences International Limited, 472–479.

[13] Anne-Kathrin Peters. 2017. *Learning Computing at University: Participation and Identity: A Longitudinal Study.* Ph.D. Thesis. Uppsala University, Sweden.

[14] Anne-Kathrin Peters and Arnold Pears. 2013. Engagement in Computer Science and IT – What!: A matter of identity? (2013), 114–121. https://doi.org/10.1109/LaTiCE.2013.42

[15] Lilian L. Pozzer and Phoebe A. Jackson. 2015. Conceptualizing Identity in Science Education Research: Theoretical and Methodological Issues. In *Sociocultural Studies and Implications for Science Education.* Springer, Dordrecht, 213–230. https://doi.org/10.1007/978-94-007-4240-6_11

[16] Henri Tajfel. 1979. Individuals and groups in social psychology*. *British Journal of Social and Clinical Psychology* 18, 2 (June 1979), 183–190. https://doi.org/10.1111/j.2044-8260.1979.tb00324.x

[17] Etienne Wenger. 1998. *Communities of practice : learning, meaning, and identity.* Cambridge University Press, Cambridge.

"I Don't Know Too Much About It": On the Security Mindsets of Future Software Creators

Mohammad Tahaei
mohammad.tahaei@ed.ac.uk
School of Informatics, University of Edinburgh

ABSTRACT

Anyone can learn to code and build software these days. But the intricate and convoluted nature of computer security means that not anyone can write proper secure code. The goal of this research is to help average software developers build secure software with little understanding of security by investigating the security and privacy perceptions, experiences, and practices of current computer science students.

CCS CONCEPTS

• **Security and privacy** → *Social aspects of security and privacy; Usability in security and privacy; Software security engineering*; • **Human-centered computing** → *Empirical studies in HCI*; • **Social and professional topics** → *Computing education; Computing education programs*; • **Software and its engineering** → *Software design engineering; Software libraries and repositories.*

KEYWORDS

Usable Security; Secure Programming; Computer Science Students; Software Developers; Software Development; Education; Security APIs

ACM Reference Format:
Mohammad Tahaei. 2019. "I Don't Know Too Much About It": On the Security Mindsets of Future Software Creators. In *Innovation and Technology in Computer Science Education (ITiCSE '19), July 15–17, 2019, Aberdeen, Scotland, UK.* ACM, New York, NY, USA, 1 page. https://doi.org/10.1145/3304221.3325592

1 MOTIVATION AND BACKGROUND

Software developers have a great deal of power to impact millions of lives with seemingly small decisions which can then have a large impact on the people using the technologies. One example is the case of the dating site Ashley Madison, where a strong cryptographic algorithm was used to store passwords but unfortunately was implemented incorrectly [5]. Basic tools such as cryptographic libraries (OpenSSL) and federated authentication (OAuth) exist partially to assist developers in integrating common security needs into their projects without needing to know all the complex details. There are also efforts to help raise awareness of common coding and design issues such as the IEEE top ten security flaws [2].

Yet, security remains a pervasive problem in deployed code. In 2013 alone, 88% of apps (out of 11,748) analysed on Google Play had at least one mistake in how the developer used a cryptographic API [3]. Non-usable APIs are a key point of failure for most developers [4, 6]. The situation is exacerbated when developers make non-obvious errors when implementing security which results in believing that code is secure when it is actually not secure [1]. The problem is a combination of the tool and the developer's misunderstanding. One potential opportunity for changing developers' security attitudes and practices is during their training. Our research questions are:

- What are computer science (CS) students' mindsets of security and privacy (SP) and security-related concepts?
- To what extent do CS students consider SP while coding, and how do they implement it?

2 METHODOLOGY AND PROGRESS

In this work, we investigate the SP mindsets of a group of twenty graduate and undergraduate *CS students* on a variety of career trajectories, and with a range of exposure to formal security training with semi-structured interviews.

Within the context of *developer-centred security*, our study highlights the extent to which both graduate and undergraduate students already have similar mindsets and practices observed in professional developers, suggesting that these may form and consolidate early. We conclude that, while early educational intervention would be ideal, we also need to provide developers with usable tools, such as APIs, and easily accessible training, which can be used both by trainees and by professionals.

REFERENCES

[1] Y. Acar, M. Backes, S. Fahl, S. Garfinkel, D. Kim, M. L. Mazurek, and C. Stransky. 2017. Comparing the Usability of Cryptographic APIs. In *2017 IEEE Symposium on Security and Privacy (SP)*. 154–171.
[2] Y. Acar, C. Stransky, D. Wermke, C. Weir, M. L. Mazurek, and S. Fahl. 2017. Developers Need Support, Too: A Survey of Security Advice for Software Developers. In *2017 IEEE Cybersecurity Development (SecDev)*. 22–26.
[3] M. Egele, D. Brumley, Y. Fratantonio, and C. Kruegel. 2013. An Empirical Study of Cryptographic Misuse in Android Applications. In *Proc. of the 2013 ACM SIGSAC Conference on Computer; Communications Security (CCS '13)*. ACM, 73–84.
[4] M. Green and M. Smith. 2016. Developers are Not the Enemy!: The Need for Usable Security APIs. *IEEE Security Privacy* 14, 5 (Sep. 2016), 40–46.
[5] S. Mansfield-Devine. 2015. The Ashley Madison Affair. *Netw. Secur.* 2015, 9 (Sept. 2015), 8–16.
[6] G. Wurster and P. C. van Oorschot. 2008. The Developer is the Enemy. In *Proc. of the 2008 New Security Paradigms Workshop (NSPW '08)*. ACM, 89–97.

ITiCSE '19, July 15–17, 2019, Aberdeen, Scotland, UK

ACM ISBN 978-1-4503-6301-3/19/07.
https://doi.org/10.1145/3304221.3325592

Utilising Game Design to Create Engaging Education

A framework for Gameful Learning

David Williams
ICT Faculty
Dublin Business School
Dublin, Ireland.
david.williams@dbs.ie

ABSTRACT

If educators were to be skilled game designers, then they would be better equipped to design engaging education scenarios. This research engages in studying commercial design of engagement in games, so educators may be able to better facilitate engaging educational design, facilitated through quantified engagement metrics (SCEQ) and game design principles (GameFlow).

CCS CONCEPTS

• CCS Concept: Social and professional topics → Student assessment
• CCS Concept: Applied computing → Education

KEYWORDS

ACM proceedings; Education; Framework; Gamification; Game Development; Flow; MDA; Pedagogy; Engagement.

ACM Reference format:
David Williams. 2019. Utilising Game Design to Create Engaging Education: A framework for Gameful Learning. In *Proceedings of Annual Conference on Innovation and Technology in Computer Science Education of ACM Annual SIG Conference (ITiCSE'19), July 15–17, 2019, Aberdeen, Scotland UK.* ACM, NY, NY, USA, 2 pages. https://doi.org/10.1145/3304221.3325594

1 CONTEXT AND MOTIVATION

In commercial game design, player engagement if a key factor for measuring success. Identified on occasion as flow [1], the balance between tedium and frustration. The games industry has become heavily dissected by academia in the search to find relatable methods to increase learner engagement [2]. Thus far however there is a visible disparity between industry standards and academic approaches.

Considering the gaming element of rewards for example, an often misunderstood concept, if we recognise that not all students are motivated by the same rewards [3]. The games industry has identified the potential negative influence of points or scores and have adapted to eliminate these as the focus of a lot of titles [4]. A fundamental principle of this research is that a focus on ludology [5] and game design principles as a tool for building are essential. Current research into games is based on dissecting games the medium to understand the principles of what make them effective [6]–[8]. Yet the game developers are using principles of game design as the method to construct their products from the first iteration. It is proposed that instead of deconstructed games, educational design would benefit from creating their material from the game design principles. This research is grounded in this approach, providing measurable outcomes in response to create a gameful engagement scenario.

ITiCSE '19, July 15–17, 2019, Aberdeen, Scotland UK

ACM ISBN 978-1-4503-6301-3/19/07.
https://doi.org/10.1145/3304221.3325594

2 LITERATURE REVIEW

Viewing education as a journey with knowledge as the destination, would be comparable to the experience of a game, exams and practical are game challenges, learning outcomes are win conditions, and as in games the aim is to change the player/learner over the journey.

It has been thoroughly studied as to why students may want to learn. In adult learning or andragogy for example it is proposed that adult learners learn due to two intrinsic factors. They want to or they need to [9], motivation is a key factor for engagement in education. This is true in the field of videogame development as to what makes a player want to play a game [10]–[12]. As such there is growing interest in the means to leverage motivational methods used in videogames within education.

A core challenge facing this transfer of motivational methods is that games, although natural learning environments fail once they no longer feel like a game [13]. The idea that a game must feel like a game [14] is not new and a lack of understanding in attempting to implement games scenarios without the core knowledge of game design can result in a contrived game environment, as most game designers will state that the game is not the experience, but rather the means to achieve the experience.

Gee and Hayes [15], who have also stated that although there is a current popular desire to allow students to develop without guidance, that this can allow students to get misdirected into answering the wrong questions, where they may find good answers, it is the role of the educator to direct the learning, as it is the role of the game designer to make sure the player finds the end of the game and completes a journey. In recent years many researchers have investigated potential frameworks for implementing gameful learning scenarios [16], [17] with many focusing on the impact these designs have on participant engagement. In game design, MDA [18] is an iterative approach to design and tuning, allowing game designers to anticipate how changes will impact each aspect of development within the framework and the resulting implementations.

3 HYPOTHESIS

This study is an investigation of the potential for educators to leverage game design mechanisms, proposing that educators would then be better equipped in designing engaging education. Subsequently this research aims to offer a framework for designing educational scenarios, based around a core principle: we must stop being educators dissecting and borrowing game elements, but rather that we are game designers building educational scenarios by mapping engagement using established game development formats like that of Mechanics, Dynamics & Aesthetics (MDA) [19]. and Flow [20] to established engagement metrics such as the Student Course Engagement Questionnaire (SCEQ) [21] providing a quantifiable outcome for use in class design.

4 RESEARCH GOALS

The primary research goal is to develop a practical framework for designing engaging classroom content that can be measured. To achieve this, secondary research goals were undertaken.

This was firstly approached by identifying appropriate game design mechanisms to apply to classroom design strategies. Whilst examining learning environments to identify measures of engagement, testing unobtrusive and unbiased observation methods of monitoring. Secondly the quantifying and approximating engagement metrics were evaluated and aligned with game design principles in live learning environment. Finally aspiring to derive scenarios where the framework could enhance, extend and improve student engagement though the application of design principles.

5 RESEARCH METHODS

The SCEQ [21] was administered, as an observational non-manipulative design, to undergraduate students in semester 1. Data was collected for the last 6 weeks of the first semester for all enrolled students.

Examining a sample snapshot of the Students sample in week 1 the Kaiser-Meyer-Olkin measure of sampling adequacy was 0.837, and the significance of the Bartlett's test of sphericity was <0.0001 – these two statistics confirm that the exploratory factor analysis technique was appropriate to use on the data.

In week 2 for the Students the Kaiser-Meyer-Olkin measure of sampling adequacy was 0.778, and the significance of the Bartlett's test of sphericity was <0.0001 confirming that the exploratory factor analysis technique was appropriate. Spearman's Rank Order Correlation for week 1 and 2 is .481 indicating a Moderate positive relationship. The student focus visibly shifts between weeks, utilising the factor descriptions a higher focus on the Emotional Engagement in week 2 in the first factor.

6 CONTRIBUTIONS

In quantifying metrics engagement, a precedent is established to justify altering the gameful scenario through controlled mechanics. It is proposed that in mapping game based heuristics, like that of GameFlow [4] to the engagement metrics a quantifiable design approaches to classroom engagement in achievable.

REFERENCES

[1] M. Csikszentmihalyi, S. Abuhamdeh, and J. Nakamura, "Flow," in *Flow and the Foundations of Positive Psychology: The Collected Works of Mihaly Csikszentmihalyi*, 2014.

[2] E. Bonsignore, V. Moulder, C. Neustaedter, D. Hansen, K. Kraus, and A. Druin, "Design Tactics for Authentic Interactive Fiction: Insights from Alternate Reality Game Designers," *Proc. 32nd Annu. ACM Conf. Hum. factors Comput. Syst. - CHI '14*, pp. 947–950, 2014.

[3] J. R. Veltsos, "Gamification in the Business Communication Course," *Bus. Prof. Commun. Q.*, vol. 80, no. 2, pp. 194–216, 2017.

[4] P. Sweetser, D. Johnson, A. Ozdowska, and P. Wyeth, "GameFlow heuristics for designing and evaluating real-time strategy games," 2012.

[5] J. Raessens, "Playful Identities, or the Ludification of Culture," *Games Cult.*, vol. 1, no. 1, pp. 52–57, 2006.

[6] J. P. Gee, E. Hayes, R. J. Torres, A. Games, K. R. Squire, and K. Salen, "Playing to learn game design skills in a game context," *ICLS'08 Proc. 8th Int. Conf. Int. Conf. Learn. Sci. - Vol. 3*, vol. 3, pp. 368–374, 2008.

[7] D. Dicheva, C. Dichev, G. Agre, and G. Angelova, "Gamification in Education: A Systematic Mapping Study Gamification in Education: A Systematic Mapping Study," *Educ. Technol. Soc.*, vol. 18, no. June, pp. 75–88, 2015.

[8] J. Downs, F. Vetere, S. Howard, and S. Loughnan, "Audience experience in social videogaming: effects of turn expectation and game physicality," *CHI '14 Proc. SIGCHI Conf. Hum. Factors Comput. Syst.*, pp. 3473–3482, 2014.

[9] M. S. Knowles, "Andragogy in Action: Applying Modern Principles of Adult Learning," *WebRef*, vol. 56, p. 707, 2003.

[10] N. Lazzaro, "Why We Play Games: Four Keys to More Emotion Without Story," *Game Dev. Conf.*, pp. 1–8, 2004.

[11] M. Tanis and J. Jansz, "Gaming for Different Reasons: What Motivates People to Play a Specific Video Game?," *Conf. Pap. -- Int. Commun. Assoc.*, pp. 1–26, 2008.

[12] J. Hamari, L. Keronen, and K. Alha, "Why do people play games? A review of studies on adoption and use," in *Proceedings of the Annual Hawaii International Conference on System Sciences*, 2015, vol. 2015–March, pp. 3559–3568.

[13] T. Bissell, *Extra Lives why video games matter*, First. Random House, 2010.

[14] J. H. Murray, "Toward a Cultural Theory of Gaming: Digital Games and the Co-Evolution of Media, Mind, and Culture," *Popular Communication*, vol. 4, no. 3. pp. 185–202, 2006.

[15] J. P. Gee and E. R. Hayes, *Language and Learning in the Digital Age*, First. USA: Routledge, 2011.

[16] O. Dele-Ajayi, J. Sanderson, R. Strachan, and A. Pickard, "Learning mathematics through serious games: An engagement framework," *Proc. - Front. Educ. Conf. FIE*, vol. 2016–Novem, 2016.

[17] L. Cooke, "Metatuning: A pedagogical framework for a generative STEM education in game design-based learning," *ISEC 2016 - Proc. 6th IEEE Integr. STEM Educ. Conf.*, pp. 207–214, 2016.

[18] R. Hunicke, M. Leblanc, and R. Zubek, "MDA: A Formal Approach to Game Design and Game Research."

[19] R. Hunicke, Robin; LeBlanc, Marc; Zubek, "MDA: A Formal Approach to Game Design And Game Research," *Work. Challenges Game AI*, 2004.

[20] M. Csikszentmihalyi, "Flow and the Foundations of Positive Psychology," pp. 21–35, 2014.

[21] M. M. Handelsman, W. L. Briggs, N. Sullivan, and A. Towler, "A Measure of College Student Course Engagement," *J. Educ. Res.*, 2005.

Direct Manipulation versus Text-based Programming

An experiment report

Michel Adam
Université Bretagne Sud
Vannes, France
Michel.Adam@univ-ubs.fr

Moncef Daoud
Université Bretagne Sud
Lorient, France
Moncef.Daoud@univ-ubs.fr

Patrice Frison
IRISA lab - Université Bretagne Sud
Vannes, France
Patrice.Frison@univ-ubs.fr

ABSTRACT

The standard approach to programming is to learn a programming language, write a program in a development environment, compile it, and run it to check how it works. Another approach is possible using direct manipulation programming. This approach makes it possible to directly manipulate the programming objects (variables, arrays, indices) to implement a given algorithm and to automatically produce the corresponding program. In this paper, we report on the results of an experiment that we performed to compare the standard approach with direct manipulation programming. The experiment was conducted with an audience of 54 beginner students divided into 2 groups. The first group programmed with Python Tutor and the second with AlgoTouch, a direct manipulation programming tool. In this article, we present the experience and detail the results obtained.

CCS CONCEPTS

• **Applied computing → Education; Interactive learning environments; • Social and professional topics → Computing education.**

KEYWORDS

programming by direct manipulation, programming for beginners, designing algorithms, visualization of algorithms

ACM Reference Format:
Michel Adam, Moncef Daoud, and Patrice Frison. 2019. Direct Manipulation versus Text-based Programming: An experiment report. In *Innovation and Technology in Computer Science Education (ITiCSE '19), July 15–17, 2019, Aberdeen, Scotland UK*. ACM, New York, NY, USA, 7 pages. https://doi.org/10.1145/3304221.3319738

1 INTRODUCTION

In many countries, programming is now taught to students from primary school to high school. The purpose is not to train programmers, but to discover the concepts of algorithm, program, coding of information, and operation of computers. These concepts are the bases for teaching a programming course according to the France Computer Society [16].

Many approaches have been proposed to teach programming. In this paper, we consider 3 categories: unplugged activities, visual programming, and textual programming.

The main goal of unplugged activities [2] is to demonstrate the steps of an algorithm through a sequence of human actions. The idea is to show that an algorithm describes a sequence of specific operations to be carried out in order to achieve a given goal. There are multiple advantages to this method since on the one hand, it can be illustrated by many concrete examples of daily life and on the other hand, it is quite simple to implement with inexpensive equipment (eg playing cards, goblets, strings, or ordinary objects). We can simulate the operation of an algorithm by asking a person to perform the actions written on a paper (see [20], [6], [14], [1], [8], [15] for experiments at different levels of education).

However, this approach is tedious, can lead to mistakes and cannot replace the experience of actually programming. It is then necessary to transform the algorithm so that it becomes a program executable by a computer. However, the transition to the programming activity is difficult [10]. Many obstacles must be overcome: learn a programming language (whose syntax is sometimes complex), and then use a programming environment to write the code, compile, run and debug. Several tools have been developed to minimize these difficulties for novices, such as ScratchJr[1], Scratch[2] and Alice[3]. These tools make it possible to carry out programs by simply animating characters. ScratchJr can be used by young children, allowing them to illustrate the notions of displacement and repetition, but does not provide conditional operators. Scratch and Alice, open many more possibilities. The user builds a program by assembling blocks representing instructions. Blocks have shapes similar to elements of a puzzle so that assembling the blocks is only possible if the blocks are compatible. The resulting program is therefore always syntactically correct and executable. On the other hand, creating this program is sometimes tedious because some operations require many manipulations. For example, a conditional statement like `if x < 0` needs to select the `IF THEN ELSE` block, then choose the comparison operator (less than <), then set the left operand (`x`), then the right operand (here the constant `0`).

Scratch and Alice are oriented towards building animation programs. In addition to the concepts found in basic programming (variables, arrays, assignment, operations, conditions, iterations, functions and procedures), the designers have added many features for animation and interaction.

[1] http://www.scratchjr.org
[2] http://scratch.mit.edu
[3] http://www.alice.org

ITiCSE '19, July 15–17, 2019, Aberdeen, Scotland UK

ACM ISBN 978-1-4503-6301-3/19/07...$15.00
https://doi.org/10.1145/3304221.3319738

In the case of traditional programming languages, most of the time, the programmer uses a text editor to write the program. However, these editors are integrated into environments that facilitate the writing of programs (Eclipse[4] was one of the precursors). Thus, many errors are detected during the editing phase. For execution, these tools typically provide a debugger to control the execution of the program (execution step by step, line by line, breakpoint, display of variables, etc.). Other environments offer what is called "live programming". The principle of these systems is that the program being edited runs continuously. Each modification of the program is therefore immediately taken into account. These environments are usually coupled to a visualization system so that the programmer can see the results. Hundhausen was a forerunner in this field with Alvis Live [11]. He introduced the concept: " What You See Is What You Code ". Alvis Live uses a dedicated language. More recently, P.Guo introduced Python Tutor [9], a tool for editing and for visualizing the operation of the Python language. Now, this system can be used also with other languages (Java, C, C++, JavaScript, Ruby). The distinguishing feature of this system is that it allows you to write code directly from a web browser, and view its execution.

However, even if these environments make it easier for beginners, the major problem remains the writing of the program. As C.Boisvert points out [3], writing a program follows a process that is rarely described in textbooks or courses. Indeed, in general, the principle of an algorithm is given, then its operation is often illustrated through a visualization system (see [19] for a bibliographic study) and finally the code is shown directly. On the other hand, experience shows that learners often have white page syndrome when it comes to translating an algorithm into a computer program. As noted by Hundhausen [12], the creator of Alvis Live, even with specific environments, novices "had trouble constructing correct loops, and referencing array elements correctly within those loops through the use of array indices".

Besides the three approaches explained above (unplugged, visual and textual), another method for the teaching of programming is called direct manipulation programming. In such a system, the user performs concrete actions on the application data, and the system automatically builds the associated program. Quite a few systems have been developed on this model since it was first proposed in 1991 [5, 13, 17, 18]. We used one of them, called AlgoTouch [7], developed since 2014.

In a first step, the learner implements an algorithm by manipulating programming elements such as variables, operators, conditional, arrays, like in the context of an unplugged activity. In a second step, having found that some operations are repeated, these operations are recorded so that they can be repeated automatically. The tool is responsible for creating the corresponding instructions. The complete program is thus built gradually by recording its different parts.

Up to now, teaching programming in our University uses the traditional text-based approach. The direct manipulation approach is recent and has not been compared with other methods. The purpose of this paper is to compare these two approaches. We present an experiment involving beginner students separated into two groups in making simple programs with these two different approaches. At first, all the students follow the same introductory programming course illustrated for one group with Python and for others with the AlgoTouch direct manipulation approach. Then, students will program with Python Tutor or AlgoTouch. In this paper we wish to answer the following questions:

- is the direct manipulation programming approach as effective as a standard text-based approach?
- what are the benefits and drawbacks for the learners in using the direct manipulation approach?

In the rest of this article, we present the two tools used for the study in more detail: Python Tutor and AlgoTouch. Then we describe the experiment conducted and the results obtained.

2 TOOLS

In this section we briefly present the tools used for the experiment. As a standard language we used Python. Actually, in recent years, Python has been chosen as a preferred language for CS1 courses across many universities all over the world. In industry too, Python is getting very popular. In our experiment we used only basic notions of programming of the Python language, so it is quite easy to learn.

Python Tutor is a widely-used code visualization and collaborative learning platform. It's been used by millions of people all over the world to visualize millions of pieces of code according to P.Guo[5]. Python Tutor was chosen for its ease of implementation because it only needs a web browser and its simplicity of use since the interface is quite explicit.

To our knowledge, the AlgoTouch system is the only manipulation programming tool we could use. It is easy to implement by launching a Java jar file and easy to use through direct manipulation interaction.

For our experiment, we chose an instruction subset common to both tools: variables, assignments, alternative, iteration, array. Indeed, these notions form the basis of the teaching of programming.

2.1 PyThon Tutor

Python Tutor is an editor/viewer program that can be used with a Web browser. The interface illustrated in Figure 1 is composed of 4 zones: an editing zone, the program execution control zone, an area for displaying the execution results and the program data display zone.

In practice, a programmer will write the program then start its execution. The execution control area contains buttons allowing code execution either line by line, or fully. It is also possible to go back one line or at the beginning of the program. At the same time, the data display area displays the data (global or local variables, arrays, lists). So, the programmer can follow the evolution of the program.

Note that Python Tutor offers other features not described here since they have not been used. Figure 1 shows an example of a completed program. It's a classical example of a dichotomic search in an array. The program uses an array `t` and five variables `n, val, left, med` and `right` where `n` is the size of the array, `val` is the

[4]https://www.eclipse.org

[5]http://pythontutor.com/

value to search for and `left, med, right` are used to index the array `t`. These data are updated as the program evolves.

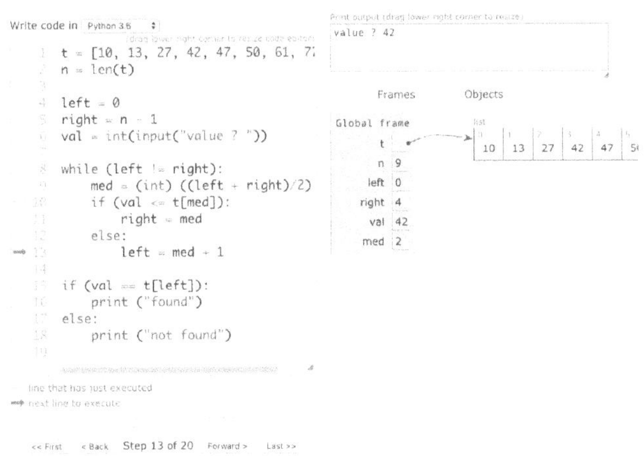

Figure 1: Python Tutor user interface

2.2 AlgoTouch

AlgoTouch uses the metaphor of the blackboard, that is to say the direct manipulation on the screen of programming objects (variables, arrays, indices). By simple gestures, the user can move these elements, drag and drop values into memory boxes (variables or arrays), increase index values, make comparisons, perform basic operations (addition, subtraction, multiplication, division). Furthermore, it allows one to record a sequence of actions, then to replay the recorded sequence, and finally to complete the construction of the algorithm by recording the different parts of the program. In fact, when the recording mode is activated, a program is created and produced as one "plays" with the elements of the algorithm. The system also handles conditional instructions, loops and macros [7].

The AlgoTouch environment screen consists of five areas as shown in figure 2: (1) the design area where the manipulation of elements occurs; (2) the console area used by the system for displaying information to the user; (3) the toolbox area with buttons; (4) the system area to manipulate the project file; and (5) the zone for displaying the generated program.

Designing a program with AlgoTouch requires a radically different approach from the standard one. The design area is where the variables, arrays, indexes and macros (explained later) are displayed and manipulated. The console area displays the instructions produced when elements are manipulated. This can be useful for users who use the tool for the first time, to view basic instructions associated with handling the objects. The toolbox area contains buttons for commands: mainly to create objects (a variable, an array of elements or an index) and for the control of execution (start the recording, stop the recording, replay the recorded sequence, save the output case, display a comparator or run the algorithm). The system area has a menu bar for managing the project being created: backup, open, create, and export the program. The program area

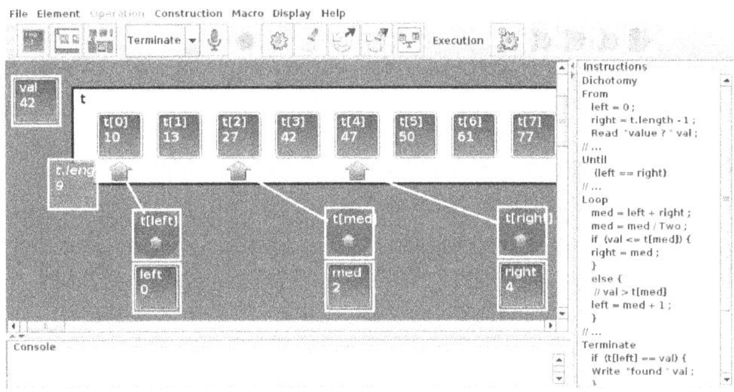

Figure 2: AlgoTouch user interface

(labeled "Instructions") contains the code produced by the user's manipulations, when recording mode is activated.

The generated code is a named macro. A macro is either a simple sequence of instructions, or an iteration with four parts: initialization (`From`), exit conditions (`Until`), a body (`Loop`) and a termination (`Terminate`).

Figure 2 shows the result of the creation of a program of dichotomic search. The program, automatically produced piece by piece, is comparable to the Python program of the figure 1. We have intentionally used the same variable names, except `n` replaced by the constant `t.length`.

2.3 Similarities and differences

These tools take two different approaches since Python Tutor allows to write a program and visualize its data while conversely, AlgoTouch allows to manipulate the data to create a program. Like Python Tutor, AlgoTouch also allows execution control with data visualization when the full program has been built.

Note that with AlgoTouch, tracking the value of a variable in an array is visual since the indexes are marked by arrows. In the example of figure 2, we easily find the value of `t[med]`, while this is not the case with Python Tutor. Indeed, as shown in figure 1, to find the value of `t[med]`, it is necessary to find the value of `med`, then look for the associated value in the array `t`. When you want to follow the evolution of the program with Python Tutor, this is rather tedious, while it's obvious with AlgoTouch.

Another difference between the two tools is the testing of the current program. AlgoTouch offers the ability to test pieces of the program during construction. For example, when the body of a loop has been created, the user can run that body several times to verify that the program iterates correctly. With Python Tutor, this is not possible, except to instrument the program by introducing additional instructions that must be removed later.

3 EXPERIMENT

We set up an experiment with first year students from an institute of technology. These new students, with different backgrounds, have a priori little or no knowledge and experience in programming. The experiment took place in several phases. The first phase involved the evaluation of knowledge via a questionnaire for 105 students before the start of the programming course. The second phase concerned the experiment with 54 selected students, divided into two homogeneous groups of the same level, one to work with AlgoTouch and the other with Python Tutor.

3.1 Preliminary evaluation of knowledge

The evaluation concerns the entire class of 105 students. It is based on a questionnaire and exercises. The questionnaire allows us to know if they have heard of the concepts of unplugged activities, of algorithms and which programming languages they "know". Then, a test exercise sequence was proposed. Participants are asked to write programs to enable us to better evaluate their level. Indeed, programming in high school is not mandatory, and thus the level of students is therefore very variable. The choice of the programming language was free. The evaluation focused on the logic of the program and not on the syntax. The series of exercises aims at verifying the acquisition of the following notions:

Sequence: enter 2 integers, calculate and display the average;
Alternative: enter 2 integers and display the greatest;
Iteration: display the numbers from 1 to n;
Iteration: enter a yes/no answer;
Array: shift the values of an array by one position.

The correction of the evaluation made it possible to select a sample of 54 students who have not been successful in the exercises. They were divided in two groups of homogeneous level. Students who have never programmed have been distributed equally in both groups. The other students were evenly distributed by skill level. The two groups were named *Py* for Python and *Agt* for AlgoTouch.

3.2 Programming Session

In a first stage, for a duration of one hour, each group took an introductory course in programming. The course content is the same for both groups. This course introduces the following basic concepts: variable, assignment, alternative, iteration, array and index. It is illustrated by the corresponding tool, AlgoTouch or Python Tutor. To explain how to create an iteration, we proposed a common method that consists of first creating the body of the loop, then defining the exit conditions and finally, programming the initialization and termination instructions.

In a second stage, lasting 30 minutes, the students learned how to use the tools. Finally, in a third stage, a session of two hours and 30 minutes of practical work was scheduled. The experiment involved the implementation of nine programs with a goal set for each exercise, as shown in the table 1. The first four exercises focus on basic programming concepts: variables, assignments, arithmetic operations, conditions, input and output. Usually these types of exercises are not difficult for the students but programming them is a necessary step for discovering the tools and creating a program for both groups. The other five exercises are dedicated to iteration starting on simple variables and then on arrays (indexed variables).

4 RESULTS

The analysis of the results is based on the programs uploaded to the university learning platform. We evaluated the exercises one after the other by applying the same criteria to judge the correctness of the programs submitted by the students. To correct the exercises we have used only three increasing levels:

Table 1: Exercises to program

Ex	Name and description	Notions to validate
Ex1	Swap: swap the values of 2 variables x and y	variable, assignment, print, execution
Ex2	Average: calculate the average of 3 variables a, b, c initialized	arithmetic operation, print
Ex3	Order: enter 2 values and display the smallest and the largest	read, condition
Ex4	FQ: enter the number of adults and children of a family, then calculate a value depending on these numbers (family-quotient)	read, condition, arithmetic operation
Ex5	GCD: calculate the GCD of 2 numbers	iteration (body, exit condition, initialisation)
Ex6	Power: calculate x to the power of n	iteration (body, exit condition, initialisation)
Ex7	Add1: increment the values of an array by 1	array, index, iteration
Ex8	Even: fill an array with successive even numbers (0,2,4,6,8, ...)	array, index, iteration
Ex9	Reverse: reverse the contents of an array (without using an intermediate array)	array, index, iteration

- Done: the student has uploaded the exercise, but it is not necessarily completed, nor operational;
- Goal: the objectives associated with the exercise are achieved, but the program may not be fully operational;
- Correct: the program is fully operational, the objectives are achieved and the results are in accordance to the specifications.

Minor issues related to optimization or display, for example, are not considered because they do not affect the execution. To illustrate the difference between achieved objectives (Goals) and expected results (Correct) let us take 3 examples:

- The objective of exercise 2 was to calculate the average of 3 numbers. In one case, a student accumulated the 3 values but divided the result by 2 instead of 3. It was considered that the objective was reached but that the program did not give the expected result (not Correct).
- For exercise 4, it was necessary to program a conditional statement with the computation of formulas in each branch. Several students have set up the conditional, but the implementation of the formulas was wrong.
- The objective of exercise 6 was to calculate x to the power n. Several students failed to treat the `n = 0` case described in the specification.

Table 2 gives the final results, for both tools and by category of exercises. Considering for example exercise 8, the table indicates that for the *Agt* group, 20 students have uploaded the exercise, but only 17 achieved the goals assigned to it and finally only 12 produced a correct program. The percentage of exercises who satisfied one of the three levels is calculated either related to the total number of exercises (Rate 1) or to the total number of uploaded exercises (Rate 2).

4.1 Interpretation of results

The analysis of the results of all the proposed exercises (see table 2) shows that we obtain for the AlgoTouch tool slightly higher rates than those of Python Tutor for the Goal and for the expected result (Correct). For Rate 1, AlgoTouch demonstrated a small advantage compared to Python Tutor: 3.7% for the Goal and 2.06% for the expected result (Correct). The Rate 2 difference was more pronounced in favor of AlgoTouch by 9.83% for the Goal and 7.26% for the expected result (Correct). The students of the *Agt* group have submitted fewer exercises, but the results are better in proportion at both Goal and Correct levels.

Table 2: Results for each exercise proposed to each group of 27 students (total of 243)

Tool	AlgoTouch			Python Tutor		
Students	27			27		
Ex	Done	Goal	Correct	Done	Goal	Correct
Ex1	27	27	27	27	23	23
Ex2	26	25	24	27	27	26
Ex3	27	24	24	27	27	23
Ex4	24	22	14	26	24	24
Ex5	23	23	23	26	18	18
Ex6	19	18	11	17	13	9
Ex7	23	20	18	24	21	21
Ex8	20	17	12	21	18	8
Ex9	12	10	10	19	6	6
Total	201	186	163	214	177	158
Rate 1	82,72%	76,54%	67,08%	88,07%	72,84%	65,02%
Rate 2		92,54%	81,09%		82,71%	73,83%

Students who used Python Tutor might seem to have an advantage because they already knew the traditional approach to reading or writing programs. Yet, students using AlgoTouch, while discovering a new approach to program building, have achieved similar or even slightly better results.

To complete our study, and knowing that learners have especially difficulties with iterations, we separated the exercises without iteration from those with iteration. The results are analyzed in the following sections.

4.2 Exercises without iterations: Ex1 to Ex4

For the first category of exercises (Ex1 to Ex 4) without iteration and requiring only a sequence of calculation instructions, the rates are quite good for both tools (see table 3). For the Python Tutor tool, we obtain slightly higher or almost similar rates to those of the AlgoTouch tool for the Goal as well as the expected result (Correct).

For Rate 1, the analysis confirms a minimal difference that favors Python Tutor of 2.78% for the Goal and 6.48% for the expected result (Correct). On the other hand, Rate 2 with an advantage to Python

Table 3: Exercises Ex1 to Ex4 without iteration: 4 exercises for each of the 27 students (total of 108)

Tool	AlgoTouch			Python Tutor		
	Done	Goal	Correct	Done	Goal	Correct
Total	104	98	89	107	101	96
Rate 1	96,30%	90,74%	82,41%	99,07%	93,52%	88,89%
Rate 2		94,23%	85,58%		94,39%	89,72%

Tutor, is almost similar for the Goal with a negligible difference of 0.16%, but more accentuated by 4.14% for the expected result (Correct).

It should be noted that these exercises are more suitable and easy to perform under Python Tutor. This is explained on the one hand by the possibility of performing a calculation with several operators in a single instruction and on the other hand, the ease of writing conditional instructions. In particular for exercise 4, students in the *Py* group outperformed those in the *Agt* group by 24 correct programs against 14. Indeed, in this exercise, the following formula had to be computed: `FQ=nbA+2+(nbC-2)/2` where `nbA` and `nbC` are respectively the numbers of adults and children. With Python, the students had only to copy the formula whereas under AlgoTouch, they had to decompose the formula using only one operator at a time. Regarding the writing of conditional statements, remember that AlgoTouch first requires the recording of the operations of the "then" clause and then, at runtime, the creation of the code missing from the "else" clause.

4.3 Exercises with iterations: Ex5 to Ex9

The second category of exercises proposed with iteration (Ex5 to Ex9), includes well known computation exercises (GCD by the subtractive method, power) and exercises for processing a collection of data of increasing degree of difficulty (see table 1).

Table 4: Exercises Ex5 to Ex9 with iteration: 5 exercises for each of the 27 students (total of 135)

Tool	AlgoTouch			Python Tutor		
	Done	Goal	Correct	Done	Goal	Correct
Total	97	88	74	107	76	62
Rate 1	71,85%	65,19%	54,81%	79,26%	56,30%	45,93%
Rate 2		90,72%	76,29%		71,03%	57,94%

The analysis of the results obtained (cf table 4) shows that the success (Goal) and validity (Correct) rates of the programs realized with the AlgoTouch tool are higher than those of the Python Tutor tool. For the Rate 1, a difference of the order of 8.8% which gives an advantage to AlgoTouch for both the Goal and the validity (Correct). For the Rate 2, a significantly higher difference in favour of AlgoTouch of 17.69% for the Goal and 18.35% for the validity (Correct).

The results show that students completed fewer exercises (97 against 107) but that the results are better. There are two reasons for this. On the one hand, a time of adaptation is necessary for learning and manipulation of the AlgoTouch tool, which generates a slower progression for the *Agt* group, and therefore this translates into a slight decrease in number of exercises completed. On the other hand, we find that the AlgoTouch method of loop construction described below and taught to the students is easier for them to implement and yields a better success rate:

- first think about the body of the loop. The user can record the operations of the loop then test it to check its operation;
- define the exit condition. By running the loop body several times, the user can determine and select an appropriate exit condition and thus record it;
- set the initialization instructions. Once the body of the iteration is created, users are able to easily determine appropriate initial values to be assigned to the variables.

With Python, the exercise is more abstract: you usually have to write the whole program by thinking of all the cases and then test it.

For the exercises addressing arrays (Ex7 to Ex9), the program debugging is facilitated with AlgoTouch through the use of visual indexes that point to values in the array. Note that for Exercise 9, although the number of programs uploaded in *Agt* group is lower than that of the *Py* group, 10 AlgoTouch programs are correct against 6 in PythonTutor.

5 CONCLUSION

We conducted a first experiment to evaluate the viability of the direct manipulation approach compared to the standard programming approach for beginners in programming. We are aware that these results are to be taken with care. Indeed, for reasons of difficulty of implementation, we worked with a rather weak corpus (2 groups of 27 students) over a limited period. However, it is remarkable to note that beginners in programming were able to carry out their first programs after only one hour of lecture and 30 minutes of training to a new tool.

Regarding Python Tutor, it was noticed that the students have easily learned how to use the tool . The dynamic display of the program data offers a certain comfort at the time of execution. The students worked faster with this tool (they did more exercises) but on the other hand, results were not as good than with AlgoTouch on iterative programs. In fact, AlgoTouch encourages the user to respect a certain method of work: record then test the loop body, take care of the exit case(s), and manage the variable intialisations. Although this same method was taught to the Python group, it is not easy to test only the loop body with Python Tutor, and on the other hand, the lack of constraints in Python Tutor allows students to edit the program as they wish.

Concerning the direct manipulation approach, these first results suggest that AlgoTouch likely facilitates the implementation of programs involving iterations (which is generally the case). Being able to visually build the loop body, and manipulate the array indexes seems to provide an answer to the problem raised by Hundhausen ("the novices have difficulties in building loops and correctly referencing elements in these loops with the use of indexes").

More specifically, with the AlgoTouch tool, this experiment has shown some limitations. Indeed, the tool that we used does not allow to edit the code produced by the tool. Currenly, in case of an error, the user must rerecord that part of the program instead of editing the code as under Python Tutor. This difficulty is characteristic of these systems as emphasized by R.Chugh comparing standard programming tools with those of direct manipulation, "Unfortunately, existing systems typically force users into just one of these two interaction modes" [4]. It would be necessary to allow for some adapted code editing, keeping the spirit of the direct manipulation; otherwise the advantage of the method disappears quickly.

Due to lack of time, the evaluation of the knowledge acquired by the students could not be carried out. It would be rewarding to carry out a new experiment with a larger population over a longer period. The experience could be complemented with an evaluation of students' knowledge and their feelings about both approaches to learning programming.

Finally, we intend to continue the experiments by focusing on classical iterative algorithms – especially algorithms on arrays – requiring simple loops and then nested loops. Indeed, given the limited time of the current experiment, it was not possible to introduce the notions of nested loops and procedures (in the case of Python), nor the notion of a macro (in the case of AlgoTouch). Would the results be of the same nature?

ACKNOWLEDGMENT

We thank Dr Dan Lewis from Santa Clara University, California, USA, for having proof read this article and added helpful comments.

REFERENCES

[1] Reem A. Alamer, Wejdan A. Al-Doweesh, Hend S. Al-Khalifa, and Muna S. Al-Razgan. 2015. Programming Unplugged: Bridging CS Unplugged Activities Gap for Learning Key Programming Concepts. In *e-Learning (econf), 2015 Fifth International Conference on*. IEEE, 97–103.

[2] Tim Bell, Jason Alexander, Isaac Freeman, and Mick Grimley. 2009. Computer science unplugged: School students doing real computing without computers. *The New Zealand Journal of Applied Computing and Information Technology* 13, 1 (2009), 20–29.

[3] Charles R. Boisvert. 2009. A Visualisation Tool for the Programming Process. In *Proceedings of the Annual ACM SIGCSE Conference on Innovation and Technology in Computer Science Education (ITiCSE '09)*. ACM, New York, NY, USA, 328–332. https://doi.org/10.1145/1562877.1562976

[4] Ravi Chugh, Brian Hempel, Mitchell Spradlin, and Jacob Albers. 2016. Programmatic and Direct Manipulation, Together at Last. *SIGPLAN Not.* 51, 6 (June 2016), 341–354. https://doi.org/10.1145/2980983.2908103

[5] Allen Cypher. 1993. *Watch what I Do: Programming By Demonstration.* MIT Press.

[6] Yvon Feaster, Luke Segars, Sally K. Wahba, and Jason O. Hallstrom. 2011. Teaching CS unplugged in the high school (with limited success). In *Proceedings of the 16th annual joint conference on Innovation and technology in computer science education.* ACM, 248–252.

[7] Patrice Frison. 2015. A Teaching Assistant for Algorithm Construction. In *Proceedings of the 2015 ACM Conference on Innovation and Technology in Computer Science Education (ITiCSE '15).* ACM, New York, NY, USA, 9–14. https://doi.org/10.1145/2729094.2742588

[8] Anna Gardeli and Spyros Vosinakis. 2017. Creating the computer player: an engaging and collaborative approach to introduce computational thinking by combining âĂŸunpluggedâĂŹactivities with visual programming. *Italian Journal of Educational Technology* 25, 2 (2017), 36–50.

[9] Philip J. Guo. 2013. Online Python Tutor: Embeddable Web-based Program Visualization for CS Education. In *Proceedings of the 44th ACM Technical Symposium on Computer Science Education (SIGCSE '13).* ACM, New York, NY, USA, 579–584. https://doi.org/10.1145/2445196.2445368

[10] Mark Guzdial. 2004. Programming environments for novices. *Computer science education research* 2004 (2004), 127–154.

[11] Christopher D. Hundhausen and Jonathan L. Brown. 2007. What You See Is What You Code: A live algorithm development and visualization environment for novice learners. *Journal of Visual Languages & Computing* 18, 1 (2007), 22 – 47. https://doi.org/10.1016/j.jvlc.2006.03.002

[12] Christopher D Hundhausen, Sean F Farley, and Jonathan L Brown. 2009. Can direct manipulation lower the barriers to computer programming and promote transfer of training?: An experimental study. *ACM Transactions on Computer-Human Interaction (TOCHI)* 16, 3 (2009), 13.
[13] Ken Kahn. 2001. How Any Program Can Be Created by Working with Examples. *Your wish is my command* (2001), 21–44.
[14] Edmund A Lamagna. 2015. Algorithmic thinking unplugged. *Journal of Computing Sciences in Colleges* 30, 6 (2015), 45–52.
[15] Brandon Rodriguez, Stephen Kennicutt, Cyndi Rader, and Tracy Camp. 2017. Assessing Computational Thinking in CS Unplugged Activities. In *Proceedings of the 2017 ACM SIGCSE Technical Symposium on Computer Science Education (SIGCSE '17)*. ACM, New York, NY, USA, 501–506. https://doi.org/10.1145/3017680.3017779
[16] SIF. 2016. Enseigner l'informatique de la maternelle à la terminale. *1024, Bulletin de la Société informatique de France* 9 (Nov. 2016), 25–33.
[17] David Canfield Smith. 1993. Pygmalion: An executable electronic blackboard. In *Watch what I do*. MIT Press, 19–48.
[18] David Canfield Smith, Allen Cypher, and Larry Tesler. 2000. Programming by Example: Novice Programming Comes of Age. *Commun. ACM* 43, 3 (March 2000), 75–81. https://doi.org/10.1145/330534.330544
[19] Juha Sorva, Ville Karavirta, and Lauri Malmi. 2013. A Review of Generic Program Visualization Systems for Introductory Programming Education. *Trans. Comput. Educ.* 13, 4, Article 15 (Nov. 2013), 64 pages. https://doi.org/10.1145/2490822
[20] Rivka Taub, Mordechai Ben-Ari, and Michal Armoni. 2009. The effect of CS unplugged on middle-school students' views of CS. *ACM SIGCSE Bulletin* 41, 3 (2009), 99–103.

Auto-Generating Visual Exercises for Learning Program Semantics

Rebecca Smith
Rice University
Houston, Texas
rjs@rice.edu

Terry Tang
Rice University
Houston, Texas
terry.tang@rice.edu

Joe Warren
Rice University
Houston, Texas
jwarren@rice.edu

Scott Rixner
Rice University
Houston, Texas
rixner@rice.edu

ABSTRACT

Understanding program execution is a challenging task for novice programmers. The semantic rules which determine how execution affects the program state are numerous and complex, and students frequently hold fundamental misconceptions about these rules. If students do not build a correct mental model of program execution early on, they will face substantial hurdles as they try to develop and debug their code. This paper presents VizQuiz, a tool for auto-generating multiple choice quizzes designed to help students gain insight into the semantic rules which govern program execution. VizQuiz provides students with an initial state and a piece of code, and tasks them with mentally tracing the execution of that code and selecting the correct final state. Reference diagrams are used to depict the initial and final states, and as feedback to help students visualize the correct behavior if they select a wrong answer. Feedback is auto-generated, so students can immediately correct their misconceptions and re-attempt.

CCS CONCEPTS

• **Social and professional topics → Computer science education**; • **Applied computing → Interactive learning environments.**

KEYWORDS

Education; Program semantics; Program mutation

ACM Reference Format:

Rebecca Smith, Terry Tang, Joe Warren, and Scott Rixner. 2019. Auto-Generating Visual Exercises for Learning Program Semantics. In *Innovation and Technology in Computer Science Education (ITiCSE '19), July 15–17, 2019, Aberdeen, Scotland UK*. ACM, New York, NY, USA, 7 pages. https://doi.org/10.1145/3304221.3319741

ITiCSE '19, July 15–17, 2019, Aberdeen, Scotland UK

ACM ISBN 978-1-4503-6301-3/19/07...$15.00
https://doi.org/10.1145/3304221.3319741

1 INTRODUCTION

The semantic rules which drive program execution are numerous, complex, and are often not intuitive to novice programmers. Students frequently hold fundamental misconceptions about the effects of program execution on the program state, and these misconceptions create substantial challenges during the development process. Therefore, it is essential to help novice programmers build correct mental models of program execution early on, so that they can effectively develop and debug their programs [2, 14–16, 18, 20].

Much past work has focused on creating tools to help students visualize the program state [5, 7, 9, 11]. These visualization tools are valuable aids to students who wish to see the current state of a program. However, such tools typically offer a passive experience. On its own, passive visualization is not enough; the scholarship of teaching and learning provides a wealth of support for the value of learning experiences that actively engage students [1, 3, 6, 10, 13]. In particular, it links the depth of mental processing that students perform to their ultimate learning and retention [3].

Several past efforts have designed tools for "active code reading" [8, 12, 17], with the goal of actively engaging students in higher orders of cognition. However, these tools largely lack support for helping students to visualize the program state. Furthermore, most existing tools offer little to no feedback to students on wrong answer selection. UUhistle does combine visualization with interactivity by presenting students with code and asking them to draw reference diagrams from scratch [19]. However, this is a challenging task for beginners, making UUhistle better suited for students that already have preliminary mental models of program execution.

To bridge the gap between the two classes of existing tools in a way that is suitable for beginners, this paper presents VizQuiz. VizQuiz is a multiple choice quiz tool which combines active code reading with program visualization. It provides students with an initial state and a piece of Python code, and asks them to mentally trace the execution of that code. After mentally executing the code, students must select the reference diagram that depicts the correct final state from amongst several distractors. The distractors are not random, nor do they require the instructor to write any code; each is an auto-generated mutation of the correct solution designed to mimic a semantic misconception that students might hold. If a student selects an incorrect state, VizQuiz offers a hint tailored to the specific misconception associated with that distractor.

Figure 1: Student Interface

Several factors contribute to the effectiveness of VizQuiz. First, it uniquely provides an interactive visualization experience that is tailored to novice programmers. Second, it scaffolds the learning experience by providing students with several states to choose from and offering automated, targeted feedback. Last, VizQuiz substantially eases the burden on the instructor by automating the tedious process of creating distractors that mimic faulty semantics. Instructors need only specify which misconceptions to target, and VizQuiz will generate the distractors as well as corresponding feedback.

VizQuiz was piloted in a controlled experiment within an introductory class on computational thinking. Students in the control group took three traditional multiple choice quizzes that had been hand-crafted by instructors and refined over several iterations of the course. Students in the experimental group used VizQuiz to take three quizzes that were designed to test the same concepts as the control quizzes. In this study, the experimental group reported average improvements in their computational thinking abilities and critical thinking skills that were greater than the corresponding gains of the control group by a statistically-significant margin, with p values of 0.023 and 0.031, respectively.

2 WORKFLOW

VizQuiz is designed to have an easy and intuitive workflow to support the goals of both students and instructors. Students are required to actively engage with the exercises, but are supported with visualizations and feedback. Instructors are given flexibility in choosing which misconceptions to target, but automation eases the task of generating exercises. Sections 2.1 and 2.2 describe the student and instructor workflows, respectively.

2.1 Student Workflow

When using VizQuiz, students are presented with three panes, as shown in Figure 1. The left pane displays a reference diagram representing the initial state of a program, and the middle pane contains the code of a program to be mentally executed on that initial state. The right pane allows the student to toggle between several different reference diagrams, each representing a possible final state. One is the correct final state that would result from applying the given program to the given initial state; the others are distractors designed to target common misconceptions. All reference diagrams — for both the initial state and the final states — are generated using code adapted from Online Python Tutor [7].

Student must mentally execute the provided code in order to select the correct final state. Upon selecting an incorrect answer, the student is presented with a hint designed to exemplify a concept about which they likely hold a misconception. This hint consists of a small piece of code and a reference diagram illustrating the correct behavior of that code. The student can then correct their misconception and re-attempt the question.

Table 1: Quiz Components

Component	Code		Reference Diagram	
	Auto-generated?	Visible?	Auto-generated?	Visible?
Init. code	No	No	Yes	Yes (left)
Applied code	No	Yes (center)	Yes	Yes (right)
Mutants	Yes	No	Yes	Yes (right)
Hints	Yes	On wrong answer	Yes	On wrong answer

2.2 Instructor Workflow

To generate quiz questions, the instructor must first write code for the initial state and the program to be executed. The initialization code is typically brief, serving only to define a few variables. For the fifteen quiz questions used in the evaluation, this code ranged from 1–5 lines. The length of the program to be executed varies according to the desired difficulty and the complexity of the concepts being tested; the programs used in the evaluation ranged from 4–23 lines.

Having written the program to be executed, the instructor can then use VizQuiz's mutation infrastructure to generate mutated variants of that program. A single mutant is created by applying one or more transformations to the program. The mutation framework will be described in greater detail in Section 3.1. Each mutant ultimately corresponds to a single distractor. The mutant code itself is not presented to students; instead, VizQuiz uses these mutants — as well as the original program — to generate reference diagrams to be displayed as possible answer choices.

Table 1 summarizes the different components that form a quiz question: initialization code, program to be executed, mutants, and hints. For each component, it indicates whether the code itself and/or its corresponding reference diagram is auto-generated or written by the instructor, as well as whether the code and/or its reference diagram are visible to the students. For components that are visible, it specifies the pane in which they appear.

3 INFRASTRUCTURE

The infrastructure of VizQuiz can be broken down into two core components. The backend auto-generates distractors and hints based on common student misconceptions. The frontend includes an instructor interface for using the results of auto-generation to build quizzes, as well as a student interface for interacting with these quizzes. While the two components are designed to complement each other, they are de-coupled in order to allow the instructor maximal flexibility. For instance, the instructor might choose to use the distractors or hints generated by the backend within a different context. Or, the instructor could choose to use the frontend framework for visualization and formative assessment, but to modify or even hand-write from scratch one or more distractors or hints.

3.1 Backend: Distractor & Hint Generation

Crafting mutants that capture semantic misconceptions is not a simple task; it often requires sophisticated, multi-line transformations. Hand-writing high quality mutants would be an onerous burden for the instructor. Therefore, VizQuiz auto-generates mutants using a modified version of `mutpy` [4]. `mutpy` is a mutation-testing tool for Python which takes an input program and randomly applies simple transformations to that program in order to generate mutants. The built-in transformations are very basic and typically affect only a single line; for instance, changing a plus sign into a minus sign, or changing the value of a constant. Such transformations are effective for `mutpy`'s original purpose of mutation testing. However, they do not reflect realistic misconceptions that students hold, and therefore are ill-suited to an educational context.

To make `mutpy` generate code that mimics semantic misconceptions, three key changes were made. First, the tool was modified to consistently apply the same transformation throughout the input program, rather than randomly selecting a single line to mutate. Second, thirty-two new, complex transformations were implemented.

Table 2: Selection of Transformations

Transformation	Student erroneously believes that...
`AndOrHigherThanNot`	and/or have higher precedence than not
`AugAssignsMutate`	Augmented assignment operations (*e.g.*, +=) mutate the lefthand side
`ChainsReferences`	References in Python can point to other references (rather than objects)
`DeleteUnusedCalls`	Functions don't have side effects, thus calls whose return values are unused can be ignored
`DivIsFractional`	Division involving two `int`s returns a `float`
`ElifIsIf`	`if` and `elif` are not mutually exclusive
`EvaluateLeftToRight`	Arithmetic expressions are evaluated left-to-right (ignoring order of operations)
`PrintIsReturn`	`print` is equivalent to `return`
`ScopeDoesNotExist`	All functions manipulate global variables

Input	Mutant	Hint
a = 10	a = 10	q = 5
b = x	b = x	r = q
c = a	c = a	q = 10
c = b	c = b	
d = a	d = a	
e = d	e = d	
x = 1	x = 1	
	c = x	
	b = x	

Figure 2: Auto-Generation Input & Outputs

Each of these was designed to target a specific misconception that is common amongst novice programmers. Effectively, these transformations serve to mimic faulty semantics. If the student holds the misconception being targeted by a given mutant, the corresponding reference diagram will reflect what they erroneously believe would be the program state after executing the input program.

The complete collection of transformations is too numerous to list here. Instead, Table 2 presents a selection of transformations as examples. These cover misconceptions on a range of topics, which include, but are not limited to, mutation (`ChainsReferences`, `AugAssignsMutate`) scope (`ScopeDoesNotExist`), order of operations (`EvaluateLeftToRight`, `AndOrHigherThanNot`) and control flow (`PrintIsReturn`, `ElifIsIf`). While the existing thirty-two transformations offer a rich variety of options to instructors, the framework is designed to be extensible, such that new transformations could easily be added to suit additional use cases.

The third change was to tag each transformation with a hint. When the instructor selects a transformation to be used to generate a distractor, the associated hint is output along with the mutant program. This hint consists of a short snippet of code that is a minimal working example of the concept underlying the misconception.

Figure 2 shows a sample input and the associated output. In this example, the instructor has selected the `ChainsReferences` misconception, which targets the case where a student erroneously believes that Python references can point to other references. Under this misconception, the student would expect re-assignment of a single variable to change the values of all aliases of that variable. Thus, the mutant code explicitly re-assigns each of these aliases to mimic this misconception. The student will not see this mutant code, but will be presented with its corresponding reference diagram. The hint involves a single re-assignment, and would be presented alongside its reference diagram to illustrate that the alias, `r`, actually remains unchanged when `q` is re-assigned. From this, the student can try to identify and correct the misconception.

3.2 Frontend: Quiz Framework

After generating each (mutant, hint) pair, the instructor is ready to use VizQuiz's instructor interface to create a new quiz. For each question, the instructor simply inputs all of the code: the initialization code, the program to be executed, the mutants and the hints. VizQuiz takes care of rendering the corresponding reference diagrams for the initial state and potential final states.

Table 3: Average Survey Responses, Spring 2018 (4-point Likert Scale)

	Question	Control Group				Experimental Group				p-value
		n	Pre-survey	Post-survey	Delta	n	Pre-survey	Post-survey	Delta	
1A	Please characterize your current level of understanding concerning how executing code affects the program state.	29	1.897	2.759	+0.862	28	1.607	2.929	+1.321	**0.013**
1B	How confident are you that you will successfully complete this course?	29	2.931	2.966	+0.034	28	2.537	2.893	+0.357	**0.034**
1C	How helpful were quizzes 1-3 in improving your understanding of how simple Python programs are executed?	29	N/A	2.690	N/A	28	N/A	2.679	N/A	0.477

Recall from Table 1 that the correct final state is the reference diagram generated from the instructor-written program, while the distractors are the reference diagrams of the mutants. If the student selects the correct final state, they proceed to the next question; otherwise, they receive the hint corresponding to the specific distractor they chose. As mentioned in Section 3.1, hints are presented as both a snippet of code and its the corresponding reference diagram, allowing students to visualize the correct behavior of the operation(s) they misunderstood.

Since VizQuiz is designed to be a formative assessment, students can make multiple attempts with no penalty. However, elements of randomness ensure that students practice mentally executing code rather than mindlessly, exhaustively trying each answer choice. Not only is the order of the answer choices shuffled between attempts, but the questions themselves may actually change slightly. Before each attempt, VizQuiz re-executes the initialization code to generate the initial state. The instructor can design this code such that the initial variables' values are randomized, resulting in a fresh challenge for the students on each subsequent attempt.

4 METHODOLOGY

VizQuiz was evaluated within an introductory course on computational thinking. This course has no prerequisites, is taken by a mix of majors and non-majors, and is offered during both semesters. The fall version is typically much larger, with multiple sections and a high proportion of intended majors. The spring version is a single section, and tends to include a greater proportion of non-majors.

A preliminary study ran in the spring of 2018, and a more in-depth follow-up study ran in the fall of 2018. At the start of each semester, students took a pre-survey which asked them to rate their confidence on a Likert scale, and also asked for a small amount of demographic information including their level of prior experience.

The study then ran during the first two weeks of the semester. The course utilizes a flipped classroom model in which students watch several brief video lectures before each class and take a multiple choice quiz on the information presented in those videos. For the purposes of this study, students were divided into a control group and an experimental group. Their group assignment determined the format they used for the first three pre-class quizzes. All students watched the same videos, and thus each pair of quizzes was designed to target the same high-level concepts: expressions, functions, and conditionals. However, the experimental group took three auto-generated quizzes within the VizQuiz framework, while the control group took three "traditional" multiple choice quizzes, composed of entirely different questions: textual questions that had been hand-crafted and refined by instructors during previous iterations of the course. All quizzes consisted of five questions.

In the initial spring study, students were randomly assigned to treatment groups. However, analyzing the results revealed that, by chance, the control group had notably higher prior experience and initial confidence than the experimental group. To avoid this issue in the fall, students were first sub-divided based on their experience level, as reported in the pre-survey. Then, each sub-group was divided randomly and evenly amongst the two treatments.

In both semesters, all students were asked to complete a post-survey. In the spring, the post-survey mirrored the confidence questions from the pre-survey. In the fall, students were also asked to rate their agreement with a series of statements regarding the quizzes. Additionally, the experimental group was given the opportunity to provide open-ended qualitative feedback on VizQuiz.

5 EVALUATION

As outlined in Section 4, both iterations of the study collected quantitative feedback using a Likert scale. In the spring semester, a 4-point Likert scale was used; in fall semester this was expanded to a 5-point scale to allow students to respond at a finer granularity. Sections 5.1 and 5.2 discuss the quantitative feedback from the spring and fall semesters, respectively. Section 5.3 presents selections from the qualitative feedback from the fall semester.

5.1 Quantitative Feedback, Spring 2018

Table 3 summarizes the quantitative results from the spring semester. This table is divided into four sections. The left section lists the questions that were asked, labeled (1A, 1B, 1C) for ease of reference. The two middle sections summarize the responses of the control and experimental groups, with sub-columns for sample size ("n"), average pre-survey response ("Pre-survey"), average post-survey response ("Post-survey"), and average intra-group change between surveys ("Delta"). The third question was only asked on the post-survey, since it pertained to the students' experience with the quizzes. Thus, its pre-survey and delta values are listed as N/A.

As stated in Section 4, despite the use of random assignment, there was a disparity in the two groups' initial confidence levels. Specifically, the control group had notably higher initial confidence. However, while the experimental group began with less confidence, they reported significantly higher deltas after using VizQuiz, and

Table 4: Average Self-Reported Confidence, Fall 2018 (5-point Likert Scale)

"Please rate your confidence in the following:"		Control Group				Experimental Group				p-value
		n	Pre-survey	Post-survey	Delta	n	Pre-survey	Post-survey	Delta	
2A	Your understanding of how executing code affects the program state (including variables and their values)	86	3.212	3.882	+0.670	104	2.942	3.779	+0.837	0.149
2B	Your ability to complete the class	87	4.314	4.291	-0.023	104	4.106	4.260	+0.154	0.072
2C	Your computational thinking abilities	54	3.679	3.660	-0.019	77	3.260	3.584	+0.324	**0.023**

Table 5: Average Agreement, Fall 2018 (5-point Likert Scale)

"Please rate your agreement with each of the following statements:"		Control Group		Experimental Group		p-value
		n	Post-survey	n	Post-survey	
3A	Quizzes 1-3 improved my understanding of the program state	88	4.00	104	4.16	0.058
3B	Quizzes 1-3 improved my ability to reason about code execution	88	3.99	105	4.14	0.067
3C	Quizzes 1-3 improved my critical thinking skills	88	3.77	105	4.01	**0.031**
3D	Quizzes 1-3 helped me learn to read simple Python programs	88	4.17	105	4.36	**0.032**
3E	Quizzes 1-3 helped me learn to think like a computer scientist	88	3.86	105	4.06	0.053

Figure 3: Agreement Distribution, Fall 2018 (5-point Likert Scale)

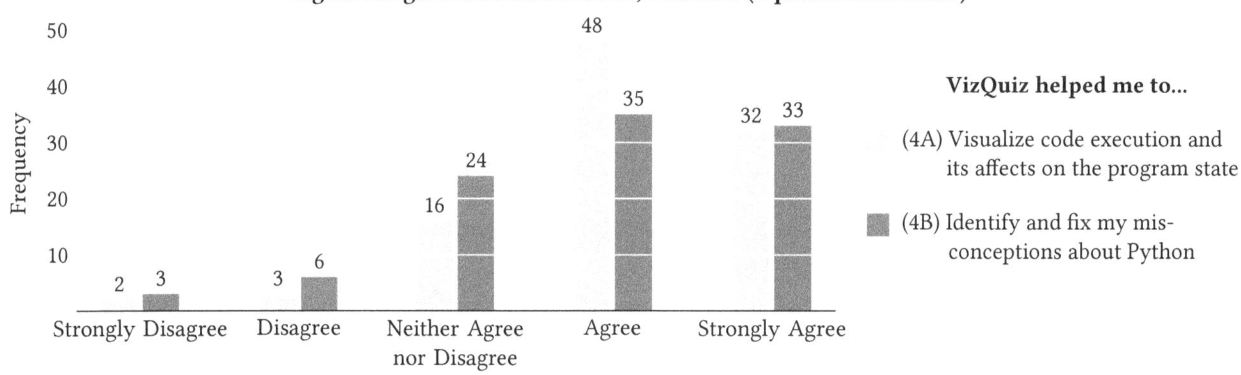

by the end of the experiment they had nearly closed the gap (as in 1B) or even surpassed the control group (as in 1A).

The rightmost column shows the results of using a one-tailed unpaired t-test to compare the two groups. For questions 1A and 1B, which appeared on both the pre- and post-surveys, significance testing was performed on the deltas. For question 1C, which only appeared on the post-survey, significance testing was performed directly on the responses to the post-survey.

The p-values for questions 1A and 1B were 0.013 and 0.034, respectively, indicating that the improvements in the experimental group's confidence were greater than those of the control group to a statistically significant degree. These results indicate that VizQuiz likely had a positive impact not only on students' confidence in the specific skills that it targeted — understanding the effects of execution on the program state (1A) —, but also on their overall confidence in their ability to complete the course (1B).

5.2 Quantitative Feedback, Fall 2018

Tables 4 and 5 present quantitative results from the fall semester. The questions in Table 4 asked students to self-report confidence, and appeared on both surveys; those in Table 5 asked students to report agreement with statements regarding the quizzes, and appeared only on the post-survey. Results are again broken down by treatment group, with the rightmost column showing the p-value from a one-tailed unpaired t-test comparing the two groups.

Interestingly, the results for questions 2A and 2B — which were nearly identical to 1A and 1B from the spring — were not statistically significant at the p=0.05 level in this iteration of the study. However, the responses to question 2C — which asked students about their confidence in their computational thinking skills — yielded a p-value of 0.023, which is considered statistically significant.

Table 5 includes two more statistically significant results at the p=0.05 level. First, students that interacted with VizQuiz found their experience to be significantly more effective in improving their critical thinking skills as compared to the control group (p=0.031). Second, it appears that VizQuiz may offer auxiliary benefits, as students in the experimental group also rated their experience as being significantly more effective in helping them learn to read simple Python programs (p=0.032).

Further, students in the experimental group were asked to rate their agreement with two statements regarding the effectiveness

Table 6: Selected Feedback, Fall 2018 (Constructive)

What was the worst part of using VizQuiz?
Sometimes the arrows were a little confusing, but it wasn't a huge issue.
When you couldn't understand the hint it was difficult to figure out what your mistake was.
At first I was confused about what we were supposed to do and what it was asking of me but I got the hang of it pretty quickly.
It was kind of boring because you couldn't write any actual code or edit anything.
It was annoying how it would change questions after a wrong answer, but it makes since why it did this.
It very time consuming.
N/A. I love VizQuiz! That love doesn't stem from easy material or a less strenuous testing format; I just think that it is a great way to learn.

Table 7: Selected Feedback, Fall 2018 (Positive)

What was the best part of using VizQuiz?
It's a good tool for furthering understanding and training you to follow and execute the code.
If I submitted an incorrect answer, [VizQuiz] would provide me with an example of correct usage of some code I misinterpreted. I could then try again and focus on correcting my mistake.
Gain a deeper understanding of the method in which code is executed. Also there are multiple attempts so if you ever don't understand something you get another chance to understand.
It was clear and easy to understand. The problems were not extremely complex and could be easily done on paper.
The hints given when you made a mistake allowed you to correct your understanding of how coding should work.
It was a great way to understand Python in a conceptual and fine-tuned way that made sure I didn't skip over crucial details about Python syntax and logic.
[VizQuiz] really helped me visualize the sequence of code and how it is like path of instructions. Since I came into the class with zero coding experience, [VizQuiz] was a nice way to visualize code without actually doing it.

VizQuiz. The average responses were 4.01 (4A) and 3.88 (4B); Figure 3 shows a full breakdown of the results. These results indicate that students largely found VizQuiz to be a valuable aid for visualizing program execution and correcting semantic misconceptions.

5.3 Qualitative Feedback, Fall 2018

Last, the post-survey in the fall semester solicited qualitative feedback from the group that interacted with VizQuiz. Students were asked to provide balanced feedback – specifically, they were asked to report both the worst and best parts of their experience with VizQuiz. Tables 6 and 7 contain a selection of responses to these two questions. The constructive criticism, in Table 6, noted that VizQuiz could be challenging and perhaps a bit confusing initially due to the unfamiliar format; however, students noted that they "got the hang of it pretty quickly", and recognized the value of certain design decisions that added difficulty (*e.g.*, questions changing between attempts). On the other hand, the positive comments underscored the value of VizQuiz in helping students to gain a deeper understanding of Python semantics through the combination of mental code execution and visualization. Many comments praised specific features of the tool, such as the visual aids, the hints, and the ability to re-attempt questions until their understanding was solidified.

6 CONCLUSION

Building correct mental models of program semantics is critical to students' success in developing and debugging programs. If semantic misconceptions are not corrected early on, they can have cascading effects as students attempt to layer increasingly complex concepts on top of a faulty foundation. Therefore, it is essential to support the development of correct mental models of program semantics from the start. To that end, this paper has presented VizQuiz, a framework for auto-generating multiple choice quizzes to help introductory students build mental models of program execution.

For students, VizQuiz was designed to provide a uniquely interactive visualization experience. It engages them in active code reading, and provides visual feedback to aid them in correcting any misconceptions they hold. Because this feedback is automated, students receive it instantaneously, so that they can immediately work to identify and correct their misconceptions. Multiple attempts create a low-stakes environment well-suited to beginners, allowing students to engage in intensive practice until they achieve mastery.

For instructors, VizQuiz was designed to balance flexibility with automation. It gives the instructor the freedom to choose which specific misconceptions they'd like to target, but automates the tedious work of crafting distractors that accurately reflect those misconceptions. Along with each distractor, it outputs a hint designed to help students correct the underlying misconception. Currently, VizQuiz supports over thirty transformations, corresponding to misconceptions on a wide range of topics such as mutation, scope, and control flow. Further, it is designed to be extensible, and additional transformations could easily be added.

VizQuiz was evaluated in a controlled experiment within an introductory course on computational thinking, where it was compared alongside a more traditional quiz model. In this study, students that interacted with VizQuiz reported significantly greater improvements in their computational thinking abilities and critical thinking skills as compared to the control group, with p-values of 0.023 and 0.031, respectively. Further, qualitative feedback highlighted the effectiveness of VizQuiz in training students to mentally execute code and helping them to correct their underlying misconceptions.

Helping students gain a firm grasp of the complex semantic rules that govern program execution is an important and challenging task. By providing instructors with an easy means of generating exercises that couple targeted practice with formative feedback, VizQuiz substantially eases this task.

ACKNOWLEDGEMENTS

This work is supported in part by NSF Award CNS-1619124.

REFERENCES

[1] Charles C. Bonwell and James A. Eison. 1991. *Active Learning: Creating Excitement in the Classroom.* ERIC.

[2] Matt Bower and Katrina Falkner. [n. d.]. Computational Thinking, the Notional Machine, Pre-service Teachers, and Research Opportunities.

[3] Fergus I.M. Craik and Robert S. Lockhart. 1972. Levels of Processing: A Framework for Memory Research. *Journal of Verbal Learning and Verbal Behavior* 11, 6 (1972), 671–684.

[4] Anna Derezinska and Konrad Halas. 2014. Experimental Evaluation of Mutation Testing Approaches to Python Programs. In *Proceedings of the 7th IEEE International Conference on Software Testing, Verification, and Validation Workshops (ICST '14).*

[5] Stephan Diehl. 2007. *Software Visualization: Visualizing the Structure, Behaviour, and Evolution of Software.* Springer Science & Business Media.

[6] Scott Freeman, Sarah L. Eddy, Miles McDonough, Michelle K. Smith, Nnadozie Okoroafor, Hannah Jordt, and Mary P. Wenderoth. 2014. Active Learning Increases Student Performance in Science, Engineering, and Mathematics. *Proceedings of the National Academy of Sciences* 111, 23 (2014).

[7] Philip J. Guo. 2013. Online Python Tutor: Embeddable Web-Based Program Visualization for CS Education. In *Proceedings of the 44th ACM Technical Symposium on Computer Science Education (SIGCSE '13).* Denver, CO.

[8] Daniel M. Hoffman, Ming Lu, and Tim Pelton. 2011. A Web-Based Generation and Delivery System for Active Code Reading. In *Proceedings of the 42nd ACM Technical Symposium on Computer Science Education (SIGCSE '11).* Dallas, TX.

[9] Jhilmil Jain, James H. Cross II, T. Dean Hendrix, and Larry A. Barowski. [n. d.]. Experimental Evaluation of Animated-Verifying Object Viewers for Java. In *Proceedings of the 3rd ACM Symposium on Software Visualization (SoftVis '06).*

[10] David W. Johnson, Roger T. Johnson, and Karl A Smith. 1998. *Active Learning: Cooperation in the College Classroom.* ERIC.

[11] Michael Kölling, Bruce Quig, Andrew Patterson, and John Rosenberg. 2003. The BlueJ System and its Pedagogy. *Computer Science Education* 13, 4 (2003).

[12] Niko Myller. 2007. Automatic Generation of Prediction Questions During Program Visualization. *Electronic Notes in Theoretical Computer Science* 178 (2007).

[13] Thomas L. Naps, Guido Rößling, Vicki Almstrum, Wanda Dann, Rudolf Fleischer, Chris Hundhausen, Ari Korhonen, Lauri Malmi, Myles McNally, and Susan Rodger. 2002. Exploring the Role of Visualization and Engagement in Computer Science Education. In *ACM SIGCSE Bulletin*, Vol. 35. ACM, 131–152.

[14] Donald A. Norman. 2014. Some Observations on Mental Models. In *Mental Models.* Psychology Press, 15–22.

[15] Andrew Ortony and David E. Rumelhart. 2017. The Representation of Knowledge in Memory. In *Schooling and the Acquisition of Knowledge.* Routledge, 99–135.

[16] Vennila Ramalingam, Deborah LaBelle, and Susan Wiedenbeck. 2004. Self-Efficacy and Mental Models in Learning to Program. In *Proceedings of the 9th ACM International Conference on Innovation and Technology in Computer Science Education (ITiCSE '04).* Leeds, UK.

[17] Takayuki Sekiya and Kazunori Yamaguchi. 2013. Tracing Quiz Set to Identify Novices' Programming Misconceptions. In *Proceedings of the 13th Koli Calling International Conference on Computing Education Research.* Koli, Finland.

[18] Juha Sorva. 2013. Notional Machines and Introductory Programming Education. *ACM Transactions on Computing Education* 13, 2 (2013).

[19] Juha Sorva and Teemu Sirkiä. 2010. UUhistle: A Software Tool for Visual Program Simulation. In *Proceedings of the 10th Koli Calling International Conference on Computing Education Research.* Koli, Finland.

[20] Lynn Westbrook. 2006. Mental Models: A Theoretical Overview and Preliminary Study. *Journal of Information Science* 32, 6 (2006), 563–579.

Identifying Predictors for Code Highlighting Skills

A Regressional Analysis of Knowledge, Syntax Abilities and Highlighting Skills

Matthias Kramer
University of Duisburg-Essen
Essen, Germany
matthias.kramer@uni-due.de

Mike Barkmin
University of Duisburg-Essen
Essen, Germany
mike.barkmin@uni-due.de

Torsten Brinda
University of Duisburg-Essen
Essen, Germany
torsten.brinda@uni-due.de

ABSTRACT

Programming comprises a multitude of involved skills and abilities. To assess these, an even larger multitude of tasks exists, ranging from very complex to basal levels. Recent demands call for the assessment of basal skills, with the aim to figure out possible problems of learners more precisely.

In order to read and interpret source code sufficiently, students must be able to recognize given concepts in a source code, e.g. to identify the objects and methods in an object-oriented program. Whether this skill relies solely on conceptual knowledge and the abilities in handling syntax is still unclear. This study gives evidence that isolated skills in these areas are outperformed by the interaction of both areas. We developed a test consisting of conceptual questions, fill-in-the-Java-keyword items and highlighting items. We investigated whether the knowledge about object orientation and the skills in handling Java syntax sufficiently predict the ability to recognize concepts in Java source code via a multiple linear regression.

We found that the model with interaction term explains the data better compared to the null model, the isolated predictors or combined predictors without interaction term. This leads to the conclusion that even though programming consists of skills in certainly different areas, it is more important to interconnect these areas with each other than to teach them in an isolated manner.

CCS CONCEPTS

• **Social and professional topics** → *Student assessment*; *K-12 education*; Computer science education.

KEYWORDS

Object-oriented programming, Conceptual knowledge, Syntactic knowledge, Assessment, Multiple linear regression

ACM Reference Format:

Matthias Kramer, Mike Barkmin, and Torsten Brinda. 2019. Identifying Predictors for Code Highlighting Skills: A Regressional Analysis of Knowledge, Syntax Abilities and Highlighting Skills. In *Innovation and Technology in Computer Science Education (ITiCSE '19), July 15–17, 2019, Aberdeen, Scotland UK*. ACM, New York, NY, USA, 7 pages. https://doi.org/10.1145/3304221.3319745

ITiCSE '19, July 15–17, 2019, Aberdeen, Scotland UK

ACM ISBN 978-1-4503-6301-3/19/07...$15.00
https://doi.org/10.1145/3304221.3319745

1 INTRODUCTION

The skills needed during programming are versatile. Identifying the problem, finding a solution, expressing the solution in a programming language and validating the solution could be a common chain of steps someone needs to follow in order to solve a given task. Thus, even small programming tasks can be very complex and difficult. This challenges teachers as well as examiners. Both need to diagnose and assess the programming ability of their students, give them an appropriate feedback and attest them some kind of ability level. But using tasks, which require multiple programming skills, can lead to false conclusions about the ability level of students as for example Petersen et al. suggest [19]. Thus, tasks which only require basal programming skills should also be used in assessments.

In recent years, researchers have tried to develop syntax-free, language independent tasks (see [18, 22]) or to isolate syntactical elements (see [15]) in order to assess the level of programming ability of students more precisely and to inspect their difficulties on a finer scale. To determine how these atomic tasks relate to "real" or "regular" tasks is the topic of this article. By investigating these relationships researchers and educators will get a deeper understanding of what is needed to be a competent programmer. Clearly, this is research work for several years. Hence, the presented results should be regarded as a small step into this direction.

In this paper, the relationship between conceptual knowledge of the object-oriented programming paradigm, syntactical knowledge of JAVA and the ability to identify certain concepts in a given JAVA source code are investigated. In section 2 it is explained, why the identification of certain concepts in a given source code is an important skill for programmers. Furthermore, the statistical methods for the decomposition of such a skill into underlying abilities by incorporation of multiple linear regression is illustrated. In section 3, the development of used items, the test situation and the data preparation are described. Following the evaluation of the results of the multiple linear regression, conclusions are drawn. Finally, section 4 gives an outlook on future studies.

2 THEORETICAL BACKGROUND

One of the most discussed aspects of educational research in the last decade is the concept of competence, see e.g., [13]. Competencies are described by Weinert [24] as the skills and abilities that enable the individual to solve problems in a certain area, along with the readiness and willingness to do so. A more recent definition, which focuses less on non-cognitive aspects, is the one of Koeppen et al. where competencies are defined as "context-specific cognitive dispositions that are acquired and needed to successfully cope with certain situations or tasks in specific domains" [9, p. 62]. Competencies are then described using different models, such as competency level models, which explain the "situational demands that can be mastered by individuals with certain levels or profiles of competencies"[9, p. 64], and competency structure models, which "deal with the relations between performances in different contexts and seek to identify common underlying dimensions. These models are especially interesting for explaining performance in specific domains in terms of underlying basic abilities, and can provide a basis for more differentiated measurement results of individual-centered assessments. The two kinds of models relate to different aspects of competence constructs. They are not mutually exclusive, but ideally complementary" [9, p. 64].

The current project of the authors aims at validating a competency structure model for object-oriented programming. It has been described in [11] and differentiates, among other aspects, between the conceptual knowledge that a person needs to be a competent programmer and the incorporated skills while handling program syntax. Theoretically, these dimensions should be empirically separable. Thus, creating items which involve only a single dimension could help assessing the skill level of a student more precisely by identifying weaknesses in a certain dimension, which then leads to better individualized support.

Typical programming tasks like translating an algorithm into a working program or inspecting and debugging code from other authors already involve skills from several theoretical dimensions at the same time. Thus, it is hypothesized that the individual competency level in each dimension should predict the overall performance in more complex tasks. To investigate such a claim, possible tasks need to be decomposed into the involved underlying dimensions.

One of the very basic tasks in programming is to read and understand source code, the own one as well as from different sources (colleague, teacher, public repository etc.). In the best case, the code is well documented and identifiers of classes, objects, methods etc. have meaningful names, making the semantics quickly accessible. If this is not the case, the textual representation of the code has to be deconstructed into its components and the interaction of these components has to be figured out, sometimes referred to as the transition between text based representation and situation model or program model and domain model [25, p. 256-257]. This transition presupposes that the reader can recognize the text based representation of a class, an object, a variable etc. as such a thing and connect it to the regarding concept.

One possibility to check whether someone is able to do that is to present source code to a person with the request to identify a certain basic element (e.g., an object identifier) or an event (e.g., an object instantiation). This can be done on paper by underlining or highlighting. How to evaluate such kind of tasks was described in [12]. To avoid guessing, several of the requested elements or incidents should be contained in the source code with the request to indicate all occurrences. In order to complete this task, a person needs knowledge about the respective syntax of the programming language as well as conceptual knowledge. Therefore it is reasonable to investigate the conceptual knowledge of persons, their syntactic skills and how these relate to their abilities in a highlighting task, i.e., a highlighting task.

In order to investigate the relationship between empirically assessed variables, an appropriate tool like linear regression is necessary. In a (multiple) linear regression, the scores of one dependent variable are modelled as a linear function of one or more independent variables, also called predictors. How well the modelled regression explains the data is expressed by the coefficient of determination R^2, a comparison of the explained variance by the model and the total variance of the data. There often is more than one hypothetical model, which could be used to explain the variance. To test which hypothetical model is statistically more likely to represent the reality, they can be compared.

If the models are nested (i.e., one is a more restricted version of the other), the difference of the R^2 values can be used in a simple ANOVA. For non-nested models information criteria such as Akaike's Information Criterion (AIC) or the Bayesian Information Criterion (BIC) [4] are suitable. A problem with multiple linear regression could be multicollinearity. Multicollinearity exists when two or more predictors correlate with each other. This can inflate the R^2 and lead to false conclusions. To detect multicollinearity the variance inflation factor can be calculated. In order to interpret the result of the multiple linear regression in a meaningful way the residuals need to be normally distributed (verified with the Shapiro-Wilk test), not autocorrelated (verified with the Durbin-Watson test) and homoscedastic (verified with the Breusch-Pagan test). Furthermore, the data needs to be inspected for potential outliers that significantly influence the result of the multiple linear regression (assessed with standardized residuals, Cook's distance, hat values and covariance ratio). Only after all the presented tests were conducted and no issues were found, the result can be interpreted in a meaningful way for the whole target population. With regard to the proposal of Benjamin et al. [3], the significance threshold in this article is set to $p = .005$.

3 THE STUDY

3.1 Item Development

In order to assess exclusively conceptual knowledge without interference of source code, the possible item formats were restricted to either open question, single choice or multiple choice format items. Due to the efficiency of automatic evaluation in contrast with guessing probability, the decision was made for the multiple choice format. Subsequently, seven concepts were chosen that are present in our competency structure model and are regarded important in the literature [1] as well as in the statewide curriculum[1] and that were intended to cover the area of conceptual school knowledge about object-orientation in a sufficient manner.

The chosen concepts were *class*, *object*, *encapsulation*, *inheritance*, *methods*, *fields/attributes* and the *constructor*. The latter one was chosen to explicitly refer to object instantiation as an integral part of object-oriented programming. In a next step, several aspects were determined that should cover each concept sufficiently. Those aspects were the *definition* (indicated by "<concept> is a <description>"), the *properties* (indicated by "<concept> has

[1] https://www.schulentwicklung.nrw.de/lehrplaene/upload/klp_SII/if/GOSt_Informatik_Endfassung.pdf

Table 1: An example for a conceptual task with its five statements.

Please determine for every statement below whether it is correct or incorrect.
A *class* is a building plan for objects.
Classes can have fields that none of their objects can access.
Classes can not be addressed by their objects during runtime.
For every *class* there needs to exist at least one object.
Class and *object* are different terms for the same concept.

one/some <properties> which <additional options>"), the *runtime behaviour* (indicated by "During runtime <concept> behaves like <description>"), the *cross-reference* (indicated by "<concept> relates to <other concept> like <description>") and the *common misconception* which was usually a statement derived from literature about common misbeliefs. For every concept five aspect statements were generated, resulting in 35 statements. All statements belonging to the same concept were presented together at the same time. By using a random generator their order and direction (formulated as positive or negative statement) was determined beforehand. Table 1 displays the five example statements for the concept *class* in the before mentioned order. It is already quite clear that neither the concepts nor the aspects are fundamentally different from each other, but lots of concepts simply relate to each other, such as classes and objects as can be seen in Table 1. Nevertheless, due to the consideration of different aspects the attempt was made to cover the conceptual knowledge to a sufficient part.

Syntactic abilities comprise the knowledge about which combinations of syntactical elements (such as keywords, identifiers, special characters etc.) are valid combinations and can therefore be compiled without error into an executable program. Whether these programs "make sense" or fulfil a task efficiently is a question of semantics, which itself presupposes syntactically correct programs and is thus currently not of interest for this study. Furthermore, the syntactic skills that are tested in this part should be as independent from the conceptual knowledge of the former part as possible. This means that, theoretically, it should be possible for a participant to score high in the conceptual scale and low in the syntactical scale (and vice versa).

To assess the syntactic abilities of the participants new items were designed in the form of *fill-in-the-gap* items. The idea is to show a program with one blank space and the description that one keyword has been deleted. This was intended to compensate for programs that would compile without the requested keyword, e.g., in case of access modifiers. The participant is asked to fill in the JAVA keyword which makes most sense to her or him. All keywords were retrieved from ORACLE's documentation[2] and then reduced according to the statewide curriculum for K12 schools. As the restriction was to only show fully compilable programs, some keywords need the presence of other keywords. Therefore, the items were constructed in a forward way, which means that items can only contain those keywords that have been assessed in former items. This guarantees that the participants do not learn from previous items. To not give possible hints towards the length of a keyword all gaps had the same length. Additionally, class, object, method and variable identifiers had obfuscated names.

[2]https://docs.oracle.com/javase/tutorial/java/nutsandbolts/_keywords.html

Table 2: An example for a fill-in-the-gap item for the keyword `else`.

Below, you can see the content of the file `Sca.java` where one JAVA keyword has been deleted. Which keyword is missing that would make the file compile without errors?

```
class Sca{
  boolean sem(boolean o){
    if(o == false){
      return true;
    } __________ {
      return false;
    }
  }
}
```

An example item for the keyword `else` is given in Table 2. Consequently, this item was only presented after previous items had asked for the keywords `class`, `boolean`, `if`, `return`, `true`, and `false`. Overall, 19 items were constructed.

Finally, six highlighting items were constructed. An example can be seen in [10]. The six different source codes consisted of 30 lines which were taken from BlueJ projects [2]. All comments were removed and, if necessary, further examples of the requested concept were inserted. One focus was explicitly on identifiers, as introductory source code often displays different concepts with the same name, e.g., `Car car = new Car()`. Hence, students were requested to highlight class identifiers, object identifiers, instantiations, field identifiers, constructors and method calls. A shortened example can be seen in Table 3.

Table 3: An example for a highlighting item.

Class identifiers in Java are those words, that refer to a specific Java class. Consider the given source code and highlight **ALL** occurences of class identifiers.

```
public class Clock
{
    private ClockDisplay clock;
    private boolean clockRunning = false;

    private void start()
    {
        clockRunning = true;
    }
}
```

At the beginning and end three questions regarding the participants self-efficacy were asked. There, the participants should estimate their abilities regarding object-orientation, programming and computer science in general. At the very end, participants were asked for sociodemographic data, interests and previous computer science and programming experience.

3.2 Participants and Test Situation

In a first step, the request for participation was distributed via a mailing list. The list is maintained by the authors and contains about 220 addresses of computer science teachers. A majority of them teaches in a secondary school located within a radius of 50 km around the authors' institution. The mail explained the content and process of the assessment. As an incentive, the teachers were promised an evaluation of their class/course results and also an anonymous comparison with all other participating classes/courses. It was stressed that all results are of importance, even if object-orientation has not been taught in all details. In a second step, those teachers, that responded to the previous mail and were willing to participate, were sent out individual credentials (assessment key and password) for their students. The used assessment tool is designed in such a way that a pair of credentials gives access to the same copy of a test, yet the results depend only on the individual session id of the browser. This implies that (accidental) reloading of the page generates a new session and leaves the old results unfinished. Yet, a whole class only needs one pair of credentials instead of one for every student. This is intended to minimize the effort for teachers and to guarantee anonymity for participants. For the teachers the authors designed a survey to provide information about the course and a manual to "standardize" instructions.

Each student got presented the same test in the same order. The assessment started with a general information about the upcoming test, a request to work on the tasks thoroughly, a note that all interaction is logged and that jumping backwards to correct former submissions was not possible. Furthermore, it was always possible to abort the test without consequences by clicking the respective button. Each new test format was introduced by a tutorial. All teachers taught courses in computer science from grade 10 to 12.

3.3 Data Preparation

An item result was considered as "aborted" when a student pressed the *ABORT* button during the assessment or when, after a considerable amount of time, there was no further action visible on server side for a specific session value, implying that the student either stopped the current session (by closing the tab or browser) or started another session. During April and July 2018, 513 results were gathered. Of those, 302 aborted results were removed. The remaining 211 students from 16 schools had finished the test from start to end. The aborted results included connection and functionality tests from the authors and from the teachers.

Since only non-aborted tests were included in the final data set, this means that every participant had actually seen every item (especially since the duration how long he or she got presented the item is saved in the logfiles). If a participant did not give any response, this means he or she got presented the item but decided to give no answer. For this reason it was decided to code every missing value as *wrong* instead of *NA*. Every concept statement was coded as 1 if it was correctly answered, 0 otherwise. Every submission of the *fill-in-the-gap* items was put in lower-case and stripped from blank spaces. An item was coded as 1 if the corresponding word matched the given solution (or one of the alternatives, see subsection 3.1), 0 otherwise. For every highlighting item the indices of highlights were retrieved in JSON format and compared with the solution. From these indices the κ value was calculated [10]. The test was then divided into a concept scale, a keyword scale and a highlight scale.

3.4 Results

All calculations were done using R version 3.5.2 [20]. The web based assessment results were prepared with the package *jsonlite*[17], the results of the highlighting data were calculated with the help of the packages *irr*[8] and *mirt*[5]. Testing the assumptions was done with a multitude of functions from the *car* package [7].

Table 4: Descriptive statistics, *** indicates significance of $p < .001$

	Scale C	Scale K	Scale H
Mean	19.51	5.17	0.93
Median	20	4	0.42
SD	6.82	5.09	1.27
Skew	−0.52	0.87	1.45
Kurtosis	0.55	−0.20	1.45
Shapiro-Wilk test	0.97^{***}	0.88^{***}	0.82^{***}

C: Concept, K: Keyword, H: Highlight

Of the participants 55% were male and 20% were female, the rest made a decision to stay anonymous. The mean age was 16.9 (SD = 1.95). Table 4 shows the descriptive statistics for the three scales and Table 5 shows the relations of the three subscales to each other in variances, covariances and Pearson correlations. The latter ones are moderate with significance values $p < .001$. Cronbach's α was computed for all subscales: The first scale provided an α of .83, an average interitem correlation of .42 and item whole correlations between .55 and .73. The second scale provided an α of .92, an average interitem correlation of .37 and item whole correlations between .37 and .73. The third scale provided an α of .83, an average interitem correlation of .44 and item whole correlations between .57 and .73.

Table 5: Relations between the subscales, upper triangle: Pearson correlations, lower triangle: covariances, diagonal: variances

	Scale C	Scale K	Scale H
Scale C	46.57	.67	.62
Scale K	23.26	25.89	.73
Scale H	5.36	4.77	1.63

C: Concept, K: Keyword, H: Highlight

3.4.1 Model selection. Both predictor scales were centered by subtracting the mean to reduce possible multicollinearity. Following the recommendations of Rouder et al. (see [21, p. 1780, Fig. 1d]) at first the models with single predictors were tested. Using solely the sum score from the concept scale to predict the sum score of the highlight scale via a simple linear regression resulted in a significant intercept of 0.93, a significant slope of 0.12 and an R^2 of

0.38. This can be interpreted as an average κ sum value of 0.93 with an increase of 0.12 points for every point in the conceptual test. Obviously, this model fits the data better than the null model which would imply no interaction at all. Using solely the sum score from the keyword scale to predict the sum score of the highlight scale via another simple linear regression resulted in a significant intercept of 0.93 as well, a significant slope of 0.18 and an R^2 of 0.54. Clearly, the second model explains far more variance than the first model. Since the models are not nested, a comparison via ANOVA makes no sense. But both AIC (605.54 for the first model and 542.39 for the second model) and BIC (615.59 for the first model and 552.44 for the second model) indicate that the first model should be dismissed.

The next regarded model was a multiple linear regression model using the sum scores from the first and the second scale as predictors without interaction term. This resulted in a significant intercept of 0.93, significant slopes of 0.04 and 0.15 as well as an R^2 of 0.56. The increased amount of explained variance already indicates that this model should be preferred over the former model with only one predictor from the keyword scale. This is also substantially supported by the significant ANOVA ($F(1, 208) = 13.37, p < .001$) as well as an AIC value of 531.24 and a BIC value of 544.65.

Finally, the multiple linear regression model with interaction term was investigated. This resulted in a significant intercept of 0.72, significant slopes of 0.06, 0.1 and 0.01 as well as an R^2 of 0.62. The increased amount of explained variance already indicates that this model should be preferred over the former model without interaction term of the predictors. This is also substantially supported by the significant ANOVA ($F(1, 207) = 29.24, p < .001$) as well as an AIC value of 505.36 and a BIC value of 522.12. To summarize, of all models investigated, the last one fits the data the best. Hence, this is the model that is further investigated. All model values are also summarized in Table 6.

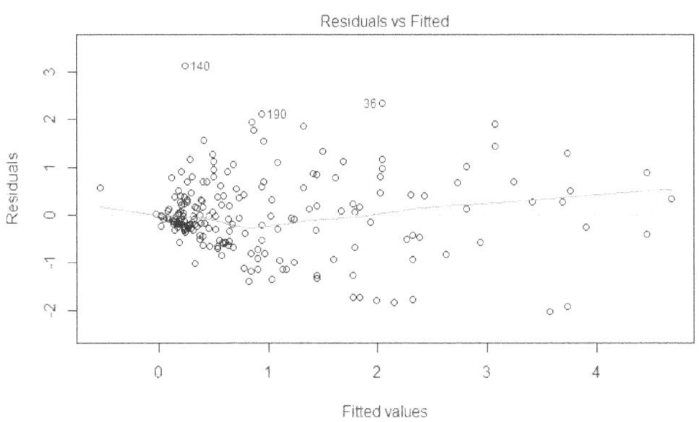

Figure 1: Distribution of residuals against the fitted values of the regression.

3.4.2 Analysis of model assumptions. Of utmost importance for the implications of a linear regression are the residuals. Hence, their distribution was inspected. It is displayed in Figure 1. Even though the data points are scattered around the fitted values, a pattern seems quite obvious, especially for the clustered points between the fitted values for 0 and 1. This is also supported by investigating the distribution. The Shapiro-Wilk test resulted in a test statistic $W = 0.97$ and a corresponding $p < .001$, hence the residuals are not considered to be normally distributed. Although an important assumption is already violated at this point, the analysis of further assumptions seems valid nonetheless. Regarding autocorrelation, the Durbin-Watson test yielded a test statistic $DW = 1.8$ and a corresponding $p = .07$, therefore no autocorrelation is assumed. Inspecting the homoscedasticity, the Breusch-Pagan test resulted in a test statistic of $\chi^2(1) = 28.2$ and a corresponding $p < .001$, which is also suggested by the plot in Figure 1 as well as the test for normal distribution. Furthermore, multicollinearity could not be detected, as the variance inflation factors resulted in 1.94 for the conceptual scale, 2.58 for the keyword scale and 1.47 for the interaction term. After inspecting the measurements for influential cases, such as standardized residuals, Cook's distance, hat values and covariance ratios (in accordance with the guidelines given by Field et al.[6, p. 292]), possible candidates for dismissal were detected. Hence, the raw data was reinspected but no substantial reasons for dismissal of these candidates could be found.

3.5 Evaluation of the Results

At first it must be said that the tasks in the presented format were surprisingly different in their difficulty for the participants to solve. The conceptual knowledge tasks in the right/wrong format seemed to be non problematic. The expected mean value for pure guessing would have been 17.5 points (which is also a considerable weakness of the scale), yet the mean, median and skewness value illustrate that a larger proportion surpassed this value than failed it. On the other hand, the keyword items seemed to be much harder, even though no code had to be interpreted for the meaning. Filling out the gap required solely syntactical knowledge, i.e., knowing which words are allowed to stand next to each other and which are not. The same way the conceptual scale was skewed to the left, this scale is skewed to the right. The large standard deviation, compared to the mean, is a further indicator for the difficulty of this task. Due to the usage of Cohen's κ for evaluating a highlight result [10], the values can range from -1 to 1 and from -6 to 6 in the aggregated score.

For all scales the Shapiro-Wilk test showed significant deviance from the normal distribution. This can stem from different factors, e.g., the participants were not used to the assessment format, the items were too hard or the instructions were unclear. The computation of Cronbach's α assumes at least essential τ−equivalency, which implies that all items assess the same latent construct in the same way apart from an additive constant. Although the τ−equivalency has not yet been analyzed for the subscales, Warrens reported how interpretations of α can still be valid even if the assumption is violated [23]. The yielded αs at least indicate good internal consistency and therefore reliability. The average interitem correlations indicate a high homogeneity in the subscales, almost close to redundancy but still in an acceptable range. The item whole correlations appear acceptable to good. None of these were below .3, hence all of these items are considered for further analyses. The Pearson correlations between the scales indicate a medium relationship. This seems obvious as usually the assessed skills are not taught isolated, especially not the syntactical aspects of a programming language.

Table 6: Model comparisons

	R^2	B	SE B	β	SE β	p	AIC	BIC
Model 1	0.38					< 0.001	605.54	615.59
Intercept		0.93	0.07			< 0.001		
Concept		0.12	0.01	0.62	0.05	< 0.001		
Model 2	0.54					< 0.001	542.39	552.44
Intercept		0.93	0.06			< 0.001		
Keyword		0.18	0.01	0.73	0.05	< 0.001		
Model 3	0.56					< 0.001	531.24	544.65
Intercept		0.93	0.06			< 0.001		
Concept		0.04	0.01	0.22	0.06	< 0.001		
Keyword		0.15	0.02	0.58	0.06	< 0.001		
Model 4	0.62					< 0.001	505.36	522.12
Intercept		0.72	0.06			< 0.001		
Concept		0.06	0.01	0.30	0.06	< 0.001		
Keyword		0.10	0.02	0.38	0.07	< 0.001		
Concept:Keyword		0.01	0.001	0.24	0.05	< 0.001		

For the choice of the model it is no surprise that one with an interaction term explains the data better than all alternative models. Obviously, a connection between pure syntax and conceptual knowledge helps to identify components in source code. In other words, recognizing elements in source code needs conceptual knowledge (students need to know what they are looking for), syntactical abilities (students need to know the language they are seeing) as well as the ability to combine both (students need to know how the thing they are looking for looks like in the given language).

This leads to possible teaching implications: students might not be able to read and understand source code correctly because they struggle with the paradigm concepts or with the syntax. Yet, it might be possible that they understood the concepts as well as the syntax, but still have problems with interconnecting both areas. Therefore, the authors recommend to explicitly exercise reading source code and explaining the meaning in terms of paradigmatic concepts as a classroom activity. Similar activities have been linked to programming proficiency [16].

Again, due to the violation of assumptions of the linear regression model, these interpretations are only valid for the assessed population and can not be generalized beyond that. From the authors point of view, at least some of the violations could be limited by including further covariates, such as the gender, previous experience in computer science or self efficacy. All of these have been assessed as well but have not been incorporated in the analysis yet.

3.6 Threats to Validity

A possible point of criticism could be the voluntary participation of the teachers and their classes. Even though it was mentioned that the results are treated anonymously and that no high expertise was expected for participation, it could still be the case that only those teachers participated which had some confidence in the performance of their group of students. Another threat for validity could result from the presented assessment format. Theoretically it would be possible for a participant to view all questions and then restart the session. This would result in a session started much later than all other sessions with the same session id and would hence point out of the data. No such data points were registered but they would be inrecognizable from sessions that were restarted involuntarily, e.g., by accidentally refreshing the page.

Furthermore, coding all missings as wrong instead of NA can be questioned. From the authors point of view, this makes sense insofar as all participants must have seen all tasks. Whether someone is unable or unwilling to give an answer was of no concern. The person would in both cases be labeled as less competent than someone who is able and willing to give the correct response. The construction of the conceptual scale could raise concerns as well. For every statement, the guessing chance is 50%, although the chance to guess all answers correct for one concept is 3.125%. A more fitting alternative could be the construction of appropriate distractors. As has been mentioned in subsection 3.5, the calculation of Cronbach's α relies on the assumption of essential $\tau-$equivalency which has not been investigated, e.g., via structural equation modeling. A last concern would be the incorporation of linear models if the response variable is restricted in its codomain to values from -6 to 6. Hence the usage of logistic regression might yield different results.

4 OUTLOOK

Based on these findings further sources of covariation will be investigated. For example, in this study the teaching approach (*objects first* vs. *objects later*) was not regarded while this could tremendously influence the outcome on our assessment. Also no detailed investigations have been done on the item level, e.g., with methods of Item Response Theory. With the help of these, the person parameters as well as the item difficulties could be estimated.

The test instrument as well as the anonymized data can be made available via the authors. The authors highly encourage other researchers to replicate their findings. While the authors will continue to do the same in the near future, a possible bias towards expected results can not be excluded. Furthermore, the sample size (after all 200 participants do not account for much statistical power) might lead to an overestimation of effects, as has been explained in the context of the ongoing replication crisis by Loken and Gelman[14].

ACKNOWLEDGMENTS

The authors express their gratitude to the whole BlueJ team under Michael Kölling for letting us use their source codes for our research as well as all the teachers who supported us with the assessment.

REFERENCES

[1] Deborah J. Armstrong. 2006. The Quarks of Object-Oriented Development. *Commun. ACM* 49, 2 (Feb. 2006), 123–128. https://doi.org/10.1145/1113034.1113040

[2] David J. Barnes and Michael Kölling. [n. d.]. *Objects First with Java: A Practical Introduction using BlueJ* (5 ed.). Pearson Education, Prentice Hall, London.

[3] Daniel J Benjamin, James O Berger, Magnus Johannesson, Brian A Nosek, E-J Wagenmakers, Richard Berk, Kenneth A Bollen, Björn Brembs, Lawrence Brown, Colin Camerer, et al. 2018. Redefine statistical significance. *Nature Human Behaviour* 2, 1 (2018), 6. https://doi.org/10.1038/s41562-017-0189-z

[4] Kenneth P. Burnham and David R. Anderson. 2004. Multimodel Inference: Understanding AIC and BIC in Model Selection. *Sociological Methods & Research* 33, 2 (2004), 261–304. https://doi.org/10.1177/0049124104268644

[5] R. Philip Chalmers. 2012. mirt: A Multidimensional Item Response Theory Package for the R Environment. *Journal of Statistical Software* 48, 6 (2012), 1–29. https://doi.org/10.18637/jss.v048.i06

[6] Andy Field, Jeremy Miles, and Zoë Field. 2012. *Discovering Statistics Using R.* Sage, Thousand Oaks CA.

[7] John Fox and Sanford Weisberg. 2011. *An R Companion to Applied Regression* (second ed.). Sage, Thousand Oaks CA. http://socserv.socsci.mcmaster.ca/jfox/Books/Companion

[8] Matthias Gamer, Jim Lemon, and Ian Fellows Puspendra Singh. 2012. *irr: Various Coefficients of Interrater Reliability and Agreement.* https://CRAN.R-project.org/package=irr R package version 0.84.

[9] Karoline Koeppen, Johannes Hartig, Eckhard Klieme, and Detlev Leutner. 2008. Current issues in competence modeling and assessment. *Zeitschrift für Psychologie/Journal of Psychology* 216, 2 (2008), 61–73.

[10] Matthias Kramer, Mike Barkmin, Torsten Brinda, and David Tobinski. 2018. Automatic Assessment of Source Code Highlighting Tasks: Investigation of Different Means of Measurement. In *Proceedings of the 18th Koli Calling International Conference on Computing Education Research (Koli Calling '18).* ACM, New York, NY, USA, Article 8, 10 pages. https://doi.org/10.1145/3279720.3279729

[11] Matthias Kramer, Peter Hubwieser, and Torsten Brinda. 2016. A Competency Structure Model of Object-Oriented Programming. In *2016 International Conference on Learning and Teaching in Computing and Engineering (LaTiCE).* 1–8. https://doi.org/10.1109/LaTiCE.2016.24

[12] Matthias Kramer, David Tobinski, and Torsten Brinda. 2016. On the Way to a Test Instrument for Object-Oriented Programming Competencies. In *Proceedings of the 16th Koli Calling International Conference on Computing Education Research (Koli Calling '16).* ACM, New York, NY, USA, 145–149. https://doi.org/10.1145/2999541.2999544

[13] Detlev Leutner, Jens Fleischer, Juliane Grünkorn, and Eckhard Klieme. 2017. *Competence Assessment in Education.* Springer, Cham. https://doi.org/10.1007/978-3-319-50030-0

[14] Eric Loken and Andrew Gelman. 2017. Measurement error and the replication crisis. *Science* 355, 6325 (2017), 584–585.

[15] Andrew Luxton-Reilly, Brett A. Becker, Yingjun Cao, Roger McDermott, Claudio Mirolo, Andreas Mühling, Andrew Petersen, Kate Sanders, Simon, and Jacqueline Whalley. 2017. Developing Assessments to Determine Mastery of Programming Fundamentals. In *Proceedings of the 2017 ITiCSE Conference on Working Group Reports (ITiCSE-WGR '17).* ACM, New York, NY, USA, 47–69. https://doi.org/10.1145/3174781.3174784

[16] Laurie Murphy, Sue Fitzgerald, Raymond Lister, and Renée McCauley. 2012. Ability to 'Explain in Plain English' Linked to Proficiency in Computer-based Programming. In *Proceedings of the Ninth Annual International Conference on International Computing Education Research (ICER '12).* ACM, New York, NY, USA, 111–118. https://doi.org/10.1145/2361276.2361299

[17] Jeroen Ooms. 2014. The jsonlite Package: A Practical and Consistent Mapping Between JSON Data and R Objects. *arXiv:1403.2805 [stat.CO]* (2014). https://arxiv.org/abs/1403.2805

[18] Miranda C. Parker, Mark Guzdial, and Shelly Engleman. 2016. Replication, Validation, and Use of a Language Independent CS1 Knowledge Assessment. In *Proceedings of the 2016 ACM Conference on International Computing Education Research (ICER '16).* ACM, New York, NY, USA, 93–101. https://doi.org/10.1145/2960310.2960316

[19] Andrew Petersen, Michelle Craig, and Daniel Zingaro. 2011. Reviewing CS1 Exam Question Content. In *Proceedings of the 42Nd ACM Technical Symposium on Computer Science Education (SIGCSE '11).* ACM, New York, NY, USA, 631–636. https://doi.org/10.1145/1953163.1953340

[20] R Core Team. 2018. *R: A Language and Environment for Statistical Computing.* R Foundation for Statistical Computing, Vienna, Austria. https://www.R-project.org/

[21] Jeffrey N. Rouder, Christopher R. Engelhardt, Simon McCabe, and Richard D. Morey. 2016. Model comparison in ANOVA. *Psychonomic Bulletin & Review* 23, 6 (01 Dec 2016), 1779–1786. https://doi.org/10.3758/s13423-016-1026-5

[22] Allison Elliott Tew and Mark Guzdial. 2011. The FCS1: A Language Independent Assessment of CS1 Knowledge. In *Proceedings of the 42Nd ACM Technical Symposium on Computer Science Education (SIGCSE '11).* ACM, New York, NY, USA, 111–116. https://doi.org/10.1145/1953163.1953200

[23] Matthijs J. Warrens. 2015. Some Relationships Between Cronbach's Alpha and the Spearman-Brown Formula. *Journal of Classification* 32, 1 (01 Apr 2015), 127–137. https://doi.org/10.1007/s00357-015-9168-0

[24] Franz E. Weinert. 2001. Concept of Competence: A Conceptual Clarification. In *Defining and Selecting Key Competencies,* Dominique S. Rychen and Laura H. Salganik (Eds.). Hogrefe & Huber Publishers, Ashland, OH, US, 45–65.

[25] Susan Wiedenbeck, Vennila Ramalingam, Suseela Sarasamma, and Cynthia L. Corritore. 1999. A comparison of the comprehension of object-oriented and procedural programs by novice programmers. *Interacting with Computers* 11, 3 (01 1999), 255–282. https://doi.org/10.1016/S0953-5438(98)00029-0

Teaching Electronics and Programming in Norwegian Schools Using the air:bit Sensor Kit

Bjørn Fjukstad
Department of Computer Science, UiT
The Arctic University of Norway

Nina Angelvik
Department of Computer Science, UiT
The Arctic University of Norway

Morten Grønnesby
Department of Medical Biology, UiT
The Arctic University of Norway

Maria Wulff Hauglann
Department of Computer Science, UiT
The Arctic University of Norway

Hedinn Gunhildrud
Science Centre of Northern Norway

Fredrik Høisæther Rasch
Department of Computer Science, UiT
The Arctic University of Norway

Julianne Iversen
Faculty of Science and Technology,
UiT The Arctic University of Norway

Margaret Dalseng
Faculty of Science and Technology,
UiT The Arctic University of Norway

Lars Ailo Bongo
Department of Computer Science, UiT
The Arctic University of Norway

ABSTRACT

We describe lessons learned from using the `air:bit` project to introduce more than 150 students in the Norwegian upper secondary school to computer programming, engineering and environmental sciences. In the `air:bit` project, students build and code a portable air quality sensor kit, and use their `air:bit` to collect data to investigate patterns in air quality in their local environment. When the project ended students had collected more than 400,000 measurements with their `air:bit` kits, and could describe local patterns in air quality. Students participate in all parts of the project, from soldering components and programming the sensors, to analyzing the air quality measurements. Following the project we conducted a survey to investigate the satisfaction of participating in the project, as well as learning outcomes in the different parts of the project to improve future versions. The results show that both teachers and students were very satisfied with participating in the project. While the students showed positive learning outcomes in electronics and simple programming parts of the project, there is room for improvement regarding more advanced programming tasks. We believe that our work provides insight for other similar maker-inspired projects, and guidelines for educators to incorporate computer programming in traditional science experiments.

CCS CONCEPTS

• **Social and professional topics** → **Computing education**; **Computational thinking**; • **Hardware** → *Sensor devices and platforms.*

KEYWORDS

computer science education, microcontrollers, STEM, air quality

ITiCSE '19, July 15–17, 2019, Aberdeen, Scotland Uk

ACM ISBN 978-1-4503-6301-3/19/07...$15.00
https://doi.org/10.1145/3304221.3325527

ACM Reference Format:
Bjørn Fjukstad, Nina Angelvik, Morten Grønnesby, Maria Wulff Hauglann, Hedinn Gunhildrud, Fredrik Høisæther Rasch, Julianne Iversen, Margaret Dalseng, and Lars Ailo Bongo. 2019. Teaching Electronics and Programming in Norwegian Schools Using the `air:bit` Sensor Kit. In *Innovation and Technology in Computer Science Education (ITiCSE '19), July 15–17, 2019, Aberdeen, Scotland Uk.* ACM, New York, NY, USA, 7 pages. https://doi.org/10.1145/3304221.3325527

INTRODUCTION

We have developed the `air:bit`, an Arduino-based air quality sensor kit that students build and program to collect air quality data in their local environment[13]. Together with the `air:bit` sensor kit, we developed teaching materials that include how to assemble the sensor kit and how to program its different sensors, and a cloud based service for students to upload and explore their collected datasets. All of which are openly available online at airbit.uit.no. We used these resources develop an interdisciplinary course for students in Norwegian upper secondary schools, which we offered to 11 different schools across Northern Norway.

From our first deployment of the `air:bit` project we identified a set of necessary improvements to scale out to even more schools. First, the initial version of the sensor kit did not provide the students with comparable data to official measurement stations. Second, because we wanted to invite more schools we had to improve how we shared resources such as programming guides to the students and teachers. Third, we had to improve the online platform for exploring the datasets to handle data from many geographically distributed locations. With these technical improvements in place, we could deploy the project to more schools, and evaluate the teaching outcomes of the participating students. Our primary goal of the evaluation was to map the difficulties of each part of the project to further improve it in future versions.

In this paper we describe the evaluation of deploying the `air:bit` project in 11 Norwegian upper secondary schools. The participating schools were all in Northern Norway, but spread over a large geographical area. We developed a survey to collect information about the experiences and teaching outcome for both students and teachers. We used this study to investigate the prior knowledge about programming and electronics, the difficulties of the different parts of the project, and to highlight areas of improvement. We describe how we redesigned the sensor kit and its accompanying resources, the online data exploration platform and the student experiences from this second deployment of the `air:bit` project. We believe our work provides insight for others that provide similar maker-inspired projects to students without any programming experience, and that it answers some questions about the effect of such projects for motivating students to engage in computer science and other STEM subjects.

THE AIR:BIT PROJECT

At The Faculty of Science and Technology at UiT The Arctic University we have a School Laboratory that is open to all local school classes, and teachers, to visit and learn about technology.[1] The school laboratory is run by academic staff at the different departments at the faculty, in addition to administrative staff at the faculty. After a teacher conference in computer programming in 2016 there was a request for a course at the school laboratory that combined computer programming with natural sciences. In 2017 we initiated the `air:bit` project with a single upper secondary school class. In our previous publication, we describe motivation behind the `air:bit` project, the first version of our `air:bit`, and our experiences from the first participating class[13].

In this paper we wish to focus on the necessary improvements to scale out the project to more schools, and what the learning outcomes for the participating students were.

Background

While programming or computational thinking is added to the school curricula in countries such as the UK, Finland or Estonia, Norway is unfortunately falling behind[11]. Initiatives such as Lær Kidsa Koding[2] are working with legislators to introduce these concepts in the Norwegian educational system, but it is a time consuming process. Fortunately, certain science subjects in the upper secondary school allow teachers to add smaller projects that combine programming with the traditional sciences.

There are a wealth of platforms and tools to introduce computer science to students of all ages. One such tool is the cheap Arduino microcontroller where users combine electronic components such as LEDs and buttons, with computer programming.[5, 8] These microcontrollers can be applied in a wide range of disciplines and application areas, from physics experiments[19] to designing wearable textiles[8, 12], or even hacking toys.[7]

Air pollution is the largest single environmental health risk, and it contributes to respiratory disease, cardiovascular disease and certain cancers.[4, 6, 14, 17, 18, 20] Air pollution originates from a wide range of sources, and especially Particulate Matter (PM) from combustion engines and cars driving with studded tires is a major problem in Norway[14, 15].

With cheaper and higher quality sensors, combined with easy-to-use microcontrollers such the Arduino UNO, it is possible to develop small sensor kits with little previous knowledge and experience with electronics. Low-cost air quality monitoring kits have already shown their effectiveness in citizen science projects, by reducing the high cost of developing such measurement stations.[3, 9, 10, 16]

[1] uit.no/skolelab
[2] kidsakoder.no

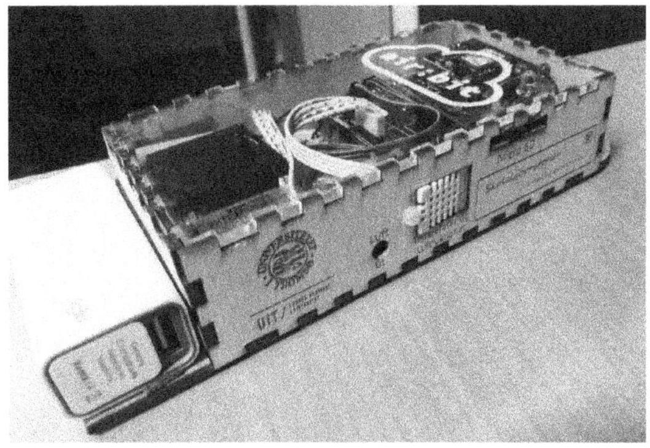

Figure 1: The second version of the air:bit sensor kit.

air:bit

The `air:bit` is a small microcontroller based data logger for measuring dust particles, air temperature, air humidity, GPS-based location, time and date. The kit is enclosed in a laser cut box, equipped with an external battery for portability. Table 1 lists the different components and their respective cost, and Figure 1 shows the assembled kit. We package and ship all components to each school in cardboard boxes.

We designed the kit as simple as possible to facilitate use in an educational setting. To simplify the assembly and soldering of the components to the microcontroller we use a custom PCB circuit board that has pre-defined pins for each sensor, and fits on top of the Arduino UNO board. New in the second version of our `air:bit` is the Nova SDS011 Dust sensor which allow students to collect data that can be compared to official measurement stations (PM2.5 and PM10). This sensor is more expensive than the previous dust sensor, but provides higher quality data. We also update the temperature and humidity sensor from the DHT11 to the DHT22. This sensor allows students to record temperatures below 0°C, which is frequent in Northern Norway. We also re-designed the box to make it easier for students to carry around.

We continue to use the standard Arduino IDE together with additional libraries to program the `air:bit`. The libraries provide the low-level functionality to retrieve data from each sensor, and students use their respective APIs to assemble a program that collects data from all sensors simultaneously and write them to a memory card. We distribute example code to interface and collect data from the individual sensors. These are small examples typically less than 100 lines of code, and students typically end up with a complete solution of around 500 lines of code. The data is recorded to the memory card using a simple CSV file format that make it simple to view and inspect the output datasets.

Improved Online Resources

To allow more schools to participate in the `air:bit` project we had to improve the online resources. We developed detailed guides on how to solder the components of the `air:bit`, how to assemble the box, and how to program each sensor. We also included a resources

Table 1: A list of the different components in the air:bit along with their cost (as of January 2018).

Component	Cost (USD)
Arduino Uno microcontroller	$3.00
NEO6MV2 GPS module	$6.00
Nova SDS011 dust sensor(PM2.5 and PM10).	$14.50
DHT22 temperature and humidity sensor	$3.50
SD Card reader and 16GB memory card	$9.00
Portable power bank	$15.00
Custom PCB circuit board	$3.00
Custom enclosure box	$5.00
USB cable	$2.00
Zip-lock bag with LEDs, resistors and spare parts	$5.00
Cardboard box	$1.50
Total:	$67.50

page with video lectures on air pollution from environmental researchers from the Norwegian Institute for Air Research (NILU) and the The Norwegian Meteorological Institute (MET). All of these are available online at airbit.uit.no. These are open to everyone.

Together with the educational resources we developed the `air:bit` platform, a system for storing, exploring and visualizing air quality data from the kits and other, external data sources.[1, 2] The system consists of three individual parts, the `air:bit` web application, a service for retrieving and uploading datasets, and a backed storage service. The web application provides students with educational resources such as instructions on how to solder each component and program the sensors, in addition to an interactive visualizations of the air quality datasets. The other two services are responsible for retrieving student data and making them available through the interactive visualizations. We host the backend services on Google Cloud Platform which makes it possible for us to scale out if we get even more participating schools. Together with student data we also retrieve data from NILU and MET through their open APIs. By developing an online service that integrates the different data sources we make it easier for students to explore the heterogeneous data.

The 2018 `air:bit` Project

We have offered our `air:bit` course twice. The pilot was held in spring 2017 at the University of Tromsø to science students at a local High School (Kongsbakken Vidergående Skole). The second round was in spring 2018 with 11 participating schools, and 164 students from across Northern Norway. In the second round, the participating teachers chose to use the `air:bit` project in four different subjects, from all three years of upper secondary school. The 164 students built in total 62 `air:bit` sensor kits.

We invited schools to participate in the second round of the project in the beginning of the fall semester of 2017. The participating schools were invited to a two-day workshop where the goal was to teach them how to assemble and program the sensor kit. Teachers from 11 schools participated and successfully built and programmed their own kits. Following the teacher workshops the teachers themselves chose how to incorporate the `air:bit` project in their classroom.

In the spring of 2018 all participating classes were invited to attend a full day workshop where they got help to finalize the assembly and programming of the `air:bit` kits. Most classes only had minor programming issues, but some student groups needed help to troubleshoot their soldering and assembly. Following the workshop, each class returned home to start data collection.

During the spring of 2018 students uploaded more than 400,000 unique measurements to our online web application. The class with the largest number of data points used their data to investigate and compare air pollution levels on the outside playgrounds of local kindergartens.

EVALUATION

The main goal of the evaluation was to get feedback from the participating students and teachers on the project for us to improve it. We aim to offer this course to Norwegian upper secondary schools in future years, both to engage students in computer programming, but also to motivate students to apply to higher education in science and technology. For us to do so, it is important to understand the difficulties of the different parts of the project, what the students learned, and areas for us to improve.

We developed two surveys to investigate learning outcomes and experiences from the `air:bit` course, one for students and another for teachers. Specifically we wanted to investigate: i) the overall satisfaction of having participated in the project; ii) how much time students spent working on the project; iii) if the students had used the online materials; iv) the difficulty of each part of the project; v) the students prior experience with programming and electronics; and vi) the programming specific learning outcomes, e.g. knowledge about variables and loops.

All questions were written in Norwegian, and we present their English translation in this paper. We have also translated the free-text responses from the students and teachers. We distributed both surveys online using a service similar to Questback.

To investigate the student perceived learning outcome and experiences from the course we asked the students to answer a questionnaire consisting of 14 multiple choice questions, and 35 statements answered on a five-level Likert scale. Of the total 164 students, we received 90 individual responses. This gives 55% answer rate. Of the 90 responses 64% were boys and 36% girls. Regarding the questionnaire for teachers, 8 of the 11 (73%) participating teachers replied to our survey.

Student Experiences

To investigate the time spent working on the project, we asked the students to report the number of weeks and hours per week spent on the project. Table 2 shows the reported number of weeks spent working on the project and Table 3 shows the reported number of hours spent every week working on the project.

We asked the students to report how they had used the online materials. 94% of the students reported that they used the online materials while they where building and programming the `air:bit`. Of these, 83% reported that these where either to a large degree or to a very large degree helpful. 14% reported that the online materials where to some extent helpful, while 4% reported that the material

Table 2: Reported number of weeks spent working on the `air:bit` project.

Less than 4 weeks	4 to 8 weeks	9 to 12 weeks	13 to 16 weeks	More than 16 weeks
4%	20%	45%	27%	4%

Table 3: Reported hours spent working on the `air:bit` project every week.

Less than 1 hour	1 to 2 hours	3 to 4 hours	More than 5 hours
10%	23%	50%	17%

was not at all or to a small degree helpful. These results back up our efforts to develop and maintain online teaching materials.

To investigate the satisfaction of the students, we asked them to rate how satisfied or dissatisfied having participated in the air:bit project. 69% of the students reported that they were satisfied or very satisfied, 23% nor satisfied or dissatisfied and 8% reported that they were very dissatisfied or dissatisfied. We are very happy with these numbers, but hope that in future editions we can further improve the satisfaction rate.

To evaluate the difficulty of each part of the project, we asked the students to evaluate the difficulty of the main tasks of the project. Table 4 shows the questions and how the students responded. From the table we clearly see that the students found it easy to get an overview of the components and solder the air:bit together. Further the students fount the LEDs, the temperature and humidity sensor, and the dust sensor relatively easy to program. These are all sensors that require minimal code, and are easy to test in the class room. However programming the GPS and memory card was a more difficult task. The most difficult task of all was to assemble all the individual parts into a single program. More than half the students answered that it was either *difficult* or *very difficult*.

Getting the GPS unit to function requires that students both write the correct code, but also take it outside for testing since it is difficult to get a GPS signal inside. We believe that the difficulties are mainly attributed to the advanced interface to the GPS library we provide, in addition to designing a program that checks for a valid GPS position and date, as well as formatting the output correctly. We hope to improve this interface in the future.

Assembling all small programs into one large program posed difficulties for most students. Since the students write separate programs for each sensor, they have to combine the flow of each program into a single piece of software. It is apparent that we failed to show how to merge two or more different Arduino programs, and this is something that we hope to improve in future versions. We have thought about developing the full program from the ground up starting with the LEDs and adding code for each component until they are all covered. This would simplify the assembly of a single program, but will make it more difficult to troubleshoot issues with each sensor since they are integrated into the same piece of software. Having one program for each sensor makes it easy to point to a faulty solder joint or incorrect usage of a software library. Remember that with Arduinos both the code and the physical sensors may cause errors.

To understand how the students' knowledge on the different parts of the project, we asked them to asses their knowledge before and after the project.

From Table 5 we see that the students reported that they knew much or very much about soldering electrical components after the projects was over. We also see a large increase in students reporting they know much or very much about programming Arduinos. Interestingly, only 40% of students report they know much or very much about measurement uncertainty in research data. By using simple off-the-shelf sensors we had hoped that we had informed the students that the sensors did not provide excellent data quality, and how to critically interpret the data. We hope to expand and improve the parts of the project where students actually perform the data analysis in future editions.

To evaluate programming specific knowledge we asked the students to rate their knowledge before and after the project. Table 6 summarizes the results. From the table we see clearly that around a third of the students reply that they know little or very little about all statements. While we see that this percentage is smaller than before the project, there is still a lot of work to do in the programming-specific parts of the `air:bit` project. We also see that the percentage of students that know little or very little is largest for the statements regarding logic tests and loops. These are fundamental in assembling the full `air:bit` program, and especially the GPS unit, and believe that these results back the results we saw in 4.

In addition to our questions, we left a text field where the students could enter free-text comments to the project. In total 17 students used this opportunity to give us comments. From these 17, two students wrote that they were given instructions that the `air:bit` kits could be used outside, and that the kits had malfunctioned from extensive outside exposure (5 days). Another student noted that the enclosing box was a bit too small for all the components. One student reported "It is a difficult project, but it's fun". Another student wrote "The project was very fun, but much of the work following the data collection it was pretty gruesome to complete. However, I learned a lot of lessons of how complicated such processes are". One student wrote that they did not get the programming guidance they needed when they visited the university. Another student wrote that the programming was too easy, and that it did not challenge the students. One student requested a guide on presenting research data.

Teacher Experiences

From the responses we got an overview of the time spent on the project, their knowledge about programming and microcontrollers prior to the project, and the learning outcomes for their students. The survey consisted of multiple choice questions and a free text field where they could enter their own comments.

Of the 8 replies, all teachers responded that their students had significant or very significant learning outcomes. All teachers also responded that they would recommend other classes to participate in the project. More than half of the teachers reported that they had much, or very much knowledge about electrical circuits, soldering,

Table 4: Survey results from reported difficulty in completing the different tasks of assembling and programming the `air:bit`.

Statement	Very easy or easy	Nor easy nor difficult	Difficult or very difficult
Solder the components	80%	18%	2%
Get an overview of the components	83%	13%	3%
Program the LEDs	73%	18%	9%
Program the temperature and humidity sensor	50%	39%	11%
Program the dust sensor	46%	41%	13%
Program the memory card and memory card reader	28%	42%	30%
Program the GPS	20%	37%	43%
Assemble the different programs into a single program	15%	32%	53%

Table 5: Survey results from the self-assessed general knowledge before and after participating in the `air:bit` project. We have combined the top and bottom categories.

Statement	Very little or Little	Neither little nor much	Much or Very much
How to solder electrical components	*23%* → 8%	*22%* → 14%	*55%* → 78%
How to plan and execute a scientific project	*24%* → 8%	*29%* → 30%	*47%* → 62%
How to collect and analyze research data	*39%* → 8%	*31%* → 30%	*30%* → 62%
What an Arduino is and how to program it	*46%* → 13%	*28%* → 28%	*26%* → 59%
How electrical circuits work	*32%* → 17%	*39%* → 33%	*29%* → 50%
How to write a computer program	*39%* → 18%	*38%* → 32%	*23%* → 50%
How to determine measurement uncertainty in research data	*36%* → 12%	*41%* → 38%	*24%* → 40%

Table 6: Survey results from the self-assessed programming knowledge before and after participating in the `air:bit` project. We have combined the top and bottom categories.

Statement	Very little or Little	Neither little nor much	Much or Very much
What a variable is and how they are used	*49%* → 29%	*17%* → 28%	*34%* → 43%
What a data type is and how they are used (e.g. `float` or `int`)	*50%* → 31%	*26%* → 28%	*24%* → 41%
What a loop is and how they are used (e.g. a `for` loop)	*56%* → 35%	*22%* → 24%	*22%* → 41%
What a logic test is and how they are used (e.g. an `if` test)	*54%* → 34%	*20%* → 25%	*36%* → 41%
How to debug a computer program	*63%* → 30%	*19%* → 29%	*18%* → 41%

programming, and how to plan and execute a scientific project. However, there were still teachers who reported that they had very little or little experience in all of these areas.

From the free text responses, one teacher reported that the students became a bit tired towards the end due to the process of writing up their findings. One teacher said that the motivation was highly variable between the students and groups, and that they did not feel any ownership to the programming due to a lot of copy-pasting.

DISCUSSION AND FUTURE WORK

Unfortunately we were unable to distribute the first set of questionnaires before the project started, and another after the project. This meant that we asked the students after completing the project to evaluate their knowledge prior to starting the project. We believe that this could have an impact on the responses.

From the feedback from the students and teachers we aim to make improvements to the `air:bit` project. The main issue we are targeting in the next round of the project is how students write the full `air:bit` Arduino program. The previous approach has been to program each sensor independently before assembling together one large program that does everything. This made it easy for students to focus on one single component at a time, making debugging both software and hardware simpler. The drawback was that most students struggled with how to assemble them together in one single program. One improvement we will incorporate in the next round is to show how we combine the individual programs for the simple sensors together into a single program. While we have developed static programming guides for students to follow, we are also experimenting with developing video guides maybe even as live streams. We hope that this will help students better understand the different computer science concepts they are introduced to, as well as simplifying the programming of the `air:bit`.

As mentioned earlier, the students had difficulties getting the GPS module to operate correctly. We have already developed a custom Arduino library for the dust sensor,[3] and aim to do the same for the GPS library. The Arduino library for the GPS module provides a low-level interface to the GPS module, but it requires extensive error handling by the calling program. We aim to develop our own fork of the original library, which provides one interface to both get a location, parse the output, return them to the user, and perform the necessary error handling.

One of the participating classes ended up not programming the `air:bit` sensor kit themselves, but sharing a complete solution. We did not make it possible to identify specific classes from individual responses, so we could not exclude the responses from these students. These students will not have completed all the different programming tasks, and we believe that they may influence the results.

One area of the project we have not discussed yet, is how to analyze the collected air pollution measurements. This has been left out to the teachers, but we are experimenting with interactive Jupyter[4] notebooks that allow students to interactively explore their data with statistical programming languages such as R or Python.

[3] Online at github.com/fjukstad/SDS011.

[4] jupyter.org

CONCLUSIONS

We have successfully deployed our `air:bit` project to schools across Northern Norway. Doing so we have introduced more students to computer programming and electronics. The new version of our sensor kit provides higher quality datasets, and together with the online resources the kits are easier to assemble and program.

The results from the surveys show that both students and teachers enjoy the project, with only 8% of students reporting that they were dissatisfied or very dissatisfied. The majority of the students spent more than 9 weeks working on the project, spending more than 3 hours each week. 94% of the students used the online materials we have developed, and 83% of the students reported that these were very helpful. Assembling the `air:bit` and programming each of the sensors were simple tasks, but combining each of the different programs into a single program that collected all the data was a difficult task for the majority of the students. While the students managed to develop the code for the sensor kit, the results show that it would be beneficial to spend more time teaching the different fundamental concepts of computer science, such as variables, logical tests, and loops.

With these results in mind, we are currently in the process of organizing a third round of the `air:bit` project with even more participating schools. We aim to continue improving the course contents based on the results we have presented, and hope other projects will benefit from our experiences.

ACKNOWLEDGEMENTS

First we would like to thank all the students and teachers who participated in the project. We would like to thank Norwegian Meteorological Institute (MET) for providing open weather observations through data.met.no and yr.no. We would like to thank Norwegian Institute of Air Research (NILU) for providing air quality measurements through their luftkvalitet.nilu.no portal. We would also like to thank Thomas Olsen, Sonja Grossberndt, and Juan Carlos Aviles Solis for their presentations and input on the projects. We would like to thank the students at the Department of Computer Science for their help teaching the course. Last, we would like to thank Monica Martinussen and Ane Sætrum for their help developing the surveys.

REFERENCES

[1] Nina Angelvik. 2018. Air Pollution Data Analysis Platform for Computer Science Education Projects. In *Proceedings of the 49th ACM Technical Symposium on Computer Science Education*. ACM, 271–271.

[2] Nina Angelvik. 2018. *Data management platform for citizen science education projects*. Master's thesis. UiT Norges arktiske universitet.

[3] Aleksandar Antonić, Vedran Bilas, Martina Marjanović, Maja Matijašević, Dinko Oletić, Marko Pavelić, Ivana Podnar Žarko, Krešimir Pripužić, and Lea Skorin-Kapov. 2014. Urban crowd sensing demonstrator: Sense the zagreb air. In *Software, Telecommunications and Computer Networks (SoftCOM), 2014 22nd International Conference on*. IEEE, 423–424.

[4] Rob Beelen, Ole Raaschou-Nielsen, Massimo Stafoggia, Zorana Jovanovic Andersen, Gudrun Weinmayr, Barbara Hoffmann, Kathrin Wolf, Evangelia Samoli, Paul Fischer, Mark Nieuwenhuijsen, et al. 2014. Effects of long-term exposure to air pollution on natural-cause mortality: an analysis of 22 European cohorts within the multicentre ESCAPE project. *The Lancet* 383, 9919 (2014), 785–795.

[5] J Dean Brock, Rebecca F Bruce, and Susan L Reiser. 2009. Using Arduino for introductory programming courses. *Journal of Computing Sciences in Colleges* 25, 2 (2009), 129–130.
[6] Robert D Brook, Sanjay Rajagopalan, C Arden Pope, Jeffrey R Brook, Aruni Bhatnagar, Ana V Diez-Roux, Fernando Holguin, Yuling Hong, Russell V Luepker, Murray A Mittleman, et al. 2010. Particulate matter air pollution and cardiovascular disease. *Circulation* 121, 21 (2010), 2331–2378.
[7] Erik Brunvand and Nina McCurdy. 2017. Making Noise: Using Sound-Art to Explore Technological Fluency. In *Proceedings of the 2017 ACM SIGCSE Technical Symposium on Computer Science Education*. ACM, 87–92.
[8] Leah Buechley, Mike Eisenberg, Jaime Catchen, and Ali Crockett. 2008. The LilyPad Arduino: using computational textiles to investigate engagement, aesthetics, and diversity in computer science education. In *Proceedings of the SIGCHI conference on Human factors in computing systems*. ACM, 423–432.
[9] Nuria Castell, Mike Kobernus, Hai-Ying Liu, Philipp Schneider, William Lahoz, Arne J Berre, and Josef Noll. 2015. Mobile technologies and services for environmental monitoring: The Citi-Sense-MOB approach. *Urban climate* 14 (2015), 370–382.
[10] Joy Dutta, Chandreyee Chowdhury, Sarbani Roy, Asif Iqbal Middya, and Firoj Gazi. 2017. Towards Smart City: Sensing Air Quality in City based on Opportunistic Crowd-sensing. In *Proceedings of the 18th International Conference on Distributed Computing and Networking*. ACM, 42.
[11] European Schoolnet. 2014. Computing our future. Computer programming and coding - Priorities, school curricula and initiatives across Europe. http://www.eun.org/c/document_library/get_file?uuid=521cb928-6ec4-4a86-b522-9d8fd5cf60ce&groupId=43887.
[12] Deborah Ann Fields, Yasmin Kafai, Tomoko Nakajima, Joanna Goode, and Jane Margolis. 2018. Putting making into high school computer science classrooms: Promoting equity in teaching and learning with electronic textiles in exploring computer science. *Equity & Excellence in Education* 51, 1 (2018), 21–35.
[13] Bjørn Fjukstad, Nina Angelvik, Maria Wulff Hauglann, Joachim Sveia Knutsen, Morten Grønnesby, Hedinn Gunhildrud, and Lars Ailo Bongo. 2018. Low-Cost Programmable Air Quality Sensor Kits in Science Education. In *Proceedings of the 49th ACM Technical Symposium on Computer Science Education (SIGCSE '18)*. ACM, New York, NY, USA, 227–232. https://doi.org/10.1145/3159450.3159569
[14] Cristina Guerreiro. 2013. Air quality in Europe: 2013 report. (2013).
[15] Jørgen A Hagen, Per Nafstad, Anders Skrondal, Sonja Bjørkly, and Per Magnus. 2000. Associations between outdoor air pollutants and hospitalization for respiratory diseases. *Epidemiology* 11, 2 (2000), 136–140.
[16] Dinko Oletic and Vedran Bilas. 2015. Design of sensor node for air quality crowdsensing. In *Sensors Applications Symposium (SAS), 2015 IEEE*. IEEE, 1–5.
[17] World Health Organization. 2015. World Health Assembly closes, passing resolutions on air pollution and epilepsy. http://www.who.int/mediacentre/news/releases/2015/wha-26-may-2015/en. [Online; Accesssed: 02.06.2017].
[18] Mathilde Pascal, Magali Corso, Olivier Chanel, Christophe Declercq, Chiara Badaloni, Giulia Cesaroni, Susann Henschel, Kadri Meister, Daniela Haluza, Piedad Martin-Olmedo, et al. 2013. Assessing the public health impacts of urban air pollution in 25 European cities: results of the Aphekom project. *Science of the Total Environment* 449 (2013), 390–400.
[19] Clovis Antonio Petry, Fernando S Pacheco, Daniel Lohmann, Gabriela A Correa, and Paulo Moura. 2016. Project teaching beyond Physics: Integrating Arduino to the laboratory. In *Technologies Applied to Electronics Teaching (TAEE), 2016*. IEEE, 1–6.
[20] Ole Raaschou-Nielsen, Zorana J Andersen, Rob Beelen, Evangelia Samoli, Massimo Stafoggia, Gudrun Weinmayr, Barbara Hoffmann, Paul Fischer, Mark J Nieuwenhuijsen, Bert Brunekreef, et al. 2013. Air pollution and lung cancer incidence in 17 European cohorts: prospective analyses from the European Study of Cohorts for Air Pollution Effects (ESCAPE). *The lancet oncology* 14, 9 (2013), 813–822.

Below C Level: A Student-Centered x86-64 Simulator

Caitlin Fanning
University of San Diego
San Diego, California
caitlinfanning@sandiego.edu

Saturnino Garcia
University of San Diego
San Diego, California
sat@sandiego.edu

ABSTRACT

Learning an assembly language introduces students to important computing concepts such as the program stack and lays the conceptual groundwork for topics such as caching. While many instructors choose a RISC language such as MIPS for teaching assembly languages, the pervasiveness of x86-64 in both the desktop and server environments has compelled many instructors to adopt it in their courses. Unfortunately, x86-64 is a complex assembly language and as a result students often have difficulty understanding and visualizing the execution of an x86-64 program. This is especially the case for introductory level students, who struggle with the concepts of control flow; the difference between registers and memory; and memory organization (e.g. the stack).

While students can use debuggers (e.g. GDB) to help them step through the execution of a program and examine the program state, these tools are challenging to learn and are therefore not an ideal fit for introductory level students. This paper introduces *Below C Level* (BCL), an x86-64 open source simulator aimed at helping novices overcome the barriers to learning this challenging language. BCL offers an intuitive interface and many features that allow students to easily simulate x86-64 code snippets or programs. During simulation BCL helps students decipher individual instructions and visualizes the program stack and register file, allowing students to quickly trace through their program and gain a deeper understanding of x86-64 code.

ACM Reference Format:

Caitlin Fanning and Saturnino Garcia. 2019. Below C Level: A Student-Centered x86-64 Simulator. In *Innovation and Technology in Computer Science Education (ITiCSE '19), July 15–17, 2019, Aberdeen, Scotland UK.* ACM, New York, NY, USA, 7 pages. https://doi.org/10.1145/3304221.3319762

1 INTRODUCTION

Students typically learn about assembly languages as part of an introductory computer organization or computer systems course. Although students are unlikely to write assembly language programs in their professional lives, learning an assembly language provides insights into the operation of processors and lays the groundwork for important topics such as the memory hierarchy, computer security, and concurrency. Students therefore stand to greatly benefit from mastering at least one assembly language.

While there are many assembly languages, only a handful are widely utilized by modern processors. Among those, x86-64 and ARM are the most widely taught in introductory computer systems/organization courses [3, 7]. Compared with x86-64, the relative simplicity of ARM makes it a more natural fit for introductory courses. However, x86-64 remains a compelling choice because of the ease with which students can connect to the language, thanks to it being the native language for most PCs and Macs. x86-64 therefore remains a popular choice for instructors, despite the pedagogical challenges it presents.

The challenges of teaching/learning x86-64 fall into two general categories: language complexity and supporting software tools. Language complexity is a product of x86-64's legacy as a CISC language. Examples of this complexity include: an abundance of operand formats, the names and sizes of registers, and large number of (sometimes) obscure instructions. Aside from this complexity, there is currently a dearth of software tools to support novice language learners. For example, x86-64 lacks a student-oriented simulator like the MARS simulator for the MIPS assembly language [9].

While there is little that can be done about language complexity (e.g. exposing students to only a subset of the instructions), new supporting tools can greatly enhance the learning experience. One area of particular need is in software to help visualize the execution of an x86-64 program. Visualization of program state is a problem that introductory level students often struggle with as they attempt to understand the operational semantics of a language. A number of tools have been developed to help CS1 students visualize Python and Java program execution [5, 6, 8], but relatively few tools have been developed for assembly languages [1, 9] and none of those have targeted x86-64. Students are therefore left to use a debugger such as GDB to help them step through an x86-64 program and examine the program state. Unfortunately, these debuggers are generally text-based, have a significant learning curve, and do not allow students to test simple snippets of code, instead forcing the user to write a complete program.

This paper introduces Below C Level (BCL), an x86-64 simulator oriented towards students. BCL offers an intuitive GUI (see Fig. 1) for visualizing program state (hardware registers and program stack) during simulation. It hides or abstracts away details of x86-64 that are non-essential for introductory computer systems courses (e.g. instruction encoding) while emphasizing and providing additional help on issues (e.g. deciphering instructions) that this paper's authors have found through years of teaching experience. BCL also provides understandable error messages for both syntactical errors and runtime errors, often providing suggested fixes for common

ITiCSE '19, July 15–17, 2019, Aberdeen, Scotland UK

ACM ISBN 978-1-4503-6301-3/19/07...$15.00
https://doi.org/10.1145/3304221.3319762

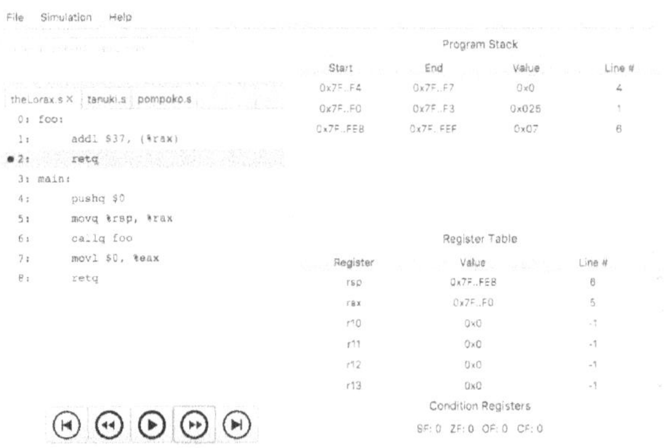

Figure 1: Below C Level (BCL) has a streamlined interface for viewing program state and managing multiple x86-64 programs.

mistakes. BCL is open source software written in Java/JavaFX, allowing for easy execution on a wide range of devices. It is available for download at https://www.github.com/usd-cs/below-c-level.

2 DESIGN OF BCL

BCL's interface (Fig. 1) was designed to ease the process of identifying critical information. Towards this goal BCL limits the data presented by its interface, prominently displaying only the program's instructions (left side) and the program's state (right side).

2.1 Simulation State Tracking

In x86-64 data is stored in the register file and memory. BCL's interface presents tabular views of both of these parts of program state. BCL displays only the stack portion of memory, which simplifies the user's view of memory while still allowing students to fully explore instructions that interact with memory. This section discusses the features available to examine program state during simulation.

2.1.1 Register Table. Students are often confused by the largely meaningless names of x86-64 registers. While there are only 16 total registers, looking through an unordered list of registers makes it difficult to track the state of the program. To combat this problem BCL introduces a novel register sorting method based on the concept of prominence. The most prominent registers are those that are used by the current instruction and those that have been used by recent instructions. For example, if the current instruction is "`incq 2(%rbx)`", the register table will display register `%rbx` at the top prior to executing it. After executing the instruction, the value stored in the register will be updated and remain near the top of the table. BCL takes into account both explicit registers (as in the previous example) as well as implicit registers (e.g. the PUSH instruction's use of the stack pointer register). By making the implicit registers prominent, students are subtly reminded of their otherwise hidden usage.

Another source of confusion when dealing with registers is the relation between a full 8-byte register and its smaller sub-registers. For example, a user may know the value stored in the 8-byte `%rax`

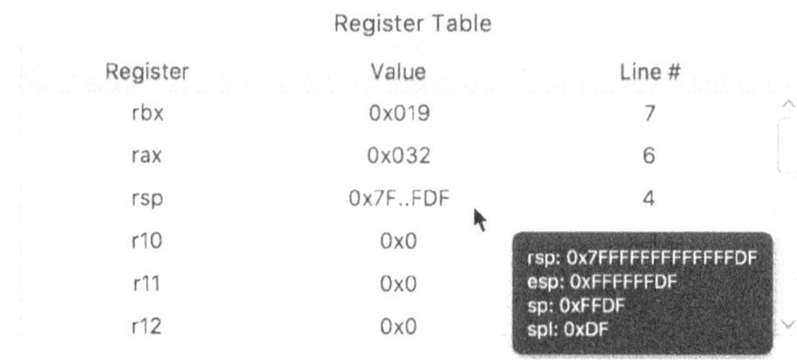

Figure 2: The register table's sub-register view provides students with the ability to see the values stored in each register's lower bits.

register but they may not know that the 4-byte `%eax` register contains the lower half of `%rax`. To visualize this relationship, users may hover over any register in the table to reveal all of its sub-registers and their contents as shown in Figure 2.

Students in an introductory computer systems course are often also new to number representation systems. BCL displays the register table values in hexadecimal by default, but allows users to switch between hexadecimal, unsigned decimal, and signed decimal representations. This is especially useful for students who struggle with two's complement representation where a small negative value (e.g. -1) may appear as a large hexadecimal value (e.g. 0xFFFFFFFF).

2.1.2 Program Stack. As previously mentioned, BCL's view of memory is limited to the program stack. This simplified view helps students focus on the many pitfalls of learning about the stack's operation, especially in regards to function calls. Students learning about the stack must successfully navigate complex x86-64 memory operands, implicit stack operations (e.g. during CALL and RET), maintaining the stack pointer, and many other issues. BCL's original motivation was to help students understand the stack, and therefore has features to address common areas of confusion.

BCL aids in deciphering the myriad of x86-64 memory operand formats by providing the user with informative instruction descriptions like the one shown in Figure 5. These instruction descriptions will be further discussed in Section 2.2.3, but this figure shows how the memory operand `8(%rax, %rbx, 2)` will be converted to an equation in the instruction description.

When dealing with larger or more complex x86-64 programs, it becomes a challenge to keep track not only of *what* is on the stack/memory but also *why* it was placed there. BCL provides several mechanisms to ease understanding the "why." First, BCL's instruction descriptions also help students uncover hidden stack operations such as the storing of the return address on the stack by a CALL instruction. Second, BCL's most prominent register sorting places the stack pointer register (i.e. `%rsp`) at the top of the register table for these hidden-stack-operation instructions. Finally, every entry in BCL's stack pane has a corresponding "Line Number" that indicates the line number of the instruction that added that entry.

BCL follows convention by having lower addresses appear lower in the view of memory. Students can easily see that instructions such as PUSH and CALL place values on the bottom the stack, helping illuminate the downward growth of the stack despite values being added to the "top." To reduce confusion, values below the stack

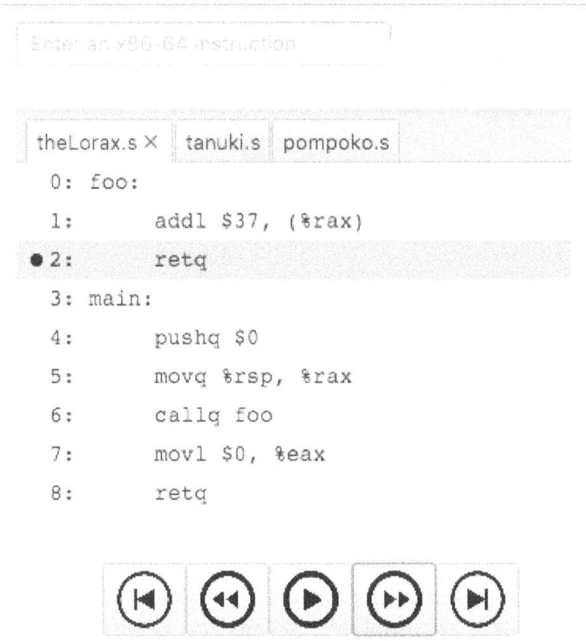

Figure 3: BCL's instruction list and simulation control buttons allow the user to easily navigate through a program.

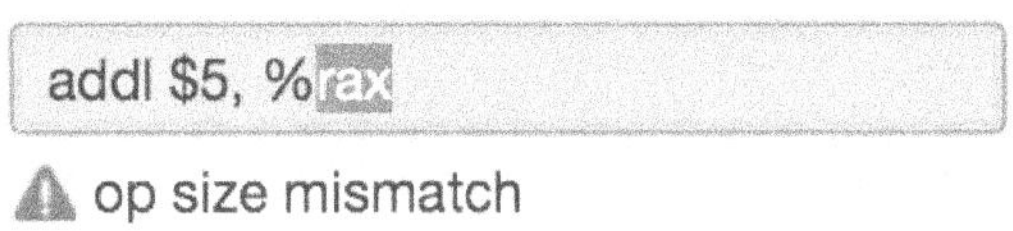

Figure 4: BCL offers guidance when syntactically incorrect instructions are entered so students may easily identify and rectify their mistakes.

pointer are not shown so when the stack pointer is incremented, students can see the stack shrink.

2.2 Program Input and Control

As shown in Figure 3, the left side of BCL's interface is dedicated to the instruction list and simulation control. The instruction list depicts the current program and allows the users to easily add, edit, or remove instructions.

2.2.1 Instruction Entry and Validation. At first novices may struggle with adding instructions due to the large number of x86-64 instructions, applicable registers, and constants. In an effort to simplify the initially daunting process and support students' learning, BCL parses entered instructions and offers informative error reporting.

BCL's error reporting is geared toward novices and the mistakes they commonly make such as: misspelled instructions, using a constant as a destination, duplicating labels, and providing the wrong number of operands. For example, students commonly struggle with selecting a correctly sized register. As shown in Figure 4, the user will be alerted to the mismatch between the declared size of the operation (the l in addl indicates a long or 4 byte operation) and the second operand (rax is an 8 byte register). The erroneous part of the instruction (the use of rax as the second operand) is automatically highlighted with the so the user can easily identify and edit it.

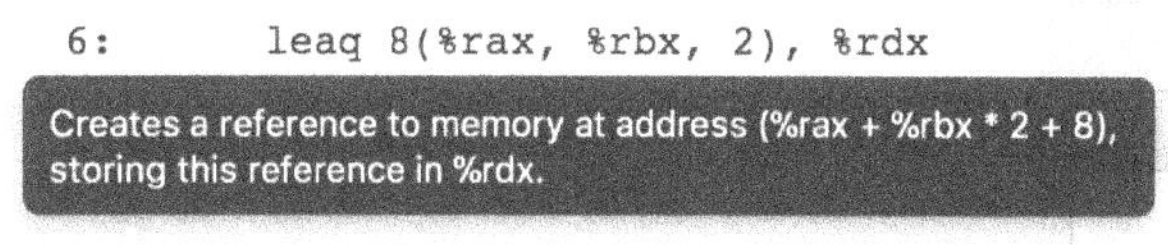

Figure 5: BCL generates instruction descriptions specific to each existing instruction. A student who has trouble understanding an instruction can hover over it in the instruction list and read the description.

BCL also provides suggested corrections for trivial errors. For example, if a user mistypes forgets the "a" in `leaq`, BCL generates the following error message: "Invalid instruction. Did you mean leaq?" In addition to identifying misspelled instructions, BCL also provides helpful suggestions for correcting invalid instruction suffixes and register names.

2.2.2 Instruction Editing and Removal. The user may right-click an existing instruction to edit or remove it. When editing an instruction, the selected instruction is highlighted blue in the list and displayed in the text entry field at the top. The user may make the changes they desire and upon hitting enter, the altered instruction is parsed and validated. It replaces the selected instruction and the simulation is restarted.

2.2.3 Instruction Descriptions. Students may desire to better understand or review a specific instruction, such as the challenging LEA instruction, the cryptically named CLT instruction, or the confusingly similar SAR and SHR instructions. BCL generates concise summaries tailored to each individual instruction. Figure 5 demonstrates a summary of the complex `leaq` instruction.

2.2.4 Runtime Error Reporting. In addition to struggling with the syntax of x86-64 programs, another difficult issue students struggle with involves errors occurring during the execution of the program. These errors are particularly tricky for students to uncover using existing tools because they usually don't cause a program to crash and therefore are easy to overlook. In particular BCL reports the following common runtime errors.

- **Improper memory alignment.** Intel has recommended alignment for all memory accesses. For example, all 8-byte values should be written to addresses that are multiples of 8. While this alignment is not strictly enforced, BCL reports this error because it is still an important consideration and one that students often overlook.
- **Reading from uninitialized memory.** Students are often used to languages that have default initial values for variables (e.g. Java). Because of this, students often assume memory is preinitialized to some value such as 0. While this will not cause an error in modern processors, it is still a misconception that often leads to buggy programs. BCL reports these reads from uninitialized memory as errors to force students to come to terms with this flawed understanding.

```
int bar(int y){
    return y + 2;
}

void foo(int *p, int x){
    *p += bar(x);
}

int main (){
    int n = 42;
    foo(&n, 19);
    return 0;
}
```

Figure 6: Case study example that demonstrates function calls and use of pointers in C.

- **Accessing an illegal part of memory.** Students are intimately familiar with the concept of segmentation faults from C and C++ programming. What they are not necessarily familiar with is the underlying cause of these errors. BCL reports accesses to memory outside of the stack to provide students with a preview of the concept of memory areas that they will encounter in operating systems courses.

BCL displays these errors above the simulation controls, informing the user of the line where the error ocurred as well as a concise description of the error.

2.2.5 Simulation Control. BCL's simulation controls allow the user to step forward or backward through a program and set a breakpoint on any instruction. Students can utilize these controls to thoroughly explore how a sequence of instructions affects program state. For example, they can set a breakpoint at an important part of the code, run to that point, then step forward or backward while examining the program state to understand the effect of each instruction.

Most students are accustomed to a "main" function acting as the beginning of a program. To facilitate this understanding, students may create a main label in their program. BCL will interpret the main label as the first instruction in the program, no matter where this label occurs in the instruction list. BCL further supports the main function abstraction by considering a return from the main function to be the end of simulation.

BCL also allows the user to have multiple concurrent simulations. The user may choose to begin a new simulation based on a blank program or a program loaded from a saved file. Each program has its own simulation state and instruction list. Switching between the programs is as simple as switching between tabs, as shown in Figure 3.

3 CASE STUDIES

In this section, we will explore several example programs to demonstrate how BCL can aid students in learning the x86-64 assembly language. These examples will highlight common sources of confusion such as function calls and conditionals, as well as demonstrate common runtime errors such as the use of uninitialized memory.

```
bar:
    addl $2, %edi
    movl %edi, %eax
    retq
foo:
    pushq %rdi
    movl %esi, %edi
    callq bar
    popq %rcx
    addl (%rcx), %eax
    retq
main:
    subq $8, %rsp
    movq $42, (%rsp)
    leaq (%rsp), %rdi
    movl $19, %esi
    callq foo
    movl $0, %eax
```

Figure 7: This x86-64 translation of Figure 6 bears little resemblance to the original code, making it difficult to decipher.

These examples, as well as others, are distributed with BCL to allow students to easily access programs that highlight important concepts.

3.1 Case 1: Function Calls and Stack Usage

Function calls are one of the most challenging assembly language concepts encountered by students. The reason for this challenge stems from the disconnect from how function calls appear in higher level languages like C and how they are implemented in assembly code. Hidden from the C version is usage of the stack and registers to pass values to functions and to receive the results. Further complicating this topic is the fact that function calling in x86-64 follows conventions rather than strictly enforced rules. It is easy for students to make a mistake in the calling convention, only to later find mysterious bugs in their code.

A small C program with several function calls as well as an x86-64 translation are shown in Figures 6 and 7. In addition to showing basic function calls, this example program also demonstrates the use of pointers and multiple parameters. As can be seen in these figures, the x86-64 code structure bears little resemblance to that of the original C code. BCL aids students in deciphering this x86-64 program in several different ways.

As described in Section 2.1, BCL visualizes the state of the program stack. Figure 8 shows BCL's stack pane view for the example program at the point where the `bar` function has just been called. Two of the main questions students have is what is on the stack and why it is there. Not only is each of the stack entries shown in the figure, answering the first question but also each entry includes the line number of the instruction that placed the value on the stack answering the second question.

Analyzing the origin of these four entries reveals many key concepts to students. For example, the first entry comes from the

Program Stack

Start	End	Value	Line #
0x7F..F0	0x7F..F7	0x02A	13
0x7F..FE8	0x7F..FEF	0x011	16
0x7F..FE0	0x7F..FE7	0x7F..F0	5
0x7F..FD8	0x7F..FDF	0x08	7

Figure 8: BCL's stack pane displays the values that have been pushed onto the stack. Students can also see the line number of the instruction that created each entry.

main function where we needed to place a value in memory so that a reference (i.e. pointer) to it could be passed to the foo function. While not shown, BCL's register table view would reveal that the %rdi register contains the address (0x7F...F0) rather than the value (42) as generated by the aforementioned leaq instruction. This single stack entry therefore highlights the utility of the LEA (load effective address) instruction as well as the use of registers for function parameters.

Continuing on we find further insights. Both the second and the fourth stack entries correspond to callq instructions. Here students are reminded of the need for the caller to indicate where the callee should return to when finished. The third entry originates from the foo function's need to save the original value of %rdi before re-purposing that register for calling the bar function. This demonstrates caller-saved register behavior as well as emphasizing the fixed location of parameters across all function calls. BCL gathers these concepts and condenses them into one simple view so students can more easily comprehend them.

3.2 Case 2: Conditionals

Students working with x86-64 will inevitably encounter several other perplexing topics, including conditional instructions (e.g. jump if equal, je) and the 1-bit condition registers/flags (e.g. the sign flag, SF). While conditional instructions themselves may be relatively easy to understand, students often struggle to grasp how these instructions use condition registers and how these registers obtain their values. For example, a CMP (compare) instruction will perform subtraction between two operands, and set the condition flags according to the result (e.g. setting SF to 1 if the result was negative). The condition registers are never explicitly named in a program, making them easy to overlook. BCL remedies this situation by displaying the contents of all four condition registers below the register table.

Users can easily understand how an instruction (e.g. CMP) utilizes the condition flags by viewing its values in the register table and stepping forward to see which flags are set in the condition registers view of the BCL window. This process is demonstrated with the simple code in Figure 9. The program uses both a conditional instruction, "jl target," and a comparison instruction, "cmpl $0, %edi". BCL aims to make interpreting this and similar code as clear as possible through several different mechanisms.

As mentioned in Section 2.1, BCL provides concise instruction summaries in order to help decipher complex conditional instructions. For the jl instruction in Figure 9, BCL provides the following

```
stoo:
    movl %esi, %eax
    cmpl $0, %edi
    jl target
    incl %eax
    jmp done
target:
    decl %eax
done:
    retq
```

Figure 9: Case study example that demonstrates the use of conditional instructions in x86-64.

Register Table

Register	Value (Signed)	Line #
rdi	-24	11
rsi	56	12
rax	56	1
rsp	-16	13
r10	0	-1
r11	0	-1

rdi: -24
edi: -24
di: -24
dil: -24

Condition Registers

SF: 1 ZF: 0 OF: 0 CF: 0

Figure 10: BCL's register table demonstrates the effects of the "cmpl $0, %edi" instruction from Figure 9. The ability to switch between hexadecimal, signed decimal, and unsigned decimal representation is useful for students learning about different number representations.

description: "Jumps to the label target if the result of the last signed comparison was less than, otherwise moves to the next line (i.e. jump if SF ^ OF == 1)." Based on this description students can quickly be reminded that the condition is based on the xor of the SF and OF condition registers.

To fully understand the operation of the jl instruction, students will need to simulate up to that point in the program. To make this easy, students can set a breakpoint at the jl instruction. At this point, students can view the values of both the condition registers and general purpose registers as shown in Figure 10. By running the simulation until the breakpoint and stepping backward through the program, the user can more easily deduce that the previous cmpl instruction sets the condition flags that jl evaluates. Students can discern from the instruction description of the cmpl instruction that zero is subtracted from the value stored in the %edi register; in this case -24.

While the result of the cmpl's subtraction is a temporary value and not stored, students can still view the value of %edi in the sub-register view. By default the register values are displayed in hexadecimal format, obscuring the fact that %edi is a negative number. However as shown in Figure 10, BCL's signed decimal view removes this confusion. Users can then step through the instruction, and track the condition registers to see whether the sign or

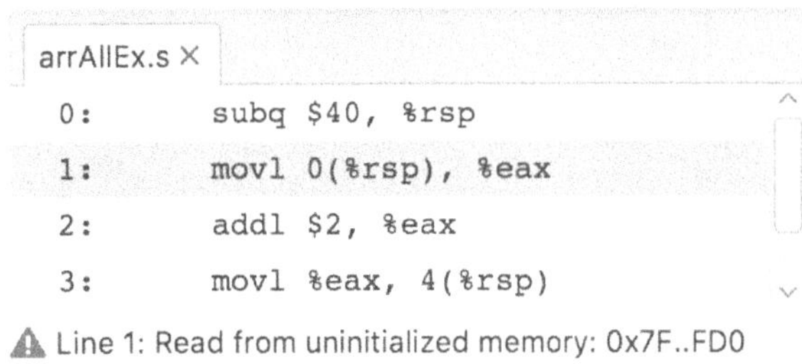

Figure 11: BCL also alerts the user to common runtime errors such as the use of uninitialized memory.

zero flag is set. They can then fully understand the logic behind the `jl` instruction's jump to the `target` label. BCL's instruction descriptions, sub-register view, and condition registers work together to clarify the oftentimes puzzling conditional instructions and the implicit operations they are based upon.

3.3 Common Runtime Errors

Many computer systems courses and their texts first introduce students to x86-64 assembly through the use of C code examples translated to a set of x86-64 instructions. As practice exercises, quizzes, or projects, students will most likely translate C code into x86-64. Although they may utilize the correct syntax for x86-64 instructions, they may not realize that their translated code may contain other types of errors as well. This subsection examines how BCL's runtime error checking can help identify these subtle errors.

3.3.1 Uninitialized Memory. Consider the following code that includes a common error made by novices, namely assuming the array is preinitialized, and therefore can be immediately read.

```
int arr[10];
arr[1] = arr[0] + 2;
```

While this error will not be evident just from running the program, it is nonetheless a serious mistake that students will need to correct. Although syntactically correct, the second line (`movl 0(%rsp), %eax`) tries to read a value from uninitialized memory. BCL prints out an error message for the user as shown in Figure 11 with the line number of the troublesome instruction, and the address it is attempting to read from. BCL forces students to confront this error which might otherwise only show up as a subtle bug when running the compiled C program.

3.3.2 Misaligned Memory. Memory alignment is a subtle concept that students often overlook when translating C code to x86-64 code. This concept is especially prominent in C structs where memory alignment often requires padding between fields. For example, in Figure 12 the struct's second field, y, is a long and therefore should be stored at an address that is a multiple of 8. If students were to translate this code directly to x86-64 without padding, then BCL will report a misaligned memory access when trying to set `foo.y` to 2800. BCL makes this mistake highly visible, forcing students to correct their misconceptions regarding memory alignment.

```
struct s {
    int x;
    long y;
} foo;
foo.x = 49;
foo.y = 2800;
```

Figure 12: Students often introduce misaligned memory errors when translating code such as this that involves structs.

4 RELATED WORK

The MARS MIPS Assembly and Runtime Simulator [9] offers students an educational tool that allows them to compile and simulate MIPS code. Besides displaying the compiled MIPS program, MARS provides a spreadsheet style display of values stored in memory and registers. BCL offers a similar environment with several important benefits over MARS. First, BCL's streamlined interface focuses students on key concepts for understanding assembly language. For example, introductory computer systems students are unlikely to need to understand x86-64 instruction encoding or know exactly where in memory instructions are located. Both of these are prominently displayed in MARS, but are abstracted away in BCL. Second, BCL has a strong focus on teaching students about the program stack. Conversely, MARS has a flat memory structure that makes following the operation of the stack more difficult.

The GNU debugger (GDB) is often used to step through assembly language programs. Again, BCL offers several important benefits over GDB. First, learning to properly utilize GDB is time-consuming and requires multiple commands to examine the values stored in the memory and registers of a program. In contrast, BCL updates and displays relevant state after each executed instruction, making it easier for students to trace their program. Second, GDB only allows users to step forward through the program: if a student accidentally goes too far, they must restart simulation and carefully step back to the same location. Finally, GDB requires a complete assembly program to begin. This introduces a huge barrier to new students who at this point are mostly trying to understand individual instructions and fragments of code. BCL easily allows individual instructions or small fragments of code to be simulated.

A number of full-system x86 or x86-64 simulators have been developed over the years, e.g. [2, 10]. While full-system simulators have an important role in education, their complexity and larger scope (e.g. focusing on I/O) greatly limit their utility in an introductory computer systems course.

5 CONCLUSION

BCL supports novice computing students by helping visualize execution of x86-64 assembly language programs. BCL's interface is designed with introductory level students in mind, with critical information easily accessible at all times while distracting details are hidden or abstracted away. BCL allows students to quickly explore even the smallest of x86-64 code fragments, with features that facilitate the learning of not only assembly language but also broader computer systems concepts. BCL is open source software and is readily available at [4].

REFERENCES

[1] [n. d.]. AL - The Assembly Language Simulator-1. https://scratch.mit.edu/projects/881462/. ([n. d.]). Accessed: 2018-08-31.

[2] Michael David Black and Priyadarshini Komala. 2011. A Full System x86 Simulator for Teaching Computer Organization. In *Proceedings of the 42Nd ACM Technical Symposium on Computer Science Education (SIGCSE '11)*. ACM, New York, NY, USA, 365–370. https://doi.org/10.1145/1953163.1953272

[3] Randal E. Bryant and David R. O'Hallaron. 2016. *Computer Systems: A Programmer's Perspective* (third ed.). Pearson.

[4] Caitlin Fanning and Saturnino Garcia. 2019. Below C Level. (April 2019). https://doi.org/10.5281/zenodo.2631956

[5] Philip J. Guo. 2013. Online Python Tutor: Embeddable Web-based Program Visualization for CS Education. In *Proceeding of the 44th ACM Technical Symposium on Computer Science Education (SIGCSE '13)*. ACM, New York, NY, USA, 579–584. https://doi.org/10.1145/2445196.2445368

[6] Juha Helminen and Lauri Malmi. 2010. Jype - a Program Visualization and Programming Exercise Tool for Python. In *Proceedings of the 5th International Symposium on Software Visualization (SOFTVIS '10)*. ACM, New York, NY, USA, 153–162. https://doi.org/10.1145/1879211.1879234

[7] David A. Patterson and John L. Hennessy. 2016. *Computer Organization and Design ARM Edition: The Hardware Software Interface* (first ed.). Morgan Kaufmann.

[8] Teemu Sirkiä. 2013. A JavaScript Library for Visualizing Program Execution. In *Proceedings of the 13th Koli Calling International Conference on Computing Education Research (Koli Calling '13)*. ACM, New York, NY, USA, 189–190. https://doi.org/10.1145/2526968.2526990

[9] Kenneth Vollmar and Pete Sanderson. 2006. MARS: An Education-oriented MIPS Assembly Language Simulator. In *Proceedings of the 37th SIGCSE Technical Symposium on Computer Science Education (SIGCSE '06)*. ACM, New York, NY, USA, 239–243. https://doi.org/10.1145/1121341.1121415

[10] Hui Zeng, Matt Yourst, Kanad Ghose, and Dmitry Ponomarev. 2009. MPTLsim: A Cycle-accurate, Full-system Simulator for x86-64 Multicore Architectures with Coherent Caches. *SIGARCH Comput. Archit. News* 37, 2 (July 2009), 2–9. https://doi.org/10.1145/1577129.1577132

Developing Course Projects in a Hack Day: An Experience Report

Kiev Gama
Centro de Informática - Universidade Federal de Pernambuco (CIn/UFPE)
Recife, Brazil
kiev@cin.ufpe.br

ABSTRACT

Some researchers are starting to point out the importance of hackathons as an alternative venue for college students practicing and learning. Many positive aspects were highlighted such as peer learning and improvements in problem-solving, project management and task priority analysis. However, this hackathon phenomena is something that is happening outside the curriculum, with scarce reports of teachers taking advantage of similar approaches in undergraduate courses. In this article, we present our experience of an undergraduate introductory course on Distributed Systems where students have to participate in a "hack day" at the end of the semester. The goal is to take advantage of the hackathon model to bring a more realistic and engaging scenario where students can develop their course project and put into practice what they have learned in the semester. With this model, they have to do face-to-face group work and also have the opportunity to share knowledge with other groups. Our experience indicates positive results with this approach. Students reported a high level of engagement and enthusiasm. There were different situations of peer learning being reported, and according to their perception, students felt they learned more in the hack day than in lectures or laboratory practice.

CCS CONCEPTS

• **Applied computing** → **Collaborative learning**; • **Software and its engineering** → *Organizing principles for web applications*; • **Computer systems organization** → Client-server architectures;

KEYWORDS

Peer learning, Project-based learning, Hackathon, Challenge-based Learning

ACM Reference Format:
Kiev Gama. 2019. Developing Course Projects in a Hack Day: An Experience Report. In *Innovation and Technology in Computer Science Education (ITiCSE '19), July 15–17, 2019, Aberdeen, Scotland UK.* ACM, New York, NY, USA, 7 pages. https://doi.org/10.1145/3304221.3319777

ACM ISBN 978-1-4503-6301-3/19/07...$15.00
https://doi.org/10.1145/3304221.3319777

1 INTRODUCTION

Recently, many new educational approaches [9, 10, 12, 18] have been proposed as means to better engage students in learning activities, improving their motivation to learn as well as their ability to build new knowledge. What all these new approaches share is an interest in catering for a new generation of students with a vast wealth of information available at the tips of their fingers. These students tend to be independent learners, as long as they are learning something that interests them. These approaches emphasize learning by doing, instead of simply knowing [7].

Challenges such as hackathons, coding marathons and the like engage students in the construction of solutions targeting real problems fostering teamwork, collaboration and complementing the formal learning that takes place in classrooms [20]. Although hackathons can be seen as venues where companies exploit cheap labor[21], for college students they have a significant and complementary role in learning and practicing programming skills [13, 19]. Hackathons allow peer learning and improvements in problem-solving, project management and task priority analysis to cite a few. Students also benefit from using face-to-face interactions that are typical of intensive collocation [16].

We support the idea that assigning projects as homework on their own may not be as effective as doing it together in co-located groups, since students have excessive distractions and waste time while doing homework, mainly due to multitasking [2]. Studies on the effect of time pressure in project groups indicate that the motivational power tends to intensify close to deadlines [8]. We, therefore, tried to motivate and engage students in one-day group projects to tackle a small challenge under time pressure where they would apply the contents they learned in the semester in the context of an undergraduate course. We called the activity a *hack day*, which is sometimes a term used interchangeably with *hackathon*.

In this paper we provide an experience report on an undergraduate course in Introduction to Distributed Systems, targeting Information System undergraduates, where the final project for the course was performed in teams during a hack-day in the university. We detail the course structure and how the hack day was put into practice. We also present the perspective of the students, with an analysis of a questionnaire answered by all class, along with some lessons learned. This paper is organized as follows: section 2 presents the background, section 3 details the course structure; section 4, 5 and 6 present evaluation, discussion and lessons learned, respectively, followed by the conclusions in section 7.

2 BACKGROUND

Challenge-based Learning [9, 14] is one of the approaches inspired on experiential learning. Under a broader perspective [20], there is a trend in students engaging in challenge-based learning activities such as hackathons and coding marathons, which are complementing the formal learning that takes place in classrooms. These activities allow them to experience "learning by doing", which has been promoted by many years [5] and supports the idea where one will only master something if actually practicing it.

Hackathons are events where software developers collaborate intensively over a short time-frame on problems to be solved by software [11]. Although not being usually held as course activity, hackathons are a good place to learn collaboratively. Peer learning can be found in college hackathons [13], where students can teach and learn from their peers. Because of the tight time and demands to quickly act, participants end up improving their skills in problem-solving, project management and task priority analysis. The aspect of learning from peers has been confirmed in a study on college hackathons [19], where learning was happening incidentally and opportunistically, with students motivated by both social and technical reasons. Warner and Guo [19] suggest hack sessions as possible models to be used in classrooms, although not many cases of hackathons or hack sessions used as part of courses are seen in the literature. Datathons (data-focused hackathons) [1] were reported as a way to have students learning and putting into practice their recently acquired data science and analytics skills. Tu et al. [17] reported the usage of a hackathon during a weekend in the middle of a Boot-Camp Style Programming Course. The goal was to give students the opportunity to consolidate their knowledge in object-oriented programming and increase their creativity and problem-solving skills. Gama et al. [6] reported a 24h hackathon in an Internet of Things course where students would prototype a connected device as a course project activity. Other approaches like coding dojos [15] are a way to learn programming in a collaborative way, with the main principles of creating a collaborative, non-competitive, inclusive and safe environment where people can be continuously learning, although they are not exactly challenge-oriented, which is an appealing way to engage students [20].

3 COURSE STRUCTURE

The Introduction to Distributed Systems course is offered as an optional course to undergraduate students of *Information Systems*. The goal is to give students an overview of distributed systems, with emphasis on the different forms of communication between applications. Instead of being just limited to lectures about distributed systems fundamental concepts, throughout the course students have contact with different technologies used in industry to build distributed applications. The following topics are covered:

- Sockets (TCP and UDP)
- RPC and RMI
- Web Services (SOAP and REST)
- Message-Oriented Middleware
- AJAX, WebSockets and HTML5 Server-Sent Events
- Complex Event Processing (CEP)

The course has a rather practical approach, balancing lectures with laboratory practice and home assignments. The lab sessions have the guidance of the teacher. In these sessions, we employ a learn-by-doing approach where students can practice what was presented in the previous lecture. The exercises in any given topic provide a scaffolding approach, bringing step-by-step instructions in introductory exercises and gradually removing details on how to solve them as the complexity evolve. The home assignments are simple scenarios where they need to employ the technology being practiced (e.g., build a Web User Interface for car price quotations consuming data from a real Web Service). At the end of the semester, students spend a whole day in a continuous 10-hour period to develop their project, working in teams during a "hack day".

3.1 Lectures and Laboratory Practice

Students begin the course by having a broad overview of distributed systems followed by classes that will focus on different approaches for communication between applications. The very basics begins with raw sockets and how to implement simple communication protocols, with laboratory practice on both TCP and UDP sockets using the Java programming language. The next topic covered is on how to abstract that type of communication with Remote Procedure Call and Remote Method Invocation, with practical exercises using Java RMI. WebServices are then explored as an interoperable way of doing RPC/RMI, with practice with Java on both SOAP and RESTful approaches. After those topics, students will be presented with different approaches to asynchronous communication. We start with Message-Oriented Middleware, with laboratory classes using RabbitMQ using both Java and Node.js. The next topic is centered around asynchronous Web Technologies (AJAX, WebSockets and HTML Server-Sent Events), where the practical lab classes involve Java and Node.js. The last topic covered consists of an introduction to stream processing approach using Complex Event Processing (CEP). The laboratory practice used Java and the Esper CEP engine.

3.2 Hack day

In the first day the teacher explained students about the 10-hour hack day that would take place in the end of the semester. The purpose is to create an environment to put students to practice together doing teamwork, organizing themselves in groups of 3 or 4. When collocation is enforced, we avoid groups working remotely or asynchronously. It allows fostering collaboration among students and having continuous support from the teacher. The event took place in a Saturday 9AM-7PM with a quick pizza pause at 1PM.

In the hack day they have a challenge proposed by the teacher where they need to combine the different concepts and technologies they learned throughout the course, to provide a solution to a practical problem taken from the real world. The challenge was focused on urban mobility data and was revealed only in the hack day. We provided CSV files containing periodic real readings of vehicles (bus and taxi) geolocation. Students were charged to read the corresponding files, simulate the streaming of data and create a user interface (UI) that allows users to monitor vehicles and get notifications. They would have to propose an architecture for the distributed application, illustrating what technologies covered by the course they would utilize. The UI functionality would be proposed by each team and validated with the teacher.

4 EVALUATION

With the objective of evaluating the students perception about this experience of using a hack day for their project assignment, we gathered feedback from all 24 male students who were enrolled in this elective course that took place in the first semester (February to June) of 2018 at the Federal University of Pernambuco (UFPE) in Recife, Brazil. They were either junior or senior level. In this section, we present a preliminary analysis of feedback provided through the survey we did. Students were informed that the responses would not affect at all their grades. To assure them about that, the questions were provided through an anonymous Google Form.

The questionnaire had 22 statements (Table 1) using a Likert scale response format where respondents would have to indicate their level of agreement (Strongly Disagree, Somewhat Disagree, Neutral, Somewhat Agree, Strongly Agree). The statements were centered around the students' perspective about learning, motivational and social aspects. There were also multiple choice questions about other aspects: previous experience in hackathons or similar events; fatigue; and the intention to enrol in another course using a similar project approach. In addition, two open-ended questions asked students about the positive and negative aspects of their hack day experience, respectively.

Each student signed an Informed Consent Form. The form detailed the objectives of the study, assuring the confidentiality of the collected data and anonymity of the participants.

Table 1: Survey questions

Survey questions
Q1. Without lectures the hack day would have been more difficult
Q2. Without laboratory practice the hack day would have been more difficult
Q3. I had a significant amount of learning in lectures
Q4. I had a significant amount of learning in lab classes
Q5. I attended to most of the lectures
Q6. I attended to most of the laboratory classes
Q7. I learned from my colleagues during lab classes
Q8. I learned by myself during the hack day
Q9. I learned from my team colleagues during the hack day
Q10. I learned from other groups during the hack day
Q11. I learned from the teacher during the hack day
Q12. I believe my team developed more things than we would do in a regular project
Q13. I learned more in the hack day than in regular lectures
Q14. I learned more in the hack day than in lab classes
Q15. I felt motivated during the hack day
Q16. I felt engaged during the hack day
Q17. The hack day allowed to establish a closer relationship with the teacher
Q18. The hack day allowed to establish a closer relationship with colleagues from my team
Q19. The hack day allowed to establish a closer relationship with colleagues from other teams
Q20. I enjoyed the experience of a hack day as a learning approach
Q21. I would prefer two rounds of 12 hours
Q22. I believe hack days could be used in other courses

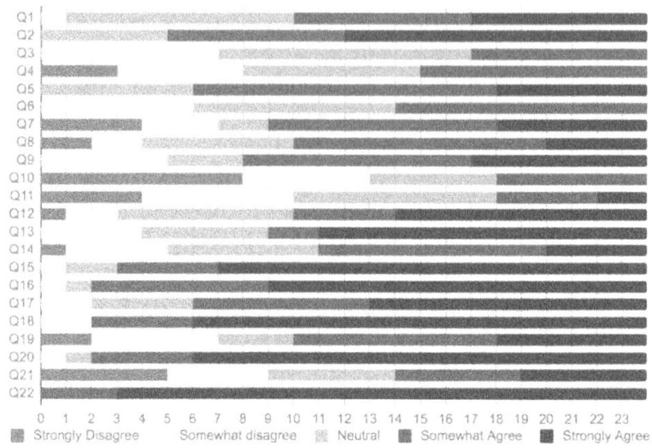

Figure 1: Results of the questionnaire in a 5-point Likert response format

4.1 Questionnaire data

Among the students, 66.7% were participating in a hackathon-like dynamic for the first time, while the other 33.3% already had some experience. Only 12.5% thought the time given was enough to finish the project, 58.3% believed they would need two additional hours to finish the project properly and 25% believed it would be better through a continuous 24-hour period while only 1 person (4.2%) believed the project would need to be broken down into two 12-hour period. When asked if they would have the intention to join other course employing a hack day for the final project, 95.8% answered "yes" while the remaining 4.2% said "no".

In general, by observing the overall trend on the responses (Figure 1) of the questionnaire, one can notice that the majority of students tend to an agreement (Somewhat Agree and Strongly Agree). Q1 and Q2 state that without lectures or laboratory practice, respectively, the hack day would have been more difficult. According to students responses, laboratory classes (79% of agreement) were of more importance than lectures (58% of agreement). However, concerning their perception about having a significant amount of learning in those classes (Q3 and Q4), there was no Strongly Agree answer for none of the two types of classes. The perception of learning in lectures (29%) was slightly less positive than laboratory classes (38%), which contrasts to the fact that students tended to agree more about having a good attendance to lectures (75% agreed) than in lab classes (42% agreed).

Questions Q7 through Q11 concerned who they mostly learned from. The agreement in responses about learning from colleagues during lab classes (Q7) was 62.5%. During the hack day, learning by themselves (Q8) had 58% of answers agreeing with that while learning from teammates (Q9) had 66.6% of agreement. In contrast to the overall trend, there is less of an agreement in questions Q10 and Q11, which correspond to learning from other groups and learning from the teacher, respectively.

Q12 concerned the perception of students about developing more things in the hack day than the team would do in a regular project. 58% of responses represented agreement (41.6% Strongly Agree and 16.6% Somewhat Agree), while 29% were neutral about that. Q13 and Q14 consisted of affirming that the student learned more in the hack day than lectures and lab classes, respectively. Although the overall agreement on those was similar (62% and 54%, respectively), there were more Strongly Agree answers (54.17%) in the former case than in the latter (16.7%).

Motivation (Q15) and engagement (Q16) were among the highest rates of agreement. In both cases, there were no Strongly Disagree answers and just one Somewhat disagree answer (4.2%). The agreement rate on those questions were 87% and 92%, respectively.

We asked if the hack day allowed establishing closer relationships with the teacher, colleagues from the same team and colleagues from other teams in questions Q17, Q18 and Q19, respectively. 92% of the responses agreed they established with closer relationships with teammates, while answers about closer relationships with teacher and colleagues were 75% and 58% of agreement, respectively.

About the hack day format, 92% of the responses indicated that students agreed that they enjoyed the experience of a hack day as a learning approach (Q20). There were no Strongly Disagree answers in this case. When asked if two rounds of 12 hours would be preferred as the hack day format (Q21), there was no consensus on that since no significant trend on responses can be found. All students agreed that hack days could be used in other courses (Q22).

4.2 Open-ended Questions

For the analysis of the students' answers to the two open-ended questions (positive and negative aspects) we performed the initial steps of the coding process suggested by Grounded Theory (open coding and axial coding) [3]. During the open coding phase we created codes that emerged from the students' comments, grouping them under categories. Later these codes were related to each other. In general, respondents used much more text to provide feedback about positive aspects than they used to comment on the negative aspects. We assigned each student with a unique identification ranging from S1 to S24, with excerpts from some of them being presented throughout the text. Six students (25%) reported they did not find any negative aspect in the hack day, with rather positive comments about it. We could verify that time was one of the key aspects. The short time and the sense of urgency generated more focus on the teams, as stated by student S8 *"A Hack day helps you keep focus on a course and devote a specific time to a task. Many people have trouble managing their own time and ranking their priorities. In this way (with a hack day) the learning happens more fluidly."*

Besides focus, the short time allows exercising task and time management as highlighted by student S23: *"With fixed and non-stop time, the student is forced in a good way to always try to maintain 100% of performance, even in the last moments, like the last reps in physical workouts. As a leader it's a good time to exercise the separation of tasks among group members. It's also a great exercise of time management."*.

The learning aspect was emphasized by some of the participants, as mentioned by S17, who mentions the benefits of the hack day approach: *"The learning in this different way was interesting. It forced us to try to get things done as fast and focused as possible. Another positive point is the possibility of discussing the project with other students or the teacher. I believe it complements very well the content, the practical classes and the exercises of the course."*

Motivating aspects of the hack day was highlighted in 7 (29%) of the comments, such as S18 *"A Hack day breaks the monotony of traditional course projects by being fun, dynamic and motivating."*. The fact of dealing with a realistic problem also engaged them in the project development, as highlighted by S23: *"A quick opportunity to apply the knowledge acquired in the course, besides the experience of building a solution for a real problem."*.

The negative aspects pointed out were not as varied as the positive ones. Most of them mentioned fatigue and time constraints. Two students reported being saturated at the end of the day while others mentioned the drowsiness after the lunch break, like S8 who said that *"At times it can be tiring. Especially after having a lunch break, students get sleepy. Not having coffee is also negative."*.

Time was indeed the aspect that was most commented, with both positive and negative feedback. One of the students (S1), clearly points that out, by saying that *"The time pressure is a double-edged sword, because sometimes it is necessary to take a break to lighten up and cool down a little, and if the time is too short, there is no way for these breaks to happen."*. It was orthogonal to other aspects, such as management, as stated by S12 *"If you do not have good planning of what will be done, you could end up wasting a lot of time."*.

A few students complaint about the difficulty of learning new things in a hack day, because there is not much time to learn and they also have the pressure of delivering the project, as stated by S17: *"I believe it only works if the students are already relatively well acquainted with the tools they will use. It was more of practicing things that I already knew than learning new things."*.

According to the statements that were collected, the participation of students in the work of each group sometimes was considered to be unbalanced and unfair. Under the perspective of S23 *"Since it is a task to be done within a short period of time if a member of the group does not know anything he will just relax. Maybe minimal participation like commits in the project code could be a solution?"*.

For the analysis of the students' answers to the two open-ended questions (positive and negative aspects) we performed the initial steps of the coding process suggested by Grounded Theory (open coding and axial coding) [3]. During the open coding phase we created codes that emerged from the students' comments, grouping them into categories. Later these codes were related to each other. We had the following categories and respectively assigned codes, resulting from axial coding:

- Practice: Application of knowledge, real cases, knowledge practice, test capacity, fixing content;
- Learning: Intensive learning, class complement, difficulty to learn something new, knowledge exchange;
- Motivation: Focus, Proactive, challenge, dynamic, productive, intensive, breaking monotony;
- Management: Time management, task organization, scope definition, team members not working;
- Social: Relationship, team integration, interaction, team work.

These categories helped to synthesize the concepts and to better understand they key aspects of the hack day, under the students perspective. The participants were highly motivated throughout activity, where they could practice the knowledge that was acquired in the course. Although the aspect of time, either under positive or negative perspective, was present in many of the complaints, it was grouped under the category of management. Learning was mentioned as positive by some of the students; however, there were opinions about the limited possibilities of learning new things due to the short time span and the pressure to deliver the project within that time. Regardless, the hack day was mostly seen as a dynamic event for practicing and learning while interacting with colleagues.

4.3 Direct observations

During the hack day, the teacher did direct observations which were immediately written down. In this section, we discuss some of these observations and bring anecdotal evidence of some findings.
Finished projects. The students organized themselves into 7 teams. Only one did not have anything properly working at the end of the hack day. That team and 3 others asked to use the time of the next class slot to give a better finishing to their project. All four teams presented the project with significant improvements. According to them, they did not spend any more time in the project over the weekend. If this is actually true, they would indeed have needed just one or two hours in the hack day.
Architectural decisions. The time was enough to reflect about changes in architectural decisions of the solutions they were creating. One group, for instance, took a natural decision toward robustness. They changed their implementation to use a message queue (RabbitMQ) instead of using a direct connection through WebSockets, which improved their solution. However, the short time forced some groups to take wrong decisions that were perceived only during the demonstration, with no time to perform changes. In another group, the system would not support more than one vehicle being monitored in the browser UI neither more than one user (e.g. different browsers) monitoring the same vehicle.
Task Management. Several groups divided activities so that each member focused on something different. For instance, a student would focus on the CSV file and latitude conversions; another one would focus on consuming data from the message queue, another student on queries in the Esper CEP Engine, etc. Although this is typical in regular project assignments, this sort of task arrangement may be undesired since can generate unbalanced learning on the different topics covered in a project if students do not rotate their responsibilities in the team.
Social interactions and Knowledge Exchange. In some groups, students who did not know each other had the opportunity to work together for the first time. In one of the groups, a student arrived late and joined a group of two people he was not acquainted with. It did not take long for him to be integrated with the group, discussing ideas and sharing tasks. In a few occasions, he was observed helping a student from another group. The collocation made easier the mutual support students gave to one another. In another example of knowledge exchange, one student took his laptop to the desk of another group and took a significant part of his time to explain something to another student. In contrast, there was a group of students with no prior friendship who did minimal interaction among them and among the other groups. They were the first ones to finish the project and provided a very simple solution.
Support from teacher. An important advantage of all students at once doing the project in the laboratory was the continuous support of the teacher. For instance, one of the groups had problems with unexpected behavior of two applications (one in Java and another in Node.JS) writing and reading on the same message queue. After discussing with the teacher, they accepted the suggestion and fixed the problem. Two group members mentioned that they did not understand quite well that concept in classes or in the lab exercise. Another group had problems understanding the WebSockets API they chose to use with Java, aiming to facilitate the combination with the Esper CEP engine, which is written in Java as well. However, the topic of WebSockets was covered with Node.JS in classes. They were about to abandon the API, but during discussion with the teacher they could clarify the differences and learn how to use WebSockets in Java.
Lack of consensus on the influence of the time frame. Student's opinions were divided about the 10-hour period being enough for the proposed project. When entering the last hour of the hack day, students were informed about the time that was left and were asked if everything was fine. While some would say the time was too short and they would still be integrating work or in the middle of development, others were about to finish their projects. Students who are interns or work part-time in industry compared this 10-hour activity to a productive day in their jobs.
Creation of a challenge-oriented culture. Although this observation was made after the event, we believe it is worth reporting. A few weeks after the course, four students registered and participated in a hackathon that took place in the university and was organized by one of this article's authors. They stated that their first experience with a hackathon dynamic was during the course, which demystified the fact of working continuous hours on a challenge and motivated them to register for the event.

5 DISCUSSION

By comparing the data collected in different ways (questionnaire and direct observations), we bring some aspects into discussion:
Perception of Learning. According to the students' perception, peer learning was instead concentrated within teams, although there was evidence through the questionnaire and through direct observations that groups would exchange knowledge and would consult the teacher as well. Their responses indicated they learned more in the hack day than in classes or laboratory practices. However, there were contradicting answers in that aspect. Some students claimed to learn new things while other did not consider they were learning but practicing what they already knew.
Social Aspects. The participants' responses indicated that spending a day together in the lab allowed establishing a closer relationship with colleagues and teacher. We confirmed that in the direct observations. The exchanges among groups reinforce the importance that collaborative environments have for learning. Besides the collaboration in the lab, we observed that during lunch, although students naturally gathered in their respective work groups to eat together they also discussed technical difficulties with other groups.
Management. There are certainly some key management issues here. This topic came up in both the open-ended answers in the questionnaire and in the direct observations. Students understood how important the time management and the division of tasks were and explicitly mentioned it. However, as it was stated in the direct

observations of the way they divided tasks and organized work may hinder the balance on the topics each team member learned.

Engagement and Motivation. Being in the university on a Saturday did not seem to bother students. The majority of them seemed to have enjoyed the activity, being open to hack days in other courses. Both their responses to the questionnaire statements and the open-ended questions confirm their motivation and engagement. The challenge-based nature of the project and the realistic nature of problems are key motivational aspects for students [20].

Hack Day Duration. There were different opinions about the duration of a hack day. Almost a third of the responses considered a 24-hour period, either straight or broken down into two 12-hour periods. Anslow et al. [1] cite the importance of making these types of event compatible with travel time and family commitments. However, half of the opinions mentioned they would need only two additional hours. As stated in the direct observations, some of the groups presented their partially completed projects and asked to finish them in an extra class, which was basically two hours. Indeed, that was enough to achieve significant improvements in all projects that had extra time. Even though in the hack day they were informed that such improvements would not increase much their final grade, they insisted in finishing the projects, which was a very positive aspect showing their engagement.

Hack day versus traditional project assignment. The fact of being an elective course attracts students from different levels (junior and senior). Therefore, many of the students did not know each other and this may affect how they work in non-collocated group projects. As some students have stated, in traditional group project assignments they usually work remotely and typically do not meet face-to-face to develop the project together. This lowers the possibility of knowledge exchange and peer learning. The intensive collocation is one of the benefits from the hackathon format [16]. Instead of reproducing the competitive environment of a hackathon, we are rather focusing on the intensive collocation aspect to foster a collaborative environment. Many comments praised the intensive collocation for several reasons (presence of all group members, exchange with other groups, support from teacher, etc). The majority of students thought this type of event was productive and believed they developed more things than they would in a regular project.

6 LESSONS LEARNED

Since this is the first time we use a hack day format in this course, many aspects were not as successful as we expected. We present below some lessons learned from this initial experience that we would likely change the next time we do a hack day in a course.

Preparation. The handling of the CSV data file was not the focus of the course contents. Students had to spend some time preparing the raw data in order to simulate the data streams. If the teacher had prepared the necessary infrastructure in advance (e.g., a stream simulator using the dump files as data sources), the teams could have used that time to focus on the project goals.

Task rotation. Some students reported that in some cases they would split their tasks in a way that they would not know in technical detail what the other team members would be doing. For instance, one team member spent the whole project with message queue while the other focused in the UI only. A mechanism to force task rotation would ensure everyone would do a little of each task and eventually practice more topics. This would also help in the case of students that did not work as much as expected, a case which was reported by a few respondents.

Pause for lunch. Although during lunch students seemed to enjoy being together, each team has its own pace and forcing them to stop for lunch would interrupt their state of total involvement (i.e. flow [4]) as some of them complained. Leaving them with the choice of when to do their break would be more appropriate in this case.

Architectural Decisions. There was little time for defining the architecture. Some groups took the wrong architectural decisions probably because of that limitation. A point for improvement would be giving them more time and more guidance in that initial phase. For instance, a joint discussion with the whole group about candidate architectures that could be proposed for a solution to their challenge asking them to indicate the advantages and disadvantages of each of the components and choices.

Challenge scope. One thing that must be well evaluated is the definition of the challenge and its scope in order to have an idea about the potential size and necessary time to build the solution. This initial experience served as a reference for future estimates of effort and scope definition. One may either reduce the scope of the challenge or convince students to reduce the scope of the proposed solution if this is the case. Another option would be using two hack days, which is our intention for the near future.

7 CONCLUSIONS

This article presented an experience report about students engaging in a *hack day* activity where they spent a whole day in the laboratory to develop their course project. It was part of an Introductory course in Distributed Systems for Information Systems undergraduates. We detailed the course structure and presented the students perspective on this activity along with observations and some lessons learned.

Overall, the allotted time was sufficient for almost all of the groups finishing the project, although some of them asked for additional time to improve it. Although the aspect of time had a positive perspective because of the pressure and focus it helped to provide, students also complained it was not enough for the scope of the challenge. Students mention learning as a valuable outcome; however, there were opinions about the limited possibilities of learning something new in such a short time frame because of the pressure to deliver the project. The participants were highly engaged and motivated during the hack day, where they could put into practice many of the topics they learned throughout the semester. The fact of being a real problem was an additional motivator to some of the students. There were different situations of peer learning being reported by students and by direct observation. According to their perception, students believed they learned more in the hack day than in lectures or laboratory practice. In future executions of this activity, we intend to address some of the drawbacks we identified in the data preparation, the limited time and scope of the projects.

ACKNOWLEDGMENTS

This work had partial support from the Brazilian National Council for Scientific and Technological Development (CNPq) - grant 315620/2018-8.

REFERENCES

[1] Craig Anslow, John Brosz, Frank Maurer, and Mike Boyes. 2016. Datathons: an experience report of data hackathons for data science education. In *Proceedings of the 47th ACM Technical Symposium on Computing Science Education*. ACM, 615–620.

[2] Charles Calderwood, Phillip L Ackerman, and Erin Marie Conklin. 2014. What else do college students "do" while studying? An investigation of multitasking. *Computers & Education* 75 (2014), 19–29.

[3] Juliet Corbin, Anselm Strauss, et al. 2008. Basics of qualitative research: Techniques and procedures for developing grounded theory. (2008).

[4] Mihaly Csikszentmihalyi and Isabella Csikszentmihalyi. 1975. *Beyond boredom and anxiety*. Vol. 721. Jossey-Bass San Francisco.

[5] John Dewey. 1938. *Experience and education*. Simon and Schuster.

[6] Kiev Gama, Breno Alencar Gonçalves, and Pedro Alessio. 2018. Hackathons in the formal learning process. In *Proceedings of the 23rd Annual ACM Conference on Innovation and Technology in Computer Science Education*. ACM, 248–253.

[7] Gerald C Gannod, Janet E Burge, and Michael T Helmick. 2008. Using the inverted classroom to teach software engineering. In *Proceedings of the 30th international conference on Software engineering*. ACM, 777–786.

[8] Josette MP Gevers, Wendelien van Eerde, and Christel G Rutte. 2001. Time pressure, potency, and progress in project groups. *European Journal of Work and Organizational Psychology* 10, 2 (2001), 205–221.

[9] Laurence F Johnson, Rachel S Smith, J Troy Smythe, and Rachel K Varon. 2009. *Challenge-based learning: An approach for our time*. Technical Report. The New Media Consortium.

[10] David A Kolb. 2014. *Experiential learning: Experience as the source of learning and development*. FT press.

[11] Marko Komssi, Danielle Pichlis, Mikko Raatikainen, Klas Kindström, and Janne Järvinen. 2015. What are Hackathons for? *IEEE Software* 32, 5 (2015), 60–67.

[12] Stephan Krusche, Bernd Bruegge, Irina Camilleri, Kirill Krinkin, Andreas Seitz, and Cecil Wöbker. 2017. Chaordic learning: a case study. In *Software Engineering: Software Engineering Education and Training Track (ICSE-SEET), 2017 IEEE/ACM 39th International Conference on*. IEEE, 87–96.

[13] Arnab Nandi and Meris Mandernach. 2016. Hackathons as an informal learning platform. In *Proceedings of the 47th ACM Technical Symposium on Computing Science Education*. ACM, 346–351.

[14] Mark Nichols, Karen Cator, and Marco Torres. 2016. Challenge Based Learner User Guide. *Redwood City, CA: Digital Promise. link-http://cbl. digitalpromise. org/2016/08/30/challenge-based-learning-guide* (2016).

[15] Danilo Toshiaki Sato, Hugo Corbucci, and Mariana Vivian Bravo. 2008. Coding dojo: An environment for learning and sharing agile practices. In *Agile, 2008. AGILE'08. Conference*. IEEE, 459–464.

[16] Erik H Trainer, Arun Kalyanasundaram, Chalalai Chaihirunkarn, and James D Herbsleb. 2016. How to hackathon: Socio-technical tradeoffs in brief, intensive collocation. In *Proceedings of the 19th ACM Conference on Computer-Supported Cooperative Work & Social Computing*. ACM, 1118–1130.

[17] Yu-Cheng Tu, Gillian Dobbie, Ian Warren, Andrew Meads, and Cameron Grout. 2018. An Experience Report on a Boot-Camp Style Programming Course. In *Proceedings of the 49th ACM Technical Symposium on Computer Science Education*. ACM, 509–514.

[18] Natasha M Costa Valentim, Williamson Silva, and Tayana Conte. 2017. The students' perspectives on applying design thinking for the design of mobile applications. In *Proceedings of the 39th International Conference on Software Engineering: Software Engineering and Education Track*. IEEE Press, 77–86.

[19] Jeremy Warner and Philip J Guo. 2017. Hack. edu: Examining How College Hackathons Are Perceived By Student Attendees and Non-Attendees. In *Proc. of the 2017 ACM Conf. on Intl Computing Education Research*. ACM, 254–262.

[20] Scooter Willis, Greg Byrd, and Brian David Johnson. 2017. Challenge-Based Learning. *Computer* 50, 7 (2017), 13–16.

[21] Sharon Zukin and Max Papadantonakis. 2017. Hackathons as Co-optation Ritual: Socializing Workers and Institutionalizing Innovation in the "New" Economy. In *Precarious Work*. Emerald Publishing Limited, 157–181.

Use, Modify, Create: Comparing Computational Thinking Lesson Progressions for STEM Classes

Nicholas Lytle
Veronica Catété
Danielle Boulden
nalytle@ncsu.edu
vmcatete@ncsu.edu
NC State University
Raleigh, North Carolina

Yihuan Dong
Jennifer Houchins
Alexandra Milliken
Amy Isvik
ydong2@ncsu.edu
NC State University
Raleigh, North Carolina

Dolly Bounajim
Eric Wiebe
Tiffany Barnes
wiebe@ncsu.edu
tmbarnes@ncsu.edu
NC State University
Raleigh, North Carolina

ABSTRACT

Computational Thinking (CT) is being infused into curricula in a variety of core K-12 STEM courses. As these topics are being introduced to students without prior programming experience and are potentially taught by instructors unfamiliar with programming and CT, appropriate lesson design might help support both students and teachers. "Use-Modify-Create" (UMC), a CT lesson progression, has students ease into CT topics by first "Using" a given artifact, "Modifying" an existing one, and then eventually "Creating" new ones. While studies have presented lessons adopting and adapting this progression and advocating for its use, few have focused on evaluating UMC's pedagogical effectiveness and claims. We present a comparison study between two CT lesson progressions for middle school science classes. Students participated in a 4-day activity focused on developing an agent-based simulation in a block-based programming environment. While some classrooms had students develop code on days 2-4, others used a scaffolded lesson plan modeled after the UMC framework. Through analyzing student's exit tickets, classroom observations, and teacher interviews, we illustrate differences in perception of assignment difficulty from both the students and teachers, as well as student perception of artifact "ownership" between conditions.

CCS CONCEPTS

• **Social and professional topics → Computational thinking**; *K-12 education*;

KEYWORDS

Use-Modify-Create, Computational Thinking, Lesson Design

ACM Reference Format:

Nicholas Lytle, Veronica Catété, Danielle Boulden, Yihuan Dong, Jennifer Houchins, Alexandra Milliken, Amy Isvik, Dolly Bounajim, Eric Wiebe, and Tiffany Barnes. 2019. Use, Modify, Create: Comparing Computational Thinking Lesson Progressions for STEM Classes. In *Innovation and Technology in Computer Science Education (ITiCSE '19), July 15–17, 2019, Aberdeen, Scotland Uk.* ACM, New York, NY, USA, Article , 7 pages. https://doi.org/10.1145/3304221.3319786

ITiCSE '19, July 15–17, 2019, Aberdeen, Scotland Uk

ACM ISBN 978-1-4503-6301-3/19/07...$15.00
https://doi.org/10.1145/3304221.3319786

1 INTRODUCTION

It is becoming increasingly necessary for every child to have experience with 21st-century Computational Thinking (CT) skills [28]. However, these skills have typically been taught within elective Computer Science classes or outside of school activities [17]. To reach *all* students, CT must be integrated into required K-12 courses, such as science and math. This CT integration will pose several challenges. First, lessons must not only focus on key CT concepts but must also include and integrate domain knowledge, though research demonstrates that CT topics can be integrated without detracting from the learning of the core domain material [3]. Further, these activities must be designed with the understanding that they may be the first introduction to programming or CT for many students and teachers. Successful integration depends on equipped and capable teachers, though many do not have the prerequisite background required to teach CT or computer science [7]. Professional development can give teachers experience with CT skills [8, 12, 21], however, to reach all students, we must develop solutions that can be readily adopted by both experienced and inexperienced teachers and that can improve student learning in both CT and course content.

This study compares two separate design implementations of a 4-day computing infused science lesson across multiple classrooms. One condition received a lesson including 3 days of coding while the other received a scaffolded curriculum modeled after Lee's Use-Modify-Create (UMC) [16]. Through our quasi-experimental design, we aim to investigate how UMC sequencing impacts:

1. Student-perceived *difficulty* of the lesson.
2. Student-perceived *ownership* of the used and developed programs.
3. Teacher-perceived *difficulty* of the lesson and *ability* to teach it.

2 RELATED WORK

As demand increases for incorporating computing into core K-12 subjects, so does the need for classroom activities that are tailored for non-computing focused teachers and students. Through adding computing activities directly into a STEM course, teachers gain improved mastery of their discipline when using new instructional approaches [26]. However, reporting suggests that teachers lose much of the control they traditionally have over the learning process and may become uncomfortable when students pose and solve open-ended integrated STEM and Computing problems [6]. For teachers to support these students engaging in self-directed collaborative processes, they require an ability to diagnose difficulties and give hints, rather than supply solutions.

A prior case study by Cateté et al. [4] on infusing CT into science classrooms highlights how teachers were hesitant to lead new programming activities, and were afraid of misguiding students, even with professional development and classroom support. These concerns are also identified in a 2017 report for UK teachers facing computing infusion [23]. The most common challenges mentioned included subject knowledge, differentiation, lack of time, approaches to teaching topics, students' understanding, and ability to problem solve. This report also lists successful teacher strategies towards teaching computing such as unplugged activities[2], computational thinking, contextual learning, and scaffolding of programming tasks. In order to improve the incorporation of computing into science classrooms, we attempt to utilize the above findings to create more supportive materials for both teachers and students facing computing.

One such approach to improving CT acquisition with reduced cognitive stress comes in the form of curricular materials that follow a scaffolded intensity of interaction. Research by Lee et al, suggests that using a Use-Modify-Create (UMC) learning progression can promote the acquisition and development of CT while also limiting the anxiety from activities that teachers may have previously perceived to be "too hard" for students [15, 16]. In the first phase, **Use**, students inspect code and run existing models acting as "consumers of someone else's creation[16]." In transitioning to the **Modify** phase, students go from solely using existing code to changing the code to suit their intended desires as designers. This act of modifying also brings about a change in perceived ownership as students move toward viewing the code as their own. In the final phase, **Create**, students end up in a state where they have created a completely new model, having full ownership of the design and agency over its development[16].

Lee promoted UMC not only as a lesson scaffolding framework, but also a way to create this sense of "ownership" in learners. It has been argued that in order to realize the full benefit of CT, students must develop a sense of ownership over the models underlying the CT concepts being taught [5]. During creation, the final step of UMC, students increase engagement in learning and perceived agency of their learning, which is associated with behavioral, emotional, and cognitive engagement [22]. UMC allows students to take increasing ownership of the learning by giving them progressively more complex tasks. This increased ownership empowers students to investigate CT and underlying assumptions behind the tasks.

Researchers have used UMC as a basis for a number of CT and CT-infused activities across the K-8 curriculum [13, 15, 27]. Werner et al. employed UMC in the creation of an elective game programming course [27], finding that students demonstrated understanding of several CT and CS concepts through developing games. Furthermore, Grizioti et al. developed a game-specific adaptation in which players first play then modify/fix a "half-baked" version of the game, and then create a new version [13]. Sentance and Waite extend UMC in their PRIMM (Predict, Run, Investigate, Modify, Make) model for teaching text-based programming[24]. Initial workshops suggest that teachers are willing to adopt this model, but like Werner and Grizioti, this work is situated in a pure CS context.

We believe the UMC framework can extend into core domains, alleviating the burden of learning to program while simultaneously learning domain material. This will allow students to ease into the activity, become familiar with the programming environment, and explore how smaller changes affect the code. We assume these same benefits extend to teachers who also might not be familiar with coding and would welcome scaffolded lessons. We finally posit that as students go from users to creators in the Use-Modify-Create lessons, their sense of ownership of the project will increase to match that of students who participate in lessons where they always create code from scratch. We test out these assumptions using an A/B study across multiple classrooms as described in the section below. If these hypotheses are supported, these benefits can reduce teachers' fears of being CT novices as well as students' frustration with the difficulty of learning to program, potentially increasing adoption of materials developed using the UMC progression.

3 METHODS

3.1 Context

The study took place in two separate middle schools (School 1, School 2) in the mid-atlantic United States. The classrooms were all 6th grade (age 11-12) science classrooms taught by one of 4 teachers (1 from School 1, 3 from School 2). None of the teachers had experience instructing programing lessons. Each teacher was responsible for multiple class *periods* with different students. Teachers in School 2 had 5 class periods each while the teacher in School 1 taught 2 class periods. Each period averaged 20 - 30 unique students. A total of 394 students participated in the study, but we only analyze data from the 160 consenting students who provided data for every day. Demographic information for these students is reported in Table 1. Chi-Square tests show no significant differences in gender or race between the two populations.

Table 1: Gender and race/ethnicity by condition.

		UMC (N=95)	Control (N=65)	Total (N=160)
Gender	Female	42.1%	41.5%	41.9%
	Male	47.4%	55.4%	50.6%
Race Ethnicity	Black	19.0%	13.9%	16.9%
	Caucasian	26.3%	26.2%	26.3%
	Hispanic	15.8%	18.5%	16.9%
	Asian	14.7%	15.4%	15.0%
	Multi-racial	3.2%	3.1%	3.1%
	N/A	21.1%	23.1%	21.9%

We further surveyed students on their previous programming experiences. Responses are shown in Table 2 ranging from Never to Daily. Chi-Square tests show no significant differences in prior programming experience between the two populations. In an open response follow up to question 1, many students reporting "Rare" or "Occasional" described participating in an Hour of Code activity [14]. Those marking "Frequent" or "Daily" report being in a computing club or technology elective course.

Table 2: Participants' computing background self-ratings.

	Never	Rare	Occasional	Frequent	Daily
Q1	Previous participation in computing activities				
UMC	7.4%	9.5%	54.7%	11.6%	6.3%
Control	6.2%	15.4%	47.7%	20.0%	7.7%
Q2	Previous experience writing a computer program				
UMC	15.8%	21.1%	41.1%	7.4%	4.2%
Control	13.8%	23.1%	40.0%	15.4%	4.6%

3.2 Curriculum

The activity was designed to be a 4-day, CT lesson. Though teachers were trained on the material, on programming days, a research team member taught the first period as part of a "Faded Instructor Scaffolding Model" designed to help teachers understand the curriculum from a student's perspective. Each programming day took place within the Cellular environment [1], an extension of the block-based programming language Snap! [10] that provides a good method for agent-based modeling and has been used in similar initiatives with infusing CT into STEM curriculum [4].

For use in the 6th grade science classroom, the topic of "Food Webs" was chosen. In the food web curriculum, students learn about how energy is transferred from producers to primary and secondary consumers. The computing-infused activity let students explore the transfer of energy in a simplified food web developed using the block-based programming environment, Cellular [1]. We describe each daily segment of the activity below, and a breakdown by condition is visualized in Figure 1. The Use-Modify-Create (UMC) version was adapted from a previous version of the food web activity used in classrooms which acts as our control lesson in this study.

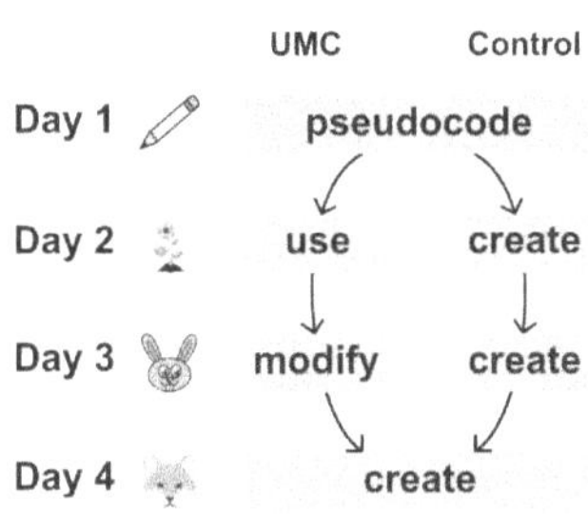

Figure 1: Programming methods for Food Web agents (plants, bunnies, foxes) by day and condition

Day 1 - Both conditions completed an "Unplugged" activity [2] in which students reviewed definitions and components of a Food Web (e.g. primary and secondary consumer, how energy is transferred through the system, etc.). This ended with completing a worksheet lead by the instructor where students described the behavior of agents in the model through pseudo-code. This was done to prepare students for developing these ideas within the programming model.

Day 2 - Day 2's focus was the "Plant" agent (the producer), which would grow based on the solar energy given by the "Sun" (code provided for both conditions). For the control condition, students had to develop code for the Plant to be able to transition between stages of its life cycle using the amount of 'Solar Energy' received over time. This was represented in code as sequential conditionals, checking both the plant's current state and energy before transitioning into the next state. The students in the UMC condition had plant code provided and instead inspected and read through the working code in order to become familiar with the different conditions. The instructor led students in exploration by changing the initial input (the solar energy intensity), the cutoff conditions (how much energy is needed to transition) and the amount of energy lost through transitioning. Students then used a worksheet to record how those changes affected the speed in which flowers changed state.

Day 3 - Day 3's focus was the "Bunny" agent (the model's primary consumer). Control condition students wrote code to add the new agent to their working model. Meanwhile, the UMC condition had Bunny code provided at the outset. However, the given bunny behavior did not conform with their idea of the actual model (e.g. bunnies never ate when they got low on energy, flowers transitioned to an incorrect state after being eaten etc.). Thus, students during this class period *modified* the existing code in order to make it conform to the existing ideas they had discussed on Day 1's activity of how the model should behave. This is similar to the activity found in prior studies of fixing the "half-baked microworld"[13].

Day 4 - The agent focus for the final lesson was on this model's secondary consumer, the "Fox". Both conditions had to develop the entire Fox code (in a sense, *creating* a new model with this additional agent) and update the "Bunny" code to react to the new agent and implement the desired final behavior in their model. Once complete, as shown in Figure 2, students were tasked with changing some functionality in their code and comparing how their new simulations behaved differently from their previous one.

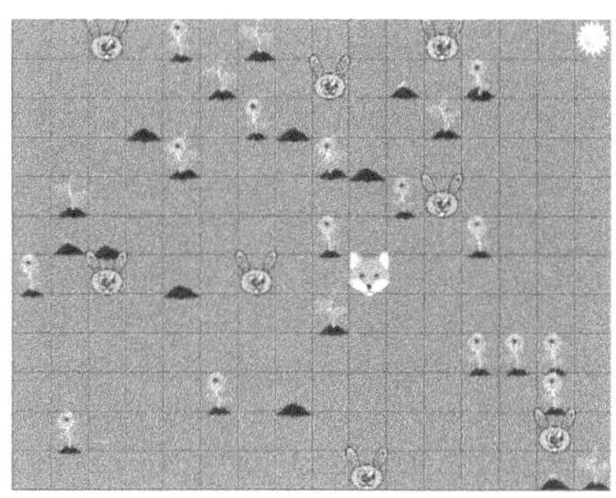

Figure 2: Food Web in Cellular showing how plant, bunny, and fox agents appear on the grid at one time step.

Although each programming day builds on previous topics, students begin with the same starter code for their condition to reduce effects from student absences or incompletion from a prior day. The topic of Food Webs and the sequencing of our curriculum affords the exploration of our research questions for a number of reasons. First, as a life science topic found in common core guidelines, Food Web is an exemplar STEM lesson that could be taught throughout the United States. Second, as the topic of Food Web focuses on the interaction between different actors in an environment, it lends itself nicely to a computing task focused on developing an agent-based model or simulation like prior UMC-developed lessons [16]. Finally, as we use a multi-day assignment, we can segment each programming day to be on a single Food Web actor, allowing us to frame the UMC conditions' activity to match each phase of UMC.

3.3 Data Collection

Evaluation of the initiative was recorded through a number of data collection methods. For every period, at least one research team member was present taking observation notes, focusing on the students' interactions within the environment as well as how the teacher was teaching the lesson. After the conclusion of each day's activity, students took an end-of-activity "Exit Ticket" in which they answered a series of questions about the activity. In order to study student-perceived difficulty, we asked students to rate the difficulty of the days' activity on a 1-5 Likert scale (Very Easy to Very Difficult). For student-perceived ownership, two questions were included that addressed the ability to express one's ideas and the belief the code was their own creation. These questions were on a 7-point Likert scale from Strongly Agree to Strongly Disagree.

For teacher-perceived difficulty, we first analyzed classroom observations that focused on the teacher's ability to teach the lesson. Additionally, a member of the research team conducted interviews using a semi-structured interview protocol with each of the participating teachers at the conclusion of the lesson sequence. The protocol consisted of questions targeted to elicit general teacher feedback about each of the days of the lesson sequence and their impact on students (e.g., What are the strengths of the lesson? Weaknesses?) Interviews lasted approximately twenty to thirty minutes and were audio recorded and transcribed for analysis. A constant comparison analysis [20] of the interview transcripts provided insights on the teachers' perceptions of the lessons from a pedagogical standpoint, comparing teacher interviews within groups and between groups.

4 RESULTS

4.1 Student-perceived difficulty

Each day, students completed the exit ticket question "Please use the [scale of 1 to 5 (Very Easy to Very Difficult)] to rate how difficult or easy the lesson was today." The daily average values for students in each condition are given in Table 3. A Friedman Test, similar to a parametric repeated measures ANOVA but for non-parametric data [9], was performed in order to determine if there were differences found in the average values for each of the days. For the Use-Modify-Create (UMC) condition, no significant difference was found among the four days $\chi^2_3 = 1.879, p = 0.598$. However, for the control condition, $\chi^2_3 = 9.984, p = 0.019$ showing significance. Therefore, a post-hoc Wilcoxon Signed Rank Test, a non-parametric equivalent to a paired T-Test [29], was performed between each of the pairwise groups. No significant differences were found between days 1 and 3, 1 and 4, nor 3 and 4. However, for each pairwise comparison with day 2, a significant difference was found (1-2: $V = 240, p = .002$; 2-3: $V = 770, p = .003$; and 2-4: $V = 218, p = .004$). An additional Mann Whitney U Test, a non-parametric test similar to an unpaired T-Test[19], was performed between groups for each of the 4 days to determine differences in difficulty responses between conditions for the same day. No significant differences were found in the comparisons between conditions for Days 1 ($W = 3187, p = 0.72$), 3 ($W = 3162, p = 0.79$), or 4 ($W = 3144, p = 0.84$). However, comparing Day 2 (the first coding day) between the two conditions found a significant difference with UMC being significantly easier ($W = 2238, p = .002$).

This difference in difficulty is backed by classroom observations. Researchers found that in the UMC classrooms, students were often able to finish their designated tasks more quickly, especially on the third day where the UMC group modified a bunny while the control group coded one from scratch. This time difference means that the UMC group had additional time to add elements or engage in teacher-led discussions about connections to class topics. Further, researchers found in some control condition classrooms (especially on Day 2 and to some degree Day 3) that students had difficulty finishing the task. As a result, teachers in the control group on Day 2 either forged ahead leaving many students behind, or slowed the lesson so all students could keep up, but were unable to complete the full lesson to add flowers. During the follow-up interviews, teachers in the control condition commented on the need for more scaffolding, while teachers in the UMC condition did not express this concern. Teachers in the UMC condition indicated that the progression of the curriculum served as an effective scaffold for students' conceptual understanding of the programming environment that better prepares them for creating their own program models. One of the teachers articulates this below:

"...like day [two], when we were on the computer. You really understand the beginning part. And then day [three] it builds a little bit more and you're building the code. You're playing with it. And day [four] is really copying the bunny code, just tweaking it a tiny bit. So at that point they've done so much with it already. They've got it. I mean, they were playing with all kinds of things."

4.2 Student-perceived ownership

Two questions were added to the coding day exit tickets (Days 2, 3, and 4) to address student-perceived ownership. These were: "To what extent do you agree with the following statement: I was able to express my ideas in the model today" and "To what extent do you agree with the following statement: The code I ended the lesson with is my own creation" both on a scale from 1 (Strongly Agree) to 7 (Strongly Disagree). The average values for these answers are shown in Table 3. A Friedman Test was performed in order to determine if there were differences found in the average values for each of the days. No significant difference was found among the three days for 'expressing ideas' for both the control group, $\chi^2_2 = 0.0231, p = 0.989$ and for the UMC group $\chi^2_2 = 1.1421, p = 0.565$. However, in performing Mann Whitney U Tests between the 2 groups, significant differences were found in Days 3 ($W = 3389, p = 0.03$) and 4 ($W = 3425, p = 0.04$) though not for Day 2 ($W = 3683, p = 0.21$). For the statement "The code I ended the lesson with is my own creation", a Friedman Test finds no significant difference in the control condition answers: $\chi^2_2 = 0.562, p = 755$. However, for the UMC condition, the Friedman Test found a significant difference among the three: $\chi^2_2 = 9.637, p = 0.008$. A follow-up pairwise Wilcoxon-Signed Rank Test was performed between each of the

Table 3: Reporting of Average and Standard Deviation for student responses to Exit Ticket questions.

	Use-Modify-Create Condition (N=95)				Control Condition (N=65)			
Likert Questions	Day 1	Day 2	Day 3	Day 4	Day 1	Day 2	Day 3	Day 4
Rate how difficult or easy the lesson was today: (Very Easy) 1 - 5 (Very Difficult).	$\overline{\chi} = 2.11$ $\sigma = 0.93$	$\overline{\chi} = 2.04$ $\sigma = 1.18$	$\overline{\chi} = 2.15$ $\sigma = 1.03$	$\overline{\chi} = 2.25$ $\sigma = 1.09$	$\overline{\chi} = 2.03$ $\sigma = 0.85$	$\overline{\chi} = 2.58$ $\sigma = 1.13$	$\overline{\chi} = 2.11$ $\sigma = 1.03$	$\overline{\chi} = 2.25$ $\sigma = 1.09$
"I was able to express my ideas in the model today." (Strongly Agree) 1 - 7 (Strongly Disagree)	N/A	$\overline{\chi} = 2.89$ $\sigma = 1.45$	$\overline{\chi} = 2.64$ $\sigma = 1.48$	$\overline{\chi} = 2.68$ $\sigma = 1.54$	N/A	$\overline{\chi} = 3.13$ $\sigma = 1.18$	$\overline{\chi} = 2.98$ $\sigma = 1.32$	$\overline{\chi} = 2.99$ $\sigma = 1.32$
"The code I ended the lesson with is my own creation." (Strongly Agree) 1 - 7 (Strongly Disagree)	N/A	$\overline{\chi} = 3.54$ $\sigma = 1.87$	$\overline{\chi} = 2.79$ $\sigma = 1.64$	$\overline{\chi} = 2.93$ $\sigma = 1.72$	N/A	$\overline{\chi} = 3.39$ $\sigma = 1.42$	$\overline{\chi} = 3.24$ $\sigma = 1.44$	$\overline{\chi} = 3.21$ $\sigma = 1.43$

days and while no significant difference was found between Days 3 and 4 ($V = 769, p = 0.38$), significant differences were found between Days 2 and 3 ($V = 1973, p < 0.001$) and Days 2 and 4 ($V = 1000, p = 0.006$) within the UMC group. Additional Mann-Whitney U Tests were performed between the two conditions. While no difference was found between Day 2 ($W = 4207, p = 0.8$) or Day 4 ($W = 3485, p = 0.07$) between the conditions, significant differences were found between the Day 3 ($W = 3284, p = 0.02$) responses between groups.

While not as direct as the student-perceived difficulty differences, there were key classroom observational differences between the conditions that corroborate the findings from the exit tickets. First, as stated before, students in the UMC condition were often able to finish tasks faster and were therefore able to explore more within the code, and add their own additional features. It is possible that adding their own touches after the guided part of the lesson led to an increased sense of artifact 'ownership'. Second, researchers observed (and teachers commented during follow-up interviews) that students in the UMC condition seemed more engaged in the activity, but it was actually difficult to keep students engaged in the control condition. This disconnect with the material and the monotony of the tasks in the control condition might have contributed to the students' sense that the code was not their own.

4.3 Teacher-perceptions

Teacher interview transcripts were analyzed using a constant comparative method [20] that entailed searching for themes amongst the teachers within each condition and then comparing data from the teachers across the two conditions. Results reflected the difficulties that teachers in the control group faced. The two teachers implementing the coding-intensive control version of the curriculum expressed concerns that their students needed more scaffolding to complete the lessons and concerns about their students' daily engagement. When asked about potential improvements to the curriculum, both teachers suggested giving students more time to "explore" and "play" with the code prior to creating their own programs. UMC provides this opportunity for students. As one of the teachers in UMC condition explains, "the kids [during the 'use' day] were understanding the coding; they were understanding why it was changing and they were starting to play around with some of that as well." Additionally, results from teacher interviews demonstrated that teachers in the control condition perceived a decrease in student engagement each day. Teachers themselves suggested changing the approach each day, e.g. "I got a lot of comments that they were bored with it because it was the same thing day after day. So I can't really think of it right now, but if there is, like some kind of way to mix it up and still have the same information, but maybe have them do it in a different way." Our data and teacher interviews suggest that approaching coding through a variety of tasks, as the UMC approach does, can improve student engagement. It is also possible that the structured UMC sequence makes the Create day more purposeful and engaging for students. One teacher explains her students' reactions to the Create day, "They're like 'day three was very fun'. They really got a chance to understand how the whole thing is connected."

The teacher interviews also corroborated that a UMC sequence offers benefits to teachers, as it supports their learning and confidence with the materials. One of the teachers revealed to us that, researcher support "wasn't needed the last day because I knew it. At this point I was like, 'I'm comfortable. I know where you're going with this.'" Both of the teachers in the code creation sequence commented that the lessons were "exhausting," as one teacher described that implementing the lessons entailed "standing in front of a room and talking and basically having you being the first person [they're] gonna ask questions to for five hours."

The findings above are supported by observations of teachers working through the curriculum. Like the teacher above noted, researchers observed that teachers gained confidence in teaching the lessons in both conditions, but this was more marked for UMC teachers. The two UMC teachers, in addition to following the guided material provided to them, were able to add new tasks to class periods where time was still available, and led students in guided discussions about the connections between the CT concepts and the scientific concepts modeled within the environment. As previously discussed, teachers in the control condition had difficulty engaging and keeping all students on task as observed by the researchers, and often needed to pause (especially on Days 2 and 3) to check which task they needed to be doing or what the code was supposed to look like. While this was also observed with one teacher of the UMC condition, this behavior was occurring later in the assignment sequence (on Days 3 and 4) and not to the same frequency.

5 DISCUSSION

For student-perceived difficulty, **students perceived the introduction to coding on Day 2 as significantly harder in the control group than any other day**. While there was the same procedure for each of the coding days in this condition (i.e. students had to create an agent on each day) having to do this for the first time might have been difficult without prior knowledge or experience in the environment. Days 1, 3, and 4 having similar reported levels of perceived difficulty, suggests that while the Day 2 activity was harder, getting through it and understanding the procedure prepared students for the Day 3 and 4 coding activities. No difficulty spike, however, was found in the sequence for the UMC condition. The benefits of this sequence can be explained using James Paul Gee's principles of good learning [11]. It could be that first "using" the new Cellular environment was "pleasantly frustrating" – challenging but perceived to be easily done, and then modifying it and then creating a new agent results in "well-ordered problems" that allow students to develop mastery [11]. In contrast, Day 2 for the control condition combined the need to learn the new environment while also learning the basics of programming and how they work within the environment, potentially increasing the cognitive load of the students [25], which could result in a higher perceived difficulty on Day 2.

Two questions were assessed to measure student perceived *ownership* of the models each day. While there are differences between conditions for the question regarding expression of ideas, the most pronounced differences between days and conditions is found for the question on whether the code was their "own creation". While the difference was not significant, the average value for the response was higher in Day 2 of the UMC condition, indicating that UMC students did not feel as much ownership over the final code as students in the control condition. This was expected, as Day 2 represents the "Use" day where students changed parameters and input variables, but did not create any new code. It is only on Day 3, where students in UMC were "Modifying" existing Bunny code, that there is a difference in perceived ownership between groups. We were somewhat surprised that students in the UMC condition felt significantly more ownership of their code, since they made fewer programmatic changes (code adds, deletes, edits) than the control group. It could be that the framing of the activity as modifying existing code to make it perform the 'correct' behaviors played into this mindset. In addition, the large number of program edits needed in the control condition may have made more creative activities, such as augmenting the model behavior, blend in with more mechanical changes, like dragging in pre-specified blocks. In some cases, these creative activities may not have even occurred, since teachers struggled to help students complete the Day 3 and Day 4 activities in the control group. The strengthening of artifact ownership in the UMC condition that began on Day 3 carried into Day 4, with the **UMC group agreeing significantly more than the control group that their final code was their own, despite both conditions doing the exact same task**.

In addition to student reported data, reflections from teachers also suggest that they would benefit from and prefer the UMC Condition. Teacher expertise is in supporting student learning, and their perceptions confirm that a strict code creation approach is not as effective for their classrooms. Since many teachers are novices to programming and CT, and their courses are focused on other topics, it is not realistic to expect disciplinary K-12 teachers to be able to support such an intensive coding approach to integrating CT. The UMC model helps teachers gradually learn how programs represent their disciplinary knowledge, enabling them to make those connections just in time with students. As stated by teachers, having time to be able to "explore" the environment by first reading and understanding code, then performing minor edits, and finally being ready to add independent features, gives both students and teachers an easier progression of tasks. This means that teachers can adopt integrated CT curricula more readily, letting them learn CT and programming along with their students.

6 CONCLUSION

In this paper, we present results from an A/B study of Use-Modify-Create (UMC) versus a control group implementation of a CT-infused Food Web activity. With student reports corroborated by classroom observations and teacher interviews, we were able to confirm previous research results showing that UMC sequencing provides students a natural progression to learn computational thinking within a science course, while giving students more ownership over the artifacts they create. We also found that teachers using our UMC curriculum felt it was easy to teach, and that it promoted student engagement and exploration, while teachers using a code-intensive control curriculum desired more scaffolding and features to improve student engagement.

Limitations of this work include potential population bias, instructor effects, and our interpretation of the UMC model. Participants are from two middle schools where many students have prior exposure to learning computing. This population bias could have improved students' ability to go through the curriculum and the ease in which they learned and experienced the topics. However, as the daily difficulty ratings are discussed in relative terms, we assume that a middle school with less access to CT and computing education would show even greater differences in perceived difficulty between the UMC and control conditions. It is not clear how more or less programming experience would impact student ownership ratings. Four teachers participated in the study, with two leading instruction in each condition. As such, there is no way for us to separate instructor effects from the curricular content/sequencing. Though Kruskal-Wallis Tests [18] and Mann-Whitney U Tests find no significant difference in student perceived difficulty by teacher group, it is still possible that instructors played a role in the student perception of difficulty and ownership. Finally, while Lee's original paper on the UMC model defined "Creation" as students making their own designs [16], we interpret it specifically to mean that students should develop all of their own code for an agent. In future studies, we hope to design activities that facilitate more open-ended student exploration and creativity.

ACKNOWLEDGMENTS

This material is based upon work supported by the National Science Foundation under grant number 1742351. Any opinions, findings, and conclusions expressed in this material are those of the authors and do not necessarily reflect the views of the NSF.

REFERENCES

[1] Bernd Meyer Aidan Lane and Jonathan Mullins. 2012. *Simulation with Cellular A Project Based Introduction to Programming* (first ed.). Monash University, Melbourne, Australia. Online: https://github.com/MonashAlexandria/snapapps.

[2] Tim Bell, Jason Alexander, Isaac Freeman, and Mick Grimley. 2009. Computer science unplugged: School students doing real computing without computers. *The New Zealand Journal of Applied Computing and Information Technology* 13, 1 (2009), 20–29.

[3] Acey Kreisler Boyce, Antoine Campbell, Shaun Pickford, Dustin Culler, and Tiffany Barnes. 2011. Experimental evaluation of BeadLoom game: how adding game elements to an educational tool improves motivation and learning. In *Proceedings of the 16th annual joint conference on Innovation and technology in computer science education*. ACM, ACM, New York, NY, 243–247.

[4] Veronica Cateté, Nicholas Lytle, Yihuan Dong, Danielle Boulden, Bita Akram, Jennifer Houchins, Tiffany Barnes, Eric Wiebe, James Lester, Bradford Mott, and Kristy Boyer. 2018. Infusing Computational Thinking into Middle Grade Science Classrooms: Lessons Learned. In *Proceedings of the 13th Workshop in Primary and Secondary Computing Education (WiPSCE '18)*. ACM, New York, NY, USA, Article 21, 6 pages. https://doi.org/10.1145/3265757.3265778

[5] Bob Coulter, Irene Lee, and Fred Martin. 2010. Computational Thinking for Youth.

[6] National Research Council et al. 2011. *Successful K-12 STEM education: Identifying effective approaches in science, technology, engineering, and mathematics*. National Academies Press, Washington, D.C.

[7] Jan Cuny. 2012. Transforming high school computing: a call to action. *ACM Inroads* 3, 2 (2012), 32–36.

[8] Yihuan Dong, Veronica Catete, Robin Jocius, Nicholas Lytle, Tiffany Barnes, Jennifer Albert, Deepti Joshi, Richard Robinson, and Ashley Andrews. 2019. PRADA: A Practical Model for Integrating Computational Thinking in K-12 Education. In *Proceedings of the 50th ACM Technical Symposium on Computer Science Education (SIGCSE '19)*. ACM, New York, NY, USA, 906–912. https://doi.org/10.1145/3287324.3287431

[9] Milton Friedman. 1937. The use of ranks to avoid the assumption of normality implicit in the analysis of variance. *Journal of the american statistical association* 32, 200 (1937), 675–701.

[10] Dan Garcia, Brian Harvey, and Tiffany Barnes. 2015. The beauty and joy of computing. *ACM Inroads* 6, 4 (2015), 71–79.

[11] James Paul Gee. 2007. *Good video games+ good learning: Collected essays on video games, learning, and literacy*. Vol. 27. Peter Lang, New York, NY.

[12] Joanna Goode, Jane Margolis, and Gail Chapman. 2014. Curriculum is not enough: the educational theory and research foundation of the exploring computer science professional development model. In *Proceedings of the 45th ACM technical symposium on Computer science education*. ACM, ACM, New York, NY, 493–498.

[13] Marianthi Grizioti and Chronis Kynigos. 2018. Game modding for computational thinking: an integrated design approach. In *Proceedings of the 17th ACM Conference on Interaction Design and Children*. ACM, New York, NY, USA, 687–692.

[14] Filiz Kalelioğlu. 2015. A new way of teaching programming skills to K-12 students: Code. org. *Computers in Human Behavior* 52 (2015), 200–210.

[15] Irene Lee, Fred Martin, and Katie Apone. 2014. Integrating computational thinking across the K–8 curriculum. *Acm Inroads* 5, 4 (2014), 64–71.

[16] Irene Lee, Fred Martin, Jill Denner, Bob Coulter, Walter Allan, Jeri Erickson, Joyce Malyn-Smith, and Linda Werner. 2011. Computational thinking for youth in practice. *Acm Inroads* 2, 1 (2011), 32–37.

[17] Jane Margolis. 2010. *Stuck in the shallow end: Education, race, and computing*. MIT Press, Cambridge, MA.

[18] Patrick E McKnight and Julius Najab. 2010. Kruskal-Wallis Test. *The corsini encyclopedia of psychology* 4 (2010), 1–1.

[19] Patrick E McKnight and Julius Najab. 2010. Mann-Whitney U Test. *The Corsini encyclopedia of psychology* 4 (2010), 1–1.

[20] Matthew B Miles, A Michael Huberman, and Johnny Saldana. 2014. *Qualitative data analysis*. Sage, Washington DC, USA.

[21] Thomas W Price, Veronica Cateté, Jennifer Albert, Tiffany Barnes, and Daniel D Garcia. 2016. Lessons Learned from BJC CS Principles Professional Development. In *Proceedings of the 47th ACM Technical Symposium on Computing Science Education*. ACM, ACM, New York, NY, 467–472.

[22] Johnmarshall Reeve and Ching-Mei Tseng. 2011. Agency as a fourth aspect of studentsâĂŹ engagement during learning activities. *Contemporary Educational Psychology* 36, 4 (2011), 257–267.

[23] Sue Sentance and Andrew Csizmadia. 2017. Computing in the curriculum: Challenges and strategies from a teacherâĂŹs perspective. *Education and Information Technologies* 22, 2 (2017), 469–495.

[24] Sue Sentance and Jane Waite. 2017. PRIMM: Exploring pedagogical approaches for teaching text-based programming in school. In *Proceedings of the 12th Workshop on Primary and Secondary Computing Education*. ACM, ACM, New York, NY, 113–114.

[25] John Sweller. 1988. Cognitive load during problem solving: Effects on learning. *Cognitive science* 12, 2 (1988), 257–285.

[26] David Weintrop, Elham Beheshti, Michael Horn, Kai Orton, Kemi Jona, Laura Trouille, and Uri Wilensky. 2014. Defining computational thinking for science, technology, engineering, and math.

[27] Linda Werner, Shannon Campe, and Jill Denner. 2012. Children learning computer science concepts via Alice game-programming. In *Proceedings of the 43rd ACM technical symposium on Computer Science Education*. ACM, ACM, New York, NY, 427–432.

[28] Jeannette M Wing. 2006. Computational thinking. *Commun. ACM* 49, 3 (2006), 33–35.

[29] RF Woolson. 2007. Wilcoxon signed-rank test. *Wiley encyclopedia of clinical trials* (2007), 1–3.

Text-based Programming in Elementary School: A Comparative Study of Programming Abilities in Children with and without Block-based Experience

Marcos J. Gomez
Universidad Nacional de Cordoba
Cordoba, Argentina
mgomez4@famaf.unc.edu.ar

Marco Moresi
Universidad Nacional de Cordoba
Cordoba, Argentina
mrc.moresi@gmail.com

Luciana Benotti
Universidad Nacional de Cordoba / CONICET
Cordoba, Argentina
benotti@famaf.unc.edu.ar

ABSTRACT

This paper describes an elementary school intervention to teach a text-based programming language to 10-11 year old students. We compare students with no previous programming experience with students with 3 semesters of experience with a block-based programming language. We analyze students' performance and learning based on detailed logs in an online programming platform and on multiple choice tests. Although both groups have a similar percentage of syntactical errors, the experienced group showed a better performance on exam scores and a lower number of test case errors. These findings suggest that, 10-11 year old students benefit from block-based experience when learning a new text-based programming language.

CCS CONCEPTS

• **Social and professional topics** → **K-12 education**; • **Applied computing** → *Computer-assisted instruction*; • **Software and its engineering** → *Imperative languages.*

KEYWORDS

Learning analytics; elementary education; text-based languages; block-based languages

ACM Reference Format:

Marcos J. Gomez, Marco Moresi, and Luciana Benotti. 2019. Text-based Programming in Elementary School: A Comparative Study of Programming Abilities in Children with and without Block-based Experience. In *Innovation and Technology in Computer Science Education (ITiCSE '19), July 15–17, 2019, Aberdeen, Scotland UK.* ACM, New York, NY, USA, 7 pages. https://doi.org/10.1145/3304221.3319734

1 INTRODUCTION

In the last years, governments, universities, companies and organizations around the world have joined forces to bring the teaching of Computer Science (CS) at elementary, middle and high schools [11, 14, 22, 29]. In this context, there is still an ongoing debate on whether elementary school children are developmentally ready to learn programming or even to use computers (see for example [6]).

While research on teaching programming in higher educational levels is vast, and there is increasing consensus on curricular designs (e.g., [15]), studies over elementary schools are not as common [8]. Research based on teaching CS in elementary school can be classified (according to [2]) in three categories: unplugged activities [3], block-based visual programming [28] and robotics [5, 21]. Most of the documented experiences use block-based platforms such as Scratch [24, 28], Snap! [16], Alice [9], Code.org [17]. Block-based languages are supposed to allow students to focus on concepts, leaving aside the syntactic complexity present when learning to program using a text-based language. But, how well can elementary school students transition from block-based languages to text-based languages? In other words, our research question Q1: *do children with block-based experience have programming abilities that make it easier to learn a text-based language?*

In order to address this question we pose two non directional hypotheses. Ha is related to syntactic errors, Hb is related to semantic errors, defined as follows. A student makes a syntactic error when her/his program does not comply with the grammar of the programming language. A student makes a semantic error when she/he holds a misconception about the program behavior. In Section 3 we formally define these two kinds of errors.

Ha (null): There is no significant difference in the amount of syntactic errors that students with and without previous block-based programming experience make.

Hb (null): There is no significant difference in the amount of semantic errors that students with and without previous block-based programming experience make.

With the purpose of testing these hypotheses and contributing to a CS curriculum selection and scope, we designed an observational study for elementary school children. We carried out programming lessons in a real school setting focusing on loops, conditionals, sequences, and parameters; and their application to programming. The main contributions of this paper are three. First, we introduce an online coding tool that logs an student learning process while programming, registering each submission made by the student along with formative feedback automatically generated by the tool. Second, we analyze comparatively how 10-11 year old children with and without previous programming experience create programs in a text-based programming language. Finally we evaluate the

ITiCSE '19, July 15–17, 2019, Aberdeen, Scotland UK

ACM ISBN 978-1-4503-6301 3/19/07...$15.00
https://doi.org/10.1145/3304221.3319734

students on fundamental programming concepts in programming challenges involving code interpretation.

The paper is organized as follows. Section 2 reviews elementary school experiences and situates this paper with respect to previous work. Section 3 presents the online coding tool, called Mumuki, as well as the text-based programming language used for our observational study. Section 4 describes the student groups involved as well as the methods for data collection. Section 5 discusses the results of our study, their implications and potential threats to validity.

2 PREVIOUS WORK

There are several tools which allow elementary school children to create, run and debug simple computer programs using specific platforms that are both challenging and attainable for most children [7, 13, 18]. Previous work [12, 18] reports that even children who are preliterate, have diverse background and different developmental stages, engage with tangible platforms, such as wooden or virtual blocks. Some implications of learning programming at such an early age have been analyzed. According to Clements [7], children who use computer assisted programs have the opportunity to analyze a situation and reflect on the properties of objects they have to manipulate. Clements concluded, that it links intuitive children knowledge (about movements and drawings) into more explicit formal ideas using programming language and "facilitates positive beliefs about the creation (of technological products)". Other studies [12] have suggested that computer programming develops higher order thinking skills such as metacognitive competencies. Students who used Logo and tangible programming could propose different methods to solve a problem and had the ability to debug a program. This means, that children are monitoring their thinking looking for the program mistakes. This is a strong indicator of metacognition.

While exploring how to teach programming to little children some researchers have found that the difficulties in children programming laid in their immature motor skills and on syntax problems [13, 25]. Thus, there has been a vast development on specific programming platforms to address the developmental traits of small children (such as Toon Talk, Scratch Jr, CHERPS, etc). In this context, block-based programming has been an interesting line of work to teach programming to little children. Morgado et al [25] propose lesson plans for preschool and elementary school children based on their extensive experiences in the classroom. They documented how elementary school children engage while learning competences and concepts such as syntax, parameter passing, compound procedures, parallelism and concurrency, communication channels, input and client and servers using Toon Talk platform. As the result of their exploratory study, they suggested different strategies to teach each concept, such as using metaphors to teach variables. Although most interventions to teach programming to preschool and elementary school children achieve high student engagement and participation, we still need to understand more how the use of these platforms promotes developing programming abilities and learning particular concepts.

There are few previous studies that explore what programming concepts children can understand at different developmental stages to establish school curricula content and scope. Martinez et al [21] found that 4 to 10 year olds could learn and apply basic programming concepts of sequencing, conditionals, and loops by engaging in a mix of unplugged activities and block-based programming. Magnenat et al [20] taught robot programming to different elementary school children using a block-based language to program a robot action for different events. Comparing the groups performance, they found that most children understood and solved simple tasks such as moving a robot upon a touch of a button or identifying robot's instructions. Both studies teach and evaluate using the same block-based language. Hence, it is not clear whether the learning is language specific or conceptual.

Dagiene et al [10] compared students from Finland, Sweden and Lithuania of ages 7 to 12 performing computational thinking tasks exercises. Using multiple choice questions, they evaluated concepts such as graph analysis, search algorithms, data structures, pattern matching, etc. They found no strong difference across age groups, but rather among student backgrounds.

The previous work more related to the research question Q1 that we posed in Section 1 are the following two. First, Armoni et al [2] found that students who learned Scratch in middle school more quickly grasped concepts in text-based languages when they reached high school, although they did not perform significantly better in the course assessments. Then, Weintrop and Wilensky [31] compared separate groups of high-school students learning basic programming constructs. One group learned a block-based language while the other learned a text-based language. Their results suggest that novice programmers' understanding of basic programming constructs (such as conditionals and loops) is better in block-based languages. Differently from us, both studies focus on high-school students.

Summing up, there is considerable enthusiasm around the world towards introducing young children to programming. However, there is a need to systematically evaluate the impact of such initiatives on the learning outcome, independently from the programming language. In this paper, we explore elementary school students' conceptual gain during their transition from block-based programming into text-based programming.

3 THE ONLINE PROGRAMMING TOOL

In this section we introduce Gobstones and Mumuki, which we use for our study. Gobstones [19] is a text-based programming language and Mumuki is an online programming environment. A screenshot of a sample programming exercise using the Gobstones language in Mumuki [4] is shown in Figure 1.

Gobstones [19] is a programming language developed for CS1 university students who do not have previous programming knowledge. Gobstones is an imperative programming language whose syntax is based on a simplified C syntax, and its output is restricted to moving color balls on a board. Martinez-Lopez et al. in [19], describe the three elements that are part of Gobstones philosophy: a graphical output, a simplified syntax and a focus on fundamental programming constructs. As can be seen in Figure 1, the graphical output is simple and concrete. It is a rectangular board of a programmable size, made of cells which can hold colored balls, such as the blue ball in the figure. The balls can be manipulated by a head that works on a single cell at a time, and is depicted as a yellow

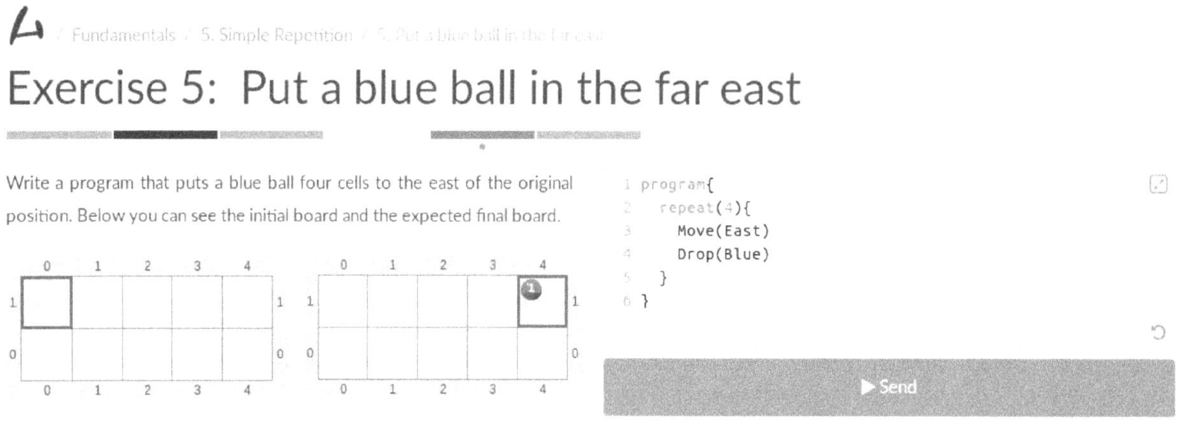

Figure 1: Mumuki screenshot with an exercise description on the left and a program written by a student on the right.

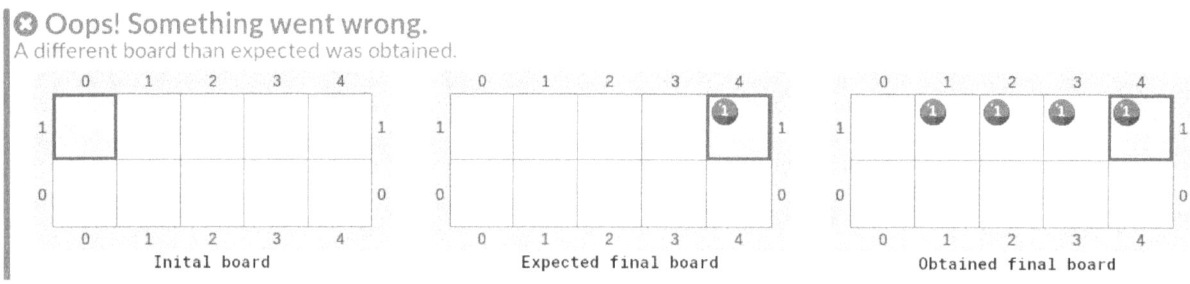

Figure 2: Feedback generated by Mumuki for the program in Figure 1, the program is executable but incorrect.

cell with a red border. Each board has only one yellow cell, which means that the head is over this cell. The head can execute the following primitives defined in [19]: (1) `Drop`, which puts a ball of a given color (for example Red, Green, Blue, or Black) on the current cell. (2) `Grab`, which takes a ball of a given color from the current cell, if it exists, and makes the board explode otherwise. (3) `Move`, which moves the head in a given direction (North, East, South, or West), if there is a cell in this direction, and makes the board explode otherwise.

Mumuki [4], as can be seen in Figure 1, includes a progress bar indicating which exercises have been solved (in green), which have been attempted but are either not executable because of a syntax error (in dark red) or incorrect because of a semantic error (in light red), and which have not been attempted yet (in grey). The students can solve the exercises in any order they want, but Mumuki suggests an order with the progress bar. The current exercise is marked with a blue dot. The figure shows the title and the description of the programming problem and makes explicit the board where the program starts running and the expected final board. Students have to write a Gobstones program that transforms the initial board into the expected final board. Given this goal, we define two possible kinds of errors. A student makes a *syntactic error* when her/his program does not comply with the grammar of Gobstones and is marked in *dark red* by Mumuki. A student makes a *semantic error* when the program reaches a different final board than that expected. That is, she/he holds a misconception about the program. Semantic errors are marked in *light red* by Mumuki. A light red program is syntactically correct but does not achieve the exercise goal. As follows we exemplify both kinds of errors.

The exercise in Figure 1 asks the student to write a program that drops a blue ball four cells to the east of the initial position. In the right hand panel, Mumuki includes an editor where the student can write the solution. In the figure, the solution is marked in light red. The feedback generated by Mumuki when the student presses send for this incorrect solution is shown in Figure 2. The feedback shows that the obtained final board is different than the expected one. Figure 3 shows a correct solution for the running example. The difference with the program in Figure 1 is that `Drop(Blue)` is outside the repeat. In Figure 4 the student made a syntactic error. The student forgot to write a closing parenthesis. In this case, the exercise is assessed as dark red because the code is not syntactically correct and therefore it cannot be executed.

Every solution submitted by a student is stored by Mumuki in its database. The timestamp, the code, and the tests results are also stored, so the full history can be reproduced. This information could be used by a teacher in order to improve the exercises, to explore common mistakes, etc. In this paper we use it in order to analyze the kinds of errors made by the students.

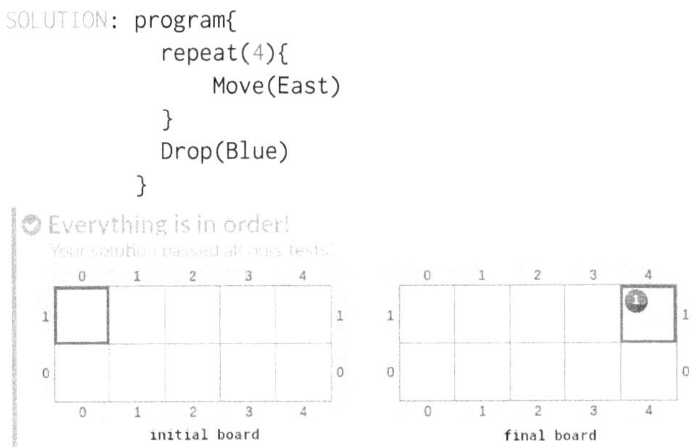

Figure 3: Correct solution for the exercise in Fig. 1.

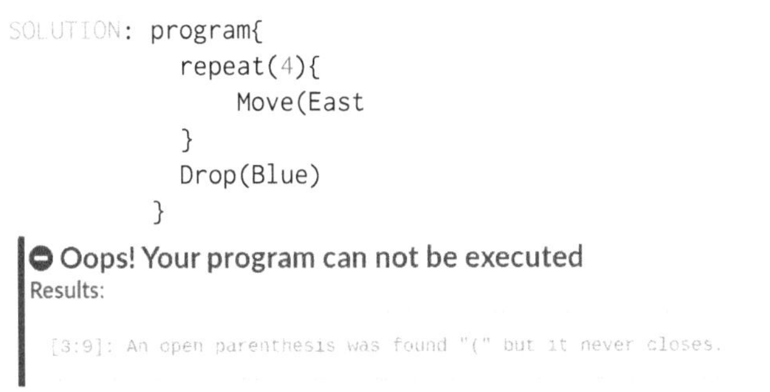

Figure 4: Non executable program for the exercise in Fig. 1.

4 STUDY DESIGN

In this section we describe our observational study designed to test the hypotheses posed in Section 1. In 4.1 we present the schools, the intervention design and the background of the students in programming. In 4.2 we describe the kinds of logs made per school using Mumuki and the multiple choice exam.

4.1 The setting for the study

We performed interventions in two different privately run primary schools receiving state public funds. There are no children below the poverty line and most children have middle class parents. The schools serve the same neighbourhood. In both of them we taught Gobstones using Mumuki. Both experiments were carried out at the schools during school hours with 10 and 11 year old students, attending 5th grade of elementary school. One of these schools is called Escuela Nueva Juan Mantovani (ENJM), and the other, Nuestra Señora de Valle (NSDV).

The complete experience lasted 5 hours in each school. While using Mumuki, students worked alone or in groups of two or three. The same teacher was in charge of the experience at both schools. Students were asked to complete 23 programming exercises organized in 2 Mumuki lessons. Through these exercises, students learned programming concepts such as sequence, conditionals, loops and parameters. After the experience, students took part of a multiple choice exam.

Students from ENJM had previous experience with fundamental programming concepts. Programming is part of the core curricula of the school. The students that participated in the experience had three semesters of previous experience learning to program. Students had 1 hour of programming per week. The 3 programming semesters were taught at ENJM following an experience based pedagogy and the curriculum was project-based. A complete description of the curricula and the didactic sequences used can be found in [1]. In short, the ENJM students were introduced to programming and other CS topics by developing their own video-games and animations with Scratch as well as unplugged activities.

Students from the other school, NSDV, did not have any previous experience in programming. Their teachers and the head of the school reported that programming was not part of the curricula. The students were asked to auto-assess their programming background previous to this experience. All of the students confirmed that they have not been exposed to programming in other settings (e.g., at home, or in some outreach program).

4.2 Programming logs and exam

In total, 129 students participated in the experiences. 63 from ENJM and 66 from NSDV. The ENJM students used Mumuki in 32 groups of 2 or 3 students and 5 groups of 1 student, while in NSDV, the students used Mumuki in 31 groups of 2 or 3 students. Each experience lasted in total 5 hours. Due to school restrictions, in the ENJM experience, 5 one hour meetings were held, while in NSDV, the experience lasted 2 two-hour-and-a-half meetings.

Groups of students that participated in the experiences produced a total of 2066 errors while attempting a median of 17 exercises per group in each school. The Table 1 presents the total of errors per school. The 31 groups of students from NSDV made 1225 errors, and the 37 groups from ENJM made 841 errors. Although there were more groups in ENJM, they made less errors than the NSDV students. The table also reports the number of exercises attempted by all the groups as well as the time on task defined as the sum of minutes between submissions for all students in a given day. The time on task for both groups was almost the same.

School	ENJM	NSDV
Number of student groups	37	31
Number of exercises attempted	607	611
Time on task (in minutes)	3046	3072
Number of syntactic errors (dark red)	305	385
Number of semantic errors (light red)	536	640
Total number of errors	841	1225

Table 1: The upper part reports basic metrics of the investment in learning comparatively for both schools. The lower part compares the types of program errors per school.

After the experience, students took part of a multiple choice exam. The exam was not mandatory. The exam was composed of 6 multiple choice questions. Each question had a program written in Gobstones and an initial board. The student had to apply the Gobstones program to the initial board, and select the correct final board from 4 possible options. A sample question from the exam[1] is shown in Figure 5. The correct answer is Option 2.

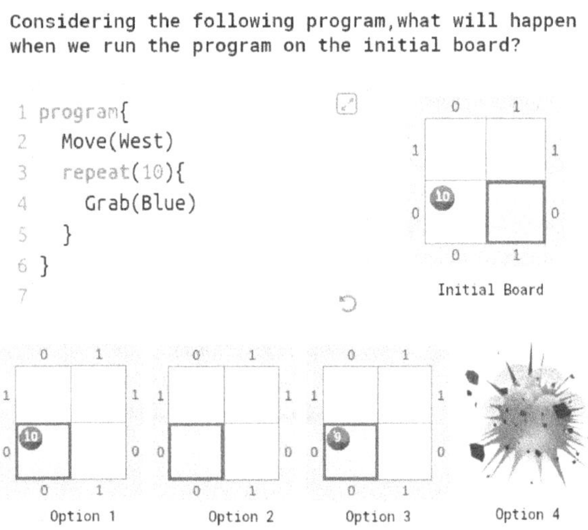

Figure 5: Sample exercise from the multiple choice exam.

All questions had the same weight on the final score. The scale of the exam score was from 0 to 10. Table 2 shows the number of students per school that participated in the experience divided by gender, and how many students took the multiple choice exam.

School	ENJM			NSDV		
Gender (F/M) and Total	F	M	T	F	M	T
Number of students participating	30	33	63	37	29	66
Number of students tested	26	31	57	18	11	29

Table 2: Participants distribution (not mandatory exam).

5 FINDINGS

In this section we describe our findings with respect to the hypotheses posed in Section 1. Using the online system logs, we first compare the amount of syntactic and semantic errors for both schools. The system logs were made by groups of 1, 2 or 3 students. Then we present the results of the multiple choice exam by school. The exam was taken individually. Finally we discuss the limitations of the study.

5.1 Programming logs findings

Table 3 shows the amount of syntactic (dark red) and semantic errors (light red) made by ENJM and NSDV schools during the experience. In order to compare schools performances while solving programming exercises in Mumuki we define two metrics. The *semantic ratio* per group is the amount of programs with semantic errors that the group submitted divided by the amount of exercises that the group attempted. The *syntactic ratio* is analogous but it considers the syntactic errors.

[1]The complete test is available here (in Spanish): url anymized

Table 3 reports the average per group (of 1, 2 or 3 students) for these two metrics for both schools, in the ratio column. It also reports the raw amount of programs in both types for both schools, in the # column.

	ENJM		NSDV		ratio t-test	
	#	ratio	#	ratio	p	t
Syntactic errors	305	0.70	385	0.62	0.588	0.543
Semantic errors	536	0.74	640	1.01*	0.024	2.31

Table 3: Average group ratios and raw amount of syntactic and semantic errors. Statistically significant differences are marked with * for unpaired t-test performed on the ratios.

The table also presents the results of applying unpaired t-tests to ENJM and NSDV average ratios for both metrics. The semantic ratio average of ENJM is 0.74 while in NSDV average is 1.01. In other words, after overcoming syntactic errors, ENJM groups make semantic errors in 7 out of 10 attempted exercises in average. In contrast, NSDV groups make semantic errors in 10 out of 10 exercises. The unpaired t-test shows that there is a difference in this metric that is statistically significant between groups from ENJM and NSDV (p=0.024). These results give evidence for rejecting the null hypothesis Hb (null) in favor of the alternative one: groups with previous programming experience make significantly less semantic errors than groups with no such experience.

The difference between schools for the syntactic ratio average is not statistically significant, based on the unpaired t-test, as can be seen in the table (p=0.588). Therefore, the Ha (null) hypothesis cannot be rejected. This is coherent with the fact that both groups do not have previous experience in text-based coding languages, so syntactic errors appear in similar proportion in both schools.

5.2 Multiple choice exam findings

Figure 6 shows a box plot of the exam marks (over a maximum mark of 10 points) for both schools. The median mark for NSDV is 6.66 and for the ENJM is 8.33 (the difference is 1.67 points). The exam was designed to include as alternative answers common programming misconceptions. For example, in Figure 5 the incorrect options (1,3 and 4) illustrate different misconceptions about the loop behavior. The difference between the median marks in both schools is statistically significant using unpaired t-tests (p=0.0014). This gives further evidence for rejecting the null hypothesis Hb (null) in favor of the alternative one.

5.3 Limitations of the study

In this section we discuss the potential threats to validity for the present study.

First, there is no formal assessment of the background of the NSDV students. Their previous background is self-reported by their teachers, directors and the students themselves as described in Section 4. All of them confirmed no previous exposure to programming.

Second, the temporal organization for both schools was not exactly the same. ENJM students were taught the material in 5 one-hour meetings while the NSDV students had 2 lessons of 2.5 hours. Meetings were held once a week for both schools. The teacher

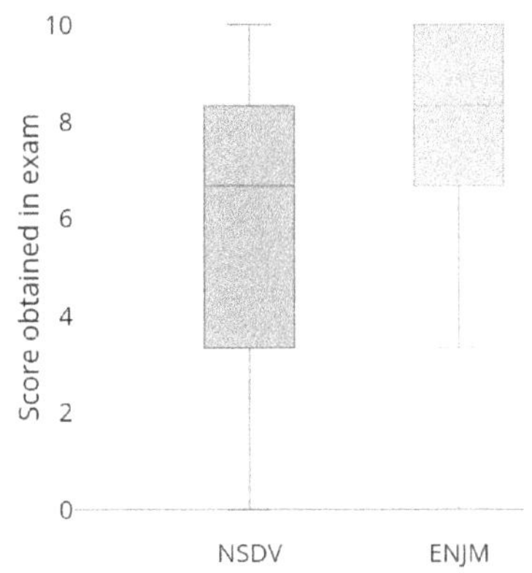

Figure 6: Box plot of the exam marks for both schools.

observed that, at the beginning of every meeting, students spent some time getting ready for the task. However, it does not seem to impact the time on task as reported in Table 1.

Finally, only 29 of the 66 students that participated in the NSDV experience decided to take part in the exam, as reported in Table 2. In the ENJM experience 57 out of 63 decided to take the exam. The exam was not mandatory at any school. While students may have different reasons not to take an exam, self-confidence in their performance is probably one of them.

6 DISCUSSION AND CONCLUSIONS

In this paper we describe an elementary school study carried out at two schools with 10-11 year old students. One of the them had 1 year and a half of experience learning programming with a block-based language. The other had no previous programming experience. In this context we explored the research question Q1: *do children with block-based experience have programming abilities that make it easier to learn a text-based language?*

We comparatively analyzed errors in a text-based programming language using logs from a programming tool and a multiple choice exam. We evaluated two non directional hypotheses Ha and Hb. Ha is related to the amount of syntactic errors and Hb to the semantic errors made in a text-based programming language new for both of them. We use logs from a programming environment called Mumuki which automatically corrects programming exercises in order to test both hypotheses.

When testing Ha we find that children make a similar amount of syntactic errors regardless of their background. This finding is coherent with previous work [26, 27] which argues that block-based languages do not address syntactic problems but merely delay them. Such previous work was performed at university level while ours is at primary school. A reason to start with block-based languages could be that not everything can be learned at the same time. Weintrop and Wilensky [31] compared separate groups of high-school students learning basic programming constructs. One group learned a block-based language while the other learned a text-based language. Their results suggest that novice programmers' understanding of basic programming constructs (such as conditionals and loops) is better in block-based languages.

We evaluate Hb using both the logs and the multiple choice exam. In the logs we find that, after overcoming syntactic errors, the children with experience make significantly less semantic errors than the children without block-based experience. In average, 7 out of 10 attempted exercises had an error for each experienced group while each group without experience made a semantic error in 10 out of 10 exercises. The Gobstones exercises, such as the one in Figure 1, allow for small changes to the code that have a strong impact on the correctness of the exercise as discussed in Section 3. It is possible than through trial-and-error the students can reach a correct solution while programming misconceptions remain. By considering the amount of semantic errors, we observe more trial-and-error in the school with no background in block-based languages.

We also evaluate the Hb hypotheses through a multiple choice exam. The exam was designed to provide common misconceptions [2, 30, 31] associated to fundamental programming constructs as alternative wrong answers. We find that the mark in the exam is significantly higher for children with block-based programming experience. Based on the logs and the exam results, we conclude that the group with previous block-based experience made less semantic errors than those without experience. Armoni et al [2] found that students who learned Scratch in middle school more quickly grasped concepts in text-based languages when they reached high school, although they did not perform significantly better in the course assessments. Differently from them, our study was done in elementary school. Moreover, we did find significant differences in the exam between our schools. This may be due to the fact that Armoni et al text-based experience was longer than ours. Our experience lasted 5 hours in total while theirs was carried out during a whole semester (total hours are not reported). As a result, in their case, the group of students with no previous block-based experience had more time to catch up.

Summing up, we have presented evidence that 10-11 year old students with block-based experience learn a new text-based language more easily than similar students with no block-based experience. In future work we will compare the schools across different kinds of programming misconceptions and analyze differences by gender.

With all the enthusiasm and effort towards introducing programming to a younger population globally [1, 2, 6–8, 21], this paper presents empirical evidence to contribute to the ongoing discussion. We explore students' actual learning gain in the eventual transition from popular teaching environments such as block-based programming into text-based programming. Further, our goal is to advance research involving elementary school, which is not as popular as research involving university or even high school. Meerbaum-Salant et al [23] pose the question: should we make things "easy" for students during their initial studies or should we teach them the "right way" from the beginning? Our empirical evidence supports the claim that children with block-based experience develop programming abilities that make it easier to learn a text-based language. When starting from elementary school, the "easy" way could be a step towards the "right way".

ACKNOWLEDGMENTS

This work was partially funded by grants PICT-2014-1833, PDTS-CIN-CONICET-2015-172.

REFERENCES

[1] Carlos Areces, Luciana Benotti, Joshep Cortez-Sanchez, Raul Fervari, E. Garcia, , Cecilia Martinez, Martin Onetti, Eduardo Rodriguez-Pesce, and Nicolas. Wolovick. 2018. *Ciencias de la Computacion para el aula: 2do ciclo de Primaria* (1 ed.). Fundacion Sadosky: Program.ar.

[2] Michal Armoni, Orni Meerbaum-Salant, and Mordechai Ben-Ari. 2015. From scratch to real programming. *ACM Transactions on Computing Education (TOCE)* 14, 4 (2015), 25.

[3] Tim Bell, Jason Alexander, Isaac Freeman, and Mick Grimley. 2009. Computer science unplugged: School students doing real computing without computers. *The New Zealand Journal of Applied Computing and Information Technology* 13, 1 (2009), 20–29.

[4] Luciana Benotti, Federico Aloi, Franco Bulgarelli, and Marcos J Gomez. 2018. The Effect of a Web-based Coding Tool with Automatic Feedback on Students' Performance and Perceptions. In *Proceedings of the 49th ACM Technical Symposium on Computer Science Education (SIGCSE '18)*. ACM, New York, NY, USA, 2–7.

[5] Luciana Benotti, Marcos J Gómez, and Cecilia Martínez. 2017. UNC++ Duino: A kit for learning to program robots in Python and C++ starting from blocks. In *Robotics in Education*. Springer, 181–192.

[6] Marina U. Bers. 2010. The Tangible Robotics Program: Applied Computational Thinking for Young Children. *Early Childhood Research & Practice* 12, 2 (2010).

[7] Douglas H Clements and Julie Sarama. 2002. Teaching with computers in early childhood education: Strategies and professional development. *Journal of Early Childhood Teacher Education* 23, 3 (2002), 215–226.

[8] K-12 Computer Science Framework Steering Committee et al. 2016. K-12 computer science framework. (2016).

[9] Stephen Cooper, Wanda Dann, and Randy Pausch. 2003. Teaching Objects-first in Introductory Computer Science. *SIGCSE Bull.* 35, 1 (Jan. 2003), 191–195.

[10] Valentina Dagiene, Linda Mannila, Timo Poranen, Lennart Rolandsson, and Par Söderhjelm. 2014. Students' Performance on Programming-related Tasks in an Informatics Contest in Finland, Sweden and Lithuania. In *Proceedings of the 2014 Conference on Innovation; Technology in Computer Science Education*. ACM, 153–158.

[11] Barbara Ericson, Mark Guzdial, and Maureen Biggers. 2007. Improving secondary CS education: progress and problems. In *ACM SIGCSE Bulletin*, Vol. 39. 298–301.

[12] Louise P Flannery and Marina Umaschi Bers. 2013. Let's Dance the "Robot Hokey-Pokey!" Children's Programming Approaches and Achievement throughout Early Cognitive Development. *Journal of Research on Technology in Education* 46, 1 (2013), 81–101.

[13] Louise P Flannery, Brian Silverman, Elizabeth R Kazakoff, Marina Umaschi Bers, Paula Bontá, and Mitchel Resnick. 2013. Designing ScratchJr: support for early childhood learning through computer programming. In *Proceedings of the 12th International Conference on Interaction Design and Children*. ACM, 1–10.

[14] A. Fowler, J. Pirker, I. Pollock, B. de Paula, M. Echeveste, and M. Gómez. 2016. Understanding the Benefits of Game Jams: Exploring the Potential for Engaging Young Learners in STEM. In *Proceedings of the 2016 ITiCSE Working Group Reports*. ACM, New York, USA, 119–135.

[15] Joanna Goode, Gail Chapman, and Jane Margolis. 2012. Beyond curriculum: the exploring computer science program. *ACM Inroads* 3, 2 (2012), 47–53.

[16] Brian Harvey, Daniel Garcia, Josh Paley, and Luke Segars. 2014. Snap!(build your own blocks). In *Proceedings of the 45th ACM technical symposium on Computer science education*. ACM, 749–749.

[17] Filiz Kalelioğlu. 2015. A new way of teaching programming skills to K-12 students: Code. org. *Computers in Human Behavior* 52 (2015), 200–210.

[18] Elizabeth R Kazakoff, Amanda Sullivan, and Marina U Bers. 2013. The Effect of a Classroom-Based Intensive Robotics and Programming Workshop on Sequencing Ability in Early Childhood. *Early Childhood Education Journal* 41, 4 (2013), 245–255.

[19] Pablo E Martínez López, Daniel Ciolek, Gabriela Arévalo, and Denise Pari. 2017. The GOBSTONES method for teaching computer programming. In *2017 XLIII Latin American Computer Conference (CLEI)*. 1–9.

[20] Stéphane Magnenat, Jiwon Shin, Fanny Riedo, Roland Siegwart, and Morderchai Ben-Ari. 2014. Teaching a Core CS Concept Through Robotics. In *Proceedings of the 2014 Conference on Innovation and Technology in Computer Science Education*. ACM, NY, USA, 315–320.

[21] Cecilia Martinez, Marcos Gomez, and Luciana Benotti. 2015. A Comparison of Preschool and Elementary School Children Learning Computer Science Concepts Through a Multilanguage Robot Programming Platform. In *Proceedings of the 2015 ACM Conference on Innovation and Technology in Computer Science Education*. 159–164.

[22] Cecilia Martinez, Marcos Gomez, Marco Moresi, and Luciana Benotti. 2016. Lessons Learned on Computer Science Teachers Professional Development. In *Proceedings of the 2016 ACM Conference on Innovation and Technology in Computer Science Education*. 77–82.

[23] Orni Meerbaum-Salant, Michal Armoni, and Mordechai Ben-Ari. 2011. Habits of programming in scratch. In *Proceedings of the 16th annual joint conference on Innovation and technology in computer science education*. ACM, 168–172.

[24] Orni Meerbaum-Salant, Michal Armoni, and Mordechai Ben-Ari. 2013. Learning computer science concepts with scratch. *Computer Science Education* 23, 3 (2013), 239–264.

[25] Leonel Morgado, Ken Kahn, and Maria GB Cruz. 2010. Preschool cookbook of computer programming topics. *Australasian Journal of Educational Technology* 26, 3 (2010), 309–326.

[26] Dale Parsons and Patricia Haden. 2007. Programming osmosis: Knowledge transfer from imperative to visual programming environments. In *Procedings of The Twentieth Annual NACCQ Conference*. 209–215.

[27] Kris Powers, Stacey Ecott, and Leanne M. Hirshfield. 2007. Through the Looking Glass: Teaching CS0 with Alice. *SIGCSE Bull.* 39, 1 (March 2007), 213–217.

[28] Mitchel Resnick, John Maloney, Andrés Monroy-Hernández, Natalie Rusk, Evelyn Eastmond, Karen Brennan, Amon Millner, Eric Rosenbaum, Jay S Silver, Brian Silverman, et al. 2009. Scratch: programming for all. *Commun. ACM* 52, 11 (2009), 60–67.

[29] David Thompson and Tim Bell. 2013. Adoption of new CS high school standards by New Zealand teachers. In *Proc of the Workshop in Primary and Secondary Computing Education*. ACM, 87–90.

[30] Ashok Kumar Veerasamy, Daryl D'Souza, and Mikko-Jussi Laakso. 2016. Identifying Novice Student Programming Misconceptions and Errors From Summative Assessments. *Journal of Educational Technology Systems* 45, 1 (2016), 50–73.

[31] David Weintrop and Uri Wilensky. 2015. Using Commutative Assessments to Compare Conceptual Understanding in Blocks-based and Text-based Programs. In *Proceedings of the Eleventh Annual International Conference on International Computing Education Research*. 101–110.

Exploring Differences in Minority Students' Attitudes towards Computing after a One-Day Coding Workshop

Michael J. Lee
New Jersey Institute of Technology
Newark, New Jersey, USA
mjlee@njit.edu

ABSTRACT

As programming continues to be an essential 21st century skill, it is critical to focus on diversity and increasing participation of underrepresented groups in computing. To address this need, we must better understand minorities' views and attitudes towards programming, especially in their youth, as literature shows that children form ideas about their interests and careers in middle school or earlier. To explore this, we provided middle school students in the U.S. with a full day (7 hours) of programming activities to learn about their initial attitudes towards computing and how a short intervention might change these attitudes. We ran two separate one-day events, serving a total of 34 minority students (21 males and 13 females; grades 6 and 7) from a low-income, urban area. We found that students' initial attitudes towards computing were high, and that one day of learning programming increased their reported attitudes in computing even more. We also found differences in attitudes by gender and ethnicity. These findings highlight the positive attitudes minority students have towards computing, and the importance of providing resources and support to help maintain their interests in computing while recognizing demographic differences.

CCS CONCEPTS

• **Social and Professional Topics → Computing Education.**

KEYWORDS

Computing education; Middle school; Minorities; Attitudes

ACM Reference Format:
Michael J. Lee. 2019. Exploring Differences in Minority Students' Attitudes towards Computing after a One-Day Coding Workshop. In *Innovation and Technology in Computer Science Education (ITiCSE '19), July 15–17, 2019, Aberdeen, Scotland, UK.* ACM, New York, NY, USA, 7 pages. https://doi.org/10.1145/3304221.3319736

1 INTRODUCTION

Software is transforming the world economy, creating significant demand for programming skills in science, technology, education, health, and other rapidly growing fields [37]. Meanwhile, programming and computing-related jobs are among the fastest growing

Figure 1: Sussex Avenue Renew School students (6th and 7th grade) playing the Gidget game for their morning activity.

career opportunities [10], growing faster than all other occupations in some parts of the world such as in the U.S. [37]. However, many of these positions will go unfilled as there are not enough people with the right training/skills to take these jobs [17, 50]. Moreover, for positions that do get filled, the diversity of both the workforce and undergraduate population continues to be dominated by certain groups (e.g., males), contributing to severe inequities and bias in software design and use [38], including disproportionately low participation by minority groups. Without new learning opportunities that both engage a wider range of the population and sustain their learning and engagement over time, we cannot adequately address the lack of diversity and low supply of technology workers.

Many youth are not choosing to pursue computing-related subject fields, further increasing the lack of representation in computing (this is particularly true for underrepresented groups in the U.S. [37]). Although many computing related enrichment activities are available to high school students, research has shown that youth begin to form ideas about future careers during their formative years in middle school [11, 15, 21].

This project attempts to address inequities in computing by learning more about low-income, minority, middle school students' initial views and attitudes towards computing and how a one day programming workshop (event) might change these attitudes. We surveyed middle school students using validated instruments, before and after they were exposed to programming with a debugging game and block programming environment. Our goal was to provide minority students a positive experience with programming, and also to share our findings about these students' attitudes towards computing so that educators and researchers can better design effective programming interventions to motivate these students who are underrepresented in computing.

ITiCSE '19, July 15–17, 2019, Aberdeen, Scotland, UK

ACM ISBN 978-1-4503-6301-3/19/07...$15.00
https://doi.org/10.1145/3304221.3319736

2 RELATED WORK

2.1 Middle Schools

Although many computing related enrichment activities target high school students, research has shown that youth begin to form ideas about future careers earlier, during their formative years in middle school [11, 15, 21]. Many educational research efforts targeting younger children have focused on how to engage them in CS by using programming environments that are user-friendly and have the potential to lower the cognitive threshold for novice programmers, such as Scratch (e.g., [32]), Alice (e.g., [25, 26]), Gidget [31], and others [19]. Overall, studies repeatedly found that these types of environments are effective in the acquisition of basic programming skills and concepts (e.g., [29, 31, 32]) and support computational thinking. For example, Meerbaum-Salant et al. [34] found that Scratch helped middle schoolers learn most of the targeted CS concepts. Lee & Ko [31] found similar results with Gidget, where users showed significant, measurable learning gains for targeted CS concepts. In our study, we aim to learn more specifically about underrepresented and minority middle students and their attitudes towards computing, both before and after working with some of the programming environments mentioned above.

2.2 Females and Minority Students

Females are underrepresented in computing [41]. Research shows that social environment influences many girls to exclude considering computing career choices by the time they enter high school, even before they have been exposed to any computing instruction [36, 43, 47]. During their formative time in middle school, girls are deeply engaged in forming confidence in STEM disciplines [1, 18, 48] but might be more risk averse [9, 22, 46] and have lower self-efficacy and self-confidence in computing than their male peers [2, 4, 8, 33]. For example, females tend to have lower confidence in computer-based problem-solving tasks like programming [2, 6], which may make them less likely to pursue computing activities on their own [33]. They also have a lower likelihood of trying new software features [2, 6] and a greater reluctance to tinker with code or programming tools [3, 6]. We aim to make our events gender-inclusive [7] to appeal to a wide range of people with different preferences and computing skill.

Members of ethnic minority groups are also largely underrepresented in computing. Availability of computing resources such as internet access has been reported to be significantly related to household income and inversely affected by minority status [24]. Even when minorities gain access to educational computing resources, they are often taught rote learning activities rather than cognitively demanding tasks [45] or patronized by their instructors, mentors, and peers [16, 20]. Young minorities that express interest in computing may stand out and be dissuaded by their friends and family [12], so they may avoid or quit pursuing computing. We hypothesize that early computing instruction in a safe and positive environment will counter many of these negative effects.

There have been numerous efforts to increase participation of young underrepresented minorities and females in computing activities. Robinson & Pérez-Quiñones, were able to change underrepresented middle school girls' initial negative perceptions of computing by teaching them human-computer interaction (HCI) methods through paper prototyping over a week-long workshop [40]. Similarly, Doerschuk et al., found that their underrepresented middle school students' self-reports of computer science knowledge increased significantly after a one-day workshops run by undergraduate students who created the programming instructional materials [14]. Denner analyzed data from middle school students on the first day of a computing after-school program and found that the strongest direct predictor of girls' interest in computing classes and careers was the extent to which they see value in computing, and perceived support from peers and adults (teachers and parents) [11]. Our experience report adds to this body of knowledge, using validated survey instruments and similar curricula to learn more about underrepresented students' attitudes towards computing and how we might be able to encourage more participation.

3 METHOD

The purpose of our experience report is to investigate what minority middle school students think of computing, and how programming—in the form of a concrete learning experience using an educational programming game and block programming environment—might change their initial attitudes. Our hypotheses were:

(1) Minority children will have positive views towards computing.
(2) Minority children's attitudes towards computing will increase (positively) after a basic educational programming experience.

3.1 Location and Recruitment

We ran two separate one-day, Saturday events during different semesters of the school year. The first took place at Sussex Avenue Renew School, a local K-8 public school in Newark, New Jersey (U.S.). The second took place at the Urban League of Essex County's office (a local non-profit organization), and included students from two other K-8 public schools from Newark. The schools' demographic makeup reflects the community they serve, composed of 52% Hispanics, 47% African Americans, and 1% others; 82% of these students are low-income—eligible for free or reduced-price lunch.

Principals recruited students from their respective schools by recommendations from their 5th and 6th grade teachers, who made announcements in their classes. Venues for both events included a classroom, equipment (e.g., laptops with WiFi access), a middle school teacher (one male technology teacher at the first event, and one female technology teacher at the second event), and two male undergraduate student instructors. The same two instructors ran both events and taught the middle school students, while the teachers were available primarily for classroom support (e.g., to help keep the children on task). All of the middle school students were dropped off and picked up by their respective parents/guardians.

3.2 Procedure

Although traditional survey measures are commonly used to understand views toward computing [29], they often ask about attitudes abstractly, or without exposing participants to actual programming. Our seven-hour day consisted of breakfast, taking a pretest, a programming game activity, lunch, a block programming activity, and then a posttest. Breakfast was 15 minutes, lunch was 45 minutes, and the surveys took 30 minutes each. The game and block programming game were each 2.5 hours. In more detail:

3.2.1 *Morning Activity.* For their opening activity, students played Gidget [30, 31] (www.helpgidget.org)—a free, online, educational programming game—to give them a positive introduction to coding, as one's first experience with code is important [28]. Jernigan et al. [23] and Lee et al. [30] demonstrated that the game is engaging for a wide range of programming novices and that it is a good introduction to (text-based) programming for after-school programs. We encouraged our middle school students to complete as many levels as they could during the scheduled 2.5 hours, as each subsequent level in Gidget covers progressively difficult introductory programming (CS1) concepts [30].

3.2.2 *Afternoon Activity.* For our afternoon closing activity, our events used the Scratch "Creative Computing" curriculum [5] to give the middle school students experience with a block programming language. Scratch has been used extensively to engage youth with block programming through animation authoring and storytelling [32, 34]. The morning session consisted of the "Unit 0: Getting Started" section of Harvard University's Creative Computing curriculum for 2.5 hours, giving students an introduction to Scratch, its features, and how to use block programming with examples that they could follow to make animations.

3.2.3 *Pre and Post Tests.* We used two existing, tested, and validated paper-based instruments to collect the data from students: 1) the Computer Attitudes Questionnaire (CAQ) v5.14 [27] (designed for middle school students), and 2) the Computing Attitudes Survey (CAS) v4.0 [42]. The former measures general computing attitudes (e.g., "I enjoy doing things on a computer.") whereas the latter specifically measures computer science programming attitudes (e.g., "After I study a topic in computer science and feel that I understand it, I have difficulty solving problems on the same topic.") and is designed to be an extension of the former.

Our pre and post tests consisted of the first 20 questions from the CAQ (labeled as "Part 1" in the original document [27]), and all 26 of the CAS questions [42]. For the CAS, we replaced all occurrences of "computer science" with "computing" to keep the scope of the questions intentionally broad and to minimize potential confusion (especially during the pretest, since students had not started the programming activities yet). We added two questions to the end of the test, Q46: "I am interested in learning more about computer programming," and Q47: "I can become a computer programmer." We also inserted one attention check question towards the end of the questionnaire, "Please choose 'agree' (number 4) for this answer," to help ensure that students were paying attention to the 48 questions. All answer choices were in the form of a 5-point Likert scale [39] to determine how agreeable students were to the statements (with 1 being least agreeable, and 5 being most agreeable).

There were three additional questions asking students if they wanted to go to college, and whether they would attend more classes *at* school or *outside* of school to learn more about programming. Then, only for the pretest (since we would not expect responses to change during the course of the day), we collected demographic information (i.e., grade level, ethnicity, gender, and eligibility for free/reduced lunch), and asked four yes/no questions examining if they: owned a smartphone, had prior programming experience, and had access to a computer and/or internet at home.

4 RESULTS

It took the middle school students approximately 30 minutes to complete each of the pre and post tests. In total, we had 34 students (n = 34) participate in our event (11-13 years old). The first event included 12 boys and 6 girls (seven 6th graders and eleven 7th graders; see Figure 1), and the second event included 9 boys and 7 girls (seven 6th graders and nine 7th graders). All of the students were underrepresented minorities in STEM, identifying as either African American (AA students; 8 each at the events) or Hispanic/Latino (HL Students; 10 at the first event, and 8 at the second event), and all were eligible for free/reduced cost lunch.

We report the median of our (ordinal) responses. Throughout this analysis, we use nonparametric Wilcoxon/Kruskal-Wallis rank sums tests (for differences between pre and post tests) and Chi-Squared likelihood ratio tests (for differences within a pretest or posttest) with $\alpha = 0.05$ confidence—as our data was not normally distributed—to compare participants' responses based on their demographic categories. We report our statistically significant results in Tables 1 through 4 with the understanding that our sample size is small and that the resulting statistics may not be widely generalizable. As both of our events used the same schedule and instructors, and all the students came from the same school district with comparable demographic distributions (i.e., grade, gender, ethnicity, and eligibility for free/reduced cost lunch), we report our results aggregating all event participants into one group.

4.1 Computing Attitude (CAQ & CAS) Results

4.1.1 *Pretest Scores (Initial Attitudes).* We examined the students pretest scores to gauge their initial attitudes towards computing before taking part in our activity. Overall, the students reported positive attitudes towards computing for on the pretest, with medians of 4 ("agree) or 5 ("strongly agree") for all positive valence questions (e.g., Q11: "I believe that it is important for me to learn how to use a computer," and Q31: "I find the challenge of solving computing problems motivating."), medians of 1 ("strongly disagree") through 3 ("neither agree nor disagree") for all negative valence questions (e.g., Q16, "Working with a computer makes me nervous," and Q45: "I worry that mistakes I make when using a computer may damage my computer."), and medians of 2 ("disagree") or 3 ("neither agree nor disagree") for all neutral valence questions (e.g., Q23: "If I want to apply a method used for solving one computing problem to another problem, the problems must involve very similar situations.").

We found some differences in response by ethnicity and gender in the pretest scores. For example, Q7 ("I know that computers give me opportunities to learn many new things.") and Q20 ("I can learn more from books than from a computer.") had significantly different responses by ethnicity, where AA students were more likely to agree with both statements compared to their HL classmates (see Table 1). Additionally, Q30 ("When working on a computing problem, I brainstorm about solution strategies before trying to solve it.") had significantly different responses on the pretest by ethnicity, where AA students were more likely to agree with this statement compared to their HL classmates (see Table 1).

For Q10 ("I believe that the more often teachers use computers, the more I'll enjoy school."), males were significantly more likely to agree with the statement over their female classmates (see Table 2).

Question (Pretest-Top/Posttest-Bottom):	Statistic	p.val
7. I know that computers give me opportunities to learn many new things.	$X^2(4,N=34)=9.988$ (AA is Higher)	*.041**
20. I can learn more from books than from a computer.	$X^2(4,N=34)=10.67$ (AA is Higher)	*.031**
30. When working on a computing problem, I brainstorm about solution strategies before trying to solve it.	$X^2(3,N=34)=8.831$ (AA is Higher)	*.032**
3. I will be able to get a good job if I learn how to use a computer.	$X^2(1,N=33)=5.405$ (AA is Higher)	*.020**
27. There are times I solve a computing problem in more than one way to help with my understanding.	$X^2(3,N=34)=9.371$ (AA is Higher)	*.025**
28. I think about the computing technologies or problems I experience in everyday life.	$X^2(3,N=34)=7.917$ (AA is Higher)	*.048**
45. I worry that mistakes I make when using a computer may damage my computer.	$X^2(4,N=34)=9.550$ (HL is Higher)	*.049**

AA = African American/Black Students; HL = Hispanic/Latino Students

Table 1: Pretest & Posttest Differences by Ethnicity

Next, Q33 ("I enjoy solving computing problems."), Q40 ("Understanding computing basically means being able to recall something you've read or been shown."), and Q44 ("To learn about computing, I only need to memorize solutions to sample problems."), male students were significantly more likely to agree with these statements than their female classmates (see Table 2).

4.1.2 Posttest Scores (Post-Activity Attitudes). Like the pretest, students reported highly positive attitudes towards computing on the posttest with some minor improvements for some questions. There were no statistically detectable differences by gender within the posttest scores. However, we did find a few question that had statistically significant difference responses by ethnicity (see Table 1).

For example, in Q3 ("I will be able to get a good job if I learn how to use a computer."), AA students were significantly more likely agree with the statement over their HL classmates. Additionally, Q27 ("There are times I solve a computing problem in more than one way to help with my understanding.") and Q28 ("I think about the computing technologies or problems I experience in everyday life.") had significantly different responses on the posttest by ethnicity, where AA students were more likely to agree with both statements compared to their HL classmates (see Table 1). Conversely, on Q45 ("I worry that mistakes I make when using a computer may damage my computer."), HL students were more likely to agree with the statement compared to their AA classmates (see Table 1).

4.1.3 Comparison between Pre and Post Test Scores. Table 3 lists the questions where statistically significant differences were detected comparing the posttest and pretest. Responses from seven questions (two of the twenty from the CAQ, and five of twenty-six from the CAS) were significantly different between the tests.

Question (Pretest):	Statistic	p.val
10. I believe that the more often teachers use computers, the more I'll enjoy school.	$X^2(3,N=34)=8.657$ (Males Rate Higher)	*.034**
33. I enjoy solving computing problems.	$X^2(2,N=34)=6.730$ (Males Rate Higher)	*.035**
40. Understanding computing basically means being able to recall something you've read or been shown.	$X^2(3,N=34)=9.890$ (Males Rate Higher)	*.020**
44. To learn about computing, I only need to memorize solutions to sample problems.	$X^2(3,N=33)=8.769$ (Males Rate Higher)	*.033**

Table 2: Pretest Differences by Gender

For example, Q3 ("I will be able to get a good job if I learn how to use a computer.") and Q4 ("I can concentrate on a computer when I use one.") having statistically higher posttest values than the pretest values in both cases (see Table 3). Negative valence questions, Q22 ("Errors made by computers are random, and when they happen, there's not much I can do to understand why."), and Q41 ("If I get stuck on a computing problem, there is no chance I'll figure it out on my own."), both had statistically significant lower posttest values than the pretest in both cases (demonstrating an improvement in attitudes). Likewise, for positive valence questions, Q25 ("When I solve a computing problem, I break it into smaller parts and solve them one at a time."), Q33 ("I enjoy solving computing problems."), and Q35 ("Learning about computing is just about learning how to think differently."), all had statistically higher posttest values compared to pretest values.

4.1.4 Comparison by Gender and Ethnicity. We also compared the difference between the posttest and pretest scores by gender and ethnicity. Although there were no statistically significant differences detected between the pretest and posttest scores by gender, we did find several differences by ethnicity (see Table 4).

We found that for Q3 ("I will be able to get a good job if I learn how to use a computer."), our AA students' scores from their pretest to their posttest increased significantly more than those of their HL classmates (Table 4). We also found several questions where HL students' scores improved significantly in their posttest over their pretest compared to their AA classmates. These included, Q4 ("I concentrate on a computer when I use one."), and Q33 ("I enjoy solving computing problems."). Q19 ("Computers are difficult to use.") has a negative valence, with the posttest score being significantly lower, meaning that HL students were more likely to report that computers were not as difficult to use in their posttest than their pretest compared to their AA classmates (see Table 4).

For negative valence questions, Q23 ("If I want to apply a method used for solving one computing problem to another problem, the

Question:	Statistic	p.val
3. I will be able to get a good job if I lean how to use a computer. Pre- Median: 4 (range 3-5) / Post- Median: 5 (range 4-5)	W=1336.5,Z=3.189 (Post is Higher)	*.001**
4. I can concentrate on a computer when I use one. Pre- Median: 4 (range 3-5) / Post- Median: 5 (range 4-5)	W=1323.5,Z=2.00 (Post is Higher)	*.045**
22. Errors made by computers are random, and when they happen, there's not much I can do to understand why. Pre- Median: 4 (range 1-5) / Post- Median: 2 (range 1-5)	W=1023,Z=-1.997 (Post is Lower)	*.046**
25. When I solve a computing problem, I break it into smaller parts and solve them one at a time. Pre- Median: 3 (range 1-5) / Post- Median: 3.5 (range 1-5)	W=1336,Z=2.044 (Post is Higher)	*.041**
33. I enjoy solving computing problems. Pre- Median: 4 (range 3-5) / Post- Median: 4 (range 1-5)	W=1335,Z=2.092 (Post is Higher)	*.036**
35. Learning about computing is just about learning how to think differently. Pre- Median: 4 (range 2-5) / Post- Median: 5 (range 3-5)	W=1280.5,Z=2.106 (Post is Higher)	*.035**
41. If I get stuck on a computing problem, there is no chance I'll figure it out on my own. Pre- Median: 3 (range 1-4) / Post- Median: 2 (range 1-5)	W=999,Z=-2.245 (Post is Lower)	*.025**
48. I can become a computer programmer. Pre- Median: 3 (range 3-5) / Post- Median: 5 (range 3-5)	W=1347,Z=2.276 (Post is Higher)	*.023**

Table 3: Comparison of Pre/Post Test (General)

Question:	Statistic	p.val
3. I will be able to get a good job if I learn how to use a computer. Pre- Median: 4 (range 3-5) / Post- Median: 5 (range 4-5)	W=336,Z=3.116 (AA Higher Post)	*.002**
4. I concentrate on a computer when I use one. Pre- Median: 4 (range 3-5) / Post- Median: 5 (range 4-5)	W=398.5,Z=2.204 (HL Higher Post)	*.028**
19. Computers are difficult to use. Pre- Median: 2 (range 1-5) / Post- Median: 1 (range 1-5)	W=265.5,Z=-2.28 (HL Higher Pre)	*.022**
23. If I want to apply a method used for solving one computing problem to another problem, the problems must involve very similar situations. Pre- Median: 3 (range 1-5) / Post- Median: 3 (range 1-5)	W=211,Z=-2.028 (AA Higher Pre)	*.043**
25. When I solve a computing problem, I break it into smaller parts and solve them one at a time. Pre- Median: 3 (range 1-5) / Post- Median: 3.5 (range 1-5)	W=314.5,Z=1.967 (AA Higher Post)	*.049**
33. I enjoy solving computing problems. Pre- Median: 4 (range 3-5) / Post- Median: 4 (range 1-5)	W=402.5,Z=2.296 (HL Higher Post)	*.022**
35. Learning about computing is just about learning how to think differently. Pre- Median: 4 (range 2-5) / Post- Median: 5 (range 3-5)	W=364,Z=2.030 (HL Higher Post)	*.042**
41. If I get stuck on a computing problem, there is no chance I'll figure it out on my own. Pre- Median: 3 (range 1-4) / Post- Median: 2 (range 1-5)	W=208,Z=-2.251 (AA Higher Pre)	*.024**
48. I can become a computer programmer. Pre- Median: 3 (range 3-5) / Post- Median: 5 (range 3-5)	W=318,Z=2.161 (AA Higher Post)	*.031**

AA = African American/Black Students; HL = Hispanic/Latino Students

Table 4: Comparison of Pre/Post Test by Ethnicity

problems must involve very similar situations."), and Q41 ("If I get stuck on a computing problem, there is no chance I'll figure it out on my own."), AA students reported statistically significant lower agreement in the posttest for all three questions (demonstrating an improvement in attitudes) compared to their HL classmates.

For the positive valence question Q25 ("When I solve a computing problem, I break it into smaller parts and solve them one at a time."), AA students reported statistically significant higher agreement in their posttest than their pretest compared to HL students. Similarly, for Q33 ("I enjoy solving computing problems.") and Q35 ("Learning about computing is just about learning how to think differently."), HL students reported statistically significant higher agreement in their posttest than their pretest compared to their AA classmates.

4.2 Additional Question Results

For Q48 ("I can become a computer programmer"), we found that the posttest scores were significantly different from the pretest (median 3), with the posttest (median 5) scoring much higher (see Table 3). Moreover, we found a statistically significant difference when comparing posttest and pretest scores for this question, where AA students were more likely to agree with the statement compared to their HL classmates (see Table 4).

All (34 of 34) students reported that they wanted to attended college, and would take more classes *at* school to learn more about computers and computer programming. All but one student (33 of 34) reported that they would want to take more classes *outside* of school to learn more about computers and computer programming.

For our pretest-only questions, 25 of 34 (73.5%) students reported that they owned a smartphone. Additionally, 27 of 34 (79.4%) students indicated they had a computer at home. These same students also had access to the Internet at home. Those 7 of 34 (20.6%) who stated not having a computer at home also did not have Internet access at home. 10 of the 34 (29.4%) students reported they had some previous programming experience (all using Scratch).

5 DISCUSSION

5.1 Initial View of Computing & Programming

We confirm our first hypothesis that our minority middle school students had initially positive attitudes towards computing and programming, before participating in our activity (Sections 4.1.1 and 4.2.1). In addition to our survey results, our students were open to talking (positively) about computing and appeared to be genuinely interested in partaking in the day's computing activities along with their classmates. This is similar to DiSalvo et al.'s findings that AA students interested in a computing activity were eager to talk about it with their peers in the context of use, but not outside [13]. Unfortunately, we are unable to determine if our students would be willing to talk to other peers about their computing activities outside, as we only interacted with them during the one day event(s). However, we observed that our students were eager to learn, and admired their peers with more experience/skill in programming. These skilled students also spent time helping their less-experienced peers with different concepts and issues throughout the day.

5.1.1 Comparison by Gender and Ethnicity. We found a total of four significantly different scores in the students' initial (i.e., pretest) computing attitudes by gender. Based on the responses, it appears that our male students had higher computing self-efficacy and wanted to use computers in their classes more often than their female classmates (see Q10 and Q33 in Table 2). However, it also appears that our male students believed that computing mostly involved rote learning (see Q40 and Q44 in Table 2). Overall, these differences found by gender are not entirely unexpected, as previous research has shown that females tend to have lower self-efficacy in computing than males [2, 3, 6].

We also found a total of three significantly different scores in the students' initial computing attitudes by ethnicity. Our AA students were more likely than their HL classmates to agree that computers provide opportunities to learn new things and that they brainstorm solutions before working on computing problems (see Q7 and Q30 in Table 1). However, these AA students were also more likely than their HL counterparts to agree that they could learn more from books than computers (Q20, Table 1). These findings on AA students' views towards success are similar to those described in the narratives of successful AA college students by Urias et al. [44], and highlight the need for educators to rethink how to deliver computing education that will both engage and set them up for success. This also highlights the need to learn more about the various, distinct perceptions that different minority groups may have towards computing, as a one-size-fits all model for teaching and engaging these different groups may not be ideal.

5.1.2 Post Views of Computing. Addressing our second hypothesis, we found an increase in several of the reported attitudes by our students towards computing after participating in our activity.

We found a total of eight questions where responses in the posttest were significantly different from the pretest. The first were related to jobs, where students agreed on their posttest that they could get a good job if they learned how to use a computer, and that they could become a computer programmer themselves (Q3 and Q48, Table 3). Students also reported on their use of computers and solving problems, where they said they can concentrate on computers when they use one, that they enjoy solving computing problems, and to do so, they can break it into smaller pieces to solve individually (Q4, Q25, and Q33, Table 3).

Additionally, these students better understood how computers worked, stating that the errors made by computers are not random (Q22), learning computing is about thinking differently (Q35), and that they can figure out on their own how to overcome difficult computing problems (Q41). For Q48 ("I can become a computer programmer."), students originally had a median of 3 ("neither agree nor disagree") (Table 3), but this increased significantly to a median of 5 ("highly agree") by the end of our event. This result was especially pronounced for our AA students (Table 4).

These results demonstrate that a short, one-day event teaching programming concepts can have significant impacts on students' understanding of computing, how to solve programming problems, and increase their confidence in becoming programmers themselves. Future work will explore how to sustain these students' interest and attitudes, and what types of activities are effective in doing so.

5.1.3 Comparison by Ethnicity and Gender. We also found several questions where responses in the posttest were significantly different from the pretest based on ethnicity and by gender. Examining the responses, it appears that our AA students became much more confident in their own ability to overcome obstacles in computing after participating in the event compared to their HL classmates.

First, AA students were more likely to agree that learning how to use a computer could get them a good job (Q3). They also became more confident in their computing abilities, understanding that computing problems can be solved in multiple ways (Q23), and that they have the capability to solve these problems on their own (Q44), using strategies such as dividing a problem into smaller parts (Q25).

Our HL students' computing self-efficacy also improved significantly between their pretest and posttest scores, but differently from their AA classmates. They reported that they concentrated on computers when they were using one (Q4), that computers are not difficult to use (Q19), that they enjoy solving computing problems (Q33), and that learning about computing is just a matter of thinking differently (Q35, Table 4).

Next, we found that the gender differences described in 5.1.1 completely disappeared by the end of the event, suggesting that something about our event raised the female students' self-efficacy and understanding of computing. We do not believe that the gender of the other participants (21 of 34; 61.8% were male), instructors (two males), or teachers (one male and one female) largely attributed to this positive change in female students, as there were fewer females overall. Instead, we suspect that the events' programming activities attributed to this effect. According to its developers, Gidget was designed using a gender-inclusive approach and was found to engage high school females in programming summer camps [7, 30]. Researchers examining Scratch also did not find any gender differences in the number of projects created [35], nor with participation patterns or project complexity [49], suggesting that Scratch provides similar opportunities and engagement across genders. We plan to examine these issues in future events to help identify specific factors that may engage (or disengage) females.

These findings demonstrate that there are major differences in the attitude changes between different minority groups and genders. Future work will further examine these differences so that educators and researchers can better understand how to create learning interventions that support different groups of learners.

5.2 Limitations and Future Work

We had significant results in several of our measures. However, we had two activities throughout the day (playing a debugging game and making animations with a block programming language), making it difficult to isolate the specific intervention or factors that affected students' responses. Future events can offer only one activity throughout the day so that we can better understand the specific intervention's effect.

We reported statistics combining participants from our two events into into one group. We believe this is acceptable, as the demographic makeup of both groups were comparable, all students attended public schools in the same school district, and both events followed the same structure/curriculum with the same instructors.

All of our students were recruited by participating schools' principals, which may have introduced a selection bias (e.g., students who signed up for a Saturday programming event are likely to have positive views of computing). Moreover, we had a fairly small number of participants overall and though we found some statistically significant results for some demographic factors, we were unable to detect anything at the intersection of these factors (e.g., the interaction between gender and ethnicity on the responses). These issues may limit the generalizability of our results. In the future, we will work with additional schools in recruiting a larger number of participants and seek to minimize effects of potential selection biases (e.g., recruiting an entire class if possible).

6 CONCLUSION

We worked with 34 minority middle school students across two Saturday events, exposing them to programming through an educational game and a block programming environment. We found that these students' initial views and attitudes towards computing were positive. We also found that the day of activities increased these positive views even further, with a significant number of them stating that they could become a computer programmer themselves.

We also found some differences by gender and ethnicity in students' initial attitudes towards computing, and also after they finished their activity. These findings highlight the need to further examine the differences between minority groups and even across different demographic factors within these groups. Better understanding of these differences can lead to more targeted and effective programming-related interventions to help increase minorities engagement and representation in computing.

ACKNOWLEDGMENTS

We thank the Newark Public Schools and the Urban League of Essex County for their contributions and participation. This work was supported in part by the National Science Foundation (NSF) under grants DRL-1837489 and IIS-1657160. Any opinions, findings, conclusions or recommendations are those of the authors and do not necessarily reflect the views of the NSF or other parties.

REFERENCES

[1] Albert Bandura. 1986. Social Foundation of Thought and Action: A Social-cognitive View. *Englewood Cliffs* (1986).

[2] Laura Beckwith, Margaret Burnett, Susan Wiedenbeck, Curtis Cook, Shraddha Sorte, and Michelle Hastings. 2005. Effectiveness of End-user Debugging Software Features: Are there Gender Issues?. In *SIGCHI Conference on Human Factors in Computing Systems*. ACM, 869–878.

[3] Laura Beckwith, Cory Kissinger, Margaret Burnett, Susan Wiedenbeck, Joseph Lawrance, Alan Blackwell, and Curtis Cook. 2006. Tinkering and Gender in End-user Programmers' Debugging. In *SIGCHI Conference on Human Factors in Computing Systems*. ACM, 231–240.

[4] Joel Brandt, Mira Dontcheva, Marcos Weskamp, and Scott R Klemmer. 2010. Example-centric Programming: Integrating Web Search into the Development Environment. In *SIGCHI Conference on Human Factors in Computing Systems*. ACM, 513–522.

[5] K Brennan, M Chung, and J Hawson. 2011. Scratch Curriculum Guide: A Design-based Introduction to Computational Thinking with Scratch. (2011).

[6] Margaret Burnett, Scott D Fleming, Shamsi Iqbal, Gina Venolia, Vidya Rajaram, Umer Farooq, Valentina Grigoreanu, and Mary Czerwinski. 2010. Gender Differences and Programming Environments: Across Programming Populations. In *ACM-IEEE International Symposium on Empirical Software Engineering and Measurement*. ACM, 28.

[7] Margaret M Burnett, Elizabeth F Churchill, and Michael J Lee. 2015. SIG: Gender-Inclusive Software: What We Know About Building It. In *ACM Conference Extended Abstracts on Human Factors in Computing Systems*. ACM, 857–860.

[8] Tor Busch. 1996. Gender, Group Composition, Cooperation, and Self-efficacy in Computer Studies. *Journal of Educational Computing Research* 15, 2 (1996), 125–135.

[9] James P Byrnes, David C Miller, and William D Schafer. 1999. Gender differences in risk taking: a meta-analysis. *Psychological Bulletin* 125, 3 (1999), 367.

[10] Anthony P Carnevale, Nicole Smith, and Michelle Melton. 2011. STEM: Science Technology Engineering Mathematics. *Georgetown University Center on Education and the Workforce* (2011).

[11] Jill Denner. 2011. What Predicts Middle School Girls' Interest in Computing? *International Journal of Gender, Science and Technology* 3, 1 (2011).

[12] Betsy DiSalvo, Mark Guzdial, Amy Bruckman, and Tom McKlin. 2014. Saving Face while Geeking Out: Video Game Testing as a Justification for Learning Computer Science. *Journal of the Learning Sciences* 23, 3 (2014), 272–315.

[13] Betsy DiSalvo, Sarita Yardi, Mark Guzdial, Tom McKlin, Charles Meadows, Kenneth Perry, and Amy Bruckman. 2011. African American Men Constructing Computing Identity. In *SIGCHI Conference on Human Factors in Computing Systems*. ACM, 2967–2970.

[14] Peggy Doerschuk, Jiangjiang Liu, and Judith Mann. 2009. INSPIRED Computing Academies for Middle School Students: Lessons Learned. In *Richard Tapia Celebration of Diversity in Computing Conference: Intellect, Initiatives, Insight, and Innovations*. ACM, 52–57.

[15] Jacquelynne S Eccles and Rena D Harold. 1993. Parent-school Involvement during the Early Adolescent Years. *Teachers College Record* (1993).

[16] Erwin Flaxman. 1992. The Mentoring Relationship in Action. *The Institute for Urban & Minority Education Briefs* 3 (1992).

[17] Gary Gereffi, Vivek Wadhwa, Ben Rissing, Kiran Kalakuntla, Soomi Cheong, Qi Weng, and Nishanth Lingamneni. 2005. Framing the Engineering Outsourcing Debate: Placing the United States on a Level Playing Field with China and India. *Duke University Report* (2005).

[18] Judith Gill. 1994. Shedding Some New Light on Old Truths: Student Attitudes to School in Terms of Year Level and Gender. (1994).

[19] Shuchi Grover, Roy Pea, and Stephen Cooper. 2016. Factors Influencing Computer Science Learning in Middle School. In *ACM Technical Symposium on Computer Science Education (SIGCSE)*. ACM, 552–557.

[20] Eleanor Guetzloe. 1997. The Power of Positive Relationships: Mentoring Programs in the School and Community. *Preventing School Failure: Alternative Education for Children and Youth* 41, 3 (1997), 100–104.

[21] Nancy E Hill and Ming-Te Wang. 2015. From Middle School to College: Developing Aspirations, Promoting Engagement, and Indirect Pathways from Parenting to Post High School Enrollment. *Developmental Psychology* 51, 2 (2015), 224.

[22] Gerald A Hudgens and Linda Torsani Fatkin. 1985. Sex Differences in Risk Taking: Repeated Sessions on a Computer-simulated Task. *The Journal of Psychology* 119, 3 (1985), 197–206.

[23] William Jernigan, Amber Horvath, Michael Lee, Margaret Burnett, Taylor Cuilty, Sandeep Kuttal, Anicia Peters, Irwin Kwan, Faezeh Bahmani, Andrew Ko, et al. 2017. General Principles for a Generalized Idea Garden. *Journal of Visual Languages & Computing* 39 (2017), 51–65.

[24] Yasmin B Kafai, Kylie A Peppler, and Grace M Chiu. 2007. High Tech Programmers in Low-income Communities: Creating a Computer Culture in a Community Technology Center. In *Communities and Technologies*. Springer, 545–563.

[25] Caitlin Kelleher and Randy Pausch. 2007. Using Storytelling to Motivate Programming. *Commun. ACM* 50, 7 (2007), 58–64.

[26] Jordana Kerr, Mary Chou, Reilly Ellis, and Caitlin Kelleher. 2013. Setting the Scene: Scaffolding Stories to Benefit Middle School Students Learning to Program. In *Visual Languages and Human-Centric Computing (VL/HCC)*. IEEE, 95–98.

[27] G Knezek and R Christensen. 1997. Attitudes Toward Information Technology at Two Parochial Schools in North Texas. *Retrieved September* 5 (1997), 2005.

[28] Andrew J Ko. 2009. Attitudes and Self-efficacy in Young Adults' Computing Autobiographies. In *IEEE Symposium on Visual Languages and Human-Centric Computing (VL/HCC)*. IEEE, 67–74.

[29] D Midian Kurland and Roy D Pea. 1985. Children's Mental Models of Recursive LOGO Programs. *Journal of Educational Computing Research* 1, 2 (1985), 235–243.

[30] Michael J Lee, Faezeh Bahmani, Irwin Kwan, Jilian LaFerte, Polina Charters, Amber Horvath, Fanny Luor, Jill Cao, Catherine Law, Michael Beswetherick, et al. 2014. Principles of a Debugging-first Puzzle Game for Computing Education. In *Visual Languages and Human-Centric Computing (VL/HCC)*. IEEE, 57–64.

[31] Michael J Lee and Andrew J Ko. 2015. Comparing the Effectiveness of Online Learning Approaches on CS1 Learning Outcomes. In *ACM International Computing Education Research (ICER)*. ACM, 237–246.

[32] John H Maloney, Kylie Peppler, Yasmin Kafai, Mitchel Resnick, and Natalie Rusk. 2008. *Programming by Choice: Urban Youth Learning Programming with Scratch*. Vol. 40. ACM.

[33] Jane Margolis and Allan Fisher. 2003. *Unlocking the Clubhouse: Women in Computing*. MIT press.

[34] Orni Meerbaum-Salant, Michal Armoni, and Mordechai Ben-Ari. 2013. Learning Computer Science Concepts with Scratch. *Computer Science Education* 23, 3 (2013), 239–264.

[35] Andrés Monroy-Hernández and Mitchel Resnick. 2015. Empowering Kids to Create and Share Programmable Media. *arXiv preprint arXiv:1507.01282* (2015).

[36] NCWIT. [n. d.]. National Center for Women and Information Technology. ([n. d.]). Retrieved April 21, 2018 from https://www.ncwit.org/

[37] U.S. Bureau of Labor Statistics. 2018. Occupational Outlook Handbook. (2018). Retrieved April 21, 2018 from https://www.bls.gov/ooh/

[38] David A Patterson. 2005. Restoring the Popularity of Computer Science. *Commun. ACM* 48, 9 (2005), 25–28.

[39] Melanie A Revilla, Willem E Saris, and Jon A Krosnick. 2014. Choosing the Number of Categories in Agree–Disagree Scales. *Sociological Methods & Research* 43, 1 (2014), 73–97.

[40] Ashley Robinson and Manuel A Pérez-Quiñones. 2014. Underrepresented Middle School Girls: On the Path to Computer Science through Paper Prototyping. In *ACM Technical Symposium on Computer Science Education (SIGCSE)*. ACM, 97–102.

[41] Jennifer A Rode, Eleanor F Toye, and Alan F Blackwell. 2004. The Fuzzy Felt Ethnography–Understanding the Programming Patterns of Domestic Appliances. *Personal and Ubiquitous Computing* 8, 3-4 (2004), 161–176.

[42] Allison Tew, Brian Dorn, and Oliver Schneider. 2012. Toward a Validated Computing Attitudes Survey. In *ACM International Computing Education Research (ICER)*. ACM, 135–142.

[43] Lisa Tsui. 2007. Effective Strategies to Increase Diversity in STEM Fields: A Review of the Research Literature. *The Journal of Negro Education* (2007), 555–581.

[44] Marissa Vasquez Urias, Vannessa Falcon, Frank Harris III, and J Luke Wood. 2016. Narratives of Success: A Retrospective Trajectory Analysis of Men of Color who Successfully Transferred from the Community College. *New Directions for Institutional Research* 2016, 170 (2016), 23–33.

[45] Mark Warschauer. 2004. *Technology and Social Inclusion: Rethinking the Digital Divide*. MIT press.

[46] Elke U Weber, Ann-Renee Blais, and Nancy E Betz. 2002. A Domain-specific Risk-attitude Scale: Measuring Risk Perceptions and Risk Behaviors. *Journal of Behavioral Decision Making* 15, 4 (2002), 263–290.

[47] Sarita Yardi and Amy Bruckman. 2007. What is Computing?: Bridging the Gap Between Teenagers' Perceptions and Graduate Students' Experiences. In *ACM International Computing Education Research (ICER)*. ACM, 39–50.

[48] L Zimmer and S Bennett. 1987. Gender Differences on the California Statewide Assessment of Attitudes and Achievement in Science. In *American Educational Research Association*.

[49] Oren Zuckerman, Ina Blau, and Andrés Monroy-Hernández. 2009. Children's Participation Patterns in Online Communities. *Interdisciplinary Journal of E-Learning and Learning Objects* 5, 1 (2009), 263–274.

[50] Stuart Zweben. 2011. 2009-2010 Taulbee Survey Undergraduate CS Degree Production Rises; Doctoral Production Steady. (2011).

A Framework for Decomposition in Computational Thinking

Peter J. Rich
Brigham Young University
Provo, Utah, United States
peter_rich@byu.edu

Garrett Egan
Brigham Young University
Provo, Utah, United States
egan.garrett@gmail.com

Jordan Ellsworth
Brigham Young University
Provo, Utah, United States
jcellswo@gmail.com

ABSTRACT

Computational Thinking has become an important cognitive skill to develop in all areas of education. Despite its increasing popularity, the construct itself is only partially understood. There are few measures currently in place that advance our understanding of computational thinking and its sub-constructs. In this article, we analyze existing measures of computational thinking (CT), looking specifically at their measures of decomposition. Decomposition is defined as the process of breaking down a problem into its sub-components. Even though most definitions of computational thinking include decomposition, few break down the decompositional process beyond a basic definition. As one of the first steps in the computational thinking process, it is important to better understand the various manners in which decomposition occurs, which methods are most effective, and under what conditions. To better understand the decompositional process, we analyze evidence of decompositional process in a variety of disciplines. We then present a framework for decomposition in computational thinking. We demonstrate how this framework may help educators to better prepare students to break down complex problems, as well as provide guidance for how decompositional ability might be measured.

CCS CONCEPTS

• **Social and professional topics → Computational thinking; Student assessment; K-12 education.**

KEYWORDS

Computational Thinking, Decomposition, Framework, Assessment

ACM Reference Format:

Peter J. Rich, Garrett Egan, and Jordan Ellsworth. 2019. A Framework for Decomposition in Computational Thinking. In *Innovation and Technology in Computer Science Education (ITiCSE '19), July 15–17, 2019, Aberdeen, Scotland Uk.* ACM, New York, NY, USA, 6 pages. https://doi.org/10.1145/3304221.3319793

1 INTRODUCTION

Wing [33] suggested that "Computational Thinking is the thought processes involved in formulating problems and their solutions so that the solutions are represented in a form that can be effectively carried out by an information-processing agent." CT is not only the process of solving problems, but also of defining them. As educators have seen the value of the thought processes involved in CT being learned at a young age, they have sought to measure and teach CT during students' formative education worldwide [7]. Though scholars are working to improve the teaching and measurement of CT, there remains a lack of consistency in the definitions used to describe CT [22, 24, 27] . These inconsistent definitions cause measurement and teaching of CT to remain a complex challenge. The K–12 Computer Science Standards promoted by the Computer Science Teachers Association (CSTA) acknowledged this difficulty: "[d]eveloping an approach to computational thinking that is suitable for K-12 students is especially challenging in light of the fact that there is, as yet, no widely agreed upon definition of computational thinking" [11].

Despite the lack of a consistent definition of CT, there are some components that researchers agree are important aspects of CT, such as abstraction, decomposition, pattern finding, algorithm building, and debugging [11, 12].

Grover and Pea [16] asked,"What . . . can we expect children to know or do better once they've been participating in a curriculum designed to develop CT and how can this be evaluated?" (p. 42). Efforts have been made to measure CT through traditional multiple-choice tests, lesson plans, analysis of computational artifacts, game design, and mobile app development. A robust measure of computational thinking ability would measure each of its sub-constructs without being conflated or confused with other sub-constructs.

One of the most consistently mentioned, but unexplored components of CT is decomposition [15, 24, 27]. Most definitions of computational thinking include decomposition as part of the process, but few provide specific details as to how decomposition is performed, ways of identifying more or less effective means of decomposing a problem, or common decompositional challenges. Considering that problem decomposition is one of the first steps of computational thinking, doing it well can potentially improve or hinder the entire CT process.

The purpose of this article is to define problem decomposition beyond a generic, "break down the problem" description [5, p. 430]. We analyze existing measures of CT, looking specifically for their measures of decomposition. We then explore examples of problem decomposition across multiple disciplines. This resulted in an emergent framework to better understand decomposition as a distinct CT skill.

2 LITERATURE REVIEW

A variety of measures, evaluations, and assessments have been developed to aid in the recognition of CT ability. These have been tested on children from four to sixteen years of age. Some measures require students to take a multiple-choice style test agnostic of a specific programming language or platform, while others involve the analysis of computational artifacts created by students. Using Google scholar and the ACM database, we searched for "measure"

ITiCSE '19, July 15–17, 2019, Aberdeen, Scotland Uk

ACM ISBN 978 1 4503 6301-3/19/07. . . $15.00
https://doi.org/10.1145/3304221.3319793

or "assess" and "computational thinking." We were specifically interested in measures created since Wing's revival of computational thinking in 2006. This resulted in 9 measures whose specific aim was to measure evidence of CT in students or their computational products. Table 1 presents these measures, the constructs they each purport to measure, and each measure's specific explanation for how it measured decomposition.

This analysis demonstrates that there are many different constructs being measured by the different measures of CT. Regarding decomposition, the most common approach was not to measure it at all. When decomposition was measured, it was often measured by counting the ways in which students 'modularized" their code. This is likely due to the fact that modularizing demonstrates a certain "breaking down" of the code into manageable "blocks." While this may be one result of decomposition, this narrow definition reveals little about how an individual went about modularizing or decided how to modularize a block of code, and completely masks the decision-making process inherent in decomposition.

Despite the value these measures bring to the educational community in measuring CT ability, there are two areas for improvement in existing measures of CT: (a) conflation of multiple aspects of CT and (b) dependence on expert review for detection of successful decomposition. Conflation occurs when a measure combines multiple aspects of CT in a single measurement. In many cases, decomposition was paired with "abstraction" in a measure's rubric. This often occurred with descriptive measures that seek to identify aspects of CT through artifact analysis. In the case of objectively-measured tests, a student only receives credit for demonstrating computational thinking by providing a correct answer. The problem with this approach is that multiple CT sub-constructs may be involved in the process of coming to a correct solution. Students could use some form of cognitive shortcut or ad hoc trial and error method in order to arrive at the correct answer, which could cause false positives for CT ability.

Some measures' attempts to assess decompositional abilities are vague and dependent on the "you know it when you see it" notion that requires expert analysis in order to detect successful CT [8, 18]. This is not to dismiss expert review. Rather, we note that the rubrics provided in the literature do little more than state, "breaking down the problem." This leaves a lot of interpretation up to the expert. In addition, it suggests that any one "breaking down" process is the same as any other. Yet, those same experts, when teaching computational thinking or programming, can identify more and less successful approaches by their students.

In order to have an effective and holistic measure of CT, we need an empirical means of measuring decomposition [8]. In order to develop an effective assessment of decomposition as a part of CT, we need to understand how decomposition is used as a problem solving tool. Due to the paucity of guidance provided by existing measures, we sought to discover the use of decomposition as a problem-solving strategy in various fields of interest.

3 DECOMPOSITION AS USED IN VARIOUS FIELDS

Decomposition is a common step in many problem-solving processes and is employed in a variety of fields [1, 13]. In order to

Table 1: Table 1: CT Measures with measured sub-constructs

Measure	CT Constructs Measured	Decomposition Definition
Computational Thinking test [25]	Sequences, loops, conditionals, functions, logical operations, testing and debugging,,reusing and remixing, abstracting and modularizing	"Modularizing"(p. 680)
Dr. Scratch [6]	Abstraction & problem decomposition, parallelism, logical thinking, synchronization, flow control, user interactivity, data representation	"Definition of blocks" (p. 46)
Computational Thinking Patterns Test [4]	Computational concepts: sequences, loops, events, parallelism, conditionals, operators and data; Computational practices: experimenting and iterating, testing and debugging, reusing and remixing, abstracting and modularizing, Computational perspectives: expressing, connecting, and questioning	"Modularizing"(p. 7)
The Fairy Performance Assessment, [3]	Comprehension, design, complex problem solving, debugging	Not measured specifically
Computational Thinking Pattern Analysis (CTPA)	Push, pull, transportation, collision, absorption, generations, cursor control, hill climbing, diffusion.	Not measured specifically
CS4Impact [5]	Data collection, data analysis, data representation, problem decomposition, abstraction, algorithms and procedures, automation, parallelization, simulation, connection to other fields	"Students are required to break the problem down on their own." (p. 430)
Progression of Early Computational Thinking (PECT) [28]	Procedures and algorithms, problem decomposition, parallelization and synchronization, abstraction, data representation	"Modularize..."(p. 63)
Evaluation of Computer Games [2]	Sequence, iteration, variables, conditional statements, lists (arrays), event handling, threads, coordination and synchronisation, keyboard input, random numbers, boolean logic, dynamic interaction, user interface design	Not measured specifically
Assessment of Mobile Computational Thinking, [26]	Naming, procedural abstraction, variables, loops, conditionals, lists, screen interface, events, component abstraction, data persistence, data sharing, public web services, accelerometer & orientation sensors, location awareness	Not measured specifically

better understand decomposition, we analyzed case studies from various fields of research to determine how decomposition is used, understood, and measured.

The fields we selected came primarily from their inherent connection to CT, such as STEM fields like Computer Science and Engineering. We searched Google Scholar, ACM, EBSCO, and Scopus for "problem decomposition," "problem setup," "breaking down the problem," "modularization," and related terms in articles that provided information on the decompositional process in these respective fields. We found little direct research on problem decomposition within these STEM fields. This could have occurred because of differences in term usage, such as the term "decomposition" when used in the context of Biology, and the broad usage of other terms, such as "problem-solving." We then broadened our search to include case studies that evaluated problem solving within these fields. In these case studies, we analyzed how the authors described their process for breaking down complex problems, and we identified principles of decomposition within their work.

After an initial investigation, we recognized connections between what we had found in these STEM fields with principles of foundational theoretical fields, such as Philosophy, Anthropology, and Design. In order to add to our theoretical understanding of decomposition as a problem-solving strategy, we searched for articles in these theoretical fields for information that would improve our understanding of decompositional processes in non-STEM fields.

In the following section, we present research from STEM and non-STEM fields that demonstrates how decomposition may be approached and understood from various perspectives. The goal of this section is to demonstrate the variety of ways individuals approach decomposition, as well as to extract common decompositional principles.

3.1 Decomposition in STEM

Common ways of decomposing the computational problems we analyzed in computer science were to break down the problem by its structure, function, sequence, and dependence [10, 19, 20, 31]. Structural decomposition consists of breaking down the problem into the sub-pieces and resolving each one separately. Functional decomposition breaks the problem down by which functions are performed by which pieces of the system, separating them so that each can be analyzed separately. Sequential decomposition determines the order of operations in a process or other sequence of steps, and dependence decomposition breaks down the problem by which parts are dependent on which other parts. Each of these ways of decomposing a problem appears to be more effective in specific situations, depending on what information is needed in order to resolve the problem.

Another important finding from the Computer Science literature is the concept of black box programming [14]. A black box is a device, process, or system whose inputs, outputs, and relationships to other processes or systems may be known, but whose internal structure is unknown. Most problems, prior to successful decomposition, are like black boxes, whose inner structures and relationships are unknown to the problem solver.

In engineering, math, science, and technology, we found the decomposition process simply defined as "the act of breaking something down into simpler constituents" [21]. Mattson Sorenson maintain that the two most common forms of breaking down problems and products in engineering are structural decomposition and functional decomposition. Those observations come from a product development perspective, focusing on how to creatively begin the product design process. Structural decomposition involves dividing the problem up into its physical components. For example, a bicycle could be broken down into the seat, wheels, brakes, gears, etc. Functional decomposition involves splitting the problem into sections based on what they perform. Sorensen and Mattson (ibid) suggest this strategy to be especially useful when "there is no established concept or preconceived structure" (p. 228). For example, if we were to need something to get us to the store and back, we could break it down into sections such as: time to arrive at store, top speed, steering method, etc. This example illustrates how an unsolved problem acts as a black box until it is broken down into a more understandable set of structures and functions that can be used to solve the larger problem.

3.2 Decomposition in Non-STEM Fields

In Ontology (i.e., the study of being) philosopher researchers have tried for centuries to categorize the types of beings, as well as the characteristics that define existence. Two common categories spoken of are substance and relation, the matter and how that matter compares and relates to other matter (Heidegger, 1927). Many sub-categories are also identified based on their relevance to a specific issue or field, such as place, time, state, sequence, and dependence. Place, as a form of categorizing types of beings, states that some objects are above other objects, or some objects are located on the ground. Some commonly used categories are sequence, relation, and substance or physical characteristics [23, 32?].

It is also important to note that philosophical understanding of problem decomposition tends to focus on breaking down a problem as a strategy for understanding the problem better [?]. This is similar to using dissection as an educational activity for better understanding animal anatomy and biology. This also relates strongly with the goal of opening up the black box and better understanding the inner workings of any given system, process, or device. The task of decomposition is not used as the goal, but rather the means of gaining some important new information that will inform the next steps of the problem solving strategy. James Spradley [30], a well-known ethnographer, outlined a series of semantic relationships that can be used to better understand how individuals interact within and relate to their cultures. Namely:

- Strict Inclusion - X is a kind of Y
- Spatial - X is a place in Y; X is a part of Y
- Cause-Effect - X is a cause/result of Y
- Rationale - X is a reason for doing Y
- Location for - X is a place for doing Y action
- Function - X is used for Y
- Means-end - X is a way to do Y
- Sequence - X is a step/stage in Y
- Attribution - X is an attribute/characteristic of Y

These semantic relationships are used as a way to meaningfully decompose and categorize parts of a culture into its relational sub-parts. For example, the "Location for" relationships help to describe where tasks are typically performed in a specific culture. This decompositional strategy is intended as an iterative process of successively approximating a solution, using problem decomposition as a means of identifying ways of reaching the next successful iterative step [29].

4 A DECOMPOSITIONAL FRAMEWORK

Before successful decomposition is performed, a problem or sub-problem is known only as a black box. The inputs, outputs, and other relationships between problems or sub-problems may be known, but the inner workings of the problem at hand are unknown. Decomposition helps the problem solver to better understand the inner function of the problem by unpacking the problem and separating it into multiple sub-problems. Often, when breaking down a problem into sub-problems, the sub-problems all begin as black boxes as well, with their inner structures unknown to the problem solver.

For example, in this article we have broken down CT into the component parts decomposition, abstraction, pattern-finding, algorithm-building, and debugging. By breaking down CT in this way, we better understand how it works, even if we do not yet have a complete understanding of the inner workings of each sub-construct. The next step is to break down each sub-construct to unpack those black boxes as well.

4.1 Decompositional Categorization

One of the key features of decomposition is the differentiating and categorizing of parts of a problem or sub-problem [12]. The goal of this activity is to divide the problem or sub-problem into more manageable pieces or to gain better understanding of the problem by breaking it down into its component parts.

Two general forms of decomposition emerged from our examination of the theoretical and practical examples found in the previously explored fields. Those two forms of decomposition are substantive decomposition and relational decomposition [17].

4.1.1 Substantive Decomposition. Substantive decomposition involves the breaking down of a problem or artifact by its componential characteristics, such as breaking down a jigsaw puzzle by its various pieces, a painting by the colors used, or an article by its paragraphs. These are attributes or parts of the object or idea being decomposed. When decomposing a problem, a person identifies a meaningful axis on which they can categorize parts of the problem, and then they divide and cluster those parts into the identified categories along the specified axis [15].

Axis selection is dependent on the problem statement and context. One such axis could be to break down a problem artifact by its component parts, separating connected pieces at their joints in order to understand each part individually. This is commonly used in the analysis of physical objects, such as in automobiles or human anatomy [9], but can also be used to better understand the component parts of an abstract concept, such as the breaking down of an argument into its premises, assumptions, and conclusions.

Figure 1 **??** shows the general case of substantive decomposition, where some component A is broken down into two sub-components B and C. These two sub-components are then considered separately and distinct of each other, and they provide additional information while separate that was not provided while combined.

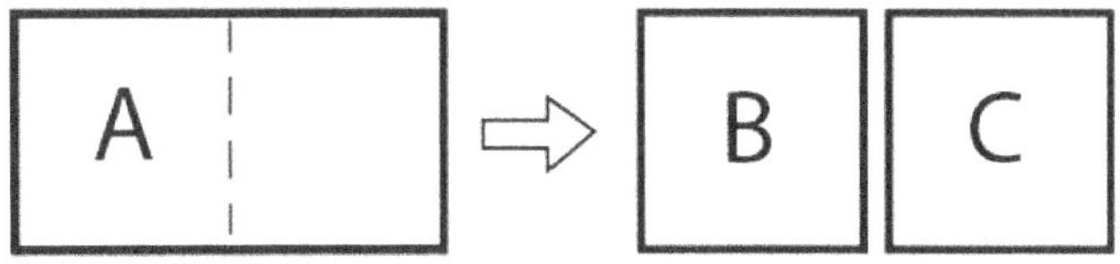

Figure 1: Substantive Decomposition Process

4.1.2 Relational Decomposition. Each component or sub-component of the problem may relate to other parts and sub-parts. Those relations could be based on time, sequence, location, dependence, function, or any of the other previously mentioned categories of relational decomposition.

Relational decomposition is performed by assigning a relation between two components or sub-components of a problem. This can be done, if desired, similar to substantive decomposition, by determining a type of relation, such as dependence, function, or sequence, and assigning all relations of that type to the various components and sub-components identified.

Figure 2 **??** shows the general case of relational decomposition, where some components A and B are assigned a relation. Prior to this relational decomposition, A and B were not considered to be related in this way.

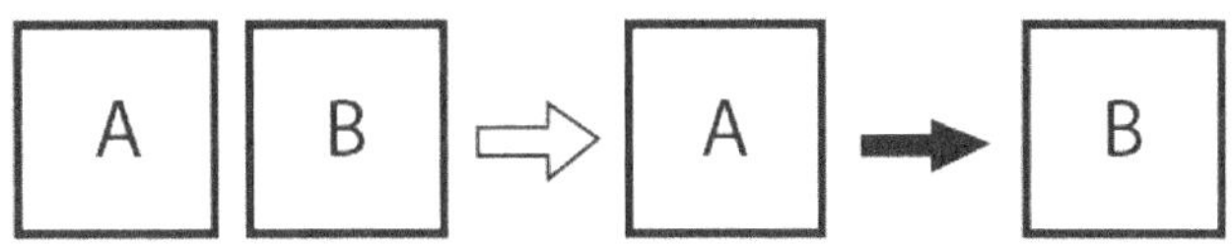

Figure 2: Relational Decomposition Process

4.1.3 Combining Substantive and Relational. Using Spradley's [30] set of semantic relationships listed earlier, we can better visualize how substantive and relational decompositions work together.

Substantive decomposition creates the "X" and "Y" of the semantic relationships. Relational decomposition creates the connection between the "X" and the "Y." For example, the semantic relationship "X is a cause/result of Y" relates two substantive parts or sub-parts of a problem using a cause-effect relationship. Each substantive part or sub-part could be understood separate from the specific relational situation, but given the current circumstance, they are related in the specified manner.

4.1.4 Resolving Functional Decomposition. In Engineering, Computer Science, Design, and other fields, we observe problems frequently broken down by their functions. We believe that functional decomposition is the result of substantive and relational processes. For example, in Computer Science, a program is often broken down into a series of objects related by the functions that they perform, and how that relates those objects to the other objects in the system. Functional decomposition is understood through this framework as a combination of a substantive and relational decomposition combined to form a decompositional semantic relationship. This includes two or more components or sub-components related by a functional relationship. An example of this is shown in Figure 3 ??, which depicts a class "Person", a class "Ball", and a relationship between them called "Kick." A function includes both substantive components and the relationship between them. This is similar to the identification of "propositions" in cognitive science, wherein memories are identified as nodes that are related to each other semantically (Anderson, 2005). Decomposing by function, then, is a parallel substantive and relational decomposition, which separates objects into their functional sub-groups and labels them with the appropriate functional relationships.

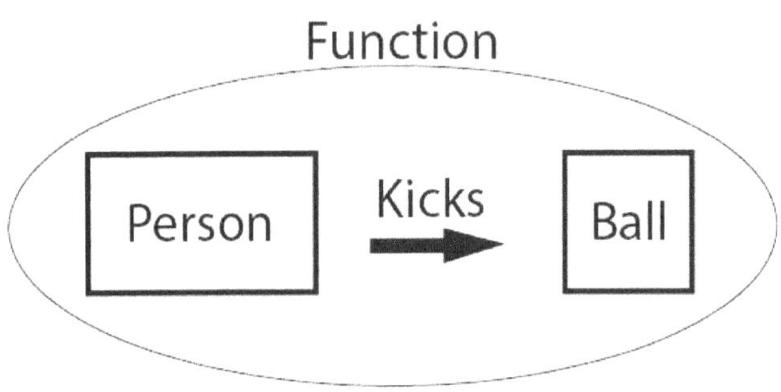

Figure 3: Functional Decomposition Process

With these two general categories of decomposition— substantive and relational—we can better understand the categorical process of decomposing a problem, and how that decompositional process helps to gain new meaningful information for solving the overall problem.

4.2 Decomposition as an Iterative Process

The act of decomposing a problem into its sub-parts appears to be an iterative process that involves a series of steps or events that contribute to the overall act of problem decomposition [29]. Similar to many design processes, such as the Engineering Design Process (EDP), instructional design processes such as the Successive Approximation Model (SAM), and others, this process includes multiple steps that can be repeated any number of times until sufficient information has been gathered to solve the problem. The generic steps we've identified are described below.

(1) *Identify an Axis*: One or more axes are identified as potential candidates to be used as part of the problem decomposition, based on their perceived potential value added toward solving the problem.
(2) *Proactively evaluate*: Each axis is evaluated for its potential to add new meaning or understanding to the problem prior to carrying at the decomposition.
(3) *Accept/Reject Axis*: Each axis is then either accepted or rejected, based on the previous evaluation. If rejected, a new axis is identified and evaluated. If accepted, the process continues.
(4) *Execute Decomposition*: The selected axis is used to categorize and label the parts and sub-parts of the problem.
(5) *Retroactively Evaluate*: The resulting decomposed version of the problem is evaluated for its ability to help solve the problem.

This decompositional process can be repeated as required in order to gain sufficient meaning and begin reconstructing the solution to the problem through patterns and algorithms. These events do not necessarily occur linearly, as various axes could be identified and decomposed in parallel to identify their related or differentiated value or meaning. This iterative approach to problem decomposition suggests that decomposition may occur at almost any point during CT. This contrasts with the belief that CT is a linear process, and that problem decomposition only occurs at one point of the process.

4.3 Decompositional Strategies

Problem decomposition is a tool that can be used as a part of a larger problem-solving strategy. We can learn many of the uses of problem decomposition as a part of CT by viewing problem decomposition through a lens of various problem-solving strategies. Below is a list of a few examples, for illustration.

- *Means-end decomposition*: Starting from the desired end solution and working backwards to break the problem into its component parts. In this approach, the last pieces decomposed become the first pieces developed.
- *Bottom-Up decomposition*: Using a specific sub-piece to identify the related axis. This most commonly occurs when a specific sub-part of the problem is known, but its relationship to the whole is unclear and relevant to resolving the whole problem.
- *Multivariate decomposition*: Using multiple axes to identify parts or sub-parts that exist in a cross-sectional category or to prove dissociation between specific parts or sub-parts.
- *Multi-level decomposition*: Decomposing the problem multiple times, categorizing sub-parts from a specific category into sub-categories.
- *Comparative decomposition*: Using multiple axes to identify similarities or differences in the clustering of parts or sub-parts based on the different axes. This can be a useful method for finding common threads in multiple arguments, definitions, etc.

5 DISCUSSION

To provide clarity for this decompositional framework, we now consider a few examples below to illustrate the practical application of this framework to computational problems.

5.1 Example 1: Coding a Queue

Our first example is of a computer science assignment to create a simple queue class.

A student might initially identify that there are component pieces required in a queue class, such as some form of data storage (array, variables, etc.) and functions to add and remove items from the queue. This is an example of substantive decomposition, identifying the parts needed in order to solve the problem.

The student might then identify that a queue adds items to the back of the line and retrieves them from the front of the line. This means that there is a sequence to the objects in the queue, as well as functional relations between the abstract queue class and the data storage object accessed by that class. This is an example of relational decomposition, identifying the ways in which the substantive parts of the problem interact and relate.

In order to organize their thoughts, the student might draw a concept map of the different objects involved in solving this problem, as well as the ways in which they relate.

A teacher could then view the students' design and assist the student to identify all of the necessary objects and relationships involved in the problem. The teacher may also assess the order in which objects/relationships were identified, grouped, and labeled, giving a more concrete way to measure successful decomposition.

5.2 Example 2: Predicting the Tides

Our second example is of an Earth Science assignment to predict the height of the ocean tides in a specific area using pre-generated data available online. A student might first identify the substantial variables that might be used to predict tide height, such as time of day, temperature, moon phase, etc. The student might then identify or test the ways these variables relate to tide height and to each other in order to identify patterns. Once the student has identified any noticeable patterns in the data, they might then mentally note the relationships between variables and remove variables that have no impact on tide height while focusing on variables that have the strongest impact. By performing this decomposition successfully, the student will be set up well to create an algorithm for accurately predicting the height of the tides. The algorithm, after all, is a series of relationships between variables that is used to predict an outcome.

Notice that some instances of decomposition occurs before pattern-finding or abstraction, while others occur after. Decomposition is also a potential part of the debugging process as well. This illustrates the iterative nature of CT, with decomposition occurring throughout the process, and not only initially in a linear fashion.

6 CONCLUSION

While there are a variety of existing measures of Computational Thinking, none of these adequately assess decomposition. By analyzing decompositional practices in a diversity of domains, we have more fully described what's inside the black box of decomposition. Namely, decomposition can be viewed of as a process of:

(1) categorizing potential elements
  (a) identifying substantive elements
  (b) identifying relationships between elements
(2) employing different strategies to execute a chosen decomposition (e.g., means-end, bottom-up, multivariate)
(3) iteratively evaluating the utility of a specific decomposition

This is a nascent framework and needs further exploration. Through highlighting these process can now ask questions about what types of categorizations or strategies do experts vs. novices utilize, or how can we more purposefully operationalize decomposition. In answering such questions, we hope to be able to formulate a more holistic measure of CT.

REFERENCES

[1] 2009. *Design science as nested problem solving.* ACM.
[2] 2012. *Evaluation of computer games developed by primary school children to gauge understanding of programming concepts.*
[3] 2012. *The fairy performance assessment: measuring computational thinking in middle school.* ACM.
[4] 2012. *New frameworks for studying and assessing the development of computational thinking.* Citeseer.
[5] 2013. *CS4Impact: measuring computational thinking concepts present in CS4HS participant lesson plans.* Vol. Proceeding of the 44th ACM technical symposium on Computer science education. ACM.
[6] 2015. *Automatic detection of bad programming habits in scratch: A preliminary study.* IEEE.
[7] 2017. *Assessing children's understanding of the work of computer scientists: the draw-a-computer-scientist test.* ACM.
[8] 2018. *Labeling Implicit Computational Thinking in Pizza Pass Gameplay.* ACM Press, New York, New York, USA.
[9] A Avolio. 1980. Multi-branched model of the human arterial system. *Medical & Biological Engineering & Computing* (1980), 709–718.
[10] P. J. Blanco, J. S. Leiva, R. A. Feijoo, and G. C. Buscaglia. 2010. Black-box decomposition approach for computational hemodynamics: One-dimensional models. *Computational Methods for Applied Mechanical Engineering* (2010), 1385–1405.
[11] CSTA. 2017. *K-12 Computer Science Standards, Revised 2017.* CSTeachers.org.
[12] J. Cuny, L. Snyder, and J. M. Wing. 2010. Demystifying computational thinking for non-computer scientists. *Unpublished manuscdript in progress* (2010).
[13] R. Davis and R. G. Smith. 1983. Negotiation as a metaphor for distributed problem solving. *Artificial Intelligence* 20, 1 (1983), 63–109.
[14] B. Du Boulay, T. O'Shea, and J. Monk. 1981. The black box inside the glass box: presenting computing concepts to novices. *International Journal of Man-Machine Studies* 14, 3 (1981), 237–249.
[15] D Fried, A. Legay, J. Ouaknine, and M. Y. Vardi. 2018. Sequential relational decomposition. *ACM/IEEE Symposium on Logic in Computer Science* (2018), 432–441.
[16] Shuchi Grover and Roy Pea. 2013. Computational Thinking in K–12: A Review of the State of the Field. *Educational Researcher* 42, 1 (2013), 38–43.
[17] M Heidegger. 1927. Neomarius Verlag. In *Sein und Zeit*, J. Macquarrie and E. Robinson (Eds.). Harper & Row, New York, 41–311.
[18] C. Ho. 2014. Some phenomena of problem decomposition strategy for design thinking. *Design Studies* 22, 1 (2014), 27–45.
[19] A. Leygue and E. Verron. 2010. A first step towards the use of proper general decomposition method for structural optimization. *Springer Link* 17, 4 (2010), 465–472.
[20] N. A. M. Maiden and A. G. Sutcliffe. 1996. A computational mechanism for parallel problem decomposition during requirements engineering. *IEEE* (1996), 159–163.
[21] C. A. Mattson and C. D. Sorenseon. 2017. *Fundamentals of Product Development.* Vol. 5th ed. Springer.
[22] Seymour Papert. 1980. *Mindstorms: Children, Computers, and Powerful Ideas.* Basic Books, Inc., New York, NY: USA.
[23] A Potesta. 2016. The fragility of the present and the task of thinking: Heidegger, thinker of the future. *Philosophy Today* 60, 4 (2016), 911–925.
[24] Noa Ragonis and Päivi Kinnunen (Eds.). 2015. *Concepts in K-9 Computer Science Education.* Vol. the 2015 ITiCSE. ACM Press, New York, New York, USA.
[25] Marcos Román-González, Juan-Carlos Pérez-González, and Carmen Jiménez-Fernández. 2017. Which cognitive abilities underlie computational thinking? Criterion validity of the Computational Thinking Test. *Computers in Human Behavior* 72 (2017), 678–691.
[26] Mark Sherman and Fred Martin. 2015. The assessment of mobile computational thinking. *Journal of Computing Sciences in Colleges* 30, 6 (2015), 53–59.
[27] Valerie J. Shute, Chen Sun, and Jodi Asbell-Clarke. 2017. Demystifying computational thinking. *Educational Research Review* (2017).
[28] Beth Simon, Alison Clear, and Quintin Cutts (Eds.). 2013. *Modeling the learning progressions of computational thinking of primary grade students.* Vol. the ninth annual international ACM conference. ACM Press, New York, New York, USA.
[29] James Spradley. 1979. *The ethnographic interview.* Harcourt Brace Jovanovich. College Publishers, Fort Worth, Texas: USA.
[30] James Spradley. 1980. *Participant observation.* Holt, Rinehart, and Winston, New York, NY: USA.
[31] A. Tarlecki, R. M. Burstall, and J. A. Goguen. 1991. Some fundamental algebraic tools for the semantics of computation: Part 3. Indexed Categories. *Theoretical Computer Science* (1991), 239–264.
[32] A. L. Thomasson. 2008. Existence questions. *Springer Science & Business Media* (2008), 63–78.
[33] Jeannette M Wing. 2006. Computational thinking. *Commun. ACM* 49, 3 (2006), 33–35.

Making Computer Science Education Mandatory: Exploring a Demographic Shift in Switzerland.

Alexander Repenning
School of Education
Northwestern Switzerland (PH FHNW)
Windisch, Switzerland
alexander.repenning@fhnw.ch

Anna Lamprou
School of Education
Northwestern Switzerland (PH FHNW)
Windisch, Switzerland
anna.lamprou@fhnw.ch

Serge Petralito
School of Education
Northwestern Switzerland (PH FHNW)
Windisch, Switzerland
serge.petralito@fhnw.ch

Ashok Basawapatna
SUNY Old Westbury
NY, USA
basawapatnaa@oldwestbury.edu

ABSTRACT

A promising approach to make K-12 Computer Science education more systemic could arise from a strategy focusing mostly on pre-service teachers educated through mandatory courses instead of self-selected in-service teachers. When employing mandatory courses, schools of education can reach all future teachers, but what are potential consequences resulting from this demographic shift? Pre-service teachers may not expect to acquire programming skills and may not be convinced of the relevance of Computer Science. In 2017, one of the first mandatory Computer Science education courses for pre-service K-12 teachers was introduced at the School of Education of northwestern Switzerland (PH FHNW). The mandatory nature of the course was possible because of the introduction of Computer Science as a subject in a new national curriculum. The course, based on Scalable Game Design, was taken by over 600, mostly female (75%), pre-service elementary school teachers. This paper explores the characteristics of this new audience and investigates the consequences of mandatory pre-service teacher Computer Science education. While our research shows that the course was successful, with regards to improving the students' skills, it reveals significant gender effects concerning attitudes towards Computer Science and self-efficacy.

CCS CONCEPTS

• Social and professional topics → Computational thinking • Social and professional topics → Computer science education • Social and professional topics → K-12 education • Social and professional topics → Gender

KEYWORDS

Computer Science Education, K-12, Pre-service teacher education, Self -efficacy, Gender issues in Computer Science Education, Mandatory Computer Science Education

ACM Reference format:

Alexander Repenning, Anna Lamprou, Serge Petralito and Ashok Basawapatna. 2019. Mandatory pre-service teacher Computer Science Education: Exploring a demographic shift in Switzerland. In *Proceedings of 24th ACM Innovation and Technology in computer Science Education, (ITiCSE'19). ACM, Aberdeen, Scotland, UK, 7 pages.* https://doi.org/10.1145/3304221.3319758

ACM ISBN 978-1-4503-6301-3/19/07...$15.00
https://doi.org/10.1145/3304221.3319758

1 INTRODUCTION

In an effort to mainstream Computer Science education (CSed) in Switzerland, pre-service elementary school teachers are being required to take CSed classes. Specifically, the Lehrplan 21 (LP21), the new common curriculum for compulsory education in the 21 German-speaking cantons, makes the introduction of CSed classes mandatory for students beginning in elementary school. In order to prepare pre-service teachers for a successful implementation of the LP21, the School of Education of northwestern Switzerland (PH FHNW), Switzerland's largest School of Education, started exploring the systemic impact on K–12 CSed through mandatory pre-service teacher education. This project engages all PH FHNW pre-service elementary school teachers in CSed, through two mandatory CSed courses. The first, which started in September of 2017, consisted of 600 students of which 75% identified as female, many with little to no prior Computer Science (CS) experience. These two courses are amongst the first of their kind and such a development has initiated the stage III of what can be characterized as the crossing of the CSed chasm [1], a notion anchored in the diffusion of innovation literature [2] and the main challenge preventing K–12 CSed to advance from teachers who are technology enthusiasts to pragmatists. It suggests it is difficult to move beyond early adopters of a new idea, such as K–12 CSed, to the early majority.

At the elementary school level, Stage III introduces two related shifts resulting in a new demography for K-12 CSed: a shift from self-selected/in-service (Stage II) to mandatory/pre-service interventions (Stage III) which suggests an audience with little or no prior knowledge and interest in the subject and a resulting shift from a male prevalent to a female prevalent pool of teachers (the majority of elementary school teachers is female[2]). To better understand these shifts, this paper poses the following research question: *What are the consequences of mandatory pre-service teacher CSed?*

We explored this question by analyzing the responses to pre and post questionnaires from the first students of the PH FHNW CSed course. The results paint a promising but also puzzling picture for K-12 CSed.

2 RELATED WORK

With CSed slowly finding a place into the K-12 curriculum, a lot of efforts has been put into providing professional development for in-service teachers [9]. Currently, K-12 CSed in most countries is undergoing stage II of the crossing of CSed chasm described in the previous section. Worldwide there are various initiatives and organizations providing professional development courses and support. For example, the Beauty and Joy of Computing (BJC), an introductory CS curriculum developed at the University of California, Berkeley and intended for non-majors, offers week long summer courses for teachers [42]. The Scalable Game Design (SGD) Summer Institutes in Colorado, brings together teachers with CS researchers to develop CT curricula [8, 43]. The Code.org a nonprofit, is dedicated to making CS accessible in schools and in increasing participation by women and underrepresented minorities. Finally, the Computer Science Teachers Association (CSTA) provides opportunities for K–12 teachers and their students to better understand and teach CS [10].

Even though there are many excellent examples of professional development initiatives, the crossing of the CSed Chasm requires finding a place for CS in pre-service teachers' educational curricula (stage III) [1]. Previous research focuses on pilot projects involving selected pre-service teachers' CS training [11, 12], and reports on early experiences providing limited empirical evidence [13], and to some extent literature about pre-service primary level teacher CSed [14]. Even though the need to educate pre-service teachers has been previously addressed in literature [15, 16], most research involving pre-service teachers and CS is focusing on questions about attitudes towards the use of computers [17]. The implementation of a national standard in Switzerland (LP21) is changing this. In anticipation of its implementation, two Schools of Education started to provide mandatory CS courses. In Schwyz, the PHSH started offering the first obligatory CSed course for its pre-service teachers [13], and in northwestern Switzerland, the PH FHNW started to offer two mandatory courses [14]. Since 2017 PH FHNW has already reached over 1000 pre-service elementary school teachers.

Switzerland's mandatory pre-service teacher CSed approach is an attempt to move from stage II to stage III and cross the CSed chasm [1]. However, mandatory pre-service teacher education reaches a different demographic. PH FHNW's first CSed course was taken by over 600, mostly female (75%) students, many with little to no prior CS experience, revealing a major and consequential shift in audience.

Research shows that women tend to have less programming experience than men [18-20]. One reason for that is that they show less interest in technology [21]. There exists a giant gender gap in CS in comparison to other professions with a very low representation of women [22- 24]. This underrepresentation is not due to lack of ability. Research has shown that women and men have equal abilities [25, 26] but women report lower self-efficacy in STEM and CS [27-32]. This research strongly suggests that mandatory K-12 pre-service CSed will have to address self-efficacy challenges resulting from this demographic shift to empower female teachers.

3 MANDATORY PRE-SERVICE TEACHER CSED - THE SCALABLE GAME DESIGN COURSE

The Scalable Game Design (SGD) courses are mandatory for all the students who study to become elementary school teachers at the PH FHNW and are taught in two consequent semesters. The first course is focused on establishing CS as a subject while the second, is focused on CS didactics. This paper is based on data collected from the first course. Most challenging for that course was the extraordinary heterogeneity regarding the background, knowledge and interests of pre-service teachers. It had to cope with a wide range of interests, ranging from intensive CS enthusiasm to complete CS apathy. Additionally, in contrast to other subject areas, the course could not assume that students had even basic CS knowledge from their previous education. Assuming that students had essentially no CS / programming background the course's goal was to establish CS as a subject area, teach students simple programming and provide them with an understanding of CT using materials addressing the LP 21 competences.

The course was built on a definition of CT heavily influenced by the needs of the primary school teachers and their future students. To that end, and for the purposes of this course, the CT definition used is a combination of mathematical -analytical thinking with natural sciences, engineering, and other disciplines. It is conceptualized as *thinking with the computer* (Denken mit dem Computer in German): joining human abilities with computer affordances. CT is regarded and employed as a way of thinking where the computer is used as an instrument that supports the human thought process [5]. Based on Wing's [33] definition, the CT process can be segmented into the three As stages: *Abstraction*: problem formulation, *Automation*:

[2] U.S. Bureau of Labor Statistics

representation of a solution and *Analysis*: execution and evaluation of the solution representation.

The course was developed based on a three-pillar approach:

1) Motivation and Learning Strategy: Scalable Game Design. The SGD pedagogy is based on the Zones of Proximal Flow theory and puts motivation at the center of the course [7, 34]. Using a project first approach, SGD offers both low threshold and high ceiling activities. The students' programming and CT skills scale up gradually [35], through a set of increasingly sophisticated game and simulation projects.

2) Tools designed specifically to teach and support CT at the elementary school level: Computational Thinking Tools. Because CT is different from programming [44], specific tools, Computational Thinking Tools, should be used to support CT learning [45]. CT Tools are educational environments that make the teaching of CT practical [3, 4]. CT Tools address cognitive challenges by acting as programming support tools that make programming more accessible [36]. They also address affective challenges by acting as creativity support tools [37] enabling students to create artifacts of personal relevance [6].

3) The 7 big ideas of Computer Science. The mapping of the SGD strategy onto the CS part of the LP 21 was straightforward. The three main LP 21 CS topics (data, algorithms, and systems) were identified as a subset of the 7 big ideas found in the AP Computer Science Principles (CSP) framework: creativity, abstraction, data, algorithms, programming, the Internet and global impact [38].

The SGD course is 14 weeks long, offering a two-hour session per week. Each week's session was divided into two parts: a theory part and an activity part. Each of the seven CSP ideas was mapped onto a two-week block in order to cover their different aspects and demonstrate their relevance to the professional function of primary school teachers. The theory part provided knowledge and competencies regarding one of the seven CSP ideas. For the activity part the students focused on creating their own projects using CT Tools. The students learned to program through a project first approach, supported by scaffolding methods and using mainly the CT Tool AgentCubes [37]. The students started to program immediately after being introduced to AgentCubes in their first session. Initially they created simple Frogger like games using step-by-step instructions, but as the course progressed they gradually moved on to program more advanced games and STEM simulations while experimenting without the use of instructions. Other tools, such as Scratch and Processing were also introduced. In the second half of the course the activity part became more prevalent and even more self-guided since the students were working on their own final projects. For the projects the students had to work in groups. Through this hands-on work, the students were able to learn how to write simple programs and to become computational thinkers. The instructors of the course had a combined background in CS and education.

4 METHODS

The study was conducted at the PH FHNW during the 2017 fall semester and participation (in the study) was anonymous and voluntary. The following sections describe in detail the methods used for the study.

4.1 Procedure

The first of the mandatory CSed courses comprised of 14 sessions. Survey data were collected from the participants during the first and last sessions. Both surveys were conducted on a computer in the classroom. The first electronic survey was completed by participants in the beginning of the first introductory lesson (N=541), which represents the baseline data of this study. The same participants completed a second electronic survey at the last session (after 14 weeks), representing the post-data (N=474). The second survey contained a number of questions that were the same as the first one, but also included a part with course evaluation questions.

4.2 Participants

The sample of this study comprises a total of 541 pre-service primary-school teachers. Participation in the SGD course was a mandatory part of their pre-service teacher education. The sample consisted of 379 female (74.02%) and 133 male (25.98%) participants. Roughly half (52.93%) of the participants were in their first semester. The majority of participants was between the ages of 18 and 23.

4.3 Measures

The baseline- and post-surveys consisted in part by identical items. The following measures were applied:

Demographics. Age, gender, and the students' semester, were assessed at the beginning of the survey.

Computer skills/experience. A first set of 4 5-point Likert-scale items (1=strongly disagree, 5=strongly agree) consisted of questions with regard to the participant's computer skills and experiences in video games and programming. E.g. *"I am good with computers."* and *"I can program."*

Attitude towards the notion of programming video games. Two items assessed whether participants would like to learn how to develop video games and whether they would like to learn programming.

Attitude towards Computer Science (CS). A subsequent set of 5-point Likert-scale items consisted of 5 items concerning the participants' attitude towards CS. This for example included items, assessing whether participants think that CS is hard or boring and whether participants like the notion of programming video games as a teaching tool for CS.

Self-efficacy indicator. Self-efficacy aspects were measured by asking five self-efficacy questions that best addressed our research focus taken from Bandura's self-efficacy scale [39, 40]. These items were rephrased to fit the context of self-efficacy concerning computers and the inclusion of computer techniques in teaching. E.g. *"If I come across technological challenges I tend to give up easily."*, *"The idea that in future schools will be more strongly influenced by technology makes me anxious."*

5 RESULTS

Descriptive statistics. Overall, our participants indicated on a Likert-Scale from 1 to 5 that they do not play video games (M = 1.87) or games on their phones/tablets (M = 2.27) often. They further indicated their computer skills to be average (M = 3.07) and that they do not know how to program (M = 1.3). The participants were however indifferent about whether they would like to learn programming (M = 2.23) or to develop a videogame (M = 3.23). Furthermore, the pre-service school-teachers thought that CS is rather difficult (M = 3.64), yet they did not find CS to be a boring subject (M = 2.31). The participants also rather liked the idea of developing a videogame for teaching CS (M = 3.46). Finally, CS is seen as a rather important factor of their job career (M = 3.78) and even more so for the future of their students (M = 4.24). As can be seen in Table 1, the five questions (Q: 12-16) that measured self-efficacy aspects were rated rather positive.

Gender differences. Table 1 depicts univariate descriptive statistics of single items, split by gender, and two-sided independent t-tests assessing gender differences for each item. Effect sizes were calculated using Cohen's d [41] for different sample sizes. A Benjamini-Hochberg adjustment to decrease the false discovery rate and assign significance was also performed [46]. Significant p-values and effect-sizes > .49 are in bold. Compared to male participants, female participants indicated that they play less video games and games on their phones/tablets. Female pre-service teachers further indicated to be less skilled with computers and programming as well as less interested in learning to program and in developing a videogame. Furthermore, female participants tend to think that CS is hard and boring and the idea of developing a video game to teach CS was less well received by female pre-service teachers. Self-efficacy was also rated worse among female participants. The tests yielded significant results for most of these differences between gender groups (grey rows in Table 1). However, female and male participants do not significantly differ concerning the notion that CS is important for their job or the future of their students (items 10 and 11 in Table 1). Also, self-efficacy items 15 and 16 (Table 1) do not significantly differ between male and female participants.

Differences between pre- and post-measurement. As we were not able to match the pre- and post-assessments, since the participation in the study was anonymous, one-sample t-test analysis was conducted in order to find out if the items were rated significantly different after the course. Our "sample" consisted of the post- data while as our baseline against which it was benchmarked we used the mean reported from the pre-data. Similar to the pre-data analysis, a Benjamini-Hochberg adjustment was performed to decrease the false discovery rate and assign significance [46]. The results are presented in Table 2. For female and male participants, self-reported ability for using computers and programming changed significantly for the better (see table 2 items 1 and 2). The notion that CS is hard (item 5, Table 2), was rated significantly lower by female participants in the post- assessment, as also did their attitude regarding learning programming. Furthermore, the notions regarding the importance of CS for their profession and their future students (items 8 and 9, Table 2) were rated significantly lower after the course for both genders. Finally, from the five self-efficacy questions (items 10-14, Table2) three, regarding basic computer skills, the idea that schools will increasingly be influenced by technology and fear that parents will think that the teachers'

Table 1: Initial self-assessment of skills, attitude and efficacy split by gender. Significant differences in grey.

Item	Female (M, SD)	Male (M, SD)	Effect size, p-value
1. I play video games on PC/console[3]	M = 1.5, SD = .99	M = 2.9, SD = 1.55	**d = 1.21, p < .00**
2. I play games on my phone/tablet[3]	M = 2.18, SD = 1.19	M = 2.53, SD = 1.33	d = .29, **p = .007**
3. I am good with computers[3]	M = 2.97, SD = .81	M = 3.32, SD = .89	d = .42, **p < .00**
4. I can program[3]	M = 1.25, SD = .61	M = 1.43, SD = .71	d = .28, **p = .008**
5. I would like to learn programming[4]	M = 3.12, SD = 1.17	M = 3.63, SD = 1.13	d = .44, **p < .00**
6. I think it would be cool to develop a video game[5]	M = 3.02, SD = 1.35	M = 3.82, SD = 1.17	**d = .61, p < .00**
7. I think CS is hard[4]	M = 3.72, SD = .98	M = 3.38, SD = .95	d = -.35, **p < .01**
8. I think CS is boring[4]	M = 2.34, SD = 1.00	M = 2.08, SD = .97	d = -.26, **p = .01**
9. I think developing video games is a great way to teach CS[5]	M = 3.35, SD = 1.06	M = 3.85, SD = .96	d = .48, **p < .00**
10. I think that CS is important for my profession as primary level teacher[4]	M = 3.78, SD = 1.02	M = 3.87, SD = 1.02	d = .09, p = .383
11. I think that CS is important for the future of my students[4]	M = 4.29, SD = .86	M = 4.32, SD = .86	d = .04, p = .281
12. If I come across a technological challenge, I tend to give up easily[6]	M = 2.88, SD = 1.09	M = 2.37, SD = 0.99	**d = -.49, p < .00**
13. I will probably never be good with technology[6]	M =2.64, SD = 1.06	M = 2.21, SD= 1.16	d =-.38, **p < .00**
14. I think my computer skills will never surpass basic knowledge[6]	M = 2.34, SD = 1.12	M = 2.03, SD = 0.98	d =-.29, **p = .003**
15. The idea that in future schools will be more strongly influenced by technology makes me anxious[6]	M = 1.99, SD = 1.05	M = 1.88, SD= 0.98	d =-.11, p= .279
16. I am afraid parents will think that my technological knowledge is not sufficient to teach their children[6]	M = 1.85, SD = 0.96	M = 1.78, SD = 0.99	d=-.07, p= .486

[3] Questions with regard to the participants' computer skills
[4] Questions with regard to participants' attitudes towards CS
[5] Questions with regard to participants' attitude towards programming video games
[6] Self-efficacy questions

skills are not good enough, yield significant negative results only for the female participants.

Table 2: Course impact split by gender. Green: significant positive; red: significant negative; orange: significant for only one gender

Item	Female participants			Male participants		
	Pre Mean	Post Mean	p-value, effect size	Pre Mean	Post Mean	p-value, effect size
1. I am good with computers[3]	2.97	3.44	**d = .59 p < .00**	3.32	3.88	**d = .67 p < .00**
2. I can program[3]	1.25	2.77	**d = 2.05 p < .00**	1.43	3.00	**d = 2.06 p < .00**
3. I would like to learn programming[4]	3.12	2.95	d = -.14 **p = .01**	3.63	3.45	d = -.18 p = .069
4. I think it would be cool to develop a video game[5]	3.02	2.91	d = -.09 p = .116	3.82	3.58	d = -.20 p = .035
5. I think CS is hard[4]	3.72	3.49	d = -.24 **p < .00**	3.38	3.30	d = -.08 p = .332
6. I think CS is boring[4]	2.34	2.24	d = -.11 p = .049	2.08	2.00	d = -.10 p = .282
7. I think developing video games is a great way to teach CS[5]	3.35	3.37	d = .02 p = .658	3.85	3.77	d = -.07 p = .37
8. I think that CS is important for my profession as primary level teacher[4]	3.78	3.23	**d = -.54 p < .00**	3.87	3.42	d = -.45 **p < .00**
9. I think that CS is important for the future of my students[4]	4.29	3.92	d = -.33 **p < .00**	4.32	4.03	d = -.31 **p = .003**
10. If I come across a technological challenge, I tend to give up easily[6]	2.88	2.91	d = .03 p=.522	2.37	2.35	d = -0.02 p=.846
11. I will probably never be good with technology[6]	2.64	2.62	d = -.02 p=.713	2.21	2.03	d = -.17 p=.034
12. I think my computer skills will never surpass basic knowledge[6]	2.34	2.51	d = .15 **p=.006**	2.03	2.03	d = - p=.965
13. The idea that in future schools will be more strongly influenced by technology makes me anxious[6]	1.99	2.28	d = .27 **p < .00**	1.88	1.87	d = -.01 p=.846
14. I am afraid parents will think that my technological knowledge is not sufficient to teach their children[6]	1.85	2.11	d = .26 **p < .00**	1.78	1.75	d = -.03 p=.752

6 DISCUSSION

The transition from self-selected/in-service to mandatory /pre-service CSed has resulted in a significant shift in demographics. The data gathered in Table 1 and 2 are discussed below to answer our research question:

What are the consequences of mandatory pre-service CS education?

Characteristics of mandatory/pre-service elementary school teachers, including skills, attitude toward game design, attitude towards CS and self-efficacy have been reported in Table 1. Twelve out of 16 measures, the gray ones, show significant gender differences. For all the questions, including the ones showing non-significant differences (questions 10, 11, 15 and 16) values are not only different but also consistently lower for females. In two cases, questions 1 and 6 the effect sizes of the difference were large. Both of these questions were related to videogames (question 1: playing them, question 6: creating them). Given the large effect sizes this suggest that a CS course based on game design aimed at a mandatory/pre-service teacher audience would have to very carefully justify the use of games and game design.

The pre-service teachers who took the course were mostly women who do not play video games, have average computer skills and no programming experience. Only a single person (N=541) strongly agreed with the statement 4 *"I can program."* Even though they were indifferent about learning programming or developing video games they indicated that they like the idea of developing video games for teaching purposes. In contrast to previous research [36], showing that there is a perception about CS being hard and boring, this particular audience did not think that CS is boring even though they found the subject rather difficult. Finally, our students displayed overall positive self-efficacy, however, as expected, and in accordance to previous research [27-32], the female students rated lower in the self-efficacy items than the male students. The female students initially self-assessed their skills, experience and interest lower than men and were also more reserved about the development of video games as teaching tools (Table 1). Despite the gender differences, both male and female responses can overall be characterized as rather positive regarding CS. The students also found CS very important for their professional future and the future of their students, something that might explain the surprising positive attitude towards the course. This unexpected result indicates that CS mandatory courses might not actually be met with resistance and skepticism.

The impact of the course has been explored through data represented in Table 2, presenting shifts in skills, attitude toward game design, attitude towards CS and self-efficacy by gender. Green rows indicate statistically significant changes and large effect sizes suggesting improvements. Red rows indicate statistically significant changes indicating regression. Orange rows indicate statistically significant changes for only one gender.

Computer skills/experience. *(questions 1-2).* The big effect sizes (d = 2.05 female, d = 2.06 male) calculated for question 2: *"I can program"* indicates that our students think that they have learned how to program. Effect sizes exceeding 0.8 are considered large [41]. An effect size larger than two suggests a massive shift in skills or at least the perception of that shift. Students perceptions were matched by other measures including a programming test and also by the programs turned in as part of their final game design project. The gender specific effect sizes were nearly identical suggesting that the positive shift in skills was equivalent. It should be noted, however, that the pre-values of *"I can program"* were significantly different and therefore the post values remained different. The large effect sizes of question 2 *"I am good with computers"* also indicate that students (males ever more than females) feel that their general computer skills have increased substantially.

Attitude towards the notion of programming video games (questions 4, 7). Question 7: "I think developing video games is a great way to teach Computer Science" did not result in significant pre/post changes. It was also gender polarizing. Females had a non-significant but positive shift, whereas males had non-significant but negative shift. The non-significant but negative drop, may be the result of realizing that programming video games can be quite labor intensive. The non-significant but positive shift for the female participants may be the result of females having a significantly lower agreement than males on the pre-values. Question 4: "I think it would be cool to develop a video game" yield a larger negative shift only for the male participants. The lack of a large positive shift may be connected to the course structure. In this first course the focus was mostly on the mechanisms of programming and game design largely ignoring pedagogical concerns such as concrete connections to the national curriculum. Establishing the connections between programming, game design and the national curriculum was part of the second course, i.e., the CS didactics course. This raises the question if a two-course structure, somewhat separating cognitive from affective concerns, consisting of an "introduction to CS" followed by a "CS didactics" is the right approach for a mandatory/in-service teacher audience.

Attitude towards Computer Science *(questions 3, 5, 6, 8, 9).* The course was able to positively impact the general perception that CS is hard and boring. Both genders lowered their values in question 5: *"I think CS is hard"* (significant drop for females) and question 6: *"I think CS is boring."* Even though both male and female students indicated that they find CS hard in the pre-questionnaire, the pre-post analysis indicated significant results only for the female participants. This means that even though the course made CS topics more accessible to all students, the effect was more prevalent for women. This is a very positive result given the fact that the majority of our students are women. However, participants were not interested in deepening their programming experiences according to question 3: *"I would like to learn programming"* (significant drop for females). Perhaps the most alarming negative and statistically significant shifts were captured by question 8: *"I think that CS is important for my profession as primary level teacher"* and question 9: *"I think that CS is important for the future of my students."* We speculate that this drop may be rooted in their initial misperception of what CS is. In a different survey many students expressed their belief, that a CS course would teach them how to use computers through applications such as Microsoft PowerPoint and Word. Realizing after the course that CS is not about application use skills but instead includes skills such as programming may have been responsible for lowering their agreement values for questions 8 and 9. Again this could be connected to the course structure which at this point in the "introduction to CS", does not take time to explain connections between programming activities and the national curriculum or explaining connections between CS and other subject areas such as STEM, languages and art. In other words, they expected computers to be useful in schools but do not fully appreciate the role of programming.

Self-efficacy *(questions 10-14)* Pre-post analysis of the self-efficacy questions has not shown a large shift. Instead, analysis revealed gender polarizing results. All but question 11 changed slightly for the worse for only the female students, while questions 12 to 14 yield significant negative results only for the female students. Even though our students scored quite high in self-efficacy and their self-efficacy remains overall positive after the course, our results indicate that the course did not strengthen our students' self-esteem. Actually, our female students appear to be slightly less confident to teach CS after taking the SGD course, while our male students appeared slightly more confident.

Overall, the course had a significant and large positive effect for both male and female participants, regarding their CS skills, which was also the main goal of the CS course. However, male participants still benefitted slightly more than female participants. It is possible that this slightly asymmetrical benefit can be overcome with the second course focusing on computer science didactics making it clearer how and why computer science including programming is relevant to teaching practice.

7 CONCLUSIONS

The CSed Chasm, can be crossed and become systemic by shifting the focus of teacher education from self-selected in-service teachers, to all pre-service teachers (mandatory). The resulting shift in demographics is likely to include a large percentage of technology skeptic teachers as well as a majority of women. At the School of Education FHNW in Switzerland, mandatory pre-service teacher education teaching CS through game design has begun at the elementary school level. This paper explored the consequences of mandatory pre-service CSed. Our research showed that all our students were able to learn to program. Additionally, the results indicated that the female students found CS less difficult after the end of the course. However, in terms of self-efficacy, female students appeared to be slightly less confident to teach CS after taking the SGD course. In light of such findings, future research should focus on developing CS courses that address efficacy issues especially in anticipation of the gender shift that mandatory pre-service teacher CSed brings about. Regardless of its large sample, our study has limitations. Our analysis depends solely on subjective data, while our inability to match pre-with post data did not allow a two-sided dependent t-test analysis, that would have been more appropriate. Future research could employ objective data such as student's grades to back up subjective data and use designs that support pre-post matching.

REFERENCES

[1] Repenning, A., *Scale or Fail: Moving beyond self-selected computer science education in Switzerland.* Communications of the ACM, 2018. **61**(5): p. 40-42.

[2] Rogers, E.M., *Diffusion of innovations (1st ed.).* 1962, New York: Free Press of Glencoe.

[3] Alexander, R., *Scalable Game Design: Broadening Participation by Integrating Game Design and Science Simulation Building into Middle School Curricula,* in *Future Directions in Computing Education, Summit Meeting.* 2014: Orlado, Florida.

[4] Repenning, A., *Transforming "Hard and Boring" into "Accessible and Exciting",* in *NordiCHI 2016, Workshop on Cultures of Participation in the Digital Age: From "Have to" to "Want to" Participate.* 2016: Gothenburg, Sweden.

[5] Papert, S., *An exploration in the space of mathematics educations.* International Journal of Computers for Mathematical Learning, 1996. **1**(1): p. 95-123.

[6] Repenning, A., *Moving Beyond Syntax: Lessons from 20 Years of Blocks Programing in AgentSheets.* Journal of Visual Languages and Sentient Systems, 2017. **3**(July): p. 68-89.

[7] Basawapatna, A., et al., *The Zones of Proximal Flow: Guiding Students Through A Space Of Computational Thinking Skills and Challenges,* in *International Computing Education Research (ICER 2013).* 2013, ACM Press.: San Diego, CA, USA.

[8] Bradshaw, P. and J. Woollard, *Computing at school: an emergent community of practice for a re-emergent subject.* 2012.

[9] Lamprou, A., A. Repenning, and N.A. Escherle, *The Solothurn Project – Bringing Computer Science Education to Primary Schools in Switzerland,* in *22nd Annual Conference on Innovation and Technology in Computer Science Education (ITiCSE 2017).* 2017: Bologna, Italy. p. 218-223.

[10] Association, C.T. 2005 [cited 2018 May 20 2018]; Available from: https://www.csteachers.org/.

[11] Huett, K.C. and M.A. Varga. *Building Pre-Service Teacher Interest in Computer Science Education through Mentoring Experiences.* in *Proceedings of the 47th ACM Technical Symposium on Computing Science Education.* 2016. ACM.

[12] Yadav, A., et al., *Computational thinking in elementary and secondary teacher education.* ACM Transactions on Computing Education (TOCE), 2014. **14**(1): p. 5.

[13] Döbeli Honegger, B. and M. Hielscher, *Vom Lehrplan zur LehrerInnenbildung-Erste Erfahrungen mit obligatorischer Informatikdidaktik für angehende Schweizer PrimarlehrerInnen.* Informatische Bildung zum Verstehen und Gestalten der digitalen Welt, 2017.

[14] Lamprou, A. and A. Repenning. *Teaching How to Teach Computational Thinking.* in *ITiCSE* 2018. Larnaca, Cyprus: ACM.

[15] Darling-Hammond, L. and J. Bransford, *Preparing teachers for a changing world: What teachers should learn and be able to do.* 2007: John Wiley & Sons.

[16] Yadav, A., C. Stephenson, and H. Hong, *Computational thinking for teacher education.* Commun. ACM, 2017. **60**(4): p. 55-62.

[17] Teo, T., *Pre-service teachers' attitudes towards computer use: A Singapore survey.* Australasian Journal of Educational Technology, 2008. **24**(4).

[18] Beyer, S. and S. Haller, *Gender differences and intragender differences in computer science students: Are female CS majors more similar to male CS majors or female nonmajors?* Journal of Women and Minorities in Science and Engineering, 2006. **12**(4).

[19] He, J. and L. Freeman, *Are men more technology-oriented than women? The role of gender on the development of general computer self-efficacy of college students.* AMCIS 2009 Proceedings, 2009: p. 672.

[20] Katz, S., et al., *Gender and race in predicting achievement in computer science.* IEEE Technology and Society Magazine, 2003. **22**(3): p. 20-27.

[21] Schmidt, F.L., *A theory of sex differences in technical aptitude and some supporting evidence.* Perspectives on psychological science, 2011. **6**(6): p. 560-573.

[22] Margolis, J. and A. Fisher, *Unlocking the clubhouse: Women in computing.* 2003: MIT press.

[23] Beyer, S., *Women and science, technology, engineering, and math (STEM).* 2015: Oxford University Press.

[24] Beyer, S., *Why are women underrepresented in Computer Science? Gender differences in stereotypes, self-efficacy, values, and interests and predictors of future CS course-taking and grades.* Computer Science Education, 2014. **24**(2-3): p. 153-192.

[25] Beyer, S., *The accuracy of academic gender stereotypes.* Sex Roles, 1999. **40**(9-10): p. 787-813.

[26] Beyer, S., *Predictors of Female and Male Computer Science Students' Grades.* Journal of Women and Minorities in Science and Engineering, 2008. **14**(4).

[27] Beyer, S., *Gender Differences and Intra-Gender Differences amongst Management Information Systems Students.* Journal of Information Systems Education, 2008. **19**(3).

[28] Durndell, A. and Z. Haag, *Computer self efficacy, computer anxiety, attitudes towards the Internet and reported experience with the Internet, by gender, in an East European sample.* Computers in human behavior, 2002. **18**(5): p. 521-535.

[29] Syzmanowicz, A. and A. Furnham, *Gender differences in self-estimates of general, mathematical, spatial and verbal intelligence: Four meta analyses.* Learning and Individual Differences, 2011. **21**(5): p. 493-504.

[30] Watt, H.M., *The role of motivation in gendered educational and occupational trajectories related to maths.* Educational Research and Evaluation, 2006. **12**(4): p. 305-322.

[31] Ziegler, A., M. Dresel, and B. Schober, *Prädiktoren des Selbstvertrauens von Mädchen und Jungen vor dem erstmaligen Chemieunterricht am Gymnasium.* Psychologie in Erziehung und Unterricht, 2000.

[32] Harrington, B., et al. *Gender, confidence, and mark prediction in CS examinations.* in *Proceedings of the 23rd Annual ACM Conference on Innovation and Technology in Computer Science Education.* 2018. ACM.

[33] Wing, J.M., *Computational Thinking.* Communications of the ACM, 2006. **49**(3): p. 33-35.

[34] Repenning, A., et al., *Scalable Game Design: A Strategy to Bring Systemic Computer Science Education to Schools through Game Design and Simulation Creation.* Transactions on Computing Education (TOCE), 2015. **15**(2): p. 1-31.

[35] Papert, S., *Instructionism versus Constructionism,* in *The Children's Machine.* 1993, BasicBooks. p. 137-156.

[36] *Women Who Choose Computer Science – What Really Matters, The Critical Role of Encouragement and Exposure.* 2014, Google: Google Report. p. 9.

[37] Repenning, A., et al., *AgentCubes: Enabling 3D Creativity by Addressing Cognitive and Affective Programming Challenges,* in *World Conference on Educational Media and Technology, EdMedia 2012.* 2012: Denver, Colorado, USA. p. 2762-2771.

[38] CollegeBoard. *AP Computer Science Principles.* 2017 [cited 2017 01.11.2017]; Available from: https://apstudent.collegeboard.org/apcourse/ap-computer-science-principles/course-details.

[39] Bandura, A., *Self-efficacy: Encyclopedia of Human behavior (Vol. 4, pp. 71-81).* 1994, New York: Academic Press.

[40] Bandura, A., *Guide for constructing self-efficacy scales.* Self-efficacy beliefs of adolescents, 2006. **5**(1): p. 307-337.

[41] Cohen, J., *Statistical power analysis for the behavioral sciences. 2nd.* 1988, Hillsdale, NJ: erlbaum.

[42] Berkeley, BJC. "The BJC Curriculum." accessed May 20 2018. https://bjc.berkeley.edu/curriculum/

[43] SGD. "Scalable Game Design Summer Institutes." accessed May 23 2018. https://sgd.cs.colorado.edu/wiki/Summer_Institutes.

[44] Duncan, C. and T. Bell, A Pilot Computer Science and Programming Course for Primary School Students, *in Proceedings of the Workshop in Primary and Secondary Computing Education.* 2015, ACM: London, United Kingdom. p. 39-48.

[45] Repenning, A., A. Basawapatna, and N. Escherle, Computational Thinking Tools, *in IEEE Symposium on Visual Languages and Human-Centric Computing.* 2016, IEEE Press: Cambridge, UK.

[46] Benjamini, Y. and Y. Hochberg, *Controlling the false discovery rate: a practical and powerful approach to multiple testing.* Journal of the royal statistical society. Series B (Methodological), 1995: p. 289-300.

Pedagogical Content for Professors of Introductory Programming Courses

Yorah Bosse*
University of Sao Paulo / Federal University of Mato Grosso do Sul
Sao Paulo / Ponta Pora, Brazil
yorah@ime.usp.br

David Redmiles
University of California
Irvine, USA
redmiles@ics.uci.edu

Marco A. Gerosa
Northern Arizona University / University of Sao Paulo
Flagstaff / Sao Paulo, USA / Brazil
marco.gerosa@nau.edu

ABSTRACT

Teaching introductory programming requires knowledge of both content and pedagogy. Pedagogy includes understanding the typical difficulties students face as they learn, as well as recognizing didactic strategies professors can use to help students to overcome these difficulties. Our research aims to improve the pedagogical knowledge instructors have to teach introductory programming courses, especially those new in this area. We conducted 16 semi-structured interviews with instructors who teach introductory programming courses and collected diaries filled by 110 students during their studies. Qualitative analysis of this data revealed a set of difficulties students faced when learning programming basics and a set of didactic strategies professors use to mitigate them. The results were reviewed by senior instructors in order to confirm them and by junior instructors to verify the importance of this material from their perspective. The main contribution of our paper is a set of difficulties faced by students learning programming, a classification of the most harmful challenges, and the didactic strategies usually used to teach and avoid them. Thus, we provide the basis for the pedagogical content necessary to junior and senior professors planning introductory programming courses.

KEYWORDS

pedagogical content; learning to program; novice learners; barriers to learning; introductory programming; strategies; computational thinking

ACM Reference Format:
Yorah Bosse, David Redmiles, and Marco A. Gerosa. 2019. Pedagogical Content for Professors of Introductory Programming Courses. In *Innovation and Technology in Computer Science Education (ITiCSE '19), July 15–17, 2019, Aberdeen, Scotland UK.* ACM, New York, NY, USA, 7 pages. https://doi.org/10.1145/3304221.3319776

*The first author is financially supported by the UFMS - Federal University of Mato Grosso do Sul.

ACM ISBN 978-1-4503-6301-3/19/07...$15.00
https://doi.org/10.1145/3304221.3319776

1 INTRODUCTION

Learners of programming around the world who are writing, running, and debugging code in introductory programming courses (CS1) inevitably run into frustrating hurdles [19], including understanding programming' basic concepts [2, 15, 16, 18, 23, 27, 31]. Though people learn to program in different ways, such as with graphical programming blocks, text, or both [17, 21, 31], and for different reasons [4], few consider it an easy task [1, 15, 18]. This can be perceived through failure and dropout rates, which reach about 28% among undergraduate students [3, 5].

Preparing new generations of professional and casual developers is a big challenge. If instructors are to overcome the difficulties students face, quell their frustrations, and help them achieve their goals, they need both knowledge of content and pedagogy [25, 29, 30]. Pedagogical knowledge includes three types of information: difficulties faced by students as they attempt to learn the content, typical paths students need to traverse to understand the content, and a set of strategies instructors can use in classes to avoid the difficulties [6].

Our research was developed to help instructors of CS1 prepare their classes and improve their teaching strategies so they can support students learning to program in C or Python. For that, we focus on two research questions:

RQ1 - What are the difficulties students face when learning how to program?

RQ2 - What didactic strategies do instructors use to overcome these difficulties?

Experienced teachers acquire knowledge of content and pedagogy and know the types of difficulties students have and how to circumvent them [6]. However, research has shown that expertise can lead to over-confidence in one's knowledge, meaning teachers can overlook details when teaching a topic they know well [13]. Even so, that knowledge can help other instructors in the task of how, for instance, to better organize the content for students [6]. Taking this into account, we collected qualitative data from two sources of data: semi-structured interviews with 16 professors from the University of Sao Paulo - USP - Brazil and diaries maintained by 110 students when taking CS1 at the same university. This data was analyzed using Grounded Theory techniques. The findings were reviewed by experienced instructors to confirm the results, in addition, it was collected the inexperienced instructors' perspectives about the importance of this material. The main contribution of this paper is a set of difficulties faced by students learning programming, a classification of the most harmful challenges, and the didactic strategies usually used to teach and avoid them. This material can guide instructors, especially inexperienced ones, to prepare their classes, helping them improve their teaching and students' learning.

2 RELATED WORK

We organize our literature review according to the difficulties students face, and then the methods and strategies instructors use to teach the content.

Difficulties: The content covered in programming courses can be difficult to understand, such as pointers and abstract data types [22, 24]. According to Mhashi and Alakeel [22], the most difficult programming concepts are repetition, recursion, lists, pointers, passing parameters, abstract data types, and the use of libraries. Some of these difficulties also appear in the research from Sevella and Lee [28]. They further show that students confuse 'For' and 'While' concepts in C and find it difficult to use functions, sometimes developing programs without ever using this feature. In addition, they point out difficulties with variables: students forget to declare them or assign wrong types. They also note difficulties with selection structures, such as writing conditional statements and nested selections. They found no difficulty with understanding lists. However, for the instructors responding to the questionnaire by Piteira and Costa [24], lists are among the most difficult topic, aside from pointers, structured data types, error handling, and parameters. Pointers and passing parameter by reference are also considered two of the most difficult topics by Lahtinen and colleagues [1]. Piteira and Costa [24] add that other difficulties for students include the use of language libraries and abstract data types. Regarding syntax, Hristova and colleagues [27] report the wrong use of '=' vs '==', '&&' vs '&', '||' vs '|', different amounts of opening and closing parentheses, brackets and quotation marks, wrong separators in 'For' loops, and so on.

Methods and strategies used to teach basic programming content: Traditional teaching methods can be inadequate for many students: teaching is not personalized, and dynamic concepts are presented with static material [14]. In contrast, Deek and colleagues [20] have developed an approach to programming courses that helps students learn concepts and their uses. In this approach, language characteristics were gradually introduced to students only in the context of specific problems. This has been shown to have positive effects on student achievement and confidence in programming. There are also programming tools that allow students to overcome the barriers to learning to program themselves [7, 17, 21], and to give automatic feedback to students about their codes [11, 12], not only feedback on syntax questions, but also on program semantic issues [26]. Another approach for increasing students' knowledge and developing their abilities is to increase the number of exercises, carefully selecting and solving them afterwards [22]. While visualization techniques to show complex concepts can help, visualizations are most often used for algorithm animation, with less emphasis on illustrating the basic structure of programs and their execution [22].

While the literature tends to focus on the content students consider difficult, we seek to identify a set of difficulties students face in CS1 in order to organize a set of strategies that instructors may use to avoid them and improve learning.

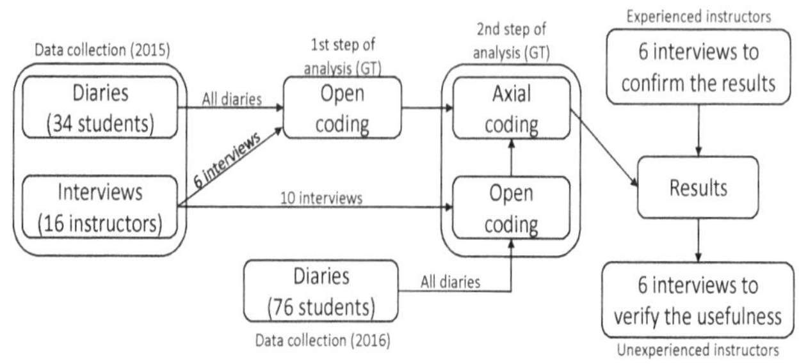

Figure 1: Scheme of the methodology.

Table 1: Instructors' data.

Professor ID	Years of Experience	Gender
P1 - P3	More than 40 years	1 F and 2 M
P4 - P5	31 to 40 years	2 M
P6 - P7	21 to 30 years	2 M
P8 - P12	11 to 20 years	2 F and 3 M
P13 - P16	1 to 10 years	4 M

3 METHODOLOGY

We conducted semi-structured interviews with 16 instructors and asked students to maintain diaries. Figure 1 shows an overview of our methodology, which is detailed below.

3.1 Data Collection

This study is motivated by a previous study conducted at the University of Sao Paulo (Brazil) from 2010 to 2014, based on data from approximately 18,500 students from various majors who enrolled in 29 CS1 courses [5]. The results showed that approximately 30% of these registrations resulted in failures and dropouts, which corroborates results obtained by Bennedsen and Caspersen [3].

In the present study, we chose to further investigate these courses and topic-related issues. We conducted interviews with instructors to delve into particulars, focusing on the topics to gain a perspective of the students' learning experiences and instructors' teaching experiences [10]. Sixteen instructors from the Computer Science Department at the University of Sao Paulo were selected for interviews. About 30 instructors from the department had taught this course at least once. The first 6 instructors interviewed were those who were teaching introductory programming for the six classes whose students were keeping diaries about the difficulties in learning how to program. The other 10 were randomly selected. Each instructor was identified with an ID comprising a P, followed by a number from 1 to 16. Table 1 shows the level of experience and gender of the subjects.

The interviews began with a very general question: 'In your view, what are the difficulties faced by students in CS1?' The instructor was then guided to talk about the following introductory topics: variables; assignment command; input and output functions; arithmetic, relational (<, >, =, ...) and logical (and, or not) expressions; selection (if...else) and repetition structures (while, for, ...); string manipulation; uni- and multi-dimensional arrays; structured data;

Table 2: Students' data.

Age	Total	%
Not informed	1	1%
15 - 24	84	76%
25 - 34	17	15%
35 - 44	6	5%
45 - 54	1	1%
55 - 64	1	1%

TACB	Total	%
0	81	74%
1	17	15%
2	6	5%
3	4	4%
4	1	1%
5	1	1%

functions; and pointers. Most of the interviews took about half an hour, but some lasted for up to an hour.

We arranged for students to fill out diaries during their studies, keeping us informed about their difficulties as they emerged. We collected data from 6 different classes in 2015 (34 students) and another 6 in 2016 (76 students), yielding a total of 110 student diaries. The diaries were arranged in shared documents (Google Docs). We asked the students to include: code snippets, especially the wrong ones; how they fixed the errors; and the doubts they had about learning the topics. To clarify possible misunderstandings about the text written by the students, the researchers sometimes posed questions in the diaries. Each student was also identified with an ID, composed by an S, followed by a number from 1 to 110. Table 2 shows the total and percentage of students by age range and the number of times they attended the course before (TACB).

3.2 Data Analysis

For the analysis of the data, we used Grounded Theory (GT) techniques, as described by Strauss and Corbin [9]. During the analysis, concepts, categories, and subcategories emerged. According to Corbin and Strauss [8], "the procedures of grounded theory are designed to develop a well-integrated set of concepts that provide a thorough theoretical explanation of social phenomena under study." The groupings of these concepts into a higher degree of abstraction are called "categories" [9].

The data was read and analyzed, and relevant information was marked with a tag, thus characterizing a concept. Grouping these concepts, categories emerged. We primarily focused on two of them: 'Difficulties with the Topics' and 'Didactic Strategies.' After that, all text highlighted with codes was read again to identify difficulties, strategies, and connections among both. To confirm the results obtained with the data analysis, the results were presented to six experienced instructors to validate the findings. Then, six other instructors were interviewed, all inexperienced with the teaching of programming, in order to verify their opinions about the importance of the results for preparing their classes.

4 FINDINGS AND DISCUSSION

In this section, we present the results obtained in two categories defined in the data analysis, Difficulties and Strategies, answering the two research questions that guided our study.

RQ1 - What are the difficulties students face when learning how to program?

The difficulties presented below are divided by topics addressed in the courses, which are listed in the methodology section. Figure 2 presents the set of difficulties reported by instructors and students, which we classified in three levels. The first level comprises difficulties considered the most impactful to learning programming, which are marked with two stars. The intermediate level is marked with a star, and the last level has no marking. After each difficulty appears the number X of times they are cited by instructors 'p' and the number Y of times cited by students 's': XpYs. The 16 interviewed instructors commented mainly on C and Python; most of the difficulties listed in the diagram are related to the C language.

We found difficulties related to 10 topics taught in CS1, namely: Variables, Expressions, Input/Output Functions, Selection and Repetition Structures, Uni- and Multidimensional Array, Function, Pointer, and String. One of the difficulties of the first level of classification is **initializing the variables**, as shown in the topic Variable of the diagram. Many students do not know if it is necessary to initialize and with what value: "*When compiling everything was fine, however, the final result (max) has a gigantic number ... problem tidy, I had not put the initial value of the variable max...*" - S18. In addition, the **difference in the treatment of variables in mathematics and programming** can generate doubt, as explained by P8: "*Then there are 'x = x + 1' and these students experiencing difficulty do not understand if you read as in math, 'x is equal to x + 1,' (student replies) that 'it is impossible for x to be equal to x + 1'.*"

Working with Expressions, the result shows difficulties related to **detecting the wrong result due to data type problems**: "*... when it is a numerical operation, it is difficult for them to perceive the error. So, for example, an algorithm to calculate, make an average, ... yields zero (as a result) and sometimes the student realizes that they used integer rather than float*" - P7. Another source of difficulty is **writing logical expressions**. According to P11, "*...something that exists in natural language and that normally does not exist in programming language is something like 'x > 3 and < 5' and in computing I cannot write like this, you have to write 'x > 3 and x < 5', then they write it wrong, they write 'x > 3 and < 5'.*" The students find it difficult to write logical expressions in the syntax of the programming language, which is usually different from that used in mathematics and natural language. And, as already cited by Hristova and colleagues [27], there is **confusion between '=' and '=='**. According to S34, this is a constant error: "*I wrote the program and noticed some difficulties I constantly face such as ... whether to use = or == within the Selections or Repetition Structures.*"

Regarding Selection Structures, the most complicated task is working with **nested selections** with a set of pairs 'IF..ELSE': "*When I had nesting, one selection within another, that caused a lot of confusion*" - P15. Similarly, the most complicated Repetition Structure to learn is the creation and use of **nested repetition** structures, that is, two or more structures of repetition, with one inside the other. A classic example of using nested repetitions is the manipulation of multidimensional arrays. Other difficulties include the creation of the **stopping condition** and manipulating the **control variable**. According to P15, students begin to use the control variable without even initializing it, "*... they use a variable in the stop condition before assigning an initial value to this variable,*" and then they misuse the increment or decrement operators so that it satisfies the desired stop condition: "*... their challenge to generate a repetition structure was to understand the concept of a stop condition,*

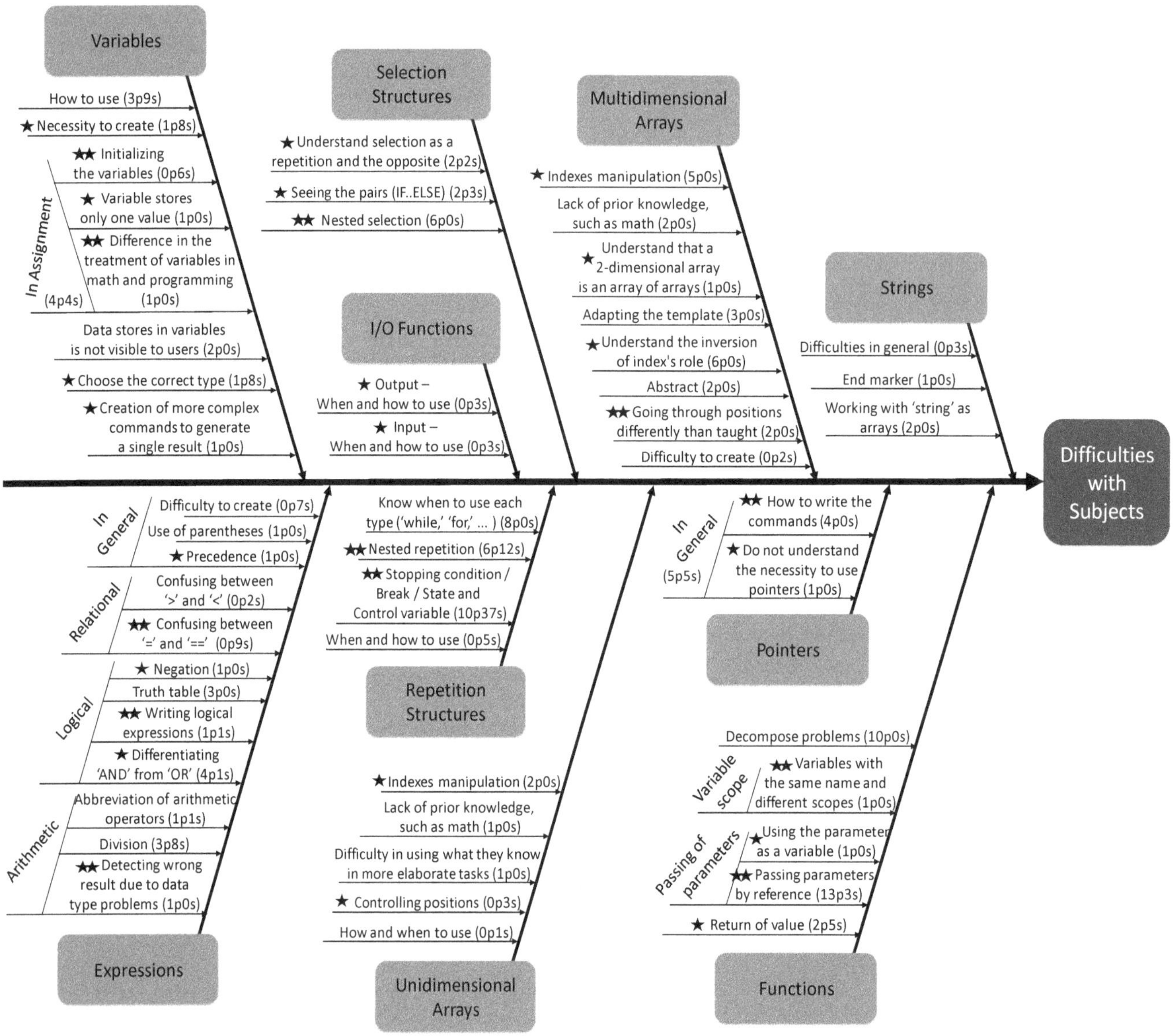

Figure 2: Diagram showing the list of difficulties per topics taught in introductory programming courses.

how to create a stop condition, and how to make an increment of a variable that satisfies this condition." Manipulating variables is also a task necessary for working with Multidimensional Arrays, where **going through positions differently than taught** is a source of difficulty, as exemplified by P14: "*... if we use a 2-dimensional array, for example, to represent a game board and ask to move diagonally, or backward, ... then things start to get confusing. Especially if the 'i' and 'j' (variables used to indicate the position in the row and column) that are there, begin to appear in a switched order.*"

Finally, for P4, when teaching Pointers, "*the trouble starts to get bigger.*" Pointers are cited by many researchers as one of the most difficult topics [22, 24, 28], and the results of this study confirmed this, as can be observed in the comment made by P14: "*But of the content of the course, I think the most difficult thing was for them to understand pointers.*" P13 reports that the students "*end up learning by heart,*" and adds "*I think they can understand, closer to the end of the second semester,*" that is, only in the subsequent course. Many even avoid teaching pointers: "*We try to avoid talking about pointers too*" - P10. Others end up showing them only because they are necessary to pass parameters by reference, and the main difficulty is **how to write the commands** using pointers. Working with Functions, besides the difficulty with **passing parameters by reference**, students confuse **variables with the same name and different scopes**.

RQ2 - What didactic strategies do instructors use to overcome these difficulties?

During the interviews, instructors mentioned many strategies they used to teach the topics and to mitigate difficulties students

Strat ID	Times cited	Strategy Name	Main difficulties that it helps
S1	16	Using visual resources	Variables. Nested repetition. Function. Uni and multidimensional array. General
S2	10	Using 'pseudocode and programming language' as a cycle for each new concept	General
S3	9	Solving together with students in class	General
S4	8	Explain using problems and similar exercises	General
S5	8	Omit some concepts and language details	Pointer - how to write the commands. Function - passing parameters by reference. Programming language - syntax issues. General
S6	8	Using "recipes"	Programming language - syntax issues. Multidimensional array - indexes manipulation and going through positions differently than taught. Pointer - do not understand the necessity to use pointers. Function – return of value. General
S7	7	Step-by-step execution	Function – variable scope. Repetition structure - stopping condition and manipulation of the control variable. General
S8	6	Making an analogy with known concepts / objects	Variables. Expressions. Function. Selection structure. General
S9	6	Intensive practice	General
S10	5	Programming on the projector screen	General

Table 3: Strategy used to avoid or minimize the difficulties faced by students to learn how to program.

face. In this paper, we present the strategies mentioned 5 times or more in the interviews. The third column of Table 3 reports the topics or difficulties linked to the strategies. If the term General is used in this column, this means that this strategy was quoted at least once in each of the topics covered.

Using visual resources (S1). Abstraction is one of the major problems of the course. It is difficult for the novice student to visualize where the data is, how it is processed, or how the commands work: "*...there is a difficulty in working with abstract concepts...*" - P9 and P15 remembered "*...classes that at first did not work, you had to have something visual too*" and cited an example "*Variable declaration needs to be visual ... explaining that declaring a variable will occupy space in memory, this abstraction is a bit difficult.*" The 'visuals'can be drawings: "*...I draw the memory...*" - P9 or made using features like arrows that represent the input and output of the data in a function, for example: "*I always do in a graphic way the inputs and outputs, with arrows*" - P8. Another form of visual presentation is "*...animations, if I needed to show that visually...*" - P15 and adds that "*...there are many visual resources on the internet....*"

Using 'pseudocode and programming language' as a cycle for each new concept (S2). Few instructors begin the course with pseudocode before progressing to a programming language, "*With the algorithm in pseudo-language, I did not see much success ... having two simultaneous languages was not going to be as effective*" - P16. Most of the interviewed instructors use pseudocode only to teach the concept and then immediately show the same concept in the programming language: "*... I give the algorithmic concept and after this, I go to the program ... I do it like this, coming and going*" - P9. According to P11, "*The programming language is a tool to teach algorithms and data structures*" and the pseudocode or pseudo language is quickly used, without many rules, only to explain the concepts.

Solving together with students in class (S3). This is another highly used strategy: to "*solve and write problems together with the students ... the idea is to let them participate and they try to develop the program together. Often times, I show the program even knowing that it is wrong and we try to find (the mistake)*" - P3. Many instructors reported using this strategy and claim it works because students participate and can see step-by-step how the program is developed.

Explain using problems and similar exercises (S4). To introduce and show the usefulness of the concepts that need to be taught in the course, one strategy is to use problems: "*I usually start explaining a content by describing a problem*" - P16. For P10, it is a way to motivate students, "*...we try to motivate by using some problems,*" because the student sees the concept's usefulness in practice and learns how it should be used. Between presenting the first problem to the student and more complex exercises, P16 advises "*...also bring to class exercises that are similar but do not solve exactly that problem.*" In this way, the student can practice what was taught, and then use it in other situations.

Omit some concepts and language details (S5). Details of the coding language can hinder the development of the code. If the instructor omits some details, they may improve initial learning: "*The idea was to abstract the language syntax somewhat*" - P15. P5 also said "*...if I have to teach in C, I do not explain an input command. I even joke: 'Look, God told you to do it like this.'*," because if you explain every detail of the syntax, the content does progress. Concepts are also omitted at times when they are not indispensable. An example of this was offered by P1, with the following statement: "*Passing parameter is also all by pointer, I do not need to speak of pointers, they do the exercise without problems ... they are hidden from them, these concepts, but they are in fact using (them).*"

Using "recipes" (S6). In content that is considered more complicated, as is the case of passing parameters by reference using pointers,: "*When we teach with C we make the passage by reference, but we provide a 'recipe', so it is (I use) '&' when I call the function and within the function '*'.*" - P12. In addition, to avoid language syntax explanations often unnecessary for the moment, such as 'scanf' and 'printf' in the C programming language, instructors use a kind of 'recipe;' that is, a step-by-step instruction of how something should be done.

Step-by-step execution (S7). Another frequently used technique is step-by-step execution, so that the student sees what is happening in the program, which also helps them find existing errors in the code. This execution is done on the board or even using the projector. Everything that happens, from change of values in the variables to the output of a repetition or change of variable scope, is line-by-line shown and analyzed during this exercise: "*I used slides that were showing repetition actually happening as a debugging of the program and going through each instruction line*" - P15. However, for more advanced students, this exercise can be a bit tedious.

Making an analogy with known concepts / objects (S8). This involves using an everyday example from the real world, with situations familiar to the student, as P3 suggested: "*make an association with a real-world problem where you have the same type* *of separation (situation). I think this makes sense, so it helps a lot."* In reference to arithmetic, logical, and relational expressions, P1 said that *"they (the students) confuse a lot... I started with day to day examples"* and P11 reinforces that *"I think this is a fundamental thing, exercises that have to do with the universe of the student."*

Intensive practice (S9). Five instructors cited intensive practice during the interviews, corroborating results presented by Mhashi and Alakeel [22]. According to P13, *"The student has to arrive, sit, study, work, exercise and solve as many exercises as possible. It is very Kumon style. It is training, training, training."* Feedback is also important, as P11 said *"I give a lot of exercises for them to do in the classroom, from there they do on paper..., if we have three solutions (made by students in the classroom), I ask the 3 students to go (to write on the board) and I show the three different solutions. Then we discuss the 3 solutions."*

Programming on the projector screen (S10). Lastly, this strategy includes developing the code during class, projecting it so that the student can see and participate, and collaboratively making changes and showing the results: *"I use blackboard and projector ... writing a program in the act and running it"* - P15 and P14 said that this *"...makes a significant difference."*

In addition, future confirmatory research could yield data beyond instructors' experiences, exploring the degree of student development in the CS1 courses that use those strategies. Linking the findings to existing pedagogical theories could be of great value to add knowledge and increase the contribution of these results.

5 VALIDATION OF THE RESULTS

After compiling the results, they were validated by 6 experienced instructors. Each of them was asked about the difficulties listed by topic and didactic strategies mentioned. During these interviews, one new idea arose: a suggestion to classify the difficulties as explained in the Findings section. Having confirmed our findings, six inexperienced instructors (Pu) were interviewed. These instructors had taught less than three CS1 courses and work in universities of different states in Brazil. We asked them to comment on the importance of this information about difficulties and strategies. The difficulties were showed to them without the classification presented in this paper. Even unaware of this suggestion given by experienced instructors, two of them commented on the importance of classification, as indicated in a comment made by Pu4: *"...the list of difficulties could help me to organize my classes, but I think that if the difficulties had a classification, showing which of them are the most harmful for students learning programming, it could be easier to use in practice..."*

All of the six inexperienced interviewed instructors said that the list of difficulties and strategies could greatly help to plan the material used with students and in explaining the topics, as commented by Pu6: *"...knowing the difficulties, I would work out the topic in the classroom so that the difficulty arise and so I would help them solve the doubts..."* Three of them commented that most of the difficulties could be minimized or eliminated depending on the programming language used, citing Python as an example. They added that the difficulties exist not only for C language, but also for many others, like Java. One important point they addressed regarded the topics and/or difficulties linked to the strategies. Even though most strategies are known , this connection could help to determine the best strategy at certain times in class.

5.1 Threats to Validity

The data was collected from experienced instructors from the same department who teach in different colleges at a single university. This factor may raise some doubts as to the accuracy of the results in other contexts. A survey could be created to confirm the results obtained and to complete the set of difficulties and didactic strategies.

6 CONCLUSION

Learning to program is not an easy task [1]. Students who study programming face many difficulties, as do their instructors. Some difficulties related to content are generally mild; they can be quickly clarified with examples of application and practical exercises, as is the case in understanding variables. Other difficulties are more complicated, requiring instructors to use several resources to improve learning and not always successfully. One such case is the topic Pointer. Many instructors shared their desire to avoid this topic in CS1, because they consider it too difficult. However, it is necessary for teaching other content, such as pass parameters by reference in C, in the topic Function. Pointer concepts are often omitted (S4) and/or used in the form of 'recipes' (S8), so there is no need to delve deeper into them in CS1. In addition, functions, uni- and multi-dimensional arrays, and repetition structures (while, for, ...) are considered the three most difficult topics in the instructors' view.

To teach CS1, inexperienced instructors consider it useful to have the list of difficulties students face and the strategies they can use to teach the content and avoid them. According to them, having knowledge of the difficulties could change the way they teach; for example, they can choose exercises that make the difficulties arise during the class, so that they can support students in solving them. About the strategies, we received good feedback from inexperienced instructors as well. Although many of them were already aware of many of the strategies on the list, they considered it important to have the list, in part because some of the strategies were linked to the difficulties that could be avoided, and also because the list tends to make them remember each one, making it easier to integrate them into a class. The contribution of our paper may improve pedagogical knowledge to better teach and consequently better learn programming.

ACKNOWLEDGMENTS

We thank the instructors and students who kindly provided us with the data that made this study possible. We also thanks to CAPES, this study was financed in part by the "Coordenacao de Aperfeicoamento de Pessoal de Nivel Superior " - Brazil (CAPES) - Finance Code 001.

REFERENCES

[1] Essi Lahtinen; Kirsti Ala-Mutka and Hannu-Matti Jarvinen. 2005. A study of the difficulties of novice programmers. *ACM SIGCSE Bulletin* 37, 3 (Sept 2005), 14. https://doi.org/10.1145/1067445.1067453

[2] Kirsti M. Ala-Mutka. 2004. Problems in learning and teaching programming-a literature study for developing visualizations in the Codewitz-Minerva project. *Codewitz Needs Analysis* (2004), 1-13.
[3] Jens Bennedsen and Michael E. Caspersen. 2007. Failure rates in Introductory Programming. *ACM SIGCSE Bulletin* 39, 2 (Jun 2007), 32-36. https://doi.org/10.1145/1272848.1272879
[4] Ilias Bergstrom and Alan F Blackwell. 2016. The practices of programming. *2016 IEEE Symposium on Visual Languages and Human-Centric Computing (VL/HCC)* (2016), 190-198. https://doi.org/10.1109/VLHCC.2016.7739684
[5] Yorah Bosse and Marco Aurelio Gerosa. 2016. Why is programming so difficult to learn? Patterns of Difficulties Related to Programming Learning. *ACM SIGSOFT Software Engineering Notes* 41, 6 (2016), 1-6. https://doi.org/10.1145/3011286.3011301
[6] John D. Bransford; Ann L. Brown and Rodney R. Cocking. 2000. How People Learn: Brain, Mind, Experience, and School. Expanded Edition. *National Academy Press* (2000), 384. https://doi.org/10.17226/9853
[7] Jill Cao; Irwin Kwan; Rachel White; Scott D. Fleming; Margaret M. Burnett and Christopher Scaffidi. 2012. From barriers to learning in the idea garden: An empirical study. *IEEE Symposium on Visual Languages and Human* (2012), 59-66. https://doi.org/10.1109/VLHCC.2012.6344483
[8] Juliet Corbin and Anselm Strauss. 1990. Grounded theory research: Procedures, canons, and evaluative criteria. *Qualitative Sociology* 13, 1 (1990), 3-21. https://doi.org/10.1007/BF00988593
[9] Juliet Corbin and Anselm Strauss. 2015. *Basics of Qualitative Research: Techniques and Procedures for Developing Grounded Theory* (4rd ed.). SAGE Publications, Inc. 456 pages. https://us.sagepub.com/en-us/nam/basics-of-qualitative-research/book235578
[10] John W. Creswell. 2014. *Research design: Qualitative, quantitative, and mixed methods approaches* (4rd ed.). SAGE Publications, Inc. 304 pages.
[11] Juan C. Rodriguez del Pino; Enrique Rubio-Royo and Zenon J. Hernandez-Figueroa. 2012. A Virtual Programming Lab for Moodle with automatic assessment and anti-plagiarism features. *Conf. e-Learning, e-Business, Entrep. Inf. Syst. e-Government* (2012).
[12] Michelle Ichinco; Yoanna Dosouto and Caitlin Kelleher. 2014. A tool for authoring programs that automatically distribute feedback to novice programmers. *IEEE Symposium on Visual Languages and Human-Centric Computing (VL/HCC)* (2014), 207-208. https://doi.org/10.1109/VLHCC.2014.6883058
[13] Matthew Fisher and Frank C. Keil. 2015. The Curse of Expertise: When More Knowledge Leads to Miscalibrated Explanatory Insight. *Cognitive Science: A Multidisciplinary Journal* 40, 5 (Sep 2015), 1251-1269. https://doi.org/10.1111/cogs.12280
[14] Anabela Gomes and Antonio Mendes. 2007. Learning to program - difficulties and solutions. *International Conference on Engineering Education - ICEE 2007* (2007). http://icee2007.dei.uc.pt/proceedings/papers/411.pdf
[15] Anabela Gomes and Antonio Mendes. 2015. A teacher's view about introductory programming teaching and learning: Difficulties, strategies and motivations. *2014 IEEE Frontiers in Education Conference (FIE) Proceedings* (Feb 2015), 1-8. https://doi.org/10.1109/FIE.2014.7044086
[16] Sandy Garner; Patricia Haden and Anthony Robins. 2005. My program is correct but it doesn't run: A preliminary investigation of novice programmers' problems. *ACE '05 Proceedings of the 7th Australasian conference on Computing education* 42 (2005), 173-180.
vfill
[17] Michelle Ichinco and Caitlin Kelleher. 2017. Towards Block Code Examples that Help Young Novices Notice Critical Elements. *2017 IEEE Symposium on Visual Languages and Human-Centric Computing (VL/HCC)* (2017), 335-336. https://doi.org/10.1109/VLHCC.2017.8103497
[18] Tony Jenkins. 2002. On the Difficulty of Learning to Program. *Language* 4 (2002), 53-58. https://doi.org/10.1109/ISIT.2013.6620675
[19] Ian Drosos; Philip J.Guo and Chris Parnin. 2017. HappyFace: Identifying and predicting frustrating obstacles for learning programming at scale. *Proceedings of IEEE Symposium on Visual Languages and Human-Centric Computing, VL/HCC* (2017), 171-179. https://doi.org/10.1109/VLHCC.2017.8103465
[20] Fadi P. Deek; Howard Kimmel and James A. McHugh. 1998. Pedagogical Changes in the Delivery of the First-Course in Computer Science: Problem Solving, Then Programming. *Journal of Engineering Education* 87, 3 (July 1998), 313-320. https://doi.org/10.1002/j.2168-9830.1998.tb00359.x
[21] Michael J. Lee. 2014. Gidget: An online debugging game for learning and engagement in computing education. *2014 IEEE Symposium on Visual Languages and Human-Centric Computing (VL/HCC)* (2014), 193-194. https://doi.org/10.1109/VLHCC.2014.6883051
[22] Mahmoud M. Mhashi and Ali M. Alakeel. 2013. Difficulties Facing Students in Learning Computer Programming Skills at Tabuk University. *Recent Advances in Modern Educational Technologies* (2013), 15-24. https://www.tib.eu/en/search/id/BLCP%3ACN084897952/Difficulties-Facing-Students-in-Learning-Computer/
[23] Iain Milne and Glenn Rowe. 2002. Difficulties in Learning and Teaching Programming - Views of Students and Tutors. *Education and Information Technologies* 7, 1 (Mar 2002), 55-66. https://doi.org/10.1023/A:1015362608943
[24] Martinha Piteira and Carlos Costa. 2013. Learning Computer Programming: Study of difficulties in learning programming. *Proceedings of the 2013 International Conference on Information Systems and Design of Communication - ISDOC '13* (2013), 75-80. https://doi.org/10.1145/2503859.2503871
[25] Edward F. Redish. 1996. Discipline-Specific Science Education and Educational Research: The Case of Physics. *Journal of Applied Developmental Psychology* 21, 1 (1996), 85-96.
[26] Alexander Repenning. 2011. Making programming more conversational. *IEEE Symposium on Visual Languages and Human-Centric Computing (VL/HCC)* (2011), 191-194. https://doi.org/10.1109/VLHCC.2011.6070398
[27] Maria Hristova; Ananya Misra; Megan Rutter and Rebecca Mercuri. 2003. Identifying and correcting Java programming errors for introductory computer science students. *ACM SIGCSE Bulletin* 35, 1 (2003), 19-23. https://doi.org/10.1145/792548.611956
[28] Pranay Kumar Sevella and Young Lee. 2013. Determining the barriers faced by novice programmers. *International Journal of Software Engineering (IJSE)* 4, 1 (2013), 10-22. https://vpn.utm.my/docview/1416417332?accountid=41678
[29] Lee S. Shulman. 1986. Those Who Understand: Knowledge Growth in Teaching. *American Educational Researcher Association* 15, 2 (Feb 1986), 4-14. http://www.jstor.org/stable/1175860
[30] Lee S. Shulman. 1987. Knowledge and Teaching: Foundations of the New Reform. *Harvard Educational Review* 57, 1 (Apr 1987), 1-23. http://hepgjournals.org/doi/10.17763/haer.57.1.j463w79r56455411
[31] David Weintrop. 2015. Blocks, text, and the space between: The role of representations in novice programming environments. *2015 IEEE Symposium on Visual Languages and Human-Centric Computing (VL/HCC)* 2015-Decem, C (2015), 301-302. https://doi.org/10.1109/VLHCC.2015.7357237

An Exploration of Novice Programmers' Comprehension of Conditionals in Imperative and Functional Programming

Claudio Mirolo
University of Udine
Udine, Italy
claudio.mirolo@uniud.it

Cruz Izu
The University of Adelaide
Adelaide, Australia
cruz.izu@adelaide.edu.au

ABSTRACT

Students of introductory programming courses are expected to develop higher-order thinking skills to inspect, understand and modify code. However, although novices can correctly write small programs, they appear to lack a more abstract, comprehensive grasp of basic constructs, such as conceiving the overall effect of alternative conditional flows. This work takes a little-explored perspective on the comprehension of *tiny* programs by asking students to reason about reversing conditionals in either an imperative or a functional context. More specifically, besides deciding if the given constructs can be reversed, students had to justify their choice by writing a *reversing* program or by providing suitable *counterexamples*.

The students' answers to four reversibility questions have been analysed through the lens of the SOLO taxonomy. 45% of students correctly identified the reversibility for the four code items; furthermore, more than 50% of each cohort were able to provide correct justifications for at least three of their four answers. Most incorrect answers were due to failures to consider border cases or to edit the conditional expressions appropriately to reverse the construct. Differences in comprehension between functional and imperative languages are explored indicating the explicit *else* paths of the functional examples facilitate comprehension compared with the implicit else (no update) of its imperative counterpart.

KEYWORDS

program comprehension; reversibility; imperative vs. functional programming; CS1; SOLO taxonomy

ACM Reference Format:

Claudio Mirolo and Cruz Izu. 2019. An Exploration of Novice Programmers' Comprehension of Conditionals in Imperative and Functional Programming. In *Innovation and Technology in Computer Science Education (ITiCSE '19), July 15–17, 2019, Aberdeen, Scotland, UK*. ACM, New York, NY, USA, 7 pages. https://doi.org/10.1145/3304221.3319746

1 INTRODUCTION

Besides introducing language constructs and examples of related code implementations, most CS1 courses focus their learning activities to cover other practical abilities such as tracing and testing programs, with little concern over how to approach computations in a comprehensive way. If we adopt the "reductionist" perspective addressed in [14], mastery of meaningful programming endeavours builds on the ability to envisage the full range of computation flows and their overall effect for each basic constituent part. The *reversibility tasks* considered here were conceived precisely to get insight into such ability, specifically for key conditional constructs.

In essence, a code block is *reversible* if we can undo its effect: in the imperative paradigm we should be able to restore the original state from its final state; in the functional paradigm we should be able to establish the function's inputs from its output. Reversibility means all possible final outputs/states can be undone, thus forcing students to reason comprehensively about the enacted computation.

Recent work [8] has exploited this concept to investigate program comprehension at introductory levels using think-aloud interviews. As an apparently trivial conditional got the lowest performance in [8], we replicated part of that work by testing students' ability to deal with reversibility of two "if" statements [7], confirming that half of the subjects did not recognise that a simple conditional like that shown in Figure 1(i) cannot be reversed. The present study elaborates further on the results of this preliminary work by analysing both "if" and "if-else" statements in an *imperative* context, as well as their corresponding constructs in a *functional* context. In imperative programs instructions may change the state of variables, while in functional programs there is no state but computations return results that may be reused.

Students were not exposed to the concept of reversibility in class. Thus the task was new to them, assessing their higher order skills instead of simple recall. After a short introduction to reversibility in the exam paper, students were asked to decide if the given conditional statements or functions can be reversed or not; they were also asked to justify their decision by writing the code/function reversal for a "Yes" or providing suitable *counterexamples* for a "No". In particular, this study addresses two research questions:

RQ1. To what extent can we assume that CS1 students are able to envisage the *overall effect* of a conditional construct?

RQ2. Are there features of the *imperative* vs. *functional* paradigm that may impact on the comprehension of conditionals?

The main contribution of this study is twofold. Firstly, it uses a new perspective to explore program comprehension, both in imperative as well as functional contexts. Secondly, it provides a first insight into novice programmers' ability to analyse basic constructs in such a way.

The rest of the paper is organised as follows: after outlining some background in Section 2, Section 3 describes how the empirical data

ITiCSE '19, July 15–17, 2019, Aberdeen, Scotland, UK

ACM ISBN 978-1-4503-6301-3/19/07...$15.00
https://doi.org/10.1145/3304221.3319746

was collected and analysed; Section 4 summarises the quantitative and qualitative results, which are further discussed in Section 5.

2 BACKGROUND

In Piaget's theory of cognitive development, reversibility is a key step toward more advanced thinking [18]. It is connected to progress from using and manipulating symbols to looking at them at a higher abstraction level and making better use of logical thinking. Moreover, according to a neo-Piagetian perspective, Piaget's learning stages are relevant independently of age when approaching new knowledge domains [22]. Thus, if this framework can also account for students' cognitive processes, reversibility should be an appropriate tool to analyse the first steps in the development of programming abilities. While the central role of "reverse thinking" in CS was highlighted in [6], tasks asking to reverse a piece of code were first proposed by Lister [11], as a device to test an "archetypal manifestation of concrete thinking" in novice programmers, and later by Teague and Lister [24] (but see also [23]) to assess students' ability to reverse short programs. More recently, as mentioned above, this idea has been developed in [8] and [7] by asking the students to reason about short programs in terms of reversibility.

More in general, reversibility can be seen as a tool to assess program comprehension. This broader topic has been addressed from a variety of perspectives, focusing on the role of different types of abstractions, including data and control flow [17]; on the divide between code tracing, reading and "chunking" abilities [5, 10, 12, 13]; on students' ways of classifying code fragments based on perceived similarities and differences [25]; on mental models of program behaviour [2, 19]; on the correlations between performance and types of annotations in the exam papers [16]; on the understanding of loops and nested loops [3]; on the issues connected with basic concepts of language notation and operational semantics [14].

That even simple conditional constructs may present a challenge to some students emerged, in particular, from the analysis of a huge dataset by Cherenkova et al., who reported that "a significant number [of students ...] exhibit the common errors of failing to check the border condition or reversing the conditional" [4].

The reference framework for the core part of our analysis is the SOLO taxonomy [1], an instrument of widespread use to assess code reading and writing tasks, e.g. [13, 21, 26], which is deemed to provide "a means of evaluating cognitive or mental models, to see if the novices are able to make connections between what they have learnt." [21]. From this perspective, the learners' achievements are classified in terms of complexity and quality of the interrelationships between parts they are able to deal with.

3 METHODOLOGY

In this section we describe the reversibility tasks and the rationale for using them in our investigation. Then, we outline the data collection process. Finally, we present the criteria underlying our analysis and our application of the SOLO taxonomy.[1]

[1]The complete text of the tasks as well as the SOLO classification of a variety of students' justifications (serving as guidelines) are available from the corresponding author, CM, upon reasonable request.

Analyse the following code fragments and determine if they are reversible:

- if your answer is *Yes, reversible* (i.e. the command is reversible), write a piece of code to restore the original state of the variables.
- If your answer is *No* (i.e. it is not always possible to undo the effect), provide examples for which we cannot recover the original state.

(i)
```
// int x
if ( x > 10 ) {
  x = x - 1;
}
```

(ii)
```
// int x
if ( x > 10 ) {
  x = x + 1;
}
```

(iii)
```
// int x
if ( x < 0 ) {
  x = x + 1;
} else {
  x = x - 1;
}
```

(iv)
```
// int x
if ( x % 2 == 0 ) {
  x = 2 * x;
}
```

Figure 1: Task on reversibility: imperative test (Java).

Analyse the following procedures and determine if they are reversible:

- if your answer is *Yes, reversible*, define the procedure for the *inverse* function.
- If your answer is *No*, provide examples showing that there cannot be an inverse function.

(i)
```
; int -> int
(define (p n)
  (if (> n 10)
      (- n 1)
      n ))
```

(ii)
```
; int -> int
(define (p n)
  (if (> n 10)
      (+ n 2)
      (+ n 1) ))
```

(iii)
```
; int -> int
(define (p n)
  (if (< n 0)
      (+ n 1)
      (- n 1) ))
```

(iv)
```
; char -> char
(define (pd c)
  (cond ((char<? c #\0) c)
        ((char<? c #\9) (integer->char (+ (char->integer c) 1)))
        ((char=? c #\9) #\0)
        (else          c)   )))
```

Figure 2: Task on reversibility: functional test (Scheme).

3.1 Tasks

The tasks examined in this paper are shown in Figure 1 (imperative programming) and Figure 2 (functional programming). Although unconventional from the students' standpoint, a peculiar feature of this type of tasks is that, to a large extent, it allows to disentangle the understanding of program behaviour from any specific application domain knowledge. For the sake of our investigation, we selected a mixed method that combines the three item formats useful in measuring higher order thinking skills: *selection*, *explanation*, and *creation* [9]. For each of the four items, students had first to identify whether a program is reversible or not (selection); then they were required either to provide a counterexample (explanation), or to write a reversing program (creation).

In the exam paper the questions were preceded by a basic introduction on reversibility, not shown here due to space limitations. Both tests were presented at the start of the exam paper when students were fresh and active. Moreover, each of the function definitions reported in Figure 2 appeared also in a second, slightly modified version and the order of the corresponding items was different in the two versions.

The operations in the branches of the conditionals are simple and individually straightforward to reverse. The key insight to decide about the reversibility of a given item is that there are different computation flows — one of which may be implicit — whose outcomes

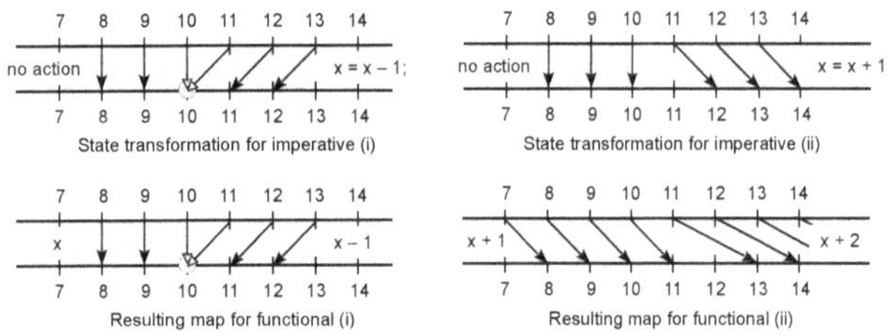

Figure 3: Depiction of the (state vs. functional) transformations for items (i) and (ii) in the two tasks.

may "overlap," as shown in Figure 3 for item (i). In order to identify similar overlaps students have to think of and carefully analyse border computations. Then, if the program is reversible, to provide a correct solution it is necessary to deal with the relationships between condition and operations in the alternate branches.

An issue identified in the imperative task was that the (correct) code to reverse (ii) could fall in two distinct categories, depending on whether the student was aware of the fact the original condition could be left unadjusted or not. From a SOLO perspective, this makes it difficult to discriminate between relational, multistructural and unistructural answers. Thus, in the functional task we modified the operations in (ii) in such a way that the condition should not be left unchanged when defining the inverse function (see Figure 3 for a visual illustration of both cases).

3.2 Data collection

We collected the exam answers from two first year undergraduate cohorts at the University of Udine, in Italy. Each exam paper was anonymised and digitized prior to analysis.

The first cohort took the imperative test in June 2017 as part of their CS1 exam. The test included six questions, of which we have analysed the first 4, and was worth 25% of the paper's marks. These 73 students had attended a full year of programming course (24 weeks: 80 lecturing hours + 60 practical hours) adopting a functional-first approach with Scheme followed by Java (imperative programming and basic notions of object-orientation).

The second cohort took the functional test in January 2018, after completing the first half year of functional programming with Scheme. The test included again six questions, worth 40% of that assessment. The class was composed not only by students enrolled in the CS degree, as in the case of the first cohort, but also by students starting a new degree on emerging computing technologies. In addition, not all students progressed towards the final exam by June 2018. Thus, to compare similar cohorts, the second dataset comprises only the 81 CS students who sat the June 2018 exam.

3.3 Analysis

To begin with, we measured the percentages of students who had chosen correct options. Then, we applied the SOLO taxonomy to conduct a qualitative analysis of the justifications — counterexamples or code — provided for each individual item. Although simple, the proposed tasks require abilities at the *relational* level that cannot be taken for granted in an introductory course.

Each individual answer has been mapped into four SOLO categories as per criteria listed in Table 1. To consistently apply these

Table 1: SOLO Classification guidelines.

SOLO Level	Answer features (reasoning or code)
Prestructural (1)	Poor answer showing either lack of understanding of the task or inadequate programming skills.
Unistructural (2)	Simplistic attempt to reverse part(s) of the code, while disregarding unequivocal interactions with other parts; attempts to reverse the code by some sort of cursory "syntactic manipulation"; flawed attempt to justify that the code cannot be reversed.
Multistructural (3)	Answer indicating that the goal of the task is clearly understood and pursued with a reasonable approach, but somehow incomplete, e.g. the reasoning may be ambiguous or the code may be affected by minor flaws.
Relational (4)	Correct and accurate answer, providing either some appropriate reversing program or a clear counterexample showing that the program cannot be reversed.

Table 2: Correct options and explanations for each item.

		Imperative			Functional		
item	reversible?	correct option	relational answer	SOLO mean	correct option	relational answer	SOLO mean
(i)	No	49.3%	37.0%	3.11	74.1%	64.2%	3.28
(ii)	Yes	97.3%	89.0%	3.73	82.7%	46.9%	2.85
(iii)	No	80.8%	58.9%	3.15	72.8%	65.4%	3.31
(iv)	Yes	94.5%	82.2%	3.66	82.7%	43.2%	2.69
both (i, iii)		47.9%	34.2%	–	63.0%	55.6%	–
both (ii, iv)		91.8%	79.5%	–	69.1%	27.2%	–

broad criteria, two researchers independently performed a deductive content analysis [15] to rate all students' answers to the imperative test. The discussions following this preliminary rating resulted into two subsequent revisions, and the overall inter-rater agreement of the second refinement was about 88%. Eventually, further discussion resolved minor rating differences and led to the final classification that is presented in section 4.2.

Based on this training, one researcher rated all functional test papers and produced detailed guidelines, including most variants of justifications, that have then been checked and approved by a second researcher.

4 RESULTS

4.1 Selected options

Table 2 shows the rate of correct options for the items presented in Figure 1 and 2. Although it may be expected that the imperative cohort would perform slightly better, as they had more instruction and practice, this turned out to be the case for (ii-iv) but not for (i). Relative to item (i), indeed, the functional group outperformed the imperative one, the ratio being about 3:2.

If we look at reversible (ii and iv) versus not reversible code (i and iii) we can see it is harder to identify non reversible items. There are two possible reasons: (1) answering *Yes* may be the default option for a number of students, and (2) it is difficult to spot an occasional flow overlap if not thinking about border values.

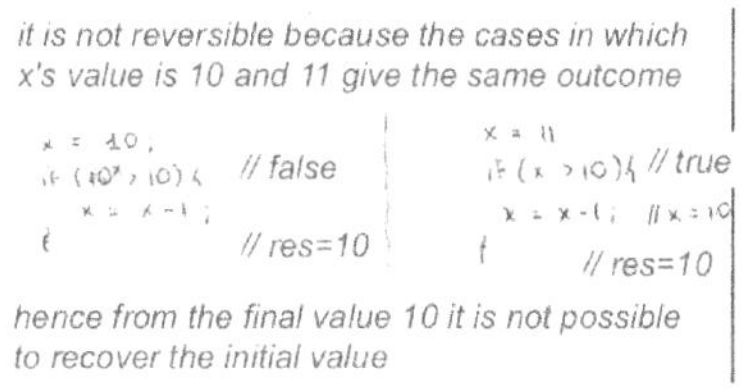

(a) Relational

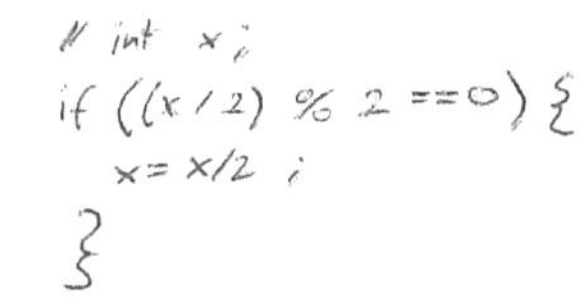

(b) Multistructural

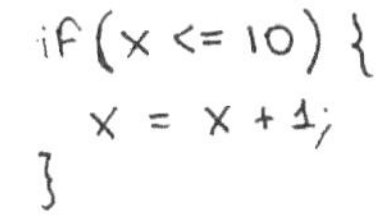

(c) Unistructural

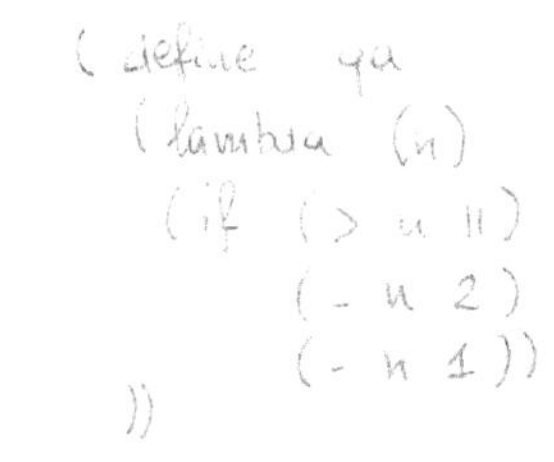

(d) Relational

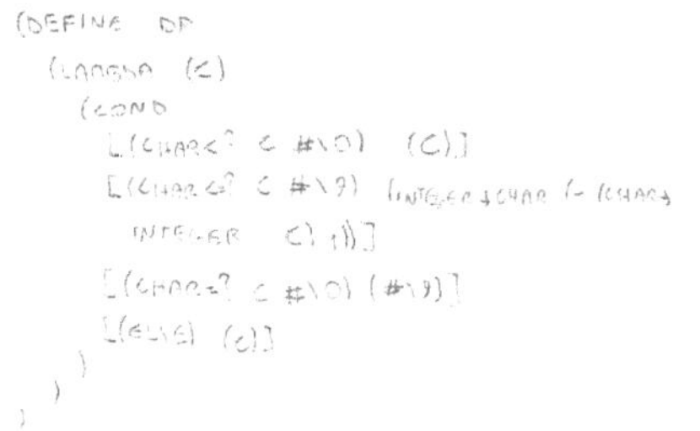

(e) Multistructural

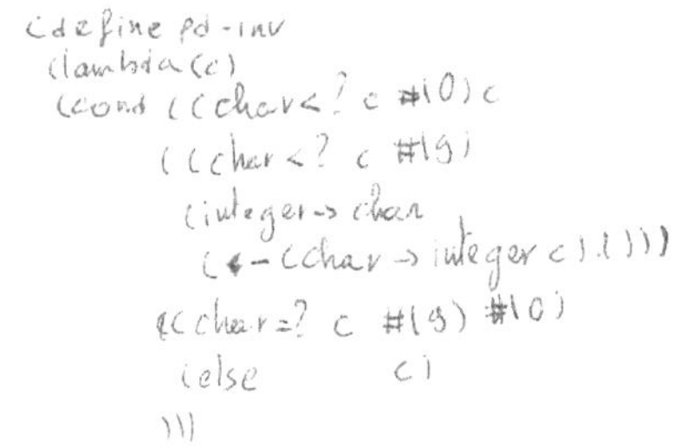

(f) Unistructural

Figure 4: Sample answers at different SOLO levels for imperative (top line) and functional (bottom line) tests.

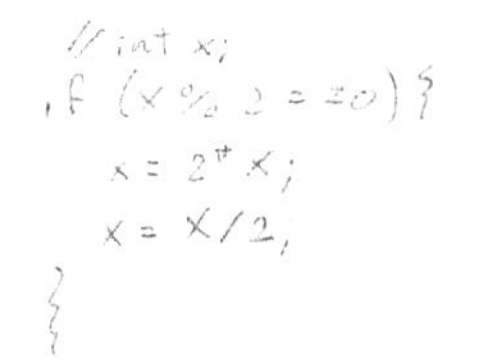

(a) Imperative

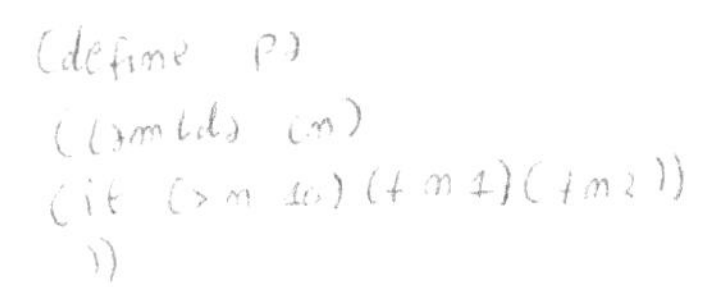

(b) Functional

Figure 5: Sample answers for pre-structural SOLO level.

4.2 SOLO analysis

We next move to the SOLO analysis. Table 2 reports the percentage of relational answers and the SOLO mean resulting from the rating process based on the criteria outlined in Table 1. As is customary, SOLO means are determined by averaging over the weights assigned to each level [20]: 4=relational, 3=multistructural, 2=unistructural, 1=prestructural, and 0=no justification. Besides presenting a few additional figures, in this subsection we will briefly describe and provide illustrative samples for each SOLO level.

Relational answers. Relational justifications, which are correct and accurate, amount to about two thirds of the answers overall for the imperative test and about 55% for the functional test. A couple of examples are shown in Figure 4.a relative to the imperative item (i) and Figure 4.d for the functional item (ii).

Table 3 shows how consistently students appear to work at the relational level, in terms of number of relational justifications.

Multistructural answers. Overall, 17% of the answers for the imperative test, but only 6% for the functional test, have been rated at this level. A representative example, relative to the imperative test, is shown in Figure 4.b: the student has tried to adjust the condition in accordance with the effect of the operation in the original code, without paying attention that it holds not only for the doubles of even numbers but also for every second odd number. In other words, the approach is reasonable, but the task is not completely mastered. An example of a multistructural attempt to reverse the functional program (iv) is shown in Figure 4.e, where each individual case has been identified and dealt with appropriately, but the order in which the conditions are evaluated is incorrect.

We classified at this level also trials to reverse the imperative code (i) by changing the assignment and reworking the condition accordingly, while however missing the state overlap.

Unistructural answers. Answers at this SOLO level — overall about 9% for the imperative test and 30% for the functional test — reflect a naive approach in which each component of the conditional construct is edited *independently* of the others. In particular, it includes functional's answers where the students reversed the operations in the *if* branches, but simply copied the original condition, so failing to coordinate *multiple* structures in order to achieve the task at hand. Another recurrent issue for item (iv) of the functional test is shown in 4.f., where the expression in the third clause is reversed, but everything else is left unaffected (contrast this to Figure 4.e).

Other unistructural answers result from attempts to reverse the program by manipulating the conditional almost syntactically, as in the example in Figure 4.c where the expression in the assignment and the condition of item (i) are carelessly reversed.

Prestructural answers. Overall, less than 6% of the answers of the imperative cohort, as well as of the *full* functional cohort, have been classified as prestructural. In the imperative test, several such answers exhibit the issue of immediately undoing the change inside the original code, as exemplified in Figure 5.a for item (iv).

A few programs result from some sort of "mechanical" manipulation of the conditional constructs, as in the example of Figure 5.b, relative to the functional item (ii), where the expressions in the two branches are simply swapped. Other prestructural answers report odd explanations or reveal a clear lack of understanding of the reversibility concept.

Table 3: Number of relational justifications vs. number of correct options per student for each cohort.

	correct options	relational justifications 4	3	2	1	0	total
imperative	4	30.1%	11.0%	4.1%	–	–	45.2%
	3		16.4%	13.7%	2.7%	–	32.9%
	2			11.0%	4.1%	5.5%	20.5%
	1				–	1.4%	1.4%
	total	30.1%	27.4%	28.8%	6.8%	6.8%	100%
functional	4	22.2%	14.8%	6.2%	1.2%	1.2%	45.7%
	3		13.6%	3.7%	7.4%	2.5%	27.2%
	2			4.9%	7.4%	8.6%	21%
	1				–	6.2%	6.2%
	total	22.2%	28.4%	14.8%	16.0%	18.5%	100%

Student's consistency. Table 3 shows the distribution of the number of correct options vs. their relational justifications within the observed groups. The dark-gray colored cells indicate consistent answers in that each correct answer is suitably justified. When the number of justifications relative to correct options drops significantly, i.e. 2 out of 3 correct options are not appropriately justified, we could infer the selection arose from partial understanding of the code or even from a random guess. The imperative cohort was overall more consistent, with less than 7% not able to provide one justification, compared to 18% for the functional cohort. We should note, though, that at least half of students in each cohort could provide 3 or more relational justifications.

Question difficulty. The SOLO means shown in Table 2 reflect the question difficulty for each cohort, while Figure 6 shows the percentages of answers at each SOLO level for each item. For the imperative cohort, item (i) shows the lowest rate of relational answers, with most students working at the multistructural level by reversing the code, which will work for all values but 10. The items (ii) and (iv) have the highest SOLO means, with more than 80% of the cohort classified at the relational level. For the functional cohort, providing counterexamples when the code is non-reversible appears to be easier (more than 85% of students that selected "No" did so) compared to working out the correct functional code in the reversible case.

In short, although the distribution of justifications shown in Table 3 are not dissimilar for the two groups, the imperative cohort obtained higher results relative to the items (ii) and (iv), which we attribute to the fact it was possible to reverse the code without editing the conditions as explained in section 3.1. We have investigated this hypothesis by performing a finer-grained analysis of the answers for the students that attempted to reverse item (ii). Table 4 distinguishes the types of treatment of the *if* condition and reports the corresponding frequency: while some students reworked the condition to compensate for the effect of the operation on the variable state or on the returned value, others simply used the given condition without changes in their reversing program. Table 4 will be interpreted and discussed in the next section.

Table 4: Analysis of justifications associated to answers reporting a correct option (*Yes*) for item (ii).

% of answers	Imperative	Functional
with correct reworked condition	52.1%	57.6%
with unedited condition	39.4%	27.3%
other	8.5%	15.1%
correct code (relational)	91.5%	57.6%

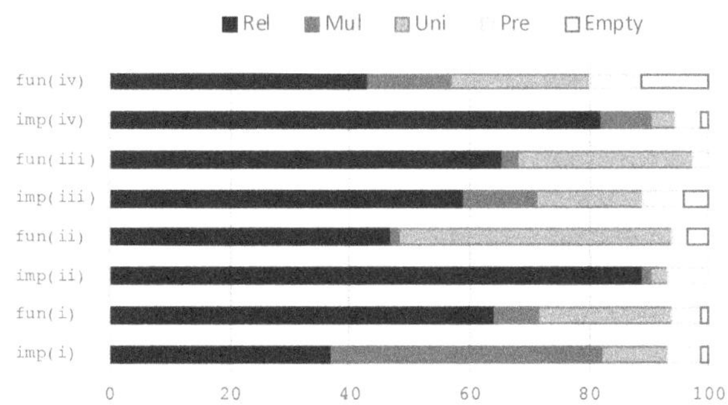

Figure 6: SOLO distribution for each item (i–iv) for either imperative or functional context.

5 DISCUSSION

We proceed now by revisiting the results presented in the previous section in light of the research questions.

In regards to RQ1, from Table 3 we can see that 45% of students in each cohort chose the right option in all four cases. However, when we look at the quality of their justifications, only 30% for the imperative test (22% for the functional test) were able to provide good counterexamples for non reversible items and correct program reversal for the reversible ones. It then appears that it is not so easy to have a comprehensive grasp of the implications of a simple conditional construct, be it imperative or functional.

Recognising that a program based on a conditional can*not* be reversed seems to be more challenging than guessing that it can. This may be explained by the difficulty to identify border computations that would suggest suitable counterexamples.

It is worth observing that the overall SOLO means, across all four items, are 3.41 and 3.03 for the imperative and functional cohorts respectively, which compares well to other studies using SOLO to assess skills of novice programmers; for instance, Sheard et al. [20] classified students' reading ability with short code fragments to swap the values of two variables, and reported a mean score of 2.39. (Note, moreover, that in our studies both the reversibility concept and the task were completely unfamiliar to the students.)

In regards to RQ2, the performances of the functional group vs. the imperative cohort diverge significantly for item (i), both in terms of chosen options as well as of correct justifications. A most likely explanation of this phenomenon brings into play the implicit *else* branch of the imperative conditional statement. Apparently, students tend to consider only the branch they can see and so ignore the overlap. Adding an explicit else as in item (iii) increases the number of correct answers from 49.3% to 80.8% in the imperative case, although the reasoning behind both statements follows a similar thought process. As instructors, we have seen novices writing *else* redundant code such as $x = x$, which may be a cue of their inaccuracy about the final state for the statement in (i).

There is also a strong divergence between the relational answers of the two groups for the reversible items (ii) and (iv), as shown in Table 2. The difference may be partly attributed to the shorter programming experience of the participants in the functional test. However, we presume that it is mostly due to the increased difficulty for items (ii, iv) in the functional test, because of the need to rework the conditions. This explanation is also substantiated by the fine-grained analysis of the justifications associated to correct options for item (ii), which is shown in Table 4. Indeed, we can observe that the percentage of correctly reworked conditions is similar for both cohorts, in the range 50–60% — as is the the overall percentage of correctly reworked and unedited conditions. Going back to Figure 3, the right side diagram shows the value 10 is not a possible final state of x for the imperative task; thus, asking "$x > 10$" or "$x > 11$" would provide the same outcome for the reversing code, therefore the unedited condition is correct. It is unclear, though, how many of the approx. 40% of the students who did not modify the condition of item (ii) in the imperative test did so intentionally. Moreover, if more students attempt to edit the condition, as needed in the functional case, we expect a higher rate of incorrectly edited conditions, which is included in the "other" row of Table 4.

Finally, many novice programmers are not at ease with coordinating operations and conditions to reverse a program. This is reflected in the number of answers classified as unistructural for each item, which ranges from 3% to 18% in the imperative test and from 22% to 46% in the functional test. Again, performance of the latter cohort is worse due to the greater difficulty of some subtasks. Students at that SOLO level can write code that is syntactically correct but does not achieve the correct result due to poor coordination.

Limitations. As with most exploratory studies, a key limitation is that the investigation involved two cohorts from one institution in consecutive years, thus it remains unclear to what extent the results can be generalised to other student populations. However, based on the findings in [7], where the performances on items (i) and (ii) of the imperative test have been compared for two cohorts from different countries, we can expect that the problems pointed out here are widespread among novice programmers.

Implications for educators. The repeated experiment has identified a recurrent weakness that concerns students' ability to carry out a comprehensive case analysis and to abstract from a *stepwise* explanation of program behaviour, failing "to see the forest for the trees" [12]. This weakness appears under both imperative and functional programming contexts. The additional semester practice does not help to reduce this weakness overall. In fact, the borderline overlap is more likely to be ignored for item (i) of the imperative test due to the implicit *empty* else.

It is then likely that we overestimate students' ability to plan testing and debugging of small programs, tasks they are usually expected to accomplish by the end of a CS1 course. This will suggest that the reversibility tasks considered here could be a helpful addition to CS1 instruction to explain and explore interactions between computation flows in conditional statements.

Using them towards the end of CS1 as a short intervention or revision may also help to improve students' higher-order thinking skills. Besides, we could scaffold this activity for weaker students, for example by giving them a reversible, say imperative, program construct and asking them to code its reversal, then revise with them the two steps required: (1) reverse each variable update and (2) adjust the conditional statement that triggers the update.

Additionally, this set of tasks provides a concrete example of what thinking in a comprehensive ways means compared with other revision tasks, such as multiple choice questions that trace a small program for a single input value and are often approached cursorily. This comprehensive reasoning can also be modelled with related tasks such as asking CS1 students to use the border case analysis to not only decide on reversibility, but also develop and document testing and debugging plans.

6 CONCLUSIONS

To contribute new insights into program comprehension, we have investigated the ability of two first year undergraduate cohorts to analyse and reverse tiny imperative and, respectively, functional programs based on conditional constructs. Their answers have been thoroughly analysed under the lens of the SOLO taxonomy. Overall, considering the task's novelty, students' performance was encouraging: more than half of the students could provide relational justifications for at least 3 of the 4 conditional examples. This translated on a high SOLO mean (both cohorts have a mean value > 3) compared to related studies, such as [20], that use this framework to evaluate their coding progress.

This analysis has provided the following **insights** about novices' mastery of conditional constructs:

(a) Building a comprehensive view of the implications of simple conditional constructs is a challenging task for novice programmers in either imperative or functional languages (first research question). In particular, students do not seem to be careful enough while dealing with border computations.
(b) The lack of an explicit *else* branch — a typical situation in an imperative context — turns out to affect remarkably students' analysis of the code behaviour (second research question).
(c) A significant fraction of students appear to face problems in order to master the coordination between conditions and operations in the reversing code.

This type of reversibility exercises could aid instructors to assess progress of novices who already have mastered the "atomic concepts" of syntax and semantics addressed in [14]. Asking for justifications as in this study provides useful insights into their mental models, which could trigger early detection of latent misconceptions.

We are currently extending our investigation on reversibility to cover different tiny programs, namely simple loops (imperative paradigm) and recursive constructs (functional paradigm), while also looking for opportunities to include other student cohorts. Furthermore, future work will aim at designing related tasks in order to gain more insight into students' mental models and ways of reasoning while deciding that a program cannot be reversed or while writing a reversing program.

REFERENCES

[1] J. B. Biggs and K. F Collis. 1982. *Evaluating the quality of learning: The SOLO taxonomy*. Academic Press, New York, USA.

[2] R. Bornat, S. Dehnadi, and D. Barton. 2012. Observing Mental Models in Novice Programmers. In *Proc. 24th Annual Workshop of the Psychology of Programming Interest Group*. Article 6, 7 pages.

[3] Ibrahim Cetin. 2015. Student's Understanding of Loops and Nested Loops in Computer Programming: An APOS Theory Perspective. *Canadian Journal of Science, Mathematics and Technology Education* 15, 2 (Feb. 2015), 155–170. https://doi.org/10.1080/14926156.2015.1014075

[4] Yuliya Cherenkova, Daniel Zingaro, and Andrew Petersen. 2014. Identifying Challenging CS1 Concepts in a Large Problem Dataset. In *Proceedings of the 45th ACM Technical Symposium on Computer Science Education (SIGCSE '14)*. ACM, New York, USA, 695–700. https://doi.org/10.1145/2538862.2538966

[5] Kevin Cox and David Clark. 1998. The Use of Formative Quizzes for Deep Learning. *Computers & Education* 30, 3-4 (April 1998), 157–167. https://doi.org/10.1016/S0360-1315(97)00054-7

[6] David Ginat and Michal Armoni. 2006. Reversing: An Essential Heuristic in Program and Proof Design. In *Proceedings of the 37th SIGCSE Technical Symposium on Computer Science Education (SIGCSE '06)*. ACM, New York, NY, USA, 469–473. https://doi.org/10.1145/1121341.1121488

[7] Cruz Izu, Claudio Mirolo, and Amali Weerasinghe. 2018. Novice Programmers' Reasoning About Reversing Conditional Statements. In *Proceedings of the 49th ACM Technical Symposium on Computer Science Education (SIGCSE '18)*. ACM, New York, USA, 646–651. https://doi.org/10.1145/3159450.3159499

[8] Cruz Izu, Cheryl Pope, and Amali Weerasinghe. 2017. On the Ability to Reason About Program Behaviour: A Think-Aloud Study. In *Proceedings of the 2017 ACM Conference on Innovation and Technology in Computer Science Education (ITiCSE '17)*. ACM, New York, USA, 305–310. https://doi.org/10.1145/3059009.3059036

[9] F.J. King, L. Goodson, and F. Rohani. 1998. Higher order thinking skills: Definitions, strategies, assessment. Florida State University - Center for Advancement of Learning and Assessment.

[10] Raymond Lister. 2007. The Neglected Middle Novice Programmer: Reading and Writing without Abstracting. In *Proceedings of the 20th Conference of the National Advisory Committee on Computing Qualifications (NACCQ'07)*, S. Mann and N. Bridgeman (Eds.). 133–140.

[11] Raymond Lister. 2011. Concrete and other neo-piagetian forms of reasoning in the novice programmer. *Conf. Res. Pract. Inf. Technol. Ser.* 114 (2011), 9–18.

[12] Raymond Lister, Beth Simon, Errol Thompson, Jacqueline L. Whalley, and Christine Prasad. 2006. Not Seeing the Forest for the Trees: Novice Programmers and the SOLO Taxonomy. In *Proceedings of the 11th Annual SIGCSE Conference on Innovation and Technology in Computer Science Education (ITICSE '06)*. ACM, New York, USA, 118–122. https://doi.org/10.1145/1140124.1140157

[13] Mike Lopez, Jacqueline Whalley, Phil Robbins, and Raymond Lister. 2008. Relationships Between Reading, Tracing and Writing Skills in Introductory Programming. In *Proc. 4th Int. Workshop on Computing Education Research (ICER '08)*. ACM, New York, USA, 101–112. https://doi.org/10.1145/1404520.1404531

[14] Andrew Luxton-Reilly, Brett A. Becker, Yingjun Cao, Roger McDermott, Claudio Mirolo, Andreas Mühling, Andrew Petersen, Kate Sanders, Simon, and Jacqueline Whalley. 2017. Developing Assessments to Determine Mastery of Programming Fundamentals. In *Proceedings of the 2017 ITiCSE Conference on Working Group Reports (ITiCSE-WGR '17)*. ACM, New York, USA, 47–69. https://doi.org/10.1145/3174781.3174784

[15] Philipp Mayring. 2014. *Qualitative content analysis: theoretical foundation, basic procedures and software solution*. Klagenfurt, Austria.

[16] Robert McCartney, Jan Erik Moström, Kate Sanders, and Otto Seppälä. 2004. Questions, Annotations, and Institutions: observations from a study of novice programmers. In *Proceedings of the 4th Koli Calling International Conference on Computing Education Research (Koli Calling '04)*. ACM, New York, USA, 11– 19.

[17] Nancy Pennington. 1987. Comprehension Strategies in Programming. In *Empirical Studies of Programmers: Second Workshop*, Gary M. Olson, Sylvia Sheppard, and Elliot Soloway (Eds.). Ablex Publishing Corp., Norwood, NJ, USA, 100–113.

[18] Jean Piaget. 1999. *The Construction of Reality in the Child*. Routledge. Original edition: La représentation du monde chez l'enfant, F. Alcan, Paris, 1926.

[19] Ian Sanders, Vashti Galpin, and Tina Götschi. 2006. Mental models of recursion revisited. In *Proceedings of the 11th Annual SIGCSE Conference on Innovation and Technology in Computer Science Education (ITICSE '06)*. ACM, New York, USA, 138–142.

[20] Judy Sheard, Angela Carbone, Raymond Lister, Beth Simon, Errol Thompson, and Jacqueline L. Whalley. 2008. Going SOLO to Assess Novice Programmers. In *Proceedings of the 13th Annual Conference on Innovation and Technology in Computer Science Education (ITiCSE '08)*. ACM, New York, USA, 209–213. https://doi.org/10.1145/1384271.1384328

[21] Shuhaida Shuhidan, Margaret Hamilton, and Daryl D'Souza. 2009. A Taxonomic Study of Novice Programming Summative Assessment. In *Proc. 11th Australasian Conf. on Computing Education - Volume 95 (ACE '09)*. Australian Computer Society, Inc., Darlinghurst, Australia, 147–156.

[22] Peter Sutherland. 1999. The application of Piagetian and Neo-Piagetian ideas to further and higher education. *International Journal of Lifelong Education* 18, 4 (1999), 286–294. https://doi.org/10.1080/026013799293702

[23] Donna Teague. 2015. *Neo-Piagetian Theory and the Novice Programmer*. Ph.D. Dissertation. Queensland University of Technology - School of Electrical Engineering & Computer Science, Brisbane City, QLD, Australia. R. Lister, C. Fidge & M. Corney supervisors.

[24] Donna Teague and Raymond Lister. 2014. Programming: Reading, Writing and Reversing. In *Proceedings of the 2014 Conference on Innovation and Technology in Computer Science Education (ITiCSE '14)*. ACM, New York, USA, 285–290. https://doi.org/10.1145/2591708.2591712

[25] Errol Thompson, Jacqueline Whalley, Raymond Lister, and Beth Simon. 2006. Code Classification as Learning and Assessment Exercise for Novice Programmers. In *Proceedings of the 19th Annual Conference of the National Advisory Committee on Computing Qualifications*, S. Mann and N. Bridgeman (Eds.). NACCQ in cooperation with ACM SIGCSE, 291–298.

[26] Jacqueline Whalley, Tony Clear, Phil Robbins, and Errol Thompson. 2011. Salient elements in novice solutions to code writing problems. *Conferences in Research and Practice in Information Technology Series* 114 (2011), 37–45.

Towards a Common Instrument for Measuring Prior Programming Knowledge

Rodrigo Duran
Aalto University
Finland
rodrigo.duran@aalto.fi

Jan-Mikael Rybicki
Aalto University
Finland
jrybicki@cc.hut.fi

Arto Hellas
University of Helsinki
Finland
arto.hellas@cs.helsinki.fi

Sanna Suoranta
Aalto University
Finland
sanna.suoranta@aalto.fi

ABSTRACT

Computing education researchers and educators use a wide range of approaches for measuring students' prior knowledge in programming. Such measurement can help adapt the learning goals and assessment tools for groups of learners at different skills levels and backgrounds. There seems to be no consensus on if and how prior programming knowledge should be measured. Traditional background surveys are often ad-hoc or non-standard, which do not allow comparison of results between different course contexts, levels, and learner groups. Moreover, surveys may yield inaccurate information and may not be useful due to lack of detail. In contrast, tests can provide much higher detail and accuracy than surveys about student knowledge or skills, but large-scale tests are typically very time-consuming or impractical to arrange. To bridge the gap between ad-hoc surveys and standardized tests, we propose and evaluate a novel self-evaluation instrument for measuring prior programming knowledge in introductory programming courses. This instrument investigates in higher detail typical course concepts in programming education considering the different levels of proficiency. Based on a sample of two thousand introductory programming course students, our analysis shows that the instrument is internally consistent, correlates with traditional background information metrics and identifies students of varying programming backgrounds.

CCS CONCEPTS

• **Social and professional topics → Computer science education**; *Model curricula*; Student assessment.

KEYWORDS

Self-evaluation, assessment, CS1, introductory programming, prior experience

ACM Reference Format:

Rodrigo Duran, Jan-Mikael Rybicki, Arto Hellas, and Sanna Suoranta. 2019. Towards a Common Instrument for Measuring Prior Programming Knowledge. In *Innovation and Technology in Computer Science Education (ITiCSE '19), July 15–17, 2019, Aberdeen, Scotland Uk.* ACM, New York, NY, USA, 7 pages. https://doi.org/10.1145/3304221.3319755

ITiCSE '19, July 15–17, 2019, Aberdeen, Scotland Uk

ACM ISBN 978-1-4503-6301-3/19/07...$15.00
https://doi.org/10.1145/3304221.3319755

1 INTRODUCTION

With the increase of computer science and programming related initiatives that seek to make computing accessible to all[1], an increasing number of students have some background in programming when they enter tertiary education. Computing education researchers share a general agreement that prior programming experience influences student performance in introductory programming courses [14, 30, 32, 38, 39, 41], while certain teaching approaches may reduce the difference [37]. Information on prior programming experience could be used to provide more challenging options for more experienced students [6].

Prior programming experience has been measured using numerous approaches [12]. Students have been asked, for example, if they have any prior programming experience [2]; how many programming languages they have used [14]; and what is the largest program they have written [26]. Furthermore, a range of approaches exist where students are asked to read code, answer a set of questions, and/or to write short programs [27, 35]; however, these are often used as tests and can thus be learned, as answers may be predictable. Researchers have also suggested using data from students' problem-solving processes to automatically infer students' programming experience [21, 36].

To address these issues, this article introduces and evaluates an instrument for measuring students' prior programming knowledge. Drawing inspiration from general scales used in language assessment, such as The Common European Framework of Reference for Languages (CEFR) [9], in which students' knowledge of a particular language can range from beginner to mastery level, we constructed an instrument for assessing elementary programming knowledge. Using the instrument, students can evaluate their programming knowledge from beginner to mastery level in topics typically taught in introductory programming courses.

While Feigenspan et al. [12] presented a work similar to ours, their work focuses on more advanced topics and self-ratings of experience, whereas our instrument is targeted at concepts within introductory programming courses. Their results, however, support our notion that self-evaluation questions can be useful for measuring experience. With our instrument, students can observe their gradual knowledge increase, which also allows them better understand course objectives and view their own progress – that is, our instrument can be used multiple times during a course. The instrument offers teachers information on students prior and current knowledge, which is useful in course design, decision making, and in guiding students towards particular content areas. In addition,

[1]Such as Code.org, CSforALL, CS Principles Project, Hour of Code, Khan Academy, and MOOCs.

the instrument can, in principle, be used at all educational levels, including open education.

This article conducts an exploratory analysis focusing on student responses in our data collection with the following research questions:

RQ1 Is the instrument internally consistent?
RQ2 What types of knowledge patterns does the instrument identify?
RQ3 How does the instrument compare with traditionally used ad-hoc measures of programming background?

This article is organized as follows. Section 2 presents the related work regarding instruments of evaluation, such as questionnaires in CS and other contexts as well as validated tests in CS. Section 3 discusses how our instrument is constructed. Section 4 describes the course and data collection methods. Section 5 outlines the results of our work, which are further discussed in Section 6. Finally, Section 7 concludes the article and suggests future research directions.

2 RELATED WORK

Self-evaluation have been researched in various contexts, including health professions [13], classroom teaching [28], language teaching [9] and MOOCs [20]. Although students with little experience in self-assessment may over- or underestimate their abilities or knowledge, self-assessment can contribute to higher student achievement, particularly when students are guided in this process. For example, rubrics provide a criterion-based self-assessment, which helps to understand the goals and requirements of a course [28].

Since self-evaluation is a skill, research has shown that the validity, accuracy, and effectiveness of self-assessment can also be improved using qualitative formative feedback, and triangulation between self-, peer- and teacher assessment [13, 20, 28]. Self-evaluation can also function as a self-reflection tool, supporting self-regulation of learning [42].

In Europe, educational institutions across different levels are encouraged to adopt the Common European Framework of Reference (CEFR) [9] for assessing the language ability of learners. The CEFR framework includes both extended descriptions of skills levels allowing instructors to reach a common understanding of language skills as well as practical self-assessment grids for common reference levels in CEFR for languages [9, p. 26-27].

In the CEFR, the language skills levels range between A1 (beginner) and C2 (mastery). The skills are categorized into separate areas, such as listening, speaking, reading and writing skills. These grids are typically translated into different languages, but skills definitions and ranges remain the same or similar. This allows both students to estimate their own skills and teachers to gain a quick understanding of each student's approximate skills. When offering standardized language tests, such as TOEFL [11] and IELTS [1], the test results can be linked with the CEFR levels, allowing instructors to understand the overall skills levels of students in different skills areas.

Prior knowledge is essential to learning, and CS is no different; perhaps, the gaps between experienced and inexperienced learners are even more pronounced. Research shows that at the beginning of the course learners with some prior knowledge in CS outperform learners with no experience by a fair margin [15, 40], and prior knowledge can be used (with moderate effects) to reduce the gap between experienced/inexperienced learners by introducing intermediate level CS1 courses [19]. Even if at the end of the course this gap is mostly closed, students with no prior experience face a great amount of psychological stress and pressure to keep the pace of experienced students. If this gap is not diagnosed at early stages, learners can feel demotivated or even drop-out from courses [17].

Most current methods used to evaluate prior knowledge in CS are questionnaires. Usually, programming experience is treated as a single construct evaluated by metrics associated with experience in generic terms [12, 16, 18]. There is little consensus on what and how to ask participants and how representative is this information. Feigenspan et al. [12] presented one of the most complete, and closest to our study, investigations of the relationship between prior knowledge and performance, examining programming experience, familiarity with programming languages and paradigms, and educational background. Their findings show that these metrics correlate highly with performance on programming tasks, suggesting that students are able to self-evaluate reliably.

While these questionnaires use metrics that show interesting correlations, richer and robust methods used in personalized learning [3] demand a deeper understanding of how prior experience translates into the comprehension of concepts present in CS1 courses. Recent work towards more reasonable and granular assessment questions [10, 25] in CS1 exams points to the importance of knowing in detail the concepts learners are familiar with. Detailed information could be used to set more realistic expectations and design assessment instruments matching learner's ability (as captured by Vygotsky's *zone of proximal development* [29]), with the difficulty of concrete programs used in assessment instruments [10]. This kind of personalized learning approach can assist learners with less prior knowledge by directing them to activities that enhance their comprehension of a particular topic.

Computer Science Education recently produced validated CS tests, such as the FCS1 [35] and SCS1 [27], which could accurately and reliably provide a high degree of insight into learner's knowledge. However, these tests still have some limitations. They are not generally available since making them public could decrease their validity. Longitudinal studies with repeated measurements of the test could be affected by its limited pool of questions and low flexibility in arranging them. Tests are time-consuming and hard to scale to very large courses. Although the FCS1 and SCS1 introduce some agnosticism with the pseudocode used in tests, these cannot be considered language independent. Students with different backgrounds (e.g. visual blocks or functional programming language users) could be disproportionately under-evaluated. These tests can also be considered difficult and not suited as a pre-test.

3 CONSTRUCTION OF THE INSTRUMENT

Our instrument for self-evaluation (at https://goo.gl/nGR9Th) was designed to resemble the self-assessment grid for common reference levels in CEFR for languages [9, p. 26-27]. For this first version of the instrument, we chose to focus on code comprehension and reading skills. While we believe that in the future it is possible to design an instrument aimed at programming writing skills, at this initial stage of development reading/comprehension can be considered a less demanding cognitive skill [10, 22, 24]. To some extent, the hierarchical structure of developing skills and knowledge also resemble Bloom's taxonomy of educational objectives [4].

To fill the gaps in earlier approaches, our instrument aims to provide a fast, easy to apply and widely available way to evaluate prior knowledge in programming that covers much of the common introductory programming course content. This instrument can be used by anyone several times, including longitudinal evaluations within the same cohort without losing its validity. The instrument can be language agnostic since it does not use or depend on concrete code written in a particular language and paradigm. Although the instrument can use of support information (e.g. guidelines, examples in concrete code, etc) that can be bound to a specific language or paradigm, its framework is flexible enough to be easily adapted and refined, accommodating different aspects of programming at different levels of ability. The self-evaluation also can benefit students at the beginning of the course by making expectations and self-reflection evident [28].

The instrument has two dimensions: concepts and levels. The vertical axis contains the concepts related to programming in a CS1 course, based on the list of content areas provided by FCS1 [35]: *variables and assignment (var), input and output (io), expressions and arithmetic operators (exp), conditional statements (sel), loops and iteration (loops), data collections (lists), functions and methods (funcs) and classes and objects (objs).* Although FCS1 does not explicitly order the areas in increasing levels of complexity, our instrument uses an order that is consistent with concepts' order of complexity of a program written in an imperative paradigm [10]. However, the order of the concepts do not necessarily impose a hierarchy (they can be used in any order) and learners with different backgrounds and knowledge in these concepts will not be affected.

The horizontal axis contains the estimated proficiency levels of programming concepts, inspired by the CEFR scale of proficiency in language skills [9] adapted to programming contexts. The levels were designed using the principles of the stage of cognitive development in the programming context [10, 23, 33]. Every level matches the description of a stage of cognitive development, complexity levels or familiarity with the concept. We defined complexity in terms of the number and quality of interacting elements [5, 10, 31], learner's expertise level and the number of available higher-order schemas [10] and ability to summarize a program [7, 10, 34]. Overall, the levels describe the path the learner takes to be fully proficient in a concept: from total unfamiliarity with the concept, to familiarity with the concept drawn from other contexts, being able to recognize and comprehend the syntax of the concept in a concrete program, tracing a program using concrete values with meaningful naming conventions and finally explain a program using abstract values in plain English without meaningful conventions. Each level is assigned with a letter to define its stage and a number for a degree. Each level has a statement (in quotes, below) to be evaluated by the learner, who self-assigns to a level.

- *"I am unfamiliar with this concept"*: unfamiliar level (A0);
- *"In general, I know what this concept means"*: At the beginner level (A1), learners are able to relate to a concept without being able to identify it in the code. For example, a learner can relate to the concept of objects without being able to recognize it in the code or be able to work with it.
- *"In general, I can recognize the syntax used by the programming language to represent this concept"*: At the elementary level (A2), learners can recognize the syntax related to a concept in the code without being able to comprehend it as a whole or transfer it overall meaning to other contexts. For example, learners can recognize the term "class" in the code without understanding how it works or be able to manipulate its functionality.
- *"I can read and trace code that uses this concept with a few elements. I can correctly predict the output of the code using concrete values, and the code uses descriptive naming conventions"*: At the intermediate level (B1), for example, learners can understand that "`for cont in range of 10`" will repeat 10 times, or the function "`uppercase('ITiCSE')`" will return the capitalized input.
- *"I can read and trace code that uses this concept with several different elements. I can correctly predict the output of the code when this concept uses concrete values, and the code uses descriptive naming conventions"*: At the upper intermediate level (B2), learners can cope with code having multiple abutted loops with inner conditional structures, for example.
- *"I can mostly recognize patterns of using this concept in different types of code even if the naming conventions are not always standard or clear. I am able to comprehend the purpose and behavior of code that uses this concept receiving a range of distinct inputs"*: At the advanced level (C1), for example, when tracing the following code snippet

```
1 def b(x):
2     n = []
3     for e in x:
4         if (e >= 0):
5             n.append(e)
6     return n
```

  learners can, after careful consideration of elements in the code, recognize lower-level patterns, such as traversing a collection (line3), checking for negative numbers (line4), and adding elements to a list (line 5).
- *"I can easily recognize and explain the logic of code using this concept even if the naming conventions are not always standard or clear. I can generalize the purpose and behavior of code using this concept receiving a range of distinct inputs. I am able to summarize the purpose of the code using this concept in plain English"*: At the mastery level (C2), using the above code snippet as an example, learners can immediately summarize in their own words that the code represents a filter function which takes a list as input and outputs all non-negative numbers.

4 CONTEXT AND DATA

This study was conducted during an open online course in programming offered at the University of *anonymous*. The course is offered free as a MOOC and covers the principles of programming in the Java language. The course is taken both by degree students and students not affiliated with the University of Helsinki. At the beginning of the course, students fill in a research consent form, our concepts instrument, a questionnaire with age, gender and metrics of their prior programming experience, similar to Feigenspan et al. [12]: elementary level school courses *(elemC)*, secondary level school courses *(secC)*, programming courses attended not at elementary or secondary levels (including online) *(otherC)*, hours programmed in total *(hpt)*, hours programmed per week *(hpw)*, programming languages *(langs)*, programming languages you consider yourself a beginner *(beginL)*, names of the programming languages you consider yourself a beginner, programming languages you consider yourself an advanced user *(advancL)*, names of the programming languages you consider yourself an advanced user, programming languages you consider yourself an expert *(expL)*, names of the programming languages you consider yourself an expert and largest program code *(lp)*.

The original instrument and questions were created in English and later translated to Finnish by an expert language instructor and an expert programming instructor. Answering the questionnaire is voluntary but includes an incentive raffle of movie tickets. Students could skip any question, and they could also choose to not to give research consent and still be included in the raffle.

From a total of 2853 course participants, 2468 answered the questionnaire[2]. From respondents, 2249 gave research consent. To curate the data, we set as exclusion criteria responses in which more than 2 variables were left unanswered in the concepts instrument, or if a value considered unreasonable (e.g. hundreds of programming courses taken) was inserted in more than two variables. If only one field fitted the exclusion criteria, a value `NA` was assigned to it. Open questions with free text were cleaned to remove typos, and the programming language names had the nomenclatures standardized. The final data set contains 2196 responses, of which 54.05% reported to be male, 43.85% female and 2.09% other. The average age of respondents is 36.93 years (ranging from 11 to 88 years old).

5 RESULTS

Data was collected using an online form and aggregated into a data set with all 23 variables (n = 2196), which were divided into three main groups: 8 variables in the concepts group, 2 in personal information group, and 13 in traditional background questions. Data was then analyzed using R Studio version 3.5.0.

Due to the nature of the course, respondents have heterogeneous backgrounds and levels of expertise. Regarding the programming languages, respondents reported knowledge in (at least) Java (n=561, 25.54%), Python (n=437, 19.89%), C/C++ (n=332, 15.11%), JavaScript (n=208, 9.47%), C# (n=137, 6.23%), Scala (n=36, 1.63%), Basic (n=35, 1.59%), Assembly (n=25, 1.13%), Lua (n=10, 0.45%), Arduino (n=6, 0.27%), and Scratch (n=3, 0.13%). To investigate if the data is normally distributed, we performed the Shapiro-Wilk test for all variables, which are not normally distributed. The concepts variables have W values equal 0.9, p-value < 0.001, except for objects with W=0.8. In background variables, W ranged from 0.3 to 0.02; thus, all tests account for such limitation. Table 1 shows basic descriptive statistics for all numeric variables from the concept instrument and background information.

To answer **RQ1**, we first investigated standard metrics of consistency. The inter-item (II) correlation was estimated using the `corr.test` function from the *psych* package using the Spearman rank method. Although the data is not normally distributed, the variances and covariances of variables are finite, making this approach appropriate. Cronbach's alpha (CA) was calculated using the `alpha` function from the *psych* package. Table 2 shows II and CA values of the concepts instrument.

[2]We consider a participant being in the course if they complete at least one programming assignment.

Table 1: Descriptive statistics for each variable in the study.

	var	io	exp	sel	loops	lists	funcs	objs
median	2.00	2.00	2.00	2.00	2.00	2.00	1.00	1.00
mean	2.36	2.27	2.33	2.41	2.26	2.03	1.89	1.53
std.dev	2.06	2.03	2.00	1.97	1.97	1.85	1.82	1.71

elemC	secC	otherC	hpt	hpw	lp	langs	beginL	advL	expL
0.00	0.00	0.00	10.00	0.00	5.00	5.00	1.00	0.00	0.00
0.15	0.33	1.51	511.80	3.32	18119.81	7.66	2.06	0.61	0.12
0.50	0.93	4.00	3290.97	35.16	539470.64	22.90	4.15	1.29	0.59

Table 2: Internal consistency metrics.

	var	io	exp	sel	loops	lists	funcs	objs	Mean
II	0.86	0.87	0.87	0.88	0.88	0.85	0.86	0.82	0.86
CA	0.98	0.98	0.98	0.98	0.98	0.98	0.98	0.98	0.98

While II correlation and CA metrics provide a good overview of the internal consistency of the instrument, we also analyzed its construct validity. To investigate the theoretical latent factors in the data, a Factor Analysis (FA) was performed using a Principal Axis Factor with Varimax rotation. The Kaiser-Mayer-Olking measure (KMO=0.944) and Bartlett's test of Sphericity (p<0.001) suggested that the sample is factorable. After three iterations, the analysis yielded a two-factor solution, when loadings less than .30 were excluded, as presented in Figure 1. The first factor contains 10 items, including all variables in the concept instrument, accounting for 65% of the variance with factor loadings from .300 to .923. The second factor contains four items, accounting for 12% of the variance with factor loadings from .362 to .708. The first factor can be labeled as "concepts" and second as "prior knowledge".

Figure 1: Factor Analysis.

		var	io	exp	sel	loops	lists	funcs	objs	otherC	hpt	advancL	expL	% of Variance
Factor	1	0.90	0.91	0.91	0.93	0.92	0.87	0.89	0.82	0.30		0.51		65.37
	2									0.53	0.71	0.36	0.62	11.95

The FA and the Principal Component Analysis (PCA) are techniques often applied in the construction of multi-scale tests to determine which items load on which scales [8]. While the FA tests a theoretical model of latent factors causing observed variables, the PCA reduces correlated observed variables to a smaller set of important independent composite variables. The PCA was performed using the `pcrcomp` function applied to all numeric variables in the data set. The first component (PC1) explains 44% of the variance, and the first nine components have a cumulative proportion of variance of 84%. The first component is composed by the concepts instrument, and the remaining components are a mix of background variables (e.g. elemC and advancL; age, expL, lp, hpt, hpw and otherC; beginL and secC).

Since the FA and PCA results suggest that the concepts instrument explains most of the variation in the data, we investigated if a set of components could emerge within the concepts instrument. The PCA of the concepts instrument shows a PC1 explaining 88% of the variance in the data, followed by a PC2 with 4.1% of the variance. Figure 2 shows the biplot of the components over the variables, indicating three distinct groups: *basic* (var, io, exp, sel, loops), *advanced* (lists, functions) and *expert concepts* (objects).

Figure 2: Component analysis of the concepts instrument. To improve clarity, the image is cropped to remove outliers.

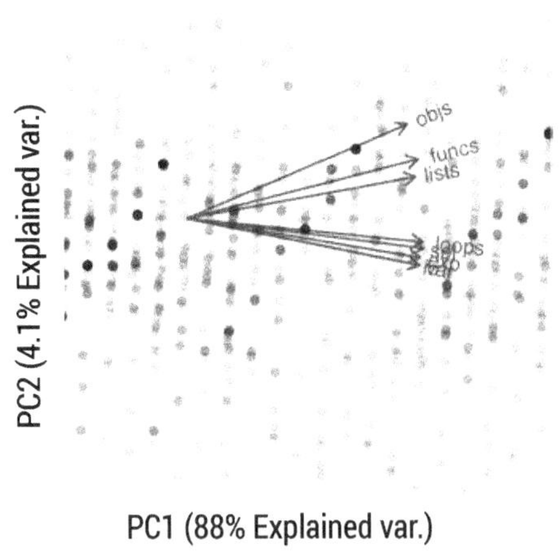

Since the PCA and FCA suggest the existence of three distinct groups of concepts in the instrument, we investigated **RQ2** by analyzing patterns arising from responses. More specifically, since these groups suggest a hierarchy of concepts (basic, advanced and expert), we investigated if the patterns of responses supported such hierarchy. While it is not possible to generalize this hierarchy to every learner (e.g. Scala learners in a functional paradigm could show higher levels of proficiency in functions and objects than loops), we aimed to identify patterns that suggest a prevalence of groups identified in the FA and PCA analysis (perhaps more akin to traditional imperative paradigm instruction).

We filtered the original data set to remove all respondents with missing values in any concept (n = 2190) and evaluated for each respondent if the sequence of answers, analyzed by each concept (labeled as *single* in Table 3), could be classified as strictly increasingly monotonic, increasingly monotonic, strictly decreasingly monotonic, decreasingly monotonic, constant or other. We hypothesized that patterns of constant, strictly decreasingly monotonic and decreasingly monotonic responses could indicate a hierarchy of concepts (basic concepts with high scores, gradually decreasing to low scores in objects). Of the 538 respondents classified as constant, 269 (50%) evaluated themselves as A0 in all concepts, 98 (18.21%) as A1, 24 (4.46%) as A2, 36 (6.50%) as B1, 24 (4.46%) as B2, 31 (5.76%) as C1, and 56 (9.85%) as C2.

Given the high amount (56.34%) of non-classified responses, we investigated if the components described in the PCA could improve the classification methods. For each respondent, we calculated the mean of variables within each of the three groups (basic, advanced and expert) and observed if this sequence of three values followed an increasing or decreasing pattern. Respondents previously classified as constant were excluded from this analysis. In Table 3, the group column represents this second analysis. The results show a decrease in the number of non-classified responses (56.34% - 28.39%) and an increase in the ratio of responses that can be classified as part of a hierarchy (43.28% - 64.53%).

Table 3: Patterns in students responses, analyzed by concepts (single) or by groups of concepts (beginner, advanced, mastery). N = 2190.

	Single	Ratio	Groups	Ratio
Monotonically increasing	29	1.32%	119	7.2%
Strictly monotonically increasing	0		0	
Monotonically decreasing	389	43.28%	490	64.53%
Strictly monotonically decreasing	0		576	
Constant	538		538	
Other	1234	56.34%	469	28.39%

To answer **RQ3**, we calculated the correlations between the concepts instrument and traditional background variables. A correlation matrix was calculated for the overall data set. For correlations, we used the Spearman rank method in the `rcorr` function. Figure 3 shows the correlations among all variables, with non-significant correlations (at p=0.05) marked as crosses. All p-values were adjusted using the Bonferroni correction method. The strongest correlations are between concepts and the weakest with age.

Figure 3: Correlation matrix of the overall data, excluding names of PL variables.

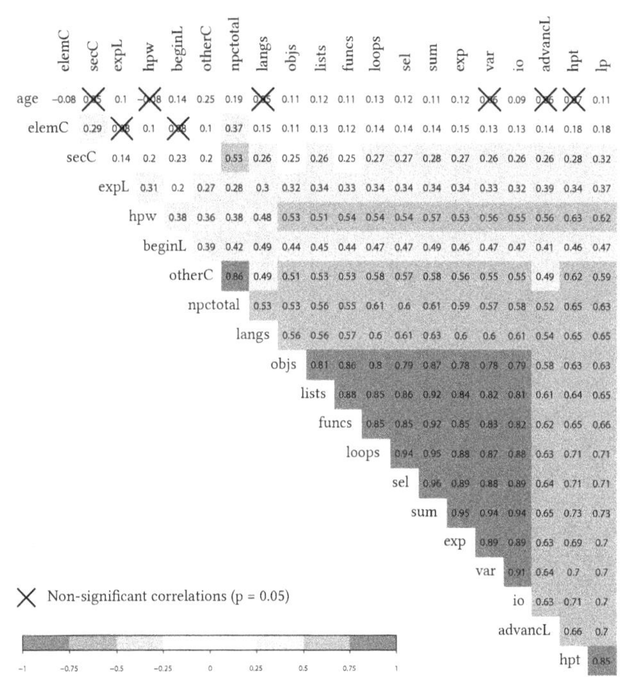

6 DISCUSSION

It is still not usual to collect previous knowledge information of students in CS courses [6]. The results presented here could support a larger adoption of prior knowledge investigation methods by providing a richer and reliable set of instruments. Internal consistency analysis provides evidence to answer RQ1, showing that the instrument is highly internally consistent. PCA and FA analysis also show that the instrument is measuring similar but distinct components of knowledge. PCA also shows that within the instrument there is fair discrimination among three groups that align very well with established notions of basic, advanced and expert concepts (at least in an imperative programming paradigm).

In RQ2, we investigated patterns of responses in the instrument. More specifically, we wanted to examine if a hierarchy of concepts (assuming an imperative paradigm with a certain style of code composition) could be extracted from data. We were able to show that, overall, responses reflected patterns matching this hierarchy (a constant or decreasing pattern in scores), matching the FA and PCA analysis that yields three distinct groups of concepts. While these findings could be useful to instructional designers and supply additional information of students evaluations of certain topics, we are careful to make strong claims of its generalization. Table 3 shows that many responses could not be classified (56.34% and 28.39%). We speculate that some responses may be incoherent (e.g. responses where the var concept was marked as A0 but all other concepts marked as C2) and can be attributed to mistakes in filling the form. Some non-classified answers could reflect different learner backgrounds (e.g functional programmers rating functions and objects higher than loops). The instrument itself can be considered agnostic (programming language and paradigm), and its data allows the investigation of more diverse patterns.

To answer RQ3, we observe that traditional metrics still have a low to moderate correlation with each other and the instrument. Within the instrument, while all variables have a high correlation, objects can be regarded as a distinct element (also supported by the PCA). Given the diverse programming languages background of respondents and the high mean of their ages, we conjecture that, in general, learners were exposed to imperative paradigms with little (or at late stage) exposure to objects. Concerning the background variables, the largest code produced and total hours of experience still have high correlations with the instrument variables and background variables.

It is worth noting how little the courses at elementary and high school levels correlate with other variables. Given the age of some respondents, it is possible that a very low number of them were actually exposed to programming at these levels. Our data also indicates a very small number of students exposed to languages currently presented at ES or HS, such as Scratch or Arduino. A number of respondents reported a very high number of courses (up to 50 courses). It is likely that the emergence of micro-courses that may take just a few hours to complete biases these results. Interestingly, the number of programming languages in which learners consider themselves as advanced users have a strong correlation with the instrument. We conjecture that learners with these levels of exposure and ability have enough knowledge to self-evaluate more reliably.

In language education, these kinds of instruments have been adopted for administrative and educational purposes. In administrative contexts, universities may require that students need to prove a certain minimum language skills level in a foreign language before accepted to begin their studies, such as B2 or C1 level. The official estimation of language skills is provided by language professionals. However, students can use a CEFR grid to self-evaluate their skills and estimate whether they should participate in language courses to obtain required skills. In educational contexts, language courses can specify a prerequisite level that students should have before entering a course. This ensures students do not enroll in courses that exceed their skills level. In computing education, a widely adopted common framework for skills levels could offer similar benefits for learners, instructors and administrators.

As limitations of this work, we acknowledge that self-evaluation can suffer from poor reliability and accuracy. It is not clear how truthful students are in their responses, how well they comprehended statements in the instrument or how much effort they devoted to answering the questions. It is also possible that learners with distinct backgrounds have different standards and self-evaluate in different ways. Learners with high competency may underestimate and learners with low competency overestimate their knowledge.

7 CONCLUSION

This article has introduced and evaluated an instrument for language independent evaluation of prior programming knowledge for introductory programming courses. The instrument was inspired by language learning self-evaluation instruments, such as CEFR. Unlike traditional approaches and instruments measuring prior programming knowledge, our instrument focuses on core areas relevant to learning programming. The instrument can provide a teacher with an overview of students' prior knowledge on core areas and gives students an opportunity to evaluate and reflect on their current level of knowledge.

Our analysis with 2196 responses suggests that the instrument is internally consistent. Principal component analysis of the responses identifies three main components: (1) basic programming concepts, (2) advanced concepts (or perhaps, functional programming concepts?), and (3) object-oriented programming concepts. Metrics used by previous studies are still relevant and correlate well with the instrument.

Our future work aims to analyze how responding to the instrument influences student behavior in introductory programming courses and how these responses correlate with other instruments for assessing programming competency, such as course grades and the SCS1 [27]. We plan to investigate if this instrument allows the detection of distinct patterns in students answers, which could be matched to backgrounds in different paradigms and programming languages, yielding distinct hierarchies. Finally, we plan to investigate pertinent issues with self-reporting, focusing on how students' self-reported knowledge evolves as they proceed in introductory programming courses. We will refine the instrument by adding detailed descriptions and examples for each concept and each level, creating statements more contextualized. We will continue to extend the instrument to include measures of code writing ability in the future.

REFERENCES

[1] [n. d.]. The International English Language Testing System (IELTS). https://www.ielts.org

[2] Alireza Ahadi, Raymond Lister, Heikki Haapala, and Arto Vihavainen. 2015. Exploring machine learning methods to automatically identify students in need of assistance. In *Proceedings of the eleventh annual International Conference on International Computing Education Research*. ACM, 121–130.

[3] Alireza Ahadi, Raymond Lister, Heikki Haapala, and Arto Vihavainen. 2015. Exploring machine learning methods to automatically identify students in need of assistance. In *Proceedings of the eleventh annual International Conference on International Computing Education Research*. ACM, 121–130.

[4] Lorin W Anderson, David R Krathwohl, Peter W. Airasian, Kathleen A. Cruikshank, Richard E. Mayer, Paul R. Pintrich, James Raths, and Merlin C. Wittrock. 2001. *A taxonomy for learning, teaching, and assessing: A revision of Bloom's taxonomy of educational objectives* (abridged ed.). Addison Wesley Longman. 302 pages.

[5] Jens F Beckmann. 2010. Taming a beast of burden–On some issues with the conceptualisation and operationalisation of cognitive load. *Learning and instruction* 20, 3 (2010), 250–264.

[6] Janet Carter, Su White, Karen Fraser, Stanislav Kurkovsky, Colette McCreesh, and Malcolm Wieck. 2010. ITiCSE 2010 working group report motivating our top students. In *Proceedings of the 2010 ITiCSE working group reports*. ACM, 29–47.

[7] Tony Clear, Anne Philpott, Phil Robbins, and Simon. 2009. Report on the Eighth BRACElet Workshop: BRACElet Technical Report 01/08. *Bulletin of Applied Computing and Information Technology* 7, 1 (2009).

[8] Andrew L Comrey. 1988. Factor-analytic methods of scale development in personality and clinical psychology. *Journal of consulting and clinical psychology* 56, 5 (1988), 754.

[9] Council of Europe. 2001. *The Common European Framework of Reference for Languages: Learning, teaching, assessment*. Strasbourg. https://rm.coe.int/1680459f97

[10] Rodrigo Duran, Juha Sorva, and Sofia Leite. 2018. Towards an Analysis of Program Complexity From a Cognitive Perspective. In *Proceedings of the 2018 ACM Conference on International Computing Education Research*. ACM, 21–30.

[11] Educational Testing Service (ETS). [n. d.]. The TOEFL®Test. https://www.ets.org/toefl

[12] Janet Feigenspan, Christian Kästner, Jörg Liebig, Sven Apel, and Stefan Hanenberg. 2012. Measuring programming experience. In *Program Comprehension (ICPC), 2012 IEEE 20th International Conference on*. IEEE, 73–82.

[13] Michael J Gordon. 1991. A review of the validity and accuracy of self assessment in health professions training. *Academic medicine* 66, 12 (1991), 762–769. http://dx.doi.org/10.1097/00001888-199112000-00012

[14] Dianne Hagan and Selby Markham. 2000. Does It Help to Have Some Programming Experience Before Beginning a Computing Degree Program?. In *Proceedings of the 5th Annual SIGCSE/SIGCUE ITiCSEconference on Innovation and Technology in Computer Science Education (ITiCSE '00)*. ACM, New York, NY, USA, 25–28. https://doi.org/10.1145/343048.343063

[15] Edward Holden and Elissa Weeden. 2003. The impact of prior experience in an information technology programming course sequence. In *Proceedings of the 4th conference on Information technology curriculum*. ACM, 41–46.

[16] Edward Holden and Elissa Weeden. 2004. The experience factor in early programming education. In *Proceedings of the 5th conference on Information technology education*. ACM, 211–218.

[17] Päivi Kinnunen and Lauri Malmi. 2006. Why students drop out CS1 course?. In *Proceedings of the second international workshop on Computing education research*. ACM, 97–108.

[18] Päivi Kinnunen, Maija Marttila-Kontio, and Erkki Pesonen. 2013. Getting to know computer science freshmen. In *Proceedings of the 13th Koli Calling International Conference on Computing Education Research*. ACM, 59–66.

[19] Michael S Kirkpatrick and Chris Mayfield. 2017. Evaluating an Alternative CS1 for Students with Prior Programming Experience. In *Proceedings of the 2017 ACM SIGCSE Technical Symposium on Computer Science Education*. ACM, 333–338.

[20] Chinmay Kulkarni, Koh Pang Wei, Huy Le, Daniel Chia, Kathryn Papadopoulos, Justin Cheng, Daphne Koller, and Scott R. Klemmer. 2013. Peer and self assessment in massive online classes. *ACM Transactions on Computer-Human Interaction* 20, 6 (2013), 1–31. https://doi.org/10.1145/2505057

[21] Juho Leinonen, Krista Longi, Arto Klami, and Arto Vihavainen. 2016. Automatic Inference of Programming Performance and Experience from Typing Patterns. In *Proceedings of the 47th ACM Technical Symposium on Computing Science Education (SIGCSE '16)*. ACM, New York, NY, USA, 132–137. https://doi.org/10.1145/2839509.2844612

[22] Raymond Lister. 2011. Concrete and Other Neo-Piagetian Forms of Reasoning in the Novice Programmer. *Proceedings of the Thirteenth Australasian Computing Education Conference* Ace (2011), 9–18.

[23] Raymond Lister. 2016. Toward a Developmental Epistemology of Computer Programming. In *Proceedings of the 11th Workshop in Primary and Secondary Computing Education*. ACM, 5–16.

[24] Mike Lopez, Jacqueline Whalley, Phil Robbins, and Raymond Lister. 2008. Relationships between reading, tracing and writing skills in introductory programming. In *Proceedings of the fourth international workshop on computing education research*. ACM, 101–112.

[25] Andrew Luxton-Reilly, Brett A Becker, Yingjun Cao, Roger McDermott, Claudio Mirolo, Andreas Mühling, Andrew Petersen, Kate Sanders, Jacqueline Whalley, et al. 2018. Developing Assessments to Determine Mastery of Programming Fundamentals. In *Proceedings of the 2017 ITiCSE Conference on Working Group Reports*. ACM, 47–69.

[26] Matthias M Müller. 2004. Are reviews an alternative to pair programming? *Empirical Software Engineering* 9, 4 (2004), 335–351.

[27] Miranda C. Parker, Mark Guzdial, and Shelly Engleman. 2016. Replication, Validation, and Use of a Language Independent CS1 Knowledge Assessment. In *Proceedings of the 2016 ACM Conference on International Computing Education Research (ICER '16)*. ACM, New York, NY, USA, 93–101. https://doi.org/10.1145/2960310.2960316

[28] John A. Ross. 2006. The Reliability , Validity , and Utility of Self-Assessment. *Practical assessment, research and evaluation* 10 (2006), 1–13. https://doi.org/10.1016/j.aspen.2014.06.014

[29] Wolfgang Schnotz and Christian Kürschner. 2007. A reconsideration of cognitive load theory. *Educational psychology review* 19, 4 (2007), 469–508.

[30] Judy Sheard, Angela Carbone, Selby Markham, A J Hurst, Des Casey, and Chris Avram. 2008. Performance and Progression of First Year ICT Students. In *Proceedings of the Tenth Conference on Australasian Computing Education - Volume 78 (ACE '08)*. Australian Computer Society, Inc., Darlinghurst, Australia, Australia, 119–127. http://dl.acm.org/citation.cfm?id=1379249.1379261

[31] John Sweller. 2010. Element interactivity and intrinsic, extraneous, and germane cognitive load. *Educational psychology review* 22, 2 (2010), 123–138.

[32] Harriet G Taylor and Luegina C Mounfield. 1994. Exploration of the relationship between prior computing experience and gender on success in college computer science. *Journal of educational computing research* 11, 4 (1994), 291–306.

[33] Donna Teague. 2015. *Neo-Piagetian theory and the novice programmer*. Ph.D. Dissertation. Queensland University of Technology.

[34] Donna Teague, Malcolm Corney, Alireza Ahadi, and Raymond Lister. 2013. A qualitative think aloud study of the early neo-piagetian stages of reasoning in novice programmers. In *Proceedings of the Fifteenth Australasian Computing Education Conference-Volume 136*. Australian Computer Society, Inc., 87–95.

[35] Allison Elliott Tew and Mark Guzdial. 2010. Developing a Validated Assessment of Fundamental CS1 Concepts. In *Proceedings of the 41st ACM Technical Symposium on Computer Science Education (SIGCSE '10)*. ACM, New York, NY, USA, 97–101. https://doi.org/10.1145/1734263.1734297

[36] Richard C. Thomas, Amela Karahasanovic, and Gregor E. Kennedy. 2005. An Investigation into Keystroke Latency Metrics As an Indicator of Programming Performance. In *Proceedings of the 7th Australasian Conference on Computing Education - Volume 42 (ACE '05)*. Australian Computer Society, Inc., Darlinghurst, Australia, Australia, 127–134. http://dl.acm.org/citation.cfm?id=1082424.1082440

[37] Phil Ventura and Bina Ramamurthy. 2004. Wanted: CS1 Students. No Experience Required. In *Proceedings of the 35th SIGCSE Technical Symposium on Computer Science Education (SIGCSE '04)*. ACM, New York, NY, USA, 240–244. https://doi.org/10.1145/971300.971387

[38] Arto Vihavainen, Jonne Airaksinen, and Christopher Watson. 2014. A systematic review of approaches for teaching introductory programming and their influence on success. In *Proceedings of the tenth annual conference on International computing education research*. ACM, 19–26.

[39] Susan Wiedenbeck, Deborah Labelle, and Vennila NR Kain. 2004. Factors affecting course outcomes in introductory programming. In *16th Annual Workshop of the Psychology of Programming Interest Group*.

[40] Chris Wilcox and Albert Lionelle. 2018. Quantifying the Benefits of Prior Programming Experience in an Introductory Computer Science Course. In *Proceedings of the 49th ACM Technical Symposium on Computer Science Education*. A, 80–85.

[41] Brenda Cantwell Wilson and Sharon Shrock. 2001. Contributing to Success in an Introductory Computer Science Course: A Study of Twelve Factors. In *Proceedings of the Thirty-second SIGCSE Technical Symposium on Computer Science Education (SIGCSE '01)*. ACM, New York, NY, USA, 184–188. https://doi.org/10.1145/364447.364581

[42] Barry J Zimmerman. 2002. Becoming a Self-Regulated Learner: An Overview. *Theory into practice* 41, 2 (2002), 64–70. https://doi.org/10.1207/s15430421tip4102

Copying Can Be Good: How Instructors Use Imitation in Teaching Programming

Carol Zander
University of Washington Bothell
Bothell, WA, USA
zander@u.washington.edu

Anna Eckerdal
Uppsala University
Uppsala, Sweden
Anna.Eckerdal@it.uu.se

Robert McCartney
University of Connecticut
Storrs, CT, USA
robert@engr.uconn.edu

Jan Erik Moström
Umeå University
Umeå, Sweden
jem@cs.umu.se

Kate Sanders
Rhode Island College (Emerita)
Providence, RI, USA
ksanders@ric.edu

Lynda Thomas
Aberystwyth University
Aberystwyth, Wales, UK
ltt@aber.ac.uk

ABSTRACT

Students' "copying" is often considered negatively. In this paper, we explore the ways in which copying and imitation are used positively by computing instructors in their teaching. We found that instructors expect their students to use these strategies in many different contexts and at many different levels.

CCS CONCEPTS

• **Social and professional topics → Computer science education.**

KEYWORDS

Mimicry; Imitation; Copying

ACM Reference Format:
Carol Zander, Anna Eckerdal, Robert McCartney, Jan Erik Moström, Kate Sanders, and Lynda Thomas. 2019. Copying Can Be Good: How Instructors Use Imitation in Teaching Programming. In *Innovation and Technology in Computer Science Education (ITiCSE '19),July 15–17, 2019, Aberdeen, Scotland UK*. ACM, New York, NY, USA, 7 pages. https://doi.org/10.1145/3304221.3319783

1 INTRODUCTION AND MOTIVATION

In computing education, "copying" generally has negative connotations. If one of your colleagues mentions over lunch that her students have been copying, likely the students have been copying from each other or from the web. Very probably, the conversation will quickly develop into a discussion of how to prevent or respond to plagiarism.

But is copying always bad? Asian education has long had the reputation of valuing the memorization and repetition of given information [12]. This practice has sometimes been dismissed as mere "rote learning" by Western educators. The Asian students may or may not be doing rote learning in the Western sense, but even if they are, how many generations of students (and how many of us) have begun to program by typing in some version of the "hello" program, character by character? Börstler et al. [2] stress the importance of giving students good code examples precisely because students (consciously or unconsciously) model their code on what they have seen.

Moreover, in other fields, the need to imitate is openly acknowledged. For instance, when you learn to speak another language, it is essential to imitate a native speaker. Similarly, in art, music, and sports, it is common for novices to imitate expert teachers.

This paper reports on the first step in an investigation of the use of imitation, copying, and mimicry in teaching introductory through advanced programming. These three terms are overlapping but not identical. In general, we use the term "copy" in relation to artifacts, "imitate" in relation to behavior, process, or attitudes, and "mimic" in the sense of Meyer and Land [26] who use the term to be synonymous with copy or imitate and also as a way that students can assume the identity of a person who has mastered a skill (see Section 2.2.) ("Mimic" is also often used to refer to imitation for the purpose of ridicule, but we do not use that meaning here.)

Specifically, we have the following research question:

RQ How are imitation, copying, and mimicry actually used by instructors in teaching students programming?

Thus, our focus is on what the instructor provides to students or does with the intention that the students will imitate all or part of what they see. The purpose of our examination is threefold:

- Identify imitation as a topic for research in computing education
- Cast some light on, and provide examples of, the fact that CS instructors do expect their students to imitate some things that they do (and NOT to imitate others)
- Produce a framework that gives some structure to the many ways in which imitation can be used, so that readers are able to consciously articulate their own practice.

The structure of the paper is as follows. Section 2 covers background and some related work. In Section 3 we describe our survey, how we collected data, and how we analyzed the responses. In Sections 4 and 5 we present the results of our analysis. In Section 6 we discuss these results in the context of a deeper discussion of related work. Finally, we conclude in Section 7.

ITiCSE '19, July 15–17, 2019, Aberdeen, Scotland UK

ACM ISBN 978-1-4503-6301-3/19/07...$15.00
https://doi.org/10.1145/3304221.3319783

2 BACKGROUND AND RELATED WORK

2.1 Rote and shallow learning

In previous educational research, mimicry has generally been related to memorization and rote learning which a number of studies have showed being less beneficial for learning [10, 15, 29].

The concepts of deep and surface learning [7, 20], which have had great impact on research in higher education, belong in this tradition. Deep learning here means learning with understanding while surface learning relate to rote learning. From computer science education Hughes and Peiris [11], for example, found strong negative correlation between how students perform in programming courses and a "surface apathetic approach" to learning, meaning students memorize and reproduce what they have seen without any deeper understanding.

This view on mimicry has, however, been challenged and has been argued to be an important step in students' learning [12, 21]. In a comparative study of Chinese and Australian students of accounting, Cooper [4] found that "While surface approaches to learning can be associated with mechanical rote learning, memorization through repetition can be used to deepen and develop understanding and help achieve good academic performance." (p. 306). This is also supported by Kember [12] who writes that "The perception that students rely upon rote-learning can be explained as a failure to realise that memorisation could be accompanied by an intention to seek understanding."

Moreover, a recent European study from mathematics education research [8] on eighth grade students compared three instructional practices: memorizing formulas and procedures, listening to the teacher, and relating mathematics to daily life (which one might expect to require deeper understanding). The study showed that memorizing formulas and processes and listening to the teacher were positive predictors for mathematics achievement, while relating mathematics to daily life was not.

2.2 Threshold concepts and liminal space

In connection with their work on threshold concepts, Meyer and Land [26] argue for the positive value of mimicry. They write that mimicry can "involve both attempts at understanding and troubled misunderstanding, or limited understanding, and is not merely intention to reproduce information in a given form." [26, p. 377]. Moreover, it can be a useful strategy: "students might well adopt what appears to be a form of mimicry as a serious attempt to come to terms with conceptual difficulty, or to try on certain conceptual novelties for size as it were. ... they may well prove to be successful routes through to understanding for certain learners." [26, p. 383].

Meyer and Land introduce the term "liminal space" for the transitional period from beginning to learn a concept to fully mastering it. Eckerdal et al. investigated the liminal space from a student perspective, doing in-depth interviews of computer science majors nearing graduation [6], and found that "many students state that at some stage during the learning process they mimic what others have done without exactly understanding what they are doing" (p. 131). But "for the interviewed students the 'mimicry' seemed to be just a stepping stone in their further learning" (p. 129).

2.3 The role of examples

The approach of increasing the complexity of examples and encouraging students to abstract essentials, which many CS instructors use almost reflexively to scaffold programming, is made explicit by Muller in Pattern Oriented Instruction (POI) [28]: "The main principles ... lie in defining Algorithmic Patterns - solutions to basic algorithmic problems - and in organizing course problem-solving activities around them."

As a foundation to their work on examples in textbooks, Börstler et al. discuss the importance of examples in learning generally [2]. They note that "By continuously exposing students to exemplary examples, important properties are reinforced. Students will eventually gain enough experience to recognize general patterns which helps them to distinguish between good and bad designs." They also point out that if examples are not carefully constructed, students will have difficulty in recognizing patterns. Students will not be able to distinguish surface properties from structurally or conceptually important properties.

Morrison et al. [27] explain that worked examples are typically a combination of a problem statement and a step-by-step description of how to solve the problem (including a concrete solution). Thus, the reader is given both a concrete solution to adapt for future use, but also a demonstration of the process by which a solution can be obtained from a problem statement.

In a study on the difficulties of novice programmers, Lahtinen et al. [13] found that "example programs were considered as the most useful type of material both by the students and the teachers." Anderson et al. [1] described how novices used example programs to acquire the knowledge needed to write recursive programs.

Reimann and Schult [30, p. 123] discuss how examples are powerful role models for many. Although when experts use examples, they then attempt to reason from a domain they understand well to the one that is puzzling. "What novices often do, however, is employ a knowledge-lean style of analogical reasoning, analogical transfer within a domain, not across domains. For instance, and most important, students use worked-out examples provided in textbooks, by the teacher, or by their peers when solving new problems" [30, p. 123].

In a study investigating the troublesome characteristic of threshold concepts, [25] we found that using examples in conjunction with practice was a common strategy students in their final year of study found useful when stuck. We also found [24] that one of the strategies used by students doing informal or self-directed learning was to use examples. Students found samples, typically on the web, and used these to scaffold to more sophisticated code.

Bransford [3] reports that the literature on transfer "suggests that the most effective transfer may come from a balance of specific examples and general principles, not from either one alone." Trafton's work [32, p. 78] agrees that using examples alone is not best, "that examples are an important way of acquiring skill, but simply studying and self-explaining examples is not the best way to understand and learn how to solve problems; studying examples and solving problems together allows more problem solving knowledge to be gained than simply studying examples." Malan and Halland [17, p. 83] argue that "the role of examples should go beyond merely illustrating concepts or principles and should 'sell' concepts to new programmers." If not done properly, "some examples can do harm by undermining the very concept they are introducing."

2.4 Variation theory and transfer

Tying in with the examples thread, from a Variation Theory [19] perspective, learning is discussed in terms of how students become aware of new critical aspects of phenomena, or relationships between such aspects. Phenomena investigated have traditionally been concepts, but it has been argued, it could also be skills [31].

Students progressively expand their knowledge through varying aspects. Typically, the teacher introduces systematic variations to highlight the different aspects of the concepts or skills. In this way, the student learns to make sense of how different situations can be managed. As the students' learning progresses and the student can discern differences, they then also are able to determine aspects to disregard. Transfer of knowledge from one context to another is also best achieved when students are exposed to differences rather than to sameness [18]. Mimicry with little variation will thus not facilitate learning.

3 METHODOLOGY

In this study we conducted semi-structured interviews with seven computer science instructors, here named A - G with no reference to their names. Participants included instructors at five institutions in Sweden (A, B, and C), the United Kingdom (D and E), and the United States (F and G). Six of these instructors were male, one female; all had over 20 years teaching experience. For analysis, the interviews were transcribed verbatim; where necessary, they were translated into English by the interviewer.

An initial email invitation was sent out asking if instructors would show us some materials they expected students to imitate. Two pilot interviews were undertaken, and then the rest of the interviews used the same interview script. In the script, after asking about what parts of the materials students were expected to imitate, instructors were asked about the context, e.g., when the imitation would occur, which course, what they wanted students to learn from the lesson, and so on. They were asked how they help the students to see what can be varied and what stays the same. Instructors discussed the effectiveness of using imitation and how imitation is used with respect to learning to program.

To analyze the interviews, we began by reading and re-reading the interview data, tagging parts that related to imitation. As a group, we decided on the kinds of information sought. See Figure 1 for the primary items (first row).

Then as a group, we filled in the table for ten examples taken from our interviews. One example is shown in Figure 1 in the second row. In addition we noted: at what level this occurred (beginner/ intermediate/ advanced), where it occurred (lab/lecture), and how the instructor communicated the information(lecture/demo/notes/video).

As we filled in the table, we discussed the kinds of examples we saw. Using content analysis [22] and grouping together the answers to the interview questions and using content analysis to tease out similar themes and ideas, we found that the examples followed more of a continuum and less of distinct categories. Nonetheless, the uses can be grouped into broad categories and organized in a framework, discussed in Results.

What instructor does	**What instructor hopes student will do**	**What instructor hopes is imitated**	**Learning goal**
Shows code for finding largest	*Write code for finding smallest*	*Structure of the code*	*Abstraction from details*

Figure 1: Information recorded with one example; headings row in boldface, entries from example in italics.

4 RESULTS – THE FRAMEWORK

Many of our subjects initially responded that they doubted that they could help with this project, but when pressed they, in fact, agreed that they used imitation extensively and in ways they had not previously thought about. Instructor A, for instance, said "The first thing I thought about when I heard 'mimic' was small thing, 'this is the way to do it', ... But you're right, what we do is to try to change/affect behavior." One subject, instructor G, agreed that teaching is "a big long set of imitation."

The instructors mainly described situations that related explicitly to code: situations in which they demonstrated code, or explained code, or expected students to copy or change code. But as the conversations developed, it became apparent that the instructors also hope that students will imitate their process, their behaviour, and even their attitude (not just to coding, but to learning).

As we organised the responses in the table shown in Figure 1, we saw a wide variety of imitation expectations ranging from exact copying to greatly abstracting from the information relayed. We also saw a wide range of sources, from code handouts and screencasts to instructors working along with students to discover a solution. We organized the different *kinds* of imitation in terms of artifact vs. process, and the *level* of copying, from exact to abstract. An example of the first distinction is copying the structure of some code vs. mimicking the process of debugging, while an example of the latter is copying code as it is, vs. using a design pattern to develop a concrete program. This continuum of mimicry, with representative examples is represented in Figure 2. The next section gives further examples.

5 RESULTS - EXAMPLES

In this section, we present a range of examples from our interviews, organized by the areas of the framework shown in Figure 2.

5.1 Copying artifacts – at most minor changes

For pedagogical purposes, instructors sometimes expect students to copy what they have given exactly. For example, the first time beginners compile and run their own program, instructor G gives them a correct program to type in: "Hello world. Here's how we go ahead and compile hello world." Providing code for students to copy literally allows them to focus on the mechanics of interacting

What is copied \ Copy level	Exact	Minor changes	Abstract
Artifact	*Hello world* (5.1)	*Given code for finding largest, find smallest* (5.1)	*Convert recursive code to iterative* (5.2)
Process	*Follow exact instructions* (5.3)	*Trace code line-by-line* (5.3)	*Approach to programming* (5.4)

Figure 2: Continuum of imitation. Examples are given in italics, numbers refer to section where discussed.

with an IDE or compiler without the added complexity of writing a syntactically correct program. Similarly, because there is so much to learn in the first weeks of programming, some code may be given to beginners to copy literally *for now*, with the promise of an explanation in the future. One example of this, taken from instructor D's Java course, is: `public static void main()`.

Asking for minor variations in code can be designed to make students think:

> *Instructor F:* [Y]ou show them a for loop that goes from one to ten, and then you ask them to do one that goes from one to twenty, say, and then you ask them to go from one to a variable ... instead of a fixed limit.

Given multiple examples such as these, this instructor hopes that students "see what elements repeat and what elements can vary", so they can imitate "visual patterns." Similar minor variations can be shown on other types of loops, if-statements, functions, classes, and so on.

If carefully designed, a sequence of examples can help students to see the difference between the invariants in code and what they can change:

> *Instructor F:* There is one way to do this is with multiple examples so [...] they can see what elements repeat and what elements can vary from one to another.

Somewhat more modification is required when students are given a method and asked to make it do a different (but fairly similar) task. One example involves searching in an array:

> *Instructor G:* I do give them a sample or a similar problem and say, hey, we found the largest one in the array. Now let's do one where you find the smallest one in the array.

Like the examples of for loops given above, these examples can be carefully sequenced. Later examples in the same sequence involves somewhat more challenging modifications like asking the student to find both the smallest and the largest item.

5.2 Copying artifacts – major changes

As students advance, they are able to make larger changes, or changes based on a more abstract understanding. Recursion is a topic that lends itself to copying based on a deeper level of understanding. Instructor C discusses how the pattern of base case and recursive calls are used in many examples - especially in linked lists: "You can do many variations on the same theme." In the teaching of this topic, instructor C makes a point of showing both the recursive and iterative solutions to many of the problems and notes that "It's good for thinking. Sometimes recursion is a good solution, sometimes it's not."

Sometimes copying code requires the student to recognize and abstract something across examples. Instructor F provides code and tasks with a recurring pattern, then asks the students to discern and use it: "I ask them to look at the pattern, run it, understand it, and then modify it to do something else."

5.3 Imitating process – at most minor changes

Sometimes students are asked to imitate a process exactly: the "Hello, world" task mentioned previously might include exact instruction on how to compile a file; students might be given step-by-step instructions to install an IDE.

Sometimes the instructor would like the student to be able to apply a process in a similar situation. Instructor D shows how to identify classes, objects, attributes in a problem text in lecture, expecting that students will learn the process.

> *Instructor D:* I put this under the document reader and get them to highlight, what they think objects, significant objects, the nouns and the verbs, basically. Then, to see if we can draw a little diagram together. [...] Then, we have this little diagram. [shows diagram modeling cars and a garage]

Later, during an assessment, the students are given a problem text involving dogs and kennels, and asked to copy the process.

> *Instructor D:* It's a different problem statement but the things that they have to do are exactly the same so they have to underline things and they have to draw a diagram at the end.

Another example is the process of "playing with code" as a way to read and understand it:

> *Instructor F:* They can look at [the screencasts] before class. It's me playing with a version of the code that they will see in the lab to illustrate something like, say, pointers.

In the lab, students are then given the code and asked to answer questions about it. Ideally, they will both understand the specific code they're given and learn something about how to read and understand code in the future.

Some processes are useful in gaining detailed understanding. Instructor G uses box and pointer diagrams as a way to illustrate what happens in memory:

> *Instructor G:* I drew boxes on the board. I labeled what the pointers were and I said okay, how many pointers do we have to reset? Let's number them and keep track of pointers that we are resetting. [...] and I know a lot of them do use the pictures to get an understanding of what their code is doing or should be doing.

Instructor E demonstrates in class how tracing code line-by-line can promote understanding.

> *Instructor E:* I'm trying to make a few points. One, understanding exactly what code does is the difference between a program that works and one that is broken. Understanding even your own code even when there's only two lines of it is nontrivial.

5.4 Imitate process, behavior, or attitude – major changes

Instructors reported demonstrating several processes beyond simple modifications that they hope their students will imitate.

Instructor G (among others) demonstrates the process of debugging with the hope that students will use a similar approach when searching for their own bugs:

> *Instructor G:* I also show them how to do debugging using the IDE [...] looking at variables and going through the code step by step.

Instructor G also teaches the students to comment out potentially problematic code:

> *Instructor G:* And so when a student comes and they can't figure out their code, and they're compiling and they're getting a whole bunch of errors, I tell them start commenting things out [...] And start with the first compilation error, fix that one [...] until you have something that at least the compiler is happy about.

Instructor F shows buggy code and goes through it systematically to find the bug, giving "an exemplar of a process" that the students can imitate.

In some cases, students are expected to imitate a process where high-level abstraction is needed. One example of that comes from an intermediate programming course involves implementing design patterns. In addition to going over the patterns, the instructor provides links to websites with sample code implementing those patterns. When asked whether he expects the students to copy the code examples, he replies:

> *Instructor F:* I would expect them more to look to abstract. So they have the abstract description, the pattern, then they have a concrete implementation which is the code, and I would really expect them to do is to look at the code and pull out an intermediate level abstraction.

This intermediate level abstraction can be used for two purposes: to guide the development of specific implementations, and to "help them understand the more abstract approach."

A goal of teaching is that the students learn the process of solving problems, rather than the solutions to specific problems.

Instructor E makes this explicit:

> *Instructor E:* Half the reason for doing these case studies is to try and explain to them what my thought process was as I went through the problem [...] hoping that they would follow a similar process to me.

Some educators take this further, into modelling an appropriate attitude to learning. An entire approach to learning is discussed by Instructor A:

> *Instructor A:* [Y]ou want to illustrate how you reason [...] 'Try this to see if, well it worked but then I ended up in this' so I have no problem in illustrating that it wasn't perhaps a good way of doing it, 'I must have another approach for solving this' [...] I think that I [exhibit] very little prestige and feel no need to prove something.

And instructor B discusses having an attitude of curiosity:

> *Instructor B:* "We would love to see them become curious enough that they really want to know how this method actually works."

6 DISCUSSION

In this paper we aim at shedding some light on the role of mimicry in computer science. The examples in Section 5 collectively illustrate the wide variety of ways in which instructors incorporate copying and imitation into their teaching.

6.1 Our results in context

We have organized our findings in a two-dimensional graph considering artifacts and process, ranging from copying exactly or with minor changes to abstract copying with major changes (as seen in Figure 2).

Copying artifacts: We find examples of literal copying and minor changes to code. These examples can be used to support novices' learning if the variation is carefully constructed so that what the teacher intends the students to learn is not disguised by too much variation. On the other hand, no variation, or too similar examples, can prevent learning rather than strengthen it. Variation Theory [19] presents patterns of variation which teachers can use as a tool box in the class room.

We also find examples where students copy code, but the changes are much deeper and students must abstract from given material. This includes examples such as when students are given code for one algorithm, and asked to write the code for a related algorithm. The students can follow the pattern of the first algorithm, but are still required to understand it in a much deeper manner to implement the second. Such examples are in line with Pattern-Oriented instruction [28] which builds on previous research on how knowledge is organized in memory.

Related to minor and abstract copying, instructor F discusses implicit and explicit mimicry. In implicit mimicry the instructor shows many examples, hoping that the students understand "the abstract concept of how does this work." The opposite is then when the instructor explicitly points to what is important in the examples. Previous research [19] shows that identifying what is important from many similar examples is very difficult. Explicit imitation is in this sense more efficient for learning than implicit imitation.

Imitating process: Examples include a wide range where students are expected to mimic processes which do not require any deeper understanding. These kinds of tasks are still common in computer science and the instructors reported a number of such examples ranging from nearly exact imitating, e.g., installing software, to mimic skills like tracing code. There exists a huge body of literature on how students learn these skills, for example, [9, 14, 16, 23]. The focus in previous research on how students learn these skills addresses how important mimicry is, even the more shallow form.

The most advanced examples of imitation are typically abstract and require a much deeper understanding. An example is provided by Instructor F, whose students are expected to learn design patterns by forming their own intermediate representations that bridge the design-pattern abstractions and the corresponding concrete implementations. Another example is when students imitate a problem solving process which usually entails many different parts that must be put together and requires reflection and thoughtfulness.

Other examples involve students being expected to mimic their instructor's behavior or attitudes, which can lead to identity, a sense of belonging, as discussed by Meyer and Land [26]. The overall goal is that our students will attain a deep level of understanding through mimicry.

6.2 Good and bad mimicry

Many previous studies report that mimicry does not support learning. For example in mathematics education research Lithner [15] writes, with reference to Hiebert [10], that there are "massive amounts of converging data" that claim negative effects of imitating given solution methods (p. 937). Dewey [5, p. 41] discusses positive and negative imitation writing that "imitation of ends ... is a superficial and transitory affair which leaves little effect upon disposition." "Imitation of ends" is in line with Lither's notion of "imitating given solution methods". Dewey, however, makes a distinction between imitation of ends and imitation of means which help to reach ends:

> Imitation of means of accomplishment is, on the other hand, an intelligent act. It involves close observation, and judicious selection of what will enable one to do better something which he already is trying to do.

When *is* mimicry beneficial for learning? The first observation from the data is that the educators in the present study as well the students in a former study [6] claim that they use mimicry in ways which seem to be in line with Dewey's description of "imitation of means".

The second observation is that few of the examples of mimicry described by the educators involve memorization and root learning. Mimicry in computer science seems to have less to do with memorization since most problems students encounter require understanding

The third observation from our data is that the educators describe their careful use of example code for students to mimic. Previous research points to the importance of carefully designed examples for students' learning [15, 27, 30]. Bransford's [3] results on the importance of "balance of specific examples and general principles" for transfer, is in line with how our educators explain how they use code examples in their teaching

Even though most of the examples of mimicry mentioned by the educators in the study support learning, we found that the educators also describe situations where mimicry is less helpful for students. An example of this, of course, is plagiarism, when the materials are not obtained from the instructor and typically little learning occurs. Other examples are where students imitate the wrong aspect of the educator's behaviour. Instructor F doesn't want to provide the students with a template for the lab reports to mindlessly fill in: "The problem with that is if I give them a template, they will imitate it, they will return the template. They will fill it in... I won't give them an example to imitate." The instructor wants the students "to understand what the requirements are and the structure is and then generate a document that is their own" and not to duplicate the surface appearance of the template. Thus avoiding types of mimicry that seem to be in line with surface learning [7].

The examples of mimicry we have identified in the present study are at different levels ranging from shallow to deep. This may be appropriate for students at different stages of their education. Verbatim copying may help novices to get started, while for more advanced students, it is the processes and behaviour of the educator which should be imitated. An example of the latter is students mimicking the educator when doing their own research. Generally the examples of abstract and deep mimicry, the right side of Figure 2, require mimicry with reflection and understanding, which is characteristic of deep learning.

7 CONCLUSIONS, IMPLICATIONS, AND FUTURE WORK

The major contribution of this paper is to identify copying, imitation, and mimicry as a topic worthy of investigation in computing education. We present examples to illustrate how educators use a wide variety of types of imitation to achieve pedagogical goals. Copying is not just plagiarism.

In addition, we present a framework for thinking about different types of mimicry: is the student copying code,imitating a process, or imitating an attitude? And in each case, is the copy exact, does it require major modifications, or is it somewhere in between?

This framework allows us to change the discussion around copying. Literal copying of code can be acceptable, but only in very limited cases. Copying code with extensive modifications is more likely to be acceptable, and the more advanced the students, the more modifications would be expected.

Imitating process, on the other hand, is much less controversial. Imitating blindly may lead to errors. For example, beginners attempting to speak the language of computing may talk about "if loops". But a student copying process is unlikely to be taken before a disciplinary board. If your students learn good object-oriented design, or skillful debugging strategies, or simply learn to love programming, does it matter whether they learn it from their instructor, or a more advanced student, or a YouTube video?

There is considerable future work to be done in this area. Some research questions include:

- What types of copying and imitation have instructors observed in their students?
- What is the students' perspective on, not just plagiarism, but the wider range of copying and imitation strategies?
- How can we communicate to students the positive value of certain types of copying and imitation while distinguishing the unacceptable types of copying?
- How can we move students from shallow to deeper forms of copying?
- What is the best approach to investigate imitation of process, which (unlike code imitation) does not leave a "trace" that can be examined?

8 ACKNOWLEDGMENTS

Thanks to Jonas Boustedt who worked with us initially and the instructors who took the time to meet with us.

REFERENCES

[1] J. Anderson, R. Farrell, and R. Sauers. 1984. Learning to program in LISP. *Cog. Sci.* 8, 2 (1984), 87–129.

[2] Jürgen Börstler, Marie Nordström, and James H. Paterson. 2011. On the Quality of Examples in Introductory Java Textbooks. *Trans. Comput. Educ.* 11, 1, Article 3 (Feb. 2011), 21 pages. http://doi.acm.org/10.1145/1921607.1921610

[3] J.D. Bransford, A.L. Brown, and R.R. Cocking. 2004. *How People Learn* (expanded edition ed.). National Academy Press.

[4] Barry J Cooper. 2004. The enigma of the Chinese learner. *Accounting Education* 13, 3 (2004), 289–310.

[5] John Dewey. 2004. *Democracy and education.* Courier Corporation.

[6] Anna Eckerdal, Robert McCartney, Jan Erik Moström, Kate Sanders, Lynda Thomas, and Carol Zander. 2007. From Limen to Lumen: Computing Students in Liminal Spaces. In *Proceedings of the Third International Workshop on Computing Education Research (ICER '07).* ACM, New York, NY, USA, 123–132. https://doi.org/10.1145/1288580.1288597

[7] Noel J Entwistle. 1991. Approaches to learning and perceptions of the learning environment. *Higher Education* 22, 3 (1991), 201–204.

[8] Kimmo Eriksson, Ola Helenius, and Andreas Ryve. 2018. Using TIMSS items to evaluate the effectiveness of different instructional practices. *Instructional Science* (2018), 1–18.

[9] Sue Fitzgerald, Gary Lewandowski, Renee McCauley, Laurie Murphy, Beth Simon, Lynda Thomas, and Carol Zander. 2008. Debugging: finding, fixing and flailing, a multi-institutional study of novice debuggers. *Computer Science Education* 18, 2 (2008), 93–116.

[10] J Hiebert. 2003. What research says about the NCTM Standards. I J. Kilpatrick, WG Martin, D. Schifter & National Council of Teachers of Mathematics.(red). *A research companion to Principles and standards for school mathematics* (2003).

[11] Janet Hughes and D Ramanee Peiris. 2006. ASSISTing CS1 students to learn: learning approaches and object-oriented programming. 38, 3 (2006), 275–279.

[12] David Kember. 2000. Misconceptions about the learning approaches, motivation, and study practices of Asian students. *Higher Education* 40 (2000), 99–121.

[13] E. Lahtinen, K. Ala-Mutka, and J. Ärvinen. 2005. A study of the difficulties of novice programmers. In *ITiCSE-05.* 14–18.

[14] Raymond Lister, Elizabeth S. Adams, Sue Fitzgerald, William Fone, John Hamer, Morten Lindholm, Robert McCartney, Jan Erik Moström, Kate Sanders, Otto Seppälä, Beth Simon, and Lynda Thomas. 2004. A Multi-national Study of Reading and Tracing Skills in Novice Programmers. In *Working Group Reports from ITiCSE on Innovation and Technology in Computer Science Education (ITiCSE-WGR '04).* ACM, New York, NY, USA, 119–150. https://doi.org/10.1145/1044550.1041673

[15] Johan Lithner. 2017. Principles for designing mathematical tasks that enhance imitative and creative reasoning. *ZDM* 49, 6 (2017), 937–949.

[16] Mike Lopez, Jacqueline Whalley, Phil Robbins, and Raymond Lister. 2008. Relationships Between Reading, Tracing and Writing Skills in Introductory Programming. In *Proceedings of the Fourth International Workshop on Computing Education Research (ICER '08).* ACM, New York, NY, USA, 101–112. https://doi.org/10.1145/1404520.1404531

[17] K. Malan and K. Halland. 2004. Examples that can do harm in learning programming. In *OOPSLA-04.* 83–87.

[18] Ference Marton. 2006. Sameness and difference in transfer. *The Journal of the Learning Sciences* 15, 4 (2006), 499–535.

[19] Ference Marton. 2015. *Necessary Conditions of Learning.* Routledge, New York & London.

[20] Ference Marton and Roger Säljö. 1976. On qualitative differences in learning: I–Outcome and process. *British journal of educational psychology* 46, 1 (1976), 4–11.

[21] Ference Marton, David Watkins, and Catherine Tang. 1997. Discontinuities and continuities in the experience of learning: An interview study of high-school students in Hong Kong. *Learning and instruction* 7, 1 (1997), 21–48.

[22] Philipp Mayring. 2000. Qualitative Content Analysis. *Forum Qualitative Sozialforschung / Forum: Qualitative Social Research* 1, 2 (2000). https://doi.org/10.17169/fqs-1.2.1089 Accessed March 16, 2019.

[23] Robert McCartney, Jonas Boustedt, Anna Eckerdal, Kate Sanders, and Carol Zander. 2013. Can First-year Students Program Yet?: A Study Revisited. In *Proceedings of the Ninth Annual International ACM Conference on International Computing Education Research (ICER '13).* ACM, New York, NY, USA, 91–98. https://doi.org/10.1145/2493394.2493412

[24] Robert McCartney, Anna Eckerdal, Jan Erik Moström, Kate Sanders, Lynda Thomas, and Carol Zander. 2010. Computing Students Learning Computing Informally. In *Proceedings of the 10th Koli Calling International Conference on Computing Education Research (Koli Calling '10).* ACM, New York, NY, USA, 43–48. https://doi.org/10.1145/1930464.1930470

[25] Robert McCartney, Anna Eckerdal, Jan Erik Mostrom, Kate Sanders, and Carol Zander. 2007. Successful Students' Strategies for Getting Unstuck. *SIGCSE Bull.* 39, 3 (June 2007), 156–160.

[26] Jan HF Meyer and Ray Land. 2005. Threshold concepts and troublesome knowledge (2): Epistemological considerations and a conceptual framework for teaching and learning. *Higher education* 49, 3 (2005), 373–388.

[27] Briana B. Morrison, Lauren E. Margulieux, and Mark Guzdial. 2015. Subgoals, Context, and Worked Examples in Learning Computing Problem Solving. In *ICER '15.* 21–29. http://doi.acm.org/10.1145/2787622.2787733

[28] Orna Muller. 2005. Pattern Oriented Instruction and the Enhancement of Analogical Reasoning. In *ICER '05.* 57–67. https://doi.org/10.1145/1089786.1089792

[29] Daniel Gil Pérez and Joaquin Martinez Torregrosa. 1983. A model for problem-solving in accordance with scientific methodology. *European Journal of Science Education* 5, 4 (1983), 447–455.

[30] P. Reimann and T.J. Schult. 1996. Turning examples into cases: acquiring knowledge structures for analogical problem solving. *Educ. Psychol.* 31, 2 (1996), 123–132.

[31] Lynda Thomas, Anna Eckerdal, Robert McCartney, Jan Erik Moström, Kate Sanders, and Carol Zander. 2014. Graduating students' designs: through a phenomenographic lens. In *Proceedings of the tenth annual conference on International computing education research.* ACM, 91–98.

[32] J.G. Trafton. 1994. *The contributions of studying examples and solving problems to skill acquisition.* Ph.D. Dissertation. Princeton University. https://search.proquest.com/docview/304138429?accountid=14784

Applying Case-Based Learning for a Postgraduate Software Architecture Course

Eng Lieh Ouh
School of Information Systems
Singapore Management University
elouh@smu.edu.sg

Yunghans Irawan
Institute of Systems Science
National University of Singapore
yirawan@nus.edu.sg

ABSTRACT

Software architecture remains a difficult subject for learners to grasp and for educators to teach given its level of abstraction. On the other hand, case-based learning (CBL) is a popular teaching approach used across disciplines especially in business, medicine and law where students work in groups apply their knowledge to solve real-world case studies, or scenarios using their reasoning skills and existing theoretical knowledge. In this paper, we provide how we apply case-based learning to address the challenge in teaching a postgraduate software architecture course. Our learners are postgraduate students taking a master's program in software engineering. We first describe our design of case-based learning for our software architecture course. We then analyse the survey ratings and learners' profile to evaluate the effectiveness of the proposed case-based design. These data are gathered from 9 class runs over a period of 8 years. Our analysis results show the effectiveness of our case-based design and significant relationships between this effectiveness to the learners' years of working experiences and the number of learners. Key contributions in this paper are our proposed case-based design for software architecture and the analysis findings.

KEYWORDS

Software architecture; curriculum design; case-based learning; pedagogical approach

ACM Reference format:

E. L. Ouh and Y. Irawan. 2019. Applying Case-Based Learning for a Postgraduate Software Architecture Course. In *Proceedings of ACM Annual Conference on Innovation and Technology in Computer Science Education (ITiCSE'19), July 15-17, 2019, Aberdeen, Scotland, UK.* ACM, NY, NY, USA. 6 pages. https://doi.org/10.1145/3304221.3319737

1 INTRODUCTION

In a software system, creating an architecture of a system comprises of designing the system's high-level building blocks within the user's environment that can exhibit the required non-functional qualities. These qualities of the system are determined by the design decisions made of an architect. The abstractness of architecture concepts poses a key challenge for learners to grasp and educators to teach.

Galster and Angelov noted in their work [1] that learners often find it challenging for them to appreciate the fuzziness of software architecture concepts and unable to switch their mindset from the concrete aspect of software programming and low-level software design to abstract architectural thinking. In addition to the vagueness of the concept of software architecture itself, Boer, Farenhorst and Vliet also commented in their work [2] that architecture problems are usually "wicked" and requires educational methodologies that deviate from the traditional active lecturer / passive student relation. For one who is used to writing code and compiles to get a deterministic result, the mindset of structuring components together in a diagram, justifying their key decisions with potential trade-offs without a concrete output and there is no one single perfect solution is a frustrating divergence from what they are doing. -

The skill set for one be a competent software architect is also multi-faceted which increase the level of difficulty of teaching it in a classroom environment. The role of a software architects entails one to have the following desired skills:

S1. *Technical skills to design and structure the software components from conceptual theoretical thinking to a practical digital solution.* Software architecture is the fundamental organisation of a system embodied in its components, their relationships to each other, and to the environment, and the principles guiding its design and evolution [1].

S2. *Analytical skills to evaluate the problems quickly, analyse the possible root causes and make significant design decisions for the project.* An architect who is unable to make significant design decisions (principles) on the components and their relationships in an environment where much is unknown is unlikely to succeed. "The life of a software architect is a long and rapid succession of suboptimal design decisions taken partly in the dark." [2].

S3. *Learning skills and motivation to keep up to date with the quickly evolving tools and technologies.* Though software architects do not need to be technology experts in all areas, it is essential that an architect is motivated to keeps abreast of the frequently changing technology trends and practices.

S4. *Effective communication skills to understand and negotiate project requirements with relevant stakeholders.* Specifically, an architect should have effective language skills, including

ITiCSE '19, July 15–17, 2019, Aberdeen, Scotland UK

ACM ISBN 978-1-4503-6301-3/19/07...$15.00 https://doi.org/10.1145/3304221.3319737

speaking, writing, and presentation abilities to address complex problems with a seemingly simple design that are easy to grasp.

The design of a software architecture course needs to incorporate elements that can effectively impart the above skills. Case-based learning's main traits are that a case is used to stimulate and underpin the acquisition of knowledge, skills, and attitudes. These cases present a disciplinary problem or problems for which students devise solutions under the guidance of the instructor. The following bullet points discuss the benefits of applying case-based learning (CBL) with respect to the desired skills of a software architect.

- (With respect to S1) CBL provides students with an opportunity to see theory in practice. This integration of knowledge and practice in real-world or authentic contexts expose students to viewpoints from multiple sources. Students can also see how a decision impact different participants, both positively and negatively.
- (With respect to S2) During the case discussion, students are required to analyse data and background information in order to reach a conclusion. Since many assignments are open-ended, students practice choosing appropriate analytic techniques as well.
- (With respect to S3) In the midst of searching answers to the case problems, students learn the importance of continuous learning to keep up to date with the solutions available. They will be motivated to search for new architectural styles and technologies for a better solution to the case problems.
- (With respect to S4) In CBL, students can develop communicative and collaborative skills along with content knowledge. In their effort to find solutions and reach decisions through discussions, students sort out factual data, articulate issues, reflect on their relevant experiences and draw conclusions they can relate to new situations. In the process, they acquire substantive knowledge and develop collaborative, and communication skills.

In this paper, we seek to investigate and validate the following two high-level research questions.

RQ1 How do we design case-based learning in software architecture for postgraduate students?

RQ2 How is the effectiveness of our case-based design for our group of learners to learn software architecture?

The rest of the paper is organised as follows: We first describe the related work in section 2. We seek to address RQ1 with our proposed case-based design in section 3 and our implementation of the case-based design in section 4. In section 5, we seek to address RQ2 by explaining our evaluation design followed by our evaluation analysis in section 6. Lastly, we explain the threats to validity in section 7 and conclude this paper in section 8.

2 RELATED WORK

Comparing Problem-Based Learning with Case-Based Learning: Effects of a Major Curricular Shift at Two Institutions: Srinivasan, Wilkes, Stevenson, Nguyen and Slavin in [3] describe their experiences in applying and comparing problem-based learning (PBL) and case-based learning (CBL) methods to the medical curriculum for students studying in two major academic medical centres. The results of their study show that learners and faculty overwhelmingly preferred guided inquiry-based of CBL over open inquiry-based of PBL for their medical curriculum. In our study, we seek to validate the effectiveness of applying CBL and the design elements of a case for a software architecture course.

Teaching adult learners on software architectural thinking skills: Ouh and Irawan [4] present their experiences to teach software architecture course to adult learners and the insights to applying both the case-based (CBL) and problem-based (PBL) methods. Their research shows that learners better appreciate the open inquiry aspect of PBL where they can learn from other learners' experiences and thinking within a short time span. PBL based approach, which does not have any pre-set goals and expected outcomes like CBL, tends to in a way works well with adult learners. On the other hand, there are also learners who appreciate the guided and structured aspects of the workshop based on the CBL method. They suspect that this difference may be due to the level of experiences of their adult learners. The learners' level of experiences of learners in their study on average is slightly higher as compared to the learners' level of experiences in our study. Besides the level of experiences, their study also compares and analyse the effectiveness of case-based learning against the other possible factors of the learner's profile.

Teaching Software Architecture to Undergraduate Students: Rupakheti and Chenoweth in [5] describe their experiences and learnings in teaching software architecture course to undergraduates. Their course design involves daily quizzes, homework, paper reviews and project work. They strongly favour a project-based version of teaching architecture, even at the undergraduate level. Ouh and Irawan [6] adopt an experiential risk learning model to design their software architecture course for undergraduates to address the challenges of teaching abstract software architecture concepts to undergraduates. The model comprises of activities to simulate risks that can happen in practical scenarios, and their role is to be able to recognise these risks, reflect on the causes and mitigate these risks.

3 PROPOSED CASE-BASED DESIGN FOR SOFTWARE ARCHITECTURE

One key artifact in case-based learning is the case, and an effective case design is essential to achieve the benefits of CBL. We review existing work in CBL and samples of software engineering case studies available in [7]. To the best of our knowledge, there is no existing work to discuss the design of a case for software architecture. In this section, we propose our case-based design for software architecture to address our first research question RQ1. We break down RQ1 into 2 specific sub-questions.

RQ1.1 What is the proposed case-based design for software architecture?

RQ1.2 How to conduct the case-based design for software architecture?

We will address RQ1.1 in this section in terms of case format, case conduct and required elements of a case. RQ1.2 will be discussed in the next section on the implementation of our case-based design.

The format of a case influences how to use it with the students and can be in the form of *bullet-cases, mini-cases and descriptive cases. Bullet-Cases* comprises of two or three sentences with a single teaching point, and students discuss them in small groups or individually. This format is used during the lectures and generally conducted in a short duration of 5-15 minutes. These cases enable the students to quickly review key concepts taught, analyse and discuss the potential problems. *Mini-Cases* are designed within a single class meeting and usually tightly focused, useful for helping students apply concept within a practical scenario. We use this format in workshops and usually incur a longer duration from 60 minutes to 2 hours. *Descriptive cases* are written up to 5 pages (1-2 paragraphs per page), and each page is disclosed to the student with discussion and development of learning goals and study questions for each part of the case. This type of cases is typically used for two or more class meetings. We use the descriptive cases for assessments where the students can review the case on a longer duration of days before giving their analysis and recommendations. The students can gain technical and analytical skills when they discuss the cases based on these formats. The descriptive cases also allow the students to learn from other sources due to the longer duration and less focused on a single concept.

The conduct of a case teaching can be in the form of *discussion, debate or public hearing*. *Discussion format* refers to the typical format when the instructor asks probing questions, and the students analyse the problem depicted in the story with clarity and brilliance. *Debate format* is well suited for cases where two diametrically opposed views are evident. *Public hearing* format is an ideal format to allow a variety of people to speak and different views to be expressed. The students can practice their communication and collaborative skills during the case conduct. We use discussion format for bullet-cases during lectures, discussion or debate formats for mini-cases during workshops and public hearing format for descriptive cases during assessments.

Based on the earlier discussion of desired skills of a software architect and a study by Clements, Kazman and Klein et al. [8] on the duties, skills and knowledge of software architects, the required elements (RE) of a case for software architecture involve:

RE1. Description of stakeholder and their requirements that require learners to investigate new architectural styles and the required components to support the style.

RE2. Description of business and technical environments, tools, technologies and other necessary components to enable the learner to describe an architecture in the form of architectural artifacts.

RE3. Description of constraints to enable the learners to reason their architectural decisions and justify the trade-offs among software qualities.

4 IMPLEMENTATIONS OF OUR CASE-BASED DESIGN FOR SOFTWARE ARCHITECTURE

In this section, we address RQ1.2 with a discussion of how we implement bullet-cases, mini-cases, and descriptive cases in lectures, workshops and assessments as shown in Table 1. We focus our cases in the typical architecture domains of the web, mobile, cloud and enterprise system architectures. We design these cases in a guided format for learners to be able to follow the steps to address specific issues identified in these cases.

4.1 Implementing Bullet-Cases in Lectures

Bullet-cases are good to discuss during a lecture for students to reflect on an important concept. We typically inject bullet cases after about 15-30 minutes of slides, which provide a good change in teaching style from passive slide-based lectures to discussion-based. Learners are typically grouped into small groups of 2-3 or individually to address the case questions.

As an example, after a lecture on ISO 25010 software qualities [9], which can be dry given the long list of software qualities, we introduce a bullet case where specific examples (e.g. online banking when one-time authentications or OTP are required) are discussed for the potential quality trade-offs and mitigation actions to minimize the trade-off. Using the same example of online banking, we highlight that the design for confidentiality trade-offs the usability of the system and can be mitigated if OTP is required only at certain transactions instead of at the login page. Students are also welcomed to give their own examples that they have experienced.

4.2 Implementing Mini-Cases in Workshops

For mini-cases, learners form larger groups of 4-5 and we use both the discussion and debate format. The learners are required to solve specific questions in these practical business cases, present and discuss with the class. The duration of the workshop can take between 60 minutes to 2 hours. Each group might be doing the same case or a different one. They are playing the role of an architect and have to address the stakeholders' concerns, played by other groups of learners in the class. We conduct a reflection session after the learners have presented which is vital for the learners to recap on their understandings and for instructors to ensure the learning outcomes are achieved.

An example of a case is a web/ mobile enterprise system integrated with some internet of things (IoT) devices that are monitoring the environment, which provides continuous environment updates such as haze and weather information. The learner's role is to design this enterprise system with efficient delivery of this information to the users in a timely manner. A point to ponder is the scalability of the design that is required to be handled situations when a large number of concurrent users are assessing the system during serious environmental conditions. We discuss the usage of caching instead of retrieving the data from the internal system to increase performance. Another case adopted is about a multi-tenant system to be built and deployed on the cloud. The learner's role is to review the requirements and designs on how to handle the multi-tenancy aspect of the system. There are design decisions and trade-offs for each of the multi-tenancy options that impact qualities. Points to ponder include the decisions of shared vs isolated designs. Deciding on a shared platform might ensure a lower cost but trade-off the security aspect. Deciding on a no-shared platform isolates the system in terms of security but at a more significant cost and maintenance for the service provider [10].

4.3 Implementing Descriptive Cases in Assessments

For descriptive cases used in assessments, learners form groups of 4-6 and we use the public hearing format. The learners are exposed to case studies that are of a broader scope and require them to make more decisions and produce more concrete architecture deliverables as in a real-life project. Each group analyse the case and provide their recommendations with justifications to the rest of the groups within 3-5 class sessions. Other groups are allowed to participate with questions during the public hearing session.

An example of a descriptive case being adopted in our course is when the learners are given a real-life integration case study, and they are required to address specific key issues on enterprise integration. In this case study, the company wishes to migrate its legacy mainframe system to a modern application architecture based on Java. During the migration phases, they wish to adopt an architecture also to migrate the subsystems integrated into the legacy system. The learner's role is to design the integration architecture for the migration of the subsystems. The learners are given the current architecture diagram and interface details of each subsystem and the legacy system with specific requirements such as minimum disruption to the subsystems. Points to ponder include the performance impact due to the additional layer of computation between the legacy system and subsystems when the learner designs an enterprise service bus (ESB) between the systems.

In another example of a descriptive case, we describe a case of a nationwide healthcare system designed with the objective to monitor students' health in primary, secondary and tertiary institutions. The learner is required to architect a distributed system that still addresses the security, performance, maintainability and scalability qualities. Decisions made on the architecture design can favour one of the qualities but likely trade-off another. For example, the learner will need to decide whether to first persist the healthcare data in the storage available in each institution during the screening process or directly access a centralised remote system to persist the data. Adopting the former can allow for better decoupling of the system but risk data inconsistency across all institutions. On the other hand, adopting the latter can achieve better maintainability of the architecture and data consistency but risks single point of failure (SPOF) at each institution. For each trade-off, the learners should be able to recommend mitigation actions. In the earlier case, the learners can propose redundancy designs to address SPOF.

We also change the style in certain classes to allow the teams to propose their own case. In this case, instructors evaluate these cases and inject specific questions to be addressed instead. This format helps the learners to be exposed to more variety of case studies but increase the difficulty for the instructors to have a standard rubric to assess their performance. We partially addressed this concern by incorporating feedbacks from other teams in the final assessments.

5 Evaluation of our Case-Based Design for Software Architecture

In this section, we seek to address our second research question RQ2. We break down RQ2 into 2 specific questions.

RQ2.1 Is our case-based design effective for our learners to learn software architecture?

RQ2.2 What are the factors in our learners' profile that impact the effectiveness of our case-based design?

We first describe our evaluation design, followed by an evaluation analysis to address RQ2.1 and RQ2.2. The evaluation of our case-based design is conducted over 9 class runs in 8 years for 386 postgraduate students taking a software architecture course with our proposed case-based design.

5.1 Evaluation Design

The learners are required to provide survey ratings based on a 5-point Likert scale to the following key survey questions:

(1) "Is the case-based sessions effective to learn software architecture?" with ratings of "1-Poor, 2-Unsatisfactory, 3-Satisfactory, 4-Good, 5-Excellent."

(2) "What is your expected grade for the case-based assessment?" with ratings of "1-F, 2-D, 3-C, 4-B, 5-A".

The survey ratings and information of the learners' profile are averaged out over the number of students in each course run. Table 2 shows these average ratings obtained from the first class in 2010 to the last class in 2017. There are two class runs in 2010 and one class run for the rest of the years.

We compile their profile based on their postgraduate admission data in terms of their years of working experiences, their basic degrees and their job domain. We categorised their basic degrees into 3 types - (1) IT-Related (e.g. Computer Science, Information Systems, and Information Technology), (2) Engineering (e.g. Electrical, Electronics Engineering) and (3) Non-IT/Engineering (e.g. Mathematics, Physics). In the column "Proportion of Learners with IT-Related Basic Degree" of Table 2, we show the percentage

Table 1. Implementation of Proposed Case-Based Design and Implementation

Case Type and Objective	Case Format	Case Conduct	Case Duration	Examples of a Case and its relationships to the required Case Required Elements
Bullet-Cases - Reinforce single teaching point	Discussion Format	Lectures	15-30 minutes	Discussion on ISO 25010 software qualities (RE3)
Mini-Cases – Apply focused concepts in a practical scenario	Discussion and Debate Formats	Workshops	60 minutes to 2 hours	Web / Mobile Architecture for a Government Agency (RE2, RE3) Multi-Tenant Cloud Architecture based on e-Commerce (RE2, RE3)
Descriptive Cases – Detailed scenarios to apply multiple concepts	Public Hearing Format	Assessments	3-5 class sessions	Distributed Architecture based on a Healthcare domain (RE1, RE2, RE3) Enterprise Integration Architecture based on Insurance domain (RE1, RE2, RE3)

of learners with a basic degree that is of IT-Related type per class run. We categorised the learner's job domain into 5 types - (1) Academic and Research, (2) Financial and Insurance, (3) Government and Medical, (4) Services and Product and (5) Others (Telecoms, Transport, Energy). Our workshop and assessment cases scenarios are based on domains of type (2) and (3). In the column "Proportion of Learners with Case-Related Job Domain" of Table 2, we show the percentage of learners with their job domains that match the domains in our case scenarios per class run.

6 Evaluation Analysis

We first explain the general trends of the survey results to address RQ2.1, followed by an analysis of these results to address RQ2.2. For RQ2.1, the effectiveness ratings for the case-based design are generally good and above (above 4) except for two years falling just below the good rating. These ratings are considered good in the 5-point scale for our department, giving us confidence that the learners are able to learn software architecture using the case-based design effectively. The expected grade rating is fairly consistent over the years ranging between 4 and 4.4 except for the year 2012 with 3.974 which is still very close to 4 (B grade). For improvements, we seek to find out the reasons for the drop of effectiveness in 2013 and 2017 by performing a correlation analysis (as shown in Table 3) between the survey ratings and the learner's profile to derive more insights to address RQ2.2. Following are the key takeaways:

- We realised that the learner's years of experiences are highly negatively co-related (-0.815) to the effectiveness of the case-based design. A regression analysis of the learners' experiences against the effectiveness also shows a statistically significant relationship with a p-value of 0.007 (<0.01). This result implies that with longer the years of working experiences, the effectiveness of our case-based design actually decreases. A possible qualitative explanation is due to the guided-inquiry aspect of our case design. For learners' with less working experiences, the case design with guided-inquiry discussions enable these learners to understand and apply the knowledge gained. However for learners' with longer years of working experiences, the case design with guided-inquiry discussion might not be as effective as these learners might already being exposed to similar case scenarios which limit what they can learn from these cases. A possible suggestion based on the study [4] is to adopt another teaching approach - Problem Based Learning with open-inquiry.
- The effectiveness of the case-based design is also negatively co-related (-0.721) with the total number of students. A regression analysis of the total number of students against the effectiveness also shows a statistically significant relationship with a p-value of 0.028 (<0.05). It might be good to hear views from diverse groups of students, but it can be ineffective when the number of students is too large, and some students are no longer involved in the discussions. One possible mitigation strategy is to assign each group to understand at least one other group and they are required to pose challenging questions to that group.
- The proportion of learners with IT-related basic degree is positively related (0.66) to the effectiveness of the case-based design. Although we expect this outcome, the co-relations are not as strong as expected with the regression analysis showing a p-value of 0.051 (>0.05). We also realised that many of these learners took other diplomas and certifications, which might have made their basic degree less relevant to the effectiveness of our case-based design.
- The proportion of learners with case-related job domain does not show significant co-relations (0.066) to the average effectiveness rating. Even though our cases primarily focus on domains of Financial and Insurance, Government and Medical, the decision to focus on these domains does not impact the effectiveness of the case-based design to learn software architecture. We believe the reason is that the learnings of our cases are to a certain extent generic enough to be applicable to many other domains.

Table 2. Survey ratings and Learners' Profile

Year/Run	Survey Ratings		Learners' Profile			
	Average Effectiveness Rating	Average Expected Grade	Years of Working Experience	Total Number of Learners	Proportion of Learners with IT-Related Basic Degree	Proportion of Learners with Case-Related Job Domain
2010 Run 1	4.265	4.317	5.47	34	73.33%	28.57%
2010 Run 2	4.244	4.333	4.36	41	66.67%	32.00%
2011 Run 3	4.212	3.974	5.30	41	68.75%	19.05%
2012 Run 4	4.255	4.304	5.45	47	77.27%	22.50%
2013 Run 5	3.977	4.386	6.26	44	54.76%	14.29%
2014 Run 6	4.27	4.243	4.80	37	61.54%	14.29%
2015 Run 7	4.152	4.25	5.86	46	54.17%	16.67%
2016 Run 8	4.14	4.43	5.86	37	68.00%	6.90%
2017 Run 9	3.9	4.4	6.69	59	57.50%	28.57%

Table 3. Relationships between Survey Ratings and Learners' Profile

	Average Effectiveness Rating	Average Expected Grade
Years of Working Experience	-0.815	0.199
Total Number of Learners	-0.721	0.191
Proportion of Learners with IT-Related Basic Degree	0.666	-0.169
Proportion of Learners with Case-Related Job Domain	0.066	0.004

- The average expected grade rating is not showing any significant co-relations to any of the factors in the learners' profile. A possible reason is that the expected grade is more related to their type of skills rather than the years of working experiences or basic degree or job domain. We realised that learners with prior job scope requiring them to make architectural design and decisions tends to be more confident of their performance when taking this course.

7 Threats to Validity

The learners' years of experiences and job domain obtained during their postgraduate admission might differ when they actually take the course. They can take this course in their first or second year and we adjust their years of experiences accordingly. Their job domain might also differ and we further verify and adjust accordingly against their LinkedIn profile if available.

Our findings are on the application of CBL with the guided-inquiry format in a postgraduate software architecture course. These findings remain to be validated in other course scenarios (e.g. software design, software testing) or other groups of learners (e.g. undergraduates) or other formats (e.g. open-inquiry).

8 Conclusion

Teaching software architecture to postgraduate students poses challenges due to its inherent level of abstraction. In this paper, we describe how we design case-based learning into our course to enable our postgraduate students to learn software architecture more effectively. This paper explains the benefits of applying case-based learning that corresponds well with the required skills of a software architect. We provide how we design our cases for software architecture and how we implement these cases in a postgraduate course over a period of 8 years.

We evaluate the effectiveness of our case-based design in software architecture based on survey ratings and analyse the relationships of the survey ratings to our learners' profile. Our survey ratings show that our proposed case-based design in software architecture is effective for our group of learners. Our analysis results show the learners' years of working experiences and the number of students have significant negative co-relationships to the effectiveness of the case-based design. On the other hand, the learners' job domain and basic degree do not have significant co-relationships with the effectiveness of the case-based design.

We hope that these findings can guide course designers to design case-based learning for courses with similar challenges and better understand the relationships of the learner's profile to the application of case-based learning. In our future work, we seek to compare and analysis our current case-based learning design with other design approaches and investigate across groups of adult learners including undergraduate and more experienced working adults to derive new insights.

REFERENCES

[1] M. Galster and S. Angelov, "What makes teaching software architecture difficult?" In IEEE/ACM International Conference on Software Engineering Companion (ICSE-C), 2016.

[2] R. C. d. Boer, R. Farenhorst and H. v. Vliet, "A community of learners approach to software architecture education." In 22nd Conference on Software Engineering Education and Training, 2009. CSEET '09, 2009.

[3] M. Srinivasan, M. Wilkes, F. Stevenson, T. Nguyen and S. Slavin, "Comparing problem-based learning with case-based learning: effects of a major curricular shift at two institutions." In Academic Medicine, 82(1), 74-82, 2007.

[4] E. L. Ouh and Y. Irawan, "Teaching Adult Learners on Software Architectural Thinking Skills." In Frontiers in Education, 2018.

[5] C. R. Rupakheti and S. V. Chenoweth, "Teaching software architecture to undergraduate students: an experience report." In IEEE/ACM 37th IEEE International Conference on Software Engineering (ICSE), 2015.

[6] E. L. Ouh and Y. Irawan, "Exploring Experiential Learning Model and Risk Management Process for an Undergraduate Software Architecture Course." In Frontiers in Education, 2018.

[7] V. Saini, P. Singh and A. Sureka, "Seabed:An open-source software engineering case-based learning database." In Computer Software and Applications Conference (COMPSAC), 2017 IEEE 41st Annual (Vol. 1, pp. 426-431). IEEE.

[8] P. Clements, R. Kazman, M. Klein, D. Devesh, S. Reddy and P. Verma, "The duties, skills, and knowledge of software architects." In Software Architecture, 2007. WICSA'07. The Working IEEE/IFIP Conference on (pp. 20-20). IEEE.

[9] "ISO/IEC 25010:2011 Systems and software engineering -- Systems and software Quality Requirements and Evaluation (SQuaRE) -- System and software quality models." 2011. [Online]. Available: https://www.iso.org/standard/35733.html.

[10] E. L. Ouh and S. Jarzabek, "An Adaptability-Driven Model and Tool for Analysis of Service Profitability." In International Conference on Advanced Information Systems Engineering. Springer, 2016.

Students' Misconceptions of Optimization Algorithms

J. Ángel Velázquez-Iturbide
Universidad Rey Juan Carlos
C/ Tulipán s/n, 28933 Móstoles, Madrid, Spain
angel.velazquez@urjc.es

ABSTRACT

There are ongoing efforts to identify students' misconceptions of computing topics, including algorithms. The paper addresses students' misconceptions of optimization problems and their corresponding algorithms. Optimization problems are an important class of problems in computer science, thus their associated misconceptions may form a relevant subset of misconceptions on algorithms. The findings presented are based on a number of evaluations conducted in past years. Assignment reports elaborated by students were used as primary materials for qualitative analysis. We present 8 misunderstandings, structured into 5 general themes. As it could be expected, some themes refer to optimization algorithms or to specific algorithm design techniques, but we also identified misconceptions of two more general themes, namely basic concepts of optimization, and basic concepts of problems and algorithms. We discuss implications of the findings for algorithm instruction and curricula.

CCS CONCEPTS

• Social and professional topics~Computer science education • Social and professional topics~Student assessment • Theory of computation~Algorithm design techniques

KEYWORDS: Computer science education; optimization problems; algorithm design techniques; students' misconceptions

ACM Reference format:

J. Ángel Velázquez-Iturbide. 2019. Students' misconceptions of optimization algorithms. In *Proceedings of the 24th Annual Conference on Innovation and Technology in Computer Science Education (ITiCSE'19). ACM, NY, NY, USA, 7 pages.* https://doi.org/10.1145/3304221.3319749

1 Introduction

There are ongoing efforts to identify students' misconceptions of computing topics [2]. Most research on students' misconceptions has been conducted in introductory programming [2]. However, a number of studies have contributed in recent years to misconceptions of algorithms. In particular, we find works reporting students' misconceptions of: algorithm analysis [6], sorting algorithms [16][18], greedy algorithms [20][21], dynamic programming [4][5][25], and computational complexity [7]. Some of these efforts yielded concept inventories [6]. Other studies report on other difficulties, such as students' attitude towards design [8] or correctness [13], but the focus of this paper is on knowledge.

According to constructivism, students receiving the same instruction may construct different mental models [1]. Therefore, we do not speak about correct mental models but about viable or unviable models, depending on whether they allow explaining and understanding the object of study. We may speak about conceptual errors or misconceptions to refer to key aspects of a mental model that make its viability difficult or impossible.

In this paper, we present students' misconceptions regarding algorithms for optimization problems. We stated and analyzed uncommon assignments which challenged students' shallow understanding of algorithmic concepts, producing cognitive conflicts to them [14][15]. Challenges come from placing activities at higher levels of Bloom's taxonomy (such as Apply or Evaluate) or of SOLO taxonomy (such as the relational level).

Focusing on optimization problems is not arbitrary. Many useful algorithms solve optimization problems, e.g. shortest paths in graphs. Many algorithm design techniques are used to solve optimization problems, e.g. the greedy technique. Finally, many theoretical results on computational complexity are established by means of optimization problems, e.g. the clique problem.

We classify our study as an experience report rather than as a research report because it was not the result of a planned research. In the academic years 2013/14, we introduced an assignment based on a new tool, called OptimEx [23], intended to experiment with optimality of algorithms. Although we thought it would be an easy assignment for students, we were surprised by the high number of unexpected mistakes. The next year, we introduced some minor corrections to remove potential sources of confusion, but results were unsatisfactory, again. We conducted a qualitative analysis of reports submitted by students and we found unexpected misconceptions and attitudes. In the following two academic years, we decided to analyze other assignments in order to obtain an enhanced understanding of students' misconceptions and to make didactic interventions.

The main contribution of the paper is a set of 8 misconceptions, grouped into 5 themes. Some misconceptions are of basic algorithmic or optimization concepts and others are of optimization algorithms or specific algorithm design techniques.

ITiCSE'19, July 15–17, 2019, Aberdeen, Scotland UK

ACM ISBN 978-1-4503-6301-3/19/07...$15.00
https://doi.org/10.1145/3304221.3319749

The list of misconceptions presented for each theme is not meant to be exhaustive of misconceptions on algorithmics.

We must warn that 2 (out of 8) misconceptions were *partially* reported in a past paper reporting the first evaluation [22]. The interest of including here both reported and unreported misconceptions is to give researchers and instructors as complete a set of misconceptions as possible. Furthermore, such misconceptions were stated in different terms, thus we present them here with the added value of reformulating them in the context of a more comprehensive understanding of students' difficulties.

The structure of the paper follows. In the following section, we present our evaluations, including educational context, materials, and analysis methods. In section 3, we present a number of misconceptions grouped into themes. The last section contains our conclusions and a short discussion.

2 Evaluation Setting

In this section, we present the course, the materials used for the analysis, and the analysis methodology. They are described in full detail in several technical reports available (in Spanish) at the following URL: http://www.lite.etsii.urjc.es/technical-reports/.

2.1 Course

The study was conducted in the "Advanced Algorithms" course, which is an elective course offered to senior students of the Computer Science Degree at Universidad Rey Juan Carlos. The course syllabus contains the following algorithm design techniques: the greedy technique, heuristic and approximate algorithms, backtracking, branch-and-bound, dynamic programming, and probabilistic algorithms. The "Advanced Algorithms" course builds on "Design and Analysis of Algorithms", a mandatory course offered to sophomore students.

2.2 Materials

Primary data were the reports elaborated by students for each assignment. The following procedure was used to solve each assignment:

1. The problem statement and any additional materials are available at the start of a 2-hour lab session. Students may address the assignment either individually or in pairs. The goal of a session is that students start solving the problem and may resolve any initial doubts.
2. Students must deliver their solutions in either 4 or 7 days, depending on the assignment difficulty. They must write a report following the instructions explained in a given outline. Typically, the sections of the report allow documenting design decisions, code, complexity analysis or experimental measures. Design decisions depend on the particular algorithm design technique, and usually are considered the most important part of the solution [10].
3. We grade the assignment a few days after the deadline. We communicate to students their grade and give them feedback about the weak parts of their solutions (and perhaps recommendations for improvement).
4. Students are given a new deadline to improve their solutions and submit a second report. The new submission is graded and feedback is given again. The second grade can be higher than the first one, but it cannot be the highest grade (i.e. grade A).

We analyzed both first and second submissions. However, we only present here the results of each first submission, given that the second submission often has the problems identified solved.

Table 1 shows the list of topics addressed in the assignments evaluated, the academic years when each evaluation was conducted, and the optimization problem addressed in each assignment. We assign fictitious numbers to the assignments for the current presentation.

The list of problems cited with acronyms in Table 1 follows: the activity selection problem (denoted AS) [3, ch. 16] [12, ch. 4], the weighted activity selection problem (WA) [12, ch. 6], the optimal office plan problem (OP) [12, p. 315], and the minimum-cost spanning-tree problem (Kruskal's algorithm, denoted K [3, ch. 5] [12, ch. 4]). Note that an important requirement to select an optimization problem for assignments 3 and 4 was that it should be solved by students with bounded effort using the algorithm design techniques addressed in the course.

Table 1: Assignments evaluated

Assignment	2013/14	2014/15	2015/16	2016/17
1: greedy			AS	K
2: backtracking, branch & bound			OP	OP
3: heuristic			OP	OP
4: comparison	WA	WA	OP	OP

Coding assignments vary from an assignment where hardly any restriction is placed on the target code (assignment 3) to an assignment where students must conform to a given coding scheme (assignment 1) to an assignment where the main emphasis is on the design decisions that underlie the resulting algorithms (assignment 2). Another assignment asks students to benchmark algorithms outcomes with respect to optimality (assignment 4). The OptimEx tool [23] supports generation of test cases and comparison of outcomes. A summary of the assignment statements follows.

1. Greedy technique. Greedy algorithms are often described assuming that input candidates are sorted according to a specific greedy criterion. For instance, Kruskal's algorithm is presented assuming that the graph is represented as an adjacency list, sorted in increasing order of arc length. However, this is a simplification, as the precondition of the problem specification does not state that input is sorted. Therefore, the given algorithm can only be considered as a working prototype, which does not fully satisfy the problem specification. In this assignment, students had to modify a given greedy algorithm based on sorted input data to handle the more realistic situation of non-sorted input data. In the given problem, input candidates were known in advance, thus

an efficient way of proceeding consisted in sorting candidates before the actual greedy process. However, the algorithm had to assure referential transparency, i.e. sorting could not produce side-effects, such as altering the contents of input data structures. See [19] for more details on this issue.

2. Backtracking and branch-and-bound techniques. Given an optimization problem, solve it by backtracking and then modify it to derive a branch-and-bound algorithm. Both algorithms must respectively include their most relevant design decisions: the search tree for backtracking, and a bounding function for branch-and-bound. For instance, the 0/1 knapsack problem can be solved with backtracking by using a permutation tree. In addition, it can be solved with branch-and-bound by using an upper bound based on the sum of the objects entered into the knapsack plus those not considered yet.
3. Heuristic algorithms. Given an informal description of several greedy criteria that can be used to solve heuristically a given optimization problem, code them and compare their relative outcomes with respect to optimality. In this assignment, we suggested for simplicity to code heuristics in a greedy style.
4. Comparing algorithms optimality. Given several alternative algorithms that solve a given optimization problem using different design techniques or design decisions, compare their outcomes with respect to optimality. Note that algorithms based on exact design techniques (such as backtracking or branch-and-bound) should always yield optimal values. However, heuristic algorithms will produce optimal or sub-optimal values, depending on the input data set.

As explained in the introduction, every evaluation was followed in the next academic year by an intervention intended to remove identified misconceptions. The nature of interventions depended on the kind of misconceptions identified, thus we sketch these interventions in Section 3, along with misconception findings.

2.3 Analysis Methodology

We conducted a qualitative content analysis of reports elaborated by students. We did not use predefined codes or categories. However, we used as guiding criteria to identify categories the features of solutions with respect to: underlying concepts, design technique elements, correctness, efficiency, and programming style. Therefore, our content analysis contains elements of the conventional and the directed approaches [11].

3 Results

We present variations on problematic issues found in students' reports. Note that each evaluation of an assignment was followed by an intervention next academic year, therefore it is common to have an increasing percentage of students performing better. Although interventions varied for the different design techniques, they typically consisted in additional lecture notes or worked examples, enhanced alignment between instruction and assignments, or reordering of assignments.

2.4.1 Assignment 1 – The greedy technique. In this assignment, students had to modify a given greedy algorithm that assumed that input candidates were sorted, and to develop a new version of the algorithm that assumed that candidates are unsorted. Input candidates (i.e. arrays) had to be sorted before proceeding with the greedy process. However, the algorithm was not allowed to modify the contents of input arrays as a side-effect of the algorithm.

Some students had a first difficulty in understanding the problem. The issues involved were explained as necessary until they were fully understood.

Modified algorithms were classified into six categories:

1. Correct algorithm.
2. Relatively inefficient algorithm. The student's algorithm contained unnecessary array declarations or array copies. Thus, it was logically correct, but it was relatively inefficient.
3. Faulty algorithm. The approach used to modify the given algorithm was correct, but severe faults were found in the code.
4. Algorithm with side-effects. The algorithm modified, as a side effect of sorting candidates, the contents of input arrays.
5. Inefficient algorithm. At each iteration, the algorithm searched for the next candidate in the unsorted array. As explained in lectures, this selection process is less efficient than a preliminary sorting phase followed by a traversal of the sorted array. Therefore, these students ignored that sorting is a coding design decision adequate for many greedy algorithms, as well as a part of the assignment statement (sorting was required).
6. Non-conformant algorithm. The student' solution did not conform to the assignment statement, typically by using different data types for parameters.

The second and third categories show relatively viable mental models. However, the two following categories exhibit severe misunderstandings of the solution, and the last category implies free interpretation (and, probably, hasty reading) of the assignment.

Table 2 shows the percentages of students in each category. Interventions consisted in stronger emphasis on this issue in lectures and development of worked examples. Most mistakes disappeared in the second academic year.

Table 2: Categories of modified greedy algorithms

Category	2015/16 (N=38)	2016/17 (N=29)
Correct	20 (53%)	24 (83%)
Inefficient	4 (10.5%)	2 (7%)
With faults	5 (13%)	1 (3%)
That alters	2 (5%)	1 (3%)
With no sorting	5 (13%)	0 (0%)
Non-conformant	2 (5%)	1 (3%)

2.4.2 Assignment 2 – Backtracking and branch-and-bound techniques. This assignment was a typical construction task, where students had to develop and document both a backtracking and a branch-and-bound algorithm for a minimization problem.

In previous years, we noticed that most students did not have major difficulties on developing a backtracking algorithm, but their explanations were unsatisfactory. Consequently, students were asked in the academic year 2015/16 to state the validity condition to be checked on partial solutions during the backtracking process. We may classify students' identification of checks as:

1. Correct.
2. Comparison between the value of a new complete solution and the best complete solution found so far. These students did not understand which check they had to identify.
3. Check on complete solutions. Note that backtracking algorithms often are efficient because validity is checked on partial solutions rather than on complete solutions. These students described an enumeration rather than a backtracking algorithm.
4. Problem precondition. Again, students misunderstood which check we were referring to.
5. No check identified.

Table 3 shows the frequency of these categories. In the academic year 2016/17, we stressed the different checks present in backtracking algorithms but we did not ask this issue again.

Table 3: Categories of validity checks in backtracking

Category	2015/16 (N=35)
Correct	17 (49%)
Comparison	5 (14%)
Complete	4 (11%)
Precondition	1 (3%)
No check	8 (23%)

We also noticed variation in the value of an initial, fictitious solution, which will be readily updated with the value of the first complete solution. We stated a minimization problem, thus the initial solution should have a very high value. Answers (N=30) can be classified into 5 categories:

1. Infinity, typically represented as the Java constant Integer.MAX_VALUE (10 reports: 33%).
2. A low, arbitrary value, e.g. -1 (8: 27%).
3. A high value computed from input data, e.g. sum of all the costs (5: 17%).
4. A high, arbitrary value, e.g. 1,000,000 (5: 17%).
5. A value computed from input data but that did not provide an upper bound, e.g. sum of some costs (1: 3%).
6. Other (1: 3%).

Note that categories 1 and 3 are valid answers. Category 4 is nearly correct. Category 2 presents an answer that would be correct for a maximization problem with positive benefits, but these students did not realize that a low value was not acceptable for a minimization problem.

We also asked students to declare the bounding function used in their branch-and-bound algorithms as well as its implementation. It was a minimization problem, therefore this function should define a lower bound. Declarations matched the following categories:

1. Correct definition.
2. Inefficient implementation. The bounding function declaration is correct, but it is computed from scratch for each partial solution.
3. Partially correct declaration. The bounding function makes sense, but it has significant deficiencies. The most common pitfall is not guaranteeing a lower bound.
4. Confusion of checks. Some students thought that comparing a new complete solution and the best solution found so far played the role of checking bounds.
5. Obscure declaration or implementation. It is given an obscure declaration of a bounding function, or an obscure implementation without an accompanying explanation.
6. No declaration.

Table 4 shows the frequency of these categories. Interventions consisted in explicit definition of bounding functions, including typical formats and worked examples.

Table 4: Categories of declarations of bounding functions

Category	2015/16 (N=34)	2016/17 (N=28)
Correct	3 (9%)	5 (18%)
Inefficient	1 (3%)	1 (4%)
Partially correct	8 (23.5%)	12 (43%)
Confusion of checks	20 (59%)	4 (14%)
Obscure	1 (3%)	3 (11%)
No declaration	1 (3%)	3 (11%)

2.4.3 Assignment 3 – Heuristic algorithms. In this assignment, a sketch of several greedy-like heuristic algorithms were given. Students had to code them and compare their outcomes.

Most students solved correctly the assignment in the academic year 2015/16, but we also found students who mixed up two issues: the greedy criterion and the cost to minimize. An intermediate category comprises students' contributions whose main design decisions are correct, but their implementation is convoluted. Table 5 shows the percentages of each category.

The intervention addressed consisted in including a revision of problem specifications in the introductory sessions of the course, with an emphasis on optimization problems. Lecture notes were also delivered to students.

Table 5: Categories of coding of heuristic algorithms

Category	2015/16 (N=37)	2016/17 (N=29)
Correct	28 (76%)	26 (90%)
Obscure	0 (0%)	3 (10%)
Incorrect	9 (24%)	0 (0%)

Given the confusion cited above, we asked in the academic year 2016/17 to decompose the problem specification into parts: precondition, post-condition (i.e. validity condition) and target function. Table 6 shows the number of parts correctly identified.

Table 6: Number of specification parts correctly identified (2016/17, N=29)

#parts	0	1	2	3
# (%) students	3 (10%)	4 (14%)	16 (55%)	6 (21%)

Most students identified the precondition, but they were unable to correctly identify the postcondition. In some cases, they just declared the return data type. It also was common to intermingle postcondition and target function. Even worse was the fact that some students stated different postconditions or target functions for the two algorithms suggested in the assignment statement.

2.4.4 Assignment 4 – Comparing algorithms optimality. Students had to run several algorithms that solved the same optimization problem and compare their outcomes. The algorithms either were given in the statement or had been constructed in previous assignments. If relative performance of algorithms was inconsistent with the predictions of theory, students had to analyze their algorithms, because it was a symptom of unnoticed bugs.

We identified three categories, based on report conclusions:

1. Correct solutions.
2. Partially correct solutions. Reports where students proposed a subset of exact algorithms.
3. Incorrect solutions. This category gathers two cases: reports where no algorithm is optimal in 100% of the test cases, and reports where some algorithms are identified as exact despite evidence that other algorithms have better optimality performance.

Many students with incorrect solutions did not notice that data gathered for some algorithms were inconsistent with their expected exactitude, according to the theory. Other students in this category noticed such a contradiction, but they did not attempt to find the source of error and fix it. (See [22] for additional details.)

Some minor interventions were made in the second year, such as revising the writing of the assignment statement, but the percentage of incorrect solutions remained very high. We considered that interpreting experimental results, and detecting and fixing the sources of error was more demanding for students than expected. Therefore, we addressed more drastic interventions. We enhanced our lecture notes and, most importantly, we trained students gradually in experimentation and interpretation of results.

In the following two years, students started comparing two heuristics algorithms in an early assignment (here, assignment 3). In the following assignments, students constructed new algorithms for the same problem using different design techniques, which were incrementally compared with algorithms developed in past assignments.

Table 7 shows the results obtained in the four academic years. For the last two years, the table only shows the results of comparing the two heuristic algorithms; subsequent submissions with additional algorithms performed increasingly better.

Table 7: Categories of comparison of algorithm optimality

Category	2013/14 (N=28)	2014/15 (N=29)	2015/16 (N=37)	2016/17 (N=29)
Correct	8 (29%)	15 (52%)	28 (76%)	26 (90%)
Partially correct	2 (7%)	0 (0%)	0 (0%)	3 (10%)
Incorrect	18 (64%)	14 (48%)	9 (24%)	0 (0%)

It also was remarkable ignorance of the difference between "optimum" and "optimal". Furthermore, optimality adjectives (optimum, optimal, maximum, minimum, etc.) were often used as comparative adjectives. In other words, they often claimed that a value or an algorithm was "more optimum" than another one.

3 Misconceptions

As a result of the analyses reported above, we identified 8 misconceptions. They state in general terms the specific findings reported above. Misconceptions often are not isolated but they can be grouped into 5 general topics or "themes" (using Zehra *et al.*'s terminology [25]). Presentation of misconceptions within themes makes more understandable the nature of students' difficulties.

Table 8 shows the relationship of misconceptions with the findings presented in the previous section for each assignment.

Table 8: Relationship assignments-misconceptions

Assignment	Misconceptions
1	4, 6
2	2, 3, 4, 7, 8
3	3, 4
4	1, 5

We briefly describe the misconceptions, as well as their specific manifestation in different assignments.

Theme 1 – Basic concepts of optimization.

1. Misunderstanding of basic concepts of order. Students had an intuitive understanding of these concepts, but they ignored more elaborate concepts, such as the difference between "optimum" and "optimal". This was also manifested in their incorrect use as comparative adjectives.
2. Misunderstanding of basic properties of order. In particular, many students are not aware of the existence of neutral elements for the max and min operations. A consequence was incorrect setting of initial values in backtracking or branch-and-bound algorithms, which either were inadequate for a minimization the target function, or were "magic numbers", or did not guarantee a lower bound.

Theme 2 – Basic concepts of problems and algorithms.

3. Misunderstanding of the parts of the specification of an optimization problem. This was manifested as inability to identify the parts of an informal statement of a problem (assignment 3), or as inability to identify the relation of the

different checks in backtracking or branch-and-bound algorithms with the parts of the specification (assignment 2).

4. Misunderstanding of the relation between specification (i.e. problem) and algorithm. When consistency was demanded between the precondition and the algorithm in assignment 1, some students did not realize that the heading of the algorithm was not altered. Furthermore, some students did not fully understand that the specification of a problem in functional terms does not allow side-effects. Confusion between specification and algorithm was also noted in assignment 2, where some students stated different post-conditions or target functions for alternative algorithms that solved the same problem. Finally, some students confused in assignment 3 the roles of target function (part of a problem specification) and greedy criterion (design decision specific of an algorithm).

Theme 3 – Optimization algorithms.

5. Misunderstanding of exact and inexact algorithms. An exact algorithm must optimally solve an optimization problem for all valid input data, while an inexact algorithm may yield optimal or suboptimal results for different input data. Misunderstanding this behavior resulted in inability to deduce from algorithm outcomes which ones were exact or inexact, and in inability to detect inconsistency, with respect to optimality, between outcomes gathered experimentally and outcomes expected for algorithms developed using specific design techniques.

Theme 4 – Greedy algorithms.

6. Misunderstanding of the design decisions underlying efficient implementation of greedy algorithms. As a consequence, some students did not implement the greedy algorithm for a problem where candidates were known in advance as an initial sorting and subsequent array traversal. Rather, they repeatedly searched the next candidate in each iteration of the greedy algorithm.

Theme 5 – Design techniques based on tree state spaces.

7. Confusion on the enumeration, backtracking and brand-and-bound techniques. It was manifested in incorrect identification of particular conditions to be checked in each technique.
8. Misunderstanding of bounds in branch-and-bound. This misunderstanding may refer to either their declaration, their role within the branch-and-bound algorithm, or their inefficient implementation. Need of a lower bound in a minimization problem, rather than an upper bound, was often not noticed.

4 Conclusions

We have presented 8 misconceptions concerning optimization problems and algorithms, integrated into 5 themes. In some cases, we were able to identify the alternative conceptions held by students, for instance, confusion of roles between specification and algorithm. However, in other cases we know students' faults without knowing students' conceptions, for instance, inability to deduce from experimental data which algorithms were exact or inexact. Knowing such alternative conceptions could shed light on how to build new, viable models from existing, unviable ones [17]. Despite ignorance of students' alternative models, didactic interventions aimed at removing misconceptions had positive effects.

Some findings are coherent with other studies. Thus, misunderstandings 1, 4 and 5 were also found in [20][21]. In those studies, students changed a problem specification to accommodate a situation to their preconception that a problem can optimally be solved by only one algorithm. Therefore, they had deficient understanding of basic optimization and algorithmic concepts. Students also were unable to interpret experimental results to identify optimal greedy algorithms.

The study has as a major limitation that it is not the result of a planned research (even though the instruments used for analysis were rigorous). Consequently, the misconceptions only represent a subset of actual students' misconceptions in algorithm courses. In particular, the misconceptions identified depend of the specific teaching approach adopted by the instructor and the problems assigned to students. However, an additional evidence in favor of the relevance of those misunderstandings reported is that they deal with issues which are not explicitly addressed in textbooks. Consequently, we should not be surprised by the fact that these issues are misunderstood by some students.

An unexpected finding was that half our misconceptions are about basic concepts of optimization (theme 1) or of problems and algorithms (theme 2). This finding suggests that more attention should be devoted to both topics in algorithm courses. On the optimization side, many textbooks contain preliminary mathematical material but it does not deal with optimization issues. Not even discrete mathematics courses address optimization topics. We suggest to accommodate these topics in the computing curriculum. On the programming side, algorithm textbooks emphasize efficiency issues, giving correctness issues for granted. However, these findings suggest that algorithm courses should devote more attention to correctness issues. In particular, students' use of terminology (misconception 1) shows that they understand optimality as a relative property, much in the same way as Kolikant described students' understanding of correctness [13].

In the future, we would like to develop a more exhaustive list of students' misconceptions of algorithms. This task can again be facilitated by the use of educational interactive tools (e.g. [24]). Furthermore, conceptual models should be enhanced in textbooks by explicitly addressing the issues identified in the study.

ACKNOWLEDGMENTS

This work was supported by research grants of the Ministry of Economy and Competitiveness (ref. TIN2015-66731-C2-1-R) and of the Regional Government of Madrid (ref. P2018/TCS-4307).

REFERENCES

[1] Ben-Ari, M. 2001. Constructivism in computer science education. Journal of Computers in Mathematics and Science Teaching 20, 1 (2001) 45-73. Available at http://www.editlib.org/p/8505/.

[2] Clancy, M. 2004. Misconceptions and attitudes that interfere with learning to program. In Computer Science Education Research, S. Fincher and M. Petre, Eds. Routledge, London, UK, 85-100.

[3] Cormen, T. H., Leiserson, C. E., Rivest, R. L., and Stein, C. 2009. Introduction to Algorithms, 3rd ed. MIT Press, Cambridge, MA.

[4] Danielsiek, H., Paul, W., and Vahrenhold, J. 2012. Detecting and understanding students' misconceptions related to algorithms and data structures. In Proc. 43rd Technical Symposium on Computer Science Education. SIGCSE 2012. ACM, New York, NY, 21-26. DOI= 10.1145/2157136.2157148.

[5] Enström, E., and Kann, V. 2017. Iteratively intervening with the "most difficult" topics of an algorithms and complexity course. ACM Trans. Computing Education 17, 1 (January 2017) article 4. DOI= 10.1145/3018109.

[6] Farghally, M. H., Koh, K. H., Ernst, J. V., Shaffer, C. A. 2017. Towards a concept inventory for algorithm analysis topics. In Proc. 2017 ACM SIGCSE Technical Symposium on Computer Science Education. SIGCSE'17. ACM, New York, NY, 207-212. DOI= 10.1145/3017680.3017756.

[7] Gal-Ezer, J., and Trakhtenbrot, M. 2016. Identification and addressing reduction-related misconceptions. Computer Science Education 26, 2-3 (2016) 89-103. DOI= 10.1080/08993408.2016.1171470.

[8] Ginat, D. 2007. Hasty design, futile patching and the elaboration of rigor. In Proc. 12th Annual Conference on Innovation and Technology in Computer Science Education. ITiCSE'07. ACM, New York, NY, 161-165. DOI= 10.1145/1268784.1268832.

[9] Glaser, B., and Strauss, A. 2011. The Discovery of Grounded Theory: Strategies for Qualitative Research. Aldine, Chicago, IL.

[10] Haberman, B., Averbuch, H., and Ginat, D. 2005. Is it really an algorithm – The need for explicit discourse. In Proc. 10th Annual Conference on Innovation and Technology in Computer Science Education. ITiCSE'05. ACM, New York, NY, 74-78. DOI= 10.1145/1067445.1067469.

[11] Hsieh, H.-F., Shannon, S. E. 2005. Three approaches to qualitative content analysis. Qualitative Health Research 15, 9 (November 2005) 1,277-1,288. DOI= 10.1177/1049732305276687.

[12] Kleinberg, J., and Tardos, É. 2006. Algorithm Design. Pearson Addison-Wesley, Boston, MA.

[13] Kolikant, Y.B-D. 2005. Students' alternative standards for correctness. In Proc. First International Workshop on Computing Education Research. ICER'05. ACM, New York, NY, 37–43. DOI= 10.1145/1089786.1089790

[14] Ma, L., Ferguson, J., Roper, M., Wood, M. 2011. Investigating and improving the models of programming concepts held by novice programmers. Computer Science Education 21, 1 (March 2011) 57-80.

[15] Moreno, A., Sutinen, E., Joy, M. 2014. Defining and evaluating conflictive animations for programming education: The case of Jeliot ConAn. In Proc. 2014 ACM SIGCSE Technical Symposium on Computer Science Education. SIGCSE'14. ACM, New York, NY, 629-634. DOI= 10.1145/538862.2538888.

[16] Simon, B., Chen, T-Y., Lewandowski, G., McCartney, R. and Sanders, K. 2006. Commonsense computing: What students know before we teach (Episode 1: sorting). In Proc. 2006 International Workshop on Computing Education Research. ICER'06. ACM, New York, NY, 29–40. DOI= 10.1145/1151588.1151594.

[17] Smith III, J.P., diSessa, A.A., and Roschelle, J. 1993-1994. Misconceptions reconceived: A constructivist analysis of knowledge in transition, The Journal of the Learning Sciences 3, 2 (1993-1994) 115-163.

[18] Taherkhani, A., Korhonen, A., and Malmi, L. 2012. Categorizing variations of student-implemented sorting algorithms. Computer Science Education 22, 2 (2012) 109–138. DOI= 10.1080/08993408.2012.692917.

[19] Velázquez-Iturbide, J. Á. 2011. The design and coding of greedy algorithms revisited. In Proc. 16th Annual Conference on Innovation and Technology in Computer Science Education. ITiCSE'11. ACM, New York, NY, 8-12. DOI= 10.1145/1999747.1999753.

[20] Velázquez-Iturbide, J. Á. 2013. An experimental method for the active learning of greedy algorithms. ACM Transactions on Computing Education 13, 4 (October 2013) article 18.

[21] Velázquez-Iturbide, J. Á. 2013. Identification and removal of misconceptions on optimization concepts underlying greedy algorithms. Journal of Research and Practice in Information Technology 45, 3/4 (August 2013) 203-217.

[22] Velázquez-Iturbide, J. Á. 2014. Difficulties, attitudes and misconceptions on experimenting with optimization algorithms. In Proc. 2014 International Symposium on Computers in Education. SIIE'14. IEEE Xplore, 17-22. DOI= 10.1109/SIIE.2014.7017698.

[23] Velázquez-Iturbide, J. Á. 2016. GreedEx and OptimEx: Two tools to experiment with optimization algorithms. International Journal of Engineering Education 32, 3 (2016) 1,097-1,106.

[24] Velázquez-Iturbide, J. Á., and Pérez-Carrasco, A. 2016. Systematic development of dynamic programming algorithms assisted by interactive visualization. In Proc. 21st Annual Conference on Innovation and Technology in Computer Science Education. ITiCSE'16. ACM, New York, NY, 71-76. DOI= 10.1145/2899415.2899450.

[25] Zehra, S., Ramanathan, A., Zhang, L.Y., Zingaro, D. 2018. Student misconceptions of dynamic programming. In Proc. 2018 ACM SIGCSE Technical Symposium on Computer Science Education. SIGCSE'18. ACM, New York, NY, 556-561. DOI= 10.1145/3159450.3159528.

AlgoBOWL: A Competition-Based Group Project for Algorithms Courses

Dinesh P. Mehta
Colorado School of Mines
Golden, CO, USA
dmehta@mines.edu

Jack Rosenthal
Colorado School of Mines
Golden, CO, USA
jrosenth@mines.edu

ABSTRACT

We describe a competition-based group project that has been in use in the Algorithms course at our institution each semester since 2012. The class is given an NP-hard optimization problem; each student group is asked to create a heuristic algorithm for the problem. The heuristic is run on a set of inputs (with each group supplying one input) and groups are ranked based on their aggregate performance within a specified time period. This paper describes our experience with this approach, including challenges, and our recent efforts to address these through a web application used to facilitate the competition.

ACM Reference Format:
Dinesh P. Mehta and Jack Rosenthal. 2019. AlgoBOWL: A Competition-Based Group Project for Algorithms Courses. In *Innovation and Technology in Computer Science Education (ITiCSE '19), July 15–17, 2019, Aberdeen, Scotland UK.* ACM, New York, NY, USA, 7 pages. https://doi.org/10.1145/3304221.3319761

1 INTRODUCTION

The 2013 "Curriculum Guidelines for Undergraduate Computer Science Programs" [13] developed by a Joint Task Force of ACM and the IEEE Computer Society describes the "Body of Knowledge" for Computer Science. The Body of Knowledge is described in terms of several Knowledge Areas, with the area most relevant to this paper being "Algorithms and Complexity (AL)." It emphasizes the importance of Algorithms in all of Computer Science stating that "Algorithms are essential in all advanced areas of computer science: artificial intelligence, databases, distributed computing, graphics, networking, operating systems, programming languages, security, and so on."

In this paper, we describe a competition-based group project that has been in use in the Algorithms course at our institution since 2012. The class is given an NP-hard optimization problem; each group is asked to create a heuristic algorithm for the problem. The heuristic is run on a set of inputs (with each group supplying one input) and groups are ranked based on their aggregate performance based on the quality of the solutions with respect to the optimization criterion. This task directly addresses the following language from the curriculum guidelines:

> An important part of computing is the ability to select algorithms appropriate to particular purposes and to apply them, recognizing the possibility that no suitable algorithm may exist.

The "possibility that no suitable algorithm may exist" is certainly applicable to NP-hard problems.

In addition, the project contains a significant testing/validation component with each group being required to verify the results of the other groups. More specifically, the project addresses several of the fine-grained learning objectives listed in the curriculum guidelines under AL as well as learning objectives associated with SDF (software development fundamentals), a few of which are listed below:

- Use a greedy approach to solve an appropriate problem and determine if the greedy rule chosen leads to an optimal solution.
- Use a heuristic approach to solve an appropriate problem.
- Explain the significance of NP-completeness.
- Apply a variety of strategies to the testing and debugging of simple programs.

This paper describes our experience with this approach, including challenges, and our recent efforts to address these through a web application used to facilitate the competition.

2 LITERATURE REVIEW

Enström et al. [8] identify dynamic programming and NP-completeness as being among the most difficult topics in an Algorithms course[1]. They emphasize the difficulty of NP-completeness reductions which they describe as "tasks [that] look similar but have a different purpose than in algorithm construction exercises." Among the activities designed to promote understanding, they propose an NP-Completeness Reduction Lab (also described in [7]), which is a programming assignment that asks students to implement a reduction as a programming exercise. The insight that NP-completeness proofs may be considered to be algorithms for pedagogical purposes is also made by Crescenzi[4], who describes the use of algorithm visualizations to aid understanding. Later Crescenzi et al. [5] describe interventions consisting of using both automatic program assessment and algorithm visualizations. Similar concerns with reductions and a variety of interventions ranging from interactive tutoring systems to student-produced videos to alternative definitions of the complexity classes are described elsewhere [10, 16, 17, 22, 24].

[1]This observation is consistent with this instructor's experience teaching Algorithms.

ITiCSE '19, July 15–17, 2019, Aberdeen, Scotland UK

ACM ISBN 978-1-4503-6301-3/19/07...$15.00
https://doi.org/10.1145/3304221.3319761

Khuri [15] describes a geometric approach to assist students to develop an understanding of P and NP problems that focuses on two specific problems. *Our paper instead focuses on what a practitioner might do if a problem turns out to be NP-complete.*

Although we are not aware of the use of Algorithms competitions (besides the well-known but substantially different ICPC competitions), the CS Ed literature describes the widespread use of competitions to achieve pedagogical objectives in software engineering and cybersecurity on one hand to helping improve diversity outcomes on the other [1–3, 9, 11, 12, 14, 21, 25].

3 BACKGROUND

"Algorithms" is a required course in our eight-semester undergraduate curriculum. Students are expected, but not required, to take the course in their sixth semester. Immediate prerequisites are our "Data Structures" (CS2) and Discrete Mathematics courses. Graduate students who have not previously taken an equivalent course are also required to take the course for graduate credit. Topics covered in the course include asymptotic analysis, data structures, sorting, unweighted and weighted graphs, dynamic programming, and NP-completeness. (Some of the material in asymptotic analysis, data structures and sorting is a review of concepts learned earlier in CS2, but a significant portion is devoted to advanced topics in these areas.) We have adopted a mixed model for teaching the course consisting of (i) traditional homework assignments and exams and (ii) four significant projects (contributing to 40% of the total grade), each of which includes a conceptual and an implementation component. While the specific content of the projects varies from one semester to the next, the theme remains the same. In general, Project 1 is to implement and measure run times for one exhaustive and one heuristic algorithm for an NP-hard optimization problem, Project 2 is AlgoBOWL (the subject of this paper), Project 3 is based on dynamic programming, and Project 4 requires students to solve a non-trivial Maze problem using graph algorithms.

Projects 1 and 4 are individual projects, while Projects 2 and 3 are group projects, with three students per group. To ensure that students are motivated to contribute substantially to their group projects, the grading rubric consists of two components to evaluate group projects. The first is a score assigned by the instructor that is based on the quality of the work. The second is based on effort percentages based on each member's contribution and as reported by the students. If there is a significant discrepancy in the group's self-assessment or if there is reason to believe that it is not accurate, the instructor reserves the right to allocate effort percentages based on an interview with the students. This approach is similar to the "bonus money" idea in [23]. An alternative approach to assigning grades in a programming project is to assign an individual student credit if his/her module works [6]. This is not feasible in Algorithms as a significant portion of the activity is conceptual.

4 ALGOBOWL OVERVIEW

The basic process of AlgoBOWL (see Figure 1) can be seen from the students group's perspective as: (1) creating an input that you think will stress the other groups' optimization algorithms, (2) running your optimization algorithm on all of the other groups' inputs and submitting all of the outputs, and finally (3) verifying all of the other groups' outputs to your input.

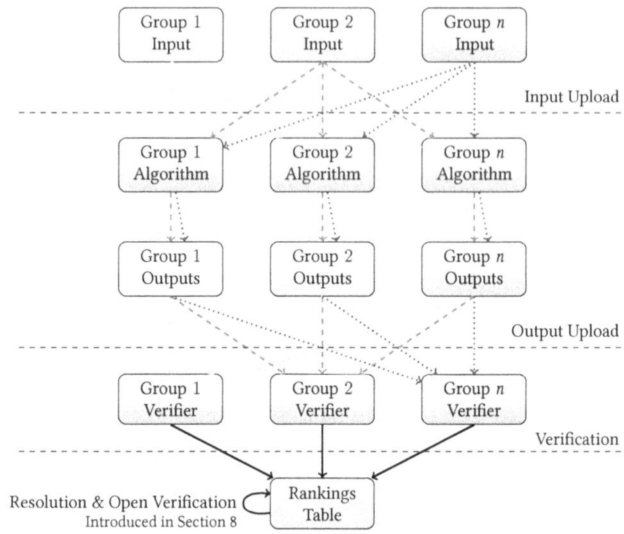

Figure 1: AlgoBOWL stages

The verified results are used to create a ranking table.

5 EXAMPLE OF AN ALGOBOWL PROBLEM

Your input is a weighted undirected graph G with an even number of vertices and a set of edges connecting pairs of distinct vertices. The objective is to design an algorithm that splits the vertices into two sets of *equal* size so that the sum of the weights of edges crossing between vertices in different sets is minimized.

Input Format:

The input will be provided in a file in the following format: the first line contains two integers: the first denotes n, the number of vertices and the second denotes m, the number of edges in the graph (n should be even). The vertices of the graph may then be denoted by integers in the range $[1, n]$. Each subsequent line in the graph denotes an edge in the graph followed by its weight.

```
6 8
1 3 1
1 4 1
1 6 1
2 3 1
2 5 1
3 5 1
4 6 1
5 6 1
```

The input above describes a graph with six vertices labeled 1 through 6, and eight undirected edges, each with a weight of one. The first of these edges joins vertices 1 and 3. The resulting graph is shown in Figure 2. Observe that a split of ({1,4,6}, {2,3,5}) results in weight 2, whereas a split of ({1,2,3}, {4,5,6}) results in weight 4, making the first split superior to the second.

Input Restrictions: No input will contain more than 1,000 vertices and 100,000 edges. Edge weights are integers in [1,50].

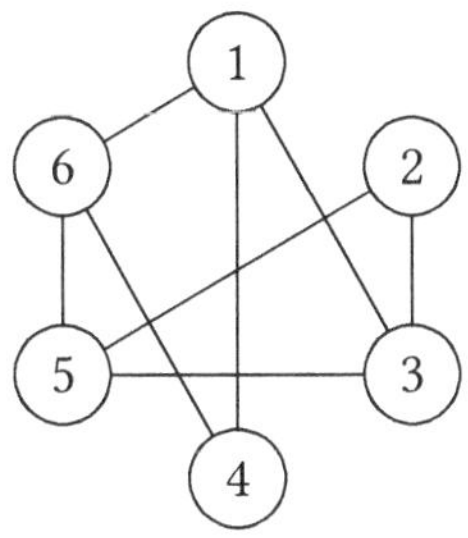

Figure 2: Example

Output Format: Line 1 of your output will contain the weight of your solution. Line 2 will contain vertex IDs assigned to the first set and Line 3 will contain vertex IDs assigned to the second set. To illustrate, the output for the second split in the example is

```
4
1 2 3
4 5 6
```

6 PEDAGOGICAL CONSIDERATIONS

(1) [Scaffolding] Prior to AlgoBOWL in our algorithms course, students have already implemented one exhaustive and one suboptimal greedy heuristic to the NP-hard TSP optimization problem. Related class discussions and worksheets on counterexamples and inputs resulting in suboptimal solutions provide additional scaffolding. Material on advanced heuristic searches such as random restart and simulated annealing is made available for groups wanting to go the extra mile.

(2) [Awareness of NP-Completeness] An algorithms course typically emphasizes problems that have polynomial-time solutions, and describes the many techniques for developing algorithms (e.g., greedy, divide and conquer, dynamic programming, etc). This leaves students with the impression that most problems are tractable within the universe of all algorithmic problems. However, there are arguably more intractable problems than tractable ones. AlgoBOWL creates awareness of this phenomenon.

(3) [NP-complete problems can be solved] In a traditional introduction to NP-completeness presented by many algorithms courses, students are left with the impression that NP-completeness is a "death sentence" in terms of their ability to solve a problem. Although NP-completeness implies that there is not a polynomial-time solution, there are in fact numerous techniques available to cope with NP-completeness such as heuristics, approximation algorithms, stochastic optimization and mathematical programming. These are typically not covered in an introductory Algorithms course, however. AlgoBOWL demonstrates that one *can* obtain near-optimal solutions to most instances with relatively little effort.

(4) [Certifying Verifiable Algorithms] Each group provides an output that not only includes the value of the quantity to be optimized, but also the solution that results in that value, allowing the verifying group to confirm correctness. This reinforces the value of software testing as an integral part of the software development process. In addition, it is an example of a *certifying algorithm* [18]:

> "A certifying algorithm is an algorithm that produces, with each output, a certificate or witness (easy-to-verify proof) that the particular output has not been compromised by a bug."

(5) [The NP Class] The notion of a fast (and relatively easy) verification algorithm also loosely introduces the concept of NP. Recall that a problem is in NP if, given a certificate, it can be verified in polynomial time. The verification process used in AlgoBOWL approximates this concept.

(6) [Benchmarking] Each group's algorithm is run on multiple (typically 15-20) inputs. It is possible that Algorithm A performs better than Algorithm B on Input 1, but worse on Input 2. We have developed a ranking scheme that determines the aggregate performance of the algorithm. In the excitement of the competition, students end up internalizing the benchmarking process we're using. This understanding is applicable to other areas of CS such as benchmarking processors (e.g., [20]).

(7) [Group Activity] AlgoBOWL is a group project with groups formed using the approach described in [19]. Students accordingly receive the well-known benefits of group projects: task allocation, communication, peer evaluation.

(8) [Applicability] The competitive nature of the AlgoBOWL project may be viewed as a microcosm of industry and academic research. Industry and academic research groups are often in an implicit or explicit competition with each other to produce better algorithms, software and products in a limited amount of time. AlgoBOWL provides students with this experience.

(9) [Constructive vs. Search Heuristics] Broadly, students must choose from two types of techniques for their AlgoBOWL implementations: (1) a constructive heuristic, typically as a greedy algorithm, or (2) a local search technique, such as simulated annealing. Based on our observations, groups utilizing local search techniques generally perform better in the competition. While this is well known in the research community, it is not as well known among undergraduate students. AlgoBOWL helps students develop this insight.

(10) [Fun!] Above all, our (anecdotal) experience is that students enjoy AlgoBOWL. The competition motivates team members to work together and perform well without creating an overly stressful atmosphere. There is a small component (15%) of the grade that depends on the algorithm's aggregate performance, with the bulk (85%) being assigned to the correct and timely completion of the various AlgoBOWL steps. This results in relatively healthy competition. Our department gives students belonging to the winning team a small cash award and recognizes them at an annual departmental event with our industrial partners. [2]

[2] One of the co-authors of this paper is a former undergraduate who participated in and enjoyed the competition and was excited to develop the AlgoBOWL software as his Masters project.

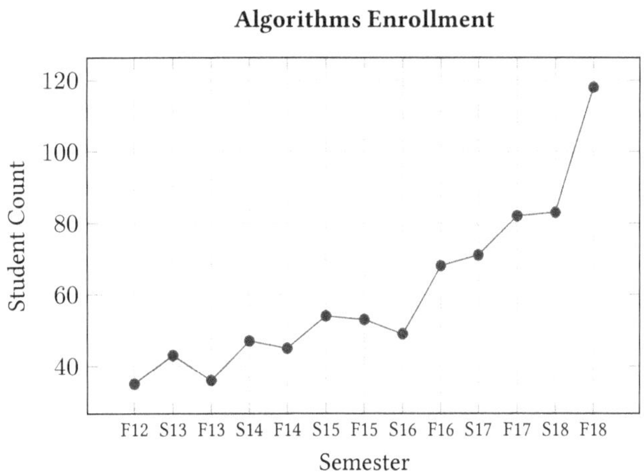

Figure 3: Increasing class sizes led to difficulty in managing the competition.

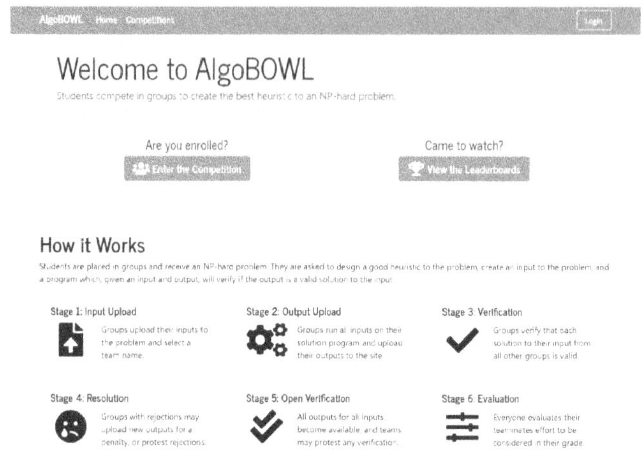

Figure 4: AlgoBOWL landing page explains competition stages and gives visitors a link for to view the rankings.

7 CHALLENGES

The original version of AlgoBOWL consisted of only three stages: each group (1) shares their input with all the other groups, (2) produces outputs for all of the inputs, and finally, (3) verifies the correctness of each output to their input.

While this model is simple, two underlying issues became apparent: (1) students were not creating inputs which matched the specification in the problem statement, resulting in havoc later on, and (2) students had little incentive to verify correctly, resulting in many false-positive or false-negative verifications.

In order to mitigate these issues, well-defined time barriers between the stages were not enforced, often resulting in race conditions. For example, one group may share their input, another group starts producing an output, and the first group changes their input. As a further mitigation technique, the competition was originally held with everyone in the same computer lab over the time span of an hour or two. As class sizes increased (shown in Figure 3), this was no longer possible, and the competition moved to an online format, making many of the issues detrimental to the competition.

Our recent work includes the development of two new stages in the competition, addressing both of the underlying issues. In addition, we developed a web application to facilitate the competition with well-defined time barriers, and allowing students to participate from wherever they wish.

8 NEW STAGES AND SOFTWARE

Our newly developed web application is open source and written in Python using the TurboGears framework. We designed the application to make the competition sustainable for the next generation of computer science students. Using our web application, instructors can:

- Run multiple competitions simultaneously, which is particularly useful if there are multiple course sections.
- Provide a rankings table which is visible to others in the department who are interested in watching the competition.
- Optionally, provide input and output verification scripts as a mechanism to ensure the students are verifying correctly, and if a different competition format is desired, can replace the student verification mechanism entirely. Additionally, this mechanism can be used to automate student protests in the Resolution and Open Verification stages.
- Customize site logins to use university single sign on, for example, with Shibboleth, or implement a custom authentication system using our extension interface.

With the added stages to the competition, a clean and simple interface is necessary to help students understand the project. The only stage that is shown at a given time is the current stage, so the student only ever needs to worry about performing one action at a time. This prevents the race conditions described previously. Each stage is live for a predetermined period of time (typically 24 hours) before moving on to the next stage.

8.1 Input Upload Stage

During the input upload stage, students upload their input files and decide upon a group name. If the instructor desires, they may create group names rather than let students choose, or even auto-assign random group names from a provided set (e.g., animals). With the instructor's input verification script, invalid inputs are prevented from being uploaded. This avoids the issue of invalid input sharing described in Section 7.

8.2 Output Upload Stage

After the input upload stage ends, groups may begin downloading the inputs from other groups and running their heuristic program on the inputs. When their program provides results, they may begin uploading their outputs for each input on the site. Currently, the competition does not consider algorithm run time with the ranking based on quality of the output. However, each group's algorithm must be fast enough to compute the output for every other group during the output upload stage (i.e., the algorithm should be able to process 15-25 inputs in a 24-hour period).

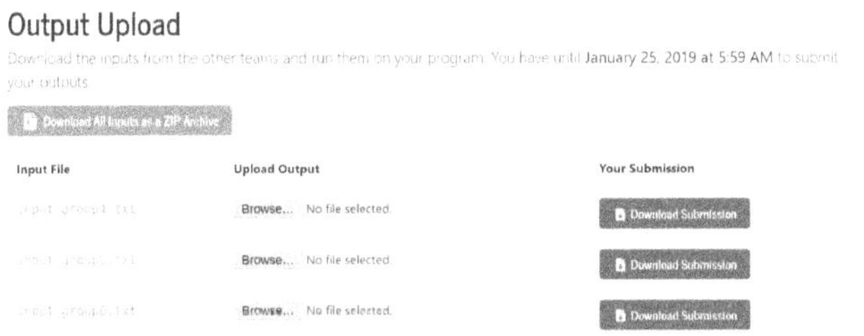

Figure 5: Students provide outputs to each input during the Output Upload Stage. As a convenience, they may download all outputs at once as a compressed ZIP folder.

This interface is shown in Figure 5.

As outputs start being uploaded, the instructors may view the results of their verification program on their private rankings table. These verification results are hidden from students, as it is the students' job to provide this data later on. The students only see the unverified rankings table fill in as groups upload outputs. If the instructor chooses to run the competition without verification stages (which may be desired for a simpler and shorter competition), these results are made available immediately to the students.

8.3 Verification Stage

During the verification stage, students are asked to download the outputs provided by other groups *for their input only*. They use their verification program to determine if the output is valid based on the specification provided in the problem statement, and mark on the web application whether they believe the output is correct or not. As the students put in their verifications using the interface shown in Figure 6, the rankings table begins to show which outputs were accepted or rejected, shown in Figure 7.

Figure 6: During the verification stage, each group either accepts or rejects each output to their input.

8.4 Resolution Stage

The purpose of the resolution stage, shown in Figure 8, is two-fold:

(1) To give students with rejected outputs a second chance to submit a new output, with a mechanism that is fair to the other students in the competition.
(2) To allow students with rejected outputs the opportunity to claim the rejection was incorrect using a *protest* mechanism.

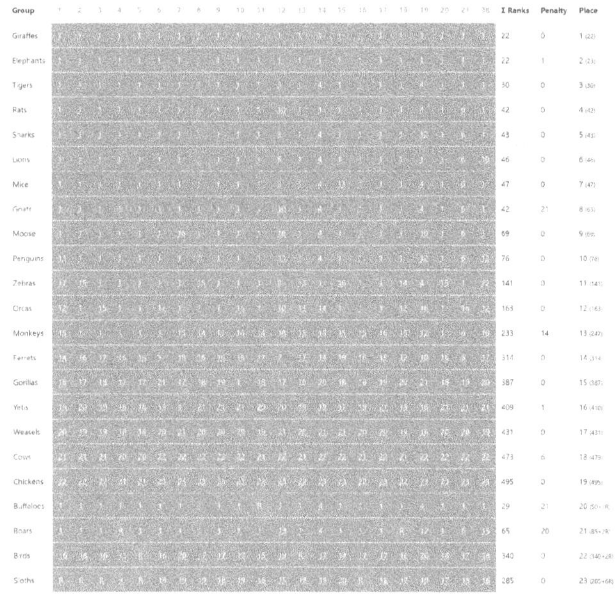

Figure 7: The rankings table, after all verifications have been submitted.

Students with rejected outputs may only choose one action. That is, they may only protest or re-upload, but not both. In either case, the new verification is done by the instructor or their verification script. To make the competition fair to groups who uploaded correct outputs the first time, groups who re-upload will have their rank in the rankings table penalized. The penalty does not affect groups who protest successfully.

There remains the case where a student may know their output should have been rejected, but instead it was accepted. For example, if their heuristic program created a mistake across all outputs, and one group decided to verify as correct. In this case, the student is allowed to re-upload (and it will be to their advantage to re-upload) an accepted output, as there will be no chance to re-upload if the group waits for open verification.

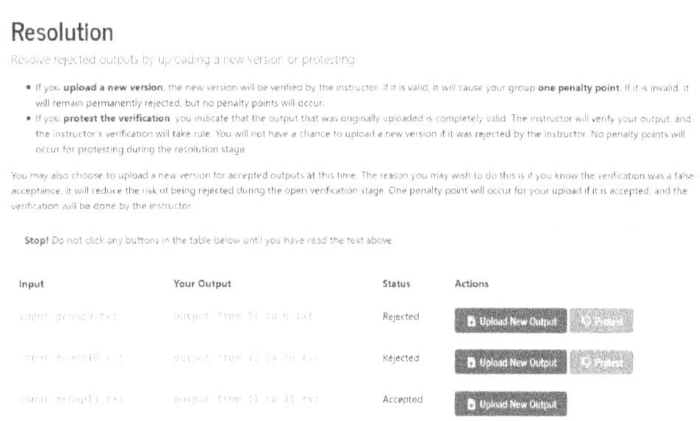

Figure 8: The resolution interface makes clear to groups with rejected outputs what their choices are.

8.5 Open Verification Stage

During open verification, all inputs and outputs become available for everyone to view. No re-uploading is allowed at this point. Any group which suspects an issue with any verification may submit a protest, requesting the instructor to verify. To discourage frivolous protests, a penalty is assessed if a group incorrectly protests another group's output. The purpose of this stage is to:

(1) Encourage groups with an accepted output they know is incorrect to re-upload during the resolution stage.
(2) Make the competition outcomes transparent to the students.

If the competition has progressed well, we expect very few protests during this time. When students know that the competition will be made fully transparent, they will take pains to ensure that their verifications are correct. This is shown to be true in Section 9.

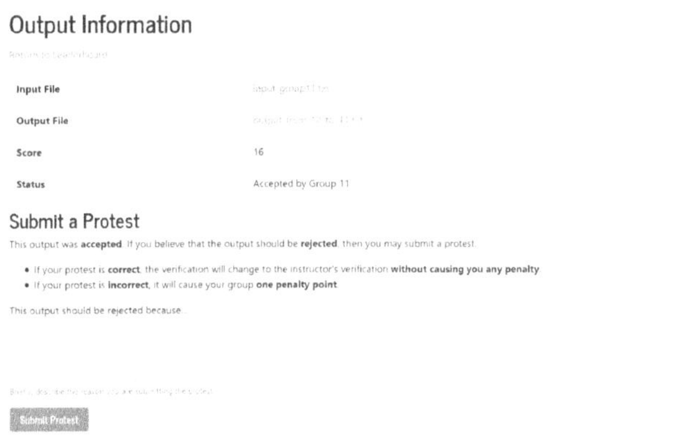

Figure 9: During open verification, all students may see the outputs for every input, and submit protests if they believe verifications to be incorrect.

8.6 Evaluation and Grading

As explained in Section 3, students are requested to submit the relative effort contribution percentages of each of their group members, including themselves. Our web application prompts the students to submit evaluations when the competition has ended using the interface shown in Figure 10.

To help ease grading on the instructor, AlgoBOWL provides an auto-generated grading table with adjustable equations, like the one shown in Figure 11. A group grade is determined based off of verification accuracy, the number of unique output scores to the submitted input, output acceptance rate, and the overall ranking in the competition. The evaluation data submitted by the students is automatically taken into account, and the group grade is multiplied by the corresponding evaluation multiplier to create the grade for each student. The application will highlight cases of evaluation data with large inequality, and the instructor should review these cases manually to assign an appropriate grade.

9 RESULTS

With the increasing class sizes shown in Figure 3, the introduction of our software and the new stages provided relief to the issues

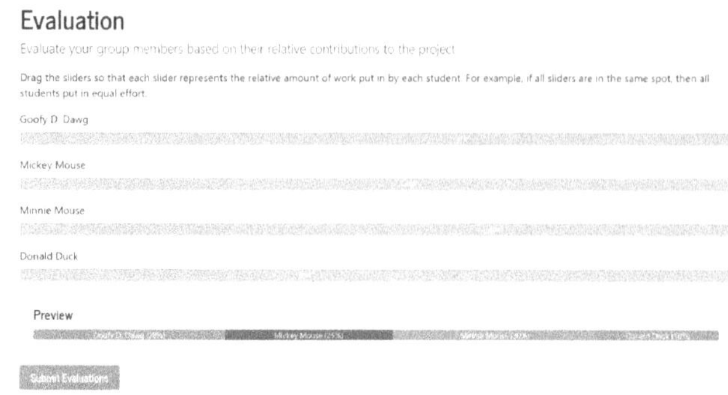

Figure 10: Student evaluation interface: dragging the sliders above scales the percentages submitted, shown in the preview below the sliders.

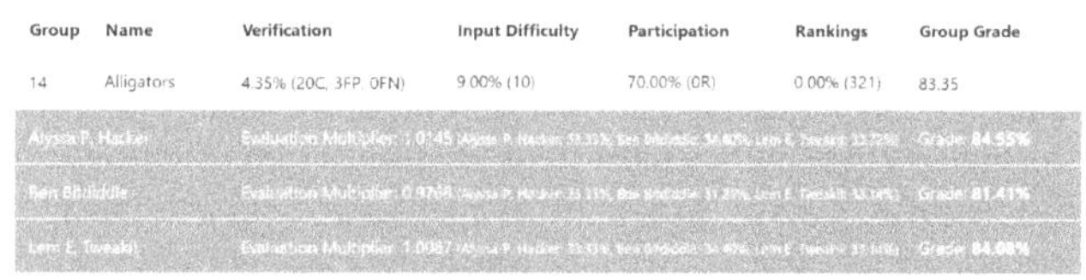

Figure 11: Grading table shown to instructor: equations used to create the group grade are adjustable by the instructor.

discussed in Section 7. This can be seen by comparing verification accuracy from Spring 2018 semester (prior to the new stages and software) to Fall 2018 semester (after the improvements) in Table 1.

Table 1: AlgoBOWL before and after the new stages/software

	Spring 2018	Fall 2018
Students Enrolled	83	118
Groups	23	38
Initial Verification Accuracy (before *resolution*, for Fall 2018)	82%	95%
Post-Resolution Verif. Accuracy	*n/a*	100%
Open Verification Protests	*n/a*	0

10 CONCLUSION

Although we have not studied AlgoBOWL formally as a pedagogical technique (e.g., by using control groups), we have high confidence that it provides the pedagogical benefits listed in Section 6 because it exposes students to ideas they were just not previously exposed to in a traditional offering of the course. AlgoBOWL has a lasting impact on students. While students might forget specific algorithms discussed in class, conversations with alumni indicate they don't forget AlgoBOWL and the lessons learned. The recent web-based software infrastructure has greatly improved the administration of the competition and improved its scalability in the face of exploding enrollments. Our project and software system is available for other algorithms instructors for deployment in their course: interested instructors should contact us for more information.

REFERENCES

[1] Arnold, J., Bort, H., Naugle, R., O'Hare, C., and Brylow, D. Multi-track programming competitions with scratch. In *Proceedings of the 47th ACM Technical Symposium on Computing Science Education* (New York, NY, USA, 2016), SIGCSE '16, ACM, pp. 228–233.

[2] Bowring, J. F. A new paradigm for programming competitions. *SIGCSE Bull. 40*, 1 (Mar. 2008), 87–91.

[3] Bryce, R., Mayo, Q., Andrews, A., Bokser, D., Burton, M., Day, C., Gonzolez, J., and Noble, T. Bug catcher: A system for software testing competitions. In *Proceeding of the 44th ACM Technical Symposium on Computer Science Education* (New York, NY, USA, 2013), SIGCSE '13, ACM, pp. 513–518.

[4] Crescenzi, P. Using avs to explain np-completeness. In *Proceedings of the Fifteenth Annual Conference on Innovation and Technology in Computer Science Education* (New York, NY, USA, 2010), ITiCSE '10, ACM, pp. 299–299.

[5] Crescenzi, P., Enström, E., and Kann, V. From theory to practice: Np-completeness for every cs student. In *Proceedings of the 18th ACM Conference on Innovation and Technology in Computer Science Education* (New York, NY, USA, 2013), ITiCSE '13, ACM, pp. 16–21.

[6] Diwan, A., Waite, W. M., and Jackson, M. H. An infrastructure for teaching skills for group decision making and problem solving in programming projects. In *Proceedings of the 33rd SIGCSE technical symposium on Computer science education* (2002), SIGCSE '02, pp. 276–280.

[7] Enström, E., and Kann, V. Computer lab work on theory. In *Proceedings of the Fifteenth Annual Conference on Innovation and Technology in Computer Science Education* (New York, NY, USA, 2010), ITiCSE '10, ACM, pp. 93–97.

[8] Enström, E., and Kann, V. Iteratively intervening with the “most difficult” topics of an algorithms and complexity course. *Trans. Comput. Educ. 17*, 1 (Jan. 2017), 4:1–4:38.

[9] Ford, V., Siraj, A., Haynes, A., and Brown, E. Capture the flag unplugged: An offline cyber competition. In *Proceedings of the 2017 ACM SIGCSE Technical Symposium on Computer Science Education* (New York, NY, USA, 2017), SIGCSE '17, ACM, pp. 225–230.

[10] Frank-Bolton, P., and Simha, R. Docendo discimus: Students learn by teaching peers through video. In *Proceedings of the 49th ACM Technical Symposium on Computer Science Education* (New York, NY, USA, 2018), SIGCSE '18, ACM, pp. 473–478.

[11] Henderson, P. B. Issac: Indiana student software awards competition. *SIGCSE Bull. 35*, 1 (Jan. 2003), 332–335.

[12] Johnson, C., Call, A., and Herrnstadt, S. Learning elsewhere: Tales from an extracurricular game development competition. In *Proceedings of the 18th ACM Conference on Innovation and Technology in Computer Science Education* (New York, NY, USA, 2013), ITiCSE '13, ACM, pp. 70–75.

[13] Joint Task Force on Computing Curricula, A. f. C. M. A., and Society, I. C. *Computer Science Curricula 2013: Curriculum Guidelines for Undergraduate Degree Programs in Computer Science*. ACM, New York, NY, USA, 2013. 999133.

[14] Kearse, I. B., and Hardnett, C. R. Computer science olympiad: Exploring computer science through competition. In *Proceedings of the 39th SIGCSE Technical Symposium on Computer Science Education* (New York, NY, USA, 2008), SIGCSE '08, ACM, pp. 92–96.

[15] Khuri, S. Intractability: A geometric representation. *SIGCSE Bull. 26*, 1 (Mar. 1994), 228–232.

[16] MacCormick, J. Seeking evidence for basing the cs theory course on non-decision problems (abstract only). In *Proceedings of the 2017 ACM SIGCSE Technical Symposium on Computer Science Education* (New York, NY, USA, 2017), SIGCSE '17, ACM, pp. 700–700.

[17] McCartin-Lim, M. Complexity tutor: Developing an interactive tutoring system for computational complexity (abstract only). In *Proceedings of the 47th ACM Technical Symposium on Computing Science Education* (New York, NY, USA, 2016), SIGCSE '16, ACM, pp. 494–494.

[18] McConnell, R. M., Mehlhorn, K., Näher, S., and Schweitzer, P. Certifying algorithms. *Computer Science Review 5*, 2 (2011), 119–161.

[19] Mehta, D., Kouri, T., and Polycarpou, I. Forming project groups while learning about matching and network flows in algorithms. In *Proceedings of the 17th ACM Annual Conference on Innovation and Technology in Computer Science Education* (New York, NY, USA, 2012), ITiCSE '12, ACM, pp. 40–45.

[20] Reguly, I. Z., Keita, A.-K., and Giles, M. B. Benchmarking the ibm power8 processor. In *Proceedings of the 25th Annual International Conference on Computer Science and Software Engineering* (Riverton, NJ, USA, 2015), CASCON '15, IBM Corp., pp. 61–69.

[21] Richard, G. T., Kafai, Y. B., Adleberg, B., and Telhan, O. Stitchfest: Diversifying a college hackathon to broaden participation and perceptions in computing. In *Proceedings of the 46th ACM Technical Symposium on Computer Science Education* (New York, NY, USA, 2015), SIGCSE '15, ACM, pp. 114–119.

[22] Rubio-Sánchez, M. An introduction to problem equivalence with combinatorics. In *Proceedings of the 13th Annual Conference on Innovation and Technology in Computer Science Education* (New York, NY, USA, 2008), ITiCSE '08, ACM, pp. 313–313.

[23] Smarkusky, D., Dempsey, R., Ludka, J., and de Quillettes, F. Enhancing team knowledge: instruction vs. experience. In *Proceedings of the 36th SIGCSE technical symposium on Computer science education* (2005), SIGCSE '05, pp. 460–464.

[24] Trakhtenbrot, M. Students misconceptions in analysis of algorithmic and computational complexity of problems. In *Proceedings of the 18th ACM Conference on Innovation and Technology in Computer Science Education* (New York, NY, USA, 2013), ITiCSE '13, ACM, pp. 353–354.

[25] Zhou, H., Zhang, H., Zhou, Y., Wang, X., and Li, W. Botzone: An online multi-agent competitive platform for ai education. In *Proceedings of the 23rd Annual ACM Conference on Innovation and Technology in Computer Science Education* (New York, NY, USA, 2018), ITiCSE 2018, ACM, pp. 33–38.

The Effectiveness of Creating Localized Content for Middle School Computing Curriculum

Huda Gedawy
Computer Science
Carnegie Mellon University Qatar
Doha, Qatar
hgedawy@cmu.edu

Saquib Razak
Computer Science
Carnegie Mellon University Qatar
Doha, Qatar
srazak@cmu.edu

Hanan Alshikhabobakr
Computer Science
Carnegie Mellon University Qatar
Doha, Qatar
halshikh@cmu.edu

ABSTRACT

The need for computing education in K-12 is growing all over the world. Several countries have created national curriculum standards to meet this growing need. In most cases, the actual implementation of the curriculum, including the technical content, is left to individual schools or teachers. In this paper, we outline our work in implementing a computing curriculum based on Alice software in the State of Qatar. We present our experience in creating the content and evaluating its effectiveness. The curriculum was developed in cooperation with schoolteachers, education professionals, and the Qatari Ministry of Education. Materials developed included lesson plans, academic calendar, assessment tools, and student textbooks. We address the issues encountered in creating this computing curriculum content.

CCS Concepts

• **Computing education** • **Critical thinking**

Keywords

Curriculum Content, K-12, Computing, Computer Science

ACM Reference format:

Huda Gedawy, Saquib Razak, and Hanan Alshikhabobakr. 2019. The Effectiveness of Creating Localized Content for Middle School Computing Curriculum. In *Proceedings of 24th Annual ACM Conference on Innovation and Technology in Computer Science Education (ITiCSE'19), July 15-17, 2019, Aberdeen, Scotland, UK.* ACM, NY, NY, USA, 7 pages. https://doi.org/10.1145/3304221.3319778

1. INTRODUCTION

The importance of computational thinking has pushed many countries to introduce computing education at an early stage in their educational systems. Although the approach varies in different countries, many have recently included Computer Science (CS) in their K-12 curriculum. The National Science Foundation (NSF) in the US, for example, funded CS 10K to introduce computer science in 10,000 high schools, aiming to train more than 10,000 teachers to prepare them to deliver the program [1]. The Department of Education in the UK also introduced their new National Curriculum in 2014, requiring K-12 to teach computing in place of the Information and Communications Technologies (ICT) curriculum. Similarly, countries like New Zealand and France have started to shift from using ICT curriculum to using CS [2] [3]. Some countries such as Poland, Korea and Germany started this process even earlier by introducing CS in K-12 more than 30 years ago [4] [5].

The success of a curriculum depends on three main factors: well-designed standards that the curriculum needs to fulfil, curriculum content that matches the standards, and proper teacher training in curriculum content and pedagogy. Computer science education researchers and education boards in various countries have spent considerable effort in defining appropriates standards in computer science and computing for middle- and high-schools. There also seems to be an understanding that most teachers lack the necessary skills to teach computer science and hence a substantial emphasis has also been placed on training the teachers to deliver these standards. Unfortunately, while there is sufficient literature in designing curricula and guidelines for CS education in K-12, there is a lack of support in the implementation of the new curricula in schools. Most of the existing work focuses on training teachers on the new tools but not assisting them in implementing the new content in a classroom setting. This results in placing the responsibility of content creation to teachers who are themselves not proficient in the field [6]. "It's really hard to convince a computer science professional to give up a job that pays up to three times more to pursue teaching" [7].

This lack of curriculum content has created difficulties for implementation and adaptation of computer science curriculum in schools [6]. The problem is more pronounced in countries where the medium of education is in languages other than English. In those countries, learning a concept as hard as programming, in a language other than the native language of the students introduces a severe cognitive overload on the students [8]. In most cases, teachers use English content with in-class explanations given in local languages [9]. The lack of online resources and textbooks in local languages cause a problem for both students and teachers [8].

Qatar is a small but resourceful country in the Middle East located in the Persian Gulf. The country's educational vision is in line with the international call to improve computing education [10]. Alice in the Middle East is a project that introduces computing education in Qatar. Throughout the last several years, this project focused on developing a computing curriculum based on the Alice programming environment [11]. Our efforts included creating a culturally relevant version of the Alice tool, collaborating with schools and the Ministry of Education (MOE) to

ITiCSE '19, July 15–17, 2019, Aberdeen, Scotland UK

ACM ISBN 978-1-4503-6301-3/19/07...$15.00
https://doi.org/10.1145/3304221.3319778

design a suitable computing curriculum, and running professional development to better prepare teachers for course delivery. As mentioned earlier, there is a disconnect between skills of local teachers and skills required to create curriculum content for Computer Science. The focus of this paper is to present our experience in working to bridge this gap. As part of this project, we worked with teachers to create a suitable CS content in Arabic and English.

In this paper, we present our experience implementing an Alice-based CS curriculum in an effort to empower students and motivate them to consider computing for their higher education and future careers. We present our experience in developing the curriculum content and report on our findings based on feedback from students and teachers, as well as students' assessments. We focused on creating curriculum content that was readily usable by teachers after we had provided them with training. We created lesson plans for each class, assessment techniques and tools, textbooks for students and teachers, and online content for student support. We also present the challenges we faced in presenting the content in Arabic while keeping a connection with the equivalent English terminology. We measured the effectiveness of our approach by evaluating student satisfaction and enhancement in their computing knowledge and performance.

2. LITERATURE REVIEW

A recent report published in ACM's *Transaction on Computing Education* journal summarized the experience of five countries that implemented CS in their K-12 schools [2]. Each of these cases reported their experience following Darmstadt framework, which was developed to allow a more practical way of transferring research results in the field of CS education [12]. Even after reviewing the case studies, questions about how to design effective curriculum still remain: "How should CS school curricula be designed? Which structure should CS school curricula have? How detailed should CS school curricula be? Who should be involved in the design process of CS school curricula?" [12]. In a study attempting to examine the role of CS and its rationales in curricula, the members of the Task Force of the Education Committee (TC3) of the International Federation of Information Processing (IFIP) concluded that most countries in their study emphasized the need for K-12 students to learn CS [13]. Moreover, this study found that more investigation on teaching methods is needed as there is inadequate information on "how students learn to think computationally and how approaches developed in one curriculum area or context may become generalized to other areas" [13].

Examining CS curriculum implementation cases from several countries, we summarize prominent cases in France, New Zealand and Australia. The France Superior Curricula Council proposed new curricula that teach computational thinking for kindergarten, elementary and middle school students. In their first pilot study, they focused on K-5 STEM subjects that also involved CS topics inspired from the Computer Science Teachers Association (CSTA) [3]. New Zealand has recently implemented a computing curriculum in high schools to include not only teaching programming, but key ideas such as algorithms, human-computer interaction, and computer graphics [2]. They introduced CS for grade 8, where they developed their curriculum based on English-language published curricula like CSTA, European Digital Competence framework (DIGCOMP), APCS course, England national curriculum, and the Australian curriculum [14]. In Australia, the curriculum was newly introduced in schools and was not purely taught as CS, but rather digital technology as a whole discipline. They attempted to balance computational thinking and human interaction with technology. They also aimed to make students well rounded users and creators of technology. This curriculum starts as early as kindergarten: "This curriculum assumes that students, even as young as five, have the capacity and the right to develop the skills and knowledge required to operate effectively and ethically in a digital world" [15].

Countries with a history of teaching CS may have struggled in retaining students, since students were not selecting the subject when offered as an elective; hence, such countries are considering reforming their curricula. Poland has had informatics in high school as an elective since 1986, but with low attendance. In their new curriculum published in 2015, they start with a clear description and course objectives that are adequately formulated to match the students' level. The curriculum will assist students in learning computational thinking in order to solve problems in various school subjects, as well as motivate students to consider computing as a career option. The new curriculum is flexible, allowing teachers to personalize the subject according to the student's level and interest [5]. Korea is another example, with a long history of implementing CS curriculum in schools. Their CS course was offered as a core subject in elementary and an elective in middle and high school as early as 1970. The curriculum incorporated unplugged activities and educational programming languages that rely less on syntax and Robotics. However, in the last 10 years, CS courses have had a high dropout rate in middle and high school and educators are now working on future plans to increase students' turnout [4].

3. CURRICULUM DEVELOPMENT AND IMPLEMENTATION

We found that supplying schools with the Alice tool and providing teachers with appropriate training was not sufficient to ensure students will acquire consistent knowledge and skills needed in computing. The MOE highly recommended that students and teachers were offered supportive materials based on their vast experience with teaching ICT in schools. Such materials included year and term plans, lecture notes, class activities, and assessments. The materials were developed in cooperation with teachers and were used as a guide to use Alice effectively in delivering the course. We observed that we could not rely on teachers to create the content since most teachers, although trained in IT fields, have been teaching computer applications for several years and are out of touch with computing and programming.

We began our process by articulating the major objectives and learning outcomes, i.e. what we want students to learn by the end of the academic year and/or term. We then created year and term plans for each week. The academic year was divided into two terms of 15 weeks. Classes met twice a week for 45-minute blocks. Students completed their assessments in weeks 14 and 15. Tables 1 and 2 show the distribution of Alice-based curriculum topics over the academic year. The sequence of topics was a major concern, since it influenced students' learning and engagement. We took extra care to make sure we alternated topics between a CS principal and Alice's features (sounds, cameras movement, etc.) that will bring the excitement back to the course.

For each concept, we created a PowerPoint presentation that teachers can use in classes, as well as a lesson plan and class activities. The lesson plans were created in close coordination with teachers in order to create activities appropriate for all students including the gifted and talented (G&T), as well as, Special Education Need (SEN) students. Lesson plans started with an overview of the lesson, and then presented the theoretical part by introducing the new concept. This was followed by an example of how the concept is applied and used to solve problems. Finally, the practical part of the lesson provided an example of the new concept in Alice animation. Students then used the new concepts for ideas of their own. Teachers were provided with solutions to all examples, exercises, sample short quizzes and tests. Students, on the other hand, were given study guides to help them prepare for exams. Each lesson was kept short enough for teachers to cover the activities during one class period. All content is available online at alice.qatar.cmu.edu.

Table 1: Term 1 Schedule

Week	Topics
1	Introduction to computing
2-3	Introduction to Alice and Alice controls
4-5	Sequential and concurrent execution
6	Adding text and using objects' properties
7	Revision and midterm
8-10	Storyboarding
11	Using built-in functions and expressions
12-13	Using camera and sound in Alice
14-15	Students' project and final

Table 2: Term 2 Schedule

Week	Topics
1	Recap, project simulation
2-4	Program decomposition, writing and using methods
5-6	Interactive programming and event handling
7-8	Boolean expressions and conditional execution
9	Revision and midterm
10-11	Repetition and randomization
12	Creating, applying and using parameters in methods
13-14	Creating functions and variables
15	Students' project and final

3.1 Piloting Stage

We introduced a computing curriculum for middle school students in Qatar that uses Alice as a tool to introduce complex programming concepts in a more accessible and engaging way. We began our collaboration with three schools (2 public schools and 1 private) in 2014-2015. More than 320 students in grade 8 used the Alice tool and the curriculum materials during ICT classes taught twice a week for 1 hour per session.

3.2 Assessment Plan

One of our major objectives was to evaluate the effectiveness of this approach with participating teachers and students. Data was collected from teachers and students in surveys. Teachers answered questions relevant to their own experiences with Alice and the curriculum materials, as well as student experiences from the teachers' perspective. For instance, we asked teachers about their experience in teaching computing, including which topics students enjoyed more and if students understand the explanations provided in the materials or do they need clarification. We also asked teachers what would they change in the curriculum, as well as what other suggestions they might have. Students were asked to evaluate the curriculum by rating their experiences with the different topics. We also asked: what would they like to learn more of; what were questions they asked their teachers that were not answered; which examples did they like more; and what difficulties did they face.

Teachers submitted feedback form at the end of each class. The data was used to evaluate the quality and suitability of the lessons and in identifying shortcomings, support mechanisms needed, and areas of improvement. Teachers answered questions about difficulties faced in teaching a topic; what worked well and what did not; did students display interest in the demonstration and exercises; and how many students finished the exercises successfully. Furthermore, we administered pre- and post-tests to targeted students to assess progress in learning logic, computational thinking, and problem-solving skills. This data was used to measure the effectiveness of the curriculum and guide revisions.

During the evaluation of the pilot-testing stage of the curriculum, we conducted school visits to get first-hand impressions of the progress. We attended classes to understand students' overall experience and to identify the extent of the usability of materials provided to teachers.

4. CURRICULUM IMPROVEMENTS

The feedback collected in the pilot stage helped us improve the quality and suitability of the curriculum, as well as to create an appropriate textbook. In light of the lessons learned and recommendations from the MOE and teachers, we found it necessary to offer students a textbook to facilitate their learning and enable them to have a better early CS education experience. Tailored textbooks were developed because of lack of suitable CS resources that accommodate for course type, as well as preserve culture and social values. Therefore, we wrote textbooks in Arabic for middle school students who were taking Alice as a regular subject. The textbook content was made to be modern, familiar and culturally acceptable by students in Qatar. Each chapter in the book included: an introduction, learning objectives, a definition and explanation of the concept, technical terminologies and some hints about designing and developing techniques. Flowcharts were developed to show how advanced programming statements execute, in addition to solved examples that promoted good programming habits. Each chapter ended with a summary of terms, a number of theoretical questions, and some practical exercises that students should be able to complete on their own.

The Arabic textbook had to be mindful that students use Alice, as a tool, in English. Furthermore, university-level computing studies are conducted in English, hence, students should be familiar with English terminology used in computing concepts. Our Arabic textbook incorporated English terminology wherever appropriate. An example of a typical book chapter is shown in figure 1.

5. CURRICULUM CHALLENGES

Initiating a computing curriculum based on students' creativity and ability was a difficult task. The curriculum was created and improved as a result of the feedback; however, it aimed to make a difference in the quality of CS education in Qatar and integrate well in schools. The lack of resources to teach CS concepts in the medium of instruction being used at the schools was a major challenge. It was also difficult to secure teacher buy-in due to a lack of trust in new materials and resistance to change. Teachers found it difficult to cope with some pedagogical and conceptual challenges in teaching Alice. Below is a list of main challenges experienced while developing and improving the curriculum.

أهداف التعلم Learning Objectives

عند نهاية هذا الفصل، يتوقع أن يكون الطالب قادراً على أن:

يُعرّف الطرائق Methods ويذكر فائدتها في كتابة برامج الحاسوب.	-1
يُعدّد أهم مميزات الطرائق.	-2
يُعرّف الطرائق الخاصة بالعالم World-Level Methods.	-3
ينشيء برامج بها طرائق خاصة بالعالم في Alice.	-4
يُعرّف الطرائق الخاصة بالكائنات Object-Level Methods.	-5
ينشيء برامج بها طرائق خاصة بالكائنات في Alice.	-6

المصطلحات الرئيسة Terminologies

Methods	الطرائق
World-level Methods	الطرائق الخاصة بالعالم
Object-level Methods	الطرائق الخاصة بالكائنات
Decomposition Strategy	استراتيجية التفكيك
Abstraction	التجريد

Figure 1: English vocabulary for key concepts embedded within the Arabic textbook.

5.1 Reading Level

We intended to present the concepts at an appropriate reading level so that middle school students could understand, follow and absorb the content easily. We also had to guarantee the suitability of the language and vocabulary selection for the target age group. We followed the approach of using real life analogies, since this is a good way to introduce advanced CS concepts. We provided examples of how the concepts exist in our daily life and looked at how to apply them to solve problems in the different aspects of life. For instance, the typical walking action we repeat everyday includes sequential and concurrent actions of taking one step at a time and moving legs and arms simultaneously. Students can model these actions, thus facilitating learning and recognition of the concepts. To ensure appropriateness of textbook content, we checked the clarity of language and selection of vocabulary with English and Arabic language experts and we reviewed the overall curriculum content in consultation with university curriculum consultants, MOE&HE and CS professors. Subsequently, we tested sample chapters on students and collected feedback before the widespread use of the curriculum in the field-testing stage.

5.2 Content Translation

It was critical to provide Arabic speaking students with a learning resource in their native language to relieve the cognitive overload of studying CS in a foreign language. We created an Arabic version for all curricular materials and the challenge was mainly in translating computing terminologies into Arabic. English is the language of technology and the language of computing and programing, hence, the computing terminology in other languages, including Arabic, is poor and not found in professional literature. We found research on computer science terminologies in Arabic to be inconvenient and not standardized.

In a study done on the vague use of computer linguistics when translated into Arabic, Khuwaileh contextualized a number of common and heavily used computer terms that have no equivalence in Arabic [16]. Their study showed that many computer terms are problematic and are classified as vague expressions and terminologies. For example, compute and calculate are translated as having identical meanings, and descriptive statistical words like mean, simultaneous and critical value were inappropriately translated in computer textbooks [16]. Furthermore, Khuwaileh found that problematic words were hard to translate because of the lack of Arabic translation resources in the computer field as well as the inefficiency of the English-Arabic dictionaries.

When translating the materials, we ensured an accurate delivery of the information while maintain a commitment to the source and target languages. The language of instruction must be clear, concise and precise. Terminologies such as loops, if/else conditions, functions, variables and modularity lost their real meaning when translated into Arabic. We needed to have a sense of language perception in order to select the most suitable term from the Arabic dictionary. In cases where no equivalence was available, we provided an explanation of the concepts as required. Also, when a denotative meaning did not express the concept well, we offered a connotative meaning. The vocabulary selection was reviewed with language exports and English terminologies were kept in the book to enrich students' computing dictionary.

5.3 Content Suitability

Qatar is a conservative country that values the preservation of religion, heritage, and tradition. To guarantee acceptance, a culturally and religiously appropriate curriculum was as important as making it academically strong. Contextualizing the materials can have a significant impact in students' attainment and interest, as well as teachers' efficacy. For instance, using examples that reflect the local environment like camel racing and pearl diving made the content more engaging for students and enabled them to absorb materials better. Moreover, we could not use examples asking students to calculate monetary amounts with nickels and dimes, since students are not familiar with the terms.

6. FIELD TESTING STAGE

Following the successful piloting of Alice curriculum in three schools, we expanded our attempts to reach more schools. In academic year 2015-2016, we collaborated with 11 schools with more than 800 students.

6.1 Implementation Plan

In this stage, students from six public schools and five private schools used the textbooks and study guides. Teachers used the improved supportive materials including term plans, lesson plans, and quizzes. Teachers followed the same pedagogical technique as in the pilot stage and introduced new concepts through storytelling. To create animations or games in Alice, students had to logically decompose the problem, develop the algorithm, and implement the code. This technique proved to work well with students, since it simplified challenging concepts like conditional execution and developed their computational thinking skills in an innovative context. Teachers also employed techniques to help students understand the importance of the concept before introducing it. For example, when students learn how to animate a cat jumping, the first comment they made was "*it's jumping only once*" or "*how can we duplicate the action?*" Most students followed the simple approach of copying and pasting the jumping code several times. At that point, teachers presented the looping concept and students understood it better [17].

6.2 Assessment Plan

Towards the end of the academic year, we evaluated the curriculum implemented in the field-testing stage in public schools in which around 460 students were involved in the study. In this process, we analyzed feedback collected from teachers and students (Satisfaction Indicators) and improvements in students' computational thinking, logical reasoning, and analytical skills (Performance Indicators).

We conducted a one-hour focus group interview in all six public schools asking teachers questions about their overall experience as well as their perceived students' experiences. Teachers completed surveys about their personal experience teaching programming and computing, and this curriculum in particular. Students answered surveys and assessments to report on their general experience with the program and curriculum materials, as well as improvements in their attainment levels.

7. FINDINGS

Data collected in the pilot and field testing stages were compiled, encoded, compared and analyzed to give us insight into the current status of the program and its future direction. The major objective of collecting this data was to evaluate and prove the effectiveness of our approach in building computing knowledge and skills, while keeping students' interest. It is important to clarify that student surveys and assessments were sent to schools and teachers were asked to encourage students to complete them. We, therefore, had no control over the quantity of responses.

7. 1 Satisfaction Indicators

Teachers' and students' satisfaction indicators were measured using feedback on their overall experience and the course contents. Comments collected from teachers, in the interviews and surveys, were coded and classified under three categories; 1) Positive: something good about the program [i.e. Students liked the book], 2) Negative: a short coming of the program [i.e. It was targeting higher achievers] and 3) Challenge: something negative beyond the program [i.e. Students were not introduced to programming before]. Students' responses, in the anonymous surveys, were also coded and divided into two categories; positive (very satisfied and satisfied) and negative (not satisfied and not satisfied at all).

Table 3: Students' Ratings of the Book's Evaluation Criteria

Criteria	%
Contents of the book were suitable.	60
I could easily understand the concepts.	63
Concepts were introduced in an engaging way.	62
I was able to complete the examples with the teacher.	64
I could implement most of the exercises in Alice.	55
The level of exercises was suitable.	62
The level of questions was suitable.	59
I needed simpler explanation to understand the topics.	51
I needed more examples.	51
I liked the book design and organization.	51
The lesson time covered the content and/or exercise.	53
I contributed in class with questions and comments.	60

7.1.1 Feedback on Overall Experience

In focus group interviews, we asked teachers about their overall experience teaching the program, as well as their perceived students' experience. After analyzing the data, we found that 50% of their comments about the program were positive (i.e. some teachers described their experience by saying; "It was surprisingly positive; we didn't expect this. We were against it from the beginning since students are suffering with other ICT tools used already" and "It was difficult in general for the majority of students, however we found that it stimulated students' minds and provoked their creative thinking"). Around 15% of teachers indicated facing some challenges (i.e. one of the teachers explained "Students' major problem was their motivation to learn not their abilities to learn and work with Alice"). Overall, 35% of the comments were negative, some of which were due to students' lack of interest in programming and the difficulty of the program. We hope that as teachers become more comfortable with teaching computing concepts, this negative sentiment will decrease.

Students were asked to report on their satisfaction with the program. Only 97 students replied to this question and 85% of those had positive responses about their experience - one student said, "Alice was interesting and easy for me, I only faced few difficulties," another said, "It was fun". Conversely, 15% of students' comments were negative - a student said, "Everything is hard in the program", another said, "The program is hard and not useful" while another explained, "Programming is hard". Complaining is culturally acceptable and encouraged in Qatar, therefore it is not surprising that students' complaints would be clearly communicated. In fact, the MOE&HE has set up emails to accept complaints about schools. Therefore, an 85% positive result is a good indicator of success.

7.1.2 Feedback on Course Content

To assess the effectiveness of our computing curriculum, we asked teachers about the content suitability for students in that age group, as well as to comment on their overall experience using the book for teaching. Teachers had more negative comments about the book than positive. Some of the negative comments were: "The book was very heavy and big" and "The theory questions were too difficult". Most of their positive comments were associated with students - "Students liked the book and liked the interactive programming the most".

In evaluating their experience with the book, students were also asked about the content suitability and whether the main concepts and contents presented were easily understood. To analyze this part, we coded students' ratings and categorized them into positive: >=3 and negative: <3. In general, 57% evaluated the book positively, which signifies that students regarded the book as good. Most of the negative comments were associated with book's big size (i.e. one of the students said, "The book was long and one semester wasn't sufficient to complete it"). Please refer to table 3 for more details on student evaluation of the book. Although the majority of students were satisfied with the book, 51% felt they needed more examples and preferred simpler explanation in order to understand the topics.

Table 4: Teachers' Satisfaction Indictor with the Book

Indicator	Average Rating
Overall experience with teaching Alice.	3.2
Students' overall experience with Alice.	2.2
Experience using the book to teach.	2.6
Topics presented in the book.	2.5
Examples and exercise in the book.	2.6
Students' use of the book.	2.8
Support to students during semester.	3.3

Although we collected data from focus group interviews, we felt it was important to collect data on teachers' individual perspectives about the program. We asked teacher to complete a survey rating their experience with the program and the curriculum. Teachers were given two rating scales of 1-4. We coded the data and categorized anything with a rating of >2 as positive. In particular, for questions 1-5 indicators were as follows: (1=poor, 2=good, 3=very good and 4=excellent) and for questions 6-7 (1=not at all, 2=somewhat, 3=mostly and 4=very much). As indicated in table 4, on average almost all of the ratings were above 2, which implies that the teachers were satisfied with their experience and the materials in general.

7.2 Performance Indicators

Student and teacher satisfaction for the program and curriculum was not sufficient to indicate the success of this initiative: an evaluation of the curriculum's quality was mandatory. We conducted pre- and post- assessments for a randomly selected group of 122 students to measure the growth in their level. The same assessment was given to a group of students of same age who took existing ICT curriculum. The schools in the second group were selected randomly by Ministry of Education. The students were required to complete the assessment during regular lessons. The assessments consisted of 15 multiple-choice questions that required no special knowledge other than thinking abilities. Students used computational and algorithmic thinking skills to analyze problems in the test and drive conclusions. In general, Alice students were able to demonstrate higher levels of logical thinking and analytical skills. The results showed that Alice students scored 7.5% higher on average than the control group. Furthermore, two Alice students scored above 70% on the assessment, compared to a highest score of 60% in the control group [18]. This result shows a lack of motivation for gifted and talented students while using the existing ICT curriculum.

8. DISCUSSION

Throughout the implementation phases of the program, we were able to collect data to help us measure the effectiveness of the curriculum. We discovered that there were more positive impressions of the curriculum materials. Students who were introduced to programming through Alice generally enjoyed the experience. Most students felt that the book had important subject matter and was relevant when applied in life. The fact that 60% of the students were contributing to lessons with comments and questions implies a high level of interest in the subject. Teachers also gave a rating of above 2 (good) for their experience with the curriculum, which means that they were comfortable teaching it. Although most of the teachers in the focus group interviews reported negative impressions about the book, it was mainly associated with the size and weight rather than the actual content.

In addition to the general positive impression received, the assessments results displayed improvements in students' computational thinking, logical reasoning, and analytical skills. The results also indicated that Alice students acquired more fundamental computing skills than the other group examined.

The findings proved our hypothesis that providing a culturally acceptable computing curriculum has a significant impact on increasing students' attainment and interest in computing and increasing teachers' interest in delivering more advanced CS courses, as per their request, which indicates its success.

9. CONCLUSIONS AND FUTURE WORK

Throughout our experience of making computing curriculum available in Qatari schools, we found that creating a tailored curriculum reflecting the local culture, language and age group of the target audience is the way forward. Creating a tailored curriculum also involved studying the educational context of Qatar that entailed assessing students' computing knowledge and teachers' experience with programing. The task was difficult to achieve considering there was no programming curriculum in place, in addition to the absence of suitable resources in teaching middle school students in Qatar.

Our future work will be to design and implement a computing curriculum that spans all three years of middle school. The curriculum will be designed with horizontal and vertical integration. This will ensure that learning is consistent with the skills that students have learned within their grade level, as well as, building on concepts incrementally across each successive grade. The curriculum will encourage inquiry based contextualized learning with design for transfer. More importantly, we will design and conduct teacher training that is intensive, on-going, and connected to practice to help teachers cope with the changes in the new computing curriculum.

10. ACKNOWLEDGMENTS

This paper was made possible by NPRP grant # 10-0205-170345 from the Qatar National Research Fund (a member of Qatar Foundation). The statements made herein are solely the responsibility of the author[s].

11. REFERENCES

[1] M. desJardins, "Creating AP CS principles: let many flowers bloom," *ACM Inroads*, vol. 6, no. 4, 2015.

[2] T. Bell, P. Andreae and A. Robins, "A Case Study of the Introduction of Computer Science in NZ Schools," *ACM Transactions on Computing Education (TOCE)*, vol. 14, no. 2, p. 10, 2014.

[3] V. Chiprianov and L. Gallon, "Introducing Computational Thinking to K-5 in a French Context," in *ACM Conference on Innovation and Technology in Computer Science Education*, 2016.

[4] J. Choi, S. An and Y. Lee, "Computing education in Korea—current issues and endeavors," *ACM Transactions on Computing Education (TOCE)*, vol. 15, no. 2, p. 8, 2015.

[5] M. M. Syslo and A. B. Kwiatkowska, "Introducing a new computer science curriculum for all school levels in Poland," in *International Conference on Informatics in Schools: Situation, Evolution, and Perspectives*, 2015.

[6] K. Bateman, "The UK's new computing curriculum is here: Are teachers ready?," *Computer Weekly*, 08 2014.

[7] Z. Ahmad, "Filling the pipeline for computer science teachers," Science, 2019.

[8] S. Raj, A. Gerald, K. Ketsuriyonk, J. M. Patel and R. Halverson, "Does Native Language Play a Role in Learning a Programming Language?," in *Proceedings of the 49th ACM Technical Symposium on Computer Science Education*, New York, NY, USA, 2018.

[9] J. R. Fennema-Bloom, "Code-scaffolding: A pedagogic code-switching technique for bilingual content instruction," *Journal of Education*, vol. 190, no. 3, pp. 27-35, 2010.

[10] "Qatar National Vision 2030," *Qatar, General Secretariat for Development*, 2008.

[11] S. Cooper, W. Dann and R. Pausch, "Alice: a 3-D tool for introductory programming concepts," *In Journal of Computing Sciences in Colleges*, vol. 15, no. 5, pp. 107-116, 2000.

[12] P. Hubwieser, M. Armoni and M. N. Giannakos, "How to implement rigorous computer science education in K-12 schools? Some answers and many questions," *ACM Transactions on Computing Education (TOCE)*, vol. 15, no. 2, 2015.

[13] M. Webb, N. Davis, T. Bell, Y. J. Katz, N. Reynolds, D. P. Chambers and M. M. Sysło, "Computer science in K-12 school curricula of the 2lst century: Why, what and when?," *Education and Information Technologies*, pp. 1-24, 2016.

[14] C. Duncan and T. Bell, "A Pilot Computer Science and Programming Course for Primary School Students," in *Proceedings of ACM Workshop in Primary and Secondary Computing Education*, 2015.

[15] M. Webb, N. Davis, T. Bell, Y. J. Katz, N. Reynolds, D. P. Chambers and M. M. Syslo, "Computer science in K-12 school curricula of the 2lst century: Why, what and when?," *Education and Information Technologies*, pp. 1-24, 2016.

[16] A. A. Khuwaileh, "IT terminology and translation: Cultural, lexicographic and linguistic problems," *LSP Journal-Language for special purposes, professional communication, knowledge management and cognition*, vol. 1, no. 2, 2010.

[17] N. Tabet, H. Gedawy, H. Alshikhabobakr and S. Razak, "From Alice to Python. Introducing Text-based Programming in Middle Schools.," in *Proceedings of the 2016 ACM Conference on Innovation and Technology in Computer Science Education*, Arequipa, 2016.

[18] S. A. Sabbagh, H. Gedawy, H. Alshikhabobakr and S. Razak, "Computing Curriculum in Middle Schools - An Expereince Report," in *ACM Conference on Innovation and Technology in Computer Sceince Education*, Bologna, 2017.

Using Action Research to Distill Research-Based Segments of Pedagogical Content Knowledge of K-12 Computer Science Teachers

Ofra Brandes
Department of Science Teaching
Weizmann Institute of Science
Rehovot, Israel
ofra.brandes@weizmann.ac.il

Michal Armoni
Department of Science Teaching
Weizmann Institute of Science
Rehovot, Israel
michal.armoni@weizmann.ac.il

ABSTRACT

Teachers' pedagogical content knowledge (PCK) is an important factor in all that concerns teaching and learning processes. As such, it plays an important role in pre-service teachers' training and in-service teachers' professional development. In line with this, the pedagogical content knowledge of computer science teachers (CS-PCK) receives considerable attention in current computing education research. However, very little is known about effective ways of extracting valid and reliable CS-PCK segments from the practical work of CS in-service teachers, and hence, only a limited reservoir of such segments is available for CS educators. Here we report on research in which we developed and investigated a new strategy for extracting research-based CS-PCK segments from the practical work of experienced high-school teachers. This strategy incorporated action research, conducted by the CS teachers in their classes, as part of a long and extensive workshop for professional development of CS teachers. Our findings show that the use of action research within the unique platform provided by the workshop yielded a rich variety of research-based CS-PCK segments. Furthermore, our findings emphasize the important role of the social context of the workshop in teachers' success in conducting reliable and valid action research. In addition, teachers' attitudes regarding the use of action research as a tool for improving their practice were positive, as well as their tendency to adopt and use this tool in their practice.

CCS CONCEPTS

• Social and professional topics → K-12 education

KEYWORDS

Action research; PCK; CS-PCK; teachers; K-12

ACM Reference format:

Ofra Brandes and Michal Armoni. 2019. Using Action Research to Distill Research-Based Segments of Pedagogical Content knowledge of K-12 Computer Science Teachers. In *Proceedings of 24th Annual ACM Conference on Innovation and Technology in Computer Science Education (ITiCSE'19), July 15-17, 2019, Aberdeen, Scotland, UK.* ACM, New York, NY, USA, 7 pages. https://doi.org/10.1145/3304221.3319773

ACM ISBN 978-1-4503-6301-3/19/07...$15.00 https://doi.org/10.1145/3304221.3319773

1 INTRODUCTION

Teachers' knowledge is a key factor in implementing any teaching program. Of special interest is the subject-dependent component of teachers' pedagogical content knowledge (PCK), which encapsulates all that the teacher has to know in order to teach a subject effectively. Portraying the PCK of in-service teachers is important for making their PCK accessible and usable for other teachers, and for using it in teacher preparation. However, eliciting the PCK of teachers is difficult, since it should rely on authentic practice, and should be reliable, as well as transferable. Focusing on the PCK of computer science K-12 teachers (CS-PCK), several endeavors have been made to conceptualize and portray the CS-PCK of in-service teachers. However, these efforts have often failed to achieve the above requirements. Since they are based on teachers' narratives and self-reports, the CS-PCK segments are often very general, dissociated from the class, and do not constitute concrete, concise and ready-to-use pieces of information. In addition, they may be unreliable, since the information provided by teachers is taken as is, without any validation. We propose a strategy for extracting concrete CS-PCK segments that stem from teachers' practice, and are research-based, hence reliable. To this end, we employ action research, a known framework for in-service teacher development. We use action research in a workshop for in-service CS teachers, in which the teachers perform action research in their classes, relying on the social context of the workshop for guidance, support, and feedback. At the end of this workshop, each action research results in a research- and experience-based segment of CS-PCK. Here we present our strategy and the study that accompanied it, to examine the effectiveness and feasibility of our strategy.

Note that we describe research within research. In our own research we study in-service teachers that conduct action research in their classrooms. For the sake of clarity, we will use the term "study" when referring to the first, and the term "action research" when referring to the second, expect for a few cases, in which any disambiguation is resolved in another way. In addition, we will hereafter use the term CS-PCK to refer to CS-PCK of K-12 teachers.

The paper is organized as follows: We provide the necessary background and related research in Section 2, and describe the research in Section 3. Section 4 presents the findings, and Section 5 discusses the results and presents our conclusions.

2 BACKGROUND

This section lays the basis for this study by discussing its three pillars: the framework of PCK, the current state of affairs regarding CS-PCK, and action research (Sections 2.1-2.3, respectively).

2.1 Pedagogical Content Knowledge (PCK)

About thirty years ago, Shulman [36, 37] coined a new concept describing the unique knowledge of in-service teachers, namely, "pedagogical content knowledge" (PCK). Until then teachers' knowledge was thought to consist of two facets: knowledge of the subject matter and pedagogical knowledge, which is common to all teachers, including, for example, class management and general learning theories. To these Shulman added PCK, as the "missing paradigm". PCK is subject dependent, constituting the teachers' expertise on this subject, and it is based on their experience, including all their knowledge that allows them to teach their subject effectively: how to make its concepts and ideas comprehensible and accessible to students of various learning styles and abilities [25].

PCK is the product of both practical work and personal experience [2, 7, 8]. Hence, it is not identical for all teachers of the same discipline [25]. It develops as experience is gained, but it has also been shown to be transferable among teachers [12, 13]. Thus, although according to Shulman's original definition, portraying PCK should be done in the context of in-service teachers, PCK is also studied in the context of pre-service teacher training [27, 5]. Indeed, the inclusion of PCK in pre-service teacher training and in-service teachers' professional development is known to be effective [1]. To allow for such inclusion, it is necessary to extract PCK from available sources. There are two types of sources: The first includes research publications, from which research-based PCK can be extracted [36]. Another is the 'wisdom of practice' of other teachers who are experienced, excellent, and expert teachers [38, 39, 15]. This is a complex task, especially since much of the PCK is concealed, even though teachers constantly use and enrich it [40]. Several tools were developed for this purpose [13, 25], among which are the CoRe and PaP-eRs. Usually information is collected from in-service teachers by asking them about their beliefs and opinions regarding the teaching of concepts and ideas of the discipline. However, such tools do not yield authentic segments that conform to the definition of PCK. An inherent disadvantage of these models is that they rely on teacher self-reports and narratives that are not validated and therefore, are potentially unreliable.

2.2 CS-PCK

When PCK was defined, the practice and research concerning it was general and common to all disciplines. Over time, it was agreed that PCK can be defined and measured only in relation to specific subject matter [40, 17, 9]. In line with this, PCK-related research became disciplinary. Research on CS-PCK is still in its preliminary stages, compared to the older disciplines, such as mathematics. However, as K-12 CS education is becoming increasingly more prevalent, and consequently, the importance of teachers' knowledge and training is increasingly acknowledged, the research on CS-PCK has increasingly evolved (see [18] for a survey of 19 papers).

Just like in any other discipline, CS-PCK is necessary and even critical in any teaching situation, even for expert teachers [30], and its positive effect on teaching has been repeatedly shown [e.g., 20, 21]. Consequently, the need for sharable CS-PCK resources to be used in pre-service CS teachers' training and in-service CS teachers' professional development has also been acknowledged [24]. As with general PCK, these resources should be based on research-based segments of CS-PCK [e.g., 41] and teachers' experience reports [24]. The first can be extracted from the many research publications on teaching CS in schools. This body of CS-PCK is not sufficiently acknowledged and covered in teacher preparation programs [31]. However, these segments of PCK are not represented in a way that makes them accessible to teachers and easy to use in authentic teaching situations. To make CS-PCK resources usable for teachers' practice and training, an adequate conceptualization of CS-PCK is needed. Several research efforts have been made to conceptualize CS-PCK and to elicit CS-PCK from CS teachers' experience. Saeli [33] used Grossman's theoretical 4-question model [14] to conceptualize CS-PCK and to identify research-based segments of CS-PCK in the CS education research literature. Then [32] she attempted to extract PCK segments from CS teachers, using CoRe, which is also based on Grossman's model, and by working with groups of teachers. Relying on Grossman's model, both studies yielded very general propositions, which were out of the classroom context and were not directly derived from teachers' practice. Therefore, they were very difficult to transfer to classroom practice, and could not be considered as a reservoir of CS-PCK segments that can be applied by others. In addition, teachers' reports were taken as is, without any validation and without considering their expertise; thus, they suffer from the inherent questionable reliability of self-reports. Another conceptualization of CS-PCK was designed by the KUI research team [19, 3], yielding a 2-dimensional category system that could serve as a model for CS-PCK. This model can be used to characterize PCK-segments, and to assess CS-PCK [29]. However, it may be less suitable as a structure for a PCK resource, since the high resolution and high fragmentation of the categories dissociate them from a holistic context, and make the PCK segments associated with them too difficult to use in authentic situations. Another study that is worth mentioning in our context, even though it deals with CS-PCK of higher-education instructors, is that of Oleson et al. [30], who aimed to uncover the PCK required to teach one specific method of inclusive design, building on the experience of the instructors. They worked with a small group of instructors who were teaching this topic, and used their reflections on their actual teaching process to elicit PCK that corresponded to issues raised by the students and through class observations, resulting in 11 pieces of PCK. Like Saeli, they appreciated the factor of collaboration, and to this end, they created a wiki, to which they and the instructors uploaded teaching materials. They too (again, like Saeli) did not control the instructors' knowledge or their ability to reflect on their practice. They presented this study as being based on action research (see Section 2.3), although apparently the only aspect of action research in their study was teachers' reflection on their teaching.

2.3 Action Research

Action research is a process by which teachers can learn about their own way of teaching and can evaluate their decisions and actions, from their own classroom practice [16]. It can be seen as a cyclic inquiry into the teachers' work and into their students' learning [28]. Reflection, which is an integral part of action research, gives the teachers an opportunity to improve their practice by reflecting on their own experiences and from feedback generated from their colleagues' insights [16, 25]. Hence, action research is considered to be meaningful for pre- and in-service teachers' professional development [23]. The process of action research starts by identifying a real need and formulating it into a research question, then continues to the next stages of planning an intervention to answer the need and implementing it while collecting data on the process. The last step involves reflection on what has been done, in order to improve results before beginning another research cycle [28]. In an optimal situation, the research has to include a full cycle, which can repeat itself, thus enabling the researchers' conclusions to be implemented. It is also necessary to hear the teachers' testimony about their own work in order to maximize the research outcomes [26].

Usually, the practice of action research does not include a full validation of the findings, since this is not considered necessary when the reflection process and its effect on the teacher's own practice is the center of attention. As described in Section 3.2, in the context of our study, we act differently.

3 THE STUDY

3.1 Our Research Question

We focus on the following research question: How effective and feasible is the use of action research methodology for distilling research-based CS-PCK segments from the practical work of in-service high-school CS teachers?

This question has two aspects: 1 (effectiveness). Does the use of action research by in-service high-school CS teachers lead to research-based CS-PCK segments? 2 (feasibility). To what extent do in-service high-school CS teachers willingly and properly utilize action research? Obviously, using action research for this purpose is useless if it cannot lead to research-based PCK. However, there is no point in using it if the teachers are reluctant to cooperate.

3.2 Our Research Method

The common research methods applied when investigating teachers' knowledge are qualitative-naturalistic; thus, the teachers' narratives and self-perceptions of the processes they undergo occupy a central place [13, 11, 17, 4]. In this framework, methods like grounded theory [10], and case studies [2, 4, 35] are used. The use of observations and multiple data from a variety of sources allows triangulation of data and enables researchers to capture the complex aspects of teaching. It also provides a glimpse into the participants' world and reflects their understanding [22, 40]. Qualitative research also enables returning to participants from a time perspective, thus enabling researchers to get their retrospective perception of the research experience [6].

In our study we implemented this using multiple research methods and multiple data sources. Thus, our study is qualitative, and involves monitoring the action research done by the teachers and evaluating its outcomes. This is achieved within the framework of a collaborative group, which is assumed to be the proper framework for performing qualitative-naturalistic research in order to reveal in-service teachers' PCK [32]. The data were collected over a few months, including a retrospective component a few months later after the workshop ended. This results in a reliable and validated interpretation of reality.

3.3 The Workshop

In order to achieve our study's goals, we had to actively guide and follow the action research conducted by the participating teachers. In addition, since the goal of the action research was to obtain research-based outcomes, we had to provide the teachers with a setting that supports validation processes. To this end, we conducted a longitudinal workshop for the participating teachers, thus creating a collaborative group [32]. The workshop provided a research environment in which the participants could design their own research and enjoy the feedback and support of their peers. The first author guided the workshop, which consisted of nine 5-hour meetings, held from June to December 2017. A last retrospective meeting took place in May 2018.

During the first two meetings, the participants were introduced to the underlying concepts of teachers' knowledge, PCK in general, and CS-PCK in particular, as well as action research. The rest of the workshop followed the phases of action research: The participants chose and rationalized the context of their research, formulated their research question, and designed the research process, including the research tools. After performing the experiment in their classrooms, the data were analyzed and the findings were presented in the workshop plenum. Throughout all these stages, the participants validated their decisions with the help of their peers, and sometimes withdrew to former stages, improving or updating goals, questions, tools, and more, as needed. All this was done while integrating several modes of work. Each phase was introduced and explained in the plenary meetings. Then the teachers used the (very active) workshop's forum for an iterative process of discussing these issues, presenting preliminary products (such as research questions and research tools) and receiving feedback from their peers and the instructor. These products were then discussed again during the meetings and their final versions were submitted through regular assignments that were given throughout the workshop. At the end of the workshop, the teachers were required to submit a final assignment, describing in detail the action research they had conducted and the CS-PCK segments that were extracted as a result of this research. All in all, the workshop was very time consuming for the teachers, who had to invest dozens of hours beyond the meeting for preparing the assignments, participating in the forum discussions, and of course, conducting the action research.

3.4 The Participants

The workshop was advertised among the CS teachers in our country, offering the teachers an opportunity for professional development that was acknowledged by the Ministry of Education. Those who were interested were interviewed by the first author, who verified that they were experienced and appreciated teachers and were willing to invest substantial work, during and outside the meetings. Twelve in-service CS teachers participated in the workshop from start to finish, and submitted all the required assignments. Among them were seven females and five males. One had an undergraduate degree in software engineering, and all the others had an undergraduate degree in CS. All but one had also a master's degree, and two of them had a Ph.D. degree. All were teaching CS at the high-school level, with varying experience (an average of 17 years). They all were aware of being part of the study and of the data collection, and gave their consent accordingly. The study was approved by the IRB and by the Ministry of Education.

3.5 The Research Tools

Various types of data were collected throughout the workshop. All nine meetings were fully recorded and transcribed. In addition, all the forum chats, as well as email correspondence and personal communication with the instructor were transcribed. The data also included the on-going assignments as well as the final assignment.

3.6 Analysis

We used two different categorical systems corresponding to the two aspects of the research question presented above, to analyze the data collected from the various sources. The cross-referencing of the data assisted in triangulation and verification of the findings, and enabled a full understanding of their meaning [34, 22]. The combination of these sources reflected multiple voices of the participating teachers, while giving expression to their views and their understanding of the processes they had undergone, thus establishing the reliability of the analysis [14].

The first categorical system focused on the aspect of effectiveness, that is, whether the use of action research by the teachers led to research-based CS-PCK segments. It included six categories aimed at examining whether the outcomes were indeed research-based (representing components conforming to the customary practice of empirical research), and another category, aimed at examining whether the outcomes represented CS-PCK segments. The resulting system is as follows: 1. the action research subject; 2. research questions; 3. The action research plan and research tools; 4. data collection; 5. Data analysis; 6. conclusions. 7. the characteristics of the outcomes. Categories 3 and 5 also refer to appropriate validation processes.

The second categorical system focused on the aspect of feasibility. We used the framework of grounded theory [10]; hence the categories were not defined in advance but instead emerged from the data, based on the participants' written and oral statements. The transcribed texts were dissected into statements, and each statement was examined for components relevant to the aspect of feasibility. Corresponding categories were defined and refined until the categorical system was stable (see Section 4.2 for the categories). The categorical system was constructed by the first author and was validated by the second author, who received about 20% of the data segments and categorized them with sufficient accuracy using the constructed system. Disagreements were discussed and resolved until full agreement was achieved. Using these categorical systems, we applied content analysis on the data set [34] and employed a similar validation process.

4 FINDINGS

We present the findings regarding the two aspects of our research question in the following two sections, respectively. In each section we refer to all relevant categories, but owing to space limitations, we present examples only for some of the categories.

4.1 Effectiveness

In order to show that the action research conducted by the teachers resulted in research-based CS-PCK segments, we needed to show that all seven categories were satisfactorily in evidence, for all teachers.

1. Choosing the action research subject. In Assignment 1, the participants had to choose a motivating personal topic for the research, based on their interest and experience, and to express the rationalization for the intervention and its description. T10 shared her motivation in the forum, requesting feedback: "I'd like to find another way to introduce this topic [efficiency]. [...] It is taught in a very technical manner. [Perhaps] some class activity, away from the computer." As shown by the outcomes of Assignment 1, this phase was completed successfully by all the teachers.

2. Research questions. The first task in Assignment 2 was to formulate the research questions. Again, the data analysis showed that all the teachers completed the task successfully. For example, the context of T7's action research was a learning unit dealing with deterministic finite automata (DFA) and regular languages. T7's research question was how the use of graphic patterns for teaching the construction of DFA affects students' learning outcomes. She refined this question using two sub-questions, referring to two kinds of outcomes: constructing automata and recognizing the language accepted by a given automaton.

3. Research plan and research tools. In Assignment 2 the teachers were also required to design the experiment, including a detailed description of the suggested teaching process and the corresponding action research tools they were planning to use. Our findings show that they successfully completed this task, again using the social context for assistance and feedback. For example, "The first part can be evaluated quantitatively using a focused questionnaire that examines the difference between passing parameters by value and by reference [...]. The second part may be evaluated using an interview with students who displayed some difficulties in performing the task [...]. I do not know how to focus my questions on understanding the reason for the difficulty, [...] my hypothesis is that it [the interview] can illuminate a wider misunderstanding" (forum, T3). Realizing the need for an interview as a research tool, T3 became aware of her lack of knowledge regarding this tool, and added: "I [want] to learn more about this research method and especially what we should ask students in order to understand the roots of their difficulties". This was addressed at the following workshop meeting.

4. *Data collection.* All participants successfully completed this phase. T3 elaborated on the process: "In the last exam I added another question [...]. Out of 24 students, 12 did not answer the questions correctly, 2 did not answer at all, and 10 answered correctly [...]. I interviewed students who usually have an excellent understanding but failed to answer this question" (forum).

5. *Data analysis.* Data analysis started at the sixth meeting. The teachers brought the data they had collected to the plenary sessions, and discussed their analysis and findings with the group. Some teachers were confident in their research process up to that point, but now became uncertain. For example, T3 was convinced that her analysis reflected a total failure of her intervention. However, T10 supported her analysis, showing her a different point of view, and then suggested that she evaluate students' understanding using another exercise that utilizes recursion (communication from the forum). At the end of this phase, all teachers successfully completed their analysis.

6. *Conclusions.* The conclusions were discussed at the meetings, verifying that they were reliably and directly derived from the findings and hence from the validated data analysis, and that they related to the research questions. T4 concluded: "[the intervention succeeded] since I saw many students who [...] used it as an aid in a recursive solution process. [...] in the coming years [...] I will combine it with the methods I have used before, to handle cases in which the students are required to analyze a given program [...]. This insight results from the individual interviews that I conducted following the intervention" (final assignment).

7. *The characteristics of the outcomes.* We have shown that the outcomes were research based, but we still have to show that they are indeed CS-PCK segments [36, 37]. Each of the 12 final assignments included a description of the resulting CS-PCK segment. Reviewing the descriptions supported our hypothesis that they are authentic CS-PCK segments. Here is a partial description of the CS-PCK segment of T8. This segment concerns the introductory unit learned in 10th grade. It deals with search algorithms and presents a strategy for introducing the topic in class. It includes 12 interactive tasks posed to the entire class. Each task is presented by a slide showing a very large collection of numbers, organized differently for each task. In each task another number is provided and the students are requested to determine whether it appears on the slide. One student keeps track of the process and records for each task the average time it took the class to reach the answer. This process is accompanied by discussions, in which the class reflects on the outcomes of each task and their meaning. This motivates students to develop searching strategies by themselves. They spontaneously realize the merit of sorting before searching. The effects last beyond the introductory session and include a better understanding of search algorithms and of efficiency of algorithms. Clearly, this is a product of the practical work of an in-service CS teacher, which includes a combination of pedagogical knowledge for learning a specific content, that is, this is a CS-PCK segment.

As can be seen by the wide variety of examples cited above, the workshop yielded a very rich variety of CS-PCK segments dealing with different learning units and with different parts of the syllabus in each unit. This scope is another indicator of the effectiveness of using action research supported by a collaborative workshop as a strategy for extracting research-based CS-PCK segments of in-service high-school teachers.

The workshop served as a natural platform for the validation processes (of the research tools and the analyses). These processes were conducted by the teachers (in the forum and the plenary meetings), who acted as content experts. Sometimes the validation process caused the teachers to withdraw to some previous stage and to plan their moves again. The participants reflected on these processes in the final assignment. Here are two examples:

Validating the research tools. "A preliminary draft of the test and the personal questionnaire were presented to the teachers at the workshop. There were several important comments that made me correct the formulations in order to better link the questionnaire to the test questions." (final assignment of T4).

Validating the data analysis. "I received many responses that enabled me to look at the type of errors and see that they were mostly not about control of objects, but other mistakes." (final assignment of T12).

4.2 Feasibility

After establishing the effectiveness of the strategy, we now turn to the aspect of feasibility, that is, do the teachers willingly and properly employ action research? Employing the grounded theory methodology resulted in a few categories that were organized under two super-categories, relating to conceptual and affective factors.

1. Conceptual super-category: Understanding of action research. It consists of two sub-categories.

a. *Effective understanding of the action research process.* A large part of the evidence that supported the aspect of effectiveness (Section 4.1) was relevant to this category as well, since it showed that the teachers succeeded in completing all phases of their action research. It was reinforced by additional evidence, mostly from the retrospective meeting.

b. *Understanding the merits of action research.* Much of the evidence under this category came from the retrospective meeting that took place at the end of the school year and concluded the entire experience from a six-month perspective. This brings credibility and validation, since teacher' conceptions did not stem from momentary enthusiasm, but rather from a long-term thoughtful examination. During this meeting, many teachers acknowledged a transformation from experience-based, intuitive, and spontaneous pedagogical decisions, to empirically-based strategies.

2. Affective super-category: attitudes towards action research and the entire experience. It consists of four sub-categories:

a. *Pleasure from the workshop.* The teachers often expressed enjoyment and satisfaction.

b. *Acknowledgement of the positive effect of action research on teachers' practice.* This category reflects positive attitudes toward the habit of reflecting, inherent to action research. For example, "This research we did [...] contributed to me and to my students. Many times, we [the teachers] work and go on. [When] you stop to look, you also see and then it's a very good opportunity to [...] get feedback." (T8, retrospective meeting). The feeling that performing the action research made them think deeply about the subject they chose was supported by substantial evidence.

c. *Acknowledgment of the positive effect on teachers' practice as a direct outcome of the enrichment of the CS-PCK practical reservoir.* Our findings indicate that the teachers' CS-PCK improved because of the new CS-PCK segment they had uncovered. For example, in the retrospective meeting T8 reported very positive effects on teaching time and performance. T1 said "It [the intervention] came out of a need I felt [...]. The action research constituted an opportunity to make the difference." The enhancement of their CS-PCK also resulted from their intense involvement in their colleagues' research. "[W]e also contributed to each other [...] we were all influenced by the [other] studies. I can testify that I used a lot of things they did here." (T1).

d. *Attitudes towards the social context.* The data included many references to the unique social context of the teachers' action-research experience. From the participants' point of view, this context was necessary to make their action research possible, as T12 summarized in the retrospective meeting: "It [the action research] is really something I think I could not have done without the guys who were here". It also gave them a feeling of community, which they often missed as sole CS teachers in their schools.

Note that our focus in this study was not on how the workshop affected the teachers' practice. However, teachers' reflections on this issue indicate their positive attitudes and overall positive impression, thus also indicating their willingness to take part in such a project, and hence, in making it feasible.

5 DISCUSSION AND CONCLUSIONS

In this study we used action research integrated into a longitudinal workshop for in-service teachers, as a tool for obtaining CS-PCK segments that are both research and experience based. Our findings demonstrate the effectiveness and feasibility of our strategy. Specifically, teachers were able to correctly perform action research, and did so willingly, while acknowledging its benefits. Our findings also point out the important role of the social context provided by this workshop. The contribution of this work is significant. It provides a novel tool for enhancing the body of documented CS-PCK, which is acknowledged as a very important task. It bridges the gap that currently exists in the area of CS-PCK, in which non-validated CS-PCK is obtained from in-service teachers. In addition, unlike existing strategies for eliciting CS-PCK, it yields concrete, concise, and ready-to-use CS-PCK segments. Our workshop was also shown to positively affect the practice of the research participants, as will be reported elsewhere. In addition, as part of our research project we intend to make the resulting segments of CS-PCK accessible to teachers by using them as a basis for a CS-PCK resource. To this end, we developed a framework for organizing CS-PCK that supports easy use of CS-PCK reservoirs. We used a preliminary version of this framework to guide the teachers in preparing their final assignments. This framework will also be reported elsewhere.

An important limitation of our study concerns the validation processes performed by the teachers as part of their action research, which did not follow a clear protocol. This was caused by time constraints, causing the workshop to be shorter than intended. However, based on our complete corpus of data, we are certain that standard formal peer validation, guided by the instructor – as originally planned – will be successfully performed. This remains to be verified in future workshops. In addition, like any qualitative study, the generalizability of its findings is limited. However, we can safely say that our goal of demonstrating the applicability and feasibility of such a strategy was achieved. Obviously, the effectiveness and feasibility depend on the participating teachers. Excellent, experienced, and collaborative teachers are needed to successfully implement our strategy, but we believe that any attempt to uncover PCK from teachers' experience should rely on such teachers.

ACKNOWLEDGMENTS

We wish to thank the teachers who participated in the workshop, for their invaluable contribution.

REFERENCES

[1] Michal Armoni. 2011. Looking at secondary teacher preparation through the lens of computer science. *ACM Transactions on Computing Education,* 11, 4, Article 23, 38 pages.

[2] Miriam Ben-Peretz. 2011. Teacher knowledge: What is it? How do we uncover it? What are its implications for schooling? *Teaching and Teacher Education,* 27, 1, 3-9.

[3] Elena Bender, Peter Hubwieser, Niclas Schaper, Melanie Margaritis, Marc Berges, Laura Ohrndorf, Johannes Magenheim, and Sigrid Schubert. 2015. Towards a competency model for teaching computer science, *Journal of Education*, 90, 4, 519-532.

[4] Amanda Berry, and Jan H. Van Driel. 2012. Teaching about teaching science: Aims, strategies and backgrounds of science teacher educators. *Journal of Teacher Education*, 64, 2, 117-128.

[5] Malte Buchholz, Mara Saeli, and Carsten Schulte. 2013. PCK and reflection in computer science teacher education. In *Proceedings of the 8th Workshop in Primary and Secondary Computing Education*, 8-16.

[6] David Clarke, and Hilary Hollingsworth. 2002. Elaborating a model of teacher professional growth. *Teaching and Teacher Education*, 18, 947–967.

[7] Michael F. Connely, Jean D. Cladinin, and Ming Fang He. 1997. Teachers' personal practical knowledge on the professional knowledge landscape. *Teaching and Teacher Education*, 13, 7, 665-674.

[8] Larry Cuban. 1993. The lure of curricular reform and its pitiful history. *Phi Delta Kappan*. 75, 2, 182-185.

[9] Fien Depaepe, Lieven Verschaffel, and Geert Kelchtermans. 2013. Pedagogical content knowledge: a systematic review of the way in which the concept has pervaded mathematics educational research. *Teaching and Teacher Education,* 34, 12-25.

[10] Barney G. Glaser, and Anselm L. Strauss. 1967. *The Discovery of Grounded Theory. Strategies for Qualitative Research*. Aldine, Chicago, Illinois, USA.

[11] Ivor Goodson, and Pat Sikes. 2001. *Life History Research in Educational Settings: Learning From Lives*. Open University Press, London, UK.

[12] Pamela L. Grossman. 1989. A study in contrast: Sources of pedagogical content knowledge for secondary English. *Journal of Teacher Education*, 40, 5, 24-31.

[13] Pamela L. Grossman. 1990. *The Making of a Teacher: Teacher Knowledge and Teacher Education*. Columbia University, New York, NY, USA and Teachers College Press, London, UK.

[14] Egon G. Guba, and Yvonna S. Lincoln. 1981. *Effective Evaluation: Improving the Usefulness of Evaluation Results Through Responsive and Naturalistic Approaches.* The Jossey-Bass higher and adult education series and the Jossey-Bass social and behavioral science series, San Francisco, CA, US.

[15] John A.C. Hattie. 2003. Teachers make a difference: What is the research evidence? In *Building Teacher Quality: What does the research tell us, Proceedings of the Australian Council for Educational Research*.

[16] James Hiebert, Anne Morris, and Brad Glass. 2003. Learning to learn to teach: an "experiment" model for teaching and teacher preparation in mathematics. *Journal of Mathematics Teacher Education*, 6, 3, 201–222.

[17] Heather C. Hill, Deborah L. Ball, and Stephen G. Schilling. 2008. Unpacking pedagogical content knowledge: Conceptualizing and measuring teachers' topic-specific knowledge. *Journal for Research in Mathematics Education*, 39, 4, 372-400.

[18] Aleata Hubbard. 2018. Pedagogical content knowledge in computing education: a review of the research literature. *Computer Science Education*, 28, 2, 117-135.

[19] Peter Hubwieser, Johannes Magenheim, Andreas Mühling, and Alexander Ruf. 2013. Towards a conceptualization of pedagogical content knowledge for computer science. In *Proceedings of the 9th International Computing Education Research Conference*, 1-8.

[20] Loannis Ioannou, and Charoula Angeli. 2013. Teaching computer science in secondary education: a technological pedagogical content knowledge perspective. In *Proceedings of the 8th Workshop in Primary and Secondary Computing Education,* 1-7.

[21] Loannis Ioannou, and Charoula Angeli. 2014. Examining the effect of an instructional intervention on destabilizing learners' misconceptions about the central processing unit .In *Proceedings of the 9th Workshop in Primary and Secondary Computing Education*, 93-99.

[22] Dona M. Kagan. 1990. Ways of evaluating teacher cognition: Inferences concerning the Goldilocks Principle. *Review of Educational Research*, 60, 3, 419-469.

[23] Joseph Keating, Rosario Diaz-Greenberg, Mark Baldwin, and Jacqueline Thousand. 1998. A collaborative action research model for teacher preparation programs. *Journal of Teacher Educion*, 49, 5, 381–390.

[24] Herman Koppelman. 2008. Pedagogical content knowledge and educational cases in computer science: an exploration. In *Proceedings of the Informing Science & IT Education Conference*, 125-133.

[25] John Loughran, Amanda Berry, and Pamela Mulhall. 2012. *Understanding and Developing Science Teachers' Pedagogical Content Knowledge* (2nd Ed.). Sense Publishers, Rotterdam, Netherlands.

[26] John Loughran, Pamela Mulhall, and Amanda Berry. 2004. In search of pedagogical content knowledge in science: developing ways of articulating and documenting professional practice. *Journal of Research in Sience Teaching,* 41, 4 , 370–391.

[27] Shirley Magnusson, Joseph Krajcik, and Hilda Borko. 1999. Nature, sources, and development of pedagogical content knowledge for science teaching. In Julie Gess-Newsom, and Norman G. Lederman (Eds.), *PCK and Science Education*. 95-132. Kluwer Academic Publishers, The Netherlands.

[28] Rachel Mamlok-Naaman, Oshrit Navon, Miriam Carmeli, and Avi Hofstein. 2003. Teachers research their students' understanding of electrical conductivity. *The Australian Journal of Education in Chemistry*, 62, 13-19.

[29] Melania Margaritis. 2014. What pedagogical content knowledge competencies do computer science pre-service teachers have? In *Proceedings of the 10th annual conference on International computing education research*, 161-162.

[30] Alannah Oleson, Christopher Mendez, Zoe Steine-Hanson, Claudia Hilderbrand, Christopher Perdriau, Margaret Burnett, and Andrew J. Ko. 2018. Pedagogical content knowledge for teaching inclusive design. In *Proceedings of the 2018 ACM Conference on International Computing Education Research*, 69-77.

[31] Mara Saeli. 2009. How to teach programming in secondary education: First results of a PhD project. In *Proceedings of the 14th annual ACM SIGCSE conference on Innovation and technology in computer science education*, 356.

[32] Mara Saeli. 2012. *Teaching Programming for Secondary School: a Pedagogical Content Knowledge Based Approach*. Unpublished PhD Dissertation, Technical University Eindhoven, Eindhoven, The Netherlands.

[33] Mara Saeli, Jacob Perrenet, Wim M. G. Jochem, and Bert Zwaneveld. 2011. Teaching programming in secondary school: a pedagogical content knowledge perspective. *Informatics in Education*, 10, 1, 73–88.

[34] Asher Shkedi. 2005. *Multiple Case Narrative: A Qualitative Approach to Studying Multiple Populations*. John Benjamins Publishing Company, Amsterdam, The Netherlands.

[35] Lee S. Shulman. 1983. Autonomy and obligation: The remote control of teaching. In Lee S. Shulman, and Gary Sykes (Eds.), *Handbook of Teaching and Policy*. Longman, New York, NY, USA.

[36] Lee S. Shulman. 1986. Those who understand: Knowledge growth in teaching. *Educational Researcher*, 15, 2, 4-14.

[37] Lee S. Shulman. 1987. Knowledge and teaching: Foundations of the new reform. *Harvard Educational Review*, 57, 1, 1-21.

[38] Lee S. Shulman. 2002. Truth and consequences? Inquiry and policy in research on teacher education. *Journal of Teacher Education*, 53, 3, 248-253.

[39] Lee S. Shulman. 2007. Practical wisdom in the service of professional practice. *Educational Researcher*, 36, 9, 560–563.

[40] Jan H. van Driel, Douwe Beijaard, and Nico Verloop. 2001. Professional development and reform in science education: The role of teachers' practical knowledge. *Journal of Research in Science Teaching*, 38, 2, 137-158.

[41] Jan H. van Driel, Nico Verloop, and Wobbe de Vos. 1998. Developing science teachers' pedagogical content knowledge. *Journal of Research in Science Teaching*, 35, 6, 673–695.

A Systems Change Approach to CS Education: Creating Rubrics for School System Implementation

Leigh Ann DeLyser
CSforALL
New York, NY, US
leighann@csforall.org

Lauren Wright
CSforALL
New York, NY, US
lauren@csforall.org

ABSTRACT

Computer science education is moving from an elective subject in K-12 schools to a more compulsory topic with a focus on all students. As a new discipline is added to education, we need to explore not only the implications and theory behind student and teacher learning and development, but also the systems change that will happen in organizations in order to produce sustainable CS education. In this paper, we explore theories of systems change, especially in education, and describe the creation of a series of rubrics to help districts self-assess their CS education supports. Early data is presented from a pilot year of workshops with 67 school districts showing a partial landscape of how school districts rate their own strengths and weaknesses and provide a discussion of initial evidence of validity for the rubrics.

CCS CONCEPTS

• **Social and professional topics → K-12 education.**

KEYWORDS

School System; Institutional Change; Computer Science Education

ACM Reference Format:

Leigh Ann DeLyser and Lauren Wright. 2019. A Systems Change Approach to CS Education: Creating Rubrics for School System Implementation. In *Proceedings of Innovation and Technology in Computer Science Education (ITiCSE '19)*. ACM, New York, NY, USA, 7 pages. https://doi.org/10.1145/3304221.3319733

1 INTRODUCTION

Computer Science education has experienced a period of increased awareness and implementation in primary and secondary schools over the past few years. Although an imperfect measure, the Advanced Placement Computer Science (CS) exam numbers over the last 10 years show a picture of increased student participation in the United States and also an increase in the number of schools offering the course[15]. Additionally, surveys of the landscape in the United States have shown increased interest by parents and students in offering Computer Science (CS) courses [37], and efforts such as the Hour of Code, standards writing, and teacher professional development have increased the number of primary schools who offer CS content. This growth is not unique to the United States, and many other countries are also expanding access to computing, or informatics, education.

In the midst of all of these efforts, the focus has been on supporting the development of teacher skills and capabilities as there is a critical need for teachers to provide CS instruction. In the US, public funding, such as grants from the National Science Foundation, allocations from individual states [28, 30], and even the federal Department of Education [29] prioritize the training of teachers for potential grantees.

Funding and focus in the US has resulted in an increase in offerings and professional development hours focused on computer science concepts and pedagogy for educators. CS teacher professional development opportunities have helped increase the teacher capacity to offer CS in schools; however, these efforts are quickly out pacing the supports necessary for school systems, specifically districts in the US, to implement CS evenly across classrooms. The US has a distributed system of education, allowing for local education agencies (states and even towns) to make choices about how and where to implement computer science instruction.

The distributed nature of education in the US, combined with a lack of knowledge by school administrators have led to teachers self-selecting professional development. Without coordination, teachers who teach the same grade, in the same building, sometimes will be teaching completely different computer science content because they self-selected into different professional development opportunities without any building or district level coordination.

In addition to a lack of alignment, the teachers who participate in professional development often need to advocate for offering a new CS class or find time to add CS content in pre-existing classes. Because the teacher has self-selected into a professional development, school administration is not always enthusiastic about CS. Many teachers who attend professional development report they are unable to implement the CS for which they were trained due to barriers within their own building [16].

Previous research in CS education, specifically the development and publication of the Darmstadt Model, has called for a focus on levels of systems and structures to support CS education in schools [22]. Systems have different learning needs than people, and so different plans for engagement and tools for assessments will need to be designed. Although the US presents a specific challenge due to the distributed nature of education, the structural components of supporting education coherence[7] are a best practice of high-functioning educational systems internationally. This paper

ITiCSE '19, July 15–17, 2019, Aberdeen, Scotland, UK

ACM ISBN 978-1-4503-6301-3/19/07...$15.00
https://doi.org/10.1145/3304221.3319733

contributes to the literature called for in [22] by detailing the creation of a framework to help schools and school systems self-assess their computer science education implementations.

In this paper, we detail the development of the framework and rubrics designed for school leader usage. To contribute to a discussion of validity, the paper also presents initial data from the usage of rubrics aligned to that framework for 67 school districts. Section 2 discusses the importance of system level supports, both from a theoretical perspective and using examples from other major curricular roll outs in K-12 education. Section 3 describes the development of the framework and rubrics, including alignment with similar tools from other academic disciplines. Section 4 describes the piloting of the rubrics at regional workshops and the data that resulted from the rubric usage, and provides a discussion of evidence for validity of the rubrics for the domain. Section 5 offers conclusions and future work.

2 LITERATURE REVIEW

In the 2011 paper by Barr and Stephenson, *Bringing Computational Thinking to K-12: What is Involved and What is the Role of The Computer Science Education Community?*, the authors suggest that sustained implementation of CS education would require both curricular resources and resources to inform policy makers. This sentiment was echoed in the 2013 paper proposing a landscape to categorize CS education research. The Darmstadt Model for CS education in schools developed by Hubweiser et. al.[22] can be used to map the focal areas of the research and highlight the relevance of research focused on more than just students.

Policy makers is a broad term and mostly is translated to mean state or national decision makers [20]; however, in the US, local district policies can be just as impactful on implementation at the classroom level as state and national policy [9]. In this section, we discuss relevant literature supporting the creation of school system level tools for CS education. Although not rigorously explored in CS education, tools that support school systems (or district in the US) have been studied in other domains, and findings from those disciplines can help inform CS education research in our attempts to scale rigorous computer science to a broad audience of students.

2.1 Support for District Level Engagement

School districts provide a central core operation in US education that not only connect schools through a fiscal umbrella, but also one of policy and priority [25]. Recent educational initiatives in the US have pushed districts to be implementers of policy and initiatives that are backed by research and evidence of student learning outcomes [2]. As CS education often does not have the education research that shows the types of student outcomes districts have been conditioned to look for in other domains such as math or science, this may be influencing some of the enthusiasm gaps we see between administrators and teachers and parents when it comes to CS education [37].

Additionally, almost all of the professional development for CS education in the US focuses specifically on teachers. There are few resources available for school leaders to not only understand what introductory CS may look like in a single classroom, but what a coherent program of CS and ongoing master teacher development would look like across multiple grades.

With the rush to put any CS into schools in the US, curriculum choices have been made based more on the availability of professional development or the availability of funding to engage teachers in a particular geographic location. Only in population dense areas, which are most likely to have funding at several different universities for different curricular options or provide a hub for curricular offerings due to the vast number of teachers available for professional development, will teachers have a reasonable choice amongst different curricular options [14]. This does not mean teachers cannot choose to implement one of the nationally available curricula such as Exploring Computer Science [18] or one of the many Advanced Placement CS Principles courses, but the professional development that makes all those new curricula accessible to new CS teachers may not be available.

The constraint on choices, combined with the sense of urgency for implementing CS [3], has lead to a landscape where the majority of courses and curricula are focused on being a student's first experience with computing, all the way up to Advanced Placement offerings. The enthusiasm around CS education is encouraging, however, the literature is full of educational reform efforts which had strong support for implementation and then faded as attempts to implement at scale were misaligned with school and district priorities [6].

One strategy for combating a scattered approach to educational implementation is to develop coherent instructional systems that cross multiple levels of stakeholders and have well-articulated purposes and visions at their centers [27]. The notion of coherent instructional systems has been further developed into a robust literature base within educational policy implementation scholarship (see [7]; [34]; [36]). The core idea is that various elements of instructional systems - teacher learning and professional development efforts, instructional approaches and assessments, and supplemental student supports - be aligned in service of the ultimate goal - student learning. CS education research literature has yet to explore these decision making processes by the schools and districts themselves, instead of focusing on the curriculum designer's perspective.

2.2 District Tools in Other K-12 Disciplines

CS education is different from other major curriculum roll outs in recent years because the discipline itself, unlike Mathematics or Science, is new to the teachers and decision makers in the school system. Yet, despite the differences inherent in CS education, it is still likely that schools and districts will need to consider many similar structural components when implementing CS.

For example, the implementation of the Next Generation Science Standards (NGSS) produced numerous studies and resource documentation for the supports schools and teachers needed in order to implement the new standards and curricula. Although Science was not a new subject for the teachers, there were still new content areas, new methods of inquiry for students, and new types of assessments of student learning that needed to be integrated into the previous practice of science in schools.

State departments of education, such as Maryland, created plans that included years of preparation for full implementation including scope and sequence, instructional material design, professional development for teachers, and technical assistance for the districts [31]. If a curricular change for an existing subject required years of planning, should not the addition of sustainable CS education also require thoughtful multi-year plans by local educational agencies? Even with the supports proposed by researchers and state departments of education and the familiarity with the overall discipline, the roll out of the NGSS was politically challenging and fraught with mixed outcomes.

In the US there have been many efforts to increase the state policies related to CS education [11]. Yet research has shown that state mandates do not often lead to equitable or rigorous educational implementation [4]. The absence of support for local change within schools, and the alignment of implementation is key for student outcomes to match desired policy goals [8]. The creation of district rubrics for CS education reflects best practices of other curricular areas in creating plans supporting policy aligned implementation. These rubrics, combined with a visioning and goal setting process (to be published separately) create the ability for school leadership teams to implement thoughtful plans regarding computer science education. Additionally, it allows districts to critically define the local efforts needed to implement an equitable approach to CS Education [35].

3 RESEARCH METHODOLOGY AND RUBRIC DEVELOPMENT

The rubrics were developed by the authors and refined using a Design Based Implementation Research approach [17]. In this section, we describe the methodology used as well as the contributing research from other educational domains that lead to the development of the rubrics.

3.1 Relevant Reviewed Materials

The efforts to add CS education to primary and secondary schools is often heralded as a unique endeavor because it is not the modification of an existing discipline, but the addition of an entirely new subject to schools [21]. In the US, the most major curricular roll outs were the Next Generation Science Standards[12] and Common Core Curriculum Standards[23]. Organizations such as Achieve, Inc. created district-facing frameworks, rubrics, and worksheets in order to facilitate discussions amongst district teams to enable change. Additionally, funding opportunities can also be used to prompt change in systems. Most recently, the competitive Race to the Top[24] grants were used to prompt change through applications for funds.

The district rubrics described in this paper were designed after a review of these support documents and the frameworks used to create them. Figure 1 shows the alignment between the NGSS Indicators from Achieve, Common Core curriculum roll out workbook, and Race to the Top indicators with the categories for the school support instruments created and used in this project.

Although an international audience may not find these rubrics immediately applicable, the connection to the Darmstadt Model shows the usefulness of this case study for an international audience [22]. As shown in Section 3.4, rubrics targeted to school districts impact both the Level of Responsibility/Range of Influence and Berlin Model/Top Dimension axis of the model. Through district participation, self assessment against the rubrics, and their subsequent usage to prompt organizational goal setting enable data collection in Preconditions and Decision Areas. The participants in the process impact schools, classrooms, and therefore students.

3.2 Design Based Implementation Research

Design Based Implementation Research (DBIR) [17] is an iterative design approach to education improvement and reform. A key component of DBIR according to Penuel et. al. (2007) is a "concern with developing capacity for sustaining change in systems"[32].

The rubrics were developed with a review of relevant documents from other domains and have been tested, with slight refinements to the document and workshop process over the last 8 months following participant feedback. The major changes to the rubrics in the iteration cycles were:

- Alterations to rubric rating labels: following participant feedback, the lowest rubric category was modified from "Not Engaged" to "Novice" and highest rating from "Exemplary" to "Highly Developed."
- Addition of explicit mentions of CS: the words "Computer Science" or "CS" were added in many rubric descriptions in order to make explicit that all the rubric areas were referring to CS.

Other changes to the workshop process included more share outs of information between districts in the workshop and early activities to focus teams on the goals and visions for CS education held by team members.

3.3 Design choices

The rubric areas were created after a review of several frameworks to support school decision making for curricular adoption and an evaluative rubric for grant applications. These documents guided the categories that were chosen and the overall structure of the rubric statements in the progression from novice to highly developed. Similar to the Next Generation Science Standards Workbook[5], the district support rubrics were built around a few "big ideas".

- *Teachers as Advocates* In many instances teachers are looked at as the key component for the implementation of CS. Organizations such as Code.org create pages specifically directed at teachers to help them advocate for CS in their district [10]. While this is a common practice and the rubrics recognize work by individual teachers, they seek to move beyond disconnected advocates to working teams of teachers supported by district leaders and policies.
- *Diversity Throughout* Initiatives that focus on CS as a literacy for all students should impact equal numbers of underrepresented students. Instead of separating diversity efforts into separate components of a rubric (and therefore making them easily ignored), diversity is woven throughout and Section 3.5 highlights the rubric components that address diversity.
- *Implementation Choice* Schools and school organizations vary greatly across the US. With this in mind, it is unlikely

Rubric Areas	NGSS Indicators	Common Core Workbook	Race to the Top
Leadership	Equity and Access Internal Communication Management Professional Learning for Teachers Student Outcomes	Organize to Implement Train Educators on Common Core and Assessments Transition Accountability and Data Reporting Systems Establish Procedures to Monitor Performance and Solve Problems	Great Teachers and Leaders Data Systems to Support Accountability State Success Measures (State Policy Climate)
Teacher Capacity	Educator Collaboration Within and Across Districts		
Materials and Curriculum Selection and Refinement	Instructional Materials Assessments Equity and Access	Align Instructional Materials Transition Technology and Assessment Systems	Standards and Assessment
Partners	Partnerships with External Organizations Educator Collaboration within and Across Districts Leadership Collaboration with Other Districts	Student Transition to Higher Education	
Community	Community Communication	Student Transition to Higher Education	
Infrastructure	School Structures	Transition Technology and Assessment Systems	

Table 1: Categories of Rubric Development

that CS education will be structurally implemented in the same way in every school. The rubrics are designed to support best practices in a variety of implementations (integrated, stand alone, etc.) and future work will explore the landscape of implementation choices made by schools.

These big ideas are reflected in the design decisions made throughout the rubrics. Table 1 shows the relationships between the NGSS Indicators [13], the common core workbook components [1], Race to the Top indicators [33], and the CS categories in the rubrics.

3.4 School Impact Areas and Rubrics

The tool was developed with five areas for self assessment. These areas are: Leadership, Teacher Capacity, Materials and Curriculum Selection and Refinement, Community, and Partners. A sixth category, Infrastructure, is planned and will be tested in the fall of 2018. These categories align with the Darmstadt Model Educational Relevant Areas of Educational System (Leadership), Socio-Cultural Related Factors (Community), Policies (Leadership), Teacher Qualification (Teacher Capacity), Intentions (Leadership: Outcomes), Knowledge (Teacher Capacity, Leadership), Curriculum Issues (Materials and Curriculum Selection and Refinement), Extracurricular Activities (Partners, Community), Outcomes/Effects (Leadership: Outcomes).

In each category, subtopics were identified to align with other school planning documents and rubric areas were described for Novice, Emerging, Developing, and Highly Developed ratings. Full rubrics can be found at www.csforall.org/script.

3.5 Diversity

With the lack of ethnic and gender diversity in post secondary CS majors, and companies in the US, diversity is an important lens to consider when addressing CS education implementation. Diversity and equity mean different things in different communities, making generic statements about diversity difficult to integrate in a tool meant to be used nationwide. Diversity is integrated throughout the rubric areas and built into the assumption that all students will be taking some form of CS and teacher working groups will use data and student artifacts to review and adjust implementation. The one exception is the inclusion of Materials for Diverse Learners in the Curriculum and Materials Selection and Refinement Rubric. "Diverse Learners" refers specifically to students with disabilities according to researchers consulted on the language and design of that particular sub-category.

4 PRELIMINARY DATA

The rubrics were tested with 67 school districts between August 2017 and June 2018. Completion of the rubric areas varied by workshop due to the on-going development and release of rubric areas during the pilot year as well as the length of the workshop. For the purposes of this paper, we will present the preliminary data from the district teams that completed Leadership, Teacher Capacity, and Materials and Curriculum rubrics. In this section, we describe the method of engagement with the districts, the preliminary data collected through team self-assessment with the rubrics, and implications for the rubrics themselves. The data is not meant to provide a means to infer a national landscape, nor was the set of districts selected to create a generalizable national image of CS education. Instead, these data are offered as evidence of validity of the rubrics.

4.1 Workshop Design and District Profiles

The school districts assembled teams and participated in SCRIPT workshops designed to engage them with the rubrics and create a goal setting process where the districts created individualized plans for CS education. Districts were recruited through a general call for participation by CSforALL for one of 7 workshops held in Yorktown Heights, NY; Ithaca, NY; Atlanta, GA; Nashville, TN, Austin, TX; Boston, MA; Detroit, MI; and St. Louis, MO. Districts were also recruited through local advocates near each workshop, such as a professional development center or post secondary institution. Once districts were identified, they were encouraged to assemble a team of at least 3 participants to attend the workshop. Districts were encouraged to include a district level administrator, school administrators, and instructional staff who had CS teaching roles. This could be a stand alone CS teacher from a high school, an elementary teacher who conducted CS or computational thinking activities in their classroom, or a library media specialist who did CS lessons in the computer lab.

Table 2 shows the characteristics of the 67 districts who participated in the SCRIPT workshops. The data in the table was retrieved from the National Center for Educational Statistics (NCES) School District Search system. Data for seven districts were omitted for Free and Reduced Lunch percentages as there was no data in NCES for those districts.

Table 2: District Participation Profiles

Metric	Min	Max	Mean	Median
Students K-12	252	387,311	21,707	5,082
Schools	1	655	36	9
Team Size	1	12	4.7	4
Students on Free or Reduced Lunch	0 %	100%	46.2%	50%

The workshops reached a very diverse set of school districts, both large and small. In order to test the rubric applicability in a wide variety of implementation environments, the portfolio of districts also included districts that were known to be just starting to implement CS and those who had more established programs.

At the workshop, districts did an icebreaker computational thinking activity, engaged in a process to identify their core values, and introduce themselves to the room. The day was then divided into sections for each of the rubric areas to be explored. As a pilot year, the rubric sections for Leadership, Teacher Capacity and Development, and Materials and Curriculum Selection and Refinement were used at all of the workshops and will be explored in this paper. The Partners and Community sections were only used in two workshops and the release of the Infrastructure rubric is scheduled after the publication of this paper; these areas will not be covered in this paper.

During an individual section, school districts were asked to self-assess their current CS program against the rubric for that area. All members of the district team had access to either an electronic or paper copy of the rubric, and each team came to consensus for the individual rating. Rubric scores were submitted once per district through an online form immediately after discussion. After completing the form, districts then were asked to view resources and example goals and write 3- and 6-month goals related to CS education and the rubric area they completed. In this paper, we are only evaluating the rubric scores and plan to study the goals set by the districts in another paper.

4.2 Rubric Data

The full rubrics completed by the districts are available online (www.csforall.org/script). For each rubric area, there were sub-categories, and descriptive text describing the characteristics of each rubric level: Novice, Emerging, Developed, or Highly Developed.

Although each rubric area has individual characteristics, there is a general pattern to the rubric levels. A rating of Novice often indicates that there is no CS efforts related to the rubric sub-category. A rating of Emerging most likely indicates there are teachers who are working independently to implement CS with no coordination with other teachers in the district. A rating of Developed indicates teams of teachers working towards a common goal, plan, or set of learning objectives that apply to all students. A rating of Highly Developed indicates that the teams of teachers use best practices and data to revisit and revise the plans and goals in a cycle of continuous improvement.

Figure 1 shows the percentage of districts at each rubric level for the sub-categories of the Leadership rubric. A majority of the districts were either Novice (25.9%) or Emerging (56.5%) across the entire area. The District Leadership sub-category had the most Developing or Highly Developed self-ratings from the district. This was surprising considering previous research showing a lack of engagement from school and district administration[37] and may be an indicator that the districts that engaged with this process were already a selective subset. This is not a threat to the validity of this paper as I am evaluating the rubrics and not claiming the 67 districts are representative of a national landscape.

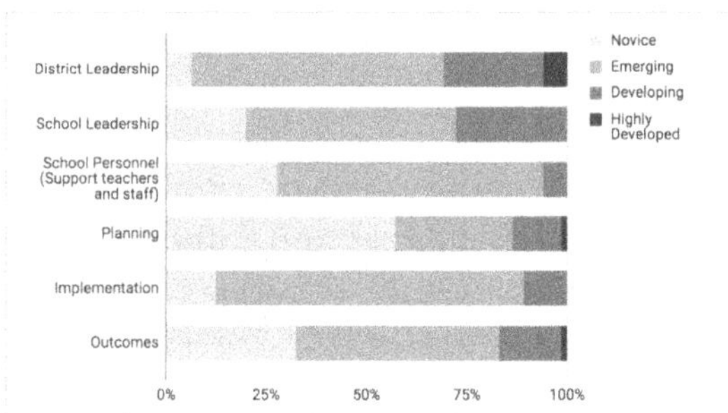

Figure 1: Leadership Rubric Data

Figure 2 shows the percentage of districts at each rubric level for the sub-categories of the Materials and Curriculum Selection and Refinement rubric. As seen in Leadership, a majority of the districts were either at the Novice (33.9%) or Emerging (50.6%) levels across the entire area. Consistent with prior CS education research[19], the sub-category with the most Novice districts was Assessment.

Figure 3 shows the percentage of districts at each rubric level for the sub-categories of the Teacher Capacity and Development rubric. Similarly to the other rubric areas, most of the districts

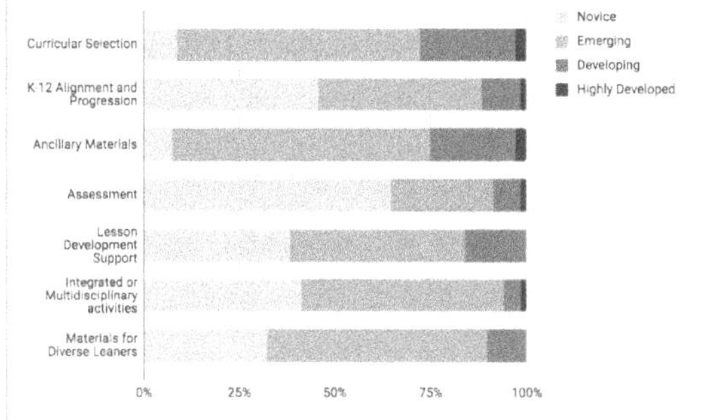

Figure 2: Materials and Curriculum Rubric Data

were either Novice(39%) or Emerging(44.1%) in this area. As with the other rubric areas, there were varied responses across the sub-components of the rubric, with the sub-component of Advanced Teacher Capacity being the most developed. This is not surprising as many school districts offer salary incentives or other grants for all teachers to pursue advanced coursework.

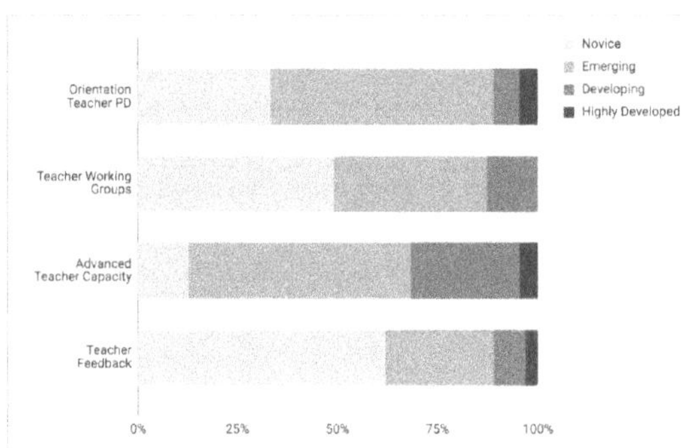

Figure 3: Teacher Capacity and Development Rubric Data

4.3 Discussion of Evidence of Validity

Moskal and Leydens (2000) [26] identify three primary areas of evidence for scoring rubrics when evaluating evidence of rubric validity. In this section, I discuss these areas with relation to the rubrics piloted with 65 districts from August 2017 to February 2018.

4.3.1 Content-Related Evidence. Content-related evidence assesses whether the rubric covers the intended subject matter it was designed to assess. The district rubrics were designed to assess CS education implementation within school districts in the US. As evidence of content alignment, I present the text of the rubrics themselves, which include the specific words "computer science" throughout the rubric descriptions. For example, the District Leadership sub-category of the rubric for Emerging says "District leadership recognizes CS education efforts but is not engaged in coordination or shared planning processes (if they exist)." Throughout the rubrics, CS is used to ensure the district teams are self-assessing their CS implementations.

4.3.2 Construct-Related Evidence. Construct-related evidence identifies the underlying reasoning or thought processes involved in the self-assessment or rubric scoring. Although the organization did not record the discussion of the district teams, the post-workshop survey (completed in the room at the end of the workshop) can be used to inform the question of construct-related evidence.

Participants felt strongly that the workshop guided them to clear next steps (95.2%). With regards to the individual rubric areas, the post-survey asked if the goals the districts set were guided by the workshop for Leadership (92.5%), Teacher Capacity and Development (92.9%), and Materials and Curriculum Selection and Refinement (95.2%). They were also asked if the goals would help advance their rubric scores for Leadership (82.5%), Teacher Capacity and Development (81.7%), and Materials and Curriculum Selection and Refinement (81.7%).

Construct related evidence also exists in Figure 1 in the alignment of rubric areas to research supported categories for school and district curricular implementations. Additional rubric (and workshop) construct related evidence will emerge in the analysis of the goals set by districts in a subsequent paper.

4.3.3 Criterion-Related Evidence. Criterion-related evidence seeks to determine if the rubric outcomes correlate with actual implementation that is happening in the schools. As the districts had no incentive to either inflate their scores or provide false information (all rubric scores were private to the teams and were only to be shared in aggregate in publications such as this one), the organization trusts that the self-assessments are accurate. Additional evidence for criterion-related validity will be presented in a separate paper focused on the analysis of goals set by participants.

5 FUTURE WORK

In this paper, we presented a description of the development of a series of rubrics for school districts to use in order to self assess and guide efforts for CS education implementation. Additionally, we shared data from the early use of the rubrics with 67 school districts from a variety of settings across the US for preliminary evidence of the validity of the rubrics for the domain.

Future work in the US is already under way, including a longitudinal study with a small number of districts. This deep dive is using qualitative and quantitative instruments to assess the alignment of their CS education efforts and monitor changes within the educational systems as a result of engaging with the organization for district-focused workshops. Additionally, an analysis of the goals set by districts is currently ongoing. The analysis will use the goals in conjunction with the rubric data to infer a landscape of not only areas where districts need support, but also where districts can use existing structures and resources to apply to CS education to increase implementation and rigor.

6 ACKNOWLEDGMENTS

The authors would like to acknowledge Dell Legacy of Good for the funding supporting the pilot workshops and rubric iteration. CSforALL would also like to acknowledge Maya Israel, Richard Ladner, and other members of the CSforALL community who have provided feedback on the rubrics and SCRIPT process.

REFERENCES

[1] Achieve and the US Education Delivery Institute. *Implementing Common Core State Standards and Assessments: A Workbook for State and District Leaders*. Achieve, 2012.

[2] S. Anderson, K. Leithwood, and T. Strauss. Leading data use in schools: Organizational conditions and practices at the school and district levels. *Leadership and Policy in Schools*, 9(3):292–327, 2010.

[3] O. Astrachan, J. Cuny, C. Stephenson, and C. Wilson. The cs10k project: mobilizing the community to transform high school computing. In *Proceedings of the 42nd ACM technical symposium on Computer science education*, pages 85–86. ACM, 2011.

[4] M. A. Bair and D. E. Bair. Failure, the next generation: Why rigorous standards are not sufficient to improve science learning. *International Journal of Education Policy and Leadership*, 9(5), 2014.

[5] J. Best and A. Dunlap. Next generation science standards: Considerations for curricula, assessments, preparation, and implementation. *McREL International*, 2014.

[6] A. S. Bryk, L. M. Gomez, A. Grunow, and P. G. LeMahieu. *Learning to Improve: How America? s Schools Can Get Better at Getting Better.* ERIC, 2015.

[7] A. S. Bryk, P. B. Sebring, E. Allensworth, J. Q. Easton, and S. Luppescu. *Organizing schools for improvement: Lessons from Chicago*. University of Chicago Press, 2010.

[8] C. E. Coburn, H. C. Hill, and J. P. Spillane. Alignment and accountability in policy design and implementation: The common core state standards and implementation research. *Educational Researcher*, 45(4):243–251, 2016.

[9] C. E. Coburn, J. Touré, and M. Yamashita. Evidence, interpretation, and persuasion: Instructional decision making at the district central office. *Teachers College Record*, 111(4):1115–1161, 2009.

[10] Code.org. Expand computer science at your school or district. Webpage, April 2018.

[11] Code.org. Promote computer science. Webpage, April 2018.

[12] N. R. Council et al. Next generation science standards: For states, by states. 2013.

[13] N. R. Council et al. *Guide to implementing the next generation science standards*. National Academies Press, 2015.

[14] L. A. DeLyser and M. Preston. A public school model of cs education. In *Proceedings of the International Conference on Frontiers in Education: Computer Science and Computer Engineering (FECS)*, page 233. The Steering Committee of The World Congress in Computer Science, Computer Engineering and Applied Computing (WorldComp), 2015.

[15] B. Ericson and M. Guzdial. Measuring demographics and performance in computer science education at a nationwide scale using ap cs data. In *Proceedings of the 45th ACM technical symposium on Computer science education*, pages 217–222. ACM, 2014.

[16] C. Fancsali, L. Tigani, P. Toro Isaza, and R. Cole. A landscape study of computer science education in nyc: Early findings and implications for policy and practice. In *Proceedings of the 49th ACM Technical Symposium on Computer Science Education*, pages 44–49. ACM, 2018.

[17] B. J. Fishman, W. R. Penuel, A.-R. Allen, B. H. Cheng, and N. Sabelli. Design-based implementation research: An emerging model for transforming the relationship of research and practice. *National society for the study of education*, 112(2):136–156, 2013.

[18] J. Goode. Increasing diversity in k-12 computer science: Strategies from the field. In *ACM SIGCSE Bulletin*, volume 40, pages 362–366. ACM, 2008.

[19] S. Grover, M. Bienkowski, and E. Snow. Assessments for computational thinking in k-12. In *Proceedings of the 46th ACM Technical Symposium on Computer Science Education*, pages 700–700. ACM, 2015.

[20] M. Guzdial. Bringing computer science to us schools, state by state. *Communications of the ACM*, 59(5):24–25, 2016.

[21] P. Hubwieser. Computer science education in secondary schools–the introduction of a new compulsory subject. *ACM Transactions on Computing Education (TOCE)*, 12(4):16, 2012.

[22] P. Hubwieser. The darmstadt model: a first step towards a research framework for computer science education in schools. In *International Conference on Informatics in Schools: Situation, Evolution, and Perspectives*, pages 1–14. Springer, 2013.

[23] C. C. S. S. Initiative et al. Common core state standards for mathematics. washington, dc: National governors association center for best practices and the council of chief state school officers, 2010.

[24] P. McGuinn. Stimulating reform: Race to the top, competitive grants and the obama education agenda. *Educational Policy*, 26(1):136–159, 2012.

[25] M. W. McLaughlin. Learning from experience: Lessons from policy implementation. *Educational evaluation and policy analysis*, 9(2):171–178, 1987.

[26] B. M. Moskal and J. A. Leydens. Scoring rubric development: Validity and reliability. *Practical assessment, research & evaluation*, 7(10):71–81, 2000.

[27] F. M. Newmann, B. Smith, E. Allensworth, and A. S. Bryk. Instructional program coherence: What it is and why it should guide school improvement policy. *Educational evaluation and policy analysis*, 23(4):297–321, 2001.

[28] A. D. of Education. Computer science education in arkansas. Website, April 2018.

[29] U. D. of Education. Supporting effective educator development program. Website, April 2018.

[30] V. D. of Education. Computer science education in virginia. Website, April 2018.

[31] N. A. of State Boards of Education. A goal without a plan is a wish. State Innovations Newsletter, March 2014.

[32] W. R. Penuel, B. J. Fishman, B. Haugan Cheng, and N. Sabelli. Organizing research and development at the intersection of learning, implementation, and design. *Educational researcher*, 40(7):331–337, 2011.

[33] B. Rabe. Race to the top: The expanding role of us state renewable portfolio standards. *Sustainable Dev. L. & Pol'y*, 7:10, 2006.

[34] B. Rowan, R. Correnti, R. J. Miller, and E. M. Camburn. School improvement by design: Lessons from a study of comprehensive school reform programs. *Consortium for Policy Research in Education*, 2009.

[35] R. Santo, L. A. DeLyser, J. Ahn, A. Pellicone, J. Aguiar, and S. Wortel-London. Equity in the who, how, and what of computer science education: K12 school district conceptualizations of equity in 'cs for all' initiatives. *Research on Equity and Sustained Participation in Engineering, Computing adn Technology (RESPECT)*, 2019.

[36] M. K. Stein and C. E. Coburn. Architectures for learning: A comparative analysis of two urban school districts. *American Journal of Education*, 114(4):583–626, 2008.

[37] J. Wang, H. Hong, J. Ravitz, and S. Hejazi Moghadam. Landscape of k-12 computer science education in the us: Perceptions, access, and barriers. In *Proceedings of the 47th ACM Technical Symposium on Computing Science Education*, pages 645–650. ACM, 2016.

Effect of Native Language on Student Learning and Classroom Interaction in an Operating Systems Course

Adalbert Gerald Soosai Raj
Department of Computer Sciences and Education
University of Wisconsin-Madison
gerald@cs.wisc.edu

Eda Zhang
Department of Curriculum and Instruction
University of Wisconsin-Madison
rzhang346@wisc.edu

Saswati Mukerjee
Department of Information Science and Technology
College of Engineering Guindy, Anna University
msaswati@auist.net

Jim Williams
Department of Computer Sciences
University of Wisconsin-Madison
jimw@cs.wisc.edu

Richard Halverson
Department of Educational Leadership and Policy Analysis
University of Wisconsin-Madison
rich.halverson@wisc.edu

Jignesh M. Patel
Department of Computer Sciences
University of Wisconsin-Madison
jignesh@cs.wisc.edu

ABSTRACT

Understanding an operating systems (OS) code base is a difficult task since it involves understanding a huge amount of low-level C and assembly code. The inherent level of difficulty associated with OS topics is high because of the high element interactivity (i.e., material consists of elements that heavily interact). The mental effort associated with learning a complex subject like OS may be higher for non-native English speakers, when the subject is taught in a natural language (i.e., English) that is not the students' native language. We were interested in finding the effect of an instructional design that combines the students' native language along with English on students' understanding of select topics in OS. We designed an experiment to teach CPU virtualization using xv6 to two groups of undergraduate students in Tamil Nadu, India. We taught the experimental group using English and Tamil (native language of students in Tamil Nadu) and the control group using only English. We conducted a pre-test and a post-test to test students' understanding of the OS topics taught, before and after our intervention respectively. We also collected data on the questions that students asked in lectures during our intervention. We found that teaching OS using native language and English is no different than teaching OS using only English with respect to student learning. We also found that the native language had an impact on the student engagement and classroom interaction by creating more dialogue within the Tamil+English (experimental) classroom when compared to the English-only (control) classroom.

ITiCSE '19, July 15–17, 2019, Aberdeen, Scotland, UK

ACM ISBN 978-1-4503-6301-3/19/07...$15.00
https://doi.org/10.1145/3304221.3319787

CCS CONCEPTS

• **Social and professional topics → Computer science education;**

KEYWORDS

Bilingual CS Education, Operating Systems, Native Language

ACM Reference format:
Adalbert Gerald Soosai Raj, Eda Zhang, Saswati Mukerjee, Jim Williams, Richard Halverson, and Jignesh M. Patel. 2019. Effect of Native Language on Student Learning and Classroom Interaction in an Operating Systems Course. In *Proceedings of Innovation and Technology in Computer Science Education, Aberdeen, Scotland, UK, July 15–17, 2019 (ITiCSE '19)*, 7 pages.
https://doi.org/10.1145/3304221.3319787

1 INTRODUCTION

Students in India learn their subjects during K-12 (kindergarten (K) through twelfth grade (12)) either in English or their native language (i.e., the language that a person has spoken from earliest childhood). This choice of language depends on whether the student studies in an English-medium school or a native-language-medium school during their K-12. The decision about which medium of instruction a child studies is made by the child's parents. The parents make these decisions mainly based on their financial status. Tamil-medium education is free of cost but English-medium education costs some money. This difference in costs forces the students from poor financial backgrounds to learn only in Tamil-medium as these students' parents are not in a position to afford an English-medium school for their children's education.

Although there are two mediums of instruction during K-12, Computer Science is taught in undergraduate institutions primarily in English. The main reason for teaching CS in English is because English is the de facto international language of programming [9]. Therefore, students who aren't very comfortable in English (e.g., students who studied in a Tamil-medium school during their K-12 and students who aren't proficient with English even though they may have studied in an English medium school) find it difficult to understand introductory programming concepts since the subject is already difficult and they are also forced to learn it in a language that they are not comfortable with [13]. As a result, these students end up failing their CS courses, and eventually develop inferiority complexes about their abilities [12].

Most of the prior work in the area of bilingual CS education have been focused mainly on teaching introductory programming [13, 20]. Although the upper-level CS courses like the operating systems are considered to be inherently more difficult than the intro programming courses, to the best of our knowledge, no previous work has been done in studying the effect of a students' native language in learning advanced subjects like the operating systems. We consider our work as a first small step in this direction.

Our research tries to answer the following two questions:

(1) *What is the effect of using the native language of non-native English speakers on student understanding of concepts/code in an upper level Computer Science course, like introduction to operating systems (using xv6 codebase)?*
(2) *What is the effect of native language on classroom interaction measured using the number and the quality of questions asked during a class?*

To answer these questions and to better understand the impact of the medium of instruction to teach upper-level CS classes, we conducted an experiment where we taught an OS course based on xv6 [4] (a simple unix-like teaching operating system) using both *Tamil and English* to a group of students (experimental group) whose native language was Tamil. We also taught the same OS course to another set of students (control group) *only in English*, even though their native language was also Tamil. We used *Tamil along with English* to teach the experimental group since we believe that even though Tamil may help students to better understand programming concepts, they should learn English too since English is the global language for programming and communication [11].

2 RELATED WORK

Soosai Raj et. al. [20] studied the effect of native language on student learning and sentiments and found that teaching linked lists in data structures using Tamil and English was no different than teaching using only English. They also found that students have expressed positive sentiments about learning using two languages, based on the student feedback data [19]. We consider our study to be an extension of this work applied to the domain of an upper-level CS class.

John Airey [1] studied undergraduate physics classes that were taught in English and Swedish to 22 students at two Swedish universities. The lectures were recorded and students were interviewed using stimulated recall. He found that when taught in English the students asked and answered fewer questions and reported being less able to simultaneously follow the lecture and take notes. Students adapted to being taught in English by; asking questions after the lecture, no longer taking notes in class, reading sections of work before class or - in the worst case - by using the lecture for mechanical note taking. Our study is an application of this work in the context of computer science education. We made classroom observations and made a note of the classroom interactions based on the questions asked by the students.

Pal and Iyer [14–16] studied the effect of using native language (Hindi) on student learning for non-native English speakers. They found that Hindi-medium students understood programming concepts better (measured using post-tests), when they were taught using Hindi compared to being taught using only-English. Our study differs from this study in the medium of instruction used for teaching programming: they used a Hindi-only approach while we used a bilingual (Tamil+English) approach.

Probyn interviewed some teachers in South Africa who use English along with Xhosa, an official South African language, to teach Science [17, 18]. The study shows that the language of learning and teaching frequently creates a barrier to learning when it is not the native language of the learners. The benefits of code-switching between the two languages for increased comprehension among students is also highlighted. We consider our study as an extension to this study where we try to find if the vernacular has any effect on learning programming, mainly by measuring student learning using pre-and-post technical tests.

3 METHODOLOGY

In this section, we explain the methodology that we used to conduct our experiment and collect our data.

3.1 Participants

The experiment was conducted in a well reputed Engineering college in Tamil Nadu. Two groups of third-year students, enrolled in two different sections of an operating systems course were selected as participants for our study. One group was treated as the control group and the other group was treated as the experimental group. The total number of students in the control and experimental group were 51 and 39 respectively. All these students have previously taken a programming and data structures course in C [10]. They have also taken an introductory course on the basic concepts of an operating systems (e.g., scheduling policies, page replacement policies, process creation APIs, concurrency using threads, etc) in which they learn policies and APIs of an OS. The course in which we conducted our intervention was the next course that students take after the basic OS course in which they learn the mechanisms and implementation details of CPU/memory virtualization, and File Systems in a unix-like OS.

3.2 Experimental Design

The experiment was conducted using a *nonrandomized control group pre-test post-test design* [5]. In this design, the participants were not randomly assigned to groups but remained in their pre-assigned groups. This was done as we conducted our experiments as part of regular classes and so were not able to randomize and regroup our participants into two new groups. This experimental design helped us to keep the details of our experimental procedure to be a secret from the students until the end of our intervention. This increases the external validity of the design by reducing the reactive effects of the experimental procedure [5]. We acknowledge that the problem with this approach is that even if there are any post-test differences between the groups, they may be attributed to characteristic difference between the groups rather than to the intervention. We take this issue into consideration in our result analysis by choosing our statistical models for pre-test post-test comparison very carefully (see Section 4 for more details). The teacher, who was the actual instructor for the two sections of this course, agreed to teach the two groups during our intervention.

The teachers introduced the researcher as a visiting faculty who will observe their classes and co-teach a few classes whenever needed. The researcher was a silent observer who took field notes during the intervention. The researcher helped the teacher answer a few questions on xv6 [4] codebase whenever the teacher needed some help. It is important to note that, as a part of our experiment, xv6 was introduced for the first time in this operating systems course, as a way to explain the concepts underlying the unix operating systems. As xv6 was a new codebase even for the instructor, the researcher who was familiar with the codebase before, helped the teacher in answering a few questions that the students asked about the codebase during the lectures.

3.3 Experimental Procedure

The following activities were performed with both the English-only (control) group and the Tamil+English (experimental) group as a part of our intervention. There was a pre-test, in-class lectures, code walkthrough sessions, and a post-test. The questions in the pre-test and the post-test were in English for both groups.

3.3.1 Pre-test. A pre-test was conducted to determine the students' understanding of the basic concepts of an OS. There were four questions on the pre-test. There was one question each on CPU scheduling policies, page replacement algorithms, creating new processes using fork and exec, and concurrency using threads. The pre-test was conducted for a total of 24 points, six points for each question. The pre-test questions were created based on the previous topics that students learned in the basic OS course, in consultation with the instructor who taught that course.

The above mentioned topics were tested in the pre-test as they would give us a baseline for understanding the students' prior knowledge about an OS before our intervention. The complete pre-test can be found at this link: http://bit.do/os_pretest.

3.3.2 Classroom Lectures. Twelve classroom-based lectures, each of 50 minutes duration, were presented for both groups. The mechanisms behind CPU virtualization were explained in those twelve lectures. Topics discussed were: process creation, limited direct execution, system calls, timer interrupt, context switch, etc. The same topics were taught to both the groups. The free online textbook, Operating Systems: Three Easy Pieces (OSTEP) [3], was used as a reference to teach these topics.

The main differences between the lectures for the two groups were the following: The lectures were taught *only in English* for the students in the control group. Also, the students in the control group were required to communicate with the instructor and their classmates during the lecture in English only.

On the other hand, the lectures were taught using both *English and Tamil* in the experimental group, and the students were free to communicate in any of those two languages, whichever they felt more comfortable with. The instructor used both English and Tamil nearly equally (i.e., 50% time in English - 50% time in Tamil) while teaching the experimental group. The instructor answered the questions during the lecture using the same language (either English or Tamil) in which they were asked.

The instructor used bilingual teaching methods like code-switching [6] and translanguaging [7] for teaching the Tamil+English (experimental) group. The instructor used *code-switching* for switching between Tamil and English in the following way. She used English to introduce a topic, to explain the basic idea behind the topic, and to explain some technical terms (e.g., context switch). She switched to Tamil whenever she felt that a particular topic needed detailed explanation in order to help the students understand the idea in a better way (e.g., How does a context switch happen?). The instructor used *translanguaging* as follows. She used Tamil only for oral explanations, discussion, and answering students' questions. She wrote all the content (e.g., topic names, definitions, explanations etc.) on the chalk-board during the lectures only in English.

3.3.3 Code Walkthrough Sessions. The instructor conducted regular code walkthrough sessions as a part of our intervention, where she helped students understand the code flow of the OS topics discussed in the lectures (e.g., system call, scheduler, context switch). xv6 code was used during these code walkthrough sessions for understanding the internal workings of a unix-like operating system. The code walkthrough sessions were conducted as a part of the twelve lectures (see Section 3.3.2). Approximately, six of the twelve classroom lectures were used for code walkthroughs and the remaining six were used for explaining OS concepts about CPU virtualization.

The only difference between the code walkthrough sessions for the two groups was the language that was used while explaining the xv6 code: Tamil and English was used for the code explanations in the experimental group while English only was used for code explanations in the control group.

3.3.4 Post-test. The post-test consisted of 7 questions on CPU virtualization. The post-test questions were open-ended and based on the following topics: (1) Process state transitions, (2) Trapping into the kernel, (3) System calls vs library functions, (4) Process Control Block (PCB) in xv6, (5) User vs kernel threads, (6) `syscall()` function in xv6, and (7) Steps in servicing a system call.

All the questions on the post-test were based on the material taught during the classroom-based lectures and the code walkthrough sessions. The post-test was conducted for a total of 25 points. The complete post-test can be found at this link: http://bit.do/os_posttest.

3.3.5 Classroom observations. The researcher observed two regular classes before our intervention. Classes were taught only in English to both the groups before our intervention. Our intervention was conducted only for 6 weeks during the regular semester (which is usually 15 weeks long).

During our intervention, the researcher acted as a silent observer and took field notes of the questions asked by the students, answers given by the instructor, and the follow-up questions that were arised and answered. The observer also made notes of the language used for asking the questions. One sample interaction in the experimental group was as follows (Q - question asked by the student; A - answer given by the teacher): *Q: Why do we save the context of process A twice during a context switch? A: We save it twice because if we are switching to a different process, then we need to save the context of both the user thread and the kernel thread of process A. Q: So, do we use different memory locations to store these two different contexts? A: Yes, we do. The context of the user thread is stored in a structure called a trap frame and the context of the kernel thread is stored in a structure called process control block in xv6.* The complete set of questions asked by students in both the groups and the answers given by the instructor can be found here: http://bit.do/os_questions

4 RESULTS

The mean of the pre-test scores and the post-test scores for the two groups are shown in Table 1 and Table 2 respectively.

Table 1: Mean of pre-test scores for the two groups

Group	N	Mean	Std. Dev.	Std. Error of Mean
Control	51	48.0	16.9	2.4
Experimental	39	58.2	14.7	2.4

Table 2: Mean of post-test scores for the two groups

Group	N	Mean	Std. Dev.	Std. Error of Mean
Control	51	55.1	20.2	2.8
Experimental	39	59.7	20.4	3.3

4.1 Analysis of Pre-test Scores

We compared the pre-test of both groups using an independent samples t-test. The following assumptions for two sample t-test were satisfied:

(1) The Central Limit Theorem (CLT) applies to each sample individually. i.e., pre-test data is normally distributed in both the groups as confirmed by the Quantile-Quantile (Q-Q) plots.

(2) The pre-test scores of both the groups are random samples that are independent of each other.

(3) The variances of the pre-test scores are approximately equal. (i.e., Standard deviation of control group (s1) = 16.9; Standard deviation of experimental group (s2) = 14.7; s1/s2 = 1.1 < 1.5).

We performed an independent samples t-test to compare the pre-test scores between the control group and the experimental group and found *a significant difference* in pre-test scores between the two groups (t(90) = -3.05, df = 88, p = 0.003). This means that the two groups differed significantly with respect to their prior knowledge on OS concepts. Therefore, we cannot directly compare the post-test scores between the two groups using independent samples t-test [5]. Instead we intend to do the following two types of analysis:

(1) Compare the gain scores (post-test - pre-test) of the two groups using an independent samples t-test (if t-test assumptions are satisfied).

(2) Compare the post-test scores of sub-groups of students having the same pre-test score between the two groups using ANalysis of COVAriance (ANCOVA) [8]. Note that post-test analysis was not possible since the assumptions for ANCOVA was not satisfied (see Section 4.3).

4.2 Analysis of Gain Scores

The mean of the gain scores for the two groups are shown in Table 3. The mean gain for the control group is higher than that of the experimental group. The assumptions for independent samples t-test (as shown in Section 4.1) were satisfied by the gain scores of both the groups. We performed independent samples t-test [8] to compare the gain scores between the control group and the experimental group and found *no significant difference* in gain scores (t(90) = 1.25, df = 88, p = 0.21).

Table 3: Mean of gain scores for the two groups

Group	N	Mean	Std. Dev.	Std. Error of Mean
Control	51	7.1	18.9	2.6
Experimental	39	1.5	22.7	3.6

4.3 Analysis of Post-test Scores

We intended to use ANCOVA to find if there was any difference in the post-test score (response variable) due to the students' group (independent variable), while controlling for the students' pre-test scores (covariate). All assumptions of ANCOVA were satisfied for our data, except the homogeneity of regression lines. Hence, we were not able to compare the post-test differences between the two groups using ANCOVA as explained below.

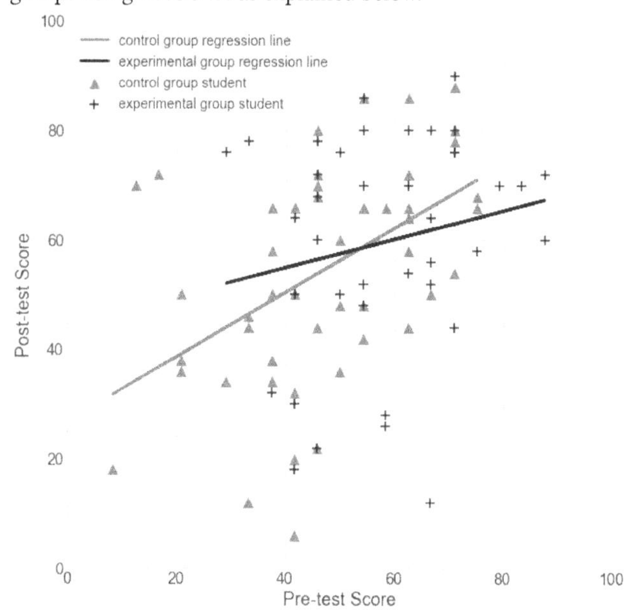

Figure 1: A scatter plot showing each student's pre-test score plotted on the x-axis and the post-test score plotted on the y-axis. The regression lines are also plotted for each group which shows the relationship between the pre-test and post-test scores.

We plot a scatter plot in Figure 1 using the pre-test and the post-test scores of the students in both the groups. In this scatter plot, the x-axis represents the pre-test scores of the students and the y-axis represents the post-test scores of the students. The two lines shown in this scatter plot are the regression lines for a particular group that summarizes the relationship between the post-test score and the pre-test score for that group.

The regression lines for both the groups have *positive slopes* (0.26 for the experimental group and 0.59 for the control group) and the regression lines are above the diagonal (i.e., the line connecting the points (0,0) and (100,100)), which means that our intervention had a similar positive effect on both the groups. But the slopes are not nearly equal since the slope of the regression line for the control group (0.59) is more than twice the slope of the regression line for the experimental group (0.26). This means that we cannot apply ANCOVA to find if there is any significant difference between the post-test scores of the two groups.

4.4 Analysis of Student Questions

The number of questions asked by the students in both the groups is shown in Table 4. The total number of questions asked by the students in the Tamil+English (experimental) group (# questions = 11) is nearly three times more than the number of questions asked by the students in the English-only (control) group (# questions = 4).

Table 4: Number of questions asked by the students in the two groups

Group	Total questions	# English	# Tamil
Control	4	4	0
Experimental	11	2	8

In the experimental group, the number of questions asked in Tamil (# questions = 8) were more than the number of questions asked in English (# questions = 2) by a factor of 4 (i.e., a ratio of 4:1 in favour of Tamil). One student asked a question in English and followed up with another question in Tamil. This student's question was not considered to be in either of the two groups and hence the number of questions in English (2) + number of questions in Tamil (8) is one less than the total number of questions (11). In the control group, there weren't any question that were asked in Tamil since the students were required to communicate only in English.

One interesting observation was that, even though there were not as many questions in the control group as there were in the experimental group during the lectures, the number of students who asked questions on a one-on-one basis after class was more in the English-only (control) group than in the Tamil and English (experimental) group.

We classify the questions asked by the students in both the groups into the following four types of knowledge dimensions based on revised Bloom's taxonomy [2]:

(1) Factual knowledge (e.g., What is an address space?)
(2) Conceptual knowledge (e.g., Why doesn't a program have stack or heap when it is on disk?)
(3) Procedural knowledge (e.g., When we switch from one process to another are there really two context switches that happens?)
(4) Metacognitive knowledge (e.g., Why do we save the context of process A twice during a context switch?)

A few questions were classified under more than one knowledge domain. For example, the following question asked by a student started as a factual question but the follow-up question was in the conceptual knowledge domain (Q - Question; A - Answer): *Q (Student): What is static data? A (Teacher): Static data is the part of the address space where global and static variables that are common for all functions are stored. Q (Student): Why can't those variables be stored on the stack? A (Teacher): Good question. They can't be stored on the stack since these variables should be accessible from any function. A stack frame for a function only stores the local variables that were created within the function and hence these local variables are accessible only from within the function that is currently executing.* Note that even though there were two questions that were asked as a part of this interaction, it was treated as only one question as follow-up questions were considered to be part of the original question.

The number of questions that are classified across the four different knowledge dimensions is shown in Table 5.

Table 5: Classification of questions across 4 knowledge domains

Group	Factual	Conceptual	Procedural	Metacog.
Ctrl	3	0	1	0
Exp	4	7	2	2

The number of factual questions in both the groups were almost equal. There were no conceptual questions in the English-only (control) group while there were seven conceptual questions in the Tamil+English (experimental) group. The number of procedural questions in the English-only and the Tamil+English group were one and two respectively. There were no metacognitive questions in the English-only group while there were two such questions in the Tamil+English group.

There were no follow-up questions in the English-only (control) group and there were five follow-up questions in the Tamil+English (experimental) group.

The questions across the four knowledge domains asked by the students in the experimental group are classified based on the language (Tamil or English) that was used to ask the question and the results are summarized in Table 6.

Table 6: Classification of questions across the four knowledge domains from the Tamil+English (experimental) group based on the language

Domain	English	Tamil
Factual	2	2
Conceptual	1	6
Procedural	0	2
Metacognitive	0	2

There were equal number of factual questions in Tamil and English. Six conceptual questions were asked in Tamil while one was asked in English. All procedural and metacognitive questions were asked in Tamil.

5 DISCUSSION

5.1 Interpretation of Results

Our study tried to find if using the native language (Tamil) along with English for teaching an upper-level CS course like the operating systems had any effect on students' learning of programming when compared to using only English. We measured the student learning in terms of gain scores and post-test scores.

The difference between the two groups with respect to the gain score is not statistically significant (see Section 4.2). This shows that teaching programming using Tamil and English is no different than teaching programming using only English. Also, we were unable to measure the difference between the two groups with respect to the post-test score (with the pre-test score as a covariate) using ANCOVA since one of the ANCOVA assumptions (i.e., homogeneity of regression slopes) was not satisfied. Therefore, we need more quantitative experiments in this area to better understand the impact of the native language on students' understanding of upper-level CS concepts.

Our finding on the effect of native language on student learning in an operating systems course matches the findings of Soosai Raj et. al. [20] which found that the use of the native language (Tamil) did not have a significant positive impact on student learning in a data structures course. We consider our findings to be a validation of the previous results from an introductory programming course to an upper-level CS course.

On the other hand, our findings contradict the findings of Pal and Iyer [13] which suggests that the native language (Hindi) had a significant positive effect on students who did their schooling in a Hindi-medium school. The main reason for this difference might be that in our study even though the native language of all students was Tamil, the majority of students studied in an English-medium school during their K-12. On the other hand, 50% of students in Pal and Iyer's study were from a Hindi-medium background.

Based on the classroom observations we conducted as part of our study, we did a frequency count of the questions that were asked in the classroom, during our intervention, in both the groups. We found that giving students the freedom to speak using either their native language (Tamil) or English increased the classroom interaction that happened during the lectures (measured using the questions that were asked by the students in-class) in the Tamil+English (experimental) group when compared to the English-only (control) group (see Table 4).

We classified the questions along four knowledge dimensions based on the revised Bloom's taxonomy [2] and found that the students in the Tamil+English (experimental) group asked more questions about conceptual and procedural knowledge while the students in the English-only (control) group asked questions mainly about factual knowledge. We also found that 80% of the questions that students asked in the Tamil+English group were in Tamil. The use of the students' native language also encouraged the students in the Tamil+English group to ask follow-up questions in their native language while such a trend of asking follow-up questions was not found in the English-only group. Our results on analyzing the student questions shows that the use of the native language had an impact on the number and the quality of questions that non-native English speakers ask in a CS classroom.

An alternative interpretation of our results is that the students in the Tamil+English (experimental) group are better students (based on the pre-test scores) when compared to the students in the English-only (control) group. Therefore, the questions that these students asked might not be due to the native language but instead due to their inherent curiosity. We argue that this might not be the case since classroom observations that were conducted before our intervention showed that the amount of interaction that happened in the two groups were minimal and similar across the two groups.

Our results on the classroom interaction matches those observed by Airey [1] while teaching physics using English and Swedish. For example, Airey found that English is a barrier for students to ask questions during a lecture because students do not want to be embarrassed before their peers by asking a question in English. We also found that students in the English-only (control) group asked a lot fewer questions than students in the Tamil+English (experimental) group, where students were free to use their native language, if needed.

5.2 Limitations and Future Work

The main limitation of our study is the use of *nonrandomized control group pre-test post-test design*. We used this design mainly because we wanted our intervention to be part of regular classes. Therefore, we weren't able to randomize students into two different groups but instead used the two pre-formed groups as our experimental and control groups. As a consequence, the two groups varied significantly with respect to their prior knowledge in OS before the start of our intervention. Although we have taken this pre-test difference into consideration in our analysis of results, we acknowledge that the results would have been more reliable if these initial differences didn't exist among these groups. To minimize the effects due to the initial differences among the two groups, as a part of our future work, we plan to conduct more controlled experiments with a *randomized control group pre-test post-test design* [5] to better understand the effects of the native language for learning upper-level CS classes. We plan to do this by conducting special topics courses (outside students' regular course schedules) where the instructor will have the flexibility to randomize students into two different groups.

Another limitation with our study is that we did not control for the students' English proficiency. This is important because if the students in the two groups differed significantly in their English skills, then this might be an important confounding factor in our experiments. As part of our future experiments we plan to control for the students' English skills by conducting tests for English proficiency prior to our intervention.

6 CONCLUSION

We found that teaching an upper-level CS course (i.e., operating systems) using a bilingual teaching methodology (in Tamil and English) is no different than teaching using only English with respect to student learning measured using pre- and post- tests. We also found that the native language had a positive impact on the classroom interaction, measured using the quantity and the quality of student questions that were asked during the class. We conclude that more studies should be conducted in bilingual CS education, across different CS courses and using different natural languages (e.g., Spanish) to truly understand and benefit from the role that native language plays in computer science education.

ACKNOWLEDGEMENTS

Our sincere thanks to Dr. Saswati Mukherjee, Ms. V. Ezhil Arasi and Mr. B. R. Yuvaraj for allowing us to work with their students and helping us conduct these experiments. We also thank all the students who took part in our experiments.

REFERENCES

[1] John Airey. 2009. *Science, language, and literacy: Case studies of learning in Swedish university physics.* Ph.D. Dissertation. Acta Universitatis Upsaliensis.

[2] Lorin W Anderson, David R Krathwohl, Peter W Airasian, Kathleen A Cruikshank, Richard E Mayer, Paul R Pintrich, James Raths, and Merlin C Wittrock. 2001. A taxonomy for learning, teaching, and assessing: A revision of BloomâĂŹs taxonomy of educational objectives, abridged edition. *White Plains, NY: Longman* (2001).

[3] Remzi H. Arpaci-Dusseau and Andrea C. Arpaci-Dusseau. 2015. *Operating Systems: Three Easy Pieces* (0.91 ed.). Arpaci-Dusseau Books.

[4] Russ Cox, M Frans Kaashoek, and Robert Morris. 2011. Xv6, a simple Unix-like teaching operating system. (2011).

[5] Dimiter M Dimitrov and Phillip D Rumrill Jr. 2003. Pretest-posttest designs and measurement of change. *Work* (2003).

[6] Jennifer R Fennema-Bloom. 2009. Code-scaffolding: A pedagogic code-switching technique for bilingual content instruction. *Journal of Education* (2009).

[7] Ofelia Garcia and Claire E Sylvan. 2011. Pedagogies and practices in multilingual classrooms: Singularities in pluralities. *The Modern Language Journal* (2011).

[8] Gene V Glass and Kenneth D Hopkins. 1970. *Statistical methods in education and psychology.* Prentice-Hall Englewood Cliffs, NJ.

[9] Philip J Guo. 2018. Non-Native English Speakers Learning Computer Programming: Barriers, Desires, and Design Opportunities. In *Proceedings of the 2018 CHI Conference on Human Factors in Computing Systems.* ACM, 396.

[10] Brian W Kernighan and Dennis M Ritchie. 2006. The C Programming Language. (2006).

[11] Thomas Andrew KIRKPATRICK. 2011. Internationalization or Englishization: Medium of instruction in today's universities. (2011).

[12] T Murugavel. 2011. The Problems of Non-English Medium Engineering Students and Possible Solutions. (2011). http://worldlitonline.net/the-problems-of-non-english.pdf

[13] Yogendra Pal. 2016. *A Framework for Scaffolding to Teach Programming to Vernacular Medium Learners.* Ph.D. Dissertation. IIT, Bombay.

[14] Yogendra Pal and Sridhar Iyer. 2012. Comparison of English versus Hindi Medium Students for Programming Abilities Acquired through Video-Based Instruction. In *T4E.* IEEE.

[15] Yogendra Pal and Sridhar Iyer. 2015. Classroom Versus Screencast for Native Language Learners: Effect of Medium of Instruction on Knowledge of Programming. In *ITiCSE.* ACM.

[16] Yogendra Pal and Sridhar Iyer. 2015. Effect of medium of instruction on programming ability acquired through screencast. In *LaTiCE.* IEEE.

[17] Margaret Probyn. 2001. Teachers voices: Teachers reflections on learning and teaching through the medium of English as an additional language in South Africa. *Bilingual Education and Bilingualism* (2001).

[18] Margaret Probyn. 2005. Learning science through two languages in South Africa. In *The 4th International Symposium on Bilingualism, Somerville, MA.*

[19] Adalbert Gerald Soosai Raj, Kasama Ketsuriyonk, Jignesh M Patel, and Richard Halverson. 2017. What Do Students Feel about Learning Programming Using Both English and Their Native Language?. In *2017 International Conference on Learning and Teaching in Computing and Engineering (LaTICE).* IEEE, 1–8.

[20] Adalbert Gerald Soosai Raj, Kasama Ketsuriyonk, Jignesh M Patel, and Richard Halverson. 2018. Does Native Language Play a Role in Learning a Programming Language?. In *Proceedings of the 49th ACM Technical Symposium on Computer Science Education.* ACM, 417–422.

Using Automated Prompts for Student Reflection on Computer Security Concepts

Hui Chen
CUNY Brooklyn College
Brooklyn, NY, U.S.A.
hui.chen@brooklyn.cuny.edu

Agnieszka Ciborowska
Virginia Commonwealth University
Richmond, VA, U.S.A.
ciborowskaa@vcu.edu

Kostadin Damevski
Virginia Commonwealth University
Richmond, VA, U.S.A.
kdamevski@vcu.edu

ABSTRACT

Reflection is known to be an effective means to improve students' learning. In this paper, we aim to foster meaningful reflection via prompts in computer science courses with a significant practical, software development component. To this end we develop an instructional strategy and system that automatically delivers prompts to students based on their commits in a source code repository. The system allows for prompts that instigate reflection in students to be timely with respect to students' work, and delivered automatically, thus easily scaling up the strategy.

In this paper, we describe the design of a rule-based prompt delivery system, including a list of security related reflection prompts. We collect preliminary evidence for the reflection strategy in a course targeting mobile development. The evaluation provides evidence that such a system can help realize a reflection-in-action instructional strategy at scale and improve students' learning.

Figure 1: An example of automated reflection-in-action where a student is encouraged to learn about the security principle of Chain of Control, as they are working on developing a secure mobile app.

CCS CONCEPTS

• **Applied computing** → **Education**; **Computer-assisted instruction**; • **Computing methodologies** → *Artificial intelligence*;

KEYWORDS

reflection; reflection prompt; automated reflection

ACM Reference Format:
Hui Chen, Agnieszka Ciborowska, and Kostadin Damevski. 2019. Using Automated Prompts for Student Reflection on Computer Security Concepts. In *Innovation and Technology in Computer Science Education (ITiCSE '19), July 15–17, 2019, Aberdeen, Scotland UK*. ACM, New York, NY, USA, 7 pages. https://doi.org/10.1145/3304221.3319731

1 INTRODUCTION

Drawn from experiential and constructivist view of learning, reflection is a process where a student contemplates and learns from current or past experiences. Instructors have strived to instigate reflection in various fields of professional practice and education for multiple decades [20], with numerous studies showing that reflection is beneficial to learning in many areas and disciplines [8]. In particular are its benefits to system design [2], including computer programming and software engineering [4–6, 25, 29]. While reflection is a diverse area of study, the focus of this paper is prompt-based reflection, where students are asked to reflect based on questions or directions provided by the instructor. The literature states that the learning outcomes of prompt-based reflection are strongly dependent on: 1) the quality of the prompts; 2) the timing of their delivery [7, 12]. Both of these characteristics are contingent on connecting the reflective prompts to individual student progress. However, *instructors closely monitoring each student's progress on numerous projects and assignments does not scale and is not realistic in most computer science programs.*

To address the challenge of scaling up prompt based reflection, in this paper, we propose and provide preliminary evidence for *automated prompt-based reflection*, an instructional strategy that applies principles from recommendation systems to suggest prompts to students based on their current activity. The recommendation system necessary to enable this instructional strategy uses as input students' ongoing work represented as changesets (or diffs) in source code management system (e.g. git), which are increasingly stored online via Web services like GitHub and BitBucket.

We evaluate the instructional strategy on reflection prompts targeting secure mobile application development. The prompts provide an opportunity to reinforce abstract security concepts introduced in lecture, by applying them to each individual student's progress on a practical project of implementing an Android app. Our results indicate that the instructional strategy is well received by students, leads to improvements in learning of security concepts, and even encourages students to revise and improve the design and implementation of the software project itself. Figure 1 shows an

ITiCSE '19, July 15–17, 2019, Aberdeen, Scotland UK

ACM ISBN 978-1-4503-6301-3/19/07...$15.00
https://doi.org/10.1145/3304221.3319731

actual interaction with a prototype prompt recommendation system, where a contextual and timely reflective prompt is delivered to a student designing an Android app with a login screen. The contributions of this paper are:

- instructional strategy for automatically instigating reflection using prompts in the course of software development assignments or projects;
- design of a recommendation system based technique for automated prompt-based reflection;
- preliminary evaluation results of the efficacy of the instructional strategy.

The rest of this paper is organized as follows. Section 2 outlines the background and related work. In Section 3 we describe the automated system for reflection and the set of prompts we defined for teaching secure mobile development. Section 4 discusses preliminary results in applying the system and instructional strategy in a mobile development focused course. Finally, we conclude the paper and discuss the future work in Section 5.

2 BACKGROUND AND RELATED WORK

The practice of reflection helps learners gain tacit knowledge [16]. Different from a novice, an expert has a larger body of tacit or experiential knowledge from which the expert can instinctively draw insights and apply them to current problem settings [17]. Software development is a discipline where the tacit knowledge is not easily captured by a set of rules and formulae. Therefore, it is difficult to be communicated by an instructor using lecture, and often requires project-based or problem-based instruction. Reflection is a key component in connecting concepts discussed in lecture, with those observed during non-trivial projects or assignments.

Encouraging learners and practitioners towards quality reflection on their experiences has been attempted and investigated by many educators and researchers. For instance, a frequently used reflection technique is for students to write reflective essays or blogs [29]. Our approach is different as it is based on prompts, which are far more specific about what is being reflected than an open-ended essay writing or blogging. Therefore, text of the prompts plays an important role in the quality of the student reflection.

Two other important characteristics that make reflective prompts effective are adaptivity and timeliness [7, 12]. Adaptivity means that reflection should be specific to the context of the current work by the student, and therefore able to influence the students future action on the project. Timeliness refers to the sensitivity of the prompts to the current actions by the students, in a way that the prompts do not completely disrupt the student at key points of their work. While adaptivity and timeliness can be obtained automatically using the system we describe in the paper, the quality of the prompts' content still requires careful tuning by the instructor.

There are numerous existing uses of reflection either in computer science education or aided by automated tools [6, 10, 13, 15, 22, 25, 27–29]. Researches have also developed automated reflection tools that help learners, more specifically, designers, reflect [22, 27]. These tools are not prompt-based, focusing instead on guiding designers to carry out open-ended reflection activities, such as, writing reflective logs, curating visual bookmarks, and visualizing creative designs [21, 27, 29].

Edwards investigated students' reflection via a test-driven development approach in lower-division programming courses, suggesting reflection's effectiveness in the fostering of comprehension, analysis, and hypothesis-testing skills across programming assignments [6]. Different from the type of reflection we describe, Edwards used reflection that is explicit and algorithmic as expressed in the program code to construct automated test cases.

Fostering effective reflection across a wide range of students is in effect a very challenging and complex topic. Although reflection's benefits are often regarded as self-evident and central to building capacity for lifelong learning, many concerns exist in applying reflective practice [8]. For instance, from the perspective of cognitive load theory, reflective practice, if not applied well, can overwhelm students and have negative impacts on students' learning [11, 26], in particular on novices. Proper scaffolding and guidance are important to reduce students' cognitive load when instigating reflection [9, 19]. This paper describes a specific approach that allows individualized delivery of prompts after students' incremental submission of their work. We also investigate whether our prompts and the automated timing of their delivery can target opportune times for reflection, which does not produce undue cognitive burden in reflection.

3 RECOMMENDING PROMPTS FOR REFLECTION

3.1 Rule-Based Recommendation System

From the educator's perspective, a typical use case of the our automated prompt-based reflection consists of a few steps. First, the instructor composes a set of reflective prompts specific to an assignment or project. The reflective prompts may reference content from lecture, or reference external documents, such as book chapters, API documentation, and research articles. The set of reflective prompts and the supporting explanation carry the reflection guidance provided to students.

Second, the instructor utilizes a prompt recommendation and delivery system, an essential component of the automated reflection approach described in this paper. This prompt recommendation and delivery scheme can range from the instructor specifying rules for the delivery of each prompt (e.g. a student invoking a method on the `Log` static class could trigger the prompt in Figure 1) to more general and automated approaches that allow for flexible expression of how prompts should be delivered.

Third, the student responses to the prompts are collected and delivered to the instructor. While directly grading the prompts is discouraged [8], their content provides valuable feedback to the instructor on students understanding of specific concepts.

In building a prompt recommendation system, there are design choices along two dimensions: 1) input data; and 2) models of student software development activity. The prompt recommendation's system input data can be static, i.e., submitted source code upon the completion of the project, episodic, i.e., versions of students' source code committed to a source code repository, or live, i.e., students' activity streaming from their IDE. From episodic data we can learn a student's progress on a project, while from interaction data we can infer what actions the student is carrying out at each moment in time. Along the second dimension, student software development

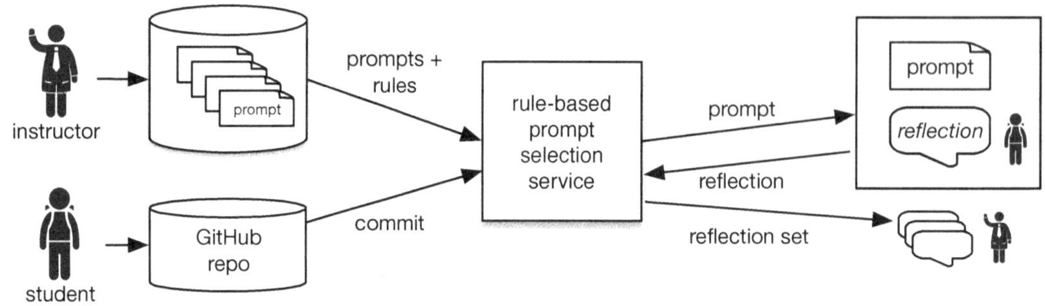

Figure 2: Design of the rule-based prompt delivery system.

activity models can be deterministic, typically consisting of a set of rules, or be probabilistic, building a probability distribution over the reflective prompts. In this paper, we concentrate on describing a a *rule-based* approach based on episodic changeset data. The advantage of a rule-based system is its simplicity, while the disadvantage that it requires the instructor express a specific rule (e.g., a regular expression over some aspect of the changeset) for the delivery of each prompt. Next, we describe the architecture of our system.

Figure 2 illustrates the major components and actors in the rule-based prompt recommendation system. We base our architecture of the rule-based prompt recommendation system on GitHub, which offers integration abilities via RESTful Web services. The instructor initially constructs reflection prompts [1], and rules for their delivery that are represented as regular expressions. The set of prompts are stored in a reflection prompt database, which we implement as a separate Web service. As students push their local commits to the central repository, GitHub's Webhook mechanism communicates their content to the rule-based prompt selection and delivery (Web) service. This selection and delivery service examines the content of each commit (or diff), executes each rule (i.e. regular expression) from the database, selecting a prompt from the set of available reflection prompts. Following the selection, the service extracts the student's e-mail address from GitHub's payload, and uses it to immediately send an e-mail to the student containing the reflection prompt and brief instructions. The e-mail uses the instructor's account, for which we use GMail's RESTful Web service, although many other general alternatives are possible. Once the prompt is delivered to students, the students compose answers to the prompts as e-mail replies that are sent to the instructor of the course.

3.2 Reflection Prompts

We designed a set of reflection prompts to help students learn secure design principles as they are applied in mobile application development. We considered two dimensions when designing reflection prompts, content relevancy and work relevancy.

To establish content relevancy, we identified a list of secure design principles, secure coding standards, and secure coding best practice. Saltzer and Schroeder devised a list of principles for information protection, such as, fail-safe default, least privilege, separation of privilege, and complete mediation [18]. These principles are often used as guidelines to develop secure systems, and discussed in well-known textbooks, such as, "Computer Security: Art and Science" by Bishop [3] and "Security in Computing" by Pfleeger and Pfleeger [14]. More recently, Smith revisited Saltzer and Schroeder's principles and gave them a contemporary treatment, yielding a list of overlapping secure principles [23]. In addition, for Android mobile app development, more specific secure development recommendations exist, such as, the Android Secure Coding Standard by the Software Engineering Institute [24] (the secure coding standard) and Android's "App Security Best Practices" [1] (the best practice).

We establish a mapping among the secure design principles, the secure coding standard, and the best practice, and write prompts aiming at providing students with opportunity to reflect on a selected list of secure design principles. Table 1 lists all the concepts, prompts and rules that we created. Although in this study we focus on secure software design principles, note that the reflective prompts and the system we described can be applied to guide students through various CS topics (e.g. operating systems, programming languages) with easy to discern patterns in the source code.

4 PRELIMINARY STUDY RESULTS

To investigate the impact of the automated prompt-based reflection on students' learning, we conducted a study with about 80 computer science students, focusing on concepts in software security. During the study we collected a set of preliminary results based on students' reflections and surveys, that we present in this section.

4.1 Method

We deployed the system and the prompts in a Fall 2018 Software Engineering course taught at one of the authors' affiliated institutions to junior and senior undergraduate students. The course is based on a large scale group project, an Android App of student's own choosing, spanning 3 graded iterations each lasting roughly 2 weeks. A lecture on secure software development was delivered in class, discussing overall principles and a set of examples extracted from real-world Android security exploits [1, 18, 23].

Students were informed about the automated prompt-based reflection project upon beginning of the study. Participation in the study was voluntary, although was encouraged with a bonus point.

We run the rule-based automatic prompt-based reflection system for the period about 5 weeks, covering 2 out of 3 project iterations, starting from October 4, 2018 to November 12, 2018. Based on

[1] An alternative to this is for the instructor to reuse existing prompts on a specific topic.

Table 1: Security-related reflection prompts targeting mobile development.

Secure Principles by Saltzer and Schroeder [18] and Smith [23]	Regex Rule	Prompt
Least Privilege	`"<uses-permission"` in AndroidManifest.xml	I noticed that your app requires the use of a new permission (defined in the Android Manifest file). Permissions may pose a risk to users' privacy so I would like you to answer these questions: 1) Is the permission necessary for the functioning of your app? 2) Does your app need to hold the permission all the time when the app is running? If not, when should you request the permission and when should you relinquish the permission? 3) Explain how does the Principle of Least Privilege that we discussed in class relate to this scenario?
Fail-safe default / Deny by default	`"<provider"` in AndroidManifest.xml	I noticed that you declared a new Content Provider in your Android Manifest file. Recall that if you do not wish to send data from your app to another app, which you probably do not, you should understand the "android:exported" attribute of the provider element and make sure the value of it is set properly. Explain how does the use of a content provider and setting this attribute relate to the the Principle of Deny by Default we discussed in class?
Least common mechanism / Chain of control	`"new\s+Intent.+ACTION"` in *.java	I noticed that you are using an implicit Intent. Think about the fact that the data we package in an implicit Intent can be received by anyone that registers for that Intent broadcast. Do you think this exploit is possible for your application? Explain how this scenario relates to the principle of Chain of Control we discussed in class?
Least common mechanism / Chain of control	`"openFileOutput\("` in *.java	I noticed that your app stores data in a file. Does the stored data contain any sensitive information? Who has access to the data (i.e. is it internal or external storage)? Explain how this scenario relates to the principle of Chain of Control we discussed in class?
Least common mechanism / Chain of control	`"Log\."` in *.java	I noticed that you wrote logging statements. This is great as logging is an important means to diagnose an application in development and in production. Consider the contents of the logged data; could it be considered sensitive to security or privacy? Explain how this scenario relates to the principle of Chain of Control we discussed in class?

the student's commit pushed to the remote repository on Github, the system automatically determines whether a security related reflection prompt should be sent. The student may receive multiple reflection prompts, however a reflection prompt is not sent twice to the same student. Upon the conclusion of each iteration, we sent an anonymous and voluntary post-reflection survey.

4.2 Data Collection

Over the course of the study, we collected data about student's reflections, including answers to the reflection prompts, the time of sending a prompt and the time of receiving an answer. Overall, we sent 35 reflective prompts and gathered 26 responses from 20 students.

At the end of an iteration, we sent the post-reflection survey via email to students that received at least one prompt during the iteration. The survey was designed to evaluate the efficacy of the proposed approach from a viewpoint of a student. The questions in the survey relates to e.g. prompts difficulty and relevancy, effort required to answer a prompt and the influence of reflection on the students' knowledge.

4.3 Analysis and Evaluation

Data collected during the automated prompt-based reflection study is depicted by Figure 3 composed of part (a) related to to the students' reflections and part (b) presenting the survey summary. Overall, the results are consistent with the literature and confirm that students benefit from the reflection practice. Most of the students that received the reflection prompt, decided to participate in the study (20 out of 29) and more than half of the provided answers were completely to the instructor's satisfaction. The voluntary post-reflection survey was completed by 15 out of 20 students, with 13 students that responded to the received prompt. The post-reflection survey indicates that students generally had positive feeling toward the reflection process. It is noteworthy that 1/3 of students (5) who answered the survey realized their violation of secure design principles only after they received the prompts, and almost equal number of students (6) indicated that they either modified or planned to modify their code in a result. The majority of these students considered the reflection process had great impact on their learning of secure design principles and practice.

In the following, we discuss a few observations from the data.

Students' reflections sizes. We measure the size of a student's reflection using word count. The distribution of words per an answer is presented in the upper part of Figure 3. The number of words in a reflection is commonly over 100 words (16 out of 26 reflections) implying that most of the students engaged in the reflection process.

Timing of the prompts. One of the objective of the study was to provide students with the reflection prompt at convenient time. Analyzing the time interval between sending the prompt and receiving the student's answer, we observe that only 10 out of 26 responses were provided within the first day of receiving the reflection prompt, although this results may have been influenced by the medium used to disseminate prompts as the frequency of checking an e-mail application may vary between students.

To evaluate the timing of prompts from students' perspective, during the survey the students were asked to assess if they were

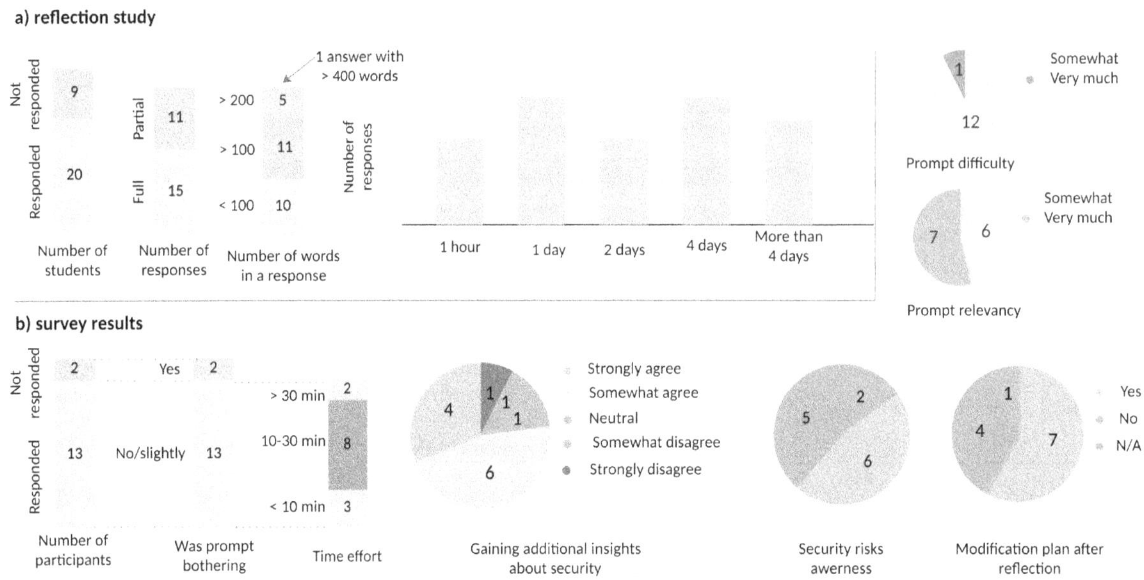

Figure 3: Overview of the data collected via the preliminary study consisting of reflection responses(a) and a post-reflection participant survey (b).

bothered by receiving the prompt while working on the project. All of 13 students that responded to the prompts answered that they were either not bothered at all or slightly bothered. However, the 2 survey participants who did not answer the prompts, indicated that the reason for not responding was that they were too busy to reflect. It seems that sending the reflection prompts when students update the remote code repository is an appropriate time only to some students *but not to all.* This also could be an indication that the students who are not bothered by the prompts may have reached a milestone in their project work.

Quality of the reflection prompts. We consider two factors when determining prompt quality: relevancy of the prompts to the course material and difficulty to answer the prompts. All the 15 survey respondents answered that prompts are *somewhat relevant* or *very relevant* to the course material. Only 1 student believed that the prompt was too difficult to answer, while 12 students indicated that the prompts were *somewhat difficult.* Based on these results, we conclude that the prompts were relevant and at a proper level of difficulty to reflect effectively.

Students' effort of reflections. Only 2 students claimed that they spent more than 30 minutes to answer the reflection prompts, while most of the students, 8 out of 13, estimated they needed between 10 and 30 minutes to provide a response. This result suggests that the prompts did not put significant additional burden on the students, while allowing them to refresh or expand their knowledge.

Impact on students' learning. Finally, we examine the impact of the automatically prompted reflection on students' learning effectiveness and outcomes. 5 out of 13 students reported they were not aware of potential security risks in their code, however, all of them indicated that they had revised or had a plan to revise the code as the result of answering the prompts. In addition, one of the students, that was aware of the risk, also decided to revise or improve the code. Most of the students, 10 out of 13, indicated that the reflection helped them gain additional insights or strengthened their knowledge of security principles.

4.4 Students' Comments and Reflection

Analyzing the student's free-text comments collected via the post-reflection survey, we noticed that students found the reflective practice to be beneficial for their learning process. For instance, one student wrote,

> *"I think it was extremely helpful as it forced me to research and refresh my mind to answer. It was also helpful in relation to our final [...]. The prompt was also good because it wasn't just a straightforward question, but it had information and terms I did not know so I was able to research and gain more knowledge before answering."*

and yet another indicated,

> *"Not logging certain information was something I never thought about being a possible security crack in a program. But it does make perfect sense that you need to be careful to not log information that could be exploited."*

These comments reveal that students, encouraged by the reflection, are able to expand their knowledge and gain new insights by conducting additional research. In addition, some of students' reflections show that the students pondered alternatives and gained practical experience by relating the reflection process to real-world applications, such as,

> *"[t]he logging statements I used were mainly for debugging purposes. However, they did print out the* `toString` *of events that the user created for the calendar. This could be considered sensitive information, as the user might not want any outside sources seeing these events. Much like the Principle of Chain Custody says, the programmer should not log anything that could be considered sensitive or private, as the log can be obtained rather easily, like by connecting an Android device to a PC. In a future iteration, I will be sure to remove logging statements that output the* `toString` *of the user's*

events before I update the repository, in order to protect the user's privacy, or ensure that I am not logging any private information."

4.5 Threats to Validity

This exploratory study aims to show that an automatic prompt-based reflection system can be applied to computer science courses to help students improve learning outcomes. While the sample size of this case study is not large enough to provide any robust and general conclusions, the collected data provides some evidence that the described intervention via the system is consistent with the literature on applying reflection.

The work suffers several threats to validity. For instance, there are a few threats to external validity. First, we informed students that we wanted to observe how they would respond to reflection prompts, which would influence students' decision whether to take part in the study. This is in effect an instance of "Hawthorne effect (attention causes differences)". Second, it might as well be that these group of students were the very first to be prompted for reflection. This is an example of "novelty and disruption effect (anything different makes a difference)". Because this intervention is new to them, the students responded to the uniqueness of the approach rather than the actual reflective practice. Third, we designed and implemented the system, and unknowingly implemented reflective intervention in a way that worked with this group of students. However, whether other educators can achieve the same results while using our system remains untested. This is in effect called "experimenter effect". We discuss in part some approaches to alleviate these threats in Section 5.

5 CONCLUSIONS AND FUTURE WORK

This paper describes a strategy for automated prompt-based reflection. Using a rule-based prompt delivery system, we instantiate this strategy for teaching secure development in mobile programming courses. We present preliminary results based on our experience in applying the system and strategy to a junior-level computer science course. The results show that the system enables us to scale-up prompt based reflection. The students were relatively positive on their experience responding to the prompts, while the quantitative data also show high rate of prompt responses.

Apart from growing the scale of this study to increase sample size and variety, we consider a few enhancement of the automatic prompt-based reflection system. First, the prompts at present are hand-written and selected by the system based a set of rigid rules. It is easy to make a mistake in the rules which results in the wrong prompt being delivered to the student. Our aim to enhance the way instructors can express the prompt delivery rules, or provide automated targeting of prompts without rules, e.g., based on past student commit histories.

Apart from this, we are also interested in improving and expanding the set of prompts targeting mobile application development. As one student commented in our post-reflection survey: *"could ask more challenging questions that we haven't covered, like those related to databases or storing passwords, etc."*

REFERENCES

[1] Android. 2018. App security best practices. (2018). available via https://developer.android.com/topic/security/best-practices, retrieved November 12, 2018.

[2] Eric P.S. Baumer, Vera Khovanskaya, Mark Matthews, Lindsay Reynolds, Victoria Schwanda Sosik, and Geri Gay. 2014. Reviewing Reflection: On the Use of Reflection in Interactive System Design. In *Proceedings of the 2014 Conference on Designing Interactive Systems (DIS '14)*. ACM, New York, NY, USA, 93–102. https://doi.org/10.1145/2598510.2598598

[3] Matt Bishop. 2003. *Computer security: art and science.* Addison-Wesley Professional.

[4] Christopher N. Bull and Jon Whittle. 2014. Supporting Reflective Practice in Software Engineering Education through a Studio-Based Approach. *IEEE Software* 31, 4 (July 2014), 44–50. https://doi.org/10.1109/MS.2014.52

[5] John W. Coffey. 2017. A Study of the Use of a Reflective Activity to Improve Students' Software Design Capabilities. In *Proceedings of the 2017 ACM SIGCSE Technical Symposium on Computer Science Education (SIGCSE '17)*. ACM, New York, NY, USA, 129–134. https://doi.org/10.1145/3017680.3017770

[6] Stephen H. Edwards. 2004. Using Software Testing to Move Students from Trial-and-error to Reflection-in-action. *SIGCSE Bull.* 36, 1 (March 2004), 26–30. https://doi.org/10.1145/1028174.971312

[7] Angela Fessl, Oliver Blunk, Michael Prilla, and Viktoria Pammer. 2017. The known universe of reflection guidance: a literature review. *International Journal of Technology Enhanced Learning* 9, 2-3 (2017), 103–125.

[8] Linda Finlay. 2008. Reflecting on reflective practice. *PBPL paper* 52 (2008), 1–27. Available: https://www.open.ac.uk/opencetl/resources/pbpl-resources/finlay-l-2008-reflecting-reflective-practice-pbpl-paper-52.

[9] Cindy E Hmelo-Silver, Ravit Golan Duncan, and Clark A Chinn. 2007. Scaffolding and achievement in problem-based and inquiry learning: A response to Kirschner, Sweller, and Clark (2006). *Educational psychologist* 42, 2 (2007), 99–107.

[10] Norio Ishii and Kazuhisa Miwa. 2005. Supporting Reflective Practice in Creativity Education. In *Proceedings of the 5th Conference on Creativity & Cognition (C&C '05)*. ACM, New York, NY, USA, 150–157. https://doi.org/10.1145/1056224.1056246

[11] Paul A Kirschner, John Sweller, and Richard E Clark. 2006. Why minimal guidance during instruction does not work: An analysis of the failure of constructivist, discovery, problem-based, experiential, and inquiry-based teaching. *Educational psychologist* 41, 2 (2006), 75–86.

[12] Äli Leijen, Kai Valtna, Djuddah AJ Leijen, and Margus Pedaste. 2012. How to determine the quality of students' reflections? *Studies in Higher Education* 37, 2 (2012), 203–217.

[13] Stephen MacNeil. 2017. Tools to Support Data-driven Reflective Learning. In *Proceedings of the 2017 ACM Conference on International Computing Education Research (ICER '17)*. ACM, New York, NY, USA, 299–300. https://doi.org/10.1145/3105726.3105745

[14] Charles P Pfleeger and Shari Lawrence Pfleeger. 2002. *Security in computing.* Prentice Hall Professional Technical Reference.

[15] Julia Prior, Samuel Ferguson, and John Leaney. 2016. Reflection is Hard: Teaching and Learning Reflective Practice in a Software Studio. In *Proceedings of the Australasian Computer Science Week Multiconference (ACSW '16)*. ACM, New York, NY, USA, Article 7, 8 pages. https://doi.org/10.1145/2843043.2843346

[16] Arthur S Reber. 1989. Implicit learning and tacit knowledge. *Journal of experimental psychology: General* 118, 3 (1989), 219.

[17] Gary Rolfe. 1997. Beyond expertise: theory, practice and the reflexive practitioner. *Journal of clinical nursing* 6, 2 (1997), 93–97.

[18] Jerome H Saltzer and Michael D Schroeder. 1975. The protection of information in computer systems. *Proc. IEEE* 63, 9 (1975), 1278–1308.

[19] Henk G Schmidt, Sofie MM Loyens, Tamara Van Gog, and Fred Paas. 2007. Problem-based learning is compatible with human cognitive architecture: Commentary on Kirschner, Sweller, and Clark (2006). *Educational psychologist* 42, 2 (2007), 91–97.

[20] Donald A. Schön. 1987. *Educating the Reflective Practitioner: Toward a New Design for Teaching and Learning in the Professions.* Wiley. https://books.google.com/books?id=qqxsQgAACAAJ

[21] Moushumi Sharmin and Brian P. Bailey. 2011. "I Reflect to Improve My Design": Investigating the Role and Process of Reflection in Creative Design. In *Proceedings of the 8th ACM Conference on Creativity and Cognition (C&C '11)*. ACM, New York, NY, USA, 389–390. https://doi.org/10.1145/2069618.2069710

[22] Moushumi Sharmin and Brian P. Bailey. 2013. ReflectionSpace: An Interactive Visualization Tool for Supporting Reflection-on-action in Design. In *Proceedings of the 9th ACM Conference on Creativity & Cognition (C&C '13)*. ACM, New York, NY, USA, 83–92. https://doi.org/10.1145/2466627.2466645

[23] Richard E Smith. 2012. A contemporary look at Saltzer and Schroeder's 1975 design principles. *IEEE Security & Privacy* 10, 6 (2012), 20–25.

[24] Software Engineering Institute. 2018. Android Secure Coding Standard. (2018). available via https://wiki.sei.cmu.edu/confluence/display/android, retrieved November 12, 2018.

[25] Jeffrey A. Stone. 2012. Using Reflective Blogs for Pedagogical Feedback in CS1. In *Proceedings of the 43rd ACM Technical Symposium on Computer Science Education (SIGCSE '12)*. ACM, New York, NY, USA, 259–264. https://doi.org/10.1145/2157136.2157216

[26] John Sweller, Paul A Kirschner, and Richard E Clark. 2007. Why minimally guided teaching techniques do not work: A reply to commentaries. *Educational psychologist* 42, 2 (2007), 115–121.
[27] Andrew M. Webb, Rhema Linder, Andruid Kerne, Nic Lupfer, Yin Qu, Bryant Poffenberger, and Colton Revia. 2013. Promoting Reflection and Interpretation in Education: Curating Rich Bookmarks As Information Composition. In *Proceedings of the 9th ACM Conference on Creativity & Cognition (C&C '13)*. ACM, New York, NY, USA, 53–62. https://doi.org/10.1145/2466627.2466636
[28] Yu-Chun Grace Yen, Steven P. Dow, Elizabeth Gerber, and Brian P. Bailey. 2017. Listen to Others, Listen to Yourself: Combining Feedback Review and Reflection to Improve Iterative Design. In *Proceedings of the 2017 ACM SIGCHI Conference on Creativity and Cognition (C&C '17)*. ACM, New York, NY, USA, 158–170.
[29] Jose P. Zagal and Amy S. Bruckman. 2007. GameLog: Fostering Reflective Game-playing for Learning. In *Proceedings of the 2007 ACM SIGGRAPH Symposium on Video Games (Sandbox '07)*. ACM, New York, NY, USA, 31–38.

Teaching Integer Security Using Simple Visualizations

James Walker
Man Wang
jwwalker@mtu.edu
manw@mtu.edu
Michigan Technological University
Houghton, MI

Steven Carr
Western Michigan University
Kalamazoo, MI
steve.carr@wmich.edu

Jean Mayo
Ching-Kuang Shene
jmayo@mtu.edu
shene@mtu.edu
Michigan Technological University
Houghton, MI

ABSTRACT

Integer errors can introduce significant vulnerabilities into C programs. We have developed a program analysis and visualization tool to help students understand integer representation and type conversions with the goal to help students avoid introducing these errors into the code they develop. The visualization is through the Integer Representation (IR) window within a larger system for analysis and visualization of security issues in C programs. The system is called the Visualization and Analysis for C Code Security (VACCS) system. In this paper, we describe our experience with teaching fundamental aspects of integer security in a junior-level systems programming course, the IR window, and an evaluation of the tool. Our results indicate that students found the tool to be useful and that it enhanced the course in which it was used.

CCS CONCEPTS

• **Social and professional topics → Computing education.**

KEYWORDS

Integer security; visualization; cybersecurity education

ACM Reference Format:

James Walker, Man Wang, Steven Carr, Jean Mayo, and Ching-Kuang Shene. 2019. Teaching Integer Security Using Simple Visualizations. In *Innovation and Technology in Computer Science Education (ITiCSE '19), July 15–17, 2019, Aberdeen, Scotland UK.* ACM, New York, NY, USA, 7 pages. https://doi.org/10.1145/3304221.3319760

1 INTRODUCTION

Naive and sloppy use of integers within a C program can introduce subtle but serious security vulnerabilities. This is especially dangerous because many systems-level programs are written in C for performance reasons and these systems-level programs are fundamental to protection of information.

While undergraduate courses in computer organization and C programming commonly cover integer representation and type conversions, we have found that even after taking these courses, many students do not deeply understand these topics and have little understanding of the serious security vulnerabilities that can be introduced by improper use. Although it has not been updated recently, integer overflow appeared in the most recent version (2011) of the twenty five most critical software vulnerabilities identified by the Common Weakness Enumeration [2], created by Mitre and the SANS Institute.

Visualization is an educational technique that is widely used to improve learning. We have developed a tool that uses visualization to help students understand integer security. The tool is part of a larger system called the Visualization and Analysis for C Code Security (VACCS) System. The VACCS system is designed to help students learn how to code securely in C. The Integer Representation (IR) component focuses on helping students to understand integer security. The IR window depicts the representation of integer types and the effects of wraparound and conversion from one integer type to another.

There are a number of pedagogical tools for visualization of security concepts, including network protocols and defenses [4, 9, 16, 18], formal models [5, 8, 15] and cryptography [3, 6, 7, 11–13]. Benham proposed a method to teach data representation using a modular clock [1]. There are also visualization systems aimed to teach computer architecture [14, 17]. Our tool focuses only on integer representation within the larger context of C program security.

This paper describes our experience with teaching integer security within a required junior-level course on systems programming in C at Michigan Technological University. Section 2 describes our experience teaching the subject matter. Section 3 describes the visualization tool. Section 4 describes our use and evaluation of the tool. Our conclusions are given in section 5. The evaluation results indicate that students felt the tool was useful and that students' knowledge of the material was improved during the course.

2 TEACHING INTEGER SECURITY

2.1 Motivation

Naive and sloppy use of integers can introduce subtle and significant security vulnerabilities into a C program. Consider the code in figure 1 [10]. (Line numbers have been added as a convenience.).

A user inputs the size of some data and the data itself as arguments one and two to the program. The program then makes a copy of the buffer.

This provides a useful motivating example when beginning a discussion on integer security. It represents code that a student is likely to write in an attempt to prevent writing beyond the bounds of a statically allocated buffer, in this program the buffer `buf`.

The code is indicative of a common failure by students to consider the entire range of values for a signed integer. For example, they

ITiCSE '19, July 15–17, 2019, Aberdeen, Scotland UK

ACM ISBN 978-1-4503-6301-3/19/07...$15.00
https://doi.org/10.1145/3304221.3319760

```
1   #define BUFF_SIZE 10
2   int main( int argc, char * argv [] ){
3   int  len;
4   char buf [BUFF_SIZE];
5   len = atoi(argv[1]);
6   if ( len < BUFF_SIZE) {
7       memcpy( buf , argv[2] , len);
8   }
9   else
10      printf("Too much data\n") ;
11  }
```

Figure 1: C Code to Copy a User Input Buffer

commonly consider only positive values where they expect positive values. If the value of `len`, set at line 5, is negative, the code at line 7 will be executed.

The code at line 7 exposes that a student may be sloppy about noting type conversions that take place on a procedure call; and may misunderstand the effect of converting between signed and unsigned types. The third argument to `memcpy` is type `size_t` (unsigned) so that the amount of data copied can far exceed the 10 bytes allocated to `buf`. This results in a classic buffer overflow in which memory beyond `buf` can be overwritten.

In order to avoid these errors, students need to understand how integers are represented, when conversions take place within a C program, how conversions are performed, and the resulting values. These topics are commonly covered in undergraduate courses in C and computer organization.

2.2 Curriculum

In order to integrate important security concepts throughout our undergraduate curriculum, we decided to cover integer security within a junior-level systems programming course. This course teaches students about processes, linking and loading, I/O, IPC and network programming through the LINUX system call interface. This course also covers buffer overflows and stack protections. Students are required to code in C. The course prerequisites are a course in C programming for Java programmers and a course in computer organization. Our curriculum had previously included the material on integer security and buffer overflows in a senior-level elective on computer security.

On the first day of class, we gave a short quiz to identify student understanding of the use of integers within a C program. There were four questions in total with one point per question. The quiz questions are given in table 1. Question 1 asked students to identify the effects of conversion from a larger signed type to a smaller signed type. It required that students recognize the binary representation of the minimum representable value for a signed integer and that this binary value would be truncated in order to perform the conversion.[1] Question 2 asked students to identify the effects of an integer overflow. Question 3 required students to understand the binary representation of the smallest representable unsigned type, the truncation on conversion, and the corresponding signed value. Question 4 required students to understand the representation of -2, identify the conversions applied (one at the division, resulting in an unsigned, and one at the assignment) and determine the effects of these conversions.

[1] Students were given the size in bytes of all types used in the quiz.

Table 1: Pre-test Questions

Q1	short int x;
	int i;
	i = INT_MIN;
	x=i;
	What is the value of *x*?

Q2	int x;
	x=INT_MAX;
	x=x+3;
	What is the value of *x*?

Q3	short int x;
	unsigned int ui;
	ui=UINT_MAX;
	x=ui;
	What is the value of *x*?

Q4	signed s;
	unsigned u;
	signed x;
	s=-2; u=2;
	x=s/u;
	What is the value of *x*?

Student performance is given in table 2. The mean represents the average score received on the one point question. It also shows the percentage of students who answered that question correctly as no partial credit was given.

Table 2: The Means (μ), Standard Deviations (σ) of the Pre-test Questions

	Q1	Q2	Q3	Q4
μ	0.28	0.06	0.05	0.08
σ	0.45	0.24	0.21	0.27

We were surprised at the class performance. Students performed poorly on all questions. This meant that our standard coverage was inadequate to root this material into the students' working knowledge. It also confirmed the utility of reviewing the material with an eye toward integer security.

The coverage roughly followed the integer security discussion in Secure Coding in C and C++, by Robert Seacord [10]. We reviewed integer representation, conversions, and operations (addition, subtraction, multiplication and division). Throughout the discussion, we included examples of security errors that result from improper use of integers.

3 INTEGER REPRESENTATION WINDOW

3.1 Design

The Visualization and Analysis for C Code Security (VACCS) system has several visualization components aimed at helping students to better understand how programs execute and coding practices that can create security vulnerabilities. A student runs an analysis program against her C code to produce a sequence of events. Each event corresponds to the execution of one source code line. These events are input to a visualization system which provides several perspectives on the execution. These perspectives include the Program Address Space (PAS), Call Graph (CG), Sensitive Data handling (SD) and File Operations (FO). Students step the visualization forward or backward through the events, or allow the system to execute the events without user intervention using a user-specified time interval between the events. This paper focuses on the Integer Representation (IR) component of the PAS perspective.

The IR window was designed to help students understand the effect of conversion from one type to another. We focused on identifying the number of bytes for a given type, changes in the number of bytes and in bit values that occur on a particular conversion, and the associated decimal value of these bit patterns when two's complement representation is used.[2] At the time the tool was designed, we felt that students would not have difficulty understanding when conversions would be applied and the resulting types.

3.2 Use

The VACCS system comes up on the PAS tab, as shown in figure 2. There are tabs for each of the visualizations as well as the source code. Any of these windows can be detached from the main window to be a standalone window for the convenience of side-by-side reference. In this depiction, the source code has already been detached. The source code window is shown in figure 3. The next line to be executed is highlighted in yellow.

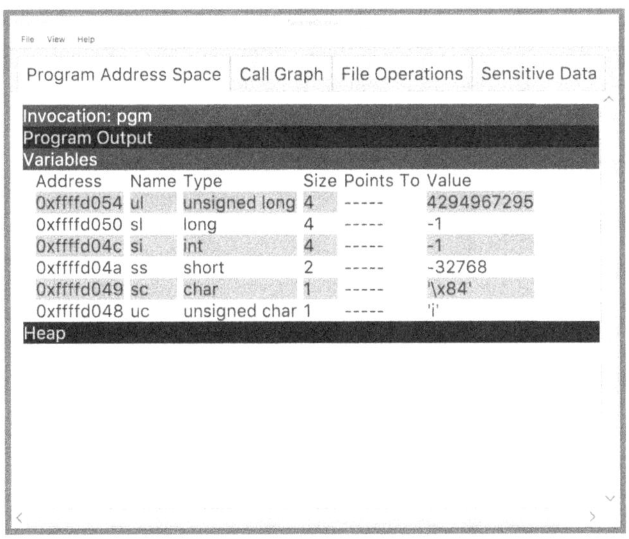

Figure 2: VACCS Program Address Space Visualization

[2]Two's complement was included in both of our lecture and tool as it is the most common method of representing signed integers on computers. Ones complement was also included in our lecture, but was not incorporated in the tool due to its less common use.

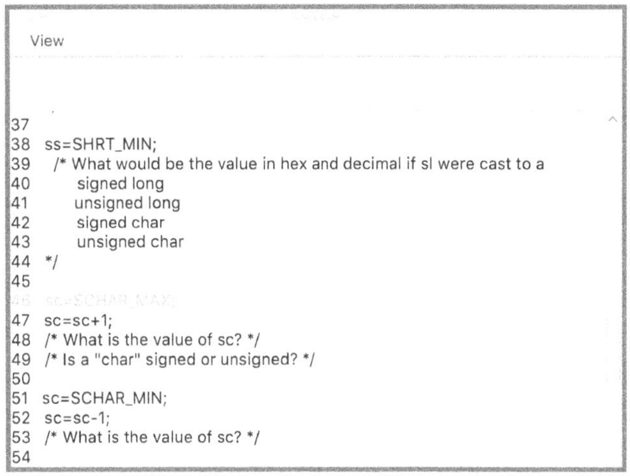

Figure 3: VACCS Source Code Window

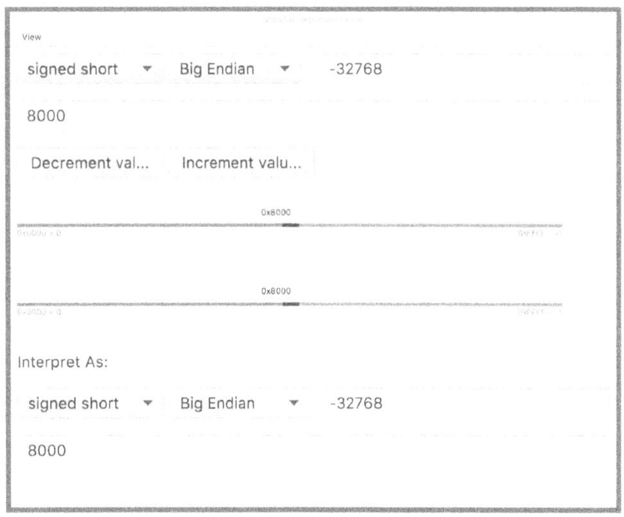

Figure 4: VACCS Integer Representation Window

A student brings up the IR window by clicking on the value of an integer variable in the PAS. Figure 4 shows the IR window that results from clicking on the value of the signed short integer variable `ss` from the main window depicted in figure 2. The value of `ss` has just been set to `SHRT_MIN` which is -32768.

The window has several features that allow a student to explore representation and conversion of the selected value. There are two representations of the chosen number, one at the top of the window and one at the bottom. Both the hexadecimal value for the corresponding bytes and the decimal value represented (`8000` and `-32768`, respectively, in figure 4) are shown. This allows a student to modify the parameters of the depicted value and look at the relevant values before and after a conversion. The endianess is also shown. Associated with each representation is a horizontal line scaled by the range of values (in hexadecimal and decimal) that can be represented by the given type. Negative values are shown in red, positive values are shown in green, and the current value is shown in blue.

The byte order defaults to big endian. Selection of little endian from the drop down menu depicts the value that results from interpreting the same bit pattern in little endian order. Figure 5 shows the IR window of figure 4 after Little Endian is selected.

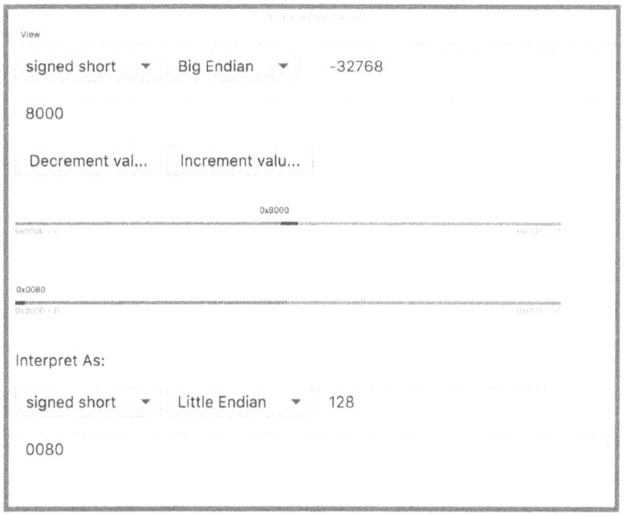

Figure 5: Big Endian and Little Endian Representations

The student can cast the value to another type by choosing a different type from the drop down menu in the representation given in the bottom half of the window. Figure 6 shows the signed short value cast to a signed int.

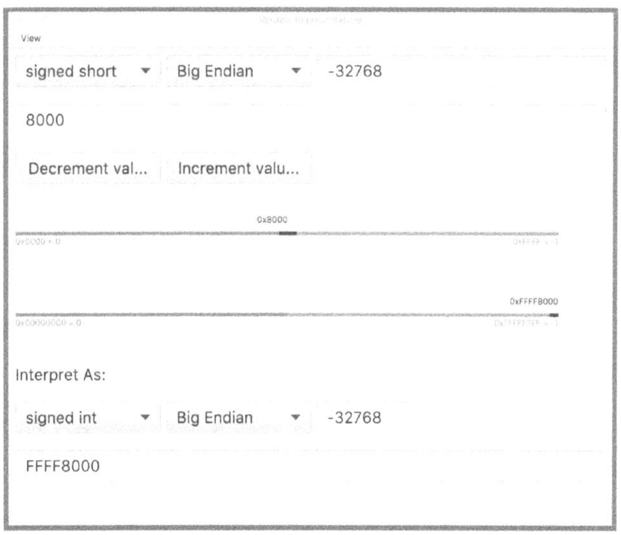

Figure 6: `Signed Short` and `Signed Int` Representations

A student can modify the depicted value in two ways. She can edit the decimal value in the upper representation or she can use the increment and decrement value buttons. All these actions operate against both the upper and lower representations. Figure 7 shows the IR window after the value shown in figure 4 is decremented.

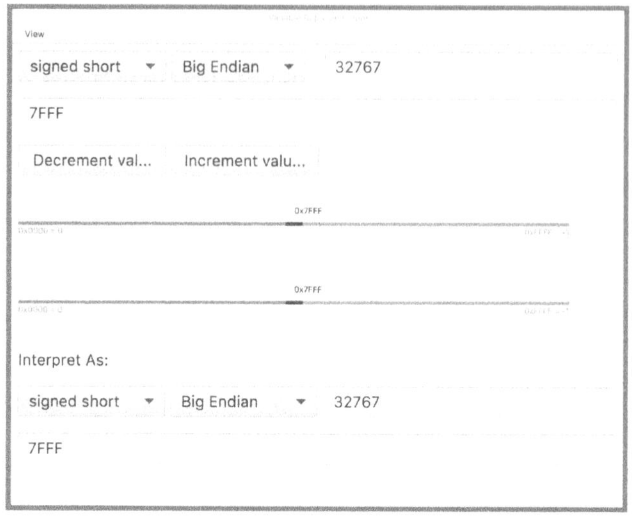

Figure 7: Decrement of `SHRT_MIN`

4 EVALUATION

4.1 Environment, Procedure and Goals

The tool was evaluated at Michigan Technological University in a required junior-level systems programming course with a total of 65 students. Students were given a pre-test on their knowledge prior to any lecture over the material.

Lectures were then given on integer representation, overflow, how and when integer type conversions are performed, common errors and methods to avoid these errors. The IR window was used during the lecture to demonstrate the mechanics of conversions between integer types: the number of bytes before and after the conversion, the bit values, and the corresponding decimal values when the representation is in two's complement. These in-class examples were similar to the questions that appeared on a post-test. Students were then given an extra credit assignment in which they used the IR window of the VACCS system to answer questions over the lecture material. After the extra credit assignment, students evaluated their experience with using the IR window. The knowledge of all students was assessed through questions on a post-test in the form of a midterm exam. We collected 59 valid pre-tests, 60 valid post-tests, and 25 valid evaluation forms.

The pre-test and post-test used essentially the same set of questions. These questions were discussed in section 2.2 and are given in table 1. The IR window was used to present all the knowledge required to answer questions Q1, Q2, and Q3. Question Q4 not only required a type conversion, like the other questions, but required that students identify when a conversion must be performed and the resulting type. We did not included this in design of the IR window, or spend much time on it during lecture, because we believed students would not have difficulty with this material.

4.2 Test Performance

Table 3 and figure 8 have the mean, standard deviation and confidence intervals (CI^- and CI^+) of each question in the pre-test and post-test. The correctness of all questions improved in the post-test.

Q1 and Q2 showed a 51% and 41% increase in correctness, respectively. Q3 showed a 72% improvement, jumping from the lowest mean in the pre-test to the second highest mean in the post-test. Q4 only improved by 2%, and has a correctness of 10% in the post-test.

Table 3: The Means (μ), Standard Deviations (σ) and 95% Confidence Intervals of the Pre- and Post-test Questions

Pre-test				
	Q1	Q2	Q3	Q4
μ	0.28	0.06	0.05	0.08
σ	0.45	0.24	0.21	0.27
CI^-	0.17	0.00	0.00	0.01
CI^+	0.39	0.12	0.10	0.14
Post-test				
	Q1	Q2	Q3	Q4
μ	0.79	0.47	0.77	0.10
σ	0.41	0.50	0.42	0.30
CI^-	0.69	0.34	0.67	0.00
CI^+	0.89	0.59	0.88	0.17

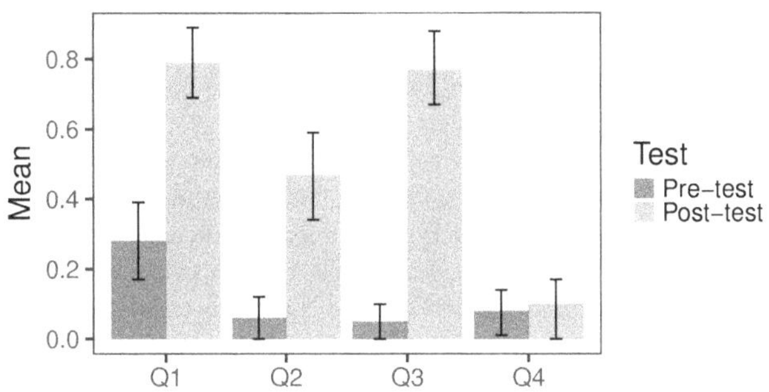

Figure 8: The Means with 95% Confidence Intervals of the Pre- and Post-test Questions

We further used ANOVA (parametric) to investigate whether students' performance throughout the tests had significantly improved and employed the Kruskal-Wallis (KW) test (non-parametric) for confirmation of the result, both at 95% significant level. The p-values from both tests had values less than 0.05 in Q1, Q2, and Q3. With their increased means from the pre-test to the post-test (table 3), this indicates that the performance on integer representation and type conversion significantly improved. Hence, students showed significant improvement in Q1, Q2 and Q3 in the post-test.

Students did not show significant improvement in Q4. We expect this is because they could not give a correct answer unless they identified the conversion to unsigned at the division. (Most students answered "-1".) We had expected that students would be able to identify when conversions take place within a C program, so we did not add it to the visualization system or spend a significant amount of lecture time on this material.

Based on the response to Q4, we believe this material merits greater attention. In order to facilitate instruction and self-learning, we are developing a new visualization to help students identify when conversions take place. This visualization will take a single equation as input. It will depict the abstract syntax tree for the equation and step through each component operation. The visualization will show operand types for each operation and the type that results from applying the rules for integer conversions. The rules for conversion will be displayed and the rule applied at each operation will be identified. This course does not require homework, so students may also need more practice with this material.

4.3 Subjective Evaluation

We used a set of questions (table 4) to collect information on student perception of the effectiveness of the tool. We also gathered information on the time spent using the IR window. The first 10 rating questions evaluated the effectiveness of the IR window. The choices were: 1:strongly disagree, 2:disagree, 3:neutral, 4:agree, and 5:strongly agree. Q11 to Q13 evaluated the time participants spent on the tool. The choices for Q11 were 1:less than 5 mins, 2:5-9 mins, 3:10-14 mins, 4:15-29 mins, and 5:more than 30 mins. The choices for Q12 are 1:once, 2:twice, 3:3-4 times, 4:5-10 times, and 5:more than 10 times. The choices for Q13 were 1:less than 5 mins, 2:5-14 mins, 3:15-29 mins, 4:30-60 mins, and 5:more than 1 hour.

Table 4: IR Window Rating and Usage Questions

Rating Questions	
Q1	The IR window helped me to see how integer type conversions are performed
Q2	I understand integer type conversions better after using the IR window
Q3	By using the IR window, I was able to identify concepts I did not understand
Q4	The IR window enhanced the course in the area of integer type conversion
Q5	The text of the IR window was easy to read
Q6	The interface for integer conversion was intuitive
Q7	The depiction of the value range for (un)signed integers was easy to read
Q8	The depiction of the value range of (un)signed integers was easy to understand
Q9	The depiction of value range of (un)signed integers helped me to understand integer type conversions
Q10	The Increment and Decrement functions were useful for exploring incrementing/decrementing an integer beyond its max or min
Usage Questions	
Q11	How long did it take to understand integer conversion using the tool
Q12	How many times did you use the software
Q13	How long did you use the software in total

Table 5 lists the mean, standard deviation and confidence intervals for each of the evaluation questions. Figure 9 depicts the means and confidence intervals for both the evaluation and usage questions.

The rating of the tool was generally positive with a mean of 4.00. Q10 received the highest rating of 4.6, which means that students believed that the Increment and Decrement functions were useful for exploring the effects of incrementing and decrementing an integer beyond its maximum and minimum. Q7, which is associated with the readability of the depiction of the range of values for (un)signed integers at the right of IR window, had the lowest rating of 3.56. Initially the system used a circular representation to depict the range of decimal values. This was changed to a line (as seen in the figures of section 3) in response to the student comments. The means of Q11, Q12 and Q13 are 2.52, 2.08 and 3.32. This indicates that students generally used the IR Window twice for 10 to 15 minutes each time and 15 to 30 minutes in total.

Table 5: The Means (μ), Standard Deviations (σ), and Confidence Intervals of Evaluation Questions

	Q1	Q2	Q3	Q4	Q5
μ	4.48	4	3.82	4.32	3.96
σ	0.59	0.76	0.80	0.56	0.93
CI^-	4.25	3.70	3.51	4.10	3.59
CI^+	4.71	4.30	4.13	4.54	4.33
	Q6	Q7	Q8	Q9	Q10
μ	4	3.56	3.64	3.64	4.6
σ	0.82	1.04	0.95	0.99	0.58
CI^-	3.68	3.15	3.27	3.25	4.37
CI^+	4.32	3.97	4.01	4.03	4.83

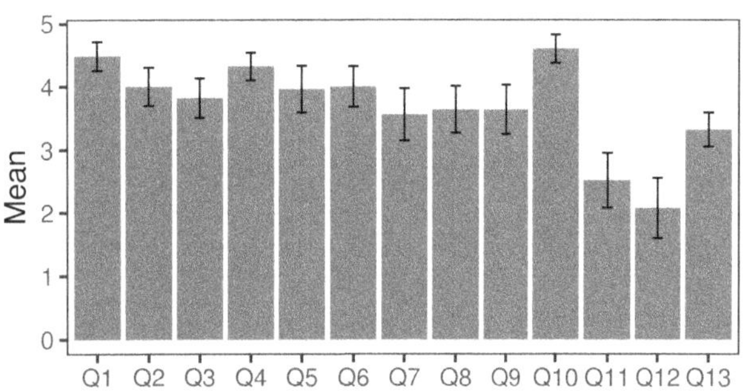

Figure 9: The Means with Confidence Intervals of Evaluation Rating and Usage Questions

The four write-in questions were used to collect information of the participants' major, their thoughts on the IR window, features to add, and problems with installation. Regarding the IR window, the feedback was generally positive in its functionality, layout and usage. Many students enjoyed the "*nice layout*" and stated that "*I like using the IR window. It made it easy to visualize when a value would roll over. It was good to be able to see when only the hex or decimal value changed and to think about why*", "*It was very helpful to have a visual that encompassed all the important aspects of int conversions and abstracted away from doing the math by hand*" and "*It is very good for showing integer type conversions. I have not seen an easier to use program that shows such important information in a GUI so perfectly designed for someone to pick up and use as they please*".

Most students did not encounter problems with the installation. A few students had an issue running Java UISplashScreen (the current tool name) on Windows machines. This could have been a Java version problem, as one student suggested. When asked to suggest features to add, the majority of students found the available features satisfying. There were also some comments for further improvements. A student suggested "*showing how mathematical operators changed a number during its process that would be great*". Some students found that "*the circle on the right side of IR window is not easy to interpret*" and suggested that "*some descriptions should be added*". We felt this was partially addressed when we changed the range depiction from a circle to a line. We are considering addition of a help button.

5 CONCLUSIONS AND FUTURE WORK

The lecture together with use of the IR window to present examples during class significantly increased students' understanding of the material as measured through a quiz. Additionally, students felt like the IR window enhanced the course. We are extending the IR window to allow students to predict or view the type changes that occur during the evaluation of a C language statement. The additions will include the ability to visualize the entire type coercion process and how intermediate values are affected by C semantics. Students will be able to step through the computations and type coercions that the compiler must implement to generate valid code.

The post-test results and evaluation were encouraging for use of the tool to improve learning. Yet many students continued to find the material difficult. We plan to create a stand-alone tool that can be easily used in earlier courses or by students that are studying the material independently. This tool will include the features of the current IR window, add the type coercion enhancement described above, and will also present a binary representation of variable values including association of bytes with increasing hardware address.

The tool was used both during lecture and to provide (extra credit) homework problems for students. The VACCS system significantly enhanced the lectures. It proved to make lecture far more convenient by providing a quick, error-free mechanism to tie the representation of an integer variable with its decimal value. It was also convenient to discuss the conversion between any integer types by simply selecting the new type in the IR window. When students asked the inevitable "what if" questions, it was quick and straightforward to both explain and then demonstrate.

The most recent version of the VACCS system is available at: http://pages.mtu.edu/~jwwalker/vaccs.html.

6 ACKNOWLEDGMENTS

This work was supported in part by the National Science Foundation under grants DGE-1523017 and DUE-1245310.

REFERENCES

[1] James W. Benham. 1992. A Geometric Approach to Presenting Computer Representations of Integers. *SIGCSE Bull.* 24, 4 (Dec. 1992), 27–28.

[2] Steve Christey (Ed.). 2011. *Common Weakness Enumeration.* http://cwe.mitre.org/top25/ (Accessed: 2018-08-31).

[3] Derek Ebeling and Rob Santos. 2007. Public Key Infrastructure Visualization. *J. Comput. Sci. Coll.* 23, 1 (Oct. 2007), 247–254.

[4] Niakam Kazemi and Shiva Azadegan. 2010. IPsecLite: A Tool for Teaching Security Concepts. In *Proceedings of the 41st ACM Technical Symposium on Computer Science Education (SIGCSE '10).* ACM, New York, NY, USA, 138–142.

[5] Yifei Li, Steve Carr, Jean Mayo, Ching-Kuang Shene, and Chaoli Wang. 2012. DTEvisual: A Visualization System for Teaching Access Control Using Domain

Type Enforcement. *Journal of Computing Science in College* 28, 1 (October 2012), 125–132.

[6] Jun Ma, Jun Tao, Melissa Keranen, Jean Mayo, Ching-Kuang Shene, and Chaoli Wang. 2014. SHAvisual: A Secure Hash Algorithm Visualization Tool. In *Proceedings of the 2014 conference on Innovation & technology in computer science education*. ACM, 338–338.

[7] Dino Schweitzer and Leemon C. Baird III. 2006. The design and use of interactive visualization applets for teaching ciphers. In *Proceedings of the 7th Annual IEEE Information Assurance Workshop*. 69–75.

[8] Dino Schweitzer, Mike Collins, and Leemon C Baird III. 2007. A visual approach to teaching formal models in security. In *Proceedings of the 11th Colloquium for Information Systems Security Education (CISSE)*. 69–75.

[9] Dino L. Schweitzer, Leemon C. Baird III, Mike D. Collins, Wayne C. Brown, and Mike Sherman. 2006. GRASP: A visualization tool for teaching security protocols. In *Proceedings of the 10th Colloquium for Information Systems Security Education*. 75–81.

[10] Robert C. Seacord. 2013. *Secure Coding in C and C++* (2nd ed.). Addison-Wesley Professional.

[11] Jun Tao, Jun Ma, Melissa Keranan, Jean Mayo, and Ching-Kuang Shene. 2012. ECvisual: A Visualization Tool for Elliptic Curve Based Ciphers. In *roceedings of the 43rd ACM technical symposium on Computer Science Education*. ACM, 571–576.

[12] Jun Tao, Jun Ma, Melissa Keranen, Jean Mayo, and Ching-Kuang Shene. 2011. DESvisual: A Visualization Tool for the DES Cipher. *Journal of Computing Science in College* 27, 1 (October 2011), 81–89.

[13] Jun Tao, Jun Ma, Melissa Keranen, Jean Mayo, Ching-Kuang Shene, and Chaoli Wang. 2014. RSAvisual: A Visualization Tool for the RSA Cipher. In *Proceedings of the 45th ACM technical symposium on Computer science education*. ACM, 635–640.

[14] Kenneth Vollmar and Pete Sanderson. 2006. MARS: An Education-oriented MIPS Assembly Language Simulator. In *Proceedings of the 37th SIGCSE Technical Symposium on Computer Science Education (SIGCSE '06)*. ACM, 239–243.

[15] Man Wang, Steve Carr, Jean Mayo, Ching-Kuang Shene, and Chaoli Wang. 2014. MLSvisual: A Visualization Tool for Teaching Access Control Using Multi-Level Security. In *Proceedings of the 2014 conference on Innovation & technology in computer science education*. ACM, 93–98.

[16] Justin Warner, David Musielewicz, G. Parks Masters, Taylor Verett, Robert Winchester, and Steven Fulton. 2010. Network Firewall Visualization in the Classroom. *J. Comput. Sci. Coll.* 26, 2 (Dec. 2010), 88–96.

[17] Cecile Yehezkel, Mordechai Ben-Ari, and Tommy Dreyfus. 2005. Computer Architecture and Mental Models. In *Proceedings of the 36th SIGCSE Technical Symposium on Computer Science Education (SIGCSE '05)*. ACM, 101–105.

[18] Xiaohong Yuan, Percy Vega, Yaseen Qadah, Ricky Archer, Huiming Yu, and Jinsheng Xu. 2010. Visualization Tools for Teaching Computer Security. *Trans. Comput. Educ.* 9, 4, Article 20 (Jan. 2010), 28 pages.

The Impact of Adding Textual Explanations to Next-step Hints in a Novice Programming Environment

Samiha Marwan
Nicholas Lytle
North Carolina State University
Raleigh, North Carolina
{samarwan,nalytle}@ncsu.edu

Joseph Jay Williams
University of Toronto
Toronto, Canada
williams@cs.toronto.edu

Thomas Price
North Carolina State University
Raleigh, North Carolina
twprice@ncsu.edu

ABSTRACT

Automated hints, a powerful feature of many programming environments, have been shown to improve students' performance and learning. New methods for generating these hints use historical data, allowing them to scale easily to new classrooms and contexts. These scalable methods often generate next-step, code hints that suggest a single edit for the student to make to their code. However, while these code hints tell the student what to do, they do not explain why, which can make these hints hard to interpret and decrease students' trust in their helpfulness. In this work, we augmented code hints by adding adaptive, textual explanations in a block-based, novice programming environment. We evaluated their impact in two controlled studies with novice learners to investigate how our results generalize to different populations. We measured the impact of textual explanations on novices' programming performance. We also used quantitative analysis of log data, self-explanation prompts, and frequent feedback surveys to evaluate novices' understanding and perception of the hints throughout the learning process. Our results showed that novices perceived hints with explanations as significantly more relevant and interpretable than those without explanations, and were also better able to connect these hints to their code and the assignment. However, we found little difference in novices' performance. Our results suggest that explanations have the potential to make code hints more useful, but it is unclear whether this translates into better overall performance and learning.

KEYWORDS

Intelligent tutoring systems, next step hints, textual hints, computer science education

ACM Reference Format:
Samiha Marwan, Nicholas Lytle, Joseph Jay Williams, and Thomas Price. 2019. The Impact of Adding Textual Explanations to Next-step Hints in a Novice Programming Environment. In *Innovation and Technology in Computer Science Education (ITiCSE '19), July 15–17, 2019, Aberdeen, Scotland UK.* ACM, New York, NY, USA, 7 pages. https://doi.org/10.1145/3304221.3319759

ITiCSE '19, July 15–17, 2019, Aberdeen, Scotland UK

ACM ISBN 978-1-4503-6301-3/19/07...$15.00
https://doi.org/10.1145/3304221.3319759

1 INTRODUCTION

Introductory programming courses often have high attrition and failure rates, with pass rates estimated as low as 68% [6, 38]. As such, there is a growing evidence to suggest that novice programming students need additional support [7, 37]. This is especially true in large classrooms and MOOCs, where instructors cannot interact with every student [17, 21]. To address this, researchers have developed intelligent systems for automatically generating support for students during programming [2, 13, 16, 31], such as hints and feedback, which have been shown to improve students' learning outcomes [8, 9]. These systems often offer next step, edit-based hints, which suggest an edit that a student should make to bring their code closer to a correct solution [10, 28]. Data-driven systems can generate these next-step hints automatically using historical students' data [31, 34], rather than with expensive expert models (e.g. [24]), allowing them to scale easily to new classrooms and contexts. These next-step hints are powerful as they can support students *during* program construction, and *automatically* adapt to the student's current code to support different student solutions. However, these data-driven, next-step hints generally show only *what* to do, not *why*. Previous work has shown this lack of explanations can make next-step hints difficult for novices to interpret and connect to their current code [29], leading to a decrease in how often students request and follow hints, and eroding their trust in the system [29, 32].

In this paper we introduce a straightforward method for generating textual explanations to accompany automated, next-step programming hints. We implement this feature in iSnap [28], an extension of the block-based *Snap!* programming environment [12, 14], which offers on-demand, data-driven, next-step hints. These hints are generated adaptively to respond specifically to a student's current code. We refer to these hints as *code hints*, since they show only the code that should be changed. We designed the textual explanations to connect these code hints to the programming exercise objectives and explain the functionality of the suggested blocks. Previous work suggests that these explanations could improve novices' programming outcomes, but that novices do not always read such explanations [11]. We therefore evaluated the impact of adding these textual explanations to code hints in iSnap through two controlled experiments with different populations.

In Experiment 1, we conducted a controlled study on novices in an introductory programming course for non-CS majors. We studied the effect of adding textual explanations to code hints, and found promising trends across multiple exercises, suggesting that explanations may increase students' willingness to use and follow the hints. However, as in previous work [1, 28], the majority of students did not use hints, so our sample size was small, and our results were inconclusive. To investigate further, we conducted a second experiment with crowd workers recruited on Amazon's Mechanical Turk platform, which has been suggested as an appropriate alternative to university participants [5, 19]. This experiment allowed us to recruit a larger number of learners, collect fine-grained survey data, and give learners different, uneven levels of support – all of which were infeasible in our first classroom experiment. In addition to analyzing learners' final outcomes, as in previous work [35], we make empirical analysis using log data, self-explanation prompts, and frequent feedback surveys to understand learners' understanding and perception of the hints throughout the learning process. Both experiments studied novices with little-to-no programming experience. We find learners who received code hints *with* textual explanations rate these hints as significantly more useful, and were more likely to follow these hints which shows similar trend to Experiment 1. In addition, learners who received textual explanations were also significantly more likely to explain the relationship between the received hints, their code and the assignment objectives. However, we found no significant difference in the two groups' programming performance.

In Experiment 1, we investigated 2 research questions: *How does adding textual explanations to code hints impact (1) The perceived usefulness of hints? (2) The hints' request rate?*. In Experiment 2, due to the fewer restrictions in this study, we collected surveys to better investigate RQ1 and investigated 2 more research questions: *How does adding textual explanations to code hints impact (3) Learners' performance on the current and future programming assignments? (4) Learners' ability to self-explain the relationships between the code hints to their own code and the assignment?*

In summary, the contributions of this work are: (1) A system that combines the scalability of adaptive, next-step programming "code hints" with textual explanations[1]. (2) An exploratory study suggesting that these explanations may increase students' willingness to follow code hints. (3) Evidence suggesting that adding these textual explanations to next-step hints increases their perceived usefulness, and learners' ability to explain the purpose of the hints.

2 RELATED WORK

Many educational programming systems provide automated, contextualized support to novices during problem solving. This support can greatly improve learning outcomes [11]. For example, Corbett et al. [9] showed that students who received various forms of feedback while using the system completed subsequent programming assessment in significantly less time with significantly fewer errors. Two common means of this automated support are next-step hints [25, 28, 31] and feedback hints [13, 23]. Next-step hints suggest a specific edit that a student should make to their code to make progress towards a solution, which can be presented through textual instructions [34] or a visual demonstration of the suggested edit [28] (see Figure 1). Automated, next-step hint generation is a rapidly growing area of research, and researchers have developed a variety of techniques, including data-driven approaches [27, 31, 34], program synthesis [26, 36], and automated program repair [39].

[1]iSnap's demo, datasets and source code are available at http://go.ncsu.edu/isnap.

Prior evaluations of next-step programming hints suggest that they may increase students' immediate performance, but the results were inconclusive due to low rates of hint-usage [32, 33]. This low rates of hint-usage might be due to the hints' lack of explanation and interpretability [28, 29].

Feedback hints offer students expert-authored help messages, often in response to specific errors in student code. For example, SQLTutor [23] and INCOM [20] are tutoring systems that use a constraint-based model to provide feedback hints to students whenever a constraint is violated. Unlike next-step hints, the feedback provided by these systems usually comes after students submit their code. However, in an evaluation of the Lambda Autograder [3], which offers such feedback, students mentioned they prefer feedback for each step rather than general feedback at the end. In [15], Head et al. proposed a system that allows teachers to write reusable feedback for programming exercises in Python. In this study, teachers expressed how useful the system was in saving time in grading. However, they mentioned that some students might still need more individualized feedback on their code. In this work, both textual explanations and code hints are adaptive to students' code and can be provided at any time during programming.

One challenge with evaluating automated support, such as next-step hints and feedback messages, is that these supports are usually part of larger programming systems, and researchers often evaluate these systems as a whole, without singling out specific support features to better understand them [18]. For example, Gerdes et al. evaluated their programming tutor, Ask-Elle [13], and its adaptive support through questionnaires. This methodology may be insufficient at analyzing the real impact of these hints on student's behavior during programming because they focus more on student's *opinion* and not their actual *behavior*. In this study, we isolate the impact of one specific element of support – textual explanations – to evaluate it directly. Another common way of evaluating these systems in literature is by checking students' performance when solving exercises with support [16, 28]. However, improved performance with support does not necessarily imply improved learning, since hints and feedback often give the student part of the correct solution [4]. In this paper, we address these issues in two ways: (1) by evaluating student performance on future tasks as a measure of learning (2) by using self-explanations as an alternative technique to measure the impact of hints on students' knowledge [22].

3 DESIGN OF AUTOMATED TEXTUAL EXPLANATIONS

We designed automated textual explanations hints for iSnap, a block-based novice programming environment that provides students with on-demand, data-driven *code hints* during programming [28]. iSnap extends *Snap!*, which is used by thousands of students in "The Beauty and Joy of Computing" AP Computer Science Principles classes [12]. iSnap's hints are generated by the SourceCheck algorithm that uses a database of correct student solutions for a given problem [31]. SourceCheck matches the current code of a hint-requesting student to the nearest correct solution in the database and suggests edits that will bring the student closer to that solution. Students request hints on iSnap by clicking a *Check My Work* button, after which their code is annotated with multiple hint buttons, each corresponding to a contextual hint generated based on their current code [28]. When a student clicks on the hint button, a hint window is shown suggesting a single edit to students' code, such as inserting a code element as shown in Figure 1.

Each of SourceCheck's next-step hints suggest a code block that students can add. That block comes from a correct solution in SourceCheck's database, corresponding to a node in that solution's abstract syntax tree (AST) [31]. We generate textual explanations for a given problem in iSnap by first identifying all common AST nodes in the database of solutions, such as the "pen down" block shown in Figure 1. We then manually annotate each of these solution AST nodes with a textual explanation for the corresponding hint. Note that in the experiments presented in this paper, we used expert-authored solutions, rather than student solutions, to generate the hints, as this has been shown to produce higher-quality hints [32], but our approach could be applied to either.

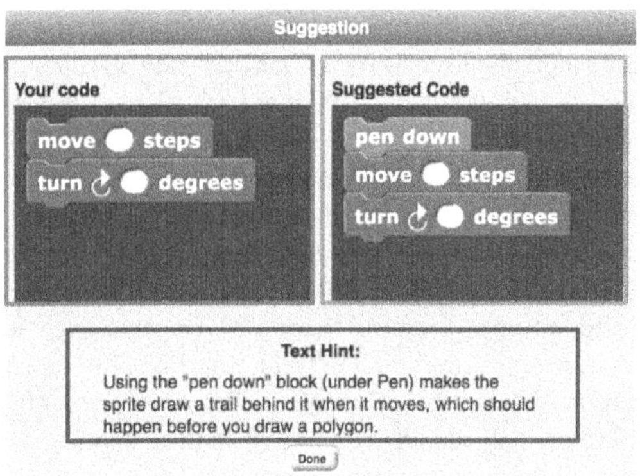

Figure 1: A next-step hint with textual explanation in iSnap. The student's code is shown in the top-left (red box), with suggested code hint in the top-right (green box), annotated with a textual explanations (blue box).

In a programming exercise that asks students to draw a polygon, if a code hint is shown visualizing the need to use the "pen down" block (needed for drawing), the textual explanation in this case will be: *"Using the "pen down" block under Pen, makes the sprite draws a trail behind it when it moves, which should happen before you draw a polygon"* as shown in Figure 1. Our textual explanations were authored to provide 3 types of information to the student: (1) where can they find the relevant block *"Using the pen down block under Pen"*; (2) the functionality of this block *"makes the sprite draws a trail behind it when it moves"*; and (3) why this block should be used in the correct solution *"which should happen before you draw a polygon"*. We related the functionality of the block to the assignment objectives, as our prior work suggested this was a point of difficulty for many students in understanding hints [29]. For the experiments described in this work, the last author, who is familiar with the assignments and classroom context, wrote the textual explanations, including the three types of information described above.

4 EXPERIMENT 1: CLASSROOM STUDY

In our first, exploratory experiment, we investigated the impact of adding textual explanations to code hints in a classroom context. We investigated our research questions by focusing on how explanations impacted students' willingness to request and follow hints. Previous work has shown that this is a good proxy for perceived hint quality and usefulness [32].

4.1 Population and Procedure

The study was conducted during an introduction to programming course for non-majors in a research university during Fall 2018. Before the first exercise, a researcher explained iSnap's hint interface to students and encouraged them to use it whenever they needed support. There was no limit to the number of hints students could request, and iSnap reminded students about the hint feature at the beginning of each exercise. Our experiment was conducted on 2 in-lab exercises, where students could request help from undergraduate teaching assistants (TAs), and on 1 homework exercise, completed independently. Since students could request help from TAs during in-lab assignments and almost all complete the homework correctly, we do not analyze the quality of their programming performance in this experiment (though we do so in Experiment 2). The total number of students was 45, and all students completed their work using iSnap.

The students were randomly assigned into two groups: Group A (G_A) and Group B (G_B). Our experiment has a crossover design, so that both groups had access to textual explanations at different times. For the first two tasks, G_A received code hints with textual explanations, while G_B received only code hints, but for the third task[2], G_A was given only code hints, while G_B was given both textual explanations and code hints. As shown in Table 1, only 15-21 students requested hints on any assignment.

4.2 Measures and Results

We used 2 measures to understand the impact of textual explanations on the perceived usefulness and quality of hints. We first looked at the number of hints requested by students in each condition. As shown in the "H" columns of Table 1, there was no consistent trend across exercises. Students who *did* ask for hints in both groups seemed to ask for similar numbers of hints. The second measure we looked at was the hint follow rate (FR), or the average number of hints followed by each student. We defined a hint as "followed" if a student created the *suggested* block in that hint before receiving a new one. As shown in the "FR" columns of Table 1, the group with textual explanations had a higher average follow rate across assignments (approaching 100% in the homework exercise), ranging from 12 to 25 percentage points. These results suggest that students who received textual explanations with their hints were more convinced to follow the hints.

Looking more closely at *which* hints were followed and not, we can see how explanations may impact students' follow rate. Remember, for any assignment, there are a fixed number of unique, possible hints (each corresponding to one code block). When shown to a student, these hints are adapted to their current code (i.e. showing where to add the block). There were 9, 10 and 14 unique possible hints on the three exercises, respectively. A given hint may be shown to different students, and a student may view the same hint

[2]This was also true for a fourth task, but due to a power outage, we were unable to collect data for this task.

Table 1: Experiment 1 Results: For each exercise, the number of students who requested any hints (n), the mean number of hints requested (H), and the mean hint follow rate (FR). * indicates the group which received textual explanations.

	Lab 1			Homework 1				Lab 2		
	n	H	FR	n	H	FR		n	H	FR
G_A^*	11	9.27	0.53	7	5.7	0.95	G_B^*	5	10	0.70
G_B	10	7.27	0.56	8	6.25	0.70	G_A	10	9.90	0.47

multiple times. We say a hint has been *ignored* if at least one student received it and chose not to follow it. For students who received code hints *only*, the number of unique, ignored hints were 7/9, 6/10, 8/14 for the 3 exercises respectively. However, for students who also received textual explanations, the number of unique, ignored hints were 3/9, 1/10, and 5/14, respectively. This suggests that while many different kinds of code hints were ignored by students, when these hints are accompanied by explanations, only a few hints are ever ignored. We hypothesized that these few ignored hints may have had inadequate explanations, which were confusing or hard to act on. For example, in the second exercise the only hint that was not followed by G_A was *"Each time your code repeats, your sprite should draw one side of the polygon"*, which explains the code hint that suggested the addition of the *"move forward"* block.

4.3 Discussion

Our results suggest that textual explanations can serve their intended purpose of improving students' ability to understand and follow hints. Students with textual explanation were more likely to follow the hints they received. With explanations, most hints were followed anytime they were seen, which was not true for hints without explanations. While this exploratory analysis suggests some promise for textual explanations, our data consists of only a few students. Though trends were consistent across 3 exercises, we cannot make strong conclusions from these results. One limitation of this experiment is that students were allowed to request hints on demand, and, as shown in previous studies, students who most need support often do not ask for hints when they need them [1, 28]. We therefore can only study a subset of the students of interest. It is worth noting that the first and third exercises were in-lab, where students might have had additional support from instructors, possibly affecting how they used hints.

To get a better understanding of why some hints were not followed, we manually inspected each hint that was not. We found two potential reasons. First, some students requested a hint and then immediately closed it and requested another (without doing any additional edits to their code), repeating this process until either they stopped requesting hints or followed one. This is possible because iSnap displays multiple hint suggestions at a time for different parts of a student's code. This behavior suggests that sometimes students were looking for help in a specific part of their code and ignored hints for other parts, resulting in a decreased follow rate. The second reason, as noted earlier, is that some of the unfollowed hints with textual explanations may not have had the clearest explanations. In our future studies we plan to rephrase them or add the option of having more than one textual explanation for the same code hint in the hope of making these explanations more understandable and effective for novices.

5 EXPERIMENT 2: CROWD WORKERS

Based on promising but inconclusive results of Experiment 1, we designed Experiment 2 to overcome some of its limitations by recruiting larger population, providing hints pro-actively (instead of on-demand) and collecting surveys and self-explanations on the hints to better understand their impact on learners' understanding and their perceived usefulness. Experiment 2 aimed to answer the following research questions: How does adding textual explanations to code hints impact: (1) Learners' perceived usefulness of the hints? (2) Learners' performance on the current and future programming assignments? (3) Learners' ability to self-explain the relationships between code hints, their own code and the assignment?

5.1 Population and Procedure

In this experiment, our learners consisted of crowd workers who were recruited from Amazon's Mechanical Turk platform which has been discussed to be as effective form of conducting large-scale user studies as using university participants [5, 19]. All learners reported that they had no prior programming experience, though we did not collect any further demographic information. We paid learners $4-7 to complete the study (varying the amount to increase speed of recruiting). The data were collected as part of a larger study on the effect of different types of hint support which included 209 learners. We focus on a subset of that data relevant to our research questions about the impact of adding textual explanations to code hints, which included just 92 learners. We also excluded 4 of them from our study: 2 learners did not write any code, 1 learner finished the exercise before receiving the first hint and the last one gave meaningless self-explanations (discussed below), leaving a total of 88 learners in our analysis.

During the study, learners completed a programming task (detailed below), during which they were provided with some form of automated help. All 88 learners received code hints. Of these, 48 were randomly assigned to receive textual explanations with their code hints (group G_T), while the other 40 received only code hints (group G_C). Additionally, approximately half of the participants were randomly assigned to self-explain each received hint, and we use this data in our evaluation, as explained below. Learners started the study by reading a short tutorial on block-based programming in iSnap for 5 minutes[3]. The tutorial explained how to use iSnap's user interface as well as all the programming concepts needed for the programming task. These concepts included input/output, loops, operators and drawing shapes, which were all explained by text and short animated videos. Afterwards, learners started to work on a programming task for 15 minutes. The programming task involved drawing a polygon based on the number of sides the user inputs.

During programming, iSnap interrupted the learners every two minutes and provided them a hint according to their condition (e.g. showing a code hint) because we wanted rich data about multiple hints, rather than biased sample when learners request it and to avoid the limitations in Experiment 1 as well. After receiving the

[3] We provided only a short time for the tutorial, since our goal was to study how students learned hints while *programming*.

hint, iSnap asked them for their thoughts on the action (Post-help survey). The 2 minute action timer restarted after learners finished the post-help survey, giving them 2 more minutes of work before being interrupted again. The 15 minute timer was not paused during these surveys, though they were identical across conditions. While offering help proactively, as we did in this study, is less common than offering on-demand help, however, results from a pre-help survey (not analyzed in this paper) showed that learners desired help the vast majority of the time when it was given. After 15 minutes, learners were stopped and then worked on a second programming task (Task 2) for 15 minutes. Task 2 asked them to create a program that draws a strip of triangles, with the number of triangles given by the user. This task uses similar programming concepts as Task 1, but is slightly more advanced. Unlike Task 1, every 2 minutes learners were given a random hint independent of their condition in Task 1. We found that each learner received 2-5 hints during each task, varying depending on how long they took on the pre-help and post-help surveys, and whether there was a reasonable hint.

5.2 Measures

We collected 3 types of data relevant to this analysis: log data, post-help survey responses, and self-explanations. To measure learners' performance, we divided each programming task into 4 objectives (e.g. "ask the user for input and use it correctly", "draw a shape," etc.). Finishing all the objectives correctly is equivalent to successful completion of the task. We developed an automatic grader to determine which objectives learners have completed, and manually verified these grades for approximately half of participants. After each hint, iSnap asked learners 4 questions in the Post-help survey to rate the support they received (e.g. code hints). These 4 questions measured: (1) Usefulness: *How useful were the action(s) that iSnap just took?*, (2) Relevance: *How well did this hint address what you were working on or stuck on?*, (3) Progress: *How well did this hint help you progress towards a correct solution?*, (4) Interpretability: *How easily could you interpret the meaning of this hint?*. We based questions 2-4 on a rubric for rating hint quality [32]. In addition, we measured the hints' *follow rate*, which is the average of hints followed by each learner, by auto-inspecting learners' log traces to know if they really have followed the hint or not.

Approximately half of participants (19 in G_T and 21 in G_C) received a self-explanation prompt after each hint with a randomized prompt (e.g. *"How would you use this hint?", "Why do you think Snap recommended this hint?"*). We used their responses to measure learners' ability to explain the purpose of the hints, evaluating a total of 125 self-explanations. Two researchers familiar with the task used a yes/no rubric to independently assess whether learners' self-explanations connected their hints to their: (1) Current Code: *Is the explanation related to the learner's current code situation?*; (2) Programming Concepts: *Does the explanation show that the learner has learned anything related to programming concepts?*; (3) Assignment: *Does the explanation show how the hint can help the learner in his assignment?*. The two researchers blindly rated learners' self-explanations, i.e. without knowing the learner's condition (e.g. received code hints). The two researchers divided the first half of the self-explanations answers into 3 rounds for rating each of the 3 questions. After each round, conflicts were discussed and resolved. We calculated Cohen's kappas for each question in each round, where 9 kappas ranged from 0.724 to 1, indicating substantial agreement. Afterwards, the second half of the self-explanations' answers was divided between the two researchers for grading.

5.3 Results

Hints' perceived usefulness and follow rate. We averaged learners' responses in the Post-help Survey across Task 1 to assign one rating per question to each learner. As shown in Table 2, we compared average ratings between G_T learners and G_C learners. We used Mann-Whitney U tests here, as in the remainder of this section, as our data were non-normal. We found that G_T learners rated iSnap's help as significantly more useful ($p = 0.021$), relevant ($p = 0.030$) and interpretable ($p = 0.018$) than G_C. Learners in G_T also rated the hints as more effective in helping them to make progress; however, the rating differences were not significant ($p = 0.109$). In addition, we found that the learners' hint follow rate was higher in G_T than G_C, as in Experiment 1. However, despite a medium effect size (Cohen's $d = 0.38$) this difference was not significant ($p = 0.137$).

Learners' Performance. We compared number of objectives that learners completed during Task1 (with hints determined by their condition) and in Task2 (with randomized help, independent of their condition). As shown in Table 2, we found no significant difference in the number of objectives completed by each group in Task1 ($p = 0.66$) or in Task2 ($p = 0.28$). One simple way we hypothesized the textual explanations might improve learners' performance is by helping students to locate code blocks, since this information was included in the explanation. We identified all hints that asked the learner to find and create a new code block, where the learner correctly followed this hint (before receiving another hint). For each learner, we calculated the average time they took to create these blocks. However, the difference in this average time for learners in G_C (Med = 28.1) and G_T (Med=24.5) was not significant ($p = 0.57$).

Learners ability to self-explain the relationships between code hints, their own code and the exercise's objectives. For learners who received self-explanation prompts after receiving hints, we rated their self-explanations, as described in Section 5.2. For each learner, we determined the percentage of their self-explanations which connected the received hint to : 1) their current code (Current Code), 2) correct programming concept(s) (Programming Concepts), and 3) the objective(s) of the programming assignment (Assignment). As shown in Table 3, we found that these percentages were much higher in G_T than G_C. A Mann-Whitney U Test shows that this difference is statistically significant for the first and third questions ($p = 0.020$, $p = 0.057$, $p = 0.023$).

5.4 Discussion

Our results suggest that textual explanations can improve code hints by increasing how useful, relevant and interpretable learners perceive them to be (RQ1) and learners' ability to self-explain the hints (RQ3). There is also some evidence that the explanations increase learners' willingness to follow hints, as suggested by Experiment 1, though the difference was not significant. This suggests that, despite concerns raised in prior work [11], learners did in fact

Table 2: Experiment 2 Results. The table gives Mean (M), Standard Deviation (SD) and Median (Med) for both groups, with the p value for comparison using a Mann-Whitney U test, and effect size, Cohen's d.

	Interpretability			Relevance			Progress			Usefulness			Follow Rate			Task 1 Perf.			Task 2 Perf.		
	M	SD	Med	M	SD	Med	M	SD	Med	M	SD	Med	M	SD	Med	M	SD	Med	M	SD	Med
$G_T(48)$	8.24	2.24	9	8.31	2.12	9	7.90	2.59	9	8.28	1.91	9	0.75	0.31	0.87	2.31	1.32	2	2.15	1.46	2
$G_C(40)$	7.53	1.82	7.22	7.46	2.13	8	7.47	1.97	7.1	7.36	2.21	7.91	0.62	0.39	0.7	2.15	1.52	2	2.48	1.35	2
p	**0.018**			**0.03**			0.109			**0.021**			0.137			0.665			0.288		
d	0.34			0.39			0.18			0.44			0.38			0.11			0.23		

Table 3: Self-Explanations Results in Experiment 2. For each question, Mean (M), Standard Deviation (SD) and Median (Med) with the p value for comparison using a Mann-Whitney U test, and effect size, Cohen's d.

	Current Code			Prog. Concepts			Assignment		
	M	SD	Med	M	SD	Med	M	SD	Med
$G_T(19)$	0.52	0.42	0.5	0.29	0.34	0.25	0.35	0.35	0.33
$G_C(21)$	0.22	0.28	0	0.12	0.27	0	0.12	0.27	0
p	**0.020**			0.057			**0.023**		
d	0.852			0.55			0.73		

read explanations and derive some benefits. Interestingly, despite these advantages, there is no evidence that textual explanations improved learners' performance on the current or future tasks (RQ2). In prior analysis of this data, we did find that learners with code hints (without textual explanations) performed better on Task 1 than those with no hints [30]. This suggests that code hints do improve learners' immediate performance, but our results indicate that the textual explanations did not contribute to this improvement. It is interesting that learners' increased ability to relate hints to programming concepts suggests a type of learning, but this did not translate into improved performance. This may be because, even with textual explanations, learners still only related 29% of hints they received to programming concepts on average.

Regarding the design of the textual explanations, recall that our goal was to provide the learner with 3 types of information: block's functionality, why it is needed in the given assignment, and the location of the block. Our analysis on learners' self-explanations show that this information helped learners to relate hints to their own code, programming concepts (e.g. definition of loops, etc.) and to the assignment objectives. For example, one learner in G_T received a hint to use the "repeat block", then they were asked: *"How would you use this hint?"*. The learner self-explained the hint *"I would use it to repeat however many sides there are in the polygon"*. The third type of information was the location of the suggested block. However, we found no evidence that this information helped learners in G_T to find blocks faster than those in G_C. This might be because iSnap blocks are already color-coded, so when a learner is given a code hint he can find its location by matching its color with the category of the same color. As a result it is possible that learners did not need this feature to be stated explicitly in text. These results show that our explanations design fulfilled 2 of its objectives.

In this Experiment, there are several limitations to our results. First, the population consists of paid crowd workers with no prior programming experience. Their motivations and prior knowledge may differ from those of other populations of learners where programming hints are used. However, this study allowed us to be flexible with the design and add as many constraints (like self-explanations and post-help surveys) which is usually hard to do in a classroom setting, like in Experiment 1, that is restricted to a specific time and format. Second, the 2-minute counter we used to time when participants received hints is different from the on-demand way that many hints are presented [13, 34], and may have been distracting for users. However, prior work shows that students who most need support often do not ask for hints when they need them [1, 28]. Our approach of offering hints proactively allowed us to study hints' impact on all learners, not just the ones who are willing to ask for help. We also note that the textual explanations were still visible to learners when they were writing self-explanations of hints. It is unclear to what extent these explanations reflect students' *understanding* of the hints, as opposed to a summary of the visible explanations. However, we found no cases where a learner directly copied a textual explanation in their self-explanation.

6 CONCLUSIONS AND FUTURE WORK

In this paper we designed complementary textual explanations for our existing code hints in iSnap, with the goal of overcoming the limitations of code hints that only tell a student what to do. We evaluated our combined support by conducting two controlled studies on different populations. In our first classroom study, we found evidence that hint explanations may improve students' willingness to follow code hints, though we did not have enough participants to confirm these results. We conducted another study on a larger population of crowd workers, allowing us to do additional empirical analysis. Our results showed that learners who received textual explanations in addition to code hints perceived iSnap's support as significantly more useful, relevant and interpretable and had a better understanding of the hints provided than learners who received only code hints. We found no contradictions in the results of the two studies, and we argue that our results from the second study should generalize to a classroom context. In our future work, we will improve the design of textual explanations by supporting not only hints that suggest *to insert* a given block, but also those that suggest *to delete* a block as well. Additionally, a larger classroom study on more difficult exercises using a pre and post tests to measure learning gain as well could confirm how well our findings from Experiment 2 generalize to a classroom setting. Finally, we aim to design an interface for iSnap for teachers to author these explanations for new assignments.

REFERENCES

[1] Vincent Aleven, Ido Roll, Bruce M. McLaren, and Kenneth R. Koedinger. 2016. Help Helps, But Only So Much: Research on Help Seeking with Intelligent Tutoring Systems. *International Journal of Artificial Intelligence in Education* 26, 1 (2016), 1–19.

[2] John R. Anderson, Frederick G. Conrad, and Albert T. Corbett. 1989. Skill Acquisition and the LISP tutor. *Cognitive Science* 13, 4 (1989), 467–505.

[3] Michael Ball. 2018. *Lambda: An Autograder for Snap!.* Technical Report. Electrical Engineering and Computer Sciences University of California at Berkeley. https://www2.eecs.berkeley.edu/Pubs/TechRpts/2018/EECS-2018-2.pdf

[4] Joseph E Beck, Kai-min Chang, Jack Mostow, and Albert Corbett. 2008. Does help help? Introducing the Bayesian Evaluation and Assessment methodology. In *International Conference on Intelligent Tutoring Systems.* Springer, 383–394.

[5] Tara S. Behrend, David J. Sharek, Adam W. Meade, and Eric N. Wiebe. 2011. The viability of crowdsourcing for survey research. *Behavior Research Methods* 43, 3 (25 Mar 2011), 800.

[6] Jens Bennedsen and Michael E. Caspersen. 2007. Failure rates in introductory programming. *ACM SIGCSE Bulletin* 39, 2 (2007), 32. https://doi.org/10.1145/1272848.1272879

[7] Xianglei Chen and Matthew Soldner. 2013. *STEM Attrition: College Students' Paths Into and Out of STEM Fields.* Technical Report. National Center for Education Statistics, Institute of Education Sciences, U.S. Department of Education. http://nces.ed.gov/pubs2014/2014001rev.pdf

[8] Albert T. Corbett. 2001. Cognitive Computer Tutors: Solving the Two-Sigma Problem. In *Proceedings of the International Conference on User Modeling.* Springer, 137–147.

[9] Albert T Corbett and John R Anderson. 2001. Locus of feedback control in computer-based tutoring: Impact on learning rate, achievement and attitudes. In *Proceedings of the SIGCHI conference on Human factors in computing systems.* ACM, 245–252.

[10] Davide Fossati, Barbara Di Eugenio, Stellan Ohlsson, Christopher Brown, and Lin Chen. 2010. Generating proactive feedback to help students stay on track. *Lecture Notes in Computer Science (including subseries Lecture Notes in Artificial Intelligence and Lecture Notes in Bioinformatics)* 6095 LNCS, PART 2 (2010), 315–317.

[11] Davide Fossati, Barbara Di Eugenio, Stellan Ohlsson, Christopher Brown, and Lin Chen. 2015. Data Driven Automatic Feedback Generation in the iList Intelligent Tutoring System. *Technology, Instruction, Cognition and Learning* 10, 1 (2015), 5–26.

[12] Dan Garcia, Brian Harvey, and Tiffany Barnes. 2015. The Beauty and Joy of Computing. *ACM Inroads* 6, 4 (2015), 71–79.

[13] Alex Gerdes, Bastiaan Heeren, Johan Jeuring, and L. Thomas van Binsbergen. 2017. Ask-Elle: an Adaptable Programming Tutor for Haskell Giving Automated Feedback. *International Journal of Artificial Intelligence in Education* 27, 1 (2017), 1–36.

[14] Brian Harvey, Daniel Garcia, Josh Paley, and Luke Segars. 2012. Snap!:(build your own blocks). In *Proceedings of the 43rd ACM technical symposium on Computer Science Education.* ACM, 662–662.

[15] Andrew Head, Elena Glassman, Gustavo Soares, Ryo Suzuki, Lucas Figueredo, Loris D'Antoni, and Björn Hartmann. 2017. Writing Reusable Code Feedback at Scale with Mixed-Initiative Program Synthesis. In *Proceedings of the ACM Conference on Learning @ Scale.* ACM, 89–98.

[16] Jay Holland, Antonija Mitrovic, and Brent Martin. 2009. J-LATTE: a Constraint-based Tutor for Java. In *Proceedings of the International Conference on Computers in Education.* University of Canterbury. Computer Science and Software Engineering, 142–146.

[17] Shalini Kaleeswaran, Anirudh Santhiar, Aditya Kanade, and Sumit Gulwani. 2016. Semi-Supervised Verified Feedback Generation. *CoRR* (2016), 739–750.

[18] Hieke Keuning, Johan Jeuring, and Bastiaan Heeren. 2016. Towards a Systematic Review of Automated Feedback Generation for Programming Exercises. In *Proceedings of the 2016 ACM Conference on Innovation and Technology in Computer Science Education - ITiCSE '16.* ACM, 41–46. https://doi.org/10.1145/2899415.2899422

[19] Aniket Kittur, Ed H Chi, and Bongwon Suh. 2008. Crowdsourcing user studies with Mechanical Turk. In *Proceedings of the SIGCHI conference on human factors in computing systems.* ACM, 453–456.

[20] Nguyen-Thinh Le, Wolfgang Menzel, and Niels Pinkwart. 2009. Evaluation of a constraint-based homework assistance system for logic programming. *Proceedings of the 17th International Conference on Computers in Education* (2009), 51–58.

[21] Victor J. Marin, Tobin Pereira, Srinivas Sridharan, and Carlos R. Rivero. 2017. Automated personalized feedback in introductory Java programming MOOCs. *Proceedings - International Conference on Data Engineering* August (2017), 1259–1270.

[22] Danielle S. McNamara. 2017. Self-Explanation and Reading Strategy Training (SERT) Improves Low-Knowledge Students' Science Course Performance. *Discourse Processes* (2017).

[23] Antonija Mitrovic. 1998. A knowledge-based teaching system for SQL. In *Proceedings of ED-MEDIA*, Vol. 98. 1027–1032.

[24] Antonija Mitrovic, Brent Martin, and Pramuditha Suraweera. 2007. Intelligent tutors for all: Constraint-based modeling methodology, systems and authoring. *IEEE Intelligent Systems* 22 (2007), 38–45.

[25] Benjamin Paaßen, Barbara Hammer, Thomas William Price, Tiffany Barnes, Sebastian Gross, and Niels Pinkwart. 2017. The Continuous Hint Factory - Providing Hints in Vast and Sparsely Populated Edit Distance Spaces. *arXiv preprint arXiv:1708.06564* 10, 1 (2017), 1–35. arXiv:1708.06564

[26] Daniel Perelman, Sumit Gulwani, and Dan Grossman. 2014. Test-driven synthesis for automated feedback for introductory computer science assignments. *Proceedings of Data Mining for Educational Assessment and Feedback (ASSESS 2014)* (2014).

[27] C Piech, J Huang, A Nguyen, M Phulsuksombati, M Sahami, and L Guibas. 2015. Learning program embeddings to propagate feedback on student code. *arXiv preprint arXiv:1505.05969* (2015), 1093–1102. arXiv:arXiv:1505.05969v1

[28] Thomas W Price, Yihuan Dong, and Dragan Lipovac. 2017. iSnap: towards intelligent tutoring in novice programming environments. In *Proceedings of the 2017 ACM SIGCSE Technical Symposium on Computer Science Education.* ACM, 483–488.

[29] Thomas W Price, Zhongxiu Liu, Veronica Cateté, and Tiffany Barnes. 2017. Factors Influencing Students' Help-Seeking Behavior while Programming with Human and Computer Tutors. In *Proceedings of the 2017 ACM Conference on International Computing Education Research.* ACM, 127–135.

[30] Thomas W. Price, Joseph J. Williams, and Samiha Marwan. 2019. A Comparison of Two Designs for Automated Programming Hints. *2nd Educational Data Mining in Computer Science Education (CSEDM) Workshop at the International Conference on Learning Analytics and Knowledge (LAK)* (2019).

[31] Thomas W. Price, Rui Zhi, and Tiffany Barnes. 2017. Evaluation of a Data-driven Feedback Algorithm for Open-ended Programming. In *Proceedings of the International Conference on Educational Data Mining.*

[32] Thomas W Price, Rui Zhi, and Tiffany Barnes. 2017. Hint generation under uncertainty: The effect of hint quality on help-seeking behavior. In *International Conference on Artificial Intelligence in Education.* Springer, 311–322.

[33] Kelly Rivers. 2017. *Automated Data-Driven Hint Generation for Learning Programming.* PhD. Carnegie Mellon University.

[34] Kelly Rivers and Kenneth R. Koedinger. 2017. Data-Driven Hint Generation in Vast Solution Spaces: a Self-Improving Python Programming Tutor. *International Journal of Artificial Intelligence in Education* 27, 1 (2017), 37–64.

[35] André L. Santos. 2012. An open-ended environment for teaching Java in context. In *Proceedings of the 17th ACM annual conference on Innovation and technology in computer science education - ITiCSE '12.* ACM Press, New York, New York, USA, 87.

[36] Rishabh Singh, Sumit Gulwani, and Armando Solar-Lezama. 2013. Automated feedback generation for introductory programming assignments. *Acm Sigplan Notices* 48, 6 (2013), 15–26.

[37] Arto Vihavainen, Jonne Airaksinen, and Christopher Watson. 2014. A systematic review of approaches for teaching introductory programming and their influence on success. *Proceedings of the tenth annual conference on International computing education research - ICER '14* (2014), 19–26.

[38] Christopher Watson and Frederick W B Li. 2014. Failure rates in introductory programming revisited. In *Proceedings of the ACM Conference on Innovation and Technology in Computer Science Education.* ACM, ACM, 39–44.

[39] Jooyong Yi, Umair Z. Ahmed, Amey Karkare, Shin Hwei Tan, and Abhik Roychoudhury. 2017. A Feasibility Study of Using Automated Program Repair for Introductory Programming Assignments. In *Proceedings of the Joint Meeting on Foundations of Software Engineering.* ACM, 740–751. https://doi.org/10.1145/3106237.3106262

Using Social Annotations to Augment the Learning Space and Learner Experience

Shaveen Singh and Bernd Meyer
Faculty of Information Technology
Monash University
Melbourne, Victoria, Australia
shaveen.singh@monash.edu

ABSTRACT

Learning has always been considered a social and collaborative activity. From the social constructivism perspective, students learn through the process of sharing experiences and build knowledge and understanding through discussion. This pilot study demonstrates the successful integration of an online social annotation tool in a Python programming workshop that allows students to discuss learning material and code segments with their fellow classmates. We investigate how the students leveraged the tool to improve their learning and to log their sentiments while reading the material and attempting the programming activities. We find that those students who had access to the annotation tool spent an above average amount of time on the material. They also had a higher completion rate and performance compared to the control group who did not have the annotation feature available to them. Feedback from the students who used the tool was very positive. Finally, we delve deeper into analysing the annotation patterns and explore how instructors can make use of fine-grained annotation data to inform and adapt the design of CS teaching and learning materials in online or blended contexts.

CCS CONCEPTS

• **Applied computing → Interactive learning environments**; *Distance learning*; *E-learning*; Collaborative learning.

KEYWORDS

annotations; digital education; engagement; situated cognition

ACM Reference Format:

Shaveen Singh and Bernd Meyer. 2019. Using Social Annotations to Augment the Learning Space and Learner Experience. In *Innovation and Technology in Computer Science Education (ITiCSE '19), July 15–17, 2019, Aberdeen, Scotland UK.* ACM, New York, NY, USA, 7 pages. https://doi.org/10.1145/3304221.3319767

1 INTRODUCTION

The aim of education should be to create autonomous learners, i.e. learning to learn. Burner discusses in [2] that the purpose of education is not just to impart knowledge, but instead to facilitate thinking and problem-solving skills which can then be transferred to a range of situations. This does not obviate the classroom teacher; it will always be necessary not only to arrange the conditions of learning but also to discuss, debrief, and encourage future explorations by asking the right questions or giving an appropriate direction at the most opportune time. Rather, the environment should stimulate interest and facilitate learning.

Learning is intrinsically linked to physically situated cognition [6]. Literature confirms that since we learn best through enactive encounters, appropriate experiences with materials assist conceptual development [1]. The four central ideas in situated cognition (the 4Es) are: (1) the embodiment thesis argues that cognition encompasses both the mind and the body; (2) the embed thesis maintains that people exploit features of the physical and social environment to increase their cognitive abilities; (3) the enactive thesis describes the cognition as dependent upon a person's interactions with the world and (4) the extended cognition thesis posits that cognition emerges from interacting with the artifacts and others.

It is well understood that environmental structure is critical to human cognition and this is evident in the physical spaces at institutions around us. It is even noticeable from the architectural perspective. For example, many universities incorporate strategies to promote social engagement, communication and collaboration by encouraging social density in so-called *attractor spaces* such as workrooms fitted with shared screens, courtyard gardens, games rooms, etc. Strategically planned seating configurations around campus and in libraries, and open office spaces for research students similarly serve the purpose of facilitating social knowledge construction. The challenge is to have similar embodied experience in the virtual learning spaces.

2 EMBODIED EXPERIENCE IN AND WITH ENVIRONMENT

The embodiment thesis maintains that cognition depends upon physical characteristics of the body [18]; its sensory and motor capabilities shape the mind [16]. A major historical influence for the embodiment thesis is Gibson's work on the theory of affordances [7]. Gibson believed that people understand the world in terms of functional relevance and possibilities for action (affordances). He defines affordances as a relationship between people and environment, dependent upon the person's intentions and physical abilities with respect to action opportunities provided by features of the environment.

This allows people to feel that tools and objects used during learning become an extension of themselves, serving to organise

ITiCSE '19, July 15–17, 2019, Aberdeen, Scotland UK

ACM ISBN 978-1-4503-6301-3/19/07...$15.00
https://doi.org/10.1145/3304221.3319767

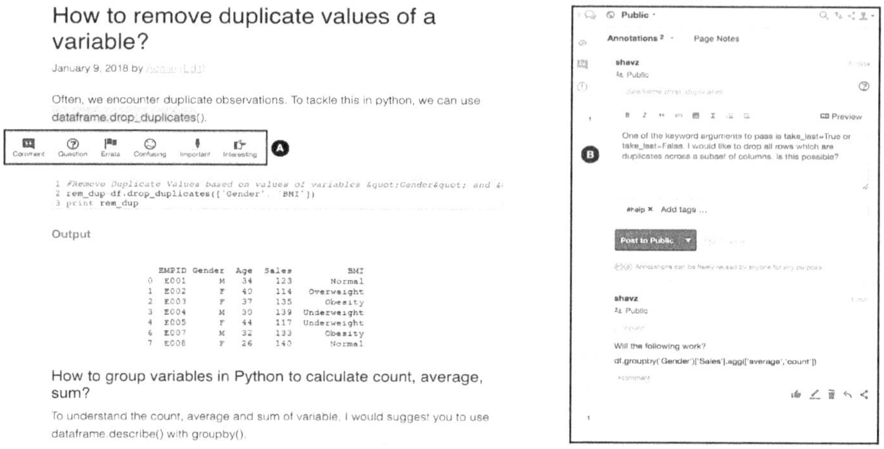

Figure 1: The annotation tool showing (A) the popup dialog when a user selects the text and (B) the annotations in the right hand pane.

their knowledge construction and understanding. Using the tools allows learners to externalise the idea and/or thought process. This, in turn, enables them to receive feedback from the environment (peers and others) in response to which they can initiate new actions.

Annotations are a tool that offers their users a means to (1) identify and process new information, (2) record interpretation and inference, (3) assist problem structuring through solution attempts and (4) reflect on the process of reading in that exact moment. Studies have shown a firm relationship between thinking and acting with tools, for example, demonstrating activation of motor processes in the brain when people think about using tools, say words associated with tool use, or watch someone else use a tool [10, 15].

Embodied and embedded cognition often go hand-in-hand and are sometimes referred to collectively as embodied, embedded cognition [3]. Where embodied cognition considers how people use their bodies to help them think, embedded cognition theory considers how people use features of their environment to improve their cognitive abilities [16]. People do not store or process information they can easily off-load to the environment, a process known as of *cognitive bootstrapping* [4]. They exploit aspects of their environments as things to think with, helping them better understand, evaluate, and elaborate on ideas.

3 THE ANNOTATION TOOL

The social annotation platform serves as a transparent tool in the knowledge-generation process. Students act using the features of the annotation tool to identify, process and organise knowledge. Annotating, then, is a method of abstracting and compressing information which can be classified as "seeing with a tool". Annotations are additionally used as a tool to off-load cognitive work to the environment (cognitive bootstrapping). Numerous studies cite annotation as a ubiquitous companion activity to responsive reading, and the ability to annotate documents is reported as an essential and often requested feature of digital reading interfaces for education [11, 13, 17, 19]. Annotations vary widely in purpose, content and desired permanence but they all share a few important common properties. Namely their creation is always interleaved with the act of reading and they are anchored, i.e. they pertain to a specific portion of the text.

In this research, we extended the Hypothesis tool [8] which allows students to asynchronously annotate learning material such as readings, lecture notes and problem sets in a chat-like fashion. We investigate two aspects of annotation use. Firstly, we explore the affordance of the tool in assisting Computing Science students' knowledge construction process. Secondly, we analyse how annotations enable educators to obtain richer and more actionable insights from the use of learning material.

The student view of the course page is shown in Figure 1. It shows what the student sees after accessing the reading material and highlighting a specific passage on a page. Six different tagging options were made available to students to categorise their annotations. Upon selecting one of the six annnotation categories, a conversation window opens in the right hand pane where the student can pose a question or post a comment. Figure 1 shows a portion of text that has been highlighted in the learning material and the six (6) annotation options being displayed below the highlight. Table 1 shows the six pre-defined annotation options that students can use when posting an annotation.

Table 1: Six different annotation categories for students

Category	Purpose
Comment	to contribute opinions and remarks
Question	to elicit information or response from peers or instructors
Errata	to report inaccuracies in the learning material
Important	to encode important concepts/terminologies
Confusing	to report material that need further clarification or elaboration.
Interesting	to identify concepts or discussion that are notable and one may want to explore in future

Students can also add their own custom tags to their annotation to categorise them and the corresponding text. These tags are searchable and can be used to connect with others working on the same topic or to follow a group's annotation activity across the material. Annotations are public by default but can be made private. If the annotation is public, other students can respond asynchronously to the conversation as shown in Figure 2. Students can upvote, share or flag annotations made by others. The search box on the top right corner of the sidebar lets students search annotations by username, tag or keyword.

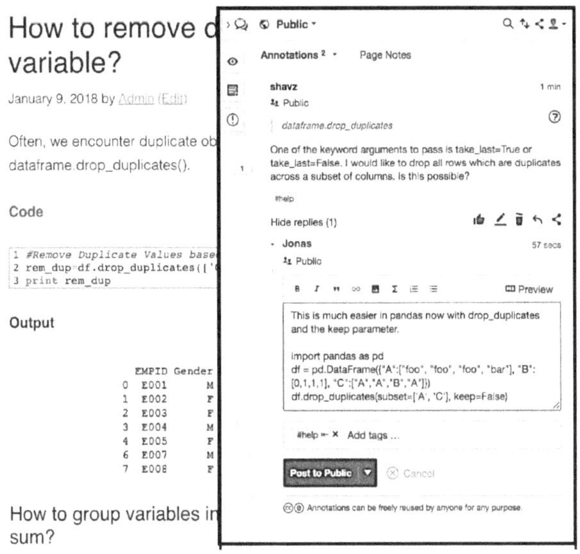

Figure 2: The annotation tools shows a user responding to an annotation in the right-hand side-bar

For instructors, the annotation platform also includes an integrated dashboard (Fig. 9), which provides real-time feedback on how students are engaging with the reading task. This is further discussed in Section 5.3.

4 METHODOLOGY

4.1 Research questions

The goal of this research is to examine the affordances of the annotation tool to augment the CS learning space and investigate how it enhances learning. We answer the following specific questions:

(1) How do students perceive and use annotations whilst engaging with learning materials?
(2) How does the social annotation platform augment student participation and performance?
(3) What useful insights does the annotation tool generate about the students learning and how can these insights be used by instructors to enhance teaching?

4.2 Participants and settings

Two workshops were advertised on "Data Visualisation using Python" during the semester break targeting undergraduate and post-graduate students of Engineering and Information Technology at Monash university. A total of 57 students enrolled in the workshops. Each workshop was divided into two phases:

(1) **Preparatory Phase:** Students were given preparatory material, i.e. a 20-page study guide comprising of readings, coding instructions and quizzes (multiple-choice and programming exercises) on data visualisation using Python. Students had to complete this task online on their own, at home, prior to the face-to-face session. The material was made available via a content delivery platform as a HTML e-book. Students could use the annotation feature on the platform to annotate the pages in their own time. All reading interactions on the platform were recorded. The choice to annotate was completely voluntary and no marks were awarded for making annotations. However, students were informed that the annotations made would be used to adapt the teaching focus (content and exercises) of the half-day face-to-face workshop session. Students could see how others were annotating and could respond to each others annotations on the learning material.
(2) **Face-to-Face Session:** A 3-hour face-to-face session was delivered to the students a week after the preparatory phase was concluded. For these, the teaching material was adapted in response to the students' experience with the learning material as captured in the annotations.

The experimental group consisted of 37 participants. These had access to the annotation feature enabled within their platform. The control group comprised of 20 students who did not have access to the annotation tool. The shared demographics of both groups is in Figure 3 . Apart from the ability to use annotations, preparatory course material, quizzes and schedule for both groups were completely identical.

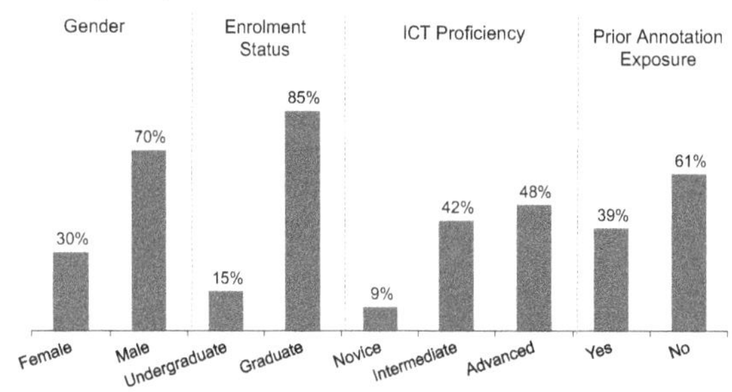

Figure 3: Characteristics of the Participants

The scenario typifies a traditional Computer Science course where students are expected to complete their reading and preparatory work at home and the actual problem-solving or coding exercises take place during the face-to-face session in the presence of an instructor. Figure 3 summarizes the characteristics of the participants who enrolled in the workshop.

4.3 Procedure

To evaluate the efficacy of the annotation tool, we performed the analysis as described below. Fine-grained data regarding annotations, the nature or category, annotation position within the document, author, posting timestamp, counts and any reply/upvote were identified as independent variables. The dependent variable in the experiment was the completion rate and quiz score. We first extracted the above-mentioned independent annotation metrics that could describe the students' annotation behaviour. We aggregated some of these data as a way of describing how much and when, relative to class, students were participating. We used the statistical software SPSS to calculate correlations between specific annotation metrics and time spent, completion rate and student performance. Finally, we report more qualitative insights into how the instructor used annotation information to adapt the teaching approaches in the classroom and the student experience of using the annotation tool.

5 RESULTS

5.1 Students use of the annotation tool

During the preparatory week 307 annotations were made by the 36 students in the twenty (20) page document. Thirty-six (36) out of thirty-seven (37) students contributed annotations during this phase.

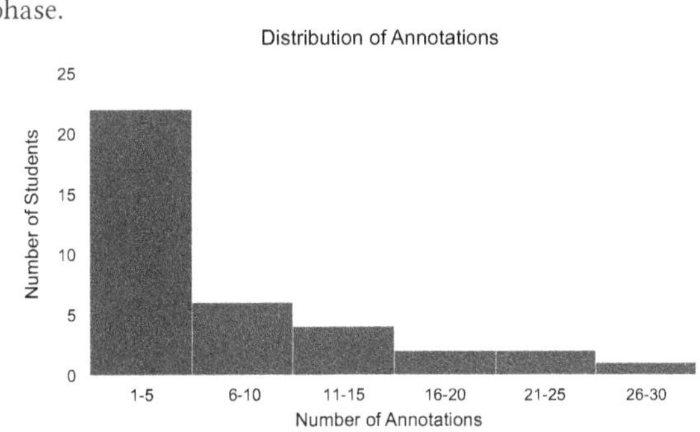

Figure 4: Distribution of the number of annotations made

Figure 4 shows the frequency of students that made particular numbers of annotations. The average number of annotations per page was 15.3 (SD = 2.2) and the average number of annotation per student was 8.57 (SD = 2.4). The average number of interactions with an annotation (clicks/views/upvote) across the whole document was 24.6 (SD = 4.3). We believe this value was low because annotating was entirely voluntary. We hope to investigate the impact of incentives in future experiments.

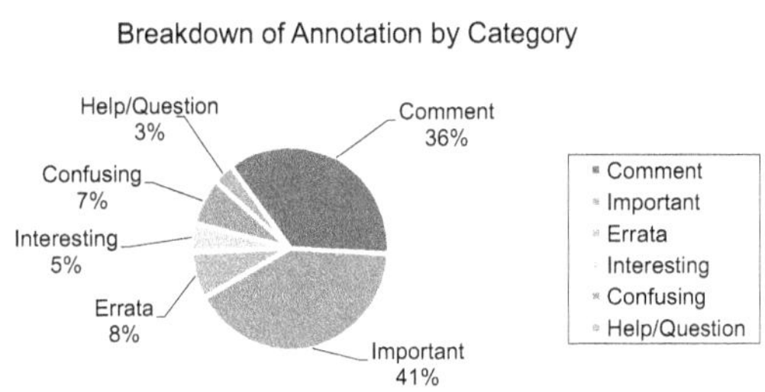

Figure 5: Proportion of annotations made by category.

Figure 5 shows the distribution of annotations by the six different annotation categories. Most of the annotations made were *comments* (summarisation and elaborations)—used to stimulate thinking and *important* tags—used to indicate key concepts (cognitive bootstrapping). These are reported as common strategies used by students to understand/summarise notes and help retention of knowledge [16] and confirmed by our student survey results in Figure 10.

5.2 Annotating increases participation and performance

We see in Figure 6 that the time spent reading online material is significantly higher for the cohort that used the annotation tool. The

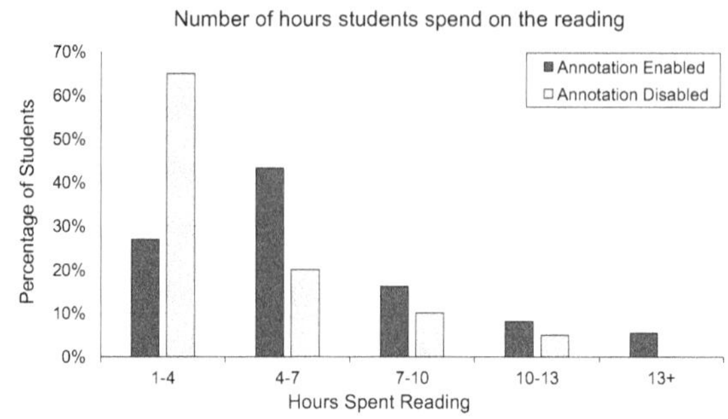

Figure 6: Reading time of experimental vs control group.

minimum preparation time for the workshop was recommended to be at least 4 hours. Approximately 73% of the students who used the annotation platform spent well above the suggested time (> $4 hours$) compared to only 35% of students from the control group.

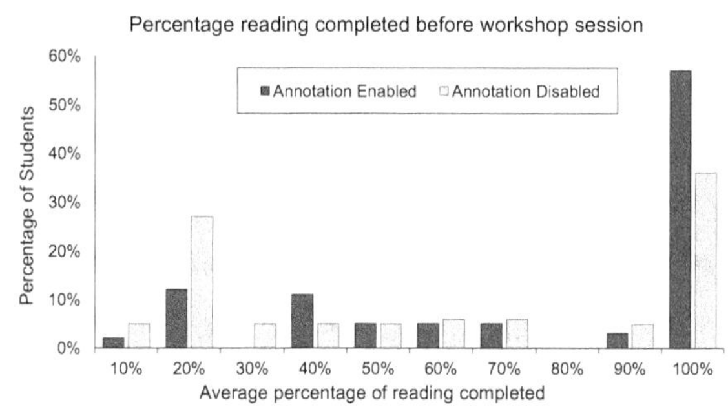

Figure 7: Completion rate of experimental vs control group.

Figure 7 shows the extent to which students completed their preparatory material from the two cohorts. Close to 57% of the students who were using annotations completed all the readings during the preparatory two weeks compared to only 36% completion rate obtained from the control group.

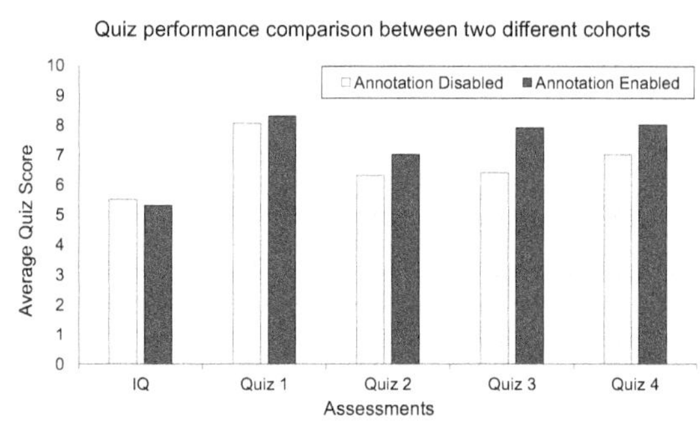

Figure 8: Performance of experimental vs control group.

Some literature reports that students only read on average 28% of the assigned pre-readings [5]. However, this was a report on psychology courses and we could not find any figures for CS courses (although anecdotal from experience, it is similarily low). At 57%, our result is considerably higher than what is reported in the literature and the observed completion rate of the control group.

Figure 8 above shows that students using the annotation tool seem generally to have done marginally better in the module quizzes. This is more pronounced for the later (more advanced quizzes). The average score for quizzes 2-4 for the cohort that used the annotation was $8-10\%$ higher when compared to the cohort where annotation tool was not being used ($p < 0.05$).

5.3 Obtaining actionable insights from annotation data

One of the benefits we foresee from using annotation as a data source is that it provides contextual and qualitative feedback to instructors for actioning interventions—something that is much needed in programming courses to understand students' difficulties with content and concepts.

The integrated dashboard (Fig. 9) provides instructors with near real-time feedback on how students are engaging with specific sections of the module. The colour of the bubble corresponds to the category of annotation it belongs to and the size of the bubble corresponds to the frequency of annotations made on that module. Clicking on the bubble leads the instructor to an itemized list of all annotations that were made on that page corresponding to the respective annotation classification.

The philosophy behind the annotation breakdown report is based on Just-in-Time-Teaching [12], which uses instant feedback from students to inform teachers on where students are routinely grappling with difficult concepts. Their reactions to the learning materials (aggregated according to the six different tagging options and learning modules) can be extremely valuable in communicating student experience in near real-time. We discuss two scenarios where this leads to useful insights for the instructor.

5.3.1 Using Annotation Data to Improve Teaching Material. Nine out of ten (9/10) annotations posted in Module 4.6 were tagged as confusing (Fig. 9). The annotation listing against the section showed that the module focused on creating *"Small Multiple"* plots using Python. This insight led the instructor to make the following improvements to the teaching material:

(1) The instructor created a guided tutorial on *"Small Multiples"* as a pre-workshop exercise for the students.
(2) Two additional slides on *"Small Multiple"* were included in the face-to-face material to be discussed during the lecture.

Although the entire class had access to this supplementary material, the interventions were to help mainly the students who reported confusion through their annotation posting. These students usually are the "at-risk" cases (non-completers or low performers) as reported by our analysis in the previous section. The survey at the end of the workshop showed positive feedback on the quick remediation action taken of the instructor. A few of the responses we got from the students included:

"This is an excellent tutorial. It clarifies all my doubts. Thank you for providing this."

"Just what I was looking for."

"Thanks. Here is another link I found useful: https://python-graph-gallery.com/125-small-multiples-for-line-chart/"

5.3.2 Using annotation data to adapt face-to-face teaching. Another benefit worth reporting is the value of annotation data for adapting the face-to-face teaching approach in the classroom. The insights received from the annotation breakdown report (Fig. 9) was valuable for the instructor to tailor their teaching strategy and time allocation for topics in the face-to-face session. Topics which had recorded a high number of confusion annotations were emphasized more during the lecture. Additionally, during the workshop session itself, students were annotating on the lecture slides and programming exercises. The instructor was able to get a real-time view of student difficulty as students progressed during the workshop. Some students preferred asking questions in writing or flagging concepts in the teaching material rather than asking orally. After examining the list of annotations, the instructor was able to revisit some of the highly annotated concepts again during the workshop.

5.4 Student Experiences with the Annotation Platform

We surveyed the students at the conclusion of the workshop to understand their experiences with the social annotation platform. Figure 10 shows that 42% of the students actively utilised the annotation platform ("Very Often" and "Always") and for most of

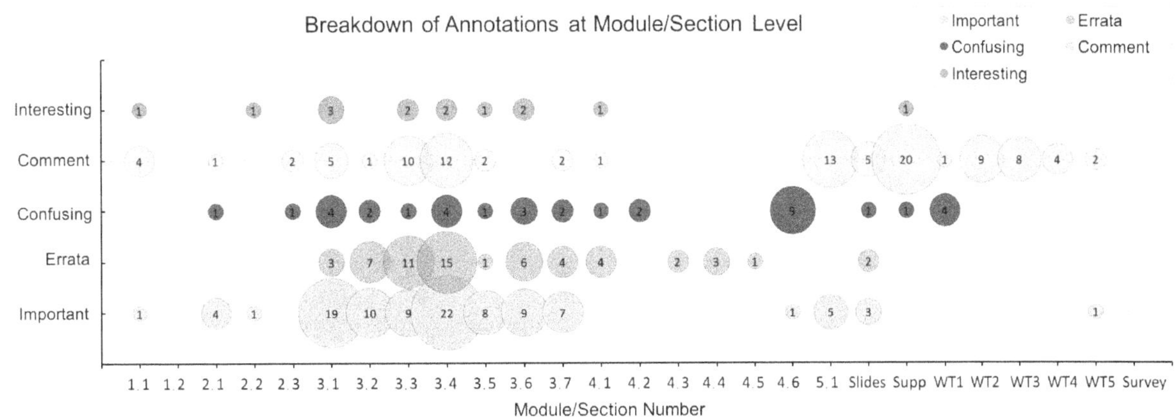

Figure 9: The annotation breakdown report

the anticipated activities—but most commonly for note taking and reporting issues (confusion or errors) with material.

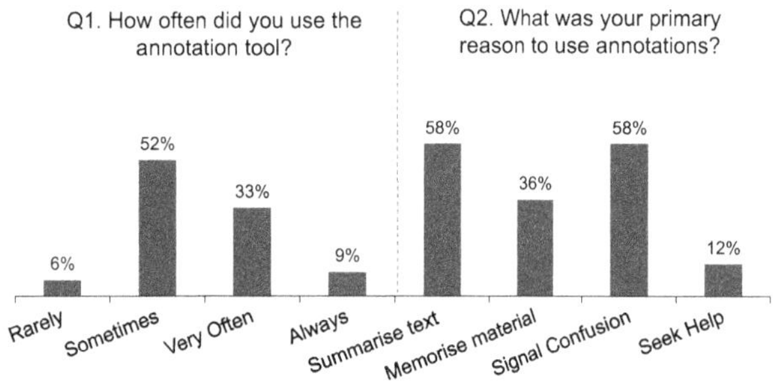

Figure 10: Student response on how often they used the annotation tool and the reason for using it

In Figure 11, students reported that the categorisation of annotations was one of the most useful features they encountered during the experiment. This was expected based on previous research on the uses of annotations [9].

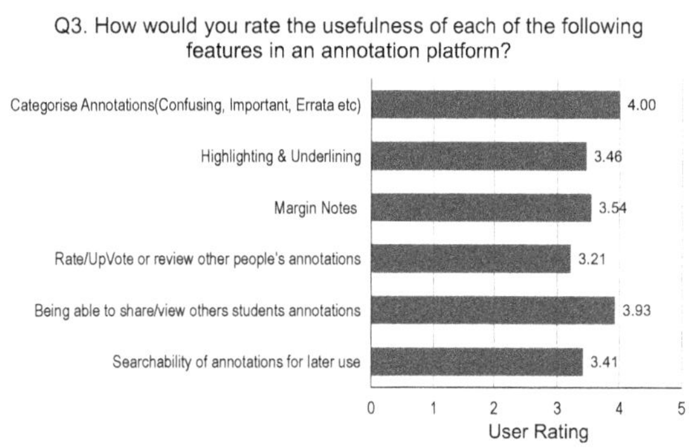

Figure 11: Students rating of usefulness of features

The annotation categories used in the tool were chosen to reflect the steps in the learning and teaching strategy framework discussed in [14]. According to this framework, effective teaching materials should be designed to address four key incremental steps in the learning process: (1) engaging interest, (2) encoding important information, (3) elaborating meaning, and (4) evaluating progress. In linking the annotation categories to these steps, we hoped that they would to some degree be indicative of these steps: (1) *Interesting*—engaging with inspiring material, (2) *Important*—encoding key concepts, (3) *Comment*—reflecting deeper thinking and elaboration and (4) *Confusion/Help*—for critical self-evaluation.

61% of the students in the experimental group had not used an online annotation tool before. We sought the group's feedback after this experiment on the effectiveness of annotations as opposed to discussion forums as a tool for learning. Figure 12 highlights that 79% of the student rated the annotation tool highly towards supporting their knowledge construction (giving Level 4 and Level 5 ratings) compared to 54% of students who regarded the discussion forum at that same level. The Level 5 rating may have been rare as we encountered a small techncial glitch in the annotation platform during the preparatory week. Even though this was fixed quickly it may have impacted on the user experience and ratings.

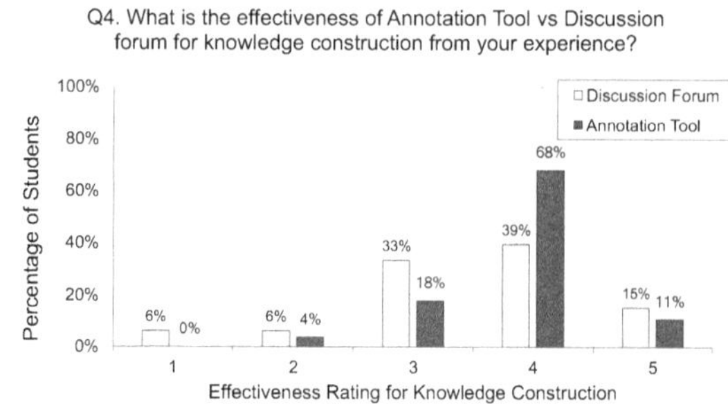

Figure 12: Students preference of Annotation Tool vs Discussion Forum

6 CONCLUSION

This study explored the efficacy of an annotation platform as a tool to empower learners in the knowledge construction process. We found that completion rate and time spent on learning was higher for students that used the annotation platform. Additionally, the performance of these students was generally higher as well.

We have also shown how an annotation platform can be a way to extend a learning environment. It can be considered as a transparent mechanism to facilitate the identification, processing and organisation of knowledge and as a tool for cognitive bootstrapping. We found that the students rated the annotation tool as highly valuable compared to the traditional alternative of a discussion forum.

Annotations give students the opportunity to comment on the learning materials provided. Thus, they can not only be seen as an indicator of whether students are struggling but also as "... *an assessment of how well the instructor was doing as an explainer*" [20]. The dashboard in Figure 9 can be used for this dual purpose. Annotation analysis thus provides valuable contextual feedback on student experience to guide content creators in improving the teaching materials.

Our next step is to run large-scale versions of our experiment in real-life university courses with enrolments in excess of 600 students for a whole semester. Fine-grained document usage and annotation data will be collected to closely examine the capabilities, uses, and limitations of this data source. In contrast to the present study, which analysed annotation use in isolation, we will perform a joint analysis of annotation use and other document usage data to analyse how these data sources can complement each other. We are specifically looking at complementing annotation use data with document traversal paths and reading time information in the hope that a joint analysis afford us insights that we cannot obtain from either data source in isolation.

User studies for students and instructors, comprising of think-aloud sessions, surveys and interviews, will be undertaken to further understand how students perceive and use annotations in real-life courses and to evaluate the usefulness of the analytics. Based on our study, we also see real potential for annotation tools beyond conventional instruction materials, namely in peer-based learning environments for collaborative coding, such as Google Colab.

6.1 Acknowledgments

The authors would like to thank Dr. Michael Wybrow for his constructive feedback on the manuscript.

REFERENCES

[1] Dor Abrahamson, John B. Black, David DeLiema, Noel Enyedy, Darin Hoyer, Cameron L. Fadjo, and Dragan Trninic. 2012. You're it! Body, action, and object in STEM learning. In *Proceedings of the International Conference of the Learning Sciences: Future of learning (ICLS 2012)*, Vol. 1. 283–290.

[2] Jerome S Bruner. 1960. The Process of Education, Harvard, Univ. *Press, Cambridge, Mass* (1960).

[3] Andy Clark. 2008. Pressing the flesh: a tension in the study of the embodied, embedded mind? *Philosophy and phenomenological research* 76, 1 (2008), 37–59.

[4] Andy Clark. 2008. *Supersizing the mind: Embodiment, action, and cognitive extension*. OUP USA.

[5] Michael A Clump, Heather Bauer, and Catherine Bradley. 2004. The Extent to which Psychology Students Read Textbooks: A Multiple Class Analysis of Reading across the Psychology Curriculum. *Journal of Instructional Psychology* 31, 3 (2004).

[6] Graham Drake. 2003. 'This place gives me space": Place and Creativity in the Creative Industries. *Geoforum* 34, 4 (2003), 511–524.

[7] James J Gibson. 1977. The theory of affordances. In Perceiving, Acting and Knowing, Eds. RE Shaw and J. Bransford.

[8] Hypothes.is. 2018. Hypothesis - The Internet, peer reviewed. https://web.hypothes.is/

[9] Jingyan Lu and Liping Deng. 2013. Examining students' use of online annotation tools in support of argumentative reading. *Australasian Journal of Educational Technology* (2013).

[10] Bradford Z Mahon and Alfonso Caramazza. 2008. A critical look at the embodied cognition hypothesis and a new proposal for grounding conceptual content. *Journal of physiology-Paris* 102, 1-3 (2008), 59–70.

[11] Catherine C Marshall and AJ Brush. 2004. Exploring the relationship between personal and public annotations. In *Proceedings of the 4th ACM/IEEE-CS joint conference on Digital libraries*. ACM, 349–357.

[12] Gregor M Novak, Evelyn T Patterson, Andrew D Gavrin, and Wolfgang Christian. 1999. Just-In-Time Teaching: Blending Active Learning with Web Technology Prentice Hall. *New Jersey* (1999).

[13] Kenton O'hara and Abigail Sellen. 1997. A comparison of reading paper and on-line documents. In *Proceedings of the ACM SIGCHI Conference on Human factors in computing systems*. ACM, 335–342.

[14] Biagio Pilato and Mark M Ulrich. 2014. Is The Case Study Method an Effective Pedagogical Method for Students to Learn the Fundamentals of Financial Accounting? *ASBBS Proceedings* 21, 1 (2014), 541.

[15] Friedemann Pulvermüller, Olaf Hauk, Vadim V Nikulin, and Risto J Ilmoniemi. 2005. Functional links between motor and language systems. *European Journal of Neuroscience* 21, 3 (2005), 793–797.

[16] Philip Robbins and Murat Aydede. 2009. A short primer on situated cognition. *The Cambridge handbook of situated cognition* (2009), 3–10.

[17] Alexander Thayer, Charlotte P Lee, Linda H Hwang, Heidi Sales, Pausali Sen, and Ninad Dalal. 2011. The imposition and superimposition of digital reading technology: the academic potential of e-readers. In *Proceedings of the SIGCHI Conference on Human Factors in Computing Systems*. ACM, 2917–2926.

[18] Margaret Wilson. 2002. Six views of embodied cognition. *Psychonomic bulletin & review* 9, 4 (2002), 625–636.

[19] L Kate Wright, Sacha Zyto, David R Karger, and Dina L Newman. 2013. Online Reading Informs Classroom Instruction and Promotes Collaborative Learning. *Journal of College Science Teaching* 43, 2 (2013), 44–53.

[20] Sacha Zyto, David Karger, Mark Ackerman, and Sanjoy Mahajan. 2012. Successful classroom deployment of a social document annotation system. In *Proceedings of the SIGCHI Conference on Human Factors in Computing Systems*. ACM, 1883–1892.

RepoBee: Developing Tool Support for Courses using Git/GitHub

Simon Larsén
KTH: Royal Institute of Technology
Stockholm, Sweden
slarse@kth.se

Richard Glassey
KTH: Royal Institute of Technology
Stockholm, Sweden
glassey@kth.se

ABSTRACT

The use of version control systems within computing education is growing in popularity. However, this is challenging because such systems are not particularly well designed to support educational situations, nor are they easy to use with confidence in teaching, as specialist knowledge and experience is required. This experience paper reports the development of the open source tool RepoBee, which assists in the use of Git/GitHub in an educational context. The tool provides a straightforward interface for managing batch tasks such as repository generation and cloning for setting and gathering assignments, opening and closing of issues to communicate with students, as well as facilitating peer reviews. Parts of RepoBee are open to integration with third party tools for additional tasks, such as running unit tests or static analysis on student repositories. We also include the perspectives of both teachers and teaching assistants who have been using the tool as part of a first year course for computer scientists.

CCS CONCEPTS

• **Social and professional topics → Computing education.**

KEYWORDS

Git/GitHub, Version Control Systems, Course Management, Computing Education

ACM Reference Format:

Simon Larsén and Richard Glassey. 2019. RepoBee: Developing Tool Support for Courses using Git/GitHub. In *Innovation and Technology in Computer Science Education (ITiCSE '19), July 15–17, 2019, Aberdeen, Scotland UK.* ACM, New York, NY, USA, 7 pages. https://doi.org/10.1145/3304221.3319784

1 INTRODUCTION

The ability to effectively use a version control system (VCS) forms an important part of a student's development towards working collaboratively with others and managing a set of resources over time [7, 14, 18]. Whilst the concept of version control is straightforward (see [17, Chapter 25]), it is a topic that can also become complicated quite quickly when adopting to a new workflow model and collaborating with others across multiple branches of a repository. Therefore it cannot be left to chance that students pick up this vital skill by themselves.

Beyond benefiting a student's development, the use of VCS can benefit teachers as well. A growing body of computing education literature has reported on the positive experiences of using different VCS to distribute assignments to students [2, 16], manage group projects [7, 15], automatically test and grade student work [8, 10, 12], and analyse repository data as a novel source of student insights [4, 5, 18].

However, despite this strong trend, the adoption of a VCS into a course depends on the teacher's confidence and ability to use the technology in a pedagogical context. For teachers who use a VCS as part of their normal practice, it is still a step up to administer potentially thousands of repositories for students who depend upon them for completing their assignments or projects. There is a clear risk that in striving to benefit from VCS integration, additional complexity and uncertainty is introduced. In contrast to most modern learning management systems, VCS are designed for industrial use, and do not come with the necessary scaffolding to support a teacher in their desire to adopt the technology.

In response to this challenge, teachers have developed their own solutions and shared them with the community as open source projects. Typically, these were developed to support a local need, such as a specific course. Whilst this is a positive step forward, there is a need to try to better generalise the most common academic tasks, such as distributing work assignments, gathering assignments for assessment, assigning peer review tasks, linking to third party tools to automate assessment tasks, and sharing feedback with students.

To move towards this goal, this paper presents RepoBee, an open source tool for managing a Git/GitHub based course. It strives to support the common academic tasks mentioned above, maintain a simple command line interface, document itself for teachers rather than software engineers, and expose a basic interface for extension in order to fit specific course needs. The remainder of the paper is as follows: Section 2 identifies the related work in this area; Sec. 3 provides a tour of the main features of RepoBee; Sec. 4 provides the teacher's perspective on using RepoBee; and finally Sec. 5 gives the perspective of the teaching assistants (TA).

2 RELATED WORK

The motivation to use a VCS within computing education has developed in parallel with the development of each new generation of VCS. Early examples that have been reported in the literature made use of the Concurrent Versions System (CVS)[1]. In [18], the historical data that is recorded by CVS was identified as useful information

[1] http://cvs.nongnu.org/

ACM ISBN 978-1-4503-6301-3/19/07...$15.00
https://doi.org/10.1145/3304221.3319784

Table 1: Comparison of open source tools for VCS support and their educational features

			GUI	Group Projects	Individual Assignments	Repository Cloning	Automatic Grading	Peer Review	Extensibility	Feedback
ACAD	UC Santa Barbara, USA	https://git.io/fxwj9		✓	✓	✓				
Classroom	GitHub Inc.	https://git.io/vGVC2	✓	✓	✓	✓				✓
GHClass	Duke University, USA	https://git.io/fxwjb		✓	✓					✓
Gitomator	MIT, USA	https://git.io/fjLZT		✓	✓	✓	✓		✓	
Rhomboid	University of British Columbia, Canada	https://git.io/fxwjh			✓		✓	✓		✓
Submit50	Harvard University, USA	https://git.io/fxree			✓		✓		✓	✓
Teacher's Pet	GitHub Inc.	https://git.io/PCz4Vg			✓					
Virtual Classroom	Simula School of Research and Innovation, Norway	https://git.io/fxref			✓			✓	✓	

for understanding how students develop software incrementally. [7] explored how students could work in group projects using a combination of the Eclipse integrated development environment and CVS to better manage group project resources, reduce their dependence on group synchronisation meetings, and resolve participation problems by allowing mentors to passively monitor activity in the CVS repository. In a similar group project setting, [16] found that beyond the usual group work benefits that CVS affords and the vital experience of using an industrial tool, teachers also noted that it was an effective means to distribute resources. Rather than have students download zip archives from the course web, the resources could be deployed *ready-to-use* on the CVS server.

2.1 Distributed Version Control Systems

Centralised VCS, such as CVS and Subversion[2], have since been superseded by distributed version control systems (Git[3] and Mercurial[4]), which combined with hosting platforms (GitHub[5], BitBucket[6], GitLab[7] etc), have continued to support educational use cases. [13] found that the cloud hosting of Git repositories greatly simplified the burden on teachers needing to manage and maintain local servers. In contrast, and reflecting the rapid development of hosting solutions in the space of VCS, [1] encountered negative feedback from students, as the GitLab hosting service was unreliable at the time that the course was occurring. However, these issues have faded as DVCS and hosting platforms have matured into stable systems that are reliable for teaching.

Whilst conceptually there is little difference between the various combinations of VCS and associated hosting platform, Git/GitHub has emerged as quite a popular combination for teachers exploring this space, as reflected by the literature [3, 6, 9, 11]. In part, this may be explained by the reputation that Git and GitHub enjoy as the de facto platform for managing and hosting open source projects, and also by the initiatives by GitHub Inc. to develop an education community with support for teachers and students (on-site training, unlimited private repositories, and engagement with the academic community across various forums).

Despite the positive findings from integrating a VCS into an academic context, they still remain as a sufficiently complicated technology for the average teacher to not only master, but also feel confident in using within their courses, where they may find themselves responsible for controlling thousands of repositories. To make matters less complicated, and to introduce more certainty, tools have been developed to help with adoption of VCS in teaching.

2.2 Tool Support for Course Management

In terms of support for teachers, there is an emerging set of open source tools to choose from, as listed in table 1. Each of these tools have attempted in their own respective way to provide basic educational features that build upon the VCS and hosting platform. In most cases the primary interface is command line based, with the only exception being Classroom, which is a web application. Typically these features include a means to distribute pre-made repositories to the students taking a course (all tools). This will either be in the form of a group project (ACAD, Classroom, GHClass & Gitomator) or an individual assignment (all tools). In order to support assessment, tools may support cloning of repositories to a local machine (ACAD, Classroom[8] & Gitomator), automatic grading (Gitomator, Rhomboid & Submit50), or assign peer reviews (Rhomboid & Virtual Classroom). As every teaching situation or course setup may be unique in some way, the support for extensibility is also important (Gitomator, Submit50 & Virtual Classroom).

[2]https://subversion.apache.org/
[3]https://git-scm.com/
[4]https://www.mercurial-scm.org/
[5]https://github.com/
[6]https://bitbucket.org/
[7]https://gitlab.com/

[8]This requires a companion desktop application to be used

Finally some of these tools also try to complete the loop by providing feedback via the VCS and hosting platform (Classroom[9], GHClass, Rhomboid and Submit50).

It is clear there is interest in this space for tool support for VCS within computing education. As this brief overview hints towards, it is difficult to find a tool that provides a complete set of distribution, assessment, automated grading, peer review and feedback. This forms the basic motivation of the RepoBee project, to build on the foundation provided by these tools, and provide a set of features that support a teacher in their use of a VCS for course management. Furthermore, it provides a plugin architecture that allows teachers to include their own custom tasks (e.g. running unit tests and statically analysing code) with a relatively low level of complexity and the possibility to share with others who also extend RepoBee. The next section will provide an overview of the basic features of RepoBee.

3 REPOBEE OVERVIEW

RepoBee is an open source project, and is freely available to use, extend or modify[10]. It was developed to fit the workflow of an introductory computer science course at KTH in which Git and GitHub[11] are integral parts. As such, large parts of RepoBee rely on the conventions we have established, and is tied into services provided by GitHub. To be able to discuss RepoBee, some concepts relating to GitHub and our workflow must first be defined. The primary GitHub concepts are as follows:

- *Repository*: In Git, a repository is a version-controlled directory structure that can be easily synchronized across multiple machines. A GitHub repository is superset of Git repository functionality, including integration with an issue tracker[12].
- *Issue*: A GitHub issue is a topic on a repository issue tracker. Issues can be opened, read and commented by anyone with read access to the repository[13].
- *Organization*: A type of shared user account used to group related repositories. For this paper, it is sufficient to think of an Organization as a collection of repositories[14].
- *Team*: A group of users that, among other things, can be used to manage access control to repositories. Members of the Team receive the same access rights to repositories as are granted to the Team[15].

The concepts that relate to the workflow, and are critical to RepoBee's operation, are as follows:

- *Master repository*: A template repository for an assignment from which student repositories are generated. Typically includes instructions and skeleton code.
- *Student repository*: A student's (or group's) copy of a master repository.
- *Target Organization*: A GitHub Organization related to a course round, housing that round's student repositories.
- *Master Organization*: An Organization for the master repositories of a single course. The Master Organization should be persistent across course rounds to allow for orderly maintenance and updating of master repositories.

Section 3.1 uses these concepts to present the main features of RepoBee, while Sec. 3.2 outlines the basic workflow for which those features were designed.

3.1 Main Features

The functionality of RepoBee can be roughly divided into three categories:

- *Repository management*: Creating student repositories and updating existing ones, as well as cloning their repositories.
- *Issue management*: Opening and closing issues, as well as listing any previously opened issues.
- *Peer review management*: Students are given read access to other repositories that they are to review. RepoBee handles allocation of reviews, simple progress tracking, and revocation of read access.

Table 2 lists the commands available in RepoBee. With the exception of `show-config`, `verify-settings` and `migrate`, which will not be discussed in this paper, all commands are designed for batch operations on student repositories. Given a list L of student usernames and a list M of master repository names, a RepoBee command will operate on the student repositories defined by the Cartesian product $L \times M$. For example, given $L = \{S1, S2\}$ and $M = \{A, B\}$, the resulting student repository names will then be $L \times M = \{S1\text{-}A,\ S1\text{-}B,\ S2\text{-}A,\ S2\text{-}B\}$, as can be seen in Fig. 1. L is typically provided as a text file in which each line is a student username, while M must be written out on the command line. There is also support for group assignments, in which case the elements of L are sets of student usernames.

Table 2: List of RepoBee commands

Command	Effect
`setup`	Setup student repositories
`update`	Update student repositories
`clone`	Clone student repositories
`open-issues`	Open issues in student repositories
`close-issues`	Close issues in student repositories
`list-issues`	List issues in student repositories
`assign-reviews`	Allocate peer reviews
`check-reviews`	Check for opened review issues
`purge-review-teams`	Revoke reviewers' read access
`migrate`*	Migrate repositories between Organizations
`show-config`*	Show the configuration file
`verify-settings`*	Verify that base settings are OK

*Not discussed in this paper.

[9]This requires a Travis CI server to be associated with the repository
[10]https://github.com/repobee/repobee
[11]RepoBee works both with self-hosted GitHub Enterprise and https://github.com
[12]https://help.github.com/articles/about-repositories/
[13]https://help.github.com/articles/about-issues/
[14]https://help.github.com/articles/about-organizations/
[15]https://help.github.com/articles/about-teams/

3.1.1 Repository management. Managing repositories is RepoBee's primary purpose, and `setup`, `update` and `clone` are the core commands to achieve this. The `setup` command creates student repositories, pushes the contents of the corresponding master repositories to them, and also gives students indirect access through Teams. The `update` command allows a teacher to push updates to already created student repositories, after having updated a master repository. A problem occurs when students have already started to work and have pushed changes to their repositories, which results in the update being rejected. The solution here is to provide an optional file to the `update` command, which is opened as an issue in repositories that reject the update. The issue could for example contain information about the change, and what students have to do to incorporate it. The final command, `clone`, is of interest to anyone correcting assignments or running data analysis on repositories. The basic functionality of `clone` is to simply clone student repositories into the current working directory, which is in itself useful. Section 3.1.4 discusses how this functionality can be expanded upon through the use of plugins.

3.1.2 Issue management. RepoBee provides three commands for managing issues: `open-issues`, `close-issues` and `list-issues`. The `open-issues` command takes a file as an argument, and opens it as an issue in student repositories. This can for example be useful to announce corrections or clarifications to an assignment when using the `update` command would be inappropriate, or to communicate assignment-specific grading criteria (see Sec. 4). We also typically provide feedback to students in issues, and some TAs prefer to open such issues using RepoBee instead of the web interface. For example, when an student has submitted a solution that does not meet all requirements, a TA may open an issue with a title like "Corrections required", detailing what the student has to fix. In order to keep communication focused on the GitHub platform, we also typically provide general "Pass" and "Fail" feedback to students by opening issues with corresponding titles. Although this may not be the most appropriate use of issues as the feedback may not require any actions from the students, it is convenient for TAs to handle all feedback on a single platform, and for students to receive feedback in proximity to their code. The `list-issues` command can then be helpful to quickly get an overview of which students have received feedback, and which are required to do corrections. The command matches issue titles against a regular expression, and results can be further filtered by status ("open", "closed" or "all") and issue author. Finally, the `close-issues` command allows a user to close any issues with titles matching a regular expression, which is useful to keep the issue tracker clean for anyone communicating for example grading criteria, peer review tasks (see Sec. 3.1.3) or feedback through issues.

3.1.3 Peer review management. Peer review management is the latest addition to RepoBee. The `assign-reviews` command creates one review Team with read access per student repository, and adds reviewers to them. The algorithm that allocates reviews is part of the plugin system discussed in Sec. 3.1.4, and RepoBee currently ships with two algorithms. The default algorithm simply allocates a specified amount of reviews at random. An alternate algorithm splits students into pairs, and possibly one triplet, that are then assigned to review their paired partner. We have found that the latter algorithm works well during exercises in the introductory courses, as the students are able to discuss their code with each other. We typically have students submit their review as an issue in the reviewed repo, and the `check-reviews` command can check which students have opened review issues. This functionality is not robust enough to use peer review as a graded task itself, as there are ways students could fool it. It can however be a powerful tool in a high-trust environment where students are motivated to learn, or in a supervised environment, such as at an exercise class. Note also that the focus is on lightweight code review that can spark discussion among the students, and there is no anonymity between parties. Once the time for reviews is deemed to be over, the `purge-review-teams` command deletes review Teams, which revokes the reviewers' access to other students' repositories.

3.1.4 Plugins - Extending RepoBee's functionality. A plugin, also called an add-on or an extension, is typically a fragment of a program that "plugs into" an existing application. A plugin architecture both allows a programmer to extend an application without modifying its internals, and lets end users customize it by simply installing plugins created by others. As an example, web browsers typically have extensive support for plugins[16]. RepoBee defines a series of hooks where plugins can hook into the execution of the application. Most of these hooks are defined in and around the `clone` command, with the intention of allowing arbitrary tasks to be run on the cloned repositories. Put simply, when a repository has been cloned, all plugins that define a certain hook are invoked and passed the path to the repository. The plugin can then do more or less whatever is possible to do in the Python programming language, and can optionally report results to RepoBee.

Plugins can also add command line arguments that are seamlessly presented like they were part of the base tool. When all plugins have finished running, RepoBee presents the results of each plugin on a per-student repository basis. A simple plugin that ships with RepoBee looks for Java source files and tries to compile them. This can be helpful when teaching introductory classes, where students often submit code that does not compile. Another more advanced plugin runs JUnit4 test classes on Java production code in student repositories and reports the results, which can be highly useful for correcting any assignments involving strictly defined APIs[17]. Anyone with basic skills in Python can write a plugin, as the process is well documented[18], and there is a template to start from[19]. Installing an existing plugin is no harder than installing any other Python package, such as RepoBee itself. A key design decision with the plugin system was to make it as transparent as possible, and it is meant to provide purely optional configurability. Users do not need to know about the plugin system to use RepoBee, even though some of the core functionality is implemented as internal plugins. The intention is to further expand the plugin system to other parts of RepoBee as new use cases that require different functionality arise.

[16] There are thousands of plugins available for the Firefox web browser: https://addons.mozilla.org/en-US/firefox/

[17] https://github.com/repobee/repobee-junit4

[18] https://repobee-plug.readthedocs.io

[19] https://github.com/repobee/repobee-plugin-cookiecutter

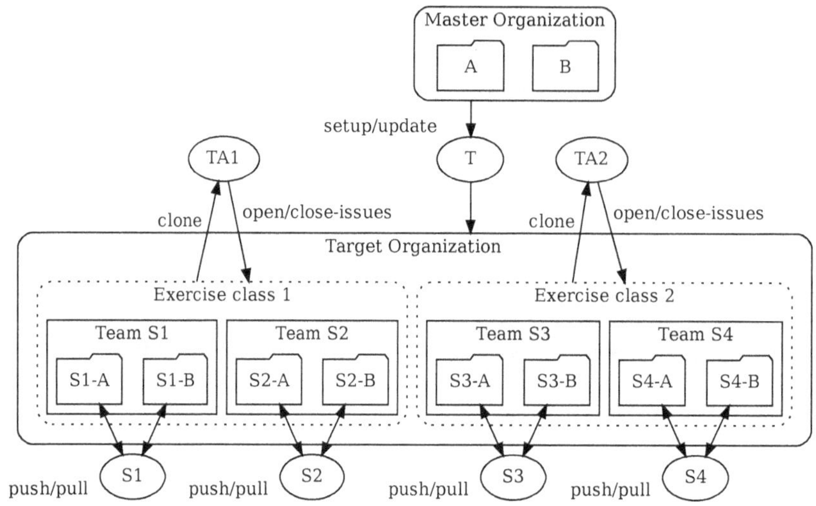

Figure 1: RepoBee workflow schematic. A and B are master repositories, T is a teacher, TAx are the teaching assistants and Sx are the students of the current course round.

3.2 Workflow

RepoBee is an opinionated tool that has been designed around a particular workflow, which may be adopted fully or partially by users of RepoBee. Repository and issue management are the primary parts of this workflow and is schematically described in Fig. 1. Rectangles with rounded corners and sharp corners represent Organizations and Teams, respectively. Ellipses represent people, where *Sx* is a student, *TAx* is a teaching assistant and *T* is a teacher. The dashed outlines represent exercise classes of students that are defined by external class lists provided to RepoBee as an argument (recall *L* as discussed in Sec. 3). Finally, folders represent repositories, where *A* and *B* are the master repositories, and e.g. *S*1-*A* is *S*1s copy of *A*.

When assignments are to be published, the teacher uses the `setup` command to create the student repositories and populate them with data pulled from the master repositories. The command also creates one Team for any student or group that does not already have one, and grants the Teams access to repositories as shown by the visual grouping of repositories in Fig. 1. A student sees only the repositories that an affiliated Team has access to, with the rest of the target Organization being completely invisible to them. On our GitHub Enterprise host, students that have created their accounts are added to their Teams automatically, giving them write access to their repositories. Stragglers can be added to their Teams at a later time. On https://github.com, students are invited to the target Organization and get added to their respective Teams upon accepting their invitations. The students can then push and pull from their repositories using only Git, and need not have any knowledge of RepoBee.

When the deadline for an assignment has passed, TAs use the `clone` command and provide it with their respective class lists to clone their students' repositories to disk. Note that as these class lists are simple files, changing them in the occurrence of swaps or dropouts is trivial, and each TA can simply maintain their own list. It is often useful to run plugins at this stage, for example to differentiate the repositories with compiling code from those with malformed or missing code. The TAs can then open issues in the students' repositories communicating pass, fail or required corrections. Some prefer GitHub's web interface to open individual issues, but it can be done with RepoBee as well by specifying a single student or group.

Peer review management is also an important part of RepoBee, but it exists as an optional addition to the workflow presented here. As described in Sec. 3.1.3, it uses Teams in a rather different way by creating one read only Team per student repository, and adding reviewers to that Team. Because of the somewhat different use of Teams, we found no way to represent it concisely in Fig. 1 alongside the core workflow.

4 TEACHER PERSPECTIVE

The use of Git and GitHub in teaching and course management has been an ongoing process over several years. The development of RepoBee was motivated in part due to the success and popularity of adopting Git/GitHub for our first year course, but also due to the concern that the existing tool we had been using, Teacher's Pet, was no longer fit for purpose. Furthermore, other courses that followed ours expressed an interest in our tool chain, and communicating the various patches and incantations required to make the former solution work was somewhat off-putting to other teachers.

In terms of weekly use as a teacher, RepoBee has succeeded in terms of reducing the fear of batch generating a large number of repositories for students. In any given year we expect to generate

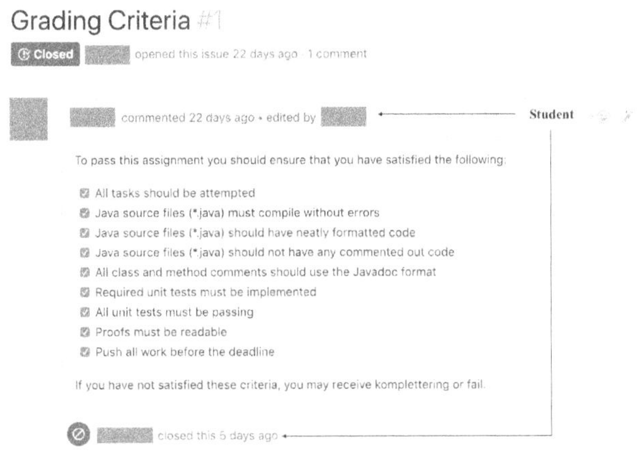

Figure 2: Grading criteria posted by a teacher on the issue tracker of a repository and checked off and closed by student

about 5000 repositories for 200 students over 25 weeks of assignments. Even though I have a working knowledge of Git, there is still a leap of faith required to take responsibility for generating so many repositories that students are expecting on a regular schedule. RepoBee takes away that stress, and has a relatively simple workflow for a teacher. Furthermore the comprehensive documentation[20] helps in two ways: (1) helping those taking the first tentative steps; and (2) to act as a gentle reminder for the forgetful teacher.

Beyond the basic job of generating the repositories, the ability to open issues up on all of the student repositories on any given week has been a really useful means to delivering simple grading criteria relevant for particular assignments. As Fig. 2 shows, students are motivated to engage with their criteria using the check box formatting that the GitHub issue tracker supports to confirm they feel they have satisfied the expectations of that particular week. Such features encourage the investigation of new and novel techniques.

5 TEACHING ASSISTANT PERSPECTIVE

One of the strong aspects of RepoBee is that TAs can also make use of it to improve their workflow, and develop an understanding of how the course is managed. We asked for some informal feedback after four months of use to get a feel for the TA perspective.

5.1 Setup and Learning Curve

As RepoBee is a new type of tool for the TAs, this was reflected in some of the feedback received. One TA stated that the initial setup was a weakness: "*It's pretty challenging to get into. Can seem too advanced at first, but it is worth it*" (TA1), yet after this there were no difficulties: "*…I've basically done the same things over and over without difficulties*" (TA1). Another TA noted simply that a weakness was, "No GUI" (TA2). As a next step in the project, we do have plans to generate a GUI from the command-line interface to further reduce the learning curve for both teachers and teaching assistants.

[20] https://repobee.readthedocs.io

5.2 General Usage

Of the three TAs that responded, all of them made use of the main features to clone repositories and run plugins for automated assessment, as reflected by one TA: "*I use the clone feature to clone repos in bulk quickly, the javac plugin to check that submissions compile, and the junit4 plugin to make automated testing easier*" (TA2). Another TA reported: "*It also greatly speeds up correcting assignments. If I would have had a tool that could clone my students' repositories and run test classes on them when I first started as a teaching assistant, the first year would have been much easier going*" (TA3). This underlines the importance of giving TAs the right tools to make their job easier when helping teachers with their courses.

5.3 Use of Peer Review

Finally, two of the TAs made use of the peer review feature. One TA reported that having support for peer review encouraged them to make use of it as a practice in their exercises, and, "*It enabled many meaningful conversations about their code*" (TA2). Whilst this result is no surprise to any teacher that has tried peer review as a practice, the additional tool support actually encouraged this practice at the TA level, as all the setup was available with a single command. The other TA reflected on the implications of the random and pairwise allocation schemes: "*While the tool did what it was supposed to, the reviews were a bit lackluster, and students were running around the classroom to ask for clarifications*" (TA3), and subsequently, "*The second time, I used the pairwise allocation scheme, and reviews were much better. Students discussed their code together without having to run back and forth, and really seemed to get something out of it. Random allocation of reviews probably works better for a home assignment*" (TA3). Here it is nice to see the ability to peer review is enabled and controlled by TAs, but it also can provoke reflection on what actually works best for a given teaching situation.

6 CONCLUSION

This experience paper has presented RepoBee, a tool for supporting teachers in their use of Git/GitHub in their courses. It has a simple command-line interface and comprehensive documentation to help teachers overcome some of the hurdles that they may face. It provides the ability to distribute repositories to students based on templates, maintain privacy between student repositories, clone repositories for assessment, run additional plugins for automated tasks such as testing or other static analysis, post issues across all student repositories for class notifications, and finally configure peer review Teams for peer assessment activities. In terms of the features outlined in Table 1, RepoBee currently provides everything but a GUI and automatic grading. The former is a planned feature, while the latter could be implemented as plugins, with the caveat that the grading process would have to be triggered manually. Additonally, future work will continue to streamline the user experience and extend the library of plugins. RepoBee owes a debt to the other tools that teachers have already contributed as open source projects, and it attempts to generalise some of the features that are required for managing a course based around a VCS. We hope that by continuing this thread of development, both students and teachers will experience the many benefits that VCS can bring to a course without the complexity and confusion.

REFERENCES

[1] Miroslav Biňas. 2013. Version Control System in CS1 Course: Practical Experience. In *IEEE 11th International Conference on Emerging eLearning Technologies and Applications (ICETA'13)*. pp. 23–28. https://doi.org/10.1109/ICETA.2013.6674398

[2] Curtis Clifton, Lisa C Kaczmarczyk, and Michael Mrozek. 2007. Subverting the Fundamentals Sequence: Using Version Control to Enhance Course Management. In *Proceedings of the 38th ACM Technical Symposium on Computer Science Education (SIGCSE'07)*. ACM Press, pp. 86–90. https://doi.org/10.1145/1227310.1227344

[3] Joseph Feliciano, Margaret-Anne Storey, and Alexey Zagalsky. 2016. Student experiences using GitHub in software engineering courses: a case study. In *Proceedings of the 38th International Conference on Software Engineering Companion (ICSE'16)*. 422–431. https://doi.org/10.1145/2889160.2889195

[4] Richard Glassey. 2018. Managing assignment feedback via issue tracking. In *Proceedings of the 23rd Annual ACM Conference on Innovation and Technology in Computer Science Education (ITiCSE 2018)*. ACM Press, p. 382. https://doi.org/10.1145/3197091.3205819

[5] Louis Glassy. 2006. Using version control to observe student software development processes. *J. of Computing Sciences in Colleges* 21, 3 (2006), pp. 99–106.

[6] Lassi Haaranen and Teemu Lehtinen. 2015. Teaching Git on the Side. In *Proceedings of the 20th Annual ACM Conference on Innovation and Technology in Computer Science Education (ITiCSE'15)*. ACM Press, 87–92. https://doi.org/10.1145/2729094.2742608

[7] Ken T. N. Hartness. 2006. Eclipse and CVS for Group Projects. *J. of Computing Sciences in Colleges* 21, 4 (2006), pp. 217–222.

[8] Jason Heckman, Sarah and King. 2018. Developing Software Engineering Skills using Real Tools for Automated Grading. In *Proceedings of the 49th ACM Technical Symposium on Computer Science Education*. ACM Press, 794—-799. https://doi.org/10.1145/3159450.3159595

[9] Ville Isomöttönen and Michael Cochez. 2014. Challenges and Confusions in Learning Version Control with Git. In *Communications in Computer and Information Science*, Zholtkevych G. (eds) Ermolayev V., Mayr H., Nikitchenko M., Spivakovsky A. (Ed.). Vol. 469. 178–193. https://doi.org/10.1007/978-3-319-13206-8_9

[10] An Ju and Armando Fox. 2018. TEAMSCOPE: Measuring Software Engineering Processes with Teamwork Telemetry. In *Proceedings of the 23rd Annual ACM Conference on Innovation and Technology in Computer Science Education (ITiCSE'18)*. ACM Press, pp. 123–128. https://doi.org/10.1145/3197091.3197107

[11] John Kelleher. 2014. Employing git in the classroom. In *World Congress on Computer Applications and Information Systems (WCCAIS'14)*. IEEE, pp. 1–4. https://doi.org/10.1109/WCCAIS.2014.6916568

[12] Andreas Krusche, Stephan and Seitz. 2018. ArTEMiS: An Automatic Assessment Management System for Interactive Learning. In *Proceedings of the 49th ACM Technical Symposium on Computer Science Education*. ACM Press, 284—-289. https://doi.org/10.1145/3159450.3159602

[13] Joseph Lawrance, S Jung, and Charles Wiseman. 2013. Git on the cloud in the classroom. In *Proceeding of the 44th ACM technical symposium on Computer science education (SIGCSE'13)*. pp. 639–644. https://doi.org/10.1145/2445196.2445386

[14] Stephen Paul Linder, David Abbott, and Michael J. Fromberger. 2006. An instructional scaffolding approach to teaching software design. *J. of Computing Sciences in Colleges* 21, 6 (2006), pp. 238–250.

[15] Ivan Milentijevic, Vladimir Ciric, and Oliver Vojinovic. 2008. Version control in project-based learning. *Computers and Education* 50, 4 (2008), pp. 1331–1338. https://doi.org/10.1016/j.compedu.2006.12.010

[16] Karen L. Reid and Gregory V. Wilson. 2005. Learning by Doing : Introducing Version Control as a Way to Manage Student Assignments. In *Proceedings of the 36th ACM technical symposium on Computer Science Education (SIGCSE'05)*. ACM Press, pp. 272–276. https://doi.org/10.1145/1047124.1047441

[17] Ian Sommerville. 2015. *Software Engineering* (10th ed.). Addison-Wesley.

[18] Ying Liu. 2004. CVS historical information to understand how students develop software. In *International Workshop on Mining Software Repositories (MSR'04). In proceedings of the 26th International Conference on Software Engineering (ICSE'04)*. ACM Press, pp. 32–36. https://doi.org/10.1049/ic:20040472

Evaluating Instructors' Classification of Programming Exercises Using the Revised Bloom's Taxonomy

Susana Masapanta-Carrión
Pontificia Universidad Católica del Ecuador
Quito, 17012184, Ecuador
s.masapanta@alumnos.urjc.es

J. Ángel Velázquez-Iturbide
Universidad Rey Juan Carlos
28933 Móstoles, Madrid, Spain
angel.velazquez@urjc.es

ABSTRACT

It is a well-known fact that different instructors understand Bloom's taxonomy differently, thus they classify given test exercises into different levels of the taxonomy. The article reports on the impact of training instructors on the use of the taxonomy for programming courses with two innovations: encouraging instructors to classify each exercise into several cognitive processes necessary to solve it, and providing them with a wide range of examples of classified programming exercises. We evaluated the impact of these innovations in two training sessions. In the first session, the revised Bloom's taxonomy was introduced to the participants, and in the second session, the innovations were presented. In both sessions, participants were asked to classify ten exercises. The results show that classification into several cognitive processes was natural to instructors. However, other results were mixed. On the one hand, accuracy was increased, and confidence was increased for experienced participants. On the other hand, variation was increased, and confidence was decreased for non-experienced participants. Results show that our approach assists instructors in classifying exercises, but higher increases of expert instructors suggest that longer training is necessary for non-expert instructors.

CCS CONCEPTS

• Social and professional topics~Computing education

KEYWORDS: Computing science education; Bloom's taxonomy; Instructors' training

ACM Reference format:

Susana Masapanta-Carrión, J. Ángel Velázquez-Iturbide. 2019. Evaluating Instructors' Classification of Programming Exercises Using the Revised Bloom's Taxonomy. In *Proceedings of 24th Annual Conference on Innovation and Technology in Computer Science Education (ITiCSE'19), July 15-17, 2019, Aberdeen, Scotland, UK. ACM, NY, NY, USA, 7 pages.* https://doi.org/10.1145/3304221.3319748

ACM ISBN 978-1-4503-6301-3/19/07...$15.00.
https://doi.org/10.1145/3304221.3319748

1 Introduction

Learning taxonomies are frequently used in computing education [4]. The original Bloom's taxonomy [2] is the most frequently used, mainly to classify assessment tests [11]. However, a number of publications report on remarkably divergent classifications of exercises by different instructors [7][13]. Other authors have reported self-difficulties in classifying given exercises [8][14][16] [17], which were solved collaboratively by multiple rounds of classification and by developing shared conventions. Gluga *et al.* [5] also report that instructors' confidence in their classification of exercises was higher than their actual accuracy.

Despite the difficulties of use of Bloom's taxonomy, it is highly popular, probably because it appeals to instructors' intuition on the different types of students' understanding [6]. Therefore, it is worth studying and evaluating ways to remove or alleviate such classification difficulties. In this paper, a few proposals intended to alleviate difficulties are presented, as well as an evaluation of their impact on instructors. The results were mixed, i.e. both positive and negative results were obtained.

The article makes several contributions. Firstly, several recommendations to enhance the use of Bloom's taxonomy are presented. Secondly, up to the authors' knowledge, it is the first evaluation regarding Bloom's taxonomy that explicitly addresses several issues: usage of the revised taxonomy, consideration of the dimension of type of knowledge, and measuring variation and decomposition in participants' classifications. Thirdly, a heterogeneous set of results are presented: some results are positive and others, negative. Overall, they form a basis for future research.

The structure of the paper is as follows. In the second section, the two issues addressed to alleviate difficulties on classifying programming exercises are presented. The third section presents the evaluation setting, and the fourth section presents the results obtained. Finally, a discussion is included, and some conclusions are summarized.

2 Addressing Reported Difficulties

According to a past review [11], several reasons have been suggested to explain the difficulties of use of Bloom's taxonomy in computer science education. We consulted the two books that describe the taxonomies [1][2], and we noticed that some problems reported in the review come from a shallow understanding of the taxonomy. We also analyzed the causes hypothesized in the review, as well as their plausibility and ways to address them. Consequently, a guide to the revised taxonomy for computing instructors was elaborated [12].

In this paper, we focus on two specific recommendations that were selected for evaluation:

- Classification of an exercise into several levels.
- Provision of computer-science specific examples.

For consistency with the definition of the revised taxonomy, we also emphasized the use of the two dimensions of the taxonomy.

Dimensions of cognitive process and type of knowledge. A major difference of the revised taxonomy with respect to the original one is that it has two dimensions. The cognitive dimension is similar to the original taxonomy, with 6 categories that group 19 cognitive processes. However, most of the contents of the Knowledge level in the original taxonomy was moved to a new dimension: type of knowledge. Four types of knowledge were defined (namely, Factual, Conceptual, Procedural and Metacognitive), including 11 subtypes. Typically, a learning goal is stated so that its verb is associated to a cognitive process and its noun to a type of knowledge. The authors of the taxonomy recommend classifying by focusing on the subcategories of both dimensions, rather than on the categories [1, p. 264].

Classification of an exercise into several levels. One of the goals of the original taxonomy was to provide a framework to classify assessment exercises. The taxonomy has a hierarchical structure, where achievement of any level of cognitive development assumes that the lower levels were also achieved. However, categories of cognitive processes do not have such a strict hierarchy in the revised taxonomy [1, p. 267].

Furthermore, solving a problem may involve several cognitive processes (and its associated types of knowledge) [1, p. 89]. Classifying an exercise implies guessing a sequence of cognitive processes that a typical student is expected to perform to solve the exercise. A prerequisite of this task is stating the student's expertise, as different degrees of expertise often lead to different problem-solving paths [1, p. 106].

The proposal presented here suggests instructors to carry out this decomposition before identifying their corresponding cognitive processes. In addition, it is suggested to mark one of the cognitive processes involved in solving a given exercise as the most relevant, since instructors typically have a main concern when they design a given exercise.

Provision of computer-science specific examples. The original taxonomy, dated 1956, did not include any computing example. The revised taxonomy included a few examples involving computer science, the most notable being an exercise where the student is asked to describe the goal of given piece of code (category Understand, cognitive process Summarizing [1, p. 73]). Drafts of programming exercises were included in our guide for each cognitive process and each subtype of knowledge.

3 Evaluation

In this section, the evaluation setting is described in detail.

3.1 Research Questions

It is useful to gather objective measures about: (a) instructors' outcomes on classifying exercises, and (b) the impact of clarifications on their outcomes. The rationale for the latter issue is obvious; the rationale for the former is that, up to our knowledge, there is no quantitative or qualitative information about instructors' difficulties or discrepancies.

Instructors' outcomes were operationalized by means of the following four measures. For each measure, a simple definition is given in terms of cognitive processes, but it is later extended to other parts of the revised Bloom's taxonomy:

Decomposition. The degree of decomposition is the number of different cognitive processes that an instructor guesses it is necessary to solve a given exercise. This definition can also be applied to the number of subtypes of knowledge, as well as to the categories of either dimension.

Variation. The degree of variation is the number of different cognitive processes guessed by a number of instructors to solve a given exercise. The degree of variation may count either all cognitive processes or only the most relevant cognitive processes. This definition can also be applied to subtypes of knowledge, as well as to the categories of either dimension.

Accuracy. Accuracy is the percentage of participants whose identification of the most relevant cognitive process in a given exercise matches researchers'. This definition can also be applied to subtypes of knowledge, as well as to the categories of either dimension.

Confidence. The degree of confidence is the subjective confidence that an instructor has on his/her classification of a given exercise.

Similar definitions of the two latter measures were used by Gluga *et al.* [5]. The definition of accuracy could be extended to consider all cognitive processes identified by researchers and conductors, but this task was not addressed to keep results relatively simple. It could be addressed in the future.

The inquiry can be formulated as research questions. Some questions inquire on instructors' behavior when they use the revised Bloom's taxonomy:

RQ1. What is the degree of variation of main cognitive process in participants' classification?

RQ2. What is the percentage of accuracy in participants' classifications (compared to ours)?

RQ3. What is participants' degree of confidence on their classifications?

A second set of research questions inquire on the effect on instructors of stressing the two factors above identified (namely, classification of an exercise into several levels, and provision of computer-science specific examples):

RQ4. What is the degree of decomposition into different cognitive processes in participants' classifications?

RQ5. Do clarifications influence participants' degree of variation?

RQ6. Do clarifications influence participants' percentage of accuracy?

RQ7. Do clarifications influence participants' confidence?

This study focuses on the first three types of knowledge of the taxonomy. Metacognitive knowledge was excluded because it is independent of computer science and focus on computing education was sought.

3.2 Participants

Eight instructors of the Universidad Rey Juan Carlos agreed to participate. They were required to be computer scientists and to have experience as instructors in programming courses. One participant was excluded after the evaluation because her classifications did not specify the subcategory level in any dimension. Therefore, the number of participants with valid answers was seven.

As a part of the first session, participants were asked to self-rate their degree of knowledge of Bloom's taxonomy. A 5-level Likert scale was used, where 1 means: no knowledge, 2: some knowledge, 3: medium knowledge, 4: much knowledge, and 5: proficient. They were also asked to identify the version of the taxonomy they were familiar with. The results show a heterogeneous population, as shown in Table 1.

Table 1: Level of knowledge of Bloom's taxonomy

Instructor's code	Level of knowledge	Taxonomy version
1	2	Revised
2	5	Both
3	4	Original
4	1	None
5	2	Original
6	4	Both
7	3	Original

3.3 Procedure

The evaluation consisted of two sessions. In the first session, the revised Bloom's taxonomy was presented in general terms. In the second session, the two factors identified above (namely, classification of an exercise into several levels, and provision of computer-science specific examples) were stressed.

The first session lasted 40 minutes. It commenced with the vision of a video presenting the revised Bloom's taxonomy, with a duration of 16 minutes. The video introduced Bloom's taxonomy, differentiating both versions and identifying the revised version as the object of the evaluation. Definitions and examples were presented for each category and subcategory in both dimensions. The video ended with an example of how to classify a simple exercise.

After watching the video, instructors were asked to classify 10 programming exercises. Each exercise had to be assigned a cognitive process and a subtype of knowledge. In addition, instructors rated for each question their degree of confidence in their classification using a 5-level Likert scale.

There was a break of 20 minutes between both sessions. The second session lasted 1 hour and 10 minutes. It also began with a video presentation of 20 minutes. Different programming exercises were presented as examples for all cognitive processes and subtypes of knowledge. Then, it was explained that solving an exercise typically involves several cognitive processes, and it was illustrated with a programming exercise.

Next, instructors were asked to classify the same 10 programming exercises of the first session. For each exercise, they were asked: (a) to identify the cognitive processes (and their associated subtypes of knowledge) necessary to solve the exercise, (b) to identify the most relevant cognitive process, from their point of view as instructors, and (c) to rate their confidence in their classification.

3.4 Materials

As explained above, the evaluation was supported by two videos. In addition, participants were given in both sessions a diagram of the categories and subcategories of the revised Bloom's taxonomy, so that they did not have to rely on their memory. They were also given a written summary (6 pages) of the taxonomy and of our suggestions, including sketches of programming exercises associated to each cognitive process and subtype of knowledge as well as a fully classified example.

An important part of our evaluation was the selection of test exercises to classify. 54 exercises were gathered from papers [4][5][9][10][14][15][16][17] cited in the systematic review [11]. Each exercise was cataloged by ourselves into multiple cognitive processes and subtypes of knowledge. We often disagreed in the division into cognitive activities or in their classification. Thus, a number of rounds was held until we agreed completely. Not surprisingly, in some cases, we also disagreed with the classification made by the authors of the papers from where the exercises were extracted.

Ten representative Java programming exercises were selected. They are summarized in Table 3. A complete statement of each exercise can be found in its corresponding reference. The classification column shows the complete set of cognitive processes determined by ourselves, with the most relevant processes in bold. Note that all exercises require recognizing Java syntax as the first cognitive process, but exercise 6, which requires recalling Java terminology.

The exercises were made available as web forms. Each exercise included the problem statement and declared that students had faced problems of the same kind. It also contained fields to introduce participant's classifications and degree of confidence.

4 Results

This section successively presents results on variation, decomposition, accuracy, and confidence.

4.1 Variation – First Session

In the first session, participants had to classify the given exercises in a traditional way, i.e. into a single cognitive process and subtype of knowledge. Table 4 shows the degree of variation in each category or subcategory for all the exercises, as well as their minimum, maximum and median. Note the high degree of variation, with the exceptions of exercise 2 for both dimensions and of exercise 9 for type of knowledge.

4.2 Decomposition and Variation - Second Session

In the second session, participants were encouraged to decompose the problem solving process of each exercise into several cognitive processes, and to identify the most relevant cognitive process.

Table 2 shows the degree of decomposition for each exercise, including the minimum, maximum and median number of cognitive processes proposed per exercise. Note that the participants' median is very similar to ours.

Table 5 shows variation in the most relevant cognitive process for each exercise. There is an increase in the three statistical measures of cognitive processes with respect to the first session. However, in the type of knowledge dimension, there are increments and decrements.

Table 2: Decomposition – session 2

Decomposition	Exercise									
	1	2	3	4	5	6	7	8	9	10
Minimum	1	1	1	1	1	1	2	1	2	2
Maximum	3	3	3	4	4	4	4	4	5	4
Median	1	3	2	2	2	2	3	3	2	3
# in our classification	1	3	2	2	3	2	3	3	2	4

Table 3: Test exercises

Exercise	Summary of the test exercise	Classification	Reference
E1	Answer a question about Java elements	**Remember (Recognizing), Factual (Terminology)**	[13, question 1]
E2	Identify the value of an expression	Remember (Recognizing), Factual (Terminology) Analyze (Organizing), Conceptual (Classifications) **Apply (Executing), Procedural (Algorithms)**	[13, question 2]
E3	Identify the generic contents of a variable after a sequence of operations	Remember (Recognizing), Factual (Terminology) **Understand (Explaining), Conceptual (Classifications)**	[13, question 4]
E4	Identify the specific contents of a variable after a sequence of operations and conditionals	Remember (Recognizing), Factual (Terminology) **Apply (Executing), Procedural (Algorithms)**	[13, question 5]
E5	Identify the string printed after a sequence of statements containing loops	Remember (Recognizing), Factual (Terminology) Analyze (Organizing), Conceptual (Classifications) **Apply (Executing), Procedural (Algorithms)**	[13, question 7]
E6	Identify a false statement about methods	Remember (Recalling), Factual (Terminology) **Understand (Explaining), Conceptual (Classifications)**	[13, question 10]
E7	Answer two questions involving constructors	A) Remember (Recognizing), Factual (Terminology) **Analyze (Differentiating), Conceptual (Classifications)** B) Apply (Executing), Procedural (Algorithms)	[15, 2nd question in category Understand]
E8	Write a method that provides a given functionality	Remember (Recognizing), Factual (Terminology) Understand (Interpreting), Conceptual (Classifications) **Create (Producing), Conceptual (Classifications)**	[15, question in the category Create]
E9	Identify a correct Java implementation of a diagram	Remember (Recognizing), Factual (Terminology) **Understand (Interpreting), Conceptual (Classifications)**	[16, question 3]
E10	Fill a given piece of code to provide a given functionality	Remember (Recognizing), Factual (Terminology) Analyze (Differentiating), Conceptual (Classifications) Analyze (Organizing), Conceptual (Classifications) **Understand (Explaining), Conceptual (Generalizations)**	[3, question 8]

Table 4: Variation– session 1

Taxonomy dimensions	Exercise										Min	Max	Median
	E1	E2	E3	E4	E5	E6	E7	E8	E9	E10			
Categories	3	1	3	3	3	3	3	4	3	4	1	4	3
Cognitive process	5	2	5	5	6	5	6	5	4	7	2	7	5
Types of knowledge	2	1	2	2	2	2	2	2	1	2	1	2	2
Subtypes of knowledge	2	2	4	4	4	4	4	4	2	4	2	4	4

Table 5: Variation– session 2

Taxonomy dimensions	Exercise										Min	Max	Median
	E1	E2	E3	E4	E5	E6	E7	E8	E9	E10			
Categories	2	4	4	4	3	2	5	4	4	4	2	5	4
Cognitive process	3	6	6	5	4	5	7	6	6	6	3	7	6
Types of knowledge	2	2	2	2	2	2	3	2	2	2	2	3	2
Subtypes of knowledge	3	3	3	3	2	3	4	3	2	5	2	5	3

Table 6: Accuracy – session 1

Dimension	Exercise									Min	Max	Median/mean
	E1	E2	E3	E4	E5	E6	E8	E9	E10			
Categories	4	7	2	3	3	3	0	1	0	0	7	3
	57%	100%	29%	43%	43%	43%	29%	14%	0%	0%	100%	40%
Cognitive process	1	6	0	3	2	0	0	1	0	0	6	1
	14%	86%	0%	43%	29%	0%	0%	14%	0%	0%	86%	21%
Types of knowledge	5	7	1	5	6	5	0	0	1	0	7	5
	71%	100%	14%	71%	86%	71%	0%	0%	14%	0%	100%	47%
Subtypes of knowledge	5	4	1	4	4	0	0	0	1	0	5	1
	71%	57%	14%	57%	57%	0%	0%	0%	14%	0%	71%	30%

Table 7: Accuracy – session 2

Dimension	Exercise									Min	Max	Median/mean
	E1	E2	E3	E4	E5	E6	E8	E9	E10			
Categories	5	2	4	3	4	5	2	3	3	2	5	3
	71%	29%	57%	43%	57%	71%	29%	43%	43%	29%	71%	49%
Cognitive process	3	2	1	3	4	0	1	2	1	0	4	2
	43%	29%	14%	43%	57%	0%	14%	29%	14%	0%	57%	27%
Types of knowledge	4	2	2	3	4	6	1	3	3	1	6	3
	57%	29%	29%	43%	57%	86%	14%	43%	43%	14%	86%	45%
Subtypes of knowledge	4	2	2	3	4	2	1	3	1	1	4	2
	57%	29%	29%	43%	57%	29%	14%	43%	14%	14%	57%	35%

Table 8: Evolution of participants' accuracy

	Session 1		Session 2		Difference	
	Little knowledge	Much knowledge	Little knowledge	Much knowledge	Little knowledge	Much knowledge
Categories	18%	22%	22%	40%	4%	18%
Cognitive process	38%	40%	40%	56%	7%	16%
Types of knowledge	26%	30%	37%	48%	11%	18%
Subtypes of knowledge	48%	40%	37%	52%	-11%	12%

4.3 Accuracy

In this section, results on question 7 are not included because it is a compound question and some participants had difficulties in introducing their respective classifications in the forms.

Results on accuracy obtained in the first session are summarized in Table 6. Regarding cognitive processes, notice that question 2 is the only one with accuracy greater than 50%. More generally, the questions with high accuracy (questions 2, 4, and 5) correspond to the Apply – Executing cognitive process. The results are similar for classifications into category of cognitive process. The large increase in accuracy for question 1 (Remember) when we consider the category rather than just the cognitive process denotes lack of clarity between the two cognitive processes of category Remember.

With respect to subtypes of knowledge, questions 1, 2, 4 and 5 obtain the highest percentages. These questions involve knowledge of type Factual (Terminology) and Procedural (Algorithms), while the rest of the questions involve different subtypes of Conceptual knowledge. At the level of type of knowledge, the results are similar but sharper (with the exception of exercise 6).

The results obtained in the second session are shown in Table 7. Most exercises involving cognitive processes Remember – Recognizing (question 1) and Apply – Executing (questions 4 and 5) obtain the highest rates. At the category of cognitive process, exercises in categories Remember (exercise 1) and Understand (3, 6, 9 and 10) experience an increase, while predictive exercises (2, 4 and 5) remain the same. The prediction exercise 2 and the creation exercise 8 always have low accuracy rates.

Results can also be analyzed for participants. They were clustered according to their familiarity with Bloom's taxonomy. Table 8 presents the mean accuracy of participants with initial little or no knowledge of Bloom's taxonomy (participants 1, 4 and 5) and of participants with great or very great familiarity (2, 3 and 6). The results of the participant with regular knowledge are not included, but they are aligned with more experienced participants. The results for each category or subcategory in both sessions are presented.

Note that experienced participants exhibit higher accuracy (with the exception of subtype of knowledge in the first session, but this advantage is lost in the second session). All participants increase their accuracy in the second session, but experienced participants have greater accuracy increases.

4.4 Confidence

Tables 9 and 10 show the mean confidence in both sessions per question and per participant, respectively. Similarly, to Gluga *et al.* [5], mean confidence is mapped into percentages.

Table 9: Confidence per exercise in both sessions

Exercise	Category of cognitive activity	S. 1	S. 2	Dif.
E1	Remember (Recognizing)	86%	86%	0%
E2	Apply (Executing)	89%	83%	-6%
E3	Understand (Explaining)	77%	80%	4%
E4	Apply (Executing)	80%	77%	-3%
E5	Apply (Executing)	77%	77%	0%
E6	Understand (Explaining)	77%	74%	-3%
E7	Analyze (Differentiating) / Apply (Executing)	77%	74%	-3%
E8	Create (Producing)	74%	74%	0%
E9	Understand (Interpreting)	69%	83%	14%
E10	Understand (Explaining)	71%	74%	3%

Table 10: Confidence per participant in both sessions

Participant	Familiarity with Bloom	S. 1	S. 2	Dif.
P1	Small	62%	84%	22%
P2	Very great	84%	92%	8%
P3	Great	80%	76%	-4%
P4	None	80%	62%	-18%
P5	Small	92%	80%	-12%
P6	Great	84%	86%	2%
P7	Regular	62%	68%	6%

In general, the difference of confidence per session is small, with the exception of question 9 (increase of 14%), which was classified as Understand – Interpreting. If questions are grouped into cognitive categories, predictive questions (2, 4, 5), corresponding to the Apply – Executing cognitive process, accumulate a decrease of confidence equal to 9%.

With respect to participants, all of them were over-confident on their classifications, as their confidence is always above 60% while their accuracy rate is almost always below 50%. Note also that instructors with little or no familiarity with Bloom's taxonomy jointly accumulate a decrease of confidence (-8%), while familiarized instructors increased their confidence (6%).

5 Discussion

The results obtained shed light to research questions on the use of Bloom's taxonomy. For instance, the median of the participants' degree of decomposition is almost equal to ours. Therefore, decomposing a given exercise into a sequence of cognitive processes to solve was a natural activity for instructors (RQ4).

Some results are consistent with previous research regarding overconfidence (RQ3) [5], as well as high degree of variation (RQ1) and low degree of accuracy (RQ2) [7][13]. An original contribution was quantifying the degree of variation. The median number of cognitive processes per exercise was 5 or 6 (depending on the session). Variation in subtypes of knowledge also was notable, with median equal to 3 or 4.

The innovations produced several effects on participants. Firstly, variation was increased (RQ5). Obviously, the total number of cognitive processes or subtypes of knowledge was expected to be higher, as decomposition was promoted. However, higher variation in the most relevant cognitive processes was not expected. Secondly, participants' accuracy increased in the second session (RQ6), but increase was higher for participants familiarized with Bloom's taxonomy. Thirdly, confidence on classification of most exercises remained equal or decreased (with the notable exception of exercise 9). Finally, there was an increase of confidence in participants with previous knowledge of the taxonomy and a decrease in participants with no or little knowledge (RQ7).

Analysis of data at the category and subcategory levels for both dimensions shows specific difficulties, such as difficulty to distinguish cognitive processes of the Remember and Understand categories, as well as the subtypes of Conceptual knowledge.

Higher increments in accuracy and confidence for participants with previous knowledge of Bloom's taxonomy suggests that mastering it has a steep learning slope. As a consequence, popular recipes such as giving a list of verbs may assist in a first contact with Bloom's taxonomy, but longer exposition to the taxonomy is necessary for minimum mastery. This conclusion is reinforced by a short, semi-structured interview held a few days later with the participant proficient in Bloom's taxonomy. He acknowledged to have been confused because of the high number of cognitive processes as well as by the type of knowledge dimension, which he had not considered before.

Threats to validity. Two main threats can be identified. Firstly, the number of participants is small and they are from the same university. Actually, it is not easy to recruit many instructors experienced in programming courses. We partly offset this threat with participants' heterogeneous expertise. Secondly, accuracy is a problematic measure, but we used it to compare our results with related works [5]. A big effort was made to achieve a consensus on decomposition and classification, but they are subjective tasks. Devising a more objective measure is an open issue for future work.

6 Conclusions

Two innovations have been presented to contribute to a more secure use of revised Bloom's taxonomy, namely classifying each exercise into several cognitive processes and providing examples of classified programming exercises. The results of their evaluation were mixed. Some results were positive: decomposing problem solving into several cognitive processes was a natural task for instructors, accuracy was increased, and confidence was increased for experienced participants. However, negative results were also obtained: variation was increased, and confidence was decreased for non-experienced participants. Overall, our approach had positive outcomes, but higher increases by expert instructors suggest that non-expert instructors need longer training.

Currently, a qualitative analysis of the cognitive processes and subtypes of knowledge proposed for each kind of exercise is being conducted in order to identify the most common sources of disagreement. As a future line of research, instructors' training should be redesigned so that they practice longer with exercises placed at the different subcategories of the taxonomy.

ACKNOWLEDGMENTS

This work was supported by research grants of the MINECO (ref. TIN2015-66731-C2-1-R) and of the CAM (ref. P2018/TCS-4307).

REFERENCES

[1] L.W. Anderson, D.R. Krathwohl, P.W. Airasian, K.A. Cruikshank, R.E. Mayer, P.R. Pintrich, R. Raths, and M.C. Wittrock. 2001. *A Taxonomy for Learning, Teaching and Assessing. A Revision of Bloom's Taxonomy of Educational Objectives.* Pearson Education Limited.

[2] B.S. Bloom, M.D. Engelhart, E.J. Furst, W.H. Hill, and D.R. Krathwohl. 1956. *Taxonomy of Educational Objectives: Handbook I: Cognitive Domain*, Longmans.

[3] S. Fitzgerald, B. Simon and L. Thomas. 2005. Strategies that students use to trace code: an analysis based in grounded theory. In *Proceedings of the First International Workshop on Computing Education*, 69-80.

[4] U. Fuller, C.G. Johnson, T. Ahoniemi, D. Cukierman, I. Hernán-Losada, J. Jackova, E. Lahtinen, T.L. Lewis, D.M. Thompson, C. Riedesel, and E. Thompson. 2007. Developing a computer science-specific learning taxonomy. In *ITiCSE-WGR '07 Working Group Reports*, , ACM DL, 152-170. DOI: 10.1145/1345443.1345438.

[5] R. Gluga, J. Kay, R. Lister, S. Kleiman, and T. Lever. 2012. Over-confidence and confusion in using Bloom in programming fundamentals assessment. In *Proceedings 43th ACM Technical Symposium on Computing Science Education*, 2012, ACM DL, 147-15. DOI: 10.1145/2157136.2157181.

[6] I. Hernán-Losada, C.A. Lázaro-Carrascosa, and J.Á. Velázquez-Iturbide. 2004. On the use of Bloom's taxonomy as a basis to design educational software on programming. In *Engineering Education in the Changing Society*, C. da Rocha Brito y M.M. Ciampi (eds.), COPEC, 2004, 351-355. Retrieved 24th April 2017 at http://copec.eu/congresses/wcete2004/

[7] C.G. Johnson and U. Fuller. 2006. Is Bloom's taxonomy appropriate for computer science? In *Proceedings of the 6th Baltic Sea Conference on Computing Education Research*, 120-123. DOI 10.1145/1315803.1315825.

[8] C.M. Lewis, H. Khayrallah and A. Tsai. 2013. Mining data from the AP CS A exam: Patterns, non-patterns, and replication failure. In *Proceedings of the 9th Annual ACM International Computing Education Research*, 115-122.

[9] R. Lister and J. Leaney. 2003. First year programming: let all the flowers bloom. In *Proceedings of the Fifth Australasian Conference on Computing Education*, 221-230.

[10] R. Lister. 2000. On blooming first year programming, and its blooming assessment. In *Proceedings of the Australasian Conference on Computing Education*, 158-162.

[11] S. Masapanta-Carrión and J.Á. Velázquez-Iturbide. 2018. A systematic review of the use of Bloom's taxonomy in computer science education. In *Proceedings 49th ACM Technical Symposium on Computing Science Education*, , ACM DL, 441-446. DOI: 10.1145/3159450.3159491.

[12] S. Masapanta-Carrión, and J.Á. Velázquez-Iturbide. Guía de uso de la taxonomía de Bloom en informática. Technical Report DLSI1-URJC, no. 2018-03, Universidad Rey Juan Carlos. Retrieved 20th August 2018 at http://www.lite.etsii.urjc.es/technical-reports/.

[13] D. Oliver, T. Dobele, M. Greber and T, Roberts. 2004. Comparing course assessments: When lower is higher and higher, lower, *Computer Science Education*, 14(4), 321-341.

[14] S. Shuhidan, M. Hamilton and D. D'Souza. 2009. A taxonomic study of novice programming summative assessment. In *Proc. of the Eleventh Australasian Conference on Computing Education*, 147-156.

[15] B. Taylor and S. Kaza. 2011. Security injections: Modules to help students remember, understand, and apply secure coding techniques. In *Proceedings of the 16th Annual Joint Conference on Innovation and Technology in Computer Science Education*, 3-7.

[16] E. Thompson, A. Luxton-Reilly, J.L. Whalley, M. Hu and P. Robbins. 2008. Bloom's taxonomy for CS assessment. In *Proceedings of the Tenth Conference on Australasian Computing Education*, 155-161.

[17] J.L. Whalley, R. Lister, E. Thompson, T. Clear, P. Robbins, P.K. Kumar and C. Prasad. 2006. An Australasian study of reading and comprehension skills in novice programmers, using the Bloom and SOLO taxonomies. In *Proceedings of the 8th Australasian Conference on Computing Education*, 243-252.

Design and Pilot Testing of Subgoal Labeled Worked Examples for Five Core Concepts in CS1

Lauren E. Margulieux
Georgia State University
Department of Learning Sciences
Atlanta, GA 30302-3978
lmargulieux@gsu.edu

Briana B. Morrison
University of Nebraska Omaha
Computer Science Department
Omaha, NE 68182
bbmorrison@unomaha.edu

Adrienne Decker
University at Buffalo
Dept. of Engineering Education
Buffalo, NY 14260-4200
adrienne@buffalo.edu

ABSTRACT

Subgoal learning has improved student problem-solving performance in programming, but it has been tested for only one-to-two hours of instruction at a time. Our work pioneers implementing subgoal learning throughout an entire introductory programming course. In this paper we discuss the protocol that we used to identify subgoals for core programming procedures, present the subgoal labels created for the course, and outline the subgoal-labeled instructional materials that were designed for a Java-based course. To examine the effect of subgoal labeled materials on student performance in the course, we compared quiz and exam grades between students who learned using subgoal labels and those who learned using conventional materials. Initial results indicate that learning with subgoals improves performance on early applications of concepts. Moreover, variance in performance was lower and persistence in the course was higher for students who learned with subgoals compared to those who learned with conventional materials, suggesting that learning with subgoal labels may uniquely benefit students who would normally receive low grades or dropout of the course.

CCS CONCEPTS

• **Social and professional topics** → *Computer science education*

KEYWORDS

CS1; subgoal learning; worked examples; problem solving

ACM Reference format:

Lauren Margulieux, Briana B. Morrison and Adrienne Decker. 2019. Design and Pilot Testing of Subgoal Labeled Worked Examples for Five Core Concepts in CS1. In *Proc. of the 24th Annual Conf. on Innovation & Technology in Computer Science Education (ITiCSE'19). July 15–17, 2019, Aberdeen, Scotland UK., ACM, New York, NY, USA,* https://doi.org/10.1145/3304221.3319756

1 Introduction

The computing education community is constantly exploring methods to improve learning outcomes and student retention in college-level introductory programming courses. Subgoal-labeled worked examples are a promising method to improve problem-solving performance for novice learning, but they have been tested only for one to two hours of instruction at a time [7, 8, 9]. The current project substantially extends this line of work by identifying the subgoals for problem-solving procedures typically taught throughout an introductory Java programming course, developing subgoal-labeled worked examples and paired practice problems to be used while teaching the course, and conducting a pilot test on the effectiveness of the materials to improve problem-solving performance across an entire semester.

The guiding questions for this work were:

1. What are the subgoals of problem-solving procedures typically taught in college-level introduction to programming courses that use an imperative programming language?
2. If students learn procedures using subgoal-oriented worked-examples and paired practice problems, do they perform better than students who learn using non-subgoal-oriented materials on course assessments?

ACM ISBN 978-1-4503-6301-3/19/07. https://doi.org/10.1145/3304221.3319756

2 Subgoal Learning in Programming Education

Subgoal learning is an instructional design framework used in programming education that improves novice problem-solving performance [3, 6, 7, 8, 9]. Subgoal learning explicitly teaches students the subgoals, or functional pieces, of a problem-solving procedure. For example, to solve a problem with a loop, students must define and initialize variables, so defining and initializing variables is a subgoal of solving a problem with a loop. The specific steps taken to achieve this subgoal varies from problem to problem, but the function remains the same. Novices solve programming problems better when they explicitly learn the subgoals of a procedure because they often do not recognize these functional pieces on their own [4].

Worked examples are commonly used to teach problem-solving procedures for well-structured problems because they demonstrate how to apply an abstract procedure to a concrete problem before the learner can solve problems independently [2, 12, 13]. The drawback of worked examples, however, is that they must include details specific to a problem. For example, to demonstrate how to solve a problem using a `for loop`, the worked example must also include a cover story, such as "write a loop that will calculate the average age of the first 100 people to take a survey." Learners tend to organize information about the procedure using these easy-to-grasp details rather than around the hard-to-conceptualize abstract procedure that they are learning, leading to difficulty transferring knowledge to new problems [2, 11]. Subgoal learning addresses this problem by pointing out shared functional features in worked examples, helping learners to organize information so that it can transfer more easily [4, 7]. Furthermore, by drawing learners' attention to the functional features and away from the superficial details, subgoal learning can help learners manage cognitive load [9].

3 Identifying Subgoals with the TAPS Protocol

Some readers might think that instructors naturally point out the subgoals of problem-solving procedures, but they often do not [4]. Unlike declarative knowledge (i.e., factual knowledge, such as 2+2=4), procedural knowledge (i.e., knowledge about how to do something, such as tying a shoe) becomes more automatized the more it is used [1]. Therefore, experts in a domain have procedural knowledge that has become automatized over years of practice, and they cannot easily recognize or verbalize it. As a result, the process of identifying subgoals is arduous because it requires accessing tacit procedural knowledge from an expert. To access tacit procedural knowledge and identify the subgoals of five core programming procedures, we employed a cognitive task analysis, specifically the Task Analysis by Problem Solving (TAPS) protocol developed by Catrambone [5].

3.1 TAPS Protocol

The TAPS protocol requires a subject-matter expert (SME) and a knowledge-extraction expert (KEE) who is unfamiliar with the problem-solving procedure. The KEE asks the SME to bring problems that exemplify the problem-solving procedure. In the following description, the SME will have female pronouns and the KEE male pronouns to help distinguish between them.

The session starts with the KEE asking the SME to solve the first problem. The SME does not provide a lecture or explanation of the problem-solving process before solving problems. Instead, the SME solves the first problem and explains what she is doing while the KEE takes notes. During the first problem, the KEE typically does not ask many questions while gaining a general sense of the procedure, but the KEE might ask the SME to repeat steps or re-explain steps that he missed or did not understand.

When the KEE is finished taking notes on the first problem, he asks the SME to solve another problem and explain what she is doing. Again, the KEE takes notes on the process, specifically looking for similarities between the problems. During the second problem, the KEE typically asks more questions, especially about 1) analogous components of the two problems, 2) why the SME did a problem-solving step, and 3) how the SME knew which step to take next. SMEs can typically answer questions about analogous steps easily. Beyond the explanation that they provide while solving the problem (i.e., the declarative knowledge that they have about the procedure), they often struggle to explain why they took a step or how they knew which step to take next (i.e., the procedural knowledge that they have automatized). Automatized procedural knowledge is often what instructors struggle to impart to their students because they think that it is common knowledge or because they think it is intuitive.

When the SME starts to struggle to explain steps of the problem-solving procedure, this is the level at which the KEE often identifies subgoals. In TAPS, it is important that the KEE be unfamiliar with the problem-solving procedure because his novice perspective will help distinguish between common knowledge and automatized procedural knowledge, both of which will seem like common knowledge to the SME. The first stage of TAPS ends when the KEE feels like he has a complete set of notes for explaining the problem-solving procedure. The number of problems that the SME solves to reach this point depends on the complexity of the procedure, the skill of the KEE at extracting knowledge, and the skill of the SME at verbalizing tacit knowledge. The first stage typically takes between one and four hours. It is a demanding task for both the KEE and SME, and we recommend taking an extended break every two hours.

During the second stage of TAPS, the KEE attempts to solve problems using his notes for guidance. When the KEE reaches an impasse, he can ask the SME for help and update his notes. The SME should not offer help. Once the KEE can reliably solve new problems using only his notes, the notes are complete.

During the final stage of TAPS, the KEE organizes and edits the complete notes to create a list of subgoals for the procedure and asks the SME for feedback. The subgoals represent only the procedural knowledge required for a problem-solving procedure, not the declarative knowledge, such as what operation `%` represents (modulus). While both types of knowledge are necessary to solve problems, instructors can easily recognize and explain declarative knowledge. Therefore, subgoal learning interventions focus on the procedural knowledge that instructors can struggle to share.

3.2 Identifying Subgoals in Introductory Programming (Java)

We used the TAPS protocol to identify subgoals of problem-solving procedures using expression (assignment) statements, selection statements, loops, object instantiation and method calls, writing classes, and arrays in Java. The SME was one of the authors, Morrison, a computing education researcher and assistant professor in the CS Department at University of Nebraska Omaha. Morrison has 23 years of experience teaching programming and over 15 years of experience specifically teaching introductory courses in Java. The KEE was another one of the authors, Margulieux, a computing education researcher and assistant professor in the Department of Learning Sciences at Georgia State University. Margulieux has 6 years of experience using the TAPS protocol and had never learned programming before serving as KEE on this project.

For each programming concept, the SME and KEE identified subgoals for evaluating code and writing code. Furthermore, after creating the list of subgoals, they received feedback from the other author, Decker, a computing education researcher with 18 years of experience teaching introductory programming. The subgoals are listed in Figure 1. Part A for each subgoal topic lists the evaluate subgoals, and part B lists the write subgoals. Some subgoals are broken down into sub-subgoals.

4 Designing Instruction

After the identification phase, we designed instructional materials to help students learn the subgoals of the problem-solving procedures. The traditional method of teaching subgoals in STEM is through subgoal-labeled worked examples (SLWEs) [4, 7, 9]. Students who study SLWEs perform better than those who study unlabeled worked examples because the subgoal labels highlight the structure of the procedure and prompts students to recognize similarities between solutions [4, 7, 9]. Therefore, we designed SLWEs for each set of subgoals with multiple levels of difficulty.

Figure 1. Subgoals identified through TAPS protocol.

Subgoals for evaluating and writing expression (assignment) statements	
A. Evaluate expression statement	B. Write expression statement
1. Determine whether data type of expression is compatible with data type of variable 2. Update variable for pre based on side effect 3. Solve arithmetic equation 4. Check data type of copied value against data type of variable 5. Update variable for post based on side effect	1. Determine expression that will yield variable 2. Determine data type and name of variable and data type of expression 3. Determine arithmetic equation with operators 4. Determine expression components 5. Operators and operands must be compatible
Subgoals for evaluating and writing selection statements	
A. Evaluate selection statement	B. Write selection statement
1. Diagram which statements go together 2. For if statement, determine whether expression is true or false 3. If true – follow true branch, if false –follow else branch or do nothing if no else branch	1. Define how many mutually exclusive paths are needed 2. Order from most restrictive/selective group to least restrictive 3. Write if statement with Boolean expression 4. Follow with true bracket including action 5. Follow with else bracket 6. Repeat until all groups and actions are accounted for
Subgoals for evaluating and writing loops.	
A. Evaluate loops	B. Write loops
1. Identify loop parts a. Determine start condition b. Determine update condition c. Determine termination condition d. Determine body that is repeated 2. Trace the loop a. For every iteration of loop, write down values	1. Determine purpose of loop a. Pick a loop structure (while, for, do_while) 2. Define and initialize variables 3. Determine termination condition a. Invert termination condition to continuation condition 4. Write loop body a. Update loop control variable to reach termination
Subgoals for calling and writing methods	
A. Call or trace method calls	B. Write methods
1. Classify method as `static` method or `instance` method a. If `static`, use the class name b. If `instance`, must have or create an instance 2. Write (instance / class) dot method name and ( ) 3. Determine whether parameter(s) are appropriate a. Number of parameters passed must match method declaration b. Data types of parameters passed must match method declaration (or be assignable) 4. Determine what the method will return (if anything: data type, void, print, change state of object) and where it will be stored (nowhere, somewhere) 5. Evaluate right hand side of assignment (if there is one). Value is dependent on method's purpose	1. Define method header based on problem 2. Define return statement at the end 3. Define method body/logic a. Determine types of logic (expression, selection, loop, etc.) b. Define internal variables c. Write statements
Subgoals for using objects and writing classes	
A. Use objects (creating instances)	B. Write classes (associated rules sheet)
1. Declare variable of appropriate class datatype. 2. Assign to variable: keyword `new`, followed by class name, followed by (). 3. Determine whether parameter(s) are appropriate (API) a. Number of parameters b. Data types of the parameters	1. Name it 2. Differentiate class-level (`static`) vs. instance/object-level variables 3. Differentiate class-level (`static`) vs. instance/object behaviors/methods 4. Define instance variables (that you want to be interrelated) 5. Define class variables (`static`) as needed 6. Create constructor (behavior) that creates initial state of object 7. Create 1 accessor and 1 mutator behaviors per attribute 8. Write toString method 9. Write equals method 10. Create additional methods as needed

Figure 1. Subgoals identified through TAPS protocol *(continued)*

Subgoals for evaluating and writing arrays	
A. Evaluate arrays	B. Write arrays
1. Set up array from 0 to size-1 2. Evaluate data type of statements against array 3. Trace statements, updating slots as you go a. Remember assignment subgoals	1. Data type plus [ ] 2. Variable name = `{initializer list}`, or `new datatype [size]`

For each topic in Figure 1, we created several SLWEs in increasing level of difficulty. The simplest version may skip some of the subgoals identified for the procedure because they are not necessary for simple problems. It may also include more sub-subgoals than later levels of SLWEs to provide more guidance at the earliest stage of learning. The difficulty level of SLWEs gradually increase, adding subgoals and reducing sub-subgoals as the problems increase in complexity. The parameters for problem complexity in each level were determined by Morrison and Margulieux after identifying the subgoals of each procedure, and Decker provided feedback. Based on the parameters, Morrison and Decker designed the first draft of the SLWE and practice problems (see Figure 2), and Margulieux provided feedback and help during iterative design.

The SLWEs were interleaved with practice problems so that after students studied a worked example, they attempted to solve at least one similar problem. Interleaving worked examples and practice problems improves learning efficiency over studying worked examples as in a block before attempting to solve problems [14]. The SLWE--practice-problem pairs were intended to be used as either a homework assignment or as instructional materials that the instructor discusses in class. If using the materials in class, other instructional techniques can be combined with the materials. For example, instructors might use a flipped classroom approach in which students learn about the problem-solving procedure conceptually before class; then class time is used to practice problem solving with the SLWE--practice-problem pairs. While students are working on practice problems, they can engage in Peer Instruction, which asks students to explain their solution to a peer and resolve differences in answers before the instructor provides the correct answer and has been effective in introductory programming courses [10].

5 Report of Pilot Test

The instructional materials were pilot tested in the introductory programming courses at University of Nebraska Omaha. There are five sections of the course taught by three full-time faculty instructors with similar experience levels and supported by six graduate teaching assistants. All sections of the course are coordinated so that they include the same topics at the same pace and have the same quizzes and exams. The course was designed as a flipped class in which students watched recorded lectures before class and then answered peer instruction questions during class and problem solved in small groups. All sections follow this format, but the online section uses a different medium for class. Two sections of the course were taught by Morrison and used the SLWE during class. Three sections of the course, including the online section, were taught with conventional, non-subgoal worked examples. All other instructional features of the sections were the same among the sections. The pilot test compares student performance (i.e., quantitative grades) on quizzes and exams across sections.

5.1 Study Methods

The total number of students across all five sections was 307 based on enrollment at the beginning of the semester. Students were excluded from analysis if they did not complete at least one exam and one quiz, effectively dropping the course, making $N = 265$. They were split across the conventional course group (n = 145) and the SLWE course group (n = 120).

Though we do not have space in the current paper to fully discuss learner characteristics, we found no correlations between group and demographic factors or learner characteristics, including reason for taking the course, expected grade, expected difficulty of the course, interest in the course content, anxiety about course performance, age, gender, full-time or part-time status, race, primary language, family socioeconomic status, academic major, high school GPA, college GPA, year in school, or prior experience with programming. There were also no correlations between these factors and quiz or exam scores. Thus, these learner characteristics were not used a covariates or random factors in the analysis.

Figure 2. Example of subgoal-labeled worked examples and practice problem pair for writing expression statements (see Figure 1).

Subgoal-Labeled Worked Example 1 – Simple arithmetic equation	**Paired Practice Problems**

Assume the following given declarations:
`int max = 100;`
`double tax = 0.5, result, bill = 26.12;`
Write the code to store max multiplied by tax in the variable result.
SG1: *Determine expression that will yield variable*
`max * tax`
SG2: *Determine data type and name of variable and data type of expression*
Result to be stored in variable `result`. That variable is a **double.** The expression `max * tax` is an **int** multiplied by a **double** yields a **double.** A **double** can be assigned to a **double.**
SG3: *Determine arithmetic equation with operators*
`result = max * tax;`
	Practice Problem 1:
	Calculate a 15% tip on the bill.
	
	Practice Problem 2:
	Determine the total amount owed including bill, tip, and tax.

5.1.1 Data collection sources. Student performance on the four exams and five quizzes was collected. We also had the initial instructor keep a weekly journal on the teaching experience. Below are the characteristics for the student performance items:

- The majority of quiz questions were either multiple choice or short answer. Exams consisted of multiple choice questions (usually 1/3 to 1/2 of the exam grade) and short answer and long answer questions.
- All exam and quiz questions were based on peer instruction questions presented in class (near transfer) or the homework assignments (far transfer).
- Exams and quizzes were scored identically across sections. All multiple choice and short answer questions were automatically graded, and all student responses were reviewed by one member of the instructional team. Rubrics for open ended questions were developed and a single member of the instructional team graded all responses for a single question.
- For exams, students were allotted 2 hours.
- Quizzes were assigned over weekends, from Friday morning until Monday at midnight and had a 20-minute time allotment.

5.2 Results and Discussion

The quiz and exam scores were each analyzed in a few ways to examine the differences in performance between students who received SLWEs and those who received conventional, non-subgoal instruction. The following values were calculated for each student:

1. **Total** score, which is out of all available points on exams or quizzes. Thus, if a student did not turn in an exam or quiz (e.g., because they dropped out of the course) this score would treat the missing grade as a zero.
2. **Average** score, which is the average score for all exams or quizzes that were submitted by a student. Thus, if a student did not turn in an exam or quiz, this score would not be affected by the missing grade.
3. **Number** of assessments completed, which is the total number of exams or quizzes taken regardless of score.

Conducting analyses with these different values allows us to examine the performance and retention differences between groups. Initially in the analyses, the online section was separate from the other non-subgoal sections in case the medium of the courses affected performance or there was a fundamental difference between students who signed up for the online or in-person courses. In all of the analyses, however, the online and in-person non-subgoal groups performed equivalently. Therefore, they were consolidated for the final analyses.

5.2.1 Quiz performance. For all three values calculated from students' quiz grades, the subgoal group performed better than the non-subgoal group. For the **total** quiz score, including zeros for missing grades, the maximum score was 31. The subgoal group (M = 12.0, SD = 5.6) performed better than the non-subgoal group (M = 9.5, SD = 6.3) with a medium effect size, d = 0.42. The SD of the subgoal group was sufficiently less than that of the non-subgoal group to violate the homogeneity test, p = .03; therefore, the non-parametric and more conservative Mann-Whitney test was used to compare groups, U = 6703, p = .001. For the **average** quiz score, not including zeros for missing grades, the maximum score was 6.2 points. The subgoal group (M = 2.98, SD = 0.9) performed better than the non-subgoal group (M = 2.57, SD = 1.0) with a medium effect size, d = 0.44, $t(264)$ = 12.03, p = .001. For the **number** of quizzes taken out of five, the subgoal group (M = 3.9, SD = 1.2) took more quizzes than the non-subgoal group (M = 3.4, SD = 1.6) with a small-medium effect size, d = 0.32. The SD of the subgoal group was less than that of the non-subgoal group, p < .01; therefore, Mann-Whitney was used, U = 7126, p = .01. This pattern of results means that the subgoal group completed more quizzes and performed better on them, regardless of whether the missing grades are factored in as zeros or not.

More detailed examination of scores on each quiz with repeated measures analysis suggests that the subgoal group consistently performed better than the non-subgoal group on each quiz. Mauchley's test of sphericity was significant, p < .01, as is common in repeated measures analyses, and the Huynh-Feldt correction was used to make the statistical values more conservative. There was no main effect of quiz, $F(5, 260)$ = 2.04, p = .11, suggesting that the subgoal intervention was equally effective across all topics. Given that each quiz was designed to test only the new concepts that had been taught, this finding means that students benefitted from the SLWEs for each new topic, despite gaining knowledge about other programming topics. This analysis could only be conducted with the total quiz score because the average quiz score would be missing data from un-submitted quizzes. Given that the effect size for the difference between groups was equivalent for the analyses with the total and average quiz scores, this analysis is expected to be representative of average quiz score as well.

5.2.2 Exam performance. Students' exam grades had a different pattern than their quiz grades. For the **total** of all exam scores, including zeros for missing grades, the maximum score was 200. The subgoal group (M = 140.3, SD = 42.4) performed better than the non-subgoal group (M = 128.2, SD = 51.6) with a small effect size, d = 0.26, $t(264)$ = 4.20, p = .04. For the **average** exam score, not including zeros for missing grades, the maximum score was 50. In this case, the subgoal group (M = 37.5, SD = 7.6) did not perform statistically better than the non-subgoal group (M = 35.8, SD = 9.1), d = 0.20. The SD of the subgoal group was less than that of the non-subgoal group, p = .02, so Mann-Whitney was used, U = 7975, p = .24. This difference in results can be explained by the different in **number** of exams taken. Out of four exams, the subgoal group (M = 3.7, SD = 0.8) took more than the non-subgoal group (M = 3.5, SD = 1.0) with a small effect size, d = 0.22. The SD of the subgoal group was less than that of the non-subgoal group, p < .01, so Mann-Whitney was used U = 7785, p = .045. The most plausible explanation for this pattern of results, based on the statistics, is that exam performance was equivalent between the subgoal and non-subgoal groups for students who took all exams. The difference in the **total** exam analysis is likely due to the zeros from students who did not take all exams. Because students in the non-subgoal group had disproportionally more zeros than the subgoal group, their mean total score would decrease more than the subgoal group's.

This pattern of results has two likely implications. First, it implies that SLWEs did not improve exam scores, which aligns with the theory behind subgoal learning. Subgoal learning has been shown to be effective because it helps learners to recognize the abstract structure of problem-solving procedures before they have enough knowledge to recognize it for themselves. Therefore, subgoal learning should be most effective at the beginning of learning a new procedure (e.g., when learners take a quiz), and as learners gain more knowledge about a procedure (e.g., by the time they take an exam), the effect should diminish. Second, the pattern of results implies that students in the subgoal group were more likely than those in the non-subgoal group to complete the semester. Especially because the subgoal group had less variance on exam scores than the non-subgoal group, subgoal learning might have helped students who would typically drop out of the course to remain in the course and be more successful. Further analysis of students who dropped out of the course and any common characteristics that they share would be needed to determine whether this is the most likely cause of the differences between groups.

5.2.3 Instructor experience. Morrison taught two sections of the introductory programming course for this study. Each section of students had a different culture. One section contained mostly computing majors, was held earlier in the day, and taught in a large auditorium classroom. The second section contained mostly students taking the course as a requirement for an engineering degree and was held late in the afternoon, allowing working professional students to attend.

The students in both sections expressed that the subgoals and the SLWEs done during class helped them to learn the material, either in anonymous comments in mid-term student surveys or through personal discussions. While working through the SLWEs during class, students were asked to state what the next subgoal to be accomplished would be, or what the code would be to accomplish a specific subgoal. By having the students continually verbalize the subgoal labels and associated code, it was hoped that the students would internalize the subgoals.

The most rewarding use of teaching with subgoal labels occurred at the end of the semester when covering arrays. While explaining the typically difficult topic of references versus primitives with shallow and deep copies, the notion of revisiting subgoals from assignment statements proved especially helpful. When walking through code and bringing back the assignment subgoal labels, the students could quickly determine what needed to be done or whether the code was correct by looking at the data types of the variables involved. Reminding the students to evaluate the data type of the variables involved in the statements allowed them to see if the action was being taken on an array element that was a primitive or reference type. This also proved beneficial on test questions that used nested [ ], such as

```
array[array[1] + array[2]] = 10
```

6 Conclusions

In this project, we used the TAPS protocol to identify the subgoals of problem-solving procedures that use expression/assignment statements, selection statements, loops, object instantiation and method calls, writing classes, and arrays in Java (see Figure 1). We then used those subgoals to design subgoal-labeled worked examples and paired practice problems to be used as the concepts were taught in an introductory programming course. To begin exploring the efficacy of the materials, we conducted a pilot test that compared quiz and exam performance of students who were taught with the subgoal materials and those who were taught with the conventional, non-subgoal materials for the course. Based on a sample of 265 students over the fall 2018 semester, we found that students who learned with the subgoal materials performed better on quizzes throughout the semester. This result suggests that the subgoal materials helped learners to solve problems using the procedure more effectively during the early stages of learning even though no performance difference between groups was found on the exams. We also found that students who learned with the subgoal materials were more likely to submit all of the exams (i.e., not drop out of the course). This finding paired with the finding that subgoal materials did not predict exam performance suggests that the subgoal materials helped more students to stay in the course and achieve equivalent exam performance as their peers. Moreover, average exam performance in the subgoal group had consistently less variance than that in the non-subgoal group, suggesting that the subgoal materials helped to equalize performance across students.

Though these results are promising, the pilot test has significant limitations. The instructor who was teaching with the subgoal materials was also part of the research team. This circumstance was necessary to fix any errors or overlooked details that would disrupt using the materials in class, but it also diminishes the validity of our results. The instructor is a veteran at teaching introductory programming and, thus, has significant prior experience, which helps to increase consistency of instruction and reduce bias. Some level of bias, however, is still likely to have been represented in the data. Now that the materials have been fully applied in a course, we will begin testing them in courses taught by instructors who are independent from the project. The promising results that we found in the pilot test suggest that further testing is worthwhile. If we can find the same pattern of results in more valid experimental settings, then we will have strong evidence that adopting the subgoal materials can improve learning in introductory programming courses. The materials are designed to be used in place of existing worked examples and practice problems, as they are currently used in a course. Thus, we expect that the barriers for adopting the materials will be low but offer substantial benefits, particularly, we hope, for students who are most likely to struggle.

7 ACKNOWLEDGMENTS

Our thanks to the reviewers who helped to improve this paper. We also thank the students who consented to be part of this study.
This work is funded in part by the National Science Foundation under grants 1712231 and 1712025. Any opinions, findings, and conclusions or recommendations expressed in this material are those of the authors and do not necessarily reflect the views of the NSF.

8 REFERENCES

[1] Anderson, J. R. (1996). ACT: A simple theory of complex cognition. *American Psychologist, 51*(4), 355.

[2] Atkinson, R. K., Derry, S. J., Renkl, A., & Wortham, D. (2000). Learning from examples: Instructional principles from the worked examples research. *Review of Educational Research, 70*(2), 181-214.

[3] Brown, N. C., & Wilson, G. (2018). Ten quick tips for teaching programming. *PLoS Computational Biology, 14*(4).

[4] Catrambone, R. (1998). The subgoal learning model: Creating better examples so that students can solve novel problems. *Journal of Experimental Psychology: General, 127*(4), 355.

[5] Catrambone, R. (2011). Task analysis by problem solving (TAPS): Uncovering expert knowledge to develop high-quality instructional materials and training. Paper presented at the 2011 Learning and Technology Symposium (Columbus, GA, June).

[6] Joentausta, J., & Hellas, A. (2018, February). Subgoal Labeled Worked Examples in K-3 Education. In *Proceedings of the 49th ACM Technical Symposium on Computer Science Education* (pp. 616-621). ACM.

[7] Margulieux, L. E., Guzdial, M., & Catrambone, R. (2012). Subgoal-labeled instructional material improves performance and transfer in learning to develop mobile applications. In *Proceedings of the Ninth Annual International Conference on International Computing Education Research* (pp. 71-78). New York, NY: ACM.

[8] Morrison, B. B., Decker, A., & Margulieux, L. E. (2016). Learning loops: A replication study illuminates impact of HS courses. In *Proceedings of the Twelfth Annual International Conference on International Computing Education Research* (pp. 221-230). New York, NY: ACM.

[9] Morrison, B. B., Margulieux, L. E., & Guzdial, M. (2015). Subgoals, context, and worked examples in learning computing problem solving. In *Proceedings of the Eleventh Annual International Conference on International Computing Education Research* (pp. 21-29). New York, NY: ACM.

[10] Porter, L., Bailey Lee, C., Simon, B., & Zingaro, D. (2011). Peer instruction: Do students really learn from peer discussion in computing?. In *Proceedings of the Seventh International Computing Education Research Conference* (pp. 45-52). ACM.

[11] Renkl, A. (1997). Learning from worked-out examples: A study on individual differences. *Cognitive Science, 21*(1), 1-29.

[12] Schwonke, R., Renkl, A., Krieg, C., Wittwer, J., Aleven, V., & Salden, R. (2009). The worked-example effect: Not an artefact of lousy control conditions. *Computers in Human Behavior, 25*(2), 258-266.

[13] Sweller, J. (2006). The worked example effect and human cognition. *Learning and Instruction.*

[14] Trafton, J. G., & Reiser, B. J. (1993). Studying examples and solving problems: Contributions to skill acquisition. In *Proceedings of the 15th Conference of the Cognitive Science Society* (pp. 1017-1022).

Syntax-based Improvements to Plagiarism Detectors and their Evaluations

Lawton Nichols
UC Santa Barbara
lawtonnichols@cs.ucsb.edu

Kyle Dewey
CSU Northridge
kyle.dewey@csun.edu

Mehmet Emre
UC Santa Barbara
emre@cs.ucsb.edu

Sitao Chen
UC Santa Barbara
sitaochen@ucsb.edu

Ben Hardekopf
UC Santa Barbara
benh@cs.ucsb.edu

ABSTRACT

Software plagiarism cheats students out of their own education and leads to unfair grading, making software plagiarism detection an important problem. However, many popular plagiarism detection tools are inaccurate, language-specific, or closed source, limiting their applicability. In this work, we seek to address these problems via a novel approach. We adapt the optimal Smith-Waterman sequence alignment algorithm to precisely measure the similarity between programs, greatly improving detection accuracy relative to competitors. Our approach is applicable to any language describable by an ANTLR grammar, which includes most programming languages. We also provide a new type of evaluation based on random program generation and obfuscation. Finally, we make our approach freely available, allowing for customizations and transparent reasoning about detection behavior.

ACM Reference Format:
Lawton Nichols, Kyle Dewey, Mehmet Emre, Sitao Chen, and Ben Hardekopf. 2019. Syntax-based Improvements to Plagiarism Detectors and their Evaluations. In *Innovation and Technology in Computer Science Education (ITiCSE '19), July 15–17, 2019, Aberdeen, Scotland UK.* ACM, New York, NY, USA, 7 pages. https://doi.org/10.1145/3304221.3319789

1 INTRODUCTION

Plagiarism cheats plagiarizers out of their own education, and can lead to unfair grading of students who do not plagiarize. As such, the detection of software plagiarism is an important problem. While there is a large existing body of work on plagiarism detection (e.g., [4–6, 8, 10, 12, 14], we observe that plagiarism detection remains an unsolved problem. Specifically, existing plagiarism detection approaches tend to be inaccurrate, language-specific, or closed source [4], limiting their practicality.

Towards solving these problems, we observe the following:

- The syntax of most languages allows programs to differ in operationally indistinguishable ways, as by varying whitespace or variable names. This sort of syntactic noise is frequently exploited to obfuscate plagiarism [4].
- Most languages have features which are related to each other (e.g., both `if` and `switch` perform conditional code execution). A common plagiarism obfuscation is to substitute these features with each other [4].
- Many kinds of plagiarism obfuscations can be phrased as code additions, deletions, or modifications.

In this work, we directly exploit these observations to inform the design of a novel plagiarism detection approach. Towards removing superfluous syntactic information, we adopt a syntax-aware approach with *filtering* refinements, which strip away anything the user considers uninteresting. As a countermeasure to language feature substitution, we define *abstraction* refinements, which allow the user to specify how similar different language features are to each other. Finally, we observe that the Smith-Waterman algorithm [13], classically from bioinformatics, is well-suited to plagiarism detection; the algorithm was was specifically designed to compare sequences in the presence of additions, deletions, and modifications. The use of these refinements, in conjunction with the Smith-Waterman algorithm, leads to a plagiarism detection solution which is accurate *by design.*

While our approach is syntax-aware, it is not tied to the syntax of any particular language. We use ANTLR [7] grammars for defining program syntax, which are commonly used when defining language parsers for compilers. Most languages can be defined with ANTLR grammars, and many already have ANTLR grammars available, making our approach applicable to most languages. While our filtering and abstraction refinements require an additional time investment to specify, this investment needs to be performed only once per language, making the specification burden overall minute.

To evaluate the accurracy of our approach, we compare it against multiple existing plagiarism detection approaches (namely, MOSS [12], JPLAG [10], and Zhang and Liu [8]) on Java programs. While designing our evaluation, we discovered that many evaluations are based on simulated plagiarized programs written by the very authors of the corresponding plagiarism detection technique (e.g., [3–5, 8, 15]). We observe that subtle biases can be introduced with this evaluation approach, as it is possible for an author to subconsciously write programs which are more liable to be caught by their own technique. To reduce such bias, we base our evaluation on randomly-generated Java programs which have been automatically obfuscated using plagiarism obfuscation approaches observed in the wild (e.g., those in Martins et al. [4]). Our evaluation shows that

ITiCSE '19, July 15–17, 2019, Aberdeen, Scotland UK

ACM ISBN 978-1-4503-6301-3/19/07...$15.00
https://doi.org/10.1145/3304221.3319789

our approach is superior to that of all competing approaches, in terms of true/false positives/negatives discovered.

Overall, our contributions are as follows:

- We introduce a novel syntax-aware plagiarism detection approach. We explain our technique in Section 3, and provide an example in Section 4.
- We introduce a new evaluation approach based on random program generation and obfuscation, and use this evaluation approach to evaluate our plagiarism detection approach. We find that our plagiarism detection approach offers superior accurracy to that of all competitors considered. Section 5 provides further details.
- We make our plagiarism detection and evaluation approaches, along with their corresponding source code, freely available[1].

2 BACKGROUND AND RELATED WORK

Plagiarism is associated with malicious intent, and students who plagiarize code will often obfuscate it to avoid detection [4]. Plagiarism detection tools (hereafter referred to as "detectors") must see through these obfuscations.

Similarity-based detectors give scores to all possible pairs of programs, where higher-scoring pairs are more similar to each other (and more indicative of plagiarism) than lower-scoring pairs. Exactly what constitutes a "high score" is relative to the listing of scores; in practice, instructors would look at the code corresponding to some of the highest-scoring pairs, in order to make a judgement call on whether or not plagiarism occurred. While this still requires instructors to perform manual code inspection to find plagiarism, it dramatically reduces the number of pairs to consider, going from hundreds to thousands of pairs to perhaps several. With this in mind, the purpose of detectors in practice is to eliminate unlikely cases of plagiarism, leaving only likely cases.

2.1 Evaluating Plagiarism Detectors

Effective detectors will consistently give high scores to plagiarism and low scores to non-plagiarism. This suggests an evaluation strategy: see how a given detector scores known cases of plagiarism and non-plagiarism, and measure how close these scores are to expectations. Ideally, this evaluation would involve real student assignment submissions, reflecting how detectors are intended to be used. However using real submissions has a problem: students must *honestly tell us* whether or not they plagiarized. Given the negative consequences of plagiarism, along with the fact that plagiarism is intentionally obfuscated to avoid detection, students cannot be relied upon to provide this information. As such, alternative evaluation strategies are frequently used.

A common alternative strategy is to manually create benchmarks which intentionally plagiarize code [3–5, 8, 15]. We argue that this is prone to bias, as authors may subconsciously write benchmarks which behave differently on their own detector. In contrast, we generate random programs and randomly perturb them in a manner consistent with plagiarism.

[1] https://github.com/lawtonnichols/plagiarism-detector

2.2 Related Work on Plagiarism Detection

Only two of the papers mentioned in a recent plagiarism detection survey [4] are open source, and each lacks widespread language support. We believe our approach fills this gap.

The most successful detector is MOSS [12], and we compare our tool against it in our evaluation. The algorithm behind MOSS (namely, Winnowing [12]) is freely available, though the MOSS tool itself is closed source. While Winnowing is language-agnostic, MOSS has language-specific modes, and setting these modes properly has dramatic impact on the results (see Section 5.3). As such, MOSS's approach is neither widely applicable nor freely available, unlike our approach. MOSS, Nayayanan et al. [6], and Chilowicz et al. [1] are all based on fingerprinting at various granularity levels, with MOSS using files, Nayayanan et al. using token sequences, and Chilowicz et al. using syntax trees.

JPLAG is a Java-specific detector which applies a string tiling algorithm at the token level [10]. Son et al.'s [14] approach, like ours, is based on comparing parse trees, though their comparison is based on convolution kernels instead of sequence alignment.

Tahaei and Noelle [16] detect plagiarism by observing multiple submissions of code and comparing the differences between those submsisions via logistic regression. In contrast, our work does not require multiple submissions of student programs. Their evaluation was done on student code labeled by the instructor.

Fu et al. [2] use a version of the TF-IDF statistic to find the most "surprising" differences on abstract syntax trees. Their evaluation was on short programs, and cases of plagiarism were generated from starter code using generators made by multiple people. This evaluation is similar to our own, but the types of program transformations performed by the generators are unclear.

Prado et al. [9] introduce a detector which uses static and dynamic analyses to perform plagiarism detection, making it reliant on existing tools and analyses for the languages that it supports. In contrast, our method only requires an ANTLR grammar and minimal work to add a new language.

Sulistiani and Karnalim [15] compare token sequences, filtering them using cosine similarity for efficiency. We observe that token sequences remove some of the underlying structure of a program, and so our detector instead works with parse trees. Their evaluation consists of handmade cases of plagiarism.

Zhang and Liu's [8] approach is arguably the most similar to our own, as they also make use of the Smith-Waterman algorithm [13]. However, Zhang and Liu's approach has several key differences from that of our own: to the best of our knowledge, they convert trees to sequences via a preorder traversal instead of a postorder traversal (Section 3.1), their scoring function is less general than that of our own (Section 3.5), they do not perform sorting (Section 3.2), and most importantly, they lack our filtering and abstraction refinements (see Section 3.3). For these reasons, we have found that Zhang and Liu's approach cannot detect plagiarism as accurately as our proposed method, as our evaluation shows (Section 5.3).

3 OUR METHOD

Figure 1 provides a graphical view of our process. In the rest of this section, we cover each part in more detail.

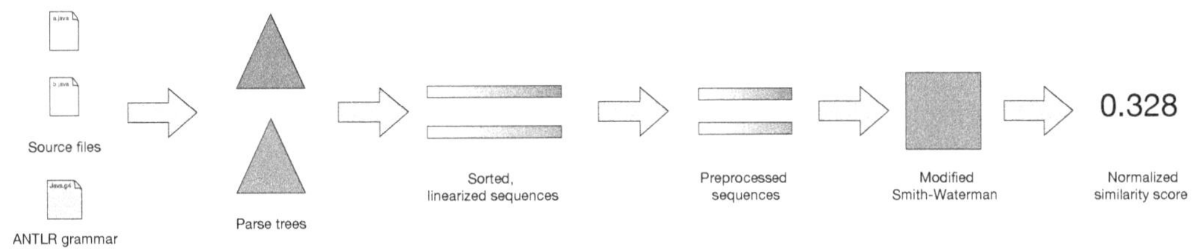

Figure 1: A graphical overview of our method.

3.1 Parsing: ANTLR Grammars to Sequences

Our method requires as input the parse tree of a program—because parse trees can be made for any programming language, every further step works exactly the same regardless of the initial language. We assume that input programs are syntactically well-formed, which is reasonably ensured via a course policy which states that only compiling programs may receive credit. To get parse trees, we use the ANTLR parser generator [7], which has existing grammars for several popular languages.

Adding support for a new language. With this in mind, to apply our approach to a new language, a user needs only to: (1) find (or create) an ANTLR grammar describing the language; (2) use the ANTLR tool to create a corresponding parser for the grammar; (3) write fairly straightforward boilerplate code to attach the parser to our tool; (4) provide minimal information for filtering (see Section 3.3). To keep things concrete, we focus on Java for the remainder of this paper, but any other language could be substituted in its place.

The parser from ANTLR produces parse trees corresponding to input programs. Once we obtain a parse tree for two given programs, we *linearize* the two trees by performing a postorder traversal and outputting the labels of each node traversed. Once we have the two programs that we wish to compare in this linearized form, we then preprocess them before performing sequence alignment on them. The first preprocessing step is sorting the functions.

3.2 Sorting

Because we are comparing entire files at a time, we must be wary of a common plagiarism operation: function rearrangement. The order of the functions should not matter when evaluating cases of plagiarism—it makes no difference if `foo()` comes before or after `bar()` if their contents are plagiarized.

The heuristic we use is to sort functions in each file by size (i.e., the number of nodes in the parse tree) before we linearize each parse tree. We found that this gives good results while avoiding the exponential blowup that would occur with trying every possible combination of functions.

After the linearized sequences are in this sorted order, we can further prune and enhance the information contained within them.

3.3 Filtering, Abstraction, and Weight

In this step, we determine which parse tree node labels to keep, what equivalence class they belong to (if any), and provide a relative score that indicates how important a given label is. Users must provide information specifying how labels are grouped, once per language. We explain each case along with its justification.

Filtering. Another common plagiarism operation is renaming variable names and other identifiers, so we cannot trust any such node in a parse tree. We have a filtering phase to get rid of these and other parse tree labels that we deem unsuitable for comparison. In fact, we found the ratio of useful to interesting nodes to be so small that we only require a list of nodes to *keep*.

As an example, consider the Java grammar rule for expressions:

```
expression
    : primary
    ...
    | methodCall
    | NEW creator
    | '(' typeType ')' expression
    | expression postfix=('++' | '--')
    | prefix=('+'|'-'|'++'|'--') expression
    ...
```

This is essentially a catch-all rule, and almost every line of Java code will contain an `expression` node in its sub-parse tree. As such, there no useful information in `expression`, and so we omit it from our output. There are many similar rules in the Java grammar.

Abstraction. Several nodes act in a similar way, and should be considered as such. For example, several `if`/`else` statements may be transformed into one `switch` statement, and vice versa. We therefore consider parse tree node labels for `if`/`else` and `switch` to be in the same equivalence class, and we consider them to "match" in our Smith-Waterman algorithm. Different kinds of loops also belong together in the same equivalence class.

This concludes our preprocessing steps. We are now ready to compare two program sequences with a modified Smith-Waterman algorithm. Before introducing our algorithm, we first discuss sequence comparison in general.

3.4 Comparing Sequences: False Start

Smith-Waterman is a relatively unfamiliar algorithm to most computer scientists, so we will briefly compare it to the more familiar and similar concept of string edit distance. Levenshtein distance is the most common string edit distance measurement algorithm.

Levenshtein distance has notions of insertion, deletion, and mismatch "costs", and the final answer is the minimized cost of performing these different string-altering operations. Overall, Levenshtein distance determines the most cost-effective way to turn one string into another. Smith-Waterman has similar computational costs, but matching is more customizable; for example, Smith-Waterman allows a *matrix* of scores, which allows a programmer to give different match/mismatch scores to different pairs of elements of a sequence. In this work, we assign higher scores to programs that match at certain key nodes, such as loops and if statements.

Levenshtein distance also computes a cost over the entire string, in what is known as a global alignment. For example, comparing the strings `A = ''cat''` and `B = ''␣␣␣cat␣␣''` results in a score of 5, because the entire string A must be transformed into the entire string B. In contrast, Smith-Waterman performs a *local* alignment and finds the largest substrings of each string that match. Local alignment is important for our purposes because we want to give a high similarity score to a pair of programs when a *portion* of one is found in the other; our method would be less accurate if we only gave high similarity scores to program pairs when they have almost everything in common.

3.5 Comparing Sequences: Smith-Waterman

The Smith-Waterman algorithm [13] is a dynamic programming-based sequence alignment algorithm. It computes a numerical value representing how similar or dissimilar two sequences are. Originally implemented with bioinformatics in mind, it is used to compare biological sequences (e.g., RNA and proteins) and to determine how closely two such sequences overlap each other. The algorithm works for sequences of any kind, not just sequences of characters; in this work, we align sequences of abstracted parse tree nodes.

Smith-Waterman is parameterized by a gap score (for insertions and deletions) and a scoring matrix (for matching and mismatching). This matrix is consulted each time nodes are compared to determine how similar they are, and so tuning this matrix has a major impact on the results. We simplify the process of constructing a scoring matrix by: (1) providing all nodes that match a default match score, and all nodes that do not match a default mismatch score; and (2) assigning relative weights to certain matches.

Weights. Experimentally, we found that some label classes are more important than others. For example, it is quite likely that several `if` statements will match in a plagiarized pair of programs, whereas assignment statements do not closely correspond. For this reason, we assign relative weights to certain equivalence classes of labels. Just like the rest of our method, these weights are completely customizable to fit any instructor's needs. The relevant portion of our weight/equivalence class file follows:

```
{"conditional": 5, "loop": 5, "return": 5,
"functioncall": 5, "assign": 2}
```

This syntax specifies that conditional statements (e.g., `if/else`, `switch`) that match are to be given 5× the match score. If such a node does not match, we perform the same multiplcation against the mismatch score.

Final steps. After obtaining a similarity score from the Smith-Waterman algorithm, we normalize the scores to be between 0.0 and 1.0. Without such a normalization, larger plagiarized program pairs (which naturally have more similar portions than shorter plagiarized program pairs) would have larger scores, rendering sorting by score useless.

4 COMPLETE EXAMPLE

This section goes through an in-depth example of our method.

Description of the programs. Figure 2 contains three example programs: A, B, and C. Programs A and B have been plagiarized using several common operations (e.g., identifier renaming, manipulation of spacing, etc.) [4], while program C is independent of A and B. We use this example to demonstrate our method, and we further elaborate on plagiarism operations in our evaluation (Section 5).

Parsing. We first parse the three programs, creating the parse trees shown in Figure 3. None of these parse trees look similar to each other, with differences in both the number of nodes and node structure. Our goal is to get Programs A and B into a format where they both "look" similar; it is for this reason that we preprocess and linearize the parse tree nodes.

Sorting. We then extract functions and sort them by their size, in terms of the number of parse tree nodes. In this example, sorting will not change the function order in Program A. However, in Program B, `func2` will be moved to come *before* `func1`. This sorting heuristic thus puts the plagiarized functions in the same order.

Linearization. We then perform a postorder traversal of the parse trees before we prune further. The contents, however, are the important part, and we want to get Programs A and B into a format where they have a lot in common. The first few nodes of Program A's `bar` function are (bold font indicating common elements):

TerminalNodeImpl, **IdentifierNonterminal**, **(**, **TerminalNodeImpl**, **)**, **TerminalNodeImpl**, FormalParameters, **{**, **TerminalNodeImpl**, **int**, **TerminalNodeImpl**, **PrimitiveType**, **TypeType**, sum, **TerminalNodeImpl**, **VariableDeclaratorId**, =, **TerminalNodeImpl**, 0, **TerminalNodeImpl**, Literal, Primary, PrimaryExpression, VariableInitializer, VariableDeclarator, VariableDeclarators, LocalVariableDeclaration, . . .

The first few nodes of Program B's `func1` function are:

TerminalNodeImpl, **IdentifierNonterminal**, **(**, **TerminalNodeImpl**, int, **TerminalNodeImpl**, PrimitiveType, TypeType, dummy1, **TerminalNodeImpl**, VariableDeclaratorId, FormalParameter, TerminalNodeImpl, **int**, **TerminalNodeImpl**, **PrimitiveType**, **TypeType**, dummy2, **TerminalNodeImpl**, **VariableDeclaratorId**, FormalParameter, FormalParameterList, **)**, **TerminalNodeImpl**, FormalParameters, {, **TerminalNodeImpl**, int, . . .

While there are similarities at the beginning, they do not last long. `func2`'s extra parameters and names, as well as the extra statements at the beginning, are taking up a substantial amount of space, so we want to remove them. Similarly, any identifier names are naturally untrustworthy, and are thus ripe for removal. Not shown are the nodes for the `while` and `for` loops, which are currently considered different; we want to treat these as being similar to each other.

Pruning and Abstraction. Beforehand, we have compiled a set of "useful" parse tree nodes which we want to keep; it is only necessary to do this once per language. In this step, we prune out any node that is not in our useful set. After performing this pruning, we are left with sequences that are typically ~33% as large as the originals. Pruning reduces both the amount of input to process downstream (improving performance), as well as the amount of irrelevant "noise" in the input (improving accurracy/precision). The final nodes of Program A's `bar` function are (bold font indicating common elements):

```
public class A {
    public void foo() {
        for (int i = 1; i < 10; i++) {
            System.out.println(i);
        }
    }

    public int bar() {
        int sum = 0;
        for (int i = 0; i < 10; i++) {
            for (int j = 0; j < 10; j++) {
                sum += i + j;
            }
        }
        return sum;
    }
}
```

(a) Program A

```
public class B
{public int func1(int dummy1, int dummy2)
    {int extraStmt1 = 5, int extraStmt2 = 42;
     int s = 0; int i = 1;
        while (11 > i)
        { int j = 1; while (11 > j) {
                s += (i - 1) + (j - 1);
                j = j + 1;
            }
            ++i;
        }
        return s;
    }
    public void func2()
    {int z = 1; while (10 > z)
    {System.out.println(z); z++;}}
}
```

(b) Program B

```
public class C {
    public void hello() {
        System.out.println("Hello, world!");
    }

    public int sum2(int x) {
        int a = 0;
        for (;;) {
            if (x <= 0) break;
            a += x;
            x--;
        }
        return a;
    }
}
```

(c) Program C

Figure 2: Three contrived example programs: A and B for a plagiarized pair, while C has no plagiarized information taken from A or B.

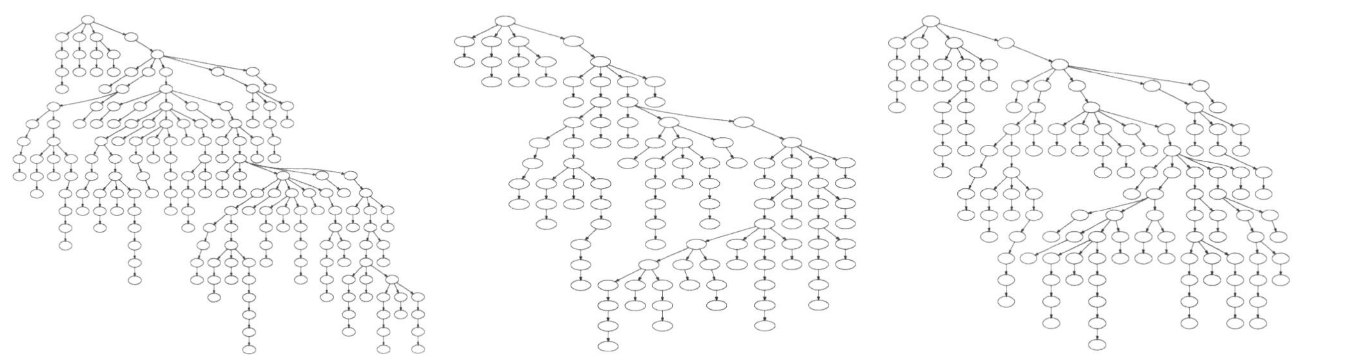

(a) Parse tree for Program A (b) Parse tree for Program B (c) Parse tree for Program C

Figure 3: A bird's eye view of the parse tree structure for Programs A, B, and C.

`..., Primary,` **`Primary`**`,` **`AdditiveExpression`**`,` **`AssignExpression`**`,` **`ForLoop`**`,` **`ForLoop`**`,` **`Primary`**`,` **`ReturnStatement`**

The last nodes of Program B's `func1` function are:

`..., Literal,` **`Primary`**`,` **`AdditiveExpression`**`,` **`AssignExpression`**`,` **`WhileLoop`**`, Primary, PrefixIncDecNegPlus,` **`WhileLoop`**`,` **`Primary`**`,` **`ReturnStatement`**

These pruned sequences share several similar elements, and sequence alignment will give a larger score on these than the originals. One final step that is not shown is abstraction, where we group similar nodes. In this example, we will end up grouping `WhileLoop` and `ForLoop` into the same equivalence class, and so we will consider them to represent the same node; this allows sequence alignment to return a larger score for these plagiarized programs.

Smith-Waterman. Running Smith-Waterman on the abstracted sequences is the last step. We run the algorithm for each pair of input programs with the scoring matrix generated by the supplied node weights. The scores are relative to each other, and are not meaningful on an absolute scale. Higher-scoring pairs are more indicative of plagiarism than lower-scoring pairs, and in practice users need only look at the several highest-scoring pairs to find plagiarism.

The final scores. After all this work has been done, we are left with a similarity score between 0 and 1 for each pair of programs:

- Program A and Program B: 0.299
- Program A and Program C: 0.193
- Program B and Program C: 0.120

In this case, our method has correctly scored the plagiarized program pair higher than the non-plagiarized program pairs.

5 EVALUATION

In this section we compare our method to existing methods.

5.1 What We Compare Against

We evaluate our method against MOSS [12] and JPLAG [10], both widely used plagiarism detection tools. We tested MOSS in Java

Table 1: Results for each method. ↓ indicates that a lower value is better, and ↑ indicates that a higher value is better

Method	Cutoff	Time (s) (↓)	True Pos. (↑)	False Pos. (↓)	True Neg. (↑)	False Neg. (↓)	Precision (↑)	Recall (↑)	F-Measure (↑)
Our method	0.15	115.9	33	16	4,884	17	0.673	0.660	0.667
Zhang and Liu	0.58	970.3	16	37	4,863	34	0.302	0.320	0.311
MOSS, Java Mode	0.44	30.8	11	33	4,867	39	0.250	0.220	0.234
MOSS, Text Mode	N/A	4.1	0	0	4900	50	∞	0.000	0.000
JPLAG	0.17	4.7	18	46	4,854	32	0.281	0.360	0.316

mode and in text mode; we did this to evaluate what would happen if MOSS was run on a language that it does not support. Both MOSS and JPLAG were run with default parameters.

We also evaluate against our implementation of Zhang and Liu's method [8]. Both our method and Zhang and Liu's method require multiple parameters, namely a tree traversal order, a match score, a mismatch score, and a gap score. We experimentally determined optimal values for each of these parameters. For our method, we use postorder traversal, a match score of 1, a mismatch score of -1, and a gap score of -2. For Zhang and Liu, we use preorder traversal, a match score of 1, a mismatch score of -1, and a gap score of -1—we also tried a gap score of -2, but -1 gave better results.

5.2 Benchmarks and Methodology

To address the bias problem discussed in Section 2.1, we employ random program generation and random program transformation to create our benchmark suite. We have created 50 pairs of original and plagiarized Java programs for a total of 100 Java programs, and we evaluate by comparing all pairs of those 100 programs. We implemented our generator to perform several popular plagiarism obfuscations observed in the wild [4]:

- Addition of random amounts of whitespace.
- Changing every identifier name (e.g., variable names, argument names, function names, etc.).
- Changing type names to equivalent ones (we overapproximate this by transforming type names into random strings).
- Changing operations to equivalent ones (e.g., replacing $A + B < C$ with $C > B + A$).
- Replacing control structures with equivalent ones (e.g., swapping while with for and vice versa).
- Changing the order of statements and functions.

Our metrics are the standard ones of precision (true positives / (true positives + false positives)) and recall (true positives / (true positives + false negatives)). These numbers are combined via F-measure [11], which provides a single number to compare the relative performance of each method.

5.3 Results

Table 1 shows the results for every method that we tried. There were 4,950 possible pairs of programs to compare, and 50 "true" cases of plagiarism; all other pairs are considered to be false positives. Each method produces a score between 0 and 1 indicating the likelihood that a pair was plagiarized. To convert this score to a binary yes/no for whether or not plagiarism was detected, we selected a cutoff value for each technique, where scores ≥ to the cutoff were considered indicative of plagiarism. Cutoff scores were picked to maximize the F-measure for each method.

Discussion. Our method has the best F-measure, and the running time is in the middle of the group.

Both ours and Zhang and Liu's methods start with the same parse trees and subsequently run an $O(n^2)$ algorithm. However, our method is nearly 8.4x faster than Zhang and Liu's method. This is because our filtering stage dramatically reduces the input size, minimizing n in the aforementioned time complexity. It is possible that pruning obviously non-matching pairs (e.g., programs of vastly different lengths) could help to further reduce our runtime, but we leave this investigation for future work.

MOSS' text mode returned no matching results, which was to be expected; all identifiers were changed, and so there would be no meaningful matches in any sliding window of results. As such, while Winnowing [12] (the technique MOSS is based on) is language-agnostic, MOSS itself is not. While some effort is needed to apply our technique to a new language, this is fundamentally impossible with MOSS, due to MOSS' closed-source nature.

MOSS' Java mode and JPLAG both had similar results. MOSS' time includes sending the files over the network and waiting for a response from the server, so it is possible that the running time of the main plagiarism detection algorithm is closer to that of JPLAG.

Threats to Validity. Our method cannot detect every kind of plagiarism. For example, it cannot currently handle obfuscation where functions are broken down into many small functions, though it would be possible to mitigate this issue (at the expense of increased runtime) by comparing all function pairs. Semantic similarity is also a research-worthy challenge: it is always possible to trick a syntax-based method by swapping the code with completely different code that does the same thing (e.g., insertion sort with quicksort).

6 CONCLUSION

In this paper we presented a plagiarism detection method based on the Smith-Waterman sequence alignment algorithm. Our method works for any language with a grammar, and converts parse trees to a linearized form. We demonstrate that preprocessing these sequences is key; through filtering, abstracting, and sorting we are able to find more true cases of plagiarism than popular, existing methods such as MOSS. Our evaluation utilizes random program generation and plagiarism obfuscations, minimizing biases subconsciously introduced when working with handwritten benchmark suites. Program generation also allows us to obtain exact ground truth, which is not obtainable from student code. We have made our tool and its source code freely available.

In the future, we would like to investigate skipping the linearization phase; there are existing *tree* alignment algorithms, and it remains to be shown whether they are able to scale and perform as well as our current method. We may also be able to improve the runtime of our method via further input pruning.

Acknowledgments

This work was supported by NSF CCF-1319060.

REFERENCES

[1] Michel Chilowicz, Etienne Duris, and Gilles Roussel. 2009. Syntax tree fingerprinting for source code similarity detection. In *Program Comprehension, 2009. ICPC'09. IEEE 17th International Conference on*. IEEE, 243–247.

[2] Deqiang Fu, Yanyan Xu, Haoran Yu, and Boyang Yang. 2017. Wastk: A weighted abstract syntax tree kernel method for source code plagiarism detection. *Scientific Programming* 2017 (2017).

[3] David Gitchell and Nicholas Tran. 1999. Sim: a utility for detecting similarity in computer programs. In *ACM SIGCSE Bulletin*, Vol. 31. ACM, 266–270.

[4] Vítor T Martins, Daniela Fonte, Pedro Rangel Henriques, and Daniela da Cruz. 2014. Plagiarism detection: A tool survey and comparison. In *OASIcs-OpenAccess Series in Informatics*, Vol. 38. Schloss Dagstuhl-Leibniz-Zentrum fuer Informatik.

[5] Lefteris Moussiades and Athena Vakali. 2005. PDetect: A clustering approach for detecting plagiarism in source code datasets. *The computer journal* 48, 6 (2005), 651–661.

[6] Sandhya Narayanan and S Simi. 2012. Source code plagiarism detection and performance analysis using fingerprint based distance measure method. In *Computer Science & Education (ICCSE), 2012 7th International Conference on*. IEEE, 1065–1068.

[7] Terence J. Parr and Russell W. Quong. 1995. ANTLR: A predicated-LL (k) parser generator. *Software: Practice and Experience* 25, 7 (1995), 789–810.

[8] Li ping Zhang and Dong sheng Liu. 2013. AST-based multi-language plagiarism detection method. In *Software Engineering and Service Science (ICSESS), 2013 4th IEEE International Conference on*. IEEE, 738–742.

[9] Bruno Prado, Kalil A Bispo, and Raul Andrade. 2018. X9: An Obfuscation Resilient Approach for Source Code Plagiarism Detection in Virtual Learning Environments.. In *ICEIS (1)*. 517–524.

[10] Lutz Prechelt, Guido Malpohl, and Michael Phlippsen. 2000. JPlag: Finding plagiarisms among a set of programs. (2000).

[11] Yutaka Sasaki et al. 2007. The truth of the F-measure. (2007).

[12] Saul Schleimer, Daniel S Wilkerson, and Alex Aiken. 2003. Winnowing: local algorithms for document fingerprinting. In *Proceedings of the 2003 ACM SIGMOD international conference on Management of data*. ACM, 76–85.

[13] T.F. Smith and M.S. Waterman. 1981. Identification of common molecular subsequences. *Journal of Molecular Biology* 147, 1 (1981), 195 – 197. https://doi.org/10.1016/0022-2836(81)90087-5

[14] Jeong-Woo Son, Seong-Bae Park, and Se-Young Park. 2006. Program Plagiarism Detection Using Parse Tree Kernels. In *PRICAI 2006: Trends in Artificial Intelligence*, Qiang Yang and Geoff Webb (Eds.). Springer Berlin Heidelberg, Berlin, Heidelberg, 1000–1004.

[15] Lisan Sulistiani and Oscar Karnalim. 2019. ES-Plag: Efficient and sensitive source code plagiarism detection tool for academic environment. *Computer Applications in Engineering Education* 27, 1 (2019), 166–182.

[16] Narjes Tahaei and David C Noelle. 2018. Automated Plagiarism Detection for Computer Programming Exercises Based on Patterns of Resubmission. In *Proceedings of the 2018 ACM Conference on International Computing Education Research*. ACM, 178–186.

Author Index

Ada, Mireilla Bikanga 259
Adam, Michel 353
Adams, Joshua 255
Aggarwal, Ashish 261, 292
Ahmed, Sherif Aly 265
Ajanovski, Vangel 267
Albert, Jennifer 278
Alharbi, Lubna 293
Almeida, Ricardo 306
Almujally, Nouf 294
Alrashidi, Huda 295
Alshaigy, Bedour 263
Alshikhabobakr, Hanan 478
Alvarado, Christine 196
An, Haokang 154
Andrews, Ashley 278
Angelvik, Nina 374
Apiola, Mikko-Ville 16
Arguelles Cruz, Amadeo Jose .. 255
Armoni, Michal 485
Arslanyilmaz, Abdurrahman 296
Azevedo, Rodolfo 23
Azhar, Mohammad 251
Ballew, William 329
Bälter, Olle 133
Barkmin, Mike 367
Barksdale, Sarah 257
Barnes, Tiffany 271, 278, 395
Barr, Matthew 203, 313
Basawapatna, Ashok 422
Becker, Brett A. 51, 58, 253
Begosso, Luiz Ricardo 297
Begosso, Luiz Carlos 297
Bennett, Casey C. 265
Benotti, Luciana 402
Berg, Tessa 126
Berry, Miles 231, 332
Bettin, Briana 182
Bhardwaj, Jyoti 85
Bhatia, Sajal 251
Bikanga Ada, Mireilla 203
Black, Michael 233
Bongo, Lars Ailo 374
Bort, Heather 269
Bosse, Yorah 429
Bouchard, Durell 253
Boulden, Danielle 395
Bounajim, Dolly 395
Bouvier, Dennis J. 253
Bowman, Nicholas A. 170, 176
Bradley, Andrew 263
Brandes, Ofra 485
Bresnihan, Nina 298
Brinda, Torsten 367
Brophy, Sean 312
Brown, David W. 309
Bryans, Emily 315
Burdge, Darci 285
Busuttil, Leonard 257
Caceffo, Ricardo 23
Cao, Yingjun 99
Cardella, Monica 312
Carr, Steven 513
Cassel, Lillian 299
Cateté, Veronica 271, 278, 395
Che, S. Megan 210
Chen, Hui 506
Chen, Sitao 555
Ciborowska, Agnieszka 506
Cody, Christa 271
Coelho, Hendi 306
Cole, Elizabeth 257
Connolly, Cornelia 269
Corpier, Kendra 296
Crosby, Ryan 300
Culver, K.C. 170, 176
Cunha, Douglas Sanches 297
Cunningham, Kathryn 37, 269
Cutts, Quintin 261, 313, 203
Dalseng, Margaret 374
Damevski, Kostadin 506
Daoud, Moncef 353
Dashti, Cameron 154
Davis, Karen C. 265
Dawkins, Hillary 301
Deb, Debzani 302
Debnath, Sourav 319
Decker, Adrienne 239, 548
DeLyser, Leigh Ann 231, 492
Denny, Paul 253
Devlin, Marie 300
Dewey, Kyle 555
Dichev, Christo 299
Dicheva, Darina 299
Diniz, Andrew 306
Diplan, Nohelia 317
DiSalvo, Betsy 161
Domínguez, César 318
Donaldson, Peter 203, 269
Dong, Yihuan 278, 395
Dorodchi, Mohsen 259
Douglas, Grant 301
Draper, Steve 203
Duran, Rodrigo 261
Duran, Rodrigo Silva 443
Eckerdal, Anna 450
Edwards, Doug 315
Egan, Garrett 416
Eisele, Victoria 259
Ellis, Heidi J. C. 285
Ellsworth, Jordan 416
Emre, Mehmet 555
Erdil, D. Cenk 255
Ericson, Barbara 37, 332
Erkan, Ali 235
Euler, Stephan 237
Fabian, Khristin 126
Fagin, Barry 303
Falkner, Katrina 189, 257
Falkner, Nickolas 269
Fanning, Caitlin 381
Feijóo-García, Pedro G. 304
Fessard, Grégoire 78
Fisher, Lorraine 298
Fjukstad, Bjørn 374
Foster, Derek 255
Fouh, Eric 267
Franco, Luis Henrique Buzzo 297
Frank-Bolton, Pablo 23
Freeman, Jason 315
Frison, Patrice 353
Fuad, Muztaba 302
Fukazawa, Yoshiaki 92
Gagne, Greg 251, 305
Gama, Kiev 306, 388
Garcia, Rita 189
Garcia, Saturnino 381
García-Izquierdo, Francisco J. ... 318
Gardner-McCune, Christina 9, 292, 304
Geck, Gaetano 307
Gedawy, Huda 478
Geissler, Markus 308, 323
Gerosa, Marco A. 429

Ghafoor, Sheikh K. 309
Glassey, Richard 168, 534
Glover-Netherton, Kevin 301
Goldstein, Seth Copen 154
Gomez, Marcos J. 402
Gonsalvez, Chris 267
Grasso, Floriana 293
Griswold, William G. 196
Groher, Iris 321
Grønnesby, Morten 374
Grossman, Sabrina 315
Gunawardena, Ananda 310
Gunhildrud, Hedinn 374
Gutica, Mirela 261, 311
Guy, Breonte 299
Guzdial, Mark 37, 161
Hainey, Brian 255
Haldimann, Jonas 307
Halverson, Richard 499
Hamouda, Sally 51
Harada, Yasunori 326
Hardekopf, Ben 555
Harrington, Brian 253
Hauser, Florian 320
Hedin, Björn 133
Heeren, Bastiaan 119
Heinemann, Birte 261
Heliotis, James 259
Hellas, Arto 44, 269, 443
Hines, Thomas 309
Hislop, Gregory W. 285
Höppner, Frank 105
Houchins, Jennifer 395
Hudec, David 301
Hughes, Janet 168
Hyman, Harvey 255
Impagliazzo, John 265
Irawan, Yunghans 457
Irwin, Keith 299
Isvik, Amy 278, 395
Iversen, Julianne 374
Izu, Cruz 261, 436
Jackson, Stoney 285
Jaime, Arturo 318
Jarratt, Lindsay 170, 176
Jeuring, Johan 119
Jimmieson, Phil 293
Jocius, Robin 278
Joshi, Deepti 278
Joy, Mike 294, 295
Kamil, Amir 253
Kann, Viggo 133
Kapoor, Amanpreet 9, 334
Kari, Chadi 251
Karkare, Amey 253
Karvelas, Ioannis 336
Kasahara, Remin 92
Ke, Shannon 37
Kennedy, Cazembe 210, 224
Keuning, Hieke 119
Kleanthous, Styliani 71
Knietzsch, Marco 320
Korhonen, Ari 140
Kraemer, Eileen T. 210, 224, 261
Kramer, Matthias 367
Krogstie, Birgit R. 263
Kumar, Amruth N. 65
Kumar, Viraj 263
Kuno, Yasushi 326
Laakso, Mikko-Jussi 16
Lamprou, Anna 422
Larsén, Simon 534
Lawson, Aubrey 210
Lee, Adam 235
Lee, Michael J. 409
Lee, Taneisha 315
Leinonen, Juho 44, 267
Lewis, Gareth 255
Liao, Soohyun Nam 99, 196
Liebe, Christine 257
Ljulin, Artur 307
Lodi, Michael 147
Lonati, Violetta 261
Lorås, Madeleine 338
Lowe, Tony 30, 312, 340
Lucarelli, Chery 332
Lunt, Sean 301
Lutz, Megan E. 259
Luxton-Reilly, Andrew 267
Lynch, Aine 298
Lytle, Nicholas 278, 395, 520
Magerko, Brian 315
Maguire, Joseph 251, 313
Mahadev, Aparna 314
Maiorana, Francesco 257, 332
Margulieux, Lauren E. 548
Marshall, Lindsay 300
Marwan, Samiha 520
Masapanta-Carrión, Susana 541
Matta, Joseph 233
May, Johannes 307
Mayo, Jean 513
McCartney, Robert 51, 450
McCuaig, Judi 301
McDonald, Chris 253
McGettrick, Andrew 265
McGill, Monica 231, 239, 241, 257
McGregor, Léon 342
McKlin, Tom 315
Meharg, Debbie 126
Mehta, Dinesh P. 471
Menasalvas, Ernestina 316
Meyer, Bernd 527
Milliken, Alexandra 271, 395
Millwood, Richard 298
Mirolo, Claudio 261, 436
Mohammed, Alliyya 301
Moreno, Ana M. 316
Moresi, Marco 402
Morreale, Patricia 317
Morrison, Briana 231, 548
Moschella, Marialaura 344
Mosley, James 301
Moström, Jan Erik 450
Mottok, Jürgen 320
Mountrouidou, Xenia 251
Mukherjee, Saswati 499
Nakar, Liat 346
Nakayama, Yuriko 326
Nazir, Sajid 255
Nguyen, Manh Van 255
Nichols, Lawton 555
Nisiotis, Louis 71
Nygren, Henrik 44
Oguamanam, Vanessa 161
Olarte, Juan J. 318
Ord, Rick 99
Osera, Peter-Michael 253
Ott, Linda 182, 263
Ouh, Eng Lieh 457
Parkinson, Jack 203, 267, 313
Parrish, Allen 265
Parzanchevski, Noam 243
Patel, Jignesh M. 499
Pearce, Janice L. 253
Peltsverger, Svetlana 319
Pereira, Teresa Susana Mendes 265
Peters, Anne-Kathrin 263
Petersen, Andrew 269
Petralito, Serge 422
Petre, Marian 331
Pettit, Raymond 253
Pointon, Michael Scott 217

Polhill, Dalton 301
Pollock, Ian 241
Pollock, Ian 263
Poole, Matthew 267
Porter, Leo 99, 196
Postner, Lori 285
Power, James F. 112
Prather, James 253
Price, Thomas 520
Quille, Keith 257
Raj, Rajendra K. 265
Rasch, Fredrik Høisæther 374
Rashed, Mostafa 301
Razak, Saquib 478
Redmiles, David 429
Renna, Ilaria 78
Repenning, Alexander 422
Reuter, Rebecca 320
Rich, Peter J. 416
Richards, Gretchen 332
Riedesel, Charles 263
Riese, Emma 133
Rixner, Scott 360
Robinson, James 269
Robinson, Richard 278
Rogers, Mike 309
Romanowski, Carol J. 265
Rosenthal, Jack 471
Rubinstein, Amir 243
Rybicki, Jan-Mikael 443
Sabitzer, Barbara 321
Sakamoto, Kazunori 92
Sakr, Majd 154, 255
Sametinger, Johannes 321
Sampangi, Raghav V. 322
Sampson, Matthew 301
Sanders, Kate 51, 450
Schmellenkamp, Marko 307
Schmidt, Jonas 307
Schulte, Carsten 261
Scott, Michael 249
Segre, Alberto Maria 170, 176
Senbel, Samah 245
Sentance, Sue 257
Servin, Christian 308, 323
Sheard, Judy 51, 269
Shene, Ching-Kuang 513
Siegel, Angela A. 168, 322
Simon 51 267
Singer, Jeremy 203
Singh, Shaveen 247, 527
Smith, Colin 2
Smith, Rebecca 360
Smith, Russell M. 302
Smith, Sally 2, 126
Solomon, Amber 161
Somerville, Derek 313
Sonnabend, Daniel 307
Soosai Raj, Adalbert Gerald 499
Souza, Renan 23
Stange, Melissa 308, 323
Stewart, Khadija 324
Stone, Kate 1
Stott, Lee 255
Strong, Glenn 298
Sundin, Lovisa 203, 265
Suoranta, Sanna 443
Swoboda, Nik 316
Szabo, Claudia 217, 269
Szynkiewicz, Justyna 348
Tahaei, Mohammad 350
Tamarov, Yossi 243
Tang, Cara 308, 323
Tang, Terry 360
Taylor-Smith, Ella 2, 126
Thai, Kevin 196
Thomas, Lynda 450
Thota, Neena 267
Touretzky, David S. 292
Townsend, Gloria 324
Tschirbs, Felix 307
Tshukudu, Ethel 259
Tucker, Cindy S. 308, 323
Tudor, Liviana 251
Ullmann, Thomas Daniel 295
Ureel, Leo 182, 259, 325
Valstar, Sander 196
Varey, Alison 126
Vehlken, Fabian 307
Velázquez-Iturbide, J. Ángel 464, 541
Vivian, Rebecca 189, 257
Vivitsou, Marianna 140
Vosen, David 251
Waldron, John 112
Walker, James 513
Wallace, Charles 263, 325
Walther, Marissa 325
Wang, Man 513
Wang, Patrick 78
Wanzer, Dana 315
Warren, Joe 360
Washizaki, Hironori 92
Watanabe, Takeshi 326
Weeda, Renske 261
White, Laurie 255
Wiebe, Eric 395
Williams, David 351
Williams, Jim 499
Williams, Joseph Jay 520
Wright, Lauren 492
Wulff Hauglann, Maria 374
York, Dustin 317
Young, Rhys 301
Young, Tiffany 327, 328, 329
Yuen, Timothy T. 251
Zander, Carol 450
Zarb, Mark 168, 249, 327, 328, 329
Zeume, Thomas 307
Zhang, Eda 499
Zhang, Hongyi 154
Zingaro, Daniel 196

www.ingramcontent.com/pod-product-compliance
Lightning Source LLC
LaVergne TN
LVHW082014200926
848481LV00010B/2859
* 9 7 8 1 4 5 0 3 7 0 6 3 9 *